Microsoft® Office 2016 IN PRACTICE

word COMPLETE

Randy Nordell

AMERICAN RIVER COLLEGE

McGraw Hill Education

MICROSOFT OFFICE 2016: IN PRACTICE WORD COMPLETE

Published by McGraw-Hill/Irwin, a business unit of The McGraw-Hill Companies, Inc., 1221 Avenue of the Americas, New York, NY, 10020. Copyright © 2017 by The McGraw-Hill Companies, Inc. All rights reserved. Printed in the United States of America. No part of this publication may be reproduced or distributed in any form or by any means, or stored in a database or retrieval system, without the prior written consent of The McGraw-Hill Companies, Inc., including, but not limited to, in any network or other electronic storage or transmission, or broadcast for distance learning.

Some ancillaries, including electronic and print components, may not be available to customers outside the United States.

This book is printed on acid-free paper.

2 3 4 5 6 7 8 9 LMN 20 19 18 17

ISBN 978-1-259-76266-6
MHID 1-259-76266-1

Chief Product Officer, SVP Products & Markets: *G. Scott Virkler*
Managing Director: *Scott Davidson*
Executive Brand Manager: *Wyatt Morris*
Executive Director of Development: *Ann Torbert*
Senior Product Developer: *Alan Palmer*
Executive Marketing Managers: *Tiffany Russell & Debbie Clare*
Director, Content Design & Delivery: *Terri Schiesl*
Program Manager: *Mary Conzachi*
Content Project Manager: *Rick Hecker*
Buyer: *Jennifer Pickel*
Designer: *Matt Backhaus*
Cover Image: *© Chris Ryan/Getty Images*
Senior Digital Product Analyst: *Thuan Vinh*
Compositor: *SPi Global*
Printer: *LSC Communications*

Library of Congress Cataloging-in-Publication Data

Names: Nordell, Randy, author.
Title: Microsoft Office 2016: in practice Word complete / Randy Nordell.
Description: New York, NY: McGraw-Hill Education, [2017]
Identifiers: LCCN 2016021656 | ISBN 9781259762666 (acid-free paper)
Subjects: LCSH: Microsoft Word. | Word processing.
Classification: LCC Z52.5.M52 N667 2017 | DDC 005.52—dc23
LC record available at https://lccn.loc.gov/2016021656

The Internet addresses listed in the text were accurate at the time of publication. The inclusion of a website does not indicate an endorsement by the authors or McGraw-Hill, and McGraw-Hill does not guarantee the accuracy of the information presented at these sites.

www.mhhe.com

dedication

Bob and Lanita, thank you for generously allowing me to use the cabin where I completed much of the work on this book. Don and Jennie, thank you for teaching me the value of hard work and encouraging me throughout the years. Kelsey and Taylor, thank you for keeping me young at heart. Kelly, thank you for your daily love, support, and encouragement. I could not have done this without you. I'm looking forward to spending more time together on our tandem!

—Randy Nordell

brief contents

■ **OFFICE**   Chapter 1: Windows 10, Office 2016, and File Management   O1-1

■ **WORD**   Chapter 1: Creating and Editing Documents   W1-2

■ **WORD**   Chapter 2: Formatting and Customizing Documents   W2-65

■ **WORD**   Chapter 3: Collaborating with Others and Working with Reports   W3-133

■ **WORD**   Chapter 4: Using Tables, Columns, and Graphics   W4-209

■ **WORD**   Chapter 5: Using Templates and Mail Merge   W5-269

■ **WORD**   Chapter 6: Using Custom Styles and Building Blocks   W6-327

■ **WORD**   Chapter 7: Advanced Tables and Graphics   W7-391

■ **WORD**   Chapter 8: Using Desktop Publishing and Graphic Features   W8-462

■ **WORD**   Chapter 9: Working Collaboratively and Integrating Applications   W9-524

■ **WORD**   Chapter 10: Automating Tasks Using Templates and Macros   W10-585

■ **WORD**   Chapter 11: Working with Forms and Master Documents   W11-642

■ **WORD**   Chapter 12: Customizing Word 2016 and Using OneDrive and Office Online   W12-695

APPENDICES

Appendix A: Office 2016 Shortcuts   A-2

See Resources in SIMnet for:
Appendix B: Business Document Formats (online only)

GLOSSARY   G-1

INDEX   I-1

contents

OFFICE

CHAPTER 1: WINDOWS 10, OFFICE 2016, AND FILE MANAGEMENT — O1-1

Chapter Overview	**O1-1**
Student Learning Outcomes (SLOs)	**O1-1**
Case Study	**O1-1**
1.1—Using Windows 10	**O1-2**
Windows 10	O1-2
Microsoft Account	O1-2
Windows Desktop and Taskbar	O1-3
Start Menu	O1-3
Add Apps	O1-4
Customize the Start Menu	O1-4
Customize the Taskbar	O1-5
File Explorer	O1-6
OneDrive	O1-7
Cortana	O1-8
Task View	O1-9
Settings	O1-9
Action Center	O1-10
1.2—Using Office 2016	**O1-10**
Office 2016 and Office 365	O1-10
Office Desktop Apps, Office Universal Apps, and Office Online	O1-11
Open an Office Desktop Application	O1-12
Office Start Page	O1-13
Backstage View	O1-14
Office Help—Tell Me	O1-14
Mouse and Pointers	O1-15
Touch Mode and Touch Screen Gestures	O1-15
1.3—Creating, Saving, Closing, and Opening Files	**O1-17**
Create a New File	O1-17
Save a File	O1-18
Create a New Folder When Saving a File	O1-19
Save As a Different File Name	O1-20
Office 2016 File Types	O1-20
Close a File	O1-20
Open an Existing File	O1-21
Pause & Practice 1-1: Use Windows 10 and Share an Office File	***O1-22***
1.4—Working with Files	**O1-25**
File Views	O1-25
Change Display Size	O1-26
Manage Multiple Open Files and Windows	O1-26
Snap Assist	O1-27
1.5—Printing, Sharing, and Customizing Files	**O1-28**
Print a File	O1-29
Export as a PDF File	O1-29
Document Properties	O1-30

Share a File	O1-31
Program Options	O1-32
1.6—Using the Ribbon, Tabs, and Quick Access Toolbar	**O1-33**
The Ribbon, Tabs, and Groups	O1-33
Ribbon Display Options	O1-33
Buttons, Drop-Down Lists, and Galleries	O1-33
Dialog Boxes, Task Panes, and Launchers	O1-34
ScreenTips	O1-35
Radio Buttons, Check Boxes, and Text Boxes	O1-35
Quick Access Toolbar	O1-35
Customize the Quick Access Toolbar	O1-36
1.7—Using Context Menus, the Mini Toolbars, and Keyboard Shortcuts	**O1-37**
Context Menu	O1-37
Mini Toolbar	O1-37
Keyboard Shortcuts	O1-37
Function Keys on a Laptop	O1-38
Pause & Practice 1-2: Modify, Export, and Share an Office File	***O1-38***
1.8—Organizing and Customizing Folders and Files	**O1-42**
Create a Folder	O1-42
Move and Copy Files and Folders	O1-42
Rename Files and Folders	O1-43
Delete Files and Folders	O1-43
Create a Zipped (Compressed) Folder	O1-44
Extract a Zipped (Compressed) Folder	O1-45
Pause & Practice 1-3: Organize Files and Folders	***O1-46***
Chapter Summary	**O1-48**
Check for Understanding	**O1-50**
Using Microsoft Windows 10 and Office 2016	**O1-51**
Guided Projects (2)	O1-51
Independent Projects (2)	O1-56
Challenge Projects (2)	O1-59

WORD

CHAPTER 1: CREATING AND EDITING DOCUMENTS — W1-2

Chapter Overview	**W1-2**
Student Learning Outcomes (SLOs)	**W1-2**
Case Study	**W1-2**
1.1—Creating, Saving, and Opening Documents	**W1-3**
Create a New Document	W1-3
Save a Document	W1-4
Save As a Different File Name	W1-5
Open a Document	W1-6
Pin a Frequently Used Document	W1-6
Share and Export Options	W1-7

1.2—Entering and Selecting Text — **W1-7**
Type Text and Use Word Wrap — W1-7
Show/Hide Formatting Symbols — W1-7
Select Text — W1-8
AutoComplete — W1-9
AutoCorrect and AutoFormat — W1-9
AutoCorrect Smart Tag — W1-9
Add Custom AutoCorrect Entry — W1-10

1.3—Using Paragraph Breaks, Line Breaks, and Non-Breaking Spaces — **W1-10**
Paragraph Breaks — W1-10
Line Breaks — W1-11
Spaces and Non-Breaking Spaces — W1-11

Pause & Practice 1-1: Create a Business Letter — *W1-12*

1.4—Moving and Copying Text — **W1-15**
Move Text — W1-15
Copy Text — W1-15
Paste Text and Paste Options — W1-16
Clipboard Pane — W1-17
Undo Change — W1-17
Redo and Repeat Change — W1-18

1.5—Changing Fonts, Font Sizes, and Attributes — **W1-18**
Font and Font Size — W1-18
Bold, Italic, and Underline Font Styles — W1-19
Other Font Style Buttons — W1-20
Change Case — W1-20
Font Dialog Box — W1-21
» Font Color — W1-21
» Underline Style and Color — W1-22
» Font Effects — W1-22
» Character Spacing — W1-23
Text Effects — W1-23
Format Painter — W1-24
Clear All Formatting — W1-25
Change Default Font and Font Size — W1-25

Pause & Practice 1-2: Customize a Business Letter — *W1-26*

1.6—Changing Text Alignment, Line Spacing, and Paragraph Spacing — **W1-28**
Default Settings — W1-29
Paragraph Alignment — W1-29
Line Spacing — W1-29
Paragraph Spacing — W1-30
Paragraph Dialog Box — W1-31
Change Default Line and Paragraph Spacing — W1-32

1.7—Using Smart Lookup and Proofreading Tools — **W1-32**
Smart Lookup and the Smart Lookup Pane — W1-32
Automatic Spelling and Grammar Notifications — W1-33
Spelling and Grammar Panes — W1-34
Customize the Dictionary — W1-34
The Thesaurus — W1-35
Word Count — W1-36

1.8—Customizing Document Properties — **W1-36**
Document Properties — W1-37
Advanced Properties — W1-37
Print Document Properties — W1-38

Pause & Practice 1-3: Finalize a Business Letter — *W1-38*

Chapter Summary — **W1-42**
Check for Understanding — **W1-43**
Using Microsoft Word 2016 — **W1-44**
Guided Projects (3) — W1-44
Independent Projects (3) — W1-55
Improve It Project (1) — W1-61
Challenge Projects (3) — W1-63

CHAPTER 2: FORMATTING AND CUSTOMIZING DOCUMENTS — W2-65

Chapter Overview — **W2-65**
Student Learning Outcomes (SLOs) — **W2-65**
Case Study — **W2-65**

2.1—Customizing Margins and Page Layout — **W2-66**
Page Layout Settings — W2-66
Margin Settings — W2-66
Page Setup Dialog Box — W2-67
Page Orientation — W2-67
Paper Size — W2-68
Vertical Alignment — W2-68
Use the Ruler — W2-69

2.2—Setting, Using, and Editing Tab Stops — **W2-69**
Set a Tab Stop — W2-70
» Set a Tab Stop Using the Tabs Dialog Box — W2-70
» Set a Tab Stop Using the Ruler — W2-71
Move a Tab Stop — W2-71
Remove a Tab Stop — W2-72
Add a Tab Leader — W2-72
Change Default Tab Stops — W2-73

2.3—Using Indents — **W2-74**
Left and Right Indents — W2-74
First Line and Hanging Indents — W2-75
Remove Indents — W2-76

Pause & Practice 2-1: Modify a Resume — *W2-77*

2.4—Inserting Page Numbers, Headers, and Footers — **W2-79**
Page Numbering — W2-79
» Insert Page Number — W2-79
» Edit Page Number in the Header or Footer — W2-79
» Different First Page — W2-80
» Page Number Format — W2-80
» Remove Page Number — W2-81
Insert Header and Footer Content — W2-81
» Number of Pages Field — W2-82
» Date and Time — W2-82
» Document Properties — W2-83
Built-In Headers, Footers, and Page Numbers — W2-84

Pause & Practice 2-2: Use Header and Page Number in a Resume — *W2-84*

2.5—Using Page and Section Breaks — **W2-86**
Page Breaks — W2-87
Section Breaks — W2-87
Edit Page and Section Breaks — W2-88

2.6—Using Bulleted, Numbered, and Multilevel Lists — **W2-88**

Create a Bulleted List W2-88
Customize a Bulleted List W2-89
Create a Numbered List W2-90
Customize a Numbered List W2-90
Multilevel Lists W2-91

2.7—Using Styles and Themes **W2-92**
Style Gallery W2-92
Apply a Built-In Style W2-93
Modify a Style W2-93
Apply a Theme W2-94

Pause & Practice 2-3: Use Bullets, a Page Break, Styles, and a Theme in a Resume *W2-95*

2.8—Using Find and Replace **W2-97**
Find W2-97
Find and Replace W2-98
Go To W2-99

2.9—Using Borders, Shading, and Hyperlinks **W2-100**
Apply Built-In Borders W2-100
Customize Borders W2-100
Apply Shading W2-101
Apply a Page Border W2-102
Insert a Horizontal Line W2-103
Create a Hyperlink W2-104
Edit or Remove a Hyperlink W2-105

Pause & Practice 2-4: Finalize a Resume *W2-106*

Chapter Summary **W2-109**

Check for Understanding **W2-110**

Using Microsoft Word 2016 **W2-111**
Guided Project (3) W2-111
Independent Project (3) W2-122
Improve It Project (1) W2-129
Challenge Project (3) W2-130

CHAPTER 3: COLLABORATING WITH OTHERS AND WORKING WITH REPORTS **W3-133**

Chapter Overview **W3-133**

Student Learning Outcomes (SLOs) **W3-133**

Case Study **W3-133**

3.1—Using Comments **W3-134**
Insert a Comment W3-134
Change User Name W3-135
Review Comments W3-135
Reply to a Comment W3-136
Resolve Comment W3-136
Edit and Delete Comments W3-136

3.2—Using Track Changes and Sharing **W3-137**
Track Changes W3-137
Display for Review Views W3-138
Accept and Reject Changes W3-138
Reviewing Pane W3-140
Share an Online File W3-140
Create a Sharing Link W3-141

Pause & Practice 3-1: Use Comments and Track Changes *W3-142*

3.3—Using Footnotes and Endnotes **W3-144**
Insert a Footnote W3-144
Insert an Endnote W3-145
View Footnotes and Endnotes W3-145
Customize Footnotes and Endnotes W3-146
» Modify Footnote and Endnote Format W3-147
» Modify Footnote and Endnote Styles W3-147
Convert Footnotes and Endnotes W3-147
Move Footnotes and Endnotes W3-149
Delete Footnotes and Endnotes W3-149

3.4—Creating a Bibliography and Inserting Citations **W3-149**
Report Styles W3-150
Bibliography Styles W3-150
Add a New Source W3-151
Insert a Citation W3-152
Insert a Placeholder W3-153
Manage Sources W3-153
Edit Citations and Sources W3-155
Insert a Bibliography W3-155

Pause & Practice 3-2: Insert and Modify Footnotes and Create a Bibliography *W3-156*

3.5—Inserting a Table of Contents **W3-161**
Use Heading Styles for a Table of Contents W3-161
Insert a Built-In Table of Contents W3-162
Insert a Custom Table of Contents W3-162
Modify a Table of Contents W3-163
Update a Table of Contents W3-163
Remove a Table of Contents W3-164

3.6—Inserting a Cover Page **W3-164**
Insert a Built-In Cover Page W3-164
Customize Cover Page Content W3-164
» Customize Document Property Content W3-165
» Add or Remove Document Property Fields W3-165
» Customize Content Control Fields W3-166
Remove a Cover Page W3-166

3.7—Using Advanced Headers and Footers **W3-167**
Page and Section Breaks W3-167
Built-In Headers, Footers, and Page Numbers W3-168
Customize Header and Footer Content W3-168
Different First Page Header and Footer W3-169
Different Odd and Even Pages W3-170
Link to Previous Header or Footer W3-170
Format Page Numbers W3-171
Navigate between Headers and Footers W3-172
Remove a Header or Footer W3-172

Pause & Practice 3-3: Add and Modify a Table of Contents and Cover Page and Use Custom Headers and Footers *W3-172*

Chapter Summary **W3-178**

Check for Understanding **W3-179**

Using Microsoft Word 2016 **W3-180**
Guided Projects (3) W3-180
Independent Projects (3) W3-195
Improve It Project (1) W3-204
Challenge Projects (3) W3-207

CHAPTER 4: USING TABLES, COLUMNS, AND GRAPHICS W4-209

Chapter Overview W4-209
Student Learning Outcomes (SLOs) W4-209
Case Study W4-209
4.1—Creating and Editing Tables W4-210
 Tables W4-210
 Navigate within a Table W4-211
 Table Tools Layout Tab W4-211
 Select Table and Text W4-211
 Add Rows and Columns W4-212
 Merge and Split Cells W4-213
 Copy or Move Columns and Rows W4-213
 Delete Columns and Rows W4-214
 Delete a Table W4-214
4.2—Arranging Text in Tables W4-214
 Resize Columns and Rows W4-214
 AutoFit a Table W4-215
 Distribute Rows and Columns W4-215
 Text Alignment W4-216
 Cell Margins W4-216
 Table Properties Dialog Box W4-217
 Sort Data in Tables W4-217
Pause & Practice 4-1: Use Tables to Customize a Brochure W4-218
4.3—Formatting and Editing Tables W4-220
 Table Tools Design Tab W4-220
 Table Borders W4-221
 View Gridlines W4-222
 Table Shading W4-222
 Table Styles W4-222
 Table Style Options W4-223
 Insert a Formula in a Table W4-223
  » Update a Formula W4-224
 Convert Text to a Table W4-224
Pause & Practice 4-2: Format a Table in a Brochure W4-225
4.4—Using Columns W4-227
 Preset Column Settings W4-227
 Customize Columns W4-228
 Convert Text to Columns W4-228
 Insert a Column Break W4-229
 Balance Columns W4-229
Pause & Practice 4-3: Use Columns to Format a Brochure W4-230
4.5—Working with Graphics W4-231
 Pictures and Online Pictures W4-231
  » Insert a Picture W4-232
  » Insert an Online Picture W4-233
 Arrange a Graphic in a Document W4-233
  » Resize a Graphic W4-234
  » Wrap Text around a Graphic W4-234
  » Position a Graphic W4-236
  » Insert a Caption W4-236
  » Group Graphic Objects W4-237
 Insert and Customize a Shape W4-238
 Insert and Customize SmartArt W4-239
 Insert and Customize WordArt W4-240
 Enhance Graphics with Styles W4-241
 Insert Symbols and Special Characters W4-241
Pause & Practice 4-4: Finalize a Brochure with Graphics W4-242
Chapter Summary W4-246
Check for Understanding W4-247
Using Microsoft Word 2016 W4-248
 Guided Projects (3) W4-248
 Independent Projects (3) W4-257
 Improve It Project (1) W4-264
 Challenge Projects (3) W4-266

CHAPTER 5: USING TEMPLATES AND MAIL MERGE W5-269

Chapter Overview W5-269
Student Learning Outcomes (SLOs) W5-269
Case Study W5-269
5.1—Using and Customizing Templates W5-270
 Word Normal Template W5-270
 Online Templates W5-271
 Insert Template Content W5-272
 Remove Template Content W5-272
 Modify Template Content and Format W5-273
Pause & Practice 5-1: Use a Word Template to Create a Fax Template W5-273
5.2—Creating Templates W5-275
 Create a Template from a Blank Document W5-276
 Save an Existing Document as a Template W5-276
 Create a Document Based upon a Template W5-277
 Edit a Template W5-278
Pause & Practice 5-2: Create a Form Letter Template from an Existing Document W5-278
5.3—Creating Envelopes and Labels W5-280
 Create an Envelope W5-280
 Envelope Options W5-280
 Envelope Printing Options W5-281
 Add an Envelope to an Existing Document W5-281
 Create Labels W5-282
 Label Options W5-282
 Create Individual Labels W5-282
 Create a Full Page of the Same Label W5-283
Pause & Practice 5-3: Create Individual Mailing Labels W5-284
5.4—Understanding Mail Merge W5-286
 Types of Mail Merge W5-286
 Main Document W5-286
 Recipients W5-286
5.5—Merging Using the Mailings Tab W5-287
 Start the Mail Merge W5-287
 Select Recipients W5-288
  » Type a New List W5-288
  » Use an Existing List W5-289
  » Select from Outlook Contacts W5-289
 Edit Recipients W5-290
 Address Block and Greeting Line Merge Fields W5-290

Match Fields W5-291
Insert an Individual Merge Field W5-292
Update Labels W5-293
Highlight Merge Fields W5-293
Preview Mail Merge W5-293
Finish and Merge W5-294
Open an Existing Merge Document W5-295

Pause & Practice 5-4: Use Mail Merge to Create Form Letters **W5-295**

5.6—Using the Mail Merge Wizard **W5-299**
Select Document Type W5-299
Select Starting Document W5-299
Select Recipients W5-300
Arrange Your Document W5-301
Preview Your Document W5-301
Complete the Merge W5-302

Pause & Practice 5-5: Use Mail Merge to Create Mailing Labels **W5-302**

Chapter Summary **W5-305**

Check for Understanding **W5-305**

Using Microsoft Word 2016 **W5-306**
Guided Projects (3) W5-306
Independent Projects (3) W5-317
Improve It Project (1) W5-323
Challenge Projects (3) W5-324

CHAPTER 6: USING CUSTOM STYLES AND BUILDING BLOCKS **W6-327**

Chapter Overview **W6-327**

Student Learning Outcomes (SLOs) **W6-327**

Case Study **W6-327**

6.1—Creating and Using Custom Styles **W6-328**
Style Gallery W6-328
Styles Pane W6-328
Types of Styles W6-329
Modify a Style W6-330
Update a Style W6-330
Create a New Style W6-331
Create a New Style from Selected Text W6-332
Modify the Style Gallery W6-332
Clear Formatting W6-333
Change Document Style Set W6-333

Pause & Practice 6-1: Create a Styles Template **W6-334**

6.2—Managing Styles **W6-337**
Manage Styles Dialog Box W6-338
» Edit a Style W6-338
» Recommended Styles W6-339
Style Pane Options W6-339
Select and Clear All Styles W6-340
Find and Replace Styles W6-341
Expand or Collapse Headings W6-342
Import and Export Styles W6-342
Styles Template W6-343
Attach a Template to a Document W6-343
Use the Organizer Dialog Box W6-344

Pause & Practice 6-2: Import and Modify Styles and Attach a Styles Template to a Document **W6-345**

6.3—Understanding and Using Building Blocks **W6-348**
Building Blocks Organizer W6-348
Create a Building Block W6-349
Insert a Building Block W6-350
Edit a Building Block W6-350
Delete a Building Block W6-351

6.4—Creating and Using AutoText Building Blocks **W6-351**
Create an AutoText Building Block W6-352
Insert an AutoText Building Block W6-352
Edit or Delete an AutoText Building Block W6-353

Pause & Practice 6-3: Create and Use Building Blocks **W6-353**

6.5—Using and Customizing Quick Parts Building Blocks **W6-357**
Create a Quick Parts Building Block W6-357
Insert a Quick Parts Building Block W6-358
Edit or Delete a Quick Parts Building Block W6-358

6.6—Using Document Property and Word Fields **W6-359**
Document Properties W6-359
Custom Document Properties W6-359
Insert a Document Property Field W6-360
Insert a Word Field W6-360
Personalize Microsoft Office W6-361
Edit and Update Fields W6-362

Pause & Practice 6-4: Use the Quick Parts Gallery and Insert Word and Document Property Fields **W6-362**

Chapter Summary **W6-366**

Check for Understanding **W6-367**

Using Microsoft Word 2016 **W6-368**
Guided Projects (3) W6-368
Independent Projects (3) W6-380
Improve It Project (1) W6-386
Challenge Projects (3) W6-389

CHAPTER 7: ADVANCED TABLES AND GRAPHICS **W7-391**

Chapter Overview **W7-391**

Student Learning Outcomes (SLOs) **W7-391**

Case Study **W7-391**

7.1—Customizing Table Content **W7-392**
Convert Text to a Table W7-392
Convert a Table to Text W7-392
Sort Text in a Table W7-393
Formulas and Functions W7-394
» Create a Formula W7-394
» Use a Function in a Formula W7-395
» Edit a Formula W7-396
» Update a Formula W7-396
Change Text Direction W7-396
Tabs and Indents in Tables W7-397
Bullets and Numbering in Tables W7-398

Pause & Practice 7-1: Create a Table from Text and Sort, Change Text Direction, and Use Formulas in a Table **W7-398**

7.2—Customizing Table Layout   **W7-401**
Table Size   W7-401
Row Height and Column Width   W7-402
Table Alignment and Position   W7-402
Cell Margins and Spacing   W7-403
Split a Table and Cells   W7-403
Nested Tables   W7-404
Repeat Header Rows   W7-404
Draw a Table   W7-405

7.3—Customizing Table Design   **W7-405**
Border Painter   W7-405
Border Styles   W7-406
Border Sampler   W7-406
Table Styles   W7-407
Modify a Table Style   W7-407
Create a New Table Style   W7-408
Quick Tables Gallery   W7-410

Pause & Practice 7-2: Split a Table, Edit Formulas, and Apply and Modify Table Styles   ***W7-411***

7.4—Working with Pictures   **W7-415**
Layout Options   W7-415
Customize Text Wrapping   W7-415
Alignment Guides and Live Layout   W7-416
Picture Wrap Points   W7-416
Picture Anchor   W7-417
Resize and Crop a Picture   W7-417
Rotate a Picture   W7-418
Format Picture Pane   W7-419
Picture Styles   W7-419
Picture Borders   W7-419
Picture Effects   W7-420
Picture Adjustments   W7-421
  » Corrections   W7-421
  » Color   W7-421
  » Artistic Effects   W7-422
  » Compress Pictures   W7-422
  » Change Picture   W7-422
  » Reset Picture   W7-423

Pause & Practice 7-3: Insert and Modify Pictures   ***W7-423***

7.5—Working with Shapes   **W7-426**
Customize Shapes   W7-427
Shape Styles   W7-427
Add Text to a Shape   W7-428
Draw a Text Box   W7-428
Selection Pane   W7-429
Order Shapes   W7-429
Align Shapes   W7-430
Group Shapes   W7-431

Pause & Practice 7-4: Insert and Customize Shapes   ***W7-431***

Chapter Summary   **W7-434**

Check for Understanding   **W7-435**

Using Microsoft Word 2016   **W7-436**
Guided Projects (3)   W7-436
Independent Projects (3)   W7-448
Improve It Project (1)   W7-456
Challenge Projects (3)   W7-459

CHAPTER 8: USING DESKTOP PUBLISHING AND GRAPHIC FEATURES   **W8-462**

Chapter Overview   **W8-462**
Student Learning Outcomes (SLOs)   **W8-462**
Case Study   **W8-462**

8.1—Using Desktop Publishing Features   **W8-463**
Custom Page Settings   W8-463
Drop Caps   W8-464
Drop Cap Options   W8-464
Page Color   W8-465
Watermarks   W8-465
  » Built-In Watermarks   W8-466
  » Custom Watermarks   W8-466
  » Create a Watermark Building Block   W8-467
  » Remove a Watermark   W8-467
Screenshots   W8-467
Hyphenation   W8-468
Line Numbers   W8-469

Pause & Practice 8-1: Apply Desktop Publishing Features   ***W8-470***

8.2—Customizing and Creating Themes   **W8-472**
Theme Colors, Fonts, and Effects   W8-472
Create Custom Theme Colors and Fonts   W8-472
Create a Custom Theme   W8-473

8.3—Using Text Boxes   **W8-473**
Built-In Text Boxes   W8-473
Customize Text Box Content   W8-474
Customize Text Box Format   W8-475
Draw a Text Box   W8-475
Text Box Building Blocks   W8-476

Pause & Practice 8-2: Work with Themes and Text Boxes   ***W8-476***

8.4—Using SmartArt   **W8-479**
Insert a SmartArt Graphic   W8-479
SmartArt Tools Tabs   W8-480
Customize SmartArt Text   W8-480
Customize SmartArt Design   W8-482
Customize SmartArt Objects   W8-482
Resize, Align, and Position SmartArt   W8-483

8.5—Using Charts   **W8-484**
Insert a Chart   W8-484
Customize Chart Data   W8-485
Chart Tools Tabs, Format Pane, and Format Buttons   W8-485
Customize Chart Layout   W8-486
Apply a Chart Style and Quick Color   W8-487
Customize Chart Elements   W8-488
Resize, Align, and Position a Chart   W8-489

Pause & Practice 8-3: Insert and Customize a Chart and SmartArt   ***W8-489***

8.6—Creating an Index   **W8-493**
Mark an Index Entry   W8-493
Mark an Index Subentry   W8-494
Cross-Reference an Index Entry   W8-494
Insert an Index Page   W8-495

Update an Index Page W8-496
Delete an Index Entry W8-496

**Pause & Practice 8-4: Mark Index Entries
and Insert and Customize an Index Page** **W8-496**

Chapter Summary **W8-500**

Check for Understanding **W8-501**

Using Microsoft Word 2016 **W8-502**
Guided Projects (3) W8-502
Independent Projects (3) W8-512
Improve It Project (1) W8-519
Challenge Projects (3) W8-522

CHAPTER 9: WORKING COLLABORATIVELY AND INTEGRATING APPLICATIONS W9-524

Chapter Overview **W9-524**

Student Learning Outcomes (SLOs) **W9-524**

Case Study **W9-524**

9.1—Advanced Collaboration Features **W9-525**
Customize Comment and Markup Color W9-525
Customize Show Markup Options W9-525
Change Tracking Options W9-526
Lock Tracking W9-527
Real-Time Collaboration on a Shared
Document W9-527
Printing Document Markup W9-528

**Pause & Practice 9-1: Use Comments and
Track Changes** **W9-529**

9.2—Using Other Collaboration Features **W9-531**
Compare Documents W9-531
Show or Hide Source Documents W9-532
Combine Documents W9-533
Check for Issues W9-534
» Inspect Document W9-534
» Check Accessibility W9-535
» Check Compatibility W9-535
Protect Document W9-536
Mark as Final W9-536
» Encrypt with Password W9-537
» Restrict Editing W9-538
» Add a Digital Signature W9-539
Manage Versions W9-539

**Pause & Practice 9-2: Combine Documents,
Check Compatibility, and Protect a Document** **W9-540**

9.3—Integrating Office Applications **W9-542**
Object Linking and Embedding W9-542
Embed an Object W9-543
Embed a File W9-544
Modify an Embedded Object W9-544
Link an Object W9-545
Open a Document Linked to an Object W9-546
Modify Linked Object Content W9-546
Modify a Link to an Object W9-546
Break a Link to an Object W9-547

**Pause & Practice 9-3: Embed, Link, and
Modify Objects** **W9-548**

9.4—Using Mail Merge Rules **W9-551**
Mail Merge Review W9-551
Mail Merge Rules W9-551
View Merge Field Codes W9-552

9.5—Using Bookmarks **W9-553**
Add a Bookmark W9-553
Display Bookmarks in a Document W9-553
Go To a Bookmark W9-554
Hyperlink to a Bookmark W9-554
Cross-Reference a Bookmark W9-554
Use a Bookmark in a Formula W9-555
Delete a Bookmark W9-555

**Pause & Practice 9-4: Perform a Mail Merge
and Use Rules to Customize the Merge** **W9-555**

Chapter Summary **W9-560**

Check for Understanding **W9-561**

Using Microsoft Word 2016 **W9-562**
Guided Projects (3) W9-562
Independent Projects (3) W9-574
Improve It Project (1) W9-581
Challenge Projects (3) W9-583

CHAPTER 10: AUTOMATING TASKS USING TEMPLATES AND MACROS W10-585

Chapter Overview **W10-585**

Student Learning Outcomes (SLOs) **W10-585**

Case Study **W10-585**

10.1—Creating and Saving Templates **W10-586**
Save a Document as a Template W10-586
Personal Templates W10-587
Online Word Templates W10-587
Edit a Template W10-588
Create a Document Based on a Template W10-588

10.2—Customizing and Using Templates **W10-589**
Customize Template Content W10-589
» Content Control Fields W10-589
» Document Property Fields W10-590
» Word Fields W10-590
Attach a Template to a Document W10-591
Styles Organizer W10-592

**Pause & Practice 10-1: Use Document
Property, Content Control, and Word
Fields in a Template** **W10-593**

10.3—Creating and Running Macros **W10-596**
Plan a Macro W10-596
Record a Keyboard-Activated Macro W10-596
Record a Button-Activated Macro W10-597
Save a Macro-Enabled Document W10-599
Macro Security Settings W10-600
Run a Macro W10-600
Create an AutoMacro W10-601
Delete a Macro W10-602

**Pause & Practice 10-2: Record a Macro and
Save a Document as a Macro-Enabled
Document** **W10-602**

10.4—Copying and Editing Macros	**W10-605**
Copy a Macro	W10-605
Edit a Macro	W10-605
Assign a Shortcut Key to a Macro	W10-606
Add a Macro Button to the Quick Access Toolbar	W10-607
Remove a Macro Button from the Quick Access Toolbar	W10-608
Pause & Practice 10-3: Copy and Edit a Macro and Assign a Shortcut and Button to a Macro	*W10-608*
10.5—Creating and Using Macro-Enabled Templates	**W10-612**
Save a Macro-Enabled Template	W10-612
Copy a Macro to Another File	W10-612
Use a Macro-Enabled Template	W10-614
Pause & Practice 10-4: Copy and Edit Macros and Create a Document Based upon a Macro-Enabled Template	*W10-614*
Chapter Summary	**W10-617**
Check for Understanding	**W10-618**
Using Microsoft Word 2016	**W10-619**
Guided Projects (3)	W10-619
Independent Projects (3)	W10-629
Improve It Project (1)	W10-637
Challenge Projects (3)	W10-640

CHAPTER 11: WORKING WITH FORMS AND MASTER DOCUMENTS W11-642

Chapter Overview	**W11-642**
Student Learning Outcomes (SLOs)	**W11-642**
Case Study	**W11-642**
11.1—Using Content Control Fields	**W11-643**
Content Control Fields	W11-643
Control Content Control Field Arrangement	W11-643
Insert a Rich Text Content Control Field	W11-643
Content Control Field Properties	W11-644
Plain Text Content Control Field	W11-645
Check Box Content Control Field	W11-646
Date Picker Content Control Field	W11-646
Picture Content Control Field	W11-647
Pause & Practice 11-1: Insert Content Control Fields	*W11-648*
11.2—Using Advanced Content Control Fields	**W11-651**
Combo Box Content Control Field	W11-651
Drop-Down List Content Control Field	W11-652
Building Block Gallery Content Control Field	W11-652
Legacy Tools	W11-653
11.3—Editing Content Control Fields	**W11-653**
Apply a Style to a Content Control Field	W11-653
Change Content Control Display and Color	W11-654
User Interaction with Content Control Fields	W11-654
Lock a Content Control Field	W11-655

Design Mode	W11-655
Delete a Content Control Field	W11-656
Pause & Practice 11-2: Insert and Customize Content Control Fields	*W11-656*
11.4—Using Forms	**W11-659**
Group Content Control Fields	W11-659
Save a Form as a Template	W11-659
Protect a Form	W11-660
Open and Fill in a Form	W11-660
Edit and Save a Form	W11-661
Pause & Practice 11-3: Group Content Control Fields and Create a Form Based on a Template	*W11-661*
11.5—Working with a Master Document	**W11-663**
Outline View	W11-663
Insert a Subdocument into a Master Document	W11-664
Create a Subdocument	W11-665
Merge Subdocuments	W11-665
Split a Subdocument	W11-666
Unlink a Subdocument	W11-666
Arrange Text in an Outline	W11-667
Lock a Subdocument	W11-667
Save and Reopen a Master Document	W11-668
Pause & Practice 11-4: Work with a Master Document and Subdocuments	*W11-669*
Chapter Summary	**W11-672**
Check for Understanding	**W11-673**
Using Microsoft Word 2016	**W11-674**
Guided Projects (3)	W11-674
Independent Projects (3)	W11-684
Improve It Project (1)	W11-690
Challenge Projects (3)	W11-693

CHAPTER 12: CUSTOMIZING WORD AND USING ONEDRIVE AND OFFICE ONLINE W12-695

Chapter Overview	**W12-695**
Student Learning Outcomes (SLOs)	**W12-695**
Case Study	**W12-695**
12.1—Customizing Word 2016	**W12-696**
Word Options	W12-696
» General	W12-696
» Display	W12-697
» Proofing	W12-697
» Save	W12-698
» Language	W12-698
» Advanced	W12-699
» Add-Ins	W12-700
» Trust Center	W12-700
Customize the Ribbon	W12-701
Customize the Quick Access Toolbar	W12-703
Remove a Command from the Quick Access Toolbar	W12-704
Remove an Item from the Ribbon	W12-705
Reset the Ribbon and Quick Access Toolbar	W12-705

12.2—Customizing Office and Installing Office Add-ins **W12-706**
Microsoft Account Information W12-706
Office Background and Theme W12-707
Connected Services W12-708
Office Add-ins W12-708
Open and Manage Office Add-ins W12-709

Pause & Practice 12-1: Customize Word 2016 Working Environment and Office Accounts Settings and Install an Office Add-in *W12-709*

12.3—Using OneDrive **W12-712**
Use OneDrive in a File Explorer Window W12-713
Use OneDrive Online W12-713
  » Create a Folder W12-714
  » Upload a File or Folder W12-715
  » Move, Copy, or Delete a File or Folder W12-716
  » Download a File or Folder W12-716

12.4—Sharing OneDrive Files and Folders **W12-717**
Share a File in Word W12-717
Create a Sharing Link W12-718
Change Sharing Permission W12-718
Other Sharing Options in Word W12-719
Share a File or Folder in OneDrive W12-720
Change OneDrive Sharing Permission W12-721

12.5—Using Office Online **W12-722**
Edit an Office Online File W12-722
Create an Office Online File W12-724
Share an Office Online File W12-724
Collaborate in Office Online W12-725
Use Comments in Office Online W12-726
Review Comments in Office Online W12-727

Pause & Practice 12-2: Use OneDrive and Office Online to Open, Edit, Save, and Share an Online Document. *W12-727*

12.6—Exploring Other Office Online Applications **W12-729**
Office Online W12-730
Excel Survey W12-730
Sway W12-731
Outlook.com W12-732
People W12-733
Calendar W12-733
OneNote Online W12-733

Pause & Practice 12-3: Create and Share a Survey in Office Online *W12-734*

Chapter Summary **W12-736**

Check for Understanding **W12-737**

Using Microsoft Word 2016 **W12-738**
Guided Projects (3) W12-738
Independent Projects (3) W12-747
Improve It Project (1) W12-753
Challenge Projects (3) W12-755

APPENDICES

Appendix A: Office 2016 Shortcuts **A-2**

See Resources in SIMnet for:
Appendix B: Business Document Formats

GLOSSARY

G-1

INDEX

I-1

about the author

RANDY NORDELL, Ed.D.

Randy Nordell is a professor of business technology at American River College in Sacramento, California. He has been an educator for over 25 years and has taught at the high school, community college, and university levels. He holds a bachelor's degree in business administration from California State University, Stanislaus, a single-subject teaching credential from Fresno State University, a master's degree in education from Fresno Pacific University, and a doctorate in education from Argosy University. Randy is the lead author of the *Microsoft Office 2013: In Practice* and *Microsoft Office 2016: In Practice* series of texts. He is also the author of *101 Tips for Online Course Success* and *Microsoft Outlook 2010*. Randy speaks regularly at conferences on the integration of technology into the curriculum. When not teaching and writing, he enjoys spending time with his family, cycling, skiing, swimming, backpacking, and enjoying the California weather and terrain.

What We're About

We wrote *Microsoft Office 2016: In Practice* to meet the diverse needs of both students and instructors. Our approach focuses on presenting Office topics in a logical and structured manner, teaching concepts in a way that reinforces learning with practice projects that are transferrable, relevant, and engaging. Our pedagogy and content are based on the following beliefs.

Students Need to Learn and Practice Transferable Skills

Students must be able to transfer the concepts and skills learned in the text to a variety of projects, not simply follow steps in a textbook. Our material goes beyond the instruction of many texts. In our content, students practice the concepts in a variety of current and relevant projects *and* are able to transfer skills and concepts learned to different projects in the real world. To further increase the transferability of skills learned, this text is integrated with SIMnet so students also practice skills and complete projects in an online environment.

Your Curriculum Drives the Content

The curriculum in the classroom should drive the content of the text, not the other way around. This book is designed to allow instructors and students to cover all the material they need to in order to meet the curriculum requirements of their courses no matter how the courses are structured. *Microsoft Office 2016: In Practice* teaches the marketable skills that are key to student success. McGraw-Hill's Custom Publishing site, **Create,** can further tailor the content material to meet the unique educational needs of any school.

Integrated with Technology

Our text provides a fresh and new approach to an Office applications course. Topics integrate seamlessly with SIMnet with 1:1 content to help students practice and master concepts and skills using SIMnet's interactive learning philosophy. Projects in SIMnet allow students to practice their skills and receive immediate feedback. This integration with SIMnet meets the diverse needs of students and accommodates individual learning styles. Additional textbook resources found in SIMnet (Resources and Library sections) integrate with the learning management systems that are widely used in many online and onsite courses.

Reference Text

In addition to providing students with an abundance of real-life examples and practice projects, we designed this text to be used as a Microsoft Office 2016 reference source. The core material, uncluttered with exercises, focuses on real-world use and application. Our text provides clear step-by-step instructions on how readers can apply the various features available in Microsoft Office in a variety of contexts. At the same time, users have access to a variety of both online (SIMnet) and textbook practice projects to reinforce skills and concepts.

Textbook Learning Approach

Microsoft Office 2016: In Practice uses the *T.I.P. approach:*
- **T**opic
- **I**nstruction
- **P**ractice

Topic

- Each Office application section begins with foundational skills and builds to more complex topics as the text progresses.
- Topics are logically sequenced and grouped by topics.
- Student Learning Outcomes (SLOs) are thoroughly integrated with and mapped to chapter content, projects, end-of-chapter review, and test banks.
- Reports are available within SIMnet for displaying how students have met these Student Learning Outcomes.

Instruction (How To)

- *How To* guided instructions about chapter topics provide transferable and adaptable instructions.
- Because *How To* instructions are not locked into single projects, this textbook functions as a reference text, not just a point-and-click textbook.
- Chapter content is aligned 1:1 with SIMnet.

Practice (Pause & Practice and End-of-Chapter Projects)

- Within each chapter, integrated Pause & Practice projects (three to five per chapter) reinforce learning and provide hands-on guided practice.
- In addition to Pause & Practice projects, each chapter has 10 comprehensive and practical practice projects: Guided Projects (three per chapter), Independent Projects (three per chapter), Improve It Project (one per chapter), and Challenge Projects (three per chapter). Additional projects can also be found in the Library or Resources section of SIMnet.
- Pause & Practice and end-of-chapter projects are complete content-rich projects, not small examples lacking context.
- Select auto-graded projects are available in SIMnet.

Chapter Features

All chapters follow a consistent theme and instructional methodology. Below is an example of chapter structure.

Main headings are organized according to the *Student Learning Outcomes (SLOs)*.

SLO 1.1 **Creating, Saving, and Opening Documen**

In Microsoft Word, you can create a variety of document types. Y
of Word enables you to create, edit, and customize high-quality an
ments. You can create Word documents from a new blank docum
plates, or from existing documents. Word allows you to save docu

amount of computer knowledge. This chapter covers the basic
Word document.

STUDENT LEARNING OUTCOMES (SLOs)

After completing this chapter, you will be able to:

SLO 1.1 Create, save, and open a Word document (p. W1-3).

SLO 1.2 Customize a document by entering and selecting text, usi
and using *AutoComplete*, *AutoCorrect*, and *AutoFormat* fe

SLO 1.3 Enhance a document using paragraph breaks, line breaks
non-breaking spaces (p. W1-10).

SLO 1.4 Edit a document using cut, copy, paste, the *Clipboard*, and
and repeat features. (p. W1-15).

SLO 1.5 Customize a document using different fonts, font sizes, an
(p. W1-18).

SLO 1.6 Enhance a document using text alignment and line and pa
(p. W1-28).

SLO 1.7 Finalize a document using Word's research and proofing t

SLO 1.8 Apply custom document properties to a document (p. W1-

A list of Student Learning Outcomes begins each chapter. All chapter content, examples, and practice projects are organized according to the chapter SLOs.

CASE STUDY

Throughout this book you have the opportunity to put into practice the application features that you are learning. Each chapter begins with a case study that introduces you to the Pause & Practice projects in the chapter. These Pause & Practice projects give you a chance to apply and practice key skills realistic and practical context. Each chapter contains three to five Pause & Practice projects.

Placer Hills Real Estate (PHRE) is a real estate company with regional offices throughout central California. PHRE encourages agents to use standard formats for their business documents. This ensures consistency in document appearance while also allowing agents to personalize their correspondence to customers and colleagues. In the Pause & Practice projects in this chapter, you create a business document related to the real estate business.

The *Case Study* for each chapter is a scenario that establishes the theme for the entire chapter. Chapter content, examples, figures, Pause & Practice projects, SIMnet skills, and projects throughout the chapter closely related to this case study content. The three to five Pause & Practice projects in each chapter build upon each other and address key case study themes.

How To instructions enhance transferability of skills with concise steps and screen shots.

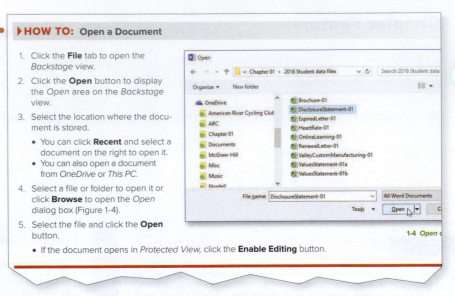

How To instructions are easy-to-follow concise steps. Screen shots and other figures fully illustrate How To topics.

Students can complete hands-on exercises in either the Office application or in SIMnet.

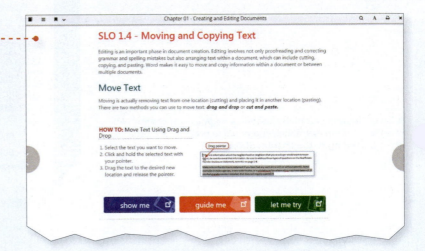

Pause & Practice 1-1: Create a business letter in block format with mixed punctuation.

Pause & Practice 1-2: Edit the business letter using copy, paste, and *Format Painter*. Modify the font, font size, color, style, and effects of selected text.

Pause & Practice 1-3: Finalize the business letter by modifying line spacing and paragraph spacing, changing paragraph alignment, translating text, using research and proofing tools, and adding document properties.

Pause & Practice projects, which each covers two to three of the student learning outcomes in the chapter, provide students with the opportunity to review and practice skills and concepts. Every chapter contains three to five Pause & Practice projects.

▶ **MORE INFO**

The *launcher* (also referred to as the *dialog box launcher*) is referred to throughout this text. Click the launcher in the bottom right corner of a group to open a dialog box or pane for additional options.

More Info provides readers with additional information about chapter content.

Another Way notations teach alternative methods of accomplishing the same task or feature such as keyboard shortcuts.

ANOTHER WAY

Press **Ctrl+Z** to undo.
Press **Ctrl+Y** to redo or repeat.

Marginal notations present additional information and alternative methods.

End-of-Chapter Projects

Ten learning projects at the end of each chapter provide additional reinforcement and practice for students. Many of these projects are available in SIMnet for completion and automatic grading.

- *Guided Projects (three per chapter):* Guided Projects provide guided step-by-step instructions to apply Office features, skills, and concepts from the chapter. Screen shots guide students through the more challenging tasks. End-of-project screen shots provide a visual of the completed project.
- *Independent Projects (three per chapter):* Independent Projects provide students further opportunities to practice and apply skills, instructing students what to do, but not how to do it. These projects allow students to apply previously learned content in a different context.
- *Improve It Project (one per chapter):* In these projects, students apply their knowledge and skills to enhance and improve an existing document. These are independent-type projects that instruct students what to do, but not how to do it.
- *Challenge Projects (three per chapter):* Challenge Projects are open-ended projects that encourage creativity and critical thinking by integrating Office concepts and features into relevant and engaging projects.

Appendix

- *Office 2016 Shortcuts:* Appendix A covers the shortcuts available in Microsoft Office and within each of the specific Office applications. Information is in table format for easy access and reference.

Additional Resources in SIMnet

Students and instructors can find the following resources in the Library or Resources sections in SIMnet.

Student Resources

- **Data Files:** Files contain start files for all Pause & Practice, Capstone, and end-of-chapter projects.
- **SIMnet Resources:** Resources provide getting started and informational handouts for instructors and students.
- **Check for Understanding:** A combination of multiple choice, matching, and short answer questions are available at the end of each SIMbook chapter in SIMnet to assist students in their review of the skills and concepts covered in the chapter.

Capstone Projects

- **Integrating Applications:** Projects provide students with the opportunity to learn, practice, and transfer skills using multiple Office applications.
- **Integrating Skills:** Projects provide students with a comprehensive and integrated review of all of the topics covered in each application (Word, Excel, Access, and PowerPoint). Available in individual application texts.

Appendices

- **Business Document Formats:** Appendix B is a guide to regularly used business document formatting and includes numerous examples and detailed instructions.

Instructor Resources

- **Instructor's Manual:** An Instructor's Manual provides teaching tips and lecture notes aligned with the PowerPoint presentations for each chapter. The manual also includes the solutions for online **Check for Understanding** questions.
- **Test Bank:** The extensive test bank integrates with learning management systems (LMSs) such as Blackboard, WebCT, Desire2Learn, and Moodle.
- **PowerPoint Presentations:** PowerPoint presentations for each chapter can be used in onsite course formats for lectures or can be uploaded to LMSs.
- **SIMnet Resources:** These resources provide getting started and informational handouts for instructors.
- **Solution Files:** Files contain solutions for all Pause & Practice, Capstone, Check for Understanding, and end-of-chapter projects.

REVIEWERS

We would like to thank the following instructors, whose invaluable insights shaped the development of this series.

Scott Straub
College of Western Idaho

Jeremy Eason
West Georgia Technical College

Linda Johnsonius
Murray State University

Barbara West
Central Georgia Technical College

Yvonne Galusha
University of Iowa

Jean Finley
Asheville Buncombe Technical Community College

Candace S. Garrod
Red Rocks Community College

Marianne Dougherty
Middlesex County College

Adam Rosen
LIM College

Peter F. Meggison
Massasoit Community College

Robert Doyle
Dona Ana Community College

Pamela Silvers
Asheville-Buncombe Technical Community College

Lisa Cady
University of Arkansas - Fort Smith

Richard Johnsen
County College of Morris

Joan Butler
Manchester Community College

Robert Nichols
College of DuPage

Anna Tsipenyuk
LIM College

Brian Fox
Santa Fe College

Leilani Benoit
Dona Ana Community College

Uma Sridharan
Presbyterian College

Marianne Daugharthy
College of Western Idaho

Tom Moore
Kapiolani Community College

Diane Morris
Tyler Junior College

Brenda McFarland
Asheville-Buncombe Technical Community College

Mitch Pendleton
LDS Business College

Tony Hunnicutt
College of the Ouachitas

Jeanine Taylor
Bryan University

Darin Bell
Treasure Valley Community College

Martha Guzman
Taller San Jose

Mary Jean Blink
Mount St. Joseph University

Ralph Dickerson
The Atlanta Workforce Development Agency

Robert LaRocca
Keiser University

Jenna Dulak
Hilbert College

Carole Eustice
Clark College

Brad West
Sinclair Community College

Gwyn Ebie
Colorado Mountain College

Susan Paulsen
Community College of Vermont

Karen A. Myers
Fisher College

Gary Judd
Trinity Baptist College

Letty Barnes
Lake Washington Institute of Technology

Tiffinee Morgan
West Kentucky Community and Technical College

Carol Lee
Central Georgia Technical College

Ronald Creel
Troy University

John Sehloff
Bethany Lutheran College

Samuel Gabay
Chicago ORT Technical Institute

Bonnie Armendariz
Bakersfield College, Bakersfield California

Sherry E. Jacob
Jefferson Community and Technical College

Tuncay Bayrak
Western New England University

Mandy Burrell
Holmes community college

Denver Riffe
American National University

Dan Lowrance
LDS Business College

Velma Latson
Bowie State University

Marilyn Mendoza
Franklin Career Institute

Lisa McCool
Alfred State College

Pamela Sorensen
Santa Rosa Junior College

Peggy Batchelor
Furman University

Larry Fudella
Erie Community College

Chet Cunningham
Madisonville Community College

Lauri Smedley
Sacramento City College

Gary Ewen
Colorado Christian University

Amanda Hardin
Mississippi Delta Community College

Rob Durrance
Keiser University

Alli Vainshtein
Riverland Community College

George C. Holder
Cloud County Community College

Colin Onita
University of Akron

Melissa Nemeth
Indiana University Kelley School of Business

Keith Conn
Cleveland Institute of Electronics

Phil Young
Baylor University

Laura Earner
Saint Xavier University

Josanne Ford
Metropolitan Career Center Computer Technology Institute

Darla Hunt
Maysville Community and Technical College

Christopher VanOosterhout
Muskegon Community College

Mark Webb
Illinois Central College

David Raney
Cuyamaca College

Christine Wolfe
Ohio University Lancaster

Dan Guerra
Community Business College

Samuel Abraham
Siena Heights University

Sandra Carriker
North Shore Community College

Shelly Smith
Valley College- Beckley

Tahir Aziz
Long Beach City College

Kin Lam
Medgar Evers College/CUNY

Sherry Grosso
University of South Carolina

Regena Aye
Allen Community College

Paul Weaver
Bossier Parish Community College

Brian McDaniel
Palo Alto College

Stephen Arney
Washburn Institute of Technology

Lynn Wermers
North Shore Community College

Lois McWhorter
Somerset Community College

J. Kirk Atkinson
Western Kentucky University

Salina Chahal
UEI College

Dana Fellows
Whiteside Area Career Center

John Golofski
Everest Institute

Eileen Dewey
Rose State College

Nasser Tadayon
Southern Utah University

Tina Denmark
Montgomery College

Delores Vance
Hazard Community and Technical College

Brad Thomas
Olivet Nazareth University

Steven Mark Sachs
Los Angeles Valley College

Andrew Smith
Marian University

Nelly Delessy
Miami Dade COllege

Richard Patterson
Peirce College

Michael Goeken
Northwest Vista College

Janice Flegle
Thomas Edison State College

Sara Rutledge
Mount Aloysius College

Seyed Roosta
Albany State University

Jim Flannery
Central Carolina Community College

Lynn Krausse
Bakersfield College

Kay Hammond
Lindenwood University

Penny Pereira
Indiana University-Purdue University Fort Wayne

Kevin Lambert
Southeast Kentucky Community and Technical College

Adam Rosen
LIM College

Cheri Whalen
Odessa College

Karr Dyal
LIM College

Shirley Birenz
New York University College of Dentistry

Jose Valdes
IBMC College

Gary DeLorenzo
California University of Pennsylvania

Kristin Roberts
Grand Rapids Community College

Michael Gray
Lane Community College

Ed Jaramillo
Peninsula College

Debasish Banerjee
Western Carolina University

Jenny Elshtain
Indiana University East

Sarah Rencher
Coconino Community College

Debbi Dybevik
Washtenaw Community College

Ann Kiefer
Chippewa Valley Technical College

Keff Lagoditz
American International College

Barbara Lave
Clark College

Morris Pondfield
Towson University

Peter Meggison
Massasoit Community College

Anne Acker
Jacksonville University

Gary Mosley
Southern Wesleyan University

Patrick J. Nedry
Monroe County Community College

Wasim A. Alhamdani
Kentucky State University

Bruce Baginski
Craven Community College

Diane Kosharek
Madison Area Technical College (Madison College)

Christina Shaner
Evergreen Valley College

Thomas Magliolo
Alvin Community College

Dmitriy Kupis
St. Joseph's College

Craig Brigman
Liberty University

Janak Shah
Berkeley college

Gary McFall
Purdue University

Phil Feinberg
Palomar College

Sheila Sicilia
Onondaga Community College

Randy Hollifield
McDowell Technical Community College

Bala R. Subramanian
Kean University

Marie Schmitz
Erie Community College

Tamar Mosley
Meridian Community College

David Bell
Pacific Union College

Jack Tan
University of Wisconsin - Eau Claire

Richard Brown
Loyola University Maryland

Narcissus Shambare
College of Saint Mary

S. E. Rouse
University of Southern Mississippi

Robert Doyle
Dona Ana Community College

David Welch
Nashville State Community College

Chen Ye
Purdue University Calumet

Bahadir Akcam
Western New England University

Frank Lucente
Westmoreland County Community College

Ted Janicki
University of Mount Olive

Kenneth R. Mayer, Jr.
Lipscomb University

Tamar Mosley
Meridian Community College

Pat McMahon
South Suburban College

Maureen Greenbaum
Union County College

Paulinus Ozor-Ilo
Gadsden State Community College

Michael Haugrud
Minnesota State University Moorhead

John Finley
Columbus State University

Philip Reaves
University of West Georgia

Cerro Coso Community College

Michael Leih
Trevecca Nazarene University

Shahla Durany
Tarrant County College - South Campus

Gary Sibbitts
St. Louis Community College at Meramec

Sandro Marchegiani
University of Pittsburgh at Johnstown

Sambit Bhattacharya
Fayetteville State University

Christine Peterson
Saint Paul College

C. Steven Hunt
Morehead State University

Shirley Nagg
Everest College

Ruth Parker
Rowan-Cabarrus Community College

Cecil Lawson
Evergreen Valley College

Adnan Turkey
DeVry College of New York

Janet Nicolaus
Mitchell Technical Institute

Mohammad Morovati
College of Dupage

Anthony Kapolka
Wilkes University

Steven Singer
Kapi'olani Community College

Bill Mills
East Texas Baptist University

Michele Schutte
Delaware Technical Community College - Terry Campus

Mark Evans
American National University

Syed Raza
Talladega College

Pam Gilmore
Reedley College

Philip Kim
Walsh University

Jeanann Boyce
Montgomery College

MaryJo Slater
Community College of Beaver County

JoAnn Brannen
Abraham Baldwin Agricultural College

Robert Patrick Sheridan
Northeast Iowa Community College

Sherry Muse
American Institute

Marcus Lacher
Minnesota State Community and Technical College

John Hupp
Columbus State University

Bernard Ku
Austin Community College

Theresa Meza
James Sprunt Community College

Jeremy A. Pittman
Coahoma Community College

LeAnne Lovering
Augusta Technical College

Lois Ann ONeal
Rogers State University

Lucy DeCaro
College of the Sequoias

Fredrick Bsharah
Cape Cod Community College

Timothy Holston
Mississippi Valley State University

Robert Balicki
Wayne County Community College District

Anita Beecroft
Kwantlen Polytechnic University

Margaret Cooksey
Tallahassee Community College

Susan Jackson
University of New Mexico-Valencia Campus

Beverly Forney
Clackamas Community College

Yves Durand
Keiser University

Cindi Nadelman
New England College

Susan Mahon
Collin College

Anthony Cameron
Fayetteville Tech Comm College

W. Randy Somsen
Brigham Young University-Idaho

Leanne Ruff
Blue Ridge Community College

Jan Wilms
Union University

Diane Bigger
LDS Business College

Michael Kurhan
Burlington County College

Vincent Yip
Umpqua Community College

Cheryl Jordan
San Juan College

Md Manzoor Murshed
Upper Iowa University

Pengtao Li
California State University, Stanislaus

George Sweiss
Governors State University Ill

Sharon M. Hope
Maria College

Ann Konarski
Baker College - Port Huron

Saiid Ganjalizadeh
Metropolitan School of Professional Studies

Brittany Bright
University of Arkansas

Iftikhar Sikder
Cleveland State University

Robin Fuller
Mississippi Gulf Coast Community College

Trude Pang
Kapiolani Community College

Tanya Patrick
Clackamas Community College

Tom Sill
Northwest University

Diane Franklin
Uintah Basin Applied Technology College

Cameron Spears
Hillsborough Community College

Kristi Smith
Allegany College of Maryland

Philip H. Nielson
Salt Lake Community College

Angela Nino
Richland College

Rajkumar Kempaiah
College of Mount Saint Vincent

Jeff Hansen
Treasure Valley Community College

J. F. Pauer
Bowling Green State University Firelands Campus

Ryan Carter
Mayland Community College

Kungwen (Dave) Chu
Purdue University Calumet

Bruce Haft
Glendale College

Tahir Aziz
J. Sargeant Reynolds Community College

Mercedes N. Alafriz
University of Phoenix/WIU

Dusty Anderson
Bluefield College

Keith Grubb
Rowan-Cabarrus Community College

Denise Reimer
Iowa Lakes Community College

Michael Sisk
Cleveland Community College

Anna Beavers
Laney College

Ted Tedmon
North Idaho College

Paulette Bell
Santa Rosa Junior College

Kevin Wyzkiewicz
Delta College

Uma Sridharan
Presbyterian College

Frank Tatum
Patrick Henry Community College

Jean Welsh
Lansing Community College

Karen Poland
Bryant and Stratton College

Aaron Tenenbaum
Brooklyn College

Susan Burden
Moberly Area Community College

Jim Patterson
Paradise Valley Community College

Richard Johnsen
County College of Morris

Ann Henry
Opportunity Center, Inc., ServiceSource - Delaware

Cathy Urbanski
Chandler-Gilbert College

Panda Jones
Gwinnett Technical College

Roni Ettleman
Atchison High School

Georgia Vanderark
Stark State College

Kevin Bradford
Somerset Community College - KCTCS

Shan Bhagoji
Monroe College

Anita Laird
Schoolcraft College

Carmen M. Aponte
Ana G. Mendez University System

Roberto Ordonez
Southern Adventist University

Marni Ferner
University of North Carolina Wilmington

Alisa Kadenic-Newman
NHTI

Andrea Langford
Ohio Valley Goodwill Industries

Barbara Schwartz
Pine Manor College

Carolyn Hill
Tallahassee Community College

Tracy Richardson
Eastern Maine Community College

Steve Nichols
Metropolitan Community College

Adell Brooks
Hinds Community College

Don Gaber
University of Wisconsin - Eau Claire

Laurie Zouharis
Suffolk University

Jill Fisher
Indian Capital Technology Center—Bill Willis Campus

Daniel Lowrance
Salt Lake Community College

Dee Hobson
Richland College

Matthew Macarty
University of New Hampshire

Jackie Porter
El Centro College

Alton Tripp
Northern Virginia Community College

Jan Repnow
Minot State University

Muhammad Obeidat
Southern Poly State University

Kirk McLean
LIM College

Saiid Ganjalizadeh
Northern Virginia Community College

Masoud Naghedolfeizi
Fort Valley State University

Kevin Fishbeck
University of Mary

Judy Smith
University District of Columbia

Mary Williams
University of Akron

Lisa Cady
University of Arkansas - Fort Smith (UAFS)

Phyllis Hutson
Southern Arkansas University Tech

Madison Ngafeeson
Northern Michigan University

Mandy Reininger
Chemeketa Community College

Lennie Alice Cooper
Miami Dade College - North Campus

Robert Pavkovich
Fortis College

Augustine Brennan
Erie Community College South

Judy Paternite
Kent State University Geauga

Brian Bradley
College of DuPage

Wilma Andrews
Virginia Commonwealth University

Anna Fitzpatrick
Rowan College at Gloucester County
Abdul Sattar
Bridgewater State University
Annette Kerwin
College of DuPage
Carolyn Barren
Macomb Community College
Matthew Marie
Aquinas College
Michael C. Theiss
University of Wisconsin Colleges
Kimberly Campbell
Eastern Maine Community College
Kamiyar Maleky
American River College
Chris Cheske
Lakeshore Technical College
Teresa Ferguson
Seattle Vocational Institute
Candace S. Garrod
Red Rocks Community College
Amiya K. Samantray
Marygrove College
Alex Morgan
DeAnza College
Howard Divins
DuBois Business College
Reshma R. Tolani
Charter College
Melinda White
Seminole State College
Michelle Thompson
Hillsborough Community College
Roy Stewart
Harris-Stowe State University
Joan Butler
Manchester Community College
Gary Moore
Caldwell Community College and Technical Institute
Brian Downs
Century College
Mitch Pendleton
LDS Business College
Meg Stoner
Santa Rosa Junior College
Orletta E. Caldwell
Grand Rapids Community College
Julia Basham
Southern State Community College
Mary Ann Culbertson
Tarrant County College Northwest Campus
Michael Carrington
Northern Virginia Community College
Freddy Barton
Tampa Vocational Institute
Sandy Keeter
Seminole State College
Harold Gress, Jr.
Wilson College
Sujing Wang
Lamar University
Brent Nabors
Clovis Community College Center
Dennis Walpole
University of South Florida
LaToya Smith
Piedmont Community College
Kyu Lee
Saint Martin's University
Lacey Lormand
University of Louisiana at Lafayette
Rebecca Bullough
College of the Sequoias
Mark Vancleve
Terronez
Raj Parikh
Westwood College
Carolyn Carvalho
Kent State University

Gerry Young
Vance Granville Community College
Marie Hartlein
Montgomery County Community College
Doug Read
Ball State University
Marie Guest
North Florida Community College
Gloria Sabatelli
Butler County Community College
Rose Steimel
Kansas Wesleyan University
Ronald Johnson
Central Alabama Community College
Eddie Bannister
Keiser University-Pembroke Pines, FL
Gustavo Diaz
Broward College
Pamela Lewis
Wilson Community College
James Schaap
Grand Rapids Community College
Gregory Latterell
Alexandria Technical and Community College
David Lewis
Bryant and Stratton College
Pamela Van Nutt
American National University - Martinsville, VA
Cheryl Miller
Bay College
James Anderson
Bay College
Darryl Habeck
Milwaukee Area Technical College
Dorvin Froseth
United Tribes Technical College
Wade Graves
Grayson College
Brenda McFarland
Asheville-Buncombe Technical Community College
Cherie M. Stevens
South Florida State College
Sandra Tavegia
The Community College of Baltimore County
Robyn Barrett
St Louis Community College - Meramec
Sharon Breeding
Bluegrass Community and Technical College
Theodore Tielens
Mt. San Jacinto
Lynda Hodge
Guilford Technical Community College
James Graves
College of Southern Maryland
Mike Michaelson
Palomar College
Kristi Parker
Baptist Bible College
Cheri Broadway
Jacksonville University
Anna Tsipenyuk
LIM College
Pamela Silvers
Asheville-Buncombe Technical Community College
Clarence Stokes
American River College
Cheryl D. Green
Delgado Community College
Kenneth N. Bryant
Kentucky State University
James Cammack
Lamar State College Port Arthur
Bryan Moss
San Jacinto College
Becky McAfee
Hillsborough Community College
David Gomillion
Northern Michigan University
Steven Bale
Truckee Meadows Community College

Julie Craig
Scottsdale Community College
Ashley Harrier
Hillsborough Community College
Brian Fox
Santa Fe College
Alicen Flosi
Lamar University
Karl Smart
Central Michigan University
David Little
High Point University
Paula Gregory
Yavapai College
Gary Sorenson
Northwest Technical College, Bemidji
Linda Lau
Longwood University
Frank Clements
State College of Florida
Keith Hood
Indiana Purdue Fort Wayne
Timothy Ely
Harcum College
Deborah Sahrbeck
North Shore Community College, Danvers, MA
Barbara West
Central Georgia Technical College
Shondra Greene
Albany State University
Amy Giddens
Central Alabama Community College
Dishi Shrivastava
University of North Florida
Patricia Frederick
Del Mar College
Bill Hammerschlag
Brookhaven College
Vinzanna Leysath
Allen University
Robert Nichols
College of DuPage
Corrine Sweet
Darton State College
Michael Magro
Shenandoah University
Vijay K Agrawal
University of Nebraska at Kearney
Timothy Ely
Harcum College
Rosie L. Inwang
Olive-Harvey College
Milledge Mosby
Prince George's Community College
Michael Torguson
Rogue Community College
Linda Phelps
Northwest Arkansas Community College
Corey DeLaplain
Keiser University Online
Lisa Lopez
Southern Wesleyan University
John Marek
Houston Community College
Lori Krei
Iowa Lakes Community College
Sharon Sneed
Eastfield Community College
Michael C. Johnson
ACD Computer College
Ben Martz
Northern Kentucky University
Russ Dulaney
Rasmussen College
Linda Johnsonius
Murray State University
Ionie Pierce
LIM College
Jo Ann Koenig
Indiana University-Purdue University Indianapolis

James Reneau
Shawnee State University
Wanda Gibson
Consolidated School of Business
David Milazzo
Niagara County Community College
John S. Galliano
University of Maryland University College
Lee Janczak
Lackawanna College
Philip Raphan
Broward College North Campus
Larry Schulze
San Antonio College
David Easton
Waubonsee Community College
Doug Baker
Kent State University
Alanna Duley
College of Western Idaho
Helen Slack
Mahoning County Career and Technical Center
Carolyn Golden
Huston-Tillotson University
Terri Tiedeman
Southeast Community College
Edwin Harris
University of North Florida
Jeff Lehman
Huntington University
Aimee Durham
Rowan-Cabarrus Community College
Denise Askew
Rowan-Cabarrus Community College
Curby Simerson
Randolph Community College
Cindi Albrightson
Southwestern Oklahoma State University
Amanda Kaari
Central Georgia Tech
Ruben Ruiz
Morton College
Riza Marjadi
Murray State University
Annette Yauney
Herkimer Couny Community College
Donna Maxson
Lake Michigan College
Benjamin White
Bainbridge State College
Joy Flanders
Central Methodist University
Jill McCollum
Southern Arkansas University Tech
Sonya Sample
Greenville Technical College
Michelle Chappell
Henderson Community College
Shawn Brown
Ashland Community and Technical College
Sherry Cox
Broward College
Bonnie J. Tuggle-Ziglar
Brookstone College of Business
Fernando Wilches
Ana G. Mendez University System
Doreen Palucci
Wilmington University
Thomas Seeley
Urbana University
Victor Wotzkow
New Professions Technical Institute
Ahmed Kamel
Concordia College, Moorhead
Marie Campbell
Idaho State University-College of Technology
Sue McCrory
Missouri State University
Somone Washington
Broward College Online
Johnnie Nixon
King's College

Gloria Hensel
Matanuska-Susitna College University of Alaska Anchorage
Gary Cotton
American River College,
Kingsley Meyer
University of Rio Grande / Rio Grande Community College
Martha Merrill
Pellissippi State Community College
Olusade Ajayi
Germanna Community College
Pat Pettit
Millikin University
Mary Evens
Clark College
Michelle Masingill
North Idaho College
Mark Douglas
Our Lady of the Lake University
Rhonda Lucas
Spring Hill College
Anita Sutton
Germanna Community College
S. E. Beladi
Broward College
Ronda Thompson
Keene State College
Lyn Snyder
Owens Community College
Mark Connell
SUNY at Cortland

Guarionex Salivia
Minnesota State University
David Arevigian
Monroe County Community College
Verlan Erickson
Western Dakota Technical Institute
John Robinson
Cumberland County College
Allan Greenberg
New York University
Debra Adams
Mott Community College
Bobbie Hawkins
Southwest TN Community College
Nancy Stephens
Chemeketa Community College
Jeremy Harris
Evangel University
Kim Mangan
Manor College
Judith Scheeren
Westmoreland County Community College
Darrelyn Relyea
Grays Harbor College
Jay F. Miller
Union College, Barbourville
Deborah Franklin
Bryant and Stratton College
Nina Fontenot
South Louisiana Community College
Jim Speers
Southeastern Oklahoma State University

Jennifer Klenke
East Central College
Young Baek
Los Angeles City College
Carl Rebman
University of San Diego
Shelly Knittle
Alaska Career College
Natunya Johnson
Holmes Community College
Linda Lemley
Pensacola State College
Ranida Harris
Indiana University Southeast
Kelly Young
Lander University
Karin Stulz
Northern Michigan University
Cathie Phillips
Lamar State College-Orange
James Brown
Central Washington University
H. Roger Fulk
Rhodes State College
Dan Britton
Chemeketa Community College
Olivia Kerr
El Centro College
Michelle Dawson
Missouri Southern State University
Dianne Hargrove
College of Health Care Professions

Shannon Shoemaker
SUNY Delhi
Bruce Caraway
Lone Star College - University Park
Richard DiRose
Hillsborough Community College - South Shore

TECHNICAL EDITORS

Karen May
Blinn College
Andrea Nevill
College of Western Idaho
Richard Finn
Moraine Valley Community College
Chris Anderson
North Central Michigan College
Gena Casas
Florida State College
Leon Blue
Pensacola State College
Mary Carole Hollingsworth
Georgia Perimeter College
Amie Mayhall
Olney Central College
Julie Haar
Alexandria Technical and Community College
Diane Santurri
Johnson & Wales University
Ramona Santa Maria
Buffalo State College

Thank you to the wonderful team at McGraw-Hill for your confidence in us and support throughout this project. Alan, Wyatt, Tiffany, Debbie, Rick, and Julianna, we thoroughly enjoy working with you all! A special thanks to Debbie Hinkle for her thorough and insightful review of the series. Thank you also to Laurie Zouharis, Amie Mayhall, Sarah Clifford, Rebecca Leveille, Jane Holcombe, and all of the reviewers and technical editors for your expertise and invaluable insight, which helped shape this book.

—Randy

Windows 10, Office 2016, and File Management

CHAPTER OVERVIEW

Microsoft Office 2016 and Windows 10 introduce many new features, including cloud storage for your files, Office file sharing, and enhanced online content. The integration of Office 2016 and Windows 10 means that files are more portable and accessible than ever when you use *OneDrive*, Microsoft's free online cloud storage. The new user interface for Office 2016 and Windows 10 allows you to work on tablet computers and smartphones in a consistent working environment that resembles that of your desktop or laptop computer.

STUDENT LEARNING OUTCOMES (SLOs)

After completing this chapter, you will be able to:

SLO Intro.1 Explore the features of Windows 10 (p. OI-2).

SLO Intro.2 Use the basic features of Office 2016 and navigate the Office 2016 working environment (p. OI-10).

SLO Intro.3 Create, save, close, and open Office files (p. OI-17).

SLO Intro.4 Customize the view and display size in Office applications and work with multiple Office files (p. OI-25).

SLO Intro.5 Print, share, and customize Office files (p. OI-28).

SLO Intro.6 Use the *Ribbon*, tabs, groups, dialog boxes, task panes, galleries, and the *Quick Access* toolbar (p. OI-33).

SLO Intro.7 Use context menus, mini toolbars, keyboard shortcuts, and function keys in Office applications (p. OI-37).

SLO Intro.8 Organize and customize Windows folders and Office files (p. OI-42).

CASE STUDY

Throughout this book you have the opportunity to put into practice the application features that you are learning. Each chapter begins with a case study that introduces you to the Pause & Practice projects in the chapter. These Pause & Practice projects give you a chance to apply and practice key skills in a realistic and practical context. Each chapter contains three to five Pause & Practice projects.

American River Cycling Club (ARCC) is a community cycling club that promotes fitness. ARCC members include recreational cyclists who enjoy the exercise and camaraderie as well as competitive cyclists who compete in road, mountain, and cyclocross races throughout the cycling season. In the Pause & Practice projects, you incorporate many of the topics covered in the chapter to create, save, customize, manage, and share Office 2016 files.

OI-1

Pause & Practice Intro-1: Customize the Windows *Start* menu and *Taskbar*, create and save a PowerPoint presentation, create a folder, open and rename an Excel workbook, and use Windows 10 features.

Pause & Practice Intro-2: Modify the existing document, add document properties, customize the Quick Access toolbar, export the document as a PDF file, and share the document.

Pause & Practice Intro-3: Copy and rename files, create a folder, move files, create a zipped folder, and rename a zipped folder.

SLO INTRO. 1

Using Windows 10

Windows 10 is the ***operating system*** that controls computer functions and the working environment. Windows 10 uses the familiar ***Windows desktop***, ***Taskbar***, and ***Start menu***, and you can customize the working environment. You can install traditional applications (***apps***), such as Microsoft Office, to your computer. Also, you can add modern apps from the Microsoft Store similar to how you add an app to your smartphone. Your ***Microsoft account*** is used to store your Microsoft settings, download apps from the Microsoft Store, and connect you to Microsoft Office, *OneDrive*, and *Office Online*.

Windows 10

The Windows 10 operating system controls interaction with computer hardware and software applications. ***Windows 10*** has a revised user interface that utilizes an updated ***Start menu***, where you can select and open a program. Alternatively, you can use the *Taskbar* on the Windows desktop, which has the familiar look of previous versions of Windows. When you log in to Windows 10 using your Microsoft account, it synchronizes your Windows, Office, and ***OneDrive*** cloud storage among computers.

Microsoft Account

In Windows 10 and Office 2016, your files and account settings are portable. In other words, your Office settings and files can travel with you and be accessed from different computers. You are not restricted to a single computer. When you sign in to Windows 10 using your Microsoft account (user name and password), Microsoft uses this information to transfer your Windows and Office 2016 settings to the computer you are

Intro-1 Create a Microsoft account

using. Your Microsoft account not only signs you in to Windows and Office but also to other free Microsoft online services, such as *OneDrive* and ***Office Online***. If you don't have a Microsoft account, you can create a free account at https://signup.live.com (Figure Intro-1).

Windows Desktop and Taskbar

The Windows desktop is the working area of Windows. When you log in to Windows, the desktop displays (Figure Intro-2). The *Taskbar* displays at the bottom of the desktop. You can open programs and folders from the *Taskbar* by clicking on an icon on the *Taskbar* (see Figure Intro-2). You can pin apps and other Windows items, such as the *Control Panel* or *File Explorer*, to the *Taskbar* (see "Customize the Taskbar" later in this section).

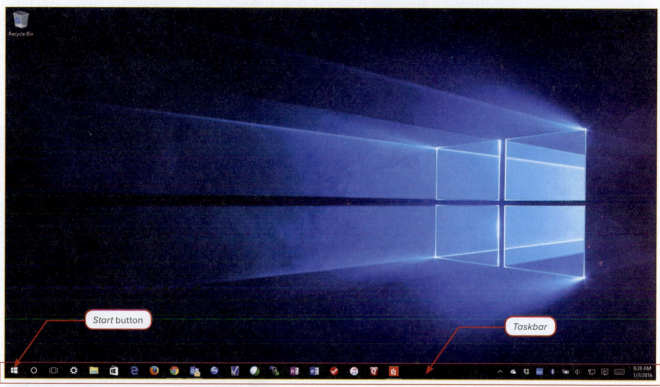

Intro-2 Windows desktop and *Taskbar*

Intro-3 Windows *Start* menu

Start Menu

Windows 10 utilizes a redesigned *Start* menu (Figure Intro-3), that you open by clicking the **Start button** located in the bottom left of the *Taskbar*. From the *Start* menu, you can open programs, files, folders, or other Windows resources. The *Start* menu is divided into two main sections. The left side of the *Start* menu displays **Most Used** items, buttons to open the **File Explorer** and **Settings** windows, the **Power** button, and **All apps**, which displays an alphabetical listing of all applications installed on your computer. The right side of the *Start* menu displays apps as tiles (large and small buttons) you can click to open an application or window.

You can customize which apps and items appear on either side of the *Start* menu, arrange and group apps on the *Start* menu, resize the *Start* menu, and display the *Start* menu as a **Start page** when you log in to Windows (similar to the *Start* page in Windows 8 and 8.1). See "Customize the Start Menu" later in this section for information about customizing the *Start* menu.

Add Apps

Windows 10 uses the term *apps* generically to refer to applications and programs. Apps include the Windows 10 Weather app, Microsoft Excel program, Control Panel, Google Chrome, or *File Explorer*. Many apps are preinstalled on a Windows 10 computer, and you can add apps to your computer. You can install an app such as Office 2016 or Quicken by downloading it from a web site or from a program DVD. These are referred to as ***traditional apps***.

The ***Microsoft Store*** app is preinstalled on Windows 10 computers. You can also install apps such as Netflix, Trip Advisor, and The Weather Channel from the Microsoft Store. These apps are referred to as ***modern apps*** and look and function similar to apps you install on your smartphone. Many apps in the Microsoft Store are free and others are available for purchase.

▶HOW TO: Add an App from the Microsoft Store

1. Click the **Start** button to open the *Start* menu.
2. Click the **Store** button (tile) to open the Microsoft Store app (Figure Intro-4).
   - If the *Store* tile is not available on the *Start* menu, click **All apps** on the *Start* menu, scroll down, and click **Store** in the alphabetic listing of all apps.
3. Select an app in the Microsoft Store (Figure Intro-5).
   - The Microsoft Store has different categories of apps.
   - You can search for apps by typing key words in the *Search* box in the upper right.
   - When you select an app, a description and screen shots of the app displays.
4. Click the **Free**, **Free trial**, or price button to install the app.
   - You must have a payment method stored in your Microsoft account to purchase apps from the Microsoft Store.
5. Click **Open** to open the installed app.
   - When you install an app, the app is listed in the *Recently added* area on the *Start* menu and *All apps* list of applications.

Intro-4 *Store* button on the *Start* menu

Customize the Start Menu

When you start using Windows 10 or after you have installed either traditional or modern apps, you can customize what appears on your *Start* menu and resize the *Start*

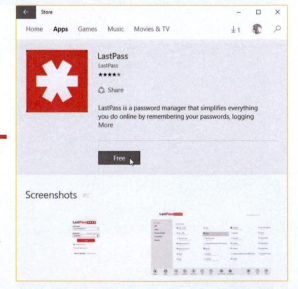

Intro-5 Install an app from the Microsoft Store

menu. When you *pin* an app to the *Start* menu, the app tile remains on the right side of the *Start* menu. Pin the apps you most regularly use, unpin the apps you don't want to display on the *Start* menu, and rearrange and resize apps tiles to your preference.

▶**HOW TO:** Customize the Start Menu

1. Move an app tile by clicking and dragging the app tile to a new location on the *Start* menu. The other app tiles shuffle to accommodate the placement of the app tile.

2. Remove an app tile from the *Start* menu by right-clicking the app tile you want to remove and selecting **Unpin from Start** from the context menu (Figure Intro-6).

   • The app tile is removed from the *Start* menu, but the program or task is not removed from your computer.

Intro-6 Unpin an app from the *Start* menu

3. Pin an app tile to the *Start* menu by clicking **All apps** at the bottom of the *Start* menu, right-clicking the app to pin, and selecting **Pin to Start** (Figure Intro-7).

   • Drag the newly added app tile to the desired location on the Start menu.

Intro-7 Pin an app to the *Start* menu

4. Resize an app tile by right-clicking the app tile, selecting **Resize**, and selecting **Small**, **Medium**, **Wide**, or **Large**.

   • Some apps only have *Small*, *Medium*, and *Wide* size options.

5. Turn on or off the live tile option by right-clicking the app tile and selecting **Turn live tile on** or **Turn live tile off**.

   • Live tile displays rotating graphics and options on the app tile. When this option is turned off, the name of the app displays on the tile.

6. Uninstall an app by right-clicking the app you want to uninstall and selecting **Uninstall**.

   • Unlike the unpin option, this option uninstalls the program from your computer, not just your *Start* menu.

7. Resize the *Start* menu by clicking and dragging the top or right edge of the *Start* menu.

8. Use a full screen *Start* menu by clicking the **Start** button to open the *Start* menu, selecting **Settings** to open the *Settings* window, clicking the **Personalization** button, clicking the **Start** option at the left, selecting **Use Start full screen**, and clicking the **X** in the upper right to close the *Settings* window (Figure Intro-8).

   • The *Start* menu expands to the full screen when opened.

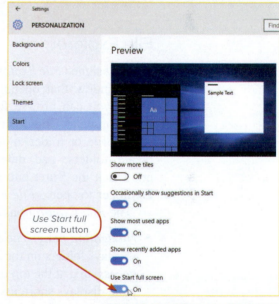

Intro-8 Use full screen *Start* menu

Customize the Taskbar

The *Taskbar* is located at the bottom of the Windows desktop, and you can quickly open an app by clicking a button on the *Taskbar* rather than opening it from the *Start* menu. You can customize the *Taskbar* by pinning, unpinning, and rearranging apps on the *Taskbar*.

▶HOW TO: Customize the Taskbar

1. Pin an app to the *Taskbar* by clicking the *Start* menu, right-clicking an app, clicking **More**, and selecting **Pin to taskbar** (Figure Intro-9).
   - You can also pin an app to the *Taskbar* from the *All apps* list in the *Start* menu.
2. Unpin an app from the *Taskbar* by right-clicking an app on the *Taskbar*, and selecting **Unpin from taskbar** (Figure Intro-10).
   - You can also unpin apps from the *Taskbar* by right-clicking the app in the *Start* menu, clicking **More**, and selecting **Unpin from taskbar**.
3. Rearrange apps on the *Taskbar* by clicking and dragging the app to the desired location on the *Taskbar* and release.

Intro-9 Pin an app to the *Taskbar*

Intro-10 Unpin an app from the *Taskbar*

> ▶ **MORE INFO**
>
> If using a touch screen, you can press and hold an app on the *Start* menu or *Taskbar* to display the app options.

File Explorer

The redesigned *File Explorer* in Windows 10 is a window that opens on your desktop where you can browse for files stored on your computer (Figure Intro-11). You can open a file or folder, move or copy items, create folders, and delete files or folders. Click the **Start** button and select **File Explorer** to open a *File Explorer* window.

The *File Explorer* has different areas:

- **Navigation pane**: The *Navigation* pane displays folders on the left. The **Quick access** area at the top of the *Navigation* pane displays shortcuts to favorite folders. You can pin or unpin folders in the *Quick access* area of the *Navigation* pane.

Intro-11 *File Explorer* window

- **Navigation buttons**: The navigation buttons (*Back*, *Forward*, *Recent location*, and *Up*) are located directly above the *Navigation* pane and below the *Ribbon*. Use these buttons to navigate a File Explorer window.
- **Folder pane**: When you select a folder in the *Navigation* pane, the contents of the folder displays in the *Folder* pane to the right of the *Navigation* pane. Double-click a folder or file in the *Folder* pane to open it.
- **Ribbon**: The *Ribbon* at the top of the *File Explorer* is collapsed by default. When you click a tab on the *Ribbon*, it expands to display the options on the tab. The main tabs of

the *Ribbon* are **File**, **Home**, **Share**, and **View**. Other context-sensitive tabs open when you select certain types of files. For example, the *Picture Tool Manage* tab opens when you select a picture file.

- **Quick Access toolbar**: The *Quick Access* toolbar is above the *Ribbon*. From the *Quick Access* toolbar, you can click the **New Folder** button to create a new folder or **Properties** to display the properties of a selected file or folder. You can add buttons, such as *Rename*, to the *Quick Access* toolbar.
- **Search**: The *Search* text box is located on the right of the *File Explorer* window below the *Ribbon*. Type key words in the *Search* text box to find files or folders.

OneDrive

OneDrive is a cloud storage area where you can store files in a private and secure online location that you can access from any computer. When you store your files in *OneDrive*, the files are actually saved on both your computer and on the cloud. *OneDrive* synchronizes your files so when you change a file it is automatically updated on the *OneDrive* cloud.

With Windows 10, the **OneDrive folder** is one of your storage location folder options, similar to your *Documents* or *Pictures* folders (Figure Intro-12). You can save, open, and edit your *OneDrive* files from a *File Explorer*
folder. Your *OneDrive* folder looks and functions similar to other Windows folders.

In addition to the *OneDrive* folder on your computer, you can also access your *OneDrive* files online using an Internet browser such as Microsoft Edge, Google Chrome, or Mozilla Firefox. When you access *OneDrive* online using a web browser, you can upload files, create folders, move and copy files and folders, and create Office files using *Office Online* (*Office Online* is discussed in *SLO Intro.2: Using Office 2016*).

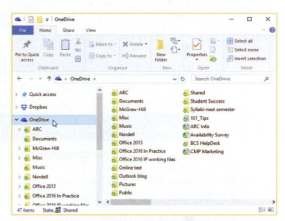

Intro-12 *OneDrive* folder in a *File Explorer* window

▶**HOW TO:** Use OneDrive Online

1. Open an Internet browser window and navigate to the *OneDrive* web site (www.onedrive.live.com), which takes you to the *OneDrive* sign in page.
   - You can use any Internet browser to access *OneDrive* (Microsoft Edge, Google Chrome, Mozilla Firefox).
2. Click the **Sign in** button, type your Microsoft account email address, and click **Next**.
3. Type your Microsoft account password and click **Sign in** (Figure Intro-13). You are taken to your *OneDrive* page.
   - If you are on your own computer, check the **Keep me signed in** box to stay signed in to *OneDrive* when you return to the page.

Intro-13 Log in to *OneDrive* online

- The different areas of *OneDrive* are listed under the *OneDrive* heading on the left (Figure Intro-14).
- Click **Files** to display your folders and files in the folder area.
- At the top of the page, buttons and drop-down menus list the different actions you can perform on selected files and folders.

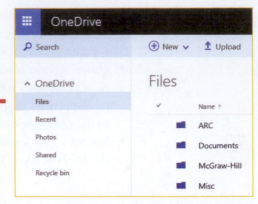

Intro-14 *OneDrive* online environment

Cortana

In addition to using the search tools in the *File Explorer*, you can also use **Cortana**, which is new in Windows 10. While the search feature in the *File Explorer* searches only for content on your computer, *Cortana* searches for content on your computer, on the Internet, and in the Microsoft Store. You can either type key words for a search or use voice commands to search for content.

When you open *Cortana*, other content, such as weather, upcoming appointments, and popular news stories, displays in the *Cortana* pane.

▶HOW TO: Search Using Cortana

1. Click the **Cortana** button on the *Taskbar* to open the *Cortana* pane (Figure Intro-15).

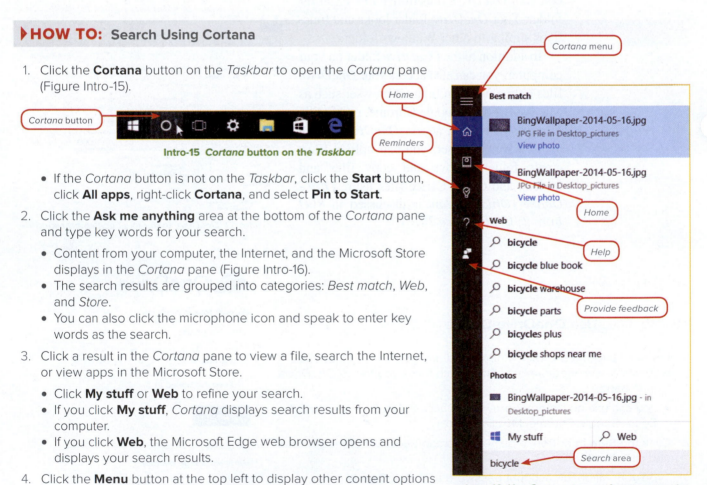

Intro-15 *Cortana* button on the *Taskbar*

- If the *Cortana* button is not on the *Taskbar*, click the **Start** button, click **All apps**, right-click **Cortana**, and select **Pin to Start**.

2. Click the **Ask me anything** area at the bottom of the *Cortana* pane and type key words for your search.

- Content from your computer, the Internet, and the Microsoft Store displays in the *Cortana* pane (Figure Intro-16).
- The search results are grouped into categories: *Best match*, *Web*, and *Store*.
- You can also click the microphone icon and speak to enter key words as the search.

3. Click a result in the *Cortana* pane to view a file, search the Internet, or view apps in the Microsoft Store.

- Click **My stuff** or **Web** to refine your search.
- If you click **My stuff**, *Cortana* displays search results from your computer.
- If you click **Web**, the Microsoft Edge web browser opens and displays your search results.

4. Click the **Menu** button at the top left to display other content options in the *Cortana* pane (see Figure Intro-16).

- The other content options are *Home*, *Notebook*, *Reminders*, *Help*, and *Feedback*.

Intro-16 Use *Cortana* to search your computer, the Internet, and the Microsoft Store

Task View

A new feature to Windows 10 is *Task View*. *Task View* displays all open apps and windows as tiles on your desktop, and you can choose which item to display or close. This feature is very helpful when you have multiple items open and want to select or close one.

Intro-17 *Task View* button on the *Taskbar*

▶**HOW TO:** Use Task View

1. Click the **Task View** button on the *Taskbar* (Figure Intro-17).
   - All open apps and windows display on the desktop (Figure Intro-18).

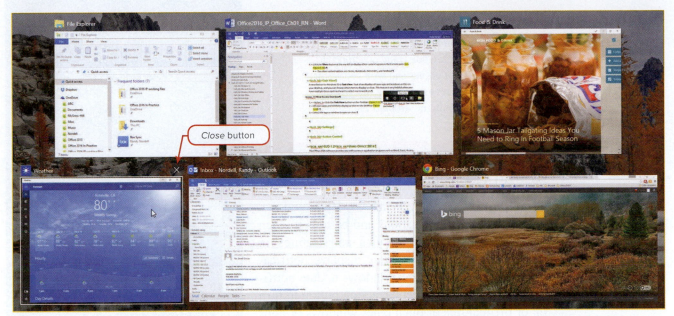

Intro-18 *Task View* with open apps and windows displayed on the desktop

2. Select the app or window to open or close.
   - Click a tile to open an app. The app opens and *Task View* closes.
   - Click the **X** in the upper right corner of an app to close an app. *Task View* remains open when you close an app.

Settings

In Windows 10, the *Settings* window is the redesigned *Control Panel* (although the *Control Panel* is still available). The *Settings* window is where you change global Windows settings, customize the Windows environment, add devices, and manage your Microsoft account. Click the **Settings** button on the *Taskbar* or *Start* menu to open the *Settings* window (Figure Intro-19). The following categories are available in the *Settings* window:

Intro-19 *Settings* window

- **System**: Display, notifications, apps, and power
- **Devices**: Bluetooth, printers, and mouse
- **Network & Internet**: Wi-Fi, airplane mode, and VPN
- **Personalization**: Background, lock screen, and colors
- **Accounts**: Your account, sync settings, work, and family
- **Time & Language**: Speech, region, and date
- **Ease of Access**: Narrator, magnifier, and high contrast
- **Privacy**: Location and camera
- **Update & Security**: Windows Update, recovery, and backup

> ### ▶ MORE INFO
>
> If you can't find an item in *Settings*, use the *Search* dialog box (*Find a setting*) in the upper right corner and type key words. If *Settings* is not available on the *Taskbar*, you can find it in the *All apps* list on the *Start* menu.

Action Center

The **Action Center** in Windows 10 provides a quick glance of notifications and buttons to open other commonly used settings and features in Windows. The *Action Center* displays notifications such as emails and Windows update notifications. Or you can click an action button to turn on or off features or open other windows or apps such as the *Settings* menu (*All Settings* button) or OneNote (*Note* button). Click the **Action Center** button on the right side of the *Taskbar* to open the *Action Center* pane on the right side of your screen (Figure Intro-20).

Intro-20 *Action Center*

Using Office 2016

Office 2016 includes common software applications such as Word, Excel, Access, and PowerPoint. These applications give you the ability to work with word processing documents, spreadsheets, presentations, and databases in your personal and business projects.

Office 2016 and Office 365

Microsoft Office is a suite of personal and business software applications (Figure Intro-21). **Microsoft Office 2016** and **Microsoft Office 365** are the same software products; the difference is how you purchase the software. Office 2016 is

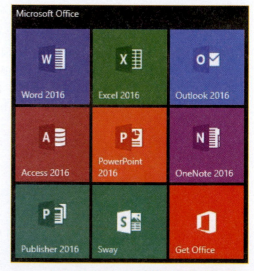

Intro-21 **Microsoft Office application tiles on the *Start* menu**

the traditional model of purchasing the software, and you own that software for as long as you want to use it. Office 365 is a subscription that you pay monthly or yearly, similar to how you purchase Netflix or Spotify. If you subscribe to Office 365, you automatically receive new versions of the software when they are released.

The common applications typically included in Microsoft Office 2016 and 365 are described in the following list:

- *Microsoft Word*: Word processing software used to create, format, and edit documents such as reports, letters, brochures, and resumes.
- *Microsoft Excel*: Spreadsheet software used to perform calculations on numerical data such as financial statements, budgets, and expense reports.
- *Microsoft Access*: Database software used to store, organize, compile, and report information such as product information, sales data, client information, and employee records.
- *Microsoft PowerPoint*: Presentation software used to graphically present information in slides such as a presentation on a new product or sales trends.
- *Microsoft Outlook*: Email and personal management software used to create and send email and create and store calendar items, contacts, and tasks.
- *Microsoft OneNote*: Note-taking software used to take and organize notes, which can be shared with other Office applications.
- *Microsoft Publisher*: Desktop publishing software used to create professional-looking documents containing text, pictures, and graphics such as catalogs, brochures, and flyers.

Office Desktop Apps, Office Universal Apps, and Office Online

Office desktop apps are the full-function Office 2016 or 365 programs installed on your computer (PC or Mac). Both Office 2016 and Office 365 are considered Office desktop apps. Because of the increased popularity and capabilities of tablets and mobile devices, Office software is also available for both tablets and smartphones. *Office universal apps* are the Office 365 programs that can be installed on tablets or other mobile devices. Office universal apps do not have the full range of advanced features available in Office desktop applications, but Office universal apps provide users the ability to create, edit, save, and share Office files using many of the most common features in the Office suite of programs.

> **MORE INFO**
>
> Office universal apps are also referred to as *Office mobile apps*.

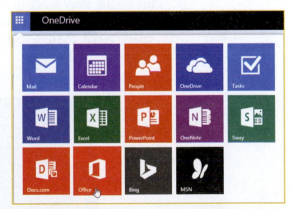

Intro-22 *Office Online*

Office Online is free online software from Microsoft that works in conjunction with your Microsoft account and *OneDrive* (Figure Intro-22). With *Office Online*, you can work with Office files online through a web browser, even on computers that do not have Office 2016 or 365 installed. This is a useful option when you use a computer at a computer lab or use a friend's computer that does not have Office installed.

You can access *Office Online* from your *OneDrive* web page to create and edit Word documents, Excel workbooks, PowerPoint presentations, and OneNote notebooks. *Office Online* is a scaled-down version of Office 2016/365 and not as robust in terms of features, but you can use it to create, edit, print, share, and collaborate on files. If you need more advanced features, you can open *Office Online* files in Office 2016.

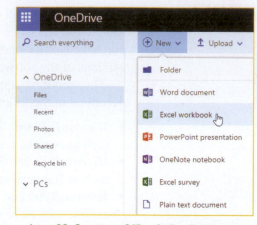

▶ **HOW TO:** Create an Office Online File

1. Open an Internet browser Window, navigate to the *OneDrive* web site (www.onedrive.live.com), and log in to *OneDrive*. If you are not already logged in to *OneDrive*, use the following steps.

   - Click the **Sign in** button, type your Microsoft account email address, and click **Next**.
   - Type your Microsoft account password and click **Sign in** to open your *OneDrive* page.

2. Click the **New** button and select the type of *Office Online* file to create (Figure Intro-23).

   - A new file is created and opens in the *Office Online* program.
   - The new file is saved in your *OneDrive* folder (both online and on your computer).

Intro-23 Create an Office Online file from your online *OneDrive* page

3. Rename the file by clicking on the file name at the top of the file, typing a new file name, and pressing **Enter** (Figure Intro-24).

   - You can also click the **File** tab to open the *Backstage* view, select *Save As*, and choose **Save As** or **Rename**.
   - Click the **OPEN IN [OFFICE APPLICATION]** button (for example **OPEN IN EXCEL**) to open the file in the Office desktop application (see Figure Intro-24).

4. Close the browser tab or window to close the file.

   - *Office Online* automatically saves the file as you make changes.

Intro-24 Rename an *Office Online* file

Open an Office Desktop Application

When using Windows 10, you open an Office desktop application by clicking the application tile on the *Start* menu or the application icon on the *Taskbar*. If your *Start* menu and *Taskbar* do not have the Office applications displayed, click the **Start** button, select **All apps**, and select **Word 2016**, **Excel 2016**, **Access 2016**, or **PowerPoint 2016** to launch the application (Figure Intro-25).

You can also use *Cortana* to quickly locate an Office desktop app (Figure Intro-26).

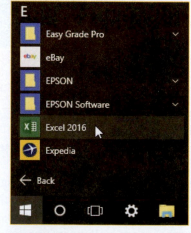

Intro-25 Open an Office desktop app from the *All apps* area on the *Start* menu

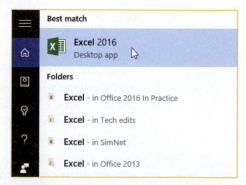

Intro-26 Use *Cortana* to find and open an app

Office Start Page

Most of the Office applications (except Outlook and OneNote) display a ***Start page*** when you launch the application (Figure Intro-27). From this *Start* page, you can create a new blank file (for example a Word document, an Excel workbook, an Access database, or a PowerPoint presentation), create a file from an online template, search for an online template, open a recently used file, or open another file. These options vary depending on the Office application.

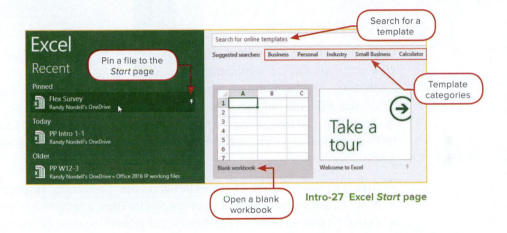

Intro-27 Excel *Start* page

▶ **HOW TO:** Use the Office Start Page

1. Open a file listed in the *Recent* area on the left side of the *Start* menu by clicking the file to open. The file opens in the working area of the Office application.

   - The *Recent* area on the left side of the *Start* page lists files you have recently used and files that are pinned to the *Start* page.

2. Open a new blank file by clicking the **Blank [*file type*]** tile (*Blank workbook*, *Blank document*, etc.) to the right of the *Recent* area.

   - You can also press the **Esc** key to exit the *Start* page and open a new blank file.

3. Open an existing file that is not listed in the *Recent* area by clicking the **Open Other Workbooks** link (Figure Intro-28). The *Open* area on the *Backstage* view displays.

   - Click the **Browse** button to open the *Open* dialog box where you can locate and open a file.
   - You can also select a different location, *OneDrive* or *This PC*, and select a file to open.

4. Open a template by clicking a template file on the right or searching for templates.

   - Search for a template by typing key words in the *Search* area on the *Start* page.
   - Click a link to one of the categories below the *Search* area to display templates in that category.

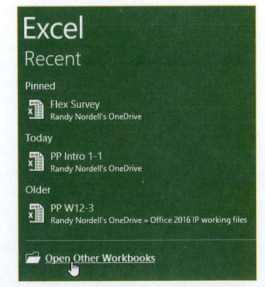

Intro-28 *Open Other Workbooks* link on the *Start* page

5. Pin a frequently used file to the *Start* page by clicking the **Pin** button.
   - The *Pin* button is on the right side of items listed in the *Recent* area and at the bottom right of templates displayed in the *Templates* area (to the right of the *Recent* area).
   - Pinned files display at the top of the *Recent* area.

Backstage View

Office incorporates the ***Backstage view*** into all Office applications (including *Office Online* apps). Click the **File** tab on the *Ribbon* to open the *Backstage* view (Figure Intro-29). *Backstage* options vary on the different Office applications. The following list describes common tasks you can perform from the *Backstage* view:

- ***Info***: Displays document properties and other protection, inspection, and version options.
- ***New***: Creates a new blank file or a new file from a template or theme.
- ***Open***: Opens an existing file from a designated location or a recently opened file.
- ***Save***: Saves a file. If the file has not been named, the *Save As* dialog box opens when you select this option.
- ***Save As***: Opens the *Save As* dialog box.
- ***Print***: Prints a file, displays a preview of the file, or displays print options.
- ***Share***: Invites people to share a file or email a file.
- ***Export***: Creates a PDF file from a file or saves as a different file type.
- ***Close***: Closes an open file.
- ***Account***: Displays your Microsoft account information.
- ***Options***: Opens the *[Application] Options* dialog box (for example *Excel Options*).

Office Help—Tell Me

In all the Office 2016/365 applications, ***Tell Me*** is the new help feature (Figure Intro-30). This new help feature displays the commands in the Office application related to your search. The *Help* feature in older versions of Office displayed articles describing the feature and how to use it. The new *Tell Me* feature provides command options that take you directly to a command or dialog box. For example if you type *PivotTable* in the *Tell Me* search box in Excel, the results include the option to open the *Create PivotTable* dialog box, as well as other options such as *Recommended PivotTables* and *Summarize with PivotTable*.

▶HOW TO: Use Tell Me

1. Place your insertion point in the **Tell Me** search box at the top of the *Ribbon* (see Figure Intro-30).

2. Type key words for the command or feature for which you are searching.

3. Select an option from the list of displayed search results (Figure Intro-31).

   • When you select a search result, it may apply a command, open a dialog box, or display a gallery of command choices.

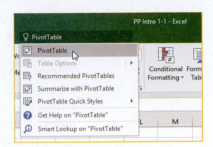

Intro-31 *Tell Me* search results

Mouse and Pointers

If you are using Office on a desktop or laptop computer, use your mouse (or touch pad) to navigate around files, click tabs and buttons, select text and objects, move text and objects, and resize objects. The following table lists mouse and pointer terminology used in Office:

Mouse and Pointer Terminology

Term	Description
Pointer	When you move your mouse, the pointer moves on your screen. A variety of pointers are used in different contexts in Office applications. The following pointers are available in most of the Office applications (the appearance of these pointers varies depending on the application and the context used): • **Selection pointer:** Select text or an object. • **Move pointer:** Move text or an object. • **Copy pointer:** Copy text or an object. • **Resize pointer:** Resize objects or table columns or rows. • **Crosshair:** Draw a shape.
Insertion point	The vertical flashing line indicating where you type text in a file or text box. Click the left mouse button to position the insertion point.
Click	Click the left mouse button. Used to select an object or button or to place the insertion point in the selected location.
Double-click	Click the left mouse button twice. Used to select text.
Right-click	Click the right mouse button. Used to display the context menu and the mini toolbar.
Scroll	Use the scroll wheel on the mouse to scroll up and down through your file. You can also use the horizontal or vertical scroll bars at the bottom and right of an Office file window to move around in a file.

Touch Mode and Touch Screen Gestures

The new user interface in Windows 10 and Office 2016 has improved touch features to facilitate the use of Windows and the Office applications on a tablet computer or smartphone. On tablets and smartphones, you use a touch screen rather than using a mouse, so the process of selecting text and objects and navigating around a file is different from a computer without a touch screen.

In Office 2016/365, **Touch mode** optimizes the Office working environment when using a computer with a touch screen to provide more space between buttons and commands. Click the **Touch/Mouse Mode** button on the *Quick Access* toolbar (upper left of the Office app window) and select **Touch** from the drop-down list to enable *Touch* mode (Figure Intro-32). To turn off *Touch* mode, select **Mouse** from the *Touch/Mouse Mode* drop-down list.

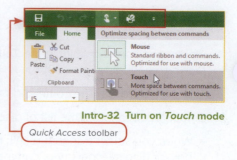

Intro-32 Turn on *Touch* mode

MORE INFO

The *Touch/Mouse Mode* button displays on the *Quick Access* toolbar when using a touch-screen computer.

The following table lists common gestures used when working on a tablet or smartphone (these gestures vary depending on the application used and the context):

Touch Screen Gestures

Gesture	Used To	How To
Tap	Select text or an object or position the insertion point. Double tap to edit text in an object or cell.	
Pinch	Zoom in or resize an object.	
Stretch	Zoom out or resize an object.	
Slide	Move an object or selected text.	
Swipe	Select text or multiple objects.	

MORE INFO

Window 10 has a **Tablet mode** that optimizes all of Windows and apps for touch screens. When you turn on the *Tablet mode* feature in Windows, the *Touch mode* in Office apps turns on automatically. Click the **Action Center** button on the Windows *Taskbar* and click the **Tablet mode** button to turn on this feature in Windows.

Creating, Saving, Closing, and Opening Files

Creating, saving, opening, and closing files is primarily done from the *Start* page or *Backstage* view of the Office application you are using. These areas provide you with many options and a central location to perform these tasks. You can also use shortcut commands to create, save, and open files.

Create a New File

When you create a new file in an Office application, you can create a new blank file or a new file based on a template (in PowerPoint, you can also create a presentation based on a theme). On the *Start* page, click **Blank [file type]** to create a new blank file in the application you are using (in Word, you begin with a blank document; in Excel, a blank workbook; in Access, a blank desktop database; and in PowerPoint, a blank presentation).

> ▶ **HOW TO:** Create a New File from the Start Page

1. Open the Office application you want to use. The *Start* page displays when the application opens (Figure Intro-33).

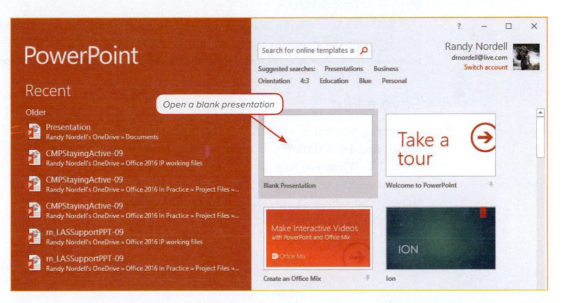

Intro-33 *Start* page in PowerPoint

2. Click **Blank [file type]** or select a template or theme to use for your new blank file. A new file opens in the application you are using.

   - The new file is given a generic file name (for example *Document1, Book1,* or *Presentation1*). You can name and save this file later.
   - When creating a new Access database, you are prompted to name the new file when you create it.
   - A variety of templates (and themes in PowerPoint only) display on the *Start* page, but you can search for additional online templates and themes using the *Search* text box at the top of the *Start* page.

> ▶ **MORE INFO**
>
> **Esc** closes the *Start* page and takes you into the Office application (except in Access).

If you have been using an application already and want to create a new file, you create it from the *Backstage* view. From the *Backstage* view, the new file options are available in the *New* area.

▶ **HOW TO:** Create a New File from the Backstage View

1. Click the **File** tab to display the *Backstage* view.
2. Select **New** on the left to display the *New* area (Figure Intro-34).
3. Click **Blank [file type]** or select a template or theme to use in your new blank file. A new file opens in the application.
   - The new file is given a generic file name (*Document1*, *Book1*, or *Presentation1*). You can name and save this file later.
   - When you are creating a new Access database, you are prompted to name the new file when you create it.

Intro-34 *New* area on the *Backstage* view in PowerPoint

▶ **ANOTHER WAY**

Ctrl+N opens a new file from within an Office application. In Access, **Ctrl+N** opens the *New* area in the *Backstage* view.

Save a File

In Access, you name a file as you create it, but in Word, Excel, and PowerPoint, you name a file after you have created it. When you save a file, you type a name for the file and select the location to save the file. You can save a file on your computer, an online storage location such as *OneDrive*, or portable device, such as a USB drive.

Click *Browse* to open the *Save* As dialog box

Intro-35 *Save As* area on the *Backstage* view in PowerPoint

▶ **HOW TO:** Save a File

1. Click the **File** tab to display the *Backstage* view.
2. Select **Save** or **Save As** on the left to display the *Save As* area (Figure Intro-35).
   - If the file has not already been saved, clicking *Save* or *Save As* takes you to the *Save As* area on the *Backstage* view.
3. Click the **Browse** button to open the *Save As* dialog box (Figure Intro-36).
   - You can also select a different location (*OneDrive* or *This PC*) and select a folder from the list of folders at the right to open the *Save As* dialog box.
4. Select a location to save the file in the *Folder* list on the left.

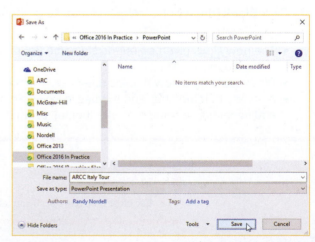

Intro-36 *Save As* dialog box

5. Type a name for the file in the *File name* area.
    • By default, Office selects the file type, but you can change the file type from the *Save as type* drop-down list.
6. Click **Save** to close the dialog box and save the file.

Create a New Folder When Saving a File

When saving files, it is a good idea to create folders to organize your files. Organizing your files in folders makes it easier to find your files and saves you time when you are searching for a specific file (see *SLO Intro.8: Organizing and Customizing Folders and Files* for more information on this topic). When you save an Office file, you can also create a folder in which to store that file.

▶**HOW TO:** **Create a New Folder When Saving a File**

1. Click the **File** tab to display the *Backstage* view.
2. Select **Save As** on the left to display the *Save As* area.
3. Click **Browse** to open the *Save As* dialog box.
4. Select a location to save the file in the *Folder* list on the left.
5. Click the **New Folder** button to create a new folder (Figure Intro-37).
6. Type a name for the new folder and press **Enter**.

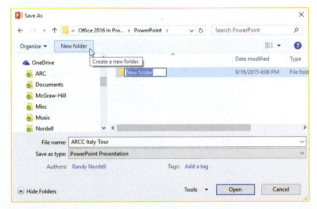

Intro-37 Create a new folder

Save As a Different File Name

After you have saved a file, you can save it again with a different file name. If you do this, you have preserved the original file, and you can continue to revise the second file for a different purpose.

▶HOW TO: Save as a Different File Name

1. Click the **File** tab to display the *Backstage* view.
2. Select **Save As** on the left to display the *Save As* area.
3. Click the **Browse** button to open the *Save As* dialog box.
4. Select a location to save the file in the *Folder* list on the left.
5. Type a new name for the file in the *File name* area.
6. Click **Save** to close the dialog box and save the file.

Office 2016 File Types

When you save an Office file, by default Office saves the file in the most recent file format for that application. You also have the option of saving files in older versions of the Office application you are using. For example, you can save a Word document as an older version to share with or send to someone who uses an older version of Word. Each file has an extension at the end of the file name that determines the file type. The *file name extension* is automatically added to a file when you save it. The following table lists common file types used in the different Office applications:

Office File Types

File Type	Extension	File Type	Extension
Word Document	.docx	Access Database	.accdb
Word Template	.dotx	Access Template	.accdt
Word 97-2003 Document	.doc	Access Database (2000-2003 format)	.mdb
Rich Text Format	.rtf	PowerPoint Presentation	.pptx
Excel Workbook	.xlsx	PowerPoint Template	.potx
Excel Template	.xltx	PowerPoint 97-2003 Presentation	.ppt
Excel 97-2003 Workbook	.xls	Portable Document Format (PDF)	.pdf
Comma Separated Values (CSV)	.csv		

Close a File

You can close a file using the following different methods:

- Click the **File** tab and select **Close** on the left.
- Press **Ctrl+W**.
- Click the **X** in the upper right corner of the file window. This method closes the file and the program if only one file is open in the application.

When you close a file, you are prompted to save the file if it has not been named or if changes were made after the file was last saved (Figure Intro-38). Click **Save** to save and close the file or click **Don't Save** to close the file without saving. Click **Cancel** to return to the file.

Intro-38 Prompt to save a document before closing

Open an Existing File

You can open an existing file from the *Start* page when you open an Office application or while you are working on another Office file.

▶**HOW TO:** Open a File from the Start Page

1. Open an Office application to display the *Start* page.

2. Select a file to open in the *Recent* area on the left (Figure Intro-39). The file opens in the Office application.

   - If you select a file in the *Recent* area that has been renamed, moved, or on a storage device not connected to the computer, you receive an error message.

3. Alternatively, click the **Open Other [file type]** (for example *Open Other Presentations*) (see Figure Intro-39) link to open the *Open* area of the *Backstage* view (Figure Intro-40).

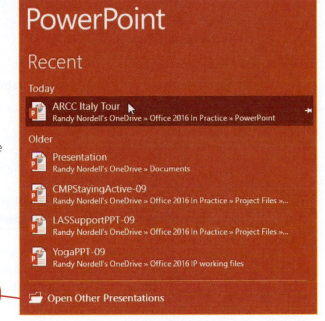

Open Other [file type] link

Intro-39 Open a file from the *Start* page

Intro-40 *Open* area on the *Backstage* view

4. Click the **Browse** button to open the *Open* dialog box (Figure Intro-41).

5. Select a location from the *Folder* list on the left.

6. Select the file to open and click the **Open** button.

   - If the file opens in *Protected View*, click the **Enable Editing** button to allow you to edit the file.

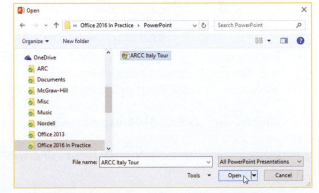

Intro-41 *Open* dialog box

When working on a file in an Office application, you might want to open another file. You can open an existing file from within an Office application from the *Open* area on the *Backstage* view.

▶ HOW TO: Open a File from the Backstage View

1. Click the **File** tab from within an open Office application to open the *Backstage* view.
2. Click **Open** on the left to display the *Open* area on the *Backstage* view (see Figure Intro-40).
3. Click the **Browse** button to open the *Open* dialog box (see Figure Intro-41).
   - You can also select a file to open from the list of *Recent* files on the right of the *Open* area on the *Backstage* view.
4. Select a location from the *Folder* list on the left.
5. Select the file to open and click the **Open** button.
   - If the file opens in *Protected View*, click the **Enable Editing** button to allow you to edit the file.

> ▶ **ANOTHER WAY**
>
> Press **Ctrl+F12** to open the *Open* dialog box when you are in the working area of an Office application (except in Access). On some laptops, you might have to press **Fn+Ctrl+F12**.

You can also open a file from a *File Explorer* folder. When you double-click a file in a *File Explorer* folder, the file opens in the appropriate Office application. Windows recognizes the file name extension and launches the correct Office application.

PAUSE & PRACTICE: INTRO-1

For this project, you log in to Windows using your Microsoft account, customize the Windows *Start* menu and *Taskbar*, create and save a PowerPoint presentation, create a folder, open and rename an Excel workbook, and use Windows 10 features.

File Needed: ***ARCC2018Budget-Intro.xlsx*** *(Student data files are available in the* Library *of your SIMnet account)*
Completed Project File Names: ***[your initials] PP Intro-1a.pptx** and **[your initials] PP Intro-1b.xlsx***

1. Log in to Windows using your Microsoft account if you are not already logged in.
   a. If you don't have a Microsoft account, you can create a free account at https://signup.live.com.
   b. If you are using a computer on your college campus, you may be required to log in to the computer using your college user name and password.

2. Customize the *Start* menu to include Office 2016 apps. If these apps tiles are already on the *Start* menu, skip steps 2a–e. You can pin other apps of your choice to the *Start* menu.
   a. Click the **Start** button at the bottom left of your screen to open the *Start* menu.

b. Click **All apps** at the bottom left of the *Start* menu (Figure Intro-42). The list of apps installed on the computer displays on the left side of the *Start* menu.

c. Locate and right-click **Access 2016** and select **Pin to Start** (Figure Intro-43). The app displays as a tile on the right side of the *Start* menu.

d. Repeat step 2c to pin **Excel 2016**, **PowerPoint 2016**, and **Word 2016** apps to the *Start* menu.

e. Display the *Start* menu and drag these Office app tiles so they are close to each other.

f. Click the **Start** button (or press the **Esc** key) to close the *Start* menu.

Intro-42 *All apps* button on the *Start* menu

3. Use *Cortana* and the *Start* menu to pin Office 2016 apps to the *Taskbar*.

a. Click the **Cortana** button (to the right of the *Start* button) on the *Taskbar* and type Access. *Cortana* displays content matching your search.

b. Right-click the **Access 2016** option near the top of the *Cortana* pane and select **Pin to taskbar** (Figure Intro-44). The app pins to the *Taskbar*.

c. Click the **Start** button to open the *Start* menu.

d. Right-click the **Excel 2016** tile on the right side of the *Start* menu, click **More**, and select **Pin to taskbar**. The app pins to the *Taskbar*.

e. Use either of the methods described above to pin the **PowerPoint 2016** and **Word 2016** apps to the *Taskbar*.

f. Drag the Office apps on the *Taskbar* to rearrange them to your preference.

Intro-43 Pin Access 2016 app to *Start* menu

Intro-44   Use *Cortana* to find an Office app and pin it to the *Taskbar*

4. Create a PowerPoint presentation and save the presentation in a new folder.

a. Click the **PowerPoint 2016** app tile on your *Start* menu to open the application.

b. Click **Blank Presentation** on the PowerPoint *Start* page to create a new blank presentation.

c. Click the **Click to add title** placeholder and type American River Cycling Club to replace the place-holder text.

d. Click the **File** tab to open the *Backstage* view and click **Save As** on the left to display the *Save As* area.

e. Click **Browse** to open the *Save As* dialog box (Figure Intro-45).

f. Select a location to save the file from the *Folder* list on the left. If the *OneDrive* folder is an option, select **OneDrive**. If it is not, select the **Documents** folder in the *This PC* folder. You can also save to a portable storage device if you have one.

g. Click the **New Folder** button to create a new folder.

h. Type American River Cycling Club as the name of the new folder and press **Enter** (Figure Intro-46).

i. Double-click the **American River Cycling Club** folder to open it.

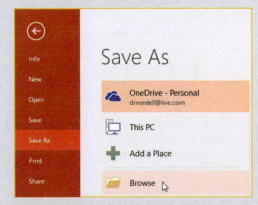

Intro-45 *Save As* area on the *Backstage* view in **PowerPoint**

j. Type [your initials] PP Intro-1a in the *File name* area.

k. Click **Save** to close the dialog box and save the presentation. Leave the file and PowerPoint open.

5. Open an Excel file and save as a different file name.

   a. Return to the Windows *Start* menu.

   b. Click the **Excel 2016** app button on the *Taskbar* to open it.

   c. Click the **Open Other Workbooks** link on the bottom left of the Excel *Start* page to display the *Open* area of the *Backstage* view.

   d. Click **Browse** to open the *Open* dialog box (Figure Intro-47).

   e. Browse to your student data files and select the *ARCC2018Budget-Intro* file.

   f. Click **Open** to open the workbook. If the file opens in *Protected View*, click the **Enable Editing** button.

   g. Click the **File** tab to open the *Backstage* view.

   h. Click **Save As** on the left to display the *Save As* area and click **Browse** to open the *Save As* dialog box.

   i. Locate the **American River Cycling Club** folder (created in step 4h) in the *Folder* list on the left and double-click the folder to open it.

   j. Type [your initials] PP Intro-1b in the *File name* area.

   k. Click **Save** to close the dialog box and save the workbook. Leave the file and Excel open.

6. Use the *Tell Me* feature in Excel to find a command.

   a. Click the **Tell Me** search box on the *Ribbon* of the Excel window and type PivotTable (Figure Intro-48).

   b. Click **PivotTable** to open the *Create PivotTable* dialog box.

   c. Click the **X** in the upper right corner of the *Create PivotTable* dialog box to close it.

7. Open the *Microsoft Store* app, the *Action Center*, and the *Settings* window.

   a. Click the **Cortana** button and type Microsoft Store.

   b. Click **Store** at the top of the *Cortana* pane to open the *Store* app.

   c. Click **Apps** in the top left and browse the available apps in the Microsoft Store.

   d. Click the **Minimize** button in the upper right corner of the *Store* window to minimize this app (Figure Intro-49). The app is still open, but it is minimized on the *Taskbar*.

   e. Click the **Action Center** button on the right side of the *Taskbar* to display the *Action Center* pane at the right (Figure Intro-50).

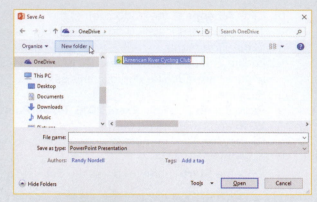

Intro-46 **Create a new folder from the *Save As* dialog box**

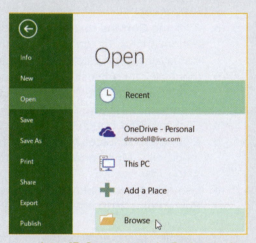

Intro-47 **Open area on the *Backstage* view**

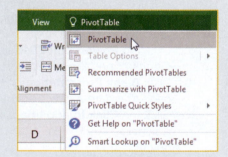

Intro-48 **Use the *Tell Me* feature to find a command**

Intro-49 ***Minimize* button on an app window**

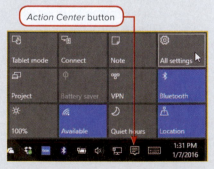

Intro-50 **Windows 10 *Action Center***

f. Click **All settings** to open the *Settings* window.

g. Click the **Find a setting** search box, type Printer, and view the search results.

h. Click the **Minimize** button to minimize the *Settings* windows to the *Taskbar*.

8. Use the *Task View* feature to open and close apps and windows.

a. Click the **Task View** button on the left side of the *Taskbar* (Figure Intro-51). All of the open apps and windows are tiled on the Windows desktop.

b. Click the **Store** app to open it. *Task View* closes and the *Store* app displays on your Windows desktop.

c. Click the **Task View** button again.

d. Click the **X** in the upper right corner to close each open app and window. You may be prompted to save changes to a file.

e. Click the **Task View** button again or press **Esc** to return to the desktop.

Intro-51 *Task View* **button on the** *Taskbar*

SLO INTRO. 4

Working with Files

When you work with Office files, a variety of display views are available. You can change how a file displays, adjust the display size, work with multiple files, and arrange the windows to view multiple files. Because most people work with multiple files at the same time, Office makes it easy and intuitive to move from one file to another or to display multiple document windows at the same time.

File Views

Each of the different Office applications provides you with a variety of ways to view your document. In Word, Excel, and PowerPoint, the different views are available on the **View tab** (Figure Intro-52). You can also change views using the buttons on the right side of the **Status bar** at the bottom of the file window (Figure Intro-53). In Access, the different views for each object are available in the *Views* group on the *Home* tab.

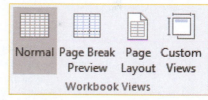

Intro-52 *Workbook Views* **group on the** *View* **tab in Excel**

Intro-53 **PowerPoint views on the** *Status* **bar**

The following table lists the views that are available in each of the different Office applications:

File Views

Office Application	Views	Office Application	Views
Word	*Read Mode* *Print Layout* *Web Layout* *Outline* *Draft*	Access (Access views vary depending on active object)	*Layout View* *Design View* *Datasheet View* *Form View* *SQL View* *Report View* *Print Preview*
Excel	*Normal* *Page Break Preview* *Page Layout* *Custom Views*	PowerPoint	*Normal* *Outline View* *Slide Sorter* *Notes Page* *Reading View* *Presenter View*

Change Display Size

You can use the *Zoom* feature to increase or decrease the display size of your file. Using *Zoom* to change the display size does not change the actual size of text or objects in your file; it only changes the size of your display. For example, if you change the *Zoom* level to 120%, you increase the display of your file to 120% of its normal size (100%), but changing the display size does not affect the actual size of text and objects in your file. You could also decrease the *Zoom* level to 80% to display more of your file on the screen.

You can increase or decrease the *Zoom* level several different ways. Your *Zoom* options vary depending on the Office application you are using.

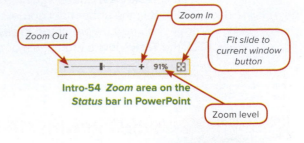

Intro-54 *Zoom* area on the *Status* bar in PowerPoint

- ***Zoom level** on the Status* bar (Figure Intro-54): Click the **+** or **−** button to increase or decrease *Zoom* level in 10% increments.
- ***Zoom group** on the View tab* (Figure Intro-55): The *Zoom* group includes a variety of *Zoom* options. The options vary depending on the Office application.
- ***Zoom dialog box*** (Figure Intro-56): Click the **Zoom** button in the *Zoom* group on the *View* tab or click the **Zoom level** on the *Status* bar to open the *Zoom* dialog box.

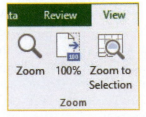

Intro-55 *Zoom* group in Excel

> **MORE INFO**
>
> The *Zoom* feature is only available in Access in *Print Preview* view when you are working with reports.

Manage Multiple Open Files and Windows

When you are working on multiple files in an Office application, each file is opened in a new window. You can ***minimize*** an open window to place the file on the Windows *Taskbar* (the bar at the bottom of the Windows desktop), ***restore down*** an open window so it does not fill the entire computer screen, or ***maximize*** a window so it fills the entire computer screen. The *Minimize, Restore Down/Maximize,* and *Close* buttons are in the upper right of a file window (Figure Intro-57).

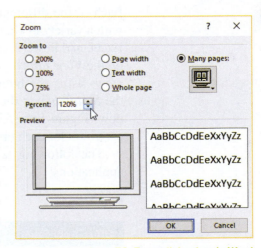

Intro-56 *Zoom* dialog box in Word

> **MORE INFO**
>
> You can open only one Access file at a time. If you open another Access file, the first one closes.

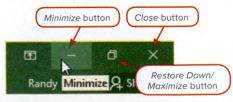

Intro-57 Window options buttons

- *Minimize*: Click the **Minimize** button (see Figure Intro-57) to hide the active window. When a document is minimized, it is not closed. It is minimized to the *Taskbar* so the window is not displayed on your screen. Place your pointer on the application icon on the Windows *Taskbar* to display thumbnails of open files. You can click an open file thumbnail to display the file (Figure Intro-58).

- *Restore Down/Maximize*: Click the **Restore Down/ Maximize** (see Figure Intro-57) button to decrease the size of an open window or maximize the window to fill the entire screen. This button toggles between *Restore Down* and *Maximize*. When a window is

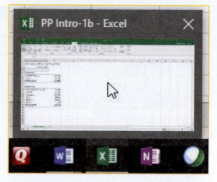

restored down, you can change the size of a window by clicking and dragging a border of the window. You can also move the window by clicking and dragging the title bar at the top of the window.

- *Close*: Click the **Close** button (see Figure Intro-57) to close the window. If there is only one open file, the Office application also closes when you click the *Close* button on the file.

  You can switch between open files or arrange the open files to display more than one window at the same time. The following are several methods to do this:

- *Switch Windows button*: Click the **Switch Windows** button [*View* tab, *Window* group] (not available in Access) to display a drop-down list of open files. Click a file from the drop-down list to display the file.

> ### ANOTHER WAY
>
> Click the Windows **Task View** button on the *Taskbar* to tile all open windows and apps on the desktop.

- *Windows Taskbar*: Place your pointer on an Office application icon on the Windows *Taskbar* to display the open files in that application. Click a file thumbnail to display it (see Figure Intro-58).

- *Arrange All button*: Click the **Arrange All** button [*View* tab, *Window* group] to display all windows in an application. You can resize or move the open file windows.

Snap Assist

The *Snap Assist* feature in Windows provides the ability to position an open window to the left or right side of your computer screen and fill half the screen. When you snap an open window to the left or right side of the screen, the other open windows tile on the opposite side where you can select another window to fill the opposite side of the computer screen (Figure Intro-59).

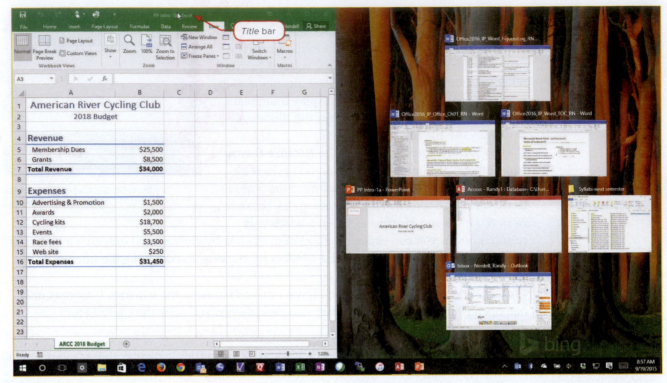

Intro-59 Windows *Snap Assist* feature

1. Click the **title bar** of an open window.

2. Drag it to the left or right edge of the computer screen and release the pointer.
   - The window snaps to the side of the screen and fills half of the computer screen (see Figure Intro-59).
   - The other open windows and apps display as tiles on the opposite side.
   - If you're using a touch screen computer, you can use *Snap Assist* by pressing and holding the title bar of an open window and dragging to either side of the computer screen.

3. Select a tile of an open window or app to fill the other half of the screen.

▶ **MORE INFO**

Snap Assist also allows you to snap a window to a quadrant (quarter rather than half) of your screen. Drag the **title bar** of an open window to one of the four corners of your computer screen.

SLO INTRO. 5

Printing, Sharing, and Customizing Files

On the *Backstage* view of any of the Office applications, you can print a file and customize how a file is printed. You can also export an Office file as a PDF file in most of the Office applications. In addition, you can add and customize document properties for an Office file and share a file in a variety of formats.

Print a File

You can print an Office file if you need a hard copy. The *Print* area on the *Backstage* view displays a preview of the open file and many print options. For example, you can choose which page or pages to print and change the margins of the file in the *Print* area. Print settings vary depending on the Office application you are using and what you are printing.

▶**HOW TO:** Print a File

1. Open the file you want to print from a Windows folder or within an Office program.
2. Click the **File** tab to open the *Backstage* view.
3. Click **Print** on the left to display the *Print* area (Figure Intro-60).
   * A preview of the file displays on the right. Click the **Show Margins** button to adjust margins or **Zoom to Page** button to change the view in the *Preview* area. The *Show Margins* button is only available in Excel.
4. Change the number of copies to print in the *Copies* area.
5. Click the **Printer** drop-down list to choose from available printers.
6. Customize what is printed and how it is printed in the *Settings* area.
   * The *Settings* options vary depending on the Office application you are using and what you are printing.
   * In the *Pages* area (*Slides* area in PowerPoint), you can select a page or range of pages (slides) to print.
   * By default all pages (slides) are printed when you print a file.
7. Click the **Print** button to print your file.

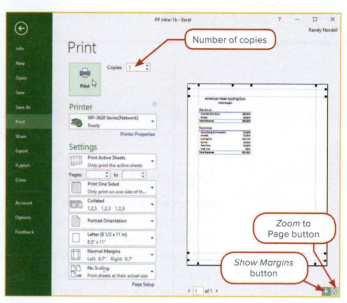

Intro-60 *Print* area on the *Backstage* view

> ▶ **ANOTHER WAY**
>
> Press **Ctrl+P** to open the *Print* area on the *Backstage* view.

Export as a PDF File

Portable document format, or *PDF*, is a specific file format that is often used to share files that are not to be changed or to post files on a web site. When you create a PDF file from an Office application file, you are actually exporting a static image of the original file, similar to taking a picture of the file.

The advantage of working with a PDF file is that the format of the file is retained no matter who opens the file. PDF files open in the Windows Reader app or Adobe Reader, which is free software that is installed on most computers. Because a PDF file is a static image of a file, it is not easy for other people to edit your files. When you want people to be able to view a file but not change it, PDF files are a good choice.

1. Open the file you want to export as a PDF file.

2. Click the **File** tab and click **Export** to display the *Export* area on the Backstage view (Figure Intro-61).

3. Select **Create PDF/XPS Document** and click the **Create PDF/XPS**. The *Publish as PDF or XPS* dialog box opens.

   • XPS (XML Paper Specification) format is an alternative to a PDF file. XPS is a Microsoft format and is not widely used.

4. Select a location to save the file.

5. Type a name for the file in the *File name* area.

6. Click **Publish** to close the dialog box and save the PDF file.

   • A PDF version of your file may open. You can view the file and then close it.

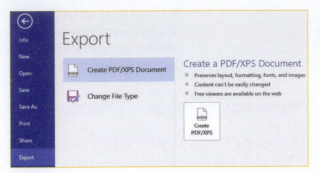

Intro-61 *Export* a file as a PDF file

Document Properties

Document properties are hidden codes in a file that store identifying information about that file. Each piece of document property information is called a ***field***. You can view and modify document properties in the *Info* area of the *Backstage* view.

Some document properties fields are automatically generated when you work on a file, such as *Size*, *Total Editing Time*, *Created*, and *Last Modified*. Other document properties fields, such as *Title*, *Comments*, *Subject*, *Company*, and *Author*, can be modified. You can use document property fields in different ways such as inserting the *Company* field in a document footer.

▶ **HOW TO:** View and Modify Document Properties

1. Click the **File** tab and click **Info**. The document properties display on the right (Figure Intro-62).

2. Click the text box area of a field that can be edited and type your custom document property information.

3. Click the **Show All Properties** link at the bottom to display additional document properties.

   • Click **Show Fewer Properties** to collapse the list and display fewer properties.
   • This link toggles between *Show All Properties* and *Show Fewer Properties*.

4. Click the **Back** arrow to return to the file.

Intro-62 **Document properties**

Share a File

Windows 10 and Office 2016 have been enhanced to help you share files and collaborate with others. The *Share* area on the *Backstage* view lists different options for sharing files from within an Office application. When you save a file to your *OneDrive*, Office provides a variety of options to share your file (Figure Intro-63). The two main sharing options are **Share with People** and **Email**. Within these two categories, you have a variety of ways to share a file with others. Your sharing options vary depending on the Office application you are using. The following list describes the sharing options available in the Office applications:

Intro-63 **Share** options on the **Backstage** view

- **Word**: *Share with People, Email, Present Online,* and *Post to Blog*
- **Excel**: *Share with People* and *Email*
- **Access**: No *Sharing* option on the *Backstage* view
- **PowerPoint**: *Share with People, Email, Present Online,* and *Publish Slides*

▶HOW TO: Share a File

1. Click the **File** tab to open the *Backstage* view and select **Share** on the left.
   - If your file is not saved in *OneDrive*, you are directed to first save the file to the cloud (*OneDrive*). Click the **Save to Cloud** button and save your file in *OneDrive*.
   - If your file is not saved to *OneDrive*, you will not have all available sharing options.

2. Share a *OneDrive* file with others by clicking **Share with People** on the left and then clicking the **Share with People** button on the right (see Figure Intro-63).

   - The *Backstage* view closes and the *Share* pane opens on the right side of the file (Figure Intro-64).
   - Alternatively, click the **Share** button in the upper right corner of the Office application window to open the *Share* pane (Figure Intro-65).
   - Type an email address in the *Invite people* text box. If you want to share the file with more than one person, separate email addresses with a semicolon.
   - Select **Can edit** or **Can view** from the permission drop-down list, which controls what others can do with your file.
   - You can include a message the recipients will receive.
   - Click the **Share** button below the message to send a sharing email to recipients.
   - Alternatively, click the **Get a sharing link** option at the bottom of the *Share* pane to create an *edit link* or *view-only link* (Figure Intro-66). You can then copy the sharing link and email it to others or post it in an online location.

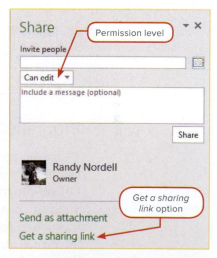

Intro-64 **Share** pane

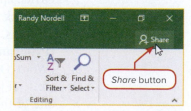

Intro-65 **The Share button** opens the **Share** pane

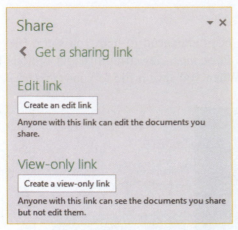

Intro-66 *Get a sharing link* options
in the *Share* pane

3. Share a file through email by clicking the **Email** button on the left side of the *Share* area on the *Backstage* view and selecting an option (Figure Intro-67).

Intro-67   *Email* share options in the *Share* area on the *Backstage* view

- These *Email* share options use Microsoft Outlook (email and personal management Office application) to share the selected file through email.
- The *Email* share options include *Send as Attachment, Send a Link, Send as PDF, Send as XPS*, and *Send as Internet Fax*.
- A description of each of these *Email* share options are provided to the right of each option.

> **MORE INFO**
>
> Sharing options are also available if you save files to other online storage locations such as Dropbox and Box.

Program Options

Using the program options, you can apply global changes to the Office program. For example, you can change the default save location to your *OneDrive* folder or you can turn off the *Start* page that opens when you open an Office application.

Click the **File** tab and select **Options** on the left to open the **[Program] Options** dialog box (Word Options, Excel Options, etc.) (Figure Intro-68). Click one of the categories on the left to display the category options on the right. The categories and options vary depending on the Office application you are using.

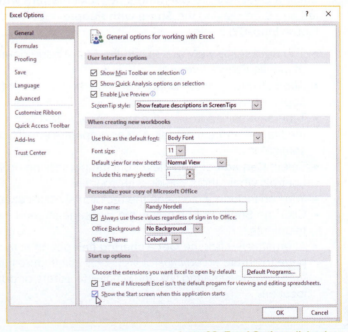

Intro-68 *Excel Options* dialog box

Using the Ribbon, Tabs, and Quick Access Toolbar

You can use the *Ribbon*, tabs, groups, buttons, drop-down lists, dialog boxes, task panes, galleries, and the *Quick Access* toolbar to modify your Office files. This section describes different tools you can use to customize your files.

The Ribbon, Tabs, and Groups

The *Ribbon*, which appears at the top of an Office file window, displays the many features available to use on your files. The *Ribbon* is a collection of *tabs*. On each tab are *groups* of features. The tabs and groups that are available on each Office application vary. Click a tab to display the groups and features available on that tab.

Some tabs always display on the *Ribbon* (for example the *File* tab and *Home* tabs). Other tabs are *context-sensitive*, which means that they only appear on the *Ribbon* when you select a specific object. Figure Intro-69 displays the context-sensitive *Table Tools Field* tab that displays in Access when you open a table.

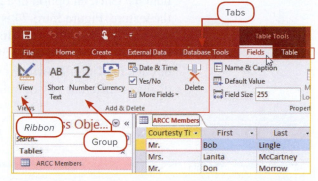

Intro-69 Context-sensitive *Table Tools Fields* tab displayed

Ribbon Display Options

The *Ribbon* displays by default in Office applications, but you can customize how the *Ribbon* displays. The **Ribbon Display Options** button is in the upper right corner of an Office application window (Figure Intro-70). Click the **Ribbon Display Options** button to select one of the three options:

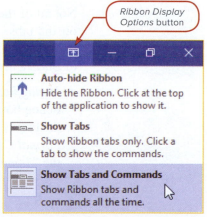

Intro-70 *Ribbon Display Options*

- *Auto-Hide Ribbon*: Hides the *Ribbon*. Click at the top of the application to display the *Ribbon*.
- *Show Tabs*: *Ribbon* tabs display. Click a tab to open the *Ribbon* and display the tab.
- *Show Tabs and Commands*: Displays the *Ribbon* and tabs, which is the default setting in Office applications.

> **MORE INFO**
>
> **Ctrl+F1** collapses or expands the *Ribbon*.

Buttons, Drop-Down Lists, and Galleries

Groups on each of the tabs contain a variety of *buttons*, *drop-down lists*, and *galleries*. The following list describes each of these features and how they are used:

- *Button*: Applies a feature to selected text or object. Click a button to apply the feature (Figure Intro-71).

- **Drop-down list**: Displays the various options available for a feature. Some buttons are drop-down lists only, so when you click one of these buttons the drop-down list of options appears (Figure Intro-72). Other buttons are **split buttons**, which have both a button you click to apply a feature and an arrow you click to display a drop-down list of options (Figure Intro-73).
- **Gallery**: Displays a collection of option buttons. Click an option in a gallery to apply the feature. Figure Intro-74 is the *Styles* gallery. You can click the **More** button to display the entire gallery of options or click the **Up** or **Down** arrow to display a different row of options.

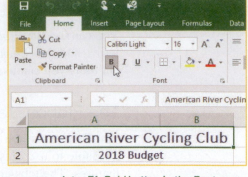

Intro-71 *Bold* button in the *Font* group on the *Home* tab

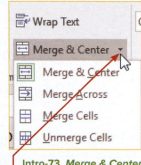

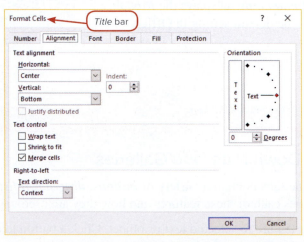

Up and *Down* buttons

More button

Intro-74 *Styles* gallery in Word

Intro-72 *Orientation* drop-down list

Intro-73 *Merge & Center* split button—button and drop-down list

Click the arrow on a split button to display the drop-down list

Dialog Boxes, Task Panes, and Launchers

Not all of the features that are available in an Office application are displayed in the groups on the tabs. Additional options for some groups display in a **dialog box** or **task pane**. A **launcher**, which is a small square in the bottom right of some groups, opens a dialog box or displays a task pane when you click it (see Figure Intro-76).

- **Dialog box**: A new window that opens to display additional features. You can move a dialog box by clicking and dragging the title bar, which is the top of the dialog box where the title is displayed. Figure Intro-75 shows the *Format Cells* dialog box that opens when you click the *Alignment* launcher in Excel.

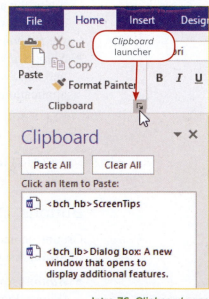

Intro-75 *Format Cells* dialog box

Intro-76 *Clipboard* pane

- *Task pane*: Opens on the left or right of the Office application window. Figure Intro-76 shows the *Clipboard* pane, which is available in all Office applications. Task panes are named according to their feature (for example *Clipboard* pane or *Navigation* pane). You can resize a task pane by clicking and dragging its left or right border. Click the **X** in the upper right corner to close a task pane.

ScreenTips

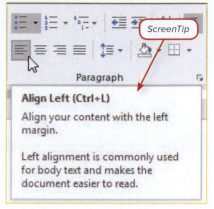

ScreenTips display descriptive information about a button, drop-down list, launcher, or gallery selection. When you place your pointer on an item on the *Ribbon*, a *ScreenTip* displays information about the selection (Figure Intro-77). The *ScreenTip* appears temporarily and displays the command name, keyboard shortcut (if available), and a description of the command.

Intro-77 *Align Left ScreenTip*

Radio Buttons, Check Boxes, and Text Boxes

Dialog boxes and task panes contain a variety of features you can apply using *radio buttons*, *check boxes*, *text boxes*, *drop-down lists*, and other buttons (Figure Intro-78).

- *Radio button*: A round button you click to select one option from a list of options. A selected radio button has a solid dot inside the round button.
- *Check box*: A square button you click to select one or more options. A check appears in a check box you have selected.
- *Text box*: An area where you can type text.

A task pane or dialog box may also include drop-down lists or other buttons that open additional dialog boxes. Figure Intro-78 shows the *Page Setup*

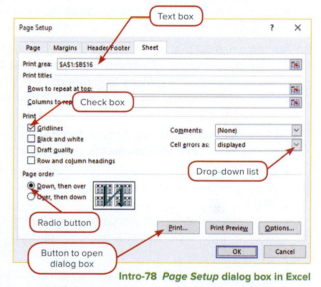

Intro-78 *Page Setup dialog box in Excel*

dialog box in Excel, which includes a variety of radio buttons, check boxes, text boxes, drop-down lists, and other buttons that open additional dialog boxes (for example the *Print* and *Options* buttons).

Quick Access Toolbar

The *Quick Access toolbar* is located above the *Ribbon* on the upper left of each Office application window. It contains buttons to apply commonly used commands such as *Save*, *Undo*, *Redo*, and *Open* (Figure Intro-79). The *Undo* button is a split button. You can click the

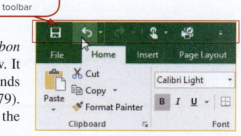

Intro-79 *Quick Access toolbar*

button to undo the last action performed or you can click the drop-down arrow to display and undo multiple previous actions.

Customize the Quick Access Toolbar

You can customize the *Quick Access* toolbar to include features you regularly use, such as *Quick Print*, *New*, and *Spelling & Grammar*. The following steps show how to customize the *Quick Access* toolbar in Word. The customization process is similar for the *Quick Access* toolbar in the other Office applications.

> **HOW TO:** Customize the Quick Access Toolbar

1. Click the **Customize Quick Access Toolbar** drop-down list on the right edge of the *Quick Access* toolbar (Figure Intro-80).

2. Select a command to add to the *Quick Access* toolbar. The command displays on the *Quick Access* toolbar.
   - Items on the *Customize Quick Access Toolbar* drop-down list with a check mark are commands that are displayed on the *Quick Access* toolbar.
   - Deselect a checked item to remove it from the *Quick Access* toolbar.

3. Add a command that is not listed on the *Customize Quick Access Toolbar* by clicking the **Customize Quick Access Toolbar** drop-down list and selecting **More Commands**. The *Word Options* dialog box opens with the *Quick Access Toolbar* area displayed (Figure Intro-81).

4. Click the **Customize Quick Access Toolbar** drop-down list on the right and select **For all documents** or the current document.
   - If you select *For all documents*, the change is made to the *Quick Access* toolbar for all documents you open in Word.
   - If you select the current document, the change is made to the *Quick Access* toolbar in that document only.

5. Select the command to add from the alphabetic list of commands on the left and click the **Add** button.
   - If you can't find the command you're looking for, click the **Choose commands from** drop-down list and select **All Commands**.
   - The list on the right contains the commands that display on the *Quick Access* toolbar.

6. Rearrange commands on the *Quick Access* toolbar by selecting a command in the list on the right and clicking the **Move Up** or **Move Down** button.

7. Click **OK** to close the *Word Options* dialog box.

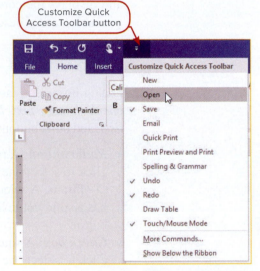

Intro-80 Add a command to the *Quick Access* toolbar

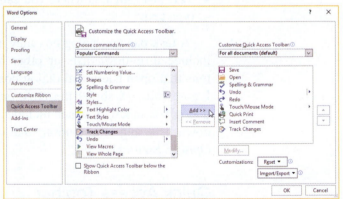

Intro-81 Customize the *Quick Access* toolbar in the *Word Options* dialog box

SLO INTRO. 7

Using Context Menus, the Mini Toolbars, and Keyboard Shortcuts

Most of the commands you use for formatting and editing your files display in groups on the tabs. But many of these features are also available using content menus, mini toolbars, and keyboard shortcuts. You can use these tools to quickly apply formatting or other options to text or objects.

Context Menu

A ***context menu*** displays when you right-click text, a cell, or an object such as a picture, drawing object, chart, or *SmartArt* (Figure Intro-82). The context menu is a vertical list of options, and the options are context-sensitive, which means they vary depending on what you right-click.

Context menus include options that perform an action (*Cut* or *Copy*), open a dialog box or task pane (*Format Cells* or *Hyperlink*), or display a drop-down list of selections (*Filter* or *Sort*).

Mini Toolbar

The ***mini toolbar*** is another context menu that displays when you right-click or select text, a cell, or an object in your file (see Figure Intro-82). The mini toolbar is a horizontal rectangular menu that lists a variety of formatting options. These options vary depending on what you select or right-click. The mini toolbar contains a variety of buttons and drop-down lists. The mini toolbar typically displays above the context menu. The mini toolbar automatically displays when you select text or an object, such as when you select a row of a table in Word or PowerPoint.

Intro-82 Context menu and mini toolbar

Keyboard Shortcuts

You can also use a ***keyboard shortcut*** to quickly apply formatting or perform commands. A keyboard shortcut is a combination of keyboard keys that you press at the same time. These can include the **Ctrl**, **Shift**, **Alt**, letter, number, and function keys (for example **F1** or **F7**). The following table lists common Office keyboard shortcuts.

Common Office Keyboard Shortcuts

Keyboard Shortcut	Action or Displays	Keyboard Shortcut	Action or Displays
Ctrl+S	Save	Ctrl+Z	Undo
F12	*Save As* dialog *box*	Ctrl+Y	Redo or Repeat
Ctrl+O	*Open* area on the *Backstage* view	Ctrl+1	Single space
Shift+F12	*Open* dialog box	Ctrl+2	Double space
Ctrl+N	New blank file	Ctrl+L	Align left
Ctrl+P	*Print* area on the *Backstage* view	Ctrl+E	Align center
Ctrl+C	Copy	Ctrl+R	Align right
Ctrl+X	Cut	F1	*Help* dialog box
Ctrl+V	Paste	F7	*Spelling* pane
Ctrl+B	Bold	Ctrl+A	Select All
Ctrl+I	Italic	Ctrl+Home	Move to the beginning
Ctrl+U	Underline	Ctrl+End	Move to the end

> **MORE INFO**
> See Appendix A for additional Office 2016 keyboard shortcuts.

Function Keys on a Laptop

Intro-83 Function key

When using a laptop computer, function keys perform specific Windows actions on your laptop, such as increase or decrease speaker volume, open Windows *Settings*, or adjust the screen brightness. So when using a numbered function key, such as **F12** as a shortcut to open the *Save As* dialog box in an Office application, you may need to press the ***function key*** (**Fn** or **fn**) on your keyboard in conjunction with a numbered function key to activate the command (Figure Intro-83). The *function key* is typically located near the bottom left of your laptop keyboard next to the *Ctrl* key.

PAUSE & PRACTICE: INTRO-2

For this project, you work with a document for the American River Cycling Club. You modify the existing document, add document properties, customize the *Quick Access* toolbar, export the document as a PDF file, and share the document.

File Needed: ***ARCCTraining-Intro.docx*** *(Student data files are available in the* Library *of your SIMnet account)*
Completed Project File Names: ***[your initials] PP Intro-2a.docx*** and ***[your initials] PP Intro-2b.pdf***

1. Open Word 2016 and open the ***ARCCTraining-Intro*** file from your student data files. If the file opens in *Protected View*, click the **Enable Editing** button.

2. Save this document as [your initials] PP Intro-2a in the *American River Cycling Club* folder in your *OneDrive* folder.
   a. In *Pause & Practice Intro-1*, you created the *American River Cycling Club* folder in *OneDrive* or other storage area. Save this file in the same location.
   b. If you don't save this file in *OneDrive*, you will not be able to complete steps 7 and 9 in this project.

3. Use a button, drop-down list, and dialog box to modify the document.
   a. Select the first heading, "**What is Maximum Heart Rate?**"
   b. Click the **Bold** button [*Home* tab, *Font* group].
   c. Click the **Underline** drop-down arrow and select **Double underline** (Figure Intro-84).
   d. Click the **launcher** in the *Font* group [*Home* tab] to open the *Font* dialog box (Figure Intro-85).
   e. In the *Size* area, select **12** from the list or type 12 in the text box.
   f. In the *Effects* area, click the **Small caps** check box to select it.
   g. Click **OK** to close the dialog box and apply the formatting changes.
   h. Select the next heading, "**What is Target Heart Rate?**"
   i. Repeat steps 3b–g to apply formatting to selected text.

4. Add document properties.
   a. Click the **File** tab to display the *Backstage* view.
   b. Select **Info** on the left. The document properties display on the right.
   c. Click the **Add a title** text box and type ARCC Training.
   d. Click the **Show All Properties** link near the bottom to display additional document properties.
   e. Click the **Specify the subject** text box and type Heart rate training.
   f. Click the **Specify the company** text box and type American River Cycling Club.
   g. Click the **Back** arrow on the upper left to close the *Backstage* view and return to the document.

5. Customize the *Quick Access* toolbar.
   a. Click the **Customize Quick Access Toolbar** drop-down arrow and select **Open** (Figure Intro-86).
   b. Click the **Customize Quick Access Toolbar** drop-down arrow again and select **Spelling & Grammar**.

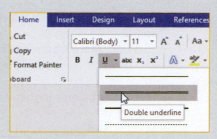

Intro-84 Apply *Double underline* to selected text.

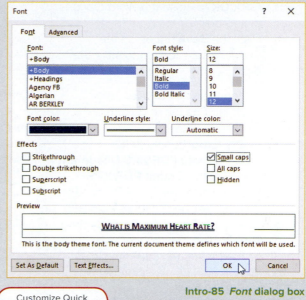

Intro-85 *Font* dialog box

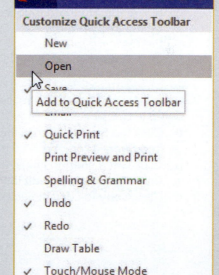

Intro-86 *Customize Quick Access Toolbar* drop-down list

c. Click the **Customize Quick Access Toolbar** drop-down arrow again and select **More Commands**. The *Word Options* dialog box opens (Figure Intro-87).

d. Select **Insert Comment** in the list of commands on the left.

e. Click the **Add** button to add it to your *Quick Access* toolbar list on the right.

f. Click **OK** to close the *Word Options* dialog box.

g. Click the **Save** button on the *Quick Access* toolbar to save the document.

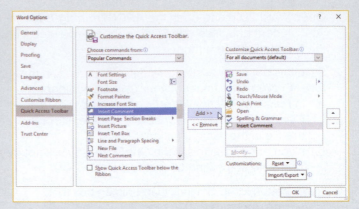

Intro-87 Customize the *Quick Access* toolbar in the *Word Options* dialog box

6. Export the file as a PDF file.

a. Click the **File** tab to go to the *Backstage* view.

b. Select **Export** on the left.

c. Select **Create PDF/XPS Document** and click the **Create PDF/XPS** button. The *Publish as PDF or XPS* dialog box opens (Figure Intro-88).

d. Select the **American River Cycling Club** folder in your *OneDrive* folder as the location to save the file.

e. Type **[your initials] PP Intro-2b** in the *File name* area.

f. Deselect the **Open file after publishing** check box if it is checked.

g. Select the **Standard (publishing online and printing)** radio button in the *Optimize for* area.

h. Click **Publish** to close the dialog box and create a PDF version of your file.

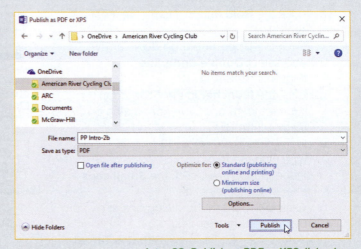

Intro-88 *Publish as PDF or XPS* dialog box

7. Get a link to share a document with your instructor. If your file is not saved in *OneDrive*, skip steps 7 and 9.

a. Click the **Share** button in the upper right of the Word window. The *Share* pane opens on the right side of your document.

b. Click **Get a sharing link** at the bottom of the *Share* pane.

c. Click the **Create an edit link** button.

d. Click **Copy** to copy the edit link (Figure Intro-89).

Intro-89 Copy a sharing link

8. Save and close the document (Figure Intro-90).

American River Cycling Club
www.arcc.org Cycling...a way of life info@arcc.org

WHAT IS MAXIMUM HEART RATE?

The maximum heart rate is the highest your pulse rate can get. To calculate your **predicted maximum heart rate**, use this formula:

(Example: a 40-year-old's predicted maximum heart rate is 180.)

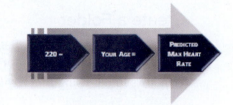

Your actual maximum heart rate can be determined by a graded exercise test. Please note that some medicines and medical conditions might affect your maximum heart rate. If you are taking medicines or have a medical condition (such as heart disease, high blood pressure, or diabetes), always ask your doctor if your maximum heart rate/target heart rate will be affected.

WHAT IS TARGET HEART RATE?

You gain the most benefits and decrease the risk of injury when you exercise in your target heart rate zone. Usually this is when your exercise heart rate (pulse) is 60 percent to 85 percent of your maximum heart rate. Do not exercise above 85 percent of your maximum heart rate. This increases both cardiovascular and orthopedic risk and does not add any extra benefit.

When beginning an exercise program, you might need to gradually build up to a level that is within your target heart rate zone, especially if you have not exercised regularly before. If the exercise feels too hard, slow down. You will reduce your risk of injury and enjoy the exercise more if you don't try to over-do it.

To find out if you are exercising in your target zone (between 60 percent and 85 percent of your maximum heart rate), use your heart rate monitor to track your heart rate. If your pulse is below your target zone (see the chart below), increase your rate of exercise. If your pulse is above your target zone, decrease your rate of exercise.

	AGE	PREDICTED MAX HEART RATE	TARGET HEART RATE (60-85% OF MAX)
MAX AND TARGET HEART RATES	20	✓ 200	120-170
	25	✓ 195	117-166
	30	✓ 190	114-162
	35	✓ 185	111-157
	40	✓ 180	108-153
	45	✓ 175	105-149
	50	✓ 170	102-145
	55	✓ 165	99-140
	60	✓ 160	96-136
	65	✓ 155	93-132
	70	✓ 150	90-128

Intro-90 PP Intro-2a completed

9. Email the sharing link to your instructor.
   a. Using your email account, create a new email to send to your instructor.
   b. Include an appropriate subject line and a brief message in the body.
   c. Press **Ctrl+V** to paste the link to your document in the body of the email.
   d. Send the email message.

SLO INTRO. 8

Organizing and Customizing Folders and Files

The more you use your computer to create and use files, the more important it is to stay organized. You can use *folders* to store related files, which makes it easier for you to find, edit, and share your files. For example, you can create a folder for the college you attend. Inside the college folder, you can create a folder for each of your courses. Inside each of the course folders you might create a folder for student data files, solution files, and group projects. Folders can store any type of files; you are not limited to Office files.

Create a Folder

In *SLO Intro.3: Creating, Saving, Closing, and Opening Files*, you learned how to create a new folder when saving an Office file in the *Save As* dialog box. You can also create a Windows folder using *File Explorer*. You can create folders inside other folders.

▶HOW TO: Create a Windows Folder

1. Click the **Start** button and select **File Explorer** to open a *File Explorer* window.
   - Your folders and computer locations are listed on the left.
2. Select the location in the *Navigation* pane on the left where you want to create a new folder.
3. Click **Home** tab, and click the **New folder** button [*New* group]. A new folder is created (Figure Intro-91).
   - The *New Folder* button is also on the *Quick Access* toolbar in the *File Explorer* window.
4. Type the name of the new folder and press **Enter**.

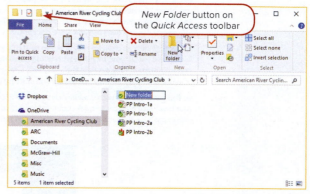

Intro-91 Create a new Windows folder

> ▶ **ANOTHER WAY**
>
> **Ctrl+Shift+N** creates a new folder in a Windows folder.

Move and Copy Files and Folders

Moving a file or folder is cutting it from one location and pasting it in another location. Copying a file or folder creates a copy of it, and you can paste in another location so the file or folder is in two or more locations. If you move or copy a folder, the files in the folder are moved or copied with the folder. Move or copy files and folders using the *Move to* or *Copy to* buttons on the *Home* tab of *File Explorer*, keyboard shortcuts (**Ctrl+X**, **Ctrl+C**, **Ctrl+V**), or the drag-and-drop method.

To move or copy multiple folders or files at the same time, press the **Ctrl** key and select multiple items to move or copy. Use the **Ctrl** key to select or deselect multiple non-adjacent files or folders. Use the **Shift** key to select a range of files or folders. Click the first file or folder in a range, press the **Shift** key, and select the last file or folder in the range to select all of the items in the range.

▶ HOW TO: Move or Copy a File or Folder

1. Click the **Start** button and select **File Explorer** to open a *File Explorer* window.
2. Select a file or folder to move or copy.
   - Press the **Ctrl** key to select multiple files or folders.
3. Click the **Home** tab in the *File Explorer* window.
4. Click the **Move to** or **Copy to** button [*Organize* group] and select the location where you want to move or copy the file or folder (Figure Intro-92).

Intro-92 Move or copy a selected file or folder

- If the folder you want is not available, select **Choose location** to open the *Move Items* or *Copy Items* dialog box.
- To use the keyboard shortcuts, press **Ctrl+X** to cut the file or folder or **Ctrl+C** to copy the file or folder from its original location, go to the desired new location, and press **Ctrl+V** to paste it.
- To use the drag-and-drop method to move a file or folder, select the file or folder and drag and drop to the new location.
- To use the drag-and-drop method to copy a file or folder, press the **Ctrl** key, select the file or folder, and drag and drop to the new location.

 ANOTHER WAY

Right-click a file or folder to display the context menu where you can select **Cut**, **Copy**, or **Paste**.

Rename Files and Folders

You can rename a file or folder in a *File Explorer* window. When you rename a file or folder, only the file or folder name changes, and the contents of the file or folder do not change.

▶ HOW TO: Rename a File or Folder

1. Click the **Start** button and select **File Explorer** to open a *File Explorer* window.
2. Select the file or folder you want to rename.
3. Click the **Rename** button [*Home* tab, *Organize* group] (see Figure Intro-92).
4. Type the new name of the file or folder and press **Enter**.

 ANOTHER WAY

Select a file or folder to rename, press **F2**, type the new name, and press **Enter**. You can also right-click a file or folder and select **Rename** from the context menu.

Delete Files and Folders

You can also easily delete files and folders. When you delete a file or folder, it is moved from its current location to the *Recycle Bin* on your computer where deleted items are stored. If a file or folder is in the *Recycle Bin*, you can restore this item to its original location or move it to a different location. You also have the option to permanently delete a file or folder; the item is deleted and not moved to the *Recycle Bin*. If an item is permanently deleted, you do not have the restore option.

► HOW TO: Delete Files and Folders

1. Open a *File Explorer* window and select the file or folder you want to delete.
   - You can select multiple files and folders to delete at the same time.
2. Click the **Delete** drop-down arrow [*Home* tab, *Organize* group] to display the list of delete options (Figure Intro-93).
   - The default action when you click the *Delete* button (not the drop-down arrow) is *Recycle*.
3. Delete a file by selecting **Recycle**, which moves it to the *Recycle Bin*.
   - *Recycle* deletes the item(s) and moves it to the *Recycle Bin*.
   - When you *Recycle* an item, you are not by default prompted to confirm the deletion. Select **Show recycle confirmation** from the *Delete* drop-down list to receive a confirmation dialog box each time you delete or recycle an item.
4. Permanently delete a file by selecting **Permanently delete**. A confirmation dialog box opens. Click **Yes** to confirm the deletion.
   - *Permanently delete* deletes the item(s) from your computer.

Intro-93 Delete selected folder

> ► **ANOTHER WAY**
>
> Press **Ctrl+D** or the **Delete** key on your keyboard to recycle selected item(s).
> Press **Shift+Delete** to permanently delete selected item(s).

Create a Zipped (Compressed) Folder

If you want to share multiple files or a folder of files with classmates, coworkers, friends, or family, you can *zip* the files into a ***zipped folder*** (also called a ***compressed folder***). For example, you can't attach an entire folder to an email message, but you can attach a zipped folder to an email message. Compressing files and folders decreases their size. You can zip a group of selected files, a folder, or a combination of files and folders, and then share the zipped folder with others through email or in a cloud storage location such as *OneDrive*.

► HOW TO: Create a Zipped (Compressed) Folder

1. Open a *File Explorer* window.
2. Select the file(s) and/or folder(s) you want to zip (compress).
3. Click the **Zip** button [*Share* tab, *Send* group] (Figure Intro-94). A zipped folder is created.
   - The name of the zipped folder is the name of the first item you selected to zip. You can rename this folder.
   - The icon for a zipped folder looks similar to the icon for a folder except it has a vertical zipper down the middle of the folder.

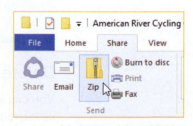

Intro-94 Create a zipped folder

Extract a Zipped (Compressed) Folder

If you receive a zipped folder via email or download a zipped folder, save the zipped folder to your computer and then you can *extract* its contents. Extracting a zipped folder creates a regular Windows folder from the zipped folder.

▶**HOW TO:** Extract a Zipped (Compressed) Folder

1. Select the zipped folder to extract.
2. Click the **Compressed Folder Tools** tab.
3. Click the **Extract all** button (Figure Intro-95). The *Extract Compressed (Zipped) Folders* dialog box opens (Figure Intro-96).
4. Click **Extract** to extract the folder.

    *   Both the extracted folder and the zipped folder display in the folder where they are located.
    *   If you check the **Show extracted files when complete** check box, the extracted folder will open after extracting.

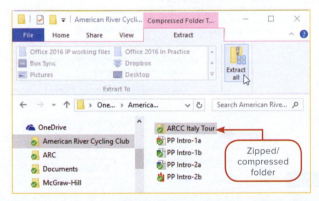

Intro-95 *Extract files from a zipped folder*

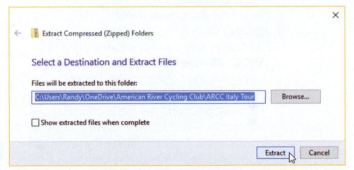

Intro-96 *Extract Compressed (Zipped) Folders dialog box*

For this project, you copy and rename files in your *OneDrive* folder on your computer, create a folder, move files, create a zipped folder, and rename a zipped folder.

Files Needed: *[your initials] PP Intro-1a.pptx*, *[your initials] PP Intro-1b.xlsx*, *[your initials] PP Intro-2a.docx*, *[your initials] PP Intro-2b.docx*, and *ARCC_Membership-Intro.accdb* *(Student data files are available in the Library of your SIMnet account)*
Completed Project File Names: *[your initials] PP Intro-1a.pptx*, *[your initials] PP Intro-1b.xlsx*, *[your initials] PP Intro-2a.docx*, *[your initials] PP Intro-2b.docx*, *[your initials]PP Intro-3.accdb*, and *ARCC Italy Tour-2018* (zipped folder)

1. Copy and rename a file.
   a. Click the Windows **Start** button and click **File Explorer** to open a *File Explorer* window. If *File Explorer* is not available on the *Start* menu, use *Cortana* to find and open a *File Explorer* window.
   b. Browse the *File Explorer* window to locate your student data files.
   c. Select the **ARCC_Membership-Intro** file.
   d. Click the **Copy to** button [*Home* tab, *Organize* group] and select **Choose location** from the drop-down list to open the *Copy Items* dialog box.
   e. Browse to locate the *American River Cycling Club* folder you created in *Pause & Practice: Intro-1*.
   f. Select the **American River Cycling Club** folder and click the **Copy** button to copy the **ARCC_Membership-Intro** file to the *American River Cycling Club* folder (Figure Intro-97). The *Copy Items* dialog box closes and the file is copied.
   g. In the open *File Explorer* window, browse to locate the *American River Cycling Club* folder and double-click the folder to open it.
   h. Click the **ARCC_Membership-Intro** file in the *American River Cycling Club* folder to select it.
   i. Click the **Rename** button [*Home* tab, *Organize* group], type [your initials] PP Intro-3 as the new file name, and press **Enter** (Figure Intro-98).

2. Create a new folder and move files.
   a. With the *American River Cycling Club* folder still open, click the **New folder** button [*Home* tab, *New* group] (see Figure Intro-98).
   b. Type ARCC Italy Tour as the name of the new folder and press **Enter**.

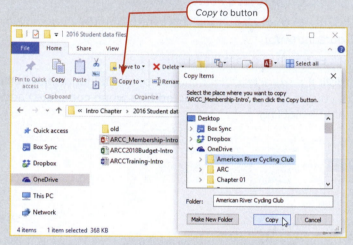

Intro-97 *Copy Items* dialog box

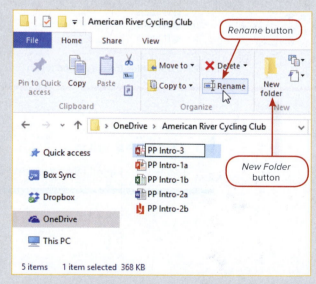

Intro-98 **Rename a file**

c. Select the *[your initials] PP Intro-1a* file.

d. Press the **Ctrl** key, select the *[your initials] PP Intro-1b*, *[your initials] PP Intro-2a*, *[your initials] PP Intro-2b*, and *[your initials] PP Intro-3* files, and release the **Ctrl** key. All five files should be selected.

e. Click the **Move to** button [*Home* tab, *Organize* group] and select **Choose location** to open the *Move Items* dialog box (Figure Intro-99).

f. Browse to locate the *ARCC Italy Tour* folder in the *Move Items* dialog box.

g. Select the **ARCC Italy Tour** folder and click the **Move** button to move the selected files to the *ARCC Italy Tour* folder.

h. Double-click the **ARCC Italy Tour** folder to open it and confirm the five files are moved.

i. Click the **Up** or **Back** arrow above the *Navigation* pane to return to the *American River Cycling Club* folder (see Figure Intro-99).

3. Create a zipped folder.

a. Select the **ARCC Italy Tour** folder.

b. Click the **Zip** button [*Share* tab, *Send* group]. A zipped (compressed) folder is created.

c. Place the insertion point at the end of the zipped folder name, type –2018, and press **Enter** (Figure Intro-100).

4. Email the zipped folder to your instructor.

a. Use your email account to create a new email to send to your instructor.

b. Include an appropriate subject line and a brief message in the body.

c. Attach the **ARCC Italy Tour-2018** zipped folder to the email message and send the email message.

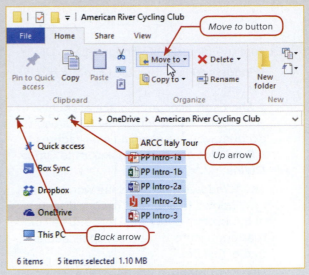

Intro-99 Move selected files to a different folder

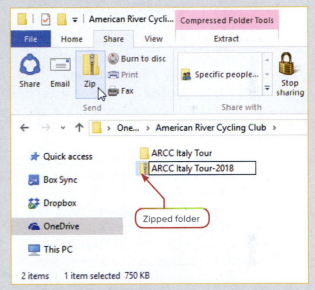

Intro-100 Create a zipped folder

Chapter Summary

Intro.1 Explore the features of Windows 10 (p. OI-2).

- *Windows 10* is a computer operating system.
- A *Microsoft account* is a free account you create. When you create a Microsoft account, you are given an email address, a *OneDrive* account, and access to *Office Online*.
- The *Windows desktop* is the working area of Windows 10 and the *Taskbar* displays at the bottom of the desktop. You can rearrange icons on and pin applications to the *Taskbar*.
- Use *Start menu* in Windows 10 to select a task. You can pin applications to the *Start* menu and customize the arrangement of apps.
- *Most Used* items, *File Explorer*, *Settings*, the *Power* button, and *All apps* options display to the left of the *Start* menu.
- *Apps* are the applications or programs installed on your computer. App buttons are arranged in tiles on the Windows 10 *Start* menu.
- The *Microsoft Store* is a Windows 10 app you use to search for and install apps on your computer.
- You can install both *traditional apps* and *modern apps* in Windows 10.
- You can customize the *Start* menu and *Taskbar* to add, remove, or arrange apps.
- The *File Explorer* is a window that displays files and folders on your computer.
- *OneDrive* is the cloud storage area where you can store files in a private and secure online location.
- In Windows 10, the *OneDrive folder* is one of your file storage location options.
- You can access your *OneDrive* folders and files using an Internet browser window.
- *Cortana* is a search tool in Windows 10 used to locate information on your computer and the Internet.
- *Task View* displays all open apps and windows as tiles on your desktop where you can select an app or window to display or close.
- *Settings* is the redesigned *Control Panel* where you change many Windows settings.

- The *Action Center* displays notifications and buttons to open many common Windows settings and features.

Intro.2 Use the basic features of Office 2016 and navigate the Office 2016 working environment (p. OI-10).

- *Office 2016* is application software that includes *Word*, *Excel*, *Access*, *PowerPoint*, *Outlook*, *OneNote*, and *Publisher*.
- *Office 2016* and *Office 365* include the same application products, but they differ in how you purchase them.
- *Office desktop apps* are the full-function Office 2016 or 365 products you install on your laptop or desktop computer.
- *Office universal apps* are a scaled-down version of Office applications you install on a tablet or mobile device.
- *Office Online* is free online software that works in conjunction with your online *Microsoft* account.
- When you open each of the Office applications, a *Start page* displays where you can open an existing file or create a new file.
- In the *Backstage view* in each of the Office applications, you can perform many common tasks such as saving, opening an existing file, creating a new file, printing, and sharing.
- *Tell Me* is the Office help feature that displays Office commands related to specific topics.
- Use the mouse (or touch pad) on your computer to navigate the pointer on your computer screen. Use the pointer or click buttons to select text or objects.
- When using Office 2016 on a touch-screen computer, use the touch screen to perform actions. You can choose between *Touch Mode* and *Mouse Mode* in Office applications.

Intro.3 Create, save, close, and open Office files (p. OI-17).

- You can create a new Office file from the *Start* page or *Backstage* view of the Office application you are using.
- When you save a file for the first time, assign the file a file name.

- You can create folders to organize saved files, and you can save a file as a different file name.
- A variety of different file types are used in each of the Office applications.
- You can close an Office file when you are finished working on it. If the file has not been saved or changes have been made to the file, you are prompted to save the file before closing.
- In each of the Office applications, you can open an existing file from the *Start* page or from the *Open* area on *Backstage* view.

Intro.4 Customize the view and display size in Office applications and work with multiple Office files (p. OI-25).

- Each Office application has a variety of display views.
- You can select an application view from the options on the **View tab** or the view buttons on the **Status bar**.
- The **Zoom** feature changes the display size of your file.
- You can **minimize**, **restore down**, or **maximize** an open Office application window.
- You can work with multiple Office files at the same time and switch between open files.
- **Snap Assist** enables you to arrange an open window on one side of your computer screen and select another window to fill the other side of the screen.

Intro.5 Print, share, and customize Office files (p. OI-28).

- You can print a file in a variety of formats. The *Print* area on the *Backstage* view lists your print options and displays a preview of your file.
- You can export a file as a **PDF (portable document format)** file and save the PDF file to post to a web site or share with others.
- **Document properties** store information about a file.
- You can share Office files in a variety of ways and allow others to view or edit shared files. To share a file with others, save the file in *OneDrive*.

- Program options are available on the *Backstage* view. You can use the program options to apply global changes to an Office application.

Intro.6 Use the *Ribbon,* tabs, groups, dialog boxes, task panes, galleries, and the *Quick Access* toolbar (p. OI-33).

- The **Ribbon** appears at the top of an Office window. It contains **tabs** and **groups** with commands to format and edit files.
- The **Ribbon Display Options** provides different ways the *Ribbon* displays in Office applications.
- Within groups on each tab are a variety of **buttons**, **drop-down lists**, and **galleries**.
- **Dialog boxes** contain additional features not always displayed on the *Ribbon*.
- Click the **launcher** in the bottom right corner of some groups to open a dialog box for that group.
- A **ScreenTip** displays information about commands on the *Ribbon*.
- Dialog boxes contain **radio buttons**, **check boxes**, **drop-down lists**, and **text boxes** you can use to apply features.
- The **Quick Access toolbar**, which contains buttons that allow you to perform commands, displays in all Office applications in the upper left.
- You can add or remove commands on the *Quick Access* toolbar.

Intro.7 Use context menus, mini toolbars, keyboard shortcuts, and function keys in Office applications (p. OI-37).

- A **context menu** displays when you right-click text or an object. The context menu contains different features depending on what you right-click.
- The **mini toolbar** is another context menu that displays formatting options.
- You can use **keyboard shortcuts** to apply features or commands.
- Some of the numbered **function keys** perform commands in Office applications. On laptops, you may have to press the function key (**Fn** or **fn**) to activate the numbered function keys.

Intro.8 Organize and customize Windows folders and Office files (p. OI-42).

- *Folders* store and organize your files.
- You can create, move, or copy files and folders. Files stored in a folder are moved or copied with that folder.
- You can rename a file to change the file name.
- When you delete a file or folder, it is moved to the *Recycle Bin* on your computer by

default. Alternatively, you can permanently delete files and folders.

- You can *zip* files and/or folders into a *zipped (compressed) folder* to email or share multiple files as a single file.
- When you receive a zipped folder, you can *extract* the zipped folder to create a regular Windows folder and access its contents.

Check for Understanding

The SIMbook for this text (within your SIMnet account) provides the following resources for concept review:

- Multiple choice questions
- Short answer questions
- Matching exercises

For these projects, you use your *OneDrive* to store files. If you don't already have a Microsoft account, see *SLO Intro.1: Using Windows 10* for information about creating a free personal Microsoft account.

Guided Project Intro-1

For this project, you organize and edit files for Emma Cavalli at Placer Hills Real Estate. You extract a zipped folder, rename files, manage multiple documents, apply formatting, and export as a PDF file.
[Student Learning Outcomes Intro.1, Intro.2, Intro.3, Intro.4, Intro.5, Intro.6, Intro.7, Intro.8]

Files Needed: **CavalliFiles-Intro** (zipped folder) *(Student data files are available in the* Library *of your* SIMnet account)
Completed Project File Names: **PHRE** folder containing the following files: **BuyerEscrowChecklist-Intro**, **CavalliProspectingLetter-Intro**, *[your initials]* **Intro-1a.accdb**, *[your initials]* **Intro-1b.xlsx**, *[your initials]* **Intro-1c.docx**, and *[your initials]* **Intro-1d.docx**

Skills Covered in This Project

- Copy and paste a zipped folder.
- Create a new folder in your *OneDrive* folder.
- Extract a zipped folder.
- Move a file.
- Rename a file.
- Open a Word document.

- Use *Task View* to switch between two open Word documents.
- Save a Word document with a different file name.
- Change display size.
- Use a mini toolbar, keyboard shortcut, context menu, and dialog box to apply formatting to selected text.
- Export a document as a PDF file.

1. Copy a zipped folder and create a new *OneDrive* folder.
    a. Click the Windows **Start** button and click **File Explorer** to open the *File Explorer* window. If *File Explorer* is not available on the *Start* menu, use *Cortana* to find and open the *File Explorer* window.
    b. Browse in the *File Explorer* window to locate your student data files.
    c. Select the **CavalliFiles-Intro** zipped folder from your student data files and press **Ctrl+C** or click the **Copy** button [*Home* tab, *Clipboard* group] to copy the folder.
    d. Select your **OneDrive** folder on the left of the *File Explorer* window, and click the **New folder** button [*Home* tab, *New* group] to create a new folder. If you don't have *OneDrive* available, create the new folder in a location where you store your files.
    e. Type PHRE and press **Enter**.
    f. Press **Enter** again to open the *PHRE* folder or double-click the folder to open it.
    g. Press **Ctrl+V** or click the **Paste** button [*Home* tab, *Clipboard* group] to paste the copied **CavalliFiles-Intro** zipped folder in the *PHRE* folder.

2. Extract a zipped folder.
    a. Select the **CavalliFiles-Intro** zipped folder.
    b. Click the **Compressed Folder Tools Extract** tab and click the **Extract all** button. The *Extract Compressed (Zipped) Folders* dialog box opens.
    c. Uncheck the **Show extracted files when complete** box if it is checked.
    d. Click the **Extract** button (Figure Intro-101). The zipped folder is extracted, and the *PHRE* folder now=contains two *CavalliFiles-Intro* folders. One folder is zipped and the other is a regular folder.

OI-51

e. Select the zipped **CavalliFiles-Intro** folder and click the **Delete** button [*Home* tab, *Organize* group] to delete the zipped folder.

3. Move and rename files.
    a. With the *PHRE* folder still open, double-click the **CavalliFiles-Intro** folder to open it.
    b. Click the first file, press and hold the **Shift** key, and click the last file to select all four files.
    c. Press **Ctrl+X** or click the **Cut** button [*Home* tab, *Clipboard* group] to cut the files from the current location (Figure Intro-102).
    d. Click the **Up** arrow to move up to the *PHRE* folder.
    e. Press **Ctrl+V** or click the **Paste** button [*Home* tab, *Clipboard* group] to paste and move the files.
    f. Select the **Cavalli files-Intro** folder and press **Delete** to delete the folder.
    g. Select the **CavalliPHRE-Intro** file and click the **Rename** button [*Home* tab, *Organize* group].
    h. Type [your initials] Intro-1a and press **Enter**.
    i. Right-click the **FixedMortgageRates-Intro** file and select **Rename** from the context menu.
    j. Type [your initials] Intro-1b and press **Enter**.

4. Open two Word documents and rename a Word document.
    a. Press the **Ctrl** key and click the **BuyerEscrowChecklist-Intro** and **CavalliProspectingLetter-Intro** files to select both files.
    b. Press the **Enter** key to open both files in Word. If the files open in *Protected View*, click the **Enable Editing** button.
    c. Press the **Task View** button on your *Taskbar* (Figure Intro-103). All open windows display as tiles on your desktop.
    d. Select the **BuyerEscrowChecklist-Intro** document.
    e. Click the **File** tab to open the *Backstage* view and select **Save As** on the left.
    f. Click the **Browse** button to open the *Save As* dialog box.
    g. Type [your initials] Intro-1c in the *File name* text box and click **Save**. The file is saved in the *PHRE* folder.
    h. Click the **X** in the upper right corner of the Word window to close the document. The *CavalliProspectingLetter-Intro* document remains open.

5. Change display size and edit and rename a Word document.
    a. Press the **Task View** button on your *Taskbar* and select the **CavalliProspectingLetter-Intro** document.

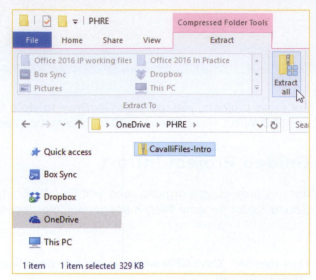

Intro-101 Extract a zipped folder

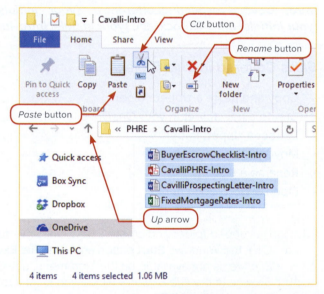

Intro-102 *Cut* files to move from a folder

Intro-103 *Task View* button on the *Taskbar*

b. Click the **Zoom In** or **Zoom Out** button in the bottom right of the document window to change the display size to **120%** (Figure Intro-104).

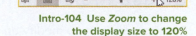

c. Select "**Placer Hills Real Estate**" in the first body paragraph of the letter and the mini toolbar displays (Figure Intro-105).

d. Click the **Bold** button on the mini toolbar to apply bold formatting to the selected text.

e. Select "**Whitney Hills resident**" in the first sentence in the second body paragraph and press **Ctrl+I** to apply italic formatting to the selected text.

Intro-105 Use the mini toolbar to apply formatting

f. Select the text that reads "**Emma Cavalli**," below "Best regards,".

g. Right-click the selected text and select **Font** from the context menu to open the *Font* dialog box.

h. Check the **Small Caps** box in the *Effects* area and click **OK** to close the *Font* dialog box.

i. With "**Emma Cavalli**" still selected, click the **Bold** button [*Home* tab, *Font* group].

j. Click the **File** tab, select **Save As** on the left, and click the **Browse** button to open the *Save As* dialog box.

k. Type [your initials] Intro-1d in the *File name* text box and click **Save**.

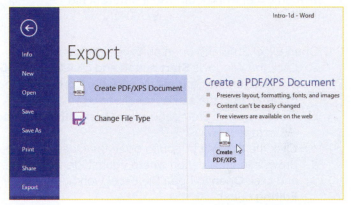

6. Export a Word document as a PDF file.
   a. With the **[your initials] Intro-1d** still open, click the **File** tab to open the *Backstage* view.
   b. Select **Export** on the left, select **Create PDF/XPS Document** in the *Export* area, and click the **Create PDF/XPS** button (Figure Intro-106). The *Publish as PDF or XPS* dialog box opens.
   c. Deselect the **Open file after publishing** check box if it is checked.
   d. Select the **Standard (publishing online and printing)** radio button in the *Optimize for* area.
   e. Type [your initials] Intro-1e in the *File name* text box and click **Publish**.
   f. Click the **File** tab to open the *Backstage* view and select **Save** on the left.
   g. Click the **X** in the upper right corner of the Word window to close the document and Word.

Intro-106 Export as a PDF file

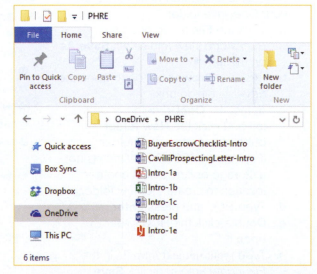

7. Your *PHRE* folder should contain the files shown in Figure Intro-107.

Intro-107 Intro-1 completed

OI-53

Guided Project Intro-2

For this project, you modify an Excel file for Hamilton Civic Center. You create a folder, rename a file, add document properties, use *Tell Me* to search for a topic, share the file, and export a file as a PDF file.
[Student Learning Outcomes Intro.1, Intro.2, Intro.3, Intro.5, Intro.6, Intro.7, Intro.8]

File Needed: ***HCCYoga-Intro.xlsx*** *(Student data files are available in the* Library *of your SIMnet account)*
Completed Project File Names: *[your initials] Intro-2a.xlsx* and *[your initials] Intro-2b.pdf*

Skills Covered in This Project

- Open Excel and an Excel workbook.
- Create a new folder.
- Save an Excel workbook with a different file name.
- Add document properties to a file.
- Use *Tell Me* to search for a topic.
- Open a Word document.
- Share a file.
- Export a file as a PDF file.

1. Open Excel 2016 and open an Excel workbook.
   a. Click the Windows **Start** button and click **Excel 2016** to open this application. If Excel 2016 is not available on the *Start* menu, click the **Cortana** button on the *Taskbar*, type Excel, and then click **Excel 2016** in the search results to open it.
   b. From the Excel *Start* page, click **Open Other Workbooks** to display the *Open* area of the *Backstage* view.
   c. Click the **Browse** button to open the *Open* dialog box.
   d. Browse to the location where your student data files are stored, select the ***HCCYoga-Intro*** file, and click **Open** to open the Excel workbook. If the file opens in *Protected View*, click the **Enable Editing** button.

2. Save a file as a different file name in your *OneDrive* folder.
   a. Click the **File** tab to open the *Backstage* view and select **Save As** on the left.
   b. Click the **Browse** button to open the *Save As* dialog box.
   c. Select the **OneDrive** folder on the left and click the **New folder** button to create a new folder (Figure Intro-108). If *OneDrive* is not a storage option, select another location to create the new folder.
   d. Type HCC and press **Enter**.
   e. Double-click the **HCC** folder to open it.
   f. Type [your initials] Intro-2a in the *File name* area and click **Save** to close the dialog box and save the file.

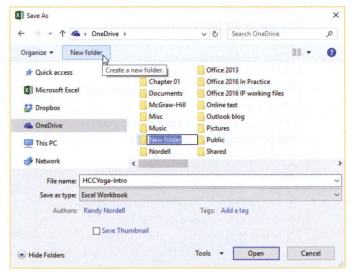

Intro-108 Create a new folder from the *Save As* dialog box

3. Add document properties to the Excel workbook.
   a. Click the **File** button to open the *Backstage* view and select **Info** on the left if it is not already selected. The document properties displays on the right.
   b. Place your insertion point in the *Title* text box ("Add a title") and type Yoga Classes as the worksheet title.

c. Click the **Show All Properties** link at the bottom of the list of properties to display more properties (Figure Intro-109).

d. Place your insertion point in the *Company* text box and type Hamilton Civic Center as the company name.

e. Click the **Back** arrow in the upper left of the *Backstage* window to return to the Excel workbook.

4. Use *Tell Me* to search for a topic.

a. Click the **Tell Me** search box at the top of the *Ribbon* and type Cell formatting (Figure Intro-110).

b. Select **Get Help on "Cell formatting"** to open the *Excel 2016 Help* dialog box.

c. Click the first result link to display information about the topic.

d. Click the **Back** arrow to return to the search list.

e. Click the **X** in the upper right corner to close the *Excel 2016 Help* dialog box.

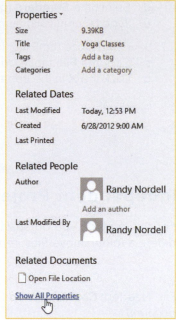

Intro-109 Add document properties

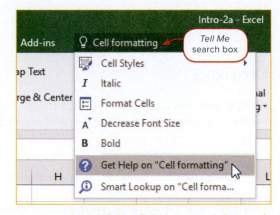

Intro-110 Use *Tell Me* to search for a topic

5. Share an Excel workbook with your instructor. If your file is not saved in *OneDrive*, skip step 5.

a. Click the **Share** button in the upper right of the Excel worksheet. The *Share* pane opens on the right side of the worksheet (Figure Intro-111).

b. Type your instructor's email address in the *Invite people* area.

c. Select **Can edit** from the drop-down list below the email address if it is not already selected.

d. Type a brief message in the body text box.

e. Click the **Share** button.

f. Click the **X** in the upper right corner of the *Share* pane to close the pane.

g. Press **Ctrl+S** to save the worksheet.

6. Export an Excel file as a PDF file.

a. Click the **File** tab to open the *Backstage* view.

b. Select **Export** on the left, select **Create PDF/XPS Document** in the *Export* area, and click the **Create PDF/XPS** button (Figure Intro-112). The *Publish as PDF or XPS* dialog box opens.

c. Deselect the **Open file after publishing** check box if it is checked.

Intro-111 *Share* pane

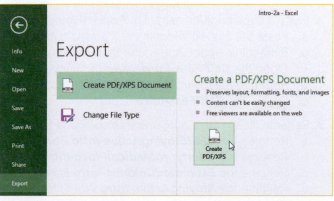

Intro-112 Export as a PDF file

    d. Select the **Standard (publishing online and printing)** radio button in the *Optimize for* area.

    e. Type [your initials] Intro-2b in the *File name* text box and click **Publish**.

7. Save and close the Excel file.

    a. Click the **File** tab to open the *Backstage* view and select **Save** on the left.

    b. Click the **X** in the upper right corner of the Excel window to close the file and Excel.

Independent Project Intro-3

For this project, you organize and edit files for Courtyard Medical Plaza. You extract a zipped folder, delete a folder, move files, rename files, export a file as a PDF file, and share a file.
[Student Learning Outcomes Intro.1, Intro.2, Intro.3, Intro.5, Intro.8]

File Needed: **CMPFiles-Intro** (zipped folder) *(Student data files are available in the* Library *of your SIMnet account)*
Completed Project File Names: *[your initials] Intro-3a.pptx, [your initials] Intro-3a-pdf.pdf, [your initials] Intro-3b.accdb, [your initials] Intro-3c.xlsx, and [your initials] Intro-3d.docx*

Skills Covered in This Project

- Copy and paste a zipped folder.
- Create a new folder in your *OneDrive* folder.
- Extract a zipped folder.
- Delete a folder.

- Move a file.
- Rename a file.
- Open a PowerPoint presentation.
- Export a file as a PDF file.
- Open a Word document.
- Share a file.

1. Copy a zipped folder and create a new *OneDrive* folder.

    a. Open a *File Explorer* window, browse to locate the **CMPFiles-Intro** zipped folder in your student data files and copy the zipped folder.

    b. Go to your *OneDrive* folder and create a new folder named Courtyard Medical Plaza within the *OneDrive* folder. If *OneDrive* is not a storage option, select another location to create the new folder.

2. Paste a copied folder, extract the zipped folder, and move files.

    a. Paste the zipped folder in the *Courtyard Medical Plaza* folder.

    b. Extract the zipped folder and then delete the zipped folder.

    c. Open the **CMPFiles-Intro** folder and move all of the files to the *Courtyard Medical Plaza* folder.

    d. Return to the *Courtyard Medical Plaza* folder to confirm the four files were moved.

    e. Delete the **CMPFiles-Intro** folder.

3. Rename files in the *Courtyard Medical Plaza* folder.

    a. Rename the **CMPStayingActive-Intro** PowerPoint file to [your initials] Intro-3a.

    b. Rename the **CourtyardMedicalPlaza-Intro** Access file to [your initials] Intro-3b.

    c. Rename the **EstimatedCalories-Intro** Excel file to [your initials] Intro-3c.

    d. Rename the **StayingActive-Intro** Word file to [your initials] Intro-3d.

4. Export a PowerPoint file as a PDF file.

    a. From the *Courtyard Medical Plaza* folder, open the *[your initials] Intro-3a* file. The file opens in PowerPoint. If the file opens in *Protected View*, click the **Enable Editing** button.

b. Export this file as a PDF file. Don't have the PDF file open after publishing and optimize for **Standard** format.

c. Save the file as [your initials] Intro-3a-pdf and save in the *Courtyard Medical Plaza* folder.

d. Close the PowerPoint file and exit PowerPoint.

5. Share a file with your instructor. If your files are not saved in *OneDrive*, skip step 5.

a. Return to your *Courtyard Medical Plaza* folder and open the **Intro-3d** file. The file opens in Word. If the file opens in *Protected View*, click the **Enable Editing** button.

b. Open the *Share* pane.

c. Type your instructor's email address and select **Can edit** from the permission drop-down list.

d. Type a brief message and **Share** the file.

e. Close the *Share* pane.

f. Save and close the document and exit Word.

6. Close the *File Explorer* window containing the files for this project (Figure Intro-113).

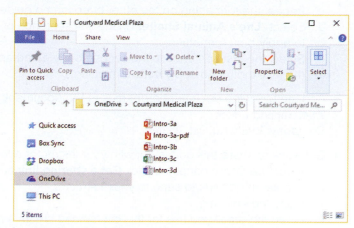

Intro-113 Intro-3 completed

Independent Project Intro-4

For this project, you modify a Word file for Life's Animal Shelter. You create a folder, rename a document, add document properties, modify a document, create a sharing link, export a document as a PDF file, and create a zipped folder.

[Student Learning Outcomes Intro.1, Intro.2, Intro.3, Intro.5, Intro.6, Intro.7, Intro.8]

File Needed: **LASSupportLetter-Intro.docx** (Student data files are available in the Library of your SIMnet account)

Completed Project File Names: **[your initials] Intro-4a.docx**, **[your initials] Intro-4b.pdf**, and **LAS files** (zipped folder)

Skills Covered in This Project

- Open a Word document.
- Create a new folder.
- Save a file with a different file name.
- Apply formatting to selected text.
- Add document properties to the file.
- Create a sharing link.
- Export a file as a PDF file.
- Create a zipped folder.

1. Open a Word document, create a new folder, and save the document with a different file name.

a. Open Word 2016.

b. From the Word *Start* page, open the **LASSupportLetter-Intro** document from your student data files. If the file opens in *Protected View*, click the **Enable Editing** button.

c. Open the **Save As** dialog box and create a new folder named LAS in your *OneDrive* folder. If *OneDrive* is not a storage option, select another location to create the new folder.

d. Save this document in the *LAS* folder and use [your initials] Intro-4a as the file name.

2. Apply formatting changes to the document using a dialog box, keyboard shortcut, and mini toolbar.
   a. Select "**To**:" in the memo heading and use the launcher to open the *Font* dialog box.
   b. Apply **Bold** and **All caps** to the selected text.
   c. Repeat the formatting on the other three memo guide words "**From**:," "**Date**:," and "**Subject**:".
   d. Select "**Life's Animal Shelter**" in the first sentence of the first body paragraph and press **Ctrl+B** to apply bold formatting.
   e. Select the first sentence in the second body paragraph ("**Would you again consider** . . .") and use the mini toolbar to apply *italic* formatting.

3. Add the following document properties to the document:
   Title: Support Letter
   Company: Life's Animal Shelter

4. Get a link to share this document with your instructor and email your instructor the sharing link.
   a. Open the *Share* pane and click **Get a sharing link** at the bottom of the *Share* pane.
   b. Create an edit link to send to your instructor.
   c. Copy the edit link.
   d. Open the email you use for this course and create a new email message to send to your instructor.
   e. Type your instructor's email address, include an appropriate subject line, and type a brief message in the body of the email message.
   f. Paste (**Ctrl+V**) the sharing link in the body of the email message and send the message.
   g. Click the **Task View** button on the Windows *Taskbar* and select the **Intro-4a** document to display this document.
   h. Close the *Share* pane.
   i. Use the **Save** command on the *Quick Access* toolbar to save the file before continuing.

7. Export this document as a PDF file.
   a. Export this file as a PDF file. Don't have the PDF file open after publishing and optimize for **Standard** format.
   b. Save the file as [your initials] Intro-4b and save in the *LAS* folder.
   c. Save and close the document and exit Word.

8. Create a zipped folder.
   a. Using *File Explorer*, open the **LAS** folder in your *OneDrive* folder.
   b. Select the two files and create a zipped folder.
   c. Rename the zipped folder LAS files.

9. Close the open *File Explorer* window (Figure Intro-114).

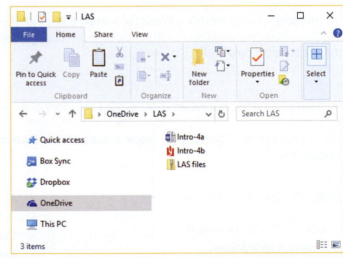

Intro-114 Intro-4 completed

Challenge Project Intro-5

For this project, you create folders to organize your files for this class and share a file with your instructor.
[Student Learning Outcomes Intro.1, Intro.5, Intro.8]

Files Needed: Student data files for this course
Completed Project File Name: Share a file with your instructor

Using *File Explorer*, create *OneDrive* folders to contain all of the student data files for this class. Organize your files and folders according to the following guidelines:

- Create a *OneDrive* folder for this class.
- Create a *Student data files* folder inside the class folder.
- Copy and paste the student data files in the *Student data files* folder.
- Extract student data files and delete the zipped folder.
- Create a *Solution files* folder inside the class folder.
- Inside the *Solution files* folder, create a folder for each chapter.
- Create a folder to store miscellaneous class files such as the syllabus and other course handouts.
- Open one of the student data files and share the file with your instructor.

Challenge Project Intro-6

For this project, you save a file as a different file name, customize the *Quick Access* toolbar, share a file with your instructor, export a file as a PDF file, and create a zipped folder.
[Student Learning Outcomes Intro.1, Intro.2, Intro.3, Intro.5, Intro.6, Intro.8]

File Needed: Use an existing Office file
Completed Project File Names: *[your initials] Intro-6a* and *[your initials] Intro-6b*

Open an existing Word, Excel, or PowerPoint file. Save this file in a *OneDrive* folder and name it [your initials] Intro-6a. If you don't have any of these files, use one from your Pause & Practice projects or select a file from your student data files.

With your file open, perform the following actions:

- Create a new folder on OneDrive and save the file to this folder using a different file name.
- Customize the *Quick Access* toolbar to add command buttons. Add commands such as *New*, *Open*, *Quick Print*, and *Spelling* that you use regularly in the Office application.
- Share your file with your instructor. Allow your instructor to edit the file.
- Export the document as a PDF file. Save the file as [your initials] Intro-6b and save it in the same *OneDrive* folder as your open file.
- Zip the files in the folder.

Microsoft® Office

IN PRACTICE

word

Creating and Editing Documents

CHAPTER OVERVIEW

Microsoft Word (Word) has been and continues to be the leading word processing software in both the personal and business markets. Word improves with each new version and is used for creating and editing personal, business, and educational documents. Word allows you to create letters, memos, reports, flyers, brochures, and mailings without a vast amount of computer knowledge. This chapter covers the basics of creating and editing a Word document.

STUDENT LEARNING OUTCOMES (SLOs)

After completing this chapter, you will be able to:

SLO 1.1 Create, save, and open a Word document (p. W1-3).

SLO 1.2 Customize a document by entering and selecting text, using word wrap, and using *AutoComplete*, *AutoCorrect*, and *AutoFormat* features (p. W1-7).

SLO 1.3 Enhance a document using paragraph breaks, line breaks, spaces, and non-breaking spaces (p. W1-10).

SLO 1.4 Edit a document using cut, copy, paste, the *Clipboard*, and the undo, redo, and repeat features. (p. W1-15).

SLO 1.5 Customize a document using different fonts, font sizes, and attributes (p. W1-18).

SLO 1.6 Enhance a document using text alignment and line and paragraph spacing (p. W1-28).

SLO 1.7 Finalize a document using Word's research and proofing tools (p. W1-32).

SLO 1.8 Apply custom document properties to a document (p. W1-36).

CASE STUDY

Throughout this book you have the opportunity to put into practice the application features that you are learning. Each chapter begins with a case study that introduces you to the Pause & Practice projects in the chapter. These Pause & Practice projects give you a chance to apply and practice key skills realistic and practical context. Each chapter contains three to five Pause & Practice projects.

Placer Hills Real Estate (PHRE) is a real estate company with regional offices throughout central California. PHRE encourages agents to use standard formats for their business documents. This ensures consistency in document appearance while also allowing agents to personalize their correspondence to customers and colleagues. In the Pause & Practice projects in this chapter, you create a business document related to the real estate business.

WORD

Pause & Practice 1-1: Create a business letter in block format with mixed punctuation.

Pause & Practice 1-2: Edit the business letter using copy, paste, and *Format Painter.* Modify the font, font size, color, style, and effects of selected text.

Pause & Practice 1-3: Finalize the business letter by modifying line spacing and paragraph spacing, changing paragraph alignment, translating text, using research and proofing tools, and adding document properties.

> **MORE INFO**
>
> *Appendix B* (online resource) contains examples of business documents.

SLO 1.1 Creating, Saving, and Opening Documents

In Microsoft Word, you can create a variety of document types. Your creativity and knowledge of Word enables you to create, edit, and customize high-quality and professional-looking documents. You can create Word documents from a new blank document, from existing Word templates, or from existing documents. Word allows you to save documents in a variety of formats.

Create a New Document

All new documents are based on the ***Normal template*** (*Normal.dotm*). When you create a new Word document, a blank document displays in the Word window. This document has default fonts, font sizes, line and paragraph spacing, and margins, all of which are controlled by the *Normal* template.

▶ **HOW TO: Create a New Document**

1. Click the **File** tab to open the *Backstage* view.
   - When you first open Word, the *Start* page is displayed. You can open a new blank document from the *Start* page.
2. Click the **New** button (Figure 1-1).
3. Select **Blank document**. A new blank document opens in Word.

1-1 Open a new blank document

> **ANOTHER WAY**
>
> **Ctrl+N** opens a new blank document.

Save a Document

When you create a blank document, Word automatically assigns a generic file name to this document, such as *Document1*. Save all your new documents using the **Save As dialog box**. You can save a Word document in a variety of file formats. By default, a Word document is saved as a *.docx* file. Other types of Word files are discussed throughout this text. The following table lists some of the more commonly used file formats.

Save Formats

Type of File	File Extension	Uses
Word Document	.docx	Standard Word 2016 document
Word Macro-Enabled Document	.docm	Word document with embedded macros
Word 97-2003 Document	.doc	Word document that is compatible with previous versions of Microsoft Word
Word Template	.dotx	Create a new document based upon a template
Word Macro-Enabled Template	.dotm	Create a new document based upon a template with embedded macros
Portable Document Format (PDF)	.pdf	Similar to a picture of a document that is used to preserve the formatting of a document
Rich Text Format (RTF)	.rtf	Generic file format that can be read by many different types of word processing programs while retaining the basic format of the document
Plain Text	.txt	Files contain only text with no special formatting and can be opened with most word processing programs
Open Document Text	.odt	Format used in the Open Office word processing program

▶ **HOW TO:** Save a New Document

1. Click the **File** tab to open the *Backstage* view.
2. Click **Save** or **Save As** to display the *Save As* area on the *Backstage* view (Figure 1-2).
3. Select the location where you want to store your document.
   - You can save to your *OneDrive*, *This PC*, or other storage device.

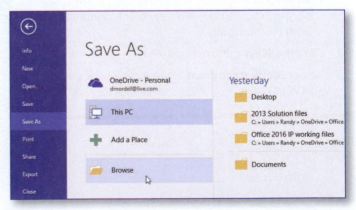

1-2 *Save As* area of the *Backstage* view

4. Click the **Browse** button or select a recently used folder in the *Folders* area on the right to open the *Save As* dialog box (Figure 1-3).

5. In the *Save As* dialog box, browse to the location on your *OneDrive*, computer, USB drive, or other storage device to save the file.

6. Type the file name in the *File name* area.

7. Click the **Save** button.

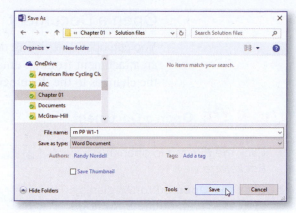

1-3 *Save As* dialog box

▶ **ANOTHER WAY**

F12 opens the *Save As* dialog box. When using a laptop computer, you might have to press the **Fn** (Function) key and the **F12** key to open the *Save As* dialog box.

After you have named and saved a document, you can save changes to the document without opening the *Save As* dialog box in the following ways:

- Press **Ctrl+S**.
- Click the **Save** button on the *Quick Access* toolbar.
- Select **Save** from the *Backstage* view.

Save As a Different File Name

You can save a document as a different name by opening the *Save As* dialog box and typing a new file name. When you save a file with a different file name, the original document is not changed and is still available. Saving with a different file name creates a new version of the original document, but the new document has a different file name.

▶ **HOW TO:** Save As a Different File Name

1. Click the **File** tab to open the *Backstage* view.

2. Click the **Save As** button to display the *Save As* area.

3. Click the **Browse** button or select a recent folder to open the *Save As* dialog box (see Figure 1-3).
   - From within Word (not the *Backstage* view), you can also press **F12** to open the *Save As* dialog box.
   - On some laptops, you might have to press the **Fn** (Function key) and the **F12** key to open the *Save As* dialog box.

4. In the *Save As* dialog box, browse to a location to save the file.

5. Type the file name in the *File name* area.

6. Click the **Save** button.

▶ **MORE INFO**

Avoid saving too many different versions of the same document. Rename only when you have a good reason to have multiple versions of a document.

Open a Document

You can open an existing document from your computer, *OneDrive*, other storage location, or an attachment from an email. After you open a document, you can edit the content and save the changes to the document.

▶ HOW TO: Open a Document

1. Click the **File** tab to open the *Backstage* view.
2. Click the **Open** button to display the *Open* area on the *Backstage* view.
3. Select the location where the document is stored.
   - You can click **Recent** and select a document on the right to open it.
   - You can also open a document from *OneDrive* or *This PC*.
4. Select a file or folder to open it or click **Browse** to open the *Open* dialog box (Figure 1-4).
5. Select the file and click the **Open** button.
   - If the document opens in *Protected View,* click the **Enable Editing** button.

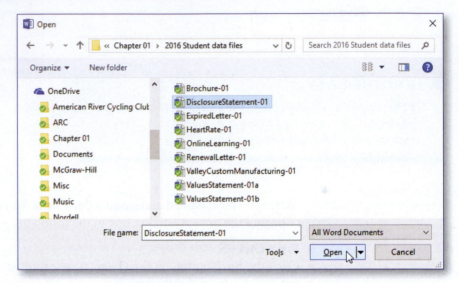

1-4 *Open* dialog box

> ▶ **ANOTHER WAY**
>
> **Ctrl+F12** opens the *Open* dialog box. Some laptops require **Fn+Ctrl+F12**.

Pin a Frequently Used Document

If you use a document frequently, you can pin it to the *Open* area on the *Backstage* view. Pinned documents appear at the top of the *Recent* documents list so you can quickly open the document. In the *Open* area on the *Backstage* view, click **Recent** and then click the **Pin** icon to the right of a file name to add the document to the *Pinned* area (Figure 1-5). Pinned files display in the *Pinned* area of the *Start* page and *Open* area of the *Backstage* view. Click the pinned file to open it.

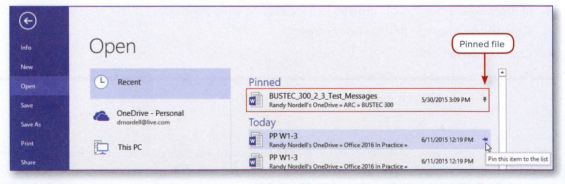

1-5 The *Pinned* area in the *Open* area on the *Backstage* view

Share and Export Options

Word 2016 provides you with sharing and export options. To share a document, you must first save the document to *OneDrive*. You can also export a Word document to PDF format.

From the **Share** (Figure 1-6) and **Export** areas of the *Backstage* view, you have the following options:

- *Share with People* [*Share* area]
- *Email* [*Share* area]
- *Present Online* [*Share* area]
- *Post to Blog* [*Share* area]
- *Create PDF/XPS Document* [*Export* area]
- *Change File Type* [*Export* area]

1-6 *Share* area of the *Backstage* view

SLO 1.2

Entering and Selecting Text

When creating or editing a document, you can type new text, insert text from another document, or copy text from a web page or another document. It is important to understand how to enter text, use word wrap, select text, show or hide formatting symbols, and use *AutoComplete* and *AutoCorrect* options to create professional-looking documents.

Type Text and Use Word Wrap

Word inserts text at the point in the document where the insertion point is flashing. By default, text is aligned at the left margin and the text wraps to the next line when it reaches the right margin, which is called **word wrap**. Press **Enter** to begin a new paragraph or line of text.

Show/Hide Formatting Symbols

The **Show/Hide** feature allows you to display or hide the formatting symbols in your document. By default, *Show/Hide* is turned off and formatting symbols do not display in your document. When the *Show/Hide* feature is turned on, you can see paragraph breaks, line breaks, spaces, tabs, and other formatting symbols that help you create clean documents and edit existing documents (Figure 1-7).

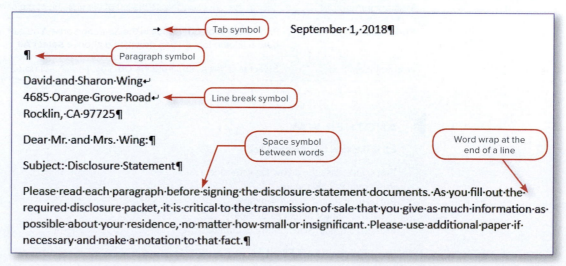

1-7 Document with *Show/Hide* turned on

Click the **Show/Hide** button in the *Paragraph* group on the *Home* tab to toggle on and off *Show/Hide* (Figure 1-8). These symbols do not print, but they allow you to see the formatting that is in the document when you view it on your screen.

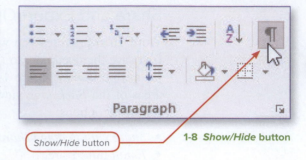

Show/Hide button

1-8 *Show/Hide* button

> **ANOTHER WAY**
>
> **Ctrl+Shift+8** turns on and off *Show/Hide*.

> **MORE INFO**
>
> When editing a document that has inconsistent formatting, begin by turning on **Show/Hide**.

Select Text

Word allows you select words, lines, sentences, paragraphs, or the entire document so you can apply formatting, copy, move, or delete selected text. You do this by clicking and dragging the pointer over the desired text, but there are a variety of additional quick methods to select text. The following table lists ways to select text.

Selecting Text

Select	Method
Word	Double-click the word.
Line	Click in the *Selection* area, which is to the left of the left margin. Your pointer becomes a right-pointing arrow.
Multiple lines of text	Click in the *Selection* area and drag up or down.
Sentence	Press **Ctrl+Click**. Hold down the **Ctrl** key and click the sentence.
Paragraph	Double-click in the *Selection* area to the left of the paragraph.
Multiple paragraphs	Click in the *Selection* area to the left of the first line of the paragraph and drag down.
Entire document	Press **Ctrl+A** or **Ctrl+Click** in the *Selection* area. You can also click the **Select** button [*Home* tab, *Editing* group] and choose **Select All**.
Non-adjacent text	Select text, press and hold the **Ctrl** key, and select non-adjacent text.

> **ANOTHER WAY**
>
> **F8** is the selection function key.
>
> Press once: Use the arrow keys to select text.
> Press twice: Select word.
> Press three times: Select sentence.
> Press four times: Select paragraph.
> Press five times: Select entire document.
>
> Press **Esc** to turn off **F8** selection.

AutoComplete

When you type a day, month, or date, Word uses the **AutoComplete** feature to automatically complete typing the day, month, or date for you, which saves you a few key strokes and allows you to be more efficient and accurate when entering dates. As you begin to type the date, Word displays the information in an **AutoComplete tag** (Figure 1-9). Press **Enter** to accept the *AutoComplete* entry. If you do not want this *AutoComplete* entry, keep typing and the *AutoComplete* entry disappears.

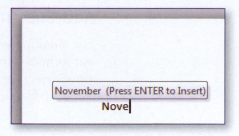

1-9 *AutoComplete* tag

AutoCorrect and AutoFormat

When you're typing, do you ever misspell a word by transposing letters or omitting a letter or adding a letter? Because we all regularly make typing mistakes, the **AutoCorrect** feature recognizes and corrects commonly misspelled words and some grammatical errors. Word automatically makes the following corrections:

- Eliminates two initial capitals in a word
- Capitalizes the first letter of a sentence
- Capitalizes the first letter of table cells
- Capitalizes the names of days
- Corrects accidental usage of the *Caps Lock* key
- Changes fractions such as 3/4 to ¾ and numbers such as 2nd to 2ⁿᵈ.

Word's **AutoFormat** controls the formatting of items such as numbered and bulleted lists, fractions, ordinal numbers, hyphens and dashes, quotes, indents, and hyperlinks. For example, when you type 3/4 followed by a space, *AutoFormat* automatically changes the format of the fraction to ¾.

AutoCorrect Smart Tag

When Word automatically makes a correction or formatting change, you have the option to accept the change, undo the change, stop Word from making the change, or control *AutoCorrect* using the *AutoCorrect Options* dialog box. If you keep typing, the change is accepted. Often when Word automatically corrects a word, you don't even recognize that a change has been made.

If you do not want to accept a change, you can click the **AutoCorrect Options smart tag** on the changed word to open the *AutoCorrect Options* menu (Figure 1-10). For example, when you type reference initials at the end of a business letter, Word automatically capitalizes the first letter. You can undo this automatic capitalization by clicking on the *AutoCorrect Options* smart tag and selecting **Undo Automatic Capitalization**.

1-10 *AutoCorrect Options* smart tag

> **ANOTHER WAY**
>
> Press **Ctrl+Z** to reverse an automatic correction made by Word.

Add Custom AutoCorrect Entry

The *AutoCorrect* dialog box allows you to customize how Word automatically corrects and formats items in a document. In this dialog box, you can also add custom items to the *AutoCorrect* menu. For example, you can add a custom entry to the *AutoCorrect* menu to correct a misspelled word or type your name every time you type your initials.

▶ **HOW TO:** Add a Custom AutoCorrect Entry

1. Click the **File** tab to open the *Backstage* view.
2. Choose the **Options** button to open the *Word Options* dialog box.
3. Click the **Proofing** button on the left.
4. Select the **AutoCorrect Options** button. The *AutoCorrect* dialog box opens (Figure 1-11).
5. Type the text you want to replace in the *Replace* box.
6. Type the word(s) to replace the original text in the *With* box.
7. Choose **Add** to add this custom *AutoCorrect* entry.
   - You can delete *AutoCorrect* entries in the *AutoCorrect* dialog box by selecting the entry and clicking **Delete**.
   - You can also add exceptions to *AutoCorrect* by clicking the **Exceptions** button.
8. Click **OK** to close the *AutoCorrect* dialog box.
9. Click **OK** to close the *Word Options* dialog box.

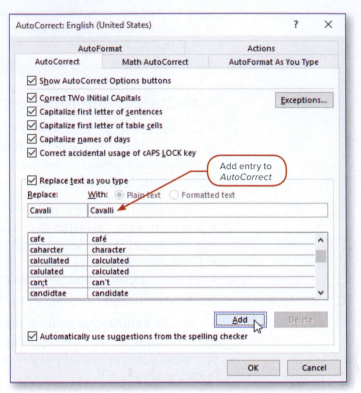

1-11 *AutoCorrect* dialog box

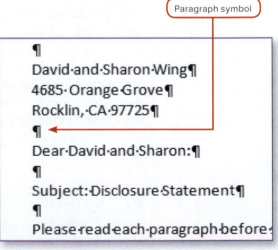

SLO 1.3

Using Paragraph Breaks, Line Breaks, and Non-Breaking Spaces

It is essential to create attractive and readable documents. Using paragraph and line breaks allows you to break up a document into more readable chunks of information. The different types of breaks can be used for different purposes when you are formatting documents.

Paragraph Breaks

The **Enter** key inserts a **paragraph break** and is marked by a **paragraph symbol** that displays at the end of each paragraph when *Show/Hide* is turned on (Figure 1-12). Use paragraph breaks to control the amount of white space between paragraphs of text within a document.

1-12 Paragraph breaks after and between lines

Many formatting features, such as indents, numbering, bullets, text alignment, line spacing, and paragraph spacing, are applied to an entire paragraph. For example, if your insertion point is within a paragraph and you change the line spacing to double space, double spacing is applied to that paragraph only. It is not applied to the entire document or just the line where the insertion point is located. For more on line and paragraph spacing, see *SLO 1.6: Changing Text Alignment, Line Spacing, and Paragraph Spacing.*

Line Breaks

*You can use **line breaks** to control breaks between lines or sentences of text. The distinction between a paragraph break and a line break is that when line breaks are used, the text separated by line breaks is treated as one paragraph. Press **Shift+Enter** to insert a line break.

You can use line breaks within a numbered or bulleted list to allow for multiple lines of text on separate lines and blank lines between the text without creating a new number or bullet (Figure 1-13). When *Show/Hide* is turned on, the line break symbol is different from the paragraph symbol.

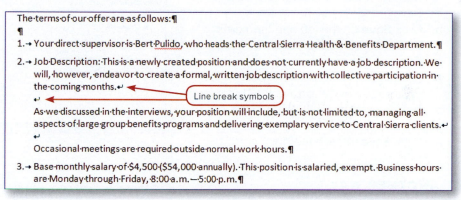

1-13 Line breaks used in a numbered list

Spaces and Non-Breaking Spaces

Spaces are included between words. Use the *spacebar* to insert a space. Current practice now dictates one space after most punctuation marks, including periods, commas, semi-colons, and ending quotation marks. Do not use spaces after a beginning quotation mark, before or after a hyphen in a hyphenated word, or when using a dash.

There might be times when you are typing a document and word wrap separates words that you want to keep together. For example, you might want to keep a person's first and last name or a date together on the same line. In this case, you can use a ***non-breaking space*** to keep these words together. To insert a non-breaking space, press **Ctrl+Shift+Spacebar** between words rather than inserting a regular space. In Figure 1-14, there is a non-breaking space between 8:00 and a.m., which keeps this information together.

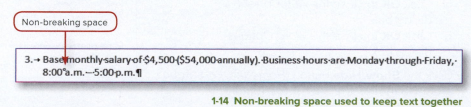

1-14 Non-breaking space used to keep text together

In this project, you create a block format business letter for Emma Cavalli, a realtor consultant for Placer Hills Real Estate. In a block format business letter, all lines begin at the left margin. For more examples of business documents, see *Appendix B* (online resource).

File Needed: None
Completed Project File Name: ***[your initials] PP W1-1.docx***

1. Open a new document.
   a. Click the **File** tab, click **New**, and click **Blank document**. You can also click **Blank document** on the *Start* page when you open Word.

2. Save the document.
   a. Click the **File** tab to open the *Backstage* view.
   b. Click **Save** on the left and then click **Browse** to open the *Save As* dialog box (Figure 1-15).
   c. Browse to the location on your computer or storage device to save the document.
   d. Type [your initials] PP W1-1 in the *File name* area.
   e. Click **Save** to save the document.

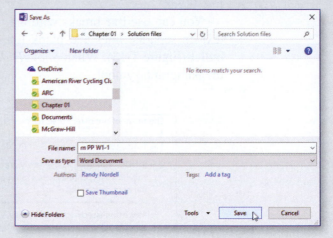

1-15 *Save As* dialog box

▶ **ANOTHER WAY**

F12 opens the *Save As* dialog box. When using a laptop computer, you might have to press the **Fn** (Function) key and the **F12** key to open the *Save As* dialog box.

3. Create an *AutoCorrect* entry.
   a. Click the **File** tab to open the *Backstage* view and select **Options** on the left to open the *Word Options* dialog box.
   b. Click the **Proofing** button on the left and select **AutoCorrect Options** to open the *AutoCorrect* dialog box (Figure 1-16).
   c. Click the **AutoCorrect** tab if it is not already selected.
   d. Type Cavali in the *Replace* area.
   e. Type Cavalli in the *With* area.
   f. Click the **Add** button to add the *AutoCorrect* entry.
   g. Click **OK** to close the *AutoCorrect* dialog box.
   h. Click **OK** to close the *Word Options* dialog box.

4. Click the **Show/Hide** button [*Home* tab, *Paragraph* group] to turn on the *Show/Hide* feature.

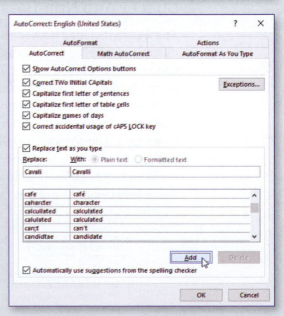

1-16 Add an *AutoCorrect* entry

5. Type the current date on the first line of the document. Type the date in month, day, year format (e.g., September 1, 2018).
   a. If the *AutoComplete* tag appears, press **Enter**, and the month is automatically inserted (Figure 1-17).
   b. Continue typing the rest of the date; press **Enter** if the *AutoCorrect* tag displays the current date.
   c. Press **Enter** two times after typing the date.

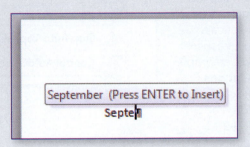

1-17 *AutoComplete* tag

6. Type the inside address, salutation, and subject line of the letter.
   a. Type David and Sharon Wing and press **Shift+Enter** to insert a line break.
   b. Type 4685 Orange Grove Road and press **Shift+Enter** to insert a line break.
   c. Type Rocklin, CA 97725 and press **Enter** to insert a paragraph break.
   d. Type Dear Mr. and Mrs. Wing: as the salutation and press **Enter**.
   e. Type Subject: Disclosure Statement as the subject and press **Enter**.

> **MORE INFO**
>
> In the salutation of a business letter, use "Dear" followed by a courtesy title (e.g., Mr., Mrs., Ms., Miss, or Dr.) and the person's last name.

7. Type the body paragraphs of the business letter and insert a non-breaking space.
   a. Type the following paragraph and press **Enter** once at the end of the paragraph. You will not need to press *Enter* at the end of each line since word wrap automatically moves text to the next line as you reach the right margin.

   Please read each paragraph before signing the disclosure statement documents. As you fill out the required disclosure packet, it is critical to the transmission of sale that you give as much information as possible about your residence, no matter how small or insignificant. Please use additional paper if necessary and make a notation to that fact.

   b. Type the following second paragraph and press **Enter** once at the end of the paragraph.

   If there is information about the neighborhood or neighbors that you as a buyer would want to know about, be sure to reveal that information. Be sure to address those types of questions on the Real Estate Transfer Disclosure Statement, item #11 on page 2.

   c. Delete the space between the words "Real" and "Estate" in the second paragraph and press **Ctrl+Shift+Spacebar** to insert a non-breaking space between.

8. Type the closing lines of the business letter.
   a. With your insertion point on the blank line below the second body paragraph, type Best regards, and then press **Enter** two times.

b. Type **Emma Cavalli** and press **Shift+Enter** to insert a line break.

c. Type **Realtor Consultant** and press **Shift+Enter** to insert a line break.

d. Type **Placer Hills Real Estate** and press **Enter** to insert a paragraph break.

e. Type your initials in lowercase letters and press **Shift+Enter** to insert a line break. Word automatically capitalizes the first letter because it is the first letter in a new paragraph.

f. Click the **AutoCorrect Options** smart tag and select **Undo Automatic Capitalization** (Figure 1-18) or press **Ctrl+Z** to undo automatic capitalization.

g. On the blank line below the reference initials, type Enclosure. An enclosure notation indicates to the reader that something is enclosed with the letter.

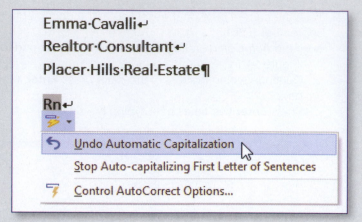

1-18 *AutoCorrect Options* smart tag

9. Press **Ctrl+S** to save the document (Figure 1-19). You can also save the document by clicking the **Save** button on the *Quick Access* toolbar or in the *Backstage* view.

10. Click the **File** tab and select **Close** (or press **Ctrl+W**) to close the document.

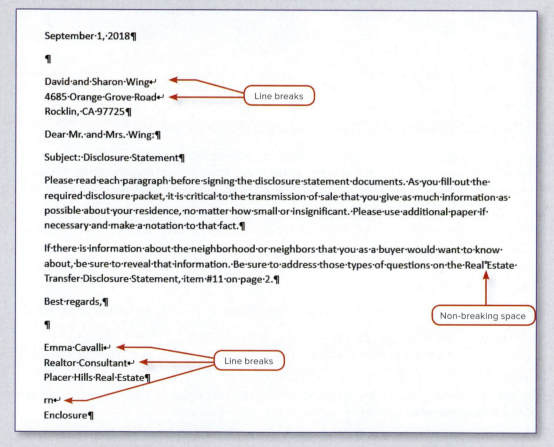

1-19 *PP W1-1 completed*

Moving and Copying Text

Editing is an important phase in document creation. Editing involves not only proofreading and correcting grammar and spelling mistakes but also arranging text within a document, which can include cutting, copying, and pasting. Word makes it easy to move and copy information within a document or between multiple documents.

Move Text

Moving is actually removing text from one location (cutting) and placing it in another location (pasting). There are two methods you can use to move text: *drag and drop* or *cut and paste*.

> ▶ **ANOTHER WAY**
>
> Press **Ctrl+C** to copy.
> Press **Ctrl+X** to cut.
> Press **Ctrl+V** to paste.

▶ HOW TO: Move Text Using Drag and Drop

1. Select the text you want to move.
   - Refer to the *Select Text* section in *SLO 1.2: Entering and Selecting Text* for methods of selecting text.
2. Click and hold the selected text with your pointer.
3. Drag the text to the desired new location and release the pointer (Figure 1-20).

Drag pointer

If there is information about the neighborhood or neighbors that you as a buyer would want to know about, be sure to reveal that information. Be sure to address those types of questions on the Real Estate Transfer Disclosure Statement, item #11 on page 2.¶

Make note on the disclosure statement if you have had any work done with or without permits. Some examples include a gas spa, a new water heater, or a wholehouse fan where a trus may have been cut. If you had granate counters installed, that does not require a permit.¶

1-20 Move using drag and drop

There are a variety of ways to move text using cut and paste:

- ***Cut and Paste buttons***: Click the **Cut** and **Paste** buttons in the *Clipboard* group on the *Home* tab.
- ***Shortcut commands***: Press **Ctrl+X** to cut and **Ctrl+V** to paste.
- ***Context menu***: Right-click the selected text to display this menu.

▶ HOW TO: Move Text Using Cut and Paste

1. Select the text you want to move.
2. Click the **Cut** button [*Home* tab, *Clipboard* group].
   - You can also press **Ctrl+X** or right-click the selected text and choose **Cut** from the context menu.
3. Place your insertion point in the desired location.
4. Click the **Paste** button [*Home* tab, *Clipboard* group].
   - You can also press **Ctrl+V** or right-click and choose from one of the *Paste Options* from the context menu. *Note: See the* Paste Text and Paste Options *section below for the different paste options available.*

Copy Text

An efficient method of inserting text into a document is to copy it from another location, such as a web page or a different document, and paste it into your document. Copying text leaves the text in its original location and places a copy of the text in a new location.

You can *copy* text by using the drag-and-drop method or the ***Copy*** and ***Paste*** buttons. Use the drag-and-drop method when copying text within the same document. The drag-and-drop method for copying is similar to the method for moving, except that you press the **Ctrl** key when dragging the text to be copied to an additional location.

▶ **HOW TO:** Copy Text Using Drag and Drop

1. Select the text you want to copy.
2. Press the **Ctrl** key and click and hold the selected text with your pointer.
   - A+ (plus sign) appears next to your pointer, indicating this text is being copied.
3. Drag to the desired new location and release the pointer (Figure 1-21). Release the **Ctrl** key after you have released the pointer.

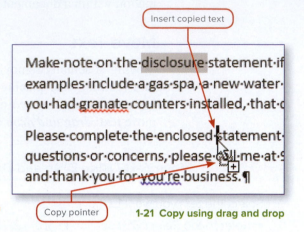

Insert copied text

Copy pointer

1-21 Copy using drag and drop

Copying text using the following copy and paste method is similar to moving text using the cut and paste method:

- ***Copy and Paste buttons***: Press the **Copy** and **Paste** buttons in the *Clipboard* group on the *Home* tab.
- ***Shortcut commands***: Press **Ctrl+C** to copy and **Ctrl+V** to paste.
- ***Context menu***: Right-click the selected text to display this menu.

Paste Text and Paste Options

You might want to paste plain text without formatting into a document, or you might want to merge the format from the source document into the new document. Word provides multiple paste options.

You have three primary paste options when you use the *Paste* button in the *Clipboard* group (Figure 1-22) or from the context menu:

- ***Keep Source Formatting***: Retains formatting from source document (the document where the text was copied)
- ***Merge Formatting***: Merges formatting from source document and current document
- ***Keep Text Only***: Pastes only unformatted text

The default paste option is *Keep Source Formatting*. In addition to these paste options, there are other context-specific paste options that are available when you paste information from lists, tables, or graphic objects.

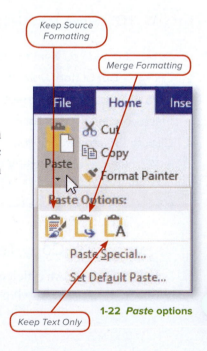

Keep Source Formatting

Merge Formatting

Keep Text Only

1-22 *Paste* options

▶ **MORE INFO**

If you have trouble with the format of pasted text, try pasting the text as plain text and formatting the text *after* you have pasted it into the document.

Clipboard Pane

When you copy or cut an item from a document, Word stores this information in the **Clipboard**. From the *Clipboard*, you can select a previously copied item and paste it into a document. When Word is open, the *Clipboard* stores multiple items copied from Word documents and also items from web pages or other documents. The *Clipboard* stores text, pictures, tables, lists, and graphics.

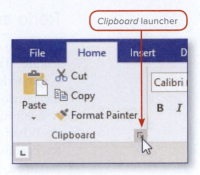

1-23 *Clipboard* launcher

The **Clipboard pane** displays all of the items stored in *Clipboard*. To display the *Clipboard* pane, click the **Clipboard** launcher in the bottom right corner of the *Clipboard* group on the *Home* tab (Figure 1-23). The *Clipboard* pane displays on the left side of the Word window and stores up to 24 copied items.

> ### MORE INFO
> The *launcher* (also referred to as the *dialog box launcher*) is referred to throughout this text. Click the launcher in the bottom right corner of a group to open a dialog box or pane for additional options.

▶ **HOW TO:** Use the Clipboard Pane to Paste Text

1. Select the text you want to copy or cut and click the **Copy** or **Cut** button [*Home* tab, *Clipboard* group].
   - You can also press **Ctrl+C** to copy or **Ctrl+X** to cut selected text.
2. Place your insertion point in the document where you want to paste the text.
3. Click the **Clipboard** launcher to open the *Clipboard* pane on the left side of the Word window (see Figure 1-23).
4. Click the item to paste or click the drop-down arrow to the right of the item and choose **Paste** (Figure 1-24). The selected content from the *Clipboard* is inserted in the document.
   - *Paste All* pastes all of the items in the *Clipboard* at the insertion point in the document.
   - *Clear All* empties the content of the *Clipboard*.
5. Click the **X** in the upper right corner of the *Clipboard* pane to close it.

1-24 *Clipboard* pane

Undo Change

You can undo, redo, or repeat previous actions. All of these commands are available on the **Quick Access toolbar**, which is above the *Ribbon* on the upper left.

When you click the **Undo** button, the last action you performed is reversed. You can undo multiple actions by clicking the **Undo** drop-down arrow to the right of the button and selecting the action to undo (Figure 1-25). For example if you select the third item in the list to undo, the previous two items will also undo.

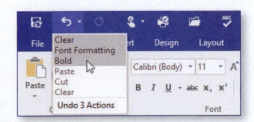

1-25 *Undo* button on the *Quick Access* toolbar

Redo and Repeat Change

The **Redo** and **Repeat** features are similar to the undo feature. The same button is used for both of these commands, and it is context sensitive. Depending on the previous action performed, the button is either *Redo* or *Repeat*.

When you use the *Undo* button, the *Redo* button is activated so you can redo the previous change (Figure 1-26).

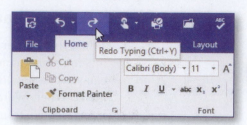

1-26 *Redo* button on the *Quick Access* toolbar

When you perform an action or apply formatting in a document, the *Repeat* button is activated (the icon changes) so you can repeat the previous action or formatting (Figure 1-27). For example, if you need to copy the date or a name into a document in multiple places, you can use the *Repeat* feature to accomplish this task quickly and accurately.

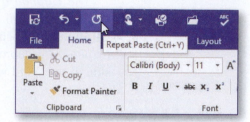

1-27 *Repeat* button on the *Quick Access* toolbar

> **ANOTHER WAY**
>
> Press **Ctrl+Z** to undo.
> Press **Ctrl+Y** to redo or repeat.

SLO 1.5

Changing Fonts, Font Sizes, and Attributes

Word has many features that you can use to customize the appearance of the text within a document. You can change the font and font size; add styles such as bold, italics, and underlining; change the case of the text; add font and text effects; adjust the scale, spacing, and position of text; and change the default font settings. You can use buttons in the *Font* group on the *Home* tab, the *Font* dialog box, and the mini toolbar to apply formatting to text.

Font and Font Size

There are two main categories of fonts: serif and sans serif. **Serif fonts** have structural details (flair) at the top and bottom of most of the letters. Commonly used serif fonts include Cambria, Times New Roman, and Courier New. **Sans serif fonts** have no structural details on the letters. Commonly used sans serif fonts include Calibri, Arial, and Century Gothic.

Font size is measured in **points** (pt.); the larger the point, the larger the font. Most documents use between 10 and 12 pt. font sizes. Titles and headings generally are larger font sizes.

When creating a new document, you can choose a font and font size before you begin typing, and it applies to the entire document. If you want to change the font or font size of existing text, you must first select the text before applying the change.

>
>
> **MORE INFO**
>
> The default font and font size in Microsoft Word are *Calibri* and *11 pt.*, respectively.
> Font size of 72 pt. is approximately 1" in height.

1. Select the text you want to change.
2. Click the **Font** drop-down list to display the list of available fonts (Figure 1-28).
   - The *Font* drop-down list has three sections: *Theme Fonts*, *Recently Used Fonts*, and *All Fonts*.
3. Select the font you want to apply to the selected text.
4. Click the **Font Size** drop-down list to display the list of available font sizes (Figure 1-29).

1-28 *Font drop-down list*

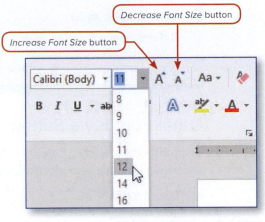

1-29 *Font Size drop-down list*

5. Select a font size to apply to selected text.
   - You can also click the **Font Size** area and type a size.
   - Click the **Increase Font Size** and **Decrease Font Size** buttons to increase or decrease the size of the font in small increments.

1-30 **Select or right-click text to display the mini toolbar**

The *mini toolbar* displays when you select or right-click text (Figure 1-30). You can use the mini toolbar to apply text formatting. Like the content menu, the mini toolbar is context-sensitive and displays different options depending on the selection you right-click.

Bold, Italic, and Underline Font Styles

You can add font styles such as **Bold**, *Italic*, and <u>Underline</u> to fonts to improve their appearance or call attention to specific text. The font style buttons for *Bold*, *Italic*, and *Underline* are available in the *Font* group on the *Home* tab.

To apply a font style, select the desired text and click the **Bold**, **Italic**, or **Underline** button in the *Font* group on the *Home* tab (Figure 1-31). You can also click a font style button to turn on a style, type the text, and click the font style button again to turn off the style.

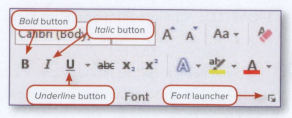

1-31 *Font* group on the *Home* tab

Other Font Style Buttons

The following are other font styles and effects in the *Font* group on the *Home* tab. Some of these style and effect features are available on the mini toolbar when you select or right-click text:

- *Strikethrough*
- *Subscript*
- *Superscript*
- *Text Effects and Typography*, which includes *Outline, Shadow, Reflection, Glow, Number Styles, Ligatures*, and *Stylistic Sets*
- *Text Highlight Color*
- *Font Color*

Change Case

The **Change Case** feature provides a quick and easy way to change the case of a single word or group of words. The *Change Case* button is in the *Font* group on the *Home* tab (Figure 1-32). The different case options are:

- *Sentence* case (capitalizes the first letter of the sentence)
- *lowercase*
- *UPPERCASE*
- *Capitalize Each Word*
- *tOGGLE cASE* (changes letters that are uppercase to lowercase and lowercase letters to uppercase)

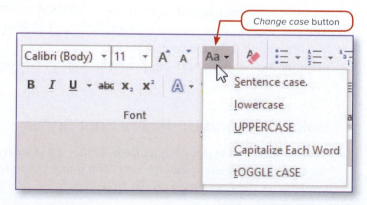

1-32 *Change Case* options

Font Dialog Box

The **Font dialog box** combines many of the font *style* and *effect options* in one location for easy access. You can open the *Font* dialog box (Figure 1-33) by clicking the **Font** launcher in the bottom right corner of the *Font* group.

In addition to the *Font*, *Font Style*, and *Size* commands on the *Font* tab, use the *Font* dialog box to change *Font Color*, *Underline Style*, *Underline Color*, and *Effects*. The *Preview* area displays a preview of selected changes, styles, and effects.

The *Advanced* tab lists *Character Spacing* options such as *Scale*, *Spacing*, *Position*, and *Kerning*. From this tab, you can also open the *Format Text Effects* dialog box.

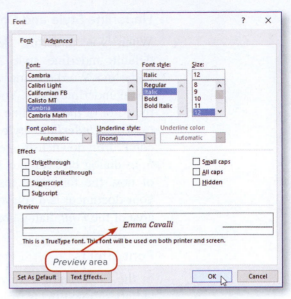

1-33 *Font* dialog box

▶ **ANOTHER WAY**

Ctrl+D opens the *Font* dialog box.

Font Color

By default, the font color in a Word document is black. You can change the font color of selected text to add emphasis. The **Font Color** drop-down list in the *Font* dialog box displays a list of available font colors.

▶**HOW TO:** Change Font Color

1. Select the text you want to be a different color.
2. Click the **Font** launcher [*Home* tab, *Font* group]. The *Font* dialog box opens (Figure 1-34).
3. Click the **Font Color** drop-down arrow to display the list of font colors.
   - The drop-down list of font color options includes *Theme Colors*, *Standard Colors*, and *More Colors*. Theme colors are those colors associated with the theme of the document. For more on themes, see *SLO 2.7: Using Styles and Themes*.
4. Choose **OK** to close the *Font* dialog box.

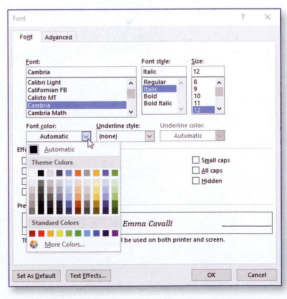

1-34 Change font color in the *Font* dialog box

▶ **ANOTHER WAY**

Change the font color by clicking the **Font Color** button [*Home* tab, *Font* group].

Underline Style and Color

When you underline selected text, the default underline style is a solid black underline. Word provides a variety of additional underline styles. You can also change the color of the underline.

The **_Underline style_** and **_Underline color_** drop-down lists are available in the _Font_ dialog box (Figure 1-35). A preview of how the formatted text will appear in your document is displayed in the _Preview_ area of the _Font_ dialog box.

Font Effects

In the _Font_ dialog box you can choose a variety of font effects from the **_Effects_** section. Some of these font effects are available in the _Font_ group on the _Home_ tab. The following table lists the different font styles and effects.

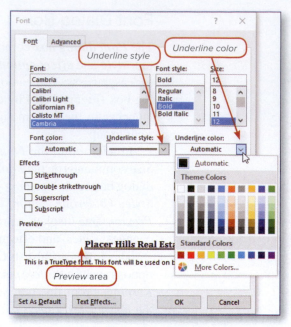

1-35 Change underline style and color

Font Styles and Effects

Style/Effect	Example
Bold	This **word** is in bold.
Italic	This _word_ is in italic.
Bold and Italic	This **_word_** is in bold and italic.
Underline	This sentence is underlined.
Double underline	This word is double underlined.
Underline Words only	This sentence is words only underlined.
Thick underline with color	This word has a thick, colored underline.
Strikethrough	This ~~word~~ has a strikethrough.
Double strikethrough	This sentence has a double strikethrough.
Subscript	H_2O uses a subscript number.
Superscript	Footnotes and endnotes use superscript numbers or letters.[1]
Small caps	Microsoft Word 2016 is in small caps.
All caps	THIS SENTENCE IS IN ALL CAPS.
Hidden	
Text Highlight Color	This word has a highlight color.
Font Color	This sentence has a font color applied.

> **MORE INFO**
>
> _Hidden_ text appears in your on-screen document, but it does not print or display in print preview.

Character Spacing

The **Character Spacing** options allow you to add more or less space between letters and words. You can also vertically raise and lower letters and words (Figure 1-36).

The **Scale** option allows you to change the horizontal spacing of a word or group of words by a percentage. You can choose from preset percentages, or you can type a custom percentage for scaling.

Spacing has three options: *Normal*, *Expanded*, and *Condensed*. For *Expanded* and *Condensed*, you can choose the amount of points by which to expand the selected text.

The **Position** option vertically raises or lowers text by a selected number of points.

Kerning adjusts the space between letters in a proportional font.

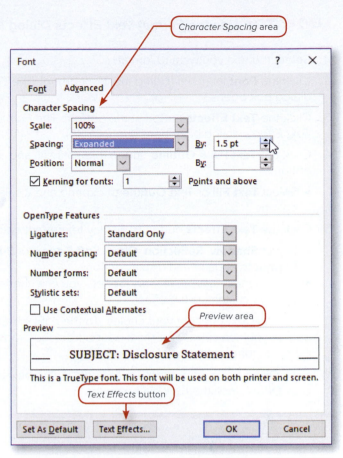

1-36 *Font* dialog box *Advanced* tab

Text Effects

Text Effects add special formatting features to selected text, such as *Outline*, *Shadow*, *Reflection*, and *Glow* (Figure 1-37). The *Text Effects* button is located in the *Font* group on the *Home* tab. There are many preset options for each of the different text effects, and there are more custom text effect options available in the *Format Text Effects* dialog box.

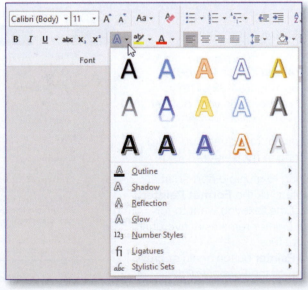

1-37 *Text Effects* button in the *Font* group

▶HOW TO: Use the Format Text Effects Dialog Box

1. Select the text you want to format.

2. Click the **Font** launcher [*Home* tab, *Font* group]. The *Font* dialog box opens.

3. Click the **Text Effects** button at the bottom. The *Format Text Effects* dialog box opens (Figure 1-38).

4. Click the **Text Fill & Outline** button to display fill and outline options.

   - Select **Text Fill** or **Text Outline** to expand and display options.

5. Click the **Text Effects** button to display text effect options.

   - Select **Shadow**, **Reflection**, **Glow**, **Soft Edges**, or **3-D Format** to expand and display options.
   - Each of these categories has *Presets* you can choose, or you can customize the effect.

6. Select the text effect of your choice. To the right of each option, you can choose a preset option from the drop-down list or customize the text effect as desired.

7. Click **OK** to close the *Format Text Effects* dialog box and click **OK** to close the *Font* dialog box.

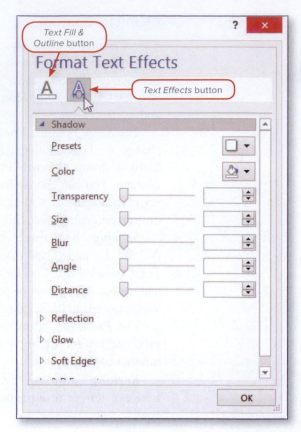

1-38 *Format Text Effects* dialog box

Format Painter

The ***Format Painter*** copies text formatting from selected text and applies the same formatting to other text in the same document or a different document. The *Format Painter* copies font, font size, line spacing, indents, bullets, numbering, styles, and other formatting features in Word. This feature saves time in applying formats and ensures consistency in document format.

▶HOW TO: Use the Format Painter

1. Select the text that has the formatting you want to copy.

2. Click the **Format Painter** button [*Home* tab, *Clipboard* group] (Figure 1-39). The *Format Painter* icon appears as your pointer (Figure 1-40).

3. Select the text you want to format, and Word applies the formatting to the selected text.

   - To apply formatting to multiple non-adjacent selections, double-click the **Format Painter** button and select the text you want to format. The *Format Painter* remains active until you turn off the feature.
   - Click the **Format Painter** button again or press the **Esc** key to turn off the *Format Painter*.

1-39 *Format Painter* button

1-40 *Format Painter* icon

Clear All Formatting

The **Clear All Formatting** feature allows you to remove all formatting for the selected text and change it back to plain text (Figure 1-41). For example, if you have applied multiple formatting styles and effects to text, you can use the *Clear Formatting* feature rather than individually deselecting all of the formatting options previously selected.

1-41 *Clear All Formatting button in the Font group*

> **MORE INFO**
>
> Be careful when using the *Clear Formatting* feature. It not only clears all text formatting but also clears line and paragraph spacing, numbering, bullets, and style formatting.

Change Default Font and Font Size

Recall that the default font in Microsoft Word is *Calibri* and the default font size is *11 pt*. This **default** setting is used on each new blank document you create. Each new document is based on the *Normal.dotm* template. This template stores the default settings for documents and controls document elements such as font, font size, line spacing, paragraph spacing, alignment, and styles.

You can change the default settings on the current document only or change the default settings in the *Normal* template. If you change the default settings for the *Normal* template, each new blank document you create uses this new default font and font size.

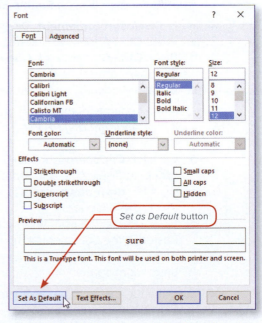

▶HOW TO: Change the Default Font and Font Size

1. Select the text you want to format.
2. Click the **Font** launcher [*Home* tab, *Font* group]. The *Font* dialog box opens (Figure 1-42).
3. Click the **Font** tab if it is not already selected.
4. Select the font and font size to set as the default.
5. Click the **Set As Default** button on the bottom left. A confirmation dialog box opens giving you two options (Figure 1-43):
   - *This document only?*
   - *All documents based on the Normal template?*
6. Select an option and click **OK** to close the dialog box.
7. Click **OK** to close the *Font* dialog box.

1-42 *Set As Default button in the Font dialog box*

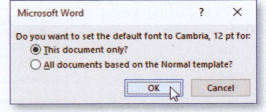

1-43 **Change default setting confirmation options**

> **MORE INFO**
>
> Be careful about changing the default settings in the *Normal* template. Do this only when you are sure you want to make this global default settings change.

In this Pause & Practice project, you customize the content of the block format letter Emma created for Placer Hills Real Estate using cut, copy, paste, and the *Clipboard*. You also enhance your document by changing the font and applying font attributes.

Files Needed: *[your initials] PP W1-1.docx* and **DisclosureStatement-01.docx** *(Student data files are available in the* Library *of your SIMnet account)*
Completed Project File Name: *[your initials] PP W1-2.docx*

1. Open the *[your initials] PP W1-1* document completed in *Pause & Practice 1-1*.
   a. Click the **File** tab to open the *Backstage* view and click **Open** on the left.
   b. Click **Browse** to open the *Open* dialog box.
   c. Browse to locate the *[your initials] PP W1-1* document, select the document, and click **Open**.

2. Save this document as *[your initials] PP W1-2*.
   a. Click the **File** tab to open the *Backstage* view and select **Save As** on the left.
   b. Click **Browse** to open the *Save As* dialog box and select the desired location to save the file.
   c. Change the file name to [your initials] PP W1-2.
   d. Click **Save** to rename the document and close the *Save As* dialog box.

3. Open the **DisclosureStatement-01** document from your student date files. Ignore any spelling and grammar errors in this document; you will fix these in *Pause & Practice 1-3*. If the document opens in *Protected View*, click the **Enable Editing** button.

4. In the **DisclosureStatement_01** document, copy both paragraphs of text to the *Clipboard*.
   a. Press **Ctrl+A** to select the text.
   b. Press **Ctrl+C** or click the **Copy** button [*Home* tab, *Clipboard* group].
   c. Close the document without saving.

5. Paste the contents of the *Clipboard* into the document.
   a. In the *[your initials] PP W1-2* document, place your insertion point to the left of "Best regards,".
   b. Click the **Clipboard** launcher [*Home* tab, *Clipboard* group] to display the *Clipboard* pane.
   c. Click the **drop-down arrow** to the right of the copied text in the *Clipboard*.
   d. Select **Paste** (Figure 1-44). The paragraphs of text are pasted in the document at the insertion point.
   e. Close the *Clipboard* pane by clicking the **X** in the upper right corner.

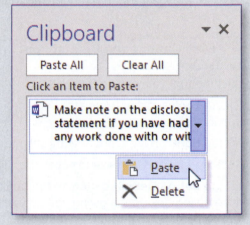

1-44 Paste text from the *Clipboard*

6. Copy the formatting of the first paragraph to the two new paragraphs.
   a. Place your insertion point in the first body paragraph of the letter.
   b. Click the **Format Painter** button [*Home* tab, *Clipboard* group].
   c. Select the last two paragraphs in the body of the letter. Be sure to include the paragraph mark at the end of the last body paragraph (Figure 1-45).

> Make note on the disclosure statement if you have had any work done with or without permits. Some examples include a gas spa, a new water heater, or a wholehouse fan where a trus may have been cut. If you had granate counters installed, that does not require a permit.¶
> Please complete the enclosed statement by [date] and return it to me. As always, if you have any questions or concerns, please call me at 916-450-3334 or email me at ecavalli@phre.com. Best wishes and thank you for you're business.¶ ᴬ⌶ ← (*Format Painter* pointer)
> Best regards,¶

1-45 Use the *Format Painter* to apply formatting to selected text

7. Copy text using the drag-and-drop method.
   a. Click the **Show/Hide** button [*Home* tab, *Paragraph* group] to display formatting symbols.
   b. Select the word **"disclosure"** in the first sentence of the third body paragraph. Double-click a word to select it.
   c. Press the **Ctrl** key and click and hold the selected text with your pointer.
   d. Drag and drop the text between the words "enclosed" and "statement" in the last body paragraph (Figure 1-46). Make sure there is one space before and after the copied word.

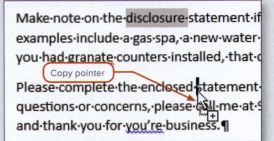

1-46 Copy text using drag and drop

8. Move a paragraph in the body of the letter.
   a. Select the entire third paragraph in the body of the letter (**"Make note . . ."**), including the paragraph mark at the end of the paragraph.
   b. Click the **Cut** button [*Home* tab, *Clipboard* group] or press **Ctrl+X**. The selected paragraph is cut from the document and stored in the *Clipboard*.
   c. Place your insertion point at the beginning of the second body paragraph.
   d. Click the top half of the **Paste** button [*Home* tab, *Clipboard* group] or press **Ctrl+V**.

9. Insert and format a date.
   a. Delete the placeholder "[date]" (including the brackets) in the last paragraph and type the date that is one week from today.
   b. Use month, day, year format (e.g., September 8, 2018).
   c. Select the date you just typed.
   d. Click the **Text Highlight Color** drop-down list button [*Home* tab, *Font* group] and choose the **Yellow** text highlight color (Figure 1-47).

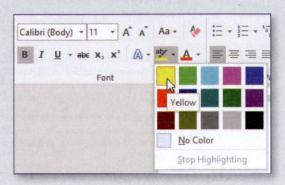

1-47 Apply text highlight color

10. Change the font and font size of the entire document.
    a. Press **Ctrl+A** to select all of the text in the document.
    b. Click the **Font** drop-down list button [*Home* tab, *Font* group] and select **Cambria**.
    c. Click the **Font Size** drop-down list button [*Home* tab, *Font* group] and select **12**.

11. Change the case and spacing of selected text.
    a. Select the word **"Subject"** in the subject line of the document.
    b. Click the **Change Case** button [*Home* tab, *Font* group] and select **UPPERCASE**. Do not use the *Font* dialog box to change the case.
    c. Select the entire subject line.
    d. Click the **Font** launcher [*Home* tab, *Font* group] to open the *Font* dialog box. **Ctrl+D** also opens the *Font* dialog box.
    e. Click the **Advanced** tab.
    f. In the *Character Spacing* area, click the **Spacing** drop-down list and select **Expanded**.
    g. In the *By* area to the right of *Spacing*, click the up arrow to change the character spacing to expanded by **1.5 pt** (Figure 1-48).
    h. Click **OK** to close the *Font* dialog box.

1-48 Change character spacing

12. Apply font styles to selected text.
    a. Select the email address **"ecavalli@phre.com"** in the last body paragraph.
    b. Click the **Font Color** drop-down list button [*Home* tab, *Font* group] and select **Dark Blue** in the *Standard Colors* area.
    c. Click the **Underline** button or press **Ctrl+U** to apply an underline to the selected email address.
    d. Select the writer's name **"Emma Cavalli"** (below "Best regards,").
    e. Click the **Font** launcher in the bottom right corner of the *Font* group to open the *Font* dialog box.
    f. Click the **Font** tab and check the **Small caps** box in the *Effects* area.
    g. Click **OK** to close the *Font* dialog box.
    h. Select the writer's title **"Realtor Consultant"** and click the **Italic** button or press **Ctrl+I**.
    i. Select the company name **"Placer Hills Real Estate"** and click the **Bold** button or press **Ctrl+B**.

13. Save and close the document (Figure 1-49).

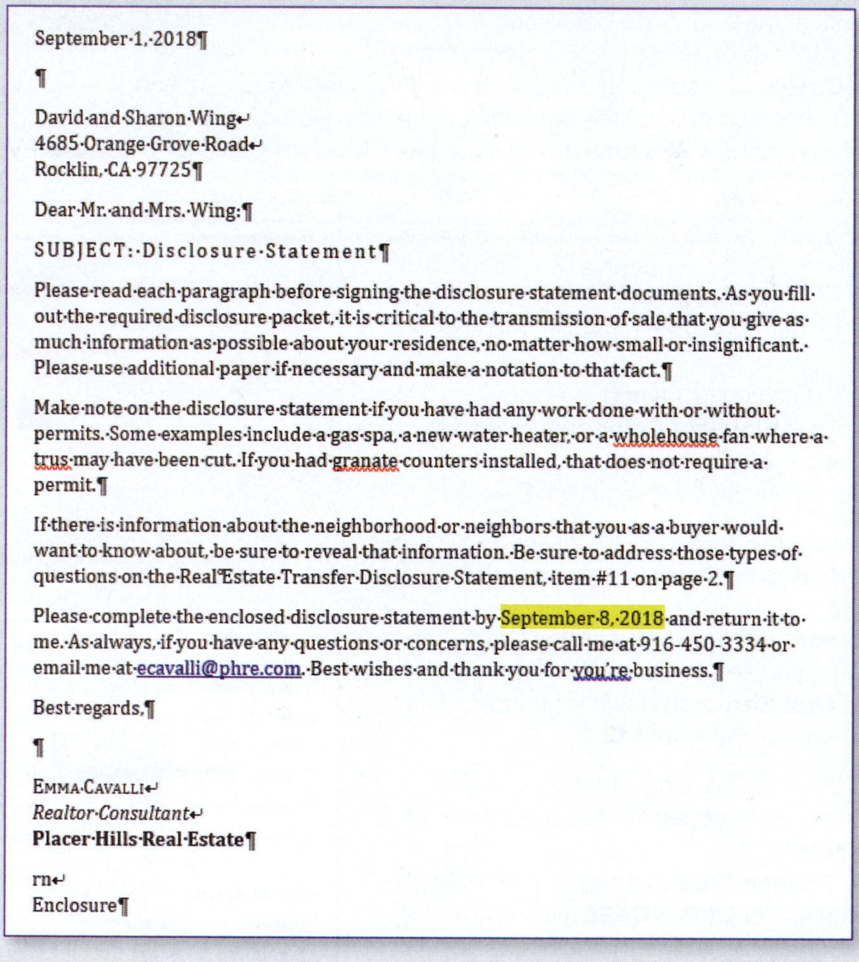

September·1,·2018¶

¶

David·and·Sharon·Wing↵
4685·Orange·Grove·Road↵
Rocklin,·CA·97725¶

Dear·Mr.·and·Mrs.·Wing:¶

SUBJECT:·Disclosure·Statement¶

Please·read·each·paragraph·before·signing·the·disclosure·statement·documents.·As·you·fill·out·the·required·disclosure·packet,·it·is·critical·to·the·transmission·of·sale·that·you·give·as·much·information·as·possible·about·your·residence,·no·matter·how·small·or·insignificant.·Please·use·additional·paper·if·necessary·and·make·a·notation·to·that·fact.¶

Make·note·on·the·disclosure·statement·if·you·have·had·any·work·done·with·or·without·permits.·Some·examples·include·a·gas·spa,·a·new·water·heater,·or·a·wholehouse·fan·where·a·trus·may·have·been·cut.·If·you·had·granate·counters·installed,·that·does·not·require·a·permit.¶

If·there·is·information·about·the·neighborhood·or·neighbors·that·you·as·a·buyer·would·want·to·know·about,·be·sure·to·reveal·that·information.·Be·sure·to·address·those·types·of·questions·on·the·Real·Estate·Transfer·Disclosure·Statement,·item·#11·on·page·2.¶

Please·complete·the·enclosed·disclosure·statement·by·September·8,·2018·and·return·it·to·me.·As·always,·if·you·have·any·questions·or·concerns,·please·call·me·at·916-450-3334·or·email·me·at·ecavalli@phre.com.·Best·wishes·and·thank·you·for·you're·business.¶

Best·regards,¶

¶

EMMA·CAVALLI↵
Realtor·Consultant↵
Placer·Hills·Real·Estate¶

rn↵
Enclosure¶

1-49 PP W1-2 completed

SLO 1.6

Changing Text Alignment, Line Spacing, and Paragraph Spacing

In addition to word wrap, line breaks, and paragraphs breaks, you can use text alignment, line spacing, and paragraph spacing to control the layout and the white space between parts of your document.

Default Settings

Just as there are default settings for font and font size, there are default settings for paragraph alignment, line spacing, and paragraph spacing. These default settings are stored in the *Normal* template on which all new blank documents are based. The following table summarizes font, line spacing, and paragraph default settings:

Normal Template Default Settings

Setting	Default Setting
Font	Calibri
Font Size	11 pt.
Horizontal Paragraph Alignment	Left
Line Spacing	1.08 lines
Paragraph Spacing—Before	0 pt.
Paragraph Spacing—After	8 pt.

Paragraph Alignment

Paragraph alignment controls how a paragraph is aligned horizontally on the page. A paragraph can be a single word, a group of words, a sentence, or multiple sentences. Paragraphs are separated by paragraph breaks. A group of words using word wrap and line breaks is considered one paragraph.

The four different paragraph alignment options are:

- *Left* (default): The paragraph is aligned on the left margin.
- *Center*: The paragraph is centered between the left and right margins.
- *Right*: The paragraph begins and is aligned on the right margin.
- *Justify*: The paragraph is aligned flush with both the left and right margins.

Change the alignment of a paragraph by clicking a paragraph alignment button in the *Paragraph* group on the *Home* tab (Figure 1-50). When changing the alignment of a single paragraph, the entire paragraph need not be selected; the insertion point only needs to be within the paragraph for the alignment to be applied. Text alignment can also be changed in the *Paragraph* dialog box, which we discuss later.

> **ANOTHER WAY**
>
> Press **Ctrl+L** to *Align Text Left*.
> Press **Ctrl+E** to *Center* text.
> Press **Ctrl+R** to *Align Text Right*.
> Press **Ctrl+J** to *Justify* text.

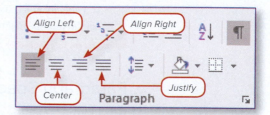

1-50 Paragraph alignment options in the *Paragraph* group

Line Spacing

Line spacing refers to the amount of blank space between lines of text within a paragraph. The default setting in Word is 1.08 lines, which is slightly more than single spacing. Most documents you type are single-spaced or 1.08 line spacing, but there are times you may want to use double-spacing (two lines), such as when typing an academic report.

As with paragraph alignment, you can apply line spacing to an individual paragraph, multiple paragraphs, or an entire document.

You change line spacing using the *Line and Paragraph Spacing* button in the *Paragraph* group on the *Home* tab (Figure 1-51). You can choose from the preset line spacing options, or you can select *Line Spacing Options* and set custom line spacing in the *Paragraph* dialog box.

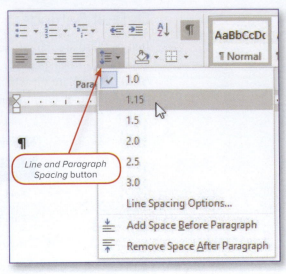

1-51 *Line and Paragraph Spacing* button in the *Paragraph* group

ANOTHER WAY

Ctrl+1 applies single-space (1 line).
Ctrl+5 applies 1.5 line spacing.
Ctrl+2 applies double-space (2 lines).

In the *Paragraph* dialog box, you see different line spacing options (Figure 1-52). The *At Least* and *Exactly* options allow you to specify points of spacing, rather than lines of spacing, between lines of text. The *Multiple* option allows you to set a line spacing option that is not a whole number, such as 1.3 or 2.25 line spacing.

1-52 *Line spacing* options in the *Paragraph* dialog box

MORE INFO

If a document has inconsistent line spacing, it looks unprofessional. Select the entire document and set the line spacing to enhance consistency and improve readability.

Paragraph Spacing

While line spacing controls the amount of space between lines of text in a paragraph, ***paragraph spacing*** controls the amount of spacing before and after paragraphs. For example, you might want the text of a document to be single-spaced, but you prefer to have more blank space before and after paragraphs. You can use paragraph spacing to accomplish this task.

Before and ***After*** paragraph spacing is set in points. The default *After* paragraph spacing is 8 pt., which is a little less than one blank line. The default *Before* paragraph spacing is 0 pt.

Change *Before* and *After* paragraph spacing from the *Paragraph* group on the *Layout* tab (Figure 1-53). You can also change *Before* and *After* paragraph spacing in the *Paragraph* dialog box and from the *Line and Paragraph Spacing* button in the *Paragraph* group on the *Home* tab.

From the *Line and Paragraph Spacing* button in the *Paragraph* group on the *Home* tab, you can **Add/Remove Space Before Paragraph** or **Add/Remove Space After Paragraph** (Figure 1-54). These options are context sensitive, depending on whether there is already *Before* or *After* paragraph spacing.

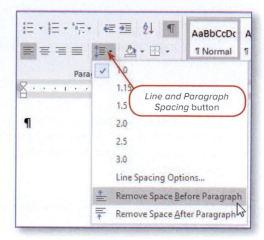

1-53 *Paragraph group on the Layout tab*

> ▶ **MORE INFO**
>
> Use line breaks to keep lines of text as a single paragraph. *Before* and *After* paragraph spacing is not applied to lines of text where line breaks are used.

Paragraph Dialog Box

1-54 *Add/Remove paragraph spacing options*

The **Paragraph dialog box** combines many of the alignment and spacing options included in the *Paragraph* groups on the *Home* and *Layout* tabs.

▶**HOW TO:** **Change Alignment and Spacing in the Paragraph Dialog Box**

1. Select the text you want to format.

2. Click the **Paragraph** launcher [*Home* or *Layout* tab, *Paragraph* group] to open the *Paragraph* dialog box (Figure 1-55).

3. Click the **Alignment** drop-down list in the *General* area and select **Left**, **Centered**, **Right**, or **Justified**.

   - The *Indentation* section of this dialog box lets you control indents. Indents are covered in *SLO 2.3: Using Indents*.

4. In the *Spacing* section, you can change paragraph spacing and line spacing.

   - Type the number of points of spacing or use the up and down arrows.
   - The *Don't add space between paragraphs of the same style* check box controls paragraph spacing between paragraphs of the same style, which is primarily used with numbered and bulleted lists and outlines.

5. Click the **Line spacing** drop-down list to select a line spacing option.

   - You can select **Multiple** and type in a specific line spacing in the *At* area.

6. Notice the *Preview* area displays how your document will look with changes.

7. Click **OK** to close the *Paragraph* dialog box.

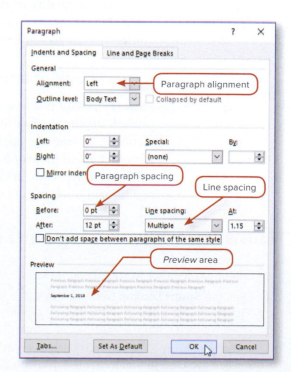

1-55 *Paragraph dialog box*

Change Default Line and Paragraph Spacing

You can set default paragraph alignment and spacing in the *Paragraph* dialog box. This process is similar to changing the font and font size default settings.

> **HOW TO:** Change the Default Paragraph Alignment and Spacing

1. Click the **Paragraph** launcher [*Home* or *Layout* tab, *Paragraph* group] to open the *Paragraph* dialog box.

2. Click the **Indents and Spacing** tab if it is not already selected.

3. Make the desired changes to paragraph and line spacing.

4. Click the **Set As Default** button on the bottom left of the dialog box. Select one of the two options in the confirmation dialog box that opens (Figure 1-56):

   - *This document only?*
   - *All documents based on the Normal template?*

5. Click **OK**.

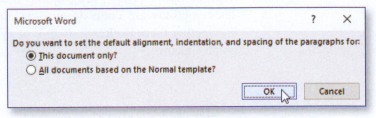

1-56 Change default setting confirmation options

SLO 1.7

Using Smart Lookup and Proofreading Tools

The words and grammar you use in a document reflect your professionalism and the reputation of your organization. Word provides you with many proofing and editing tools to improve the quality of the documents you produce. The *Smart Lookup* feature allows you to search for information on the Internet without leaving Word. The spelling, grammar, and thesaurus features help you to produce high-quality and professional-looking documents.

Smart Lookup and the Smart Lookup Pane

Smart Lookup is a new research feature in Word 2016. This feature uses Bing, an Internet search engine, to find information about a selected word or words in a Word document without leaving the application. The ***Smart Lookup pane*** displays information from the Internet about the words you select. You have the option to find additional information by clicking a hyperlink in the *Smart Lookup* pane, which opens an Internet browser displaying additional Internet content.

> **HOW TO:** Use Smart Lookup and the Smart Lookup Pane

1. Select the word or words to research.

2. Click the **Smart Lookup** button [*Review* tab, *Insights* group] (Figure 1-57) to open the *Smart Lookup* pane on the right side of the Word window (Figure 1-58).

   - By default, the *Explore* area is displayed in the *Smart Lookup* pane.
   - Click the **Define** button at the top of the *Smart Lookup* pane to display a definition of the selected word(s).
   - A privacy notice appears in the Smart Lookup pane upon first use.

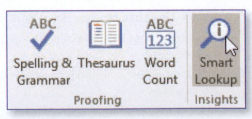

1-57 *Smart Lookup* button

3. View the research results in the *Smart Lookup* pane.
   - To view additional information about a research result, click the result title, which is a hyperlink that will open an Internet browser window displaying additional information about the topic.
   - To perform additional research on a different word, select the word in the document and click the **Smart Lookup** button again. The new results appear in the *Smart Lookup* pane.
4. Click the **X** in the upper right corner of the *Smart Lookup* pane to close the pane.

1-58 *Smart Lookup* pane

> ### ANOTHER WAY
> Right-click a word or selected word and select **Smart Lookup** from the context menu.

Automatic Spelling and Grammar Notifications

Recall that Word uses *AutoCorrect* to automatically correct many commonly misspelled words. But there are many **spelling errors** that Word does not automatically correct. When you are typing a document, Word is constantly checking the words you type against the words in its dictionary. When Word doesn't recognize a word, it marks it with a -Dot-dash **red wavy underline**.

Word also checks the grammar of your document and marks potential word choice or **grammatical errors** with a **blue wavy underline**.

> ### MORE INFO
> When Word marks a word as a possible spelling or grammatical error, it does not necessarily mean that the word is misspelled. Many proper nouns are not included in the dictionary.

▶ HOW TO: Correct Spelling and Grammatical Errors

1. Right-click a word that has a red or blue wavy underline. A context menu opens that provides different editing options (Figure 1-59).

2. Select the correct word from the list to replace the misspelled word. You can also choose from the following editing options:
   - Select **Ignore All** to ignore all instances of this spelling throughout the document.
   - Select **Ignore Once** to ignore a potential grammar error.
   - Select **Add to Dictionary** to add the word to the Word dictionary.

3. Right-click the next item with a wavy red or blue underline to repeat the editing process.

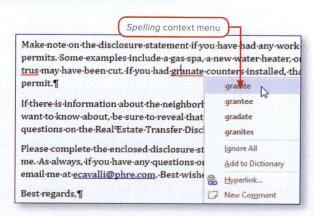

1-59 Correct a spelling error

Spelling and Grammar Panes

When finalizing a document, it is important to proofread it one last time and use the spelling and grammar check. This is especially true with longer documents. You can use the **Spelling and Grammar panes** to check your entire document for potential spelling and grammatical errors.

The *Spelling* and *Grammar* panes are context sensitive. The name of the pane (*Spelling* or *Grammar*) and the available options change depending on whether a potential spelling or grammatical error is detected.

▶**HOW TO:** Use the Spelling and Grammar Panes

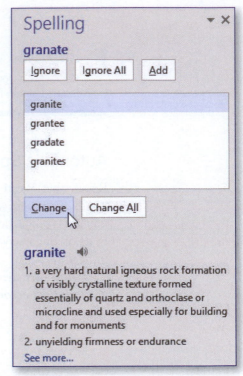

1. Click the **Spelling & Grammar** button [*Review* tab, *Proofing* group] to open the *Spelling* pane (Figure 1-60).
   - The first potential spelling or grammatical error is displayed in the *Spelling* or *Grammar* pane.
2. If the word does not need to be changed, select **Ignore**, **Ignore All**, or **Add**.
   - If you select *Add*, the selected word is added to the dictionary so it is not detected as a potential error in the future.
3. If the word needs to be changed, select the correct word and select **Change** or **Change All**.
   - *Change* changes the word and *Change All* changes all instances of the misspelled word.
   - A definition of the selected word is displayed below the list of word options.
   - If no word options are available, retype the word in the body of the document.
4. Click **OK** to finish when the dialog box opens indicating the spell and grammar check is complete.

1-60 *Spelling* pane

▶ **ANOTHER WAY**

F7 opens the *Spelling and Grammar* pane.

Customize the Dictionary

When you spell check a document, you can easily add a word to the **Word Dictionary**. When you add a word to the dictionary, Word actually creates a custom dictionary for you. You can manually add or delete words from the custom dictionary. Many proper nouns are marked as a misspelled word. You can add proper nouns you commonly use to the dictionary so they won't be marked as a misspelled word.

▶**HOW TO:** Add Words to the Custom Dictionary

1. Click the **File** tab to open the *Backstage* view.
2. Click the **Options** button to open the *Word Options* dialog box.

3. Click the **Proofing** button.

4. Click the **Custom Dictionaries** button. The *Custom Dictionaries* dialog box opens (Figure 1-61).

5. Select the dictionary to edit in the *Dictionary List*.

   - The *RoamingCustom.dic* is typically the default custom dictionary.

6. Click the **Edit Word List** button. Your custom dictionary dialog box opens (Figure 1-62). The words that have been previously added to your dictionary are displayed in the *Dictionary* area.

7. Click in the **Word(s)** area, type a word to add to your dictionary, and click the **Add** button to add the word to your dictionary.

   - To delete a word from the dictionary, select the word and click the **Delete** button.

8. Click **OK** when finished to close the *RoamingCustom.dic* dialog box.

9. Click **OK** to close the *Custom Dictionaries* dialog box.

10. Click **OK** to close the *Word Options* dialog box.

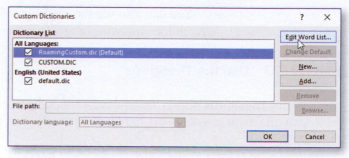

1-61 *Custom Dictionaries* dialog box

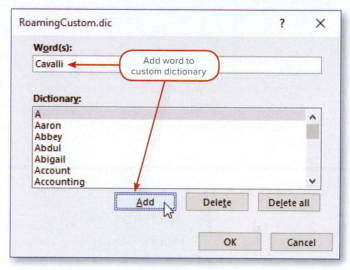

1-62 Add word to custom dictionary

The Thesaurus

Word provides a *Thesaurus* feature that you can use to find *synonyms* of words to add variety to your writing. A varied vocabulary indicates a more educated and professional writer.

There are two ways to use the *Thesaurus* to find synonyms. The first and quickest way is to select a word in the document and use the context menu (right-click) to replace a selected word with an appropriate synonym.

▶**HOW TO:** Find Synonyms Using the Context Menu

1. Right-click the word you want to replace with an appropriate synonym. The context menu displays.

2. Place your pointer on **Synonyms**. Another context menu appears with a list of synonym choices.

3. Select the synonym you prefer (Figure 1-63). The selected synonym replaces the selected word in the text and the menus close.

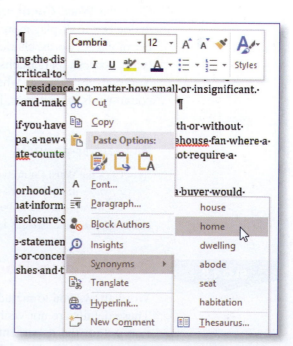

1-63 Use *Thesaurus* to find synonyms

You can also use the *Thesaurus* feature in the *Thesaurus* pane. This method allows you to search for synonyms of any word, not just a selected word in your document.

▶**HOW TO:** Use the Thesaurus

1. Click the **Thesaurus** button [*Review* tab, *Proofing* group]. The *Thesaurus* pane opens on the right side of the Word window (Figure 1-64).

2. Type a word in the *Search* text box and press **Enter** or click the **Search** button (magnifying glass icon). A list of synonyms appears in the *Thesaurus* area.

3. Choose from the synonyms listed.
   - Click the **arrow** to the right of the word to display the drop-down list. You have options to *Insert* or *Copy* the synonym.
   - You can also click a synonym in the list to look up synonyms for that word. Click the **Back** arrow to return to the previous synonym list.

4. Click the **X** in the upper right corner of the *Thesaurus* pane to close this pane.

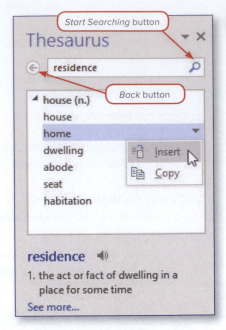

1-64 *Thesaurus* pane

> ▶ **ANOTHER WAY**
>
> **Shift+F7** opens the *Thesaurus* pane.

Word Count

Word provides a running ***word count*** in each document, which is displayed on the *Status* bar in the bottom left corner of the Word window (Figure 1-65). Click the **Word Count** area to open the *Word Count* dialog box to display more detailed information: number of pages, words, characters (no spaces), characters (with spaces), paragraphs, and lines (Figure 1-66). You can also choose whether or not to have Word count words in textboxes, footnotes, and endnotes.

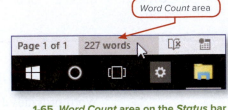

1-65 *Word Count* area on the *Status* bar

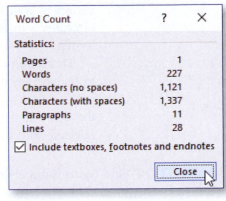

1-66 *Word Count* dialog box

> ▶ **ANOTHER WAY**
>
> Click the **Word Count** button in the *Proofing* group *on the Review* tab to open the *Word Count* dialog box.

SLO 1.8

Customizing Document Properties

Word allows you to include details about a document, which are called ***document properties***. These details are not visible in the text of the document but are included as hidden information within the document. These include fields such as *Title*, *Author*, *Comments*, *Subject*, *Company*, *Created*, and *Last Modified*. Some of the document properties are automatically generated, such as *Words*, *Total Editing Time*, and *Last Modified*, whereas other document property details can be edited individually.

Document Properties

The document properties can be viewed and edited in the *Info* area on the *Backstage* view. Document properties are saved within the document and can be viewed by others who view or use the document.

▶ **HOW TO:** Add Document Properties

1. Click the **File** tab to display the *Backstage* view.
2. Click the **Info** button if it is not already selected.
3. Review the document properties on the right side of the window (Figure 1-67).
   - Document property field names are listed on the left, and the information in these fields is listed on the right.
4. Click in a field and type information to edit the document property.
   - Some properties cannot be changed. These properties are automatically generated by Word.
5. Click the **Show All/Fewer Properties** link at the bottom to display more or fewer document property fields.
6. After entering and reviewing document properties, click the **Back** arrow in the upper left corner of the *Backstage* view to return to the document.

1-67 Document properties on the *Backstage* view

Advanced Properties

In addition to viewing and editing the document properties on the *Backstage* view, you can also display document properties in the ***Properties dialog box*** (Figure 1-68). In the *Info* area on the *Backstage* view, click the **Properties** button and select **Advanced Properties** to open the *Properties* dialog box.

You can modify the document properties on the *Summary* tab. The title of the *Properties* dialog box is context sensitive. The file name is displayed before *Properties* in the title bar of the dialog box.

1-68 *Properties* dialog box

Print Document Properties

After customizing document properties, you can print the document properties included in a document. When you print document properties, only a page listing the document properties prints, not the document itself.

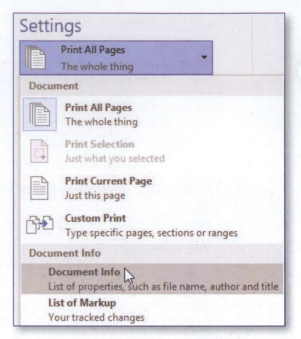

▶ HOW TO: Print Document Properties

1. Click the **File** tab to open the *Backstage* view.
2. Select **Print** on the left.
3. Click **Print All Pages** and select **Document Info** from the drop-down list (Figure 1-69).
4. Click the **Print** button to print the document properties.

1-69 Print document properties

PAUSE & PRACTICE: WORD 1-3

In the final Pause & Practice project in this chapter, you add the finishing touches on a document for Placer Hills Real Estate. You customize paragraph and line spacing, change paragraph alignment, and use spelling and grammar checkers to produce an error-free document. You also modify the document properties.

File Needed: *[your initials] PP W1-2.docx*
Completed Project File Name: *[your initials] PP W1-3.docx*

---

1. Open the *[your initials] PP W1-2* document completed in *Pause & Practice 1-2*.
   a. Click the **File** tab to open the *Backstage* view and click **Open** on the left.
   b. Click **Browse** to open the *Open* dialog box.
   c. Browse to locate the *[your initials] PP W1-2* document, select the document, and click **Open**.

2. Save this document with a different file name.
   a. Click the **File** tab to open the *Backstage* view and select **Save As** on the left.
   b. Click **Browse** to open the *Save As* dialog box and select the desired location to save the file.
   c. Change the file name to [your initials] PP W1-3.
   d. Click **Save** to save the document with a different file name and close the *Save As* dialog box.

3. Change the line and paragraph spacing on the entire document.
   a. Press **Ctrl+A** to select the entire document.
   b. Click the **Paragraph** launcher [*Home* or *Layout* tab, *Paragraph* group] to open the *Paragraph* dialog box (Figure 1-70).

c. Change the *Line spacing* to **Single**.
d. Change the *After* spacing to **12 pt**. Use the up arrow or type in the amount of spacing.
e. Click **OK** to close the dialog box.

> **ANOTHER WAY**
>
> Change line spacing in the *Paragraph* group on the *Home* tab. Change *Before* and *After* paragraph spacing in the *Paragraph* group on the *Layout* tab.

4. Add paragraph spacing before the date line of the business letter.
   a. Select or place your insertion point in the first line (date line) of the business letter.
   b. Click the **Layout** tab.
   c. Change the *Before* spacing to **72 pt**. (Figure 1-71). *Note: 72 pt. is approximately 1", which is commonly used as the spacing before the date line on business letters.*

5. Change the paragraph alignment of selected text.
   a. Select or place your insertion point in the subject line of the business letter.
   b. Click the **Center** button [*Home* tab, *Paragraph* group] or press **Ctrl+E**.

6. Use the *Thesaurus* to find synonyms for selected words.
   a. Select the word **"reveal"** in the third body paragraph.
   b. Click the **Thesaurus** button [*Review* tab, *Proofing* group]. The *Thesaurus* pane opens on the right with a list of synonyms for the selected word (Figure 1-72).
   c. Click the **drop-down arrow** to the right of the word "divulge" and choose **Insert**. The word "reveal" is replaced with "divulge."
   d. Click the **X** in the upper right corner of the *Thesaurus* pane to close the pane.
   e. Right-click the word **"residence"** in the first body paragraph. A context menu opens.
   f. Point to **Synonyms** and a list of synonyms appears.
   g. Select **"home"** from the list of synonyms. The word "residence" is replaced with "home."

7. Add a word to the custom dictionary.
   a. Click the **File** tab to open the *Backstage* view.
   b. Click the **Options** button to open the *Word Options* dialog box.
   c. Click **Proofing** on the left.
   d. Click the **Custom Dictionaries** button in the *When correcting spelling in Microsoft Office programs* area. The *Custom Dictionaries* dialog box opens.

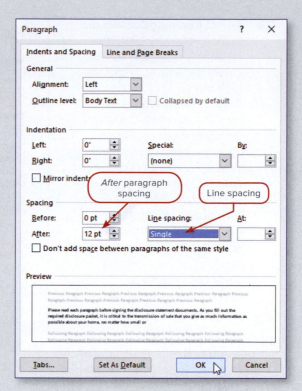

1-70 Change *Line spacing* and *After* paragraph spacing in the *Paragraph* dialog box

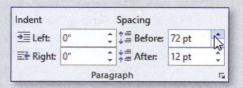

1-71 Change *Before* paragraph spacing in the *Paragraph* group

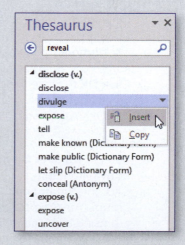

1-72 Insert a synonym from the *Thesaurus* pane

e. Select **RoamingCustom.dic** in the *Dictionary List*. If this dictionary is not available, select the available custom dictionary.

f. Click the **Edit Word List** button. The *RoamingCustom.dic* dialog box opens (Figure 1-73)

g. Type your last name in the *Word(s)* area and click the **Add** button. If your last name is already in the dictionary, the *Add* button is shaded gray.

h. Click **OK** to close the *RoamingCustom.dic* dialog box.

i. Click **OK** to close the *Custom Dictionaries* dialog box.

j. Click **OK** to close the *Word Options* dialog box.

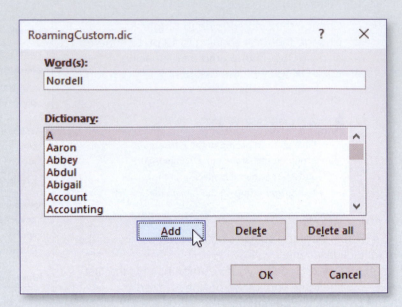

1-73 Add a word to the custom dictionary

8. Spell and grammar check the document.

a. Right-click the word **"wholehouse"** in the second paragraph. A context list of words appears (Figure 1-74).

b. Select **"whole house."** The correctly spelled word replaces the incorrectly spelled word.

c. Click the **Spelling & Grammar** button [*Review* tab, *Proofing* group] or press **F7** to open the *Spelling* pane on the right (Figure 1-75).

d. Select **"truss"** in the *Spelling* pane and click the **Change** button.

e. Continue spell checking the remainder of the document. Change "granate" to **"granite"** and "you're" to **"your."**

f. Click **Add** for "Cavalli" if it is marked as incorrect.

g. Click **Ignore** for your reference initials if it is marked as incorrect.

h. Click **Ignore** for the capitalization grammar error (lowercase reference initials).

i. Click **OK** to close the dialog box that opens and informs you that the spelling and grammar check is complete. The *Spelling* pane closes.

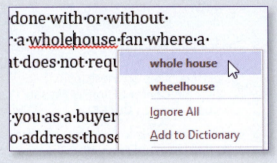

1-74 Correct spelling using the context menu

9. Use *Smart Lookup* to research selected words.

a. Select **"Transfer Disclosure Statement"** in the third body paragraph.

b. Click the **Smart Lookup** button [*Review* tab, *Insights* group]. The *Smart Lookup* pane opens on the right. If you are using this feature for the first time, you might receive a message about privacy and have to click the **Got it** button before data is displayed.

c. Review the research results on the *Smart Lookup* pane.

d. Click the **X** in the upper right of the *Smart Lookup* pane to close the pane.

1-75 *Spelling* pane

10. Add document properties to your letter.
    a. Click the **File** tab to open the *Backstage* view.
    b. Click **Info** on the left if it is not already selected. The document properties are displayed on the right side of the *Backstage* view (Figure 1-76).
    c. Click in the *Title* field and type Disclosure Statement.
    d. In the *Author* area, right-click the existing author and select **Remove Person**.
    e. In the *Author* area, click **Add an author**, type Emma Cavalli, and press **Tab**.
    f. Click the **Show All Properties** link at the bottom. More document properties are displayed.
    g. Click in the *Company* area and type Placer Hills Real Estate.
    h. Click the **Properties** drop-down list at the top of the *Properties* area and choose **Advanced Properties**. The document properties display in the *Summary* tab of the *Properties* dialog box.
    i. Click **OK** to close the *Properties* dialog box and click the **Back** arrow to return to the document.

11. Save and close the document (Figure 1-77).

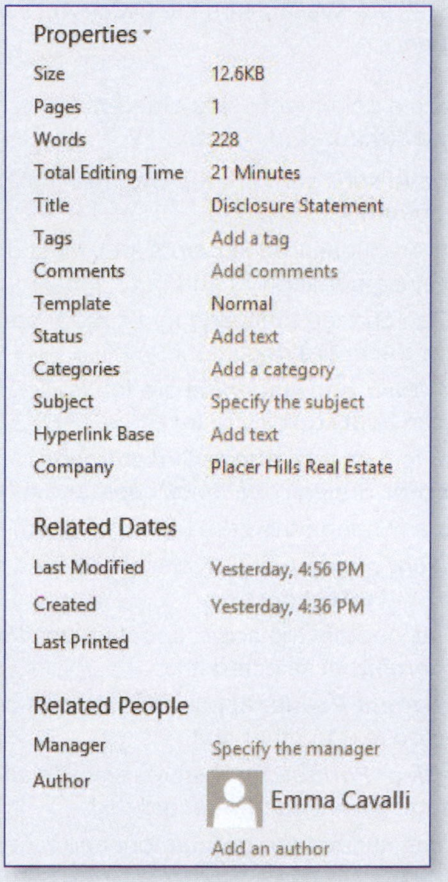

Properties ▾

Size	12.6KB
Pages	1
Words	228
Total Editing Time	21 Minutes
Title	Disclosure Statement
Tags	Add a tag
Comments	Add comments
Template	Normal
Status	Add text
Categories	Add a category
Subject	Specify the subject
Hyperlink Base	Add text
Company	Placer Hills Real Estate

Related Dates

Last Modified	Yesterday, 4:56 PM
Created	Yesterday, 4:36 PM
Last Printed	

Related People

Manager	Specify the manager
Author	Emma Cavalli
	Add an author

1-76 Document properties on the Backstage view

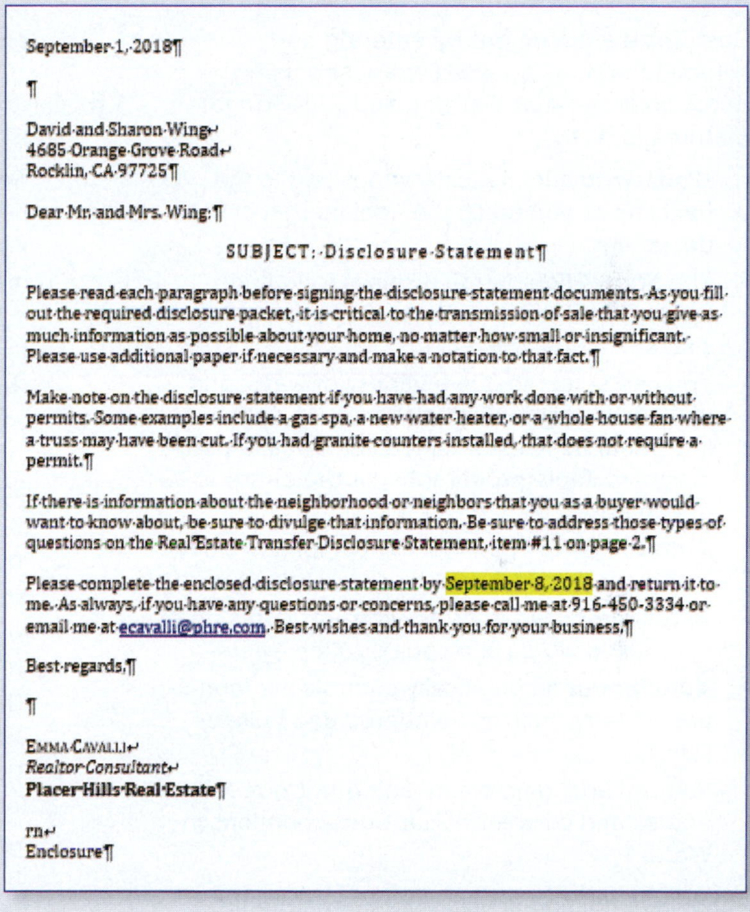

September·1,·2018¶

¶

David·and·Sharon·Wing↵
4685·Orange·Grove·Road↵
Rocklin,·CA·97725¶

Dear·Mr.·and·Mrs.·Wing:¶

SUBJECT:·Disclosure·Statement¶

Please·read·each·paragraph·before·signing·the·disclosure·statement·documents.·As·you·fill·out·the·required·disclosure·packet,·it·is·critical·to·the·transmission·of·sale·that·you·give·as·much·information·as·possible·about·your·home,·no·matter·how·small·or·insignificant.·Please·use·additional·paper·if·necessary·and·make·a·notation·to·that·fact.¶

Make·note·on·the·disclosure·statement·if·you·have·had·any·work·done·with·or·without·permits.·Some·examples·include·a·gas·spa,·a·new·water·heater,·or·a·whole·house·fan·where·a·truss·may·have·been·cut.·If·you·had·granite·counters·installed,·that·does·not·require·a·permit.¶

If·there·is·information·about·the·neighborhood·or·neighbors·that·you·as·a·buyer·would·want·to·know·about,·be·sure·to·divulge·that·information.·Be·sure·to·address·those·types·of·questions·on·the·Real·Estate·Transfer·Disclosure·Statement,·item·#11·on·page·2.¶

Please·complete·the·enclosed·disclosure·statement·by·September·8,·2018·and·return·it·to·me.·As·always,·if·you·have·any·questions·or·concerns,·please·call·me·at·916-450-3334·or·email·me·at·ecavalli@phre.com.·Best·wishes·and·thank·you·for·your·business.¶

Best·regards,¶

¶

EMMA·CAVALLI↵
Realtor·Consultant↵
Placer·Hills·Real·Estate¶

rn↵
Enclosure¶

1-77 PP W1-3 completed

Chapter Summary

1.1 Create, save, and open a Word document (p. W1-3).

- New Word documents are based on the **Normal template** (*Normal.dotx*).
- You can save documents with the existing file name or with a different file name.
- A **Word document** (**.docx**) is the standard file format. There are a variety of Word file formats in which to save a document.
- You can open, edit, and save existing Word documents.

1.2 Customize a document by entering and selecting text, using word wrap, and using *AutoComplete*, *AutoCorrect*, and *AutoFormat* features (p. W1-7).

- **Word wrap** automatically wraps text to the next line as you reach the right margin of the document.
- The **Show/Hide** button displays formatting symbols in the document to properly and consistently format documents.
- You can select text in a variety of ways, and you can select individual words, an entire line, multiple lines of text, a sentence, a paragraph, multiple paragraphs, or the entire document.
- **AutoComplete** automatically completes a day, month, or date for you.
- **AutoCorrect** automatically corrects commonly misspelled words and capitalization errors.
- **AutoFormat** automatically controls the formatting of items such as numbered and bulleted lists.
- You can add, delete, and edit *AutoCorrect* entries and customize *AutoCorrect* options in Word.

1.3 Enhance a document using paragraph breaks, line breaks, spaces, and non-breaking spaces (p. W1-10).

- The **Enter** key on the keyboard inserts a **paragraph break**. The **paragraph symbol** is visible when *Show/Hide* is turned on.
- **Line breaks** control breaks between lines or sentences to retain paragraph formatting between lines.
- **Non-breaking spaces** keep related words together.

1.4 Edit a document using cut, copy, paste, the *Clipboard*, and the undo, redo, and repeat features (p. W1-15).

- You can move or copy selected text within a document. There are a variety of methods to **cut**, **copy**, and **paste** text in a document.
- The **Clipboard** stores text that you have cut or copied. You can use the *Clipboard* to paste text into your document.
- You can **Undo**, **Redo**, and **Repeat** previous actions when working on a document. These features are available on the **Quick Access toolbar**.

1.5 Customize a document using different fonts, font sizes, and attributes (p. W1-18).

- **Serif** and **sans serif** are the two main categories of **fonts**.
- Fonts are measured in **points** (pt.). Most documents use between 10 and 12 pt. font size.
- You can change fonts and font size for specific text or the entire document.
- **Bold**, **Italic**, and **Underline** are font styles that you can apply quickly to text.
- Other font effects include **Strikethrough**, **Subscript**, **Superscript**, **Small caps**, and **All caps**.
- You can change the case of text in Word.
- The **Font dialog box** provides many **font**, **size**, **style**, and **effect options**.
- You can modify the **scale**, **spacing**, **position**, and **kerning** of selected text.
- The **Format Painter** applies formatting from selected text to other text.
- The **Clear Formatting** feature removes all formatting applied to selected text.
- You can change the **default** font and font size in Word.

1.6 Enhance a document using text alignment and line and paragraph spacing (p. W1-28).

- **Paragraph alignment** describes how text is aligned horizontally between the margins of a document: **Left**, **Center**, **Right**, or **Justified**.
- **Line spacing** refers to the amount of blank space between lines of text in a paragraph.
- **Paragraph spacing** is the amount of space between paragraphs. Paragraph spacing is measured in points.

- You can modify alignment, line spacing, and paragraph spacing on the *Home* or *Layout* tab or in the **Paragraph dialog box**.
- You can change the default line and paragraph spacing in Word.

1.7 Finalize a document using Word's research and proofing tools (p. W1-32).

- **Smart Lookup** is used to research selected word(s) without leaving Word. Research results display in the **Smart Lookup pane**.
- By default, Word automatically checks documents for **spelling** and **grammatical errors**.
- Word marks potential spelling, incorrect word, or grammatical errors with a colored wavy line under the words. You can correct errors by selecting from options in the context menu.

- You can manually spell and grammar check a document using the *Spelling and Grammar* pane.
- You can customize the **Word dictionary** by adding, deleting, or modifying words in the word list.
- The **Thesaurus** finds synonyms for words in your document.
- Word also provides you with a **Word Count**.

1.8 Apply custom document properties to a document (p. W1-36).

- You can add **document properties**, such as *Title, Author, Company, Subject, Created*, and *Last Modified*, into a document.
- You can add document properties on the *Backstage* view or in the *Properties* dialog box.

Check for Understanding

The SIMbook for this text (within your SIMnet account) provides the following resources for concept review:

- Multiple choice questions
- Matching exercises
- Short answer questions

Guided Project 1-1

In this project, Jennie Owings at Central Sierra Insurance is writing a business letter to Hartford Specialty regarding the renewal of the insurance policy for Valley Custom Manufacturing. This business letter is typed in block format and uses open punctuation. See *Appendix B* (online resource) for examples of business document formats and mixed and open punctuation.
[Student Learning Outcomes 1.1, 1.2, 1.3, 1.4, 1.5, 1.6, 1.7, 1.8]

File Needed: ***ValleyCustomManufacturing-01.docx*** *(Student data files are available in the* Library *of your SIMnet account)*
Completed Project File Name: *[your initials] Word 1-1.docx*

Skills Covered in This Project

- Add document properties.
- Use block business letter format using open punctuation.
- Change line spacing.
- Change paragraph spacing.
- Use *AutoComplete*.
- Use paragraph breaks for proper spacing between the parts of a business letter.

- Copy and paste text from another document using the *Clipboard*.
- Use *Show/Hide*.
- Undo automatic capitalization.
- Change font size.
- Apply font styles.
- Use *Smart Lookup*.
- Use spelling and grammar checker.
- Add words to the dictionary.

1. Open a new Word document.
   a. Click the **File** tab to open the *Backstage* view.
   b. Click **New** on the left and click **Blank document**. You can also click **Blank document** from the *Start* page when you first open Word.

2. Save the document as *[your initials] Word 1-1*.
   a. Click the **File** tab to open the *Backstage* view and select **Save As** on the left.
   b. Click **Browse** to open the *Save As* dialog box and select the desired location to save the file.
   c. Change the file name to [your initials] Word 1-1.
   d. Click **Save** to rename the document and close the *Save As* dialog box.

3. Add document properties.
   a. Click the **File** tab to open the *Info* area on the *Backstage* view and click the **Show All Properties** link.
   b. Type Valley Custom Manufacturing in the *Title* field.
   c. Type Central Sierra Insurance in the *Company* field.
   d. Click the **Back** arrow in the upper left of the *Backstage* view to return to the document.

4. Change the line and paragraph spacing of the document.
   a. Click the **Paragraph** launcher [*Home* or *Layout* tab, *Paragraph* group] to open the *Paragraph* dialog box (Figure 1-78).
   b. Change the *Line spacing* to **Single**.

c. Change the *After* paragraph spacing to **0 pt**.

d. Choose **OK** to close the *Paragraph* dialog box.

5. Use *AutoComplete* to type a date.

   a. Turn on **Show/Hide** [*Home* tab, *Paragraph* group] if it is not already turned on.

   b. Type the current date using month, day, year format (e.g., September 1, 2018). As you begin typing the date, *AutoComplete* completes the month and current date. Press **Enter** to accept the *AutoComplete* date.

   c. Press **Enter** four times (quadruple space) after the date.

6. Type the inside address, salutation, and subject line.

   a. Type Mrs. Cammie Speckler and press **Enter** once at the end of the line.

   b. Type Hartford Specialty and press **Enter** once.

   c. Type 4788 Market Street, Suite A205 and press **Enter** once.

   d. Type San Francisco, CA 95644 and press **Enter** two times.

   e. Type Dear Mrs. Speckler as the salutation and press **Enter** two times. No colon is used after the salutation when using open punctuation.

   f. Type RE: Valley Custom Manufacturing as the subject line and press **Enter** two times.

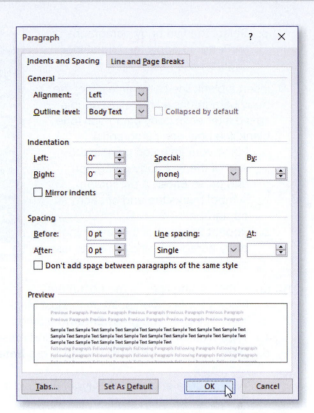

1-78 *Paragraph* dialog box

7. Copy text from another document and paste it into the current document.

   a. Open the ***ValleyCustomManufacturing-01*** document from your student data files. If the document opens in *Protected View*, click the **Enable Editing** button.

   b. Press **Ctrl+A** to select the entire document.

   c. Click the **Copy** button [*Home* tab, *Clipboard* group] or press **Ctrl+C**.

   d. Close ***ValleyCustomManufacturing-01*** without saving the document.

   e. In the ***[your initials] Word 1-1*** document, place your insertion point on the last blank line of the document.

   f. Click the **Clipboard** launcher [*Home* tab, *Clipboard* group] to open the *Clipboard* pane (Figure 1-79).

   g. Click the **drop-down arrow** to the right of the copied text in the *Clipboard* and click **Paste**. The paragraphs of text are pasted in the body of the document.

   h. Click the **X** in the upper right corner of the *Clipboard* pane to close it.

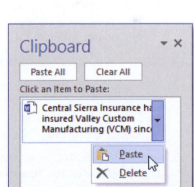

1-79 Paste from the *Clipboard*

8. Use the *Format Painter* to format the inserted paragraphs.

   a. Place your insertion point on the first line of the document (date line).

   b. Click the **Format Painter** button [*Home* tab, *Clipboard* group] to turn on the *Format Painter*.

c. Select the five body paragraphs of the letter to apply the formatting (Figure 1-80).

9. Insert a blank line between each of the body paragraphs so there is a double space after each body paragraph (one blank line between paragraphs).

a. Place your insertion point at the end of the first body paragraph and press **Enter**. A paragraph symbol marks the end of each paragraph.

b. Repeat for each of the remaining body paragraphs including the last body paragraph.

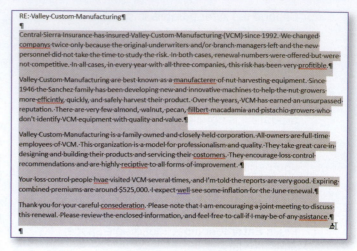

RE:·Valley·Custom·Manufacturing¶
¶
Central·Sierra·Insurance·has·insured·Valley·Custom·Manufacturing·(VCM)·since·1992.·We·changed· companys·twice·only·because·the·original·underwriters·and/or·branch·managers·left·and·the·new· personnel·did·not·take·the·time·to·study·the·risk.·In·both·cases,·renewal·numbers·were·offered·but·were· not·competitive.·In·all·cases,·in·every·year·with·all·three·companies,·this·risk·has·been·very·profitible.¶

Valley·Custom·Manufacturing·are·best·known·as·a·manufacterer·of·nut·harvesting·equipment.·Since· 1946·the·Sanchez·family·has·been·developing·new·and·innovative·machines·to·help·the·nut·growers· more·efficintly,·quickly,·and·safely·harvest·their·product.·Over·the·years,·VCM·has·earned·an·unsurpassed· reputation.·There·are·very·few·almond,·walnut,·pecan,·fillbert·macadamia·and·pistachio·growers·who· don't·identify·VCM·equipment·with·quality·and·value.¶

Valley·Custom·Manufacturing·is·a·family·owned·and·closely·held·corporation.·All·owners·are·full·time· employees·of·VCM.·This·organization·is·a·model·for·professionalism·and·quality.·They·take·great·care·in· designing·and·building·their·products·and·servicing·their·costomers.·They·encourage·loss·control· recommendations·and·are·highly·reciptive·to·all·forms·of·improvement.·¶

Your·loss·control·people·hvae·visited·VCM·several·times,·and·I'm·told·the·reports·are·very·good.·Expiring· combined·premiums·are·around·$525,000.·I·expect·well·see·some·inflation·for·the·June·renewal.¶

Thank·you·for·your·careful·consederation.·Please·note·that·I·am·encouraging·a·joint·meeting·to·discuss· this·renewal.·Please·review·the·enclosed·information,·and·feel·free·to·call·if·I·may·be·of·any·asistance.¶
¶

1-80 Use the *Format Painter* to copy formatting

10. Enter the closing lines of the document.

a. Place your insertion point on the last blank line below the body of the letter.

b. Type Sincerely and press **Enter** four times.

c. Type Jennie Owings, Vice President and press **Enter**.

d. Type Central Sierra Insurance and press **Enter** two times.

e. Type your reference initials (your first and last initials in lowercase letters with no punctuation).

f. Press **Enter**. *AutoCorrect* automatically capitalizes the first letter of your reference initials.

g. Click the **AutoCorrect Options** smart tag (Figure 1-81). The *AutoCorrect Options* smart tag appears when you place your pointer below your reference initials.

h. Select **Undo Automatic Capitalization** to undo the automatic capitalization of your reference initials.

i. Place your insertion point on the blank line below your reference initials and type Enclosure as an enclosure notation.

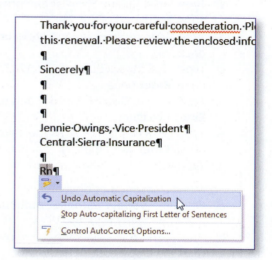

Thank·you·for·your·careful·consederation.·Pl
this·renewal.·Please·review·the·enclosed·info
¶
Sincerely¶
¶
¶
¶
Jennie·Owings,·Vice·President¶
Central·Sierra·Insurance¶
¶
Rn¶
↶
    ↶ Undo Automatic Capitalization
        Stop Auto-capitalizing First Letter of Sentences
    ⚡ Control AutoCorrect Options...

1-81 *AutoCorrect Options* smart tag

11. Select the entire document (**Ctrl+A**) and change the font size to **10 pt**. [*Home* tab, *Font* group].

12. Add *Before* paragraph spacing to the date line.

a. Select or place your insertion point in the date line.

b. Change the *Before* spacing to **72 pt**. [*Layout* tab, *Paragraph* group] (Figure 1-82).

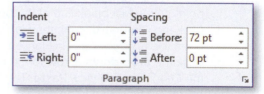

Indent		Spacing	
⫬ Left:	0"	↑⫤ Before:	72 pt
⫥ Right:	0"	↓⫤ After:	0 pt
Paragraph			

1-82 Change *Before* paragraph spacing on the date line

13. Apply a font style to selected text.

a. Select the words **"Central Sierra Insurance"** in the first paragraph.

b. Click the **Underline** button [*Home* tab, *Font* group] or press **Ctrl+U**.

c. Select the words **"Valley Custom Manufacturing (VCM)"** in the first paragraph.

d. Click the **Bold** button [*Home* tab, *Font* group] or press **Ctrl+B**.

14. Use *Smart Lookup* to research selected words.

a. Select **"harvesting equipment"** in the second body paragraph.

b. Click the **Smart Lookup** button [*Review* tab, *Insights* group]. The *Smart Lookup* pane opens on the right.

c. Review the research results on the *Smart Lookup* pane.
d. Click the **X** in the upper right of the *Smart Lookup* pane to close the pane.

15. Spell and grammar check the entire document.
   a. Press **Ctrl+Home** to move to the top of the document.
   b. Click the **Spelling & Grammar** button [*Review* tab, *Proofing* group]. The *Spelling* pane opens (Figure 1-83).
   c. If "Cammie" and "Speckler" are marked as potential spelling errors, click **Add** to add each of these names to the dictionary.
   d. For the remaining spelling and grammatical errors, select the correct word in the *Spelling* (or *Grammar*) pane and click **Change**.
   e. If prompted to continue checking the document from the beginning, choose **Yes**.
   f. Click **Ignore** if your reference initials are marked as a potential spelling or grammatical error.
   g. Click **OK** to close the dialog box that informs you the spelling and grammar check is complete.

16. Save and close the document (Figure 1-84).

1-83 Add word to the dictionary

1-84 Word 1-1 completed

Guided Project 1-2

Sierra Pacific Community College District is a multi-campus community college district. In this project, you format an informational handout regarding online learning.
[Student Learning Outcomes 1.1, 1.2, 1.3, 1.4, 1.5, 1.6, 1.7, 1.8]

File Needed: ***OnlineLearning-01.docx*** *(Student data files are available in the* **Library** *of your SIMnet account)*
Completed Project File Name: ***[your initials] Word 1-2.docx***

Skills Covered in This Project

- Open and edit an existing document.
- Change line spacing.
- Change paragraph spacing.
- Use *Show/Hide*.
- Change font size and apply color, styles, and effects.

- Cut and paste to move a paragraph.
- Use drag and drop to move a paragraph.
- Apply a shadow text effect.
- Use the *Format Painter*.
- Use spelling and grammar checker.
- Add document properties.

1. Open the ***OnlineLearning-01*** document from your student data files.
   a. Click the **File** tab to open the *Backstage* view and click **Open** at the left.
   b. Click **Browse** to open the *Open* dialog box.
   c. Browse to locate the ***OnlineLearning-01*** document, select the document, and click **Open**. If the document opens in *Protected View*, click the **Enable Editing** button.

2. Save the document as ***[your initials] Word 1-2***.
   a. Click the **File** tab to open the *Backstage* view and select **Save As** on the left.
   b. Click **Browse** to open the *Save As* dialog box and select the desired location to save the file.
   c. Change the file name to [your initials] Word 1-2.
   d. Click **Save** to rename the document and close the *Save As* dialog box.

3. Change the line and paragraph spacing of the entire document.
   a. Press **Ctrl+A** to select the entire document.
   b. Click the **Paragraph** launcher [*Home* or *Layout* tab, *Paragraph* group] to open the *Paragraph* dialog box (Figure 1-85).
   c. In the *Line spacing* area, select **Multiple** from the drop-down list.
   d. In the *At* area, type 1.2.
   e. Change the *After* paragraph spacing to **12 pt**.
   f. Click **OK** to close the *Paragraph* dialog box.

4. Turn on **Show/Hide** [*Home* tab, *Paragraph* group] and delete the one extra blank line between each paragraph including after the title.

5. Change the font and font size of the entire document.
   a. Select the entire document (**Ctrl+A**).
   b. Change the font to **Cambria** [*Home* tab, *Font* group].

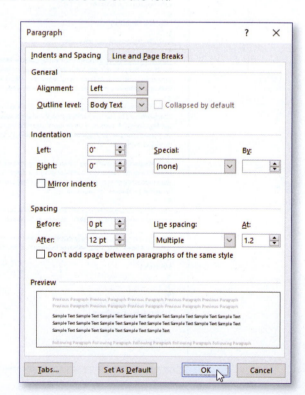

1-85 Change *Line spacing* and *After* paragraph spacing

6. Change the paragraph spacing, alignment, font size, styles, effects, and color of the title.
   a. Select the title of the document (**Online Learning Information**).
   b. Click the **Layout** tab.
   c. Change the *Before* spacing to **36 pt**. and the *After* spacing to **18 pt** [*Paragraph group*].
   d. Click the **Center** button [*Home* tab, *Paragraph* group].
   e. Click the **Font** launcher [*Home* tab, *Font* group]. The *Font* dialog box opens (Figure 1-86).
   f. Change the *Font* style to **Bold** and change the *Font Size* to **24**.
   g. In the *Effects* area, click the **Small caps** check box.
   h. Click the **Font color** drop-down list and choose **Blue-Gray, Text 2** from the *Theme Colors*.
   i. Click the **Advanced** tab.
   j. Click the **Spacing** drop-down list and select **Expanded**. Change the *By* to **1.2 pt**.
   k. Click **OK** to close the *Font* dialog box.

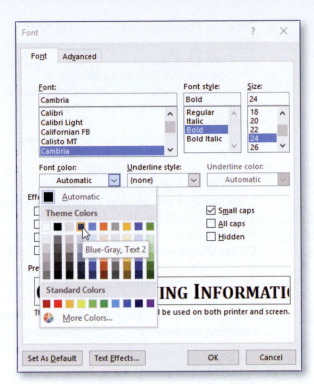

1-86 Change font style, size, effects, and color

7. Move paragraphs in the document and insert a heading.
   a. Select the last paragraph in the document, including the paragraph mark at the end of the document.
   b. Click the **Cut** button [*Home* tab, *Clipboard* group] or press **Ctrl+X**.
   c. Place your insertion point before the second line of the document ("Definition of Online Learning Modalities").
   d. Click the top half of the **Paste** button [*Home* tab, *Clipboard* group] or press **Ctrl+V**.
   e. Click at the beginning of the pasted paragraph and type Where are we now with Online Learning? and press **Enter**.
   f. Select the paragraph that begins "Hybrid Course:," including the paragraph mark at the end of the paragraph.
   g. Move this paragraph using the drag-and-drop method (click, hold, and drag) so it appears before the paragraph that begins with "Television or Tele-Web Course:" (Figure 1-87).

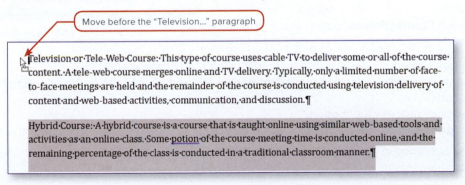

1-87 Move paragraph using drag and drop

8. Format section headings in the document and use the *Format Painter*.
   a. Select the first section heading ("**Where are we now with Online Learning?**").

b. Click the **Font** launcher [*Home* tab, *Font* group] to open the *Font* dialog box and click the **Font** tab (Figure 1-88).

c. Change the font *Size* to **12 pt**.

d. Change the *Font color* to **Blue-Gray, Text 2**.

e. Change the *Underline style* to **Double underline**.

f. Change the *Underline color* to **Blue-Gray, Text 2**.

g. In the *Effects* area, click the **All caps** check box.

h. Click **OK** to close the *Font* dialog box.

i. Click the **Text Effects and Typography** button [*Home* tab, *Font* group].

j. Place your pointer on **Shadow** and select **Offset Diagonal Bottom Right** (Figure 1-89).

k. With the formatted heading still selected, click the **Format Painter** button [*Home* tab, *Clipboard* group].

l. Select the next heading (**"Definition of Online Learning Modalities"**) to apply formatting.

9. Format paragraph headings in the document.

a. Select the first paragraph heading (**"Online Course:"**), including the colon.

b. Click the **Font** launcher [*Home* tab, *Font* group] to open the *Font* dialog box.

c. Change the *Font style* to **Bold**.

d. Change the *Font color* to **Blue-Gray, Text 2**.

e. In the *Effects* area, click the **Small caps** check box.

f. Click **OK** to close the *Font* dialog box.

10. Use the *Format Painter* to copy formatting to the other paragraph headings.

a. With the **"Online Course:"** heading still selected, double click the **Format Painter** button.

b. Select the other paragraph headings (**"Hybrid Course:"**, **"Television or Tele-Web Course:"**, and **"Web-Enhanced Course:"**) to apply the formatting.

c. Click the **Format Painter** button again to turn off the *Format Painter*.

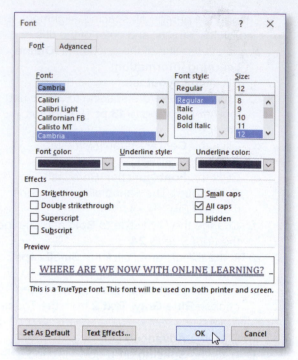

1-88 Format heading using the *Font* dialog box

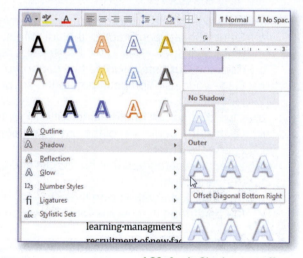

1-89 Apply *Shadow* text effect

11. Correct spelling and grammar in the document using the context menu.

a. Right-click the first misspelled word (**"managment"**) and choose the correct spelling from the list of options.

b. Repeat this process for **"potion."**

c. Click **Ignore All** or **Ignore Once** if there are other words that are marked as potentially incorrect.

12. Select the sentence in parentheses at the end of the document, including the parentheses, and click the **Italic** button [*Home* tab, *Font* group] or press **Ctrl+I**.

13. Add document properties using the *Properties* dialog box.

a. Click the **File** tab to open the *Backstage* view and click the **Info** button if it is not already selected.

b. Click the **Properties** button on the right and choose **Advanced Properties**. The *Properties* dialog box opens.

c. In the *Title* area, type **Online Learning Information**.

d. In the *Subject* area, type **Online Learning**.

e. In the *Author* area, delete the existing author name and type **Tanesha Morris** as the author.

f. Click **OK** to accept changes and close the *Properties* dialog box.

g. Click the **Back** arrow in the upper left of the *Backstage* view to return to the document.

14. Save and close the document (Figure 1-90).

ONLINE·LEARNING·INFORMATION¶

WHERE·ARE·WE·NOW·WITH·ONLINE·LEARNING?¶

SPCCD·was·a·pioneer·in·online·education·and·was·one·of·the·first·community·colleges·in·California·to·offer·fully·online·courses·in·1998.·However,·over·the·next·few·years·there·was·limited·growth·in·online·offerings·and·only·15·course·sections·were·taught·online·during·Fall·2000.·The·adoption·of·a·learning·management·system·in·Spring·2001,·and·the·availability·of·training·to·teach·online,·and·recruitment·of·new·faculty·interested·in·teaching·online·resulted·in·a·rapid·increase·in·online·offerings.¶

DEFINITION·OF·ONLINE·LEARNING·MODALITIES¶

All·online·learning·modes·offered·at·SPCCD·will·be·considered·in·the·plan.·Currently,·these·include·the·following:·online,·hybrid,·television,·and·tele-web.¶

ONLINE·COURSE:·An·online·course·is·a·course·that·is·offered·over·the·Internet.·Typically,·content·is·presented·through·web·pages·and·class·discussions·using·a·combination·of·email,·mailing·lists,·bulletin·boards,·chat·rooms,·or·newsgroups.·All·class·meetings,·assignments,·lectures,·and·assessments·are·online·(with·the·exception·of·orientation·meetings·or·other·face-to-face·examinations·as·determined·by·the·professor).¶

HYBRID·COURSE:·A·hybrid·course·is·a·course·that·is·taught·online·using·similar·web-based·tools·and·activities·as·an·online·class.·Some·portion·of·the·course·meeting·time·is·conducted·online,·and·the·remaining·percentage·of·the·class·is·conducted·in·a·traditional·classroom·manner.¶

TELEVISION·OR·TELE-WEB·COURSE:·This·type·of·course·uses·cable·TV·to·deliver·some·or·all·of·the·course·content.·A·tele-web·course·merges·online·and·TV·delivery.·Typically,·only·a·limited·number·of·face-to-face·meetings·are·held·and·the·remainder·of·the·course·is·conducted·using·television·delivery·of·content·and·web-based·activities,·communication,·and·discussion.¶

WEB-ENHANCED·COURSE:·This·type·of·course·is·taught·face-to-face·for·100%·of·the·course·meeting·time,·but·classroom·assignments·and·materials·are·supplemented·with·web-based·activities.·Examples·are:·online·projects,·handouts·and·materials,·online·discussion,·or·online·testing·(Note:·this·is·a·definition·of·a·non-online·learning·course·which·uses·online·learning·tools).¶

1-90 Word 1-2 completed

Guided Project 1-3

In this project, you create a memo for American River Cycling Club about using heart rate to increase the effectiveness of training. See *Appendix B* (online resource) for examples of business document formats. **[Student Learning Outcomes 1.1, 1.2, 1.3, 1.5, 1.6, 1.7, 1.8]**

File Needed: ***HeartRate-01.docx*** *(Student data files are available in the* Library *of your SIMnet account)*
Completed Project File Name: *[your initials]* **Word 1-3.docx**

Skills Covered in This Project

- Open and edit an existing document.
- Change line spacing.
- Change paragraph spacing.
- Use *Show/Hide.*
- Add a memo heading to a document.
- Change paragraph alignment.

- Change font size and apply styles and effects.
- Use the *Format Painter.*
- Add text highlight color.
- Use non-breaking space.
- Use *Thesaurus.*
- Add words to the dictionary.
- Add document properties.

1. Open the **HeartRate-01** document from your student data files.
   a. Click the **File** tab to open the *Backstage* view and click **Open** on the left.
   b. Click **Browse** to open the *Open* dialog box.
   c. Browse to locate the **HeartRate-01** document, select the document, and click **Open**. If the document opens in *Protected View*, click the **Enable Editing** button.

2. Save the document as *[your initials]* **Word 1-3**.
   a. Click the **File** tab to open the *Backstage* view and select **Save As** on the left.
   b. Click **Browse** to open the *Save As* dialog box and select the desired location to save the file.
   c. Change the file name to [your initials] Word 1-3.
   d. Click **Save** to rename the document and close the *Save As* dialog box.

3. Change the line and paragraph spacing of the entire document and insert a paragraph break between each paragraph.
   a. Press **Ctrl+A** to select the entire document.
   b. Click the **Paragraph** launcher [*Home* or *Layout* tab, *Paragraph* group]. The *Paragraph* dialog box opens.
   c. In the *Line spacing* area, select **Single** from the drop-down list.
   d. Change the *After* paragraph spacing to **0 pt**.
   e. Click **OK** to close the *Paragraph* dialog box.
   f. Turn on **Show/Hide** [*Home* tab, *Paragraph* group] if it is not already on.
   g. Click at the end of each paragraph and press **Enter** once to add a blank line between each of the paragraphs. Don't press *Enter* after the last body paragraph. A paragraph symbol marks the end of each paragraph.

4. Add a memo heading to the document.
   a. Place your insertion point at the beginning of the first paragraph and press **Enter**.
   b. Place the insertion point on the blank line above the first paragraph.
   c. Type TO: and press **Tab** two times.
   d. Type All ARCC Club Members and press **Enter** two times.
   e. Type FROM: and press **Tab** two times.
   f. Type Taylor Mathos, ARCC Coach and press **Enter** two times.
   g. Type DATE: and press **Tab** two times.
   h. Type the current date in month, day, year format (e.g., October 1, 2018) and press **Enter** two times.
   i. Type SUBJECT: and press **Tab** once.
   j. Type Heart Rate Training and press **Enter** two times.

5. Change the paragraph alignment and font styles of selected text.
   a. Select the second and third paragraphs in the body of the memo (beginning with **"220 – Your Age . . ."** and ending with **". . . heart rate is 180.)"**), including the paragraph mark at the end of the third paragraph.
   b. Click the **Center** button [*Home* tab, *Paragraph* group] or press **Ctrl+E**.
   c. Select the paragraph beginning **"220 – Your Age . . ."** and click the **Bold** button [*Home* tab, *Font* group] or press **Ctrl+B**.
   d. Select the next paragraph and click the **Italic** button [*Home* tab, *Font* group] or press **Ctrl+I**.
   e. Delete the blank line between the second and third paragraphs (Figure 1-91).

6. Change the font and style of selected text.
   a. Press **Ctrl+A** to select the entire document.

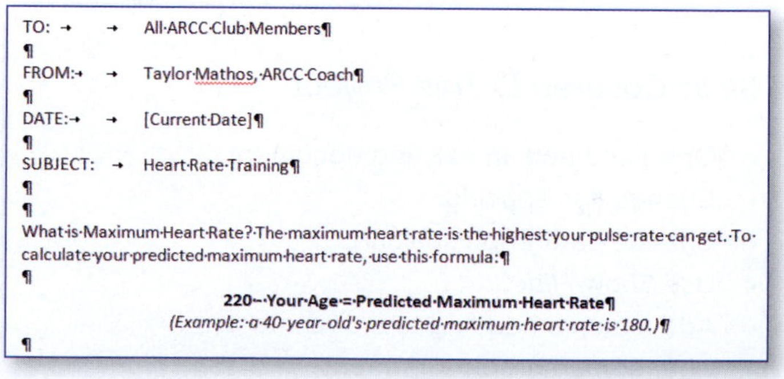

TO: →   →   All·ARCC·Club·Members¶
¶
FROM:→   →   Taylor·Mathos,·ARCC·Coach¶
¶
DATE:→   →   [Current·Date]¶
¶
SUBJECT: →   Heart·Rate·Training¶
¶
¶
What·is·Maximum·Heart·Rate?·The·maximum·heart·rate·is·the·highest·your·pulse·rate·can·get.·To·
calculate·your·predicted·maximum·heart·rate,·use·this·formula:¶
¶
         220·–·Your·Age·=·Predicted·Maximum·Heart·Rate¶
         (Example:·a·40-year-old's·predicted·maximum·heart·rate·is·180.)¶
¶

1-91 Memo heading added and paragraphs formatted

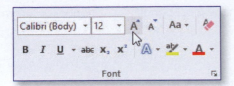

1-92 *Increase Font Size* button

b. Click the **Increase Font Size** button [*Home* tab, *Font* group] to increase the font size to 12 pt. (Figure 1-92).

c. Select the words **"Maximum Heart Rate?"** in the first sentence of the first body paragraph.

d. Click the **Font** launcher [*Home* tab, *Font* group] to open the *Font* dialog box (Figure 1-93).

e. Change the *Font style* to **Bold**.

f. Change the *Underline style* to **Words only** and change the *Underline color* to **Green, Accent 6**.

g. In the *Effects* area, select the **Small caps** check box.

h. Click **OK** to close the *Font* dialog box.

i. With the words still selected, click the **Format Painter** button [*Home* tab, *Clipboard* group].

j. Select the words **"Target Heart Rate Zone"** in the first sentence of the fifth paragraph in the body ("You gain the most benefits . . ."). The *Format Painter* applies the formatting to the selected words.

k. Select the last two sentences of the fifth body paragraph (**"Do not exercise above 85 percent . . ."**) including the period at the end of the second sentence.

l. Click the **Text Highlight Color** drop-down arrow [*Home* tab, *Font* group] (Figure 1-94) and select **Gray-25%** text highlighting.

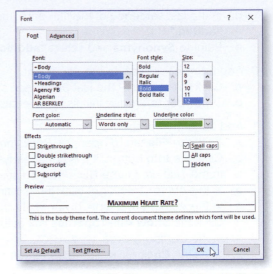

1-93 Change font style and effects

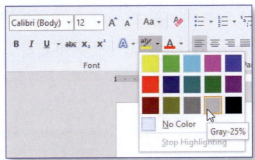

1-94 *Text Highlight Color* drop-down list

7. Use a non-breaking space to keep words together.
   a. In the first sentence of the fifth paragraph in the body ("You gain the most benefits . . ."), delete the space between the words "Target" and "Heart."
   b. Place your insertion point between these two words and press **Ctrl+Shift+Spacebar** to insert a non-breaking space. "Target" is wrapped to the next line so the words do not break between lines.

8. Add *Before* paragraph spacing to the first line of the memo heading.
   a. Place the insertion point in the first line of the memo heading (**"TO: . . ."**).
   b. Change the *Before* spacing to **72 pt**. [*Layout* tab, *Paragraph* group].

9. Use the *Thesaurus* to find synonyms for selected words.
   a. Right-click the word **"medicines"** in the third sentence of the fourth body paragraph ("Your actual maximum . . .").
   b. Point to **Synonyms** to display a list of synonyms.
   c. Select **"medications"** as the synonym (Figure 1-95).

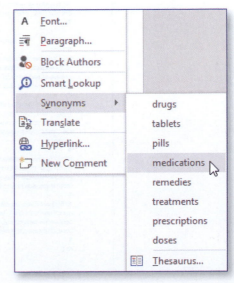

1-95 Select synonym from context menu

    d. In the last sentence of the fifth paragraph ("You gain the most benefits . . ."), right-click the word **"added."**

    e. Point to **Synonyms** and select **"additional."**

10. Add reference initials to the document.

    a. Click at the end of the last paragraph and press **Enter** two times.

    b. Type your reference initials in lowercase letters.

11. Add document properties.

    a. Click the **File** tab to open the *Backstage* view.

    b. Click the **Info** button, if it is not already selected, to display the document properties on the right.

    c. In the *Title* area, type Heart Rate Training.

    d. In the *Author* area, right-click the existing author and select **Remove Person**.

    e. In the *Author* area, type Taylor Mathos.

    f. Click the **Show All Properties** link at the bottom of the document properties.

    g. In the *Company* area, type ARCC.

    h. Click the **Back** arrow in the upper left of the *Backstage* view to return to the document.

12. Add words to the dictionary.

    a. Right-click the word **"Mathos"** in the second line of the memo heading.

    b. Choose **Add to Dictionary** from the context menu.

    c. If your reference initials are marked as incorrectly spelled (red wavy underline), right-click them and choose **Add to Dictionary**.

13. Save and close the document (Figure 1-96).

AMERICAN RIVER CYCLING CLUB

www.arcc.org   Cycling…a way of life   info@arcc.org

TO: All·ARCC·Club·Members¶
¶
FROM: Taylor·Mathos,·ARCC·Coach¶
¶
DATE: October·1,·2018¶
¶
SUBJECT: Heart·Rate·Training¶
¶
¶
WHAT·IS·MAXIMUM·HEART·RATE?·The·maximum·heart·rate·is·the·highest·your·pulse·rate·can·get.·To·calculate·your·predicted·maximum·heart·rate,·use·this·formula:¶
¶

        220·–·Your·Age·=·Predicted·Maximum·Heart·Rate¶
        (Example:·a·40-year-old's·predicted·maximum·heart·rate·is·180.)¶

¶
Your·actual·maximum·heart·rate·can·be·determined·by·a·graded·exercise·test.·Please·note·that·some·medical·conditions·might·affect·your·maximum·heart·rate.·If·you·are·taking·medications·or·have·a·medical·condition·(such·as·heart·disease,·high·blood·pressure,·or·diabetes),·always·ask·your·doctor·if·your·maximum·heart·rate/target·heart·rate·will·be·affected.¶
¶
You·gain·the·most·benefits·and·decrease·the·risk·of·injury·when·you·exercise·in·your·TARGET·HEART·RATE·ZONE.·Usually·this·is·when·your·exercise·heart·rate·(pulse)·is·60·percent·to·80·percent·of·your·maximum·heart·rate.·Do·not·exercise·above·85·percent·of·your·maximum·heart·rate.·This·increases·both·cardiovascular·and·orthopedic·risk·and·does·not·add·any·additional·benefit.¶
¶
When·beginning·an·exercise·program,·you·might·need·to·gradually·build·up·to·a·level·that·is·within·your·target·heart·rate·zone,·especially·if·you·have·not·exercised·regularly·before.·If·the·exercise·feels·too·hard,·slow·down.·You·will·reduce·your·risk·of·injury·and·enjoy·the·exercise·more·if·you·don't·try·to·over-do·it.¶
¶
To·find·out·if·you·are·exercising·in·your·target·zone·(between·60·percent·and·80·percent·of·your·maximum·heart·rate),·use·your·heart·rate·monitor·to·track·your·heart·rate.·If·your·pulse·is·below·your·target·zone,·increase·the·intensity·of·your·exercise.·If·your·pulse·is·above·your·target·zone,·decrease·the·intensity·of·your·exercise.¶
¶
rn¶

1-96 Word 1-3 completed

Independent Project 1-4

In this project, you format a business letter for Emma Cavalli to send to clients whose current home listings are expiring. See *Appendix B* (online resource) for examples of business document formats and mixed and open punctuation.
[Student Learning Outcomes 1.1, 1.2, 1.3, 1.4, 1.5, 1.6, 1.7, 1.8]

File Needed: ***ExpiredLetter-01.docx*** *(Student data files are available in the* Library *of your SIMnet account)*
Completed Project File Name: ***[your initials] Word 1-4.docx***

Skills Covered in This Project

- Open and edit an existing document.
- Change line spacing.
- Change paragraph alignment and spacing.
- Change font and font size.
- Use *Show/Hide*.

- Format document as a block format business letter with mixed punctuation.
- Move text.
- Change font styles and effects.
- Use *Smart Lookup*.
- Add document properties.
- Use spelling and grammar checker.

1. Open the ***ExpiredLetter-01*** document from your student data files.

2. Save this document as ***[your initials] Word 1-4***.

3. Apply the following formatting changes to the entire document:
   a. Select the entire document.
   b. Change the *Before* and *After* paragraph spacing to **0 pt**.
   c. Change the line spacing to **Single**.
   d. Change the paragraph alignment to **Left**.
   e. Change the font and font size to **Calibri** and **11 pt**.

4. Turn on **Show/Hide** and press **Enter** at the end of each paragraph to add a blank line after each paragraph (including the last paragraph).

5. Type and format the opening lines of the business letter.
   a. Press **Ctrl+Home** to move your insertion point to the top of the document.
   b. Type the current date (use August 15, 2018 format) and press **Enter** four times.
   c. Type the following inside address and press **Enter** two times after the last line:

      Mr. Rick Hermann
      9035 Masi Drive
      Fair Oaks, CA 95528

   d. Type Dear Mr. Hermann: as the salutation and press **Enter** two times after the salutation. There should be one blank line between the salutation and the body of the letter.
   e. Add **72 pt**. *Before* paragraph spacing to the date line.

6. Type the closing lines of the business letter.
   a. Place your insertion point on the blank line below the last body paragraph and press **Enter**.
   b. Type Best regards, and press **Enter** four times.
   c. Type the following closing lines:

      Emma Cavalli
      Realtor Consultant
      Placer Hills Real Estate

   d. Press **Enter** two times after the company name and type your reference initials in lowercase letters.

7. Move a paragraph and sentence.
   a. Move the third body paragraph so it appears before the second body paragraph. Make sure there is one blank line between each of the body paragraphs. If there is a blank space in front of the first word in the third paragraph, delete it.
   b. In the new second body paragraph ("There was a lot of detail . . ."), move the last two sentences to the beginning of the paragraph. Make sure there is proper spacing between sentences.

8. Apply formatting to text in the business letter.
   a. Select **"Placer Hills Real Estate"** in the first body paragraph and make the company name **Bold, Underline** (single line), and **Small caps**.
   b. Select the first sentence in the third paragraph including the period ("The service and experience . . .") and apply **Italic** formatting.
   c. Select the writer's name at the bottom and apply **Small caps** formatting.
   d. Select the writer's title and apply **Italic** formatting.
   e. Select the company name below the writer's title and apply **Bold** formatting.

9. Use *Smart Lookup* to research selected words.
   a. Select **"Placer Hills Real Estate"** in the first body paragraph.
   b. Click the **Smart Lookup** button [*Review* tab, *Insights* group]. The *Smart Lookup* pane opens on the right.
   c. Review the research results in the *Smart Lookup* pane.
   d. Click the **X** in the upper right of the *Smart Lookup* pane to close the pane.

10. Add the following document properties:
    a. *Title*: Expired Letter
    b. *Company*: Placer Hills Real Estate
    c. *Manager*: Kelsey Kroll
    d. *Author*: Emma Cavalli (right-click and choose **Remove Person** to remove existing author)

11. Spell and grammar check the entire document, make changes where necessary, and ignore proper nouns.

12. Save and close the document (Figure 1-97).

1-97 Word 1-4 completed

Independent Project 1-5

In this project, you combine information from different documents to create a memo for Sierra Pacific Community College District. This memo is a draft of the values statement for the district. See *Appendix B* (online resource) for examples of business document formats.
[**Student Learning Outcomes 1.1, 1.2, 1.3, 1.4, 1.5, 1.6, 1.7, 1.8**]

File Needed: ***ValuesStatement-01a.docx*** and ***ValuesStatement-01b.docx*** (*Student data files are available in the* Library *of your SIMnet account*)
Completed Project File Name: *[your initials]* **Word 1-5.docx**

Skills Covered in This Project

- Open and edit an existing document.
- Change line spacing.
- Change paragraph spacing.
- Change font and font size.
- Use *Show/Hide*.

- Format document as a memo.
- Use spelling and grammar checker.
- Change font styles and effects.
- Use the *Format Painter*.
- Move text.
- Add document properties.

---

1. Open the ***ValuesStatement-01a*** document from your student data files.

2. Save this document as *[your initials]* **Word 1-5**.

3. Copy text from another document and paste it into the current document.
   a. Open the ***ValuesStatement-01b*** document from your student data files.
   b. Select all of the text in this document and copy to the *Clipboard*.
   c. Close the ***ValuesStatement-01b*** document without saving.
   d. In the *[your initials]* **Word 1-5** document, press **Enter** at the end of the document and paste the copied text from the *Clipboard*.
   e. **Delete** the extra paragraph breaks between the first four paragraphs and at the end of the document.

4. Select the entire document and apply the following formatting changes:
   a. Change *After* paragraph spacing to **12 pt**.
   b. Change the line spacing to **1.15**.
   c. Change the font and font size to **Calibri** and **10 pt**.

5. Type and format the heading lines in the memorandum.
   a. Turn on **Show/Hide**.
   b. Place your insertion point at the beginning of the document and press **Enter**.
   c. Place your insertion point on the blank line at the beginning of the document and type the following memo information. Press **Tab** (once or twice) after the guidewords to line up information at 1" and press **Enter** once at the end of the first three lines of the memo heading.

TO:	All SPCCD Faculty, Staff, and Managers
FROM:	Lanita Morrow, Chancellor
DATE:	type current date (use November 1, 2018 format)
SUBJECT:	Draft of SPCCD Values Statement

   d. On the first line of the memo heading, change the *Before* paragraph spacing to **24 pt**.
   e. On the "SUBJECT" line of the memo heading, change the *After* paragraph spacing to **18 pt**.

6. Spell and grammar check the entire document.
   a. Add the chancellor's first and last names to the dictionary if they are marked as potential spelling errors.
   b. Correct other spelling and grammar errors as necessary.

7. Apply formatting to a paragraph heading and use the *Format Painter* to copy formatting.
   a. Select the first paragraph heading (**"Access"**) in the body of the memo and apply the following formatting:

   > *Font style*: **Bold**
   > *Font color*: **Blue-Gray, Text 2**
   > *Underline*: **Double Underline**
   > *Underline color*: **Blue-Gray, Text 2**
   > *Effects*: **Small caps**

   b. Use the *Format Painter* to apply these styles to each of the other paragraph headings in the body of the memo.

8. Move body paragraphs.
   a. Use cut and paste or drag and drop to move the body paragraphs so they are ordered alphabetically by paragraph heading. Exclude the first body paragraph. Be sure to include the paragraph symbol at the end of each paragraph when cutting or dragging.
   b. Verify there are not extra *Enters* (paragraph marks) between paragraphs at the end of the document. This document will fit on one page.
   c. Verify there are not extra spaces before the first word in each of the paragraphs.

9. Delete any extra blank lines at the end of the document so this document fits on one page.

10. Add the following document properties:
    a. *Title*: SPCCD Values Statement
    b. *Company*: Sierra Pacific Community College District
    c. *Author*: Yoon Soo Park (right-click and choose **Remove Person** to remove existing author)

11. Save and close the document (Figure 1-98).

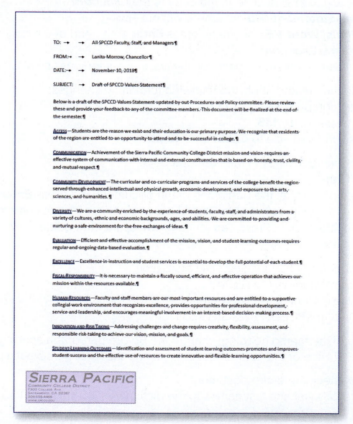

1-98 Word 1-5 completed

Independent Project 1-6

In this project, you use formatting features in Word to create a professional and appealing brochure for Emma Cavalli at Placer Hills Real Estate.
[Student Learning Outcomes 1.1, 1.2, 1.3, 1.4, 1.5, 1.6, 1.7, 1.8]

File Needed: **Brochure-01.docx** *(Student data files are available in the* Library *of your SIMnet account)*
Completed Project File Name: *[your initials]* **Word 1-6.docx**

Skills Covered in This Project

- Open and edit an existing document.
- Change font and font size.
- Change paragraph spacing.
- Change line spacing.
- Use *Show/Hide*.
- Change paragraph alignment.
- Change font styles and effects.
- Use the *Format Painter*.
- Move text.
- Use the thesaurus to find synonyms.
- Use *Smart Lookup*.
- Add document properties.

1. Open the **Brochure-01** document from your student data files.

2. Save this document as *[your initials]* **Word 1-6**.

3. Select the entire document and apply the following formatting changes:
   a. Change the font and font size to **Cambria** and **10 pt**.
   b. Change the *After* paragraph spacing to **6 pt**.
   c. Change the line spacing to **Single**.

4. Apply formatting to the opening lines of the document.
   a. Select the first five lines of the document (**"Emma Cavalli"** to **"Email: ecavalli@phre.com"**) and change the *After* paragraph spacing to **2 pt**.
   b. Select the first six lines of the document (**"Emma Cavalli"** to **"Web: www.phre.com/ecavalli"**) and **Center** these lines.
   c. Select the first line of the document (**"Emma Cavalli"**) and apply the following changes:
      Font size: **12 pt**.
      Font style: **Bold**
      Font color: **Green, Accent 6, Darker 50%**
   d. Select the second line of the document ("**Realtor Consultant**") and apply **Bold** formatting.
   e. Select the third line of the document (**"Putting Your Needs First"**) and apply **Italic** formatting.

5. Apply formatting to a section heading and use the *Format Painter*.
   a. Select the first section heading, **"Personal Statement,"** and apply **Bold**, **Underline**, and **Small Caps** formatting.
   b. On the first section heading, change the *Before* paragraph spacing to **12 pt**. and the *After* paragraph spacing to **3 pt**.
   c. Use the *Format Painter* to copy this formatting to the other section headings:

      "Real Estate Experience"
      "Why I am a Real Estate Agent"
      "What Clients are Saying"
      "Professional Credentials"
      "Education & Training"

6. In the "Why I Am a Real Estate Agent" section, combine the four sentences into one paragraph, deleting paragraph marks and inserting spaces as needed. Turn on **Show/Hide**.

7. In the "What Clients are Saying" section, make the following changes:
   a. Select the second paragraph ("It was a pleasure . . ."), make it **Italic**, and change the *After* spacing to **0 pt**.
   b. Select the source of the quote ("**-Rod & Luisa Ellisor, Rocklin, CA**") and right-align this text.
   c. Repeat the above two steps for the second quote ("Emma is conscientious . . .") and the source of the quote ("-Jon & Robin Anderson . . .").

8. Move the third section heading and the paragraph below it ("Why I Am a Real Estate Agent") so it appears before the second section ("Real Estate Experience").

9. Select the lines of text in the "Professional Credentials" section (don't include the heading) and change the *After* paragraph spacing to **3 pt**.

10. Use the *Format Painter* to repeat the above formatting to the lines of text (excluding the heading) in the "Education & Training" section.

11. Use the thesaurus to find an appropriate synonym for the following words:
    a. Replace "surpass" (in the "Personal Statement" section) with **"exceed."**
    b. Replace "emotions" (in the "Why I Am a Real Estate Agent" section) with **"sentiments."**

12. Use *Smart Lookup* to research selected words.
    a. Select **"University Nevada, Reno"** in the "Education & Training" section.
    b. Click the **Smart Lookup** button [*Review* tab, *Insights* group]. The *Smart Lookup* pane opens on the right.
    c. Review the research results in the *Smart Lookup* pane.
    d. Click the **X** in the upper right of the *Smart Lookup* pane to close the pane.

13. Add the following document properties:
    a. *Title*: Brochure
    b. *Company*: Placer Hills Real Estate
    c. *Author*: Emma Cavalli (right-click and choose **Remove Person** to remove existing author)

14. Save and close the document (Figure 1-99).

1-99 Word 1-6 completed

Improve It Project 1-7

In this project, you create a block format business letter for Margaret Jepson, an insurance agent at Central Sierra Insurance. You improve the formatting and text in this document and add opening and closing lines to create a properly formatted business letter. For more information on creating a correctly formatted block format business letter, see *Appendix B*.
[Student Learning Outcomes 1.1, 1.2, 1.3, 1.5, 1.6, 1.7, 1.8]

File Needed: ***RenewalLetter-01.docx*** *(Student data files are available in the* Library *of your SIMnet account)*
Completed Project File Name: *[your initials] Word 1-7.docx*

Skills Covered in This Project

- Open and edit an existing document.
- Change font and font size.
- Change paragraph spacing.
- Change line spacing.
- Use spelling and grammar checker.

- Format a business letter.
- Change paragraph alignment.
- Change font styles and effects.
- Use the *Format Painter*.
- Add document properties.

1. Open the ***RenewalLetter-01*** document from your student data files.

2. Save this document as *[your initials] Word 1-7*.

3. Select the entire document and apply the following formatting:
   a. *Line spacing*: **Single**
   b. *Before* and *After paragraph spacing*: **0 pt**.
   c. *Font*: **Calibri**
   d. *Font size*: **11 pt**.

4. Correct spelling and grammar as needed.

5. Type the opening lines of the business letter.
   a. Turn on **Show/Hide** if it is not already on.
   b. Place your insertion point at the top of the document and press **Enter**.
   c. On the blank line at the beginning of the document, type the current date (e.g., September 1, 2018) and press **Enter** four times.
   d. Type the following inside address and press **Enter** two times after the last line:

   Mr. Rick DePonte
   8364 Marshall Street
   Granite Bay, CA 95863

   e. Type Dear Mr. DePonte: as the salutation press **Enter** two times.
   f. Type Subject: Policy HO-2887-5546-B as the subject line and press **Enter** once.
   g. Apply **72 pt**. *Before* paragraph spacing on the date line.

6. Type the closing lines of the business letter.
   a. On the last blank line of the document, type Best regards, as the complimentary close and press **Enter** four times.
   b. Type the following information below as the writer's name, title, and company and press **Enter** two times after the last line:

Margaret Jepson, ARM, CIC, CRM
Insurance Agent
Central Sierra Insurance

 c. Type your initials in lowercase letters as the reference initials and press **Enter** once. Undo the automatic capitalization of your reference initials.

 d. Type Enclosure as the enclosure notation at the end of the business letter.

7. Apply formatting to the renewal premium information.

 a. **Center** the four lines of renewal premium information in the body of the letter.

 b. Apply **Bold** and **Small caps** formatting to the headings (not including the colons) for each of these four lines of renewal premium information.

 c. Format the "Total Premium" dollar amount as **Bold**, **Italic**, and **Double Underline**.

8. In the second body paragraph, type Hartford Specialty to replace the "*[Company Name]*" placeholder.

9. In the last body paragraph, type Rick to replace the "*[First Name]*" placeholder.

10. Add the following document properties:

 a. *Title*: Renewal Letter

 b. *Company*: Central Sierra Insurance

 c. *Author*: Margaret Jepson (right-click and choose **Remove Person** to remove existing author)

11. Save and close the letter (Figure 1-100).

1-100 Word 1-7 completed

Challenge Project 1-8

Create a cover letter for a job application. A cover letter typically accompanies a resume to introduce an applicant to a prospective employer. You can use and modify an existing cover letter, or you can create a new one. It is important to customize each cover letter for each job for which you are applying.

There are many online resources available to help you with both content and format. One of the best online resources for writing is the Online Writing Lab (OWL) from Purdue University (http://owl.english .purdue.edu/owl/). You can search this site for helpful information about cover letters.
[**Student Learning Outcomes 1.1, 1.2, 1.3, 1.4, 1.5, 1.6, 1.7, 1.8**]

File Needed: None
Completed Project File Name: *[your initials] Word 1-8.docx*

Open a new document and save this document as *[your initials] Word 1-8*.

Type this document as a personal business letter in block format. For more information on formatting a personal business letter, see *Appendix B*. Modify your document according to the following guidelines:

- Move sentences and paragraphs as needed to produce a well-organized cover letter.
- Add words to the dictionary as needed.
- Use the *Thesaurus* to find synonyms as needed.
- Include document properties, and spell and grammar check the document.

Challenge Project 1-9

Create a list of five places you would like to visit in the next five years. For each of the places you list, compose a short paragraph about that place and why it is interesting to you. Research each of the places you choose on the Internet. Use your own words when composing the paragraphs about each place.
[**Student Learning Outcomes 1.1, 1.2, 1.3, 1.4, 1.5, 1.6, 1.7, 1.8**]

File Needed: None
Completed Project File Name: *[your initials] Word 1-9.docx*

Open a new document and save it as *[your initials] Word 1-9*. Modify your document according to the following guidelines:

- Create and format a title for the document.
- Format each of the headings by modifying the font, style, and attributes.
- Change line and paragraph spacing as needed to create an attractive and readable document.
- Use consistent line and paragraph spacing throughout the document.
- Use the *Format Painter* to keep formatting consistent throughout the document.
- Move the paragraphs so the places are listed in order of your preference.
- Include document properties, and spell and grammar check the document.

Challenge Project 1-10

Create a flyer for an upcoming event for an organization to which you belong. Be sure to include all the relevant information for this event and arrange it attractively and professionally on the page.
[Student Learning Outcomes 1.1, 1.2, 1.3, 1.5, 1.6, 1.7, 1.8]

File Needed: None
Completed Project File Name: ***[your initials] Word 1-10.docx***

Open a new document and save it as ***[your initials] Word 1-10***. Modify your document according to the following guidelines:

- Create and format a title for the document.
- Format the information by modifying the fonts, styles, and attributes.
- Change line and paragraph spacing as needed to create an attractive and readable document.
- Change the text alignment as desired.
- Use the *Format Painter* to keep formatting consistent throughout the document.
- Include document properties, and spell and grammar check the document.

Formatting and Customizing Documents

CHAPTER OVERVIEW

In addition to giving you the ability to create common business documents, Microsoft Word 2016 provides formatting and editing tools you can use to customize a variety of documents. Formatting features such as custom margins, tab stops, indents, page numbering, headers, footers, breaks, lists, styles, themes, borders, and shading help you to produce readable and attractive professional and personal documents.

STUDENT LEARNING OUTCOMES (SLOs)

After completing this chapter, you will be able to:

SLO 2.1   Format a document by customizing margins, page orientation, paper size, and vertical alignment (p.W2-66).

SLO 2.2   Improve alignment and page layout by setting, using, and editing tab stops in a document (p. W2-69).

SLO 2.3   Apply indents to control text alignment (p. W2-74).

SLO 2.4   Enhance document layout by inserting page numbers, headers, and footers (p. W2-79).

SLO 2.5   Control pagination with page and section breaks (p. W2-86).

SLO 2.6   Use customized bulleted and numbered lists to effectively present information (p. W2-88).

SLO 2.7   Apply styles and themes to improve consistency in document format (p. W2-92).

SLO 2.8   Use find and replace to edit a document (p. W2-97).

SLO 2.9   Improve overall document design and format with borders, shading, horizontal lines, and hyperlinks (p. W2-100).

CASE STUDY

Courtyard Medical Plaza has a preschool for its employees' children. The preschool is currently looking for qualified applicants to fill a vacant teacher position. In the Pause & Practice projects, you modify a résumé for Richelle Wilkinson. You apply features covered in this chapter to create an attractive and informative résumé.

Pause & Practice 2-1: Edit the résumé to change margins and set tab stops and indents.

Pause & Practice 2-2: Modify the résumé to include a header with text and a page number.

Pause & Practice 2-3: Enhance the résumé by using bulleted lists, a page break, and a theme.

Pause & Practice 2-4: Finalize the résumé by using find and replace, borders, shading, horizontal line, and hyperlinks.

Customizing Margins and Page Layout

You can use margins to create *white space* around the edges of a document. White space improves the readability of a document and prevents the document from appearing cluttered. The document type and content influence the margins you use. You can also customize a document by changing the page orientation, page size, or vertical alignment.

Page Layout Settings

When you open a new Word document, the default settings control margins, page orientation, paper size, and vertical alignment. The following table lists the default page layout settings for a new document:

Default Page Layout Settings

Page Layout Option	Default Setting
Margins	1" top, bottom, left, and right
Page Orientation	Portrait
Paper Size	8.5" × 11" (Letter)
Vertical Alignment	Top

These settings are applied to the entire Word document, and you can easily change all of these settings in Word.

Margin Settings

Margin settings are measured in inches; the default margin settings for a new Word document are 1". Word provides you with a variety of *preset margin settings*. You can choose and change margins from the *Margins* drop-down list.

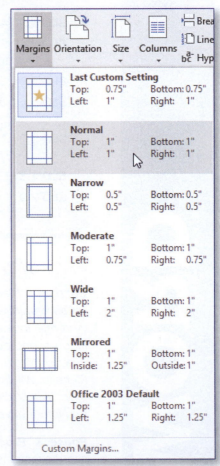

2-1 *Margins* drop-down list

▶HOW TO: Change Margin Settings

1. With a document open in Word, click the **Layout** tab.
2. Click the **Margins** button [*Page Setup* group]. Preset margin options appear in the *Margins* drop-down list (Figure 2-1).
3. Select the desired margin settings from the drop-down list of options.

The *Margins* drop-down list provides preset margin options. You are not limited to these preset options; you can also create your own custom margin settings in the *Page Setup* dialog box.

▶ MORE INFO

At the top of this *Margins* list, the **Last Custom Setting** option displays the most recent custom margin settings you have used.

Page Setup Dialog Box

If you want margin settings that are not listed in the preset margin settings in the *Margins* drop-down list, use the **Page Setup dialog box** (Figure 2-2) to change one or more of the margin settings and to create custom margins.

▶ HOW TO: Set Custom Margins

1. Click the **Layout** tab.

2. Click the **Margins** button [*Page Setup* group] and select **Custom Margins**. The *Page Setup* dialog box opens (see Figure 2-2).

3. Click the **Margins** tab if it is not already selected.

4. Change the *Top*, *Bottom*, *Left*, and *Right* margin settings as desired. You can do this the following ways:

   • Click the **Top**, **Bottom**, **Left**, or **Right** margin box and type your desired margin setting.
   • Click the **up** or **down arrow** to increase or decrease the margin size. Each click of the up or down arrow increases or decreases the margins by 0.1".
   • Press **Tab** to move from one box to another in the *Margins* area.

5. View the *Preview* area to see how the margin settings appear when applied to the document.

6. Click the **Apply to** drop-down list and select the area to apply margin settings: **Whole document**, **This point forward**, or **This section**.

7. Click **OK** to apply the custom margin settings.

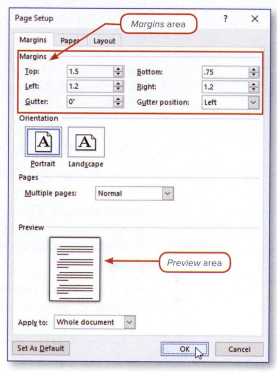

2-2 *Page Setup* dialog box

MORE INFO

Margin settings apply to the entire document by default. However, you can apply different margin settings to different sections of a document. Sections and section breaks are covered later in this chapter.

Page Orientation

Page orientation refers to the direction of the page. The two different orientation options in Word are **Portrait** and **Landscape**. Portrait is the tall orientation (8.5" × 11"), which is the default page orientation in Word. Landscape is the wide orientation (11" × 8.5"). You can change page orientation by clicking the **Orientation** button in the *Page Setup* group on the *Layout* tab (Figure 2-3).

▶ ANOTHER WAY

You can also change page orientation in the *Page Setup* dialog box.

2-3 Page orientation settings

Paper Size

Paper size refers to the actual size of the paper of your final printed document. A new document in Word is standard letter size, which is 8.5" × 11" by default. Word also provides other preset paper size settings, some of which are displayed in Figure 2-4.

You can change paper size by clicking the **Size** button in the *Page Setup* group on the *Layout* tab. When a different paper size is set, the margins of the document do not change. You may need to adjust the margin setting when you change the paper size. You can also set a custom paper size in the *Page Setup* dialog box.

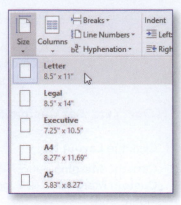

2-4 Paper size preset options

Vertical Alignment

If you are creating a flyer or a title page for a report, you might want to vertically center the information on the page. *Vertical alignment* controls the position of text between the top and bottom margins. Changing the vertical alignment of a page, section, or document is a much more effective method than using paragraph breaks (pressing *Enter* multiple times) to align information vertically. Word has four different vertical alignment options.

- *Top*: Text begins at the top margin of the document.
- *Center*: Text is centered vertically between the top and bottom margins.
- *Justified*: Space is automatically added between lines to fill the entire vertical space between the top and bottom margins.
- *Bottom*: Text begins at the bottom margin of the document.

▶ HOW TO: Change Vertical Alignment

1. Click the **Layout** tab.
2. Click the **Page Setup** launcher [*Page Setup* group]. The *Page Setup* dialog box opens.
3. Click the **Layout** tab.
4. In the *Page* area, click the **Vertical alignment** drop-down list (Figure 2-5).
5. Select the vertical alignment option of your choice.

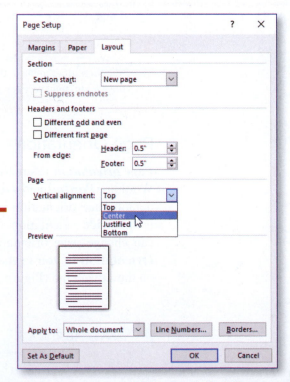

2-5 Change vertical alignment

Use the Ruler

Microsoft Word provides horizontal and vertical *rulers* that display both the typing line length and the vertical typing space available in a document. The rulers are broken into 1/8" increments. Half-inch markers are longer vertical or horizontal lines (depending on the ruler) and inch markers are numerical. On the rulers, the typing area is displayed in white, while the margin area is shaded (Figure 2-6). To display the rulers, check the **Ruler** box on the *View* tab in the *Show* group. This check box toggles on and off the display of the rulers.

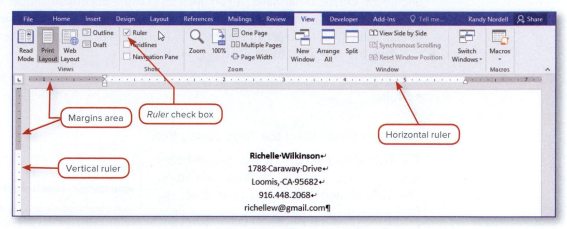

2-6 Horizontal and vertical rulers displayed

> **MORE INFO**
>
> The rulers are increasingly important and useful as you begin using tab stops, indents, columns, tables, and section breaks.

SLO 2.2   Setting, Using, and Editing Tab Stops

Tabs are useful tools to control the alignment of text. A tab is often used to indent the first line of a paragraph. A *tab stop* is where your insertion point stops when you press the *Tab* key. Tabs can also be used, for example, to align text in columns, or to begin the date at the horizontal midpoint on a modified block business letter.

The five different types of tabs stops that you can set and use in your documents are described in the following table:

Types of Tab Stops

Type of Tab Stop	Description	Tab Stop Indicator	Tab Stop in Use
Left	Text is left aligned at the tab stop	⌞	Left tab
Center	Text is centered on the tab stop	⊥	Center tab
Right	Text is right aligned at the tab stop	⌟	Right tab
Decimal	Decimal point is aligned at the tab stop	⊥	Decimal tab 620.50 8.375
Bar	A vertical bar (line) is inserted at the tab stop	▮	There is a bar | tab between these words |

Set a Tab Stop

Tabs are different from margins because tab stops apply to a paragraph or selected paragraphs rather than an entire document or sections of a document. This is important to keep in mind when setting, using, and editing tab stops.

By default in a Word document, there is left tab stop every 0.5". You can set tab custom stops in a new document before text is typed, or you can set tab stops in existing text. If you open a new blank document and set a left tab stop at 3.25", that tab stop applies to the entire document. On the other hand, if you open an existing document and set a tab stop on the first line, the tab stop is only set for that paragraph. When setting a tab stop in existing documents or text, remember to select all the text or paragraphs where you want the tab settings to apply.

There are two ways to set a tab stop in Word.

- *Tabs* dialog box
- Ruler

Set a Tab Stop Using the Tabs Dialog Box

The ***Tabs dialog box*** is an effective and easy method to set single or multiple tab stops. The *Tabs* dialog box is available from the *Paragraph* dialog box, which you can open from the *Paragraph* group on either the *Home* or *Layout* tabs.

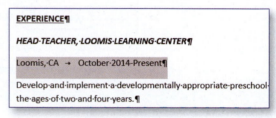

2-7 Select text before setting tab stops

▶ HOW TO: Set a Tab Stop Using the Tabs Dialog Box

1. Select the text where you want to set a tab stop (Figure 2-7).
2. Click the **Home** tab.
3. Click the **Paragraph** launcher to open the *Paragraph* dialog box.
4. Click the **Tabs** button (Figure 2-8) to open the *Tabs* dialog box.
5. Click in the **Tab stop position** area and type the desired tab stop position.
6. In the *Alignment* area, select the type of tab stop radio button you want to set.
7. Click the **Set** button (Figure 2-9). The tab stop appears in the list of tab stops below the *Tab stop position* area.
8. Click **OK** to close the *Tabs* dialog box.
   - The tab stop is applied to the selected text.
   - The tab stop is visible on the ruler.

2-8 *Tabs* button in the *Paragraph* dialog box

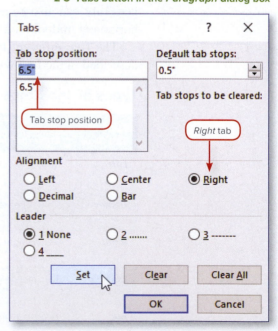

2-9 Set a right tab stop in the *Tabs* dialog box

▶ MORE INFO

Set and use tab stops to align and balance columns of text rather than pressing *Tab* multiple times between columns.

Set a Tab Stop Using the Ruler

Using the ruler to set tab stops is a quick way to add them to a document. You can also easily move or remove tab stops using the ruler. Use the **Tab selector** to select the type of tab stop you want to insert. The *Tab* selector is located at the top of the vertical ruler on the left side of the Word window. When setting tab stops in an existing document, it is very important to select the text or paragraphs where you want the tab stop to apply before setting the tab stop.

▶ **HOW TO:** Set a Tab Stop Using the Ruler

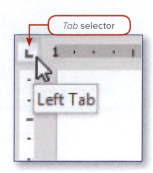

Tab selector

1. Select the text where you want to set the new tab stop(s).
   - If the rulers are not displayed, check the **Ruler** box [*View* tab, *Show* group].
2. Click the **Tab** selector to select the type of tab stop to set (Figure 2-10).
3. Click the ruler to set a tab stop.
   - When setting tab stops using the ruler, click the bottom edge of the ruler to set a tab stop (Figure 2-11).

2-10 *Tab* selector

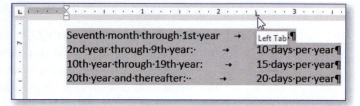

> ▶ **MORE INFO**
>
> Use the **Format Painter** to copy tab stops from one area of your document to another area.

2-11 Set a left tab stop at 2.5" on the ruler

Move a Tab Stop

It can be challenging to align text correctly and balance space between columns. But as you set and use tab stops more regularly, you become more comfortable selecting the correct type of tab stop to use, adjusting the settings of existing tab stops, and removing tab stops. When using multiple columns, adjust tab stops so you have about the same amount of white space between columns.

The easiest way to move tab stops is by using the ruler. When using the ruler to adjust a tab stop, be sure to select the appropriate text before moving a tab stop.

▶ **HOW TO:** Move a Tab Stop

1. Select the text or paragraphs where the tab stops you want to edit are set.
2. Left-click the **tab stop** on the ruler and drag it to the new location (Figure 2-12).
   - As you click the tab stop to be moved, a vertical alignment guide appears on your document. This alignment guide displays where your text aligns.

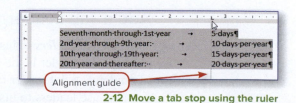

2-12 Move a tab stop using the ruler

- Press the **Alt** key when you are moving a tab stop to display a vertical guide that allows you to place the tab stop at a specific measurement (Figure 2-13).

3. Release the pointer to set the tab stop in the new location.

4. Repeat this process until you are satisfied with the placement of your tab stops.

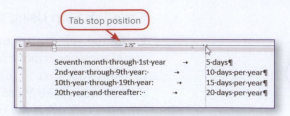

2-13 Use the *Alt* key to adjust a tab stop

Remove a Tab Stop

ANOTHER WAY

Adjust tab stops in the *Tabs* dialog box by clearing an existing tab stop and setting a new tab stop.

Occasionally, when setting tab stops using the ruler, you unintentionally add an unwanted tab stop. Or sometimes you might just want to remove unwanted tab stops. To remove tab stops from existing text, it is very important to select the text or paragraphs before deleting the tabs. When you remove or clear a tab stop, the tabbed text realigns to the default 0.5" tab stop or nearest remaining custom tab stop. Following are three different ways to remove tab stops:

- Drag a tab stop off (below) the ruler.
- Clear a single tab stop in the *Tabs* dialog box.
- Clear all tab stops in the *Tabs* dialog box.

To clear a single tab stop using the ruler, select the text or paragraphs, select the tab stop you want to remove, drag the tab stop down below the ruler, and release the pointer.

When using the *Tabs* dialog box to remove tab stops, you can clear a single tab stop or clear all existing tab stops on the selected text or paragraphs.

▶**HOW TO:** Clear a Tab Stop Using the Tabs Dialog Box

1. Select the text or paragraphs that contain the tab stops you want to remove.

2. Click the **Paragraph** launcher [*Home* or *Layout* tab] to open the *Paragraph* dialog box.

3. Click the **Tabs** button to open the *Tabs* dialog box.

4. To remove a single tab stop, select the tab stop to remove in the list of existing tab stops and click the **Clear** button (Figure 2-14). Repeat on any other tab stops you want to remove.

5. To clear all tab stops, click the **Clear All** button.

6. Click **OK** to close the *Tabs* dialog box.

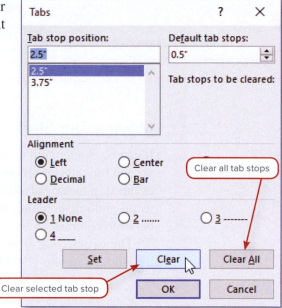

2-14 Clear a tab stop in the *Tabs* dialog box

Add a Tab Leader

You can use *leaders* to insert dots or a line between text when using tab stops. The most common type of leader is the dot leader, which is regularly used in a table of contents. In a table of contents, a dot leader is inserted between the text and the right aligned page number. You can also use leaders to insert a dashed line in the blank space between columns or to create a solid underline when creating a printed form.

Word has three different types of leaders. Examples of each of these are in the following table:

Types of Leaders

Leader	Example of Use
Dot	Chapter 1 4
Dash	Vacation Days -------- 10 days per year
Solid underline	Name_____

You can add leaders to existing or new tab stops, but they can only be added in the *Tabs* dialog box.

▶**HOW TO:** Add a Tab Leader

1. Select the text or paragraphs where you want to add a tab leader.
2. Click the **Paragraph** launcher [*Home* or *Layout* tab] to open the *Paragraph* dialog box.
3. Click the **Tabs** button to open the *Tabs* dialog box.
4. Select an existing tab stop or type a number in the *Tab stop position* text box to set a new tab stop.
5. Select the type of leader to apply in the *Leader* area.
6. Click **Set**. Figure 2-15 is an example of a dash leader.
7. Click **OK** to close the *Tabs* dialog box.

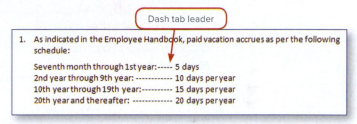

Dash tab leader

1. As indicated in the Employee Handbook, paid vacation accrues as per the following schedule:

Seventh month through 1st year:----- 5 days
2nd year through 9th year: ------------ 10 days per year
10th year through 19th year:---------- 15 days per year
20th year and thereafter: ------------- 20 days per year

2-15 Tab stop with a dash leader

Change Default Tab Stops

By default, Word has a left tab stop every 0.5". When you set a tab stop in Word, this custom tab stop overrides all preceding default tab stops. The default tab stops after your custom tab stop still remain. For example, if you set a left tab stop at the horizontal midpoint (typically 3.25") and press **Tab** to move to the horizontal midpoint, your insertion point will move to the midpoint, not 0.5". But if you press **Tab** again, your insertion point will stop at the next default tab stop, which would be 3.5".

You can customize the interval for default tab stops. If you change the default tab stop setting, this change affects only the current document, not all new documents.

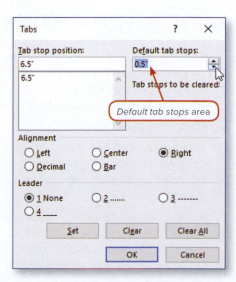

2-16 Change default tab stops

▶**HOW TO:** Change Default Tab Stops

1. Click the **Paragraph** launcher [*Home* or *Layout* tab] to open the *Paragraph* dialog box.
2. Click the **Tabs** button to open the *Tabs* dialog box.
3. In the *Default tab stops* area, use the up or down arrow to change the default tab stops (Figure 2-16).
4. Click **OK** to close the *Tabs* dialog box.

Using Indents

Indents are another powerful tool to help you control how text aligns between the left and right margins. Indents can be thought of as temporary margins, which apply to selected paragraphs. You can use indents to indent the first line of each paragraph, set off a long quote in a report, or indent the carry-over lines when creating bulleted or numbered lists.

Similar to setting tab stops, it is important to select the text where you want to apply indent settings. You can set indents using the ruler, the *Paragraph* group on the *Layout* tab, or the *Paragraph* dialog box. The four different types of indents that you can set and use in your document are described in the following table:

Types of Indents

Indent	Example of Use	Ruler Indent Marker
Left Indent	This line has a left indent.	Left Indent
Right Indent	This line has a right indent.	Right Indent
First Line Indent	This line has a first line indent.	First Line Indent
Hanging Indent	This line has a hanging indent.	Hanging Indent

Left and Right Indents

Indents apply to an entire paragraph or multiple paragraphs, not just lines of text within a paragraph. When setting an indent, select the paragraph(s) on which to apply the indent. If your insertion point is in a paragraph, the indent you set applies to that paragraph only.

▶ **HOW TO:** Set a Left and Right Indent Using the Ribbon

1. Select the text or paragraph where you want to apply the indent. If it is just one paragraph, place your insertion point in that paragraph.

2. Click the **Layout** tab.

3. Change the *Left* and *Right* indent settings [*Paragraph* group]. This change is applied to the selected text (Figure 2-17).

   • When an indent is set on a paragraph and you press *Enter* at the end of the paragraph, the indent carries over to the next paragraph.

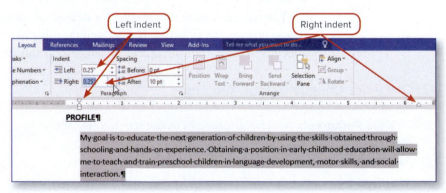

2-17 Change left and right indents

Indents can also be set using the ruler by dragging the indent marker to the desired location after you select the text you want to indent. As you drag the indent marker, an alignment guide displays the location where your text aligns.

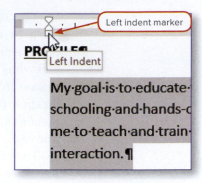

2-18 Change left indent using the ruler

1. Select the text or paragraph you want to indent. If it is just one paragraph, place your insertion point in that paragraph.
2. Left click the **left indent marker** (bottom square), drag to the desired location, and release the pointer. The left indent is applied to the text (Figure 2-18).
3. Left click the **right indent marker**, drag to the desired location, and release the pointer. The right indent is applied to the text (Figure 2-19).

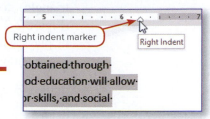

2-19 Change right indent using the ruler

> **ANOTHER WAY**
>
> Set left and right indents using the *Paragraph* dialog box. Click the **Paragraph** launcher to open the *Paragraph* dialog box.

The *Decrease Indent* and *Increase Indent* buttons in the *Paragraph* group on the *Home* tab increase or decrease the left indent in increments of 0.5" (Figure 2-20). Remove a left indent by clicking at the beginning of the paragraph and pressing **Backspace** or clicking the **Decrease Indent** button.

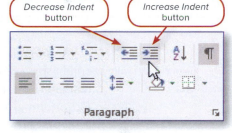

2-20 *Decrease Indent* and *Increase Indent* buttons

First Line and Hanging Indents

You can use a *First line indent* to indent the first line of a paragraph instead of using a tab. A *Hanging indent* is typically used with bulleted and numbered lists but can be used effectively to indent text that wraps to a second or more lines, such as a references page. You can use the *Paragraph* dialog box to set first line and hanging indents.

1. Select the paragraph(s) you want to indent.
2. Click the **Paragraph** launcher [*Home* or *Layout* tab] to open the *Paragraph* dialog box.
3. Click the **Special** drop-down list in the *Indentation* area and choose the type of indent: **First line** or **Hanging** (Figure 2-21).
4. In the *By* area, type the indent amount or use the up or down buttons to increase or decrease the amount of the indent.
   - The *Preview* area displays the text with the indent applied.
5. Click **OK** to close the *Paragraph* dialog box.

You can also use the ruler to set a first line indent. Select the paragraph(s) you want to indent and drag the first line indent marker (top triangle) to the desired location (Figure 2-22). The alignment guide displays where the first line of each paragraph align.

To set a hanging indent using the ruler, select the paragraph(s) you want to indent and drag the hanging indent marker (bottom triangle) to the desired location (Figure 2-23). The alignment guide displays where the carryover lines of the paragraph align.

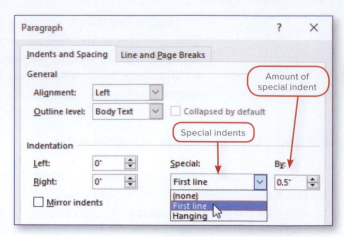

2-21 Set first line or hanging indent using the *Paragraph* dialog box

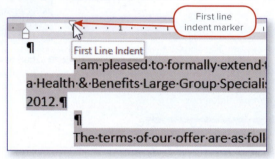

2-22 Set a first line indent using the ruler

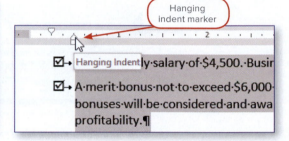

2-23 Set a hanging indent using the ruler

An ***outdent*** aligns text outside the left or right margins. Outdents are sometimes used to emphasize section headings so they are slightly to the left of the left margin. To apply an outdent, set a ***negative value*** (−0.25") in the indents area in the *Paragraph* dialog box or *Paragraph* group on the *Layout* tab or by dragging the indent marker outside of the left or right margins.

Remove Indents

Removing indents moves the indent markers back to either the left or right margin, so the margins control the alignment of text rather than the indents. Remember to select the paragraph or paragraphs before removing the indents. You can remove indents using the *Paragraph* dialog box or the *Paragraph* group on the *Layout* tab. When using either of these methods, set the indent value to 0" (Figure 2-24).

The ruler can also be used to remove indents. When using this method, select the text or paragraphs on which to remove the indents, and drag the indent marker(s) to the margin.

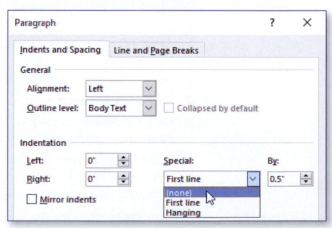

2-24 Remove indents using the *Paragraph* dialog box

In this Pause & Practice project, you format a résumé for Richelle Wilkinson. This résumé is a two-page document, and you change the margins, set tab stops and leaders, and use indents.

File Needed: **Resume-02.docx** *(Student data files are available in the* Library *of your SIMnet account)*
Completed Project File Name: **[your initials] PP W2-1.docx**

1. Open the **Resume-02** document from your student data files.

2. Save this document as [your initials] PP W2-1.

3. Change the margins of the résumé.
   a. Click the **Layout** tab.
   b. Click the **Margins** button [*Page Setup* group] and select **Custom Margins** from the drop-down list. The *Page Setup* dialog box opens.
   c. In the *Margins* area (Figure 2-25), click in the **Top** box, delete the existing margin, and type .75.
   d. Click in the **Bottom** box, delete the existing margin, and type .75.
   e. Click the **down arrow** to the right of the *Left* box to change the left margin to **1"**.
   f. Click the **down arrow** to the right of the *Right* box to change the right margin to **1"**.
   g. Click the **Apply to** drop-down list at the bottom of the dialog box and select **Whole document** if it is not already selected.
   h. Click **OK** to apply the new margin settings and close the dialog box.

2-25 Change margins in the *Page Setup* dialog box

4. Set a right tab stop with a dash leader.
   a. Select the **"Loomis, CA October 2014 Present"** text below "*HEAD TEACHER, LOOMIS LEARNING CENTER.*"
   b. Click the **Paragraph** launcher [*Layout* or *Home* tab] to open the *Paragraph* dialog box.
   c. Click the **Tabs** button in the bottom left of the *Paragraph* dialog box to open the *Tabs* dialog box (Figure 2-26).
   d. Type 6.5 in the *Tab stop position* area.
   e. Select the **Right** radio button in the *Alignment* area.
   f. Select the **3** (dash leader) radio button in the *Leader* area.
   g. Click the **Set** button to set this tab stop and leader.
   h. Click the **OK** button to close the dialog box.

5. Use the *Format Painter* to apply the tab setting to multiple areas of the résumé.
   a. Place the insertion point in the line you just formatted.
   b. Double-click the **Format Painter** button [*Home* tab, *Clipboard* group].

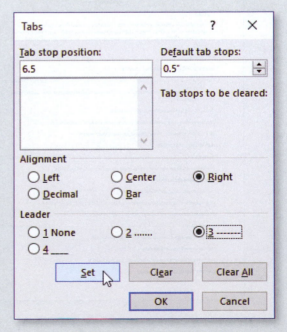

2-26 Set a right tab stop with a dash leader

c. Click each of the city, state, and date lines in the "EXPERIENCE" and "EDUCATION" sections to apply the tab settings as shown in Figure 2-27.

d. Click the **Format Painter** button to turn off copy format.

6. Remove an existing tab stop and set a left tab stop.

a. On the second page, select the lines of text below the "REFERENCES" heading.

b. Click the **Paragraph** launcher [*Layout* or *Home* tab] to open the *Paragraph* dialog box.

c. Click the **Tabs** button in the bottom left of the *Paragraph* dialog box to open the *Tabs* dialog box.

d. In the *Tab stop position* area, select the existing tab stop (**2.5"**) and click the **Clear** button to remove the existing tab.

e. Type **3.75** in the *Tab stop position* area.

f. Select the **Left** radio button in the *Alignment* area if it is not already selected.

g. Select the **1 None** radio button in the *Leader* area if it is not already selected.

h. Click the **Set** button to set this left tab stop (Figure 2-28).

i. Click the **OK** button to close the dialog box.

7. Apply a left and right indent to selected text.

a. Place the insertion point in the paragraph below the "PROFILE" heading on the first page.

b. Click the **Layout** tab.

c. Click the **Left** indent area [*Paragraph* group], type **.25** to replace the existing setting, and press **Enter**.

d. Click the **Right** indent area, type **.25** to replace the existing setting, and press **Enter**.

8. Save and close this document (Figure 2-29).

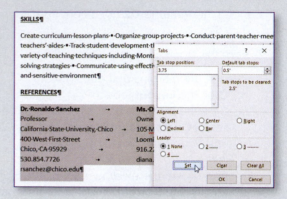

2-27 Use the *Format Painter* to apply tab settings

2-28 Set a left tab stop on selected text

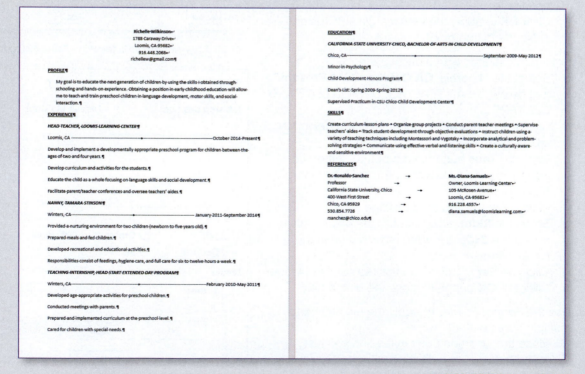

2-29 PP W2-1 completed

Inserting Page Numbers, Headers, and Footers

Page numbering, **headers**, and *footers* are regularly used in multiple-page documents. You can set the header, footer, or page number to appear on each page of the document, which means you only have to type the information once, and Word repeats that information on each subsequent page. The header area of a document is above the top margin, and the footer area is below the bottom margin.

Page Numbering

When you use Word to insert page numbers, a ***page number field*** is inserted in the header or footer of the document. This page number field automatically displays the current page number. You can control the page number location and the page number format.

Insert Page Number

Word gives you a variety of page number locations, horizontal alignment options, and number format options. The following is a list of the basic page number placement options:

- *Top of Page*
- *Bottom of Page*
- *Page Margins*
- *Current Position*

▶ **HOW TO:** Insert a Page Number

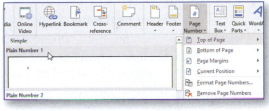

1. Click the **Insert** tab.
2. Click the **Page Number** button [*Header & Footer* group]. A drop-down list of options appears (Figure 2-30).
3. Click either **Top of Page** or **Bottom of Page**. Another drop-down list of page number options appears.
   - The top three options in this list are simple page numbers aligned at the left, center, or right.
   - Further down this list there are custom page number options.
4. Click one of the page number options to insert the current page number. The header or footer area opens with the page number inserted, and the *Header & Footer Tools Design* tab opens (Figure 2-31).
5. Click the **Close Header and Footer** button [*Close* group].

2-30 Insert page number

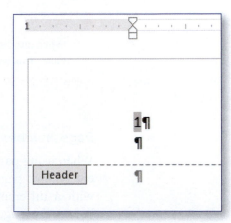

2-31 Page number inserted in the header on the left

▶ **ANOTHER WAY**

Close the header and footer by pressing the **Esc** key or double-clicking in the body of the document.

Edit Page Number in Header or Footer

When you close the header or footer, the page number appears in gray rather than black like the text of the document. The header and footer areas are outside the boundaries of the margins. If you want to edit the page number or contents of the header or footer, you have to open the header or footer. There are three ways to do this:

- Right-click the header or footer and select **Edit Header** or **Edit Footer**.
- Click the **Insert** tab, click the **Header** or **Footer** button in the *Header & Footer* group, and choose **Edit Header** or **Edit Footer**.
- Double-click the header or footer area of the document.

Different First Page

There are times when you might not want the page number and header or footer to print on the first page, but you want it to appear on the second and continuing pages. For example, on both multiple-page business letters and reports, the page number is typically not on the first page but is on the second and subsequent pages. Word gives you the option to set a ***different first page***.

▶**HOW TO:** Set a Different First Page Header and Footer

1. Go to the first page of the document.
2. Open the header or footer if it is not already open. Use one of the following methods to open the header or footer if it is not already open:

   - Right-click the header or footer and select **Edit Header** or **Edit Footer**.
   - Click the **Insert** tab, click the **Header** or **Footer** button in the *Header & Footer* group, and choose **Edit Header** or **Edit Footer**.
   - Double-click in the header or footer area of the document.

3. Click the **Different First Page** check box [*Header & Footer Tools Design* tab, *Options* group] (Figure 2-32).
4. Click the **Close Header and Footer** button [*Close* group]. The page number, header, and footer no longer appear on the first page but do appear on the second and continuing pages.

2-32 *Different First Page* check box

▶ **MORE INFO**

When inserting a page number, header, or footer, it is best to insert it on the first page of the document. This becomes increasingly important as you add section breaks to a document.

Page Number Format

When using page numbering, you might want a different type of page number format, numbering to begin with a different page number, or a chapter number before the page number. The *Page Number Format* dialog box provides you with page numbering options (Figure 2-33).

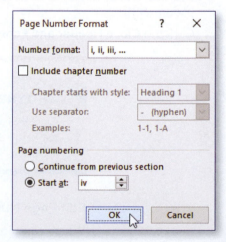

2-33 *Page Number Format* dialog box

▶**HOW TO:** Format Page Numbers

1. After inserting a page number, click the **Page Number** button [*Header & Footer Tools Design* or *Insert* tab, *Header & Footer* group] and select **Format Page Numbers**. The *Page Number Format* dialog box opens (see Figure 2-33).
2. Click the *Number format* **drop-down list** and select a page number format. There are six preset page numbering options from which to choose.
3. Select an option in the *Page numbering* section to *Continue from previous section* (default setting) or *Start at* a different page number.
   - Click the **Start at** radio button to set a different starting page number.
   - Type in the starting page number or use the up or down arrow to set the starting page number.
4. Click **OK** to close the *Page Number Format* dialog box.
5. Click the **Close Header and Footer** button [*Close* group].

Remove Page Number

If you want to remove the page numbering from a document, there are two different ways to do this.

- Select **Remove Page Numbers** from the *Page Number* drop-down list (Figure 2-34).
- Open the header or footer and manually delete the page number.

Insert Header and Footer Content

In addition to inserting page numbers into the header or footer of a document, you might want to include the number of pages in the document, date or time, title of the document, company name, or other custom content. You can enter information manually into the header or footer, or you can have Word insert document property fields.

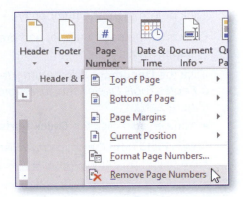

2-34 Remove page numbers

▶**HOW TO:** Insert Custom Header and Footer Content

1. Click the **Insert** tab.
2. Click the **Header** button and choose **Edit Header** in the drop-down list, or double-click in the *Header* area of the document (above the top margin). The header of the document opens and the *Header & Footer Tools Design* tab displays.
   - When you edit a header or footer, both the header and footer open and the *Header & Footer Tools Design* tab displays.
   - On this tab, there is a *Navigation* group to help you move between the header and footer and move through the different headers and footers in the document (Figure 2-35).
3. Type your information in the *Header* area (Figure 2-36).
   - You can change the formatting and alignment as desired.
   - You can insert a page number with the header or footer open.
4. Click the **Close Header and Footer** button [*Close* group].

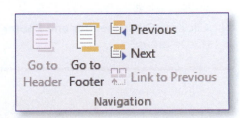

2-35 *Navigation* group on the *Header & Footer Tools Design* tab

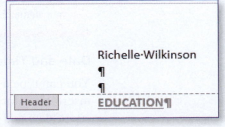

2-36 Enter custom information in the header

Number of Pages Field

In addition to inserting the current page number in a document, you can add a field code to automatically insert the total number of pages in a document (*NumPages* field).

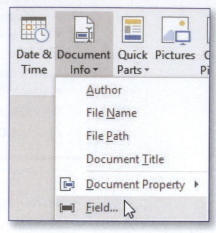

2-37 Insert field code

HOW TO: Insert the Number of Pages Field

1. Open the header or footer. The page number should already be inserted in the document.

2. Click before the page number, type **Page**, and press the **spacebar**.

3. Click after the page number and press the **spacebar**, type *of*, and press the **spacebar**.

4. Click the **Document Info** button [*Header & Footer Tools Design* tab, *Insert* group] (Figure 2-37).
   - You can also click the **Quick Parts** button.

5. Select **Field** from the drop-down list. The *Field* dialog box opens (Figure 2-38).

6. In the *Field names* area, scroll down and select **NumPages**. The description of the field is displayed in the *Description* area.

7. In the *Format* area, select a page number format.

8. Click **OK** to close the *Field* dialog box. The number of pages in the document displays (Figure 2-39).

9. Click the **Close Header and Footer** button [*Close* group].

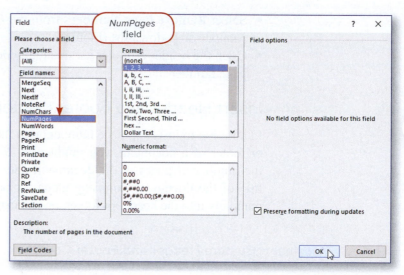

2-38 Insert *NumPages* field from the *Field* dialog box

2-39 Page number and number of pages field inserted into the header

Date and Time

You can type a date or the time in the header or footer of a document, or you can have Word insert this information. The advantages of inserting the date and time are that you have a variety of date and time formats from which to choose, and you can choose to have the date and time update automatically each time you open the document.

▶ HOW TO: Insert the Date and Time

1. Open the header or footer area and position the insertion point at the position where you want the date inserted.

2. Click the **Date & Time** button [*Header & Footer Tools Design* tab, *Insert* group]. The *Date and Time* dialog box opens (Figure 2-40).

3. Select the date or time format to use in the *Available formats* area.

4. Check the **Update automatically** check box if you want the date to update automatically.
   - Do not check *Update automatically* on time-sensitive documents where the date should remain constant.

5. Click **OK** to close the *Date and Time* dialog box. The date displays the header.

6. Click the **Close Header and Footer** button [*Close* group].

2-40 *Date and Time* dialog box

MORE INFO

Inserting a date or time is not limited to headers and footers. You can insert the date or time in the body of a document by clicking **Date & Time** [*Insert* tab, *Text* group].

Document Properties

When you have entered document properties in a Word document, you can automatically insert this information in the header or footer. For example, you might want to include the title of the document, name of the author, or date last modified. One of the advantages of inserting document properties rather than typing this information is that when you update the document properties, these fields automatically update in the header or footer and throughout the document.

▶ HOW TO: Insert Document Properties

1. Open the header or footer and place the insertion point at the location where you want the document property inserted.

2. Click the **Document Info** button [*Header & Footer Tools Design* tab, *Insert* group] (Figure 2-41).

3. Select the document property field or click **Document Property** and select the document property of your choice from the drop-down list. The document property displays in the document (Figure 2-42).
   - You can also click the **Quick Parts** button [*Header & Footer Tools Design* tab, *Insert* group] and select **Document Property**.
   - Press the **right arrow** key on your keyboard to deselect a document property field.

4. Click the **Close Header and Footer** button [*Close* group].

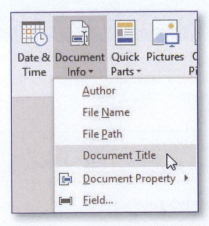

2-41 Insert document property field

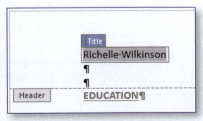

2-42 *Title* document property field inserted in the header

Built-In Headers, Footers, and Page Numbers

In addition to inserting basic page numbers, manually adding header or footer content, and inserting date and time, Word provides you with a variety of built-in custom header, footer, and page number format options. Many of the header and footer options include document properties that are automatically inserted and updated.

▶**HOW TO:** Insert a Built-In Header, Footer, or Page Number

2-43 List of built-in headers

1. Click the **Insert** tab.
2. Click the **Header**, **Footer**, or **Page Number** button [*Header & Footer* group] and select a built-in header, footer, or page number from the choices in the drop-down list (Figure 2-43). The selected content displays into the document.
   - Document property fields update automatically with document property information.
   - Some fields, such as *Pick the date*, require you to input or select information.
3. Click the **Close Header and Footer** button [*Close* group].

Keep in mind when you are using built-in headers, footers, and page numbers that many of these use tables, graphics, and advanced formatting, which makes editing more challenging without a thorough understanding of this type of content.

PAUSE & PRACTICE: WORD 2-2

In this Pause & Practice project, you modify the résumé from *Pause & Practice 2-1*. You add a header that appears only on the second page of this document and insert a document property field, page number, and Word field into the header.

File Needed: *[your initials] PP W2-1.docx*
Completed Project File Name: *[your initials] PP W2-2.docx*

1. Open the *[your initials] PP W2-1* document completed in *Pause & Practice 2-1*.
2. Save this document as [your initials] PP W2-2.

3. Edit the document properties.
   a. Click the **File** tab to open the *Backstage* view.
   b. In the *Info* area, click in the **Title** document property text box and type Richelle Wilkinson.
   c. Click the **Back** arrow to return to the résumé.

4. Insert a document property field in the header of the résumé.
   a. Place the insertion point at the beginning of the first page.
   b. Click the **Insert** tab.
   c. Click the **Header** button [*Header & Footer* group] and select **Edit Header** from the drop-down list. The header on the first page opens.
   d. Click the **Document Info** button [*Header & Footer Tools Design* tab, *Insert* group] and select **Document Title** from the drop-down list. The *Title* document property displays in the header.
   e. Leave the header open for the next instructions.

5. Insert a page number and number of pages field in the header and set it to display only on the second page.
   a. With the header still open, press the **right arrow** key once to deselect the document property field you just inserted.
   b. Press **Tab** two times to move to the right margin, type Page and **space** once.
   c. Click the **Page Number** button [*Header & Footer* group], select **Current Position** from the drop-down list, and select **Plain Number**. The page number displays in the header.
   d. **Space** once, type of, and **space** once.
   e. Click the **Document Info** (or **Quick Parts**) button [*Header & Footer Tools Design* tab, *Insert* group] and select **Field** from the drop-down list. The *Field* dialog box opens.
   f. Select **NumPages** in the *Field names* area (this is the field code to insert the total number of pages in the document) (Figure 2-44).

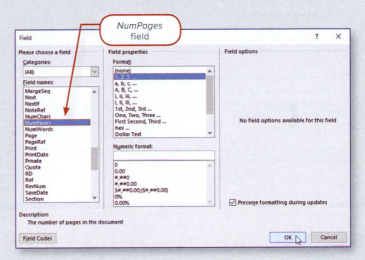

2-44 Insert *NumPages* field

   g. Select **1**, **2**, **3** in the *Format* area and click **OK** to insert the number of pages in the header.
   h. Press **Enter** two times to insert two blank lines after the header.
   i. Check to ensure that there are spaces between each of the words and page numbers.
   j. Check the **Different First Page** check box [*Header & Footer Tools Design* tab, *Options* group]. This removes the header content from the first page, but the header content displays on the second page (Figure 2-45).

2-45 Header with document property field, page number, and number of pages field

   k. Click the **Close Header and Footer** button [*Close* group] to close the header and return to the document.

6. Save and close the document (Figure 2-46).

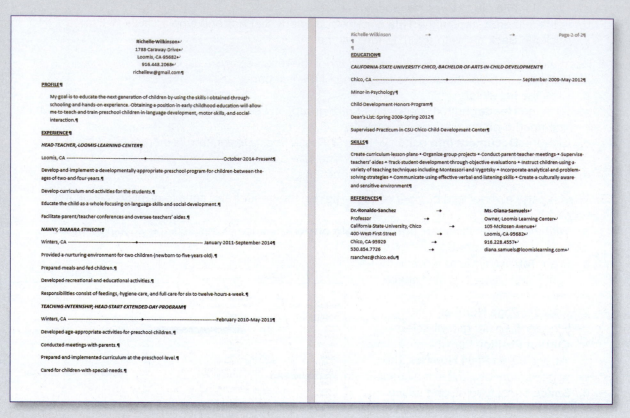

2-46 PP W2-2 completed

Using Page and Section Breaks

As you're typing a document and you get to the bottom of the page, Word automatically moves to the top of the next page so you can continue typing; this is referred to as a *soft page break*. The document's content and margins determine how much information fits on a page and what information flows to a new page.

There may be times when you want to start a new page before you get to the bottom margin or you might want different margins or page orientation in a different section of your document. Word provides options for page and section breaks to control page endings and formatting (Figure 2-47).

> ▶ **MORE INFO**
>
> Turn **Show/Hide** [*Home* tab, *Paragraph* group] on when working with page and section breaks, so you can view the placement of these breaks.

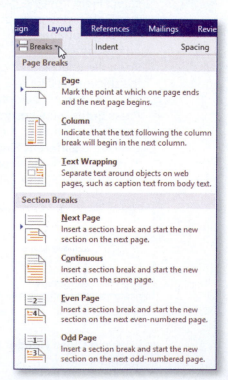

2-47 Page and section breaks

Page Breaks

Page breaks end one page and begin a new page. When you insert a *Page* break, you control where one page ends and a new page begins. There are three different types of page breaks: *Page*, *Column*, and *Text Wrapping*.

▶HOW TO: Insert a Page Break

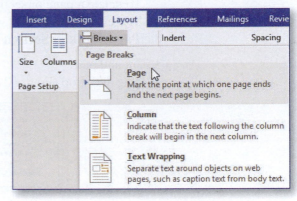

2-48 Insert *Page* break

1. Position the insertion point at the point in your document where you want to end one page and begin a new page.
2. Click the **Layout** tab.
3. Click the **Breaks** button [*Page Setup* group]. A drop-down list appears.
4. Select **Page** from the drop-down list. A page break displays in the document (Figure 2-48).
   - Turn on **Show/Hide** [*Home* tab, *Paragraph* group].
   - The *Page Break* indicator is visible and displays where the page breaks (Figure 2-49).

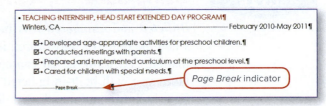

2-49 *Page* break inserted in a document

Section Breaks

Section breaks allow you even more formatting control over your document than page breaks. Section breaks can be used to format different headers, footers, and page numbering in different sections of your document. For example, if you want one page in your document to be landscape orientation, you can use a section break to control the format of an individual section. There are four different types of section breaks:

- ***Next Page***: Insert a section break and start the new section on the next page.
- ***Continuous***: Insert a section break and start the new section on the same page.
- ***Even Page***: Insert a section break and start the new section on the next even-numbered page.
- ***Odd Page***: Insert a section break and start the new section on the next odd-numbered page.

▶HOW TO: Insert a Next Page Section Break

1. Position the insertion point at the point in your document where you want to end one page and begin new section on a new page.
2. Click the **Layout** tab.
3. Click the **Breaks** button [*Page Setup* group]. A drop-down list appears.
4. Select **Next Page** from the drop-down list. A next page section break displays in the document.
   - Turn on **Show/Hide** [*Home* tab, *Paragraph* group].
   - The *Section Break (Next Page)* indicator is visible and displays where the next page section break occurs (Figure 2-50).

2-50 *Next Page* section break inserted in a document

Edit Page and Section Breaks

When finalizing a document, you might need to change the placement of a page or section break or remove a page or section break from the document. You can delete and move breaks in the same way you delete and move text from a document.

To delete a page or section break, select the break and press **Delete**.

There are two different ways to move a section or page break to a new location. First select the **Page Break** or **Section Break**, and then use one of the move options below:

- Cut and paste
- Drag and drop (Figure 2-51)

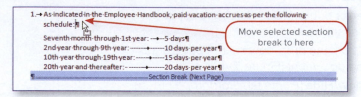

2-51 Move section break using drag and drop

SLO 2.6

Using Bulleted, Numbered, and Multilevel Lists

Bulleted and *numbered lists* highlight important information. Generally, use bulleted lists when the order of information is not important, and use numbered lists for sequential information. A *Multilevel list* can combine a variety of numbers, letters, and bullets. Word provides you with built-in bulleted, numbered, and multilevel lists, but you can also customize how the information in the list displays and aligns.

> **MORE INFO**
>
> When using bulleted and numbered lists, do not use a period at the end of lists containing only words or short phrases. If you are using complete sentences in your list, use a period at the end of each sentence.

Create a Bulleted List

You can create a bulleted list from existing text or you can create a new bulleted list. You choose the type of bullet to use from the *Bullet Library* in the *Bullets* drop-down list.

▶**HOW TO:** Create a Bulleted List

1. Select the text to be converted to a bulleted list, or, if you are beginning a new bulleted list, place the insertion point at the location where you want to begin the list.

2. Click the **Bullets** drop-down arrow [*Home* tab, *Paragraph* group] to open the library of bullet options (Figure 2-52).
   - If you click the *Bullets* button (not the *Bullets* drop-down arrow), the most recently used bullet is used for the bulleted list.

3. Select a bullet from the list of options.

4. Type your information after the bullet if you are typing a new bulleted list.

5. Press **Enter** after a bulleted item to add another bullet.

6. Press **Enter** two times after the last bullet, or click the **Bullets** button to turn off bullets.

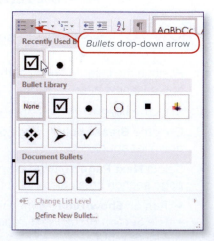

2-52 *Bullets* drop-down list

By default, bulleted lists are formatted using a hanging indent. The first line is indented 0.25" and the hanging indent is set at 0.5". You can adjust the indent using the *Decrease Indent* or *Increase Indent* buttons, ruler, or *Paragraph* dialog box.

You can add new bulleted items in the middle or at the end of the list by pressing **Enter** in front of or at the end of an existing bulleted item. To add a bulleted item before the first item in the list, click at the beginning of the first item and press **Enter**.

> ### MORE INFO
> You can use a line break (**Shift+Enter**) at the end of a bulleted sentence to add a blank line between bulleted items.

Customize a Bulleted List

In addition to using the bullets listed in the *Bullets Library*, you can select and use a custom bullet. You have the option of using a symbol from one of the font groups, or you can use a picture. If you use a picture, you can select one from the Bing Image Search or import a graphic of your own to use as a bullet.

▶ **HOW TO: Customize a Bulleted List**

1. Select the bulleted list.
2. Click the **Bullets** drop-down arrow [*Home* tab, *Paragraph* group] and select **Define New Bullet**. The *Define New Bullet* dialog box opens (Figure 2-53).
3. Click the **Symbol** or **Picture** button to open the *Symbol* or *Picture* dialog box.
   - If you click the **Symbol** button, the *Symbol* dialog box opens (Figure 2-54). From the *Font* drop-down list, you can select a symbol from any of the font sets (the most common are *Symbol*, *Wingdings*, and *Webdings*) or from *Recently used symbols*.
   - Each symbol has a character code to identify the symbol (see Figure 2-54).
   - If you click the **Picture** button, the *Insert Pictures* dialog box opens. You can import your own picture bullet from a file or use Bing Image Search to locate a picture to use as a bullet.
4. Select the bullet to use and click **OK** (or **Insert** or **Open** depending on the open dialog box) to close the dialog box.
5. Click **OK** to close the *Define New Bullet* dialog box.

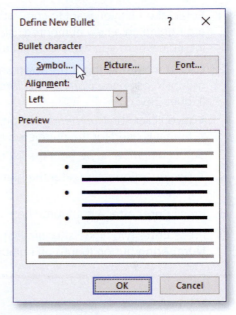

2-53 *Define New Bullet* dialog box

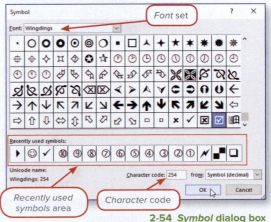

2-54 *Symbol* dialog box

You also have the option of having multiple levels of bullets with a different bullet for each level. Each subsequent bullet level is indented to distinguish it from the previous level. There are a few ways to increase or decrease the bullet level.

- Click the **Bullets** drop-down arrow [*Home* tab, *Paragraph* group] and select a bullet list level from the **Change List Level** drop-down list (Figure 2-55).
- Select or click at the beginning of a bulleted item and press **Tab** to increase bullet level.
- Select or click at the beginning of a bulleted item and click the **Increase Indent** button [*Home* tab, *Paragraph* group] to increase bullet level.
- Press **Shift+Tab** or click the **Decrease Indent** button to decrease the bullet level.

2-55 Change bulleted list level

Create a Numbered List

Creating a numbered list is similar to creating a bulleted list. The **Numbering Library** in the *Numbering* drop-down list contains number format options.

▶HOW TO: Create a Numbered List

1. Select the text you want to convert to a numbered list, or, if you are beginning a new numbered list, place the insertion point at the location where you want to begin the list.
2. Click the **Numbering** drop-down arrow [*Home* tab, *Paragraph* group] to open the *Numbering Library* of number format options (Figure 2-56).
   - If you click the *Numbering* button, the most recently used number format is used for the numbered list.
3. Select a number style from the list of options.
4. Type your information after the number if you are typing a new numbered list.
5. Press **Enter** after a numbered item to add another numbered item.
6. Press **Enter** two times after the last numbered item, or click the **Numbering** button to turn off numbering.

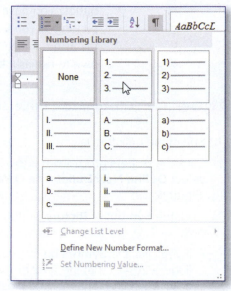

2-56 Numbering format options

> ▶ **ANOTHER WAY**
>
> Both the *Numbering* and *Bullets* drop-down lists are available from the mini toolbar when you select or right-click text.

Customize a Numbered List

In addition to being able to select a format from the *Numbering Library*, you also have the options to *Change List Level*, *Define New Number Format*, and *Set Numbering Value*.

The **Change List Level** option in the *Numbering* drop-down list allows you to select the level of the list. The numbering of each subsequent level of the list is dependent upon the number format you select.

You are not limited to the numbering formats available in the *Numbering* drop-down list. The **Define New Number Format** option allows you to customize how the numbered list displays.

▶HOW TO: Customize a Numbered List

1. Select the text where you want to change the number format, or, if you are beginning a new numbered list, place the insertion point at the location where you want to begin the list.

2. Click the **Numbering** drop-down arrow [*Home* tab, *Paragraph* group], and select **Define New Number Format**. The *Define New Number Format* dialog box opens (Figure 2-57).

3. Click the **Number style** drop-down arrow to select a number format from the list of options.
   - You can also change the numbering font by clicking the **Font** button and selecting a font, size, and style to apply to the numbered list.

4. In the *Number format* area, customize how the numbers display.
   - Typically, a period follows the numbers, but you can change this to an ending parenthesis, hyphen, other character, or no punctuation.

5. Click the **Alignment** drop-down arrow to change number alignment.
   - Numbers align on the left by default, but you can change the number alignment to center or right.

6. The *Preview* area displays how your number format will appear in your document.

7. Click **OK** to apply the number format and close the dialog box.

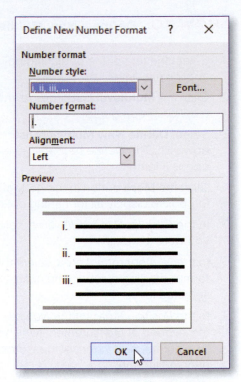

2-57 *Define New Number Format* dialog box

The ***Set Numbering Value*** dialog box includes options to *Start new list* or *Continue from previous list*. You can also set the number value to begin a new list. Open the *Set Numbering Value* dialog box from the *Numbering* drop-down list or right-click a numbered list and select *Set Numbering Value* from the context menu (Figure 2-58).

When using numbering, the context menu lists options to *Adjust List Indents*, *Restart at 1*, *Continue Numbering*, and *Set Numbering Value* (Figure 2-59).

2-58 *Set Numbering Value* dialog box

> ▶ **MORE INFO**
>
> Use the *Format Painter* to copy numbered or bulleted list formatting to other areas in a document.

2-59 Context menu numbering options

Multilevel Lists

Multilevel lists allow you to customize a list using a combination of numbers, letters, or bullets. Word provides you with a *List Library* from which to select a multilevel list. You can customize an existing multilevel list or define your own list.

As you define a new multilevel list, you have the following options to customize each level of the list:

- Number format including font and starting number
- Number style, which can be a number, letter, Roman numeral, or bullet
- Position of the number and the text that follows

▶ HOW TO: Define a New Multilevel List

1. Select the text or the beginning point on which to apply a multilevel list.

2. Click the **Multilevel List** drop-down arrow [*Home* tab, *Paragraph* group].

3. Select **Define New Multilevel list** from the drop-down list. The *Define new Multilevel list* dialog box opens (Figure 2-60).

4. Click the **More** button in the bottom left of the dialog box to display all formatting options.

5. In the *Click level to modify* area, select the level you want to modify.

6. In the *Number format* area, select the number format, starting number, and number style for the selected level.

7. In the *Position* area, set the *Number alignment*, the *Aligned at* measurement (which is the first line indent), *Text indent at* measurement (which is the hanging indent).

8. Click the **Set for All Levels** button to open the *Set for All Levels* dialog box where you to set the indents for all levels (Figure 2-61).

9. Click **OK** to apply the multilevel list settings.

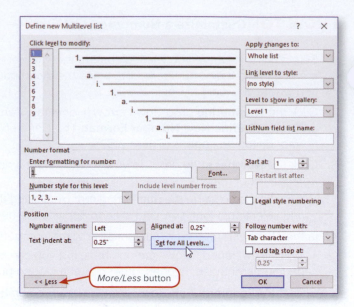

2-60 *Define new Multilevel list* dialog box

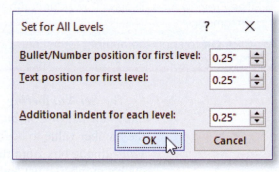

2-61 *Set for All Levels* dialog box

SLO 2.7

Using Styles and Themes

Styles are a collection of preset formatting that you can apply to a paragraph or selected text. A style can control the font, font size, style, color, effects, indents, line spacing, paragraph spacing, and borders applied to text. You can use styles to apply this preset formatting to titles, section headings, paragraph headings, text, lists, and tables. *Themes* are a collection of fonts, colors, and effects that you can apply to an entire document. Both styles and themes keep the formatting consistent throughout a single document or multiple documents.

Style Gallery

The *Style gallery* in the *Styles* group on the *Home* tab provides you with numerous built-in styles to apply to selected text in a document (Figure 2-62). The *Style* gallery does not display all of the available styles but rather displays the more commonly used styles.

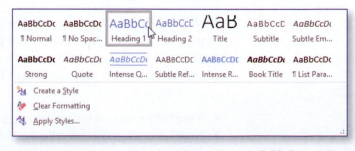

2-62 *Style* gallery

Apply a Built-In Style

You can quickly preview or apply styles to selected text or paragraphs. To preview a style, place the pointer on a style in the *Style* gallery. A live preview of the style displays on the selected text or paragraph. You can apply a style to the text by clicking a style in the *Style* gallery.

▶ HOW TO: Apply a Built-In Style from the Style Gallery

1. Select the text or paragraph where you want to apply the style.
2. Select a style from the *Style* gallery [*Home* tab, *Styles* group].
   - To see all of the styles in the *Style* gallery, click the **More** button (Figure 2-63).
   - To see the next row of styles available in the *Style* gallery, click the **down arrow** at the right side of the gallery.

2-63 Click the *More* button to display more styles

▶ ANOTHER WAY

Apply a style to selected text by selecting or right-clicking text, choosing **Styles** from the mini toolbar, and selecting the style to apply.

Modify a Style

Once a style has been applied to the text, you can change the formatting of this text. One way to do this is to make changes to font, font size, color, style, effects, etc., to the selected text without actually changing the style.

The other option is to modify the style. The advantage of modifying a style when you make a change is that the style will be consistent when applied to other text in a document. When you modify a style, text formatted with the modified style automatically updates to match the modified style. There are two ways to modify a style:

- *Update [style name] to Match Selection*
- *Modify* style

▶ HOW TO: Update Style to Match Selection

1. Apply a style to selected text.
2. Make formatting changes on the text where the style was applied.
3. Select the text you changed.
4. Right-click the style in the *Style* gallery and choose **Update [style name] to Match Selection** (Figure 2-64).
   - The style updates to match the selected text.
   - All other text with this style applied updates automatically.

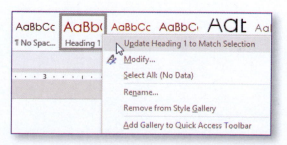

2-64 Update style to match selected text

You can also modify a style using the *Modify Style* dialog box.

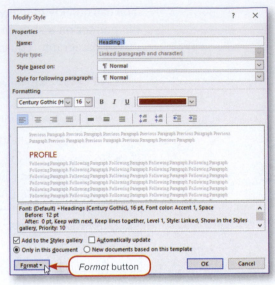

2-65 *Modify Style* dialog box

▶HOW TO: Modify an Existing Style

1. Right-click the style to modify in the *Style* gallery and select **Modify**. The *Modify Style* dialog box opens (Figure 2-65).
2. Make desired changes to the style. You can make basic formatting changes in the *Formatting* area of this dialog box.
3. Click the **Format** button at the bottom left to open other dialog boxes, such as *Font*, *Paragraph*, *Tabs*, *Borders*, etc.
   - Make desired formatting changes to the style and click **OK** to apply changes.
   - The formatting changes display in the *Preview* area.
4. Click **OK** to apply the style change and to close the *Modify Style* dialog box.

Apply a Theme

A theme is a collection of fonts, colors, and effects. Themes are similar to styles, but instead of just applying format to selected text, themes apply to an entire document. All documents have a theme; the default theme for a new document is *Office*. You can change the theme of a document or you can individually change the *Theme Colors*, *Theme Fonts*, or *Theme Effects* set in a document.

▶HOW TO: Apply a Document Theme

1. Click the **Design** tab.
2. Click the **Themes** button [*Document Formatting* group].
3. Select the theme to apply from the *Themes* gallery (Figure 2-66).
4. Click the **Colors**, **Fonts**, or **Effects** buttons [*Design* tab, *Document Formatting* group] to change each of these individually within the existing theme.

2-66 Change the *Theme* of a document

In this Pause & Practice project, you modify the résumé you edited in *Pause & Practice 2-2*. You add a bulleted list, customize the bulleted list, insert a page break, apply and modify styles, and apply a document theme.

File Needed: ***[your initials] PP W2-2.docx***
Completed Project File Name: ***[your initials] PP W2-3.docx***

---

1. Open the ***[your initials] PP W2-2*** document completed in *Pause & Practice 2-2*.

2. Save this document as [your initials] PP W2-3.

3. Convert text to a bulleted list and customize the bullet.
   a. Select the four paragraphs of text below the "EXPERIENCE" heading and the city, state, and date line.
   b. Click the **Bullets** button [*Home* tab, *Paragraph* group]. The selected text converts to a bulleted list (Figure 2-67).
   c. With the bulleted paragraphs still selected, click the **Bullets** drop-down arrow and select **Define New Bullet**. The *Define New Bullet* dialog box opens.
   d. Click the **Symbol** button. The *Symbol* dialog box opens (Figure 2-68).
   e. Click the **Font** drop-down list and scroll down to select **Wingdings**.
   f. Scroll down the list of symbols and select the **check box** symbol (*Character code* 254).
   g. Click **OK** to close the *Symbol* dialog box.
   h. Click **OK** to close the *Define New Bullet* dialog box.

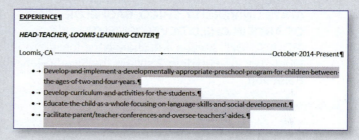

2-67 Apply bullets to selected text

4. Use the *Format Painter* to apply this bullet format to lines of text in the other "EXPERIENCE" sections and the "EDUCATION" section. Don't apply bullet formatting to the city, state, and date lines where the tab stops and leaders are applied.

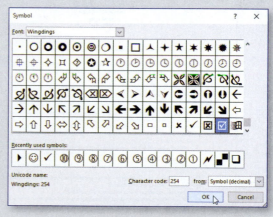

2-68 *Symbol* dialog box

5. Insert a page break in the document.
   a. Turn on **Show/Hide** [*Home* tab, *Paragraph* group].
   b. Place the insertion point in front of the "EDUCATION" heading.
   c. Select the **Layout** tab and click the **Breaks** button [*Page Setup* group].
   d. Select **Page** from the drop-down list. A page break displays at the bottom of the first page, and the "EDUCATION" section moves to the next page.

6. Change the theme and theme color of the document.
   a. Click the **Design** tab.
   b. Click the **Themes** button [*Document Formatting* group] and select **Ion** from the *Themes* gallery.
   c. Click the **Colors** button [*Document Formatting* group] and select **Red** from the *Theme Colors* drop-down list.

7. Apply styles from the *Style* gallery to selected text.
   a. On the first page of the résumé, select **"Richelle Wilkinson"** and click the **Title** style from the *Style* gallery [*Home* tab].
   b. With this text still selected, change the font size to **20 pt**.
   c. Apply the **Heading 1** style to each of the main headings ("PROFILE," "EXPERIENCE," "EDUCATION," "SKILLS," and "REFERENCES").
   d. Apply the **Heading 2** style to each of the bold and italicized subheadings in the "EXPERIENCE" and "EDUCATION" sections.

8. Modify a style.
   a. Select the **"PROFILE"** heading.
   b. Change the *Before* paragraph spacing to **16 pt**.
   c. Right-click the **Heading 1** style in the *Style* gallery and select **Update Heading 1 to Match Selection** (Figure 2-69). This style change is applied to all text with *Heading 1* style.

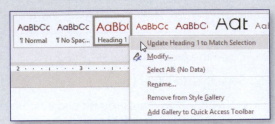

2-69 Update style to match selection

   d. On the second page, select **"CALIFORNIA STATE UNIVERSITY CHICO, BACHELOR OF ARTS IN CHILD DEVELOPMENT"** in the "EDUCATION" section and change the font size to **11 pt**.
   e. Right-click the **Heading 2** style in the *Style* gallery and select **Update Heading 2 to Match Selection**.

9. Save and close the document (Figure 2-70).

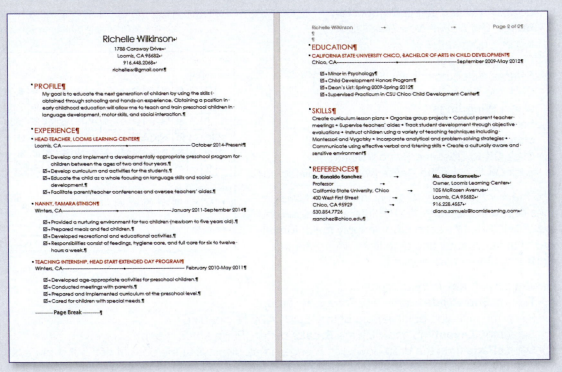

2-70 PP W2-3 completed

Using Find and Replace

Find and *Replace* are two extremely useful and powerful tools in Word. The *Find* feature allows you to search for and locate words and phrases in a document. The *Replace* feature allows you to search for a word or phrase and replace it with other text. You can also use *Find* and *Replace* to search for a specific type of formatting in a document and replace it with different formatting. These features are particularly useful in longer documents. When using *Find* or *Replace*, it is best to position your insertion point at the top of the document so Word searches from the beginning of your document.

Find

You can use the **Navigation pane** in Word to search for text and display all instances of the matching text. Word also highlights in yellow each instance of the matching text in the document. You are able to navigate through the document, see each instance, and edit as desired.

> ▶ **HOW TO:** Use Find in the Navigation Pane

1. Place your insertion point at the beginning of the document.
2. Click the **Find** button [*Home* tab, *Editing* group]. The *Navigation* pane opens on the left side of the Word window.
3. Click the **Search document** text box at the top of the *Navigation* pane and type the text you want to search.
   - The matching results display below the text box.
   - Word highlights the matching text in the document.
4. Click the **Next** or **Previous** search result buttons to move through each matching instance in the document (Figure 2-71).
   - You can also click the matching instances below the *Search document* text box to go to a specific occurrence of the matching text.

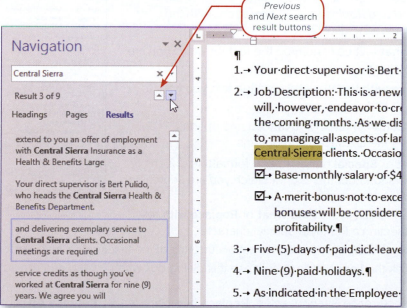

2-71 Use *Find* in the *Navigation* pane

5. Edit the highlighted text in the document if you want to make changes.
6. Click the **X** to the right of the *Search Document* text box to clear the current search.
7. Click the **X** in the upper right of the *Navigation* pane to close the pane.

▶ **ANOTHER WAY**

Ctrl+F opens the *Find* feature in the *Navigation* pane.

Find and Replace

The ***Find and Replace*** dialog box provides you three different advanced options for searching your document:

- *Find*
- *Replace*
- *Go To*

The *Find* tab of the *Find and Replace* dialog box not only searches for text in your document but also searches for specific formatting (such as font styles, line spacing, or paragraph spacing). For example, you can search for all text that is bold or italic, or that has 6 pt. *After* paragraph spacing.

Use the *Replace* feature to search for text, formatting, or a combination of text and formatting and to replace the matching text with other text, formatting, or formatted text. This feature is a quick and efficient way to find and replace text in a document.

▶ **HOW TO:** Use Replace

1. Place your insertion point at the beginning of the document.

2. Click the **Replace** button [*Home* tab, *Editing* group] or press **Ctrl+H**. The *Find and Replace* dialog box opens with the *Replace* tab displayed (Figure 2-72).

3. Click the **Find what** text box and type the text for which you are searching.

4. Click the **Replace with** text box and type the text you want to replace the found text.

5. Click the **More** button to display advanced find options. The *Less* button hides the advanced find options.

6. Click the **Format** or **Special** button to add formatting options or special characters to either the text for which you are searching or the replacement text.
   - Put the insertion point in the **Find what** or **Replace with** text box before selecting a format or special character.

2-72 Replace text

7. Click the **Find Next** button to locate the first occurrence of the text (and formatting) for which you are searching.
   - It is best to click the **Less** button to collapse this dialog box when finding and replacing content in your document.

8. When the first occurrence is found, select **Replace** (this occurrence), **Replace All** (all occurrences), or **Find Next** (skip this occurrence without replacing and move to the next).

9. Click the **Find Next** button to move to the next occurrence of the matching text and formatting.

10. When you finish finding and replacing text in the document, a dialog box opens informing you that Word has finished searching the document. Click **OK** to close this dialog box.

11. Click the **X** in the upper right corner to close the *Find and Replace* dialog box.

When using *Find* or *Replace*, wildcards can be used to help find information. You can use wildcards before, after, or between words.

- *Question mark (?):* A wildcard for a single character. For example, **w???** finds any words that begins with "w" and contains four letters (e.g., when, with, warm, or wish).
- *Asterisk (*):* A wildcard for a string of characters. For example, **search*** finds any form of the word "search" (e.g., searches, searching, or searched).

▶ **ANOTHER WAY**

Ctrl+H opens the *Find and Replace* dialog box with the *Replace* tab selected.

▶ **MORE INFO**

It is a good idea to use *Match Case* when replacing acronyms (capital letters) with words so the replaced words will not be all upper case. Also, use *Find whole words only* to refine your search.

Go To

The ***Go To*** feature allows you to go quickly to specific items or locations in your document. This feature is different from *Find* in that *Go To* moves you to specific objects or locations in your document such as a page, section, or bookmark. This feature is available in the *Find and Replace* dialog box.

▶ **HOW TO:** Use the Go To Feature

1. Click the **Find** drop-down arrow [*Home* tab, *Editing* group].
2. Select **Go To**. The *Find and Replace* dialog box opens with the *Go To* tab displayed (Figure 2-73).
3. In the *Go to what* area, select the item to go to from the list of options: *Page, Section, Line, Bookmark, Comment, Footnote,* etc.
   - The text box to the right is context sensitive and changes depending on the item chosen.
4. In the text box to the right, type in a page number, section, line, bookmark, etc.
5. Click the **Go To** button.
6. Click **Close** to close this dialog box.

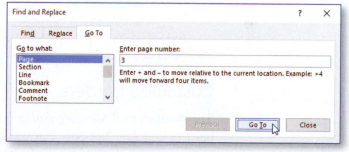

2-73 Go To in the *Find and Replace* dialog box

▶ **ANOTHER WAY**

Ctrl+G or **F5** opens the *Find and Replace* dialog box with the *Go To* tab selected.

Using Borders, Shading, and Hyperlinks

Borders and *shading* are excellent ways to highlight or emphasize important information in a document. In Word, there are many different border and shading options including preset border options. You also have the option of applying custom borders and shading to selected text or paragraphs of your document.

A *hyperlink* functions like a button and is used to take a reader to a web page, open an existing or new document, open an email message, or move to another location in the current document. You can add a hyperlink to text or a graphic in a document.

Apply Built-In Borders

You can use the ***Borders drop-down list*** in the *Paragraph* group on the *Home* tab to quickly apply borders to selected text. Borders are typically applied to paragraphs, but they can also be applied to other selected text. Borders, by default, apply to the paragraph where your insertion point is unless you select specific text. Figure 2-74 shows the different types of built-in borders.

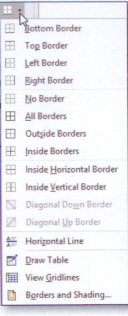

2-74 *Borders drop-down list*

▶**HOW TO: Apply Built-In Borders**

1. Select the paragraph or place the insertion point in the paragraph where you want to apply the border.
2. Click the **Home** tab.
3. Click the **Borders** drop-down arrow [*Paragraph* group] (see Figure 2-74).
4. Click the border option to apply to the selected paragraph.

> ▶ **MORE INFO**
>
> You can remove borders by selecting the paragraph or text on which the borders are applied and clicking the **No Border** option in the *Borders* drop-down list.

Customize Borders

The ***Borders and Shading dialog box*** provides many more options to customize the type of borders you use. Not only can you customize the style, width, and color of border line, but also you can customize where the border is placed in relation to the selected text. The *Borders and Shading* dialog box is available from the *Borders* drop-down list in the *Paragraph* group on the *Home* tab.

▶**HOW TO: Apply Custom Borders**

1. Select the paragraph(s) where you want to apply a border.
2. Click the **Borders** drop-down arrow [*Home* tab, *Paragraph* group] and choose the **Borders and Shading** option at the bottom of the list. The *Borders and Shading* dialog box opens (Figure 2-75).
   - In the *Apply to* area, select where you want to apply the borders. Your options are *Text* and *Paragraph*.

3. In the *Setting* area, select the type of border to use. Your options are *None*, *Box*, *Shadow*, *3-D*, and *Custom*.

4. In the *Style* area, select a style of the line from the list of options.

5. Click the **Color** drop-down arrow and select line color.

6. Click the **Width** drop-down arrow and select the width of the border line. The width of the line is measured in points.

7. View the *Preview* area to see how the border will appear in your document.

   - In the *Preview* area, you can customize how the borders appear by clicking the *Top*, *Bottom*, *Left*, or *Right* border buttons to turn on or off a border (see Figure 2-75).

8. Click the **Options** button to open the *Border and Shading Options* dialog box (Figure 2-76).

   - This dialog box includes the option to add in additional space (padding) between the border and the text at the *Top*, *Bottom*, *Left*, and *Right*.
   - The spacing is measured in points.
   - Click **OK** to close the *Border and Shading Options* dialog box.

9. Click **OK** to close the *Borders and Shading* dialog box.

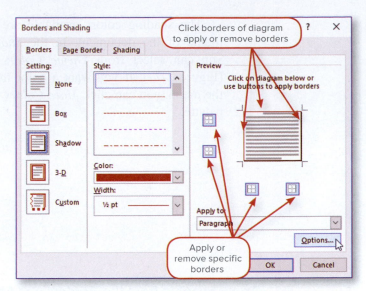

2-75 *Borders and Shading* dialog box

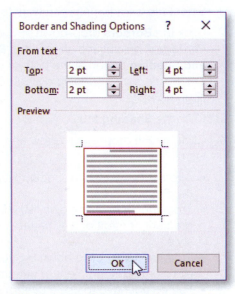

2-76 *Border and Shading Options* dialog box

Apply Shading

Applying shading to a paragraph or text is very similar to applying borders. ***Shading*** applies a background color to selected text. *Shading* color options are available from the *Shading* drop-down list in the *Paragraph* group on the *Home* tab or in the *Borders and Shading* dialog box on the *Shading* tab.

The shading colors available are dependent upon the theme of the document. In the *Shading* drop-down list, you can select from *Theme Colors* or *Standard Colors* (Figure 2-77). If you want a color that is not available in the menu, you can click *More Colors* to select from a color palette.

2-77 Shading color options from the *Shading* drop-down list

▶ **HOW TO:** Apply Shading from the Borders and Shading Dialog Box

1. Select the paragraph(s) you want to shade.
2. Click the **Borders** drop-down arrow [*Home* tab, *Paragraph* group] and choose the **Borders and Shading** option at the bottom of the list. The *Borders and Shading* dialog box opens (Figure 2-78).
3. Click the **Shading** tab.
4. Click the **Fill** drop-down arrow and select a shading fill color.
   - Alternatively, select a shading *Style* and *Color* in the *Patterns* area.
   - From the *Style* drop-down list, you can select a gradient percent or a fill pattern as the shading style.
   - From the *Color* drop-down list, you can select a fill color for the gradient or pattern you selected.
   - You do not have to use a pattern style or color for shading. Usually just a fill color is sufficient.
5. Click **OK** to close the *Borders and Shading* dialog box.

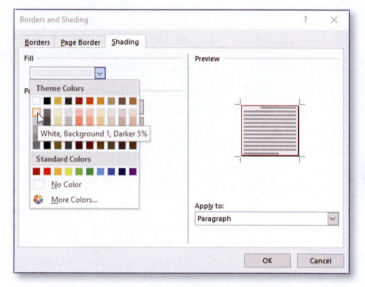

2-78 Shading options in the *Borders and Shading* dialog box

Apply a Page Border

Page borders are different from paragraph or text borders. A page border is around the entire page rather than selected paragraphs or text. Page borders are useful and attractive when creating flyers or handouts. A page border can be a line with varying styles, widths, and colors, or you can use art graphics as a page border.

▶ **HOW TO:** Apply a Page Border

1. Click the **Design** tab.
2. Click the **Page Borders** button [*Page Background* group]. The *Borders and Shading* dialog box opens with the *Page Border* tab displayed (Figure 2-79).

3. In the *Setting* area, select the type of page border you want to apply.
4. From the *Style* list, select a border style.
   - Alternatively, you can select an art to apply as the border from the **Art** drop-down list.
5. Select a border color and width from the **Color** and **Width** drop-down lists.
6. In the *Preview* area, customize how the page border appears by clicking the **Top**, **Bottom**, **Left**, or **Right** border buttons to turn on or off borders.

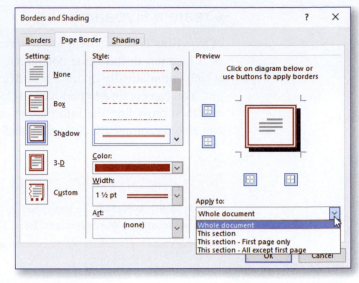

2-79 Apply a page border

7. In the *Apply to* area, select the page(s) where you want to apply the page border. Your options are:
   - *Whole document*
   - *This section*
   - *This section—First page only*
   - *This section—All except first page*
8. Click **OK** to close the *Borders and Shading* dialog box.

> ### MORE INFO
> When you apply a page border, the text in the document is not affected because the page border is placed outside the margin boundaries.

Insert a Horizontal Line

In addition to being able to insert top and bottom borders on selected text, you can also insert a ***horizontal line*** to use as a border to separate information on a page. A horizontal line is actually a graphic object that is inserted into the document. When you insert a horizontal line, the line is the width of the page. More information about using and customizing graphics is covered in *SLO 4.5: Working with Graphics*.

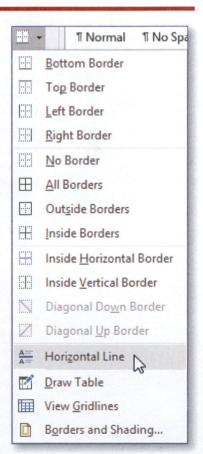

▶HOW TO: Insert a Horizontal Line

1. Place your insertion point in the document where you want a horizontal line.
2. Click the **Borders** drop-down arrow [*Home* tab, *Paragraph* group].
3. Select **Horizontal Line** from the drop-down list (Figure 2-80).
   - The horizontal line is treated as a separate paragraph and has a paragraph mark to the right.

2-80 Insert a horizontal line

Create a Hyperlink

A hyperlink is an excellent way to direct users to information on a web site, another document, or a location in the same document. You can also create a hyperlink for an email address, which automatically opens a new Microsoft Outlook email message addressed to the recipient. You can create a hyperlink by selecting the text or figure you want to turn into a hyperlink and then providing the information about the location where the user will be directed. You can also customize the *ScreenTip* and the target frame.

The *ScreenTip* is the text that displays when you place your pointer over the hyperlink in the document. The *target frame* is the window where the hyperlink document or web site opens. There are many different target frame options from which to choose. Usually it is best to choose **New window** if the link is to a different document or a web page. An email hyperlink always opens in a new window.

▶**HOW TO:** Create a Hyperlink

1. Select the text or graphic where you want to create a hyperlink.
2. Click the **Insert** tab.
3. Click the **Hyperlink** button [*Links* group]. The *Insert Hyperlink* dialog box opens (Figure 2-81).

    • The text you selected in the document as the hyperlink is displayed in the *Text to display* area. If you type other text in this text box, it will replace the text you selected in the document.

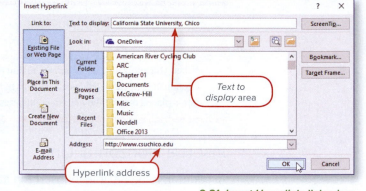

2-81 *Insert Hyperlink* dialog box

4. In the *Link to* area, select the type of hyperlink you want to create. Your options are *Existing File or Web Page, Place in This Document, Create New Document,* or *E-mail Address.*

    • If you are linking to a file, browse your computer in the *Look in* area to locate and select the file.
    • If you are linking to a web page, or type or paste (**Ctrl+V**) a web address in the *Address* area
    • If you are linking to a place in the document, a list of headings from which to choose displays.
    • If you are inserting a link to create a new document, options for the new document display.
    • If you are linking to an email address, you type in the email address and have the option to create a subject line for the email.

5. Click the **ScreenTip** button to insert text that displays when you place pointer over the hyperlink (Figure 2-82).

6. Type the *ScreenTip* text and click **OK** to close the *Set Hyperlink ScreenTip* dialog box.

7. Click the **Target Frame** button to open the *Set Target Frame* dialog box (Figure 2-83).
   - From the drop-down list of options, select where the hyperlink destination will be opened.
   - The *Set as default for all hyperlinks* check box allows you to make your target frame selection the default for all hyperlinks in your document.

8. Click **OK** to close the *Set Target Frame* dialog box.

9. Click **OK** to insert the hyperlink and close the *Insert Hyperlink* dialog box.

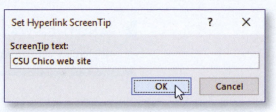

2-82 *Set Hyperlink ScreenTip dialog box*

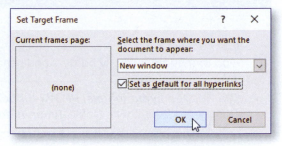

2-83 *Set Target Frame dialog box*

ANOTHER WAY

Ctrl+K opens the *Insert Hyperlink* dialog box.

Edit or Remove a Hyperlink

There might be times when you have incorporated text from a web site or another document that includes hyperlinks to a document, or you might want to edit a hyperlink in an existing document. Word allows you to quickly edit hyperlinks to change hyperlink information, add a *ScreenTip*, or change the target frame.

You can quickly remove a hyperlink from a document without deleting the text in the document. When you remove a hyperlink from existing text, the text in your document is not deleted. Only the hyperlink attached to the text is removed.

▶**HOW TO:** Edit or Remove a Hyperlink

1. Select or click the hyperlink to edit.

2. Click the **Hyperlink** button [*Insert* tab, *Links* group]. The *Edit Hyperlink* dialog box opens.
   - You can also press **Ctrl+K** or right-click the selected hyperlink and select **Edit Hyperlink**.

3. Change hyperlink information or options as needed.

4. Click the **Remove Link** button to remove an existing hyperlink (Figure 2-84).
   - When you remove a hyperlink, the *Edit Hyperlink* dialog box closes automatically.

5. Click **OK** to close the *Edit Hyperlink* dialog box if necessary.

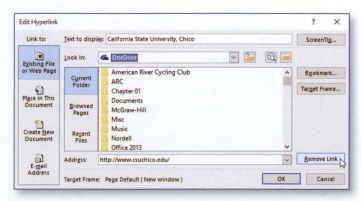

2-84 **Edit or remove a hyperlink**

PAUSE & PRACTICE: WORD 2-4

In this Pause & Practice project, you finalize the résumé you worked on in *Pause & Practice 2-3*. You use *Find and Replace*, apply borders and shading to selected text, and add hyperlinks to the document.

File Needed: *[your initials] PP W2-3.docx*
Completed Project File Name: *[your initials] PP W2-4.docx*

1. Open the *[your initials] PP W2-3* document completed in *Pause & Practice 2-3*.

2. Save this document as [your initials] PP W2-4.

3. Use *Find and Replace* to replace the hyphen between dates with an en dash.
   a. Press **Ctrl+Home** to move to the top of the document.
   b. Click the **Replace** button [*Home* tab, *Editing* group] or press **Ctrl+H** to open the *Find and Replace* dialog box.
   c. In the *Find what* text box, type – (hyphen).
   d. Place the insertion point in the *Replace with* text box.
   e. Click the **More** button if the *Search Options* are not already displayed.
   f. Click the **Special** button and select **En Dash** (Figure 2-85).
   g. Click the **Less** button to collapse the **Find and Replace** dialog box (Figure 2-86).
   h. Click the **Find Next** button to locate the first instance of a hyphen.
   i. Choose **Find Next** to skip the hyphenated word in the first paragraph.
   j. Click the **Replace** button to replace each occurrence of a hyphen between the dates with an en dash; choose **Find Next** to skip and not replace each occurrence of a hyphenated word.

2-86 Use *Find and Replace*

2-85 Select *En Dash* as the special character to replace a hyphen

   k. Click **OK** when Word has finished searching the document.
   l. Click **Close** to close the *Find and Replace* dialog box.

4. Add borders and shading to a paragraph.
   a. Select the paragraph after the "PROFILE" heading on the first page. Be sure to include the paragraph mark at the end of the paragraph.

b. Click the **Borders** drop-down arrow [*Home* tab, *Paragraph* group] and select **Borders and Shading** to open the *Borders and Shading* dialog box.

c. Select **Shadow** in the *Setting* area.

d. Select the **solid line** in the *Style* area.

e. Click the **Color** drop-down list and select **Dark Red**, **Accent 1** (Figure 2-87).

f. Select **½ pt** in the *Width* area.

g. Select **Paragraph** in the *Apply to* area.

h. Click the **Options** button to open the *Border and Shading Options* dialog box and change *Top* and *Bottom* to **2 pt**.

i. Click **OK** to close the *Border and Shading Options* dialog box.

j. Click the **Shading** tab.

k. Click the **Fill** drop-down list and select **White**, **Background 1**, **Darker 5%** (Figure 2-88).

l. Click **OK** to close the *Borders and Shading* dialog box.

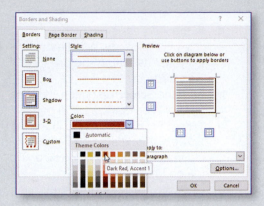

2-87 **Select border color in the *Borders and Shading* dialog box**

5. Add a bottom border to the header.

a. Right-click the header on the second page and select **Edit Header** to open the header area on the second page.

b. Place the insertion point in the first line of the header.

c. Click the **Borders** drop-down arrow [*Home* tab, *Paragraph* group].

d. Select **Bottom Border**. A bottom border displays below the header text.

e. Click the **Close Header and Footer** button [*Header & Footer Tools Design* tab, *Close* group].

2-88 **Apply shading to selected text**

6. Insert a hyperlink to an email address.

a. Select the email address in the heading information on the first page.

b. Click the **Hyperlink** button [*Insert* tab, *Links* group] or press **Ctrl+K** to open the *Insert Hyperlink* dialog box (Figure 2-89).

c. Click the **E-mail Address** button in the *Link to* area.

d. Type richellew@gmail.com in the *Text to display* area.

e. Type richellew@gmail.com in the *E-mail address* area. Word automatically inserts "mailto:" before the email address.

f. Click the **ScreenTip** button. The *Set Hyperlink ScreenTip* dialog box opens (Figure 2-90).

g. Type Email Richelle in the *ScreenTip text* area and click **OK** to close the *Set Hyperlink ScreenTip* dialog box.

h. Click **OK** to close the *Insert Hyperlink* dialog box.

2-89 **Insert hyperlink to an email address**

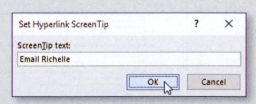

2-90 *Set Hyperlink ScreenTip* dialog box

7. Insert a hyperlink to a web site.

a. In the "REFERENCES" section on the second page, select **"California State University**, **Chico."** Don't select this text in the "EDUCATION" section.

b. Click the **Hyperlink** button or press **Ctrl+K** to open the *Insert Hyperlink* dialog box (Figure 2-91).

c. Select **Existing File or Web Page** in the *Link to* area. The *Text to display* area has *California State University, Chico* already filled in.

d. In the *Address* area, type **www.csuchico.edu**. Word automatically inserts "http://" before the web address.

e. Click the **ScreenTip** button. The *Set Hyperlink ScreenTip* dialog box opens.

f. Type **CSU Chico web site** in the *ScreenTip text* area and click **OK** to close the *Set Hyperlink ScreenTip* dialog box.

g. Click the **Target Frame** button in the *Insert Hyperlink* dialog box to open the *Set Target Frame* dialog box.

h. Select **New window** from the drop-down list and check the **Set as default for all hyperlinks** check box (Figure 2-92).

i. Click **OK** to close the *Set Target Frame* dialog box and click **OK** to close the *Insert Hyperlink* dialog box.

8. Automatically add hyperlinks to email addresses.

a. Place the insertion point after "rsanchez @chico. edu" in the "REFERENCES" section on the second page.

b. Press the **spacebar** once to automatically add a hyperlink to the email address.

c. Place the insertion point after "diana.samuels@loomislearning.com" in the "REFERENCES" section on the second page and press the **spacebar** once to automatically add a hyperlink to the email address.

9. Save and close the document (Figure 2-93).

2-91 Insert hyperlink to a web page

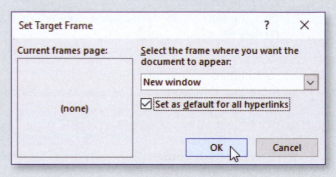

2-92 *Set Target Frame* dialog box

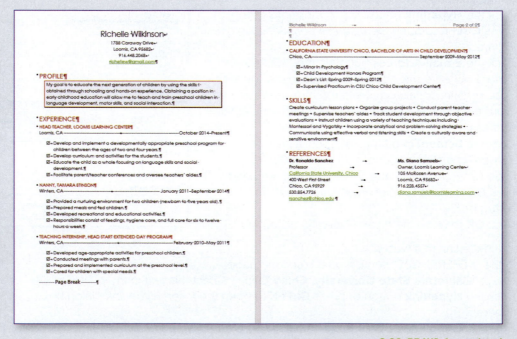

2-93 PP W2-4 completed

Chapter Summary

2.1 Format a document by customizing margins, page orientation, paper size, and vertical alignment (p. W2-66).

- Adjust the *margins* of a document to increase or decrease the *white space* surrounding the text. You can adjust the top, bottom, left, and right margins of a document.
- *Landscape* and *Portrait* are the two *page orientation* options.
- A standard sheet of paper is 8½" × 11". Select other paper sizes or create a custom paper size.
- *Vertical alignment* controls how text aligns between the top and bottom margins. By default, text aligns vertically at the top of the document. You can also use center, justified, or bottom vertical alignment.
- Use horizontal and vertical *rulers* to display the typing area on a document.
- You can change default page settings in the *Page Setup dialog box*.

2.2 Improve alignment and page layout by setting, using, and editing tab stops in a document (p. W2-69).

- There are five different types of *tab stops: Left, Center, Right, Decimal,* and *Bar*.
- Set, modify, or remove tab stops using the ruler or the *Tabs dialog box*.
- Use the *Tab selector* on the left side of the ruler to select a type of tab stop to set.
- *Leaders* can be used with tab stops. There are three different types of leaders: *Dot, Dash,* and *Solid underline*.
- In a Word document, default tab stops are set every 0.5". You can change the default tab stops.

2.3 Apply indents to control text alignment (p. W2-74).

- *Indents* can function as temporary margins and allow you to arrange paragraphs horizontally between the margins.
- There are four different types of indents: *left, right, first line,* and *hanging*.
- You can apply, modify, and remove indents with the ruler, *Layout* tab, or *Paragraph* dialog box.

2.4 Enhance document layout by inserting page numbers, headers, and footers (p. W2-79).

- You can insert a *page number* into the header or footer in various locations.

- *Headers* and *footers* are areas above and below a document's top and bottom margins.
- The *Different First Page* option allows you to remove or have different first page content in the header or footer.
- You type header and footer content once and it appears on subsequent pages.
- You can customize headers and footers with text, page numbers, the date, and other document property fields.
- You have a variety of built-in header, footer, and page numbering options.

2.5 Control pagination with page and section breaks (p. W2-86).

- Use *page breaks* to control the ending and beginning of pages in a document.
- Use *section breaks* to allow for different page setup formatting on different sections of a document.
- There are four different options for section breaks: *Next Page, Continuous, Even Page,* and *Odd Page*.
- Section breaks are visible in a document when the *Show/Hide* feature is turned on.

2.6 Use customized bulleted and numbered lists to effectively present information (p. W2-88).

- Use *bulleted* and *numbered lists* to emphasize important information.
- You can customize lists by using different symbols or pictures as bullets.
- Use numbering to display an ordered list.
- You can customize number format and levels.
- *Multilevel lists* allow you to customize a list using a combination of numbers, letters, or bullets.

2.7 Apply styles and themes to improve consistency in document format (p. W2-92).

- A *style* is a collection of preset formatting that you can apply to selected text.
- The *Style gallery* is a collection of built-in styles available in a document.
- You can modify existing styles.
- A *theme* is a collection of fonts, colors, and effects that you can apply to a document.

2.8 Use find and replace to edit a document (p. W2-97).

- The *Find* feature in Word allows you to search for specific text or format in a document.

- The **Navigation pane** displays all occurrences of the text for which you are searching.
- The **Replace** feature allows you to search for specific text in a document and replace it with other text.
- Both *Find* and *Replace* allow you to search for and replace formatting in a document.
- Use the **Go To** feature to go directly to a page, section, line, or other area in your document.

2.9 Improve overall document design and format by using borders, shading, horizontal lines, and hyperlinks (p.W2-100).

- *You can apply* **borders** *and* **shading** to text and paragraphs in a document.

- Word provides a variety of built-in border and shading options that you can apply to text, or you can customize borders and shading using the **Borders and Shading dialog box**.
- You can apply **page borders** to an individual page or all pages in a document.
- A **horizontal line** is a graphic that you can insert into a document.
- A **hyperlink** takes readers to a web page, a different document, a different location in a document, or an email address. An email hyperlink opens Microsoft Outlook and places the recipient's email address in the email message.

Check for Understanding

The SIMbook for this text (within your SIMnet account) provides the following resources for concept review:

- Multiple choice questions
- Matching exercises
- Short answer questions

Guided Project 2-1

In this project, you create a form for contractors seeking insurance coverage at Central Sierra Insurance. You apply a theme, styles, a multilevel list, tab stops, leaders, indents, borders and shading, a page break, and page numbering.
[**Student Learning Outcomes 2.1, 2.2, 2.3, 2.4, 2.5, 2.6, 2.7, 2.9**]

File Needed: **InsuranceQuestionnaire-02.docx** (*Student data files are available in the* Library *of your* SIMnet account)
Completed Project File Name: **[your initials] Word 2-1.docx**

Skills Covered in this Project

- Modify an existing document.
- Change margins.
- Apply a document theme and theme color.
- Change font size, line spacing, and paragraph spacing.
- Apply a style to selected text.
- Modify an existing style.
- Apply borders and shading to selected text.
- Set and use a tab stop with an underline leader.
- Apply and modify a multilevel list.
- Insert a page break.
- Insert a built-in page number in the footer.

1. Open the **InsuranceQuestionnaire-02** document from your student data files.

2. Save this document as [your initials] Word 2-1.

3. Change the margins of the document.
   a. Click the **Margins** button [*Layout* tab, *Page Setup* group] and select **Custom Margins**. The *Page Setup* dialog box opens.
   b. Change the *Left* and *Right* margins to **0.75"**.
   c. Click **OK** to close the *Page Setup* dialog box.

4. Change the theme and theme color of the document.
   a. Click the **Themes** button [*Design* tab, *Document Formatting* group].
   b. Select **Integral** from the drop-down list.
   c. Click the **Colors** button [*Document Formatting* group] (Figure 2-94).
   d. Select **Aspect** from the drop-down list.

5. Change the font size, paragraph spacing, and line spacing of the entire document.
   a. Press **Ctrl+A** to select the entire document.
   b. Change the font size to **11 pt**.
   c. Change the line spacing to **Single (1.0)**.
   d. Change the *After* paragraph spacing to **6 pt**.

6. Apply styles to selected text.
   a. Place the insertion point in the first line of text ("Contractor's Insurance Questionnaire").

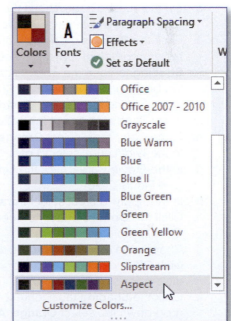

2-94 *Theme Colors* **drop-down list**

b. Click the **Title** style [*Home* tab, *Styles* group] in the *Style* gallery.

c. Select the second line of the document (**"Please carefully . . . "**).

d. Right-click the selected text, click **Styles** on the mini toolbar, and select **Book Title** from the *Style* gallery.

e. With this text still selected, click the **Change Case** button [*Home* tab, *Font* group] and select **UPPERCASE**.

f. Select **"Applicant's Instructions"** and apply the **Intense Quote** style from the *Style* gallery.

g. In the next paragraph ("Please answer ALL questions . . ."), apply the **Strong** style to the three words in all caps (**"ALL," "NONE,"** and **"NONE"**).

h. On the second page of the document, select **"Insurance Application Disclaimer"** and apply the **Intense Quote** style.

7. Modify an existing style.

a. Click the **More** button [*Home* tab, *Styles* group] to display all of the styles in the *Style* gallery.

b. Right-click the **Intense Quote** style in the *Style* gallery and select **Modify** (Figure 2-95). The *Modify Style* dialog box opens.

c. In the *Formatting* area, change the font size to **12 pt**.

d. Click the **Format** button on the bottom left and select **Paragraph**. The *Paragraph* dialog box opens.

e. Change the *Left* and *Right* indent to **0**.

f. Click **OK** to close the *Paragraph* dialog box.

g. Click the **Only in this document** radio button if it is not already selected to apply the style changes to only this document.

h. Click **OK** to close the *Modify Style* dialog box. The style changes apply to all text formatted with the *Intense Quote* style on both the first and second pages.

8. Add borders and shading to selected text.

a. On the second page, select the first three paragraphs below "Insurance Application Disclaimer."

b. Click the **Borders** drop-down arrow [*Home* tab, *Paragraph* group] and select **Borders and Shading** to open the *Borders and Shading* dialog box (Figure 2-96).

c. In the *Setting* area, select **Custom**.

d. In the *Style* area, select the **solid line** border.

e. In the *Color* area, select **Orange, Accent 1**.

f. In the *Width* area, select **1 pt**.

g. In the *Preview* area, click the **Left** and **Right** border buttons (see Figure 2-96).

h. In the *Apply to* area, select **Paragraph**.

i. Click the **Options** button to open the *Border and Shading Options* dialog box.

j. Change the *Left* and *Right* settings to **5 pt**. and click **OK** to close the *Border and Shading Options* dialog box.

k. Click the **Shading** tab (Figure 2-97), and from the *Fill* drop-down list, select **Orange, Accent 1, Lighter 80%**.

l. Click **OK** to close the *Borders and Shading* dialog box.

2-95 Modify an existing style

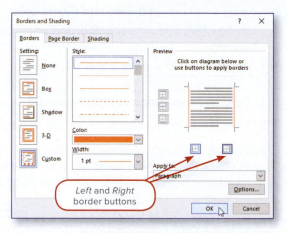

2-96 Apply a left and right border

2-97 Select shading *Fill* color

9. Change the paragraph spacing and add a tab stop with an underline leader to selected text.
   a. On the second page, select the last three lines of text.
   b. Click the **Paragraph** launcher [*Home* or *Layout* tab] to open the *Paragraph* dialog box.
   c. Change the *Before* paragraph spacing to **12 pt**.
   d. Click the **Tabs** button to open the *Tabs* dialog box (Figure 2-98).
   e. Type 7 in the *Tab stop position* area.
   f. Click the **Right** radio button in the *Alignment* area.
   g. Click the **4** (solid underline) radio button in the *Leader* area.
   h. Click the **Set** button to set this tab stop and click **OK** to close the *Tabs* dialog box.
   i. Click at the end of the "Name and Title of the Insured" line and press **Tab**. A solid underline displays across the page to the right margin.
   j. Repeat step i on the next two lines.

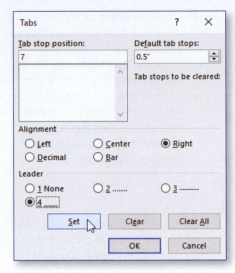

2-98 Set a right tab stop with an underline leader

10. Add a multilevel list to selected text and modify lists settings.
    a. Select the lines of text beginning with **"Applicant"** on the first page and ending with the last **"If yes, please explain:"** on the second page.
    b. Click the **Multilevel List** button [*Home* tab, *Paragraph* group] and select the **1)**, **a)**, **i)** option.
    c. With the text still selected, click the **Multilevel List** button again and select **Define New Multilevel List**. The *Define new Multilevel list* dialog box opens.
    d. Click the **Set for All Levels** button to open the *Set for All Levels* dialog box (Figure 2-99).
    e. Set the *Bullet/Number position for first level* to **0"**.
    f. Set the *Text position for first level* to **0.3"**.
    g. Set the *Additional indent for each level* to **0.3"**.
    h. Click **OK** to close the *Set for All Levels* dialog box and click **OK** to close the *Define new Multilevel list* dialog box.

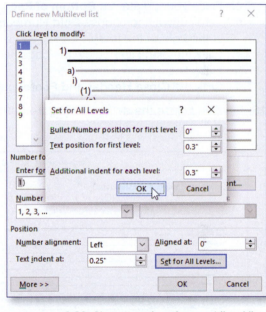

2-99 Change settings for a multilevel list

11. Increase indent on selected lines.
    a. Click anywhere on the list to deselect it.
    b. Place your insertion point in 13 in the numbered list ("If yes, . . .") and click **Increase Indent** [*Home* tab, *Paragraph* group]. This line is now letter *a)*.
    c. Repeat step b on each of the lines in the list that begin with "If yes, . . ." There should be 28 numbered items in the list when you finish this process.

12. Change paragraph spacing on the multilevel list and add a right tab stop with an underline leader.
    a. Select the entire multilevel list.
    b. Click the **Paragraph** launcher [*Home* or *Layout* tab] to open the *Paragraph* dialog box.
    c. Deselect the **Don't add space between paragraphs of the same style** check box (Figure 2-100).
    d. Click the **Tabs** button to open the *Tabs* dialog box.
    e. In the *Tab stop position* area, type 7.

W2-113

f. Click the **Right** radio button in the *Alignment* area.

g. Click the **4** (solid underline) radio button in the *Leader* area.

h. Click the **Set** button to set this tab stop and click **OK** to close the *Tabs* dialog box.

i. Click at the end of the first numbered item ("Applicant:") and press **Tab**. A solid underline displays across the page to the right margin.

j. Repeat step i on each of the numbered and lettered paragraphs.

13. Save the document.

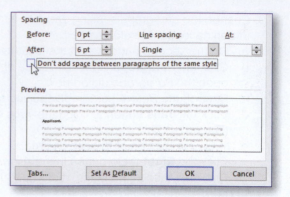

2-100 Add spacing between lines of text with the same style

14. Insert a page break in the document.
    a. Place the insertion point before the text in number 22 in the multilevel list.
    b. Press **Ctrl+Enter** to insert a page break.

15. Add a page number in the footer of the document.
    a. Press **Ctrl+Home** to move to the top of the document.
    b. Click the **Page Number** button [*Insert* tab, *Header & Footer* group].
    c. Place your pointer on **Bottom of Page** to display the drop-down list.
    d. Scroll down and choose **Bold Numbers 3** in the *Page X of Y* section. The page numbers display at the right of the footer.
    e. Click the blank line below the page numbers in the footer and press **Backspace** to delete the blank line.
    f. Click the **Close Header and Footer** button [*Header & Footer Tools Design* tab, *Close* group].

16. Save and close the document (Figure 2-101).

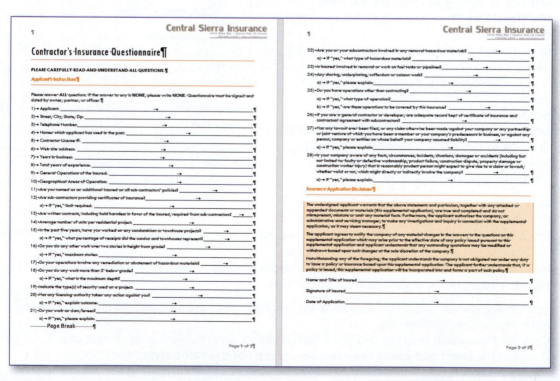

2-101 Word 2-1 completed

Guided Project 2-2

In this project, you create a checklist for employees at Placer Hills Real Estate to track the tasks they need to complete when a house enters escrow. You create a bulleted list, modify a bullet in a list, set and modify tab stops, apply and modify styles, and insert document properties in the footer.
[Student Learning Outcomes 2.1, 2.2, 2.3, 2.4, 2.6, 2.7, 2.9]

File Needed: **SellerEscrowChecklist-02.docx** (Student data files are available in the Library of your SIMnet account)
Completed Project File Name: **[your initials] Word 2-2.docx**

Skills Covered in this Project

- Modify an existing document.
- Change margins, line spacing, font, and font size.
- Set a tab stop using the ruler.
- Set a tab stop with leader.
- Apply a style to selected text.
- Modify an existing style.
- Apply and customize a bulleted list.
- Use the *Format Painter*.
- Insert a document property field and date in the footer.
- Apply a border in the footer.

1. Open the **SellerEscrowChecklist-02** document from your student data files.

2. Save this document as [your initials] Word 2-2.

3. Change margins, vertical alignment, line spacing, and font and font size, and delete blank lines.
   a. Click the **Margins** button [*Layout* tab, *Page Setup* group] and select **Normal** from the drop-down list.
   b. Click the **Page Setup** launcher to open the *Page Setup* dialog box and click the **Layout** tab.
   c. In the *Page* area, change *Vertical alignment* to **Center** and click **OK** to close the *Page Setup* dialog box.
   d. Press **Ctrl+A** to select the entire document.
   e. Change the font to **Calibri** and change the font size to **12 pt**.
   f. Change the line spacing to **2.0** (Double).
   g. Turn on **Show/Hide**.
   h. Delete all of the blank lines between the lines of text.

4. Add text to the document.
   a. In the second line of the document, place the insertion point after "Seller" and press **Tab** once.
   b. Type Property Address.
   c. Place the insertion point after "Escrow Company" and press **Tab** once.
   d. Type Escrow #.
   e. Place the insertion point after "Tasks to be Completed" and press **Tab** once.
   f. Type Date Completed.

5. Set tab stops using the ruler to align information. If the ruler is not displayed, check the **Ruler** box [*View* tab, *Show* group].
   a. Select the second and third lines of text (beginning with **"Seller"** and ending with **"Escrow #"**).
   b. Verify that the **Left Tab** is selected in the *Tab* selector area to the left of the horizontal ruler.
   c. Click the ruler at **3.5"** to set a left tab stop. If you click the wrong location on the ruler, drag the tab stop to the correct location (Figure 2-102).

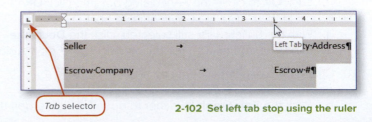

Tab selector

2-102 Set left tab stop using the ruler

    d. Select the fourth line of text (beginning with "Tasks").

    e. Click the **Tab** selector to change to a **Center Tab** stop (Figure 2-103).

    f. Click the ruler at **5.5"** to set a center tab stop.

2-103 Center tab stop

6. Set tab stops and add leaders to create lines for users to fill in information.

    a. Select the second and third lines of text (beginning with "Seller").

    b. Click the **Paragraph** launcher to open the *Paragraph* dialog box.

    c. Click the **Tabs** button to open the *Tabs* dialog box.

    d. Type 3 in the *Tab stop position* area.

    e. Click the **Right** radio button in the *Alignment* area.

    f. Click the **4** (solid underline) radio button in the *Leader* area.

    g. Click the **Set** button to set this tab stop.

    h. Type 6.5 in the *Tab stop position* area.

    i. Click the **Right** radio button in the *Alignment* area.

    j. Click the **4** (solid underline) radio button in the *Leader* area.

    k. Click the **Set** button to set this tab stop and click **OK** to close the *Tabs* dialog box.

7. Use tab stops to align text and insert underline leader.

    a. Place the insertion point before "Property Address" and press **Tab** once.

    b. Place the insertion point to the right of "Property Address" and press **Tab** once.

    c. Place the insertion point before "Escrow #" and press **Tab** once.

    d. Place the insertion point to the right of "Escrow #" and press **Tab** once.

8. Apply styles to selected text and update a style.

    a. Place the insertion point in the first line of text ("Seller Escrow Checklist").

    b. Select **Title** style in the *Style* gallery [*Home* tab, *Styles* group].

    c. Change the *After* paragraph spacing to **24 pt**. [*Layout* tab, *Paragraph* group].

    d. Click the **Center** alignment button [*Home* tab, *Paragraph* group] to center the title.

    e. Select **"Tasks to be Completed"** and apply the **Book Title** style from the *Style* gallery.

    f. Change the font size of the selected text to **14 pt**. and apply a **Double underline**.

    g. Right-click the **Book Title** style in the *Style* gallery and select **Update Book Title to Match Selection**. The *Book Title* style is updated.

    h. Select "**Date Completed**" and apply the **Book Title** style.

9. Create a bulleted list to selected text and apply a custom bullet.

    a. Select the lines of text beginning with **"Open Escrow . . . "** and ending with **"Disclosures Sent to Agent."**

    b. Click the **Bullets** drop-down arrow [*Home* tab, *Paragraph* group] and select **Define New Bullet**. The *Define New Bullet* dialog box opens.

    c. Click the **Symbol** button to open the *Symbol* dialog box (Figure 2-104).

    d. Click the **Font** drop-down arrow and select **Wingdings**.

    e. Scroll down the list and select the **open square** bullet (Character code 113).

    f. Click **OK** to close the *Symbol* dialog box.

    g. Click the **Font** button in the *Define New Bullet* dialog box. The *Font* dialog box opens.

    h. Change the *Size* to **14 pt**.

    i. Click **OK** to close the *Font* dialog box and click **OK** to close the *Define New Bullet* dialog box.

    j. With the bulleted list still selected, click the **Decrease Indent** button to align the bulleted list at the left margin.

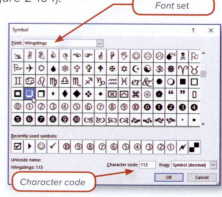

2-104 Select a symbol for a custom bullet

10. Change the hanging indent and add tab stops.

    a. Select the bulleted list.

    b. Click the **Paragraph** launcher to open the *Paragraph* dialog box.

c. Change the *Hanging* indent to **0.3"**.
d. Click the **Tabs** button to open the *Tabs* dialog box (Figure 2-105).
e. Type **4.5** in the *Tab stop position* area.
f. Click the **Left** radio button in the *Alignment* area, click the **1 None** radio button in the *Leader* area, and click the **Set** button to set this tab stop.
g. Type **6.5** in the *Tab stop position* area.
h. Click the **Right** radio button in the *Alignment* area, click the **4** (solid underline) radio button in the *Leader* area, and click the **Set** button to set this tab stop, and click **OK** to close the *Tabs* dialog box.
i. Place the insertion point after "Open Escrow with Escrow Company" and press **Tab** two times. A solid underline displays between 4.5" and 6.5".
j. Repeat step i on the remaining lines in the bulleted list.

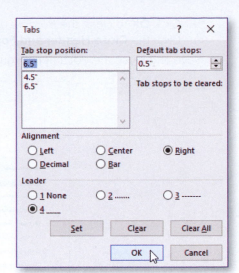

2-105 *Tabs* dialog box

11. Add text to the document.
    a. Press **Enter** after the solid underline in the last line of text in the document.
    b. Click the **Bullets** button [*Home* tab, *Paragraph* group] to turn off the bullet on this line.
    c. Type **Fax/Email Clear Pest Report** and press **Enter**.
    d. Type **Title** and press **Enter**.
    e. Type **Lender** and press **Enter**.
    f. Type **Buyer's Agent**.

12. Apply a style to selected text and use the *Format Painter*.
    a. Select **"Fax/Email Clear Pest Report"** and apply the **Subtle Reference** style.
    b. Place the insertion point in one of the bulleted items.
    c. Click the **Format Painter** button [*Home* tab, *Clipboard* group] to copy the formatting of this bulleted item.
    d. Select the last three lines of text (beginning with **"Title . . ."**). The *Format Painter* copies the bullet formatting and tab settings to these lines of text.
    e. Press **Tab** two times after each of these last three lines to insert the tabs and leaders.

13. Insert a document property field, the date, and a border in the footer of the document.
    a. Click the **Footer** button [*Insert* tab, *Header & Footer* group] and select **Edit Footer** from the drop-down list to open the footer.
    b. Click the **Document Info** button [*Header & Footer Tools Design* tab, *Insert* group], click **Document Property**, and select **Company**. The *Company* document property field displays in the footer.
    c. Press the **right arrow** key once to deselect the *Company* field.
    d. Press **Tab** two times, type **Last updated:**, and **space** once. The text aligns at the right side of the footer.
    e. Click the **Date & Time** button [*Header & Footer Tools Design* tab, *Insert* group] to open the *Date and Time* dialog box.
    f. Select the spelled out month, day, year option (e.g., January 1, 2018), check the **Update automatically** box, and click **OK** to insert the date and close the dialog box.
    g. Select all of the text in the footer and change the font to **Calibri** and the font size to **10 pt**.
    h. Click the **Borders** drop-down arrow [*Home* tab, *Paragraph* group] and select **Borders and Shading** to open the *Borders and Shading* dialog box.
    i. Click the **Color** drop-down list and select **Black**, **Text 1**.
    j. Click the **Width** drop-down list and select **1 pt**.
    k. In the *Preview* area, click the **Top** border button to apply a top border to the footer.

l. Click **OK** to close the *Borders and Shading* dialog box.

m. Click the **Close Header and Footer** button [*Header & Footer Tools Design* tab, *Close* group].

14. Save and close the document (Figure 2-106).

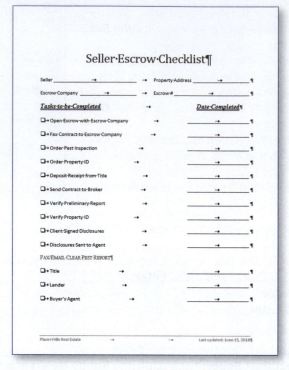

2-106 Word 2-2 completed

Guided Project 2-3

In this project, you edit and format the personal training guide for the American River Cycling Club to improve readability and effectiveness. You use find and replace, apply a document theme, modify styles, customize numbered and bulleted lists, apply borders and shading, and insert headers, footers, and document properties.

[**Student Learning Outcomes 2.1, 2.3, 2.4, 2.6, 2.7, 2.8, 2.9**]

File Needed: ***PersonalTrainingProgram-02.docx*** *(Student data files are available in the* Library *of your SIMnet account)*

Completed Project File Name: *[your initials] **Word 2-3.docx***

Skills Covered in this Project

- Modify an existing document.
- Apply a document theme.
- Change margins.
- Change line spacing and paragraph spacing.
- Apply a style to selected text.
- Apply borders and shading to selected text.
- Update an existing style.
- Customize a multilevel bulleted list.
- Use *Find*.
- Use *Find* and *Replace*.
- Insert a hyperlink.
- Insert header, footer, page number, and document properties.

1. Open the **PersonalTrainingProgram-02** document from your student data files.

2. Save this document as [your initials] Word 2-3.

3. Apply a document theme and change the line and paragraph spacing.
   a. Click the **Themes** button [*Design* tab, *Document Formatting* group] and select **Slice** from the drop-down list of theme options.
   b. Click the **Margins** button [*Layout* tab, *Page Setup* group] and select **Custom Margins** to open the *Page Setup* dialog box.
   c. Change the *Left* and *Right* margins to **1"** and click **OK** to close the *Page Setup* dialog box.
   d. Press **Ctrl+A** to select the entire document.
   e. Change the line spacing to **1.15** and change the *After* paragraph spacing to **10 pt**.
   f. Turn on **Show/Hide**.

4. Apply styles to the title, subtitle, and section headings.
   a. Select the title (first line) of the document.
   b. Apply the **Title** style from the *Style* gallery [*Home* tab, *Styles* group].
   c. Change the font size to **20 pt**. and apply **bold** and **center** alignment.
   d. Select the subtitle (second line) of the document.
   e. Apply the **Subtitle** style from the *Style* gallery.
   f. Change the font size to **16 pt**. and **center** it.
   g. Select the first section heading (**"General Guidelines"**).
   h. Apply the **Heading 1** style from the *Style* gallery.
   i. Apply the **Heading 1** style to the remaining section headings in the document (**"Personal Training Program Guidelines," "More About Long Rides," "Training Intensity and Heart Rate," "Tracking Training Miles versus Hours,"** and **"Using a Training Log"**).

5. Update a style in the document.
   a. Select the first section heading (**"General Guidelines"**) including the paragraph mark at the end of the line.
   b. Change the *Before* paragraph spacing to **12 pt**. and the *After* paragraph spacing to **6 pt**.
   c. Click the **Borders** drop-down arrow [*Home* tab, *Paragraph* group] and select **Borders and Shading**. The *Borders and Shading* dialog box opens.
   d. In the *Setting* area, select **Shadow**.
   e. In the *Style* area, select the **solid line**.
   f. In the *Color* area, select **Dark Blue, Accent 1, Darker 50%** (Figure 2-107).
   g. In the *Width* area, select **1 pt**.
   h. In the *Apply to* area, select **Paragraph**.
   i. Click the **Shading** tab, and in the *Fill* area, select **Dark Blue, Accent 1, Lighter 80%**.
   j. In the *Apply to* area, select **Paragraph**, and click **OK** to close the *Borders and Shading* dialog box.
   k. With the heading still selected, right-click the **Heading 1** style in the *Style gallery* and select **Update Heading 1 to Match Selection**. All of the headings in the document with the *Heading 1* style applied update automatically.

6. Customize the bullets and indents for the bulleted list.
   a. Right-click the first bulleted item on the first page and select **Adjust List Indents**. The *Define new Multilevel list* dialog box opens.
   b. Click **1** in the *Click level to modify* area.
   c. In the *Number style for this level* area, select **New Bullet** from the drop-down list (Figure 2-108). The *Symbol* dialog box opens.

2-107 Select border line color

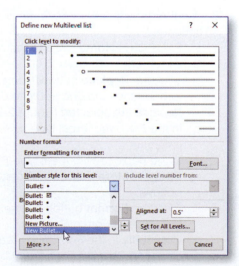

2-108 Customize bulleted list

d. In the *Font* area, select **Webdings** from the drop-down list, click the **right pointing triangle** (Character code 52), and click **OK** to close the *Symbol* dialog box (Figure 2-109).

e. Click **2** in the *Click level to modify* area in the *Define new Multilevel list* dialog box.

f. In the *Number style for this level* area, select **New Bullet** from the drop-down list. The *Symbol* dialog box opens.

g. In the *Font* area, select **Webdings** from the drop-down list, click the **double right pointing triangle** (Character code 56), and click **OK** to close the *Symbol* dialog box.

h. Click the **Set for All Levels** button in the *Define new Multilevel list* dialog box. The *Set for All Levels* dialog box opens (Figure 2-110).

i. Change the *Bullet/Number position for first level* to **0.25"**, change the *Text position for first level* to **0.5"**, and change *Additional indent for each level* to **0.25"**.

j. Click **OK** to close the *Set for All Levels* dialog box and click **OK** to close the *Define new Multilevel list* dialog box. All of the first and second level bullets and indents in the entire document are changed.

2-109 Select bullet from *Webdings* font set

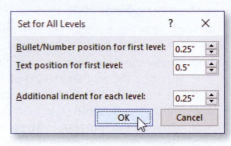

2-110 Set indents for all levels

7. Use the *Find* feature to find text in the document.

a. Press **Ctrl+Home** to go to the beginning of the document.

b. Click the **Find** button [*Home* tab, *Editing* group] or press **Ctrl+F** to open *Find* in the *Navigation* pane.

c. Type personal training program in the *Search Document* area. All instances of this text appear in the *Navigation* pane.

d. Click after "personal training program" in the first body paragraph on the first page and type (PTP). Make sure there is one space before and after "(PTP)".

e. Select **"PTP"** (not the parentheses) and apply **italic** format.

f. Click the **X** in the upper right of the *Navigation* pane to close this pane.

8. Use the replace feature to find and replace text in the document.

a. Press **Ctrl+Home** to go to the beginning of the document.

b. Click the **Replace** button [*Home* tab, *Editing* group] to open the *Find and Replace* dialog box with the *Replace* tab selected (Figure 2-111).

c. In the *Find what* area, type personal training program.

d. In the *Replace with* area, type PTP.

e. Click the **More** button to display more search options.

f. Click the **Format** button and select **Font** to open the *Replace Font* dialog box.

g. Click **Italic** in the *Font style* area and click **OK** to close the *Replace Font* dialog box.

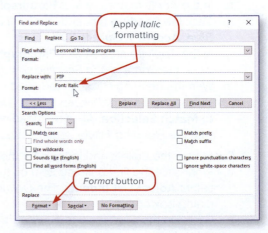

2-111 Replace text with text and formatting

h. Click the **Less** button to collapse the *Find and Replace* dialog box.

i. Click the **Find Next** button to find the first occurrence of "personal training program" in the document.

j. Do not replace this text in the title, first body paragraph, or section heading. Replace all other occurrences of "personal training program" with "*PTP*". Click the **Replace** button to replace the highlighted occurrence or click the **Find Next** button to skip and not replace an occurrence.

k. Click **OK** when you are finished searching the document and click **Close** to close the *Find and Replace* dialog box.

9. Add a hyperlink to the document.

   a. Select the subtitle of the document (**"American River Cycling Club"**).

   b. Click the **Hyperlink** button [*Insert* tab, *Links* group] or press **Ctrl+K** to open the *Insert Hyperlink* dialog box.

   c. Click the **Existing File or Web Page** button in the *Link to* area.

   d. Type www.arcc.org in the *Address* area. Word automatically inserts "http://" before the web address.

   e. Click the **ScreenTip** button to open the *Set Hyperlink ScreenTip* dialog box.

   f. Type American River Cycling Club in the *ScreenTip text* area and click **OK** to close the *Set Hyperlink ScreenTip* dialog box.

   g. Click the **Target Frame** button to open the *Set Target Frame* dialog box.

   h. Select **New window** from the drop-down list.

   i. Click **OK** to close the *Set Target Frame* dialog box and click **OK** to close the *Insert Hyperlink* dialog box.

10. Insert header and footer on the second and continuing pages.

    a. Press **Ctrl+Home** to move to the beginning of the document.

    b. Click the **Page Number** button [*Insert* tab, *Header & Footer* group].

    c. Click **Top of Page** and select **Accent Bar 2** from the drop-down list. The page number displays in the header area.

    d. Check the **Different First Page** check box [*Header & Footer Tools Design* tab, *Options* group] to remove the header from the first page so it only displays on the second and continuing pages.

11. Insert document property fields in the footer.

    a. With the header still open, click the **Go to Footer** button [*Navigation* group].

    b. Click the **Next** button [*Navigation* group] to move to the footer on the second page.

    c. Click the **Document Info** button [*Insert* group], click **Document Property**, and select **Company** to insert the company document property field.

    d. Press the **right arrow** key once to deselect the property field.

    e. Press **Tab** two times to move the insertion point to the right margin in the footer.

    f. Click the **Document Info** button [*Insert* group] and select **Document Title** to insert the title document property field.

    g. Press **Ctrl+A** to select all of the text in the footer.

    h. Apply **bold** and **italic** formatting and change the font size to **10 pt**.

    i. Click the **Go to Header** button [*Header & Footer Tools Design* tab, *Navigation* group] to move to the header on the second page.

    j. Press **Ctrl+A** to select all of the text in the header and change the font size to **10 pt**.

    k. Click the **Close Header and Footer** button [*Header & Footer Tools Design* tab, *Close* group]. The header and footer information should appear on the second and continuing pages in the document.

12. Save and close the document (Figure 2-112).

CREATING A PERSONAL TRAINING PROGRAM¶

American River Cycling Club¶

There are as many cycling training programs as there are trainers, but certain basic "rules of thumb" can be used to help you develop your own personal training program for that upcoming event, which could be a road race, criterium, time trial, or century.¶

General Guidelines¶

Each cyclist has different goals, abilities, and available time. Use these guidelines to help you plan your PTP and stick to a training schedule.¶

- Before beginning a regimented training program, develop a base of at least 500 miles of easy rides. (If you have a good winter or off season training program, you can pare down this recommendation.)¶
- Once you have your training base, calculate your average weekly mileage, and then plan to increase it by no more than 10 to 12 percent per week. This includes both total weekly mileage as well as the distance of your long ride.¶
- You can estimate the length of your training program by using your "average" long ride from your 500-mile base training period, increasing it by 10 percent a week, and repeating this until you arrive at a figure that is 75 percent of the length of the event for which you are training.¶
- Be flexible and adjust your program to your lifestyle. A rigid PTP is destined to fail.¶

Personal Training Program Guidelines¶

As you are developing your PTP, realize that it will change throughout the year as your fitness increases and days get longer. The time of year and busyness of life will influence your training program. Below are some suggestions to help you develop your PTP.¶

- The pace of your rides.¶
  - The long ride should match your own planned century speed.¶
  - The short "recovery" ride should be a leisurely pace at no more than 50 to 60 percent of your maximum heart rate.¶
- Two of the intermediate rides should be at the planned century pace.¶

Page 1¶

- One of the intermediate rides, preferably prior to your day off the bike, should be at a brisk pace 2 to 3 mph faster than your planned century speed.¶
- It's important to ride at least 5 days a week, and take at least one day off. Depending on your level of training (or evidence of overtraining) the seventh day is an additional intermediate mileage day or an additional rest day. For example:¶
  - one high mileage day equal to the event distance¶
  - one long slow recovery day¶
  - 3 intermediate mileage days¶
  - 1 or 2 rest days (off the bike or short recovery rides)¶
- Plan a short mileage day or rest day to follow the high mileage day. It should be at least 1/4 of the length of your long ride and ridden at a leisurely pace to help loosen up your muscles after the long ride of the week.¶
- The three intermediate mileage days should be midway between the short ride and the long ride of the week in mileage and should be ridden at a good training pace (85 to 90 percent of maximum heart rate). One or two of these may be interval training rides.¶
- The longest mileage day is keyed to the length of your event or ride and ridden at the pace you hope to maintain for the event. Many coaches suggest you work up to the length (or even 125 percent of the length) of the event while others are comfortable if you can ride 75 percent of the event distance comfortably.¶
- There should be an additional long mileage, recovery day during the training week.¶

More About Long Rides¶

Are long training rides necessary? Early in the spring when you're building endurance, longer rides have a role to be played in a training program. But during the competitive season conventional wisdom says not to ride significantly farther than your longest event.¶

So if you do 40K time trials and road races up to, say, 50 miles, your longest training rides don't need to be longer than 40 to 60 miles. Early-season long rides build aerobic conditioning. But once the season is underway, distance may detract from the power and speed you need to do well in your goal events.¶

American River Cycling Club → → *Personal Training Program*¶

2-112 Word 2-3 completed (pages 1 and 2 of 5)

Independent Project 2-4

In this project, you use styles, indents, lists, tab stops, the replace feature, footers, and document properties to customize the Emergency Procedures document for Sierra Pacific Community College District. [Student Learning Outcomes 2.1, 2.2, 2.3, 2.4, 2.6, 2.7, 2.8, 2.9]

File Needed: **EmergencyProcedures-02.docx** *(Student data files are available in the Library of your SIMnet account)*
Completed Project File Name: **[your initials] Word 2-4.docx**

Skills Covered in this Project

- Modify an existing document.
- Apply a document theme and theme color.
- Change margins and font size.
- Apply and modify a style.
- Apply a border to selected text.
- Apply and customize a numbered and bulleted list.
- Use the *Format Painter*.
- Set and modify tab stops.
- Use *Replace*.
- Insert a footer with document properties and current date.
- Insert a page border.
- Center text vertically.

1. Open the ***EmergencyProcedures-02*** document from your student data files.

2. Save this document as [your initials] Word 2-4.

3. Change the theme to **Integral** and the theme color to **Red**.

4. Change the top, bottom, left, and right margins to **0.75"**.

5. Select the entire document and change the font size to **12 pt**.

6. Format the title of the document.
   a. Select the title of the document and apply **Heading 1** style.
   b. Open the *Font* dialog box, apply **All caps** effect, and change the font size to **16 pt**.
   c. Change the *Before* paragraph spacing to **0 pt**.
   d. Add a **bottom border** to the title using the **Borders** drop-down list.

7. Select each of the bold section headings and apply the **Heading 2** style.

8. Modify the *Heading 2* style.
   a. Select the first section heading (**"Emergency Telephones [Blue Phones]"**).
   b. Change *Before* paragraph spacing to **12 pt**. and *After* paragraph spacing to **3 pt**.
   c. Apply **small caps** effect and **underline**.
   d. Update **Heading 2** style to match this heading. All of the section headings are updated.

9. Turn on **Show/Hide** and delete all of the blank lines in the document.

10. Select the bulleted list in the first section and change it to a numbered list.

11. Apply numbering format, make formatting changes, and use the *Format Painter*.
    a. Apply numbering to the text in the following sections: "*Assaults, Fights, or Emotional Disturbances*"; "*Power Failure*"; "*Fire*"; "*Earthquake*"; and "*Bomb Threat*."
    b. Select the numbered list in the "Bomb Threat" section.
    c. Open the *Paragraph* dialog box, set before and after paragraph spacing to **2 pt**., and deselect the **Don't add space between paragraphs of the same style** check box.
    d. Use the *Format Painter* to copy this numbering format to each of the other numbered lists.
    e. Reset each numbered list so it begins with **1** (right-click the first item in each numbered list and select **Restart at 1** from the context menu).

12. Customize a bulleted list and use the *Format Painter*.
    a. Select the text in the "Accident or Medical Emergency" section.
    b. Use a **solid square bullet** (*Wingdings*, Character code 110).
    c. Confirm the left indent is **0.25"** and hanging indent is **0.25"**. If they are not, make these changes.
    d. Set *Before* and *After* paragraph spacing to **2 pt**.
    e. Deselect the **Don't add space between paragraphs of the same style** check box (*Paragraph* dialog box).
    f. Use the *Format Painter* to apply this bulleted list format to the following text in the following sections: "*Tips to Professors and Staff*" and "*Response to Students*."

13. Change indent and paragraph spacing and apply a style.
    a. Select the text below the "Emergency Telephone Locations" heading.
    b. Set a **0.25"** left indent.
    c. Set *Before* and *After* paragraph spacing to **2 pt**.
    d. Confirm the **Don't add space between paragraphs of the same style** box is unchecked.
    e. In the "Emergency Telephone Locations" section, apply **Book Title** style to each of the telephone locations. Select only the location, not the text in parentheses or following text.

14. Change left indent and paragraph spacing and set a tab stop with a dot leader.
    a. Select the text below the "Emergency Phone Numbers" heading.
    b. Set a **0.25"** left indent for this text.
    c. Set *Before* and *After* paragraph spacing to **2 pt**.

d. Confirm the **Don't add space between paragraphs of the same style** box is unchecked.

e. With the text still selected, set a right tab stop at **7"** and use a **dot leader (2)**.

f. Press **Tab** before the phone number on each of these lines. The phone numbers align at the right margin with a dot leader between the text and phone number.

15. Apply the **Intense Reference** style to the paragraph headings in the "Accident or Medical Emergency" section (*"Life-Threating Emergencies"* and *"Minor Emergencies"*). Don't include the colon when selecting the paragraph headings.

16. Use the *Replace* feature to replace all instances of "Phone 911" with "PHONE 911" with **bold** font style.

17. Insert a footer with document property fields and the current date that appears on every page.

a. Edit the footer and use the ruler to move the center tab stop to **3.5"** and the right tab stop to **7"**.

b. Insert the **Title** document property field on the left. Use the **right arrow** key to deselect the document property field.

c. Insert the **Company** document property field at center. Use the center tab stop for alignment. Use the **right arrow** key to deselect the document property field.

d. Insert a date (use January 1, 2018 format) that updates automatically on the right. Use the right tab stop for alignment.

e. Change the font size of all the text in the footer to **10 pt**.

f. Add a **top border** to the text in the footer using the **Borders** drop-down list.

18. Insert a page border on the entire document. Use **Shadow** setting, **solid line** style, **Dark Red, Accent 1** color, and **1 pt**. line width.

19. Center the entire document vertically.

20. Save and close the document (Figure 2-113).

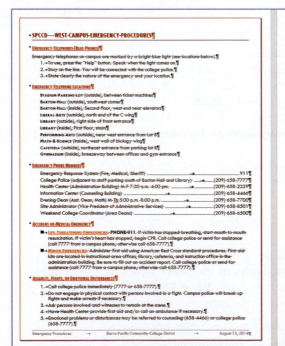
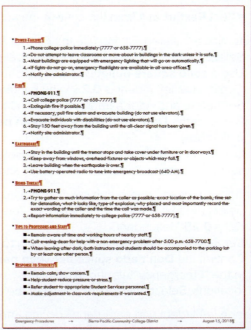

2-113 Word 2-4 completed

Independent Project 2-5

In this project, you format a bank authorization letter for Placer Hills Real Estate. You modify the formatting of an existing document, apply a theme, apply and modify styles, set tab stops, apply borders, and insert and edit hyperlinks.
[Student Learning Outcomes 2.1, 2.2, 2.7, 2.9]

File Needed: **BankAuthorization-02.docx** (*Student data files are available in the* Library *of your SIMnet account*)
Completed Project File Name: *[your initials] Word 2-5.docx*

Skills Covered in this Project

- Modify an existing document.
- Apply a document theme.
- Change margins.
- Insert an automatically updated date.
- Apply and modify a style.

- Expand font spacing.
- Change paragraph spacing.
- Use the *Format Painter*.
- Set and use tab stops.
- Apply borders and shading to selected text.
- Insert a hyperlink.
- Edit a hyperlink.

1. Open the **BankAuthorization-02** document from your student data files.
2. Save this document as [your initials] Word 2-5.
3. Change the theme to **Wisp**.
4. Change the margins to **Normal**.
5. Select the entire document and change the *After* paragraph spacing to **18 pt**.
6. Press **Enter** after the first line of the document, insert (don't type) the current date (use January 1, 2018 format), and set it to update automatically.
7. Click at the end of the document, press **Enter**, and type the following information. Use line breaks (**Shift+Enter**) after the first three lines. (*Note: The email address is automatically converted to a hyperlink; you will edit this later.*)

   Emma Cavalli
   Placer Hills Real Estate
   ecavalli@phre.com
   916-450-3334

8. Select the date line and change the *After* paragraph spacing to **30 pt**.
9. Use the *Format Painter* to copy the date line format to the **"Sincerely,"** line.
10. Apply styles and use the *Format Painter*.
    a. Apply the **Title** style to the first line of the document and change the *Before* paragraph spacing to **36 pt**.
    b. Select **"Authorization Letter to Lender,"** apply the **Intense Reference** style, and expand the font *Spacing* to **1 pt**.
    c. Select the five lines of text beginning with **"Bank/Financial Institution:"** and ending with **"Borrower Name(s):"** and apply the **Book Title** style.
    d. Use the *Format Painter* to copy the "Bank/Financial Institution" format to **"Seller/Borrower Signature(s)"**.
11. Set a tab stop with a leader.
    a. Select the five lines of text beginning with **"Bank/Financial Institution:"** and ending with **"Borrower Name(s):."**

b. Set a right tab stop at **6.5"** with a **solid underline leader**.

c. Press **Tab** after each of these five lines to insert the solid underline leader to the right margin.

12. Apply a border and shading to the paragraph.

a. Select the paragraph beginning **"Please consider . . . "**.

b. Apply a border with **Shadow** setting, **solid line** style, **Black, Text 1, Lighter 50%** color, and **1½ pt.** line width.

c. Change the border options so there is **4 pt.** from text on the top, bottom, left, and right.

d. Set the shading fill color to **White, Background 1, Darker 5%**.

13. Select the "**Seller/Borrower Signature(s)**" line and apply a custom border that is **solid line, Black, Text 1**, and **2¼ pt.** width, and apply it to the **top** of the selected paragraph.

14. Insert and customize a hyperlink.

a. Select "**Placer Hills Real Estate**" in the closing lines and insert a hyperlink.

b. Type www.phre.com as the web page address.

c. Type Placer Hills Real Estate as the *ScreenTip*.

d. Set the target frame to **New window** and make this the default for all hyperlinks.

15. Edit the "ecavalli@phre.com" email hyperlink and type Email Emma Cavalli as the *ScreenTip*.

16. Save and close the document (Figure 2-114).

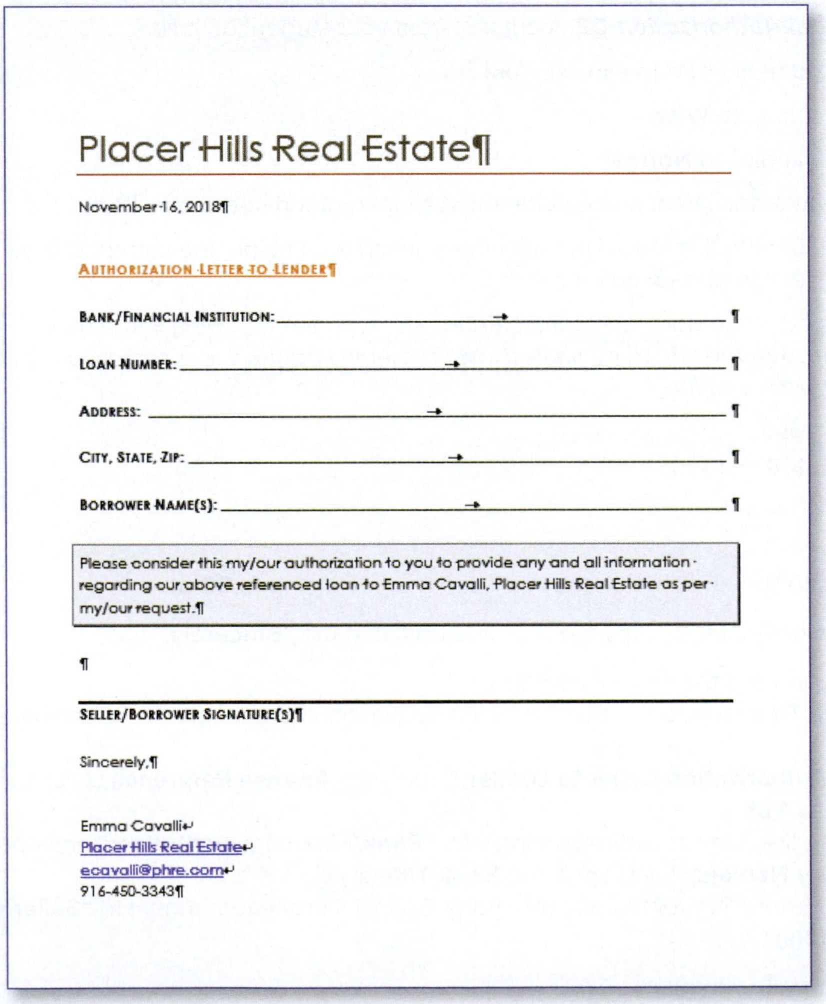

Placer Hills Real Estate¶

November 16, 2018¶

AUTHORIZATION LETTER TO LENDER¶

BANK/FINANCIAL INSTITUTION: _____ → _____¶

LOAN NUMBER: _____ → _____¶

ADDRESS: _____ → _____¶

CITY, STATE, ZIP: _____ → _____¶

BORROWER NAME(S): _____ → _____¶

> Please consider this my/our authorization to you to provide any and all information regarding our above referenced loan to Emma Cavalli, Placer Hills Real Estate as per my/our request.¶

¶

SELLER/BORROWER SIGNATURE(S)¶

Sincerely,¶

Emma Cavalli↵
Placer Hills Real Estate↵
ecavalli@phre.com↵
916-450-3343¶

2-114 Word 2-5 completed

Independent Project 2-6

In this project, you edit, format, and customize the conference registration form for Central Sierra Insurance's Agriculture Insurance Conference. You use a continuous section break, find and replace, tab stops and leaders, styles, bullets, indents, borders, shading, and hyperlinks.
[Student Learning Outcomes 2.1, 2.2, 2.3, 2.4, 2.5, 2.6, 2.7, 2.8, 2.9]

File Needed: **ConferenceRegistrationForm-02.docx** (*Student data files are available in the* Library *of your* SIMnet account)
Completed Project File Name: **[your initials] Word 2-6.docx**

Skills Covered in this Project

- Modify an existing document.
- Change margins, font, font size, line spacing, and paragraph spacing.
- Insert a header.
- Apply a style.
- Use *Find and Replace*.

- Insert a continuous section break.
- Insert a horizontal line.
- Set different margins for different sections.
- Customize a bulleted list and indents.
- Set and use tab stops and leaders.
- Apply borders and shading to selected text.
- Insert hyperlinks.

1. Open the **ConferenceRegistrationForm-02** document from your student data files.

2. Save this document as [your initials] Word 2-6.

3. Change the top and bottom margins to **0.5"**.

4. Select all of the text in the document and change the font size to **10 pt.**, line spacing to **1** (Single), and *After* paragraph spacing to **6 pt**.

5. Apply styles to title and subtitle.
   a. Select and cut the first line of the document and paste it in the header.
   b. Delete the blank line below the text in the header.
   c. Select the text in the header, apply **Title** style, align **center**, change the *After* paragraph spacing to **6 pt.**, and close the header.
   d. In the body of the document, select the first two lines beginning with "Central Sierra Insurance," apply **Subtitle** style, align **center**, and change the *After* paragraph spacing to **6 pt**.

6. Use *Find* and *Replace*.
   a. Use *Find* to locate all occurrences of "Agriculture Insurance Conference."
   b. Apply **italic** formatting to each occurrence except in the header.
   c. Use *Replace* to find all occurrences of "Oct." (include the period) and replace with **"May"**.
   d. Use *Replace* to find all occurrences of "Westfield Hotel & Spa" and replace with **"Northgate Resort"** with **Bold Italic** font style.

7. Click at the end of the second body paragraph ("Please help us to determine . . .") and insert a **continuous** section break.

8. On the blank line below the section break, insert a **Horizontal Line** from the **Borders** drop-down list (see "Insert a Horizontal Line" in *SLO 2.9: Using Borders, Shading, and Hyperlinks*).

9. Click in the document below the section break and change the left and right margins to **1.25"** and apply to **This section**.

10. Set a tab stop with a leader.
    a. Select the first two lines of text below the horizontal line.
    b. Set a right tab stop at **6"** with a **solid underline leader**.
    c. Press **Tab** after each of these lines to insert the solid underline leader to the right margin.

11. Define a new multilevel list and customize bullets and indents.
    a. Press the **Ctrl** key and select the four different bulleted lists in the document. The *Ctrl* key allows you to select non-adjacent text in the document. Don't select the text between each of the bulleted lists, and make sure all bulleted items are selected.
    b. Open the *Define new Multilevel list* dialog box (in the *Multilevel List* drop-down list).
    c. On the first, second, and third levels, change the bullet to a shaded open square bullet (*Wingdings*, Character code 113).
    d. Change the font size of the bullets on each of the first three levels to **12 pt**.
    e. Set the indents for all levels so that the first level begins at **0"**, the text for the first level begins at **0.25"**, and additional indent for each level is **0.25"**.

12. Set tab stops with a leader.
    a. Select the **"Flying—Arrival time:"** line.
    b. Set a **right** tab stop at **3"** with a **solid underline leader**.
    c. Press **Tab** after this line to insert the leader.
    d. Select the **"I need directions to *Northgate Resort* from:"** line.
    e. Set a **right** tab stop at **5"** with a **solid underline leader**.
    f. Press **Tab** after this line to insert the leader.

13. Change indents and apply custom borders and shading to selected text.
    a. Select the last two lines of the document, align **center**, and change the left and right indents to **1"**.
    b. With these two lines selected, apply a top and bottom **double line** border, **¾ pt**. width, and **Dark Blue**, **Text 2** color.
    c. Apply **Dark Blue**, **Text 2**, **Lighter 80%** shading to the selected text.

14. Insert and customize hyperlinks to email addresses.
    a. Use *Find* to locate the first occurrence of "apelandale@centralsierra.com."
    b. Select this email address and insert a hyperlink.
    c. Type apelandale@centralsierra.com as the *Text to display* and *E-mail address*. In the *E-mail address* text box, "mailto:" is automatically inserted in front of the email address.
    d. Type Email Asia Pelandale as the *ScreenTip*.
    e. Repeat steps b–d above on the second occurrence of this email address.

15. Save and close the document (Figure 2-115).

Agriculture·Insurance·Conference¶

Central·Sierra·Insurance¶

May·10-12¶

You·are·cordially·invited·to·join·us·for·Central·Sierra·Insurance's·*Agriculture·Insurance·Conference*,·May·10-12·at·***Northgate·Resort***·in·North·Kansas·City,·Missouri.¶

Please·help·us·to·determine·the·final·attendance·count·by·completing·this·form·for·each·individual·attending·from·your·agency.·Complete·this·form·and·fax·or·email·(apelandale@centralsierra.com)·to·Asia·Pelandale·by·February·23.·Print·a·copy·for·your·records.::::::::::Section Break (Continuous)::::::::::

¶

Name:· → ¶

Agency·Name:· → ¶

❑→No,·I·won't·be·able·to·make·it·to·this·year's·*Agriculture·Insurance·Conference*.¶

❑→Yes,·I·plan·to·attend·the·*Agriculture·Insurance·Conference*·in·Kansas·City·and·will·arrive·on·the·following·date:¶

❑→May·10¶

❑→May·11¶

❑→May·12¶

Please·reserve·the·following·type·of·room·for·me:¶

❑→Non-Smoking¶

❑→Smoking¶

❑→King¶

❑→Two·Doubles¶

I·will·use·the·following·transportation·to·get·to·Kansas·City:¶

❑→Flying—Arrival·time:· → ¶

❑→I·need·a·shuttle·to·***Northgate·Resort***·from·the·airport.¶

❑→Driving¶

❑→I·need·directions·to·***Northgate·Resort***·from:· → ¶

Arrangements·have·been·made·for·afternoon·golf,·for·those·interested.·Please·indicate·below·if·you·wish·to·participate·in·the·golf·outing.·If·you·do·not·care·to·join·us·for·golf,·the·afternoon·is·open·to·do·whatever·you·choose.¶

❑→Yes,·I·would·like·to·participate·in·the·golf·outing.¶

❑→No,·I·will·not·be·participating·in·golf.¶

If·you·have·any·questions·about·this·conference,·please·feel·free·to·contact·either·Asia·Pelandale·or·Richard·Rhodes.·We·appreciate·your·help!¶

¶

FAX·OR·EMAIL·THIS·FORM·TO·ASIA·PELANDALE·AT:¶

FAX:·(505-519-8630)·or·EMAIL:·apelandale@centralsierra.com¶

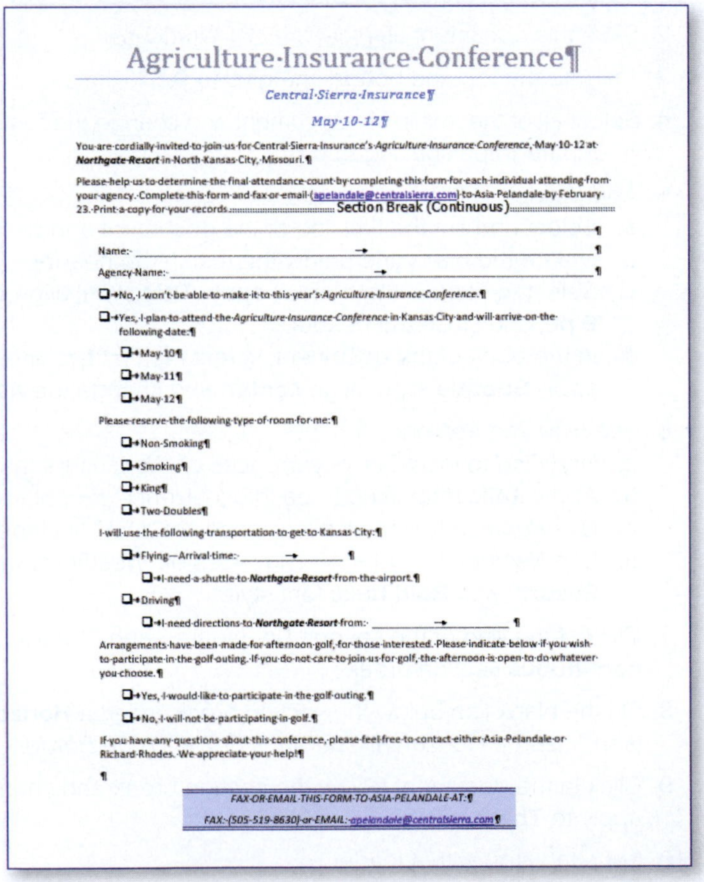

2-115 Word 2-6 completed

Improve It Project 2-7

In this project, you clean up a document that contains shortcuts for Microsoft Outlook. Courtyard Medical Plaza wants to make this document available to all of its employees. You use tab stops, styles, and many other page layout features that you have learned in this chapter to create a professional and attractive reference document.
[Student Learning Outcomes 2.1, 2.2, 2.4, 2.5, 2.7, 2.9]

File Needed: **OutlookShortcuts-02.docx** *(Student data files are available in the Library of your SIMnet account)*
Completed Project File Name: *[your initials] Word 2-7.docx*

Skills Covered in this Project

- Modify an existing document.
- Change margins, line spacing, and paragraph spacing.
- Apply and modify a style.

- Apply borders and shading to selected text.
- Set and modify tab stops and leaders.
- Use the *Format Painter*.
- Insert a page break.
- Edit footer content and tab stops.

---

1. Open the **OutlookShortcuts-02** document from your student data files.

2. Save this document as [your initials] Word 2-7.

3. Change the page orientation to **Landscape**.

4. Change the top margin to **0.5**" and the bottom, left, and right margins to **0.75**".

5. Select the entire document and change the line spacing to **1.0** (or **Single**) and the *After* paragraph spacing to **4 pt**.

6. Remove the bottom border from the title and change the *After* paragraph spacing to **0 pt**.

7. Apply custom borders and shading, change paragraph spacing, and modify the *Heading 1* style.
   a. Select "**Global Outlook Commands**."
   b. Apply a custom **single line** top and bottom border with **1 pt**. width and **Dark Blue**, **Text 2** color, and apply **White**, **Background 1**, **Darker 5%** shading.
   c. Change the *Before* paragraph spacing to **12 pt**. and the *After* spacing to **0 pt**.
   d. Update **Heading 1** to match selected text.
   e. Apply the **Heading 1** style to each of the remaining section headings ("*Mail*," "*Calendar*," "*Contacts*," "*Tasks*," "*Notes*," "*Journal*," and "*Formatting*").

8. Change paragraph spacing, set tab stops, and modify the *Heading 2* style.
   a. Select the third line of text on the first page ("Activity Shortcut . . .") and change the *Before* paragraph spacing to **6 pt**. and the *After* spacing to **3 pt**.
   b. Apply **Small caps** formatting to the selected text.
   c. Set **left** tab stops on the selected text at **3"**, **5"**, and **8.25"**.
   d. Update **Heading 2** to match selected text.
   e. Apply the **Heading 2** style to the first line of text ("Activity Shortcut . . .") after each section heading to create column headings.

9. Set tab stops and leaders to align text under the column headings and use the *Format Painter* to copy formatting.
   a. In the first section ("Global Outlook Commands") below the column headings ("ACTIVITY SHORTCUT . . ."), select all of the tabbed text beginning with "**Go to Mail**" and ending with "**Delete selected item**."

b. Set the following tabs stops:
      3" left tab stop with **dot leader (2)**
      5" left tab stop with **no leader (1)**
      8.25" left tab stop with **dot leader (2)**
   c. Use the *Format Painter* to apply the tab settings to the remaining text below the column headings ("ACTIVITY SHORTCUT . . .") in the other sections.
   d. Turn on **Show/Hide** and delete any blank lines in the document.

10. Remove the existing footer and insert a custom footer.
   a. Place your insertion point at the beginning of the document.
   b. Edit the footer and remove all content.
   c. Open the *Tabs* dialog box and **Clear All** existing tab stops.
   d. Set a center tab stop at **4.75"** and the right tab stop at **9.5"**.
   e. Insert the **Company** document property field on the left side of the footer.
   f. Press the **right arrow** key to deselect the document property field, **tab** to the center tab stop, and insert the **Title** (or **Document Title**) document property field.
   g. Press the **right arrow** key to deselect the document property field, **tab** to the right tab stop.
   h. Type Page, **space** once, insert a plain page number in the current position.
   i. **Space** once, type of, **space** once, and insert the *NumPages* field (use **1,2,3**. . . format).
   j. Apply a **single line** top border in the footer with **1 pt**. width, **Dark Blue**, **Text 2** color.
   k. Change the font size of all of the text in the footer to **10 pt**.
   l. Set the footer so it does not appear on the first page.

11. On the third page, insert a **page break** before the "Formatting" heading. This document fits on four pages.

12. Save and close the document (Figure 2-116).

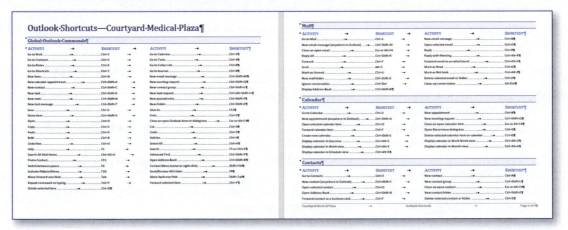

2-116 Word 2-7 completed (pages 1 and 2 of 4)

Challenge Project 2-8

Create an agenda for an upcoming meeting for an organization you are a member of, such as a club, church, volunteer organization, student group, or neighborhood association. Research online to find the common components of agendas. Robert's Rules of Order is a good source of information about meetings and guidelines for meeting protocol.
[Student Learning Outcomes 2.1, 2.2, 2.3, 2.6, 2.7, 2.9]

File Needed: None
Completed Project File Name: *[your initials] Word 2-8.docx*

Create a new document and save it as [your initials] Word 2-8. An agenda can include, but is not limited to, the following items:

- Organization name as the title
- Meeting date, start time, and end time
- Meeting location
- Meeting attendees
- Topic headings
- Topic subheadings (include details for each topic heading)
- The time each topic is expected to last

Modify your document according to the following guidelines:

- Apply styles.
- Use a multilevel list for the agenda items and subheadings.
- Customize number or bullet format and indents as needed.
- Use a right tab stop with a leader to line up the amount of time allocated for each main topic heading.
- Apply borders, shading, and/or a horizontal line to create an attractive agenda.
- Adjust margins as needed.
- Include an appropriate header and/or footer.

Challenge Project 2-9

Update your résumé using some of the document formatting features learned in this chapter. Edit your résumé so it is consistently formatted, easy to read, and professional looking. Research résumés online to get ideas about formatting and content.
[Student Learning Outcomes 2.1, 2.2, 2.3, 2.4, 2.5, 2.6, 2.7, 2.8, 2.9]

File Needed: None
Completed Project File Name: *[your initials] Word 2-9.docx*

Open your existing résumé or create a new document and save it as [your initials] Word 2-9. Modify your document according to the following guidelines:

- Apply a document theme.
- Apply styles to headings and subheadings to improve consistency in format.
- Adjust margins as needed.
- Use bulleted lists with customized bullets and indents to attractively arrange information.
- Set and use tab stops and indents as necessary to align information.
- Apply borders, shading, and/or a horizontal line to emphasize information in your résumé.
- Use page or section breaks as needed.
- Use *Find and Replace* as needed.
- Insert hyperlinks for appropriate information (e.g., email address and company names).
- If your résumé is more than one page, include a header and/or footer on the second and continuing pages.

Challenge Project 2-10

Format your favorite recipe using some of the formatting features learned in this chapter. You can look up recipes online on the Food Network, Epicurious, Simply Recipes, or other food web sites.
[Student Learning Outcomes 2.1, 2.2, 2.3, 2.6, 2.7, 2.9]

File Needed: None
Completed Project File Name: *[your initials] Word 2-10.docx*

Create a new document and save it as [your initials] Word 2-10. Your recipe should include, but is not limited to, the following:

- Recipe title
- Descriptive paragraph about the recipe
- Tab stops to arrange quantity and ingredients (and special instructions if needed)
- Numbered, step-by-step instructions
- Recipe source and/or additional information

Modify your document according to the following guidelines:

- Apply a document theme.
- Apply styles.
- Adjust margins as needed.
- Set and use a combination of tab stops (e.g., left, right, center, decimal, bar, and leaders) as necessary to attractively line up information.
- Use a numbered list for instructions.
- Use left, right, first line, and/or hanging indents as necessary.
- Apply borders, shading, page border, and/or a horizontal line to set off information in your recipe.
- Insert hyperlinks to appropriate information (e.g., link to online recipe).

CHAPTER 3

Collaborating with Others and Working with Reports

CHAPTER OVERVIEW

Creating a long report with a table of contents, citations, footnotes or endnotes, a reference page, and headers and footers can be a challenging task. Word 2016 has numerous tools that automatically create these components in a report or a multipage document. Using these tools not only saves you time when you are working on this type of document but also improves consistency within your documents. Word also provides you with a variety of collaboration tools to help you more efficiently and effectively work with others on documents.

STUDENT LEARNING OUTCOMES (SLOs)

After completing this chapter, you will be able to:

SLO 3.1 Insert, review, edit, and customize comments (p. W3-134).

SLO 3.2 Modify and review a document using *Track Changes* and share an online document (p. W3-137).

SLO 3.3 Insert and edit footnotes and endnotes in a document (p. W3-144).

SLO 3.4 Create a bibliography with properly formatted sources and insert citations into a document (p. W3-149).

SLO 3.5 Create and edit a table of contents based on headings (p. W3-161).

SLO 3.6 Insert a cover page and modify content and content control fields (p. W3-164).

SLO 3.7 Apply and customize headers and footers in a multipage document (p. W3-167).

CASE STUDY

American River Cycling Club (ARCC) is a community cycling club that promotes fitness for the entire region. ARCC members include recreational cyclists who enjoy the exercise and camaraderie and competitive cyclists who compete in road, mountain, and cyclocross races throughout the cycling season.

For the Pause & Practice projects, you create a report for club members about how to develop a personal training program. In this report, you incorporate many of the report features covered in the chapter to produce a professional-looking and useful report.

Pause & Practice 3-1: Review a report that includes comments and edits marked with tracked changes.

Pause & Practice 3-2: Insert endnotes into the report, convert endnotes to footnotes, add reference sources, insert citations, and create a bibliography page.

Pause & Practice 3-3: Apply styles to headings, create a table of contents based on the headings in the document, modify the table of contents, insert a cover page, customize headers and footers in the report, and share an online file.

W3-133

Using Comments

When you are collaborating with other people on a report or document, you can use *comments* to provide feedback in the document without making changes to the text of the document. For example, you might use comments to ask a question, make a suggestion, or provide additional information. You can also use comments when working alone on a document to make notes to yourself. You can customize how comments appear in a document, review comments in a document, edit comments, and delete comments.

Insert a Comment

When you insert a comment, the comment appears in a ***balloon*** in the ***Markup area***, which is the area to the right of a document. The *Markup* area opens when a document has comments or tracked changes (we discuss tracking changes in *SLO 3.2: Using Track Changes and Sharing*). Comments in a document are marked with the name of the author of the comment and time or date the comment was created. The text of the comment appears below the author's name in the balloon. You can insert a comment on a single word or a group of words.

▶ HOW TO: Insert a Comment

1. Select the text where you want to insert a comment.
   - When you place your insertion point at the beginning of a word or within a word, the comment is attached to the entire word.
2. Click the **New Comment** button [*Review* tab, *Comments* group] (Figure 3-1).
   - Alternatively, click the **Comments** button in the upper right of the Word window and select **New Comment**.
   - The comment balloon appears in the *Markup* area to the right of the Word window.
   - The comment time or date displays as either minutes or hours ago (e.g., 4 minutes ago), or, if it was created more than 24 hours ago, the date displays.
   - The word or words in the document with the comment attached are highlighted.
3. Type comment text in the balloon (Figure 3-2).

3-1 New Comment button

3-2 Comment in a balloon in the Markup area

4. Click the document to return to the document.

> ▶ **MORE INFO**
>
> The *Display for Review* view [*Review* tab, *Tracking* group] determines how comments display in the document. *Display for Review* views are covered in the next section, *SLO 3.2: Using Track Changes and Sharing*.

Change User Name

Each comment made in Word is attributed to the user name stored in Office. When you are signed in to Word with your Microsoft Account, Word uses this information as the **user name**. Word uses your user name as the **author** of each new document you create. Each person editing a document is referred to as a **reviewer**.

If you are using a public computer, such as in a computer lab on your college campus, the user name is a generic name given to Office on that computer. To make sure comments you make in a document are attributed to you, you can change your user name and initials in Office.

▶ **HOW TO:** Change User Name

1. Click the **Tracking** launcher [*Review* tab, *Tracking* group] to open the *Track Changes Options* dialog box.

2. Click the **Change User Name** button to open the *Word Options* dialog box (Figure 3-3).

3. Type your name in the *User name* text box.

4. Type your initials in the *Initials* text box.

5. Check the **Always use these values regardless of sign in to Office** box.

6. Click **OK** to close the *Word Options* dialog box.

7. Click **OK** to close the *Track Changes Options* dialog box.

▶ **ANOTHER WAY**

Click the **File** tab to open the *Backstage* view and click **Options** to open the *Word Options* dialog box where you can change user name and initials.

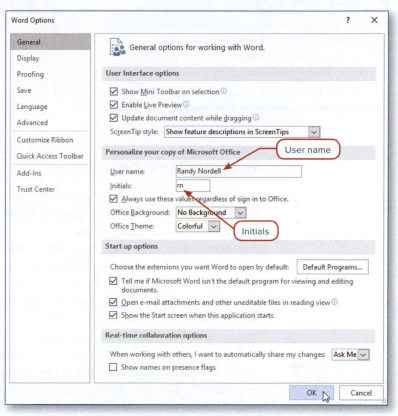

3-3 Change user name and initials in the *Word Options* dialog box

Review Comments

Each comment in a document is attributed to the reviewer who made the comment. When you place your pointer on text in a document where a comment is attached, a tag displays with the reviewer's name, the date and time of the comment, and the comment text (Figure 3-4).

If you are working on a long document with multiple comments, Word provides navigation tools to move to the next or previous comment in the document. Click the **Next** or **Previous** button in the *Comments* group on the *Review* tab

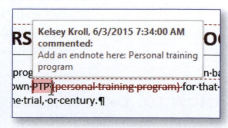

3-4 Comment details displayed in a tag

(Figure 3-5) to move to the next or previous comment in your document.

Reply to a Comment

3-5 Move to the next comment

To reply to a comment, click the **Reply** button on the right side of the comment in the *Markup* area (Figure 3-6). A reply area opens within the existing comment where you can type a reply below the original comment.

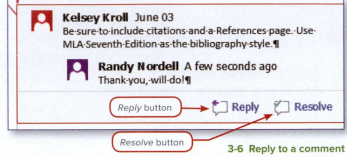

3-6 Reply to a comment

Resolve Comment

You can also resolve a comment when you have taken action on a comment but don't want to delete the comment. When a comment is resolved, the text of the comment changes to a light gray color, and the highlighted text in the document where the comment is attached is a lighter shade of the comment color.

To resolve a comment, click the **Resolve** button on the comment (see Figure 3-6). Alternatively, right-click a comment in the *Markup* area or the highlighted text in a document where the comment attached and select **Resolve Comment** from the context menu

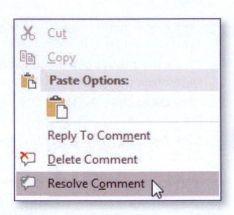

3-7 *Resolve Comment* from the context menu

(Figure 3-7). You can reopen a resolved comment by clicking the **Reopen** button on the comment or right-clicking the comment and selecting **Reopen Comment**.

Edit and Delete Comments

You can edit comments by clicking the comment balloon and editing existing text or typing new text. You can also right-click highlighted text in your document that has a comment attached and select **Edit Comment** from the context menu.

Once you have finished reviewing comments, you can delete them. You can delete comments individually or delete all the comments in the document.

> **HOW TO: Delete Comments**

1. Click the comment balloon or the highlighted comment text in the document.
   - You can also click **Next** or **Previous** [*Review* tab, *Comments* group] to select a comment (see Figure 3-5).
2. Click the top half of the **Delete** button [*Review* tab, *Comments* group] to delete the selected comment.
   - You can also right-click a comment and select **Delete Comment** from the context menu.

3. Click the bottom half of the **Delete** button for more delete options.
   - Click the **Delete All Comments in Document** button to delete all the comments in the document (Figure 3-8).

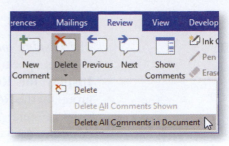

3-8 Delete all comments in the document

SLO 3.2

Using Track Changes and Sharing

Track Changes is a valuable editing tool in Word that marks changes you and others insert in a document so all reviewers can see these changes. This feature is very useful when working with a group on a report or project. As you review tracked changes in a document, you can accept, reject, or skip the marked changes. You have different options for viewing how tracked changes display in the document. Word also gives you the ability to share online documents with others and use real-time collaboration.

Track Changes

To mark editing changes in a document, you must first turn on *Track Changes*. Once you have turned on *Track Changes*, you can add, delete, and change text and formatting in the document. These changes are tracked in the body of the document and in balloons in the *Markup* area. Each line in the document that has a change is marked with a vertical gray or red line (depending on *Display for Review* view, which is covered in the next section) to the left of the line so reviewers can easily tell where changes have been made.

▶**HOW TO:** Use Track Changes

1. Click the **Track Changes** button [*Review* tab, *Tracking* group] (Figure 3-9).
   - When *Track Changes* is turned on, this button is highlighted.
   - You can also click the bottom half of the **Track Changes** button and select **Track Changes** to turn on *Track Changes*.
2. Edit, delete, insert, or format text in the document.
   - The *Display for Review* view determines how editing changes appear in the document. The *Display for Review* views are covered in the next section.
3. Click the **Track Changes** button to turn off *Track Changes*.

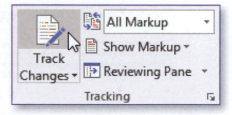

3-9 Turn on *Track Changes*

▶ **ANOTHER WAY**

Ctrl+Shift+E toggles *Track Changes* on and off.

Display for Review Views

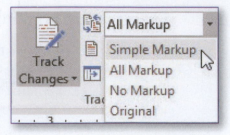

The ***Display for Review*** view determines how editing changes appear when using *Track Changes*. Click the **Display for Review** drop-down list in the *Tracking* group on the *Review* tab to select a *Display for Review* view (Figure 3-10). The following table lists and describes each of these different views:

3-10 *Display for Review* views

Display for Review Views

Display for Review View	Description
Simple Markup	Displays a final version of the document with the proposed changes incorporated. A red line to the left of a line marks changed lines in the document. Click the **Show Comments** button [*Review* tab, *Comments* group] to display or hide comments in the document.
All Markup	Displays added, deleted, and edited text in the body of the document. Formatting changes and comments display in balloons on the right. A gray line to the left of a line marks changed lines in the document.
No Markup	Displays a final version of the document with the proposed changes incorporated. All editing changes and comments are hidden.
Original	Displays the original document with proposed changes not incorporated. All editing changes and comments are hidden.

All Markup is the view people typically use when reviewing a document with changes tracked (Figure 3-11). If you view your document in ***Simple Markup***, ***No Markup***, or ***Original*** view, the tracked changes are still in the document, but they are hidden so you can view a clean (without markup) final or original version of the document. It is important to understand and use these different views when using *Track Changes* to edit a document.

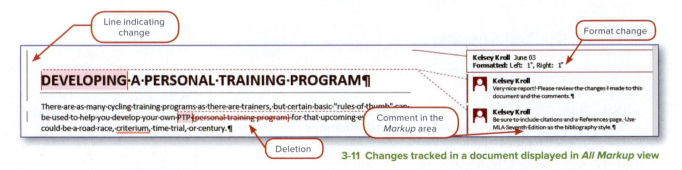

3-11 Changes tracked in a document displayed in *All Markup* view

> **MORE INFO**
>
> The **Show Comments** button [*Review* tab, *Comments* group] is only active in *Simple Markup* view where you choose how comments display. In *All Markup* view, comments always display. In *No Markup* and *Original* views, comments do not display.

Accept and Reject Changes

After a document has been marked up with editing changes, you can review each proposed change and either accept or reject the change. It's best to work in *All Markup* view when reviewing a document with changes tracked. When you accept an editing or formatting change, the change is applied to the document, and the inline markup and/or balloon is removed. When you reject an editing or formatting change, the text and formatting revert back to their original form.

Similar to comments, each editing change is attributed to a reviewer. When you place your pointer on a change in the body of the text or on a balloon, a tag displays the reviewer's name, the date and time of the change, and a description of the change (Figure 3-12).

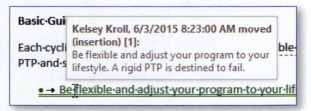

3-12 Tracked changes details displayed in a tag

▶HOW TO: Accept and Reject Changes

1. Place the insertion point at the beginning of the document (**Ctrl+Home**).

2. Click the **Display for Review** drop-down list [*Review* tab, *Tracking* group] and select **All Markup** if this is not the current view.

3. Click the **Next** button [*Review* tab, *Changes* group] to select the next change made to the document (Figure 3-13).

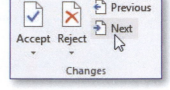

3-13 Move to the next revision in the document

   - Click the **Previous** button to select the previous revision.
   - If you are in *No Markup* or *Original* view and press the *Next* or *Previous* button, the view automatically changes to *All Markup*.

4. Click the **Accept** or **Reject** button [*Review* tab, *Changes* group] to accept or reject the change and move to the next revision.

   - If you click the bottom half of the **Accept** button, there are additional options: *Accept and Move to Next, Accept This Change, Accept All Changes Shown, Accept All Changes,* and *Accept All Changes and Stop Tracking* (Figure 3-14).
   - If you click the bottom half of the **Reject** button, there are additional options: *Reject and Move to Next, Reject Change, Reject All Changes Shown, Reject All Changes,* and *Reject All Changes and Stop Tracking.*
   - When accepting and rejecting changes, Word also stops on comments. Click **Accept** to leave the comment in the document or **Reject** to delete the comment.
   - You can also click **Next** to skip a comment or revision in the document.

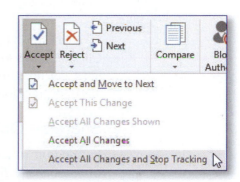

3-14 *Accept All Changes and Stop Tracking* option

5. Continue accepting or rejecting changes in the document.

6. After you reach the last change in the document, a dialog box opens confirming there are no more comments or tracked changes in the document. Click **OK** (Figure 3-15).

   - When all changes have been accepted or rejected, there will be no vertical lines to the left of the text in the body of the document.

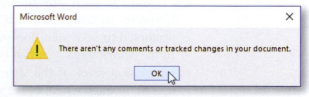

3-15 Dialog box that appears after reviewing the document

> ### ANOTHER WAY
>
> Right-click a change and select **Accept "description of change"** or **Reject "description of change"** from the context menu.

Reviewing Pane

If you are working with a document that has many editing changes marked with tracked changes or comments, the **Reviewing pane** is a useful tool. The *Reviewing* pane is a separate pane that includes all tracked changes and comments, and it can be displayed vertically on the left side of the Word window or horizontally at the bottom of the Word window (Figure 3-16). If there are a lot of changes and comments in a document and all of the balloons cannot fit in the *Markup* area, the *Reviewing* pane automatically opens.

To open the *Reviewing* pane, click the **Reviewing Pane** button in the *Tracking* group on the *Review* tab and select either **Reviewing Pane Vertical** or **Reviewing Pane Horizontal**.

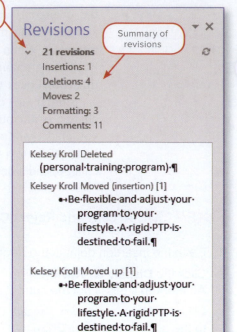

Arrow to display/hide revision details

Summary of revisions

3-16 *Reviewing* pane displayed vertically

> **MORE INFO**
>
> When the *Reviewing* pane is open, the title of the pane is *Revisions*. This book refers to this pane as the *Reviewing* pane.

At the top of the *Reviewing* pane, a summary displays the number of revisions in the document. Click the arrow to the left of the revision summary to display a breakdown of the number of insertions, deletions, moves, formatting changes, and comments in the document. You can right-click any of the revisions in the *Reviewing* pane and accept or reject changes from the context menu.

Share an Online File

In addition to collaborating with others on a document using *Comments* and *Track Changes*, Word also provides you with the option of sharing an online file with others. Sharing an online file gives you the ability to work with others on the same file at the same time, which is called ***real-time collaboration***.

You can share any files you have saved in your *OneDrive*. If you try to share a file that is not saved in *OneDrive*, you are prompted to save your document to *OneDrive* before sharing it. In the **Share** pane, you can type or select the recipients, set the permission level of the shared file, type a message recipients receive through email, or get a sharing link.

Click to open *Share* pane

Permission drop-down list

Get a *sharing link* option

3-17 Share a *OneDrive* file

▶ **HOW TO:** Share an Online File

1. Open the file you want to share.
   - If the file is not saved in *OneDrive*, save the file to *OneDrive*.
2. Click the **Share** button in the upper right of the Word window to open the *Share* pane to the right of the Word window (Figure 3-17).

- You can also open the *Share* pane from the *Backstage* view. Click the **File** button to open the *Backstage* view, click **Share** on the left, select **Share with People**, and click the **Share with People** button. The *Backstage* view closes and the *Share* pane opens in the Word document.

3. Type or select the email address of the person with whom you are sharing the file in the *Invite people* area.

- If you are using Outlook as your email program, you can select recipients from your *Outlook Contacts*. Click the **Address Book** button to the right of the *Invite people* text box, select recipients, and click **OK** to close the *Address Book* dialog box.
- If typing multiple email addresses, separate each with a semi-colon.

4. Select **Can edit** or **Can view** from the *Permission* drop-down list.

5. Type a message to recipient(s) in the *Message* area.

6. Click the **Share** button. An email is sent to people you invited.

7. Click the **X** to close the *Share* pane.

Create a Sharing Link

You can also choose to create a sharing link (hyperlink) to share a file with others rather than sending an email through Word. You can get a sharing link, copy it, and email it to others as another way of sharing. You have the option of generating an ***Edit link*** or a ***View-only link***.

▶ **HOW TO:** Create a Sharing Link

1. Open the file you want to share.
- If the file is not saved in *OneDrive*, save the file to *OneDrive*.

2. Click the **Share** button in the upper right of the Word window to open the *Share* pane to the right of the Word window.

3. Click **Get a sharing link** at the bottom of the *Share* pane (see Figure 3-17).
- Alternatively, you can click **Send as attachment**, and email the file as a Word document or PDF file.

4. Click the **Create an edit link** or **Create a view-only link** button (Figure 3-18). A link is created that you can copy and give to others.

5. Click the **Copy** button to copy the sharing link (Figure 3-19).
- You can paste the copied sharing link in an email, Word document, or other online location.

6. Click the **Back** arrow to the left of *Get a sharing link* at the top of the *Share* pane to return to the main *Share* pane, or click the **X** to close the *Share* pane.

3-18 Create a sharing link

3-19 Copy a sharing link

For this Pause & Practice project, you modify the *Developing a Personal Training Program* report for American River Cycling Club using comments and *Track Changes*.

Files Needed: ***PersonalTrainingProgram-03.docx*** *(Student data files are available in the* Library *of your* SIMnet account)
Completed Project File Names: ***[your initials] PP W3-1.docx***

1. Open the ***PersonalTrainingProgram-03*** document from your student data files.

2. Save the document as [your initials] PP W3-1.

3. Change user name and initials.
   a. Click the **Tracking** launcher [*Review* tab, *Tracking* group] to open the *Track Changes Options* dialog box.
   b. Click the **Change User Name** button to open the *Word Options* dialog box.
   c. In the *Personalize your copy of Microsoft Office* area, type your first and last name in the *User name* text box.
   d. Type your first and last initials in lowercase letters in the *Initials* text box.
   e. Check the **Always use these values regardless of sign in to Office** box.
   f. Click **OK** to close the *Word Options* dialog box.
   g. Click **OK** to close the *Track Changes Options* dialog box.

4. Change *Display for Review* view.
   a. Click the **Display for Review** drop-down list [*Review* tab, *Tracking* group] and select **Original** to view the original document without changes (Figure 3-20).
   b. Click the **Display for Review** drop-down list again and select **No Markup** to view the final document with proposed changes applied.
   c. Click the **Display for Review** drop-down list again and select **Simple Markup** to view the document with proposed changes applied. A red line on the left indicates changes in the document.
   d. If the comment text displays in the balloons, click the **Show Comments** button [*Review* tab, *Comments* group] to hide comment text and display only comment balloons.
   e. Click the **Display for Review** drop-down list again and select **All Markup** to view the final document with proposed changes visible inline and comments in balloons in the *Markup* area.

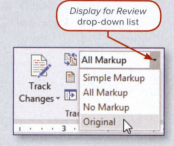

Display for Review drop-down list

3-20 Change *Display for Review* view

5. Turn on the *Reviewing* pane and reject changes.
   a. Click the **Reviewing Pane** drop-down arrow [*Review* tab, *Tracking* group] and select **Reviewing Pane Vertical**. The *Reviewing* pane displays on the left side of the Word window.
   b. In the *Reviewing* pane, find where a bulleted item was moved ("Kelsey Kroll Moved (insertion) [1]").
   c. Right-click **"Kelsey Kroll Moved (insertion) [1]"** and select **Reject Move** from the context menu (Figure 3-21).
   d. Click the **X** in the upper right corner of the *Reviewing* pane to close it.

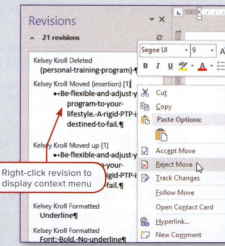

Right-click revision to display context menu

3-21 Reject moved text in the *Reviewing* pane

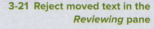

6. Accept changes in the document.
   a. Move to the top of the document (**Ctrl+Home**).
   b. Click the **Next** button [*Review* tab, *Changes* group] to select the first change.
   c. Click the top half of the **Accept** button [*Review* tab, *Changes* group] to accept the change and move to the next change.
   d. Click the **Next** button [*Review* tab, *Changes* group] three times to move through the first three comments and to locate the next tracked change ("personal training program" deleted).
   e. Click the top half of the **Accept** button to accept the change and move to the next change.
   f. Click the bottom half of the **Accept** button and select **Accept All Changes** from the drop-down list (Figure 3-22). All of the remaining changes in the document are accepted. Only comments are remaining in the *Markup* area.

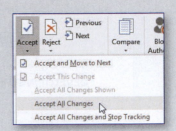

3-22 Accept all changes in the document

7. Resolve a comment and reply to a comment.
   a. Move to the top of the document and click the **Next** button [*Review* tab, *Comments* group] to move to the first comment.
   b. Click the **Resolve** button on the comment in the *Markup* area or right-click the comment and select **Resolve Comment** from the context menu (Figure 3-23). A resolved comment becomes grayed out.
   c. Click the **Next** button to move to the next comment.
   d. Click the **Reply** button on the comment in the *Markup* area (see Figure 3-23).
   e. Type Thank you, will do!

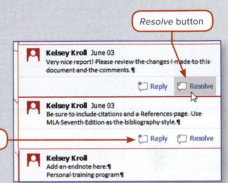

3-23 Resolve and reply to comments

8. Delete selected comments in the document.
   a. Click the **Next** button [*Review* tab, *Comments* group] to move to the next (third) comment.
   b. Click the top half of the **Delete** button [*Review* tab, *Comments* group] to delete the comment.
   c. Continue clicking **Next** and **Delete** to delete the remaining comments. Don't delete the first two comments on the first page.

9. Add comments to the document.
   a. Place the insertion point at the top of the document (**Ctrl+Home**).
   b. Click the **New Comment** button [*Review* tab, *Comments* group] to insert a new comment.
   c. Type Also insert a cover page and table of contents in the new comment.
   d. Select the first word in the first body paragraph ("**There**").
   e. Click the **New Comment** button and type Proofread this report one more time in the new comment.

10. Use *Track Changes* to revise the document.
    a. Click the top half of the **Track Changes** button [*Review* tab, *Tracking* group] to turn on track changes (or press **Ctrl+Shift+E**).
    b. Select the word **"Basic"** in the first section heading below the first body paragraph.
    c. Type General to replace the selected word. Make sure there is one space after the word (turn on **Show/Hide**, if necessary).
    d. Place your insertion point after "Training" in the second section heading on the first page ("Personal Training Guidelines").
    e. **Space** once and type Program to insert the word between "Training" and "Guidelines." Make sure there is one space between the words.
    f. Click the **Track Changes** button to turn off *Track Changes*.

11. Save and close the document (Figure 3-24).

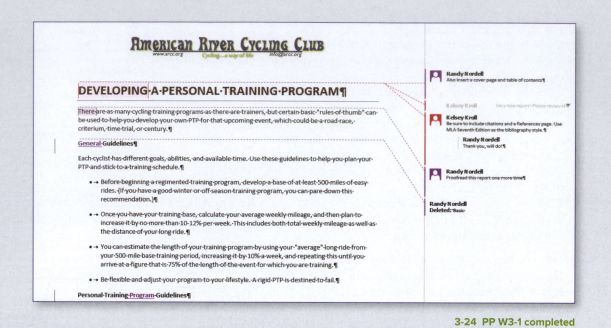

3-24 PP W3-1 completed

SLO 3.3

Using Footnotes and Endnotes

Footnotes and *endnotes* cite reference sources used in a document. You can also use them to include additional notational information. Footnotes display at the bottom of each page, while endnotes display at the end of the document.

As you insert footnotes and endnotes into your document, Word numbers them consecutively. If you insert a footnote or endnote before or between existing notes, Word automatically reorders notes. You can also customize number format and convert footnotes to endnotes or endnotes to footnotes.

Insert a Footnote

When a footnote is inserted into a document, a *reference marker*, which is a number or letter in superscript format (smaller font size and slightly raised above the typed line), displays directly after the word. Word then places the insertion point at the bottom of the page to insert the text of the footnote. A thin top border above the note separates the note from the text in the body of the document.

Footnotes display in the body of the document at the bottom of the page, not in the footer, and the text on a page with a footnote adjusts to allow space for the footnote.

▶ **HOW TO:** Insert a Footnote

1. Position the insertion point directly after the word where the footnote is to be inserted.
2. Click the **References** tab.
3. Click the **Insert Footnote** button [*Footnotes* group] (Figure 3-25).
   A reference marker is inserted in the body of the document (Figure 3-26),

3-25 *Insert Footnote* button

and the insertion point is positioned after the corresponding reference marker in the footnote area of the page.

4. Type the footnote text in the footnote area of the page (Figure 3-27).

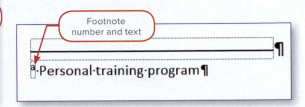

DEVELOPING·A·PERSONAL

There·are·as·many·cycling·training·programs·as·the
be·used·to·help·you·develop·your·own·PTP¶·for·tha
criterium,·time·trial,·or·century.¶

Footnote reference marker

Footnote number and text

¹·Personal·training·program¶

3-26 Footnote reference marker in the body of the document

3-27 Footnote text at the bottom of the page

5. Click in the body of the document to leave the footnote area and to return to the document.

Insert an Endnote

Inserting endnotes is similar to inserting footnotes. The main difference is the text for the endnote displays after the text at the end of the document rather than at the bottom of the page where the note appears.

▶ **HOW TO:** Insert an Endnote

1. Position the insertion point directly after the word where the endnote is to be inserted.
2. Click the **References** tab.
3. Click the **Insert Endnote** button [*Footnotes* group] (Figure 3-28). The reference marker displays in the body of the document and the insertion point is positioned after the corresponding reference marker at the end of the document.
4. Type the endnote text.
5. Click in the body of the document to leave the endnote area and to return to the document.

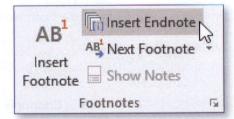

3-28 *Insert Endnote* button

▶ **ANOTHER WAY**

Alt+Ctrl+F inserts a footnote. **Alt+Ctrl+D** inserts an endnote.

View Footnotes and Endnotes

Once you have inserted footnotes or endnotes in your document, it is easy to see the footnote or endnote text at the bottom of a page or at the end of the document, but you might have a difficult time locating the reference markers in the body of the document. Word provides you with a tool to easily locate footnote reference markers in your document.

Click the **Next Footnote** button in the *Footnotes* group on the *References* tab to move to the next footnote (Figure 3-29). Click the **Next Footnote** drop-down arrow to display a list of options to move to the next or previous footnote or endnote. Click the **Show Notes** button in the *Footnotes* group to toggle between the note reference markers (in the body of the document) and the note text (in the footnote or endnote area).

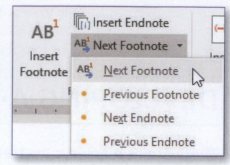

3-29 *Next Footnote* drop-down list

Word also displays the text of the footnote or endnote when you put your pointer over a reference marker (Figure 3-30).

> **ANOTHER WAY**
>
> Use the *Go To* feature in the *Find and Replace* dialog box to go to a specific note. Press **Ctrl+G** to open the *Find and Replace* dialog box with the *Go To* tab displayed.

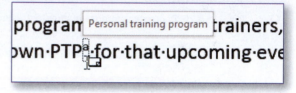

3-30 Footnote text displayed as a tag

Customize Footnotes and Endnotes

By default, footnotes are numbered consecutively with numbers (1, 2, 3) and endnotes are numbered with lowercase roman numerals (i, ii, iii). Letters or symbols such as an asterisk (*), section mark (§), or number symbol (#) are other reference marker options. You can customize how notes are numbered and where they display in a document.

▶ HOW TO: Customize Footnotes and Endnotes

1. Click the **Footnotes** launcher [*Reference* tab, *Footnotes* group] to open the *Footnote and Endnote* dialog box (Figure 3-31).

2. Select the **Footnotes** or **Endnotes** radio button in the *Location* area.
   - In the drop-down list for *Footnotes*, you have the option to position the footnote text at the *Bottom of page* (default) or *Below text*.
   - In the drop-down list for *Endnotes*, you have the option to position the endnote text at the *End of document* (default) or *End of section*.

3. In the *Format* area, you can change any of the following: *Number format*, *Custom mark*, *Start at*, or *Numbering*.

4. In the *Apply changes* area, you can apply changes to the *Whole document* or *This section* (if there are sections in your document).

5. Click **Apply** to close the dialog box and apply the changes. Do not press *Insert*, which inserts a footnote or endnote in the document.

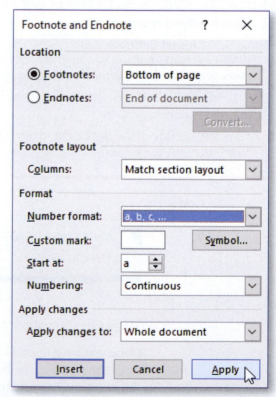

3-31 *Footnote and Endnote* dialog box

Modify Footnote and Endnote Format

In addition to customizing note placement and format, you can also change the format of footnote and endnote text. You do this the same way you format regular text in the document.

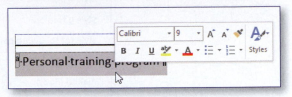

3-32 Apply formatting to footnote text

Select the footnote or endnote text and apply any formatting changes such as font, font size, style, line or paragraph spacing, or text effects (Figure 3-32). You can apply changes using the buttons on the *Home* or *Layout* tab, the context menu (right-click selected text), the mini toolbar, or keyboard shortcuts.

Modify Footnote and Endnote Styles

The appearance of the footnotes and endnotes in your document is determined by styles. Styles control the font, font size, text styles and effects, and paragraph formatting. When you insert a footnote in your document, Word applies the *Footnote Text* style.

You can modify the *Footnote Text* or *Endnote Text* style, which automatically updates all of your footnote or endnote text to reflect the changes you made to the style.

▶ **HOW TO:** Modify the Footnote or Endnote Style

1. Right-click the footnote or endnote text and select **Style** from the context menu. The *Style* dialog box opens and the name of the style displays in the *Styles* area (Figure 3-33).

2. Click the **Modify** button to open the *Modify Style* dialog box.

3. Change the basic font formatting in the *Formatting* area.

4. Click the **Format** button to display a list of other formatting options (Figure 3-34).

   • When you select a format option, another dialog box opens.
   • Make any desired formatting changes and click **OK** to close the dialog box.

5. Click **OK** to close the *Modify Style* dialog box.

6. Click **Apply** to apply changes to the style and close the *Style* dialog box.

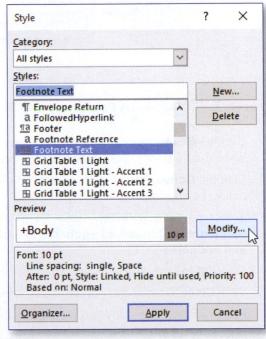

3-33 *Style* dialog box

Convert Footnotes and Endnotes

There might be times when you want to convert footnotes to endnotes or endnotes to footnotes. Rather than deleting and recreating the notes, you can use the ***Convert Notes*** feature. When you convert notes, Word automatically renumbers the reference markers and moves the note text to the correct location in the document.

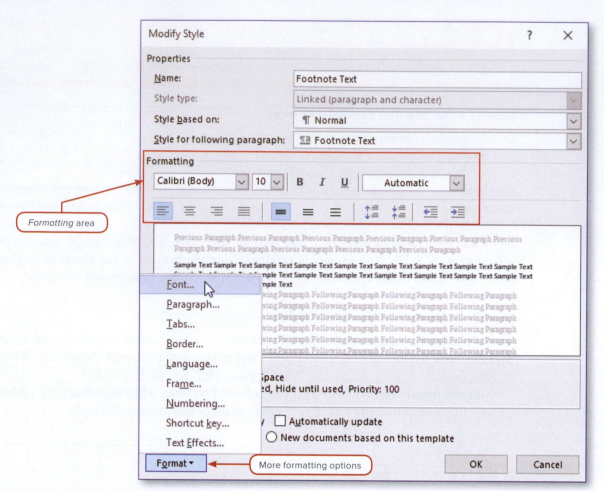

3-34 *Modify Style* dialog box

▶ HOW TO: Convert Footnotes and Endnotes

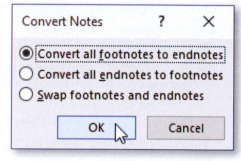

1. Click the **Footnotes** launcher [*References* tab, *Footnotes* group] to open the *Footnote and Endnote* dialog box.

2. Cick the **Convert** button in the *Location* area. The *Convert Notes* dialog box opens (Figure 3-35).

3. Select from one of the three convert options: **Convert all footnotes to endnotes**, **Convert all endnotes to footnotes**, or **Swap footnotes and endnotes**.

4. Click **OK** to close the *Convert Notes* dialog box.

5. Click **Close** to close the *Footnote and Endnote* dialog box.

   - Do not click *Insert* or Word will insert a footnote or endnote.

3-35 *Convert Notes* dialog box

▶ MORE INFO

All three of the convert options are active *only* if you have both footnotes and endnotes in your document. Otherwise, only one option is active.

You can convert individual notes using the context menu. Right-click a footnote or endnote (*not* the reference marker in the text of the document) and select **Convert to Endnote** or **Convert to Footnote** (Figure 3-36).

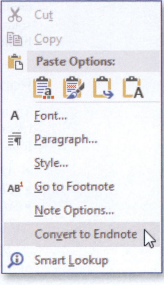

3-36 Convert individual note

Move Footnotes and Endnotes

You can move footnotes and endnotes in the same way you move text in a document. To move a note, select the **reference marker** in the body of the document (Figure 3-37) and use one of the following methods:

- Drag and drop
- **Ctrl+X** to cut and **Ctrl+V** to paste
- **Cut** and **Paste** buttons [*Home* tab, *Clipboard* group]
- **Cut** and **Paste** options in the context menu

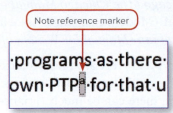

Note reference marker

·programs·as·there·
own·PTP·for·that·u

3-37 Select note reference marker to move

> **MORE INFO**
>
> When moving a note, select the note carefully to ensure that you are only moving the note and not any spaces, text, or paragraph marks.

Delete Footnotes and Endnotes

When you delete a note, Word removes the reference marker and the text of the note. Your remaining notes renumber and remain in consecutive order. To delete a note, always delete the note reference marker in the body of the document, which also deletes the note text in the footnote or endnote area.

▶ **HOW TO:** Delete a Note

1. Select the **reference marker** in the body of the document (*not* the text of the footnote or endnote at the bottom of the page or end of the document).
2. Press **Delete** on the keyboard.
   - Deleting footnote or endnote text in the footnote or endnote area will not delete the note reference marker in the body of the document.
3. Check to ensure proper spacing around text where the note was deleted.

SLO 3.4

Creating a Bibliography and Inserting Citations

Typically, the most tedious and time-consuming aspect of writing a research paper is compiling sources, creating a bibliography page, and citing sources in the body of the report. A *source* is the complete bibliographic reference for a book, journal article, or web page. A *citation* is the abbreviated source information that you place in the body of the report to credit the source of the information you use. A *bibliography* or *works cited* page lists the sources used in the report. Word includes tools to create sources, insert citations, and create a bibliography or works cited page at the end of your report.

Report Styles

There are a variety of report styles, and each differs not only in the overall format of the report but also in the format for sources and citations. The most common report styles are the following:

- *APA* (American Psychological Association)
- *Chicago* (*The Chicago Manual of Style*)
- *MLA* (Modern Language Association)
- *Turabian* (*Manual for Writers of Research Papers, Theses, and Dissertations*)

MLA and APA are the two most common report formats. The following table lists some of the general characteristics of each of these two report styles. Within each of these report formats, there can be much variance depending on the preference of your college or instructor. Always follow the formatting instructions your instructor provides.

Common Report Styles

Report Features	APA	MLA
Font	11 or 12 pt.	11 or 12 pt.
Line Spacing	Academic APA is double-spaced and business APA is single spaced.	Double-space.
Margins	For an unbound report, use 1" for all margins. For a left bound report, use 1.5" left margin and 1"top, bottom, and right margins.	Use 1" margins.
Heading Information	Heading information is typically typed on a title page.	Left align at the top of the first page and include author's name, instructor's name, class, and date on separate lines.
Title	The title is either on the title page or horizontally centered on the first page of the report.	Center on the first page of the report.
Header	Include report title and page number on the right.	Include author's last name and page number on the right.
Uses	Typically use in social and behavioral sciences, business, and nursing.	Typically use in humanities.

Bibliography Styles

As you begin compiling the sources for your report, the first thing you need to do is select the *bibliography style* of the report. The bibliography style determines how citations display in the body of the report and how references appear on a references, bibliography, or works cited page.

▶HOW TO: Select the Bibliography Style of the Report

1. Click the **Reference** tab.
2. Click the **Style** drop-down arrow [*Citations & Bibliography* group].
3. Select the style of the report from the drop-down list of report styles (Figure 3-38).

3-38 Select bibliography style

> **MORE INFO**
>
> The report style you select controls the formatting of sources and citations; it does not control the overall formatting of your report. To do that, you must apply the correct formatting to the body of your report.

Add a New Source

As you are writing a report, you should gather bibliographic information about sources used in your report (author; title of book, journal, or article; publication date and edition; publisher or online location). When you use the **Add New Source** feature, Word inserts a citation in your report at the insertion point and stores this source information. You then can access stored sources to insert additional citations and to create a bibliography page.

▶HOW TO: Add a New Source

1. Position the insertion point in your document at the point where you want to insert a citation.
2. Click the **Insert Citation** button [*References* tab, *Citations & Bibliography* group].
3. Select **Add New Source**. The *Create Source* dialog box opens (Figure 3-39).

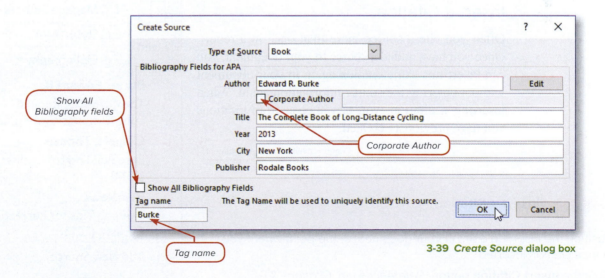

3-39 *Create Source* dialog box

4. Click the **Type of Source** drop-down list and select the type of source.
   - The fields for the source change depending on the type of source you choose.

5. Type the author information in the *Author area*. You will enter this information differently depending on the author(s) of the source.
   - *Individual Author*: In the *Author* field, type first name, middle initial, and last name (with no commas).
   - *Multiple Authors*: Click the **Edit** button to the right of the *Author* area to open the *Edit Name* dialog box. Type the author information in the *Add name* fields. Click the **Add** button to add additional authors. You can also reorder multiple authors by selecting an author in the *Names* area and clicking the **Up** or **Down** button. Click **OK** to close the *Edit Name* dialog box (Figure 3-40).
   - *Corporate Author* (e.g., USA Cycling or Velo News): Click the **Corporate Author** check box in the *Create Source* dialog box and type the corporate author.

6. Type other source information as needed (see Figure 3-39).
   - As you type in other source information, Word automatically creates a *Tag name* for your source.
   - You can edit the *Tag name* if desired.

7. Click the **Show All Bibliography Fields** check box to display more fields. For example, you might need to type the edition of the book.

8. Click **OK** to close the *Create Source* dialog box.
   - The citation displays in the document in the report style you selected (Figure 3-41).

Edit Name dialog box

Add name
Last: Burke
First: Edward
Middle: R.

Click to add additional authors → Add

Names

Up
Down
Delete

OK   Cancel

3-40 *Edit Name* dialog box

General·Guidelines¶

Each·cyclist·has·different·goals,·abilities,·and·available·
PTP·and·stick·to·a·training·schedule·(Burke,·2013).¶

Citation

3-41 Citation inserted in text

Insert a Citation

Often you cite a source more than once in a report. Once you have added a source to your document, you can insert this same citation again in your document without entering the source information again. When inserting a citation, you can choose from citations you have previously created.

Citations available in the document

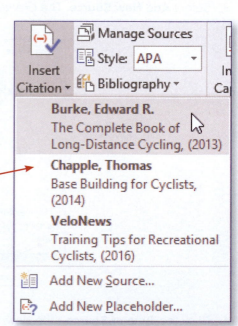

Manage Sources
Style: APA
Bibliography ▾
Insert Citation ▾

Burke, Edward R.
The Complete Book of
Long-Distance Cycling, (2013)

Chapple, Thomas
Base Building for Cyclists,
(2014)

VeloNews
Training Tips for Recreational
Cyclists, (2016)

Add New Source...

Add New Placeholder...

3-42 Insert citation from a previously created source

▶**HOW TO:** Insert a Citation

1. Position the insertion point in your document at the point where you want a citation inserted.

2. Click the **Insert Citation** button [*References* tab, *Citations & Bibliography* group].
   - A list of previously used or created sources is displayed in the drop-down list (Figure 3-42).

3. Select from your list of sources.
   - The citation is inserted in the document.
   - When you insert a citation, Word automatically inserts a space between the citation and the preceding word.

Insert a Placeholder

There might be times when you need to insert a citation but do not have all of the bibliographic information to create the source. You can insert a *placeholder* in the report to temporarily mark a spot where a citation needs to be completed. Later, you can add bibliographic source information for any placeholders inserted in the document.

▶ HOW TO: Insert a Placeholder

1. Position the insertion point in your document at the point where you want a placeholder inserted.
2. Click the **Insert Citation** button [*References* tab, *Citations & Bibliography* group].
3. Select **Add New Placeholder**. The *Placeholder Name* dialog box opens (Figure 3-43).
4. Type the name of the placeholder.
   - You can't use spaces between words in the placeholder text because the placeholder name is the tag name of the source.
   - Use can use an underscore between words when naming a placeholder.
5. Click **OK**. The placeholder displays in the document and looks similar to a citation (Figure 3-44).

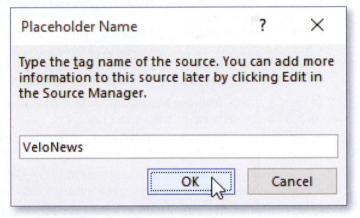

3-43 Insert a placeholder

• → One·of·the·intermediate·rides,·preferably·prior·to·your·day·off·the 2-3·mph·faster·than·your·planned·century·speed·(VeloNews).¶

Placeholder

3-44 Placeholder in the body of the document

Manage Sources

The **Source Manager** dialog box allows you to edit existing sources, add bibliographic information to placeholders, create new sources, and copy sources that were created and used in other documents. The *Source Manager* dialog box displays the sources used in your report, the placeholders that need bibliographic information, and a master list of all sources you have previously used.

1. Click the **Manage Sources** button [*References* tab, *Citations & Bibliography* group]. The *Source Manager* dialog box opens (Figure 3-45).

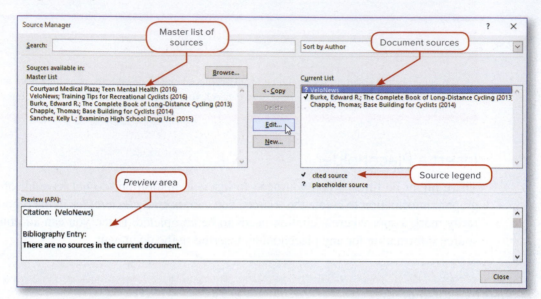

3-45 *Source Manager* dialog box

- The *Master List* of sources on the left displays *all* available sources. Some of these may have been created in other Word documents.
- The *Current List* displays the sources available in your current document.
- Sources that are cited in the document have a check mark next to them.
- Sources that are placeholders have a question mark next to them and require additional information.
- The *Preview* area displays the contents of your source.

2. To copy a source from the *Master List* to the *Current List*, select the source and press the **Copy** button. The copied source remains on the *Master List*.

3. To edit a source from either list, select the source and click the **Edit** button (see Figure 3-45). The *Edit Source* dialog box opens.

   - Make changes to the source and press **OK**.
   - Word automatically updates any citations in your document if you make changes to the source.

4. To add bibliographic information to a placeholder, select the placeholder and click the **Edit** button. The *Edit Source* dialog box opens.

   - Add bibliographic information to the placeholder and press **OK**.
   - When bibliographic information is added to a placeholder, it becomes a complete source and the question mark next to it changes to a check.
   - Word automatically replaces the placeholder with a citation in your document when you add bibliographic information to a placeholder.

5. To create a new source, click the **New** button. The *Create Source* dialog box opens.

   - Type in the bibliographic information and press **OK**.
   - This source is now available as a citation to insert in your document.
   - This source is also added to the *Master List*.

6. To delete a source from either list, select the source and click the **Delete** button.

   - You cannot delete a source from the *Current List* if it is cited in the document. You must first delete the citation in the document before deleting a source in the *Source Manager* dialog box.
   - If a source is in both lists and you delete it from one list, it is not deleted from the other list.

7. Click **Close** to close the *Source Manager* dialog box and apply any changes made.

Edit Citations and Sources

After citations and placeholders are inserted into the document, you can edit the citation or source without using the *Source Manager* dialog box. When you click a citation or placeholder in your document, you see a drop-down list of editing options (Figure 3-46):

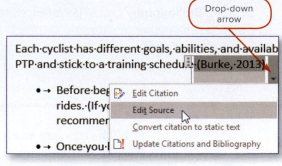

3-46 Edit citation and source options

- *Edit Citation*: This option opens the *Edit Citation* dialog box and allows you to add a page number to the citation or suppress any currently displayed information.
- *Edit Source*: This option opens the *Edit Source* dialog box and allows you to update source bibliographic information.
- *Convert citation to static text*: This option changes the citation from a Word field that is automatically generated and updated to static text that is not updated.
- *Update Citations and Bibliography*: This option updates your bibliography page to reflect any changes you have made to citations or sources.

> **MORE INFO**
>
> You can edit citations and placeholders using either the drop-down list or the context menu.

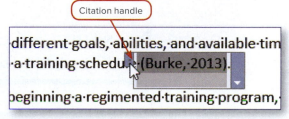

Citation handle

You can move or delete a citation or placeholder in the body of the text by clicking the citation or placeholder handle on the left and dragging it to a new location (to move) or by pressing **Delete** (to delete) on your keyboard (Figure 3-47).

3-47 Select a citation to move or delete

Insert a Bibliography

Once you have created your sources and inserted citations in the body of the report, you are ready to create a bibliography page. The bibliography page is automatically generated from the sources in your document and is formatted according to the *Bibliography Style* you selected. Word provides you with a few bibliography options.

The *Bibliography*, *References*, and *Works Cited* built-in options insert a title before the sources. The *Insert Bibliography* option just inserts the sources; you can add a title of your choice. If you plan to include a table of contents in your report, it is best to use one of the built-in options because Word applies a style for the bibliography title, which allows the bibliography page to automatically be included in the table contents.

▶ **HOW TO:** Insert a Bibliography

1. Position the insertion point in your document at the point where you want the bibliography to begin.
   - It is usually best to insert a page break (**Ctrl+Enter**) at the end of the document and begin the bibliography on a new page.

2. Click the **Bibliography** button [*References* tab, *Citations & Bibliography* group] to display the list of options (Figure 3-48).

3. Select your bibliography option. The bibliography is inserted in the document.

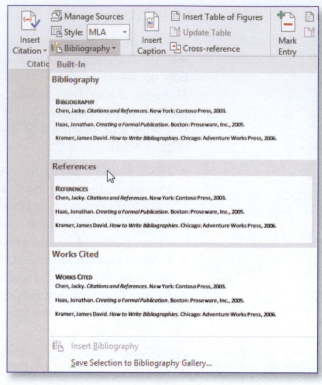

If changes are made to sources after the bibliography page has been inserted, you have to update the bibliography. Click one of the references on the bibliography page to select the entire bibliography and click **Update Citations and Bibliography** (Figure 3-49).

Click to update citations and bibliography

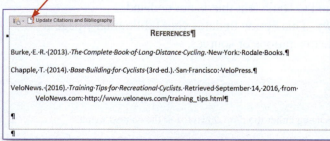

3-48 Insert *References* page

3-49 *References* page inserted into the document

> ▶ **ANOTHER WAY**
> Right-click the bibliography and choose **Update Field** or press **F9** to update the bibliography.

PAUSE & PRACTICE: WORD 3-2

For this Pause & Practice project, you modify the *Developing a Personal Training Program* report for American River Cycling Club. You accept tracked changes, delete comments, add and modify notes, select the report style, add sources and citations, and insert a bibliography page.

File Needed: *[your initials] PP W3-1.docx*
Completed Project File Name: *[your initials] PP W3-2.docx*

1. Open the *[your initials] PP W3-1* document completed in *Pause & Practice 3-1*.

2. Save this document as [your initials] PP W3-2.

3. Accept tracked changes and delete all comments in the document.
   a. Click the bottom half of the **Accept** button [*Review* tab, *Changes* group] and select **Accept All Changes**.
   b. Click the bottom half of the **Delete** button [*Review* tab, *Comments* group] and select **Delete All Comments in Document**.

4. Insert endnotes into the report.
   a. Position the insertion point after "PTP" and before the space (first page, first body paragraph). Turn on **Show/Hide**, if necessary.
   b. Click **Insert Endnote** [*References* tab, *Footnotes* group]. Word moves the insertion point to the endnote area on the last page.
   c. Type Personal training program in the endnote area.
   d. Position the insertion point after the first instance of "Max VO2" and before the space (third page, second sentence in the "Training Intensity and Heart Rate" section).

> **MORE INFO**
>
> Use the *Find* feature in the *Navigation* pane to locate specific words.

   e. Click **Insert Endnote** [*References* tab, *Footnotes* group] and type The highest rate of oxygen consumption attainable during maximal or exhaustive exercise in the endnote area.
   f. Position the insertion point after "RPM" and before the period (third page, "Sample Session" section).
   g. Click **Insert Endnote** [*References* tab, *Footnotes* group] and type Revolutions per minute in the endnote area.
   h. Apply **bold** and **italic** formatting to the words "maximal" and "exhaustive" in the second endnote (Figure 3-50).

i·Personal·training·program¶
ii·The·highest·rate·of·oxygen·consumption·attainable·during·*maximal*·or·*exhaustive*·exercise¶
iii·Revolutions·per·minute¶

3-50 Endnotes added to report

5. Convert endnotes to footnotes and change numbering.
   a. Click the **Footnotes** launcher [*References* tab, *Footnotes* group]. The *Footnote and Endnote* dialog box opens.
   b. Click the **Convert** button to open the *Convert Notes* dialog box (Figure 3-51).
   c. Select **Convert all endnotes to footnotes** if it is not already selected and click **OK**.
   d. Click **Close** to the close the *Footnote and Endnote* dialog box.
   e. Click the **Footnotes** launcher again to open the *Footnote and Endnote* dialog box.
   f. Click the **Footnotes** radio button if it is not already selected.
   g. Click the **Number format** drop-down arrow and select **a, b, c . . .** (Figure 3-52). Don't change any of the other *Format* settings.
   h. Choose **Apply** to close the *Footnote and Endnote* dialog box and apply the changes.
   i. Check your document to confirm that endnotes have been converted to footnotes and that the number format has been changed.

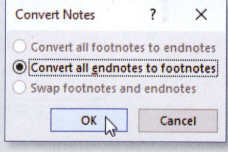

3-51 Convert endnotes to footnotes

6. Change the style of the footnotes.
   a. Right-click the footnote text at the bottom of the first page.
   b. Select **Style** from the context menu (not mini toolbar). The *Style* dialog box opens.
   c. Click the **Modify** button to open the *Modify Style* dialog box (Figure 3-53).
   d. Change the font size to **9 pt**.
   e. Change line spacing to **1.5** (see Figure 3-53).
   f. Click **OK** to close the *Modify Style* dialog box.
   g. Choose **Apply** to close the *Style* dialog box.

7. Select the report style for sources and citations.
   a. Click the **Style** drop-down list [*References* tab, *Citations & Bibliography* group].
   b. Select **MLA Seventh Edition**.

8. Add a new source and insert a citation.
   a. On the first page, position the insertion point after the word "schedule" and before the period (end of first paragraph, "General Guidelines" section).
   b. Click the **Insert Citation** button [*References* tab, *Citations & Bibliography* group].

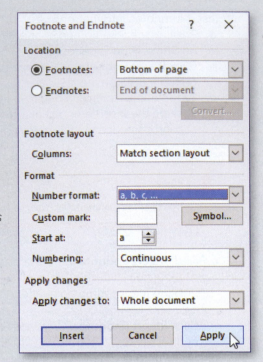

3-52 Change number format of footnotes

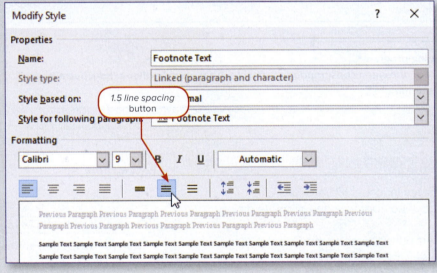

3-53 Modify *Footnote Text* style

   c. Select **Add New Source**. The *Create Source* dialog box opens (Figure 3-54).
   d. Select **Book** as the type of source.
   e. Type Edward R. Burke in the *Author* field.
   f. Type the following source information in the *Create Source* dialog box:

   Title: The Complete Book of Long-Distance Cycling
   Year: 2013
   City: New York
   Publisher: Rodale Books
   Tag name: Burke

   g. Click **OK** to add the source, insert the citation, and close the dialog box.

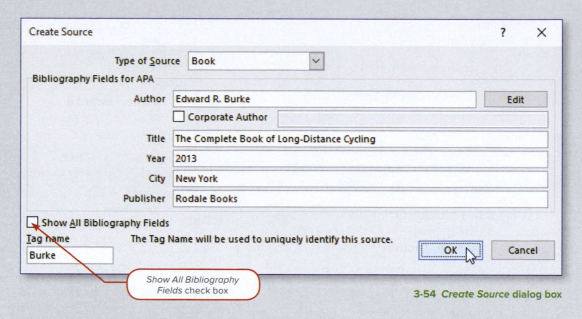

9. Add a placeholder to the report.
   a. Go the first page and position the insertion point after the word "speed" and before the period (last bulleted item, "Pace of Rides" section). You can also press **Ctrl+G** to open the *Go To* tab in the *Find and Replace* dialog box where you can quickly go to a specific page.
   b. Click the **Insert Citation** button [*References* tab, *Citations & Bibliography* group].
   c. Select **Add New Placeholder**. The *Placeholder Name* dialog box opens.
   d. Type VeloNews (no space between words) as the placeholder text.
   e. Press **OK** to insert the placeholder and close the dialog box.

10. Manage sources to add a new source and complete bibliographic information for the placeholder.
    a. Click the **Manage Sources** button [*References* tab, *Citations & Bibliography* group]. The *Source Manager* dialog box opens.
    b. Select **VeloNews** in the *Current List* area and click the **Edit** button to open the *Edit Source* dialog box.
    c. Check the **Show All Bibliography Fields** box and type the following source information:

    Type of Source: **Document from Web site**
    Corporate Author (check **Corporate Author** check box): VeloNews
    Name of Web Page: Training Tips for Recreational Cyclists
    Name of Web Site: VeloNews.com
    Year: 2016
    Year Accessed: 2016
    Month Accessed: September
    Day Accessed: 14
    URL: http://www.velonews.com/training_tips.html

    d. Click **OK** to close the *Edit Source* dialog box. The placeholder is updated as a complete source.
    e. Click the **New** button to create a new source.
    f. Check the **Show All Bibliography Fields** box and type the following source information:

    Type of Source: **Book**
    Author: Thomas Chapple
    Title: Base Building for Cyclists
    Year: 2014

City: San Francisco
Publisher: VeloPress
Edition: 3rd
Tag name: Chapple

g. Click **OK** to close the *Create Source* dialog box.
h. Click **Close** to close the *Source Manager* dialog box.

11. Insert citations into the report.
    a. Go to the second page and position the insertion point after "rest day" and before the period (second sentence of first paragraph, "Number of Rides per Week" section).
    b. Click the **Insert Citation** button [*References* tab, *Citations & Bibliography* group] (Figure 3-55).
    c. Select the **Chapple, Thomas** source. The citation displays in the report.
    d. Use the **Insert Citation** button to insert the following citations:

    Burke, Edward, R.: after "training week" and before the period (page 2, last bulleted item in the "Duration of Rides" section).
    Chapple, Thomas: after "maximum heart rate" and before the period (page 3, first paragraph in "Training Intensity and Heart Rate" section).
    VeloNews: after "overtraining" and before the period (page 3, at the end of "Other Heart Rate Factors" section).

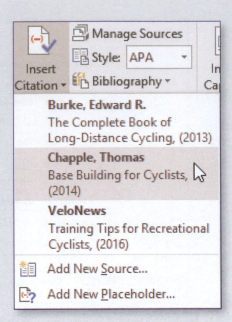

3-55 Insert a citation

12. Insert a bibliography and change report style.
    a. Position the insertion point on the blank line at the end of the document and press **Ctrl+Enter** to insert a page break.
    b. Click the **Bibliography** button [*References* tab, *Citations & Bibliography* group] and select **References** from the drop-down list. The *Reference* page is inserted on the blank page at the end of the document.
    c. **Center** the *References* title and apply **10 pt**. after paragraph spacing.
    d. Click the **Style** drop-down list [*References* tab, *Citations & Bibliography* group] and select **APA Sixth Edition**.

13. Save and close the document (Figure 3-56).

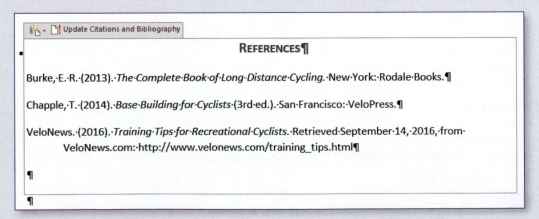

3-56 PP W3-2 References page

Inserting a Table of Contents

Most long reports have a **table of contents** to provide readers with an overview of the material covered in the report. The table of contents reflects the headings in the report; some tables of contents list only the main headings while others might list second- and third-level headings. Typically, a table of contents lists headings on the left and page numbers on the right with a dot leader separating them.

You can create a table of contents manually by typing headings, using a tab with a dot leader, and then typing the page number. But with Word, you can automatically generate a table of contents based upon the headings in your report, which saves you time. If you generate your table of contents this way, it automatically updates if topics are changed or moved or if page numbering changes in the report.

Use Heading Styles for a Table of Contents

Word can automatically generate a table of contents listing the headings in your report if you apply **heading styles** to each heading. Styles control the appearance of text by applying a specific font, font size, color, font styles and effects, and spacing to the text on which a style is applied. The document **theme** determines the appearance of the styles. The *Styles* gallery displays many of the commonly used styles.

> **MORE INFO**
>
> Styles and themes were introduced in Chapter 2 (see *SLO 2.7: Using Styles and Themes*).

The first step in automatically generating a table of contents in a report is to apply a heading style to each heading in the document. Word provides you with multiple levels of heading styles (e.g., Heading 1, Heading 2, etc.).

▶ HOW TO: Apply Heading Styles

1. Select the heading where you want to apply a style.
2. Click the heading style to apply [*Home* tab, *Styles* group] (Figure 3-57). The style is applied to the heading.

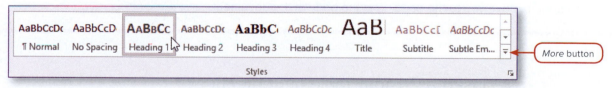

3-57   Document styles displayed in the *Style* gallery

- Apply *Heading 1* to main headings, *Heading 2* to second level headings, and other heading styles as needed.
- When you place the insertion point on a style, Word displays a live preview of the style and temporarily applies the style to the selected text.
- Click the **More** button to expand the *Style* gallery to display additional styles.

3. Continue to select headings and apply styles. Every heading you want in your table of contents must have a style.

- When a heading style has been applied to text, there is an *Expand/Collapse* button to the left of the heading (Figure 3-58). Click the **Expand/Collapse** button to expand or collapse the text below the heading.

> **GENERAL·GUIDELINES¶**
> Each·cyclist·has·different·goals,·abilities,·and·available·time.
> PTP·and·stick·to·a·training·schedule·(Burke,·2013).¶

Expand/Collapse button

3-58   Expand or collapse text below heading

Insert a Built-In Table of Contents

You can insert a built-in table of contents that includes the headings in your document. Word inserts the table of contents at the point in your report where the insertion point is located. It is a good idea to insert a blank page before the first page of your report for your table of contents.

> **HOW TO:** Insert a Built-In Table of Contents

1. Place the insertion point before the first line of the report and press **Ctrl+Enter** to insert a page break.
2. Position the insertion point at the top of the new first page.
3. Click the **References** tab.
4. Click the **Table of Contents** button [*Table of Contents* group] (Figure 3-59).
5. Select a built-in table of contents to insert. The table of contents displays in your report (Figure 3-60).

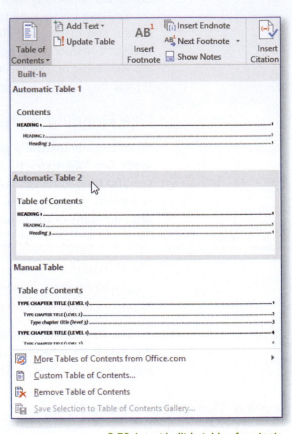

3-59 Insert built-in table of contents

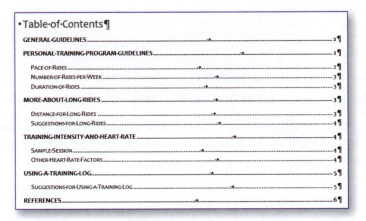

3-60 Table of contents inserted into the report

- Each heading in the table of contents is a hyperlink. Press the **Ctrl** key and click a heading in the table of content to move you to the heading in the body of the document.

Insert a Custom Table of Contents

You can insert a custom table of contents and modify the format and appearance of the table. When you insert a custom table of contents, the "Table of Contents" title is not automatically inserted as it is when you insert a built-in table of contents. If you want a title on your custom table of contents page, you should type it before inserting your table of contents.

> **MORE INFO**
>
> It is usually best to just apply font formatting (not a heading style) to the table of contents title. If you apply a heading style to the table of contents title, the table of contents title is included as an item in the table of contents when it is updated.

▶ HOW TO: Insert a Custom Table of Contents

1. Place the insertion point before the first line of your report and press **Ctrl+Enter** to insert a page break.

2. Position the insertion point at the top of the new first page.
   - If desired, type a title for the table of contents and press **Enter**.
   - Do not apply a heading style to the title.

3. Click the **Table of Contents** button [*References* tab, *Table of Contents* group].

4. Select **Custom Table of Contents**. The *Table of Contents* dialog box opens (Figure 3-61).
   - A preview of the table of contents appears in the *Print Preview* area.

5. Click the **Formats** drop-down list in the *General* area and select a table of contents format.

6. Select the number of heading levels to display in the *Show levels* area.

7. Below the *Print Preview* area, you can choose to not show page numbers, choose to not right align page numbers, and select the type of tab leader to use with right-aligned page numbers.

8. Click **OK** to insert the table of contents.

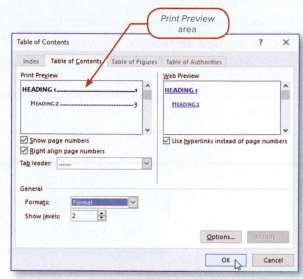

3-61 *Table of Contents* dialog box

Modify a Table of Contents

After inserting a table of contents, you might decide that you want a different format or to change the levels of headings that are displayed. When you update a table of contents, you are actually replacing the old table of contents with a new one.

▶ HOW TO: Modify a Table of Contents

1. Click anywhere in the table of contents.

2. Click the **Table of Contents** button [*References* tab, *Table of Contents* group].

3. Select **Custom Table of Contents**. The *Table of Contents* dialog box opens.

4. Make changes to the table of contents.

5. Click **OK**. A dialog box opens, confirming you want to replace the existing table of contents (Figure 3-62).

6. Click **Yes** to replace the table of contents.

3-62 **Replace existing table of contents**

Update a Table of Contents

When you make changes to your report such as adding or modifying headings, content, or page breaks, the content and page numbers in the table of contents may no longer be accurate. You need to update the table of contents to reflect these changes. You have the option of updating only page numbers or updating the entire table of contents, which includes both headings and page numbers.

1. Click anywhere in the table of contents.
2. Click the **Update Table** button [*References* tab, *Table of Contents* group]. The *Update Table of Contents* dialog box opens (Figure 3-63).
3. Select either **Update page numbers only** or **Update entire table**.
4. Click **OK** to update the table of contents.

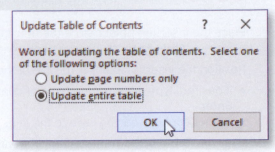

3-63 Update table of contents

▶ **ANOTHER WAY**

Press **F9** or right-click the table of contents and select **Update Field** to update the table of contents.

Remove a Table of Contents

If you no longer want a table of contents in your report, you can easily remove it. Click the **Table of Contents** button in the *Table of Contents* group on the *References* tab and select **Remove Table of Contents**. The table of contents is removed from your document (Figure 3-64).

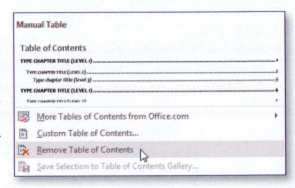

3-64 Remove table of contents

SLO 3.6

Inserting a Cover Page

Some reports have a title page as the cover or introduction. If you're writing a formal report in APA style, there is a specific way you must organize the title page. But if you're presenting a market analysis or product feasibility report at work, you might want a ***cover page*** to introduce the report with professional appeal. Word provides you with a variety of cover page options.

Insert a Built-In Cover Page

When you insert a cover page into a document, Word automatically inserts it at the beginning of the document and inserts a page break to move the existing first page content to the second page.

To insert a cover page, click the **Cover Page** button in the *Pages* group on the *Insert* tab and select one of the built-in cover pages from the drop-down list (Figure 3-65). More custom cover pages are available on Office.com. Select **More Cover Pages from Office.com** to display a list of additional cover pages.

Customize Cover Page Content

The built-in cover pages in Word are arrangements of graphics, text boxes, and Word fields. Some of the fields are ***document property fields*** and some are ***content control fields***, fields where you can type custom information. You can customize the content of the fields, delete

3-65 Insert built-in cover page

unwanted fields, and modify the graphics and text boxes on the cover page. The theme of your document controls the format of cover pages. Colors and fonts in a cover page change based on the selected theme.

Customize Document Property Content

If you have added information to the document properties of your document, Word automatically populates the document properties fields in the cover page. When you type information into a document property field on the cover page, Word adds this information to your document properties.

3-66 Document properties on the *Backstage* view

▶ **HOW TO:** Customize Document Properties

1. Click the **File** tab to open the *Backstage* view and select **Info** to display document properties (Figure 3-66).
2. Click the **Show All Properties** link at the bottom.
   - This link toggles between *Show All Properties* and *Show Fewer Properties*.
3. Add or modify document property content.
   - Some fields, such as *Last Modified* and *Created*, cannot be modified.
   - To remove the *Author*, right-click the author and select **Remove Person**.
4. Click the **Back** arrow to return to the document. Word updates the document property fields on the cover page.

Add or Remove Document Property Fields

You can also add document property fields to the cover page or remove them. When you add a document property field to a cover page, the content of this field is automatically populated with the information from your document properties.

▶ HOW TO: Add Document Property Fields

1. Position the insertion point at the place where you want to insert the document property field.
2. Click the **Insert** tab.
3. Click the **Quick Parts** button [*Text* group] (Figure 3-67).
4. Choose **Document Property**.
5. Select a document property field from the drop-down list. The document property field is inserted into the document.

> ▶ **MORE INFO**
>
> You can insert document property fields anywhere in a document.

3-67 Insert document property field

To remove a document property field, click the **field handle** to select the field and press **Delete** (Figure 3-68). Make sure to check for proper spacing and paragraph breaks when you delete a document property field.

3-68 Select and delete document property field

> ▶ **MORE INFO**
>
> Deleting the contents of a document property or content control field does not delete the field. To remove a field, click the **field handle** to select the field and press **Delete**.

Customize Content Control Fields

When you insert a cover page into a document, many of the fields are content control fields, which are fields where you type or select custom content (Figure 3-69). You may want to add content to some of these fields and remove others. You can remove Word content control fields the same way you remove a document property field (see Figure 3-68).

To insert custom content into a content control field, click in the field and type the information. You can type whatever information you want into a content control field. For example, you can type a web address into the *Address* field (see Figure 3-69).

3-69 Type text into a content control field

Remove a Cover Page

You might decide that you no longer want a cover page or that you want to insert a different one. Removing a cover page is similar to removing a table of contents. Click the **Cover Page** button on the *Insert* tab and select **Remove Current Cover Page** (Figure 3-70).

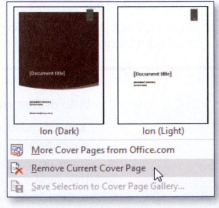

3-70 Remove cover page

When you remove a cover page, Word deletes the entire contents of the cover page and removes the page break.

SLO 3.7 Using Advanced Headers and Footers

You can use headers and footers to include page numbers and document information at the top or bottom of each page in a report or multipage document. Headers appear at the top of the page and footers appear at the bottom. You type headers and footers just once, and they automatically display on subsequent pages. You can automatically insert page numbers in the header or footer. You can also add custom content such as text, document property fields, the date, or borders.

Page and Section Breaks

For multipage documents, it is a good idea to insert page or section breaks to control page endings or special formatting in different sections. A *Page* break controls where one page ends and another begins. Use a *Next Page* section break when special document layout formatting is applied to a whole page or multiple pages of a document, such as landscape orientation to one page of the document. Use a *Continuous* section break when you apply special formatting to a section of the document, such as two-column format to specific text on one page.

> **MORE INFO**
>
> Don't use a section break to control page endings where a page break will suffice.

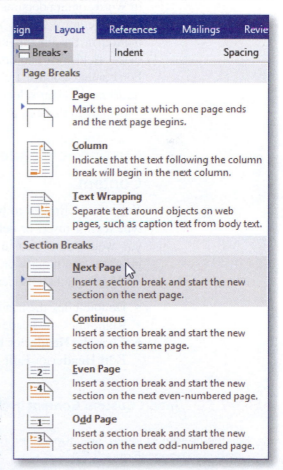

3-71 Insert page or section break

▶ HOW TO: Insert a Page or Section Break

1. Place the insertion point in the document at the point where you want the page or section break.
   - If you are inserting a continuous section break, it is best to select the text on which to apply the section break.
   - When you insert a continuous break on selected text, Word inserts a continuous section break before and after the selected text.
2. Click the **Breaks** button [*Layout* tab, *Page Setup* group] (Figure 3-71).
3. Select the type of break from the drop-down list.

> **ANOTHER WAY**
>
> **Ctrl+Enter** inserts a page break.

When working with page and section breaks, it is best to have the *Show/Hide* feature turned on so you can see where these breaks are located in a document. To delete a page or section break, select the break and press **Delete**.

Built-In Headers, Footers, and Page Numbers

Word provides you with a variety of built-in headers, footers, and page numbering options that you can insert into a document. You can also customize this built-in content. You can insert this content with the header or footer open or while you are in the main document.

> **HOW TO:** Insert a Built-In Header, Footer, or Page Number

1. Click the **Insert** tab.
2. Click the **Header**, **Footer**, or **Page Number** button [*Header & Footer* group].
3. Select the built-in header, footer, or page number from the drop-down list (Figure 3-72). The content displays and the header or footer area opens.
   - If you're inserting a page number, select the position (*Top of Page*, *Bottom of Page*, *Page Margins*, or *Current Position*) to insert the page number.
   - Additional built-in headers, footers, and page numbers display when you place your pointer on *More Headers (Footer or Page Numbers) from* Office.com.

Many of the built-in headers and footers in Word contain document property fields or content control fields. You can enter information in the document property area and these fields are automatically populated. For content control fields such as *Date* or *Address*, you can select or type the content to display in these fields (see Figure 3-69).

3-72 Insert built-in header

Customize Header and Footer Content

You are not limited to built-in content in the header and footer of your document. You can type text or insert or delete content control fields. You can format header and footer text as you would other text in your document; you can apply font formatting and borders, insert graphics, and modify or set tabs for alignment.

You can edit a header or footer in the following ways:

- Double-click the header or footer area of the document.
- Right-click the header or footer area and select **Edit Header** or **Edit Footer**.
- Click the **Header** or **Footer** button [*Insert* tab, *Header & Footer* group] and select **Edit Header** or **Edit Footer**.

> **HOW TO:** Insert Custom Content in the Header or Footer

1. Edit the header or footer. See above for different ways to edit the header or footer. The *Header & Footer Tools Design* tab opens (Figure 3-73).

3-73 *Header & Footer Tools Design* tab

2. Insert content from the *Header & Footer Tools Design* tab.

3. Type content or select a document property field to display in the header or footer.

4. Align information in the header or footer (Figure 3-74).

3-74 Built-in footer and document property field inserted in the footer

- By default, a center tab stop is set at the midpoint between the left and right margins and a right tab stop is set at the right margin.
- You can insert a tab by clicking the **Insert Alignment Tab** button [*Position* group].
- You can modify, add, or remove tabs on the ruler or in the *Tabs* dialog box [*Paragraph* dialog box, *Tabs* button].

5. Change the position of the header and footer in the *Position* group.

- By default, the header and footer are positioned 0.5" from the top and bottom of the page.
- You can change these settings in the *Page Setup* dialog box on the *Layout* tab.

6. Click **Close Header and Footer** to return to the main document.

Different First Page Header and Footer

On many reports, you don't include a page number or header and footer content on the first page, but this information is included on subsequent pages. When you select the ***Different First Page*** option, Word removes existing content from the header and footer on the first page. You can choose to leave the first page header and footer blank, or you can insert content that is different from the header and footer on second and subsequent pages.

▶**HOW TO:** Insert a Different First Page Header and Footer

1. Edit the header or footer on the first page of the document.

2. Check the **Different First Page** check box [*Header & Footer Tools Design* tab, *Options* group] (Figure 3-75).

- When the *Different First Page* check box is checked, the header (or footer) tab displays *First Page Header* (or *First Page Footer*) to distinguish it from other headers and footers in the

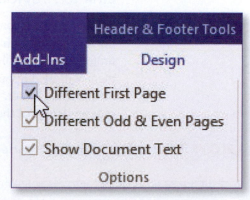

3-75 Apply *Different First Page* header and footer

document, which are labeled *Header*
(or *Footer*) (Figure 3-76).

- The header (or footer) tab label changes when you apply other header and footer formatting such as odd and even pages or have different headers for different sections of your document.

3. Click **Close Header and Footer**.

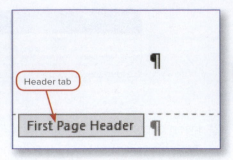

3-76 First page header

Different Odd and Even Pages

Just as you can have different header and footer content on the first page, Word provides you with the option of having ***different odd and even pages*** header and footer content on a multipage document. For example, you might want the title of the report to appear on all even pages in the footer and the page number and a company name to appear on odd pages.

> ▶ **MORE INFO**
>
> It is best to insert header and footer content on the first page of your document and then make any desired header and footer option changes.

▶ **HOW TO:** Insert Different Odd and Even Headers and Footers

1. Edit the header or footer on the first page of the document.
2. Check the **Different Odd & Even Pages** check box [*Header & Footer Tools Design* tab, *Options* group] (see Figure 3-75).
   - When the *Different Odd & Even Pages* check box is checked, the header (or footer) tab displays *Odd* (or *Even) Page Header* (or *Footer*) to distinguish it from other headers and footers in the document (Figure 3-77).
3. Click **Close Header and Footer**.

3-77 Odd page footer

Link to Previous Header or Footer

Section breaks separate your document into different sections. When you have different sections in your document, the headers and footers are by default linked to previous headers and footers. For example, a page number that appears in the footer of the first section of a document will also appear in the same position in the next section footer because it is linked to the previous footer. You can break this link to format header and footer content in one section independently of the header or footer in another section.

▶ **HOW TO:** Link or Unlink a Header or Footer

1. Edit the header or footer to be unlinked from the previous section.
   - By default the *Link to Previous* button is on (shaded).
   - The *Same as Previous* label displays on the right of the header or footer.

2. Click the **Link to Previous** button [*Header & Footer Tools Design* tab, *Navigation* group] to unlink it from the previous section (Figure 3-78).

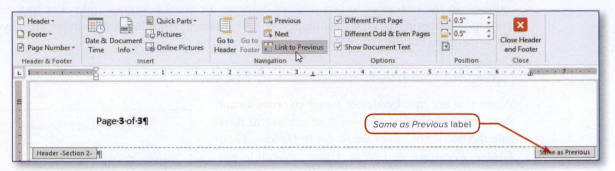

3-78 **Link to Previous** button

- The *Same as Previous* label is no longer displayed.
- The header or footer content still displays, but you can now change it without it changing the header or footer content in the previous section.

3. Click the **Link to Previous** button if you want to link header or footer content to a previous section after it has been unlinked.

   - Click **Yes** in the dialog box that opens asking if you want to link the header or footer to the previous section (Figure 3-79).

4. Click the **Close Header and Footer** button.

3-79 **Link header or footer to previous section**

Format Page Numbers

When you number the pages in your document, you can change the page number format and starting page number. For example, on a report you might want to number the front matter pages (title page, table of contents, executive summary) with roman numerals and number the body pages with regular numbers. If you are using different numbering for different sections of a document, you need to insert a next page section break between sections. This allows you to format the page numbering of each section differently.

▶**HOW TO:** Format Page Numbers

1. Select the page number to format in the header or footer.

2. Click the **Page Number** button [*Header & Footer Tools Design* tab, *Header & Footer* group].

3. Select **Format Page Numbers** from the drop-down list. The *Page Number Format* dialog box opens (Figure 3-80).

4. Click the **Number format** drop-down list and select the number format.

5. Select either the **Continue from previous section** or **Start at** radio button in the *Page numbering* area.

   - If you select *Continue from previous section*, the numbering continues consecutively from the previous section.
   - If you select *Start at*, you select the starting page number for the section.

6. Click **OK** to close the *Page Number Format* dialog box.

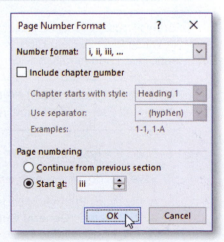

3-80 *Page Number Format* dialog box

When you include a Word cover page in a multipage document, the cover page is *not* considered the first page. Word considers the cover page as "page 0" when inserting page numbers in the header or footer, table of contents, or cross-reference links. For this reason, the page numbering in your document might be different from the page number displayed in the *Status* bar (bottom left of the Word window) of the document.

Navigate between Headers and Footers

When you are in a header or footer of a document, there are a variety of buttons you can use to navigate the header or footer areas: *Go to Header*, *Go to Footer*, *Previous*, and *Next*. These navigation buttons are in the *Navigation* group on the *Header & Footer Tools Design* tab (Figure 3-81).

3-81 Header and footer navigation buttons

Remove a Header or Footer

To remove all header or footer content from a document, you can open the header or footer and manually delete the content. All linked header or footer content is also removed when you do this. Word can also automatically remove the header or footer from a document.

▶**HOW TO:** Remove a Header or Footer

1. Click the **Insert** button.
2. Click the **Header or Footer** button [*Header & Footer* group].
3. Select **Remove Header** or **Remove Footer** from the drop-down list (Figure 3-82). The header or footer content is removed.

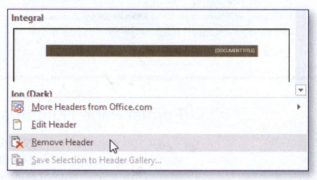

3-82 Remove header

PAUSE & PRACTICE: WORD 3-3

For this Pause & Practice project, you continue to modify the *Personal Training Program* report for the American River Cycling Club. You apply styles to headings in the report, insert and modify a table of contents, insert and modify a cover page, and insert customized footers.

File Needed: *[your initials] PP W3-2.docx*
Completed Project File Name: *[your initials] PP W3-3.docx*

---

1. Open the *[your initials] PP W3-2* document completed in *Pause & Practice 3-2*.
2. Save this document as [your initials] PP W3-3.
3. Apply styles to the headings in the report.
   a. Select the **"General Guidelines"** heading on the first page.
   b. Click the **Heading 1** style [*Home* tab, *Styles* group] to apply this style to the selected heading (Figure 3-83). If the *Heading 1* style is not visible, click the **More** button to display the entire *Styles* gallery.

c. Apply the **Heading 1** style to the following headings (bolded headings in the document):

Personal Training Program Guidelines
More about Long Rides
Training Intensity and Heart Rate
Using a Training Log

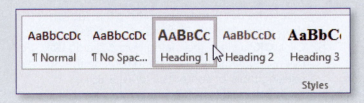

3-83 Apply *Heading 1* style

d. Apply the **Heading 2** style to the following subheadings (underlined headings in the document):

Pace of Rides
Number of Rides per Week
Duration of Rides
Distance for Long Rides
Suggestions for Long Rides
Sample Session
Other Heart Rate Factors
Suggestions for Using a Training Log

4. Add a table of contents at the beginning of the report.
   a. Turn on **Show/Hide** [*Home* tab, *Paragraph* group].
   b. Position the insertion point at the beginning of the document before the title ("Developing a Personal Training Program") and press **Ctrl+Enter** to insert a page break.
   c. Position the insertion point before the page break on the new first page.
   d. Click the **Table of Contents** button [*References* tab, *Table of Contents* group] (Figure 3-84).
   e. Select **Automatic Table 2** from the drop-down list. The table of contents displays on the first page of the report.

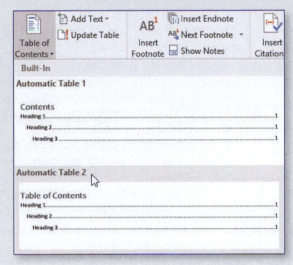

3-84 Insert table of contents

5. Customize the table of contents.
   a. Position the insertion point anywhere in the body of the table of contents.
   b. Click the **Table of Contents** button [*References* tab, *Table of Contents* group].
   c. Select **Custom Table of Contents** to open the *Table of Contents* dialog box (Figure 3-85).
   d. Click the **Formats** drop-down list and select **Formal**.
   e. Set the number of levels to **2** in the *Show levels* area.
   f. Check the **Show page numbers** and **Right align page numbers** boxes if they are not already checked.

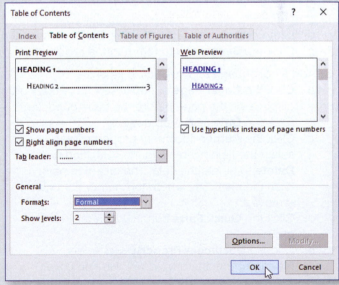

3-85 Customize table of contents

g. Select the dot leader option from the *Tab leader* drop-down list if it is not already selected.

h. Click **OK** to close the dialog box. A dialog box opens, confirming you want to replace the existing table of contents (Figure 3-86).

i. Click **OK** to replace the existing table of contents.

6. Insert page breaks and update table of contents.

a. On the second page, position the insertion point in front of the "Number of Rides per Week" heading and press **Ctrl+Enter** to insert a page break and move this heading to the next page.

b. Repeat this process on the following headings:
Suggestions for Long Rides
Using a Training Log

c. Press **Ctrl+Home** to move to the beginning of the document.

d. Click the **Update Table** button [*References* tab, *Table of Contents* group]. The *Update Table of Contents* dialog box opens.

e. Select the **Update entire table** radio button and click **OK** (Figure 3-87).

f. If there is a blank line above the table of contents, select the **paragraph mark** and press **Delete**.

g. Select the entire table of contents (including the heading) and change the font to **Calibri**.

7. Customize document properties.

a. Click the **File** tab to open the *Backstage* view and select **Info** to display document properties.

b. Click the **Show All Properties** link in the document properties area.

c. Add the following document properties:

Title: Developing a Personal Training Program
Company: American River Cycling Club
Manager: Olesia Sokol

d. In the *Author* area, right-click the author's name and select **Remove Person**.

e. Click the **Back** arrow to return to the report.

8. Add a cover page and customize fields.

a. Click the **Cover Page** button [*Insert* tab, *Pages* group] and select **Semaphore**. The cover page displays on the page before the table of contents.

b. Click the **Date** field drop-down arrow to display the calendar and select the current date.

c. Click the **Author** document property field, select the field handle (Figure 3-88), and press **Delete** to delete the field. The insertion point is on the blank line where the *Author* field was removed.

d. Click the **Quick Parts** button [*Insert* tab, *Text* group].

e. Choose **Document Property** and select **Manager** from the drop-down list. The cover page includes the *Manager* document property field.

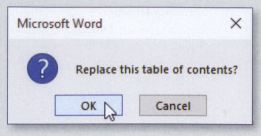

3-86 Replace existing table of contents

3-87 Update entire table of contents

3-88 Select and delete document property field

f. Click the **Company Address** field and type www.arcc.org in the field.

g. Right-click the **Subtitle** field ("[Document Subtitle]") and select **Remove Content Control** from the context menu.

h. Click the **Title** field and apply **bold** format. Bold formatting applies to the entire *Title* field.

i. Save the document.

9. Insert odd page and even page footers.

a. Press **Ctrl+Home** to move to the top of the document.

b. Click the **Footer** button [*Insert tab, Header & Footer* group] and select **Edit Footer** to open the footer area.

c. Check the **Different First Page** (if it is not already checked) and the **Different Odd & Even Pages** boxes [*Header & Footer Tools Design* tab, *Options* group].

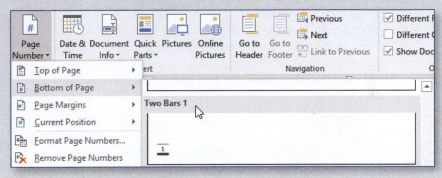

3-89 Go to the next footer

d. Click the **Next** button [*Navigation* group] to move to the odd page footer on the second page (Figure 3-89).

e. Click the **Page Number** button [*Header & Footer* group].

f. Select **Bottom of Page** and select **Two Bars 1** from the drop-down list (Figure 3-90). The page number "1" displays on the second page.

3-90 Select built-in page number

> **MORE INFO**
>
> Word considers the cover page as page 0.
> The table of contents page is page 1.

g. Click the **Next** button [*Navigation* group] to move to the even page footer on the next page.

h. Click the **Page Number** button [*Header & Footer* group], select **Bottom of Page**, and select **Two Bars 2** from the drop-down list. The page number "2" displays on the right.

i. Leave the footer open to add custom content in the next step.

10. Add custom content to the odd and even footers.

a. Place the insertion point in the even page footer.

b. Press **Ctrl+R** or click the **Align Right** button to position the insertion point on the right.

c. Click the **Document Info** button [*Header & Footer Tools Design* tab, *Insert* group] (Figure 3-91).

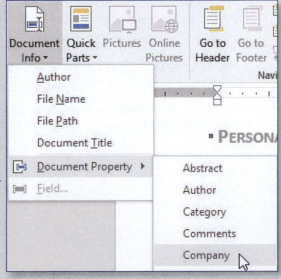

3-91 Insert document property field

d. Select **Document Property** and choose **Company** from the drop-down list. The *Company* document property field displays on the right side of the footer area.

e. Select the **Company** document property field, change the font size to **10 pt.**, and apply **bold** formatting.

f. Click the **Previous** button [*Header & Footer Tools Design* tab, *Navigation* group] to move to the odd page footer on the previous page. The insertion point should be on the left after the page number "1."

g. Click the **Document Info** button [*Header & Footer Tools Design* tab, *Insert* group] and select **Document Title** from the drop-down list. The *Title* document property field displays in the footer.

h. Select the **Title** document property field, change the font size to **10 pt.**, and apply **bold** formatting.

i. Click the **Close Header and Footer** button [*Header & Footer Tools Design* tab, *Close* group].

11. Review the document to ensure correct page numbering.
    a. There should be no header or footer on the cover page of the document.
    b. The table of contents page should be numbered "1" in the footer on the left with the title of the report following the page number.
    c. The first body page of the report should be numbered "2" in the footer on the right with the company name preceding the page number.
    d. Each subsequent page should be numbered consecutively with odd and even footers.

12. Create a sharing link to share this file with your instructor.
    a. Save this document on *OneDrive* if you haven't already. If you don't have the ability to save to *OneDrive*, skip all of step 12.
    b. Click the **Share** button in the upper right of the Word window. The *Share* pane opens on the right (Figure 3-92).
    c. Click **Get a sharing link** at the bottom of the *Share* pane.
    d. Click the **Create an edit link** button (Figure 3-93).
    e. Click **Copy** to copy the edit link.
    f. Use your email account to create a new email to your instructor.
    g. Include an appropriate subject line and a brief message in the body.
    h. Press **Ctrl+V** to paste the link to your document in the body of the email and send the email message.

13. Return to the Word document and click the **X** in the upper right corner of the *Share* pane to close it.

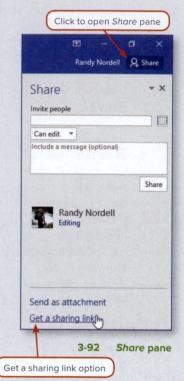

Click to open *Share* pane

3-92 *Share* pane

Get a sharing link option

3-93 Create an edit link

14. Save and close the document (Figure 3-94).

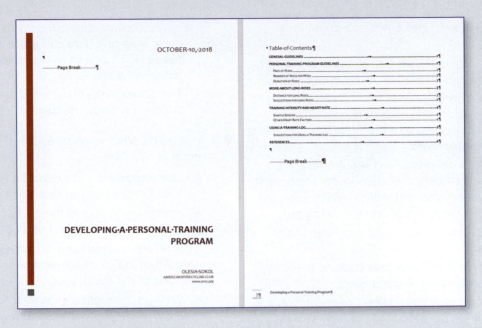

3-94 PP W3-3 completed (pages 1-4 of 7)

Chapter Summary

3.1 Insert, review, edit, and customize comments (p. W3-134).

- You can use **comments** to insert a note or provide feedback in a document without changing the content or format of the document.
- Users can add, edit, or delete comments. Comments appear to the right of the document in the **Markup area**.
- Comments are numbered sequentially in a document and are associated with a Microsoft Office **user name** and **initials**, which you can customize in the *Word Options* dialog box.
- Multiple reviewers can add comments to a document.
- Use the **Next** and **Previous** buttons to review the comments in the document.
- When you place your pointer on a comment, a tag provides details about the user name and date and time of the comment.
- You can delete comments individually or delete all comments in the document.

3.2 Modify and review a document using *Track Changes* and share an online document (p. W3-137).

- **Track Changes** is a collaboration tool that allows reviewers to make and track changes made in a document.
- There are four different **Display for Review views** to display changes in a document: **All Markup**, **Simple Markup**, **No Markup**, and **Original**.
- When *Track Changes* is on, each change is attributed to a reviewer and his or her user name.
- You can review changes using the **Previous** and **Next** buttons.
- You can accept or reject individual changes in the document, or you can accept or reject all of the changes in the document.
- The **Reviewing pane**, which can be displayed vertically on the left side of the document or horizontally at the bottom of the document, displays all of the changes in the document.
- You can customize which markups display in the document.
- Use the *Track Changes Options* dialog box to customize how tracked changes appear in your document.

- You can share online files with others, and more than one user can edit an online file at the same time, which allows **real-time collaboration** on documents.
- The **Share pane** provides different options for sharing an online document.

3.3 Insert and edit footnotes and endnotes in a document (p. W3-144).

- Use **footnotes** and **endnotes** to include additional information or reference sources.
- Footnotes appear at the bottom of the page and endnotes appear at the end of the document.
- A **reference marker** is a number, letter, or symbol that indicates a footnote or endnote in the body of the document.
- Change the location, number format, and starting number for footnotes and endnotes in the *Footnote and Endnote* dialog box.
- Word styles control the format of footnotes and endnotes. Change these styles to modify how your footnote and endnote text appears in the document.
- Convert footnotes to endnotes or endnotes to footnotes using the **Convert Notes** dialog box.
- Move footnotes and endnotes using the drag and drop method or using cut and paste.
- When you delete a footnote or endnote reference marker in the body of the document, the associated footnote and endnote text is also deleted. Footnotes and endnotes automatically renumber if one is deleted or inserted.

3.4 Create a bibliography with properly formatted sources and insert citations in a document (p. W3-149).

- A **source** is the complete bibliographic information for a reference (e.g., book, web page, journal article) used in a report.
- A **citation** is the abbreviated source information used in the body of a report.
- The **bibliography style** controls the format of the sources on the bibliography page and citations in the body of the document.
- Add a **placeholder** to temporarily mark a citation in the body of a report.
- Use the **Source Manager** dialog box to create and edit sources, edit placeholders, and view available sources.

- Insert a *bibliography* or *works cited* page to list the sources in your document.

3.5 Create and edit a table of contents based on headings in a document (p. W3-161).

- Word can automatically generate a *table of contents* for a document.
- *Heading styles* (e.g., Heading 1, Heading 2) determine the content for a table of contents.
- You can use built-in table of contents formats or customize the format of the table of contents.
- Use the *Table of Contents* dialog box to customize the format and the number of levels displayed in the table of contents.
- When document headings or pagination change, you can automatically update the table of contents to reflect these changes.

3.6 Insert a cover page and modify content and content control fields (p. W3-164).

- There are a variety of built-in *cover pages* available to add to your documents.
- A cover page has graphics, colors, text boxes, and Word fields that you can customize. The document theme controls the colors and fonts on the cover page.

- Use *document property* and *content control fields* to display information on the cover page. You can customize or delete this content.

3.7 Apply and customize headers and footers in a multipage document (p. W3-167).

- *Headers* and *footers* provide information and page numbers in a document. Headers are located at the top and footers are located at the bottom of a document.
- *Page* and *section breaks* control pagination and page numbering in a document.
- You can insert a variety of built-in headers, footers, and page numbers into a document.
- You can customize content and page numbering in headers and footers.
- *Different first page* headers and footers allow you to include different information on the first page of a document.
- *Use odd and even page* headers and footers to display different information on odd and even pages in a document.
- Change the page number format and starting page number in the *Page Number Format* dialog box.

Check for Understanding

The SIMbook for this text (within your SIMnet account) provides the following resources for concept review:

- Multiple choice questions
- Matching exercises
- Short answer questions

Guided Project 3-1

For this project, you customize the *Online Learning Plan* for Sierra Pacific Community College District. You review comments and tracked changes, add document properties, apply styles, create a table of contents, insert and modify footnotes, insert headers and footers, and add a customized cover page. [**Student Learning Outcomes 3.1, 3.2, 3.3, 3.5, 3.6, 3.7**]

File Needed: **OnlineLearningPlan-03.docx** *(Student data files are available in the* Library *of your SIMnet account)*
Completed Project File Name: *[your initials]* **Word 3-1.docx**

Skills Covered in this Project

- Modify user name and initials.
- Reject and accept tracked changes.
- Reply to a comment and resolve a comment.
- Customize document properties.
- Apply styles to selected text.
- Insert page breaks.

- Insert a table of contents.
- Insert footnotes.
- Modify footnote number format.
- Insert built-in page numbers and document property fields in the footer.
- Insert a cover page and remove and add document property fields.
- Update a table of contents.

1. Open the **OnlineLearningPlan-03** document from your student data files.
2. Save this document as [your initials] Word 3-1.
3. Change user name and initials.
   a. Click the **Tracking** launcher [*Review* tab, *Tracking* group] to open the *Track Changes Options* dialog box.
   b. Click the **Change User Name** button to open the *Word Options* dialog box.
   c. In the *Personalize your copy of Microsoft Office* area, type your first and last name in the *User name* text box.
   d. Type your first and last initials in lowercase letters in the *Initials* text box.
   e. Check the **Always use these values regardless of sign in to Office** box.
   f. Click **OK** to close the *Word Options* dialog box and click **OK** to close the *Track Changes Options* dialog box.
4. Display the *Reviewing* pane and reject changes.
   a. Click the **Display for Review** drop-down list [*Review* tab, *Tracking* group] and select **All Markup** to view the document with comments and proposed changes visible.
   b. Click the **Reviewing Pane** drop-down arrow [*Review* tab, *Tracking* group] and select **Reviewing Pane Vertical**. The *Reviewing* pane displays on the left side of the Word window.
   c. In the *Reviewing* pane, find where "Hasmik Kumar Deleted **Television or Tele-Web Course—**."
   d. Right-click this deletion and select **Reject Deletion** from the context menu (Figure 3-95).
   e. Click the **X** in the upper right corner of the *Reviewing* pane to close it.

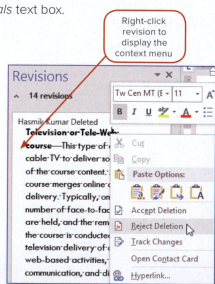

Right-click revision to display the context menu

3-95 Reject a deletion in the *Reviewing* pane

5. Accept changes in the document.
   a. Move to the top of the document (**Ctrl+Home**).
   b. Click the **Next** button [*Review* tab, *Changes* group] to select the first change.
   c. Click the top half of the **Accept** button [*Review* tab, *Changes* group] to accept the change and move to the next change.
   d. Click the top half of the **Accept** button again to accept the next change.
   e. Click the bottom half of the **Accept** button and select **Accept All Changes** from the drop-down list (Figure 3-96). All of the remaining changes in the document are accepted. Only comments are remaining in the *Markup* area.

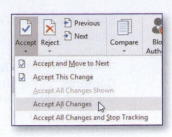

3-96 Accept all changes in the document

6. Reply to a comment, resolve a comment, and delete a comment.
   a. Move to the top of the document and click the **Next** button [*Review* tab, *Comments* group] to move to the first comment.
   b. Click the **Reply** button on the comment in the *Markup* area.
   c. Type Done!
   d. Click the **Resolve** button on the comment in the *Markup* area (Figure 3-97). The comment and reply becomes grayed out.
   e. Click the **Next** button [*Review* tab, *Comments* group] to move to the second comment (not the reply to the first comment).
   f. Click the top half of the **Delete** button [*Review* tab, *Comments* group] to delete the comment.
   g. Click the **Display for Review** drop-down list [*Review* tab, *Tracking* group] and select **No Markup** so comments are not visible.

3-97 *Resolve* **button on a comment**

7. Add document properties.
   a. Click the **File** tab to open the *Backstage* view.
   b. Click **Show All Properties** in the *Properties* area.
   c. Add the following document properties:

   Title: Online Learning Plan
   Company: Sierra Pacific Community College District
   Manager: Hasmik Kumar

   d. Click the **Back** arrow to return to the document.

8. Apply styles to the document.
   a. Go to the first page of the document, select the title (**"Online Learning Plan"**), and apply the **Title** style.
   b. Select the subtitle (**"Sierra Pacific Community College District"**) and apply the **Subtitle** style.
   c. Apply the **Heading 1** style to all of the main headings (those in all caps and bold) in the document.
   d. Apply the **Heading 2** style to all subheadings (those underlined) in the document.

9. Insert a table of contents into the report.
   a. Click in front of the first main heading in the document ("Purpose of this Plan") and press **Ctrl+Enter** to insert a page break.
   b. On the new first page of the document, place the insertion point directly after the subtitle and press **Enter**.
   c. Click the **Table of Contents** button [*References* tab, *Table of Contents* group] (Figure 3-98).

d. Select **Automatic Table 2**. The table of contents displays below the subtitle.
e. Select the words **"Table of Contents"** in the table of contents and apply **Black, Text 1** font color.
f. If there is a blank line between the subtitle and "Table of Contents," delete it.

10. Insert footnotes into the document.
a. Go to the second page of the document and position the insertion point after "Web-Enhanced course" and before the dash.
b. Click the **Insert Footnote** button [*References* tab, *Footnotes* group]. A footnote reference marker is inserted after the text and the insertion point is positioned at the bottom of the page in the *Footnotes* area.
c. Type This is a non-OL course that uses OL tools. in the footnote area.
d. On the second page of the document, position the insertion point after "(OL)" and before the space (first body paragraph, second sentence).
e. Click the **Insert Footnote** button and type Online learning is referred to as OL throughout this report. in the footnote area. This footnote becomes footnote 1 and the other footnote automatically becomes number 2.

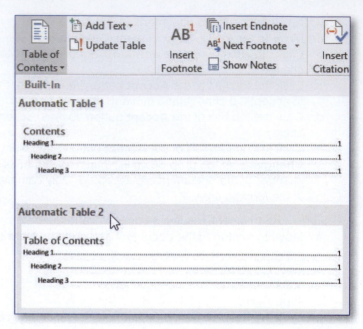

3-98 Insert table of contents

11. Modify footnote number format.
a. Click the **Footnotes** launcher to open the *Footnote and Endnote* dialog box (Figure 3-99).
b. Select **i, ii, iii**, . . . from the *Number format* drop-down list.
c. Click **Apply** to close the dialog box and apply the number format change.

12. Insert and modify content in the footer.
a. Press **Ctrl+Home** to move to the top of the document.
b. Click the **Footer** button [*Insert* tab, *Header & Footer* group] and select **Edit Footer**.
c. Click the **Document Info** button [*Header & Footer Tools Design* tab, *Insert* group] and select **Document Title** from the drop-down list to insert the *Title* document property field.
d. Press the **right arrow** once to deselect the document property field and press **Tab** to move to the center preset tab stop.
e. Click the **Document Info** button, select **Document Property**, and select **Company** from the drop-down list.
f. Press the **right arrow** once to deselect the document property field and press **Tab** to move to the right preset tab stop.

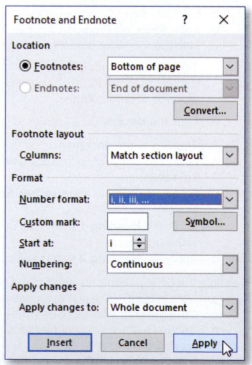

3-99 Modify footnote number format

g. Click the **Page Number** button [*Insert* tab, *Header & Footer* group], select **Current Position**, and select **Bold Numbers** from the drop-down list.

h. Select all of the text in the footer and change the font size to **10 pt**. (Figure 3-100).

3-100 Document properties and built-in page number inserted into the footer

i. Click the **Close Header and Footer** button [*Header & Footer Tools Design* tab, *Close* group].

13. Insert a page break.
   a. Position the insertion point before the last subheading ("How are Courses and Programs Selected for Online Learning Delivery?") on page 2 of the report.
   b. Press **Ctrl+Enter** to insert a page break.

14. Insert a cover page and modify content control fields.
   a. Press **Ctrl+Home** to move to the top of the document.
   b. Click the **Cover Page** button [*Insert* tab, *Pages* group].
   c. Select the **Retrospect** built-in cover page from the drop-down list. The cover page is inserted before the first page of the document.
   d. Click the **Subtitle** ("Document Subtitle") content control field handle and press **Delete** (Figure 3-101).
   e. Click the **Author** content control field handle and press **Delete**.
   f. With the insertion point on the blank line where the *Author* field was deleted, click the **Quick Parts** button [*Insert* tab, *Text* group].
   g. Select **Document Property** and select **Manager** from the drop-down list.
   h. Apply **bold** formatting to the *Company* document property field.
   i. Type www.spccd.edu in the *Address* ("Company Address") field. The web address displays in all caps; you will fix this in the next step.
   j. Select the **Address** document property field, open the *Font* dialog box, deselect the **All caps** check box, and click **OK**. The web address changes to lowercase (Figure 3-102).

3-101 Select and delete content control field

3-102 Document property fields modified on the cover page

15. Update the table of contents.
    a. Click in the table of contents.
    b. Click the **Update Table** button [*References* tab, *Table of Contents* group]. The *Update Table of Contents* dialog box opens (Figure 3-103).
    c. Select the **Update entire table** radio button.
    d. Click **OK** to close the dialog box and update the table.

16. Save and close the document (Figure 3-104).

3-103 *Update Table of Contents* **dialog box**

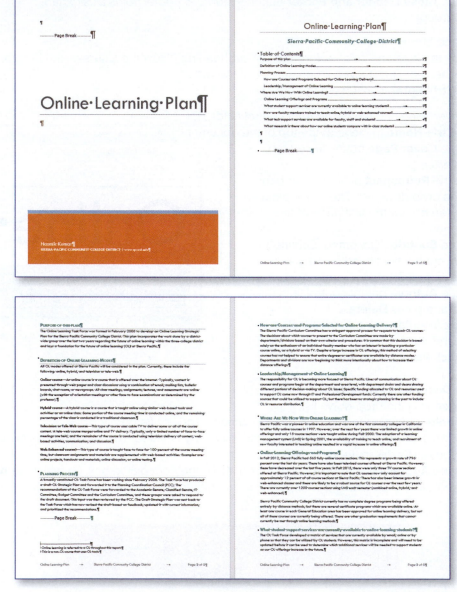

3-104 Word 3-1 completed (pages 1-4 of 6)

Guided Project 3-2

For this project, you create a multipage insurance renewal letter that Central Sierra Insurance will send on behalf of Valley Custom Manufacturing. You review comments and tracked changes, use *Track Changes*, format this document as a business letter, insert a document property field, insert and customize header content, use footnotes and endnotes, and insert a page and section break.
[Student Learning Outcomes 3.1, 3.2, 3.3, 3.7]

File Needed: ***ValleyCustomManufacturing-03.docx*** *(Student data files are available in the Library of your SIMnet account)*
Completed Project File Name: ***[your initials] Word 3-2.docx***

Skills Covered in this Project

- Review tracked changes and comments.
- Use *Track Changes*.
- Change *Display for Review* view.
- Format the document as a block format business letter.
- Insert a next page section break.
- Change margins and header location on a section of a document.
- Use a different first page header.

- Insert a document property, date, and page number in the header.
- Format the page number in the header.
- Apply a bottom border.
- Insert footnotes.
- Convert footnotes to endnotes and change number format.
- Insert a page break to control pagination.
- Accept tracked changes.
- Share a document.

1. Open the ***ValleyCustomManufacturing-03*** document from your student data files.

2. Save this document as [your initials] Word 3-2.

3. Review a comment, accept tracked changes, and delete a comment.
   a. Click the **Display for Review** drop-down list [*Review* tab, *Tracking* group] and select **All Markup**.
   b. Read the comment in the *Markup* area at the top of the document and review the tracked changes in the document.
   c. Click the **Next** button [*Review* tab, *Changes* group] to move to the first tracked change (not comment).
   d. Click the bottom half of the **Accept** button [*Review* tab, *Changes* group] and select **Accept and Move to Next**.
   e. Click the bottom half of the **Accept** button and select **Accept All Changes**.
   f. Click the bottom half of the **Delete** button [*Review* tab, *Comments* group] and select **Delete All Comments in Document**.

4. Change user name and initials.
   a. Click the **Tracking** launcher [*Review* tab, *Tracking* group] to open the *Track Changes Options* dialog box.
   b. Click the **Change User Name** button to open the *Word Options* dialog box.
   c. In the *Personalize your copy of Microsoft Office* area, type your first and last name in the *User name* text box.
   d. Type your first and last initials in lowercase letters in the *Initials* text box.
   e. Check the **Always use these values regardless of sign in to Office** box.
   f. Click **OK** to close the *Word Options* dialog box and click **OK** to close the *Track Changes Options* dialog box.

5. Turn on *Track Changes* and format the first page of the document as a block format business letter.
   a. Click the **Track Changes** button [*Review* tab, *Tracking* group] to turn on *Track Changes* and turn on **Show/Hide**. All of the changes you make will be tracked.
   b. Place your insertion point in front of "LIABILITY" on the first page.
   c. Click the **Breaks** button [*Layout* tab, *Page Setup* group] and select **Next Page** section break from the drop-down list.
   d. Move to the last blank line on the first page (in front of the section break), type Sincerely, and press **Enter** four times.
   e. Type Jennie Owings, Vice President and press **Enter** once.
   f. Type Central Sierra Insurance and press **Enter** two times.
   g. Type your initials in lowercase letters with no spaces or punctuation and press **Enter**. Word automatically capitalizes the first letter of your initials. Use the **smart tag** to undo automatic capitalization (Figure 3-105).

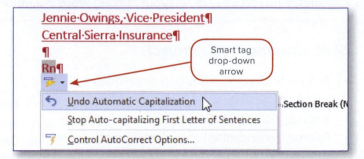

   h. Type Enclosure on the line after your reference initials.
   i. Press **Ctrl+Home** to go to the top of the document and press **Enter** four times.

3-105 Use the smart tag to undo automatic capitalization

   j. Place the insertion point on the first blank line at the top and click the **Date & Time** button [*Insert* tab, *Text* group]. The *Date and Time* dialog box opens.
   k. Select the date in proper business letter format (e.g., January 1, 2018), check the **Update automatically** box, and click **OK** to close the dialog box and insert the date.
   l. Select the dateline and apply **24 pt**. *Before* paragraph spacing.

6. Modify the margins and header position in the second section of the document.
   a. Place your insertion point in the second section of the document (page 2 or 3).
   b. Click the **Margins** button [*Layout* tab, *Page Setup* group] and select **Custom Margins** from the drop-down list. The *Page Setup* dialog box opens.
   c. Change the *Top* margin to **1.5"** and the *Left* and *Right* margins to **1.25"**.
   d. Click the **Layout** tab (Figure 3-106).
   e. In the *Headers and footers* area, change the *From edge Header* setting to **1"**.
   f. Click the **Apply to** drop-down list and select **This section**.
   g. Click **OK** to close the dialog box and apply the settings.

7. Insert header content on the second and continuing pages.
   a. Press **Ctrl+Home** to move to the top of the document.

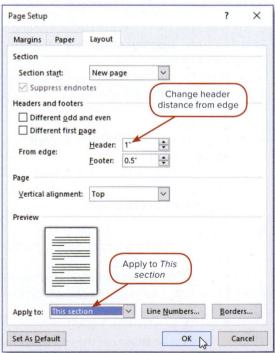

3-106 Change header position in this section of the document

b. Click the **Header** button [*Insert* tab, *Header & Footer* group] and select **Edit Header** from the drop-down list.

c. Check the **Different First Page** box [*Header & Footer Tools Design* tab, *Options* group].

d. Click the **Next** button [*Header & Footer Tools Design* tab, *Navigation* group] to move to the header in section 2.

e. Click the **Document Info** button [*Header & Footer Tools Design* tab, *Insert* group] and select **Document Title**.

f. Press the **right arrow** on the keyboard to deselect the document property field and press **Enter**.

g. Click the **Date & Time** button [*Header & Footer Tools Design* tab, *Insert* group]. The *Date and Time* dialog box opens.

h. Select the date in proper business letter format (e.g., January 1, 2018), check the **Update automatically** check box, and click **OK** to close the dialog box and insert the date.

i. Leave the header open for the next instructions.

8. Insert page number in the header and format page number.

a. With the header still open, press **Enter** after the date.

b. Type Page and **space** once.

c. Click the **Page Number** button [*Header & Footer Tools Design* tab, *Header & Footer* group], click **Current Position**, and select **Plain Number** from the drop-down list of page number options.

d. Click the **Page Number** button and select **Format Page Numbers** to open the *Page Number Format* dialog box (Figure 3-107).

e. Click the **Start at** radio button in the *Page numbering* area and change the page number to **2**.

f. Click **OK** to close the dialog box.

g. Place the insertion point after the page number and press **Enter** two times.

h. Select the page number line, click the **Borders** drop-down list [*Home* tab, *Paragraph* group], and select **Bottom Border**.

i. Click the **Close Header and Footer** button [*Header & Footer Tools Design* tab, *Close* group]. The header appears on the second and continuing pages.

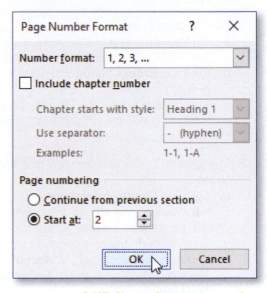

3-107 Change *Start at* page number

9. Insert footnotes.

a. Go to page 4 and place the insertion point after the period at the end of the last line of text (after "reports are included.").

b. Click the **Insert Footnote** button [*References* tab, *Footnotes* group].

c. Type A list of drivers was faxed as a separate attachment. in the footnotes area.

d. Go to the first page and place the insertion point after the period at the end of the fourth body paragraph (after "2018 renewal.").

e. Click the **Insert Footnote** button and type Inflation is anticipated to be 2 percent. in the footnotes area.

10. Convert footnotes to endnotes and change number format.

a. Click the **Footnotes** launcher to open the *Footnote and Endnote* dialog box.

b. Click the **Convert** button. The *Convert Notes* dialog box opens (Figure 3-108).

c. Select the **Convert all footnotes to endnotes** radio button and click **OK** to close the *Convert Notes* dialog box.

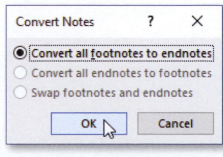

3-108 Convert footnotes to endnotes

d. Click **Close** to close the *Footnote and Endnote* dialog box.
e. Click the **Footnotes** launcher again to open the *Footnote and Endnote* dialog box (Figure 3-109).
f. Select the **Endnotes** radio button if it is not selected.
g. Click the **Number format** drop-down list and select **a, b, c, ...**
h. Click the **Apply changes to** drop-down list and select **Whole document**.
i. Click **Apply** to close the dialog box and apply the changes.

11. Insert a page break.
a. Go to page 2 and place the insertion point in front of the "PROPERTY" heading.
b. Click the **Breaks** button [*Layout* tab, *Page Setup* group].
c. Select **Page** in the *Page Breaks* area. A page break is inserted, and the "PROPERTY" heading and following text are moved to page 3.

12. Change *Display for Review* view and accept all tracked changes.
a. Click the **Display for Review** drop-down list [*Review* tab, *Tracking* group] and select **Simple Markup**. A red line on the left indicates where changes were made.
b. Scroll through the four pages to review the document.
c. Click the bottom half of the **Accept** button [*Review* tab, *Tracking* group] and select **Accept All Changes and Stop Tracking**.

13. Share the document with your instructor.
a. Save this document on *OneDrive* if you haven't already. If you don't have the ability to save to *OneDrive*, skip all of step 13.
b. Click the **Share** button in the upper right of the Word window to open the *Share* pane (Figure 3-110).
c. Type your instructor's email address in the *Invite people* text box.
d. Select **Can edit** in the drop-down list below the email address.
e. Type a brief message to your instructor and click the **Share** button.
f. Click the **X** in the upper right corner of the *Share* pane to close it.

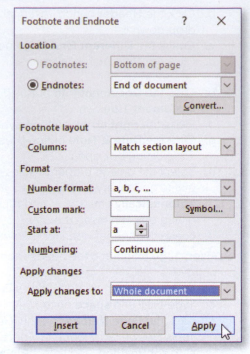

3-109 Change endnote number format

3-110 Share a document

14. Save and close the document (Figure 3-111).

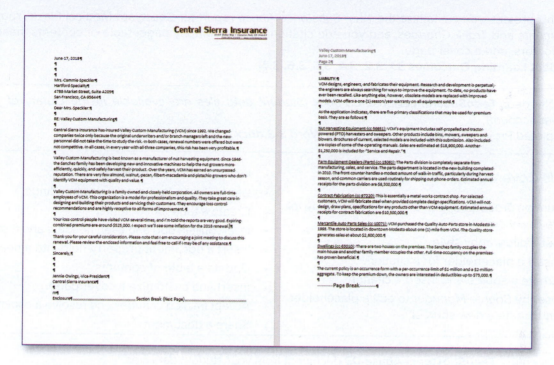

Guided Project 3-3

For this project, you customize the *Teen Substance Abuse* report for Courtyard Medical Plaza. You use *Comments* and *Track Changes*, and you add citations, a bibliography page, table of contents, headers and footers, and a cover page.
[**Student Learning Outcomes 3.1, 3.2, 3.4, 3.5, 3.6, 3.7**]

File Needed: ***TeenSubstanceAbuse-03.docx*** *(Student data files are available in the* Library *of your SIMnet account)*
Completed Project File Name: ***[your initials] Word 3-3.docx***

Skills Covered in this Project

- Turn on *Track Changes* and change *Display for Review* view.
- Set bibliography style.
- Insert a placeholder for a citation.
- Create a source and insert a citation.
- Use the *Source Manager* to edit a placeholder and create a new source.

- Insert a bibliography page.
- Use styles to format title and headings.
- Create a table of contents.
- Insert built-in odd and even headers and footers.
- Insert a document property field into a header.
- Update a table of contents.
- Insert and customize a cover page.
- Accept tracked changes and resolve a comment.
- Share a document.

1. Open the ***TeenSubstanceAbuse-03*** document from your student data files.
2. Save this document as [your initials] Word 3-3.
3. Change user name and initials.
   a. Click the **Tracking** launcher [*Review* tab, *Tracking* group] to open the *Track Changes Options* dialog box.
   b. Click the **Change User Name** button to open the *Word Options* dialog box.
   c. In the *Personalize your copy of Microsoft Office* area, type your first and last name in the *User name* text box.
   d. Type your first and last initials in lowercase letters in the *Initials* text box.
   e. Check the **Always use these values regardless of sign in to Office** box.
   f. Click **OK** to close the *Word Options* dialog box and click **OK** to close the *Track Changes Options* dialog box.
4. Turn on *Track Changes* and change the *Display for Review* view.
   a. Click the **Track Changes** button [*Review* tab, *Tracking* group] to turn on *Track Changes* and turn on **Show/Hide**. All of the changes you make will be tracked.
   b. Click the **Display for Review** drop-down list [*Review* tab, *Tracking* group] and select **Simple Markup**. Tracked changes are indicated by a red line on the left.
5. Select the report style and insert placeholders for a citation.
   a. Click the **Style** drop-down list [*References* tab, *Citations & Bibliography* group].
   b. Select **Chicago Sixteenth Edition**.
   c. On the first page in the "What Problems Can Teen Substance Abuse Cause?" section, place the insertion point at the end of the last sentence in the second paragraph ("unsafe substances") and before the period.
   d. Click the **Insert Citation** button [*References* tab, *Citations & Bibliography* group] and select **Add New Placeholder**. The *Placeholder Name* dialog box opens.
   e. Type Foundation and click **OK**. The placeholder for the citation displays in the report.
   f. On the second page in the "Can Teen Substance Use And Abuse Be Prevented?" section, place the insertion point at the end of the last sentence in the first paragraph ("and drugs") and before the period.

g. Click the **Insert Citation** button and select the **Foundation** placeholder from the drop-down list (Figure 3-112).

6. Insert a citation into the report.

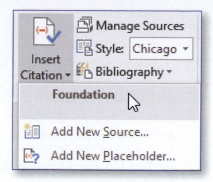

a. On the first page in the "What Is Teen Substance Abuse?" section, place the insertion point at the end of the last sentence in the second paragraph ("most often") and before the period.

b. Click the **Insert Citation** button and select **Add New Source**. The *Create Source* dialog box opens (Figure 3-113).

3-112 Insert placeholder for a citation

c. Check the **Show All Bibliography Fields** box and create a new source with the following information:

Type of Source: **Journal Article**
Author: Kelly L. Sanchez
Title: Examining High School Drug Use
Journal Name: Journal of Secondary Education
Year: 2015
Pages: 22-26
Volume: XXI
Issue: 2
Tag Name: Sanchez

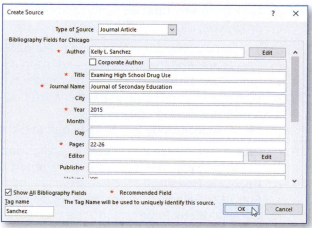

d. Click **OK** to close the dialog box and insert the citation. The citation is inserted into the report.

3-113 *Create Source* dialog box

7. Use the *Source Manager* to create a new source and provide source information for a placeholder.

a. Click the **Manage Sources** button [*References* tab, *Citations & Bibliography* group] to open the *Source Manager* dialog box.

b. In the *Current List* area, select the **Foundation** placeholder and click **Edit**. The *Edit Source* dialog box opens.

c. Use the following information to edit the placeholder source:

Type of Source: **Web site**
Corporate Author: Foundation for Teen Health
Name of Web Page: Making Good Choices
Year: 2014
Year Accessed: 2016
Month Accessed: June
Day Accessed: 25
URL: http://www.foundationforteenhealth.org/choices.htm

d. Click **OK** to close the dialog box and update the placeholders. The placeholders in the report are updated with the proper citation from the source information.

e. With the *Source Manager* dialog box still open, click the **New** button. The *Create Source* dialog box opens.

f. Create a new source with the following information:

Type of Source: **Document From Web site**
Corporate Author: Courtyard Medical Plaza
Name of Web Page: Teen Mental Health
Name of Web Site: Courtyard Medical Plaza

Year: 2016
Month: March
Day: 6
URL: http://www.cmp.com/Teen_Mental_Health.pdf
Tag Name: CMP

    g. Click **OK** to close the dialog box and click **Close** to close the *Source Manager* dialog box.

8. Insert citations into the report.
   a. On the first page in the "Why Do Teens Abuse Drugs And Alcohol?" section, place the insertion point at the end of the last sentence in the second paragraph ("increased risk") and before the period.
   b. Click the **Insert Citation** button and select the **Courtyard Medical Plaza** citation from the drop-down list.
   c. On the second page in the "What Should You Do If You Find Out That Your Teen Is Using?" section, place the insertion point at the end of the last sentence in the second paragraph ("or both") and before the period.
   d. Click the **Insert Citation** button and select the **Sanchez, Kelly L**. citation from the drop-down list.

9. Insert a bibliography page at the end of the document.
   a. Press **Ctrl+End** to move to the end of the document.
   b. Press **Ctrl+Enter** to insert a page break.
   c. With the insertion point on the blank last page, click the **Bibliography** button [*References* tab, *Citations & Bibliography* group].
   d. Select **Bibliography** to insert the built-in bibliography into the document.

10. Apply styles to the title and section headings and insert a table of contents.
    a. Apply the **Title** style to the title of the report on the first page.
    b. Apply the **Heading 1** style to each of the bold section headings in the report.
    c. Press **Ctrl+Home** to move the insertion point to the beginning of the report.
    d. Click the **Blank Page** button [*Insert* tab, *Pages* group] to insert a blank page before the first page of the report.
    e. Place your insertion point at the top of the new first page, type Teen Substance Abuse, and press **Enter**. The text should be formatted as *Title* style. If it's not, apply the **Title** style.
    f. Click the **Table of Contents** button [*References* tab, *Table of Contents* group] and select **Automatic Table 1** from the drop-down list. The table of contents is inserted below the title.

11. Insert odd and even page headers and customize content.
    a. With the insertion point still on the first page, click the **Header** button [*Insert* tab, *Header & Footer* group].
    b. Select **Motion (Odd Page)** from the drop-down list of built-in headers.
    c. Delete the existing text to the left of the page number.
    d. Click the **Document Info** button, click **Document Property**, and select **Company** from the drop-down list.
    e. Delete the page number in the colored bar in the header and place the insertion point on the blank line below the text in the header.
    f. Check the **Different Odd & Even Pages** check box [*Header & Footer Tools Design* tab, *Options* group] (Figure 3-114).

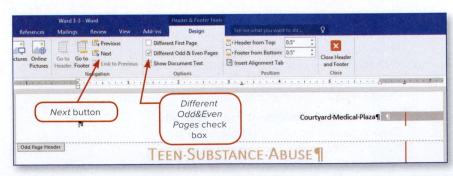

3-114 Odd page header inserted and content customized

g. Click the **Next** button to move to the *Even Page Header*.

h. Click the **Header** button [*Header & Footer Tools Design* tab, *Header & Footer* group] and select **Motion (Even Page)** from the drop-down list.

i. Delete the page number in the colored bar in the header and leave the header open.

12. Insert odd and even page footers.

a. With the *Even Page Header* still open, click the **Go to Footer** button [*Header & Footer Tools Design* tab, *Navigation* group] to move to the *Even Page Footer*.

b. Click the **Page Number** button [*Header & Footer* group], click **Bottom of Page**, and select **Brackets 2**.

c. Click the **Previous** button [*Navigation* group] to move to the *Odd Page Footer*.

d. Click the **Page Number** button [*Header & Footer* group], click **Bottom of Page**, and select **Brackets 2**.

e. Click the **Close Header and Footer** button [*Close* group].

13. Insert page breaks to control page endings.

a. Go to page 2, click in front of the last section heading ("What Are The Signs Of Substance Abuse"), and insert a **page break**.

b. Go to page 3, click in front of the last section heading ("Can Teen Substance Use And Abuse Be Prevented"), and insert a **page break**.

14. Update the table of contents.

a. Click the table of contents on the first page.

b. Click the **Update Table** button at the top of the content control field. The *Update Table of Contents* dialog box opens (Figure 3-115).

c. Select the **Update entire table** radio button and click **OK**.

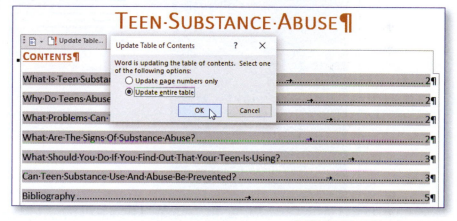

3-115 Update table of contents

15. Insert and customize a cover page.

a. Press **Ctrl+Home** to move to the top of the document.

b. Click the **Cover Page** button [*Insert* tab, *Pages* group].

c. Select the **Slice (Dark)** built-in cover page from the drop-down list. The cover page is inserted before the first page of the document.

d. Select the **Title** document property field, apply **Bold** formatting, and change the font size to **40 pt**.

e. Click the **Subtitle** content control field handle and press **Delete**.

f. Press **Ctrl+Home** to move the insertion point to the top of the cover page.

g. Click the **Quick Parts** button [*Insert* tab, *Text* group], select **Document Property**, and select **Company** from the drop-down list.

h. Select the **Company** document property field, apply **Bold** and **Small Caps** formatting, and change the font size to **24 pt**.

16. Review comments and track changes.

a. Click the **Display for Review** drop-down list [*Review* tab, *Tracking* group] and select **All Markup**.

b. Right-click the comment in the *Markup* area at the top of the third page and select **Resolve Comment**.

c. Click the bottom half of the **Accept** button and select **Accept All Changes and Stop Tracking**.

d. Click the **Display for Review** drop-down list [*Review* tab, *Tracking* group] and select **No Markup**.

17. Share the document with your instructor.
   a. Save this document on *OneDrive* if you haven't already. If you don't have the ability to save to *OneDrive*, skip all of step 17.
   b. Click the **Share** button in the upper right of the Word window to open the *Share* pane (Figure 3-116).
   c. Type your instructor's email address in the *Invite people* text box.
   d. Select **Can edit** in the drop-down list below the email address.
   e. Type a brief message to your instructor and click the **Share** button.
   f. Click the **X** in the upper right corner of the *Share* pane to close it.

18. Save and close the document (Figure 3-117).

3-116 Share a document

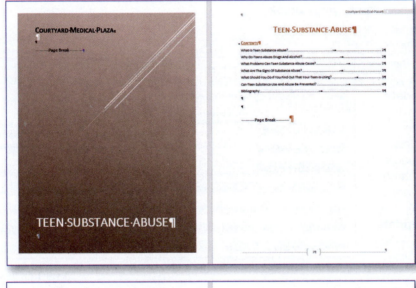

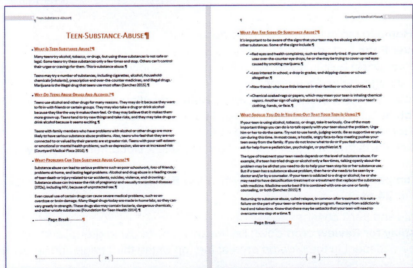

3-117 Word 3-3 completed (pages 1-4 of 6)

Independent Project 3-4

For this project, you modify the *Tips for Better Heart Rate Monitor Training* document from the American River Cycling Club. You use *Track Changes* and comments, insert and modify endnotes, insert placeholders, create sources, insert a bibliography page, insert a table of contents and cover page, and use custom headers and footers.
[Student Learning Outcomes 3.1, 3.2, 3.3, 3.4, 3.5, 3.6, 3.7]

File Needed: ***HeartRateMonitorTraining-03.docx*** *(Student data files are available in the* Library *of your SIMnet account)*
Completed Project File Name: ***[your initials] Word 3-4.docx***

Skills Covered in this Project

- Use comments and *Track Changes*.
- Insert endnotes.
- Insert a placeholder for a citation.
- Use the *Source Manager* to edit placeholders and create a new source.
- Change the bibliography style.
- Insert a bibliography page.

- Convert endnotes to footnotes.
- Insert a table of contents.
- Insert and modify a cover page.
- Insert custom headers and footers.
- Insert page breaks.
- Change footnote number format.
- Resolve a comment.
- Accept tracked changes.

1. Open the **HeartRateMonitorTraining-03** document from your student data files.
2. Save this document as [your initials] Word 3-4.
3. Change user name and initials.
   a. Open the *Track Changes Options* dialog box (**Tracking** launcher) and click the **Change User Name** button to open the *Word Options* dialog box.
   b. In the *Personalize your copy of Microsoft Office* area, type your first and last name in the *User name* text box and your first and last initials in lowercase letters in the *Initials* text box.
   c. Check the **Always use these values regardless of sign in to Office** box, click **OK** to close the *Word Options* dialog box, and click **OK** to close the *Track Changes Options* dialog box.
4. Turn on *Track Changes* and insert a comment.
   a. Turn on **Track Changes** and change the *Display for Review* view to **Simple Markup** if it is not already selected.
   b. Select the title, insert a **New Comment**, and type Insert endnotes, citations, a references page, a table of contents, and a cover page in the new comment.
   c. Click the **Show Comments** button to close the *Markup* area on the right and display only the comment balloon and not the comment text.
5. Insert endnotes.
   a. Insert an endnote at the end of the first body paragraph on the first page (after the period).
   b. Type See the References page for related book and articles. in the endnote area.
   c. Insert an endnote at the end of the paragraph (after the period) in the "Analyze Your Heart Rate Data" section on the first page.
   d. Type See the ARCC web site (www.arcc.org) for information about specific heart rate monitors. in the endnote area.
   e. Insert an endnote at the end of the second paragraph (after the period) in the "Comparing Heart Rate Values with Others" section on the second page.
   f. Type 220-age is an estimate of maximum heart rate. in the endnote area.
6. Insert placeholders for citations.
   a. Place the insertion point at the end of the second paragraph and before the period in the "Know Your Resting Heart Rate" section and insert a placeholder named **RoadCycling**.

b. Place the insertion point at the end of the second paragraph and before the period in the "Perform a Threshold Test" section and insert a placeholder named **Segura**.

c. Place the insertion point at the end of the body paragraph and before the period in the "Not Analyzing Heart Rate Data" section and insert a placeholder named **Wallace**.

7. Use the *Source Manager* dialog box to provide source information for the three placeholders. Check the **Show All Bibliography Fields** box, if necessary.

a. Edit the *RoadCycling* placeholder to include the following information.

Type of Source: **Document from Web site**
Corporate Author: Road Cycling
Name of Web Page: Training with a Heart Rate Monitor
Name of Web Site: RoadCycling.com
Year: 2015
Year Accessed: 2016
Month Accessed: August
Day Accessed: 25
URL: http://www.roadcycling.com/heart_rate.html

b. Edit the *Segura* placeholder to include the following information.
Type of Source: **Article in a Periodical**

Author: Manuel A. Segura
Title: Maximizing Threshold Training
Periodical Title: Cycling Weekly
Year: 2016
Month: March
Day: 1
Pages: 35-41

c. Edit the *Wallace* placeholder to include the following information.
Type of Source: **Book**
Author: Ingrid L. Wallace
Title: Understanding Heart Rate
Year: 2014
City: Chicago
Publisher: Penguin Books

8. Convert all endnotes to footnotes.

9. Change the bibliography style and insert a references page at the end of the document.
a. Change the bibliography style of the report to **APA**.
b. Place your insertion point on the blank line at the end of the document and insert a **page break**.
c. Insert the built-in **References** page on the last page.
d. **Center** the *References* heading and apply **10 pt**. *After* paragraph spacing.

10. Insert a table of contents.
a. Place the insertion point at the top of the document and insert a **page break**.
b. Place the insertion point at the top of the new first page and type Table of Contents.
c. Change the font size to **14 pt**., apply **bold** and **small caps** formatting, and press **Enter**.
d. Insert a **Custom Table of Contents** and use **Simple** format, show 2 levels of headings, show page numbers, right align page numbers, and use a dot tab leader.

11. Insert a cover page.
a. Insert the **Ion (Dark)** built-in cover page.
b. Select the **Year** field and choose the current date.
c. Select the **Title** field, change the font size to **44 pt**., apply **bold** formatting, and align **center**.
d. Delete the **Subtitle** and **Author** fields. Be sure to delete the entire fields, not just the text.
e. Select the **Company** field, change the font size to **12 pt**., and apply **bold** formatting.
f. Select the **Company Address** field and type www.arcc.org.

12. Insert a header and footer.
   a. Place the insertion point in the table of contents on the second page of the document.
   b. Edit the header, type Page, **space** once, and insert a plain page number in the current position.
   c. **Align Right** the header information (use **Align Right**, not a tab).
   d. Go to the footer on the second page, type American River Cycling Club on the left and www.arcc.org on the right (use tabs to align the text on the right).
   e. Apply a **solid line**, **Black, Text 1** color, ¾ **pt**. width, **top** and **bottom border** to the information in the footer.
   f. Change the font size of the information in the header and footer to **10 pt**.
   g. Close the header and footer. No header or footer should appear on the cover page.

13. Insert a **page break** before the "Analyze Your Heart Rate Data" and "Not Being Aware of Factors Affecting Heart Rate" headings.

14. Change the footnote number format to **A, B, C**.

15. Resolve a comment and accept all tracked changes.
   a. Click the **Show Comments** button to display comments.
   b. **Resolve** the comment near the top of the third page.
   c. Accept all changes in the document and stop tracking changes.
   d. Click the **Show Comments** button again so the text of the comment does not display.

16. **Update** the entire table of contents.

17. Save and close the document (Figure 3-118).

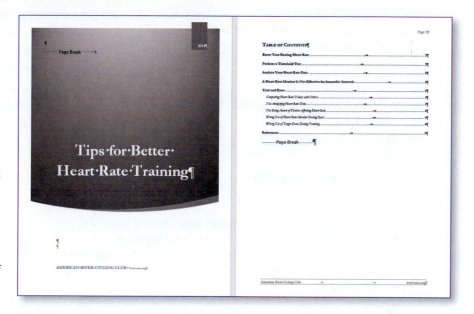

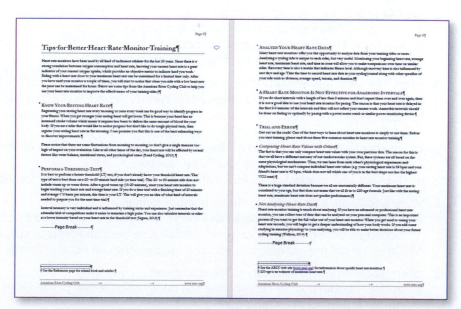

3-118 Word 3-4 completed (pages 1-4 of 6)

Independent Project 3-5

Sierra Pacific Community College District gives incoming college students a *Student Success Tips* document. For this project, you review comments and tracked changes, apply heading styles, and insert footnotes, placeholders, and a works cited page, table of contents, and cover page.
[**Student Learning Outcomes 3.1, 3.2, 3.3, 3.4, 3.5, 3.6, 3.7**]

File Needed: ***StudentSuccess-03.docx*** *(Student data files are available in the* Library *of your SIMnet account)*
Completed Project File Name: ***[your initials] Word 3-5.docx***

Skills Covered in this Project

- Review and delete a comment.
- Reject and accept tracked changes.
- Apply title and heading styles.
- Insert and modify footnotes.
- Insert a placeholder.
- Use the *Source Manager* to update a reference.
- Change the bibliography style.

- Insert a works cited page.
- Insert a table of contents.
- Use different odd and even page footers.
- Insert page numbers and a document property field into the footer.
- Insert and customize a cover page.
- Insert a page break.
- Update a table of contents.
- Share a document.

---

1. Open the ***StudentSuccess-03*** document from your student data files.

2. Save this document as [your initials] Word 3-5.

3. Review and delete selected comments and tracked changes.
   a. Change the *Display for Review* view to **All Markup**.
   b. Read the comment at top of the document and then **delete** the comment.
   c. Find the first tracked change in the document (left, right, and top margin changed) and **Reject Format Change**.
   d. Review the changes in the document and then **Accept All Changes** in the document.

4. Apply styles to the title and headings.
   a. Apply the **Title** style to the title on the first page.
   b. Apply the **Heading 1** style to all the bold headings
   c. Apply the **Heading 2** style to all the underlined headings.

5. Insert footnotes and apply text formatting.
   a. On the first page, insert a footnote after "Weekly Schedules" in the "Schedule Your Time" section.
   b. Type Weekly Schedules are available from your counselor or in the college bookstore. as the footnote text.
   c. Insert a footnote at the end of "Be sure to schedule your time for all these in your 119 hours." (after the period) in the "Schedule Your Time" section.
   d. Type Be sure to schedule recreational time in your 119 hours. as the footnote text.

6. Move a footnote and modify footnote number format.
   a. Select the first footnote reference marker (in the body) and move it so it appears after "Weekly Schedule" in the "Track Your Time" section (use drag and drop or cut and paste).
   b. Deselect the moved footnote and change the footnote number format to **a, b, c**.

7. Insert placeholders in the body of the document.
   a. In the "Introduction" section on the first page, insert a new placeholder named Navarro at the end of the body paragraph (and before the period).

b. In the "Test Anxiety" section on the second page, insert a new placeholder named Sierra at the end of the body paragraph (and before the period).

c. In the "Goal Setting" section on the fourth page, insert the Navarro placeholder (not a new place-holder) at the end of the intro paragraph (and before the period).

8. Use the *Source Manager* to update placeholder reference information.
   a. Open the *Source Manager* and edit the *Navarro* placeholder to include the following information. Check the **Show All Bibliography Fields** box, if necessary.

   Type of Source: **Book**
   Author: Tessa C. Navarro
   Title: Study Skills for College Students
   Year: 2017
   City: Chicago
   Publisher: McGraw-Hill

   b. Edit the *Sierra* placeholder to include the following information.

   Type of Source: **Document from Web site**
   Corporate Author: Sierra Pacific Community College District
   Name of Web Page: Tips for Student Success
   Name of Web Site: spccd.edu
   Year: 2016
   Year Accessed: 2016
   Month Accessed: September
   Day Accessed: 2
   URL: http://www.spccd.edu/tips4success.pdf

9. Change bibliography style and insert a works cited page.
   a. Change the bibliography style to **MLA**.
   b. Place your insertion point on the blank line at the end of the document and insert a **page break**.
   c. Insert a **Works Cited** page.

10. Insert a table of contents.
    a. Place your insertion point at the beginning of the document and insert a **page break**.
    b. Type Student Success Tips on the first line on the new first page (before the page break) and press **Enter**.
    c. On the blank line below "Student Success Tips," insert the **Automatic Table 1** table of contents.
    d. Apply the **Title** style to "Student Success Tips" on the new first page.

11. Insert a footer and add custom content.
    a. Edit the footer on the first page of the document (table of contents).
    b. Check the **Different Odd & Even Pages** box.
    c. Insert the **Accent Bar 2** from the *Page Number, Current Position* drop-down list.
    d. Press **Tab** two times and insert the **Document Title** (or **Title**) document property field.
    e. Go to the even page footer and insert the **Accent Bar 2** from the *Page Number, Current Position* drop-down list.
    f. Press **Tab** two times and insert the **Company** document property field.
    g. Change the font size to **10 pt**. and apply **bold** formatting to the footer content in both the even and odd page footers.
    h. Close the footer.

12. Insert and customize a cover page.
    a. Insert the **Slice (Light)** cover page.
    b. Delete the **Subtitle** ("Document subtitle") and **Course** ("Course title") document property fields.
    c. Change the font size of the title on the cover page to **40 pt**. and apply **bold** formatting.

13. Insert a **page break** before the "Physical Signs of Test Anxiety" heading.

14. Update the entire table of contents.

15. Share the document with your instructor.
    a. Save this document on *OneDrive* if you haven't already. If you don't have the ability to save to *OneDrive*, skip all of step 15.
    b. Click the **Share** button in the upper right of the Word window to open the *Share* pane.
    c. Type your instructor's email address in the *Invite people* text box.
    d. Select **Can edit** in the drop-down list below the email address.
    e. Type a brief message to your instructor and click the **Share** button.
    f. Click the **X** in the upper right corner of the *Share* pane to close it.

16. Save and close the document (Figure 3-119).

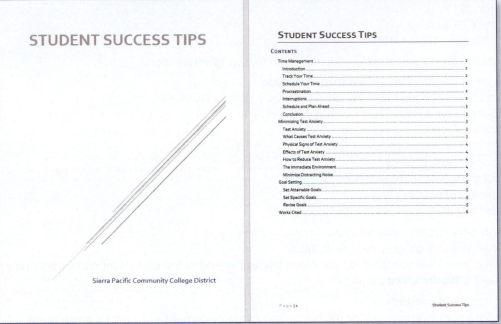

3-119 Word 3-5 completed (pages 1-4 of 7)

Independent Project 3-6

Courtyard Medical Plaza works closely with the Skiing Unlimited winter ski program. For this project, you modify the *Skiing Unlimited Training Guide* using *Track Changes* to include footnotes, a table of contents, cover page, and headers and footers.
[**Student Learning Outcomes 3.1, 3.2, 3.3, 3.5, 3.6, 3.7**]

File Needed: ***SkiingUnlimitedTrainingGuide-03.docx*** *(Student data files are available in the* Library *of your SIMnet account)*
Completed Project File Name: *[your initials]* **Word 3-6.docx**

Skills Covered in this Project

- Review and delete a comment.
- Change the *Display for Review* view.
- Modify a document using *Track Changes.*
- Change margins.
- Apply title and heading styles.
- Insert a custom table of contents.
- Insert a page number in the header.
- Insert a document property field into the footer.
- Insert page breaks.
- Insert a cover page.
- Customize cover page content and insert a document property field.
- Review and accept tracked changes.
- Update a table of contents.

1. Open the ***SkiingUnlimitedTrainingGuide-03*** document from your student data files.

2. Save this document as [your initials] Word 3-6.

3. Change user name and initials.
   a. Open the *Track Changes Options* dialog box (**Tracking** launcher) and click the **Change User Name** button to open the *Word Options* dialog box.
   b. In the *Personalize your copy of Microsoft Office* area, type your first and last name in the *User name* text box and your first and last initials in lowercase letters in the *Initials* text box.
   c. Check the **Always use these values regardless of sign in to Office** box, click **OK** to close the *Word Options* dialog box, and click **OK** to close the *Track Changes Options* dialog box.

4. Change *Display for Review* view, review and delete a comment, and turn on *Track Changes.*
   a. Change the *Display for Review* view to **All Markup** and review tracked changes in the document.
   b. Read the comment on the first page and then **delete** the comment.
   c. Turn on **Track Changes** and change the *Display for Review* view to **Simple Markup.**

5. Change the left and right margins to **1".**

6. Apply styles to the title and headings.
   a. Apply the **Title** style to the title on the first page.
   b. Apply the **Heading 1** style to all the bold headings.
   c. Apply the **Heading 2** style to all the underlined headings.
   d. Apply the **Heading 3** style to all the italicized headings.

7. Insert and customize footnotes.
   a. Insert a footnote after the "Skiing Procedures" heading on the first page.
   b. Type Skiing procedures vary depending on the clients' needs. as the footnote text.
   c. Insert a footnote after the "Guiding Techniques" heading on the second page.
   d. Type A minimum of two guides is required for all clients. as the footnote text.
   e. Change the footnote *Number format* to **A, B, C** and change *Numbering* to **Continuous.**

8. Insert a custom table of contents.
   a. Place your insertion point at the beginning of the document and insert a **page break**.
   b. Type Table of Contents on the first line on the new first page and press **Enter**.
   c. Apply the **Title** style to "Table of Contents" on the new first page.
   d. Place the insertion point on the blank line below the "Table of Contents" heading and before the page break.
   e. Insert a **Custom Table of Contents**, use **Fancy** format, show 2 levels of headings, show page numbers, right align page numbers, and do not include a tab leader.

9. Insert header and footer.
   a. On the first page (table of contents), insert the **Bold Numbers 3** built-in page number at the top of the page.
   b. Remove the extra line in the header.
   c. In the footer on the same page, insert the **Title** document property field on the left. Use the right arrow key to deselect the document property field.
   d. Insert the **Company** field on the right. Use tabs to align the field on the right.
   e. **Bold** the text in the footer and close the footer.

10. Insert page breaks to keep headings with the text below.
    a. Insert a **page break** before the "Beginning Wedge Christie Turns" heading (page 4).
    b. Insert a **page break** before the "Introduction to Equipment" heading (page 5).

11. Insert and modify a cover page.
    a. Insert the **Grid** cover page.
    b. Delete the **Subtitle** field.
    c. On the blank line between the *Title* and *Abstract* fields, insert the **Company** document property field.
    d. Delete the **Abstract** field.
    e. Select the **Company** document property field, change the font size to **20 pt.**, apply **bold** formatting, and change the text color to **Blue-Gray, Text 2**.

12. Change *Display for Review* view, accept tracked changes, and turn off **Track Changes**.
    a. Change the *Display for Review* view to **All Markup** and review the changes in the document.
    b. Turn off **Track Changes** and accept all tracked changes in the document.

13. Update the entire table of contents.

14. Save and close the document (Figure 3-120).

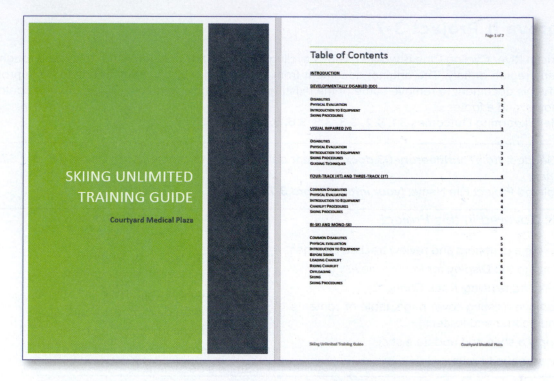

3-120 Word 3-6 completed (pages 1-4 of 8)

Improve It Project 3-7

American River Cycling Club is working with a cycling tour company to set up a trip to cycle through the Tuscany region of Italy. The original document from the cycling tour company needs to be improved. Modify this document to remove some of the existing content and add a cover page, table of contents, footnotes, and a footer.
[Student Learning Outcomes 3.1, 3.2, 3.3, 3.5, 3.6, 3.7]

File Needed: *ItalyTourItinerary-03.docx* (Student data files are available in the Library of your SIMnet account)
Completed Project File Name: *[your initials] Word 3-7.docx*

Skills Covered in this Project

- Delete a comment and review tracked changes.
- Change the *Display for Review* view.
- Make edits using *Track Changes*.
- Remove existing cover page, table of contents, and header and footer.
- Apply a style and update a style.
- Insert page breaks.

- Move and delete an endnote.
- Convert endnotes to footnotes.
- Insert and customize footnotes.
- Insert a custom table of contents.
- Edit document properties.
- Insert and modify a cover page.
- Insert custom footer content.
- Review and accept tracked changes.
- Share a document.

1. Open the *ItalyTourItinerary-03* document from your student data files.

2. Save this document as [your initials] Word 3-7.

3. Change user name and initials.
   a. Open the *Track Changes Options* dialog box (**Tracking** launcher) and click the **Change User Name** button to open the *Word Options* dialog box.
   b. In the *Personalize your copy of Microsoft Office* area, type your first and last name in the *User name* text box and your first and last initials in lowercase letters in the *Initials* text box.
   c. Check the **Always use these values regardless of sign in to Office** box, click **OK** to close the *Word Options* dialog box, and click **OK** to close the *Track Changes Options* dialog box.

4. Change *Display for Review* view, review and delete a comment, and turn on *Track Changes*.
   a. Change the *Display for Review* view to **All Markup** and review the changes in the document.
   b. Read the comment on the first page and then delete the comment.
   c. Turn on **Track Changes** and change the *Display for Review* view to **Simple Markup**.

5. Remove existing content.
   a. Click the **Cover Page** button (*Insert* tab, *Pages* group] and select **Remove Current Cover Page**.
   b. Click the **Table of Contents** button (*References* tab, *Table of Contents* group] and select **Remove Table of Contents**.
   c. Remove the existing headers and footers on all pages of the itinerary.

6. Change the page orientation to **Landscape**.

7. Apply a heading style and update a style.
   a. Apply the **Day** style to the "Day 1: . . ." heading on the first page.
   b. Select the "Day 1" heading and **Update Heading 1 to Match Selection**. The new *Heading 1* style applies to all day headings in the document.

8. Insert page breaks.
   a. Click in front of "Day 3" and insert a **page break**.
   b. Repeat this on each of the odd numbered days so only two days appear on each page.

9. Add text and apply style.
   a. Place your insertion point on the blank line after the distance in the "Day 2" section.
   b. Press **Enter** and type Notes and Questions at the insertion point.
   c. Apply **Day** style to the text you just typed.
   d. Repeat steps b and c to insert this information at the end of the "Day 4" and "Day 6" sections.
   e. In the "Day 8" section, place your insertion point on the blank line below the "Kilometers to Miles Conversion" information and above the endnotes.
   f. Press **Enter**, type Notes and Questions, and apply **Day** style to the text you just typed.

10. Move and delete endnotes and convert endnotes to footnotes.
    a. Move the first endnote marker (after the distance on "Day 3") to appear in the "Day 2" section after the distance ("83 km").
    b. Change the text to Day 2 is the longest day of the tour. in the endnote text area.
    c. Delete the second endnote reference marker after "Day 4." The endnote text is removed when you delete the reference marker.
    d. Convert all endnotes to footnotes.

11. Insert and customize footnotes.
    a. After the "Day 4" distance ("0-26 km"), insert a footnote and type Day 4 is an optional riding day. in the footnote text area. *Note: The footnote number may not be consecutive until you accept tracked changes.*
    b. After the "Day 5" distance ("42-58 km"), insert a footnote and type Day 5 has two routes from which to choose. in the footnote text area.
    c. After the "Day 6" distance ("52-68 km"), insert a footnote and type Day 6 has three routes from which to choose. in the footnote text area.
    d. Change the footnote *Number format* to **a, b, c** and change *Numbering* to **Continuous** if it is not already selected.

12. Insert a custom table of contents.
    a. Place your insertion point at the beginning of the document and insert a **page break**.
    b. Type Contents on the first line on the new first page (before the page break) and press **Enter**.
    c. Insert a **Custom Table of Contents**, use **Distinctive** format, show 1 level of headings, show page numbers, right align page numbers, and include a solid line tab leader.
    d. Select the "Day 1" through "Day 8" lines of text in the table of contents and apply **12 pt**. *After* paragraph spacing.

13. Edit the following document properties.
    Title: Cycling Classic Tuscany: Tour Itinerary
    Company: American River Cycling Club

14. Insert and modify a cover page.
    a. Insert the **Semaphore** cover page.
    b. Select the current date as the date.
    c. Change the font size of the *Title* field to **48 pt**. and apply **bold** format.
    d. Delete the **Subtitle** (*Document Subtitle*) and **Author** fields.
    e. Change the font size of the *Company* field to **14 pt**. and apply **bold** format.
    f. Select the *Address* field and type www.arcc.org in the field.

15. Insert footers on the second and continuing pages.
    a. On the second page of the document (table of contents), edit the footer.
    b. Change the alignment to **right**, insert the **Company** document property field, deselect the field (right arrow key), and **space** once.
    c. Type | (press **Shift+** to type a vertical line) and **space** once.
    d. Type Page and **space** once.
    e. Insert a plain page number in the current position.
    f. **Bold** all of the text in the footer and close the footer.

16. Change *Display for Review* view, accept tracked changes, and turn off *Track Changes*.
    a. Change the *Display for Review* view to **All Markup**.
    b. Review the tracked changes in the document.
    c. Turn off **Track Changes** and accept all tracked changes in the document.

17. Share the document with your instructor.
    a. Save this document on *OneDrive* if you haven't already. If you don't have the ability to save to *OneDrive*, skip all of step 17.
    b. Click the **Share** button in the upper right of the Word window to open the *Share* pane.
    c. Type your instructor's email address in the *Invite* people text box.
    d. Select **Can edit** in the drop-down list below the email address.
    e. Type a brief message to your instructor and click the **Share** button.
    f. Click the **X** in the upper right corner of the *Share* pane to close it.

18. Save and close the document (Figure 3-121).

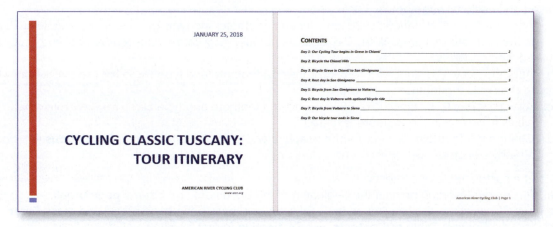

3-121 Word 3-7 completed (pages 1-4 of 6)

Challenge Project 3-8

Modify a report you have written for another class to include citations, a bibliography or works cited page, table of contents, cover page, and headers and footers. Use comments and *Track Changes*.
[Student Learning Outcomes 3.1, 3.2, 3.4, 3.5, 3.6, 3.7]

File Needed: None
Completed Project File Name: ***[your initials] Word 3-8.docx***

Open an existing report you have created and save it as [your initials] Word 3-8.

Modify your document according to the following guidelines:

- Turn on *Track Changes* and insert comments where necessary.
- Select the citation style to use for your report (e.g., APA, MLA, Chicago).
- Add citations to the body of your report and create sources.
- Add placeholders for citations in the body of your report.
- Insert a bibliography or works cited page at the end of your report.
- Use the *Source Manager* to edit placeholders and sources and add new sources, if necessary.
- Insert other citations in the body as necessary.
- Update the bibliography page.
- Apply headings styles and insert a table of contents.
- Insert a cover page and customize content.
- Insert a header, footer, and page number from the built-in list of options.
- Use different first page headers and footers.
- Insert page breaks to control pagination as necessary.

Challenge Project 3-9

Add footnotes and endnotes, heading styles, a table of contents, a cover page, and headers and footers to a multipage document that you have written. Use comments and *Track Changes*.
[Student Learning Outcomes 3.1, 3.2, 3.3, 3.5, 3.6, 3.7]

File Needed: None
Completed Project File Name: ***[your initials] Word 3-9.docx***

Open an existing report you have written for another class and save it as [your initials] Word 3-9.

Modify your document according to the following guidelines:

- Turn on *Track Changes* and insert comments where necessary.
- Add endnotes to the document.
- Convert endnotes to footnotes.
- Change the number format for footnotes.
- Move a footnote to a new location and delete a footnote.

- Insert a custom header or footer in your document.
- Add a page number in the header or footer of the document.
- Insert page breaks to control pagination as necessary.
- Apply headings styles and insert a table of contents.
- Insert a cover page and customize content.
- Insert custom header and footer content.
- Use different first page or odd and even page headers and footers.
- Insert page breaks to control pagination as necessary.

Challenge Project 3-10

Modify a report or multipage document you have written for another class to include a table of contents, a cover page, and headers and footers. Use comments and *Track Changes*.
[**Student Learning Outcomes 3.1, 3.2, 3.5, 3.6, 3.7**]

File Needed: None
Completed Project File Name: ***[your initials] Word 3-10.docx***

Open an existing report or multipage document and save it as [your initials] Word 3-10.

Modify your document according to the following guidelines:

- Turn on *Track Changes* and insert comments where necessary.
- Apply *Heading 1* and *Heading 2* styles to the headings of your document. If the document does not have headings, add two levels of headings to the document.
- Insert a built-in or custom table of contents as the first page of your document.
- Include two levels of headings in the table of contents.
- Customize the *Title*, *Company*, and *Author* document property fields.
- Insert a cover page of your choice.
- Customize the cover page by adding or removing a document property or content control fields.
- Add custom information to content control fields.
- Insert a header, footer, and page number from the built-in list of options.
- Use different first page or odd and even page headers and footers.
- Insert page breaks to control pagination as necessary.
- Update the table of contents.

Using Tables, Columns, and Graphics

CHAPTER OVERVIEW

Tables, columns, and graphics enhance the appearance and readability of your Word documents. For example, you can use tables to attractively arrange and align information in column and row format, and columns improve readability and provide additional white space in a document. You can also insert and manipulate graphics to add attention-grabbing visual elements to your documents. This chapter introduces you to the Word tools that allow you to add and customize tables, columns, and graphics.

STUDENT LEARNING OUTCOMES (SLOs)

After completing this chapter, you will be able to:

SLO 4.1 Improve the design and readability of a document by using tables to present and arrange information (p. W4-210).

SLO 4.2 Modify a table by changing column and row size, aligning text, using the *Table Properties* dialog box, sorting data, and using *AutoFit* (p. W4-214).

SLO 4.3 Enhance the appearance and function of a table by applying borders and shading, using table styles, inserting formulas, and converting text into a table (p. W4-220).

SLO 4.4 Modify the layout and design of a document using columns to present information (p. W4-227).

SLO 4.5 Enrich a document by adding and modifying graphic elements such as pictures, shapes, *SmartArt*, and *WordArt* (p. W4-231).

CASE STUDY

For the Pause & Practice projects in this chapter, you modify a brochure for Emma Cavalli, a realtor consultant with Placer Hills Real Estate (PHRE). In the past, Emma distributed brochures that were poorly designed and negatively impacted the effectiveness of her message. You modify one of Emma's brochures to include tables, columns, and graphics to improve the overall layout and effectiveness of the document.

Pause & Practice 4-1: Modify an existing brochure to include a table that presents information attractively.

Pause & Practice 4-2: Enhance the table in the brochure by using borders, shading, and table styles.

Pause & Practice 4-3: Improve the readability of the brochure by arranging text in columns.

Pause & Practice 4-4: Add visual elements to the brochure to improve the overall design of the document.

WORD

SLO 4.1 Creating and Editing Tables

In Chapter 2, you learned about aligning information into column and row format using tab stops. *Tables* are another tool that you can use to organize information into column and row format. In addition to lining up information, tables allow you more formatting options than tabs.

> ### MORE INFO
>
> On web pages, most of the information is organized into table and row format even though you might not see table borders or structure.

Tables

You can insert tables almost anywhere in a Word document. A table consists of individual *cells* where you enter information. Cells are grouped into *columns* and *rows*. When using tables, it is important to distinguish between cells, columns, and rows (Figure 4-1).

- *Cell*: The area where a column and row intersect
- *Column*: A vertical grouping of cells (think of vertical columns that support a building)
- *Row*: A horizontal grouping of cells (think of horizontal rows of seating in a stadium or auditorium)

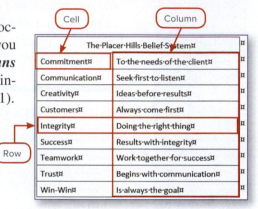

4-1 Table

▶ HOW TO: Insert a Table

1. Place your insertion point in your document where you want to insert a table.
2. Click the **Insert** tab.
3. Click the **Table** button [*Tables* group] to open the drop-down list.
4. Click and drag across the *Insert Table* grid to select the number of columns and rows you want in the table (Figure 4-2). The table is inserted into your document.
   - As you drag across the grid, the *Insert Table* label changes to display the size of the table (e.g., *3×7 Table*).

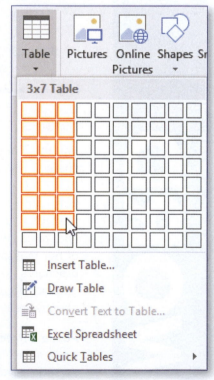

> ### MORE INFO
>
> Word lists table dimensions in column and row format. For example, a three-column and seven-row table is a 3×7 table.

When you insert a table using the *Insert Table* grid, the table size is limited depending on the size and resolution of your computer screen. You can also insert a table using the *Insert Table* dialog box.

4-2 *Insert Table* drop-down list

1. Click the **Insert** tab.
2. Click the **Table** button [*Tables* group] to open the drop-down list.
3. Select **Insert Table**. The *Insert Table* dialog box opens (Figure 4-3).
4. Select the desired number of columns and rows in the *Table size* area.
5. Select how the table is distributed horizontally between the left and right margins in the *AutoFit behavior* area.
6. Choose **OK** to insert the table.

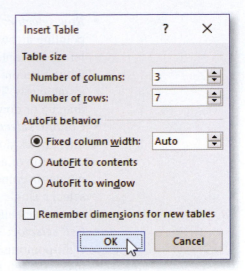

4-3 *Insert Table* dialog box

Navigate within a Table

To move the insertion point within a table, press **Tab** (or the **right arrow** key on your keyboard) to move forward one cell in the current row. When you get to the end of a row and press *Tab*, the insertion point moves to the first cell in the next row. **Shift+Tab** (or the **left arrow** key) moves you back one cell at a time. You can also use your pointer and click in a cell to insert the insertion point.

Table Tools Layout Tab

When you insert a table into a document, the **Table Tools tabs** display on the *Ribbon*. There are two *Table Tools* tabs: **Design** and **Layout**. These context-sensitive toolbars display whenever you place the insertion point in the table or select a region of the table. The *Table Tools Layout* tab provides a variety of formatting options (Figure 4-4). For more on the *Table Tools Design* tab, see *SLO 4.3: Formatting and Editing Tables*.

4-4 *Table Tools Layout* tab

Select Table and Text

When working with tables, you can select the entire table, a cell, column, or row, or multiple cells, columns, or rows to apply formatting changes. Word provides a variety of table selection tools.

- *Table selector handle*: This handle appears in the upper left of the table when the pointer is on the table (Figure 4-5). Click the **table selector** to select the entire table.

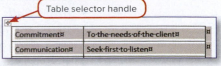

4-5 **Table selector handle**

- *Row selector*: The row selector is the right-pointing arrow when your pointer is just to the left of the table row (Figure 4-6). When the pointer becomes the row selector, click to select a single row. To select multiple rows, click and drag up or down.

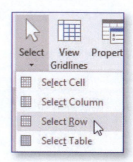

| Commitment¤ | To·the·needs·of·the·client¤ |
| Communication¤ | Seek·first·to·listen¤ |

Row selector

4-6 Row selector

- *Column selector*: The column selector is the thick, black down arrow when your pointer is on the top of a column (Figure 4-7). When the pointer becomes the column selector, click to select a single column. To select multiple columns, click and drag left or right.

Column selector

| Commitment¤ | To·the·needs·of·the·client¤ |
| Communication¤ | Seek·first·to·listen¤ |

4-7 Column selector

- *Cell selector*: The cell selector is the thick, black right-pointing arrow when your pointer is just inside the left border of a cell (Figure 4-8). When the pointer becomes the cell selector, click to select a single cell. To select multiple cells, click and drag left, right, up, or down. When the cell selector displays, double-click to select the entire row.

| Commitment¤ | To·the·needs·of·the·client¤ |
| Communication¤ | Seek·first·to·listen¤ |

Cell selector

4-8 Cell selector

- *Select button*: The select button is on the *Table Tools Layout* tab in the *Table* group. Click the **Select** button to access a drop-down list of table selection options (Figure 4-9).

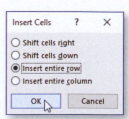

Select   View   Propert
         Gridlines

☐ Select Cell
☐ Select Column
☐ Select Row
☐ Select Table

4-9 *Select* drop-down list

Add Rows and Columns

When you insert a table into a document, you are not locked into your original table dimensions; you can always add columns and rows to the table in a variety of ways.

- *Insert Control*: Place your pointer on the left outside edge of a row or top outside edge of a column to display the insert row or column control (plus sign). Click the **insert control** to add a row or column (Figure 4-10). Select multiple rows or columns and click the insert control to add the number or rows or columns selected.

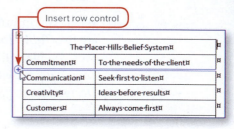

Insert row control

The·Placer·Hills·Belief·System¤	
Commitment¤	To·the·needs·of·the·client¤
Communication¤	Seek·first·to·listen¤
Creativity¤	Ideas·before·results¤
Customers¤	Always·come·first¤

4-10 Insert row control

- *Table Tools Layout tab*: In the *Rows & Columns* group, you can insert a row above or below the current row or a column to the left or right of the current column (see Figure 4-4).

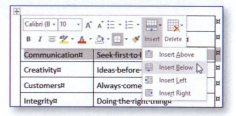

Communication¤	Seek·first·to·l
Creativity¤	Ideas·before·
Customers¤	Always·come
Integrity¤	Doing·the·right·thing¤

Insert Delete

☐ Insert Above
☐ Insert Below
☐ Insert Left
☐ Insert Right

4-11 Use the mini toolbar to insert a row

- *Mini toolbar*: Select a cell, row, column, or table to display the mini toolbar. You can also right-click the table to display the mini toolbar. Click the **Insert** button to display a list of insert options (Figure 4-11).
- *Insert Cells dialog box*: Open this dialog box by clicking the **Rows & Columns** launcher on the *Table Tools Layout* tab (Figure 4-12).
- *Tab*: When your insertion point is in the last cell in the last row, you can press **Tab** to insert a new row below the last row.

Insert Cells   ?   ✕

○ Shift cells right
○ Shift cells down
◉ Insert entire row
○ Insert entire column

  OK   Cancel

4-12 *Insert Cells* dialog box

Merge and Split Cells

Many times when you use tables you want to span information across multiple columns, such as when you are inserting a title or subtitle in a table. You can do this by merging columns, rows, and cells.

▶ **HOW TO:** Merge Cells

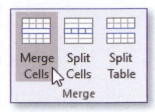

1. Select the cells to merge.
2. Click the **Table Tools Layout** tab.
3. Click the **Merge Cells** button [*Merge* group] (Figure 4-13). The cells merge into one cell.

4-13 *Merge Cells* button

Word also allows you to split a cell into multiple cells. You can split cells that were previously merged or split a single cell into multiple columns and rows. When you are splitting cells, the *Split Cells* dialog box prompts you to specify the number of columns and rows.

▶ **HOW TO:** Split Cells

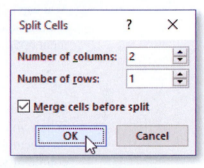

1. Select the cell(s) to split.
2. Click the **Table Tools Layout** tab.
3. Click the **Split Cells** button [*Merge* group]. The *Split Cells* dialog box opens (Figure 4-14).
4. Select the number of columns and rows that you want in the split cell.
   - By default, the *Merge cells before split* check box is selected. When you select this check box, Word merges the selected cells before splitting them into the desired number of columns and rows.
5. Click **OK** to split the cells.

4-14 *Split Cells* dialog box

> ▶ **ANOTHER WAY**
>
> Both *Merge Cells* and *Split Cells* are available from the context menu.

Copy or Move Columns and Rows

You can copy or move columns and rows in a table similar to how you copy or move text in a document. Select the column or row to copy or move, and use one of the following methods:

- *Keyboard Shortcuts*: **Ctrl+C** (copy), **Ctrl+X** (cut), and **Ctrl+V** (paste).
- *Context menu*: Right-click the selected column or row and select **Cut, Copy**, or **Paste**.

- ***Drag and drop***: Drag and drop the column or row in the new location to move it. Hold the **Ctrl** key while dragging and dropping to copy a column or row.
- ***Clipboard group on the Home tab***: Use the **Cut, Copy**, and **Paste** buttons in this group.

Delete Columns and Rows

At some point, you may need to remove columns or rows from your table. Removing columns and rows is very similar to inserting columns and rows. Click the **Delete** button in the *Rows & Columns* group on the *Table Tools Layout* tab or the mini toolbar to remove cells, columns, rows, or an entire table. You have the following options (Figure 4-15):

4-15 *Delete* options

- *Delete Cells . . .* : Opens the *Delete Cells* dialog box.
- *Delete Columns*
- *Delete Rows*
- *Delete Table*

Delete a Table

If you select an entire table and press *Delete* on your keyboard, only the information in the table is deleted; the blank table remains in your document. To delete a table, you select the **Delete Table** option from the *Delete* drop-down on the *Table Tool Layout* tab or mini toolbar (see Figure 4-15). The **Delete Table** option is also available on the context menu when you select and right-click a table.

 SLO 4.2

Arranging Text in Tables

You can adjust the width of columns and the height of rows and control how text is aligned within the cells of a table. Word provides you with a variety of table resizing and text alignment options. You also can sort information automatically within a table.

Resize Columns and Rows

Many times you need to adjust columns and rows to better fit the information in the table. When you insert a table into a document, the default size for the table is the width of the document. You can manually adjust the width of columns and the height of rows in a couple of ways.

Drag the column or row borders to increase or decrease the size of a column or row. When you place your pointer on the vertical border of a column, the pointer changes to a ***resizing pointer*** (Figure 4-16). Drag the column border to the left or right to adjust the size of the column. You can use the same method to adjust the height of a row by dragging the top or bottom border of a row up or down.

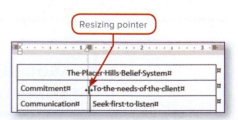

4-16 Manually adjust column width

> ▶ **MORE INFO**
>
> When you manually adjust the height of a row, it adjusts the height of the selected row only. Usually, you want to keep the height of rows consistent.

Word also allows you to type a specific size for columns and rows. It is best to adjust the size of columns and rows before merging cells. After cells are merged, it is difficult to adjust column and row sizes of a table. If you're adjusting the size of columns or rows after merging cells, be very specific about the cells you select.

▶**HOW TO:** Resize Columns and Rows

1. Select the cells, columns, or rows you want to resize.
2. Click the **Table Tools Layout** tab.
3. Change the height or width to the desired size [*Cell Size* group] (Figure 4-17).
   - Manually type the specific size or use the up or down arrows (spinner box) to resize.

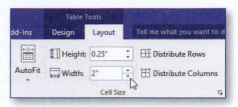

4-17 Set cell *Height* and *Width*

AutoFit a Table

When you insert a table into a document, the table is automatically set to the width of the document (inside the left and right margins). Word has three different *AutoFit* options to adjust the column width of the table. Click the **AutoFit** button in the *Cell Size* group on the *Table Tools Layout* tab to display the *AutoFit* options (Figure 4-18).

- ***AutoFit Contents***: Adjusts column widths to fit the contents of the table
- ***AutoFit Window***: Distributes the column widths so the table fits across the width of the page (this is the default setting when you insert a table into a document)
- ***Fixed Column Width***: Adjusts columns to a fixed column width

4-18 *AutoFit* options

> **MORE INFO**
>
> When you insert a table, the table has the same formatting as the text in the document. If your rows seem too high, it might be because your document contains *Before* or *After* paragraph spacing that is controlling the height of the rows in your table.

Distribute Rows and Columns

Word provides you with features to evenly distribute rows and columns, which is useful when the sizes of columns and rows in a table are uneven. ***Distribute Rows*** and ***Distribute Columns*** are on the *Table Tools Layout* tab in the *Cell Size* group (Figure 4-19).

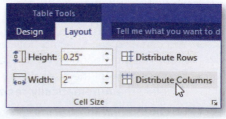

- ***Distribute Rows***: This feature evenly distributes the rows based on the height of the existing table, making all rows a consistent height.
- ***Distribute Columns***: This feature evenly distributes the columns based on the width of the existing table, making all columns the same width.

4-19 Distribute rows and columns

Text Alignment

In Chapter 1, you learned about paragraph alignment and how to left align, right align, center, or justify text. In Chapter 2, you learned how to change the vertical alignment of a page or section. Similarly, when using tables, you have both horizontal and vertical alignment options. Text can be aligned vertically and horizontally within a cell and can be aligned independently of other cells. There are nine alignment options within the cell of a table. The following alignment options are in the *Alignment* group on the *Table Tools Layout* tab (Figure 4-20):

- *Align Top Left*
- *Align Top Center*
- *Align Top Right*
- *Align Center Left*
- *Align Center*
- *Align Center Right*
- *Align Bottom Left*
- *Align Bottom Center*
- *Align Bottom Right*

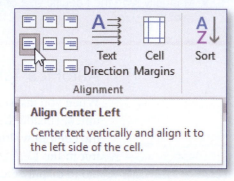

4-20 Text alignment options within a table

Cell Margins

In addition to being able to change alignment in cells, you can also adjust **cell margins**. Just like the margins on a Word document, the cells of a table have top, bottom, left, and right margins. Cell margins add space around text within a cell. The default cell margins are 0" top and bottom, and 0.08" left and right.

▶**HOW TO:** Change Cell Margins

1. Select the entire table to change the cell margins for all cells in the table.
   - You can also change cell margins on individual cells.
2. Click the **Table Tools Layout** tab.
3. Click the **Cell Margins** button [*Alignment* group]. The *Table Options* dialog box opens (Figure 4-21).
4. Enter the desired changes to the *Top*, *Bottom*, *Left*, and *Right* cell margins.
   - You can also add spacing between cells in the *Default cell spacing* area. This puts padding (space) around the outside of the cells.
   - If you don't want the size of your table to be automatically adjusted, deselect the **Automatically resize to fit contents** check box.
5. Click **OK** to apply the cell margin settings.

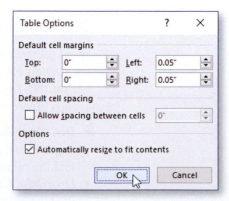

4-21 *Table Options* dialog box

Table Properties Dialog Box

The **Table Properties** dialog box consolidates many table sizing and alignment options in one location. In the dialog box, there are separate tabs for *Table*, *Row*, *Column*, *Cell*, and *Alt Text*. To open the *Table Properties* dialog box, click the **Properties** button in the *Table* group on the *Table Tools Layout* tab (Figure 4-22). You can also open the *Table Properties* dialog box from the context menu.

- **Table tab**: Adjusts the size of the table, alignment, text wrapping, positioning, borders and shading, and cell margins
- **Row tab**: Adjusts the height of rows and controls how rows break between pages
- **Column tab**: Adjusts the width of columns
- **Cell tab**: Adjusts the width of cells, vertical alignment of information in cells, and cell margins
- **Alt Text tab**: Alternative text (Alt text) is an information tag that displays when place your pointer on the table. Screen readers use Alt text in tables to accommodate those with visual impairments. Alt text is very common on web pages.

4-22 *Table Properties* dialog box

Sort Data in Tables

A very useful feature in Word is the ability to sort information within a table. You might want to arrange the text in the first column of a table alphabetically or sort numbers in descending order. When you use the *Sort* feature on a table, rows of information rearrange according to how you specify the sort.

▶**HOW TO: Sort Data in a Table**

1. Place your insertion point in the table.
2. Select the **Table Tools Layout** tab.
3. Click the **Sort** button [*Data* group]. The entire table is selected and the *Sort* dialog box opens (Figure 4-23).
4. Click the **Sort by** drop-down list and select the column to use to sort the table.
   - You can sort by any of the columns in the table.
5. Click the **Type** drop-down list and select the type of sort to perform.
   - You can sort by *Text*, *Number*, or *Date*.
6. Click the **Using** drop-down list and select the cell information to use in the sort.
   - *Paragraphs* is the default option and usually this is the only option available.

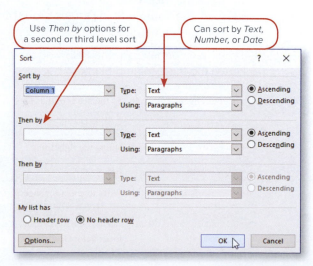

4-23 *Sort* dialog box

7. Select **Ascending** (A to Z or 1 to 10) or **Descending** (Z to A or 10 to 1) for the sort order.
   - Add a second or third sort on different columns if desired. Click the **Then by** drop-down list to add additional sorts.
   - If your table has a header row (title or column headings), click the **Header row** radio button to omit this row from the sort.
8. Click **OK** to perform the sort. Your table is sorted according to your settings.

> **MORE INFO**
>
> If your table has both a title and column headings, select the rows of the table to be sorted before clicking the **Sort** button so that only the data in the table is sorted.

> **ANOTHER WAY**
>
> Manually sort rows using copy (**Ctrl+C**), cut (**Ctrl+X**), and paste (**Ctrl+V**), or the drag and drop method.

PAUSE & PRACTICE: WORD 4-1

For this Pause & Practice project, you begin modifying Emma Cavalli's brochure. You add a table to the end of this document and then modify the table.

File Needed: **Brochure-04.docx** (Student data files are available in the Library of your SIMnet account)
Completed Project File Name: **[your initials] PP W4-1.docx**

1. Open the **Brochure-04** document from your student data files.

2. Save this document as [your initials] PP W4-1.

3. Move to the end of the document and insert a table.
   a. Press **Ctrl+End** to move to the end of the document.
   b. Click the **Insert** tab.
   c. Click the **Table** button [*Tables* group] and select a **3×7** table using the table grid. The table displays in the document.

4. Type the information in the following table. Press **Tab** to move from one cell to the next cell in the row. Leave the third column blank.

Commitment	To the needs of the client	
Communication	Seek first to listen	
Integrity	Doing the right thing	
Customers	Always come first	
Teamwork	Work together for success	
Success	Results with integrity	
Creativity	Ideas before results	

5. Delete a column and insert rows.
   a. Place the insertion point in any cell in the last column.
   b. Click the **Delete** button [*Table Tools Layout* tab, *Rows & Columns* group] and select **Delete Columns**.
   c. Place the insertion point in the second row and click the **Insert Below** button [*Table Tools Layout* tab, *Rows & Columns* group]. A blank row is inserted below the second row.
   d. Type the following information in the new third row:

Trust	Begins with communication

   e. Click the last cell of the table (bottom right cell) and press **Tab** to insert a new row at the bottom of the table.
   f. Type the following information in the new last row:

Win-Win	Is always the goal

6. *AutoFit* the table and adjust column and row size.
   a. Place your insertion point in the table.
   b. Click the **AutoFit** button [*Table Tools Layout* tab, *Cell Size* group] and select **AutoFit Contents**. The column widths adjust to fit the contents of the table.
   c. Place the insertion point in the first column.
   d. Change the *Width* to **1.2"** [*Table Tool Layout* tab, *Cell Size* group]
   e. Place the insertion point in the second column.
   f. Change the *Width* to **2"**.
   g. Use the table selector handle to select the entire table.
   h. Click the **Properties** button [*Table Tool Layout* tab, *Table* group] to open the *Table Properties* dialog box (Figure 4-24).
   i. Click the **Row** tab and check the **Specify height** box.
   j. Type **.25** in the *Specify height* field and select **Exactly** in the *Row height is* drop-down list.
   k. Click **OK** to close the *Tables Properties* dialog box and apply these settings.

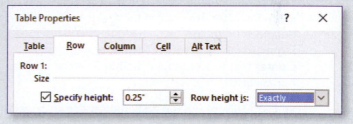

4-24 Change row height on the selected table

7. Insert a row and merge cells.
   a. Click anywhere in the table so the entire table is no longer selected.
   b. Select the first row of the table.
   c. Click the **Insert** button on the mini toolbar and select **Insert Above** to insert a new row at the top of the table.
   d. Select the new first row (if it is not already selected) and click the **Merge Cells** button [*Table Tools Layout* tab, *Merge* group]. The cells in the first row merge into one cell.
   e. Type **The Placer Hills Belief System** in the merged first row.

8. Sort the table by text in the first column.
   a. Select the **second through tenth (last) rows** of the table. Don't select the first merged row.
   b. Click the **Sort** button [*Table Tools Layout* tab, *Data* group]. The *Sort* dialog box opens (Figure 4-25).

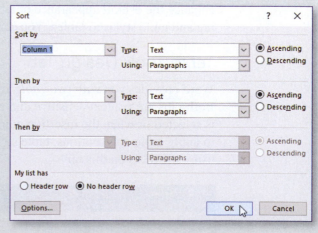

4-25 Sort table by first column in ascending order

c. Sort by **Column 1** in **Ascending** order. Leave *Type* as **Text** and *Using* as **Paragraphs**.
   d. Click **OK** to sort the rows below the title in alphabetical order.

9. Change cell margins and text alignment.
   a. Select the entire table.

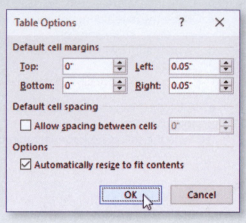

4-26 **Change cell margins**

> **MORE INFO**
>
> Click the **table selector** handle in the upper left of the table or click the **Select** button in the *Table* group on the *Table Tool Layout* tab and choose **Select Table**.

   b. Click the **Cell Margins** button [*Table Tools Layout* tab, *Alignment* group]. The *Table Options* dialog box opens (Figure 4-26).
   c. Change the *Left* and *Right* cell margins **0.05"**.
   d. Check the **Automatically resize to fit contents** box (if it is not already checked) and click **OK**.
   e. With the table still selected, click the **Align Center Left** button (first alignment button in the second row) [*Table Tools Layout* tab, *Alignment* group].
   f. Place the insertion point in the first row of the table to deselect the table.
   g. Right-click the first row of the table and click the **Center** button on the mini toolbar. The title centers horizontally.

10. Save and close this document (Figure 4-27).

The Placer Hills Belief System¤		¤
Commitment¤	To the needs of the client¤	¤
Communication¤	Seek first to listen¤	¤
Creativity¤	Ideas before results¤	¤
Customers¤	Always come first¤	¤
Integrity¤	Doing the right thing¤	¤
Success¤	Results with integrity¤	¤
Teamwork¤	Work together for success¤	¤
Trust¤	Begins with communication¤	¤
Win-Win¤	Is always the goal¤	¤

4-27 **PP W4-1 completed (table only displayed)**

SLO 4.3

Formatting and Editing Tables

In addition to the ability to adjust the structure of tables, Word provides you with many tools to enhance the overall appearance of tables. For example, you can add custom borders and shading and table styles to tables. You can also add formulas to tables and convert text into tables.

Table Tools Design Tab

Word provides you with two *Table Tools* tabs when you work with tables: *Design* and *Layout*. Both tabs are context-sensitive and are only displayed when the table or portion of the table is selected or when the insertion point is in the table. The ***Table Tools Design tab*** allows you to apply table style options, table styles, and borders (Figure 4-28). You can also draw tables using the tools on this tab.

4-28 *Table Tools Design* tab

Table Borders

By default, when you insert a table, Word formats the table with borders. You can apply borders to an individual cell, a group of cells, or an entire table. When applying borders, it is important to be very specific when selecting the area of the table on which to apply the borders.

The *Borders* button is in the *Borders* group on the *Table Tools Design* tab, in the *Paragraph* group on the *Home* tab or on the mini toolbar. The *Borders* drop-down list displays a variety of border options (Figure 4-29). You can also apply borders using the *Borders and Shading* dialog box.

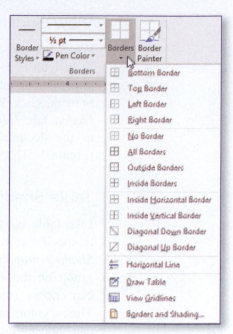

4-29 *Borders* drop-down list

▶ **HOW TO:** Apply Borders to a Table Using the Borders and Shading Dialog Box

1. Select the entire table or the desired area of the table where you want borders.

2. Click the **Borders** button [*Table Tools Design* tab, *Borders* group] and select **Borders and Shading** to open the *Borders and Shading* dialog box (Figure 4-30).

   - Alternatively, click the **Borders** button [*Home* tab, *Paragraph* group] or the **Borders** button on the mini toolbar.
   - The selection in the *Apply to* area depends on whether you are applying borders to the entire table or selected cells or rows.

3. In the *Setting* area, select the type of border from the list of options.

   - You can remove all borders by selecting **None**.

4. Select the *Style* of the border from the list of options.

5. Click the **Color** drop-down list and select the color of the border.

6. Click the **Width** drop-down list and select the width of the border.

7. In the *Preview* area, you can see how your borders will be applied to your table.

   - In the *Preview* area, you can also apply or deselect borders on specific areas of your table.
   - Click the border buttons in the *Preview* area or click the diagram borders to turn borders on or off.

8. Click **OK** to apply the border settings and close the *Borders and Shading* dialog box.

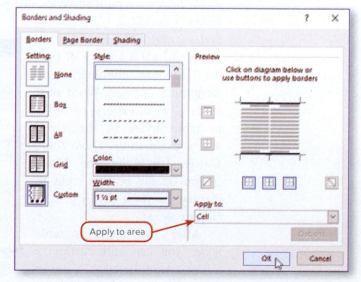

4-30 *Borders and Shading* dialog box

View Gridlines

When borders are removed from a table, it is difficult to see the column and row structure of your table. If you don't have table borders, click **View Gridlines** [*Table Tools Layout* tab, *Table* group]. Gridlines display in the document only; they do not print (Figure 4-31).

Table Shading

Like table borders, you can apply shading to specific cells or to an entire table. In the *Shading* drop-down list in the *Table Styles* group on the *Table Tools Design* tab, you can choose from *Theme Colors* or *Standard Colors* (Figure 4-32). Theme colors change depending on the theme of your document. You can choose a custom color by selecting **More Colors**, which opens the *Colors* dialog box. You can remove shading by selecting **No Color**.

You can also apply, change, or remove shading from the *Shading* tab in the *Borders and Shading* dialog box.

THE·PLACER·HILLS·BELIEF·SYSTEM¤		¤
COMMITMENT¤	To·the·needs·of·the·client¤	¤
COMMUNICATION¤	Seek·first·to·listen¤	¤
CREATIVITY¤	Ideas·before·results¤	¤
CUSTOMERS¤	Always·come·first¤	¤
INTEGRITY¤	Doing·the·right·thing¤	¤
SUCCESS¤	Results·with·integrity¤	¤
TEAMWORK¤	Work·together·for·success¤	¤
TRUST¤	Begins·with·communication¤	¤
WIN-WIN¤	Is·always·the·goal¤	¤

4-31 Table displayed with *View Gridlines* and no borders

4-32 Table *Shading* options

> ▶ **ANOTHER WAY**
>
> Apply borders and shading from the mini toolbar by right-clicking the table or a portion of the table.

Table Styles

Table Styles are built-in styles that you can apply to your tables, which are similar to text styles (see *SLO 2.7: Using Styles and Themes*). Table styles include a variety of borders, shading, alignment, and formatting options. Word provides a wide variety of built-in table styles in the *Table Styles* group on the *Table Tools Design* tab. Click the **More** button on the bottom right to display the *Table Styles* gallery (Figure 4-33).

After you apply a table style, you can still customize all aspects of the table. You can also remove all formatting of a table by selecting the **Clear** option at the bottom of the *Table Styles* gallery.

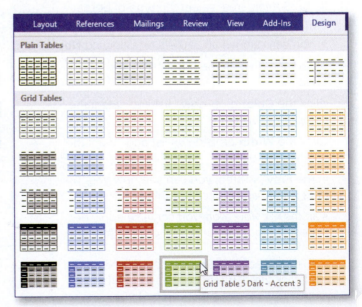

4-33 *Table Styles* gallery

Table Style Options

Word offers a variety of **Table Style Options** to customize tables (Figure 4-34). For example, many tables have a header row or column, or a total or last row, where you might want to apply special formatting for emphasis. When you select any of these *Table Style Options*, Word applies special formatting to the table style you select. Select your table style options before applying a table style.

4-34 *Table Style Options* group

> **MORE INFO**
>
> *Banded Rows* apply shading to every other row. You can also apply *Banded Columns* in the *Table Style Options* group.

▶ **HOW TO:** Apply a Table Style and Table Style Options

1. Select the table on which to apply a table style.
2. Click the **Table Tools Design** tab.
3. Select the *Table Style Options* you want to apply to the table [*Table Style Options* group] (see Figure 4-34).
   - Consider the content of your table when deciding which table style options to choose.
   - When you select or deselect table style options, the thumbnails of the table styles in the *Table Styles* gallery change to reflect the options you have chosen.
4. Click the **More** button to display the *Table Styles* gallery (see Figure 4-33).
   - You can scroll down in the *Table Styles* gallery to view more table styles.
5. Choose a table style. Word applies the style and options to your table.
   - When you point to a table style in the *Table Styles* gallery, Word provides a live preview of the table style so you can preview the style on your table.

Insert a Formula in a Table

In addition to making your tables more attractive and easier to read with formatting and style options, you can add *formulas* to tables to automatically calculate amounts. For example, you can add a formula in a total row of the table to total the numbers in the rows above (Figure 4-35).

Formula that adds the numbers above

4-35 Formula in a table

> **MORE INFO**
>
> Remember, it's best to align amount figures on the right in a table.

Most formulas used in tables in Word are simple formulas that calculate numbers in a column or row. When you insert a formula, Word, by default, inserts the *SUM* formula and adds the range of numbers in the column or row. Word also allows you to insert formulas that are more complex.

1. Place the insertion point in the cell where you want to insert the formula.
2. Click the **Table Tools Layout** tab.
3. Click the **Formula** button [*Data* group]. The *Formula* dialog box opens (Figure 4-36).
4. The formula appears in the *Formula* box.
   - You can select different formula functions from the *Paste function* drop-down list.
5. Click the **Number format** drop-down list and select a number format.
6. Click **OK** to insert the formula.

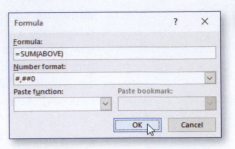

4-36 *Formula* **dialog box**

Update a Formula

A formula automatically adds values in a table, and you can automatically update a formula if values in the table change. The following are two ways to update a formula:

- Right-click the formula and select **Update Field**.
- Select the formula and press the **F9** function key (you might have to press **Fn+F9** if using a laptop).

Convert Text to a Table

You will not always create a table from scratch. You may want to create a table from existing text. For example, you might want to convert text that is arranged using tabs into a table, or you might want to convert a table into text. Word provides you with options to ***convert text to a table*** or ***convert a table to text***.

When converting text into a table, the selected text must be separated by tabs, commas, paragraph breaks, or other characters. Word uses these characters to separate text into individual cells in the table.

▶ **HOW TO:** Convert Text to a Table

1. Select the text to be converted to a table.
2. Click the **Insert** tab.
3. Click **Tables** [*Tables* group] and select **Convert Text to Table**. The *Convert Text to Table* dialog box opens (Figure 4-37).
4. In the *Table size* area, select the number of columns or rows.
   - Word automatically detects the size of the table you need.
   - You might not be able to change one or both of the values, depending on the text you selected.
5. In the *AutoFit behavior* area, select an *AutoFit* option.
   - The default setting is *Fixed column width*.
6. In the *Separate text at* area, select how you want Word to separate columns and rows.
   - Word automatically picks an option based on the text you have selected.
7. Click **OK** to convert the text to a table.

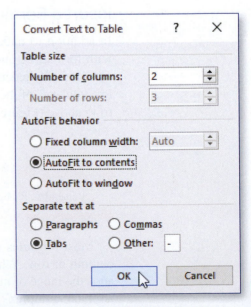

4-37 *Convert Text to Table* **dialog box**

PAUSE & PRACTICE: WORD 4-2

For this Pause & Practice project, you continue to modify Emma's brochure. You apply a table style and table style options to the table you created in the previous Pause & Practice project. You also convert text to a table and apply borders and shading.

File Needed: ***[your initials] PP W4-1.docx***
Completed Project File Name: ***[your initials] PP W4-2.docx***

1. Open the ***[your initials] PP W4-1*** document completed in *Pause & Practice 4-1*.

2. Save this document as [your initials] PP W4-2.

3. Apply table style options and a table style.
   a. Select the table at the end of the document.
   b. Click the **Table Tools Design** tab.
   c. Select **Header Row, Banded Rows**, and **First Column** [*Table Style Options* group] if they are not already selected. The other check boxes should not be selected.
   d. Click the **More** button in the *Table Styles* group to open the *Table Styles* gallery.
   e. Select the **Grid Table 5 Dark – Accent 3** style (Figure 4-38) to apply the style to the table.

4-38 Select table style

4. Apply a custom top and bottom border to the table.
   a. Select the **first row** (title) of the table.
   b. Click the **Borders** button [*Table Tools Design* tab, *Borders* group or on the mini toolbar] and select **Borders and Shading**. The *Borders and Shading* dialog box opens.
   c. In the *Setting* area, select **Custom**.
   d. Click the **Color** drop-down list and select **Black**, **Text 1**.
   e. Click the **Width** drop-down list and select **1½ pt**
   f. In the *Style* area, select the **solid line** (first line style in the list) if it is not already selected.
   g. In the *Preview* area, click the **top boundary** of the cell to add a top border (Figure 4-39).
   h. Click **OK** to close the dialog box and add the border.

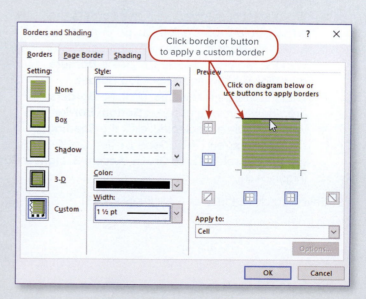

4-39 Apply custom borders

i. Select the entire **bottom row** of the table.
  j. Open the *Borders and Shading* dialog box and apply the same custom border to the bottom of the selected row (**Black, Text 1; 1½ pt.; solid line**).
  k. Click **OK** to add the border and close the dialog box.

5. Vertically align text in cells.
  a. Select the entire table and click the **Properties** button [*Table Tools Layout* tab, *Table* group] to open the *Table Properties* dialog box.
  b. Click the **Cell** tab and select **Center** in the *Vertical alignment* area.
  c. Click **OK** to close the dialog box.

6. Apply formatting changes to the text in the table.
  a. Select the first row.
  b. Open the *Font* dialog box, change *Size* to **12** and *Font color* to **Black, Text 1**, and check **All caps** in the *Effects* area.
  c. Click **OK** to close the *Font* dialog box.
  d. Select the first column, not including the title.
  e. Open the *Font* dialog box and check **Small caps** in the *Effects* area.
  f. Click **OK** to close the *Font* dialog box.

7. Convert text to a table.
  a. On the first page, select the three lines of text after "Realtor Consultant" ("**Phone**" through "**www.phre.com/ecavalli**"). Be sure to include the paragraph mark at the end of the third line, but don't select the blank line below the three lines of text.
  b. Click the **Insert** tab.
  c. Click the **Table** button [*Tables* group] and select **Convert Text to Table**. The *Convert Text to Table* dialog box opens (Figure 4-40).
  d. Change the *AutoFit behavior* to **AutoFit to contents**.
  e. Click **OK** to convert selected text to a table.

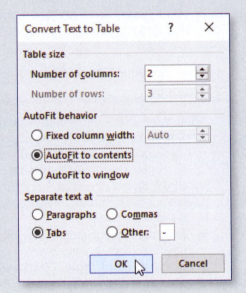

4-40 *Convert Text to Table* **dialog box**

8. Remove all borders and add custom borders and shading.
  a. With the table selected, click the **Borders** drop-down arrow [*Table Tools Design* tab, *Borders* group].
  b. Select **No Border** to remove all borders.
  c. With the table still selected, click the **Borders** drop-down arrow and select **Top Border**.
  d. With the table still selected, click the **Borders** drop-down arrow and select **Bottom Border**.
  e. With the table still selected, click the **Shading** drop-down arrow [*Table Tools Design* tab, *Table Styles* group] and select **Olive Green, Accent 3, Lighter 80%** (Figure 4-41).

9. Save and close the document (Figure 4-42).

4-41 Select *Shading* **color**

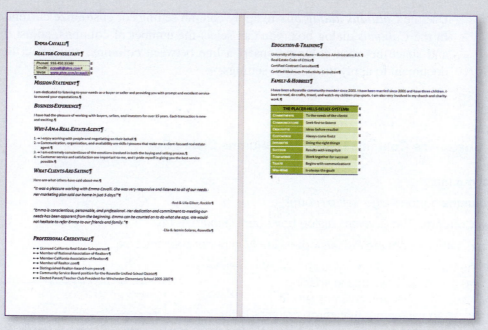

4-42 PP W4-2 completed

SLO 4.4

Using Columns

You can use columns to arrange text and tables into narrower widths and improve the readability, layout, and design of a document. In a normal Word document, text is arranged in a single column. You can apply columns to an entire document or to selected sections of a document. Word has preset column setting options, or you can customize column settings to meet your needs. You can use column and section breaks to control column endings and balance columns.

Preset Column Settings

You can apply column settings to a new document or to a document with existing text. To apply preset column settings, click the **Columns** button on the *Layout* tab in the *Page Setup* group (Figure 4-43). The *Two* and *Three* column options set columns with equal width, while the *Left* and *Right* column options arrange your document in two columns of unequal width.

When you apply columns to a document, the column settings apply only to that section of the document. If there are no section breaks, columns apply to the entire document.

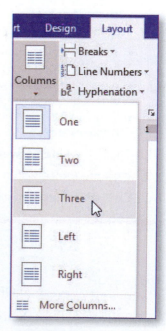

4-43 Preset column options

Customize Columns

Use the *Columns dialog box* to apply column settings or customize current column settings. In the *Columns* dialog box, you can select the number of columns, adjust the column width and space between columns, insert a line between columns, and select the portion of the document to apply the column settings.

> ▶ **HOW TO:** Customize Columns Using the Columns Dialog Box

1. Click the **Layout** tab.
2. Click the **Columns** button [*Page Setup* group].
3. Select **More Columns**. The *Columns* dialog box opens (Figure 4-44).
4. Select column settings from the *Presets* options or *Number of columns* box.

   - Based on the number of columns you choose, Word automatically sets the column width and spacing.
   - The default spacing between columns is 0.5".
   - You can choose to have more than three columns in the *Number of columns* area.

5. In the *Width and spacing* area, adjust the column widths and spacing as desired.

6. Deselect the **Equal column widths** check box to apply unequal column widths.

   - When *Equal column width* is deselected, you can adjust the width and spacing of each column individually.
   - When *Equal column width* is selected, you can adjust the width and spacing to apply to all columns.

7. Click the **Apply to** drop-down list and select the portion of the document where you want to apply column settings.

   - You can apply column settings to the *Whole document* or from *This point forward*.
   - When *This point forward* is selected, Word inserts a continuous section break at the insertion point in the document and applies column settings to the text after the continuous section break.
   - If you select text, you will be given the option to apply column settings to *Selected text* in the *Apply to* area.

8. Check the **Line between** check box to insert a vertical line between columns.

9. View the *Preview* area to see a diagram of how your columns will appear.

10. Click **OK** to apply column settings.

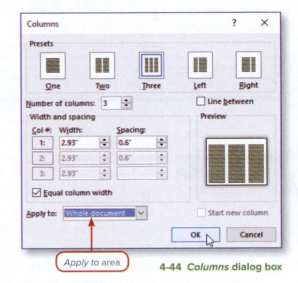

4-44 *Columns* dialog box

Convert Text to Columns

You can apply column settings to the *Whole document*, from *This point forward*, or to *Selected text*. Depending on the portion of the document where you are applying column settings, Word applies the column settings and inserts any needed section breaks. The *Apply to* drop-down list in the *Columns* dialog box displays these options (see Figure 4-44). The following table describes how Word handles each of the options:

Apply to Column Options

Columns Applied to	Actions
Whole Document	Word applies column settings to the entire document. No section breaks are added.
This point forward	Word inserts a continuous section break before the insertion point in the document and applies the column setting beginning at the insertion point, which becomes a new section of the document.
Selected text	When text is selected and column settings are applied, Word inserts a continuous section break before and after the selected text. The column settings apply only to that section.

Insert a Column Break

Column widths control the horizontal text wrapping, while the top and bottom margins or section breaks control where a column ends and wraps to the next column. You can insert *column breaks* to end a column and move subsequent text to the next column.

▶ HOW TO: Insert a Column Break

1. Place the insertion point where you want the column to end or the next column to begin.
2. Click the **Layout** tab.
3. Click the **Breaks** button [*Page Setup* group].
4. Select **Column** in the *Page Breaks* options (Figure 4-45).
   - You see a column break indicator when *Show/Hide* is turned on (Figure 4-46).

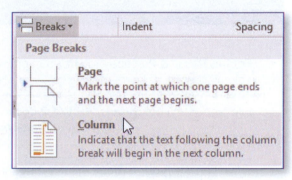

4-45 Insert *Column* break

▶ ANOTHER WAY

Ctrl+Shift+Enter inserts a column break.

▶ MORE INFO

Always turn on **Show/Hide** (**Ctrl+Shift+8**) when using page, section, or column breaks to help you see these elements in your document.

WHY·I·AM·A·REAL·ESTATE·AGENT¶

1.→ I·enjoy·working·with·people·and·negotiating·on·their·behalf.¶
2.→ Communication,·organization,·and·availability·are·skills·I·possess·that·make·me·a·client·focused·real·estate·agent.¶
3.→ I·am·extremely·conscientious·of·the·emotions·involved·in·both·the·buying·and·selling·process.¶
4.→ Customer·service·and·satisfaction·are·important·to·me,·and·I·pride·myself·in·giving·you·the·best·service·possible.¶

······················ Column Break ·····················

4-46 *Column* break inserted

Balance Columns

Column breaks are one way to balance columns on a page. Another way is to use a *continuous section break*. To make columns approximately equal in length on a page, insert a continuous section break at the end of the last column on the page. Word automatically adjusts your columns so they are about the same length.

▶ HOW TO: Balance Columns Using a Continuous Section Break

1. Place the insertion point at the end of the last column in your document.
2. Click the **Layout** tab.
3. Click the **Breaks** button [*Page Setup* group].
4. Select **Continuous** in the *Section Breaks* options.
   - You see a continuous section break indicator when *Show/Hide* is turned on.

▶ MORE INFO

Balancing columns using a continuous section break works only if there are no other column breaks controlling column endings on that page.

PAUSE & PRACTICE: WORD 4-3

For this Pause & Practice project, you apply columns to Emma's brochure. With the use of columns and column breaks, you arrange the columns and make the document fit on one page.

File Needed: ***[your initials] PP W4-2.docx***
Completed Project File Name: ***[your initials] PP W4-3.docx***

1. Open the ***[your initials] PP W4-2*** document completed in *Pause & Practice 4-2*.
2. Save this document as [your initials] PP W4-3.
3. Change the page orientation and margins.
   a. Click the **Orientation** button [*Layout* tab, *Page Setup* group] and select **Landscape**.
   b. Click the **Margins** button and choose **Custom Margins**.
   c. Change the *Top* margin to **1.2"**, and the *Bottom, Left,* and *Right* margins to **0.5"**.
   d. Click **OK** to close the dialog box and apply the margin settings. If a dialog box opens informing you that the margins are outside the printable area, click **Ignore**.
4. Arrange the text in columns and customize columns.
   a. Move to the top of the document.
   b. Click the **Columns** button [*Layout* tab, *Page Setup* group] and choose **Two**. The text displays in two columns.
   c. Click the **Columns** button again [*Layout* tab, *Page Setup* group] and choose **More Columns**. The *Columns* dialog box opens (Figure 4-47).
   d. Select **Three** in the *Presets* area.
   e. In the *Width and spacing* area, change the *Spacing* to **0.6"**.
   f. Click the **Apply to** drop-down list and select **Whole document**.
   g. Click **OK** to apply custom column settings.
5. Use column breaks to control column endings.
   a. Place the insertion point in front of "What Clients Are Saying."

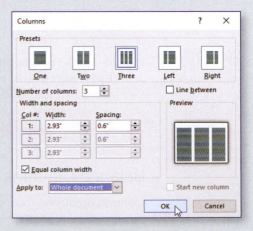

4-47 Customize column settings

b. Click the **Breaks** button [*Layout* tab, *Page Setup* group] and select **Column** to insert a column break.
c. Place the insertion point in front of "Education & Training."
d. Press **Ctrl+Shift+Enter** to insert a column break.

6. Save and close the document (Figure 4-48).

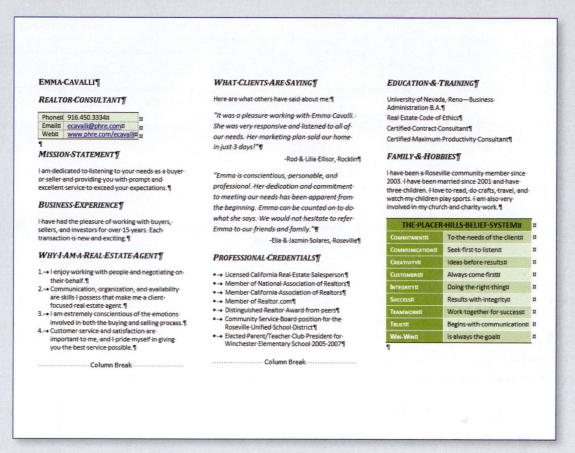

4-48 PP W4-3 completed

![SLO 4.5]

Working with Graphics

You can use graphics to visually present information and enhance a document. Graphics can be pictures stored on your computer, online pictures, shapes, *SmartArt*, and *WordArt*. You can insert and customize graphic images to meet your specific needs and effectively present information visually.

Pictures and Online Pictures

You can use pictures and graphics to enhance your documents with a visual element. You can add your own pictures and graphics to Word documents. In addition to using your own pictures and graphics, Word uses Bing images to find a wide variety of online pictures to add to your documents. Word uses the term *picture* generically to refer to any type of visual image that is saved as a graphic file. Below is a table of common types of graphic formats:

Types of Graphics

Format	Full Name	Extension	Details
PNG	Portable Network Graphics	.png	Used with pictures and editing pictures; high-quality resolution
JPEG	Joint Photographic Experts Group	.jpeg or .jpg	Relatively small file size; many pictures are saved and distributed in JPEG format
TIFF	Tagged Image File Format	.tiff	Used with high-quality digital photos and has a larger file size than JPEG or PNG
GIF	Graphics Interchange Format	.gif	Used with graphics with fewer colors
WMF	Windows Metafile	.wmf	Windows format used with many graphic images
BMP	Windows Bitmap	.bmp	Proprietary Windows format used with many Microsoft graphic images

Insert a Picture

To enhance a document, insert your own picture or a picture you have saved. See the steps below to insert a picture into a document.

▶ HOW TO: Insert a Picture

1. Place the insertion point in the document at the approximate area where you want the picture inserted.
2. Click the **Insert** tab.
3. Click the **Pictures** button [*Illustrations* group]. The *Insert Picture* dialog box opens (Figure 4-49).

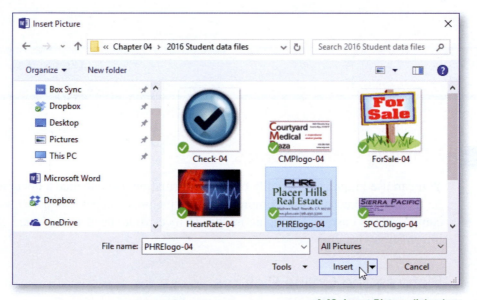

4-49 *Insert Picture* dialog box

4. Browse to the location on your computer and select a picture.
5. Click the **Insert** button to insert the picture and close the *Insert Picture* dialog box.

You might find a picture on the Internet and want to include it in a document. You can either save the picture and insert it as explained above or copy the picture and paste it into your document. Press **Ctrl+C** to copy the picture and **Ctrl+V** to paste the picture.

Include pictures obtained from the web only if you have permission from the image owner to avoid copyright infringement. For academic purposes, you may include images if you reference their sources as you would any other research citation.

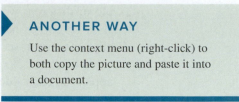

> ▶ **ANOTHER WAY**
>
> Use the context menu (right-click) to both copy the picture and paste it into a document.

Insert an Online Picture

Word provides a variety of online picture choices using ***Bing Image Search***. When using an image from *Bing Image Search*, make sure you have the permission of the image owner to avoid copyright infringement.

▶ **HOW TO:** Search for and Insert an Online Picture

1. Place the insertion point in the document where you want the picture inserted.
2. Click the **Insert** tab.
3. Click the **Online Pictures** button [*Illustrations* group] to open the *Insert Pictures* dialog box.
4. Click the *Bing Image Search* text box, type the keywords for the image you want to find, and press **Enter**.

   - Thumbnails of the pictures appear in the list below (Figure 4-50).
   - The light yellow information bar explains that some images require a license or fee to use.
   - Click **X** in the upper right of this information bar to display only those images requiring no license or fee. Click **Show all web results** to display all images, some of which require a license or fee.

5. Select the picture to insert into your document.

   - Click the **View Larger** button in the bottom right corner of a graphic to view a larger picture.
   - Click the **X** in the upper right corner to close the larger image.

6. Click the **Insert** button to insert the picture into your document.

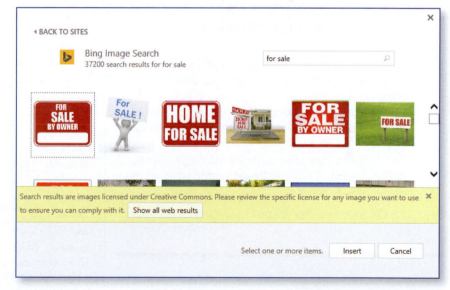

4-50 Insert an online picture

Arrange a Graphic in a Document

Once you have inserted an image into a document, you can adjust its size and position in the document. Word provides you with a number of options to resize, align, wrap text around, insert a caption, and group graphics in your document.

Resize a Graphic

In most cases, you will need to resize your graphic to fit properly in your document. You can do this a couple of different ways. You can drag the top, bottom, side, or corner handles to resize the graphic manually, or you can set a specific size for the graphic.

When you select (click) a graphic, *sizing handles* appear on each side and in each corner (Figure 4-51). To resize the graphic, click and hold one of the handles and drag in or out to decrease or increase the size of the graphic. Use the corner handles to keep the resized image proportional. If you use the side, top, or bottom handles to resize, the proportions of the image may become distorted.

4-51 Resize graphic using the sizing handles

You can also resize the image to a specific size or to a percentage of its original size.

▶ HOW TO: Resize an Image

1. Click the image to select it. The *Picture Tools Format* tab displays on the *Ribbon*.

2. Click the **up** or **down** arrows in the *Height* or *Width* area [*Size* group] to increase or decrease the size (Figure 4-52).

   • Resizing in this manner keeps the graphic proportional.

3. Alternatively, click the **Size** launcher to open the *Layout* dialog box with the *Size* tab displayed (Figure 4-53).

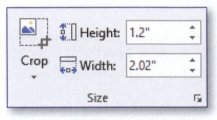

4-52 *Size* group on the *Picture Tools Format* tab

4. Change the size of the graphic to a specific size in the *Height* and *Width* areas.

   • You can also scale the graphic to make it a percentage of its original size in the *Scale* area.
   • Check the **Lock aspect ratio** box selected to prevent the graphic from becoming distorted in size.
   • The *Original size* area displays the original size of the graphic. Click the **Reset** button to reset the graphic to its original.

5. Click **OK** to resize the graphic and close the dialog box.

> ▶ **ANOTHER WAY**
>
> Open the *Layout* dialog box by right-clicking the graphic and selecting **Size and Position**.

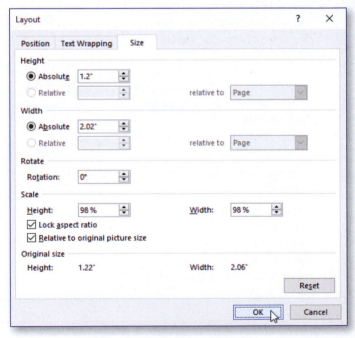

4-53 *Size* options in the *Layout* dialog box

Wrap Text around a Graphic

You can select how the text aligns or wraps around your graphic with a variety of *text wrapping* options. You can control how the text wraps around the graphic and choose to position the graphic in front of or behind the text.

▶ HOW TO: Wrap Text around a Graphic

1. Click the graphic to select it.
2. Click the **Wrap Text** button [*Picture Tools Format* tab, *Arrange* group] (Figure 4-54).
3. Select a text wrapping option.
4. Select **More Layout Options** to open the *Layout* dialog box with the *Text Wrapping* tab displayed (Figure 4-55).
   - Use the *Layout* dialog box to customize text wrapping [*Text Wrapping* tab], specify the position of the graphic [*Position* tab], and resize the graphic [*Size* tab].
5. In the *Wrap text* area, you can choose *Both sides*, *Left only*, *Right only*, or *Largest only*.
6. In the *Distance from text* area, set a specific distance from the graphic to wrap text.
7. Click **OK** to close the *Layout* dialog box.

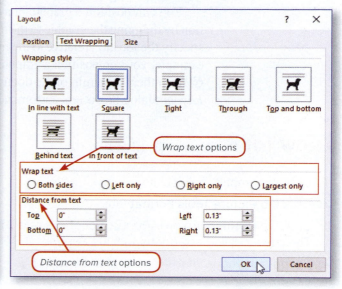

4-54 *Wrap Text* options

4-55 *Text Wrapping* tab in the *Layout* dialog box

You can also click the **Layout Options** button to the right of a selected graphic and select a text wrapping option (Figure 4-56). Click the **See more** link to open the *Layout* dialog box.

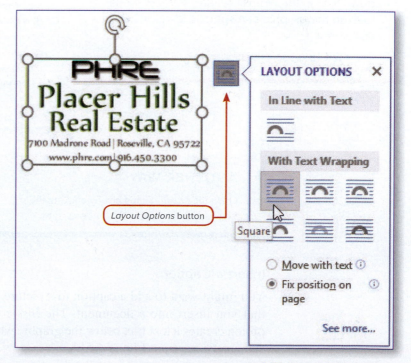

4-56 *Layout Options* menu

> ### MORE INFO
>
> *In Line with Text* is the default option when you insert a graphic into a document.

Position a Graphic

In addition to adjusting the size of a graphic and specifying how text wraps around a graphic, you can also specify the position of the graphic in your document. You can align a graphic left, right, or center by selecting the graphic and clicking the **Align** button in the *Arrange* group on the *Picture Tools Format* tab (Figure 4-57).

You can position a graphic in a document in a specific location by dragging the graphic to the desired location. You can also specify the location relative to the margins, page, or column. For example, you can position a graphic 5" from the left margin and 6" from the top margin of the document. The *Position* tab in the *Layout* dialog box offers customization options (Figure 4-58).

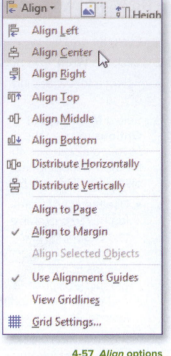

4-57 *Align* options

▶HOW TO: Position a Graphic

1. Click the graphic to select it.
2. Click the **Picture Tools Format** tab.
3. Click the **Position** button [*Arrange* group] and select **More Layout Options**. The *Layout* dialog box opens with the *Position* tab selected (see Figure 4-58).
4. Set both the horizontal and vertical alignment of the graphic.
   - In the *Horizontal* area, you have the following positioning options: *Alignment*, *Book layout*, *Absolute position*, and *Relative position*.
   - In the *Vertical* area, you have the following positioning options: *Alignment*, *Absolute position*, and *Relative position*.
5. Use the radio buttons, text boxes, and drop-down lists in the *Horizontal* and *Vertical* areas to align the graphic at a specific location in the document.
6. Click **OK** to close the dialog box.

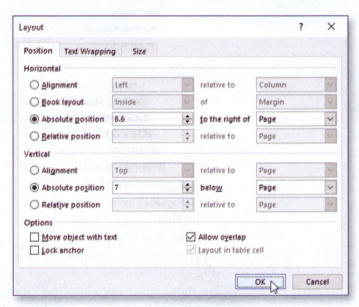

4-58 *Position* tab in the *Layout* dialog box

▶ ANOTHER WAY

Open the *Layout* dialog box by clicking the **Size** launcher [*Picture Tools Format* tab].

Insert a Caption

You might want to add a caption to a picture or chart that you insert into a document. The *Insert Caption* option creates a text box below the graphic where you can enter a caption (Figure 4-59).

4-59 Graphic with caption below

▶ HOW TO: Insert a Caption

1. Select the graphic that needs a caption.

2. Right-click the graphic and select **Insert Caption** from the context menu. The *Caption* dialog box opens (Figure 4-60).

   - Word automatically creates a caption for the object you have selected.
   - In the *Caption* text box, you can add a description after the label, but you cannot delete the label.
   - After you add a caption to a graphic, you can delete the label and number and customize the caption text.

3. Click the **Label** drop-down list and choose **Equation, Figure,** or **Table**.

   - You can add a custom label by clicking the **New Label** button and typing a custom label.
   - You can remove the label (but not the number) by checking the **Exclude label from caption** option.

4. Click the **Position** drop-down list and select the location of the caption.

5. Click **OK** to insert the caption.

6. You can edit the caption in the text box after it is added to the graphic (Figure 4-61). You can also customize the size and color of the caption text and adjust the size and positioning of the text box.

4-60 *Caption* dialog box

4-61 **Caption added to graphic**

▶ **ANOTHER WAY**

Insert a caption by clicking the **Insert Caption** button [*References* tab, *Captions* group].

Group Graphic Objects

When you work with graphics, you may want to ***group*** together related graphics and objects. For example, you might want to group a picture and caption. The advantage of doing this is that the grouped graphics become one object that you can be resize and position together.

▶ HOW TO: Group and Ungroup Graphics

1. Press the **Ctrl** key and click the graphics to be grouped (Figure 4-62).

2. Click the **Group** button [*Picture Tools Format* tab, *Arrange* group].

3. Select **Group**. The selected objects become one grouped object (Figure 4-63).

4. To ungroup grouped items, select the grouped object, click the **Group** button in the *Arrange* group on the *Picture Tools Format* tab, and select **Ungroup**.

4-62 **Multiple objects selected to be grouped together**

4-63 **Grouped objects**

Insert and Customize a Shape

In addition to pictures, you can insert other types of graphic items into your Word documents. For example, Word provides a variety of *shapes* that you can insert into your document.

When you insert a shape or line into your document, you are actually drawing the object in your document. Word's *Shapes* gallery groups shapes into categories (Figure 4-64). Once you draw a shape in your document, you can edit the size, position, alignment, and text wrapping of the object.

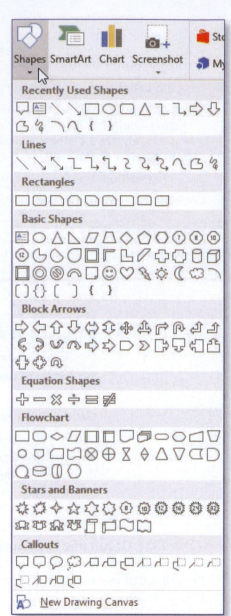

4-64 *Shapes* drop-down list

▶ HOW TO: Insert a Shape

1. Click the **Insert** tab.
2. Click the **Shapes** button [*Illustrations* group] to display the gallery of shape options.
3. Select the shape you want to use. Your pointer becomes a drawing crosshair (large, dark plus sign) when you position the pointer in the document.
4. Click and drag to create the shape (Figure 4-65). When you release the pointer, the shape is inserted into the document.
   - You don't have to be perfectly accurate when you create the shape because you can easily resize the shape after you draw it.
   - You can change the text wrapping on a shape so the shape appears on top of or behind the text, or you can have text wrap around a shape.

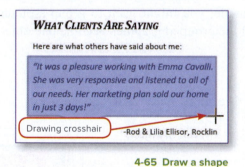

4-65 Draw a shape

Once a shape has been inserted into a document, you can move or resize it. Also, you can change the line size, color, and fill of the shapes. See Figure 4-66 and its callouts for examples of the available selection and sizing handles. The following is a list of those options:

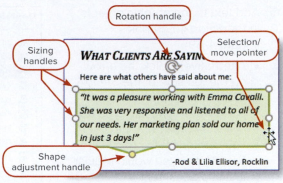

4-66 Shape selected with handles displayed

- *Selection/move pointer*: This pointer (four-pointed arrow) allows you to select and move objects. Select multiple objects by pressing the **Ctrl** key and selecting the objects.
- *Sizing handles*: Eight sizing handles are located on corners and sides of the shape. When you select one of these, the pointer becomes a sizing pointer (two-pointed arrow).
- *Rotation handle*: The rotation handle is the circular arrow at the top of the selected shape. Rotate a shape by clicking and dragging this handle to the left or right.
- *Shape Adjustment handle*: This handle is the yellow circle. You can use this handle to change the shape of an object (not all shapes have this handle available). You can also use this handle to change the size or location of a callout, corner roundness, and other shape elements.

You can change the *Shape Fill, Shape Outline*, and *Shape Effects* of a shape. Each of these areas includes many customization options to enhance shapes. When you select a shape, the *Drawing Tools Format* tab displays on the *Ribbon* (Figure 4-67).

4-67 *Drawing Tools Format* tab

Insert and Customize SmartArt

SmartArt allows you to graphically present information in your document in a visually attractive way. *SmartArt* includes a variety of categories, and within each category, numerous options are available (see Figure 4-68).

SmartArt graphics are a combination of shapes and text boxes. Once you insert a *SmartArt* graphic into a document, you can use *SmartArt Tools Design* and *SmartArt Tools Format* tabs to customize the text content and the graphic's structure.

▶**HOW TO:** Insert and Customize SmartArt

1. Position your insertion point in your document where you want to insert the *SmartArt*.
2. Click the **Insert** tab.
3. Click the **SmartArt** button [*Illustrations* group]. The *Choose a SmartArt Graphic* dialog box opens (Figure 4-68).
4. Select a *SmartArt* graphic. A preview and description of the *SmartArt* displays on the right of the dialog box.
5. Click **OK** to insert the *SmartArt* into the document.

6. Add text to the graphic objects in the *SmartArt* graphic (Figure 4-69).

- Alternatively, click the arrow on the left side of the *SmartArt* graphic to display the *Text* pane where you can type text in the *SmartArt* graphic.
- You can format the text in the *SmartArt* as you would regular text in a document.
- You can also format text in the *SmartArt* using *Text Fill*, *Text Outline*, and *Text Effects* on the *SmartArt Tools Format* tab.

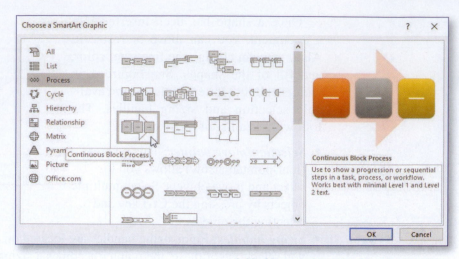

4-68 *Choose a SmartArt Graphic* dialog box

7. Customize the graphic objects in a *SmartArt* graphic using the *SmartArt Tools Design* and *Format* tabs.

- The *SmartArt Tools Design* tab controls the overall design and colors of the *SmartArt* objects.
- The *SmartArt Tools Format* tab allows you to customize the shape of objects, colors, borders, fill, and effects.

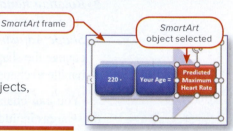

4-69 *SmartArt* with text inserted

Insert and Customize WordArt

WordArt can visually enhance a title of a document or add emphasis to certain text within a document. When you insert *WordArt*, you are actually inserting a text box in the document that can then be manipulated as a graphic. Once you insert *WordArt* in a document, you can resize and move it, and you can change the color, fill, and effects of this object.

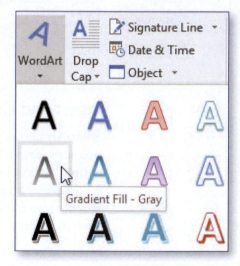

4-70 *WordArt* gallery

▶ **HOW TO:** Insert WordArt

1. Position your insertion point in your document where you want to insert the *WordArt*.

- Alternatively, select text in the document to convert to a *WordArt* object.

2. Click the **Insert** tab.

3. Click the **WordArt** button [*Text* group] and select a *WordArt* style from the gallery of options (Figure 4-70). The *WordArt* text box displays in your document.

4. Type the text you want to format as *WordArt*.

- The placeholder text (*Your text here*) is selected when you insert the *WordArt* (Figure 4-71). Type to replace the placeholder text. If the placeholder text is deselected, select it before typing your text.

5. Click anywhere in your document away from the text box to deselect the *WordArt* graphic.

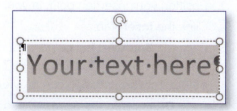

4-71 *WordArt* inserted into a document

Customizing *WordArt* is similar to customizing other graphic objects in Word. When you select the *WordArt* text box, the **Drawing Tools Format** tab displays (Figure 4-72). From this tab, you can change the style of the *WordArt*, add a border to the text box, and change the fill, outline, and effects of the *WordArt* text.

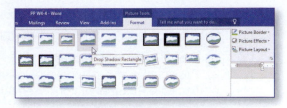

4-72 *Drawing Tools Format* tab

Resize *WordArt* by using the sizing handles on the corners and sides. Rotate the *WordArt* text box with the rotation handle. You can change the position and text wrapping of the *WordArt* in the same way you manipulate other graphics.

Enhance Graphics with Styles

Each of the different types of graphics has a variety of styles, fills, outlines, and effects that you can apply. Context-sensitive tabs appear when you select a graphic object. These context-sensitive tabs contain a variety of **style galleries** (Figure 4-73).

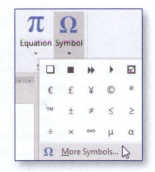

4-73 *Picture Styles* gallery

When applying styles to graphics, Word provides you with a **live preview**. When you place your pointer on a style from one of the style galleries, Word temporarily applies the style to the selected graphic to preview how it will appear in the document.

Insert Symbols and Special Characters

In addition to pictures, *WordArt*, shapes, *SmartArt*, and other types of graphic objects, Word has a variety of symbols and other special characters that you can insert into a document (Figure 4-74). The *Symbols*, *Wingdings*, and *Webdings* font sets have an assortment of characters and symbols you can insert into a document. Additional special characters available, such as the em dash, en dash, and copyright and trademark symbols.

▶HOW TO: Insert a Symbol

1. Click the **Insert** tab.
2. Click the **Symbol** button [*Symbols* group] to display a drop-down list of recently used symbols.
3. Select **More Symbols** (see Figure 4-74). The *Symbol* dialog box opens (Figure 4-75).
4. Click the **Font** drop-down list on the *Symbols* tab to select the font set.
   - Or, click the **Special Character** tab to display the list of available special characters.
5. Click a symbol or special character to insert.
   - Each character has a numerical code that identifies it. The *Character code* area displays this code.
6. Click **Insert** to insert the symbol in the document.
7. Click **Close** to close the dialog box.

4-74 *Symbol* button on the *Insert* tab

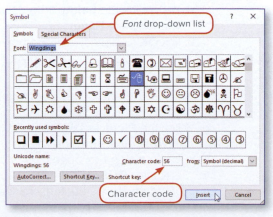

4-75 *Symbol* dialog box

For this Pause & Practice project, you finalize Emma's brochure by inserting a picture, shapes, and *WordArt*. You format and arrange these graphic objects attractively in the document.

Files Needed: ***[your initials] PP W4-3.docx, PHRElogo-04.png***, and ***ForSale-04*** *(Student data files are available in the* Library *of your SIMnet account)*
Completed Project File Name: ***[your initials] PP W4-4.docx***

1. Open the ***[your initials] PP W4-3*** document completed in *Pause & Practice 4-3*.

2. Save this document as [your initials] PP W4-4.

3. Insert the Placer Hills Real Estate logo at the bottom right corner of the document.
   a. Position the insertion point below the table in the third column.
   b. Click the **Pictures** button [*Insert* tab, *Illustrations* group]. The *Insert Picture* dialog box opens.
   c. Select the ***PHRElogo-04*** file from the student data files and click **Insert**.

4-76 Adjust the size of a graphic

4. Arrange and format the logo.
   a. With the logo selected, click the **Wrap Text** button [*Picture Tools Format* tab, *Arrange* group] and choose **In Front of Text**.
   b. In the *Height* box [*Size* group], type 1.2 and press **Enter** (Figure 4-76). The width automatically adjusts to keep the picture proportional.
   c. Click the middle of the picture and drag the graphic near the bottom right corner of the document.
   d. Click the **Picture Border** button [*Picture Styles* group] and select **Olive Green, Accent 3** (Figure 4-77).
   e. Click the **Picture Border** again, click **Weight**, and select **1½ pt**.
   f. Click the **Position** button [*Arrange* group] and select **More Layout Options**. The *Layout* dialog box opens with the *Position* tab displayed (Figure 4-78).
   g. In the *Horizontal* area, select the **Absolute position** radio button, type 8.6, click the **to the right of** drop-down list, and select **Page**.
   h. In the *Vertical* area, select the **Absolute position** radio button, type 7, click the **below** drop-down list, and select **Page**.
   i. Click **OK** to close the dialog box.

4-77 Select *Picture Border* color

5. Add a picture near the bottom of the first column.
   a. Click at the end of the fourth numbered item in the first column.
   b. Click the **Pictures** button [*Insert* tab, *Illustrations* group]. The *Insert Picture* dialog box opens.
   c. Select the ***ForSale-04*** picture from the student data files and click **Insert**.
   d. With the picture selected, change the *Height* [*Picture Tools Format* tab, *Size* group] to **1.2"** and press **Enter**.

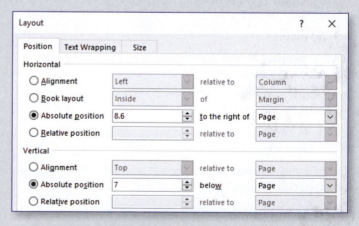

4-78 Customize position of the logo

e. Right-click the picture, choose **Wrap Text**, and select **Square**.

f. Click the middle of the picture and drag it so it is to the right of the fourth numbered item in the first column (see Figure 4-79).

6. Insert a caption for the picture.

a. Right-click the picture and choose **Insert Caption**. The *Caption* dialog box opens.

b. Click **OK** to close the *Caption* dialog box and insert the caption.

c. Delete the placeholder text in the caption text box and type Meeting Your Needs as the caption. If the caption covers the bottom of the graphic, select the border of the caption and use the down keyboard arrow to move it down slightly.

d. Press **Ctrl+E** or click the **Center** button [*Home* tab, *Paragraph* group] to center the text in the caption.

e. With the caption still selected, press the **Ctrl** key and click the picture to select it also. Both the picture and the caption should be selected.

f. Click the **Group** button [*Picture Format Tools* tab, *Arrange* group] and choose **Group**. The two objects group into one object (Figure 4-79).

4-79 Picture and caption grouped

7. Change the paragraph spacing on the two quotes in the second column.

a. Place your insertion point in the first quoted paragraph in the second column (beginning with "It was a pleasure . . .").

b. Change the *After* paragraph spacing to **12 pt**.

c. Place your insertion point in the second quoted paragraph in the second column (beginning with "Emma is conscientious . . .").

d. Change the *After* paragraph spacing to **12 pt**.

8. Add and format a shape to the quoted text.

a. Click the **Shapes** button [*Insert* tab, *Illustration* group] and select **Rectangular Callout** (Figure 4-80). Your pointer changes to a crosshair (dark plus sign).

b. On the first quote in the second column, drag from the upper left to the lower right to draw the shape over the quoted text (Figure 4-81).

c. With the shape still selected, click the **Send Backward** drop-down arrow [*Drawing Tools Format* tab, *Arrange* group] and select **Send Behind Text** (Figure 4-82). The text displays on top of the shape.

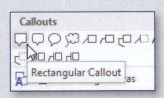

4-80 Select shape

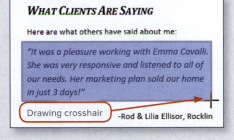

4-81 Draw rectangular shape

d. Click the *Shape Styles* **More** button [*Drawing Tools Format* tab, *Shape Styles* group] to display the gallery of shape styles.

e. Select **Colored Outline – Olive Green, Accent 3** (Figure 4-83).

f. Click the **Shape Fill** button [*Drawing Tools Format* tab, *Shape Styles* group] and select **Olive Green, Accent 3, Lighter 80%**.

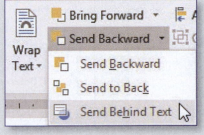

4-82 Send Behind Text

4-83 Apply a shape style

g. Click the **Shape Effects** button [*Drawing Tools Format* tab, *Shape Styles* group], select **Shadow**, and choose **Offset Diagonal Bottom Right** (Figure 4-84).

h. Change the *Shape Height* to **0.9"** and the *Shape Width* to **3"** [*Drawing Tools Format* tab, *Size* group].

i. Drag the shape to position it evenly behind the text. You can also use the keyboard arrow keys to position a selected shape.

9. Replicate and align the callout shape.
   a. With the shape still selected, press **Ctrl+C** to copy it and **Ctrl+V** to paste the copy of the shape into the document.
   b. Drag the new shape over the second quote.
   c. With the second shape still selected, change the *Shape Height* to **1.4"** [*Drawing Tools Format* tab, *Size* group].
   d. Drag the shape to position it evenly behind the text (Figure 4-85).
   e. With the second shape selected, press the **Shift** key and click the right edge of the first shape to select both shapes.
   f. Click the **Align** button [*Drawing Tools Format* tab, *Arrange* group] and select **Align Center**.
   g. Use the up or down arrow keys to adjust the vertical position of the selected shape.

10. Add *WordArt* to the brochure and customize it.
    a. At the top of the first column, select the text "**Emma Cavalli**" (including the paragraph mark).
    b. Click the **WordArt** button [*Insert* tab, *Text* group].
    c. Select **Gradient Fill – Gray** to convert the selected text to *WordArt* (Figure 4-86).
    d. With the *WordArt* selected, change the *Shape Height* to **0.8"** and the *Shape Width* to **3.6"** [*Drawing Tools Format* tab, *Size* group].
    e. Click the **Text Effects** button [*Drawing Tools Format* tab, *WordArt Styles* group], click **Reflection**, and select **Tight Reflection, touching** (Figure 4-87).

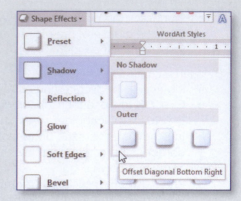

4-84 Select a shape *Shadow* option

4-85 Shapes positioned behind text

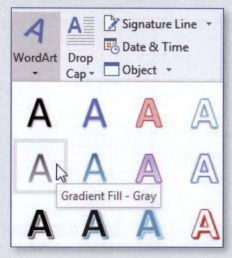

4-86 Select *WordArt* style

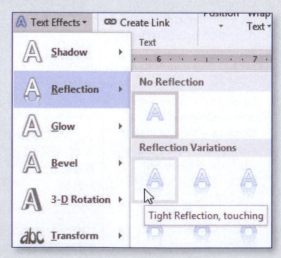

4-87 Apply a *Reflection* text effect

f.   Click the **Position** button [*Drawing Tools Format* tab, *Arrange* group] and select **More Layout Options**. The *Layout* dialog box opens.

g.   In the *Horizontal* area, change the *Absolute position* to **0.2" to the right of Page**.

h.   In the *Vertical* area, change the *Absolute position* to **0.2" below Page**.

i.   Click **OK** to close the *Layout* dialog box.

11. Save and close the document (Figure 4-88).

Emma Cavalli

REALTOR CONSULTANT

Phone	916.450.3334
Email	ecavalli@phre.com
Web	www.phre.com/ecavalli

MISSION STATEMENT

I am dedicated to listening to your needs as a buyer or seller and providing you with prompt and excellent service to exceed your expectations.

BUSINESS EXPERIENCE

I have had the pleasure of working with buyers, sellers, and investors for over 15 years. Each transaction is new and exciting.

WHY I AM A REAL ESTATE AGENT

1.   I enjoy working with people and negotiating on their behalf.
2.   Communication, organization, and availability are skills I possess that make me a client-focused real estate agent.
3.   I am extremely conscientious of the emotions involved in both the buying and selling process.
4.   Customer service and satisfaction are important to me, and I pride myself in giving you the best service possible.

Meeting Your Needs

WHAT CLIENTS ARE SAYING

Here are what others have said about me:

"It was a pleasure working with Emma Cavalli. She was very responsive and listened to all of our needs. Her marketing plan sold our home in just 3 days!"

-Rod & Lilia Ellisor, Rocklin

"Emma is conscientious, personable, and professional. Her dedication and commitment to meeting our needs has been apparent from the beginning. Emma can be counted on to do what she says. We would not hesitate to refer Emma to our friends and family."

-Elia & Jazmin Solares, Roseville

PROFESSIONAL CREDENTIALS

- Licensed California Real Estate Salesperson
- Member of National Association of Realtors
- Member California Association of Realtors
- Member of Realtor.com
- Distinguished Realtor Award from peers
- Community Service Board position for the Roseville Unified School District
- Elected Parent/Teacher Club President for Winchester Elementary School 2005-2007

EDUCATION & TRAINING

University of Nevada, Reno—Business Administration B.A.

Real Estate Code of Ethics

Certified Contract Consultant

Certified Maximum Productivity Consultant

FAMILY & HOBBIES

I have been a Roseville community member since 2003. I have been married since 2001 and have three children. I love to read, do crafts, travel, and watch my children play sports. I am also very involved in my church and charity work.

THE PLACER HILLS BELIEF SYSTEM	
COMMITMENT	To the needs of the client
COMMUNICATION	Seek first to listen
CREATIVITY	Ideas before results
CUSTOMERS	Always come first
INTEGRITY	Doing the right thing
SUCCESS	Results with integrity
TEAMWORK	Work together for success
TRUST	Begins with communication
WIN-WIN	Is always the goal

PHRE
Placer Hills Real Estate
7100 Madrone Road | Roseville, CA 95722
www.phre.com | 916.450.3300

4-88 PP W4-4 completed

Chapter Summary

4.1 Improve the design and readability of a document by using tables to present and arrange information (p. W4-210).

- **Tables** organize information in column and row format. A **column** is a vertical grouping of cells, and a **row** is a horizontal grouping of cells.
- A **cell** is where a column and row intersect.
- Use **Tab** to move forward to the next cell and **Shift+Tab** to move to the previous cell.
- **Table Tools Layout** and **Table Tools Design** tabs provide you with many table formatting features.
- You can copy or move columns or rows in a table.
- You can add or delete columns and rows from existing tables.
- When working with tables, you can select individual cells, a range of cells, rows, columns, or an entire table.
- A group of cells can be merged to create one cell. Cells can also be split into multiple cells.

4.2 Modify a table by changing the column and row size, aligning text, using the *Table Properties* dialog box, sorting data in tables, and using *AutoFit* (p. W4-214).

- You can resize columns and rows in a table.
- Use the **AutoFit** feature to automatically resize the table to fit the contents of the table, the window, or a fixed width.
- Text in a cell can be aligned both horizontally and vertically.
- **Cell margins** control the amount of spacing around the text within a cell.
- The **Table Properties** dialog box provides size and alignment options for cells, rows, columns, or an entire table.
- You can sort table information in ascending or descending order.

4.3 Enhance the appearance and function of a table by applying borders and shading, using table styles, inserting formulas, and converting text into a table (p. W4-220).

- You can apply borders and shading to parts of a table or to the entire table.

- **Table Styles** are collections of borders, shading, and formatting that you can apply to a table. Word provides a gallery of table styles.
- You can apply **Table Style Options** to a header row, total row, banded rows, first column, last column, or banded columns.
- **Formulas** in a table perform mathematical calculations.
- You can convert existing text into a table or convert an existing table to text.

4.4 Modify the layout and design of a document by using columns to present information (p. W4-227).

- You can arrange text in a document in columns.
- You can choose from preset column settings or you can customize column settings and space between columns using the **Columns dialog box**.
- **Column breaks** control column endings.
- Balance columns with column breaks or a **continuous section break**.

4.5 Enrich a document by adding and modifying graphic elements such as pictures, shapes, *SmartArt*, and *WordArt* (p. W4-231).

- Pictures and graphics add visual appeal to a document. Word can insert a variety of graphic file types.
- You can resize a graphic and position it at a specific location in a document.
- **Text wrapping** controls how text wraps around graphics.
- The Layout dialog box has options to change the position, text wrapping, and size of graphic objects.
- You can insert customized captions for graphics.
- Graphic objects can be **grouped** together to create one graphic object, which makes resizing and positioning easier.
- **Shapes** can be inserted into a document and resized and customized. You can change fill color, outline color and width, and shape effects.
- **SmartArt** graphically presents information in a document.

- **WordArt** is special text formatting that you can insert into a document.
- Word provides a variety of formatting options and styles for *SmartArt*, *WordArt*, and other graphic objects.
- You can insert a variety of symbols and special characters into documents. Use the *Symbols* dialog box to select different symbols and characters.

Check for Understanding

The SIMbook for this text (within your SIMnet account) provides the following resources for concept review:

- Multiple choice questions
- Matching exercises
- Short answer questions

Guided Project 4-1

For this project, you modify the values statement document for Sierra Pacific Community College District to arrange text in columns, insert the company logo, and use shapes.
[Student Learning Outcomes 4.4, 4.5]

Files Needed: **ValuesStatement-04.docx** and **SPCCDlogo-04.png** *(Student data files are available in the* Library *of your SIMnet account)*
Completed Project File Name: **[your initials] Word 4-1.docx**

Skills Covered in This Project

- Change page orientation.
- Change margins.
- Apply columns to text.
- Modify column settings.
- Insert a column break.

- Insert a picture.
- Change picture color.
- Modify picture size and position.
- Insert a shape.
- Modify shape size and position.
- Modify shape fill and outline.

1. Open the **ValuesStatement-04** document from your student data files.

2. Save this document as [your initials] Word 4-1.

3. Change the orientation and margins of the document.
   a. Change the orientation of the document to **Landscape**.
   b. Change the top and bottom margins to **0.5"**.
   c. Change the left and right margins to **0.75"**.

4. Apply column formatting to the text in the body of the document.
   a. Place the insertion point in front of the first paragraph heading ("Access").
   b. Click the **Columns** button [*Layout* tab, *Page Setup* group] and select **More Columns**. The *Columns* dialog box opens (Figure 4-89).
   c. Select **Three** in the *Presets* area.
   d. Change the *Spacing* to **0.4"** in the *Width and spacing* area.
   e. Click the **Apply to** drop-down list and select **This point forward**.
   f. Click **OK** to close the *Columns* dialog box.

5. Insert a column break to balance the columns on the page.
   a. Place the insertion point in front of the "Student Learning Outcomes" paragraph heading.
   b. Click the **Breaks** button [*Layout* tab, *Page Setup* group] and select **Column**.

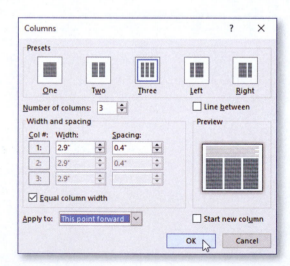

4-89 *Columns dialog box*

6. Insert, resize, and position the company logo on the bottom left of the document.
    a. Click at the end last paragraph in the first column.
    b. Click the **Pictures** button [*Insert* tab, *Illustrations* group].
    c. Select the **SPCCDlogo-04** file from the student data files and click **Insert**.
    d. Click the **Wrap Text** button [*Picture Tools Format* tab, *Arrange* group] and select **Behind Text**.
    e. Right-click the logo and choose **Size and Position**. The *Layout* dialog box opens (Figure 4-90).
    f. In the *Scale* area on the *Size* tab, change the *Height* to **120%** and press **Tab**. The width automatically adjusts to keep the logo proportional.
    g. Click the **Position** tab.
    h. In the *Horizontal* area, change the *Absolute position* to **0.3"** *to the right of* **Page**.
    i. In the *Vertical* area, change the *Absolute position* to **7.2"** *below* **Page**.
    j. Click **OK** to close the *Layout* dialog box.

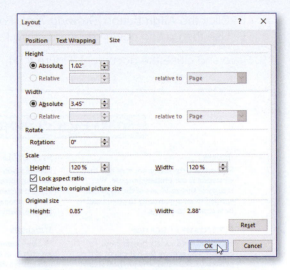

4-90 Resize logo as a percentage of its original size

7. Change the color of the logo.
    a. With the logo selected, click the **Color** button [*Picture Tools Format* tab, *Adjust* group].
    b. Select **Saturation: 0%** in the *Color Saturation* area (Figure 4-91).

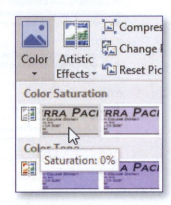

4-91 Change *Color Saturation*

8. Add a shape around the title, resize the shape, and modify the outline and fill.
    a. Click the **Shapes** button [*Insert* tab, *Illustrations* group].
    b. Select **Snip Single Corner Rectangle** from the *Shapes* gallery (*Rectangles* area). Your pointer becomes a crosshair (dark plus sign) (Figure 4-92).
    c. Click and drag the crosshair over the title and then release the pointer (Figure 4-93).

4-93 Draw shape around the title

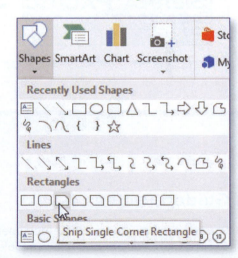

4-92 Select shape

    d. Click the **Shape Fill** button [*Drawing Tools Format* tab, *Shape Styles* group] and select **White, Background 1, Darker 15%**.
    e. Click the **Shape Outline** button [*Drawing Tools Format* tab, *Shape Styles* group] and select **White, Background 1, Darker 50%**.
    f. Click the **Shape Outline** button again, select **Weight**, and select **1½ pt**.
    g. Click the **Send Backward** drop-down arrow [*Drawing Tools Format* tab, *Arrange* group] and select **Send Behind Text** from the drop-down list.
    h. Change the *Shape Height* [*Drawing Tools Format* tab, *Size* group] to **0.4"** and the *Shape Width* to **6.3"**.

i. Click the **Align** button [*Drawing Tools Format* tab, *Arrange* group] and select **Align Center**.

j. Use the up and down keyboard arrow keys to vertically center the shape behind the title.

9. Save and close the document (Figure 4-94).

SIERRA PACIFIC COMMUNITY COLLEGE DISTRICT VALUES

ACCESS

Students are the reason we exist and their education is our primary purpose. We recognize that residents of the region are entitled to an opportunity to attend and to be successful in college.

BENEFITS OF EDUCATION

Individuals and society benefit from citizens who achieve the full extent of their personal, intellectual, and physical ability; engage in critical and creative thinking; exhibit responsible citizenship; succeed in a competitive global work environment; and participate in lifelong learning.

EXCELLENCE

Excellence in instruction and student services is essential to develop the full potential of each student.

LEADERSHIP

Responsible leadership and service among all Sierra Pacific Community College District faculty, staff, and students are nurtured and encouraged so the college will be a leader for positive change, growth, and transformation in student-oriented educational practices.

STUDENT LEARNING OUTCOMES

Identification and assessment of student learning outcomes promotes and improves student success and the effective use of SPCCD resources to create innovative and flexible learning opportunities.

DIVERSITY

We are a community enriched by the experience of students, faculty, staff, and administrators from a variety of cultures, ethnic and economic backgrounds, age is and abilities. We are committed to providing and nurturing a safe environment for the free exchanges of ideas.

COMMUNITY DEVELOPMENT

The curricular and co-curricular programs and services of the college benefit the region served through enhanced intellectual and physical growth, economic development, and exposure to the arts, sciences, and humanities.

HUMAN RESOURCES

Faculty and staff members are our most important resources and are entitled to a supportive, collegial work environment that recognizes excellence, provides opportunities for professional development, service and leadership, and encourages meaningful involvement in an interest-based decision-making process.

COMMUNICATION

Achievement of the Sierra Pacific Community College District mission and vision requires an effective system of communication with internal and external constituencies that is based on honesty, trust, civility, and mutual respect.

INNOVATION AND RISK TAKING

Addressing challenges and change requires creativity, assessment, flexibility, and responsible risk-taking to achieve our vision, mission and goals.

FISCAL RESPONSIBILITY

It is necessary to maintain a fiscally sound, efficient, and effective operation that achieves our mission within the resources available.

EVALUATION

Efficient and effective accomplishment of the ARC mission, vision, and student learning outcomes requires regular and ongoing data-based evaluation.

SIERRA PACIFIC
COMMUNITY COLLEGE DISTRICT
7300 COLLEGE AVE
SACRAMENTO, CA 92387
209.658.4466
WWW.SPCCD.EDU

4-94 Word 4-1 completed

Guided Project 4-2

For this project, you modify a document about maximum and target heart rate for the American River Cycling Club. You arrange text in a table and insert and modify *SmartArt* and a picture.
[**Student Learning Outcomes 4.1, 4.2, 4.3, 4.5**]

File Needed: ***MaximumHeartRate-04.docx*** and ***HeartRate-04.png*** (*Student data files are available in the* Library *of your SIMnet account*)
Completed Project File Name: *[your initials] Word 4-2.docx*

Skills Covered in This Project

- Insert and resize *WordArt*.
- Position and modify *WordArt*.
- Convert text to a table.
- Apply a table style.
- Modify table and text alignment.
- Change cell margins in a table.
- Insert and add text to a *SmartArt* graphic.
- Resize, position, and format *SmartArt*.
- Insert, resize, and position a picture.
- Insert a caption.
- Align and group graphic objects.

---

1. Open the **MaximumHeartRate-04** document from your student data files.

2. Save this document as [your initials] Word 4-2.

3. Insert *WordArt* as the title of the document and modify the *WordArt* object.
   a. Select the title of the document, **"American River Cycling Club"** (including the paragraph mark).
   b. Click the **WordArt** button [*Insert* tab, *Text* group].
   c. Select **Fill – Red, Accent 2, Outline – Accent 2** from the *WordArt* gallery (Figure 4-95).
   d. Change the *Shape Width* [*Drawing Tools Format* tab, *Size* group] to **6.5"**.

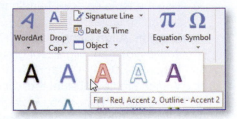

4-95 Insert *WordArt*

   e. Click the **Position** button [*Drawing Tools Format* tab, *Arrange* group] and select **More Layout Options**. The *Layout* dialog box opens (Figure 4-96).
   f. In the *Horizontal* area, select **Alignment** and **Centered** *relative to* **Margin**.
   g. In the *Vertical* area, select **Absolute position** and enter **0.2"** *below* **Page**.
   h. Click **OK** to close the *Layout* dialog box.
   i. Click the **Text Effects** button [*Drawing Tools Format* tab, *WordArt Styles* group] and select **Reflection**.
   j. Select **Tight Reflection, touching** (Figure 4-97).

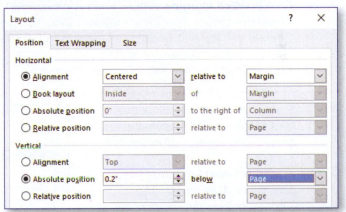

4-96 Adjust position of *WordArt*

4. Convert text into a table and format the table.
   a. Select all of the tabbed text at the bottom of the document.
   b. Click the **Table** button [*Insert* tab, *Tables* group] and select **Convert Text to Table**. The *Convert Text to Table* dialog box opens.
   c. Click the **AutoFit to contents** radio button in the *AutoFit behavior* area.
   d. Click **OK** to close the dialog box.
   e. Click the **Table Tools Design** tab.
   f. Check the **Header Row** and **Banded Rows** boxes [*Table Style Options* group] and deselect the other check boxes.
   g. In the *Table Styles* group, click the **More** button to display the *Table Styles* gallery.

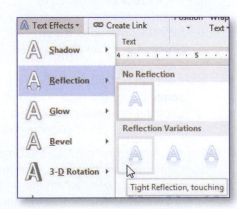

4-97 Apply *Reflection* option

h. Select **Grid Table 4 – Accent 2** (Figure 4-98).

i. In the second column of the first row, place the insertion point before "Zone," press **Backspace** to delete the space between words, and press **Enter**.

j. In the third column of the first row, place the insertion point before "Heart," press **Backspace** to delete the space between words, and press **Enter**.

5. Adjust the size and alignment of the table.
   a. Use the table selector handle to select the entire table.
   b. Click the **Align Center** button [*Table Tool Layout* tab, *Alignment* group] (Figure 4-99).
   c. With the table still selected, click the **Properties** button [*Table Tools Layout* tab, *Table* group].
   d. Click the **Table** tab, select **Center** in the *Alignment* area, and click **OK** to close the dialog box.
   e. Click the **Cell Margins** button [*Table Tools Layout* tab, *Alignment* group]. The *Table Options* dialog box opens.
   f. Change the *Top* and *Bottom* cell margins to **0.03"** and the *Left* and *Right* cell margins to **0.1"**.
   g. Click **OK** to close the *Table Options* dialog box.

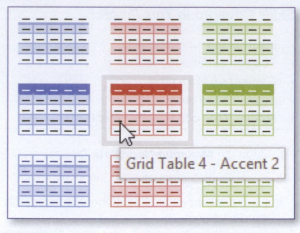

4-98 *Table Styles* gallery

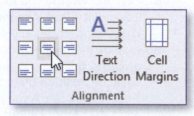

4-99 *Align Center* the text in the table

6. Insert and modify a *SmartArt* graphic.
   a. Place the insertion point at the end of the second body paragraph, "(*Example*: . . .)," in the first section.
   b. Click the **SmartArt** button [*Insert* tab, *Illustrations* group]. The *Choose a SmartArt Graphic* dialog box opens (Figure 4-100).
   c. Click **Process** in the list of *SmartArt* types.
   d. Select **Continuous Block Process** and click **OK** to insert the *SmartArt*.
   e. Click the first placeholder text (*[Text]*) and type 220, **space** once, and type − (hyphen or minus).
   f. Click the next placeholder text and type Your Age, **space** once, and type =.
   g. Click the last placeholder text and type Predicted Maximum Heart Rate.

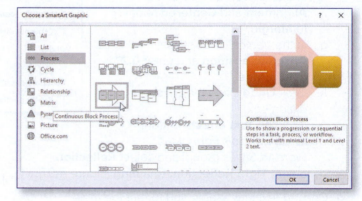

4-100 *Choose a SmartArt Graphic* dialog box

7. Format, resize, and position the *SmartArt*.
   a. Click the outside frame of the *SmartArt* graphic. *Note: Make sure the entire* SmartArt *is selected and not an object within the graphic.*
   b. In the *Size* group [*SmartArt Tools Format* tab], change the *Shape Height* to **1.5"** and the *Shape Width* to **2.6"**.
   c. Click the **Wrap Text** button [*SmartArt Tools Format* tab, *Arrange* group] and select **Square**.
   d. Click the **Position** button [*SmartArt Tools Format* tab, *Arrange* group] and select **More Layout Options**. The *Layout* dialog box opens (Figure 4-101).

e. In the *Horizontal* area, change the *Absolute position* to **4.5"** *to the right of* **Margin**.

f. In the *Vertical* area, change *Absolute position* to **0.4"** *below* **Margin**.

g. Click **OK** to close the *Layout* dialog box.

h. With the *SmartArt* still selected, select **Intense Effect** as the *SmartArt* style [*SmartArt Tools Design* tab, *SmartArt Styles* group] (Figure 4-102).

i. Click the edge of the first text box to select it, and press **Ctrl+B** to apply bold format. Repeat this format on the other two text boxes.

j. Select the last text box (if it is not already selected) and click the **SmartArt Tools Format** tab.

k. Click the **Shape Fill** button and select **Red, Accent 2** as the fill color (Figure 4-103).

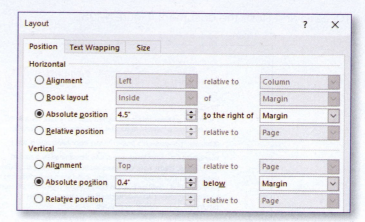

4-101 Adjust *SmartArt* position

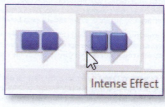

4-102 Apply *SmartArt* style

4-103 Change *Shape Fill* color

8. Insert a picture and resize and position the graphic.

a. Place the insertion point at the end of the second section heading ("Target Heart Rate").

b. Click the **Pictures** button [*Insert* tab, *Illustrations* group] to open the *Insert Picture* dialog box.

c. Locate the **HeartRate-04** picture from your student data files and click **Insert**.

d. Change the *Height* [*Picture Tools Format* tab, *Size* group] to **1"** (the width adjusts automatically).

e. Click the **Wrap Text** button [*Picture Tools Format* tab, *Arrange* group] and select **Tight**.

f. Click the **Align** button [*Picture Tools Format* tab, *Arrange* group] and select **Align Right**.

9. Format the picture and insert a caption.

a. With the picture selected, click the **More** button in the *Pictures Styles* group [*Picture Tools Format* tab] to display the gallery of styles.

b. Select the **Bevel Rectangle** picture style (Figure 4-104).

c. Right-click the picture and select **Insert Caption** from the context menu. The *Insert Caption* dialog box opens.

d. Click **OK** to insert the caption.

e. Select the caption text, click the **Text Fill** button [*Drawing Tools Format* tab, *WordArt Styles* group], and select **Red, Accent 2** as the text color.

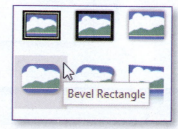

4-104 Apply *Picture Style*

f. With the caption text still selected, type Know your target heart rate to replace the caption placeholder text.

g. In the *Size* group [*Drawing Tools Format* tab], change the caption *Height* to **0.2"** and the *Width* to **1.5"**.

h. Press the **Ctrl** key and click the picture. Both the caption and picture should be selected.

i. Click the **Align** button [*Drawing Tools Format* tab, *Arrange* group] and select **Align Center**.

j. Click the **Group** button [*Arrange* group] and select **Group**. The picture and caption are grouped into one object.

10. Save and close the document (Figure 4-105).

American River Cycling Club

WHAT IS MAXIMUM HEART RATE?

The maximum heart rate is the highest your pulse rate can get. To calculate your **predicted maximum heart rate**, use this formula:

(Example: a 40-year-old's predicted maximum heart rate is 180.)

Your actual maximum heart rate can be determined by a graded exercise test. Please note that some medicines and medical conditions might affect your maximum heart rate. If you are taking medicines or have a medical condition (such as heart disease, high blood pressure, or diabetes), always ask your doctor if your maximum heart rate/target heart rate will be affected.

TARGET HEART RATE

You gain the most benefits and decrease the risk of injury when you exercise in your target heart rate zone. Usually this is when your exercise heart rate (pulse) is 60 percent to 80 percent of your maximum heart rate. Do not exercise above 85 percent of your maximum heart rate. This increases both cardiovascular and orthopedic risk and does not add any extra benefit.

know your target heart rate

When beginning an exercise program, you might need to gradually build up to a level that is within your target heart rate zone, especially if you have not exercised regularly before. If the exercise feels too hard, slow down. You will reduce your risk of injury and enjoy the exercise more if you don't try to over-do it.

To find out if you are exercising in your target zone (between 60 percent and 80 percent of your maximum heart rate), use your heart rate monitor to track your heart rate. If your pulse is below your target zone (see the chart below), increase your rate of exercise. If your pulse is above your target zone, decrease your rate of exercise.

Age	Target Heart Rate (HR) Zone (60-85%)	Predicted Maximum Heart Rate
20	120-170	200
25	117-166	195
30	114-162	190
35	111-157	185
40	108-153	180
45	105-149	175
50	102-145	170
55	99-140	165
60	96-136	160
65	93-132	155
70	90-128	150

4-105 Word 4-2 completed

Guided Project 4-3

For this project, you format a buyer escrow checklist for Placer Hills Real Estate. You convert text to a table, format the table, and insert a picture.
[**Student Learning Outcomes 4.1, 4.2, 4.3, 4.5**]

Files Needed: ***BuyerEscrowChecklist-04.docx***, ***Check-04.png***, and ***PHRElogo-04.png*** (Student data files are available in the Library of your SIMnet account)
Completed Project File Name: *[your initials]* ***Word 4-3.docx***

Skills Covered in This Project

- Convert text to a table.
- Add columns to a table.
- Apply bullets and modify alignment.
- *AutoFit* a table.
- Apply table styles and borders.
- Modify row width and column height.
- Center text vertically in a table.
- Insert, resize, and position a picture.
- Change picture color.
- Use absolute position and text wrapping.
- Apply border and effects to a picture.

---

1. Open the ***BuyerEscrowChecklist-04*** document from your student data files.

2. Save this document as [your initials] Word 4-3.

3. Convert text to a table.
   a. Select the text beginning with **"Task"** through **"Verify Preliminary Report with Lender."**
   b. Click the **Table** button [*Insert* tab, *Tables* group].
   c. Click the **Convert Text to Table** button. The *Convert Text to Table* dialog box opens.
   d. Click **OK** to accept the default settings. The text converts to a table with 1 column and 14 rows.

4. Add columns and column headings to the table.
   a. With the table selected, click the **Table Tools Layout** tab.
   b. Click the **Insert Right** button [*Rows & Columns* group] to insert a blank column to the right of the existing column.
   c. Click the **Insert Right** button two more times to insert two more columns. Your table should now have four columns.
   d. Type the following column headings in the first row:
      Column 2: Date Completed
      Column 3: Initials
      Column 4: Notes

5. Add bullets to selected text.
   a. Select all of the text in the first column below "Task."
   b. Apply an **open square bullet** to these items (*Wingdings*, Character code 111).
   c. Click the **Decrease Indent** button once so the first line indent is at 0" and the hanging indent is at 0.25".

6. Apply table style and apply formatting.
   a. Place your insertion point in the first cell in the first column.
   b. Click the **AutoFit** button [*Table Tools Layout* tab, *Cell Size* group] and select **AutoFit Contents**.
   c. Click the **Table Tools Design** tab.
   d. In the *Table Style Options* group, select **Header Row** and **Banded Rows**. The other options should be unchecked.
   e. Click the **More** button in the *Table Styles* group to open the gallery of table styles.
   f. Select **Grid Table 5 Dark** style (Figure 4-106).
   g. Select the column headings (first row of the table).
   h. **Bold** and **center** the column headings. You might have to click the **Bold** button more than once to bold all column headings.

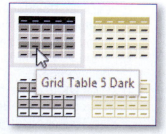

4-106 Apply table style

7. Modify cell size and alignment.
   a. Use the table selector handle to select the entire table, or use the **Select** button [*Table Tools Layout* tab, *Table* group] and click **Select Table**.
   b. Change the *Height* [*Table Tools Layout* tab, *Cell Size* group] to **0.35"**. The row height changes on the entire table.
   c. With the table still selected, click the **Properties** button [*Table Tools Layout* tab, *Table* group]. The *Table Properties* dialog box opens.

d. Click the **Cell** tab, select **Center** in the *Vertical alignment* area, and click **OK** to close the *Table Properties* dialog box.

e. Place your insertion point in the fourth column and change the *Width* [*Table Tools Layout* tab, *Cell Size* group] to **1.5"**.

8. Insert a picture and position it in the document.

a. Place your insertion point at the end of the "Buyer(s):" line after the solid underline tab leader.

b. Click the **Pictures** button [*Insert* tab, *Illustrations* group]. The *Insert Pictures* dialog box opens.

c. Locate the **Check-04** file from your student data files and click **Insert**.

d. In the *Size* group [*Picture Tools Format* tab], change the *Height* to **1.5"** (the width adjusts automatically).

e. Click the **Wrap Text** button [*Picture Tools Format* tab, *Arrange* group] and select **Tight**.

f. Click the **Color** button [*Picture Tools Format* tab, *Adjust* group] and select **Olive Green, Accent color 2 Dark** in the *Recolor* area (Figure 4-107).

4-107 Change picture color

g. Click the **Position** button [*Picture Tools Format* tab, *Arrange* group] and select **More Layout Options** to open the *Layout* dialog box (Figure 4-108).

h. In the *Horizontal* area, change the *Absolute position* to **5.5"** *to the right of* **Margin**.

i. In the *Vertical* area, change the *Absolute position* to **0.7"** *below* **Margin**.

j. Click **OK** to close the *Layout* dialog box.

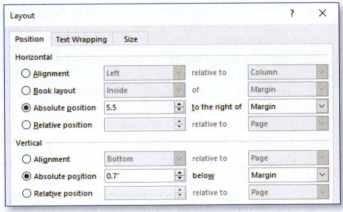

4-108 Position picture

9. Insert a picture in the upper right of the document.

a. Place your insertion point at the end of the title.

b. Click the **Pictures** button [*Insert* tab, *Illustrations* group]. The *Insert Picture* dialog box opens.

c. Select the **PHRElogo-04** file from the student data files and click **Insert**.

d. Right-click the picture, select **Wrap Text**, and choose **In Front of Text**.

e. Click the **Position** button [*Picture Tools Format* tab, *Arrange* group] and select **More Layout Options** to open the *Layout* dialog box.

f. In the *Horizontal* area, change the *Absolute position* to **6.2"** *to the right of* **Page**.

g. In the *Vertical* area, change the *Absolute position* to **0.2"** *below* **Page**.

h. Click **OK** to close the *Layout* dialog box.

i. Click the **Picture Border** button [*Picture Tools Format* tab, *Picture Styles* group] and select **Olive Green, Accent 2** (Figure 4-109).

j. Click the **Picture Border** button, click **Weight**, and select **1 ½ pt**.

k. Click the **Picture Effects** button [*Picture Tools Format* tab, *Picture Styles* group], select **Shadow**, and select **Offset Bottom** (middle option in first row).

4-109 Apply *Picture Border* color

10. Save and close the document (Figure 4-110).

BUYER·ESCROW·CHECKLIST¶

Buyer(s):· _____ → _____ ¶

Phone/Fax:· _____ → _____ ¶

Email:· _____ → _____ ¶

Agent:· _____ → _____ ¶

Property·Address:· _____ → _____ ¶

Task¤	Date·Completed¤	Initials¤	Notes¤	¤
□→Fax·Contract·to·Buyer(s)¤	¤	¤	¤	¤
□→Fax·Contract·to·Lender¤	¤	¤	¤	¤
□→Verify·Property·ID·with·Buyer(s)¤	¤	¤	¤	¤
□→Verify·Property·ID·with·Lender¤	¤	¤	¤	¤
□→Turn·in·new·sale·to·PHRE¤	¤	¤	¤	¤
□→Send·check·to·Title·Company¤	¤	¤	¤	¤
□→Notified·Buyer·of·EM·deposit¤	¤	¤	¤	¤
□→Fax/Email·Pest·Report·to·Buyer(s)¤	¤	¤	¤	¤
□→Fax/Email·Pest·Report·to·Lender¤	¤	¤	¤	¤
□→Fax/Email·*Clear*·Pest·Report·to·Buyer(s)¤	¤	¤	¤	¤
□→Fax/Email·*Clear*·Pest·Report·to·Lender¤	¤	¤	¤	¤
□→Verify·Preliminary·Report·with·Buyer(s)¤	¤	¤	¤	¤
□→Verify·Preliminary·Report·with·Lender¤	¤	¤	¤	¤

¶

Emma·Cavalli → → Placer·Hills·Real·Estate¶
916.450.3334 7100·Madrone·Road,·Roseville,·CA·95721¶
ecavalli@phre.com www.phre.com¶

4-110 Word 4-3 completed

Independent Project 4-4

For this project, you format a vaccination schedule for Courtyard Medical Plaza by converting text to a table, formatting the table, and inserting a picture.
[**Student Learning Outcomes 4.1, 4.2, 4.3, 4.5**]

Files Needed: ***VaccinationSchedule-04.docx, CMPLogo-04.png***, and ***Vaccination-04.png*** *(Student data files are available in the* Library *of your SIMnet account)*
Completed Project File Name: *[your initials]* **Word 4-4.docx**

Skills Covered in This Project

- Convert text to a table.
- Apply a table style.
- *AutoFit* table and change row height.
- Center text vertically.
- Sort text in a table.
- Insert rows and add information.
- Merge cells.
- Apply custom borders.
- Apply a style to text.
- Insert and position a picture.
- Adjust size and position of a picture.
- Apply a picture effect.
- Add and format a caption.
- Group a caption and picture.

1. Open the **VaccinationSchedule-04** document from your student data files.

2. Save this document as [your initials] Word 4-4.

3. Select the tabbed text in the middle of the document and convert it to a table (accept default settings). Don't include the blank line below the tabbed text.

4. Select the entire table and apply the following changes:
   a. Select **Banded Rows** in the *Table Style Options* group [*Table Tools Design* tab] and deselect all other check boxes.
   b. Apply the **List Table 1 Light – Accent 2** table style (Figure 4-111).
   c. Change the font size on all of the text in the table to **10 pt**.
   d. Choose **AutoFit Window**.
   e. Change row height to **0.25"**.
   f. Center all text vertically within each cell. *(Hint: Use the* Cell *tab in the* Table Properties *dialog box.)*
   g. Sort the table in **Ascending** order by **Name of Vaccine**. Be sure to select **Header row** in the *My list has* area of the *Sort* dialog box.

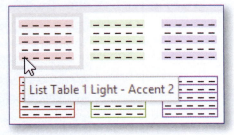

4-111 Apply table style

5. Make the following changes to the table:
   a. Insert a row above the first row.
   b. Merge the three cells in the new first row and type the following:
      RECOMMENDED VACCINATION SCHEDULE
   c. **Bold** and **center** the first row and change the font size to **11 pt**.
   d. **Bold** and **italicize** the second row.
   e. Select the first row, apply a **solid line, Black, Text 1** color, **1½ pt**. width **top** and **bottom** border.
   f. Select the second row, apply a **solid line, Black, Text 1** color, **1½ pt**. width **bottom** border.
   g. Select the last row, apply a **solid line, Black, Text 1** color, **1½ pt**. width **bottom** border.
   h. **Align Center** [*Table Tools Layout* tab, *Alignment* group] the column headings and the text in the third column.

6. Insert the following information alphabetically into the table. Insert rows where needed.

Meningococcal conjugate (MCV)	At 11-12 years	1
Hepatitis B (HepB)	At birth, 1-2 months, and 6 months	3

7. Modify the title of the document ("Vaccination Schedule").
   a. Apply **Title** style to the title of the document.
   b. Change the *After* paragraph spacing to **8 pt**.
   c. **Center** the title horizontally.
   d. Apply **small caps** and **bold** formatting to the title.

8. Insert and modify a picture.
   a. Place the insertion point after the title and insert the **CMPLogo-04** picture from you student data files.
   b. Change text wrapping to **Top and Bottom**.
   c. Change the height of the logo to **1"**. Verify the logo remains proportional.
   d. Apply the **Offset Diagonal Bottom Right** shadow picture effect.
   e. Set the horizontal and vertical absolute position at **0.2"** to the right of and below page.

9. Insert a picture and add a caption.
   a. Place the insertion point after the first body paragraph and insert the **Vaccination-04** picture from your student data files.
   b. Change the text wrapping to **Square**.
   c. Change the height of the picture to **1.3"**. Verify the graphic remains proportional.
   d. Drag the picture so it is to the right of the first and second paragraphs.
   e. Insert a caption and type Don't neglect your vaccinations! as the caption text.
   f. **Center** the caption text, change the font color to **Red, Accent 2**, and turn off italics if it is applied to the text.
   g. Select the caption and the picture and **Align Center**.
   h. **Group** the caption and the picture.
   i. Set the horizontal absolute position at **6"** to the right of margin.
   j. Set the vertical absolute position at **0.8"** below margin.

10. Save and close the document (Figure 4-112).

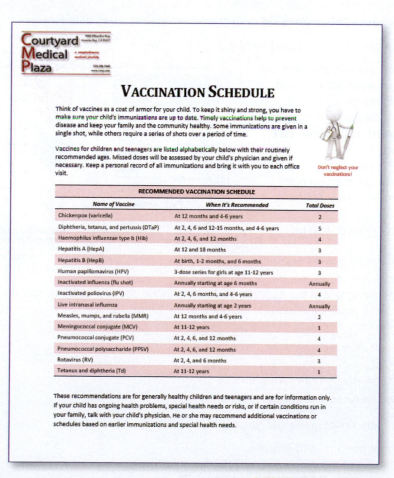

4-112 Word 4-4 completed

Independent Project 4-5

For this project, you create an emergency telephone information sheet for Sierra Pacific Community College District (SPCCD). You add and modify a *SmartArt* graphic, convert text to a table, insert a new table, format the tables, and insert the company logo.
[**Student Learning Outcomes 4.1, 4.2, 4.3, 4.5**]

Files Needed: ***EmergencyTelephones-04.docx*** and ***SPCCDlogo.png*** *(Student data files are available in the* Library *of your SIMnet account)*
Completed Project File Name: *[your initials] Word 4-5.docx*

Skills Covered in This Project

- Modify an existing document.
- Insert a *SmartArt* graphic.
- Add text to a *SmartArt* graphic.
- Resize, change color of, and apply a style to *SmartArt*.
- Convert text to a table and *AutoFit*.
- Sort text in a table.

- Insert a row, merge cells, and add information.
- Apply a table style.
- Change cell margins and alignment.
- Apply a style to text.
- Insert a table and type text.
- Insert a picture.
- Adjust a picture size and position.
- Insert a symbol and the current date.

1. Open the ***EmergencyTelephones-04*** document from your student data files.

2. Save this document as [your initials] Word 4-5.

3. Insert a *SmartArt* graphic and add text.
   a. Place your insertion point in front of the second section heading ("Emergency Telephone Locations").
   b. Insert the **Vertical Chevron List** *SmartArt* graphic from the *List* category (Figure 4-113).
   c. Type 1 in the graphic text box in the upper left of the *SmartArt* graphic.
   d. Type 2 in the graphic text box below.
   e. Type 3 in the third graphic text box in the first column of the graphic.

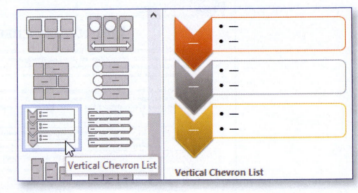

4-113 Insert *SmartArt* graphic

   f. Type the following text in the bulleted text boxes in the second column. You do not need to add bullets because bullets are already included in the *SmartArt*.

   - Press the "Help" button
   - Speak when the light comes on

   - Stay on the line
   - You will be connected with the college police

   - State clearly the nature of the emergency and your location
   ---

   g. Delete the extra bullet in the last graphic in the second column.

4. Resize and format the *SmartArt* graphic.
   a. Select the frame of the graphic to select the entire graphic.
   b. Change the height to **2.5"** and the width to **4.2"**.
   c. Change the text wrapping to **Top and Bottom**.

d. Change the color of the entire *SmartArt* graphic to **Dark 2 Fill** (Figure 4-114).

e. Apply the **Intense Effect** *SmartArt* style.

5. Convert text to a table.
   a. Select the tabbed text below the second section heading ("Emergency Telephone Locations"). Do not select the paragraph mark below the last row.
   b. Convert this text to a table and select **AutoFit to contents**.

6. Sort the table text in ascending order by the first column.

7. Add a title row and insert text.
   a. Add a row above the first row.
   b. Merge the cells in this row.
   c. Type Blue Emergency Telephones in the merged first row.

4-114 Change *SmartArt* colors

8. Format the table.
   a. Select **Header Row, First Column**, and **Banded Rows** in the *Table Style Options* group. Deselect all other options.
   b. Apply the **List Table 2** table style.
   c. Select the entire table and change the top and bottom cell margins to **0.04"** and the left and right cell margins to **0.1"**.
   d. Vertically **center** all text in the table. *(Hint: Use the* Cell *tab in the* Table Properties *dialog box.)*
   e. Horizontally **center** the text in the first row. This text should be centered vertically and horizontally.

9. Insert, resize, and position the SPCCD logo.
   a. Insert the **SPCCDlogo_04** picture (from your student data files) at the top of the document.
   b. Change the width to **3"** and keep the size proportional.
   c. Change the text wrapping to **Top and Bottom** and drag the logo above the title.
   d. Set the horizontal and vertical absolute position at **0.3"** to the right of the page and below the page.
   e. Change the *Color [Picture Tools Format* tab, *Adjust* group] to **Saturation: 0%**.

10. Modify the footer to include a symbol and the current date.
    a. Edit the footer and **space** once at the end of the text on the right side of the footer.
    b. Insert a **solid circle** symbol from the *Symbol* font set (Character code 183) and **space** once after it.
    c. Type Revised: and **space** once.
    d. Insert the current date in MM/DD/YY format and set it so that it does not update automatically.

11. Save and close the document (Figure 4-115).

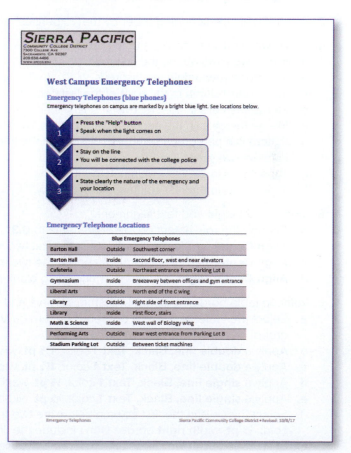

4-115 Word 4-5 completed

Independent Project 4-6

For this project, you modify a memo for Life's Animal Shelter. You edit an existing table, add rows and a column, format the table, insert formulas into the table, and insert and modify *WordArt*.
[Student Learning Outcomes 4.1, 4.2, 4.3]

File Needed: ***WeeklyExpenses-04.docx*** (*Student data files are available in the* Library *of your SIMnet account*)
Completed Project File Name: *[your initials] Word 4-6.docx*

Skills Covered in This Project

- Modify an existing document.
- Modify a table row height.
- Change cell alignment.
- Add rows and a column to a table.
- Merge table rows.
- Modify borders and shading of the table.
- Insert formulas into a table.
- Set formula number format.
- Update formulas.
- Format selected text.
- Insert *WordArt*.
- Modify and position *WordArt*.
- Change paragraph spacing.
- Insert a date.

1. Open the ***WeeklyExpenses-04*** document from your student data files.

2. Save this document as [your initials] Word 4-6.

3. Sort the table in ascending order by the "Expenses" column (the table has a header row).

4. Add rows, a column, and text to the table.
    a. Insert two rows above the first row.
    b. Insert one row below the last row.
    c. Insert one column to the right of the last column.
    d. Merge the cells in the first row and type Life's Animal Shelter.
    e. Merge the cells in the second row and type Weekly Expenses.
    f. If there is a paragraph symbol at the end of the title and subtitle text, delete the paragraph symbol in these two rows.
    g. Type Totals in the last column in the third row.
    h. Type Totals in the first column in the last row.

5. Modify row height and text alignment.
    a. Change the row height on the entire table to **0.3"**.
    b. **Align Center** (vertical and horizontal) the first two rows.
    c. **Align Center Left** the first column below the two merged rows.
    d. **Align Center Right** columns 2–9 (including blank cells) below the two merged rows.

6. Remove table borders and apply custom borders and shading.
    a. Select the table, remove all borders, and turn on **View Gridlines** [*Table Tools Layout* tab, *Table* group].
    b. Apply a **double line, Black, Text 1** color, **1½ pt.** width **top** border to the first row.
    c. Apply a **double line, Black, Text 1** color, **1½ pt.** width **bottom** border to the last row.
    d. Apply a **single line, Black, Text 1** color, **½ pt.** width **top** and **bottom** border to the third row.
    e. Apply a **single line, Black, Text 1** color, **½ pt.** width **top** border to the last row.
    f. Select the cells in the first column below the two merged rows and add a **single line, Black, Text 1** color, **½ pt.** width **right** border. Don't include the first two rows (title and subtitle).
    g. Select the cells in the last column below the two merged rows, and add a **single line, Black, Text 1** color, **½ pt.** width **left** border to the last column. Don't include the first two rows (title and subtitle).

h. Apply **Orange, Accent 6, Lighter 60%** shading fill to the first two rows.

i. Apply **Orange, Accent 6, Lighter 60%** shading fill to the last row.

j. Apply **Orange, Accent 6, Lighter 60%** shading fill to the last column.

k. Turn off **View Gridlines**.

7. Insert formulas into the table.

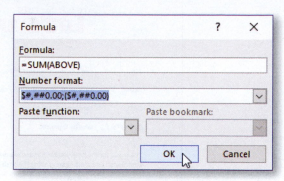

4-116 Insert a formula into the table

a. In the last row of the second column, insert a formula [*Table Tools Layout* tab, *Data* group] to add the figures above. The formula should be **=SUM(ABOVE)**. Use the **$#,##0.00;($#,##0.00)** number format (Figure 4-116).

b. Insert the same formula and number format in remaining cells in the last row, except for the last column.

c. In the last column of the fourth row, insert a formula to add the figures to the left. The formula should be **=SUM(LEFT)**. Use the **$#,##0.00;($#,##0.00)** number format.

d. Insert the same formula and number format in remaining rows in the last column. Make sure to insert the correct formula in each of these cells **=SUM(LEFT)**. Replace "ABOVE" with "LEFT" in the formula, if needed.

8. Change expense data and update formulas.

a. Change the wages for Wednesday to 592.75.

b. Right-click the total amounts in this column and row and select **Update Field** from the context menu to update the totals.

c. Update the formula for grand total (bottom right cell).

9. Format text in the table.

a. Apply **bold**, **small caps**, and **12 pt**. font size to the text in the first two rows.

b. **Bold** and **italicize** text in the third row.

c. **Bold** and **italicize** text and totals in the last row.

d. **Bold** and **italicize** totals in the last column.

e. **Italicize** the expense categories in the first column.

f. Select the table and **AutoFit Contents**.

10. Insert and customize *WordArt* for the company logo.

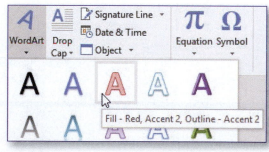

4-117 Insert *WordArt*

a. At the top of the document, insert **WordArt** and use **Fill – Red, Accent 2, Outline – Accent 2** (Figure 4-117).

b. Type Life's Animal Shelter as the text for the *WordArt*.

c. Change the text to **small caps** and **40 pt**.

d. Change the text fill to **Orange, Accent 6**.

e. Change the **Shadow** text effect to **Offset Right**.

f. Use the *Layout* dialog box to change the horizontal **Alignment** to **Centered** relative to **Margin** and change vertical **Absolute position** to **0.2"** below **Page**.

11. Modify the heading lines of the memo.

a. Add **36 pt**. before paragraph spacing on the first line of the memo heading ("TO: . . .").

b. Insert the current date on the date line in the memo heading to replace the placeholder text and set it to update automatically (use January 1, 2018 format).

12. Save and close the document (Figure 4-118).

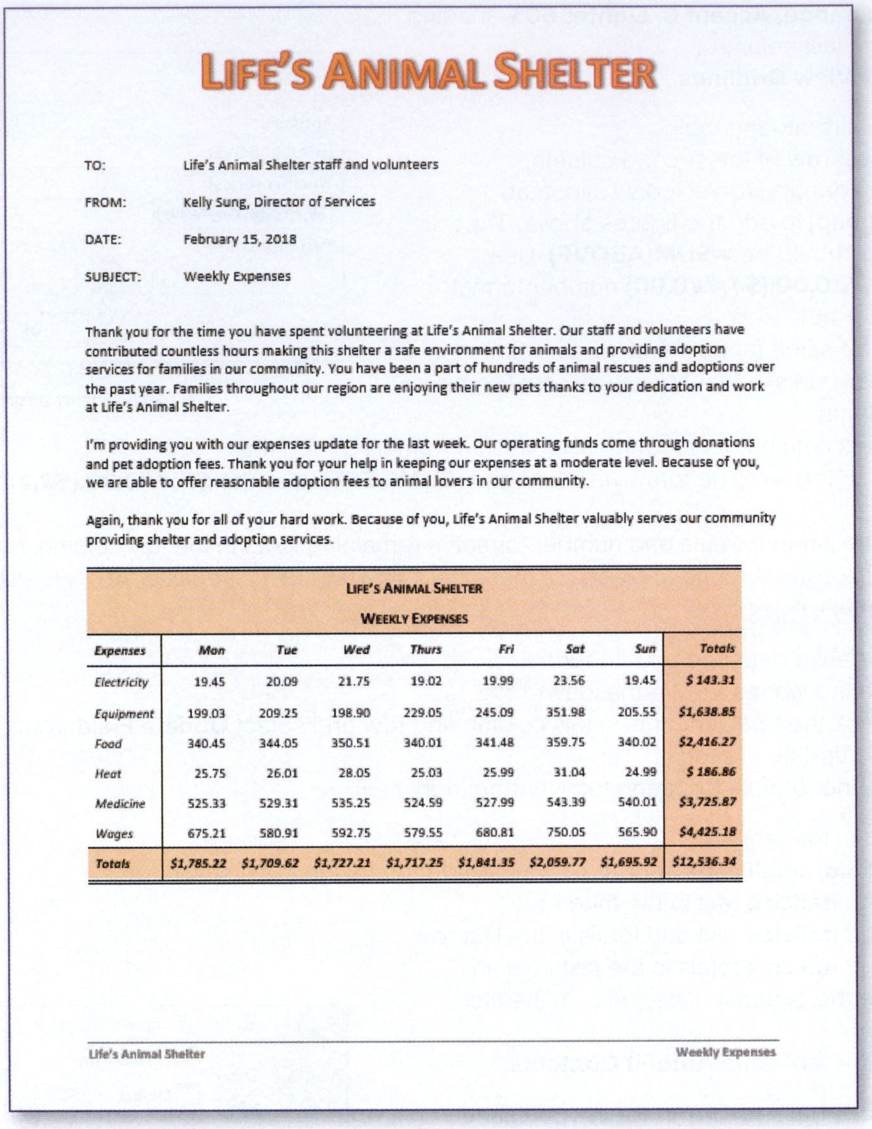

LIFE'S ANIMAL SHELTER

TO: Life's Animal Shelter staff and volunteers

FROM: Kelly Sung, Director of Services

DATE: February 15, 2018

SUBJECT: Weekly Expenses

Thank you for the time you have spent volunteering at Life's Animal Shelter. Our staff and volunteers have contributed countless hours making this shelter a safe environment for animals and providing adoption services for families in our community. You have been a part of hundreds of animal rescues and adoptions over the past year. Families throughout our region are enjoying their new pets thanks to your dedication and work at Life's Animal Shelter.

I'm providing you with our expenses update for the last week. Our operating funds come through donations and pet adoption fees. Thank you for your help in keeping our expenses at a moderate level. Because of you, we are able to offer reasonable adoption fees to animal lovers in our community.

Again, thank you for all of your hard work. Because of you, Life's Animal Shelter valuably serves our community providing shelter and adoption services.

LIFE'S ANIMAL SHELTER
WEEKLY EXPENSES

Expenses	Mon	Tue	Wed	Thurs	Fri	Sat	Sun	Totals
Electricity	19.45	20.09	21.75	19.02	19.99	23.56	19.45	$ 143.31
Equipment	199.03	209.25	198.90	229.05	245.09	351.98	205.55	$1,638.85
Food	340.45	344.05	350.51	340.01	341.48	359.75	340.02	$2,416.27
Heat	25.75	26.01	28.05	25.03	25.99	31.04	24.99	$ 186.86
Medicine	525.33	529.31	535.25	524.59	527.99	543.39	540.01	$3,725.87
Wages	675.21	580.91	592.75	579.55	680.81	750.05	565.90	$4,425.18
Totals	$1,785.22	$1,709.62	$1,727.21	$1,717.25	$1,841.35	$2,059.77	$1,695.92	$12,536.34

Life's Animal Shelter   Weekly Expenses

4-118 Word 4-6 completed

Improve It Project 4-7

For this project, you edit a document for Courtyard Medical Plaza. You arrange text in columns, position the company logo, and apply formatting to improve the overall layout of the document.
[Student Learning Outcomes 4.4, 4.5]

Files Needed: *StayingActive-04.docx* and *CMPlogo.png (Student data files are available in the* Library *of your SIMnet account)*
Completed Project File Name: *[your initials] Word 4-7.docx*

Skills Covered in This Project

- Modify an existing document.
- Apply style formatting to the title and headings.
- Change font size and alignment.
- Change paragraph spacing.
- Arrange text in columns.
- Change spacing between columns.
- Use a column break to balance columns.
- Insert a picture.
- Update formulas.
- Format selected text.
- Insert *WordArt*.
- Modify and position *WordArt*.
- Change paragraph spacing.
- Insert a date.

1. Open the **StayingActive-04** document from your student data files.

2. Save this document as [your initials] Word 4-7.

3. Modify the title of the document.
   a. Apply **Intense Reference** style to the title ("Tips for Staying Active").
   b. Change to **18 pt**. font size.
   c. Align **center**.
   d. Change the *Before* paragraph spacing to **36 pt**. and *After* paragraph spacing to **12 pt**.

4. Modify section headings of the document.
   a. Apply **Subtle Reference** style to the section headings ("Try Some of the Following Suggestions" and "To Keep Exercise Fun and Interesting").
   b. Format both section headings to **14 pt**. font size and align **center**.
   c. Format both section headings to change *Before* paragraph spacing to **12 pt**. and *After* paragraph spacing to **6 pt**.

5. Format the last line of the document to make it part of the bulleted list that precedes it and format it consistently with the other bulleted items.

6. Apply column format to the multilevel list following the first section heading.
   a. Select the multilevel list in the first section and apply two-column format. Do not include the section heading. If the section break above the list has a number, turn off numbering on this line.
   b. Use **0.75"** space between columns.

7. Apply column format to the bulleted list following the second section heading.
   a. Select the bulleted list in the second section and apply two-column format. Do not include the section heading. If the section break above the list has a bullet, turn off bullets on this line.
   b. Modify the columns to use **0.75"** space between columns.
   c. Insert a **column break** before the third bulleted item to balance the columns.

8. Place the insertion point at the end of the first section heading ("Try Some of the Following Suggestions") and **delete** the paragraph mark.

9. Place the insertion point at the end of the second section heading ("To Keep Exercise Fun and Interesting") and **delete** the paragraph mark.

10. Insert, resize, and position a picture.
    a. Insert the **CMPlogo-04** picture at the top of the document.
    b. Change the width to **2.5"** and keep the size proportional.
    c. Change the text wrapping to **In Front of Text**.
    d. Change the horizontal and vertical absolute position to **0.2"** to the right of and below page.

11. Save and close the document (Figure 4-119).

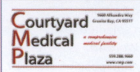

TIPS FOR STAYING ACTIVE

Almost any activity that gets you moving and strengthens your muscles is good for your health and can help you meet your fitness and weight goal. If you haven't been exercising regularly, start out slowly and gradually increase duration, frequency, and intensity. If you have been exercising regularly, keep it up!

TRY SOME OF THE FOLLOWING SUGGESTIONS:

1) AIM FOR AT LEAST 30 TO 60 MINUTES OF MODERATE INTENSITY ACTIVITY ON MOST DAYS.
   a) You can get your exercise all at once, or spread it out during the day.
      i) For example, exercising for three 10-minute periods is just as effective as exercising for 30 minutes at a time.
   b) The more physical activity you do, the more calories you burn and the greater the health benefit.

2) IF YOU DON'T LIKE COUNTING CALORIES, TRY COUNTING YOUR STEPS! WALKING 10,000 STEPS A DAY CAN HELP YOU MANAGE YOUR WEIGHT.
   a) Use a pedometer (an easy-to-wear device that senses your body's motion) to count your steps and motivate you to increase your activity.
   b) Use a journal to track your walking.

3) USE BOTH AEROBIC AND STRENGTHENING ACTIVITIES ARE IMPORTANT TO LOSING WEIGHT AND KEEPING IT OFF.
   a) As you grow older, your body slows down and your metabolism—the rate at which your body burns calories—naturally decreases.
   b) Taking a brisk walk will boost your metabolism and keep you burning calories for hours afterward.

4) REMEMBER THAT ANY FORM OF EXERCISE IS GOOD FOR YOU.
   a) Household chores
      i) Cleaning windows
      ii) Vacuuming
      iii) Folding clothes
   b) Yard work and gardening
   c) Using stairs rather than an elevator
   d) Getting up and moving regularly at work

TO KEEP EXERCISE FUN AND INTERESTING:

✓ PICK ONE OR MORE ACTIVITIES YOU ENJOY. Regular exercise is more likely to become a healthy habit when it's fun as well as rewarding. Varying your activities can help prevent boredom.

✓ EXERCISE WITH A FRIEND. The support and companionship will help keep you going.

✓ THINK ABOUT THE PAYOFFS. Exercise not only helps control weight, it is beneficial to the body and mind in a number of ways. It improves health, boosts your immune system, helps control appetite, helps you feel more energetic and relaxed, and raises your self-confidence!

✓ SET REALISTIC EXERCISE GOALS. Reward yourself in healthy ways when you achieve them.

4-119 Word 4-7 completed

Challenge Project 4-8

A budget can help you track actual or anticipated spending and compare the amount you spend with your earnings. For this project, you use skills you learned in this chapter to create a weekly or monthly budget.
[Student Learning Outcomes 4.1, 4.2, 4.3, 4.5]

File Needed: None
Completed Project File Name: *[your initials] Word 4-8.docx*

Create a new document and save it as [your initials] Word 4-8.

A budget can include, but is not limited to, the following elements:

- Document title
- Time frame of the budget
- Expenditure categories
- Days in the week or weeks in the month
- Row and column totals

Modify your document according to the following guidelines:

- Format your budget in a table.
- Use column headings for days or weeks.
- Use row headings for expense categories.
- Use formulas to total rows and columns.
- Sort table by expenditure amounts.
- Apply table style formatting.
- Adjust shading and borders as needed.
- Adjust column width and row height.
- Modify cell margins.
- Format row and column totals.
- Insert a picture.
- Format, resize, and position a picture.
- Adjust document margins as needed.
- Include an appropriate header and/or footer.

Challenge Project 4-9

Most newspapers and magazines arrange text in column format to improve readability and overall attractiveness of the document. For this project, you arrange an existing document you have written (e.g., an essay, blog entry, article for a newspaper, or posting for Craigslist) in column format.
[Student Learning Outcomes 4.4, 4.5]

File Needed: None
Completed Project File Name: *[your initials] Word 4-9.docx*

Open an existing document you have created and save it as [your initials] Word 4-9.

A document in column format can include, but is not limited to, the following elements:

- Document title
- Byline
- Section headings
- Graphics

Modify your document according to the following guidelines:

- Format your article in column format. Don't include the title as part of the columns.
- Change space and/or add a line between columns.
- Use a column or continuous section break to balance the columns.
- Insert a graphic.
- Adjust size, wrapping, and position of the graphic.
- Add a caption to the graphic.
- Adjust margins as needed.
- Include an appropriate header and/or footer.

Challenge Project 4-10

A weekly schedule can help you organize and manage work, school, family, and personal time more effectively. For this project, use a table to create a weekly schedule and calculate the time you spend on each daily activity.
[Student Learning Outcomes 4.1, 4.2, 4.3, 4.5]

File Needed: None
Completed Project File Name: *[your initials] Word 4-10.docx*

Create a new document and save it as [your initials] Word 4-10.

A weekly schedule can include, but is not limited to, the following elements:

- Document title
- Days of the week
- Time commitment categories
- Row and column totals

Modify your document according to the following guidelines:

- Format your weekly schedule in table.
- Use column headings for days of the week.
- Use row headings for time commitment categories.
- Use formulas to total rows and columns.
- Apply table style formatting.
- Adjust shading and borders as needed.
- Adjust column width and row height.
- Adjust cell margins as needed.
- Format row and column totals.
- Insert a picture.
- Format, resize, and position a picture.
- Adjust document margins as needed.
- Include an appropriate header and/or footer.

Using Templates and Mail Merge

CHAPTER OVERVIEW

Templates and mail merge are two valuable, time-saving features in Microsoft Word. **Templates** are documents on which other documents are based, such as memos, form letters, and fax cover sheets. Using a template, you can create a new document based upon the template, which you can edit and customize, and which leaves the original template unchanged.

The **Mail Merge** features allow you to create form letters, labels, or envelopes without having to retype or create separate documents for each recipient. For example, you might want to create mailing labels for an annual holiday card list or send a yearly letter to volunteers at an organization. Mail merge allows you to merge existing information, such as a letter or labels, with addresses and other information from Access, Outlook, or Excel data files.

STUDENT LEARNING OUTCOMES (SLOs)

After completing this chapter, you will be able to:

SLO 5.1 Create and customize a template based on a Word sample template (p. W5-270).

SLO 5.2 Create and use a template from a blank document or an existing Word document (p. W5-275).

SLO 5.3 Use Word to create envelopes and mailing labels (p. W5-280).

SLO 5.4 Understand the types of merges and how to select or create a recipient list (p. W5-286).

SLO 5.5 Create a merged document using the *Mailings* tab (p. W5-287).

SLO 5.6 Use the *Mail Merge Wizard* to create a merged document (p. W5-299).

CASE STUDY

Kelly McFarland is the community services coordinator for Courtyard Medical Plaza (CMP). She is also the director of volunteers for Skiing Unlimited, an adaptive snow ski program for disabled children and adults. CMP is a proud sponsor of the Skiing Unlimited program and encourages its employees to volunteer for this valuable community outreach program.

In the Pause & Practice projects in this chapter, you create a fax template, form letter template, a merged form letter, and mailing labels for Ms. McFarland.

Pause & Practice 5-1: Use a Word template to create a fax template.

Pause & Practice 5-2: Create a form letter template from an existing document.

Pause & Practice 5-3: Create mailing labels from a recipient list.

Pause & Practice 5-4: Use mail merge to create a form letter.

Pause & Practice 5-5: Use the *Mail Merge Wizard* to create mailing labels.

Using and Customizing Templates

All documents created in Word are based upon a template. Template files contain default fonts, margins, line and paragraph spacing, styles, themes, and other preset formatting options. Templates provide consistency and efficiency in creating documents. Another advantage of using a template is that the original template remains unchanged when you create and edit a new document based upon the template.

Word Normal Template

All new Word documents are based upon the ***Normal template***. The *Normal* template defines one-inch margins, Calibri font, 11 pt. font size, left alignment, and line and paragraph spacing formatting. A template file is a different type of file and has a different ***file name extension*** than a regular Word document. A file name extension follows the name of the file and typically consists of a period and three to five letters. A regular Word document has a ***.docx*** extension (for example "*Document1.docx*"), while a template file has a ***.dotx*** extension (for example "*Document1.dotx*"). See the following table for a list of file types and file name extensions.

Word File Types

File Name Extension	File Type	Sample File Name
.docx	Word Document	*Document1.docx*
.dotx	Word Template	*Document1.dotx*
.doc	Word 97-2003 Document	*Document1.doc*
.dot	Word 97-2003 Template	*Document1.dot*

> **MORE INFO**
>
> Although many other types of files are available in Word, (such as .pdf, .rtf, .txt, and .xml), documents (.docx) and templates (.dotx) are most commonly used.

Usually, the document extension for a Word file does not display in the *Title* bar of Word nor does it display in a *File Explorer* window. However, you can change the settings of *File Explorer* so the file name extension displays after the file name.

▶**HOW TO:** Display File Name Extensions in a File Explorer Window (for Windows 8 and 10)

1. Click the **Start** menu and select **File Explorer** to open a *File Explorer* window.
   - The *File Explorer* button may also display on the Windows *Taskbar* or *Desktop*.
2. Click the **View** tab.
3. Select the **File name extensions** check box [*Show/hide* group] (Figure 5-1).
   - The file name extension displays after the file name in the *File Explorer* window (Figure 5-2).

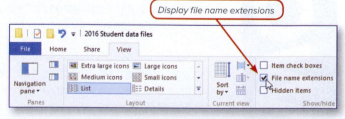

5-1 Display file name extensions in a *File Explorer* window

- In the *Layout* group [*View* tab], you can change how files display in the folder (see Figure 5-1).
- Depending on the display view, you may have to widen the column to display the file name extension.

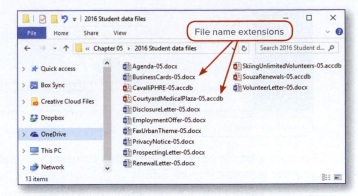

5-2 *File Explorer* window with file name extensions displayed

In Chapter 1, we discussed changing default settings on a document such as font, size, margins, and line spacing or paragraph spacing. When you change the default settings for a document, you are actually making changes to the *Normal* template (Figure 5-3). All new blank Word documents are based upon the *Normal* template, and changes made to this template are applied to all new blank Word documents.

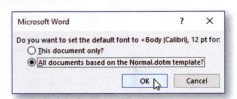

5-3 Options for changing default document settings

Online Templates

In addition to the *Normal* template, Word has a variety of online templates you can download and customize. Some of these templates display in the *New* area on the *Backstage* view. Online templates are grouped into categories, and each category contains a variety of templates. Click one of the *Suggested searches* links or use *Search for online templates* to locate and use an online template.

You can create a document based upon a fax, letter, agenda, resume, or other online template. A template provides the basic structure and formatting for the document, and you can customize it to meet your needs.

▶ **HOW TO:** Open an Online Template in Word

1. Click the **File** tab to display the *Backstage* view.
2. Click the **New** button on the left. Sample templates display in the *New* area.
3. Click one of the template category links in the *Suggested searches* area, or type key words to search for a template in the *Search for online templates* text box (Figure 5-4).

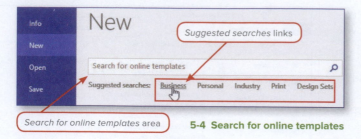

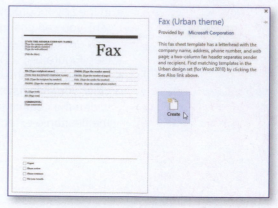

5-4 Search for online templates

4. Click a template to open a window that contains information about the template (Figure 5-5).
5. Click the **Create** button. A document (.docx) based on the Word template opens in a new Word window.

5-5 Create a document from an online template

> **MORE INFO**
>
> After creating a document based upon a template, you can save the document as a document (.docx) or a template (.dotx).

Insert Template Content

Online templates include a combination of text, tables, document property fields, and content control fields. The text functions as headings or content descriptions, while the document property and content control fields are areas where you enter your personalized text. After you create a document based upon an online template, you can insert content, modify the format of the template, and remove content fields that are not needed.

▶ HOW TO: Insert Content in a Template

1. Click the **File** tab to open the *Backstage* view and select **New** on the left.
2. Select an online template and click the **Create** button. A document based on the template opens in a new Word window.
3. Customize the text or formatting as desired.
4. Select a content control field and enter the desired text (Figure 5-6). Repeat for other control fields in the template.

5-6 Insert content in a template

   - If you have entered document properties such as *Author* or *Company* already in your document, the document property fields in the template are automatically populated with this information.
   - You can change document property information in the *Info* area on the *Backstage* view.

Remove Template Content

When you download a Word template, you may need to delete one or more of the content control fields in the template. The following are two methods to remove the unneeded content control fields.

   - Click the content control field handle to select the entire field and press **Delete** (Figure 5-7).

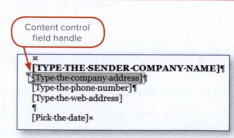

5-7 Select content control field

- Right-click the middle of the content control field and select **Remove Content Control** from the context menu (Figure 5-8).

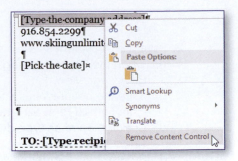

5-8 Remove content control field

Modify Template Content and Format

After creating a document based on an online template, you can add content control fields and remove any unnecessary fields. In addition to adding and removing fields, you can also change or remove any of the descriptive text used in the document. Knowledge of line and paragraph spacing, indents, tables, and borders and shading helps when you modify your template format.

Before modifying a template, ask yourself the following questions:

- Are there tables in my template? (Use the grabber handle to select each table in your template.)
- How many columns and rows are in each table? (Use *View Gridlines* [*Table Tools Format* tab, *Table* group] to display gridlines to better view the table structure.)
- Are any of the cells merged?
- How is the text aligned within each cell?
- Are there borders and/or shading in the table or template?
- Are there tabs and indents in the template? (Turn on *Show/Hide*.)
- What is the line and paragraph spacing?

If you take the time to ask yourself these questions, you will understand the structure and format of the template, which will help you modify the template to meet your needs.

PAUSE & PRACTICE: WORD 5-1

In this Pause & Practice project, you create a fax template for Kelly McFarland's Skiing Unlimited correspondence. You create a fax template from a sample template, edit the content and structure, and save the revised template.

File Needed: *Urban Fax.dotx* (from online templates) or ***FaxUrbanTheme-05.docx*** (*student data files are available in the* Library *of your SIMnet account*)
Completed Project File Name: ***[your initials] PP W5-1 template.dotx***

1. Create a template based on a Word sample template.
   a. Click the **File** button to open the *Backstage* view.
   b. Click the **New** button on the left.
   c. Type Fax in the *Search for online templates* text box and press **Enter**. Online fax templates display in the *New* area.
   d. Select **Fax (Urban theme)** and click **Create** (Figure 5-9). A document based on the template opens in a new Word window. If this online template is not available, open the ***FaxUrbanTheme-05*** document from your student data files.

2. Save the document as a *Word Template* file.
   a. Open the *Save As* dialog box from the *Backstage* view.
   b. Save the document as a template named [your initials] PP W5-1 template.
   c. Click the **Save as type** drop-down list and select **Word Template**.
   d. Browse to the folder on your computer where you save your completed projects. Be very specific about the save location when saving Word template files.
   e. Click **Save** to save the template and to close the dialog box. If a dialog box opens informing you the document will be upgraded to the newest file format, click **OK**.

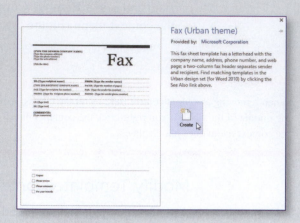

5-9 Create document based on *Fax (Urban theme)* template

3. Modify document property and type text in content control fields.
   a. Click the **File** tab to open the *Backstage* view and click **Info** on the left if it is not already selected.
   b. Remove the existing author in the *Properties* area if there is one, and type Kelly McFarland in the *Author* document property field.
   c. Click the **Back** arrow to return to the document.
   d. Fill in some of the content control fields with the following information:

Content Control Field	Enter Content
Type the sender company name	SKIING UNLIMITED
Type the phone number	916.854.2299
Type the web address	www.skiingunlimited.org
Type the sender fax number	916.854.2288
Type the sender phone number	916.854.2299

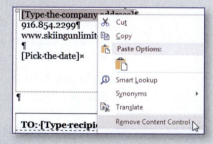

5-10 Remove content control field

4. Remove content control fields.
   a. Right-click the **Type the company address** field and select **Remove Content Control** from the context menu (Figure 5-10). The field is removed leaving a blank line between "SKIING UNLIMITED" and the phone number.
   b. Place your insertion point anywhere in the "CC: [Type text]" row.
   c. Click the **View Gridlines** button [*Table Tools Layout* tab, *Table* group].
   d. Click the **Delete** button [*Table Tools Layout* tab, *Rows & Columns* group] and select **Delete Rows** (Figure 5-11). The content control field and the entire row are removed.

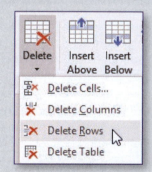

5-11 Delete row

5. Modify table format.
   a. Select the second table in the template (beginning "TO: [Type recipient name"]).
   b. Change the row height to **0.3"** [*Table Tools Layout* tab, *Cell Size* group] (Figure 5-12).
   c. Change the alignment to **Align Center Left** [*Table Tools Layout* tab, *Alignment* group].

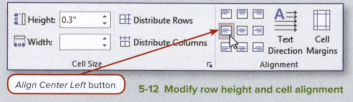

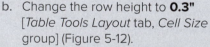
Align Center Left button

5-12 Modify row height and cell alignment

6. Modify template format and content.
   a. Select the field containing "**SKIING UNLIMITED**" and change the font size to **16 pt**.
   b. Select "**Fax**" and apply **small caps**.
   c. In the third table at the bottom of the template, delete "**Please comment**" and type Please complete and return.

7. Save and close this template (Figure 5-13).

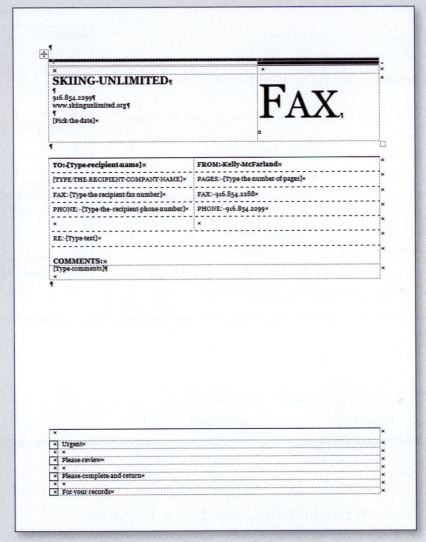

5-13 **PP W5-1 template completed**

Creating Templates

Word provides you with a variety of online templates you can customize to meet your needs, but you may want to create a template from a blank document or use an existing document. For example, you can create a template from a letter you use on a regular basis, or create a new template for a monthly travel report. The main advantage of using templates is that you can create a standardized document to use and customize it without modifying the original template file.

Create a Template from a Blank Document

When you create a new blank document in Word, it is a Word document based upon the *Normal* template. You can convert a blank document into a template by saving it as a *Word Template*.

▶ **HOW TO:** Create a Template from a Blank Document

1. Click the **File** tab to open the *Backstage* view.
2. Click the **New** button on the left.
3. Click the **Blank document** button. A new blank document opens in the Word window.
4. Open the *Save As* dialog box from the *Save As* area on the *Backstage* view.
   - You can also press **F12** to open the *Save As* dialog box.
5. Type the file name in the *File name* area.
6. Click the **Save as type** drop-down list and select **Word Template** (Figure 5-14).
   - When viewing files in a *File Explorer* window, the document icon for a *Word Template* is different from a *Word Document*.
7. Browse to the location where you want to save the file.
8. Click **Save** to close the dialog box and save the template.

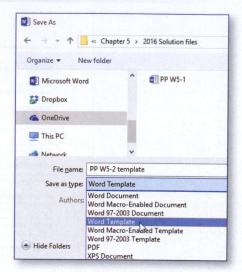

5-14 Save as a *Word Template*

▶ **ANOTHER WAY**

Press **Ctrl+N** to create a new blank document.

Save an Existing Document as a Template

There are times when you may want to save an existing file as a template. For example, you might save a course assignment sheet with your name, course title, and professor's name in the header as a template. Saving an existing document as a template is similar to saving a new document as a template.

▶ **HOW TO:** Save an Existing Document as a Template

1. Open an existing Word document.
2. Open the *Save As* dialog box from the *Save As* area on the *Backstage* view.
3. Type the file name in the *File name* area.

4. Click the **Save as type** drop-down list and select **Word Template** (see Figure 5-14).

5. Browse to the location where you want to save the file.

6. Click **Save** to close the dialog box and save the template. The Word document is saved as a *Word Template*.

Create a Document Based upon a Template

One of the most confusing aspects of using templates is determining how to open each of the different files. You can create a new Word document based upon an existing template, or you can open and edit an existing template file. When you create a document based upon a template, open the file from a *File Explorer* folder.

Open a *File Explorer* window from the *Start* menu or *Taskbar*

> **HOW TO:** Create a Document Based upon a Template

1. Click the Windows **Start** menu and select **File Explorer** (Figure 5-15).
   - The *File Explorer* might also be available on the *Taskbar* or in the *Most used* area of the *Start* menu.

5-15 Open a *File Explorer* window

2. Open the *File Explorer* folder containing the template file (Figure 5-16).

3. Double-click the template file to create a document based upon that template, or select the template file (click once) and press **Enter**.
   - When you create a document based upon a template file, Word assigns the document a generic file name, such as *Document1,* which displays in the *Title* bar of the Word window.

4. Save the document.
   - When you save the document based upon a template, the *Save As* dialog box opens so you can type a unique name for the document.
   - Notice that *Word Document* is already selected in the *Save as type* area of the *Save As* dialog box.

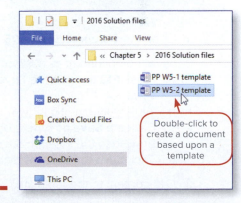

Double-click to create a document based upon a template

5-16 Create a document based upon a template

Edit a Template

You can also edit a template file. Opening a template so you can edit it is different from opening a document based upon a template. There are two different ways to open a template to edit it.

- *Open the template file from within Word*. Click the **Browse** button in the *Open* area on the *Backstage view* to open the *Open* dialog box. Browse to find and select the template file and click **Open**.
- *Open the template file from a File Explorer window*. Right-click the template file and select **Open** from the context menu.

When you open a template file to edit it, the template file name displays in the Word *Title* bar rather than the generic document name (*Document1*) that Word generates when you open a document based upon a template.

> **MORE INFO**
>
> When editing a template, open the template from within Word. When creating a document based upon a template, locate the template in a *File Explorer* window and double-click the template file.

PAUSE & PRACTICE: WORD 5-2

For this Pause & Practice project, you create a volunteer letter template file from an existing document for Kelly McFarland to send to all the Skiing Unlimited program volunteers. You then modify the template and create a document based upon this template.

The document you create based upon this template is used in *Pause & Practice 5-4*. This document contains placeholder text that you will replace when you perform a mail merge in *Pause & Practice 5-4*.

File Needed: ***VolunteerLetter-05.docx*** *(student data files are available in the* Library *of your SIMnet account)*
Completed Project File Names: ***[your initials] PP W5-2 template.dotx*** and ***[your initials] PP W5-2.docx***

1. Open the ***VolunteerLetter-05*** document from your student data files.

2. Save the document as a *Word Template* file.
   a. Press **F12** to open the *Save As* dialog box or open the *Save As* dialog box from the *Backstage* view.
   b. Type [your initials] PP W5-2 template as the file name in the *File name* area.
   c. Click the **Save as type** drop-down list and select **Word Template**.
   d. Browse to the location on your computer where you save your solution files.
   e. Click **Save** to close the dialog box and save the template.

3. Add content to the template.
   a. Place your insertion point at the beginning of the first paragraph, insert the current date [*Insert* tab, *Text* group] (use January 1, 2018 format), and set to update automatically.
   b. Press **Enter** four times.
   c. Type [Address Block] and press **Enter** two times.
   d. Type [Greeting Line] and press **Enter** two times.
   e. Press **Ctrl+End** or place your insertion point at the end of the document (at the end of the last bulleted item) and press **Enter** three times. The bulleting is turned off.
   f. Type Sincerely, and press **Enter** four times.

g. Type Kelly McFarland and press **Enter** once.

h. Type Community Services Coordinator.

4. Apply formatting changes to the template.

  a. Place your insertion point in the date line at the top of the document and change the *Before* paragraph spacing to **24 pt**.

  b. Select "**Courtyard Medical Plaza**" in the first body paragraph and apply **bold** and **italic** formatting.

  c. Use the **Find** feature to find all occurrences of "Skiing Unlimited" and apply **italic** formatting.

  d. Compare your document with Figure 5-18.

5. Save and close the template.

6. Open a document based upon the *[your initials] PP W5-2 template* file (Figure 5-17).

  a. Open the *File Explorer* folder containing the *[your initials] PP W5-2 template* file.

  b. Double-click the *[your initials] PP W5-2 template* file or select the file (click once) and press **Enter** to create a document based on the template. A new document based upon the template opens, and it has a generic file name such as *Document 1*.

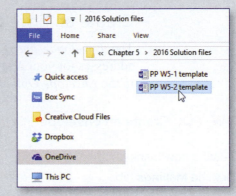

5-17 Create a document based upon a template

7. Save the document as a Word document named [your initials] PP W5-2 (Figure 5-18).

8. Close the document. If prompted to save the *[your initials] PP W5-2 template* file, click **No**.

5-18 PP W5-2 completed

Creating Envelopes and Labels

In your professional or personal life, you may need to create *envelopes* or *mailing labels* for letters, cards, or packages. If you only have a couple to do, it's not a problem to write them by hand. But, if you are sending invitations to 100 people for a grand opening of a new store or to 50 friends for a graduation party, it can be very time consuming to address envelopes by hand. Also, printed envelopes and labels look more professional. Word provides you with mailing features to quickly create envelopes and mailing labels.

Create an Envelope

The *Envelopes and Labels* dialog box provides an area to type the delivery and return addresses for your envelope. You can select the type of envelope or a specific size of envelope in the *Envelope Options* dialog box.

▶ HOW TO: Create an Envelope

1. Create a new blank document.
2. Click the **Mailings** tab.
3. Click the **Envelopes** button [*Create* group] (Figure 5-19). The *Envelopes and Labels* dialog box opens and the *Envelopes* tab displays (Figure 5-20).

5-19 Create an envelope

5-20 *Envelopes and Labels* dialog box

4. Type the mailing address in the *Delivery address* area.
5. Type the return address in the *Return address* area.
   - To change the font, size, and style of the text for both the delivery and return addresses, select the text, right-click the selected text, and select **Font** from the context menu. The *Font* dialog box opens, and you can make the desired changes.
6. Click the **Print** button.
   - If prompted to save the return address as the default return address, click **No**.
   - You may be prompted to load an envelope in the printer prior to printing.

Envelope Options

When creating and printing envelopes, you need to specify the type or size of envelope. Word provides you with an *Envelope Options* dialog box to select the type or size of the envelope, the font and size of the delivery and return address, and the position of the addresses on the envelope (Figure 5-21).

In the *Envelopes and Labels* dialog box, click the **Options** button to open the *Envelope Options* dialog box. Click the **Envelope size** drop-down list and select the envelope you will use. You can also format and adjust the position of the addresses.

5-21 *Envelope Options* dialog box

Envelope Printing Options

A *Printing Options* tab is also available in the *Envelope Options* dialog box (Figure 5-22). Use this tab to specify how the envelope is fed into the printer. Word provides you with a recommended setting for printing, but you might need to select a different feed method depending on the printer you are using.

Add an Envelope to an Existing Document

Word also gives you the option of adding an envelope to an existing document. For example, Word can create an envelope based upon a letter you are sending to a potential client. Word uses the delivery address from the letter to automatically populate the *Delivery address* field in the envelope.

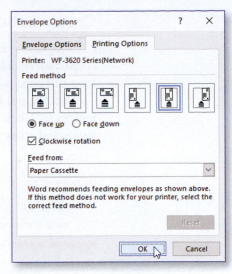

5-22 Envelope printing options

▶ **HOW TO:** Add an Envelope to a Document

1. Open a letter document where you want to add an envelope.
2. Click the **Envelopes** button [*Mailings* tab, *Create* group]. The *Envelopes and Labels* dialog box opens (Figure 5-23).
   - If the letter contains a delivery address, it displays in the *Delivery address* area.
   - If the letter does not have a delivery address, type the address in the *Delivery address* area.
3. Type the return address in the *Return address* area.
4. Click the **Options** button to set the envelope size and printing options and click **OK**.
5. Click the **Add to Document** button.
   - A dialog box opens asking if you want to set the return address as the default return address (Figure 5-24).

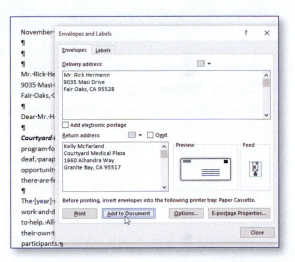

5-23 Add an envelope to an existing document

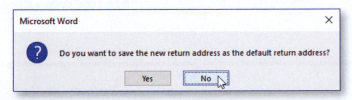

5-24 Set the default return address

- Click **Yes** if you want to save this address as the default return address or click **No** if you do not want this address as the default return address.
- The envelope is added as a separate page before the existing document (Figure 5-25).
6. Save and close the document.

5-25 Envelope added to an existing document

Create Labels

Creating and printing labels saves time and produces professional-looking documents. You can create individual labels by typing the delivery address or other information on each label or create a full page with the same information on every label, such as a page of return address labels.

You are not limited to mailing labels only. Labels can also be used for conference name badges or labels to identify project folders. Most office supply stores offer a variety of label styles and sizes to meet your needs.

> **MORE INFO**
>
> Labels and envelopes can also be merged with a database or other data sources rather than typing each label or envelope individually. Merging is covered later in this chapter.

Label Options

Before creating and printing labels, it is important to select the correct type and size of label in the *Label Options* dialog box.

> ▶ **HOW TO:** Set Label Options

1. Create a new blank document and click the **Labels** button [*Mailings* tab, *Create* group]. The *Envelopes and Labels* dialog box opens and the *Labels* tab displays.
2. Click the **Options** button to open the *Label Options* dialog box (Figure 5-26).
3. Select the type of printer and the printer tray you are using in the *Printer information* area.
4. Click the **Label vendors** drop-down list and select the vendor of the labels you are using.
5. Select the specific label product number in the *Product number* list.

   - If you can't find your specific label, click the **Find updates on Office.com** link for an updated list of labels.
   - Click the **Details** button to change the label dimensions.
   - Alternatively, click the **New Label** button and type the label dimensions to create a custom label.
6. Click **OK** to close the *Label Options* dialog box.

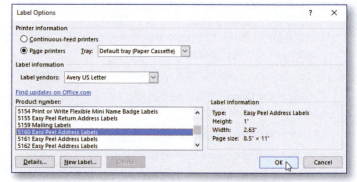

5-26 *Label Options* **dialog box**

> **MORE INFO**
>
> Avery 5160 is one of the most common types of labels used for delivery and return address labels.

Create Individual Labels

When you are creating individual labels, Word opens a new document where you can type the information for each label. Based on the type of label you select, Word inserts a table in a new document. You type the information for each label in the cells of the table.

▶ HOW TO: Create Individual Labels

1. Create a new blank document and click the **Labels** button [*Mailings* tab, *Create* group]. The *Envelopes and Labels* dialog box opens with the *Labels* tab selected (Figure 5-27).
2. Click the **Options** button and select the type of label you want to use.
3. Click **OK** to close the *Label Options* dialog box.
4. Leave the *Address* area blank.
5. Select the **Full page of the same label** radio button in the *Print* area.
   - This option creates a full page of blank labels where you type the information for each label.
6. Click the **New Document** button. A new document opens with a table inserted in the document.
7. Type the information for each label (Figure 5-28).

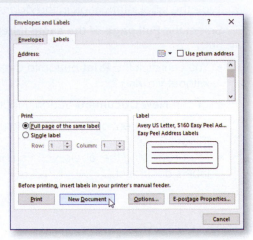

5-27 Create individual labels

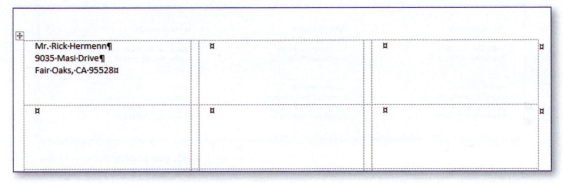

5-28 Type individual labels

- Press **Enter** after each line of the label.
- Press **Tab** twice to move to the next label. A blank column is added between each label to allow for spacing between labels.
- After typing the labels, you can print, save, and close the labels document.

▶ **MORE INFO**

After creating labels, you can adjust the left indent, line spacing, and *Before* and *After* paragraph spacing to arrange the label content.

Create a Full Page of the Same Label

You can also print a full sheet of the same label. This saves you the time of typing the same label over and over or copying and pasting the same label information in each cell.

▶ HOW TO: Create a Full Page of the Same Label

1. Create a new blank document and click the **Labels** button [*Mailings* tab, *Create* group]. The *Envelopes and Labels* dialog box opens and the *Labels* tab displays.
2. Click the **Options** button and select the type of label to use.

3. Click **OK** to close the *Label Options* dialog box.

4. Type the label information in the *Address* area.

5. Select the **Full page of the same label** radio button in the *Print* area.

   - You can click the **Print** button to directly print the document without viewing it.

6. Click the **New Document** button (Figure 5-29).

   - A new document opens containing a full page of the same label (Figure 5-30).
   - After reviewing the labels, you can print, save, and close the labels document.

5-29 **Create a full page of the same label**

5-30 **Full page of the same label**

> **MORE INFO**
>
> If you previously saved your return address, you can use this address for labels by checking the **Use return address** check box in the upper right corner of the *Envelopes and Labels* dialog box.

PAUSE & PRACTICE: WORD 5-3

In this Pause & Practice project, you create mailing labels for Kelly McFarland to use when sending out volunteer letters for the Skiing Unlimited program. You also create individual labels for delivery addresses and a full page of the same label for return addresses.

File Needed: None
Completed Project File Names: *[your initials] PP W5-3a.docx* and *[your initials] PP W5-3b.docx*

---

1. Create a new Word document.

2. Select the mailing label format.
   a. Click the **Labels** button [*Mailings* tab, *Create* group].
   b. Click the **Options** button. The *Label Options* dialog box opens.

c. Click the **Label vendors** drop-down list and select **Avery US Letter**.

d. Select **5160 Easy Peel Address Labels** in the *Product number* area (Figure 5-31).

e. Click **OK** to close the *Label Options* dialog box.

3. Create individual mailing labels.

a. Leave the *Address* area blank (Figure 5-32).

b. Click the **Full page of the same label** radio button in the *Print* area.

c. Click the **New Document** button. A new Word document opens with the labels table inserted.

4. Save the document as [your initials] PP W5-3a.

5. Type individual mailing labels.

a. Use the information in the following table to type six mailing labels.

b. Press **Tab** two times after each label to move to the next label cell on the same row. At the end of the row, press **Tab** once to move to the label cell in the new row.

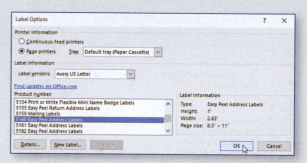

5-31 Select label type

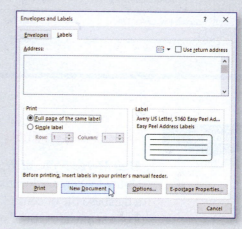

5-32 Create individual mailing labels

Mr. Rick Hermenn 9035 Masi Drive Fair Oaks, CA 95528	Dr. Karen Draper 784 Ehrlich Road Carmichael, CA 96774	Mr. Ty Han 1272 Eastwood Court Auburn, CA 95236
Dr. Seth Uribe 8263 Wales Avenue Roseville, CA 95722	Mr. Sawyer Petrosky 2741 Lake Road Granite Bay, CA 95517	Ms. Kallyn Nickols 7336 Ebony Way Auburn, CA 95236

6. Save and close this document (Figure 5-33).

7. Return to the open blank Word document.

8. Create a full page of the same label for return address labels.

a. Click the **Labels** button [*Mailings* tab, *Create* group]. The *Envelopes and Labels* dialog box opens.

b. Confirm that **Avery US Letter** and **5160 Easy Peel Address Labels** are selected. If not, click the **Options** button and select this label.

c. Type the following information in the *Address* area:

Kelly McFarland

Courtyard Medical Plaza

1660 Alhandra Way

Granite Bay, CA 95517

d. Click the **Full page of the same label** radio button in the *Print* area.

e. Click the **New Document** button (Figure 5-34). A new Word document opens and a full page of the same label displays in the labels table (Figure 5-35).

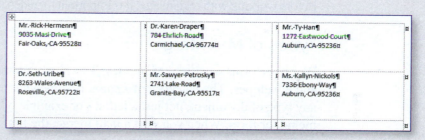

5-33 PP W5-3a completed

5-34 Create a full page of the same label

9. Save the document as [your initials] PP W5-3b and close the document.

Kelly·McFarland¶ Courtyard·Medical·Plaza¶ 1660·Alhandra·Way¶ Granite·Bay,·CA·95517¤	Kelly·McFarland¶ Courtyard·Medical·Plaza¶ 1660·Alhandra·Way¶ Granite·Bay,·CA·95517¤	Kelly·McFarland¶ Courtyard·Medical·Plaza¶ 1660·Alhandra·Way¶ Granite·Bay,·CA·95517¤
Kelly·McFarland¶ Courtyard·Medical·Plaza¶ 1660·Alhandra·Way¶ Granite·Bay,·CA·95517¤	Kelly·McFarland¶ Courtyard·Medical·Plaza¶ 1660·Alhandra·Way¶ Granite·Bay,·CA·95517¤	Kelly·McFarland¶ Courtyard·Medical·Plaza¶ 1660·Alhandra·Way¶ Granite·Bay,·CA·95517¤
Kelly·McFarland¶ Courtyard·Medical·Plaza¶ 1660·Alhandra·Way¶ Granite·Bay,·CA·95517¤	Kelly·McFarland¶ Courtyard·Medical·Plaza¶ 1660·Alhandra·Way¶ Granite·Bay,·CA·95517¤	Kelly·McFarland¶ Courtyard·Medical·Plaza¶ 1660·Alhandra·Way¶ Granite·Bay,·CA·95517¤

5-35 PP W5-3b completed

SLO 5.4

Understanding Mail Merge

Mail Merge is one of Word's most helpful and time-saving features. Mail merge provides you the ability to merge a document, such as a form letter, labels, or envelopes, with a data source such as a database file or contact records from Microsoft Outlook. Merges can be very simple or complex. You can create a list of mailing labels from your Outlook contacts or create a more sophisticated merge where you merge address and account information for a client's insurance renewal letter. Before working with mail merge, it is important to understand the different components of a merge.

Types of Mail Merge

Word performs a variety of merges. The most common types of merges are letters, labels, and envelopes. The category of *Letters* is somewhat misleading because you can merge into any type of document, not just a letter. For example, you can merge information into a report, memo, or form. When you start a mail merge, the first step is to select the type of merge to be performed (e.g., *Letters, Envelopes, Labels*).

Main Document

The *main document* is the Word document into which you merge recipient information from a secondary source. Main documents include text and other information that does not change when the merge is performed, such as the date and body of the letter. When you perform a letter mail merge, you can begin with an existing document, such as a business letter, or start with a blank document. When you perform a labels or envelopes mail merge, you specify the type of label or envelope to use.

Recipients

Recipients refer to a data source that can contain names, addresses, and other variable information. A mail merge combines a main document and the recipient information from the data source. The recipients can be from an existing data source such as a Microsoft Access or Excel file or existing contacts from Microsoft Outlook. You can also create a new recipient list to merge into the main document.

The data source used for mail merge is essentially a database of information. It is important to understand the database terminology used in the mail merge process.

- **Field:** A field is an individual piece of information such as title, first name, last name, or street address.
- **Record:** A record is a collection of related fields. A record is all of the information about one recipient, such as name, address, and other contact information.
- **File**, **Table**, or **Contacts Folder:** A file, table, or Microsoft Outlook *Contacts* folder is a group of related records.

Figure 5-36 is a Microsoft Access table. The information in each cell is a *field*. Each column heading is a *field name*. A row of information is a *record*. All of the information displayed is a *table*.

When you select recipients for a merge, you use a file, table, or *Contacts* folder as your data source of recipient information. You insert **merge fields** into the main document that function as placeholders for the variable information. During the merge, Word inserts fields from the data source into the main document.

5-36 *Microsoft Access database table*

SLO 5.5

Merging Using the Mailings Tab

One method to perform a mail merge is to use the *Mailings* tab. Another method is to use the *Mail Merge Wizard*. In this section, we walk through the steps to perform a mail merge using the *Mailings* tab (Figure 5-37). The *Mail Merge Wizard* is discussed in the next section.

5-37 *Mailings* tab

Start the Mail Merge

The first step in performing a mail merge is to select the type of merge to be performed.

▶**HOW TO:** Start the Mail Merge

1. Click the **Mailings** tab.
2. Click the **Start Mail Merge** button [*Start Mail Merge* group] and select the type of merge to be performed (Figure 5-38).
   - If you are performing a mail merge using an existing document, make sure the document is open before clicking the *Start Mail Merge* button.
   - If you are performing a labels or envelopes mail merge, you are prompted to select the type of labels or envelopes in the *Labels Options* or *Envelope Options* dialog box.

5-38 Types of mail merges

Select Recipients

The next step in the mail merge process is to select the recipients, which is the data source to be merged into the main document. Word enables you to use a variety of database files, type a new list as the source data, or use Outlook Contacts.

Click the **Select Recipients** button [*Mailings* tab, *Start Mail Merge* group] and select the type of data source to be used as the recipients (Figure 5-39). A list of options with specific information about each type follows.

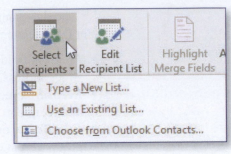

5-39 **Select recipient source file**

> **MORE INFO**
>
> It is a good idea to proofread and edit your data source before beginning a mail merge.

Type a New List

The *Type a New List* option allows you to type the recipients' information if you do not already have an existing data source. The data source is saved, and you can edit it later and use it in other mail merges.

▶**HOW TO:** Type a New Recipient List for Mail Merge

1. Click the **Select Recipient** button [*Mailings* tab, *Start Mail Merge* group].

2. Select **Type a New List**. The *New Address List* dialog box opens (Figure 5-40).

   - Word provides you with default fields (*Title, First Name, Last Name*). Edit these fields by clicking the **Customize Columns** button.

3. Type recipients' information.

   - Press **Tab** to move from field to field.
   - You do not have to type information in every field.
   - Click the **New Entry** button to begin a new record or press **Tab** after typing the last field of information.

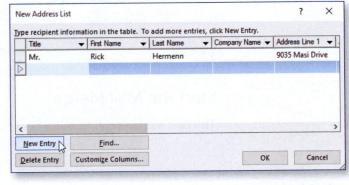

5-40 *New Address List* dialog box

4. Click **OK** after typing all recipient information. The *Save Address List* dialog box opens.

5. Type a name for the new address list, browse to the location where you want to save the file, and click **Save**.

> **MORE INFO**
>
> When creating a new address list for a mail merge, Word will save the document as a *Microsoft Office Address Lists* file (.mdb), which you can edit and use for other mail merges.

Use an Existing List

When you use an existing list for the recipients of a mail merge, you select the source file containing the recipients' information. You can use a variety of database file types for a mail merge.

> ▶ **HOW TO:** Use an Existing List for Mail Merge

1. Click the **Select Recipient** button [*Mailings* tab, *Start Mail Merge* group].
2. Select **Use an Existing List**. The *Select Data Source* dialog box opens (Figure 5-41).
3. Browse to locate the data source file, select the data source file, and click **Open**.
   - If your data source is a database file with multiple tables, a dialog box opens and prompts you to select the table to use in the merge.

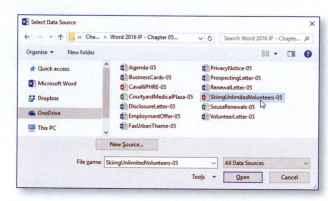

5-41 *Select Data Source* dialog box

Select from Outlook Contacts

If you use Microsoft Outlook, you probably have many contacts saved in Outlook. You can use information stored in an Outlook contacts folder to perform a mail merge.

> ▶ **HOW TO:** Select from Outlook Contacts for Mail Merge

1. Click the **Select Recipient** button [*Mailings* tab, *Start Mail Merge* group].
2. Select **Choose from Outlook Contacts**.
   - If the *Choose Profile* dialog box opens (Figure 5-42), select the Outlook profile to use and click **OK**. The *Select Contacts* dialog box opens.
   - Typically, people only have one Outlook profile, but if you have more than one Outlook profile setup on your computer, choose the correct profile to use.
3. In the *Select Contacts* dialog box, select the contacts folder to use for the mail merge (Figure 5-43).
4. Click **OK** to close the *Select Contacts* dialog box. The *Mail Merge Recipients* dialog box opens.
   - From within this dialog box, you can select the recipients to include in the merge, sort recipients, and filter recipients.
   - You can also perform these actions in the next step of the mail merge, which is to edit the recipient list.
5. Click **OK** to close the *Mail Merge Recipients* dialog box.

5-42 Select *Outlook* profile

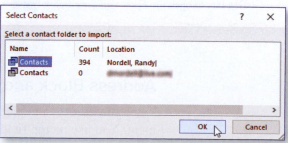

5-43 Select Outlook *Contacts* folder

Edit Recipients

After selecting or creating the recipient list, the next step in the mail merge process is to edit your recipient list. During this process you can select which records (recipients) to include in the merge, *sort* the records, and *filter* the records. Sorting arranges records in alphabetic order by a specific field, such as last name. Filtering enables you to display only those records that match a specific condition, such as from a specific town or zip code.

▶ HOW TO: Edit Recipient List for Mail Merge

1. Click the **Edit Recipient List** button [*Mailings* tab, *Start Mail Merge* group] to open the *Mail Merge Recipients* dialog box (Figure 5-44).

2. Check or uncheck the boxes in the second column to select or deselect recipients.

   - By default, all recipients in the data source file are included in the merge.

3. Sort the recipient list by clicking a column heading drop-down arrow and selecting **Sort Ascending** or **Sort Descending** (Figure 5-45).

   - Alternatively, click the **Sort** link in the *Refine recipient list* area to open the *Filter and Sort* dialog box.

4. Filter the recipient list by clicking a column heading drop-down arrow and selecting a criterion by which to filter the recipient list.

   - Alternatively, click the **Filter** link in the *Refine recipient list* area to open the *Filter and Sort* dialog box.
   - When you filter a data source, only those recipient records that match the filter criterion display in the recipient list. To display all of the recipient records, select **(All)** from the column heading drop-down list.

5. Click **OK** to close the *Mail Merge Recipients* dialog box.

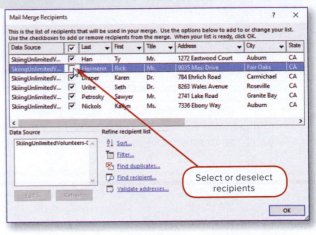

5-44 *Mail Merge Recipients* dialog box

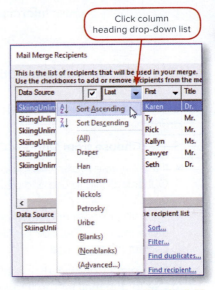

5-45 Sort or filter by field

▶ MORE INFO

It's best to use the *Filter and Sort* dialog box if you're performing a sort or filter on more than one field. Click the **Sort** or **Filter** link in the *Mail Merge Recipients* dialog box to open the *Filter and Sort* dialog box.

Address Block and Greeting Line Merge Fields

After you edit the recipient list, the next step is to insert *merge fields* into your main document. You use merge fields to insert recipient information into the main document. You can insert an address block, greeting line, or individual merge fields from your data source into the main document. Both the *Address Block* and *Greeting Line* merge fields combine individual merge fields to create an acceptable mailing address and greeting line.

▶ **HOW TO:** Insert the Address Block and Greeting Line Merge Fields

1. Open the main document for the mail merge and position the insertion point at the location to insert the address block merge field.

2. Click the **Address Block** button [*Mailings* tab, *Write & Insert Fields* group]. The *Insert Address Block* dialog box opens.

3. Select the format for the recipient's name in the *Specify address elements* area (Figure 5-46).
   - A preview of the address block appears in the *Preview* area on the right.
   - In the *Preview* area, you can view other recipients by clicking the **Next** or **Previous** arrow.

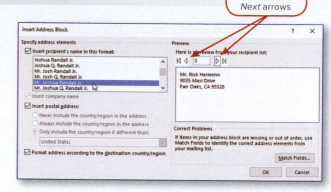

4. Click **OK** to close the *Insert Address Block* dialog box and to insert the address block merge field (<< *AddressBlock* >>) into the document (Figure 5-47).
   - Merge fields are shaded in gray when selected.

5. Position the insertion point at the location where you want to insert the greeting line merge field.

6. Click the **Greeting Line** button [*Write & Insert Fields* group]. The *Insert Greeting Line* dialog box opens (Figure 5-48).

7. Select the format for the greeting line in the *Greeting line format* area.
   - In the *Greeting line for invalid recipient names* area, you can specify a generic greeting to use if a recipient name has an invalid format.
   - In the *Preview* area, click the **Next** or **Previous** arrow to preview the greeting line for each of your recipients.

8. Click **OK** to close the *Insert Greeting Line* dialog box and to insert the greeting line merge field (<< *GreetingLine* >>) into the document (Figure 5-49).

5-46 Insert Address Block dialog box

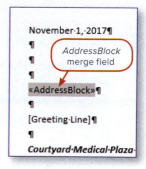

5-47 AddressBlock merge field in the main document

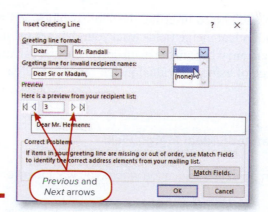

5-48 Insert Greeting Line dialog box

5-49 GreetingLine merge field in the main document

You can manually build your address block and greeting line by using individual merge fields from your data source. To build an address block, Word typically uses the following merge fields: *Courtesy Title, First Name, Last Name, Address 1, Address 2, City, State,* and *Postal Code.*

To build a greeting line, Word typically uses the following merge fields: *Courtesy Title* and *Last Name.* Type the word "Dear" or "To" before the recipient's name and punctuation after (colon) if needed.

Match Fields

What if Word does not correctly build your address block or greeting line? If your data source uses field names that Word does not recognize or correctly match with a corresponding Word field, you can use the **Match Fields** feature to manually match the field names from your data source to those field names recognized by Word.

▶ HOW TO: Match Fields

1. Click the **Match Fields** button [*Mailings* tab, *Write & Insert Fields* group]. The *Match Fields* dialog box opens (Figure 5-50).

   - The fields on the left are Word merge fields.
   - The fields on the right are from your data source.

2. Select a field at the right to match the Word field at the left.

   - Not all of the fields at the right have to be matched. Word ignores fields that are not matched.
   - Each field drop-down list displays the available fields in your data source.

3. Click **OK** to close the *Match Fields* dialog box.

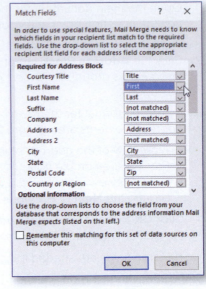

5-50 *Match Fields* dialog box

> **ANOTHER WAY**
>
> Click the **Match Fields** button in the *Insert Address Block* or *Insert Greeting Line* dialog box.

Insert an Individual Merge Field

In addition to inserting the address block and greeting line merge fields, you can also insert individual merge fields from your data source into the main document. You can insert a merge field anywhere in the main document and can use a merge field more than one time. An advantage of using individual merge fields is to create a more personalized mail merge document.

▶ HOW TO: Insert an Individual Merge Field

1. Position the insertion point at the location where you want to insert the merge field.

2. Click the **Insert Merge Field** drop-down arrow [*Mailings* tab, *Write & Insert Fields* group] to display a list of merge fields from your data source (Figure 5-51).

   - If you click the top half of the *Insert Mail Merge* button, the *Insert Merge Field* dialog box opens where you can select a merge field to insert.

3. Select the merge field to insert into the main document. The merge field displays in the document (Figure 5-52).

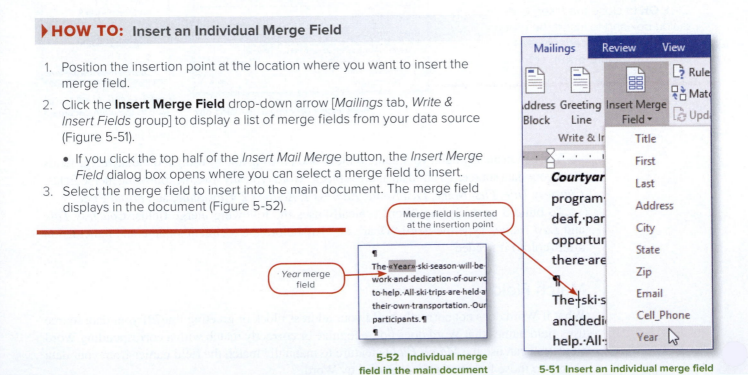

5-52 Individual merge field in the main document

5-51 Insert an individual merge field

Update Labels

When creating a labels mail merge, Word inserts the address block or merge field only in the first cell (label) of the labels main document. The ***Update Labels*** feature automatically updates each label with the merge field. Click the **Update Labels** button in the *Write & Insert Fields* group to automatically update each label. Word inserts a next record (<< *NextRecord* >>) merge field code when performing a labels merge (Figure 5-53). When you perform the mail merge, Word inserts recipient content from the data source into each subsequent label until all records are merged into the labels.

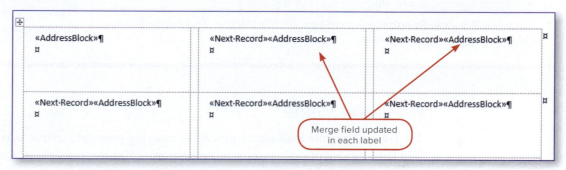

5-53 Labels updated in the main document

Highlight Merge Fields

When inserting merge fields into a main document, it can sometimes be difficult to locate the merge fields unless they are selected. Word enables you to highlight merge fields in a document so you can easily locate each merge field.

Click the **Highlight Merge Fields** button in the *Write & Insert Fields* group to highlight each merge field in your main document (Figure 5-54). When you highlight the merge fields, you can verify proper spacing and punctuation around each merge field. Toggle this feature on or off by clicking the **Highlight Merge Fields** button.

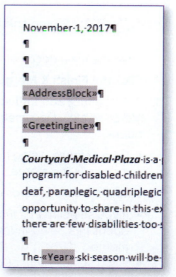

5-54 Merge fields highlighted in main document

Preview Mail Merge

Before finishing the mail merge, you can preview the merge. Preview displays your final document with data from the source file displayed in merge fields, and you can make any needed changes to the main document. Word can also automatically check your mail merge for potential errors.

1. Click the **Preview Results** button [*Mailings* tab, *Preview Results* group] (Figure 5-55). The merge fields from the first record of your data source displays in the main document.

2. Click the **Next Record** arrow to preview the next record from your data source.

3. Click the **Check for Errors** button [*Preview Results* group] to check for errors in the mail merge.

   - You are given three error checking options from which to choose (Figure 5-56). The first and third options display merge errors in a new document. The second option pauses the merge and displays merge errors as they occur.
   - Select an error checking option and press **OK**.
   - Word displays any errors found, and you can correct the errors in the data source before finalizing the merge.
   - If Word opened a new document, close this document.

4. Click the **Preview Results** button to turn off this feature. The merge fields display in your main document.

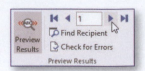

5-55 Preview next record in the main document

5-56 Checking and Reporting Errors **dialog box**

Finish and Merge

The final step in the mail merge process is merging your data source into the main document. You have two main options to finish your merge. You can merge into a new document where you can edit individual documents and save this file or print the merged document.

▶ **HOW TO:** Finish the Mail Merge

1. Save the main document before beginning the merge.

2. Click the **Finish & Merge** button [*Mailings* tab, *Finish* group].

3. Select either **Edit Individual Documents** or **Print Documents**. The *Merge to New Document* (Figure 5-57) or *Merge to Printer* dialog box opens.

   - Both of these dialog boxes allow you to choose which records to include in the merge.

4. Select a *Merge records* radio button and click **OK**.

   - If you selected *Edit Individual Documents,* your completed merge opens in a new window. You can edit, save, or print the completed merge.
   - If you selected *Print Document,* your completed merge is sent to your printer.

5. Save and close any open documents.

5-57 Merge to New Document **dialog box**

> ▶ **MORE INFO**
>
> The third *Finish & Merge* option is *Send Email Messages*, which requires the use of Microsoft Outlook. This option sends an email to each recipient.

Open an Existing Merge Document

When working on a mail merge document, you may have to save and close it and come back to it later. When you open a document that is linked to data source file, Word alerts you with a dialog box where you have three options (Figure 5-58):

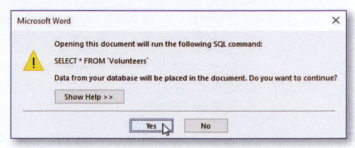

- *Yes:* This option opens your merge document and keeps it linked to the data source file. If Word cannot locate your data source, the *Select Data Source* dialog box opens.

5-58 Alert dialog box when opening a merge document

- *No:* This option opens your merge document; select the data source file by clicking the *Select Recipients* button.
- *Show Help:* This option displays the *Word Help* information in the dialog box.

> **MORE INFO**
>
> If the data source file linked to your merge main document was moved or deleted, you are prompted to select a data source for the main document.

PAUSE & PRACTICE: WORD 5-4

In this Pause & Practice project, you merge the Skiing Unlimited volunteer letter you created for Kelly McFarland in *Pause & Practice 5-2* with a Microsoft Access database to create a merged form letter. You select and edit the data source, insert merge fields into the main document, and finish the merge.

Files Needed: *[your initials] PP W5-2.docx* and *SkiingUnlimitedVolunteers-05.accdb (student data files are available in the Library of your SIMnet account)*
Completed Project File Names: *[your initials] PP W5-4 main.docx* and *[your initials] PP W5-4 merge.docx*

1. Open the *[your initials] PP W5-2* document completed in *Pause & Practice 5-2*. Do not open the *[your initials] PP W5-2 template* file.
2. Save the document as [your initials] PP W5-4 main.
3. Begin the merge and select recipients.
   a. Click the **Mailings** tab.
   b. Click the **Start Mail Merge** button [*Start Mail Merge* group] and select **Letters** (Figure 5-59).
   c. Click the **Select Recipients** button [*Start Mail Merge* group] and select **Use an Existing List**. The *Select Data Source* dialog box opens.
   d. Locate your student data files, select *SkiingUnlimited Volunteers-05* (Access database file), and click **Open**.

5-59 Select type of mail merge

4. Select recipients and sort the recipient list.
   a. Click the **Edit Recipient List** button [*Start Mail Merge* group]. The *Mail Merge Recipients* dialog box opens.
   b. Confirm that the check box for each recipient is checked.
   c. Click the **Last** column heading drop-down arrow and select **Sort Ascending** (Figure 5-60).
   d. Click **OK** to close the **Mail Merge Recipients** dialog box.

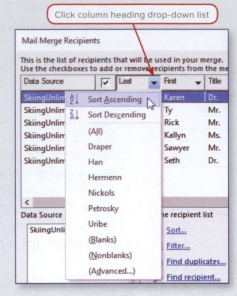

5. Insert the address block merge field into the main document.
   a. Turn on **Show/Hide** [*Home* tab, *Paragraph* group] if it is not already on.
   b. Select the "**[AddressBlock]**" placeholder text, not including the paragraph mark, and delete it.
   c. With your insertion point at that location, click the **Address Block** button [*Mailings* tab, *Write & Insert Fields* group]. The *Insert Address Block* dialog box opens (Figure 5-61).
   d. Select **Mr. Joshua Randall Jr.** as the format for the recipient's name in the *Specify address elements* area.
   e. Click the **Next** arrow in the *Preview* area to view the address block for each of the six recipients.

5-60 Sort the recipient list

   f. Click **OK** to close the *Insert Address Block* dialog box. There should be three blank lines above and one blank line below the << *AddressBlock* >> merge field in the main document.

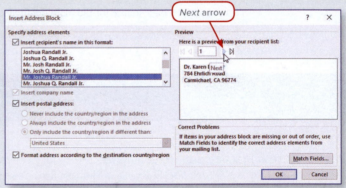

6. Insert the greeting line merge field into the main document.
   a. Select the "**[GreetingLine]**" placeholder text, not including the paragraph mark, and delete it.
   b. With your insertion point at that location, click the **Greeting Line** button [*Mailings* tab, *Write & Insert Fields* group]. The *Insert Greeting Line* dialog box opens (Figure 5-62).
   c. Select **Dear**, **Mr. Randall** and **:** (colon) in the *Greeting line format* area.
   d. Click the **Next** or **Previous** arrow in the *Preview* area to view the greeting line for each of the six recipients.
   e. Click **OK** to close the *Insert Greeting Line* dialog box. There should be one blank line above and below the << *GreetingLine* >> merge field in the main document.

5-61 Insert address block into main document

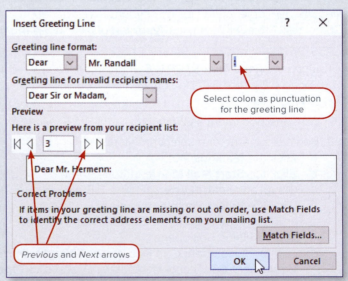

7. Insert individual merge fields into the main document.

5-62 Insert greeting line into main document

a. Delete the "**[year]**" placeholder text in the second body paragraph. Do not delete the spaces before and after the placeholder text.

b. With your insertion point at that location, click **Insert Merge Field** drop-down list [*Mailings* tab, *Write & Insert Fields* group] to display the list of merge fields (Figure 5-63).

c. Select **Year** to insert the << *Year* >> merge field. Confirm one space displays before and after the merge field.

d. Repeat this process to insert the << *Year* >> merge field to replace the other "[year]" placeholder text before the bulleted list.

e. Click the **Highlight Merge Fields** button [*Write & Insert Fields* group] to highlight the merge fields in the main document.

f. Select the second occurrence of the **<< *Year* >>** merge field and **italicize** the field.

g. Click the **Highlight Merge Fields** button again to turn off this feature.

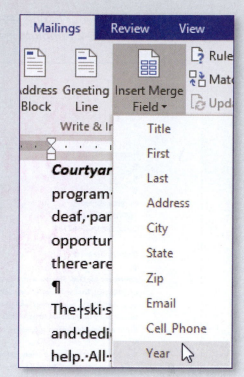

8. Replace the placeholder text (including brackets) in the bulleted list with the following dates:
   January 20
   January 27
   February 10
   February 17
   February 24

5-63 Insert an individual merge field into main document

9. Preview the merge results and check for errors.
   a. Click the **Preview Results** button [*Mailings* tab, *Preview Results* group] to display the recipient information in the main document.
   b. Click the **Next Record** or **Previous Record** arrow [*Preview Results* group] to view each of the six recipients.
   c. Click the **Check for Errors** button. The *Checking and Reporting Errors* dialog box opens (Figure 5-64).
   d. Select the **Simulate the merge . . .** radio button and click **OK**. If no errors are found in the merge, a dialog box opens to verify there are no errors. If errors are found, a new document opens with the errors displayed. Fix errors if needed.
   e. Click **OK** to close the dialog box that informs you of no errors in the merge.
   f. Click the **Preview Results** button [*Mailings* tab, *Preview Results* group] to display the merge fields in the main document.

5-64 Checking and Reporting Errors dialog box

10. Save the document. If prompted to save the *[your initials] PP W5-2 template* file, click **No**.

11. Finish the mail merge and save merged document.
    a. Click the **Finish & Merge** button [*Mailings* tab, *Finish* group] and select **Edit Individual Documents**. The *Merge to New Document* dialog box opens.
    b. Select the **All** radio button and click **OK**. The mail merge opens in a new document.
    c. Scroll through the document to make sure each of the six letters are correct.

12. Save the merged document as [your initials] PP W5-4 merge and close the document (Figure 5-65). If prompted to save the *[your initials] PP W5-2 template* file, click **No**.

13. Save and close the *[your initials] PP W5-4 main* document. If prompted to save the *[your initials] PP W5-2 template* file, click **No**.

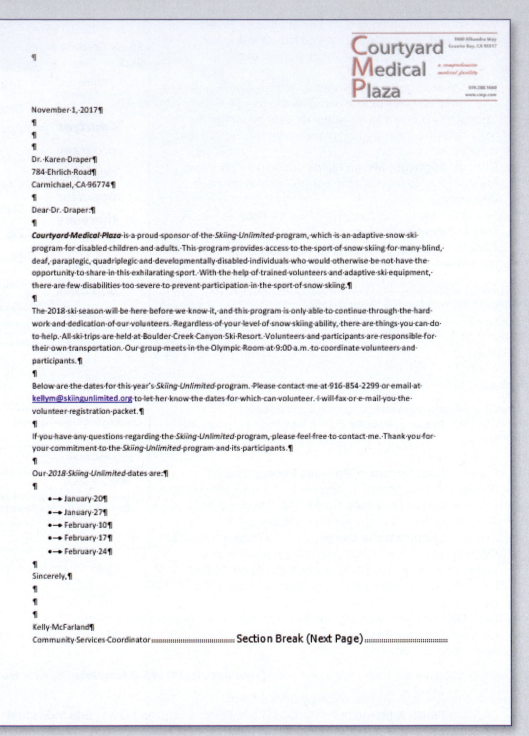

5-65 PP W5-4 merge completed (page 1 of 6)

Using the Mail Merge Wizard

Instead of using the *Mailings* tab to perform a mail merge, you can use the **Mail Merge Wizard**, which walks you through the mail merge process step by step. Using the *Mail Merge Wizard* is similar to using the *Mailings* tab. When you select the *Mail Merge Wizard* option, the *Mail Merge* pane opens on the right side of the Word window. There are six main steps to performing a mail merge:

- *Step 1:* Select document type.
- *Step 2:* Select starting document.
- *Step 3:* Select recipients.
- *Step 4:* Arrange your document. Note that the name of this step varies depending on the type of document you are merging and whether you are using an existing or new document.
- *Step 5:* Preview your document.
- *Step 6:* Complete the merge.

The following *How To* instructions and figures provide an example of using the *Mail Merge Wizard* to create mailing labels from a blank document. This example uses an Access database as the data source for the recipients. The options for each of the steps vary depending on the type of mail merge you perform with the *Mail Merge Wizard*.

Select Document Type

First, select the type of mail merge you want to perform.

▶ **HOW TO:** Select Document Type

1. Create a new blank Word document.
2. Click the **Start Mail Merge** button [*Mailings* tab, *Start Mail Merge* group].
3. Select **Step-by-Step Mail Merge Wizard**. The *Mail Merge* pane opens on the right (Figure 5-66).
4. Select the radio button for the type of document to merge in the *Select document type* area.
   - A description of the type of document appears in a section below the radio buttons.
5. Click the **Next: Starting document** link at the bottom of the *Mail Merge* pane.

5-66 *Mail Merge Wizard:* **Step 1**

Select Starting Document

Next, select your starting document. Your main document can be a new document or you can use an existing document. Depending on the type of merge you are performing, you might have to select the document options, such as changing label or envelope options.

▶ **HOW TO:** Select Starting Document

1. Click the **Change document layout** radio button in the *Select starting document* area if it is not already selected (Figure 5-67).
   - If you select *Start from existing document,* you are asked to select the document on which to perform the merge.

2. Click the **Label options** link in the *Change document layout* area. The *Label Options* dialog box opens.

3. Select the type of label to use.

4. Click **OK** to close the *Label Options* dialog box. The table of labels displays in the document.

5. Click the **Next: Select recipients** link to move to the next step in the *Mail Merge Wizard*.

   - You can click the **Previous** link in *the Mail Merge Wizard* to return to the previous step if necessary.

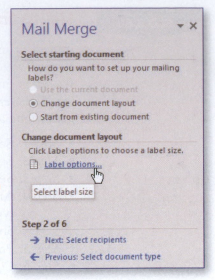

5-67 *Mail Merge Wizard: Step 2*

Select Recipients

Next, select the recipients to merge into your main document. You can use an existing data source, use contacts from a Microsoft Outlook Contacts folder, or type a new recipient list.

▶**HOW TO:** Select Recipients

1. Click the **Use an existing list** radio button in the *Select recipients* area (Figure 5-68).

   - If you choose *Select from Outlook contacts,* you are asked to select the Outlook *Contacts* folder.
   - If you select *Type new list,* you click the *Create* link and type the list of recipients.

2. Click the **Browse** link. The *Select Data Source* dialog box opens.

3. Select the data source file and click **Open**. The *Select Data Source* dialog box closes and the *Mail Merge Recipients* dialog box opens (Figure 5-69).

5-68 *Mail Merge Wizard: Step 3*

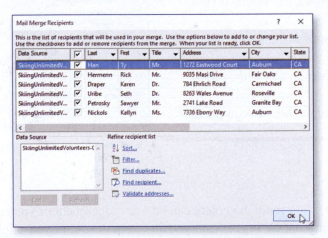

5-69 **Edit the mail merge recipients**

4. Select the recipients to be included in the merge, sort by a field in the data source, or filter the data source by specific criteria.

5. Click **OK** to close the *Mail Merge Recipients* dialog box when you have finished editing the recipient list.

6. Click the **Next: Arrange your labels** link to move to the next step.

Arrange Your Document

In the next step, insert merge fields into your document. You can insert an address block, greeting line, or other merge fields from your data source.

▶ **HOW TO:** Arrange Your Document

1. Click the **Address block** link to insert the merge field into your main document. The *Insert Address Block* dialog box opens.
   - You can also insert individual merge fields into the label. Click the **More items** link in the *Arrange your labels* area to open the *Insert Merge Field* dialog box where you can insert one or more merge fields to the label.
2. Select the address block format, confirm that the address block structure is correct, and preview the recipients in the *Preview* area.
   - If the address block is not displayed correctly, click the **Match Fields** button to match the fields from your data source with the Word merge fields used in the address block.
3. Click **OK** to close the *Insert Address Block* dialog box and to insert the << *AddressBlock* >> merge field into the first label in your document.
4. Click the **Update all labels** button in the *Replicate labels* area (Figure 5-70) to insert the << *AddressBlock* >> merge field into each of the labels in your document (Figure 5-71).
5. Click the **Next: Preview your labels** link to move to the next step.

5-70 *Mail Merge Wizard: Step 4*

5-71 **Address block inserted and labels updated**

Preview Your Document

The next-to-last step is previewing your mail merge to verify that the information from the recipient data source is correctly merged into your main document. In this step, the recipient information displays in the main document. Before completing your merge, you can preview each of the recipients, find a specific recipient, or edit the recipient list (Figure 5-72). Click the **Next: Complete the merge** link in the *Mail Merge* pane to finish the mail merge.

5-72 *Mail Merge Wizard: Step 5*

Complete the Merge

You have two options to complete the merge: *Print* or *Edit individual labels (*or *letters* or *envelopes)* (Figure 5-73). If you select *Print,* your merged document is sent directly to the printer. If you select *Edit individual labels (*or *letters* or *envelopes*), Word opens a new document with the merge performed, and you can then save and print this document.

5-73 *Mail Merge Wizard:* Step 6

PAUSE & PRACTICE: WORD 5-5

In this Pause & Practice project, you create mailing labels for Kelly McFarland to use when she sends the volunteer letters for the Skiing Unlimited program. You create individual labels for delivery addresses using information from an Access database for the recipient list.

File Needed: **SkiingUnlimitedVolunteers-05.accdb** *(student data files are available in the* Library *of your SIMnet account)*
Completed Project File Names: *[your initials]* **PP W5-5 labels.docx** and *[your initials]* **PP W5-5 labels merge.docx**

---

1. Create a new blank Word document.

2. Save the document as [your initials] PP W5-5 labels.

3. Start the *Mail Merge Wizard* (Figure 5-74).
   a. Click the **Mailings** tab.
   b. Click the **Start Mail Merge** button [*Start Mail Merge* group] and select **Step-by-Step Mail Merge Wizard**. The *Mail Merge* pane opens on the right side of the Word window.

4. Select the document type and starting document.
   a. Click the **Labels** radio button in the *Select document type* area.
   b. Click the **Next: Starting document** link at the bottom of the *Mail Merge* pane to move to *Step 2 of 6.*

5-74 **Open the** *Mail Merge Wizard*

c. Click the **Change document layout** radio button in the *Select starting document* area.

d. Click the **Labels options** link in the *Change document layout* area. The *Labels Options* dialog box opens (Figure 5-75).

e. Select **Avery US Letter** from the *Label vendors* drop-down list.

f. Select **5160 Easy Peel Address Labels** in the *Product number* list.

g. Click **OK** to close the *Label Options* dialog box.

h. Click the **Next: Select recipients** link at the bottom of the *Mail Merge* pane to move to *Step 3 of 6*.

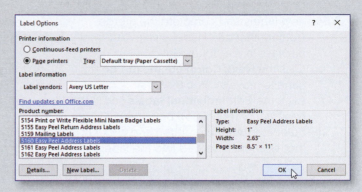

5-75 *Label Options* dialog box

5. Select recipients for the labels.

a. Click the **Use an existing list** radio button in the *Select recipients* area.

b. Click the **Browse** link in the *Use an existing list* area. The *Select Data Source* dialog box opens.

c. Browse to the location on your computer containing your student data files.

d. Select the ***SkiingUnlimitedVolunteers-05*** database and click **Open**. The *Mail Merge Recipients* dialog box opens (Figure 5-76).

e. Click the **Last** column heading drop-down arrow and select **Sort Ascending** from the drop-down list.

f. Click **OK** to close the *Mail Merge Recipients* dialog box.

g. Click the **Next: Arrange your labels** link at the bottom of the *Mail Merge* pane to move to *Step 4 of 6*.

5-76 Sort mail merge recipients

6. Insert an address block to arrange labels.

a. Place your insertion point in the first label cell and click the **Address block** link in the *Arrange your labels* area. The *Insert Address Block* dialog box opens (Figure 5-77).

b. Select the **Mr. Joshua Randall Jr.** option in the *Specify address elements* area.

c. Confirm that the **Insert postal address** check box is checked.

d. Click **OK** to close the *Insert Address Block* dialog box and to insert the merge field.

e. Click the **Update all labels** button in the *Replicate labels* area of the *Mail Merge* pane to automatically insert the *<<AddressBlock>>* field code in each of the labels in the document.

f. Click the **Next: Preview your labels** link at the bottom of the *Mail Merge* pane to move to *Step 5 of 6*.

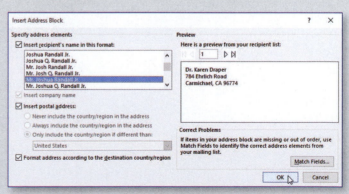

5-77 Insert address block into labels document

7. Preview labels and complete the merge.
   a. Confirm that each label displays correctly. A preview of the labels displays in the document.
   b. Click the **Next: Complete the merge** link at the bottom of the *Mail Merge* pane to move to *Step 6 of 6.*
   c. Click the **Edit individual labels** link in the *Merge* area. The *Merge to New Document* dialog box opens (Figure 5-78).
   d. Select the **All** radio button and click **OK**. A new document opens with the recipients merged into the labels.

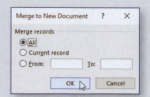

5-78 *Merge to New Document* dialog box

8. Save the completed merged document as [your initials] PP W5-5 labels merge and close the document (Figure 5-79).

9. Save and close the *[your initials] PP W5-5 labels* document.

Dr. Karen Draper¶	Mr. Ty Han¶	Mr. Rick Hermenn¶
784 Ehrlich Road¶	1272 Eastwood Court¶	9035 Masi Drive¶
Carmichael, CA 96774¶	Auburn, CA 95236¶	Fair Oaks, CA 95528¶
¤	¤	¤
Ms. Kallyn Nickols¶	Mr. Sawyer Petrosky¶	Dr. Seth Uribe¶
7336 Ebony Way¶	2741 Lake Road¶	8263 Wales Avenue¶
Auburn, CA 95236¶	Granite Bay, CA 95517¶	Roseville, CA 95722¶
¤	¤	¤

5-79 PP W5-5 labels merge completed

Chapter Summary

5.1 Create and customize a template based on a Word sample template (p. W5-270).

- **Templates** control default font and size, margins, line and paragraph spacing, themes, and other formatting options.
- All new blank Word documents are based upon the **Normal** template.
- Word template files have a **.dotx** extension after the filename.
- You can change and save defaults in the *Normal* template; all new documents based upon this template incorporate these changes.
- Word also has a variety of templates from Office.com available in the *Backstage* view.
- Insert, delete, or customize template content to meet your needs.

5.2 Create and use a template from a blank document or an existing Word document (p. W5-275).

- You can save a new Word document or an existing document (.docx) as a template (.dotx).
- You can open a new document based upon a template and edit this new document without affecting the content and format of the template.
- Templates can also be edited.

5.3 Use Word to create envelopes and mailing labels (p. W5-280).

- Create individual **envelopes** in Word or add an envelope to an existing document.
- Select the type or specific size of envelope to create and select how the envelope will print.
- Create **mailing labels** in Word by typing individual labels or creating a full sheet of the same label.

5.4 Understand the types of merges and how to select or create a recipient list (p. W5-286).

- **Mail Merge** allows you to combine a document with a **data source** such as an Access database or Outlook Contacts.
- The **main document** is the document into which information from a data source is merged.
- The data source consists of fields and records. A **field** is an individual piece of information, and a **record** is a group of related fields.

5.5 Create a merged document using the *Mailings* tab (p. W5-287).

- Use the **Mailings** tab to create and customize a mail merge job.
- Begin the mail merge by selecting the type of merge to perform.
- Select the **recipients** from an existing data source or type a new list of recipients.
- The recipient list can be **sorted**, **filtered**, or specific recipients selected.
- You can insert an **Address Block** or **Greeting Line** merge field into a document. These blocks combine individual fields from the data source to create a standard address block or greeting line for a letter or labels.
- You can insert individual **merge fields** from the data source into the main document.
- Preview the results of the merge in the main document before finalizing the merge.
- Send the finished merge results to the printer or to a new document where you can edit or save them.

5.6 Use the *Mail Merge Wizard* to create a merged document (p. W5-299).

- The **Mail Merge Wizard** is another method to create and customize a mail merge.
- The **Mail Merge pane** appears on the right side of the Word window.
- The *Mail Merge Wizard* walks you through each step of the merge process providing you with links and buttons to customize your merge.

Check for Understanding

The SIMbook for this text (within your SIMnet account) provides the following resources for concept review:

- Multiple choice questions
- Matching exercises
- Short answer questions

Guided Project 5-1

For this project, you create a disclosure statement form letter for Emma Cavalli. You merge this letter with a Microsoft Access database containing a recipient list table. You also use the *Mail Merge Wizard* to create mailing labels.
[**Student Learning Outcomes 5.3, 5.4, 5.5, 5.6**]

Files Needed: ***DisclosureLetter-05.docx*** and ***CavalliPHRE-05.accdb*** *(student data files are available in the* Library *of your SIMnet account)*
Completed Project File Names: *[your initials]* **Word 5-1 letter.docx**, *[your initials]* **Word 5-1 letter merge. docx**, *[your initials]* **Word 5-1 labels.docx**, and *[your initials]* **Word 5-1 labels merge.docx**

Skills Covered in This Project

- Use the *Mailings* tab to create merged letters.
- Use an Access database table as the data source.
- Filter and sort a data source.
- Insert an address block and greeting line merge fields.
- Insert an individual merge field.

- Apply bold and italic formatting to a merge field.
- Highlight merge fields.
- Preview and complete a merge.
- Use the *Mail Merge Wizard* to create labels.
- Select label type and recipients.
- Filter and sort label recipients.
- Insert an address block and update labels.
- Preview and complete a label merge.

1. Open the ***DisclosureLetter-05*** document from your student data files.

2. Save the document as [your initials] Word 5-1 letter.

3. Start the mail merge and select recipients.
   a. Click the **Mailings** tab.
   b. Click the **Start Mail Merge** button [*Start Mail Merge* group] and select **Letters**.
   c. Click the **Select Recipients** button [*Start Mail Merge* group] and select **Use an Existing List**. The *Select Data Source* dialog box opens.
   d. Browse to locate your student data files, select the ***CavalliPHRE-05*** database file, and click **Open**. The *Select Table* dialog box opens (Figure 5-80).
   e. Select **Current Clients** and click **OK**.

4. Filter and sort the recipient list.
   a. Click the **Edit Recipient List** button [*Start Mail Merge* group]. The *Mail Merge Recipients* dialog box opens.
   b. Click the **City** column heading drop-down arrow and select **Roseville** (Figure 5-81). Only the records that match the filter (City = Roseville) display.

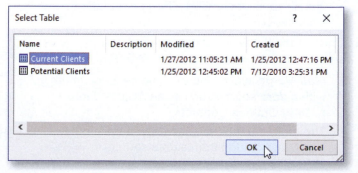

5-80 Select the database table to use as recipient list

c. Click the **Last** column heading drop-down arrow and select **Sort Ascending** to sort the filtered records by last name.

d. Click **OK** to close the *Mail Merge Recipients* dialog box.

5. Insert address block and greeting line merge fields.

a. Turn on **Show/Hide** [*Home* tab, *Paragraph* group] if it is not already on.

b. Delete the "**[Address]**" placeholder text in the letter. Don't delete the paragraph mark at the end of the line.

c. Click the **Address Block** button [*Mailings* tab, *Write & Insert Fields* group]. The *Insert Address Block* dialog box opens (Figure 5-82).

d. Select the **Mr. Joshua Randall Jr.** option in the *Specify address elements* area.

e. Click **OK** to close the *Insert Address Block* dialog box and to insert the << *AddressBlock* >> merge field in the document.

f. Delete the "**[Salutation]**" placeholder text in the letter. Don't delete the paragraph mark at the end of the line.

g. Click the **Greeting Line** button [*Write & Insert Fields* group]. The *Insert Greeting Line* dialog box opens (Figure 5-83).

h. Select **Dear**, **Mr. Randall**, and **(none)** from the three drop-down lists in the *Greeting line format* area.

i. Click **OK** to close the *Insert Greeting Line* dialog box and to insert the <<*GreetingLine*>> merge field in the document.

6. Insert an individual merge field in the body of the document.

a. In the first sentence of the fourth body paragraph, delete the "**[date]**" placeholder text. Don't delete the space before or after the placeholder text.

b. Click the **Insert Merge Field** drop-down arrow [*Write & Insert Fields* group] and select **ReturnDate** from the drop-down list to insert the << *ReturnDate* >> merge field.

c. Verify there is one space before and after the << *ReturnDate* >> merge field.

d. Select the << **ReturnDate >>** merge field and apply **bold** and **italic** formatting.

e. Click the **Highlight Merge Fields** button [*Write & Insert Fields* group] to highlight the merge fields in the document.

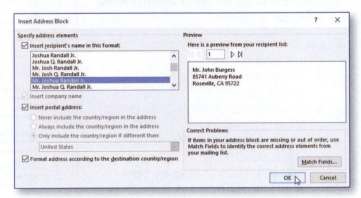

Apply filter

5-81 Filter recipient list

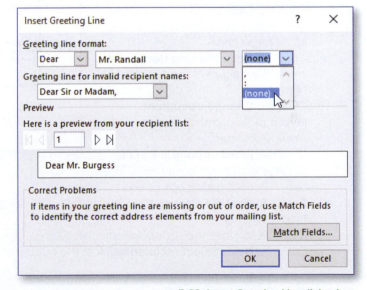

5-82 Insert Address Block dialog box

5-83 Insert Greeting Line dialog box

7. Preview and finish the merge.
   a. Click the **Preview Results** button [*Preview Results* group]. The recipient information displays in the merge fields in the document.
   b. Click the **Next Record** button to view the next recipient. Repeat this for each of the five recipients.
   c. Click the **Preview Results** and **Highlight Merge Fields** buttons to turn off these features.
   d. Click the **Finish & Merge** button [*Finish* group] and select **Edit Individual Documents**. The *Merge to New Document* dialog box opens.
   e. Click the **All** radio button and click **OK** to complete the merge. The completed merge opens in a new document.

8. Save the completed merge as [your initials] Word 5-1 letter merge and close this document (Figure 5-84).

9. Save and close the *[your initials] Word 5-1 letter* document.

10. Create mailing labels using the *Mail Merge Wizard*.
    a. Create a new blank Word document.
    b. Save the document as [your initials] Word 5-1 labels.
    c. Click the **Start Mail Merge** button [*Mailings* tab, *Start Mail Merge* group] and select **Step-by-Step Mail Merge Wizard**. The *Mail Merge* pane opens on the right side of the Word window.
    d. Click the **Labels** radio button in the *Select document type* area of the *Mail Merge* pane.
    e. Click the **Next: Starting document** link at the bottom of the *Mail Merge* pane.
    f. Click the **Change document layout** radio button if it is not already selected.
    g. Click the **Label options** link in the *Change document layout* area. The *Label Options* dialog box opens.
    h. Select **Avery US Letter** as the *Label vendor* and select **5160 Easy Peel Address Labels** as the *Product number*.
    i. Click **OK** to close the *Label Options* dialog box.
    j. Click the **Next: Select recipients** link at the bottom of the *Mail Merge* pane.

5-84 Word 5-1 letter merge completed (page 1 of 5)

11. Select and edit recipient list.
    a. Click the **Use an existing list** radio button in the *Select recipients* area.
    b. Click the **Browse** button in the *Use an existing list* area. The *Select Data Source* dialog box opens.
    c. Browse to your student data files, select the ***CavalliPHRE-05*** database, and click **Open**. The *Select Table* dialog box opens.
    d. Select **Current Clients** and click **OK**. The *Mail Merge Recipients* dialog box opens.
    e. Click the **Filter** link in the bottom half of the *Mail Merge Recipients* dialog box. The *Filter and Sort* dialog box opens (Figure 5-85).

f. On the *Filter Records* tab, click the **Field** drop-down arrow and select **City**.

g. Click the **Comparison** drop-down arrow and select **Equal to**.

h. Type Roseville in the *Compare to* field.

i. Click the **Sort Records** tab (Figure 5-86).

j. Click the **Sort by** drop-down arrow and select **Last**.

k. Click the **Ascending** radio button.

l. Click **OK** to close the *Filter and Sort* dialog box and click **OK** to close the *Mail Merge Recipients* dialog box.

m. Click the **Next: Arrange your labels** link at the bottom of the *Mail Merge* pane.

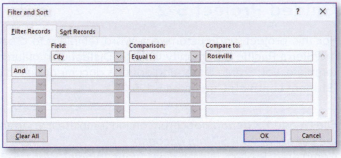

5-85 *Filter and Sort dialog box*

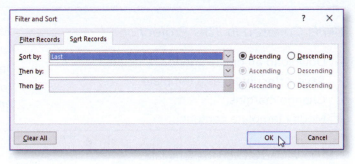

5-86 **Sort records**

12. Insert merge field and update labels.

a. Click the **Address block** link in the *Arrange your labels* area. The **Insert Address Block** dialog box opens.

b. Select the **Mr. Joshua Randall Jr.** option in the *Specify address elements* area.

c. Click **OK** to close the *Insert Address Block* dialog box and to insert the << *AddressBlock* >> merge field in the first label in the document.

d. Click the **Update all labels** button in the *Replicate labels* area to automatically insert the << *AddressBlock* >> merge field in each label in the document.

e. Click the **Next: Preview your labels** link at the bottom of the *Mail Merge* pane.

13. Preview and finish the merge.

a. Preview the recipients in the labels document. Five labels display with client information.

b. Click the **Next: Complete the merge** link at the bottom of the *Mail Merge* pane.

c. Click the **Edit individual labels** link in the *Complete the merge* area. The *Merge to New Document* dialog box opens.

d. Click the **All** radio button and click **OK** to complete the merge. The completed merge opens in a new document.

14. Save the completed merge as [your initials] Word 5-1 labels merge and close this document (Figure 5-87).

15. Save and close the *[your initials] Word 5-1 labels* document.

5-87 **Word 5-1 labels merge completed**

Guided Project 5-2

For this project, you customize a Word template to create a curriculum meeting agenda template for the Sierra Pacific Community College District Curriculum Committee. After customizing and saving this template, you create a meeting agenda document based upon this template.
[Student Learning Outcomes 5.1, 5.2]

File Needed: **Agenda.dotx** (from online templates) or **Agenda-05.docx** (student data files are available in the Library of your SIMnet account)
Completed Project File Names: **[your initials] Word 5-2 template.dotx** and **[your initials] Word 5-2 agenda.docx**

Skills Covered in This Project

- Download an online agenda template.
- Save a document as a template.
- Change margins.
- Modify template content.

- Delete a column in a table.
- AutoFit table contents.
- Open a document based upon a template.
- Add content to a document based upon a template.

1. Download an agenda template.
   a. Click the **File** tab to open the *Backstage* view in Word.
   b. Click the **New** button.
   c. Click the **Search for online templates** text box, type agenda, and press **Enter**. A list of agenda templates displays.
   d. Select **Agenda** and click **Create** (Figure 5-88). A document based upon this agenda template opens in a new Word window. If this template is not available, open the **Agenda-05** file from your student data files.

2. Save the document as a template.
   a. Open the *Save As* dialog box.
   b. Type [your initials] Word 5-2 template in the *File name* area.
   c. Click the **Save as type** drop-down list and select **Word Template**.
   d. Browse to the location on your computer to save this template.
   e. Click **Save** to save the document as a Word template. If a dialog box opens informing you the document will be upgraded to the newest file format, click **OK**.

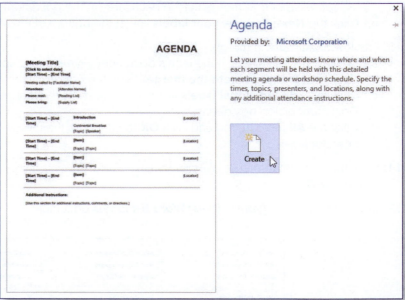

5-88 Create document based on online template

3. Customize the template content and format.
   a. Turn on **Show/Hide** [*Home* tab, *Paragraph* group].

b. Change the top and bottom margins to **0.5"**.

c. Place your insertion point before the title ("AGENDA"), type **SPCCD CURRICULUM**, **space** once, and **left** align this line.

d. Click the **Meeting Title** field and type Full Curriculum Committee Meeting.

e. Click the **Start Time** field and type 3.

f. Click the **End Time** field and type 5 p.m.

g. Click the **Facilitator Name** field and type Dr. Manuel Chavez.

h. Click the **Attendee Names** field and type Melissa Rogan, Roietta Jones, Tony Parsons, Ravi Singh, Rachel Salazar, Rebecca Frank, Kai Sung, and Heidi Anderson.

i. Click the **Reading List** field and type Curriculum printouts.

j. Delete the third row of the first table ("Please bring").

k. Replace "Additional Instructions:" near the bottom with Follow-up Notes:.

4. Customize the second table content and format.

a. Delete the third column of the second table.

b. Select the entire second table and **AutoFit Window**.

c. Select and remove the **Continental Breakfast** field in the second column in the first row and delete the blank line above the *Topic* field.

d. Select and remove the **Speaker** field in the second column in the first row and delete the tab after the *Topic* field.

e. In the second through fourth rows, select and delete the second **Topic** fields and delete the tabs after the first *Topic* fields.

f. Type the following information in the *Start Time, End Time, Introduction,* and *Item* content control fields. Don't remove or type any content in the *Topic* fields. Word automatically converts "1st" and "2nd" to superscript format.

Start Time	End Time	Introduction/Item
3:00	3:10	Preliminaries
3:10	4:00	1st Readings
4:00	4:40	2nd Readings
4:40	5:00	Degrees and Certificates

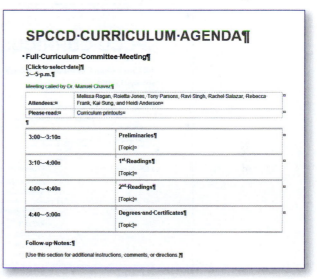

5-89 Word 5-2 template completed

5. Save and close the template (Figure 5-89).

6. Create a document based upon the *[your initials] Word 5-2 template*. *Note: Do not open this template from within Word; open from a File Explorer window.*

a. Browse to the *File Explorer* folder on your computer containing the *[your initials] Word 5-2 template* file.

b. Double-click the *[your initials] Word 5-2 template* file to create a new document based upon this template.

c. Save this Word document as [your initials] Word 5-2 agenda. Confirm that *Save as type* is **Word Document;** if it's not, change it. If prompted to save the template file, click **No**.

7. Insert content into the agenda.

a. Click the **Click to select date** field and select the next Wednesday.

b. In the *Topic* field below the "Preliminaries" heading, type the following content. Press **Enter** after the first line, but don't press *Enter* after the last item.
Approve minutes
State Curriculum Committee updates

c. Click the **Topic** field below the "1ˢᵗ Readings" heading and type the following and press **Enter** after each line except the last line:

BIO 334
BUS 300
FITN 120
PSCH 310

d. Click the **Topic** field below the "2ⁿᵈ Readings" heading and type the following and press **Enter** after each line except the last line:

HUM 330
HUM 335
PSCH 315
PSCH 320

e. Click the **Topic** field below the *Degrees and Certificates* field and type the following and press **Enter** after each line except the last line:

ACCT Accounting Degree
BUSTEC Office Professional Degree
ARTNM Animation Certificate

f. Click the field below the "Follow-up Notes" heading, type the following:

State Curriculum Committee Conference applications due next Wednesday.

8. Save and close the document (Figure 5-90). If prompted to save the template file, click **No**.

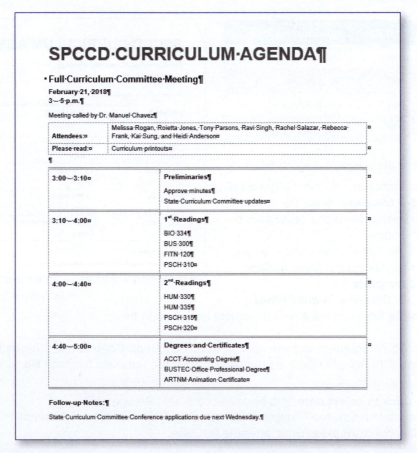

5-90 Word 5-2 agenda completed

Guided Project 5-3

For this project, you create an insurance renewal letter template for Gretchen Souza at Central Sierra Insurance. You then create a renewal letter based upon the template and merge the letter with recipients and renewal information from an Excel file.
[Student Learning Outcomes 5.1, 5.2, 5.4, 5.5]

Files Needed: **RenewalLetter-05.docx** and **SouzaRenewals-05.xlsx** (student data files are available in the Library of your SIMnet account)
Completed Project File Names: **[your initials] Word 5-3 template.dotx**, **[your initials] Word 5-3 renewals. docx**, and **[your initials] Word 5-3 renewals merge.docx**

Skills Covered in This Project

- Open an existing document and save as a template.
- Insert date and set date to update automatically.
- Create a new Word document based upon a template.
- Use the *Mailings* tab to create merged letters.

- Use an Excel file as a data source.
- Sort and filter a data source.
- Deselect recipients.
- Insert address block and greeting line merge fields.
- Insert individual merge fields.
- Highlight merge fields.
- Preview a merge and check for errors.
- Complete the merge.

1. Open the **RenewalLetter-05** document from your student data files.

2. Save the document as a template.
   a. Open the *Save As* dialog box.
   b. Type [your initials] Word 5-3 template in the *File name* area.
   c. Click the **Save as type** drop-down list and select **Word Template**.
   d. Browse to the location on your computer to save this template.
   e. Click **Save** to save the document as a Word template.

3. Insert a current date field into the letter.
   a. Delete the "**[Insert current date]**" placeholder text. Don't delete the paragraph mark at the end.
   b. Click the **Date & Time** button [*Insert* tab, *Text* group] to open the *Date and Time* dialog box.
   c. Select the date option (use January 1, 2018 format), check the **Update automatically** box, and click **OK** to insert the current date and to close the dialog box.
   d. Save and close the template.

4. Create a document based upon the **[your initials] Word 5-3 template**. *Note: Do not open this template from within Word; open from a File Explorer window.*
   a. Browse to the folder on your computer containing the **[your initials] Word 5-3 template** file.
   b. Double-click the **[your initials] Word 5-3 template** file to create a new Word document based upon this template.
   c. Save this Word document as [your initials] Word 5-3 renewals. Confirm that the *Save as type* is **Word Document**; if it's not, change it. If prompted to save the template file, click **No**.

5. Start the mail merge and select the recipients.
   a. Click the **Start Mail Merge** button [*Mailings* tab, *Start Mail Merge* group] and select **Letters**.
   b. Click the **Select Recipients** button [*Start Mail Merge* group] and select **Use an Existing List**. The *Select Data Source* dialog box opens.

c. Browse to locate your student data files, select the **SouzaRenewals-05** Excel file, and click **Open**. The *Select Table* dialog box opens.

d. Select the **Renewals$** table, verify the **First row of data contains column headers** box is checked, and click **OK**.

e. Click the **Edit Recipient List** button [*Start Mail Merge* group] to open the *Mail Merge Recipients* dialog box.

f. Click the **Last Name** column heading drop-down arrow and select **Sort Ascending**. The records are sorted by last name.

g. Deselect the check box on the last four recipients so they are not included in the merge (Figure 5-91).

h. Click **OK** to close the *Mail Merge Recipients* dialog box.

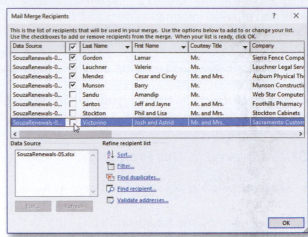

6. Insert the address block and greeting line merge fields into the letter.

a. Turn on **Show/Hide** [*Home* tab, *Paragraph* group].

b. Delete the "[**Address**]" placeholder text in the letter. Don't delete the paragraph mark at the end of the line.

c. Click the **Address Block** button [*Write & Insert Fields* group] to open the *Insert Address Block* dialog box.

d. Select the **Mr. Joshua Randall Jr.** option in the *Specify address elements* area. Click through each of the four recipients in the *Preview* area.

5-91 Deselect recipients

e. Click **OK** to close the *Insert Address Block* dialog box and to insert the << *AddressBlock* >> merge field in the document.

f. Delete the "[**Greeting**]" placeholder text in the letter. Don't delete the paragraph mark at the end of the line.

g. Click the **Greeting Line** button [*Write & Insert Fields* group] to open the *Insert Greeting Line* dialog box (Figure 5-92).

h. Select **Dear**, **Mr. and Mrs. Randall**, and **:** (colon) from the three drop-down lists in the *Greeting line format* area.

i. Click **OK** to close the *Insert Greeting Line* dialog box and to insert the <<*GreetingLine*>> merge field in the document.

5-92 *Insert Greeting Line* dialog box

7. Insert other merge fields in the body and table of the document.

a. Click the **Highlight Merge Fields** button [*Write & Insert Fields* group] to highlight the merge fields in the document.

b. Delete the "[**Policy Number**]" placeholder text in the subject line. Don't delete the space before or after the placeholder text.

c. Click the **Insert Merge Field** drop-down arrow [*Write & Insert Fields* group] and select **Policy_Number** from the drop-down list.

d. Verify there is one space before and after the << *Policy_Number* >> merge field.

e. Continue inserting merge fields in the document to replace the placeholder text using the information in the following table. Verify proper spacing and punctuation around merge fields (Figure 5-93).

Placeholder Text	Location	Merge Field
[Company]	First body paragraph	**Company**
[Insurance Company]	Second body paragraph	**Insurance_Company**
[Policy Description]	First column of table	**Policy_Description**
[Premium Basis]	Second column of table	**Premium_Basis**
[Rate per $1000]	Third column of table	**Rate_per_1000**
[Total Premium]	Fourth column of table	**Total_Premium**
[First Name]	Last body paragraph	**First_Name**

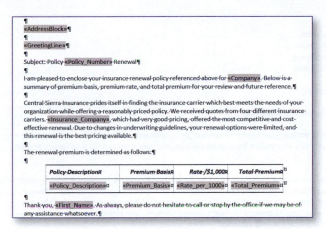

5-93 Merge fields inserted into the letter

8. Preview and check for errors in the merge.
   a. Click the **Preview Results** button [*Preview Results* group] to display the recipient information in the merge fields in the document.
   b. Click the **Next Record** or **Previous Record** button to preview all four recipients.
   c. Click the **Preview Results** button to turn off the previewing and to display the merge fields in the document.
   d. Click the **Highlight Merge Fields** button to turn off this feature.
   e. Click the **Check for Errors** button [*Preview Results* group]. The *Checking and Reporting Errors* dialog box opens (Figure 5-94).
   f. Click the **Simulate the merge . . .** radio button and click **OK**. A dialog box opens confirming that there are no errors (Figure 5-95). If there are errors, the errors are reported in a new document.
   g. Click **OK** to close the dialog box.
   h. Save the document.

9. Finish and save the merge.
   a. Click the **Finish & Merge** button [*Finish* group] and select **Edit Individual Documents**. The *Merge to New Document* dialog box opens.

5-94 *Checking and Reporting Errors* dialog box

5-95 Dialog box confirming no errors in the merge

b. Click the **All** radio button and click **OK** to complete the merge. The completed merge opens in a new document.

c. Save the completed merge as [your initials] Word 5-3 renewals merge and close this document (Figure 5-96). If prompted to save the template file, click **No**.

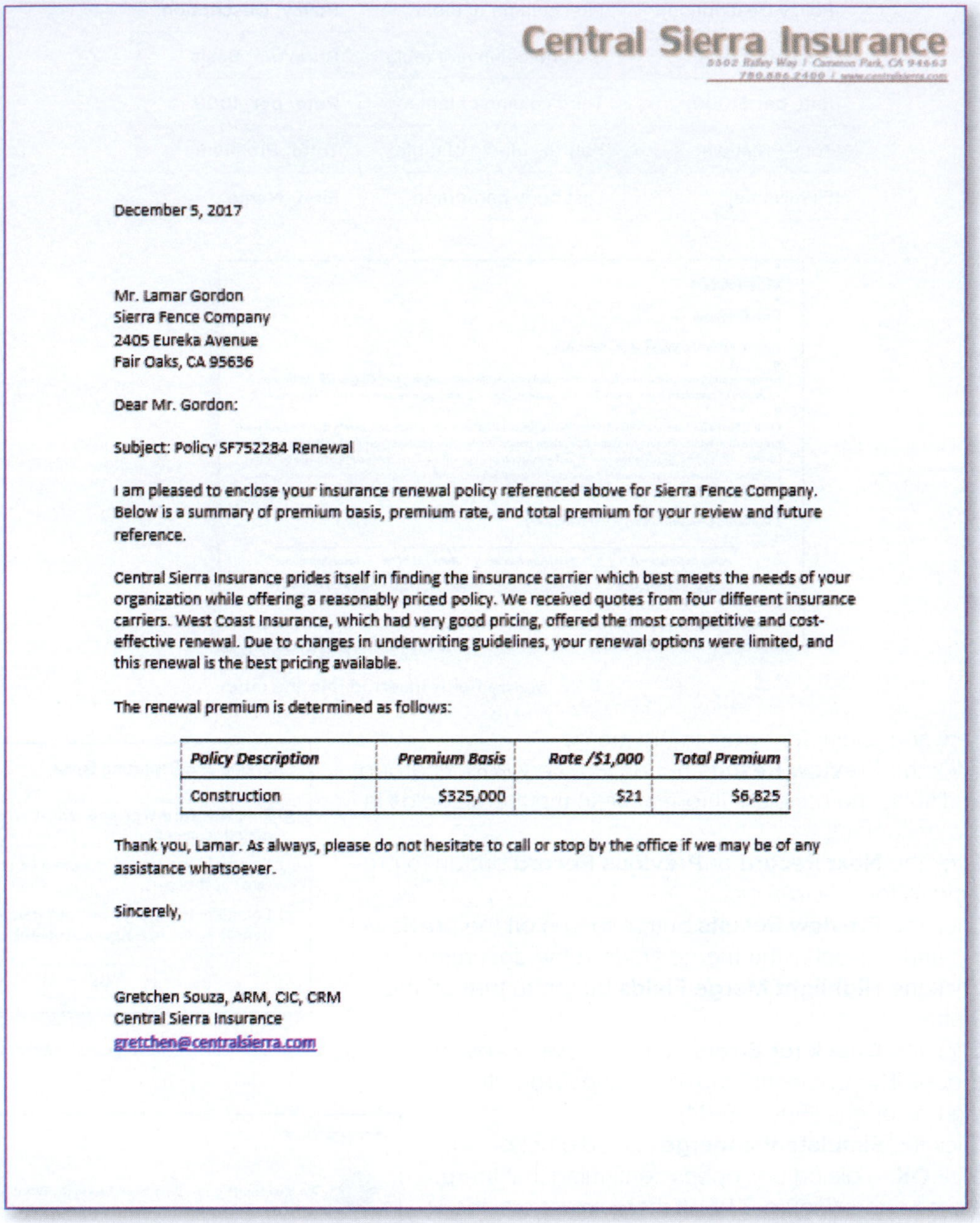

Central Sierra Insurance
5502 Ridley Way / Cameron Park, CA 94663
780.886.2400 / www.centralsierra.com

December 5, 2017

Mr. Lamar Gordon
Sierra Fence Company
2405 Eureka Avenue
Fair Oaks, CA 95636

Dear Mr. Gordon:

Subject: Policy SF752284 Renewal

I am pleased to enclose your insurance renewal policy referenced above for Sierra Fence Company. Below is a summary of premium basis, premium rate, and total premium for your review and future reference.

Central Sierra Insurance prides itself in finding the insurance carrier which best meets the needs of your organization while offering a reasonably priced policy. We received quotes from four different insurance carriers. West Coast Insurance, which had very good pricing, offered the most competitive and cost-effective renewal. Due to changes in underwriting guidelines, your renewal options were limited, and this renewal is the best pricing available.

The renewal premium is determined as follows:

Policy Description	Premium Basis	Rate /$1,000	Total Premium
Construction	$325,000	$21	$6,825

Thank you, Lamar. As always, please do not hesitate to call or stop by the office if we may be of any assistance whatsoever.

Sincerely,

Gretchen Souza, ARM, CIC, CRM
Central Sierra Insurance
gretchen@centralsierra.com

5-96 Word 5-3 renewals merge completed (page 1 of 4)

10. Save and close the *[your initials] Word 5-3 renewals* document. If prompted to save the template file, click **No**.

Independent Project 5-4

For this project, you create a letter for Emma Cavalli at Placer Hills Real Estate to send to prospective clients. You merge this letter with recipient information from an Access database and create mailing labels.
[Student Learning Outcomes 5.3, 5.4, 5.5, 5.6]

Files Needed: ***ProspectingLetter-05.docx*** and ***CavalliPHRE-05.accdb*** *(student data files are available in the Library of your SIMnet account)*
Completed Project File Names: *[your initials] Word 5-4 letter.docx*, *[your initials] Word 5-4 letter merge.docx*, *[your initials] Word 5-4 labels.docx*, and *[your initials] Word 5-4 labels merge.docx*

Skills Covered in This Project

- Insert date and set to update automatically.
- Use the *Mailings* tab or *Mail Merge Wizard* to create merged letters and labels.
- Use an Access database table as the data source for the merged letters and labels.
- Filter and sort a recipient list.
- Insert address block and greeting line merge fields.
- Insert individual merge fields.
- Highlight merge fields.
- Preview a merged document.
- Complete a letter and label merge.

1. Open the ***ProspectingLetter-05*** document from your student data files.

2. Save the document as [your initials] Word 5-4 letter.

3. Insert the current date.
   a. Delete the "**[Current date]**" placeholder text (don't delete the paragraph mark).
   b. Insert the current date (use January 1, 2018 format) and set the date to update automatically.

4. Use either the *Mailings* tab or the *Mail Merge Wizard* to start a letters mail merge.

5. Select the ***CavalliPHRE-05*** database as the existing recipient list.
   a. Use the **Potential Clients** table in this database.
   b. Edit the recipient list and filter for those recipients who live in the city of **Rocklin**.
   c. Sort the recipients by last name in ascending order.

6. Replace the "**[Address]**" placeholder text with an address block merge field.
   a. Use the **Mr. Joshua Randall Jr.** format.
   b. Scroll through the recipients in the *Preview* area to make sure the address block is formatted correctly.

7. Replace the "**[Salutation]**" placeholder text with a greeting line merge field.
   a. Use **Dear Mr. and Mrs. Randall:** format.
   b. Scroll through the recipients in the *Preview* area to make sure the greeting line is formatted correctly.

8. Insert merge fields in the body of the letter.
   a. Replace the "**[City]**" placeholder text with the **City** merge field.
   b. Replace the "**[First name]**" placeholder text with the **First** merge field.
   c. Turn on **Highlight Merge Fields** and verify spacing and punctuation around merge fields.

9. Replace "xx" with your reference initials at the end of the document.

10. Preview the merged letters. After previewing the letters, turn off both preview and highlight merge fields.

11. Finish the merge and save the documents.

a. Select **Edit Individual Documents** to finish the merge.

b. Save the merged letters as [your initials] Word 5-4 letter merge and close the document (Figure 5-97).

c. Save and close the *[your initials] Word 5-4 letter* document.

12. Create a new blank Word document and save the document as [your initials] Word 5-4 labels.

13. Use either the *Mailings* tab or the *Mail Merge Wizard* to start a labels merge.

a. Use **Avery US Letter**, **5160 Easy Peel Address Labels** as the label type.

b. Select the *CavalliPHRE-05* database as the existing recipient list.

c. Use the **Potential Clients** table in this database.

d. Edit the recipient list and filter for those recipients who live in the city of **Rocklin**.

e. Sort the recipients by last name in ascending order.

f. Insert address block merge field. Use the **Mr. Joshua Randall Jr.** format.

g. **Update Labels** so the address block merge field appears in each of the label cells.

14. Preview the merged labels. After previewing the labels, turn off preview.

15. Finish the merge to edit individual labels and save and close the documents.

a. Save the merged document as [your initials] Word 5-4 labels merge and close the document (Figure 5-98).

b. Save and close the *[your initials] Word 5-4 labels* document.

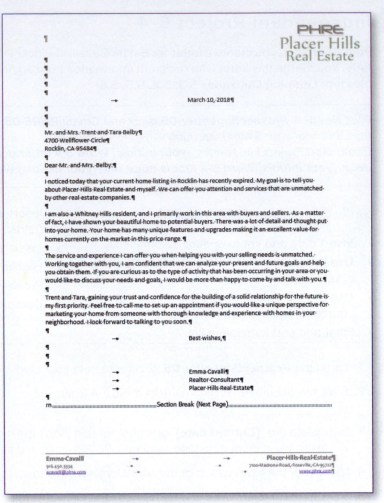

5-97 Word 5-4 letter merge completed (page 1 of 4)

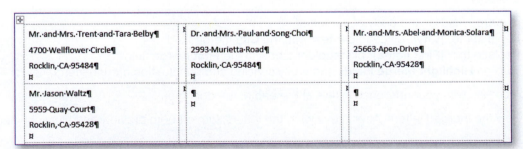

5-98 Word 5-4 labels merge completed

Independent Project 5-5

For this project, you create a business card template for the members of the American River Cycling Club. You use an online business card template, customize it, and save the document as a template. You then create a document based upon this template and customize the business cards for Kelsey Kroll. **[Student Learning Outcomes 5.1, 5.2]**

Files Needed: ***Business card (general format).dotx*** (from online templates) or ***BusinessCards-05.docx*** (*student data files are available in the* Library *of your SIMnet account*)
Completed Project File Names: ***[your initials] Word 5-5 template.dotx*** and ***[your initials] Word 5-5 business cards.docx***

Skills Covered in This Project

- Download an online business card template.
- Save a document as a template.
- Modify template content.
- Remove a content control field.
- Open a document based upon a template.
- Add content to a document based upon a template.

1. Create a document based on a business card template.
   a. Display the *New* area on the *Backstage* view and search for business cards.
   b. Select the **Business cards (Burgundy Wave design, 10 per page)** business card format as shown in Figure 5-99.

5-99 Create business cards from an online template

   c. Create a document based on this business card template. If this template is not available, open the ***BusinessCards-05*** document from your student data files.

2. Save the document as a Word template, name it **[your initials] Word 5-5 template**, and select the specific location to save the template. If prompted, update the file to the newest file format.

3. Customize template content.
   a. Turn on the **Show/Hide** feature and **View Gridlines** [*Table Tools Layout* tab, *Table* group].
   b. Click the **Company Name** field on the first business card (upper left), type American River Cycling Club, and press **Tab**. The *Company Name* fields on each business card update automatically.

c. Apply **bold**, **small caps**, and **10 pt**. font size formatting to "American River Cycling Club" on the first business card.

d. Use the **Format Painter** to apply this formatting to "American River Cycling Club" on each of the other business cards.

e. Select "**Telephone: Telephone**" (including the paragraph mark at the end of the line) on the first business card and delete the selected label and content control field. Delete this information on each of other the business cards.

f. Click the **Website** field at the bottom of the first business card, type www.arcc.org, and press **Tab**. The *Website* fields on each business card update automatically.

4. Save and close the template (Figure 5-100). If a dialog box opens and prompts you to save styles and building blocks, click **Don't Save**.

5-100 Modified business card template

5. Create a document based upon a template and save the document.

a. Open a *File Explorer* window, browse to the folder containing the *[your initials] Word 5-5 template* file, and double-click the file to create a document based upon the template file. Do not open the template file from within Word.

b. Save the Word document as [your initials] Word 5-5 business cards. Make sure you save the document as a Word document. If prompted to save the template file, click **No**.

6. Customize the first business card (upper left).

a. Click the **Your Name** field on the first business card, type Kelsey Kroll, and press **Tab**. The other business cards update automatically.

b. Type ARCC Coach in the *Position Title* field.

c. Tpe 916.522.7741 in the *Mobile . . .* field (select the second instance of the word "Mobile," which is the content control field).

d. Type kelsey.kroll@arcc.org in the *Email* field. If Word automatically capitalizes the first letter in the email address, undo this automatic capitalization.

7. Verify each business card displays the same information.

8. Save and close the document (Figure 5-101). If prompted to save the template file, click **No**. If a dialog box opens and prompts you to save styles and building blocks, click **Don't Save**.

5-101 Word 5-5 business cards completed

Independent Project 5-6

For this project, you customize a privacy notice for Courtyard Medical Plaza that includes merge fields for recipients' names and employee information. You also create file folder labels for individual employees.
[**Student Learning Outcomes 5.3, 5.4, 5.5, 5.6**]

Files Needed: ***PrivacyNotice-05.docx*** and ***CourtyardMedicalPlaza-05.xlsx*** *(student data files are available in the* Library *of your SIMnet account)*
Completed Project File Names: *[your initials] **Word 5-6.docx**, [your initials] **Word 5-6 merge.docx**, [your initials] **Word 5-6 labels.docx**,* and *[your initials] **Word 5-6 labels merge.docx***

Skills Covered in This Project

- Edit an existing document.
- Set a left tab stop.
- Use the *Mailings* tab or *Mail Merge Wizard* to create merged letters and labels.
- Use an Excel file as the data source for merged letters and labels.
- Filter and sort a recipient list.
- Insert individual merge fields.
- Apply formatting to merge fields.
- Insert date and set to update automatically.
- Preview merge documents.
- Complete a letter and label merge.

1. Open the ***PrivacyNotice-05*** document from your student data files.

2. Save the document as [your initials] Word 5-6.

3. Use either the *Mailings* tab or the *Mail Merge Wizard* to start a letters mail merge.

4. Select the ***CourtyardMedicalPlaza-05*** Excel file as the recipient list and select the **Employees$** table in this file. Verify the **First row of data contains column headers** box is checked.

5. Edit the recipient list.
   a. Filter for those recipients who are in the **Accounting** or **Marketing** departments. *Hint: Use the* Filter and Sort *dialog box.*
   b. Sort the recipients by last name in ascending order.
   c. Verify five recipients display in the *Mail Merge Recipients* dialog box.

6. Set a tab stop to align the merge fields.
   a. Select the four lines at the beginning of the document ("Name" through "Date") and set a **1.25"** left tab stop.
   b. Press **Tab** once at the end of each of these four lines.

7. Insert merge fields.
   a. Insert the **Title**, **First**, and **Last** merge fields after the tab on the "Name:" line. Ensure proper spacing between fields.
   b. Select these three merge fields and apply **bold** formatting.
   c. Insert the **EmpNumber** merge field after the tab on the "Employee Number:" line.
   d. Insert the **Department** merge field after the tab on the "Department:" line.

8. Insert the current date after the tab after "Date:" (use January 1, 2018 format) and set the date so it does not update automatically.

9. Preview the results.
   a. Check to ensure proper spacing between employee name merge fields.
   b. Preview each of the five recipients. After previewing the documents, turn off preview.

10. Complete the merge to edit individual documents.

11. Save the merged document as [your initials] Word 5-6 merge (Figure 5-102) and close the document.

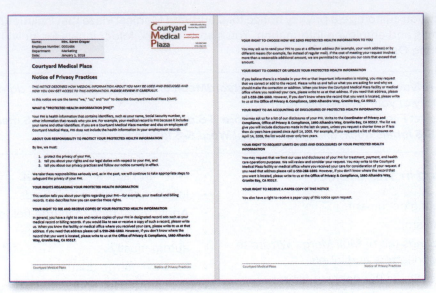

5-102 Word 5-6 merge completed (recipient 1 of 5)

12. Save and close the *[your initials] Word 5-6* document.

13. Create a new blank Word document and save the document as [your initials] Word 5-6 labels.

14. Use either the *Mailings* tab or the *Mail Merge Wizard* to start a labels mail merge.
    a. Select **Avery US Letter**, **45366 EcoFriendly Filing Labels**.
    b. Select the **CourtyardMedicalPlaza-05** Excel file as the recipient list and select the **Employees$** table in this file. Verify the **First row of data contains column headers** box is checked.
    c. Sort the recipients by last name in ascending order.
    d. Select the entire document and change the font to **Cambria** and the size to **10 pt**.

15. Insert merge fields and text in the labels.
    a. In the first cell (upper left) in the labels table, insert the **Last** and **First** fields. Separate the last and first name merge fields with a comma and space.
    b. Press **Enter** and type Employee Number:
    c. **Space** once and insert the **EmpNumber** merge field.
    d. Press **Enter** and insert the **Department** merge field.
    e. **Space** once and type Department.
    f. Select the first line of the label (<< Last>> , << First>>) and apply **bold**, **italic**, and **small caps** formatting.

16. **Update Labels** and preview the merge. After previewing the labels, turn off preview.

17. Complete the merge to edit individual documents. There are ten labels with merged information.

18. Save the merged document as [your initials] Word 5-6 labels merge (Figure 5-103) and close the document.

19. Save and close the *[your initials] Word 5-6 labels* document.

DRAPER, KAREN¶		*FALLON, TRISHA¶*
Employee·Number:·0001484¶		Employee·Number:·0001736¶
Marketing·Department¶		Medicine·Department¶
FAN, KAI¶		*HAN, TY¶*
Employee·Number:·0001984¶		Employee·Number:·0001325¶
Medicine·Department¶		Accounting·Department¶
HERMANN, RICK¶		*KIM, JAMIE¶*
Employee·Number:·0000552¶		Employee·Number:·0000954¶
Personnel·Department¶		Accounting·Department¶
NICKOLS, KALLYN¶		*PETROSKY, SAWYER¶*
Employee·Number:·0000746¶		Employee·Number:·0001080¶
Accounting·Department¶		Marketing·Department¶
SOLARA, RAMON¶		*URIBE, SETH¶*
Employee·Number:·0000825¶		Employee·Number:·0006985¶
Personnel·Department¶		Medicine·Department¶
Employee·Number:·¶		Employee·Number:·¶
·Department¶		·Department¶

5-103 Word 5-6 labels merge completed

Improve It Project 5-7

For this project, you create an employment letter template from an existing employment letter from Central Sierra Insurance. You delete specific employment information, insert placeholder text, and modify the structure of the letter.
[Student Learning Outcomes 5.1, 5.2]

File Needed: **EmploymentOffer-05.docx** (student data files are available in the Library of your SIMnet account)
Completed Project File Name: **[your initials] Word 5-7 template.dotx**

Skills Covered in This Project

- Save an existing document as a template.
- Delete numbered and lettered items from a document.
- Move numbered and lettered items.

- Change the level of an item in a multilevel list.
- Delete and insert a page break.
- Insert date.
- Delete text and insert placeholder text.
- Apply text highlight color.
- Modify header content.

---

1. Open the **EmploymentOffer-05** document from your student data files.

2. Save the document as a Word template named [your initials] Word 5-7 template. Select the specific location to save the template.

3. Delete text from the employment letter. Be sure to delete the paragraph mark at the end of the paragraphs being deleted and delete items in the order they are listed below.
   a. Delete item **16**.
   b. Delete item **11** including the three lettered items below the number.
   c. Delete items **7–9** including the lettered item on item **8**.
   d. Delete the page break at the end of the second page.

4. Move text from the employment letter. Be sure to include the paragraph mark at the end of the items being moved.
   a. Move item **5** so it displays before item 7 ("Eligibility for health benefits. . .").
   b. Move item **9** so it displays before item 8 ("Your retirement benefits") and click the **Increase Indent** button to make this the third lettered item (c) of item 7.

5. Insert a **page break** at the beginning of item 7.

6. Delete the date, insert the current date (use January 1, 2018 format), and set the date so it updates automatically.

7. Delete text and insert placeholder text. Be sure to include appropriate spacing and punctuation around placeholder text.
   a. Delete all three lines of the inside address and type [Employee's name and address] as the placeholder text. There should be three blank lines above and one blank line below this placeholder text.
   b. Delete "**Mrs. Skaar**" in the salutation (do not delete the colon) and type [Employee].
   c. In the first body paragraph, delete "**Health & Benefits Large Group Specialist**" and type [Job title].
   d. In the first body paragraph, delete "**Cameron Park**" and type [Office location].
   e. In the first body paragraph, delete "**April 1, 2018**" and type [Start date].
   f. On item 1, delete "**Bert Pulido**" and type [Supervisor].
   g. On item 1, delete "**Central Sierra Health & Benefits**" and type [Department].

    h. On item 2, delete all of the text after "Job Description:" (don't delete the period or paragraph mark at the end of the paragraph) and type **[Job description]**.

    i. On item 3, delete "**$4,500**" and type **[Salary]**. Don't delete the period after "$4,500".

8. Apply yellow text highlight color (not text color) to all of the placeholder text. Highlight only the placeholder text and brackets, not the spaces or punctuation around the placeholder text.

9. In the header on the second page, delete the date, insert the current date (use January 1, 2018 format), and set the date so it updates automatically.

10. Proofread the document to check for proper business letter formatting, spacing between parts, and spacing and punctuation around placeholder text.

11. Save and close the template (Figure 5-104).

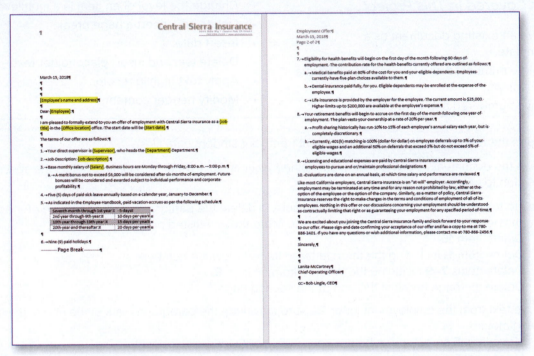

5-104 Word 5-7 template completed

Challenge Project 5-8

For this project, you create a form letter to use in a mail merge. You can merge information from a data source into any kind of document. The following is a list of examples for potential mail merge projects (you are not limited to these examples):

- A letter to your instructors informing them of an upcoming project and soliciting their input.
- A letter to family and friends inviting them to an upcoming event.
- A letter to your college's alumni soliciting scholarship donations.

Use an existing database as your data source or type a new list with recipient information. Complete the merge to a new document to edit individual documents.
[Student Learning Outcomes 5.4, 5.5, 5.6]

File Needed: None
Completed Project File Names: *[your initials] Word 5-8 main.docx*, *[your initials] Word 5-8 data.accdb*, and *[your initials] Word 5-8 merge.docx*

Create a new document and save it as [your initials] Word 5-8 main. Modify your document according to the following guidelines:

- Use proper business letter formatting if applicable.
- Change line and paragraph spacing as needed to create an attractive and readable document. Use consistent line and paragraph spacing throughout the document.
- Insert placeholder text where the merge fields are inserted.
- Select recipients or create a new list for recipients. Save the data source as [your initials] Word 5-8 data.
- Sort and/or filter the merge. Include at least five recipients in your merge.
- Insert merge fields as needed. Check for proper spacing and punctuation around merge fields.
- Highlight merge fields in the main document.
- Apply font formatting to at least one of the merge fields.
- Complete the mail merge to a new document and save as [your initials] Word 5-8 merge.

Challenge Project 5-9

For this project, you create a Word template based upon one of the Word templates on Office.com. Choose from a brochure, business cards, an invitation, a schedule, or any of the other templates available from Office.com on the *Backstage* view.
[Student Learning Outcomes 5.1, 5.2]

File Needed: None
Completed Project File Names: *[your initials] Word 5-9 template.dotx* and *[your initials] Word 5-9.docx*

Open a Word template of your choice and save the document as a Word template named [your initials] Word 5-9 template. Modify the template according to the following guidelines:

- Customize the template to meet your needs adding text and placeholder text.
- Delete any placeholder text not needed.
- Apply formatting as needed.
- Save and close the template.
- Create a Word document based upon the template and save this document as [your initials] Word 5-9.
- Replace placeholder text with custom content.
- Check for consistent and attractive formatting.

Challenge Project 5-10

For this project, you create a full sheet of return mailing labels and merged labels.
[Student Learning Outcomes 5.3, 5.4, 5.5, 5.6]

File Needed: None
Completed Project File Names: *[your initials] Word 5-10 return labels.docx*, *[your initials] Word 5-10 mailing labels.docx*, and *[your initials] Word 5-10 mailing labels merge.docx*

Create a full sheet of return mailing labels.

- Select the types of labels to be used for your return labels. Look online to find specific label information.
- Type the information to be included on the return labels and create a full page of the same label.
- Save the return labels as [your initials] Word 5-10 return labels.

Use an existing database as your data source or type a new list with recipient information. Complete the merge to a new document to edit individual labels. Modify your document according to the following guidelines:

- Select the types of labels to be used for your return labels.
- Select and sort recipients.
- Insert address block or individual merge fields.
- Change font and size as desired.
- Update all labels.
- Preview the labels.
- Save the document as [your initials] Word 5-10 mailing labels.
- Complete the merge to edit individual documents.
- Save the merged mailing labels as [your initials] Word 5-10 mailing labels merge.

CHAPTER

6

Using Custom Styles and Building Blocks

CHAPTER OVERVIEW

In Chapter 2, you learned about styles. In this chapter, you learn more about creating and managing custom styles. You also create building blocks, which allow you to save and use blocks of information. Building blocks, like styles, save you time and help you produce documents that are consistent in format and easier to read and understand. This chapter also covers *Quick Parts* building blocks, *AutoText* building blocks, document property fields, and Word fields.

CASE STUDY

In the Pause & Practice projects in this chapter, you create a styles template and a document detailing flexibility exercises for the American River Cycling Club. In these documents, you apply many of the features you learn in this chapter to create, save, and insert information in a document.

Pause & Practice 6-1: Create, save, and modify styles in a new document.

Pause & Practice 6-2: Create a style template to create, save, and manage styles, and attach a styles template to a document.

Pause & Practice 6-3: Use the *Building Blocks Organizer* and *AutoText* entries to save information and insert it into a document.

Pause & Practice 6-4: Customize the *Quick Parts* gallery and use document property fields in a document.

WORD

Creating and Using Custom Styles

Recall from *SLO 2.7: Using Styles and Themes* that **styles** are a collection of preset formatting that you apply to selected text. You can use styles to apply preset formatting to titles, section headings, paragraph headings, text, lists, and tables. You can apply or modify existing Word styles or create new styles. When you modify a style, Word automatically updates all text where that style is applied, creating a consistently formatted document and saving you time.

Themes are a collection of fonts, colors, and effects that apply to an entire document. Use styles and themes to apply consistent formatting throughout a single document or multiple documents. The default theme of a new document is *Office*. When you change the theme of a document, the font, size, color, and other attributes of each style change.

Style Gallery

The **Style gallery** is located in the *Styles* group on the *Home* tab and contains commonly used styles. Click the **More** button in the *Style* gallery to display all of the styles in the gallery (Figure 6-1). Use the **Styles** down arrow to scroll through the styles in the *Style* gallery.

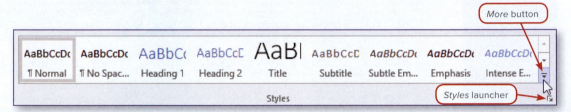

6-1 *Style* gallery

Apply a style to selected text or a paragraph by clicking a style in the *Style* gallery. When you place your pointer on a style, Word temporarily applies the style to the selected text so you can preview how the text will appear with the style applied.

> **ANOTHER WAY**
>
> Apply a style from the mini toolbar when you select or right-click text.

Styles Pane

The **Styles pane** lists many of the available styles in the document and those displayed in the *Style* gallery. By default, this pane does not list all of the available styles in a document. You can apply a style, modify a style, or create a new style from the *Styles* pane.

> **HOW TO:** Use the Styles Pane

1. Select the text where you want to apply a style.
2. Click the **Styles** launcher [*Home* tab, *Styles* group] (see Figure 6-1) to open the *Styles* pane (Figure 6-2).

3. Place your pointer on a style to display the attributes of the style.
   - Check the **Show Preview** box to display a preview of styles in the *Styles* pane
4. Click a style to apply to selected text.
5. Resize the *Styles* pane by clicking and dragging the top, bottom, left, or right edge.
6. Move the *Styles* pane by clicking and dragging the top bar of the pane.
   - You can also click the **Styles** drop-down arrow to move, size, or close the *Styles* pane.
   - Drag the *Styles* pane to the right edge of the Word window to dock the *Styles* pane at the right.
7. Click the **X** in the upper right corner to close the *Styles* pane.

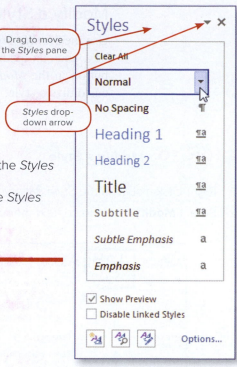

6-2 *Styles* pane

> **ANOTHER WAY**
>
> Press **Alt+Ctrl+Shift+S** to open the *Styles* pane.

Types of Styles

Word documents contain different types of styles. Some styles apply to selected text, while others apply to an entire paragraph. You can also create styles for lists and tables. The following table lists the different types of styles and a description of each type:

Types of Styles

Style Type	Description
Paragraph	Style applies to the entire paragraph.
Character	Style applies to selected text.
Linked	Style applies to selected text or an entire paragraph.
Table	Style applies to an entire table. Table styles are in the *Table Styles* gallery on the *Table Tools Design* tab.
List	Style applies to a paragraph or selected paragraphs.

An icon to the right of the style in the *Styles* pane indicates the type of style (Figure 6-3).

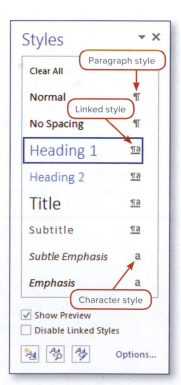

6-3 *Styles* pane with *Show Preview* turned on

> **MORE INFO**
>
> By default, table and list styles are not displayed in the *Styles* pane.

Modify a Style

Use the *Modify Style* dialog box to easily modify or update a style. In the *Modify Style* dialog box, you can quickly change the name of the style, font format, and alignment. The *Format* button in the *Modify Style* dialog box displays a list of other formatting options to further customize a style.

▶ **HOW TO:** Modify a Style

1. Right-click a style in the *Style* gallery or the *Styles* pane.
2. Select **Modify** from the context menu (Figure 6-4). The *Modify Style* dialog box opens (Figure 6-5).

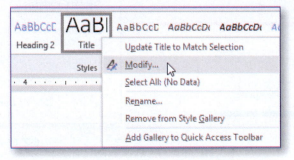

6-4 Modify a style

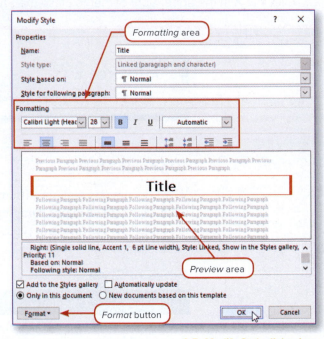

6-5 *Modify Style* dialog box

3. Type a new name for the style in the *Name* area if you want to rename the style.
4. In the *Formatting* area, change the font, size, color, style, alignment, and line spacing of the text as desired.
   - The *Preview* area displays how text appears in your document.
5. Click the **Format** button to display a list of additional formatting options (Figure 6-6).
   - When you select one of the options from the *Format* drop-down list, a dialog box opens where you can make additional changes to the style.
   - If you open and apply changes in one of these dialog boxes, click **OK** to close the dialog box and to return to the *Modify Style* dialog box.
6. Click **OK** to close the *Modify Style* dialog box.

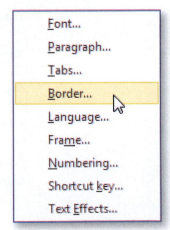

6-6 Style formatting options available from the *Format* button

Update a Style

When you update a style, the style updates based on the formatting of the selected text. For example, if you change the font, size, color, and paragraph spacing of selected text, you can update the *Heading 1* style to match the format of the selected text. When you update or modify a style, all text in the document formatted with the style updates automatically.

▶ HOW TO: Update a Style

1. Make formatting changes to selected text.
2. Right-click the style to update in the *Style* gallery or the *Styles* pane.
3. Select **Update *[Style Name]* to Match Selection** from the context menu to update the style to match the selected text (Figure 6-7).

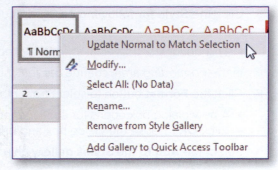

6-7 **Update a style**

▶ **ANOTHER WAY**

Right-click selected text to update a style from the *Styles* context menu on the mini toolbar.

Create a New Style

You can create a new style from scratch or create a new style based upon text that is already formatted. When you create a new style, you name the style and select a style type (*Paragraph, Character, Linked, Table,* or *List*). You have the option to base the new style on an existing style, which uses the formatting of the existing style as a starting point for the new style. You also set the style for the paragraph following the text with a style applied. For example, when you press *Enter* after a *Heading 1* style, you can set *Normal* to be the style of the next paragraph.

▶ HOW TO: Create a New Style

1. Click the **Styles** launcher to open the *Styles* pane.

2. Click the **New Style** button on the bottom left of the *Styles* pane (Figure 6-8). The *Create New Style from Formatting* dialog box opens (Figure 6-9).

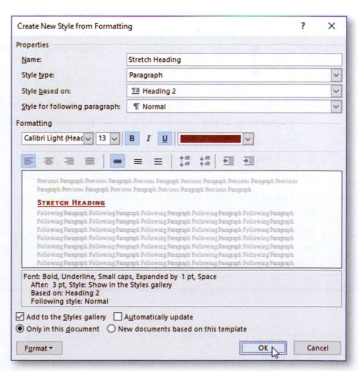

6-8 **Create a new style**

3. Click the **Name** text box and type the name of the style.

4. Click the **Style type** drop-down list and select the type of style.

5. Click the **Style based on** drop-down list and select a style as the starting point for the new style.

6-9 ***Create New Style from Formatting* dialog box**

6. Click the **Style for following paragraph** drop-down list and select the style for the paragraph following the style.

   - This option controls what style is applied to the next paragraph when you press *Enter* after text.

7. In the *Formatting* area, change the font, size, style, color, and alignment as desired.

8. Click the **Format** button to select from other formatting options.

   - A new dialog box opens for each format option you choose.
   - Click **OK** to close the dialog box and to return to the *Create New Style from Formatting* dialog box.

9. Select the **Add to the Styles gallery** check box to add the new style to the *Style* gallery.

   - By default, this box is checked when you create a new style.

10. Select the **Only in this document** radio button.

    - If you select **New documents based upon this template**, this style is added to the *Normal* template and is available on all new documents you create.

11. Click **OK** to close the dialog box.

▶ **MORE INFO**

Recall from Chapter 1 that each new document is based on the *Normal.dotx* template. This template stores the default settings for documents and controls document elements such as font, size, line spacing, paragraph spacing, alignment, and styles.

Create a New Style from Selected Text

You can also create a style based on existing text format in a document. When you do this, Word uses the existing text format to create the new style, and you have the option to modify the format of this style.

▶ **HOW TO:** Create a New Style from Selected Text

1. Select the text from which to create a new style.

2. Click the **More** button in the *Styles* group [*Home* tab] and select **Create a Style**. The *Create New Style from Formatting* dialog box opens (Figure 6-10).

3. Click the **Name** text box and type the name of the new style.

4. Click **OK** to close the dialog box and to create the new style. The new style also displays in the *Style* gallery.

   - You can also click the **Modify** button to open the *Create New Style from Formatting* dialog box that displays additional customization options (see Figure 6-9).

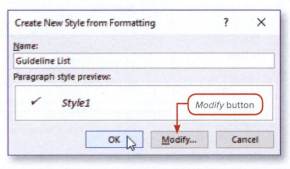

6-10 *Create New Style from Formatting* dialog box

Modify the Style Gallery

You can customize the styles that display in the *Style* gallery by adding or removing styles from the *Style* gallery. When you create a new style, you have the option to add it to the *Style* gallery by checking the **Add to the Styles gallery** box. If you didn't check this box when you created the style, you can add a style to the *Style* gallery two different ways.

- Click the style drop-down list or right-click a style in the *Styles* pane and select **Add to Style Gallery** (Figure 6-11).
- Click the style drop-down list or right-click a style in the *Styles* pane and select **Modify** to open the *Modify Style* dialog box. Check the **Add to the Styles gallery** box and click **OK**.

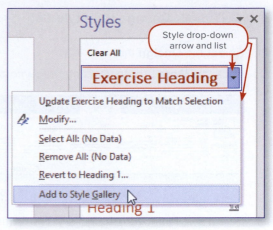

6-11 Add a style to the *Style* gallery

To remove a style from the *Style* gallery, right-click the style in the *Style* gallery or in the *Styles* pane and select **Remove from Style Gallery**.

Clear Formatting

After you create, modify, and apply styles, you might need to remove the style formatting from text in your document. You could change or remove all of the specific formatting (font, size, style, color, borders, etc.), but this would take too much time. Word allows you to quickly *clear formatting* on selected text. When you clear formatting, *Normal* style is applied to the text.

Select the text where you want to remove formatting and clear the formatting in one of the following ways:

- Click the **Clear All Formatting** button [*Home* tab, *Font* group] (Figure 6-12).
- Click the **More** button in the *Styles* group [*Home* tab] and select **Clear Formatting** (Figure 6-13).
- Click the **Clear All** option in the *Styles* pane (Figure 6-14).
- Select **Styles** from the mini toolbar and choose **Clear Formatting**.

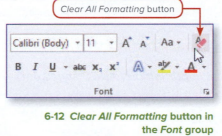

6-12 *Clear All Formatting* button in the *Font* group

6-13 *Clear Formatting* from the *Style* gallery

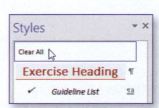

6-14 Clear formatting from the *Styles* pane

Change Document Style Set

In addition to individual styles, Word provides *style sets*, which are groups of styles. When you change the style set of your document, the format of all the styles in your document changes based on the style set you select. Style sets display in the *Style Sets* gallery in the *Document Formatting* group on the *Design* tab. Style sets control the font, size, styles, colors, borders, and line and paragraph spacing of a document. By default, a new Word document uses the *Word* style set.

1. Select the **Design** tab.
2. Click the **More** button [*Document Formatting* group] to display the *Style Sets* gallery (Figure 6-15).

6-15 *Style Sets* in the *Document Formatting* group

3. Select a style set from the gallery. The format of styles in your document changes based on the style set you choose.

You can also select different ***theme colors***, ***theme fonts***, and ***paragraph spacing*** to apply to your document. Click the **Colors**, **Fonts**, or **Paragraph Spacing** button in the *Document Formatting* group on the *Design* tab to display options on these drop-down lists (see Figure 6-15). Changing these options modify the existing theme in your document.

PAUSE & PRACTICE: WORD 6-1

In this Pause & Practice project, you create a Word template, modify existing styles, and create new styles. You also customize the *Style* gallery and change theme colors. You use the styles you modify and create in this template in *Pause & Practice 6-2*.

File Needed: None
Completed Project File Name: *[your initials] **ARCC** styles.dotx*

1. Create a new Word document.

2. Save the document as a Word template.
   a. Open the *Save As* dialog box.
   b. Type [your initials] ARCC styles in the *File name* text box.
   c. Select **Word Template** in the *Save as type* drop-down list. By default, Word changes the save location to a templates folder when you select *Word Template* as the file type.
   d. Browse to the location where you save your completed files.
   e. Click **Save** to close the dialog box and save the template.

3. Change the theme color of the document.
   a. Click the **Colors** button [*Design* tab, *Document Formatting* group].
   b. Select **Orange Red** from the drop-down list.

4. Type the following text, pressing **Enter** after each line (including the last line):
   Title
   Normal
   Subtle Emphasis
   Exercise Heading
   Stretch Heading
   Guideline List

5. Apply styles to selected text.
    a. Select the word "**Title**" and click the **Title** style in the *Style* gallery [*Home* tab, *Styles* group].
    b. Select "**Subtle Emphasis**," click the **Styles** button on the mini toolbar, and select **Subtle Emphasis** from the drop-down list.

6. Modify an existing style.
    a. Select the word "**Title**" and click the **Styles** launcher to open the *Styles* pane.
    b. Right-click the **Title** style in the *Styles* pane and select **Modify** to open the *Modify Style* dialog box.
    c. Click the **Format** button and select **Border** to open the *Borders and Shading* dialog box (Figure 6-16).
    d. Click the **Color** drop-down list and select **Orange, Accent 1**.
    e. Click the **Width** drop-down list and select **1 pt**.
    f. Click the **Top Border** and **Bottom Border** buttons in the *Preview* area to apply a **1 pt**. top and bottom border.
    g. Click the **Width** drop-down arrow and select **6 pt**.
    h. Click the **Left Border** and **Right Border** buttons in the *Preview* area to apply a **6 pt**. left and right border.
    i. Click **OK** to close the *Borders and Shading* dialog box and to return to the *Modify Style* dialog box.
    j. Click the **Format** button and select **Paragraph** to open the *Paragraph* dialog box.
    k. Change the *After* paragraph spacing to **24 pt**. and click **OK** to close the *Paragraph* dialog box and to return to the *Modify Style* dialog box.
    l. In the *Formatting* area, click the **Bold** button and the **Center** alignment button (Figure 6-17).
    m. Click **OK** to close the *Modify Style* dialog box.

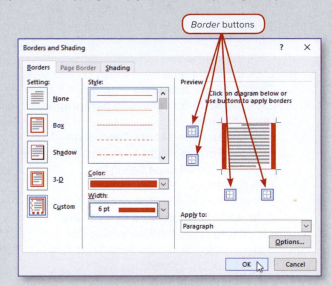

6-16 *Borders and Shading* dialog box

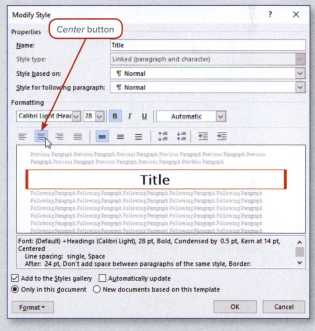

6-17 *Modify the Title style*

7. Modify text and update styles to match.
    a. Select the word "**Normal**" and change the line spacing to **single** and the *After* paragraph spacing to **10 pt**.
    b. Right-click the **Normal** style in the *Style* gallery and select **Update Normal to Match Selection** (Figure 6-18).
    c. Select the words "**Subtle Emphasis**" and apply **bold** formatting.
    d. Right-click the **Subtle Emphasis** style in the *Styles* pane and select **Update Subtle Emphasis to Match Selection**.

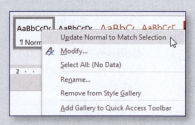

6-18 **Update style to match selection**

8. Create a new style.
    a. Select the "**Stretch Heading**" text in your document.
    b. Click the **New Style** button at the bottom left of the *Styles* pane (Figure 6-19) to open the *Create New Style from Formatting* dialog box.
    c. Click the **Name** text box and type Stretch Heading.
    d. Click the **Style type** drop-down list and select **Paragraph**.
    e. Click the **Style based on** drop-down list and select **Heading 2**.
    f. Click the **Style for following paragraph** drop-down list and select **Normal**.
    g. Click the **Bold** and **Underline** buttons in the *Formatting* area.
    h. Click the **Format** button and select **Font** to open the *Font* dialog box.
    i. Check the **Small caps** box in the *Effects* area.
    j. Select the *Advanced* tab and set the *Spacing* to be **Expanded** by **1 pt**. and click **OK** to close the *Font* dialog box and return to the *Create New Style from Formatting* dialog box.
    k. Click the **Format** button and select **Paragraph** to open the *Paragraph* dialog box.
    l. Change the *After* paragraph spacing to **3 pt**. and click **OK** to close the *Paragraph* dialog box and return to the *Create New Style from Formatting* dialog box.
    m. Confirm the **Add to Styles gallery** box is checked and click **OK** to close the dialog box and to create the new style. The *Stretch Heading* style applies to the selected text, and the style appears in the *Style* gallery and the *Styles* pane (Figure 6-20).

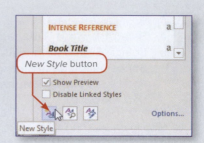

6-19 *New Style* button in the *Styles* pane

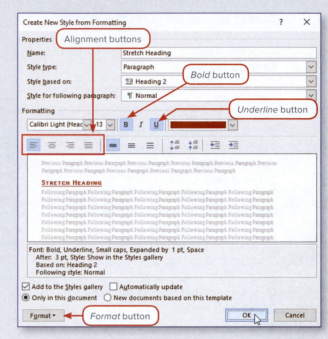

6-20 Create a new style

9. Create another new style.
    a. Select the "**Exercise Heading**" text in your document and click the **New Style** button in the *Styles* pane. The *Create New Style from Formatting* dialog box opens.
    b. Enter the following information to create the new style:

    Name: Exercise Heading
    Style type: **Paragraph**
    Style based on: **Heading 1**
    Style for following paragraph: **Stretch Heading**
    Formatting area: **Bold** and **Center** alignment

    c. Click the **Format** button and select **Border** to open the *Borders and Shading* dialog box.
    d. Change the border *Color* to **Orange**, **Accent 1**, the *Width* to **½ pt**., and click the **Top Border** and **Bottom Border** buttons in the *Preview* area.
    e. Click the **Shading** tab, change the *Fill* to **White**, **Background 1**, **Darker 5%**, and click **OK** to close the *Borders and Shading* dialog box.
    f. Click the **Format** button and select **Paragraph** to open the *Paragraph* dialog box.
    g. Change the *After* paragraph spacing to **12 pt**. and click **OK** to close the *Paragraph* dialog box.
    h. Click **OK** to close the *Create New Style from Formatting* dialog box and to create the new style.

10. Create a new style based on formatted text.
    a. Select the "**Guideline List**" text in your document and apply **italic** formatting.
    b. Click the **Bullets** drop-down arrow [*Home* tab, *Paragraph* group] and select **Define New Bullet** to open the *Define New bullet* dialog box.
    c. Click the **Symbol** button to open the *Symbol* dialog box and select **Wingdings** from the *Font* drop-down list.
    d. Select the **check mark** symbol (*Character code* 252), click **OK** to close the *Symbol* dialog box, and click **OK** to close the *Define New Bullet* dialog box.
    e. Open the *Paragraph* dialog box, confirm that the *Left* and *Hanging* indents are **0.25"** (change them if they are not), change the *After* paragraph spacing to **12 pt.**, and click **OK** to close the dialog box.
    f. Click the **More** button [*Home* tab, *Styles* group] to display the *Style* gallery, and select **Create a Style**. The *Create New Style from Formatting* dialog box opens (Figure 6-21).
    g. Click the **Name** text box, type Guideline List, and click **OK** to close the dialog box.

6-21 *Create New Style from Formatting* dialog box

11. Remove styles from the *Style* gallery.
    a. Right-click the **Heading 1** style in the *Style* gallery and select **Remove from Style Gallery** from the context menu (Figure 6-22).
    b. Right-click the **Heading 2** style in the *Styles* pane and select **Remove from Style Gallery** from the context menu.

12. Save and close the document (Figure 6-23).

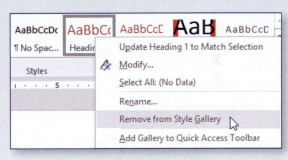

6-22 *Remove a style from the* Style *gallery*

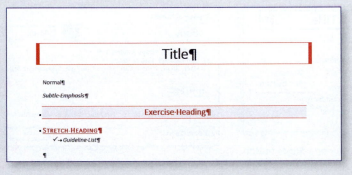

6-23 *ARCC styles* completed

Managing Styles

After you create and modify styles, you can manage your styles and determine which styles display in the *Styles* pane, delete styles from a document, modify or rename styles, and reorder styles in the *Styles* pane and *Style* gallery. You can also import styles from or export styles to another document. Recall from Chapter 5 that you can use templates to store styles you have created or modified, and you can attach templates to other Word files.

Manage Styles Dialog Box

In the previous section of this chapter, you modified existing styles in the *Style* gallery and *Styles* pane and added new styles. Word documents contain many styles that do not display in the *Style* gallery or *Styles* pane. The ***Manage Styles dialog box*** enables you to customize how styles are displayed and organized in a document.

Edit a Style

The following options are available on the *Edit* tab in the *Manage Styles* dialog box:

- Change sort order.
- Preview a style.
- Modify a style.
- Delete a style.
- Create a new style.
- Import and export styles.

▶**HOW TO:** Edit Styles in the Manage Styles Dialog Box

1. Click the **Styles** launcher to open the *Styles* pane.
2. Click the **Manage Styles** button at the bottom of the *Styles* pane (Figure 6-24). The *Manage Styles* dialog box opens.
3. Click the **Edit** tab if it is not already selected (Figure 6-25).
4. Click the **Sort order** drop-down list and select a sort option.
   - The sort options are *Alphabetical, As Recommended, Font, Based on,* and *By type*.
   - To display more styles, deselect the **Show recommended styles only** check box.
   - On the *Recommend* tab, you can change which styles are recommended.
5. Select a style to modify or delete in the *Select a style to edit* area.
   - When you select a style, a preview and description of the style displays in the *Preview* area.
   - Click the **Modify** or **Delete** button to modify or delete the selected style.
6. Click the **New Style** button to create a new style.
7. Click the **Only in this document** or **New documents based on this template** radio button to specify where these styles are available.
8. Click the **Import/Export** button to open the *Organizer* dialog box where you can import styles from or export styles to another Word document.
   - Importing and exporting styles is covered later in this section.
9. Click **OK** to close the *Manage Styles* dialog box.

6-24 *Manage Styles* button in the *Styles* pane

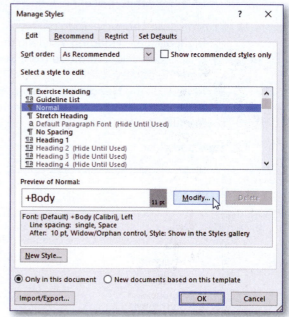

6-25 Edit styles in the *Manage Styles* dialog box

Recommended Styles

Recommended styles are those styles that display in the *Style* gallery and *Styles* pane by default. You can modify the recommended styles list.

▶ **HOW TO:** Modify the Recommended Styles List

1. Click the **Styles** launcher to open the *Styles* pane.
2. Click the **Manage Styles** button to open the *Manage Styles* dialog box.
3. Select the **Recommend** tab (Figure 6-26).
4. Deselect the **Show recommended styles only** check box to display all available styles.
5. Reorder styles by selecting a style and clicking the **Move Up** or **Move Down** button.
   - Sort order determines the order of styles displayed in the *Styles* gallery and *Styles* pane.
6. Modify the recommended styles list by selecting a style and clicking the **Show**, **Hide until used**, or **Hide** button.
   - When you click *Hide until used* on a selected style, the style does not display until you apply the previous style. For example, the *Heading 2* style does not display in the *Style* gallery or *Styles* pane until you apply the *Heading 1* style in a document.
7. Click the **Only in this document** or **New documents based on this template** radio button to determine where these styles are available.
8. Click **OK** to close the *Manage Styles* dialog box.

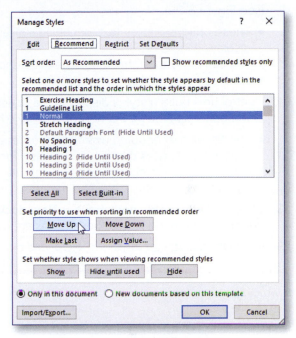

6-26 Recommended styles in the *Manage Styles* dialog box

Style Pane Options

Use the ***Style Pane Options dialog box*** to control which styles display and their order. The options in this dialog box control only the styles in the *Styles* pane, not those in the *Style* gallery. If you display additional styles in the *Styles* pane, you can always add a style to the *Style* gallery (see *SLO 6.1: Creating and Using Custom Styles*).

▶ **HOW TO:** Modify Style Pane Options

1. Click the **Styles** launcher to open the *Styles* pane.
2. Check the **Show Preview** box in the *Styles* pane to display a preview of the format of each style.
3. Click the **Options** link (Figure 6-27) to open the *Style Pane Options* dialog box (Figure 6-28).

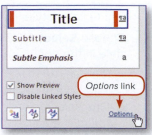

6-27 *Options* link in the *Styles* pane

4. Click the **Select styles to show** drop-down list and select which styles to display in the *Styles* pane.

   - The available options are *Recommended, In use, In current document,* and *All styles.*

5. Click the **Select how list is sorted** drop-down list and select how to sort the styles in the *Styles* pane.

   - The sort options are *Alphabetical, As Recommended, Font, Based on,* and *By type.*

6. Display text formatting as a style in the *Styles* pane by selecting one or more of the options in the *Select formatting to show as styles* area: **Paragraph level formatting, Font formatting,** or **Bullet and numbering formatting** (see Figure 6-28).

   - These options display text formatting similar to how a style displays (Figure 6-29).
   - You can apply this formatting style to selected text from the *Styles* pane as you would apply a style.

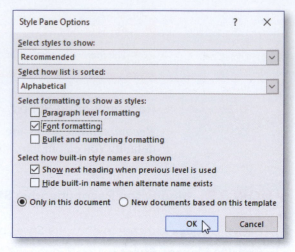

6-28 *Style Pane Options* dialog box

7. Control how built-in styles display in the *Styles* pane by selecting one or more of the options in the *Select how built-in style names are shown* area.

   - The *Show next heading when previous level is used* check box controls the availability of styles that are marked as *Hide until used.*
   - If the *Hide built-in name when an alternate name exists* box is checked, built-in styles that have been renamed are not listed in the *Styles* pane.

8. Click the **Only in this document** or **New documents based on this template** radio button to determine where these styles are available.

9. Click **OK** to close the *Style Pane Options* dialog box.

6-29 Formatting displayed as styles

Select and Clear All Styles

In a document, you might want to replace all of one style with another style or you might want to clear all formatting of one style. Word allows you to select all instances of a specific style in your document, which is an excellent way to modify all text formatted with a specific style at one time rather than change each occurrence individually.

▶**HOW TO:** Select All Formatting

1. Right-click a style in the *Style* gallery or *Styles* pane.

2. Choose **Select All** (Figure 6-30) to select all instances of the style in the document.

   - The number of instances this style is used in the document displays after the words "*Select All.*"
   - If the selected style is not used in the document, the *Select All* option is not active.

3. Apply a different style, change formatting and update the style, or clear formatting for the selected style.

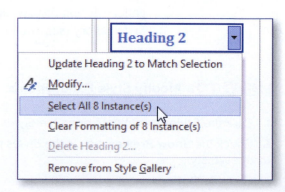

6-30 Select all instances of a style in a document

4. Remove all formatting on all instances of a specific style by selecting **Clear Formatting of Instances** (Figure 6-31).
   - The *Clear Formatting* option is also available from the *Styles* drop-down list on the mini toolbar and in the *Styles* pane.

5. Click anywhere in the document to deselect all of the selected text.

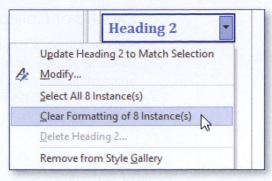

6-31 Clear formatting on all instances of a style

Find and Replace Styles

Recall from Chapter 2 that you use *Find and Replace* to find text or formatting in a document and replace it with different text or formatting. You can also use *Find and Replace* to find a specific style and replace it with a different one.

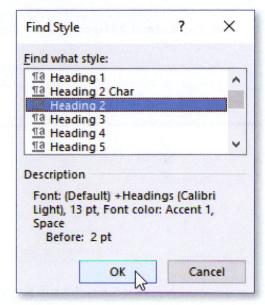

6-32 *Find Style* dialog box

▶ HOW TO: Find and Replace Styles

1. Click the **Replace** button [*Home* tab, *Editing* group] to open the *Find and Replace* dialog box.

2. Click the **More** button to display additional search options if they are not already displayed.

3. Click the **Find what** text box.

4. Click the **Format** button and select **Styles** to open the *Find Style* dialog box (Figure 6-32).

5. Select the style to find and click **OK** to close the *Find Style* dialog box.

6. Click the **Replace with** text box.

7. Click the **Format** button and select **Style** to open the *Replace Style* dialog box.

8. Select the style you want to find and click **OK** to close the dialog box.

9. Click the **Find Next** button to highlight the first occurrence of the style in the document (Figure 6-33).

10. Click the **Replace** or **Replace All** button to replace an individual occurrence or all of the occurrences of a style with a different style.

11. Click **Cancel** (or the **X** in the upper right corner) when you are finished.

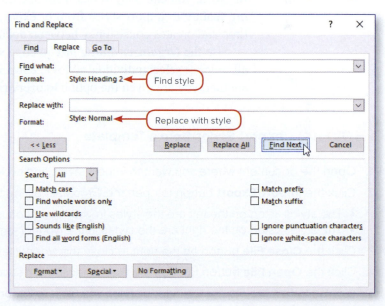

6-33 Find and replace styles

Expand or Collapse Headings

After you apply styles to the headings in your document, you can use the *Expand/Collapse* feature to display or hide the text below headings. When you collapse a heading, you hide information below the heading. You can collapse or expand a single heading or all headings in the document. This feature is useful to collapse a multi-page document and display only the headings in the document.

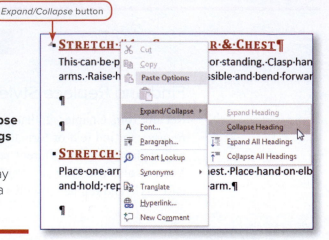

Expand/Collapse button

▶ HOW TO: Expand or Collapse Headings

1. Right-click the heading to collapse.

2. Click **Expand/Collapse** from the context menu.

3. Select from the available options: **Expand Heading**, **Collapse Heading**, **Expand All Headings**, and **Collapse All Headings** (Figure 6-34).

   - Alternatively, click the **Expand/Collapse** button (small gray triangle) to the left of the heading to collapse or expand a heading (see Figure 6-34).

6-34 Collapse Heading option

> **MORE INFO**
>
> When *Show/Hide* is turned on, a small black square displays to the left of heading where a style has been applied. This indicator helps you locate heading styles in your document.

Import and Export Styles

In Word, you can copy styles from one document to another. Use the *importing and exporting* feature to import styles from or export styles to a different document. This feature saves time and creates consistency between documents.

Use the *Organizer dialog box* to copy styles from one document to another. You can copy all styles or select individual styles to copy. When you copy built-in styles from one document to another, you are given the option to overwrite the existing built-in styles with the copied styles.

▶ HOW TO: Import Styles from a Template

1. Open the document where you want to import styles and click the **Manage Styles** button in the *Styles* pane.

2. Click the **Import/Export** button to open the *Organizer* dialog box.

   - The styles listed on the left are the styles in your open document.
   - The styles listed on the right are the styles in the *Normal* template.

3. Click the **Close File** button on the right to close the *Normal* template.

4. Click the **Open File** button to open the file containing the styles to import. The *Open* dialog box displays.

5. Browse to find the file containing the styles you want to import and click **Open**.

   - If you are importing from a regular Word document (.docx) or a file other than a template file, select the appropriate file type from the list of options available to the right of the *File name* text box.

6. Select the styles from the list on the right to copy (import) into your open document (style list on the left) (Figure 6-35).

7. Click the **Copy** button.

   - If you are importing styles with the same names as the styles in the open document, a dialog box opens asking if you want to overwrite the existing styles. Select **Yes to All** to overwrite existing styles (Figure 6-36).

8. Click **Close** to close the *Organizer* dialog box.

   - The imported styles display in the *Style* gallery and the *Styles* pane (Figure 6-37).

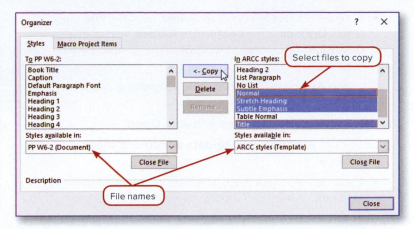

6-35 Copy styles using the *Organizer* dialog box

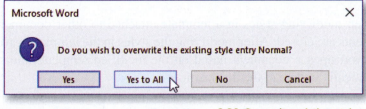

6-36 Overwrite existing styles

6-37 Imported styles displayed in the *Styles* pane

The process to export styles is similar to the importing process. When you are importing or exporting, always verify files you are using to import and export styles. The name of the file displays above each of the styles lists in the *Organize* dialog box (see Figure 6-35).

Styles Template

In *Pause & Practice 6-1*, you created a template containing new styles and modified styles. This is called a ***styles template***. When you attach a styles template to a document, the styles in the template are available in that document. The advantage of using a styles template is that, when you update styles in the styles template, these changes automatically update in all the documents where the styles template is attached.

Attach a Template to a Document

All new Word documents are, by default, based on the *Normal* template, which contains the theme and styles for the document. You can attach a different template to a document. You can also set the styles from the template to update automatically in the document(s) where the template is attached.

▶ **HOW TO:** Attach a Template to a Document

1. Open the document where you want to attach a template.

2. Click the **Document Template** button [*Developer* tab, *Templates* group] to open the *Templates and Add-ins* dialog box (Figure 6-38).

- If the *Developer* tab is not available, click the **File** tab, select **Options**, click **Customize Ribbon**, and check the **Developer** box under *Main Tabs* in the *Customize the Ribbon* area.

3. Click the **Attach** button. The *Attach Template* dialog box opens.

4. Browse to find the template and click **Open**.

5. Check the **Automatically update document styles** check box.

   - If you do not check this box, styles in the document will not update when you modify styles in the template.

6. Click **OK** to close the *Templates and Add-ins* dialog box.

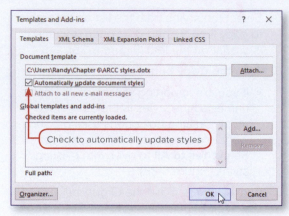

6-38 Attach a template to a document

When modifying styles in a template attached to other documents, make sure the other documents are closed. After modifying the styles in the template, save and close the template. When you open a document based on the modified template, the styles from the template automatically update in the document.

Use the Organizer Dialog Box

Use the *Organizer* dialog box to organize styles in documents that have a template attached. Similar to the method used to import styles, you can use the *Organizer* dialog box to copy, delete, or rename styles.

▶**HOW TO:** Use the Organizer Dialog Box

1. Open the document that has a template attached.

2. Click the **Document Template** button [*Developer* tab, *Templates* group] to open the *Templates and Add-ins* dialog box (see Figure 6-38).

3. Click the **Organizer** button to open the *Organizer* dialog box.

4. Click the **Styles available in** drop-down arrow on the left to select from the available documents and templates Figure 6-39).

5. Select a style from the style list and **Copy**, **Rename**, or **Delete** the style.

6. Click **Close** to close the *Organizer* dialog box.

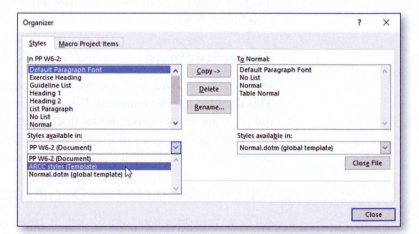

6-39 *Organizer* dialog box

> **MORE INFO**
>
> If you accidentally create a style and add it to the *Normal* template, you can delete the style in the *Organizer* dialog box.

For this Pause & Practice project, you modify a document about flexibility exercises for the American River Cycling Club. You import styles from a template, attach a styles template to a document, replace and modify styles, manage styles, and change options in the *Styles* pane.

Files Needed: **FlexibilityExercises-06.docx** and **[your initials] ARCC styles.dotx** *(student data files are available in the Library of your SIMnet account)*
Completed Project File Name: **[your initials] PP W6-2.docx**

1. Open the **FlexibilityExercises-06** document from your student data files.

2. Save the document as [your initials] PP W6-2.

3. Import styles from the **[your initials] ARCC styles** template you created in *Pause & Practice 6-1*.
   a. Click the **Styles** launcher to open the *Styles* pane.
   b. Click the **Manage Styles** button at the bottom of the *Styles* pane to open the *Manage Styles* dialog box.
   c. Click the **Import/Export** button to open the *Organizer* dialog box.
   d. Click the **Close File** button at the right to close the *Normal* template.
   e. Click the **Open File** button to open the *Open* dialog box.
   f. Browse to find the **[your initials] ARCC Styles** template and click **Open**.
   g. In the list of styles on the right, press the **Ctrl** key and select the following styles to copy (import) into your document (Figure 6-40):

      Exercise Heading
      Guideline List
      Normal
      Stretch Heading
      Subtle Emphasis
      Title

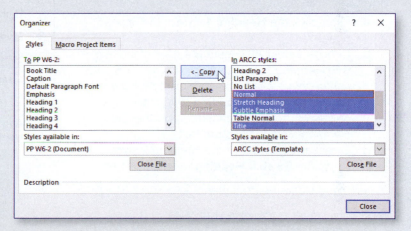

6-40 Copy styles using the *Organizer* dialog box

> **MORE INFO**
>
> Use the **Ctrl** key to select multiple, non-adjacent items in a list.

   h. Click the **Copy** button. A dialog box opens asking if you want to overwrite the existing styles.
   i. Select **Yes to All** to overwrite existing styles.
   j. Click **Close** to close the *Organizer* dialog box.

4. Attach the **[your initials] ARCC styles** template to your document.
   a. Click the **Document Template** button [*Developer* tab, *Templates* group] to open the *Templates and Add-ins* dialog box (Figure 6-41). If the *Developer* tab is not available, click the **File** tab, select **Options**, click **Customize Ribbon**, and check the **Developer** box under *Main Tabs* in the *Customize the Ribbon* area.

b. Click the **Attach** button. The *Attach Template* dialog box opens.

c. Browse to find the *[your initials] ARCC styles* template and click **Open**.

d. Check the **Automatically update document styles** box.

e. Click **OK** to close the *Templates and Add-ins* dialog box.

5. Change the theme color and apply styles.

a. Click the **Colors** button [*Design* tab, *Document Formatting* group] and choose **Orange Red**.

b. Select "**static stretches**" in the second paragraph on the first page.

c. Click the **Subtle Emphasis** style from the *Style* gallery or the *Styles* pane.

d. Select the entire paragraph that begins "Here are some general guidelines . . ." on the first page.

e. Click the **Intense Reference** style from the *Style* gallery or the *Styles* pane.

f. Select the list of guidelines below the "Here are some general guidelines . . ." paragraph.

g. Click the **Guideline List** style from the *Style* gallery or the *Styles* pane.

6. Select instances of styles and replace with different styles.

a. Right-click the **Heading 1** style in the *Styles* pane.

b. Choose **Select All** (Figure 6-42). All of the text with *Heading 1* style is selected. *Note: This selection might be displayed as "Select All: (No Data)."*

c. Click the **Exercise Heading** style in the *Style* gallery or the *Styles* pane to apply the *Exercise Heading* style to selected text.

d. Select all instances of the *Heading 2* style.

e. Apply the **Stretch Heading** to selected text.

7. Save and close the document.

8. Modify a style in the styles template.

a. Display the *Open* dialog box in Word.

b. Browse to find the *[your initials] ARCC styles* template and click **Open**.

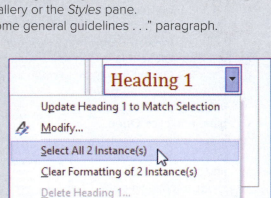

6-41 Attach the styles template to the document

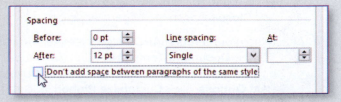

6-42 Select all instances of the *Heading 1* style

> **MORE INFO**
>
> To edit a template, open it from Word. If you open a template from a *File Explorer* window, it will open as a document based on the template.

---

c. Select the "**Guideline List**" text.

d. Open the **Paragraph** dialog box.

e. Deselect the **Don't add space between paragraphs of the same style** check box (Figure 6-43).

f. Click **OK** to close the *Paragraph* dialog box.

6-43 Apply formatting changes to the bulleted list

g. Right click the **Guideline List** style in the *Style* gallery and select **Update Guideline List to Match Selection** to update the style (Figure 6-44).

h. Save and close the template.

9. Open a document and change options in the *Styles* pane.

a. Open the ***[your initials] PP W6-2*** document. Notice that *12 pt. After* paragraph spacing now applies to the bulleted list on the first page.

b. Open the *Styles* pane if it is not already open.

c. Click the **Options** link in the *Styles* pane to open the *Style Pane Options* dialog box (Figure 6-45).

d. Click the **Select how list is sorted** drop-down list and select **Alphabetical**.

e. Click **OK** to close the dialog box.

f. Verify the changes in the *Styles* pane.

10. Save and close the document (Figure 6-46). If prompted to save changes to the template, click **No** (or **Don't Save**).

6-44 Update style to match selection

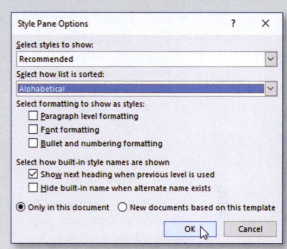

6-45 Change sort order in the *Style Pane Options* dialog box

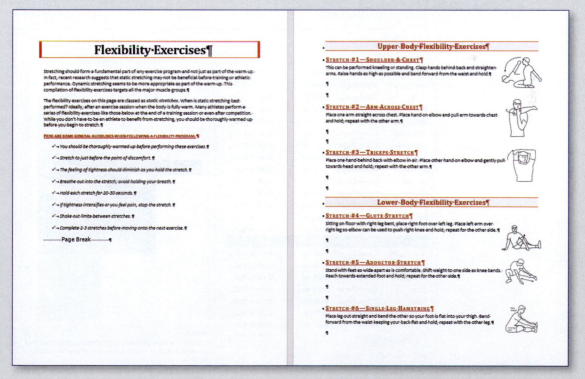

6-46 PP W6-2 completed (pages 1 and 2 of 3 pages)

Understanding and Using Building Blocks

Building blocks are stored pieces of information you insert in your documents. The built-in headers and footers, page numbers, cover pages, tables of contents, and bibliographies that you have used in your projects are examples of building blocks. In addition to using Word's built-in building blocks, you can also create and save your own custom building blocks such as company logos, paragraphs of text, closing lines of a business letter, letterhead information, or footers.

Building Blocks Organizer

Building blocks are grouped into galleries. The following built-in *building block galleries* are available in Word:

- *Bibliography* gallery
- *Cover Pages* gallery
- *Equations* gallery
- *Footers* gallery
- *Headers* gallery
- *Page Numbers* gallery
- *Table of Contents* gallery
- *Tables* gallery
- *Text Boxes* gallery
- *Watermarks* gallery

> **MORE INFO**
>
> *Quick Parts* and *AutoText* building block galleries are covered later in this chapter.

Within a gallery, building blocks are organized by *categories*. For example, in the *Page Numbers* gallery, each page number format (building block) is assigned to a category such as *Simple, Page X,* or *Page X of Y.*

The **Building Blocks Organizer** displays existing building blocks (Figure 6-47). Using the *Building Blocks Organizer,* you can preview, insert, delete, or change the properties of building blocks.

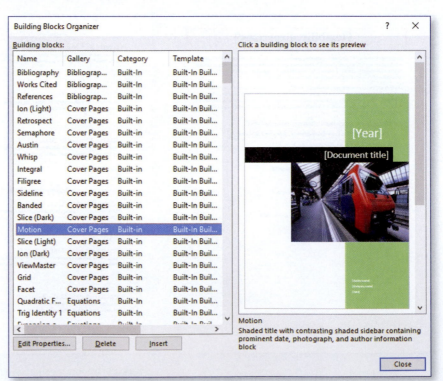

6-47 *Building Blocks Organizer* **dialog box**

1. Click the **Insert** tab.
2. Click the **Quick Parts** button [*Text* group].
3. Select **Building Blocks Organizer** to open the *Building Blocks Organizer* dialog box (see Figure 6-47).
   - The *Name, Gallery, Category,* and *Template* of each building block display.
   - By default, building blocks display in alphabetical order by gallery.
   - Click a column heading to change the sort order.
4. Select a building block to preview it on the right side of the dialog box.
   - You can change the properties of a building blocks or delete or insert a building block by clicking the **Edit Properties**, **Delete**, or **Insert** button.
5. Click **Close** to close the *Building Blocks Organizer*.

Create a Building Block

By default, built-in building blocks are stored in the *Building Block* template. The built-in building blocks are available in all new documents. You can create your own building block, add it to a gallery, assign it to a category, and select the template where you want to save it.

When you create a new building block, it is important to decide where to save it. If you are using a styles template and attaching it to other documents, you can save your custom building blocks in this template. These custom building blocks are then available in all documents where you attach the styles template.

▶ **HOW TO:** Create a Building Block

1. Select the information you want to save as a building block (Figure 6-48).
2. Click the button of the gallery where you want to save the building block.
   - For example, if you are saving a footer building block to the *Footer* gallery, click the **Footer** button [*Header & Footer* group].
3. Select **Save Selection to [gallery name] Gallery** (Figure 6-49). The *Create New Building Block* dialog box opens (Figure 6-50).
4. Click the **Name** text box and type a name for the building block.
5. Click the **Gallery** drop-down list and select the gallery where you want to store the building block.
   - This step is only necessary if you want to save the building block in a different gallery.
6. Click the **Category** drop-down list and select a category for the building block.
   - By default, new building blocks are saved in the *General* category.
   - You can create a new category or choose a different category.

6-48 Select information to save as a building block

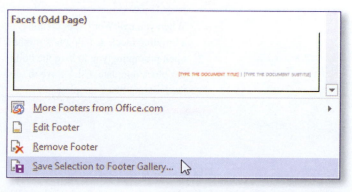

6-49 Save selection to *Footer Gallery*

7. Type a description in the *Description* text box if desired; a description is optional.

8. Click the **Save in** drop-down list and choose where to save the building block.

   - Typically, your *Save in* options are *Building Blocks* or the *Normal* template.
   - If you are working on a document that has a template attached, this template is also a *Save in* option.

9. Click the **Options** drop-down list and select how you want to insert content into a document.

   - The three options are *Insert content only, Insert content in its own paragraph,* and *Insert content in its own page.*

10. Click **OK** to save the new building block.

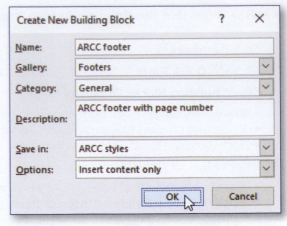

6-50 *Create New Building Block* dialog box

Insert a Building Block

After you save a building block, you can insert it by selecting the building block in the gallery where you saved it. For example, if you saved a *Footer* building block in the *Footers* gallery, it is available in the *Footer* drop-down list (Figure 6-51).

To insert a building block from the *Building Blocks Organizer,* place your insertion point in the document where you want to insert the building block, open the *Building Blocks Organizer,* select the building block to insert, and click the **Insert** button. The building block content is inserted in the document and the *Building Blocks Organizer* closes (Figure 6-52).

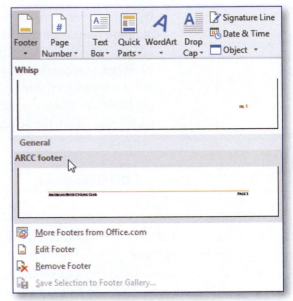

6-51 Insert *Footer* building block

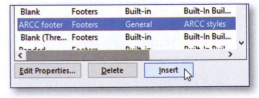

6-52 Insert building block from the *Building Blocks Organizer*

Edit a Building Block

Edit the properties of a building block to change the name, assign it to a different gallery or category, or save it in a different location. Use the *Building Blocks Organizer* to change building block properties. You can also create a new category within a gallery.

1. Click the **Quick Parts** button [*Insert* tab, *Text* group] and select **Building Blocks Organizer**.
2. Select the building block to edit and click the **Edit Properties** button to open the *Modify Building Block* dialog box.
3. Edit the building block properties as desired.
4. Click the **Category** drop-down list (Figure 6-53) and select **Create New Category**. The *Create New Category* dialog box opens (Figure 6-54).
5. Type a name for the new category and click **OK**.
6. Click **OK** to close the *Modify Building Block* dialog box and to save the changes to the building block.
7. Click **Yes** in the dialog box that asks if you want to redefine the building block (Figure 6-55).
8. Click **Close** to close the *Building Blocks Organizer.*

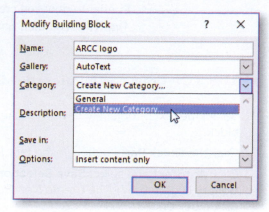

6-53 Create a new category

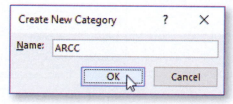

6-54 Create *New Category* dialog box

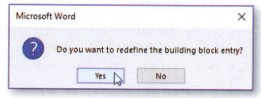

6-55 Redefine a building block

Delete a Building Block

When you no longer need a building block, you can delete it using the *Building Blocks Organizer.* You cannot change the content of a building block, but you can delete the existing building block and recreate it as a new building block.

▶**HOW TO:** Delete a Building Block

1. Click the **Quick Parts** button [*Insert* tab, *Text* group] and select **Building Blocks Organizer**.
2. Select a building block to delete.
3. Click the **Delete** button (Figure 6-56). A dialog box opens confirming you want to delete the building block.
4. Click **Yes** to delete the building block.
5. Click **Close** to close the *Building Blocks Organizer.*

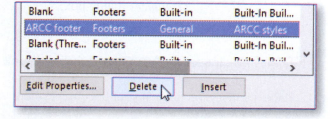

6-56 Delete a building block

SLO 6.4

Creating and Using AutoText Building Blocks

AutoText is another gallery where you save building blocks you want to use in other documents. Use the *AutoText* gallery when the information you want to store does not fit into other building block galleries such as the *Footers* gallery or *Page Numbers* gallery. For example, you might want to save specific text or a graphic that you regularly use in documents, such as a company logo graphic, the closing lines of a business letter, the opening lines of a memo, or a paragraph of text.

Create an AutoText Building Block

Similar to how you created other building blocks, select the text or object you want to save as *AutoText*. You then save this selection as an *AutoText* building block in the *AutoText* gallery.

▶ HOW TO: Create an AutoText Building Block

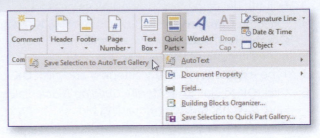

1. Select the text or object to save as an *AutoText* building block.

2. Click the **Quick Parts** button [*Insert* tab, *Text* group].

3. Click **AutoText** and select **Save Selection to AutoText Gallery** (Figure 6-57). The *Create New Building Block* dialog box opens (Figure 6-58).

   - The selection is assigned to the *AutoText* gallery.

6-57 Save selection in the *AutoText* gallery

4. Click the **Name** text box and type a name for the *AutoText*.

5. Click the **Category** drop-down list and select a category or create a new category.

6. Click the **Description** text box and type a description of the *AutoText*. A description is optional.

7. Click the **Save in** drop-down list and select the location where you want to save the *AutoText*.

8. Click **OK** to close the dialog box and save the *AutoText*.

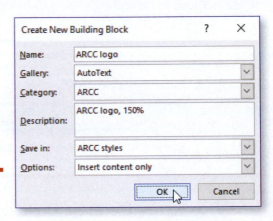

6-58 *Create New Building Block* dialog box

Insert an AutoText Building Block

AutoText building blocks are saved in the *AutoText* gallery, which is available from the *Quick Parts* drop-down list. You can also insert an *AutoText* building block from the *Building Blocks Organizer* dialog box.

▶ HOW TO: Insert an AutoText Building Block

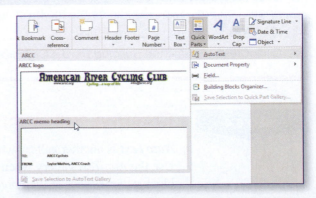

1. Place the insertion point in your document where you want to insert the *AutoText*.

2. Click the **Quick Parts** button and select **AutoText**. The *AutoText* gallery displays (Figure 6-59).

   - The category and name of the *AutoText* building blocks display above the building block.
   - Place your pointer on the *AutoText* building block to display its description.

3. Click the *AutoText* building block to insert it into the document.

6-59 Insert *AutoText* building block from the *AutoText* gallery

Edit or Delete an AutoText Building Block

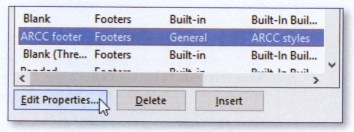

The process of editing or deleting an *AutoText* building block is similar to the process of editing other building blocks. Open the *Building Blocks Organizer,* and the *AutoText* building blocks display with all of the other building blocks. Select the building block to edit or delete and click the **Edit Properties** or **Delete** button (Figure 6-60).

6-60 Edit *AutoText* building block properties

> ▶ **ANOTHER WAY**
>
> Right-click an *AutoText* building block and select **Edit Properties** to open the *Modify Building Block* dialog box or select **Organize and Delete** to open the *Building Blocks Organizer.*

PAUSE & PRACTICE: WORD 6-3

For this Pause & Practice project, you modify the **[your initials] ARCC styles** template you created in *Pause & Practice 6-1* to include building blocks and *AutoText* building blocks. You also insert building blocks into the flexibility document you modified in *Pause & Practice 6-2.*

Files Needed: **[your initials] ARCC styles.dotx, [your initials] PP W6-2.docx**, and **ARCC-logo-06.png** *(student data files are available in the* Library *of your SIMnet account)*
Completed Projaect File Name: **[your initials] PP W6-3.docx**

1. Open the **[your initials] ARCC styles** template you created in *Pause & Practice 6-1* and modified in *Pause & Practice 6-2.* Open the template from within Word, not from a *File Explorer* folder, so the template file opens, not a document based on the template.

2. Create a *Footer* building block.
   a. Click the **Footer** button [*Insert* tab, *Header & Footer* group] and select **Edit Footer** from the drop-down list.
   b. Type American River Cycling Club at the left margin and press **Tab** two times.
   c. Type Page and **space** once.
   d. Insert a plain page number in the current position.
   e. Select all of the text in the footer and apply **bold**, **small caps**, and **10 pt**. formatting.
   f. Apply a **½ pt**. top border in **Orange**, **Accent 1** color.
   g. Select all of the text in the footer if it is not already selected (Figure 6-61).

6-61 Select text to save as a *Footer* building block

h. Click the **Footer** button [*Header & Footer Tools Design* tab, *Header & Footer* group] and select **Save Selection to Footer Gallery**. The *Create New Building Block* dialog box opens.

i. Enter the following properties for the building block (Figure 6-62):

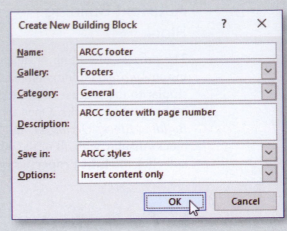

6-62 *Create New Building Block* dialog box

Name: ARCC footer
Gallery: **Footers**
Category: **General**
Description: ARCC footer with page number
Save in: *[your initials]* **ARCC styles**
Options: **Insert content only**

j. Click **OK** to close the dialog box and to save the building block.

k. Close the footer.

3. Create a memo heading.

a. Place the insertion point on the blank line after "Guideline List." If there is not a blank line after this line, press **Enter** after this line.

b. Apply the **Normal** style to the blank line.

c. Type **TO:**, press **Tab**, type ARCC Cyclists, and press **Enter**.

d. Type **FROM:**, press **Tab**, type Taylor Mathos, ARCC Coach, and press **Enter**.

e. Type **DATE:**, press **Tab**, insert (don't type) current date (use January 1, 2018 format), and set to update automatically.

f. Press **Enter** after the inserted date.

g. Type **SUBJECT:** and press **Tab**.

h. Select the first line of the memo heading and change the *Before* paragraph spacing to **72 pt**.

i. Select the last line of the memo heading and change the *After* paragraph spacing to **24 pt**.

j. Select all four lines of the memo heading and set a **1"** left tab stop.

4. Save a memo heading as an *AutoText* building block.

a. Select all four lines of the memo heading.

b. Click the **Quick Parts** button [*Insert* tab, *Text* group], click **AutoText**, and select **Save Selection to AutoText Gallery**. The *Create New Building Block* dialog box opens (Figure 6-63).

c. Enter the following properties for the building block:

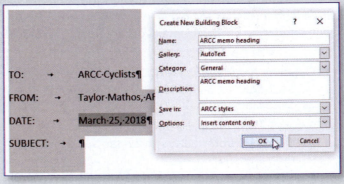

6-63 *Create New Building Block* dialog box

Name: ARCC memo heading
Gallery: **AutoText**
Category: **General**
Description: ARCC memo heading
Save in: *[your initials]* **ARCC styles**
Options: **Insert content only**

d. Click **OK** to close the dialog box and to save the building block.

5. Insert a picture in the document.

a. Place the insertion point after the tab on the last line of the memo heading and press **Enter**.

b. Insert as a picture the ***ARCC-logo-06*** file from your student data files.

c. Click the **Size** launcher [*Picture Tools Format* tab, *Size* group] to open the *Layout* dialog box.

d. In the *Scale* area on the *Size* tab, change the *Height* and *Width* to **150%**.

e. Click the **Text Wrapping** tab and change the *Wrapping style* to **Tight**.

f. Click the **Position** tab (Figure 6-64) and change the *Horizontal* position to **Alignment**, **Centered** *relative to* **Page**.

g. Change the *Vertical* position to **Absolute position**, **0.3** *below* **Page**.

h. Click **OK** to close the *Layout* dialog box.

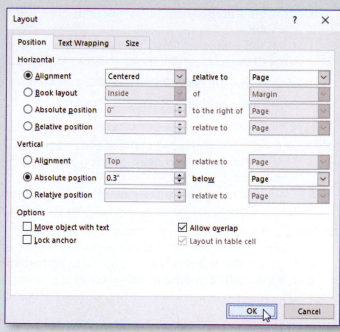

6-64 *Layout* dialog box

6. Save a graphic as an *AutoText* building block.

a. With the graphic selected, click the **Quick Parts** button [*Insert* tab, *Text* group], click **AutoText**, and select **Save Selection to AutoText Gallery**. The *Create New Building Block* dialog box opens.

b. Enter the following properties for the building block:
   Name: ARCC logo
   Gallery: **AutoText**
   Category: **General**
   Description: ARCC logo, 150%
   Save in: **[your initials] ARCC styles**
   Options: **Insert content only**

c. Click **OK** to close the dialog box and save the building block.

7. Edit building blocks to create a category.

a. Click the **Quick Parts** button [*Insert* tab, *Text* group] and select **Building Blocks Organizer**. The *Building Blocks Organizer* dialog box opens.

b. Select the **ARCC logo** *AutoText* building block and click the **Edit Properties** button to open the *Modify Building Block* dialog box.

c. Click the **Category** drop-down list and select **Create New Category** (Figure 6-65). The *Create New Category* dialog box opens.

d. Type ARCC and click **OK** to close the *Create New Category* dialog box (Figure 6-66).

e. Click **OK** to close the *Modify Building Block* dialog box.

f. Click **Yes** when the dialog opens confirming you want to redefine the building block.

g. With the *Building Blocks Organizer* still open, select the **ARCC memo heading** *AutoText* building block and click the **Edit Properties** button.

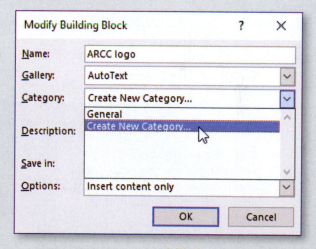

6-65 Create a new category

6-66 Name the new category

h. Click the **Category** drop-down list and select **ARCC**.
   i. Click **OK** to close the *Modify Building Block* dialog box.
   j. Click **Yes** when the dialog box opens confirming you want to redefine the building block.
   k. Click **Close** to close the *Building Blocks Organizer.*

8. Save and close the *[your initials] ARCC styles* template.

9. Open the *[your initials] PP W6-2* file you created in *Pause & Practice 6-2.*

10. Save the document as [your initials] PP W6-3.

11. Move the first page heading to the second page.
    a. Select "**Flexibility Exercises**" heading (including the paragraph mark) and cut (**Ctrl+X**) from the first page.
    b. Place the insertion point before "Upper-Body Flexibility Exercises" on the second page.
    c. Paste (**Ctrl+V**) the heading you cut from the first page.

12. Insert building blocks into the document.
    a. Place the insertion point at the beginning of the first page.
    b. Click the **Quick Parts** button [*Insert* tab, *Text* group] and select **AutoText**.
    c. Click the **ARCC memo heading** *AutoText* building block to insert it into the document (Figure 6-67). The memo heading displays at the top of the document.

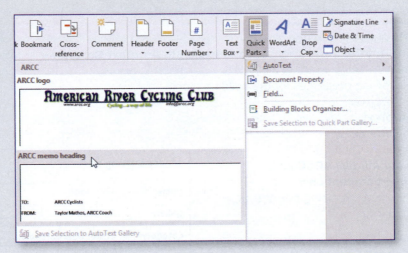

6-67 Insert *ARCC memo heading* building block

   d. Place the insertion point at the beginning of the first body paragraph below the memo heading lines if it is not already at that location.
   e. Insert the **ARCC logo** *AutoText* building block into the document. The logo displays at the top of the document.
   f. Click the **Footer** button [*Insert* tab, *Header & Footer* group].
   g. Scroll down the list of footers and select the **ARCC footer** building block (Figure 6-68).
   h. Delete the blank line below the footer text and close the footer.

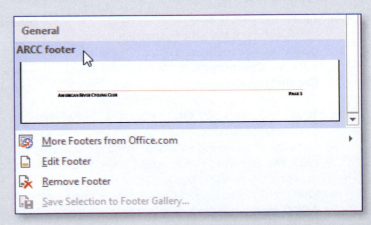

6-68 Insert *ARCC footer* building block

13. Save and close the document (Figure 6-69). If prompted to save changes to the template, click **No** (or **Don't Save**).

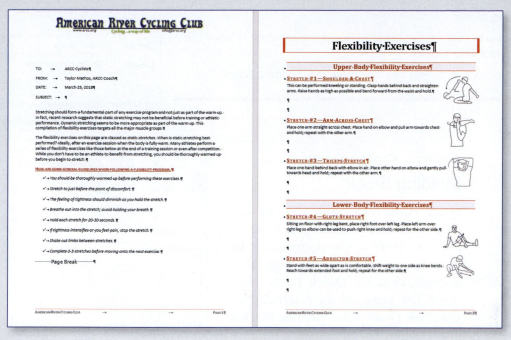

6-69 PP W6-3 completed (pages 1 and 2 of 3 pages)

Using and Customizing Quick Parts Building Blocks

Quick Parts is an additional gallery of building blocks available in Word. You can use the *Quick Parts* gallery to store information you commonly use in documents. The advantage of saving a building block in the *Quick Parts* gallery is this gallery is very easy to access. *Quick Parts* building blocks are available from the *Quick Parts* drop-down list on the *Insert* tab.

Create a Quick Parts Building Block

Creating a *Quick Parts* building block is similar to creating other building blocks such as *AutoText, Footer,* or *Header* building blocks. When you create a *Quick Parts* building block, it displays in the *Quick Parts* drop-down list and in the *Building Blocks Organizer*.

▶ **HOW TO:** Create a Quick Parts Building Block

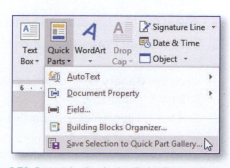

1. Select the text or object you want to save as a *Quick Parts* building block.
2. Click the **Quick Parts** button [*Insert* tab, *Text* group].
   - The selection is assigned to the *Quick Parts* gallery.
3. Select **Save Selection to Quick Part Gallery** (Figure 6-70). The *Create New Building Block* dialog box opens (Figure 6-71).

6-70 Save selection in the *Quick Parts* gallery

4. Click the **Name** text box and type a name for the *Quick Parts* build-ing block.

5. Click the **Category** drop-down list and select a category or create a new category.

6. Click the **Description** text box and type a description of the *Quick Parts* building block.

7. Click the **Save in** drop-down list and select the location to save the *Quick Parts* building block.

8. Click **OK** to close the dialog box and save the building block.

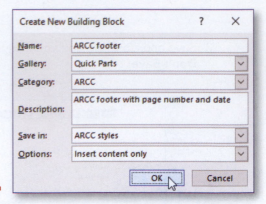

6-71 *Create New Building Block* dialog box

Insert a Quick Parts Building Block

Quick Parts building blocks are eas-ily inserted into a document. Place the insertion point in the document at the position you want the building block inserted, click the **Quick Parts** button in the *Text* group on the *Insert* tab, and select the *Quick Parts* building block to insert (Figure 6-72).

Edit or Delete a Quick Parts Building Block

You edit and delete *Quick Parts* building blocks the same way you edit and delete other building blocks. You can also edit regularly used building blocks stored in other galleries to make them available in the *Quick Parts* gallery.

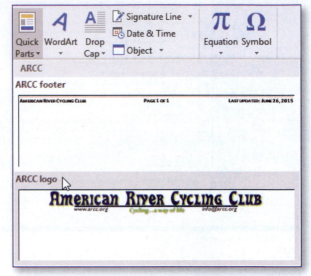

6-72 Insert *Quick Parts* building block from the *Quick Parts* gallery

---

▶ **HOW TO:** Add a Building Block to the Quick Parts Gallery

1. Click the **Quick Parts** button [*Insert* tab, *Text* group] and select **Building Blocks Organizer**. The *Building Blocks Organizer* dialog box opens.

2. Select the building block to add to the *Quick Parts* gallery.

3. Click the **Edit Properties** button to open the *Modify Building Block* dialog box.

4. Click the **Gallery** drop-down list and select **Quick Parts** (Figure 6-73).

5. Edit the building block properties as desired.
   - You can create a new category in *Quick Parts*.
   - You can have multiple *Quick Parts* categories, and *Quick Parts* are grouped by the categories in the drop-down list.

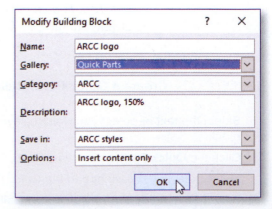

6-73 Add a building block to the *Quick Parts* gallery

6. Click **OK** to save the changes to the *Quick Parts* building block.

7. Click **Yes** when the dialog box opens asking you to confirm that you want to redefine the style.

8. Click **Close** to close the *Building Blocks Organizer* dialog box.

 SLO 6.6

Using Document Property and Word Fields

Each document you create and save includes ***document properties***. Document properties are a category of Word ***fields***. Word fields are special codes that you can insert into a document. Word fields, such as the *Company* document property field, the *NumPages* field (number of pages in the document), or a formula field, automatically insert content into a document.

> **MORE INFO**
>
> Chapter 7 describes how to insert a custom formula field.

6-74 Document properties on the *Backstage* view

Document Properties

To view and edit document properties, use the *Backstage* view. You can edit document properties such as *Title, Company,* and *Comments,* while others are automatically generated such as *Size, Pages, Words,* and *Last Modified.*

▶ **HOW TO: Edit Document Properties**

1. Click the **File** tab to open the *Backstage* view (Figure 6-74).
   - By default, the *Info* area displays and the document properties display on the right.
2. Click a document property field text box to add or edit information.
3. Click the **Show All Properties** link at the bottom to display all document properties.
   - When all properties display, the link changes to *Show Fewer Properties.*
4. Click the **Back** arrow or press **Esc** to return to the document.

Custom Document Properties

You can also view and edit document properties in the ***Properties dialog box***. This dialog box displays document information on five different tabs: *General, Summary, Statistics, Contents,* and *Custom.* The *General, Statistics,* and *Contents* tabs display document information. Use the *Summary* tab to add or edit document properties.

On the *Custom* tab, you can add a custom document property field. For example, you might want to add a document property field that is not normally available in a document such as *Department.* You can then insert this field into a document.

▶ **HOW TO: Add a Custom Document Property Field**

1. Click the **File** tab to display the *Info* area on the *Backstage* view.
2. Click the **Properties** button and select **Advanced Properties**. The *[File name] Properties* dialog box opens.

3. Click the **Custom** tab.

4. Select the custom document property field to add from the list in the *Name* area.

5. Click the **Type** drop-down list and select the type of information to store in this field: **Text**, **Date**, **Number**, or **Yes or no**.

6. Click the **Value** text box and type the information you want to store in this field.

7. Click **Add** to add the custom document property field (Figure 6-75). The custom field displays in the *Properties* area.

8. Click **OK** to close the *[File name] Properties* dialog box and click the **Back** arrow to return to the document.

6-75 Add custom document properties in the *[File name] Properties* dialog box

> **MORE INFO**
>
> Insert a custom document property field using the *Field* dialog box, which is discussed in the *Insert a Word Field* section in this chapter.

Insert a Document Property Field

You can insert document property fields in the body of a document or in the header or footer. When you insert a document property field into your document, Word displays the content stored in that field in your document. If you edit the contents of a document property field on the *Backstage* view or in the *Properties* dialog box, Word automatically updates the document property field in your document.

▶ **HOW TO:** Insert a Document Property Field

1. Place the insertion point in your document where you want to insert the document property field.

2. Click the **Quick Parts** button [*Insert* tab, *Text* group].

3. Select **Document Property** (Figure 6-76).

4. Select the document property from the list of document properties. The document property field is inserted in the document at the insertion point (Figure 6-77).

6-76 Insert document property field

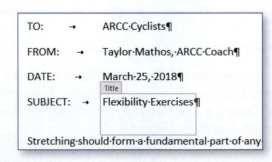

6-77 Document property field inserted into document

Insert a Word Field

You can also insert Word fields into a document. Insert a Word field using the ***Field dialog box***. The following table lists commonly used fields.

Commonly Used Fields

Field	Description
DocProperty	Inserts a document property or custom document property field.
FileName	Inserts the document file name.
NumPages	Inserts the number of pages in a document.
SaveDate	Inserts the date the document was last saved.
UserInitials	Inserts your initials from your Office personalization options.
UserName	Inserts your name from your Office personalization options.

In the *Field* dialog box, the available fields are grouped in categories. Many of the fields have field properties, which determine how the content of the field display in the document.

> **HOW TO: Insert a Word Field**

1. Place the insertion point in your document where you want to insert the field.

2. Click the **Quick Parts** button [*Insert* tab, *Text* group].

3. Select **Field** to open the *Field* dialog box (Figure 6-78).

4. Select the field to insert from the list in the *Field names* area.

   - Fields are grouped into categories. Click the **Categories** drop-down list to view the available categories.
   - The fields in a category display in the *Field names* area.

5. Select the format of the field from the list in the *Field properties* area.

   - Some fields also have *Field options* where you can further customize fields.

6. Click **OK** to close the dialog box and insert the field into the document (Figure 6-79).

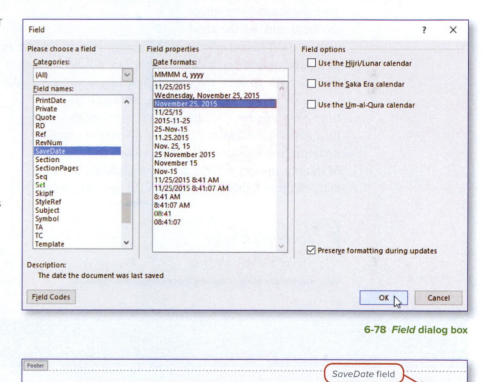

6-78 *Field* dialog box

6-79 Field inserted into the footer

Personalize Microsoft Office

When you originally install and register Microsoft Office on your computer, you are prompted to provide your user name and initials to personalize Microsoft Office. These pieces of information are Word fields that can be used in your documents. You can change this personalization information after Microsoft Office has been installed on your computer.

1. Click the **File** tab to open the *Backstage* view.

2. Click the **Options** button to open the *Word Options* dialog box (Figure 6-80).

3. Click the **General** button.

4. Type your information in the *User name* and *Initials* text boxes in the *Personalize your copy of Microsoft Office*.

5. Click **OK** to close the *Word Options* dialog box.

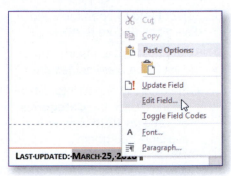

6-80 Personalize Microsoft Office

Edit and Update Fields

When you insert a field in your document, you select the field and set the field properties. You can edit a field to change how it displays in your document, such as the format of a page number or a date. Right-click a field and select **Edit Field** from the context menu (Figure 6-81) to open the *Field* dialog box where you make changes to the field properties.

Fields in a document update automatically each time you open a document, but you might need to update a field after editing a document, such as updating a formula field when values are changed. Manually update a field by right-clicking the field and selecting **Update Field** from the context menu.

▶ **ANOTHER WAY**

Press **F9** to update a field.

6-81 Select *Edit Field* from the context menu

PAUSE & PRACTICE: WORD 6-4

For this Pause & Practice project, you delete and modify existing building blocks, add building blocks to the *Quick Parts* gallery, customize and insert document properties, and insert Word fields to finalize the flexibility document for the American River Cycling Club.

File Needed: ***[your initials] PP W6-3.docx***
Completed Project File Name: ***[your initials] PP W6-4.docx***

1. Open the ***[your initials] PP W6-3*** document completed in *Pause & Practice 6-3*.

2. Save the document as [your initials] PP W6-4.

3. Delete and modify building blocks.
   a. Click the **Quick Parts** button [*Insert* tab, *Text* group] and select **Building Blocks Organizer** to open the *Building Blocks Organizer* dialog box.
   b. Select the **ARCC footer** *Footers* building block, click the **Delete** button, and click **Yes** when the dialog box opens asking if you want to delete the building block.
   c. Select the **ARCC memo heading** *AutoText* building block, click the **Delete** button, and click **Yes** in the dialog box that asks if you want to delete the building block.
   d. Select the **ARCC logo** *AutoText* building block and click the **Edit Properties** button. The *Modify Building Block* dialog box opens.
   e. Click the **Gallery** drop-down list and select **Quick Parts** to move this building block to the *Quick Parts* gallery.
   f. Click the **Category** drop-down list and select **Create New Category**. The *Create New Category* dialog box opens.
   g. Type **ARCC** and click **OK** to create the new category.
   h. Select **ARCC** from the *Category* drop-down list if it is not already selected (Figure 6-82).
   i. Click **OK** to close the *Modify Building Block* dialog box and click **Yes** when the dialog box opens asking if you want to redefine the building block.
   j. Click **Close** to close the *Building Blocks Organizer* dialog box.

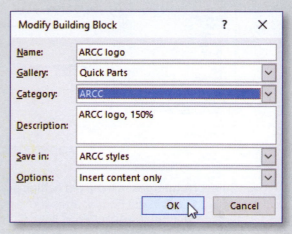

6-82 *Modify Building Block* dialog box

4. Customize and insert document properties.
   a. Click the **File** tab to open the *Backstage* view and click **Info** on the left if it is not already selected.
   b. Type **Flexibility Exercises** in the *Title* document property field.
   c. Click the **Show All Properties** link at the bottom of the document properties.
   d. Type **American River Cycling Club** in the *Company* document property field.
   e. Click the **Back** arrow to close the *Backstage* view and to return to the document.
   f. Place the insertion point after the tab on the subject line of the memo heading.
   g. Click the **Quick Parts** button [*Insert* tab, *Text* group], click **Document Property**, and select **Title** from the list of document properties to insert the *Title* document property field (Figure 6-83).

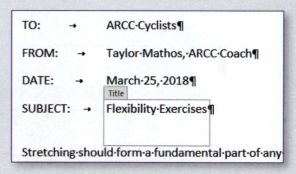

6-83 *Title* document property inserted

5. Modify the footer to include document properties and Word fields.
   a. Edit the footer on the first page of the document.
   b. Select "**American River Cycling Club.**"
   c. Click the **Document Info** button [*Header & Footer Tools Design* tab, *Insert* group], click **Document Property**, and select **Company** from the list of document properties. The *Company* document property field replaces the selected text.
   d. Place the insertion point directly before "Page" in the footer and press **Backspace** to remove one tab.
   e. Place the insertion point after the page number, **space** once, type **of**, and **space** once.
   f. Click the **Quick Parts** button and select **Field**. The *Field* dialog box opens (Figure 6-84).

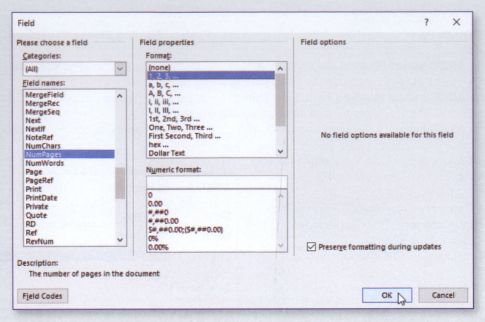

6-84 Insert *NumPages* field in the footer

g. Select **NumPages** in the *Field* names area.

h. Select **1, 2, 3** in the *Format* area and click **OK** to close the *Field* dialog box and to insert the field.

i. Press **Tab** after the *NumPages* field, type **Last updated:** and **space** once.

j. Click the **Quick Parts** button and select **Field**. The *Field* dialog box opens.

k. Select **SaveDate** in the *Field* names area, select the date format (use January 1, 2018 format) in the *Date formats* area, and click **OK** to close the *Field* dialog box and to insert the field.

6. Add the footer and memo heading to the *Quick Parts* gallery.

a. Select the entire footer (Figure 6-85).

> **MORE INFO**
>
> When you insert document property and Word fields, include proper spacing before and after the field.

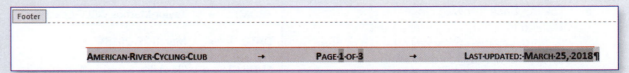

6-85 Select footer to save in the *Quick Parts* gallery

b. Click the **Quick Parts** button and select **Save Selection to Quick Part Gallery**. The *Create New Building Block* dialog box opens.

c. Enter the following properties for the building block (Figure 6-86):

  Name: ARCC footer
  Gallery: **Quick Parts**
  Category: **ARCC**
  Description: ARCC footer with page number and date
  Save in: **[your initials] ARCC styles**
  Options: **Insert content only**

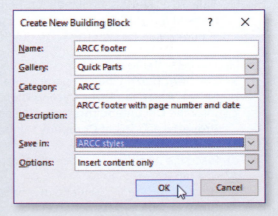

6-86 Create a new building block

d. Click **OK** to close the dialog box and save the building block.

e. Close the footer.

f. Select the four memo heading lines.

g. Click the **Quick Parts** button and select **Save Selection to Quick Part Gallery**. The *Create New Building Block* dialog box opens.

h. Enter the following properties for the building block:

   Name: ARCC memo heading
   Gallery: **Quick Parts**
   Category: **ARCC**
   Description: ARCC memo heading
   Save in: *[your initials]* **ARCC styles**
   Options: **Insert content only**

i. Click **OK** to close the dialog box and to save the building block.

7. Save and close the document. Click **Yes** if a dialog box opens asking if you want to save changes to the **ARCC styles** template file (Figures 6-87 and 6-88).

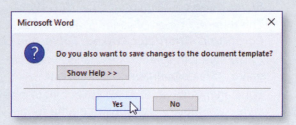

6-87 Save changes in template file

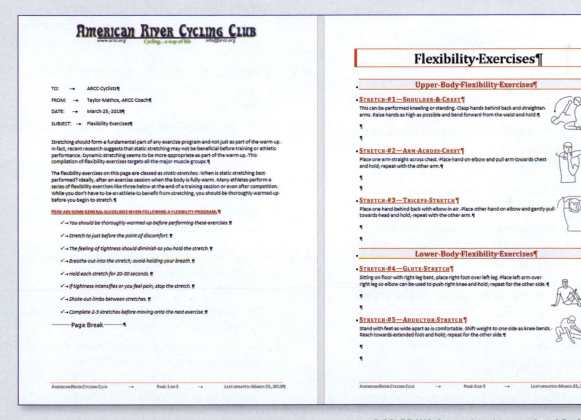

6-88 PP W6-4 completed (pages 1 and 2 of 3 pages)

Chapter Summary

6.1 Create and modify styles using the *Style gallery* and *Styles pane* (p. W6-328).

- A **style** is a set of formatting commands that are grouped together and applied to text. Use styles to apply consistent formatting in documents.
- The **Style gallery** on the *Home* tab and the **Styles pane** contain commonly used styles.
- The different types of styles available are **Paragraph**, **Character**, **Linked**, **Table**, and **List**.
- Apply styles to selected text using the *Style* gallery, *Styles* pane, or context menu.
- You can modify an existing style, create a new style, or update a style based on the formatting of selected text.
- Styles can be added to or removed from the *Style* gallery.
- Clear all of the formatting on text by selecting the **Clear Formatting** button [*Home* tab, *Font* group] or selecting **Clear Formatting** in the *Style* gallery or from context menu. You can also apply the *Clear All* style from the *Styles* pane.
- Change the **Style Set** or **theme fonts**, **theme colors**, and **paragraph spacing** to control the formatting of your document.

6.2 Customize a document by managing styles and using a styles template (p. W6-337).

- Use the **Manage Styles dialog box** to customize which styles display, change the display order of styles, edit and create styles, and import and export styles.
- **Recommended styles** display in the *Style* gallery and the *Styles* pane.
- The **Style Pane Options dialog box** also controls which styles display and the order they display in the *Styles* pane.
- You can select all instances or clear formatting of instances of styles in a document. When you select all instances of a style, you can apply formatting to these instances or replace each instance with another style.
- Use the *Find and Replace* dialog box to find and replace styles in a document.
- **Import** or **export** styles from a template or document to another template or document.
- A **styles template** contains styles that can be attached or imported to other documents.

- Use the **Organizer dialog box** to copy styles from one document to another.

6.3 Use the *Building Blocks Organizer* to create and save information in a document (p. W6-348).

- A **building block** is information that is saved and can be inserted into other documents.
- Building blocks are grouped into a variety of **building block galleries**. Commonly used building block galleries include **Footers gallery**, **Headers gallery**, and **Page Numbers gallery**.
- You create a building block by saving selected text or an object, such as a graphic or table, to a gallery.
- Use the **Building Blocks Organizer** to edit, insert, or delete building blocks.
- You can edit the properties of a building block and create a **category** to group building blocks.

6.4 Create *AutoText* building blocks to save text and objects and insert them into a document (p. W6-351).

- Use the **AutoText gallery** to store specialized text or objects.
- Modify, insert, and delete **AutoText building blocks** using the *Building Blocks Organizer*.
- Display the *AutoText* gallery by clicking the **Quick Parts** button [*Insert* tab, *Text* group] and selecting **AutoText**.

6.5 Use the *Quick Parts* gallery to store building blocks and insert them into a document (p. W6-357).

- The **Quick Parts gallery** is an easy access area to store building blocks.
- Modify, insert, and delete **Quick Parts building blocks** using the *Building Blocks Organizer*.
- Display the *Quick Parts* gallery by clicking the **Quick Parts** button [*Insert* tab, *Text* group].

6.6 Customize and use document property and Word fields in a document (p. W6-359).

- **Document property fields** are included in each document you create.
- Create custom document properties that you can insert into a document.
- View and customize document properties from the *Backstage* view or **Properties dialog box**.

- **Word fields** are special codes that can be used to insert content in a document.
- Use Word fields to insert a file name, user name, save date, and number of pages in a document.
- Insert Word fields using the **Field dialog box**.
- The *Field* dialog box lists available fields. You can customize the properties of many fields, which determines how the field displays in the document.
- Edit fields using the context menu and update fields using the context menu or by pressing **F9**.

Check for Understanding

The SIMbook for this text (within your SIMnet account) provides the following resources for concept review:

- Multiple choice questions
- Matching exercises
- Short answer questions

Guided Project 6-1

In this project, you modify the *Staying Active* document from Courtyard Medical Plaza to create new styles, modify existing styles, create a building block, and customize and insert document property and Word fields.
[**Student Learning Outcomes 6.1, 6.2, 6.3, 6.5, 6.6**]

Files Needed: ***StayingActive-06.docx*** and ***CMP-logo-06.png*** *(student data files are available in the Library of your SIMnet account)*
Completed Project File Name: ***[your initials] Word 6-1.docx***

Skills Covered in This Project

- Change the theme color set.
- Modify existing styles.
- Select all instances of a style.
- Replace an existing style with a different style.

- Create a new style based on selected text.
- Update styles to match a selection.
- Insert and position a picture.
- Save a picture as a *Quick Parts* building block.
- Insert a footer.
- Add a Word field to a footer.

1. Open the **StayingActive-06** document from your student data files.

2. Save the document as [your initials] Word 6-1.

3. Change the color set of the document.
   a. Click the **Colors** button [*Design* tab, *Document Formatting* group].
   b. Select **Red** from the drop-down list of colors.

4. Modify existing styles.
   a. Right-click **Title** in the *Style* gallery [*Home* tab, *Styles* group] or *Styles* pane and select **Modify** to open the *Modify Style* dialog box.
   b. Click the **Center** alignment button in the *Formatting* area.
   c. Click the **Format** button and select **Font** to open the *Font* dialog box.
   d. Apply **Bold** font style, change the font size to **20 pt**., and apply **All Caps** text effect.
   e. Click **OK** to close the *Font* dialog box.
   f. Click **OK** to close the *Modify Style* dialog box (Figure 6-89).
   g. Right-click the **Heading 1** style in the *Style* gallery or *Styles* pane and select **Modify** to open the *Modify Style* dialog box.

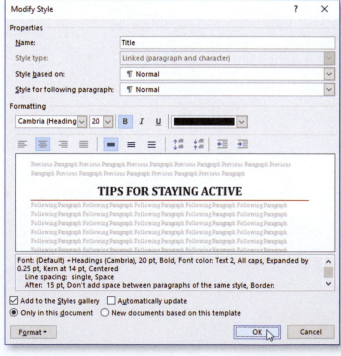

6-89 Modify *Title* style

h. Click the **Underline** button in the *Formatting* area.

i. Open the *Font* dialog box, apply **Small Caps**, and click **OK** to close the *Font* dialog box.

j. Open the *Paragraph* dialog box and apply the following changes:

   Before paragraph spacing: **12 pt**.
   After paragraph spacing: **3 pt**.
   Line spacing: **Single**

k. Click **OK** to close the *Paragraph* dialog box.

l. Click **OK** to close the *Modify Styles* dialog box.

5. Select all instances of a style and apply a different style.
   a. Click the **Styles** launcher [*Home* tab, *Styles* group] to open the *Styles* pane if it is not already open.
   b. Right-click the **Heading 2** style in the *Styles* pane and choose **Select All** to select all of the text with the *Heading 2* style applied (Figure 6-90).
   c. Click the **Heading 1** style in the *Styles* panes or *Style* gallery to replace the *Heading 2* style with the *Heading 1* style.

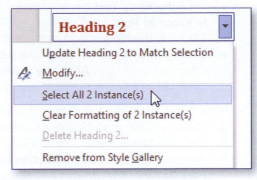

6-90 Select all instances of the *Heading 2* style

6. Create a new style based on selected text.
   a. Select all of the text after the "Keep Exercise Fun and Interesting" heading.
   b. Apply a **check mark bullet** to the selected text. If this bullet is not available from the *Bullet* drop-down list, define a new bullet, and select the check mark from the *Wingdings* font set (character code: 252).
   c. With the bulleted list still selected, click the **More** button in the *Styles* group [*Home* tab] and select **Create a Style**. The *Create New Style from Formatting* dialog box opens.
   d. Click the **Modify** button to view more formatting options.
   e. Use the following information to create the new style (Figure 6-91):

      Name: Bullet List
      Style type: **Paragraph**
      Style based on: **List Paragraph**
      Style for following paragraph: **Bullet List**

   f. Click the **Format** button and select **Paragraph**.
   g. Change the *Left* indent to **0"**, deselect the **Don't add space between paragraphs of the same style** check box, and click **OK** to close the *Paragraph* dialog box.
   h. Click **OK** to close the dialog box and to create the new style.

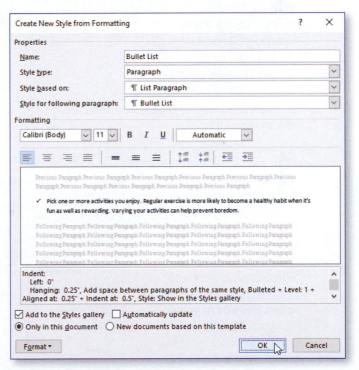

6-91 Create a new style from selected text

7. Update styles to match a selection and apply a style.
   a. Select the paragraph after the title of the document.
   b. Change the font size to **10 pt**.

c. With the paragraph still selected, right-click the **Normal** style in the *Style* gallery and choose **Update Normal to Match Selection**. All of the body text, including the numbered and bulleted lists, changes to 10 pt.

d. Select the title and change the *Before* paragraph spacing to **48 pt**.

e. Right-click the **Title** style in the *Styles* pane and select **Update Title to Match Selection**.

8. Insert a picture and change text wrapping and position.
   a. Place the insertion point at the beginning of the document.
   b. Insert the **CMP-logo-06** picture from your student data files.
   c. Click the **Wrap Text** button [*Picture Tools Format* tab, *Arrange* group] and select **In Front of Text**.
   d. Click the **Position** button and select **More Layout Options** to open the *Layout* dialog box.
   e. Change the *Horizontal* **Absolute position** to **0.3"** to the right of **Page**.
   f. Change the *Vertical* **Absolute position** to **0.3"** below **Page**.
   g. Click **OK** to close the *Layout* dialog box.

9. Save the CMP logo in the *Quick Parts* gallery.
   a. Click the **CMP logo** picture to select it.
   b. Click the **Quick Parts** button [*Insert* tab, *Text* group] and select **Save Selection to Quick Part Gallery**. The *Create New Building Block* dialog box opens (Figure 6-92).
   c. Add the following properties for the new building block:

      Name: CMP logo
      Gallery: **Quick Parts**
      Category: **General**
      Description: Insert CMP logo
      Save in: **Building Blocks**
      Options: **Insert content only**

   d. Click **OK** to close the dialog box and create the new building block.

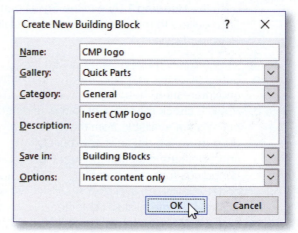

6-92 Save the CMP logo in the *Quick Parts* gallery

10. Insert a Word field in the footer.
    a. Edit the footer.
    b. Press **Tab** two times to move to the right margin.
    c. Type Last modified: and **space** once.
    d. Click the **Quick Parts** button and select **Field**. The *Field* dialog box opens.
    e. Select **SaveDate** in the *Field names* area and select the short number date format (e.g., 1/1/18) in the *Date formats* area (Figure 6-93).
    f. Click **OK** to close the *Field* dialog box.

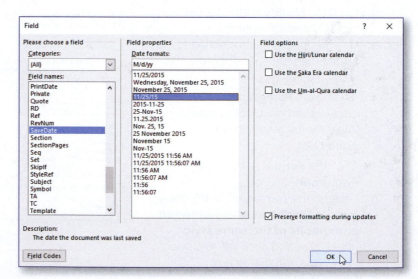

6-93 Insert the *SaveDate* field

g. Select all of the text in the footer and apply **Italic** font style.

h. Close the footer.

11. Save and close the document (Figure 6-94). When you exit Word after creating and saving building blocks, you might be prompted to save these changes. Click **Save** to save changes.

TIPS·FOR·STAYING·ACTIVE¶

Almost·any·activity·that·gets·you·moving·and·strengthens·your·muscles·is·good·for·your·health·and·can·help·you·meet·your·fitness·and·weight·goal.·If·you·haven't·been·exercising·regularly,·start·out·slowly·and·gradually·increase·duration,·frequency,·and·intensity.·If·you·have·been·exercising·regularly,·keep·it·up!¶

STAYING·ACTIVE¶

1)→ Aim·for·at·least·30·to·60·minutes·of·moderate·intensity·activity·on·most·days.·¶
   a)→ You·can·get·your·exercise·all·at·once,·or·spread·it·out·during·the·day.·¶
      i)→ For·example,·exercising·for·three·10-minute·periods·is·just·as·effective·as·exercising·for·30·minutes·at·a·time.·¶
   b)→ The·more·physical·activity·you·do,·the·more·calories·you·burn·and·the·greater·the·health·benefit.·¶
2)→ If·you·don't·like·counting·calories,·try·counting·your·steps!¶
   a)→ Walking·10,000·steps·a·day·can·help·you·manage·your·weight.·¶
   b)→ Use·a·pedometer·(an·easy·to·wear·device·that·senses·your·body's·motion)·to·count·your·steps·and·motivate·you·to·increase·your·activity.·¶
   c)→ Use·a·journal·to·track·your·walking.¶
3)→ Use·both·aerobic·and·strengthening·activities·are·important·to·losing·weight·and·keeping·it·off.·¶
   a)→ As·you·grow·older,·your·body·slows·down·and·your·metabolism—the·rate·at·which·your·body·burns·calories—naturally·decreases.·¶
   b)→ Taking·a·brisk·walk·will·boost·your·metabolism·and·keep·you·burning·calories·for·hours·afterward.·¶
4)→ Remember·that·any·form·of·exercise·is·good·for·you.¶
   a)→ Household·chores¶
      i)→ Cleaning·windows¶
      ii)→ Vacuuming¶
      iii)→ Folding·clothes¶
   b)→ Yard·work·and·gardening¶
   c)→ Using·stairs·rather·than·an·elevator¶
   d)→ Getting·up·and·moving·regularly·at·work¶

KEEP·EXERCISE·FUN·AND·INTERESTING¶

✓→ Pick·one·or·more·activities·you·enjoy.·Regular·exercise·is·more·likely·to·become·a·healthy·habit·when·it's·fun·as·well·as·rewarding.·Varying·your·activities·can·help·prevent·boredom.¶

✓→ Exercise·with·a·friend.·The·support·and·companionship·will·help·keep·you·going.¶

✓→ Think·about·the·payoffs.·Exercise·not·only·helps·control·weight,·it·is·beneficial·to·the·body·and·mind·in·a·number·of·ways.·It·improves·health,·boosts·your·immune·system,·helps·control·appetite,·helps·you·feel·more·energetic·and·relaxed,·and·raises·your·self-confidence!¶

✓→ Set·realistic·exercise·goals.·Reward·yourself·in·healthy·ways·when·you·achieve·them.¶

→   →   *Last·modified:·1/12/18*¶

6-94 Word 6-1 completed

Guided Project 6-2

For this project, you create a styles template for Sierra Pacific Community College District. You modify existing styles, create new styles, and create building blocks. You attach this styles template to the *Emergency Procedures* document, import styles, apply styles to text, and insert building blocks.
[Student Learning Outcomes 6.1, 6.2, 6.3, 6.5, 6.6]

Files Needed: ***SPCCDstyles-06.dotx*** and ***EmergencyProcedures-06.docx*** (student data files are available in the Library of your SIMnet account)
Completed Project File Names: ***[your initials] Word 6-2 styles.dotx*** and ***[your initials] Word 6-2.docx***

Skills Covered in This Project

- Edit a styles template.
- Modify text and update styles to match selected text.
- Create a new style based on selected text.
- Save a picture as a *Quick Parts* building block.
- Create a footer and insert document properties and a Word field.
- Create a *Footer* building block.
- Modify a document style set.
- Attach a template to a document.
- Insert a *Quick Parts* building block.
- Insert a footer from *Footer* gallery.
- Import styles from the styles template.
- Apply styles.
- Modify before and after paragraph spacing.

1. Open the ***SPCCDstyles-06*** template from your student data files. Open this template from within Word, not from a *File Explorer* window.

2. Save this template as [your initials] Word 6-2 styles. Be sure to save as a template.

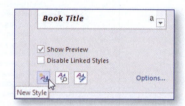

3. Modify text and update styles.
   a. Select the "**Heading 1**" text.
   b. Using the *Font* dialog box, change the font size to **14 pt.** and apply **All caps** formatting.
   c. Right-click the **Heading 1** style in the *Style* gallery and select **Update Heading 1 to Match Selection**.

6-95 *New Style* button in the *Styles* pane

4. Create new styles.
   a. Select "**Text with Tab**" including the tab.
   b. Click the **Styles** launcher [*Home* tab, *Styles* group] to open the *Styles* pane.
   c. Click the **New Style** button in the *Styles* pane (Figure 6-95). The *Create New Style from Formatting* dialog box opens.
   d. Enter the following properties for the new style (Figure 6-96):

   Name: Text with Tab
   Style type: **Paragraph**
   Style based on: **Normal**
   Style for following paragraph: **Text with Tab**

   e. Click the **Format** button and select **Tabs** to open the *Tabs* dialog box.
   f. Set a **6.5" right** tab stop with a **dot leader** (2).

6-96 Create a new style from selected text

g. Click **OK** to close the *Tabs* dialog box and click **OK** to close the *Create New Style from Formatting* dialog box.

h. Select the "**Number List**" text.

i. Click the **More** button in the *Style* gallery [*Home* tab, *Styles* group] and select **Create a Style** to open the *Create New Style from Formatting* dialog box.

j. Type Number List in the *Name* text box.

k. Click **OK** to close the dialog box and to create the new style.

5. Save the Sierra Pacific logo in the *Quick Parts* gallery.

   a. Click the **Sierra Pacific logo** picture to select it.

   b. Click the **Quick Parts** button [*Insert* tab, *Text* group] and select **Save Selection to Quick Part Gallery**. The *Create New Building Block* dialog box opens (Figure 6-97).

   c. Enter the following properties for the new building block:

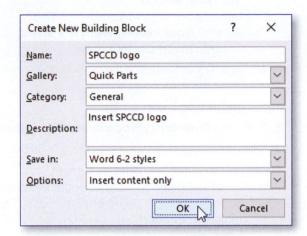

   Name: SPCCD logo
   Gallery: **Quick Parts**
   Category: **General**
   Description: Insert SPCCD logo
   Save in: **[your initials] Word 6-2 styles**
   Options: **Insert content only**

6-97 Save the SPCCD logo in the *Quick Parts* gallery

   d. Click **OK** to close the dialog box and to create the new building block.

6. Create a footer and insert document property and Word fields.

   a. Edit the footer.

   b. Click the **Document Info** button [*Header & Footer Tools Design* tab, *Insert* group] and select **Document Title** to insert this document property field in the footer.

   c. Press the **right arrow** key once to deselect the document property field and press **Tab**.

   d. Insert the **Company** document property field.

   e. Press the **right arrow** key once to deselect the document property field and press **Tab**.

   f. Type Revised and **space** once.

   g. Click the **Quick Parts** button and select **Field** to open the *Field* dialog box.

   h. Select **SaveDate** in the *Field names* area and select the date format in the *Date formats* area (use January 1, 2018 format).

   i. Click **OK** to close the *Field* dialog box.

   j. Select all of the text in the footer, change the font size to **10 pt.**, and apply a **Top Border** from the *Borders* drop-down list [*Home* tab, *Paragraph* group] (Figure 6-98).

   k. Leave the footer open and text selected.

6-98 Footer with document property and Word fields

7. Create a *Footer* building block.

   a. With the footer text still selected, click the **Footer** button [*Header & Footer Tools Design* tab, *Header & Footer* group] and select **Save Selection to Footer Gallery**. The *Create New Building Block* dialog box opens.

b. Click the **Category** drop-down list and select **Create New Category**. The *Create New Category* dialog box opens (Figure 6-99).

c. Type SPCCD and click **OK** to create the new category.

d. Enter the following properties for the new building block:

   Name: SPCCD footer
   Gallery: **Footers**
   Category: **SPCCD**
   Description: SPCCD footer
   Save in: **[your initials] Word 6-2 styles**
   Options: **Insert content only**

6-99 Create a new building block category

e. Click **OK** to close the dialog box and create the new building block.

f. Close the footer.

8. Save and close the template.

9. Open the ***EmergencyProcedures-06*** document from your student data files.

10. Save the document as [your initials] Word 6-2.

11. Change the style set of the document.
    a. Click the **Design** tab and click the **More** button [*Document Formatting* group] to display *Style Set* gallery.
    b. Select the **Shaded** style set from the list of options (Figure 6-100).

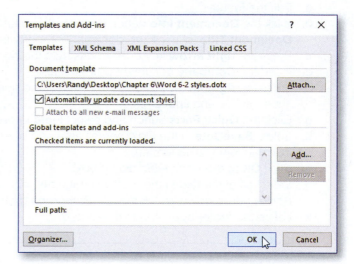

6-100 Select a style set

12. Customize the following document properties on the *Backstage* view:

    Title: Emergency Procedures
    Company: Sierra Pacific Community College District

13. Attach a template to the document.
    a. Click the **Document Template** button [*Developer* tab, *Templates* group] to open the *Template and Add-ins* dialog box (Figure 6-101). If the *Developer* tab is not available, click the **File** tab, select **Options**, click **Customize Ribbon**, and check the **Developer** box under *Main Tabs* in the *Customize the Ribbon* area.
    b. Click the **Attach** button, browse to find and select the ***[your initials] Word 6-2 styles*** template, and click **Open** to attach the template.
    c. Check the **Automatically update document styles** box.
    d. Click **OK** to close the *Templates and Add-ins* dialog box.

6-101 Attach styles template to document

14. Insert building blocks.
    a. Place the insertion point at the beginning of the document.
    b. Click the **Quick Parts** button [*Insert* tab, *Text* group] and select the **SPCCD logo** to insert the picture at the top of the document.
    c. Click the **Footer** button [*Header & Footer* group].
    d. Select the **SPCCD footer** from the drop-down list (bottom of the list) to insert the footer with the document property fields into the document.
    e. Delete the blank line below the text in the footer.
    f. Close the footer.

15. Import styles from a template.
    a. Click the **Styles** laucher [*Home* tab, *Styles* group] to open the *Styles* pane.
    b. Click the **Manage Styles** button in the *Styles* pane to open the *Manage Styles* dialog box (Figure 6-102).
    c. Click the **Import/Export** button to open the *Organizer* dialog box.
    d. Click the **Close File** button at the right to close the *Normal* template.
    e. Click the **Open File** button, browse to find and select the *[your initials] Word 6-2 styles* template, and click **Open**.
    f. Copy the following styles from the *[your initials] Word 6-2 styles* template (list on the right). Press the **Ctrl** key to select multiple non-adjacent styles (Figure 6-103):

       Bullet List
       Heading 1
       Heading 2
       Normal
       Number List
       Text with Tab

    g. Click the **Copy** button.

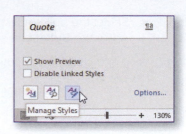

6-102 *Manage Styles* button in the *Styles* pane

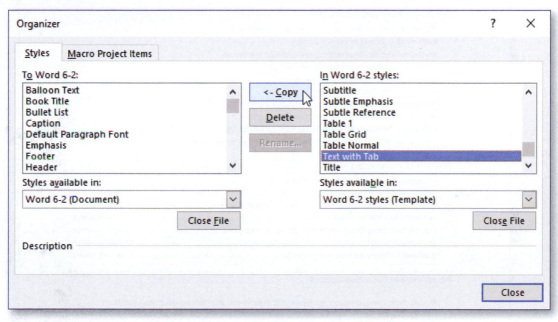

6-103 Import styles from styles template

    h. Click **Yes to All** in the dialog box that asks if you want to overwrite existing styles.
    i. Click **Close** to close the *Organizer* dialog box.

16. Apply styles to selected text.
    a. Select the bulleted list in the "Emergency Telephones [Blue Phones]" section.
    b. Apply the **Number List** style.
    c. Select the lines of text below the "Emergency Telephone Locations" heading.
    d. Change the *Before* and *After* paragraph spacing to **0 pt**.
    e. Select the lines of text below the "Emergency Phone Numbers" heading.
    f. Apply the **Text with Tab** style.
    g. With this text still selected, change the *Before* and *After* paragraph spacing to **0 pt**.

h. Select the bulleted list in the last section ("Accident or Medical Emergency").
i. Apply the **Bullet List** style.
17. Save and close the document (Figure 6-104). If prompted to save changes in the template, select **Yes** to save changes.

SPCCD—WEST·CAMPUS·EMERGENCY·PROCEDURES¶

EMERGENCY·TELEPHONES·[BLUE·PHONES]¶

Emergency·telephones·on·campus·are·marked·by·a·bright·blue·light·(see·locations·below).¶

1.→ To·use,·press·the·"Help"·button.·Speak·when·the·light·comes·on.¶
2.→ Stay·on·the·line.·You·will·be·connected·with·the·college·police.¶
3.→ State·clearly·the·nature·of·the·emergency·and·your·location.¶

EMERGENCY·TELEPHONE·LOCATIONS¶

Stadium·Parking·Lot·(outside),·between·ticket·machines¶
Barton·Hall·(outside),·southwest·corner¶
Barton·Hall·(inside),·Second·floor,·west·end·near·elevators¶
Liberal·Arts·(outside),·north·end·of·the·C·wing¶
Library·(outside),·right·side·of·front·entrance¶
Library·(inside),·First·floor,·stairs¶
Performing·Arts·(outside),·near·west·entrance·from·Lot·B¶
Math·&·Science·(inside),·west·wall·of·biology·wing¶
Cafeteria·(outside),·northeast·entrance·from·parking·lot·B¶
Gymnasium·(inside),·breezeway·between·offices·and·gym·entrance¶

EMERGENCY·PHONE·NUMBERS¶

Emergency·Response·System·(Fire,·Medical,·Sheriff) ....→............................. 911¶
College·Police·(adjacent·to·staff·parking·south·of·Barton·Hall·and·Library) ....→........ (209)·658-7777¶
Health·Center·(Administration·Building)·M-F·7:30·a.m.-4:00·pm. ....→............. (209)·658-2239¶
Information·Center·(Counseling·Building) ....→........ (209)·658-4466¶
Evening·Dean·(Asst.·Dean,·Math)·M-Th·5:00·p.m.-8:00·p.m. ....→............. (209)·658-7700¶
Site·Administrator·(Vice-President·of·Administrative·Services) ....→........ (209)·658-8501¶
Weekend·College·Coordinator·(Area·Deans) ....→............. (209)·658-6500¶

ACCIDENT·OR·MEDICAL·EMERGENCY¶

■→ Life-Threatening·Emergencies:·Phone·911.·If·victim·has·stopped·breathing,·start·mouth-to-mouth·resuscitation.·If·victim's·heart·has·stopped,·begin·CPR.·Call·college·police·or·send·for·assistance·(call·7777·from·a·campus·phone;·otherwise·call·658-7777).¶
■→ Minor·Emergencies:·Administer·first·aid·using·American·Red·Cross·standard·procedures.·First·aid·kits·are·located·in·instructional·area·offices,·library,·cafeteria,·and·instruction·office·in·the·administration·building.·Be·sure·to·fill·out·an·accident·report.·Call·college·police·or·send·for·assistance·(call·7777·from·a·campus·phone;·otherwise·call·658-7777).¶

Emergency·Procedures →   Sierra·Pacific·Community·College·District →   Revised·February·2,·2018¶

6-104 Word 6-2 completed

Guided Project 6-3

For this project, you revise an insurance renewal form letter for Wayne Reza at Central Sierra Insurance. You modify existing styles, modify the *Styles* pane, create *AutoText* and *Quick Parts* building blocks, and insert document property and Word fields.
[Student Learning Outcomes 6.1, 6.2, 6.3, 6.4, 6.5, 6.6]

File Needed: ***RenewalLetter-06.docx*** *(student data files are available in the* Library *of your SIMnet account)*
Completed Project File Name: ***[your initials] Word 6-3.docx***

Skills Covered in This Project

- Change the *Styles* pane options.
- Add a style to the *Style* gallery.
- Modify a style.
- Update a style to match selected text.
- Customize the document properties.

- Insert a document property field into the letter.
- Create a footer and insert a Word field.
- Create a *Quick Parts* building block.
- Create *AutoText* building blocks.
- Create an *AutoText* category.
- Assign *AutoText* building blocks to a category.

1. Open the ***RenewalLetter-06*** document from your student data files.

2. Save the document as [your initials] Word 6-3.

3. Modify the *Styles* pane and *Style* gallery.
   a. Click the **Styles** launcher to open the *Styles* pane.
   b. Click the **Options** link in the *Styles* pane to open the *Style Pane Options* dialog box.
   c. Click the **Select styles to show** drop-down list and select **In use**.
   d. Click the **Only in this document** radio button if it is not already selected.
   e. Click **OK** to close the dialog box and apply the changes. Only styles in use display in the *Styles* pane.
   f. Right-click the **Footnote Text** style in the *Styles* pane and select **Add to Style Gallery**.

4. Modify and update styles.
   a. Right-click the **Normal** style in the *Style* gallery or *Styles* pane and select **Modify**. The *Modify Style* dialog box opens.
   b. Click the **Format** button and select **Paragraph** to open the *Paragraph* dialog box.
   c. Change the *Line spacing* to **Single** and click **OK** to close the *Paragraph* dialog box.
   d. Click **OK** to close the *Modify Style* dialog box.
   e. Select the footnote text at the bottom of the letter ("**Note: the premium basis . . .**"); don't select the footnote number that precedes the text.
   f. Change the font to **Cambria** and apply **italic** formatting.
   g. Change the before and after paragraph spacing to **3 pt**.
   h. Right-click the **Footnote Text** style in the *Style* gallery and select **Update Footnote Text to Match Selection** to update this style.

5. Customize and insert document properties.
   a. Click the **File** tab to open the *Backstage* view.
   b. Customize the following document properties:

      Title: Renewal Letter
      Subject: type policy #
      Company: Central Sierra Insurance

   c. Click the **Back** arrow to return to the letter.
   d. Select "**Number**" in the subject line of the letter.
   e. Click the **Quick Parts** button [*Insert* tab, *Text* group].
   f. Click **Document Property** and select **Subject** to insert this field (Figure 6-105). Deselect the document property field and verify there is one space before and after the *Subject* field.

6. Create a footer and insert a Word field.
   a. Edit the footer.
   b. Click the **Align Right** button [*Home* tab, *Paragraph* group], type File name:, and **space** once.
   c. Click the **Quick Parts** button [*Header & Footer Tools Design* tab, *Insert* group] and select **Field** to open the *Field* dialog box (Figure 6-106).
   d. Select **FileName** in the *Field* names area.
   e. Select **(none)** in the *Format* area.
   f. Click **OK** to close the dialog box and insert the field.
   g. Select all of the text in the footer and change the font size to **9 pt**.
   h. Close the footer.

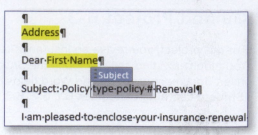

6-105 Insert *Subject* document property field

7. Add the Central Sierra Insurance logo to the *Quick Part* gallery.
   a. Edit the header and select the **Central Sierra Insurance logo**.
   b. Click the **Quick Parts** button and select **Save Selection to Quick Part Gallery**. The *Create New Building Block* dialog box opens (Figure 6-107).
   c. Enter the following properties for the new building block:

   Name: CSI logo
   Gallery: **Quick Parts**
   Category: **General**
   Description: Insert CSI logo
   Save in: **Building Blocks**
   Options: **Insert content only**

   d. Click **OK** to close the dialog box and to save the *Quick Part* building block.
   e. Close the header.

8. Create new *AutoText* building blocks.
   a. Select the opening lines of the letter beginning with the date and ending with the blank line after the subject line.
   b. Click the **Quick Parts** button [*Insert* tab, *Text* group], select **AutoText**, and choose **Save Selection to AutoText Gallery**. The *Create New Building Block* dialog box opens.
   c. Enter the following properties for the new building block:

   Name: CSI letter opening
   Gallery: **AutoText**
   Category: **General**
   Description: Insert opening lines of letter
   Save in: **Building Blocks**
   Options: **Insert content only**

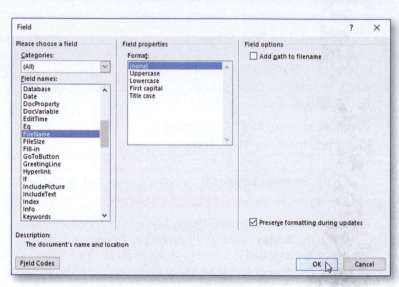

6-106 Insert *FileName* field in the footer

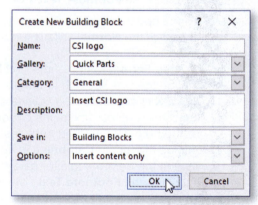

6-107 Save picture to *Quick Parts* gallery

d. Click **OK** to close the dialog box and to save the *AutoText* building block.

e. Select the closing lines of the letter beginning with "**Sincerely**" and ending with the email address.

f. Click the **Quick Parts** button, select **AutoText**, and choose **Save Selection to AutoText Gallery**. The *Create New Building Block* dialog box opens.

g. Enter the following properties for the new building block:

> *Name:* CSI letter closing
> *Gallery:* **AutoText**
> *Category:* **General**
> *Description:* Insert closing lines of letter
> *Save in:* **Building Blocks**
> *Options:* **Insert content only**

h. Click **OK** to close the dialog box and to save the *AutoText* building block.

9. Create a new *AutoText* category and assign *AutoText* building blocks to this category.

a. Click the **Quick Parts** button and select **Building Blocks Organizer** to open the *Building Blocks Organizer* dialog box.

b. Select the **CSI letter closing** in the *Building blocks* area and click the **Edit Properties** button to open the *Modify Building Block* dialog box.

c. Click the **Category** drop-down list and select **Create New Category**. The *Create New Category* dialog box opens (Figure 6-108).

d. Type CSI and click **OK** to create the new category and assign this category to the *AutoText* building block.

e. Click **OK** to close the *Modify Building Block* dialog box and click **Yes** in the dialog box that opens asking if you want to redefine the building block.

f. With the *Building Blocks Organizer* still open, edit the properties of the **CSI letter opening** *AutoText* building block and assign this building block to the **CSI** category.

g. Close the *Building Blocks Organizer* dialog box.

10. Save and close the document (Figure 6-109). When you exit Word after creating and saving building blocks, you might be prompted to save these changes. Click **Save** to save changes.

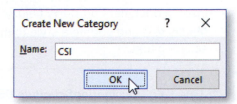

6-108 Create new *AutoText* category

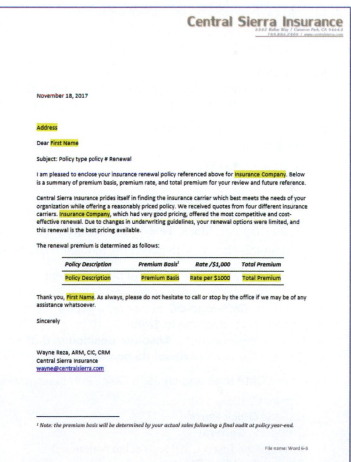

6-109 Word 6-3 completed

Independent Project 6-4

For this project, you revise the vaccination schedule for Courtyard Medical Plaza. You update an existing style, create *AutoText* and *Quick Parts* building blocks, and insert document property and Word fields.
[Student Learning Outcomes 6.1, 6.3, 6.4, 6.5, 6.6]

Files Needed: ***VaccinationSchedule-06.docx*** and ***CMP-logo-06.png*** *(student data files are available in the* Library *of your SIMnet account)*
Completed Project File Name: ***[your initials] Word 6-4.docx***

Skills Covered in This Project

- Customize document properties.
- Insert a document property field.
- Modify text and update a style to match selected text.

- Insert and position a picture.
- Create a *Quick Parts* building block.
- Create an *AutoText* building block.
- Create a new *AutoText* category.
- Assign *AutoText* building blocks to a category.
- Create a footer and insert a Word field.

1. Open the ***VaccinationSchedule-06*** document from your student data files.

2. Save the document as [your initials] Word 6-4.

3. Customize the following document properties:

   > *Title:* Vaccination Schedule
   > *Company:* Courtyard Medical Plaza

4. Insert a document property field and apply style.
   a. Insert the **Title** document property field on the blank line at the beginning of the document.
   b. Apply the **Title** style to the *Title* document property field.

5. Modify text and update a style.
   a. Make the following changes to the title of the document:

      > *Alignment:* **Center**
      > *Font style:* **Bold**
      > *Font effects:* **Small Caps**
      > *Font color:* **Red**, **Accent 2**
      > *Bottom border:* **Black**, **Text 1** color, **2¼ pt.** width

   b. Update the *Title* style to match the formatted title text.

6. Insert a picture at the bottom left of the document.
   a. Place the insertion point at the end of the document.
   b. Insert the ***CMP-logo-06*** picture from your student data files.
   c. Change text wrapping to **Tight**.
   d. Change the *Horizontal* **Absolute position** to **0.3"** to the right of **Page**.
   e. Change the *Vertical* **Absolute position** to **9.6"** below **Page**.

7. Select the **CMP logo** and create a *Quick Part* building block using the following properties:

   > *Name:* CMP logo bottom
   > *Gallery:* **Quick Parts**
   > *Category:* **General**
   > *Description:* Insert CMP logo at the bottom left
   > *Save in:* **Building Blocks**
   > *Options:* **Insert content only**

8. Select the entire table and save it as an *AutoText* building block using the following properties:

    Name: Vaccination table
    Gallery: **AutoText**
    Category: **CMP** (create new category)
    Description: Insert Vaccination table
    Save in: **Building Blocks**
    Options: **Insert content only**

9. Edit the footer and insert a Word field.
   a. Edit the footer, change alignment to **Align Right**, type Last updated:, and **space** once.
   b. Insert the **SaveDate** field (use January 1, 2018 format).
   c. Change the font size of all the information in the footer to **10 pt**. and apply **italic** formatting.
   d. Close the footer.

10. Save and close the document (Figure 6-110). When you exit Word after creating and saving building blocks, you might be prompted to save these changes. Click **Save** to save changes.

VACCINATION SCHEDULE

Think of vaccines as a coat of armor for your child. To keep it shiny and strong, you have to make sure your child's immunizations are up to date. Timely vaccinations help to prevent disease and keep your family and the community healthy. Some immunizations are given in a single shot, while others require a series of shots over a period of time.

Don't neglect your vaccinations!

Vaccines for children and teenagers are listed alphabetically below with their routinely recommended ages. Missed doses will be assessed by your child's physician and given if necessary. Keep a personal record of all immunizations and bring it with you to each office visit.

RECOMMENED VACCINATION SCHEDULE		
Name of Vaccine	*When It's Recommended*	*Total Doses*
Chickenpox (varicella)	At 12 months and 4-6 years	2
Diphtheria, tetanus, and pertussis (DTaP)	At 2, 4, 6 and 12-15 months, and 4-6 years	5
Haemophilus influenzae type b (Hib)	At 2, 4, 6, and 12 months	4
Hepatitis A (HepA)	At 12 and 18 months	3
Hepatitis B (HepB)	At birth, 1-2 months, and 6 months	3
Human papillomavirus (HPV)	3-dose series for girls at age 11-12 years	3
Inactivated influenza (flu shot)	Annually starting at age 6 months	Annually
Inactivated poliovirus (IPV)	At 2, 4, 6 months, and 4-6 years	4
Live intranasal influenza	Annually starting at age 2 years	Annually
Measles, mumps, and rubella (MMR)	At 12 months and 4-6 years	2
Meningococcal conjugate (MCV)	At 11-12 years	1
Pneumococcal conjugate (PCV)	At 2, 4, 6, and 12 months	4
Pneumococcal polysaccharide (PPSV)	At 2, 4, 6, and 12 months	4
Rotavirus (RV)	At 2, 4, and 6 months	3
Tetanus and diphtheria (Td)	At 11-12 years	1

These recommendations are for generally healthy children and teenagers and are for information only. If your child has ongoing health problems, special health needs or risks, or if certain conditions run in your family, talk with your child's physician. He or she may recommend additional vaccinations or schedules based on earlier immunizations and special health needs.

Courtyard Medical Plaza
a comprehensive medical facility

Last updated: June 1, 2018

6-110 Word 6-4 completed

Independent Project 6-5

For this project, you create a styles template for Sierra Pacific Community College District, attach the styles template to a document, and import styles from a template into a document. You modify and update existing styles, create new styles, create a *Quick Parts* building block, and insert document property and Word fields.
[**Student Learning Outcomes 6.1, 6.2, 6.3, 6.5, 6.6**]

Files Needed: new template file, *OnlineLearningPlan-06.docx*, and *SPCCD-logo-06.png* (*student data files are available in the* Library *of your SIMnet account*)
Completed Project File Names: *[your initials] Word 6-5 styles.dotx* and *[your initials] Word 6-5.docx*

Skills Covered in This Project

- Create a styles template.
- Modify a style set and theme colors.
- Update styles to match selected text.
- Create new styles based on selected text.
- Save a picture as a *Quick Parts* building block.
- Create a footer and insert document properties and a Word field.
- Create a *Footer* building block.
- Attach a template to the document.
- Insert a *Quick Parts* building block.
- Insert a footer from the *Footer* gallery.
- Import styles from the styles template.
- Select all instances of a style and replace with a different style.

1. Create a new blank document and save it as a **Word Template** named [your initials] Word 6-5 styles.

2. Change the *Style Set* to **Shaded** and the *Theme Colors* to **Grayscale** [*Design* tab, *Document Formatting* group].

3. Type the following lines of text and press **Enter** after each line:

    Heading 1
    Heading 2
    Learning Mode
    Bullet List

4. Apply the **Heading 1** style to the "Heading 1" text and the **Heading 2** style to the "Heading 2" text.

5. Update styles.
    a. Select the "**Heading 1**" text, change the font size to **12 pt**. and the font color to **Black, Text 1**, and apply **bold** formatting.
    b. Update the **Heading 1** style to match the selected text.
    c. Select the "**Heading 2**" text and change to **12 pt**. font size and **small caps**.
    d. Update the **Heading 2** style to match the selected text.

6. Modify the *Normal* style and set line spacing to **single**.

7. Create new styles.
    a. Select the "**Learning Mode**" text and apply the following changes:

        Font style: **Bold** and **underline**
        Font effect: **Small caps**
        Character spacing (Advanced tab): **Expanded** by **1pt**.

    b. Select the "**Learning Mode**" text, create a new style, name the new style Learning Mode, and select **Linked (paragraph and character)** as the *Style type* if it is not already selected. Don't change any other settings.
    c. Select the "**Bullet List**" text in the template and apply a **solid square bullet** (Wingdings, character code 110).

d. Select the "**Bullet List**" text, create a new style, name the new style Bullet List, and select **Linked (paragraph and character)** as the *Style type* if it is not already selected. Don't change any other settings.

8. Insert a picture, position it, and create a *Quick Parts* building block.
   a. Place the insertion point on the blank line below the bulleted list. If there is not a blank line below the bulleted list, position the insertion point at the end of the bulleted list, press **Enter** two times, and apply the **Normal** style.
   b. Insert the *SPCCD-logo-06* picture from your student data files.
   c. Change text wrapping to **Top and Bottom**.
   d. Change the *Horizontal* **Absolute position** to **0.3"** to the right of **Page**.
   e. Change the *Vertical* **Absolute position** to **0.3"** below **Page**.
   f. Select the logo and create a *Quick Parts* building block with the following properties:

   Name: SPCCD logo top
   Gallery: **Quick Parts**
   Category: **General**
   Description: Insert SPCCD logo
   Save in: **[your initials] Word 6-5 styles**
   Options: **Insert content only**

9. Add document property and Word fields to the footer and create a footer building block.
   a. Edit the footer.
   b. Insert the **Title** document property field on the left side of the footer. Use the right arrow key to deselect the document property field.
   c. **Tab** to the center and insert the **Company** document property field. Use the right arrow key to deselect the document property field.
   d. **Tab** to the right, type Page, **space** once, and insert a plain page number in the current position.
   e. **Space** once, type of, **space** once, and insert **NumPages** field. Use **1**, **2**, **3** as the format for the *NumPages* field.
   f. Apply a **½ pt.**, **Black**, **Text 1**, **top border** to the footer.
   g. Select the entire footer and save selection to the *Footers* gallery using the following information:

   Name: SPCCD footer
   Gallery: **Footers**
   Category: **General**
   Description: Footer with document properties
   Save in: **[your initials] Word 6-5 styles**
   Options: **Insert content only**

   h. Close the footer.

10. Save and close the template.

11. Open the *OnlineLearningPlan-06* document from your student data files.

12. Save the document as [your initials] Word 6-5.

13. Customize the following document properties:

   Title: Online Learning Plan
   Company: Sierra Pacific Community College District

14. Change *Theme Colors* [*Design* tab, *Document Formatting* group] to **Grayscale**.

15. Attach the *[your initials] Word 6-5 styles* template to the document and set it to automatically update styles.

16. Insert building blocks on the first page of the document.
   a. Insert the **SPCCD logo top** building block from the *Quick Parts* gallery.
   b. Insert the **SPCCD footer** building block from the *Footer* gallery.
   c. Delete the blank line below the footer text and close the footer.

17. Import styles from the *[your initials] Word 6-5 styles* template and copy the following styles (**Yes to All** to overwrite existing styles):

   Bullet List
   Heading 1
   Heading 2
   Learning Mode
   Normal

18. Select all instances of the **Intense Reference** style and apply the **Learning Mode** style.

19. Select the bulleted list on the last page and apply the **Bullet List** style.

20. Save and close the document (Figure 6-111).

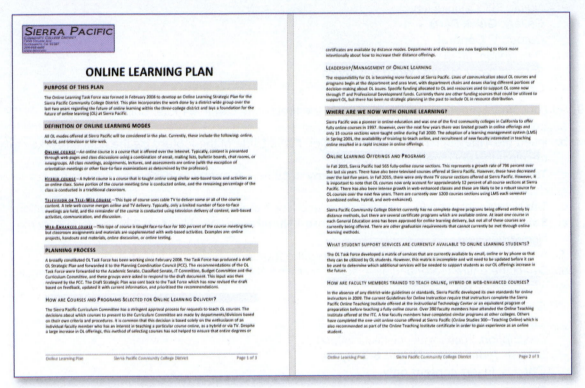

6-111 Word 6-5 completed (pages 1 and 2 of 3 pages)

Independent Project 6-6

For this project, you revise a brochure for Emma Cavalli at Placer Hills Real Estate. You update existing styles, create new styles, apply styles, and create *Header, AutoText,* and *Quick Parts* building blocks.
[Student Learning Outcomes 6.1, 6.2, 6.3, 6.4, 6.5, 6.6]

File Needed: **CavalliBrochure-06.docx** *(student data files are available in the* Library *of your SIMnet account)*
Completed Project File Name: *[your initials] Word 6-6.docx*

Skills Covered in This Project

- Add document properties.
- Modify text and update a style to match selected text.
- Create new styles.
- Apply styles to selected text.
- Create a *Quick Parts* building block.
- Create an *AutoText* building block.
- Insert a document property field.
- Create a *Header* building block.
- Create a new *Header* category.
- Assign *AutoText* building blocks to a category.
- Modify the *Styles* pane options.

1. Open the **CavalliBrochure-06** document from your student data files.

2. Save the document as [your initials] Word 6-6.

3. Customize the following document properties:

   Title: Brochure
   Company: Placer Hills Real Estate
   Author: Emma Cavalli (remove existing author)

4. Update and apply styles.
   a. Select "**Emma Cavalli**" and update the *Heading 1* style to match the selected text.
   b. Select "**Realtor Consultant**" and change the *After* paragraph spacing to **6 pt**.
   c. Update the *Heading 2* style to match the selected text.
   d. Apply the **Heading 2** style to the other section headings in the document.

5. Modify a bulleted list, create a new style, and apply a style.
   a. Select the bulleted list in the second column.
   b. Change the bullet to a **check mark** (Wingdings, character code 252).
   c. Create a style based on the selected text and name the style Check Bullet.
   d. Apply the **Check Bullet** style to the numbered list in the first column.
   e. Apply the **Check Bullet** style to the lines of text in the "Education & Training" section.

6. Save the PHRE logo (bottom right) as a *Quick Parts* building block with the following properties:

   Name: PHRE logo bottom right
   Gallery: **Quick Parts**
   Category: **General**
   Description: Insert PHRE logo
   Save in: **Building Blocks**
   Options: **Insert content only**

7. Select the entire table in the third column and save as an *AutoText* building block with the following properties:

   Name: PHRE beliefs
   Gallery: **AutoText**
   Category: **General**
   Description: Insert PHRE table
   Save in: **Building Blocks**
   Options: **Insert content only**

8. Edit the header, select "**Placer Hills**," and replace it with the **Company** document property field.

9. Select the table in the header and save it in the *Headers* gallery with the following properties:
   Name: PHRE header landscape
   Gallery: **Headers**
   Category: **PHRE** (create new category)
   Description: Insert PHRE header
   Save in: **Building Blocks**
   Options: **Insert content only**

10. Modify the *Styles Pane Options* to show only those styles in use, sort styles alphabetically, and apply these settings only in this document.

11. Save and close the document (Figure 6-112). When you exit Word after creating and saving building blocks, you might be prompted to save these changes. Click **Save** to save changes.

6-112 Word 6-6 completed

Improve It Project 6-7

For this project, you revise an existing weekly expense memo for Life's Animal Shelter to convert it into a form. You update an existing style, create *AutoText, Quick Parts,* and *Footer* building blocks, and insert document property and Word fields.
[**Student Learning Outcomes 6.1, 6.2, 6.3, 6.4, 6.5, 6.6**]

File Needed: ***LASWeeklyExpenses-06.docx*** *(student data files are available in the* Library *of your SIMnet account)*
Completed Project File Name: *[your initials]* **Word 6-7.docx**

Skills Covered in This Project

- Modify a style.
- Find all instances of a style and replace with another style.
- Apply a style to selected text.
- Modify a memo heading.
- Insert a date.

- Update Word fields.
- Create a footer and insert document property and Word fields.
- Create a *Footer* building block.
- Customize document properties.
- Create a *Quick Parts* building block.
- Create an *AutoText* building block.
- Create a new *AutoText* category.

---

1. Open the ***LASWeeklyExpenses-06*** document from your student data files.

2. Save the document as [your initials] Word 6-7.

3. Modify a style and replace a style.
   a. Modify the *Normal* style to apply **0 pt**. *After* paragraph spacing.
   b. Select all instances of the **No Spacing** style and replace with **Normal** style.

4. Modify the memo heading.
   a. Apply **36 pt**. *Before* spacing on the first line of the memo heading.
   b. Select the four memo heading lines and set a **1"** left tab stop.
   c. Delete extra tabs so all info after the memo guide words aligns at 1".
   d. Apply the **Strong** style to each of the memo heading guide words (TO:, FROM:, DATE:, SUBJECT:).
   e. Delete "**[Insert Current Date]**", insert the date (use January 1, 2018 date format), and set it to update automatically.

5. Delete the expense values in the table. Don't delete the formulas in the *Totals* column or row.

6. Update each of the formulas in the table.

7. Customize document properties using the following information:

   > *Title:* Weekly Expenses
   > *Company:* Life's Animal Shelter

8. Create a footer with document property and Word fields and save it as a *Footer* building block.
   a. Edit the footer and insert the **Company** document property field on the left. Use the right arrow key to deselect the document property field.
   b. **Tab** to the center tab stop, insert the **Title** document property field, and deselect the document property field.
   c. **Tab** to the right tab stop, type Updated:, **space** once, and insert the **SaveDate** Word field (use January 1, 2018 date format).
   d. Change the font of all footer text to **10 pt**.
   e. Apply a **1 pt**., **Black**, **Text 1**, **top border**.
   f. Select the entire footer and save it in the *Footers* gallery using the following properties:

      > *Name:* LAS footer
      > *Gallery:* **Footers**
      > *Category:* **LAS** (create new category)
      > *Description:* Insert LAS footer
      > *Save in:* **Building Blocks**
      > *Options:* **Insert content only**

9. Save the *WordArt* at the top of the document as a *Quick Parts* building block with the following properties:

   > *Name:* LAS WordArt
   > *Gallery:* **Quick Parts**
   > *Category:* **General**

Description: Insert LAS WordArt
Save in: **Building Blocks**
Options: **Insert content only**

10. Select the memo heading lines (include the two blank lines after) and save as an *AutoText* building block with the following properties:

Name: LAS memo heading
Gallery: **AutoText**
Category: **General**
Description: Insert memo heading
Save in: **Building Blocks**
Options: **Insert content only**

11. Replace "xx" at the end of the document with your initials in lower case.

12. Save and close the document (Figure6-113). When you exit Word after creating and saving building blocks, you might be prompted to save these changes. Click **Save** to save changes.

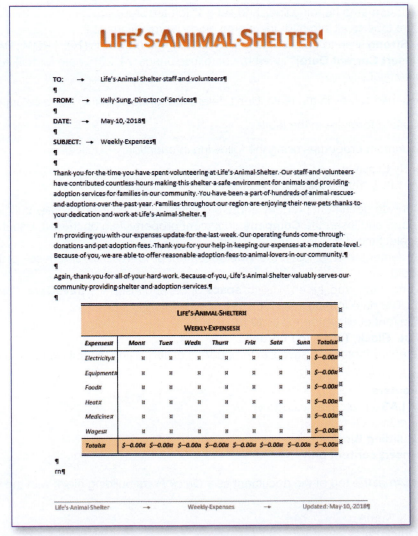

6-113 Word 6-7 completed

Challenge Project 6-8

Update your résumé using document formatting features learned in this chapter. If you don't have an existing résumé, create a new one based on an online résumé template or use a blank document to create a résumé. Incorporate styles, building blocks, and document properties. Edit your résumé so it is consistently formatted, easy to read, and professional looking. Research résumés online to get ideas about formatting and content. **[Student Learning Outcomes 6.1, 6.2, 6.3, 6.4, 6.5, 6.6]**

File Needed: Existing résumé, online résumé template, or new document
Completed Project File Name: *[your initials] Word 6-8.docx*

Open your existing résumé or create a new résumé and save it as [your initials] Word 6-8. Modify your document according to the following guidelines:

- Modify and apply existing styles to headings, subheadings, and lists to improve consistency in your resume.
- Update or create new styles based on selected text.
- Modify *Styles* pane options to include only those styles used in your cover letter.
- Modify the *Style* gallery to include styles used in your cover letter.
- Create building blocks from content in your résumé.
- Create a new category to group building blocks.
- Customize document properties.
- Insert document property and Word fields.

Challenge Project 6-9

Update an existing cover letter, use an online cover letter template, or create a new one from a blank document. Research cover letters online to learn about proper format for a personal business letter. Incorporate styles, building blocks, and document properties. Edit your cover letter so it is consistently formatted, easy to read, and professional looking.
[Student Learning Outcomes 6.1, 6.2, 6.3, 6.4, 6.6]

File Needed: Existing cover letter, online cover letter template, or new document
Completed Project File Name: *[your initials] Word 6-9.docx*

Open your existing cover letter or create a new one and save it as [your initials] Word 6-9. Modify your document according to the following guidelines:

- Modify the *Normal* style.
- Update or create new styles based on selected text.
- Modify *Styles* pane options to include only those styles used in your résumé.
- Modify the *Style* gallery to include styles used in your résumé.
- Create *AutoText* building blocks from the opening and closing lines of your cover letter.
- Save paragraphs of text as *AutoText* building blocks.
- Create a new category to group the *AutoText* building blocks.
- Customize document properties.
- Insert document property fields.

Challenge Project 6-10

Create an agenda or meeting outline for an upcoming meeting for an organization you belong to, such as a club, church, volunteer organization, student group, or neighborhood association. Incorporate styles, building blocks, and document property and Word fields. Use the Internet to research required and optional components of a meeting agenda. Robert's Rules of Order is a good source of information about meetings and guidelines for meeting protocol.
[Student Learning Outcomes 6.1, 6.2, 6.3, 6.4, 6.5, 6.6]

File Needed: None
Completed Project File Name: *[your initials] Word 6-10.docx*

Create a new document and save it as [your initials] Word 6-10. Agendas or meetings can include, but are not limited to, the following items:

- Organization name as the title
- Meeting date, start time, and end time
- Meeting location
- Meeting attendees
- Topic headings
- Topic subheadings (include details for each topic heading)
- The time each topic is expected to last

Modify your document according to the following guidelines:

- Modify and apply existing styles to headings, subheadings, and lists to improve consistency in format.
- Update or create new styles based on selected text.
- Modify *Styles* pane options to include only those styles used in your document.
- Modify the *Style* gallery to include styles used in your document.
- Create building blocks from content in your document.
- Create a new category to group building blocks.
- Customize document properties.
- Insert document property and Word fields.

Advanced Tables and Graphics

CHAPTER OVERVIEW

In Chapter 4, we covered the basics of tables, columns, and graphics. This chapter introduces the advanced features that are available when you work with tables, columns, and graphics. The advanced topics in this chapter allow you to effectively customize table content, layout, and styles. The final two sections in this chapter introduces advanced features to customize pictures and shapes.

STUDENT LEARNING OUTCOMES (SLOs)

After completing this chapter, you will be able to:

SLO 7.1 Customize table content using sorting, formulas, bullets and numbers, tabs and indents, and text direction (p. W7-392).

SLO 7.2 Customize table layouts using table properties, cell margins, the split table feature, nested tables, and a repeated header row (p. W7-401).

SLO 7.3 Enhance a table design using shading, borders, and a table style (p. W7-405).

SLO 7.4 Modify a picture using advanced layout and picture format options (p. W7-415).

SLO 7.5 Create, group, align, and modify a shape in a document (p. W7-426).

CASE STUDY

In the Pause & Practice projects, you modify a document about maximum and target heart rates for the American River Cycling Club. You use tables, columns, graphics, and shapes to effectively communicate this information.

Pause & Practice 7-1: Customize table content by converting text to a table, sorting information in the table, adding formulas, and changing text direction.

Pause & Practice 7-2: Enhance tables in the document by customizing the table layout and applying, modifying, and creating table styles.

Pause & Practice 7-3: Insert, modify, and arrange pictures in the document.

Pause & Practice 7-4: Insert, modify, arrange, and group shapes to present information graphically in the document.

Customizing Table Content

Tables are an excellent way to succinctly and attractively present information in a document. This section reviews the basics of formatting table content and covers the advanced features to customize tables, such as sorting table content, using custom formulas, adding bullets and numbering, modifying tab stops and indents, and changing text direction.

When your insertion point is in a table or when you select a table, two context-sensitive *Table Tools* tabs display on the *Ribbon*: **Table Tools Design tab** and **Table Tools Layout tab**. The *Table Tools Layout* tab provides many options to customize the layout and table content. The *Table Tools Design* tab includes options to apply and customize table styles and borders, which are covered in *SLO 7.3: Customizing Table Design*.

Convert Text to a Table

When creating a table, you can type the text into the table, or, if the text is already in the document, you can convert existing text into a table. When converting text to a table, Word uses the existing structure of the text to create a table. You can then modify the table to meet your needs.

▶ HOW TO: Convert Text into a Table

1. Select the text to convert to a table.
2. Click the **Table** button [*Insert* tab, *Tables* group] and select **Convert Text to Table**. The *Convert Text to Table* dialog box opens (Figure 7-1).
3. Adjust the number of columns and rows as necessary in the *Table size* area.
   - Word automatically determines the number of columns and rows based upon the structure of the text you select to convert to a table.
   - You can modify the number of columns and rows in this area.
4. Select from the radio buttons in the *AutoFit behavior* area to determine how the column widths of the table are set.
5. Select from the radio buttons in the *Separate text at* area to determine how the columns and rows are separated.
   - Word automatically selects a separation option based upon the structure of the text you select to convert to a table.
6. Click **OK** to close the dialog box and convert the text to a table.

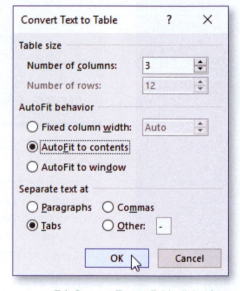

7-1 *Convert Text to Table* dialog box

Convert a Table to Text

You can also convert an existing table into text. The procedure for converting a table to text is similar to the process for converting text to a table.

▶ HOW TO: Convert a Table to Text

1. Select the table to convert to text.
2. Click the **Convert to Text** button [*Table Tools Layout* tab, *Data* group] (Figure 7-2). The *Convert Table to Text* dialog box opens.

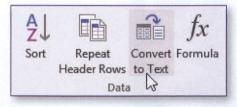

7-2 *Convert to Text* button

3. Select from the radio buttons in the *Separate text with* area to determine how the text will be separated (Figure 7-3).

- Word inserts paragraph marks, tabs, commas, or a custom separator, such as a hyphen or other symbol, to separate the text when converting a table to text.
- Tabs are the most commonly used separator when converting a table to text.

4. Click **OK** to close the dialog box and convert the table to text.

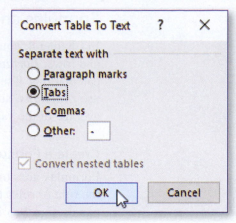

7-3 *Convert Table to Text* **dialog box**

Sort Text in a Table

Sorting text in a table is a common method of reorganizing the content of a table. You can sort any of the columns in a table in ascending or descending order. Word automatically moves entire rows of information when you perform a sort. You can also perform a multi-level sort, such as sorting a table by city and then within each city sorting by last name.

▶ **HOW TO:** Sort Text in a Table

1. Place the insertion point in the table or select the entire table.
2. Click the **Sort** button [*Table Tools Layout* tab, *Data* group]. The *Sort* dialog box opens (Figure 7-4).
3. Determine whether or not the table has a header row (column headings) and select the appropriate radio button in the *My list has* area.

- If your table has a header row, the *Sort by* options are the column headings.
- If your table does not have a header row, the *Sort by* options are the column numbers (*Column 1, Column 2*, etc.).

4. Click the **Sort by** drop-down list and select the column heading or column to sort.
5. Click the **Type** drop-down list and select **Text**, **Number**, or **Date**.

- When you sort text in a table, the text is sorted using paragraphs, which means entire rows are moved rather than individual cells.

6. Click the **Ascending** or **Descending** radio button to select the sort order.
7. Perform a secondary sort by clicking the **Then by** drop-down list, selecting the column heading or column to sort, and selecting the type and sort order.
8. Click **OK** to close the dialog box and perform the sort.

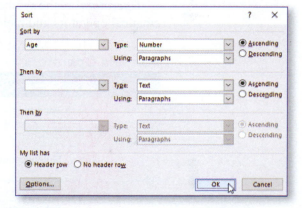

7-4 *Sort* **dialog box**

> ▶ **MORE INFO**
>
> The *Sort* feature is not limited to tables. You can also sort selected paragraphs of information or a bulleted list.

Formulas and Functions

In Chapter 4, you learned how to insert a simple formula into a table to add values in columns and rows. *Formulas* can be used in tables to perform simple or more complex mathematical calculations. Use formulas to add, subtract, multiply, or divide values in a table. You can also use *functions*, such as *SUM* (add values) or *AVG* (average values), to calculate the sum or average of the values in a column or row.

Create a Formula

Formulas are constructed in a specific way, which is called *syntax*. The formula syntax is the rule or rules that dictate how the various parts of a formula are written. For example, the equals sign (=) is always the first character you enter when creating a formula. The other parts of a formula can include cell references, operators, and values.

Remember that tables are grouped into columns (vertical) and rows (horizontal). Columns are referenced with letters and rows are referenced with numbers. For example, the first column is A, the second column is B, the first row is 1, and the second row is 2. These column and row references are not visible in Word tables as they are in Excel.

A *cell* is where a column and row intersect. Each cell has a *cell address*, which is the column and row reference. In the table at the right, the cell address displays in each cell. When creating a formula, you refer to a cell using its cell address, which is called a *cell reference* in a formula.

A1	B1	C1
A2	B2	C2
A3	B3	C3

Operators are the symbols for mathematical operations. The following table lists the mathematical operators and their order of precedence (the order they are performed in a formula):

Formula Operators

Operator	Operator Name	Order of Precedence
()	Parenthesis	First
^	Exponent	First
*	Multiplication	Second
/	Division	Second
−	Subtraction	Third
+	Addition	Third

You can also use *values* in formulas. For example, you can multiply a cell reference by 85% or subtract a cell reference from 220. The following table displays the proper syntax for formulas that use cell references, operators, and values:

Formula Syntax

Formula	Explanation
=A1+B1	Adds cells A1 and B1
=220−B3	Subtracts cell B3 from 220
=B3*85%	Multiplies cell B3 by 85% (0.85)
=(A1+A2)/2	Adds cells A1 and A2 and then divides by 2

▶HOW TO: Create a Formula

1. Place the insertion point in the cell where you want to insert a formula.

2. Click the **Formula** button [*Table Tools Layout* tab, *Data* group] to open the *Formula* dialog box (Figure 7-5).

3. Delete the existing formula in the *Formula* area.
   - Word typically inserts a function in the *Formula* area.

4. Type **=** followed by the new formula.
   - Don't include spaces between the parts of the formula.

5. Click the **Number format** drop-down list to select the format for the output of the formula.

6. Click **OK** to close the dialog box and insert the formula.

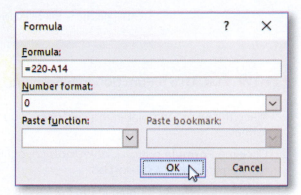

7-5 *Formula* dialog box

▶ **ANOTHER WAY**

Click **Quick Parts** [*Insert* tab, *Text* group] and select **Field** to open the *Field* dialog box. Click **Formula** to open the *Formula* dialog box.

▶ **MORE INFO**

Formulas created in Word tables are similar to formulas in Excel with a few exceptions. One difference is you cannot select a cell in Word to automatically insert a cell reference in a formula as you can in Excel. Another difference is that formulas in Word do not update automatically when data changes.

Use a Function in a Formula

Functions are built-in formulas created for common types of calculations, such as *SUM* and *AVERAGE*. Functions require a specific syntax and save you time once you understand how to build them. Functions typically are performed on a ***range*** of values. A range contains more than one cell. For example, you can use a function to add or average the values in a column or row. The following table displays the syntax for the *SUM* and *AVERAGE* functions.

Formula Syntax

Function	Explanation
=SUM(B1:B5)	Adds values in cells B1 through B5. The colon between cell references is the syntax to represent a range of cells.
=SUM(above)	Adds all of the values in the column above. "*Above*" is the syntax used to reference all of the cells in the column above the formula.
=AVERAGE(A2:A5)	Averages the values in cells A2 through A5. The colon between cell references is the syntax to represent a range of cells.
=AVERAGE(left)	Averages all of the values in the row to the left. "*Left*" is the syntax used to reference all of the cells in the row to the left of the formula.

▶ HOW TO: Use a Function in a Formula

1. Place the insertion point in the cell where you want to insert a formula.

2. Click the **Formula** button [*Table Tools Layout* tab, *Data* group] to open the *Formula* dialog box.

3. Delete the existing formula in the *Formula* area.

4. Type **=** and click the **Paste function** drop-down list and select the function (Figure 7-6).

   - You can also type the function after the equals sign using the proper syntax.

5. Type the range in the parentheses.

   - Use a colon (:) between cell references to create a range.
   - Type **above** or **left** to use the cells above or to the left of the formula.

6. Click the **Number format** drop-down list to select the format for the output of the formula.

7. Click **OK** to close the dialog box and insert the formula.

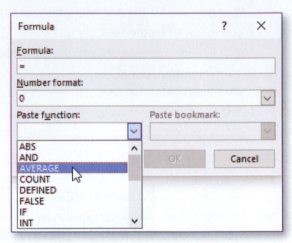

7-6 Insert *AVERAGE* function

Edit a Formula

You might need to edit a formula to change the formula or the number format. The following are two ways to edit a formula:

- Select the formula and click the **Formula** button [*Table Tools Layout* tab, *Data* group] to open the *Formula* dialog box.
- Right-click the formula, select **Edit Field** from the context menu to open the *Field* dialog box, and click the **Formula** button to open the *Formula* dialog box.

Update a Formula

Each time you open a document, all of the Word fields in the document update automatically (a formula is a Word field). But when a document is open and you change the values in a table, formulas do not update automatically; you must update the formulas manually. The following are two ways to update a formula:

- Right-click the formula and select **Update Field** from the context menu.
- Select the formula and press **F9**.

Change Text Direction

You can change the direction of text in a cell of the table. For example, you might have a title column on the left side of the table and want to change the direction of the text to vertical.

▶ HOW TO: Change Text Direction

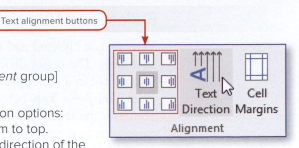

1. Select the cell or cells to change the text direction.
2. Click the **Text Direction** button [*Table Tools Layout* tab, *Alignment* group] (Figure 7-7).
   - The *Text Direction* button cycles through the three text direction options: horizontal, vertical from top to bottom, and vertical from bottom to top.
   - The text on the *Text Direction* button changes to indicate the direction of the text in the cell.
   - Merging cells may be necessary before changing text direction.
3. Use the alignment buttons [*Table Tools Layout* tab, *Alignment* group] to adjust text alignment in the cell.

7-7 Change text direction

Tabs and Indents in Tables

Using the *Tab* key in a table functions differently from using tab in paragraph text or a list. When you press the **Tab** key in a table, your insertion point moves to the next cell. But what if you need to align text or numbers in a cell using a tab stop? To move to a tab stop in the cell of a table, press **Ctrl+Tab**, which moves your insertion point to the next tab stop rather than to the next cell. Set tab stops in a table the same way you set tab stops in the body of a document using the ruler or the *Tabs* dialog box. Tabs were covered in Chapter 2 in *SLO 2.2: Setting, Using, and Editing Tab Stops*.

▶ HOW TO: Set and Use Tab Stops in a Table

1. Select the entire table or the cells in the table where you want to set a tab stop.
2. Click the **Paragraph** launcher [*Layout* tab, *Paragraph* group] to open the *Paragraph* dialog box.
   - You can also use the ruler to set tab stops. Select the type of tab stop from the *Tab* selector on the left side of the ruler. Click the ruler to set a tab stop.
3. Click the **Tabs** button to open the *Tabs* dialog box (Figure 7-8).
4. Type the tab stop position, select the alignment, and click **Set**.
5. Click **OK** to close the dialog box.
6. Press **Ctrl+Tab** to move to the tab stop in the cell.

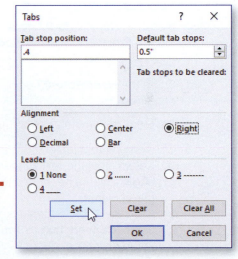

7-8 Set a tab stop in a table

You can also use indents in tables to control text alignment and alignment of carryover lines the same way you use indents in the body of a document. Set or modify indents in a table using one of the following methods:

- *Paragraph* group on the *Layout* tab
- *Paragraph* dialog box
- *Ruler*

> ▶ **MORE INFO**
>
> When setting or modifying tab stops or indents in a table, select the area of the table to change before modifying tab stops or indents.

Bullets and Numbering in Tables

You can use bulleted and numbered lists in tables like you use them in the body of a Word document. The major difference when using lists in tables is the use of the *Tab* key. In lists that are not in a table, use the *Tab* key to increase the level of the list. For example, in a list when you press **Tab** before typing the text, the list indents to the next level (**Shift+Tab** decreases the level), but in a table, pressing **Tab** moves you to the next cell and **Shift+Tab** moves you to the previous cell.

The following are two ways to adjust the level of a list in a table:

- Press the **Increase Indent** or **Decrease Indent** button [*Home* tab, *Paragraph* group].
- Click the **Bullets** or **Numbering** button [*Home* tab, *Paragraph* group], select **Change List Level**, and select the level.

> ▶ **ANOTHER WAY**
>
> Options to change the list level are available from the context menu when you right-click text in a list.

PAUSE & PRACTICE: WORD 7-1

For this Pause & Practice project, you modify a document from the American River Cycling Club about maximum and target heart rates. You convert text to a table, sort information in a table, change text direction, and create formulas.

File Needed: ***HeartRate-07.docx*** (*student data files are available in the* Library *of your SIMnet account*)
Completed Project File Name: ***[your initials] PP W7-1.docx***

1. Open the ***HeartRate-07*** document from your student data files.

2. Save the document as [your initials] PP W7-1.

3. Convert text to a table.
   a. Select all of the text aligned with tabs beginning with the "**Age**" column heading and ending with "**120-170**" in the third column.
   b. Click the **Table** button [*Insert* tab, *Tables* group] and select **Convert Text to Table** to open the *Convert Text to Table* dialog box (Figure 7-9).
   c. Confirm the number of columns in the *Table size* area is **3**.
   d. Click the **AutoFit to contents** radio button in the *AutoFit behavior* area.
   e. Click the **Tabs** radio button in the *Separate text at* section if it is not already selected.
   f. Click **OK** to close the dialog box and convert the text to a table.

7-9 **Convert selected text to a table**

4. Sort the table in ascending order by age.
   a. With the entire table still selected, click the **Sort** button [*Table Tools Layout* tab, *Data* group]. The *Sort* dialog box opens (Figure 7-10).
   b. Select the **Header row** radio button in the *My list has* area.
   c. Click the **Sort by** drop-down list and select **Age**.
   d. Click the **Type** drop-down list and select **Number**.
   e. Click the **Using** drop-down list and select **Paragraphs**.
   f. Click the **Ascending** radio button.
   g. Click **OK** to close the dialog box and sort the table.

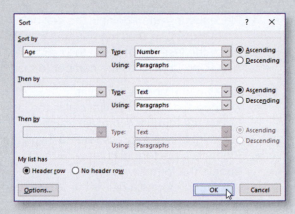

7-10 Sort the table in ascending order by age

5. Add a column, merge cells, add text, and change text direction.
   a. Place the insertion point in the first column of the table.
   b. Click the **Insert Left** button [*Table Tools Layout* tab, *Rows & Columns* group] to insert a column to the left of the first column.
   c. With the new first column selected, click the **Merge Cells** button [*Table Tools Layout* tab, *Merge* group] to merge all the cells in the first column.
   d. Type Max and Target, press **Enter**, and type Heart Rates in the first column.
   e. Click the **Text Direction** button [*Table Tools Layout* tab, *Alignment* group] two times to change the text to vertical from the bottom (Figure 7-11).
   f. Click the **Align Center** button [*Table Tools Layout* tab, *Alignment* group] to align the text vertically and horizontally in the cell.
   g. Change the font size of the text in the first column to **20 pt.** and the format to **small caps**.

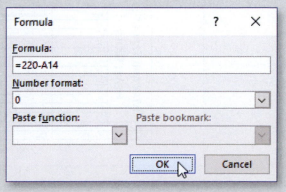

Align Center button

7-11 Change text direction

6. Add rows to the table and insert text.
   a. Place the insertion point in the last cell of the last row and press **Tab** to insert a new row.
   b. Type the following information in the new row:

| Age | Max Heart Rate | 60% of Max | 85% of Max |

   c. Press **Tab** at the end of the row to insert a new row.
   d. Type 28 in the *Age* column and press **Tab**.
   e. Select the next to the last row in the table and apply **bold** format.

7. Create and insert three formulas.
   a. Place the insertion point in the cell below "Max Heart Rate" in the last row of the table.
   b. Click the **Formula** button [*Table Tools Layout* tab, *Data* group]. The *Formula* dialog box opens (Figure 7-12).
   c. Delete the existing formula in the *Formula* area and type =220–A14. A14 is the cell reference for age.
   d. Click the **Number format** drop-down list and select **0**.
   e. Click **OK** to close the dialog box and insert the formula.

7-12 Insert a formula

    f. Place the insertion point in the cell below "60% of Max" and create the following formula: =B14*60%. Use **0** as the number format.

    g. Place the insertion point in the cell below "85% of Max" and create the following formula: =B14*85%. Use **0** as the number format.

8. Edit a value and update formulas.

    a. Change the age in the first cell in the last row to 33.

    b. Select the formula in the last row below "Max Heart Rate" and press **F9** to update the formula. You might have to press **Fn+F9** if you are using a laptop computer.

    c. Right-click the formula below "60% of Max" and select **Update Field** from the context menu to update the formula.

    d. Update the formula below the "85% of Max" heading using one of the update methods.

9. Add bullets to selected text and adjust indents.

    a. Select the numbers in the column below the "Predicted Max Heart Rate" column heading. Don't include the text in the last two rows.

    b. Apply a **check mark** bullet (Wingdings, character code 252).

    c. With the bulleted list still selected, change the left indent to **0"** [*Layout* tab, *Paragraph* group].

    d. Use the **Format Painter** to apply this bullet format to the value below "Max Heart Rate" in the last row of the table.

10. Save and close the document (Figure 7-13).

WHAT IS MAXIMUM HEART RATE?

The maximum heart rate is the highest your pulse rate can get. To calculate your **predicted maximum heart rate,** use this formula:

(Example: a 40-year-old's predicted maximum heart rate is 180.)

Your actual maximum heart rate can be determined by a graded exercise test. Please note that some medicines and medical conditions might affect your maximum heart rate. If you are taking medicines or have a medical condition (such as heart disease, high blood pressure, or diabetes), always ask your doctor if your maximum heart rate/target heart rate will be affected.

WHAT IS TARGET HEART RATE?

You gain the most benefits and decrease the risk of injury when you exercise in your target heart rate zone. Usually this is when your exercise heart rate (pulse) is 60 percent to 85 percent of your maximum heart rate. Do not exercise above 85 percent of your maximum heart rate. This increases both cardiovascular and orthopedic risk and does not add any extra benefit.

When beginning an exercise program, you might need to gradually build up to a level that is within your target heart rate zone, especially if you have not exercised regularly before. If the exercise feels too hard, slow down. You will reduce your risk of injury and enjoy the exercise more if you don't try to over-do it.

To find out if you are exercising in your target zone (between 60 percent and 85 percent of your maximum heart rate), use your heart rate monitor to track your heart rate. If your pulse is below your target zone (see the chart below), increase your rate of exercise. If your pulse is above your target zone, decrease your rate of exercise.

	Age	Predicted Max Heart Rate	Target Heart Rate (60-85% of Max)
MAX AND TARGET HEART RATES	20	✓ 200	120-170
	25	✓ 195	117-166
	30	✓ 190	114-162
	35	✓ 185	111-157
	40	✓ 180	108-153
	45	✓ 175	105-149
	50	✓ 170	102-145
	55	✓ 165	99-140
	60	✓ 160	96-136
	65	✓ 155	93-132
	70	✓ 150	90-128
	Age	Max Heart Rate	60% of Max	85% of Max
	33	✓ 187	112	159

7-13 PP W7-1 completed

Customizing Table Layout

After customizing the content of a table, you can customize the table layout, such as adjusting the size of the table, columns, or rows. You can also modify how the table aligns on the page and how text aligns within the cells. Cell margins and spacing control space around the text in cells. Tables can be split into multiple tables or combined into nested tables, which are tables within tables.

Table Size

You can set a specific table width and row height in the *Table Properties* dialog box. Use the *Table* tab in the *Table Properties* dialog box to set the table width, and use the *Row* tab to set row height.

▶ **HOW TO:** Resize a Table Using the Table
Properties Dialog Box

1. Select the table.
2. Click the **Properties** button [*Table Tools Layout* tab, *Table* group] to open the *Table Properties* dialog box (Figure 7-14).
3. Click the **Table** tab, check the **Preferred width** box, and type the width of the table.
4. Click the **Row** tab, check the **Specify height** box, and type the row height.

   • This changes the height of all rows in the table.
   • Click the **Previous Row** or **Next Row** button to individually set the height of each row.

5. Click **OK** to close the *Table Properties* dialog box.

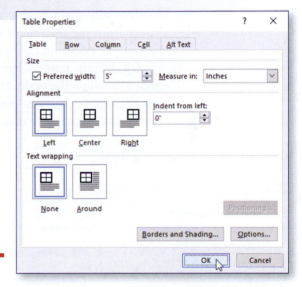

7-14 Change the width of a table

Manually resize a table by dragging the table sizing handle in bottom right corner to adjust the height or width of a table.

▶ **HOW TO:** Manually Resize a Table

1. Select the entire table using one of the following methods:

   • Click the **table selector** in the upper left corner of the table (Figure 7-15).
   • Click the **Select** button [*Table Tools Layout* tab, *Table* group] and select **Table**.

2. Click and drag the **table sizing handle** in the bottom right corner of the table.

   • Your pointer becomes a diagonal sizing pointer.
   • You can increase or decrease the height and width of the table using the table sizing handle.

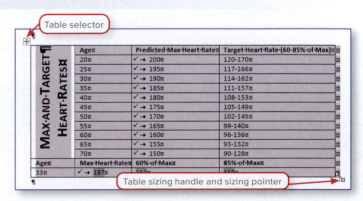

7-15 Resize a table using the table sizing handle

Row Height and Column Width

In addition to resizing the entire table, resize rows and columns individually using the following methods:

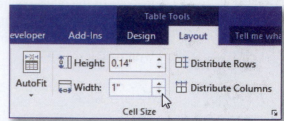

- Select the row or column to resize and change the size in the *Height* or *Width* area [*Table Tools Layout* tab, *Cell Size* group] (Figure 7-16).
- Use the *Row* and *Column* tabs in the *Table Properties* dialog box to change the height or width of specific columns and rows.
- Click and drag the right cell border to resize a column.
- Click and drag the bottom cell border to resize a row.

7-16 Resize columns and rows

Table Alignment and Position

Horizontally align a table the same way you align text in a document. Select the table and select from the alignment buttons in the *Paragraph* group on the *Home* tab. You can also change the horizontal alignment of a table in the *Table Properties* dialog box (Figure 7-17).

By default, tables display in line with the text, which means the paragraph text aligns above or below the table. However, you can modify the table position to wrap paragraph text around a table. You can position a table anywhere in a document and specify how paragraph text wraps as you have done with graphics (see *SLO 4.5: Working with Graphics*).

▶ HOW TO: Position a Table

1. Select the table or place the insertion point in the table.

2. Click the **Properties** button [*Table Tools Layout* tab, *Table* group] to open the *Table Properties* dialog box (see Figure 7-17).

3. Click the **Table** tab and click the **Around** button in the *Text wrapping* area.

   - The *Positioning* button becomes active when you select *Around*, but it is not active if *None* is selected.

4. Click the **Positioning** button. The *Table Positioning* dialog box opens (Figure 7-18).

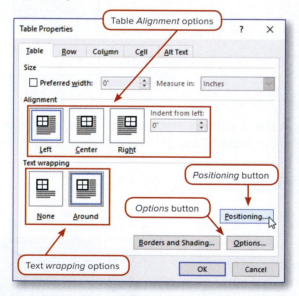

7-17 Set table to wrap around text

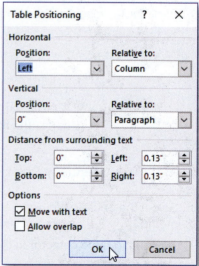

7-18 *Table Positioning* dialog box

5. Set the **Horizontal** and **Vertical** position.

6. Set the **Distance from surrounding** text.

7. Click **OK** to close the *Table Positioning* dialog box.

8. Click **OK** to close the *Table Properties* dialog box.

Cell Margins and Spacing

In Chapter 4 you learned about cell margins, which are the margins in a cell around the text (see *SLO 4.2: Arranging Texts in Tables*). **Cell spacing** refers to the space between cells. Both cell margins and spacing can be changed in the *Table Options* dialog box.

▶ **HOW TO:** Change Cell Margins and Spacing

1. Select the table or place the insertion point in the table.
2. Click the **Cell Margins** button [*Table Tools Layout* tab, *Alignment* group] to open the *Table Options* dialog box (Figure 7-19).
3. Set the **Top**, **Bottom**, **Left**, and **Right** cell margins in the *Default cell margins* area.
4. Check the **Allow spacing between cells** box and set the amount of space between cells.
5. Check the **Automatically resize to fit contents** box so that the table is resized based on the new cell margins and spacing.
6. Click **OK** to close the dialog box and apply the settings.

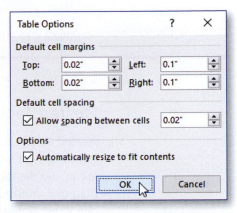

7-19 *Table Options* dialog box

▶ **ANOTHER WAY**

Click the **Options** button on the *Table* tab in the *Table Properties* dialog box to open the *Table Options* dialog box where you can change cell margins and spacing.

Split a Table and Cells

The **split table** feature divides a table into one or more tables. When you split a table, it is split between rows, not columns. Position the insertion point in or select the row that will become the first row in the new table and click the **Split Table** button in the *Merge* group on the *Table Tools Layout* tab (Figure 7-20). The table becomes two tables with a blank line between the two tables.

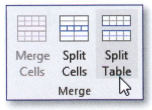

7-20 *Split Table* button

▶ **MORE INFO**

When you split a table containing formulas with cell references, the cell references in the formulas in the split table may be incorrect. Edit the formulas and change the cell references if necessary.

You can also split cells into multiple rows or columns. You can do this on a merged cell, an individual cell that has not been merged, or a range of cells in a table.

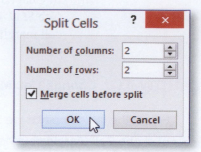

▶ HOW TO: Split a Cell

1. Select the cell or cells to be split.
2. Click the **Split Cells** button [*Table Tools Layout* tab, *Merge* group] to open the *Split Cells* dialog box (Figure 7-21).
3. Set the number of columns and rows.
   - If you are splitting a range of cells, the *Merge cells before split* check box is activated. Select this check box if you want to merge the cells before splitting the cells.
4. Click **OK** to close the dialog box and split the cells.

7-21 *Split Cells* dialog box

Nested Tables

Nested tables are tables within tables. You can insert a table into a cell of another table the same way you insert a table into a document. In nested tables, the main table is called the ***parent table***, and the table within the parent table is the ***child table***. A parent table can contain more than one child table. Figure 7-22 displays an example of nested tables: the parent table has one column and two rows with only the gridlines visible, and the parent table contains two child tables.

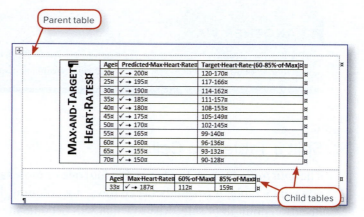

7-22 Nested tables

Repeat Header Rows

If a table spans multiple pages, improve readability by displaying column headings at the top of the second and continuing pages. The ***repeat header rows*** feature automatically displays the header row or rows at the beginning of each page. You can choose to have one or more rows repeat as the header row or rows.

The advantage of using this feature rather than inserting a heading row at the top of each page is that the repeated header row inserts automatically at the top of each page regardless of pagination. If information is inserted into or deleted from the table and page endings change, the header row still displays at the top of each page.

To use the feature, select the row or rows of the table to repeat at the top of each page and click the **Repeat Header Rows** button in the *Data* group on the *Table Tools Layout* tab

(Figure 7-23). You can turn off this feature by selecting the header row or rows and clicking the **Repeat Header Rows** button.

7-23 *Repeat Header Rows* button

Draw a Table

Another way to insert a table into a document is to use the **draw table** feature. Word provides you with a table drawing tool to create a table or add cells, rows, or columns to an existing table. When you draw a table, your pointer becomes a **pen**. Using the pen, you can draw a table and split cells into rows and columns. You can also use the **eraser** to erase cells, rows, or columns.

▶**HOW TO:** Draw a Table

1. Click the **Table** button [*Insert* tab, *Tables* group] and select **Draw Table**. Your pointer becomes a pen.
2. Click and drag to draw the outside border of the table.
3. Draw vertical lines to create columns and horizontal lines to create rows (Figure 7-24).
   - Draw rows and columns outside the border of the table to increase the size of the table.
   - If you draw diagonally within a table, a new table is created inside the existing table.
4. Click the **Draw Table** button [*Table Tools Layout* tab, *Draw* group] or press **Esc** to turn off the draw table feature.
5. Click the **Eraser** button [*Table Tools Layout* tab, *Draw* group] and your pointer becomes an eraser.
   - Drag the eraser to remove row or column borders.
   - Click the **Eraser** button again to turn it off.

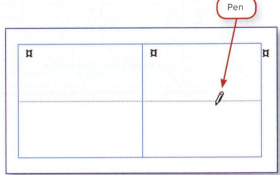

7-24 Create rows and columns using the pen

| SLO 7.3 | **Customizing Table Design** |

After modifying the content and layout of your table, customize the table design to create a more attractive table. Use shading, borders, and table styles to improve the appearance and readability of your table. A **table style** is a collection of borders, shading, and fonts. You can apply table styles, modify table styles, and create custom table styles. You can also insert tables from the *Tables* building blocks gallery or add your own table to this gallery.

Border Painter

Use the **Border Painter** feature to draw borders on your table rather than selecting borders from the *Borders* drop-down list. The *Border Painter* is similar to drawing a table, except it draws borders on the table rather than creating new rows and columns.

▶**HOW TO:** Use the Border Painter

1. Place your insertion point in the table to activate the context-sensitive *Table Tools* tabs.
2. Select the **Table Tools Design** tab.

3. Click the **Border Painter** button [*Borders* group] (Figure 7-25).

   • When you click the *Border Painter* button, your pointer becomes a pen you use to draw borders.

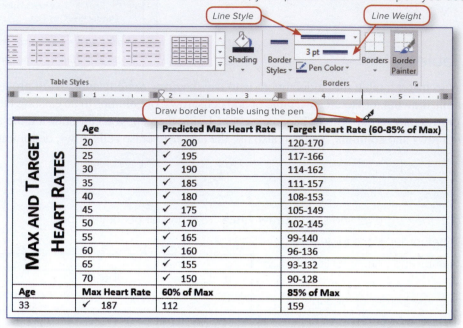

7-25 Draw a border using the *Border Painter*

4. Click the **Line Style** drop-down list and select a border line style.
5. Click the **Line Weight** drop-down list and select a border line weight.
6. Click the **Pen Color** drop-down list and select border color.
7. Click a border of the table to apply the selected border formatting.

   • Click and drag to apply the border across multiple columns or rows.

8. Click the **Border Painter** button or press **Esc** to turn off this feature.

Border Styles

The **Border Styles** gallery provides you with a variety of built-in border styles and colors (Figure 7-26). When you select a border style from the *Border Styles* gallery, the *Border Painter* turns on so you can draw borders on your table. Customize the border style using the *Line Style*, *Line Width*, and *Pen Color* drop-down lists.

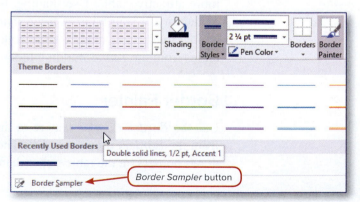

7-26 *Border Styles* gallery

Border Sampler

You previously used the *Format Painter* to copy text formatting and apply it to other text. The **Border Sampler** works like the *Format Painter*. Use the *Border Sampler* to select a border format from a table and apply it to other areas of the table or to a different table.

1. Place your insertion point in the table to activate the context-sensitive *Table Tools* tabs.

2. Click the **Border Styles** button [*Table Tools Design* tab, *Borders* group] and select **Border Sampler**.

   • Your pointer becomes an eyedropper.

3. Click the **eyedropper** on a border of your table to select a border format (Figure 7-27).

   • After you select a border format, the *Border Painter* turns on and the eyedropper becomes a pen.

4. Use the pen to apply the selected border format on other areas of the table or on a different table.

5. Click the **Border Painter** button or press **Esc** to turn off this feature.

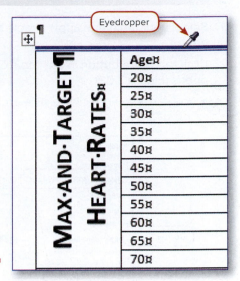

7-27 Use the eyedropper to select a border format

> ▶ **MORE INFO**
>
> Click the **Borders** launcher to open the *Borders and Shading* dialog box.

Table Styles

Table styles enhance the appearance of your tables with borders, shading, and font formatting. The **Table Styles gallery** on the *Table Tools Design* tab displays the available table styles. To apply a table style to a selected table, click the **More** button to display the *Table Styles* gallery and select a style (Figure 7-28).

The **Table Styles Options** group provides options for special formatting in specific areas of your table, such as a first column, a header row, or banded rows. After applying a table style and selecting table style options, further customize a

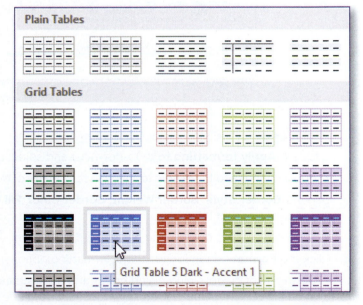

7-28 *Table Styles* gallery

table with borders, shading, font formatting, and paragraph formatting.

Modify a Table Style

In Chapter 6, you learned how to modify and create text styles (see *SLO 6.1: Creating and Using Custom Styles*). Similarly, you can also modify and create table styles. You can modify a table style after applying it to a table or modify a table style that has not yet been applied to a table. When you modify a table style, the changes apply to the tables in the document that already have that table style applied.

▶ HOW TO: Modify a Table Style

1. Select your table and apply a table style from the *Table Styles* gallery [*Table Tools Design* tab, *Table Styles* group].
2. Click the **More** button in the *Table Styles* gallery and select **Modify Table Style**. The *Modify Style* dialog box opens (Figure 7-29).
   - You can also right-click a style and select **Modify Table Style**.

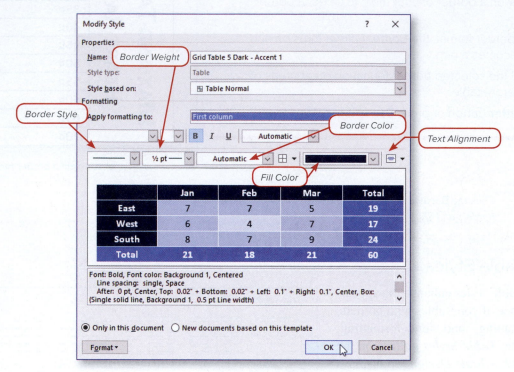

7-29 *Modify Style* dialog box

3. Type a name for the style in the *Name* area if you want to rename the style.
4. Click the **Apply formatting to** drop-down list and select an area of the table to modify formatting.
   - Apply changes to the *Whole table* or specific parts of the table, such as *Header row* or *First column*.
5. Use the **Border Style**, **Border Weight**, **Border Color**, **Fill Color**, and **Text Alignment** drop-down lists to modify the selected part of the table.
   - The *Preview* area displays the customized table style.
6. Click the **Format** button for additional formatting options.
   - Open any of the following dialog boxes and apply changes to the table style: *Table Properties*, *Borders and Shading*, *Banding*, *Font*, *Paragraph*, *Tabs*, and *Text Effects*.
   - Click **OK** to close any dialog box you opened and to return to the *Modify Style* dialog box.
7. Click **OK** to close the *Modify Style* dialog box and apply the changes to the table style.

Create a New Table Style

Creating a new table style is similar to creating a text style. Most table styles are based on the *Table Normal* style. When you create a new style, you can base the style on any of the existing table styles and then apply changes as desired.

▶ HOW TO: Create a New Table Style

1. Click the **More** button in the *Table Styles* gallery and select **New Table Style**. The *Create New Style from Formatting* dialog box opens (Figure 7-30).
   - You can also right-click a style and select **New Table Style**.
   - By default, the *Only in this document* radio button is selected, which means this new style is only available in this document.
   - If you want this style available in other documents, select the *New documents based on this template* option.

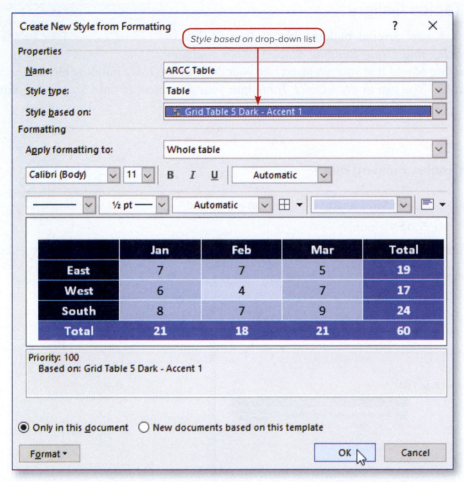

7-30 Create new table style

2. Type a name for the style in the *Name* area.
3. Confirm the *Style type* is **Table**.
4. Click the **Style based on** drop-down list and select the table style on which to base the new style.
5. Click the **Apply formatting to** drop-down list and select an area of the table to modify formatting.
   - Apply changes to the *Whole table* or specific parts of the table, such as *Header row* or *First column*.
6. Use the **Border Style**, **Border Weight**, **Border Color**, **Fill Color**, and **Text Alignment** drop-down lists to modify the selected part of the table.
   - The *Preview* area displays the new table style.
7. Click the **Format** button for more formatting options.
   - Open any of the following dialog boxes and apply changes to the table style: *Table Properties*, *Borders and Shading*, *Banding*, *Font*, *Paragraph*, *Tabs*, and *Text Effects*.
   - Click **OK** to close any dialog box you opened and to return to the *Create New Style from Formatting* dialog box.

8. Click **OK** to close the *Create New Style from Formatting* dialog box and apply the changes to the table style.

- The new style is available in the *Table Styles* gallery in the *Custom* section (Figure 7-31).

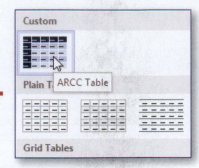

7-31 New custom style in the *Table Styles* gallery

Quick Tables Gallery

In Chapter 6, we covered building blocks (see *SLO 6.3: Understanding and Using Building Blocks*). Word contains *Table building blocks* that you can insert into your documents. *Table* building blocks are called *Quick Tables*. You can insert a *Quick Table* into your document or save an existing table in the *Quick Tables* gallery.

▶ HOW TO: Insert a Quick Tables Building Block

1. Place the insertion point in the document where you want the table inserted.
2. Click the **Table** button [*Insert* tab, *Tables* group].
3. Select **Quick Tables** to display the list of *Quick Tables* (Figure 7-32).

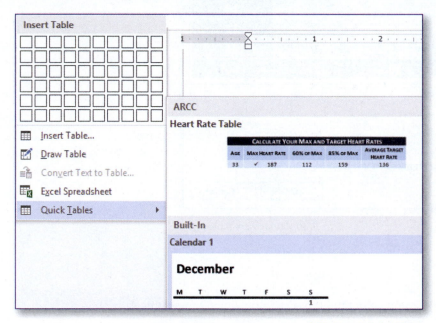

7-32 Insert *Quick Table*

4. Select a *Quick Table* to insert into your document.

▶

ANOTHER WAY

Insert a *Quick Table* using the *Building Blocks Organizer*.

You can save a table you use regularly as a *Table* building block, and the table will be available in the *Quick Tables* gallery. Saving a table as a building block is similar to saving a *Header*, *Footer*, *AutoText*, or *Quick Part* building block.

▶**HOW TO:** Save a Table to the Quick Tables Gallery

1. Select the table you want to save to the *Quick Tables* gallery.

2. Click the **Table** button [*Insert* tab, *Tables* group] and select **Quick Tables**.

3. Select **Save Selection to Quick Tables Gallery** at the bottom of the *Quick Tables* gallery. The *Create New Building Block* dialog box opens (Figure 7-33).

4. Fill in or select *Name*, *Gallery*, *Category*, *Description*, and *Save in* information.

5. Click the **Options** drop-down list and select **Insert content in its own paragraph**.

6. Click **OK** to close the dialog box.

   • The new *Table* building block is available in the *Quick Tables* gallery and the *Building Blocks Organizer*.

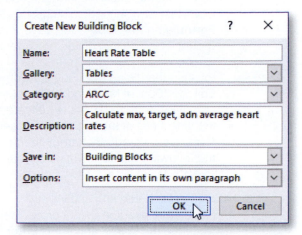

7-33 Save table as a building block in the *Quick Tables* gallery

---

PAUSE & PRACTICE: WORD 7-2

For this Pause & Practice project, you continue working with the document about maximum and target heart rates for the American River Cycling Club. You split a table, edit and create formulas, apply table styles, modify a table style, create a new table style, apply a custom table style, and save a table in the *Quick Tables* gallery.

File Needed: ***[your initials] PP W7-1.docx***
Completed Project File Name: ***[your initials] PP W7-2.docx***

1. Open the ***[your initials] PP W7-1*** document you completed in *Pause & Practice 7-1*.

2. Save the document as [your initials] PP W7-2.

3. Split the table into two tables.
   a. Place the insertion point in the next to the last row of the table.
   b. Click the **Split Table** button [*Table Tools Layout* tab, *Merge* group]. The last two rows split into a separate table.

4. Modify the new (second) table.
   a. Add a column to the right of the last column in the new (second) table.
   b. In the last cell in the first row, type Average Target, press **Enter**, and type Heart Rate.
   c. Add a row above the first row.

    d. Merge the cells in the first row.

    e. Turn on **Show/Hide** if it is not on, and if there is a paragraph mark in the merged row, delete the paragraph mark.

    f. Type Calculate Your Max and Target Heart Rates in the merged first row.

5. Edit existing formulas and create a new formula.

    a. Select the maximum heart rate formula (second table, last row, second column) and click the **Formula** button [*Table Tools Layout* tab, *Data* group]. The *Formula* dialog box opens.

    b. Change the cell reference to **A3** and click **OK** to close the dialog box (Figure 7-34).

    c. Edit the "60% of Max" and "85% of Max" formulas and type **B3** as the cell reference.

    d. In the last cell of the last column, insert a formula to average the target heart rates. Use the following function syntax for your formula and use **0** number format.
      =AVERAGE(C3:D3)

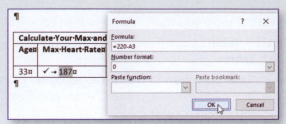

7-34 Edit existing formula

6. Modify the first table and apply a style.

    a. Place your insertion point before "Heart" in the first table (first row, third column), press **Backspace** to delete the space, and press **Enter** to make a two-line column heading.

    b. Place the insertion point before "(60-85% of Max)" (first row, fourth column), press **Backspace** to delete the space, and press **Enter** to make a two-line column heading.

    c. Select the first table.

    d. Check the **Header Row**, **Banded Rows**, and **First Column** boxes in the *Table Styles Options* group [*Table Tools Design* tab] if they are not already checked. The other options should not be selected.

    e. Click the **More** button in the *Table Styles* gallery and select the **Grid Table 5 Dark - Accent 1** table style (Figure 7-35).

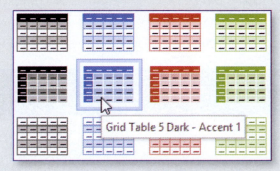

7-35 Apply a table style

7. Modify a table style.

    a. With the first table still selected, click the **More** button in the *Table Styles* gallery and select **Modify Table Style**. The *Modify Style* dialog box opens.

    b. Click the **Format** button and select **Table Properties** to open the *Table Properties* dialog box.

    c. Click the **Options** button to open the *Table Options* dialog box.

    d. Change the *Top* and *Bottom* cell margins to **0.02"** and the *Left* and *Right* cell margins to **0.1"**.

    e. Click **OK** to close the *Table Options* dialog box.

    f. Select **Center** in the *Alignment* area on the *Table* tab of the *Table Properties* dialog box.

    g. Click **OK** to close the *Table Properties* dialog box.

    h. Click the **Text Alignment** drop-down list and select **Align Center** (Figure 7-36).

    i. Click the **Apply formatting to** drop-down list and select **Header row**.

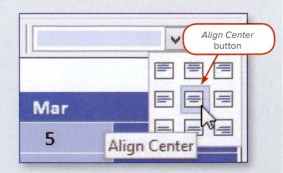

7-36 Change text alignment to *Align Center*

j. Click the **Fill Color** button and select **Dark Blue, Text 2, Darker 50%** (Figure 7-37).

k. Apply the same fill color to the **First column**.

l. Click **OK** to close the *Modify Style* dialog box.

8. Save your document, which saves the document and the table style you modified.

9. Create a new table style.

   a. Select the first table, click the **More** button in the *Table Styles* gallery and select **New Table Style**. The *Create New Style from Formatting* dialog box opens (Figure 7-38).

   b. Type **ARCC Table** in the *Name* area.

   c. Click the **Style based on** drop-down list and select **Grid Table 5 Dark - Accent 1**.

   d. Click **OK** to close the dialog box and create the new table style.

10. Apply custom table style and modify tables.

    a. Select the first table.

    b. Click the **More** button in the *Table Styles* gallery.

    c. Select the **ARCC Table** in the *Custom* area to apply the custom table style to the first table (Figure 7-39).

    d. Select the text in the first row (don't include the first column) of the first table and apply **bold** and **small caps** formatting to the text.

    e. Select the second table.

    f. Deselect the **First Column** check box in the *Table Style Options* group [*Table Tools Design* tab]. *Header Row* and *Banded Rows* should be checked.

    g. Apply the **ARCC Table** custom table style.

    h. Select the first and second rows of the second table and apply **bold** and **small caps** formatting to the text.

    i. Select the first row of the second table and change the font size to **12 pt**.

11. Save a table to the *Quick Tables* gallery.

    a. Select the second table.

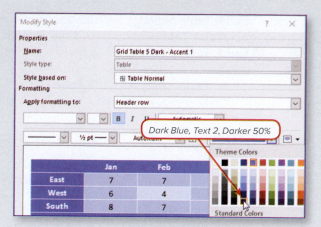

7-37 Change *Fill Color* of the header row

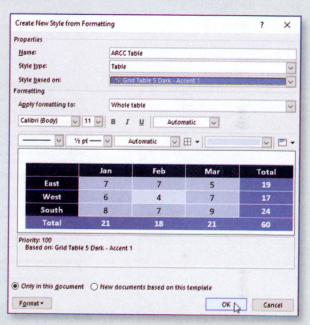

7-38 Create new table style

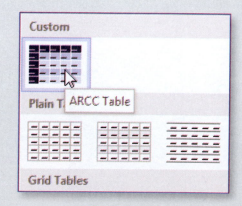

7-39 Apply custom table style

b. Click the **Table** button [*Insert* tab, *Tables* group], select **Quick Tables**, and select **Save Selection to Quick Tables Gallery** at the bottom of the *Quick Tables* list. The *Create New Building Block* dialog box opens (Figure 7-40).

c. Enter the following properties for the building block:
Name: Heart Rate Table
Gallery: **Tables**
Category: ARCC (create new category)
Description: Calculate max, target, and average heart rates
Save in: **Building Blocks**
Options: **Insert content in its own paragraph**

d. Click **OK** to close the *Create New Building Block* dialog box.

12. Save and close the document (Figure 7-41). If prompted to save changes to building blocks, click **Save**.

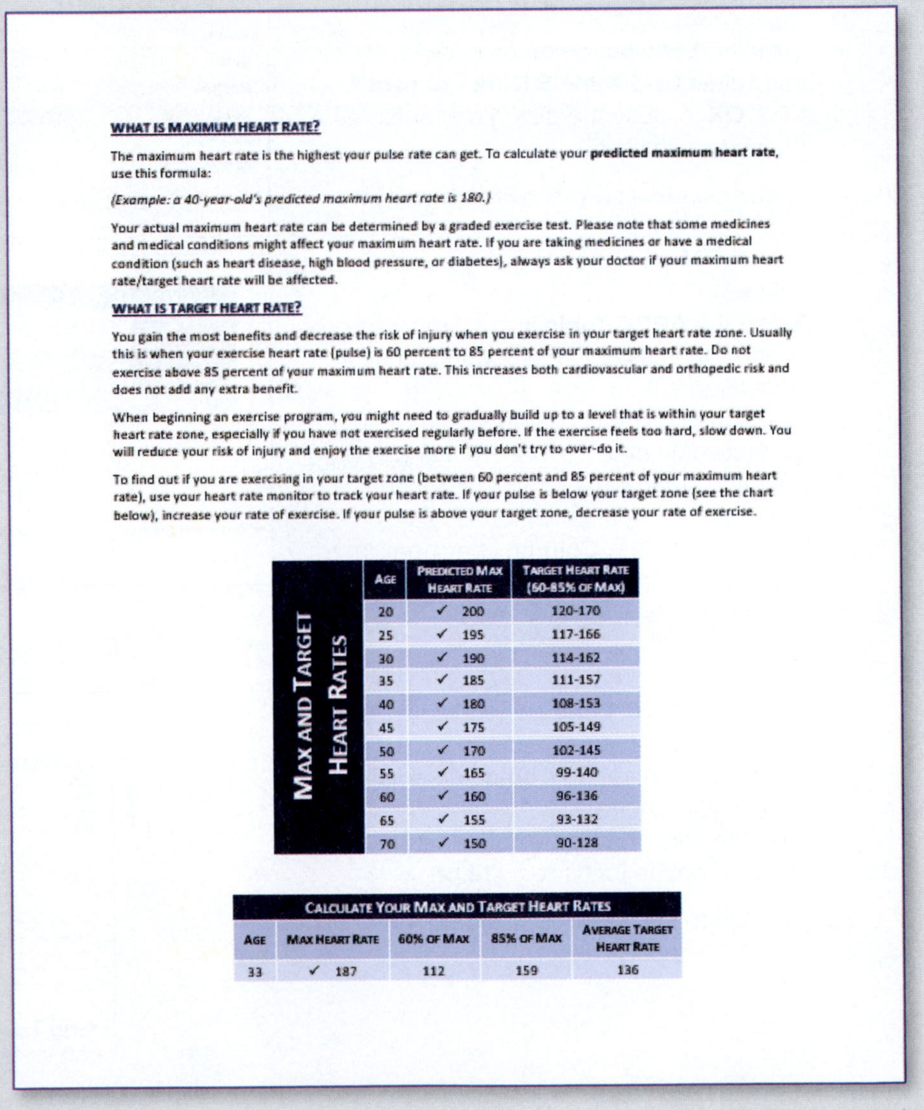

Create New Building Block

Name:	Heart Rate Table
Gallery:	Tables
Category:	ARCC
Description:	Calculate max, target, adn average heart rates
Save in:	Building Blocks
Options:	Insert content in its own paragraph

OK Cancel

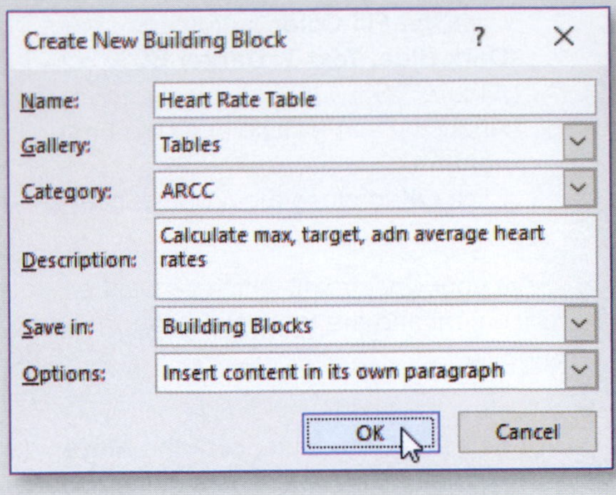

7-40 Create new table building block

WHAT IS MAXIMUM HEART RATE?

The maximum heart rate is the highest your pulse rate can get. To calculate your **predicted maximum heart rate**, use this formula:

(Example: a 40-year-old's predicted maximum heart rate is 180.)

Your actual maximum heart rate can be determined by a graded exercise test. Please note that some medicines and medical conditions might affect your maximum heart rate. If you are taking medicines or have a medical condition (such as heart disease, high blood pressure, or diabetes), always ask your doctor if your maximum heart rate/target heart rate will be affected.

WHAT IS TARGET HEART RATE?

You gain the most benefits and decrease the risk of injury when you exercise in your target heart rate zone. Usually this is when your exercise heart rate (pulse) is 60 percent to 85 percent of your maximum heart rate. Do not exercise above 85 percent of your maximum heart rate. This increases both cardiovascular and orthopedic risk and does not add any extra benefit.

When beginning an exercise program, you might need to gradually build up to a level that is within your target heart rate zone, especially if you have not exercised regularly before. If the exercise feels too hard, slow down. You will reduce your risk of injury and enjoy the exercise more if you don't try to over-do it.

To find out if you are exercising in your target zone (between 60 percent and 85 percent of your maximum heart rate), use your heart rate monitor to track your heart rate. If your pulse is below your target zone (see the chart below), increase your rate of exercise. If your pulse is above your target zone, decrease your rate of exercise.

MAX AND TARGET HEART RATES	AGE	PREDICTED MAX HEART RATE	TARGET HEART RATE (60-85% OF MAX)
	20	✔ 200	120-170
	25	✔ 195	117-166
	30	✔ 190	114-162
	35	✔ 185	111-157
	40	✔ 180	108-153
	45	✔ 175	105-149
	50	✔ 170	102-145
	55	✔ 165	99-140
	60	✔ 160	96-136
	65	✔ 155	93-132
	70	✔ 150	90-128

CALCULATE YOUR MAX AND TARGET HEART RATES				
AGE	MAX HEART RATE	60% OF MAX	85% OF MAX	AVERAGE TARGET HEART RATE
33	✔ 187	112	159	136

7-41 PP W7-2 completed

Working with Pictures

Picture is a broad term that can refer to many types of graphical images including photos and clip art. You can insert and customize pictures to enhance document layout and present information in a graphical format. When you insert a picture into a document, the ***Picture Tools Format tab*** displays on the *Ribbon*. Many of the picture formatting features are available on this tab. In this section, you learn the advanced graphic features in Word to resize, arrange, and enhance pictures.

Layout Options

When you select a picture in your document, the ***Layout Options*** button appears in the upper right corner of the selected picture (Figure 7-42). Click the **Layout Options** button to open the *Layout Options* menu where you can select a text wrapping option. In this menu, you can also select whether the picture moves as text is rearranged (*Move with text*) or is located in a fixed position on the page (*Fix position on page*).

Click the **See more** link to open the *Layout* dialog box where you have *Position*, *Text Wrapping*, and *Size* tabs to further customize your picture.

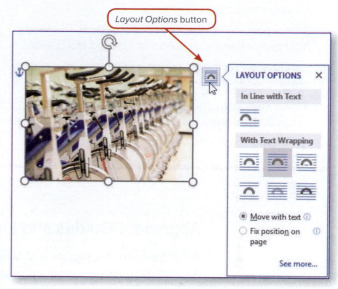

Layout Options button

7-42 *Layout Options menu*

> **MORE INFO**
>
> *In Line with Text* is the default option when you insert a picture. To change the default wrapping option, right-click a wrapping option in the *Layout Options* menu and select **Set as Default**.

Customize Text Wrapping

Click the **Wrap Text** button in the *Arrange* group on the *Picture Tools Format* tab to display a drop-down list of text wrapping options (Figure 7-43). Click the **Bring Forward** or **Send Backward** drop-down list in the *Arrange* group to further customize how your picture is arranged with text and other graphics. The *Layout* dialog box contains additional customization options to control text wrapping.

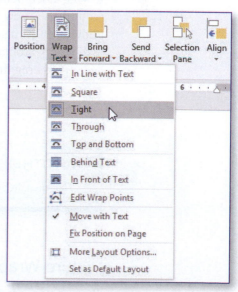

7-43 Text wrapping options from the *Wrap Text* drop-down list

▶HOW TO: Customize Text Wrapping Options

1. Select the picture.

2. Click the **Wrap Text** button [*Picture Tools Format* tab, *Arrange* group] and select **More Layout Options**. The *Layout* dialog box opens and displays the *Text Wrapping* tab (Figure 7-44).

3. Select a *Wrapping style* to specify how the text wraps around the picture.

4. Select one of the *Wrap text* radio buttons to specify how the text wraps around the sides of the graphic.

5. Set the specific distance for text to wrap around the graphic in the *Distance from text* area.

   • The *Wrapping style* option you chose controls which options are available in the *Distance from text* area.

6. Click **OK** to close the *Layout* dialog box.

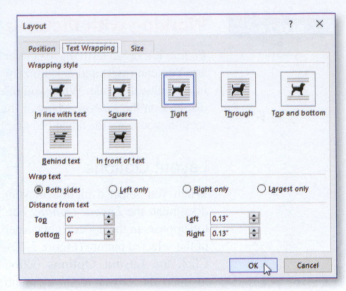

7-44 Text wrapping options in the *Layout* dialog box

Alignment Guides and Live Layout

After you insert a picture and select a text wrapping option, you can drag the picture to the desired location in your document. Word 2016 provides you with features to help you accurately position pictures. **Alignment guides** are vertical and horizontal green lines that display to guide alignment (Figure 7-45). As you drag the picture to a location, the vertical alignment guide displays at the left and right margins and the center of the document. The horizontal alignment guide displays at the top and bottom margins and on lines of text.

Click the **Align** button in the *Arrange* group on the *Picture Tools Format* tab and select **Use Alignment Guides** from the drop-down list to turn on the alignment guides.

Live layout automatically rearranges text and other objects in your document as you drag a picture to a new location. This allows you to instantly see how text wraps around your picture as you are dragging the picture.

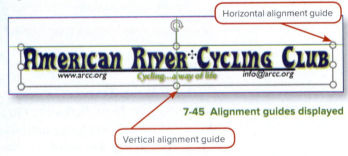

7-45 Alignment guides displayed

> ▶ **ANOTHER WAY**
>
> The *Align* drop-down list is also available in the *Arrange* group on the *Layout* tab.

Picture Wrap Points

Wrap points are the points on the picture that the text wraps around. You can edit these wrap points to more precisely customize how text wraps around the picture.

▶ **HOW TO:** Edit Picture Wrap Points

1. Select the picture.
2. Click the **Wrap Text** button and select **Edit Wrap Points**. The selected picture displays the wrap point handles (Figure 7-46).
3. Click and drag a wrap point handle to customize how the text wraps around the picture.
4. Click the **Wrap Text** button and select **Edit Wrap Points** to accept changes and turn off the *Edit Wrap Points* feature.

   - You can also click away from the picture to accept changes and turn off the *Edit Wrap Points* feature.

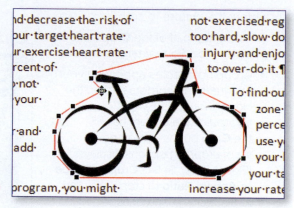

7-46 Edit wrap points

Picture Anchor

The ***picture anchor*** is a blue anchor icon and displays where the picture is anchored to the text (Figure 7-47). The picture anchor allows a picture to move with selected text if a document is modified and the text moves on the page. The picture anchor displays when you select a picture.

When you insert a picture, the picture anchor is automatically placed to the left of the paragraph closest to the picture. The picture anchor always displays at the beginning of a paragraph. Click and drag the **picture anchor** icon to anchor the picture to a different location.

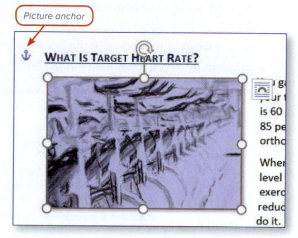

7-47 Picture anchor

Resize and Crop a Picture

The following are different ways to resize a picture:

- ***Sizing handles***: Drag the sizing handles to increase or decrease the size of the picture.
- ***Size group***: Type a specific size in the *Height* and *Width* areas in the *Size* group on the *Picture Tools Format* tab.
- ***Layout dialog box***: Click the **Size** launcher to open the *Layout* dialog box. Click the **Size** tab and type a specific height and width or scale the picture to a percentage of its original size.

When resizing a picture, it is best to keep the picture proportional to its original size, which is its ***aspect ratio***. This prevents distortion of the image. By default, when you change the size in the *Size* group or in the *Layout* dialog box, the aspect ratio is locked to keep the picture proportional to its original size. When you resize a picture using the sizing handles, the corner sizing handles resize the picture proportionally. However, the side sizing handles do not resize the picture proportionally.

Cropping is different from resizing a picture. While cropping does resize a picture, it does so by cutting out part of the picture. Use cropping to remove unwanted portions of a picture.

1. Select the picture to crop.

2. Click the top half of the **Crop** button [*Picture Tools Format* tab, *Size* group].

    *   Cropping handles appear on your picture in the corners and on the sides (Figure 7-48).
    *   If you click the bottom half of the **Crop** button, a drop-down list of cropping options displays (Figure 7-49). Select **Crop to Shape** or **Aspect Ratio** to crop a picture to a specific shape or aspect ratio. Select **Fill** or **Fit** to crop a picture to a specific size.

3. Drag a cropping handle to edit the picture.

4. Click the **Crop** button again or press **Esc** to accept the changes and to turn off cropping.

    *   Alternatively, click away from the picture to accept the changes and to turn off cropping.

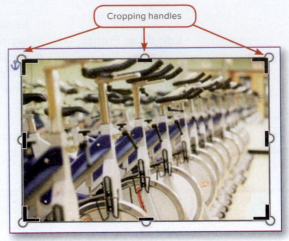

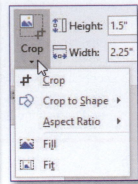

7-48 Picture with cropping handles displayed   7-49 Cropping options

---

Rotate a Picture

You can rotate a picture in a document to enhance its placement. Select the picture and then use one of the following methods to rotate the picture:

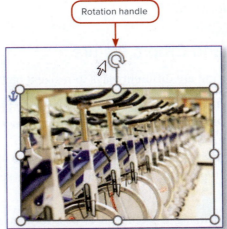

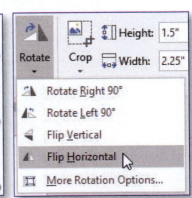

7-50 Picture with rotation handle displayed   7-51 Rotation options

*   ***Rotation handle***: Click the rotation handle at the top and drag to the left or right to rotate the picture (Figure 7-50).
*   ***Rotate drop-down list***: Click the **Rotate** button in the *Arrange* group on the *Picture Tools Format* tab to display the drop-down list of rotate options (Figure 7-51).
*   ***Layout dialog box***: Click the **Rotate** button and select **More Rotation Options** to open the *Layout* dialog box. Click the **Size** tab and change the degree of rotation in the *Rotate* area.

Format Picture Pane

Use the *Format Picture pane* to modify and enhance your pictures (Figure 7-52). This pane contains many of the picture formatting features that are available on the *Picture Tools Format* tab. Click the **Picture Styles** launcher to open the *Format Picture* pane. You can also open this pane from many of the drop-down lists on the *Picture Tools Format* tab.

The formatting categories display at the top of this pane. When you click one of the category buttons, the options in that category display below. The four main formatting categories and the different areas in each category are listed below:

- **Fill & Line**: *Fill* and *Line*
- **Effects**: *Shadow, Reflection, Glow, Soft Edges, 3-D Format, 3-D Rotation,* and *Artistic Effects*
- **Layout & Properties**: *Text Box* and *Alt Text*
- **Picture**: *Picture Corrections, Picture Color,* and *Crop*

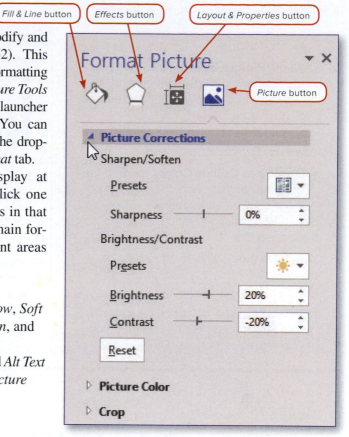

7-52 *Format Picture* pane

Picture Styles

Similar to text and table styles, ***picture styles*** apply preset borders and effects. The ***Picture Styles gallery*** contains the picture styles available in Word. Click the **More** button in the

Picture Styles gallery to display the entire *Picture Styles* gallery (Figure 7-53). Select a picture and click a picture style to apply it to the picture. When you place your pointer on the picture style, the picture style temporarily applies to the picture, allowing you to preview the picture with the style.

7-53 *Picture Styles* gallery

> **ANOTHER WAY**
>
> Right-click a picture and select a picture style from the mini toolbar.

Picture Borders

You can apply a border to your pictures and customize the color of the border, the border weight (size of the border), and the type of border line.

1. Select the picture.

2. Click the **Picture Border** button [*Picture Tools Format* tab, *Picture Styles* group] to display the drop-down list of picture border options (Figure 7-54).

3. Select the border color in the *Theme Colors* or *Standard Colors* area.

   • Click **More Outline Colors** to open the *Colors* dialog box and choose from more border color options.

4. Select **Weight** and select the thickness of the border line.

5. Select **Dashes** and select the type of border line.

   • If you select *More Lines* from the *Weight* or *Dashes* drop-down list, the *Format Picture* pane opens and provides you with more line options (Figure 7-55).

7-54 Picture border options

7-55 Picture border line options in the *Format Picture* pane

You can also apply a picture border from the *Format Picture* pane. Click the **Picture Styles** launcher to open the *Format Picture* pane (see Figure 7-55). Click the **Fill & Line** button at the top to customize the picture border. Click **Fill** or **Line** to display the customization options below each of these categories.

Picture Effects

Use **picture effects** to apply *Preset, Shadow, Reflection, Glow, Soft Edges, Bevel,* or *3-D Rotation* effects to a picture. When you click a picture effect category, a drop-down list of picture effect options displays (Figure 7-56).

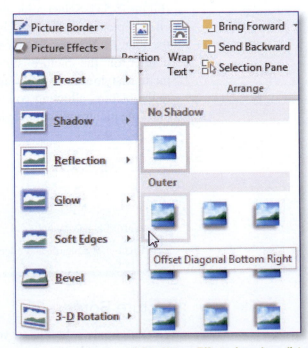

7-56 *Picture Effects* drop-down list

At the bottom of each drop-down list is an options button (for example *Shadow Options*). Click an options button to open the *Format Picture* pane. The *Format Picture* pane contains the *Shadow*, *Reflection*, *Glow*, *Soft Edges*, *3-D Format*, *3-D Rotation*, and *Artistic Effects* categories.

Picture Adjustments

Apply corrections, change colors, or add artistic effects to adjust pictures. You can also compress pictures to reduce the file size, change a picture in the document, or reset a picture to its original size and appearance. Apply these adjustments from the *Adjust* group on the *Picture Tools Format* tab.

> ▶ **ANOTHER WAY**
>
> You can also apply these adjustments in the *Format Picture* pane.

Corrections

Apply picture corrections to sharpen or soften a picture and change picture brightness and contrast. Click the **Corrections** button in the *Adjust* group on the *Picture Tools Format* tab to display a drop-down list of correction options (Figure 7-57).

The *Corrections* drop-down list displays two categories of correction options: *Sharpen/Soften* and *Brightness/Contrast*. Each of the options in both categories changes the picture by a percentage of the original picture. Click **Picture Corrections Options** to open the *Format Picture* pane for additional correction options.

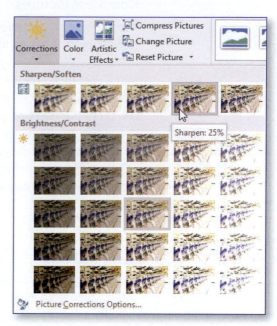

7-57 Picture correction options

Color

Adjust the color tone and color saturation of the picture or you can recolor the picture. Click the **Color** button in the *Adjust* group on the *Picture Tools Format* tab to display a drop-down list of color options (Figure 7-58).

The *Color* drop-down list displays three categories of color options: *Color Saturation*, *Color Tone*, and *Recolor*. Click **Picture Color Options** to open the *Format Picture* pane for additional correction options. Click **More Variations** for additional color options.

You can also change a color in the picture to be transparent. Click **Set Transparent Color** and select the color or colors in the picture you want to be transparent.

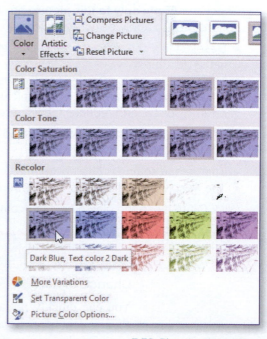

7-58 Picture color options

Artistic Effects

Word provides you with a variety of artistic effects to apply to pictures. Click the **Artistic Effects** button in the *Adjust* group on the *Picture Tools Format* tab to display a drop-down list of options (Figure 7-59). Click **Artistic Effects Options** to open the *Format Picture* pane to view additional artistic effect options.

7-59 Artistic picture effects

Compress Pictures

The file size of a picture can range from a few kilobytes (KB) up to a few megabytes (MB) or more. When you insert pictures into a document, the file size of the document increases. Word provides options to compress the file size of pictures in your document to keep the document from becoming too large (larger files are harder to send via email, for example). When you compress a picture, it changes the picture *resolution*, which determines the picture quality. Compressed picture files have lower resolution and are of lesser quality.

▶ **HOW TO:** Compress Pictures

1. Select the picture you want to compress.
2. Click the **Compress Pictures** button [*Picture Tools Format* tab, *Adjust* group]. The *Compress Pictures* dialog box opens (Figure 7-60).
3. Check the **Apply only to this picture** box in the *Compression options* area to apply compression only to the selected picture.
   - Deselect this check box to apply the settings to all pictures in the document.
   - The *Delete cropped areas of pictures* is checked by default. This removes the cropped area of pictures, which have been cropped, and reduces the file size.
4. Select one of the picture resolution radio buttons in the *Resolution* area.
   - The default setting is *Use document resolution*.
   - The *Resolution* options available depend on the picture type and its original resolution.
5. Click **OK** to close the dialog box and compress the picture or pictures.

7-60 *Compress Pictures* dialog box

Change Picture

You can quickly replace a picture with another picture in a Word document. The *Change Picture* feature removes an existing picture and replaces it with a different picture while retaining the picture size and formatting

▶ HOW TO: Change a Picture in a Document

1. Select the picture to change.

2. Click the **Change Picture** button [*Picture Tools Format* tab, *Adjust* group] to open the *Insert Pictures* dialog box (Figure 7-61). Select from the following options:

   - Select **From a file** to open the *Insert Picture* dialog box.
   - Select **Bing Image Search** or **OneDrive** to search for and select a picture.
   - You can also insert a picture from *Facebook* or *Flickr*. Both of these options require you to have an account to connect to their service.

3. Browse or search to find and select the picture you want to insert to replace the selected picture.

4. Click the **Insert** button to insert the new picture.

   - The size and formatting of the original picture applies to the new picture.

Insert Pictures

🖼️	**From a file** Browse files on your computer or local network	Browse ▸
Ⓑ	**Bing Image Search** Search the web	Bike ✕ 🔍
☁️	**OneDrive - Personal** dmordell@live.com	Browse ▸

Also insert from:

[f] [●●]

7-61 Insert Pictures dialog box

Reset Picture

After making changes to a picture, you might decide to discard the changes and return to the original picture. Click the **Reset Picture** drop-down arrow in the *Adjust* group on the *Picture Tools Format* tab and select from the following options (Figure 7-62):

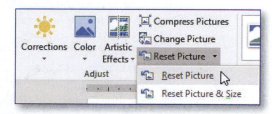

7-62 Reset Picture options

- **Reset Picture**: Discards all formatting changes
- **Reset Picture & Size**: Discards all formatting and sizing changes

---

PAUSE & PRACTICE: WORD 7-3

For this Pause & Practice project, you work with the American River Cycling Club document to insert two pictures and modify the size, arrangement, borders, and effects. You also apply adjustments to the pictures and compress the pictures.

Files Needed: ***[your initials] PP W7-2.docx, ARCC-logo-07.png***, and ***Bikes-07.png*** *(student data files are available in the* Library *of your SIMnet account)*
Completed Project File Name: ***[your initials] PP W7-3.docx***

1. Open the ***[your initials] PP W7-2*** document you completed in *Pause & Practice 7-2*.

2. Save the document as [your initials] PP W7-3.

3. Change the top and bottom margins to **0.5"** and the left and right margins to **0.75"**.

4. Select the "**What Is Maximum Heart Rate?**" heading and change the *Before* spacing to **12 pt**.

5. Insert, resize, and arrange a picture.
   a. Place the insertion point at the beginning of the document.
   b. Insert the **ARCC-logo-07** picture from your student data files.
   c. Click the **Size** launcher to open the *Layout* dialog box.
   d. Click the **Height** text box in the *Scale* area, type 150% to replace the existing setting, and press **Tab**. The *Width* automatically changes.
   e. Click the **Text Wrapping** tab and change the text wrapping to **Top and Bottom**.
   f. Click **OK** to close the *Layout* dialog box.
   g. Drag the picture so it is positioned at the top and center of the document. Use the alignment guides to position the picture accurately (Figure 7-63). If the alignment guides don't display, click **Align** [*Picture Tools Format* tab, *Arrange* group] and select **Use Alignment Guides**.

7-63 Use the alignment guides to position the picture

6. Use the *Format Picture* pane to modify a picture.
   a. Select the logo and click the **Picture Styles** launcher to open the *Format Picture* pane.
   b. Click the **Fill & Line** button at the top of the pane and select **Line** to open the *Line* settings (Figure 7-64).
   c. Select the **Solid line** radio button.
   d. Click the **Color** drop-down list and select **Dark Blue, Text 2, Darker 50%**.
   e. Change the *Width* to **1.5 pt**.
   f. Click the **Picture** button at the top of the pane and select **Picture Color** to open the *Picture Color* settings.
   g. Click the **Recolor** drop-down list and select **Blue, Accent color 1 Dark** (Figure 7-65).

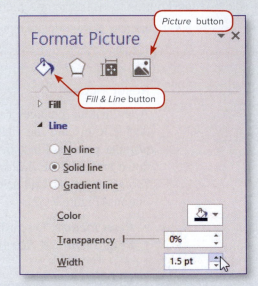

7-64 *Fill & Line* area of the *Format Picture* pane

7-65 Recolor picture

   h. Click **Picture Corrections** category in the *Format Picture* pane to display the options.
   i. Change the *Brightness* to **20%** and the *Contrast* to **−20%** in the *Brightness/Contrast* area. Use the up and down arrows or type the settings (Figure 7-66).
   j. Click the **X** in the upper right corner to close the *Format Picture* pane.

7. Insert, resize, and arrange a picture.
   a. Place the insertion point in front of the "What Is Target Heart Rate?" heading.
   b. Insert the **Bikes-07** picture from your student data files.

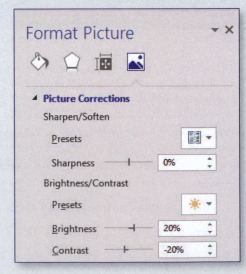

7-66 Adjust picture brightness and contrast

c. Type **1.5** in the *Height* area [*Picture Tools Format* tab, *Size* group] and press **Enter**. The width automatically adjusts to maintain the aspect ratio.

d. Click the **Wrap Text** button [*Picture Tools Format* tab, *Arrange* group] and select **Tight**.

e. Click the **Align** button [*Picture Tools Format* tab, *Arrange* group] and select **Align Right**.

f. Drag the picture anchor to the first paragraph below "What Is Target Heart Rate?" (Figure 7-67).

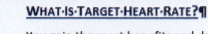

7-67 Move picture anchor

8. Modify the picture.

a. With the bike picture selected, click the **Picture Effects** button [*Picture Tools Format* tab, *Picture Styles* group], select **Shadow**, and select **Offset Diagonal Bottom Right** in the *Outer* section (Figure 7-68).

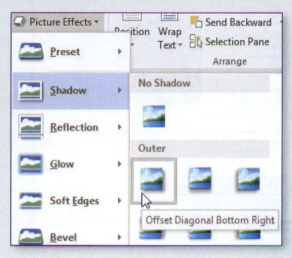

7-68 Apply shadow picture effect

b. Click the **Artistic Effects** button [*Picture Tools Format* tab, *Adjust* group] and select **Pencil Grayscale** from the drop-down list (Figure 7-69).

c. Click the **Color** button [*Picture Tools Format* tab, *Adjust* group] and select **Dark Blue, Text color 2 Dark** in the *Recolor* area (Figure 7-70).

7-69 Apply artistic effect

7-70 Apply picture color

9. Compress the picture.

a. Select the bikes picture.

b. Click the **Compress Pictures** button [*Picture Tools Format* tab, *Adjust* group] to open the *Compress Pictures* dialog box.

c. Select the **Print (220 ppi)** radio button in the *Resolution* area.

d. Click **OK** to close the dialog box and compress the picture.

10. Save and close the document (Figure 7-71).

WHAT IS MAXIMUM HEART RATE?

The maximum heart rate is the highest your pulse rate can get. To calculate your **predicted maximum heart rate**, use this formula:

(Example: a 40-year-old's predicted maximum heart rate is 180.)

Your actual maximum heart rate can be determined by a graded exercise test. Please note that some medicines and medical conditions might affect your maximum heart rate. If you are taking medicines or have a medical condition (such as heart disease, high blood pressure, or diabetes), always ask your doctor if your maximum heart rate/target heart rate will be affected.

WHAT IS TARGET HEART RATE?

You gain the most benefits and decrease the risk of injury when you exercise in your target heart rate zone. Usually this is when your exercise heart rate (pulse) is 60 percent to 85 percent of your maximum heart rate. Do not exercise above 85 percent of your maximum heart rate. This increases both cardiovascular and orthopedic risk and does not add any extra benefit.

When beginning an exercise program, you might need to gradually build up to a level that is within your target heart rate zone, especially if you have not exercised regularly before. If the exercise feels too hard, slow down. You will reduce your risk of injury and enjoy the exercise more if you don't try to over-do it.

To find out if you are exercising in your target zone (between 60 percent and 85 percent of your maximum heart rate), use your heart rate monitor to track your heart rate. If your pulse is below your target zone (see the chart below), increase your rate of exercise. If your pulse is above your target zone, decrease your rate of exercise.

MAX AND TARGET HEART RATES

AGE	PREDICTED MAX HEART RATE	TARGET HEART RATE (60-85% OF MAX)
20	✓ 200	120-170
25	✓ 195	117-166
30	✓ 190	114-162
35	✓ 185	111-157
40	✓ 180	108-153
45	✓ 175	105-149
50	✓ 170	102-145
55	✓ 165	99-140
60	✓ 160	96-136
65	✓ 155	93-132
70	✓ 150	90-128

CALCULATE YOUR MAX AND TARGET HEART RATES

AGE	MAX HEART RATE	60% OF MAX	85% OF MAX	AVERAGE TARGET HEART RATE
33	✓ 187	112	159	136

7-71 PP W7-3 completed

SLO 7.5

Working with Shapes

When working with shapes, you can modify their size, arrangement, style, fill color, border color, and effects. The process is similar to the way you modify pictures, but instead of using the *Picture Tools Format* tab you use when working with pictures, you use the ***Drawing Tools Format tab*** when working with shapes.

Customize Shapes

As you learned in Chapter 4, you can insert a shape by clicking the **Shapes** button on the *Insert* tab (see *SLO 4.5: Working with Graphics*). The *Shapes* gallery includes a variety of shapes that you can draw and customize in a document.

▶ HOW TO: Insert and Customize a Shape

1. Click the **Shapes** button [*Insert* group, *Illustrations* tab] and select a shape from the gallery.
   - When you select a shape from the *Shapes* gallery, your pointer becomes a drawing crosshair (large plus sign).
2. Use the drawing crosshair to draw a shape in your document.
   - After you have drawn a shape in your document, use the *Drawing Tools Format* tab or *Format Shapes* pane to customize the shape.
   - Use the *Size* and *Align* groups, the *Layout* menu, and the *Layout* dialog box to change the size, text wrapping, and position of the shape.
   - The size and arrangement options available are the same options available when working with a picture.
3. Select a shape in your document to edit. Shape handles appear on the selected shape (Figure 7-72).
   - Edit a shape using the sizing handles (white circles) on the sides and corners.
   - Use the shape rotation handle (circle with arrow) at the top to rotate a shape.
   - Use the shape adjustment handle (yellow circle) to adjust parts of a shape.
4. Click the **Edit Shape** button in the *Insert Shapes* group to *Change Shape* or *Edit Points* of a shape (Figure 7-73).
   - When you click *Edit Points*, shape editing handles display on a shape. Use these handles to further customize a shape.

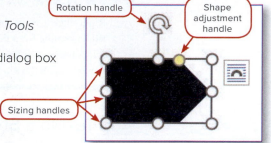

7-72 Selected shape with handles displayed

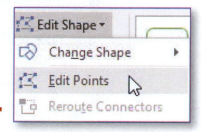

7-73 Edit Shape drop-down list

Shape Styles

In the *Shape Styles* group on the *Drawing Tools Format* tab, you can apply a shape style or customize the *Shape Fill, Shape Outline,* and *Shape Effects*. The *Shape Styles* gallery contains a variety of built-in styles to apply a preset outline, fill color, and effects to shapes. The document theme controls the colors of built-in shape styles in a document. Click the **More** button in the *Shape Styles* gallery to display the available shape styles (Figure 7-74).

In addition to the built-in shape styles, you can customize shapes using the *Shape Fill, Shape Outline,* and *Shape Effects* drop-down lists in the *Shape Styles* group on the *Drawing Tools Format* tab. The following list details the options available in each of these areas:

7-74 Shape Styles gallery

- **Shape Fill**: Customize and apply *Theme Colors, Standard Colors, No Fill, More Fill Colors, Picture, Gradient,* or *Texture* to a shape.

- **Shape Outline**: Customize and apply *Theme Colors*, *Standard Colors*, *No Outline*, *More Outline Colors*, *Weight*, *Dashes*, or *Arrows* to a shape.
- **Shape Effects**: Apply built-in *Preset*, *Shadow*, *Reflection*, *Glow*, *Soft Edges*, *Bevel*, or *3-D Rotation* effects to a shape.

You can also apply and customize shape fill, outline, and effects using the *Format Shape* pane. This pane is similar to the *Format Picture* pane and provides additional shape customization options. Click the **Shape Styles** launcher to open the *Format Shape* pane (Figure 7-75).

> **ANOTHER WAY**
>
> Right-click a shape and select a style, fill, or outline from the mini toolbar or select **Format Shape** from the context menu to open the *Format Shape* pane.

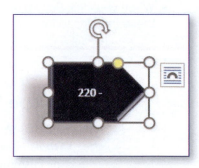

7-75 *Format Shape* pane

Add Text to a Shape

After drawing a shape, you can add text to a shape. When you add text to a shape, the text becomes part of the shape. Format the text in a shape the same way you format other text in your documents.

▶ **HOW TO:** Add Text to a Shape

1. Select a shape where you want to add text and type the text in the shape (Figure 7-76).
   - Alternatively, right-click a shape and select **Add Text** from the context menu. The insertion point displays in the shape.
2. Select the text and apply formatting changes to font, size, styles, and effects.
   - The text added to a shape is *Normal* style text by default.
   - Adjust line and paragraph spacing to vertically center text in the shape.
3. Click the **Align Text** button [*Drawing Tools Format* tab, *Text* group] and select **Top**, **Middle**, or **Bottom** to align the text vertically on the shape.
   - Text on a shape is centered horizontally by default.

7-76 Add text to shape

Draw a Text Box

You can also add text to a shape by drawing a text box on a shape and typing text in the text box. A text box is a separate object that you can modify independently of the shape.

▶ **HOW TO:** Draw a Text Box

1. Click the **Draw Text Box** button [*Drawing Tools Format* tab, *Insert Shapes* group]. Your pointer becomes a drawing crosshair.
2. Draw a text box on a shape.
3. Type text in the text box (Figure 7-77).

7-77 Type text in a text box

4. Format and arrange the text box.

- Select the text in the text box and customize the text font, size, style, and effects.
- Select the border of the text box and customize the outline, fill, and arrangement.
- You can group a text box and a shape so they become one object. Grouping objects is covered in the *Group Shapes* section, which is covered later in this chapter.

When using text with shapes, you can change the text direction, change the vertical text alignment, or add a hyperlink to text using the options in the *Text* group on the *Drawing Tools Format* tab (Figure 7-78).

7-78 *Text group on the Drawing Tools Format tab*

> **MORE INFO**
>
> To add a caption to a shape or picture, right-click the shape or picture and select **Insert Caption** from the context menu.

Selection Pane

When you are using shapes and pictures in your document, the **Selection pane** helps you view, select, and order these objects in your document. The *Selection* pane displays on the right side of the Word window, and it displays all of the objects in your document.

▶**HOW TO:** Use the Selection Pane

1. Select a shape or picture.
2. Click the **Selection Pane** button [*Drawing Tools Format* or *Layout* tab, *Arrange* group]. The *Selection* pane displays on the right side of the Word window (Figure 7-79).

   - All of the pictures and shapes in the document display in the *Selection* pane.
   - Each object has a default name.

3. Click an object in the *Selection* pane to select it. The object is also selected in the document.

   - Click the object name to rename the object.
   - Use the **Ctrl** key and your pointer to select multiple objects.
   - Click the **Hide** button (eye) to the right of the object name to hide the object in the document.

4. Select an object and click the **Bring Forward** (up arrow) or **Send Backward** (down arrow) button to re-order objects.

   - Ordering determines which object appears in front of or behind other objects. (Ordering is covered later in this section of the chapter.)

5. Click the **Selection Pane** button or the **X** in the upper right corner of the *Selection* pane to close it.

Send Backward button

Bring Forward button

Selection

Show All   Hide All

Group 6
  Pentagon 5
  Pentagon 4
  Pentagon 2
Striped Right Arrow 7
Picture 1
Picture 3

Hide button

7-79 *Selection pane*

Order Shapes

Ordering is important when you are working with multiple shapes and pictures. It determines how objects display in front of or behind other objects. Use the *Selection* pane to change the order of objects in your document. Alternatively, you can use the **Bring Forward** and **Send Backward** buttons in the *Arrange* group on the *Drawing Tools Format* tab.

Select the object or objects you want to re-order and click the **Bring Forward** or **Send Backward** button (Figure 7-80). The following options are available on these buttons:

- **Bring Forward**: *Bring Forward, Bring to Front*, and *Bring in Front of Text*
- **Send Backward**: *Send Backward, Send to Back*, and *Send Behind Text*

Align Shapes

Word provides a variety of options to precisely align shapes (or pictures) in your document. When you align multiple objects, use the **Shift** key and your pointer to select multiple objects or use the **Ctrl** key and your pointer to select multiple objects in the *Selection* pane. Click the **Align** button in the *Arrange* group and select from the alignment options (Figure 7-81). The following table describes each of the alignment options:

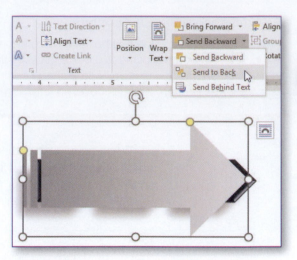

7-80 Re-order object

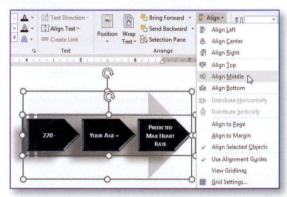

7-81 Align selected shapes

Shape Alignment Options

Alignment Option	Description
Align Left	Horizontally aligns selected objects on the left edge of objects.
Align Center	Horizontally aligns selected objects in the center of objects.
Align Right	Horizontally aligns selected objects on the right edge of objects.
Align Top	Vertically aligns selected objects on the top edge of objects.
Align Middle	Vertically aligns selected objects in the middle of objects.
Align Bottom	Vertically aligns selected objects on the bottom edge of objects.
Distribute Horizontally	Equally distributes horizontal space between selected objects.
Distribute Vertically	Equally distributes vertical space between selected objects.
Align to Page	Aligns objects in relation to the page of the document. Turn on this option and then select one of the horizontal or vertical alignment options.
Align to Margin	Aligns objects in relation to document margins. Turn on this option and then select one of the horizontal or vertical alignment options.
Align Selected Objects	Automatically turns on when you select multiple objects to align.
Use Alignment Guides	Displays vertical and horizontal alignment guides to help you align objects when dragging an object.
View Gridlines	Displays gridlines in the document to help you precisely align objects.
Grid Settings	Opens the *Drawing Grid* dialog box where you can customize how gridlines appear in the document.

Group Shapes

After modifying and aligning objects in your document, you can combine multiple objects into one object so you can easily modify it as one object rather than individual objects. Use the *group* feature to combine multiple objects into one grouped object that you can resize, arrange, and modify. Also, you can use the group feature to group a text box with a shape or group a caption with a picture.

▶ **HOW TO:** Group Multiple Objects

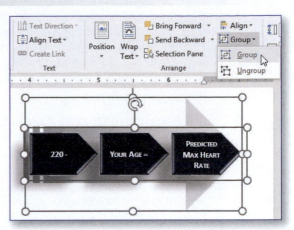

1. Select the objects you want to group.
   - In the document, use the **Shift** key and your pointer to select the objects.
   - In the *Selection* pane, use the **Ctrl** key and your pointer to select the objects.
2. Click the **Group** button [*Drawing Tools Format* tab, *Arrange* group] (Figure 7-82).
3. Select **Group**.
   - The individual objects become one grouped object.
   - To ungroup objects, select the grouped object, click the **Group** button, and select **Ungroup**.

7-82 *Group* selected shapes

PAUSE & PRACTICE: WORD 7-4

For this Pause & Practice project, you finalize the heart rate document for American River Cycling Club. You insert and customize shapes, add text to shapes, align and group shapes, and arrange the grouped object.

File Needed: *[your initials] PP W7-3.docx*
Completed Project File Name: *[your initials] PP W7-4.docx*

1. Open the *[your initials] PP W7-3* document you completed in *Pause & Practice 7-3*.

2. Save the document as [your initials] PP W7-4.

3. Insert, resize, and customize a shape.
   a. Click the **Shapes** button [*Insert* tab, *Illustrations* group].
   b. Select the **Pentagon** shape in the *Block Arrows* category (Figure 7-83). Your pointer becomes a drawing crosshair.
   c. Draw a shape approximately **1" square** on the right side of the text in the "What Is Maximum Heart Rate?" section. The shape displays on top of the text; you will modify text wrapping later.
   d. Select the shape and change the *Height* to **0.6"** and the *Width* to **1"** [*Drawing Tools Format* tab, *Size* group].
   e. Click the **Shape Fill** button [*Shape Styles* group] and select **Dark Blue, Text 2, Darker 50%**.

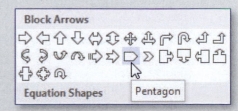

7-83 Select *Pentagon* shape

f. Click the **Shape Outline** button [*Shape Styles* group] and select **No Outline**.

g. Click the **Shape Effects** button [*Shape Styles* group], select **Preset**, and select **Preset 5** (Figure 7-84).

4. Add text to a shape and modify text.
    a. Right-click the shape and select **Add Text** from the context menu. The insertion point displays in the shape.
    b. Type 220, **space** once, and type - (hyphen).
    c. Select the text in the shape, change the font size to **9 pt.**, and apply **bold** and **small caps** formatting.
    d. Change the line spacing to **single (1.0)** and the *After* paragraph spacing to **0 pt**.
    e. Move the shape so it is approximately in the middle of the page horizontally.

5. Copy shapes and modify text in shapes.
    a. Click the edge of the shape to select it.
    b. Press **Ctrl+C** to copy the shape, and press **Ctrl+V** to paste the shape.
    c. Drag the copied shape so it is to the right of the first shape.
    d. Copy and paste the second shape and drag the third shape to the right of the second shape.
    e. Select the text in the second shape and type Your Age, **space** once, and type = to replace the existing text.
    f. Select the text in the third shape and type Predicted Max Heart Rate to replace the existing text.

6. Align and group shapes.
    a. Manually move the shapes horizontally so they are almost touching each other, leaving only a little white space between each. Press the **Ctrl** key and use the **right** or **left** arrow key to move the shapes in small increments.
    b. Click the **Selection Pane** button [*Drawing Tools Format* tab, *Arrange* group] to display the *Selection* pane.
    c. Press the **Ctrl** key and select the three **Pentagon** shapes in the *Selection* pane.
    d. Click the **Align** button [*Drawing Tools Format* tab, *Arrange* group] and select **Align Selected Objects** (if it is not already checked).
    e. Click the **Align** button and select **Align Middle** to vertically center the selected shapes (Figure 7-85).
    f. Click the **Align** button again and select **Distribute Horizontally** to place equal space between the selected shapes.
    g. Click the **Group** button [*Arrange* group] and select **Group** to group the selected shapes.

7. Draw another shape and resize and position it.
    a. Click the **Shapes** button [*Insert* tab, *Illustrations* group] (Figure 7-86).
    b. Select the **Striped Right Arrow** shape in the *Block Arrows* category. Your pointer becomes a drawing crosshair.
    c. Draw a shape approximately **3"** wide over the grouped shapes in your document.
    d. With the new shape selected, change the *Height* to **1.6"** and the *Width* to **3"** [*Drawing Tools Format* tab, *Size* group].
    e. Right-click the new shape, click the **Outline** button on the mini toolbar, and select **No Outline**.

7-84 Select *Preset* shape effect

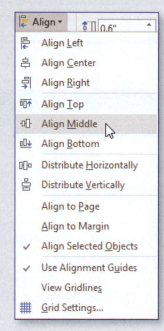

7-85 Align selected shapes

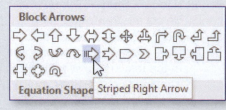

7-86 Select *Striped Right Arrow* shape

f. Click the **Fill** button on the mini toolbar and select **Dark Blue, Text 2, Darker 50%**.

g. Click the **Fill** button on the mini toolbar, select **Gradient**, and select **Linear Right** (Figure 7-87).

8. Order, align, and group shapes.

a. With the striped right arrow shape selected, click the **Send Backward** button [*Drawing Tools Format* tab, *Arrange* group] to order the arrow behind the grouped shapes.

b. Press the **Ctrl** key and click the **Group** and **Striped Right Arrow** in the *Selection* pane to select both objects (Figure 7-88). The number to the right of the object name will vary.

c. Click the **Align** button [*Arrange* group] and select **Align Middle** to vertically center the selected objects.

d. Click the **Align** button again and select **Align Right**.

e. Click the **Group** button [*Arrange* group] and select **Group** to group the selected shapes.

f. Click the **Selection Pane** button to close the *Selection* pane.

9. Adjust text wrapping and the position of grouped shape.

a. With the grouped shape selected, click the **Wrap Text** button [*Drawing Tools Format* tab, *Arrange* group] and select **Tight**.

b. Click the **Position** button [*Arrange* group] and select **More Layout Options** to open the *Layout* dialog box.

c. In the *Horizontal* area, change the **Absolute position** to **5"** to the right of **Page**.

d. In the *Vertical* area, change the **Absolute position** to **1.6"** below **Page**.

e. Click the **Text Wrapping** tab.

f. In the *Distance from text* area, change *Top* and *Bottom* to **0.2"** and *Left* and *Right* to **0"**.

g. Click **OK** to close the *Layout* dialog box.

10. Save and close the document (Figure 7-89).

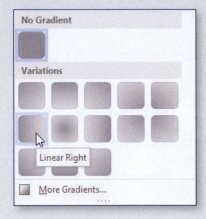

7-87 Select a *Gradient* shape fill

7-88 Select objects in the *Selection* pane

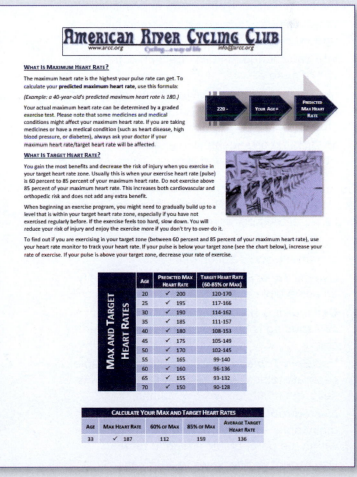

7-89 PP W7-4 completed

Chapter Summary

7.1 Customize table content using sorting, formulas, bullets and numbers, tabs and indents, and text direction (p. W7-392).

- You can convert text to a table or convert a table to text.
- The **Table Tools Layout tab** includes options to customize the layout and contents of tables.
- Sort text in a table in ascending or descending order.
- Use *formulas* in tables to perform calculations.
- The *syntax* of a formula is the structure of a formula. All formulas begin with = and include a combination of *cell references*, *operators*, and *values*.
- The *cell address* is the column letter and row number where a column and row intersect. A cell reference is a cell address used in a formula.
- *Functions*, such as *SUM* and *AVERAGE*, are built-in formulas used in common calculations.
- When values in a table change, manually update the formula.
- You can change the text direction of text in a cell of a table.
- Modify text arrangement in a table using tabs and indents. Press *Ctrl+Tab* to move to a tab stop in the cell of a table.
- Modify text arrangement in a table using bulleted and numbered lists.

7.2 Customize table layouts using table properties, cell margins, the split table feature, nested tables, and a repeated header row (p. W7-401).

- Customize table layout by modifying the size, alignment, and position of a table.
- Use the *Table Properties* dialog box to modify an entire table, rows, columns, or individual cells.
- *Cell margins* place space around text in a cell; *cell spacing* is the amount of space between cells.
- Use *Split Table* to divide a table into multiple separate tables, and use *Split Cells* to divide cells into multiple rows or columns.
- *Nested tables* are tables within tables. The main table is the *parent table*, and tables within the parent table are *child tables*.
- Use *repeat header rows* to automatically display a header row or rows at the top of each page when a table spans more than one page.
- Draw a table using the table drawing tools.

7.3 Enhance a table design with shading, borders, and a table style (p. W7-405).

- Use the *Table Tools Design* tab to customize table style options, **table styles**, and borders and shading.
- Use the **Border Painter** to draw borders on a table.
- Use the **Border Sampler** to select an existing border from a table and use the *Border Painter* to apply the border format to other areas of the table or to a different table.
- Modify an existing table style or create a new table style.
- Built-in tables are available in the **Quick Tables gallery** and are stored as building blocks. You can also create your own **Table building blocks**.

7.4 Modify a picture using advanced layout and picture format options (p. W7-415).

- Modify pictures using the **Picture Tools Format** tab or the **Format Picture** pane.
- Text wrapping controls how text wraps around a picture. Modify a picture's **wrap points** to customize how text wraps around a picture.
- *Alignment guides* and *live layout* help you arrange a picture in a document.
- The *picture anchor* determines the text the picture is anchored to in the document. The picture anchor allows the picture to move with text when a document is modified.
- After inserting a picture into a document, resize the picture using the sizing handles, the *Size* group on the *Picture Tools Format* tab, or the *Layout* dialog box.
- *Aspect ratio* refers to the picture being proportional to its original size when it is resized.
- *Crop* a picture to remove an unwanted portion of a picture.
- Crop a picture to a shape or a specific aspect ratio, or crop a picture to fit or fill a size.
- You can *rotate* a picture in a document.
- *Picture styles* are built-in styles that you can use to apply borders and effects to pictures.
- Customize a picture by applying *picture borders* and *picture effects*.
- *Adjustments* can be made to a picture to apply corrections, change the color, apply artistic effects, compress the file size, change the picture to a different picture, or reset the picture to its original form.

7.5 Create, group, align, and modify a shape in a document (p. W7-426).

- Use the drawing crosshair to draw a shape and customize its size and rotation using the *shape handles*.
- Use *edit points* of the shape to further customize the shape.
- Use built-in *shape styles* to apply *shape fill*, *shape outline*, and *shape effects* to shapes.
- Add text to a shape using the context menu or by drawing a text box on a shape.
- The *Selection pane* displays all objects in your document. Use the *Selection* pane to select and reorder objects.
- The order of shapes determines which shape appears in front of or behind other shapes.
- When working with multiple shapes, align them vertically and horizontally in relation to each other, the page, or the margins.

- *Group* multiple shapes into one object and then resize, align, position, or modify the grouped object as one object.
- *Ungroup* shapes to separate a grouped object into individual objects.

Check for Understanding

The SIMbook for this text (within your SIMnet account) provides the following resources for concept review:

- Multiple choice questions
- Matching exercises
- Short answer questions

Guided Project 7-1

For this project, you modify a document from Sierra Pacific Community College. You convert text to tables, modify tables, apply a table style, modify a style, create a new style, draw and format a shape, and insert and format a picture.
[**Student Learning Outcomes 7.1, 7.2, 7.3, 7.4, 7.5**]

Files Needed: ***EmergencyTelephones-07.docx*** and ***SPCCD-logo-07.png*** *(student data files are available in the* Library *of your SIMnet account)*
Completed Project File Name: ***[your initials] Word 7-1.docx***

Skills Covered in This Project

- Convert text to a table.
- Sort information in a table.
- Modify a table and change text direction.
- Apply a table style.

- Modify a table style.
- Create a table style.
- Apply a custom table style.
- Draw, resize, and modify a shape.
- Insert, resize, and modify a picture.

1. Open the ***EmergencyTelephones-07*** document from your student data files.

2. Save the document as [your initials] Word 7-1.

3. Convert text to a table and sort information in a table.
   a. Select the tabbed text in the "Emergency Phone Locations" section.
   b. Click the **Table** button [*Insert* tab, *Tables* group] and select **Convert Text to Table**. The *Convert Text to Table* dialog box opens (Figure 7-90).

7-90 Convert Text to Table **dialog box**

c. Enter the following settings to convert the text to a table:
   Number of columns: **3**
   AutoFit behavior: **AutoFit to contents**
   Separate text at: **Tabs**
d. Click **OK** to close the dialog box.
e. Select the table and click the **Sort** button [*Table Tools Layout* tab, *Data* group] to open the *Sort* dialog box (Figure 7-91).
f. Select the **Header row** radio button in the *My list has* area.
g. In the *Sort by* area, select **Building** in **Ascending** order, and in the *Then by* area, select **Inside/Outside** in **Ascending** order.
h. Click **OK** to close the dialog box.

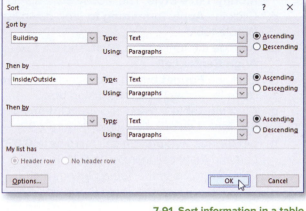

7-91 Sort information in a table

4. Convert text to a table and sort information in the table.
   a. Select the tabbed text in the "Emergency Phone Numbers" section.
   b. Click the **Table** button and select **Convert Text to Table**. The *Convert Text to Table* dialog box opens.
   c. Enter the following settings to convert the text to a table:
      Number of columns: **4**
      AutoFit behavior: **AutoFit to contents**
      Separate text at: **Tabs**
   d. Click **OK** to close the dialog box.
   e. Select the table and click the **Sort** button to open the *Sort* dialog box.
   f. Select the **Header row** radio button.
   g. In the *Sort by* area, select **Emergency Contact** in **Ascending** order.
   h. Click **OK** to close the dialog box.

5. Modify tables and change text direction.
   a. In the first table, insert a column to the left of the first column and merge the cells in the new first column.
   b. Type Emergency Phone Locations in the first column.
   c. Click the **Text Direction** button [*Table Tools Layout* tab, *Alignment* group] two times to change the text direction to vertical from bottom to top.
   d. Click the **Align Center** button [*Table Tools Layout* tab, *Alignment* group].
   e. In the second table, insert a column to the left of the first column and merge the cells in the new first column.
   f. Type Emergency Phone Numbers in the first column.
   g. Click the **Text Direction** button two times to change the text direction to vertical from bottom to top, and click the **Align Center** button. Not all of the text in the first column displays; you will fix this later in the project.

6. Apply a table style and modify the table.
   a. Select the first table and check the **Header Row**, **Banded Rows**, and **First Column** boxes in the *Table Style Options* group [*Table Tools Design* tab]. The other check boxes should not be checked.
   b. Apply the **List Table 4 - Accent 1** table style from the *Table Styles* gallery (Figure 7-92).

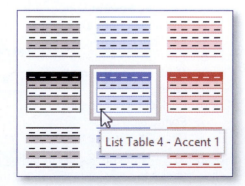

7-92 Apply a table style

c. With the first table selected, click the **More** button in the *Table Styles* gallery [*Table Tools Design* tab] and select **Modify Table Style**. The *Modify Style* dialog box opens.

d. Click the **Apply formatting to** drop-down list and select **Whole table**.

e. Change the font size to **10 pt**. and the text alignment to **Align Center Left**.

f. Click the **Format** button and select **Table Properties** to open the *Table Properties* dialog box.

g. Click the **Table** tab and click the **Options** button to open the *Table Options* dialog box (Figure 7-93).

h. Set the *Top* and *Bottom* cell margins to **0.03"** and the *Left* and *Right* cell margins to **0.1"**.

i. Click **OK** to close the *Table Options* dialog box.

j. Click **OK** to close the *Table Properties* dialog box.

k. Click **OK** to close the *Modify Style* dialog box.

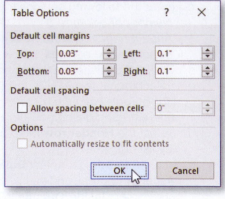

7-93 Change cell margins

7. Save the document.

8. Create a table style.

a. Place the insertion point in the first table.

b. Right-click one of the table styles in the *Table Styles* gallery and select **New Table Style**. The *Create New Style from Formatting* dialog box opens (Figure 7-94).

c. Type SPCCD table in the *Name* area.

d. Click the **Style based on** drop-down list and select **List Table 4 - Accent 1**.

e. Click the **Apply formatting to** drop-down list and select **First column**.

f. Click the **Format** button and select **Font** to open the *Font* dialog box.

g. Change the font size to **11 pt**. and apply **small caps**.

h. Click **OK** to close the *Font* dialog box.

i. Click **OK** to close the *Create New Style from Formatting* dialog box and create the new style.

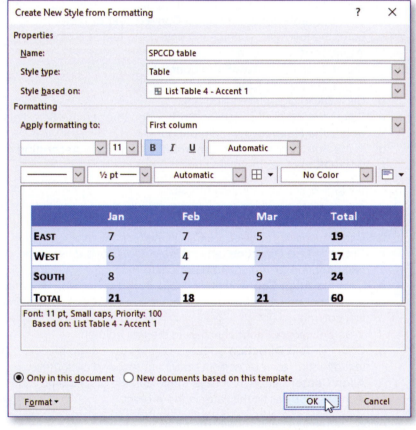

7-94 Create a new table style

9. Apply a custom table style to tables and delete text headings.

a. Select the first table and apply the **SPCCD table** style from the *Custom* area in the *Table Styles* gallery.

b. Select the second table and apply the **SPCCD table** style.

   c. Select and delete the "**Emergency Phone Locations**" and "**Emergency Phone Numbers**" headings above the tables, but don't delete the paragraph marks.

   d. Apply the **Normal** text style to the blank line above each table.

10. Draw a shape around the numbered list and resize, modify, and arrange the shape.

   a. Click the **Shapes** button [*Insert* tab, *Illustrations* group] and select the **Double Bracket** shape in the *Basic Shapes* area (Figure 7-95).

   b. Draw a shape around the numbered list.

   c. Select the shape and change the *Height* to **0.8"** and the *Width* to **4.8"** [*Drawing Tools Format* tab, *Size* group].

   d. Click the **Shape Fill** button [*Drawing Tools Format* tab, *Shape Styles* group] and select **Blue, Accent 1, Lighter 80%**.

   e. Click the **Shape Outline** button, select **Weight**, and select **2¼ pt**.

   f. Click the **Shape Effects** button, select **Shadow**, and select **Offset Diagonal Bottom Right** (Figure 7-96).

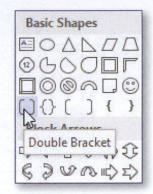

7-95 **Select shape to draw**

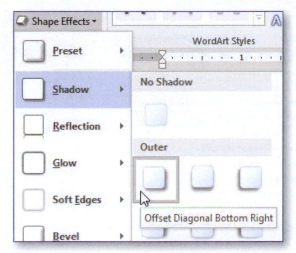

7-96 **Apply a *Shadow* shape effect**

   g. Click the **Send Backward** drop-down list [*Drawing Tools Format* tab, *Arrange* group] and select **Send Behind Text** so the shape appears behind the text.

   h. Use the keyboard arrow keys to position the shape evenly around the numbered list.

11. Insert, resize, position, and modify the company logo.

   a. Place the insertion point at the beginning of the document and insert the ***SPCCD-logo-07*** picture.

   b. Click the **Wrap Text** button [*Picture Tools Format* tab, *Arrange* group] and select **Tight**.

   c. Click the **Size** launcher [*Picture Tools Format* tab, *Size* group] to open the *Layout* dialog box.

   d. On the *Size* tab, change the *Scale* to **120%** of its original height and width.

   e. Click the **Position** tab.

   f. In the *Horizontal* area, set **Absolute position** to **0.3"** *to the right of* **Page**.

   g. In the *Vertical* area, set **Absolute position** to **0.3"** *below* **Page**.

   h. Click **OK** to close the *Layout* dialog box.

   i. With the logo selected, click the **Corrections** button and select **Picture Corrections Options** to open the *Format Picture* pane with *Picture Corrections* area opened.

j. Change the *Brightness* to **25%** and the *Contrast* to **25%**.

k. Click the **X** in the upper right of the *Format Picture* pane to close the pane.

12. Save and close the document (Figure 7-97).

SIERRA PACIFIC
COMMUNITY COLLEGE DISTRICT
7300 COLLEGE AVE
SACRAMENTO, CA 92387
209.658.4466
WWW.SPCCD.EDU

SPCCD—WEST CAMPUS EMERGENCY TELEPHONES

EMERGENCY PHONE [BLUE PHONES] PROCEDURES

1. To use, press the "Help" button. Speak when the light comes on.

2. Stay on the line. You will be connected with the college police.

3. State clearly the nature of the emergency and your location.

	Building	Inside/Outside	Location
EMERGENCY PHONE LOCATIONS	Barton Hall	Inside	Second floor, west end near elevators
	Barton Hall	Outside	Southwest corner
	Cafeteria	Outside	Northeast entrance from parking lot B
	Gymnasium	Inside	Breezeway between offices and gym entrance
	Liberal Arts	Outside	North end of the C wing
	Library	Inside	First floor, stairs
	Library	Outside	Right side of front entrance
	Math & Science	Inside	West wall of biology wing
	Performing Arts	Outside	Near west entrance from Lot B
	Stadium Parking Lot	Outside	Between ticket machines

	Emergency Contact	Days	Hours	Phone Number
EMERGENCY PHONE NUMBERS	College Police	M-Su	7:00 p.m. – 7:00 p.m.	(209) 658-7777
	Emergency Response System	M-Su	Available 24 hrs.	911
	Evening Dean	M-Th	5:00 p.m. – 8:00 p.m.	(209) 658-7700
	Health Center	M-F	7:30 a.m. – 4:00 pm.	(209) 658-2239
	Information Center	M-F	8 a.m. – 5 p.m.	(209) 658-4466
	Site Administrator	M-F	8:00 a.m. – 5:00 p.m.	(209) 658-8501
	Weekend College Coordinator	S	8:00 a.m. – 5:00 p.m.	(209) 658-6500

Emergency Telephones   Sierra Pacific Community College District   Revised July 1, 2017

7-97 Word 7-1 completed

Guided Project 7-2

For this project, you modify an insurance renewal letter from Eva Skaar at Central Sierra Insurance. You create a table and insert text, insert formulas in the table, apply a table style, customize table borders, create a table building block, insert and format a picture, and update formulas.
[Student Learning Outcomes 7.1, 7.2, 7.3, 7.4]

Files Needed: ***InsuranceRenewal-07.docx*** and ***CSI-logo-07.png*** *(student data files are available in the Library of your SIMnet account)*
Completed Project File Name: ***[your initials] Word 7-2.docx***

Skills Covered in This Project

- Insert a table and add text to a table.
- Insert formulas in a table.
- Apply a table style.
- Change cell margins and spacing.

- Change table and text alignment.
- Use the *Border Sampler* and *Border Painter*.
- Save a table as a building block.
- Insert, resize, and modify a picture.
- Update formulas in a table.

1. Open the ***InsuranceRenewal-07*** document from your student data files.

2. Save the document as [your initials] Word 7-2.

3. Insert a table into the document and type text into the table.
   a. Place the insertion point on the blank line below the "The renewal premium is . . ." paragraph and press **Enter**.
   b. Click the **Table** button [*Insert* tab, *Tables* group] and insert a **6×2** table (six columns and two rows) using the *Insert Table* grid.
   c. Type the following information in the table. Press **Enter** to create two-line column headings as shown in the following table:

Policy Description	Premium Basis	Rate per $1,000	Premium	Discount	Discounted Premium
Construction	$325,000	$21			

4. Insert formulas in the table to calculate the premium, discount, and discounted premium.
   a. Place the insertion point in the fourth column of the second row and click the **Formula** button [*Table Tools Layout* tab, *Data* group]. The *Formula* dialog box opens (Figure 7-98).
   b. Delete the existing formula in the *Formula* area and type =B2/1000*C2.
   c. Click the **Number format** drop-down list and select **$#,##0.00;($#,##0.00)**.
   d. Click **OK** to insert the formula.

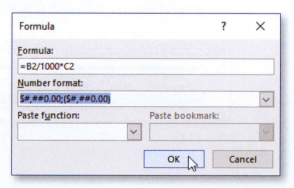

Formula	? X

Formula:
`=B2/1000*C2`

Number format:
`$#,##0.00;($#,##0.00)`

Paste function: Paste bookmark:

OK   Cancel

7-98 *Formula* dialog box

e. Place the insertion point in the fifth column and second row, create the following formula, and use the **$#,##0.00;($#,##0.00)** number format:
=D2*15%

f. Place the insertion point in the sixth column and second row, create the following formula, and use the **$#,##0.00;($#,##0.00)** number format:
=D2−E2

5. Apply a table style and modify the table style.
   a. Select the table and **AutoFit Contents**.
   b. Check the **Header Row**, **Banded Rows**, and **Last Column** boxes in the *Table Style Option* group [*Table Tools Design* tab]. The other boxes should not be checked.
   c. Apply the **Grid Table 2** table style from the *Table Styles* gallery (Figure 7-99).
   d. Click the **Cell Margins** button [*Table Tools Layout* tab, *Alignment* group] to open the *Table Options* dialog box.
   e. Change the *Top* and *Bottom* margins to **0.05"** and the *Left* and *Right* margins to **0.15"** and click **OK** to close the dialog box.
   f. With the table selected, click the **Properties** button [*Table Tools Layout* tab, *Table* group] to open the *Table Properties* dialog box and click the **Table** tab.
   g. Click the **Center** button in the *Alignment* area and click **OK** to close the *Table Properties* dialog box.
   h. Select the first row of the table and change text alignment to **Align Bottom Center** [*Table Tools Layout* tab, *Alignment* group].
   i. Select the second row of the table and change text alignment to **Align Center**.

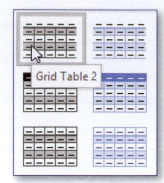

7-99 Apply a table style

6. Use the *Border Sampler* and *Border Painter* to apply borders to the table.
   a. Place the insertion point in the table and click the **View Gridlines** button [*Table Tools Layout* tab, *Table* group] to display table gridlines if they do not already display.
   b. Click the **Border Styles** drop-down list [*Table Tools Design* tab, *Border* group] and select **Border Sampler** from the drop-down list. Your pointer becomes an eyedropper.
   c. Using the eyedropper, click the horizontal border between the first and second rows (Figure 7-100). The eyedropper copies the border style, the *Border Painter* turns on, and the eyedropper becomes a pen.
   d. Use the pen to draw a horizontal border on the table gridline above the first row (Figure 7-101).

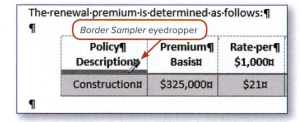

7-100 Use the *Border Sampler*

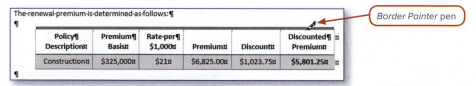

7-101 Use the *Border Painter*

   e. Use the pen to draw a horizontal border on the table gridline below the second row.

f. Click the **Border Painter** button [*Table Tools Design* tab, *Border* group] to turn off the *Border Painter.*

g. Click the **View Gridlines** button [*Table Tools Layout* tab, *Table* group] to turn off table gridlines.

7. Save the table as a building block in the *Quick Tables* gallery.
   a. Select the table.
   b. Click the **Table** button [*Insert* tab, *Tables* group], select **Quick Tables**, and then select **Save Selection to Quick Tables Gallery**. The *Create New Building Block* dialog box opens (Figure 7-102).
   c. Enter the following information to create a new table building block:
      Name: CSI Premium table
      Gallery: **Tables**
      Category: CSI (*create new category*)
      Description: Calculates insurance premium
      Save in: **Building Blocks**
      Options: **Insert content in its own paragraph**
   d. Click **OK** to close the *Create New Building Block* dialog box.

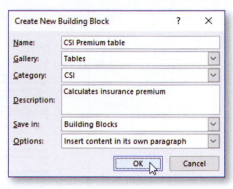

7-102 Create a new building block

8. Insert, resize, position, and modify company logo.
   a. Place the insertion point at the beginning of the document and insert the *CSI-logo-07* picture.
   b. Click the **Wrap Text** button [*Picture Tools Format* tab, *Arrange* group] and select **Square**.
   c. Change the *Width* to **4"** [*Picture Tools Format* tab, *Size* group].
   d. Drag the logo to align with the right and top margins of the document. Use the alignment guides to position the picture.
   e. Click the **Position** button [*Picture Tools Format* tab, *Arrange* group] and select **More Layout Options** to open the *Layout* dialog box.
   f. In the *Horizontal* area, set **Absolute position** to **4.2"** *to the right of* **Page**.
   g. In the *Vertical* area, set **Absolute position** to **0.3"** *below* **Page**.
   h. Click **OK** to close the *Layout* dialog box.
   i. With the logo selected, click the **Color** button [*Picture Tools Format* tab, *Adjust* group] and select **Red, Accent color 2 Dark** in the *Recolor* area (Figure 7-103).

7-103 Change picture color

9. Change a value in the table and update formulas.
   a. Change the "Premium Basis" amount in the table to $350,000.
   b. Right-click the "Premium" amount and select **Update Field** from the context menu to update the formula.
   c. Select the "Discount" amount and press **F9** to update the formula (if you're using a laptop, you might have to press **Fn+F9** to update the formula).
   d. Update the "Discounted Premium" formula using one of the two methods described above.
   e. Select the "Discounted Premium" formula and apply **bold** formatting.

10. Save and close the document (Figure 7-104). If prompted to save changes to building blocks, click **Save**.

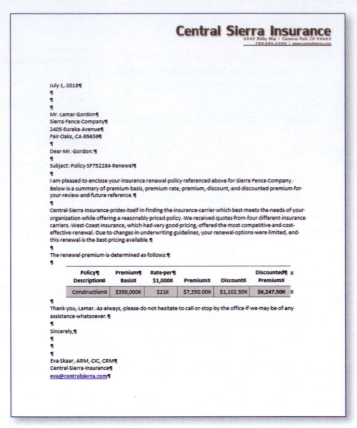

7-104 Word 7-2 completed

Guided Project 7-3

For this project, you modify the Tuscany cycling tour itinerary for the American River Cycling Club. You convert text to a table, modify the table, insert pictures, crop and modify pictures, and insert and modify a shape.
[Student Learning Outcomes 7.1, 7.2, 7.3, 7.4, 7.5]

Files Needed: *CyclingTuscany-07.docx*, *Day1-07.jpg*, *Day2-07.jpg*, *Day3-07.jpg*, *Day4-07.jpg*, *Day5-07.jpg*, *Day6-07.jpg*, *Day7-07.jpg*, and *Day8-07.jpg* (*student data files are available in the* Library *of your SIMnet account*)
Completed Project File Name: *[your initials] Word 7-3.docx*

Skills Covered in This Project

- Convert text to a table.
- Insert a column and merge cells.
- Remove borders from a table.
- Insert and resize a picture.
- Crop a picture to a shape and apply a shadow.
- Align pictures in a table.
- *AutoFit* a table to contents.
- Draw, resize, modify, and arrange a shape.

---

1. Open the **CyclingTuscany-07** document from your student data files.

2. Save the document as [your initials] Word 7-3.

3. Change margins, convert text to a table, and modify the table.
   a. Change the top, bottom, left, and right margins to **0.5"**.
   b. Select the entire document.
   c. Click the **Table** button [*Insert* tab, *Tables* group] and select **Convert Text to Table**. The *Convert Text to Table* dialog box opens (Figure 7-105).
   d. Set *Number of columns* to **1** in the *Table size* area.
   e. Select the **AutoFit to window** radio button in the *AutoFit behavior* area.
   f. Select the **Paragraphs** radio button in the *Separate text at* area.
   g. Click **OK** to close the dialog box and convert the selected text to a table.
   h. With the table selected, click the **Borders** drop-down arrow [*Table Tools Design* tab, *Borders* group] and select **No Border** to remove all of the table borders.
   i. Click the **View Gridlines** button [*Table Tools Layout* tab, *Table* group] to display the table gridlines.

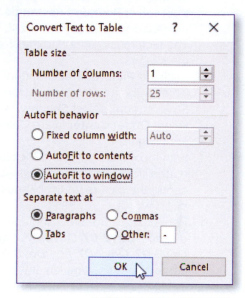

7-105 Convert text to a table

4. Insert a column and merge cells.
   a. Insert a column to the right of the existing column.
   b. Select the entire second column and apply the **Normal** text style.
   c. Select the two cells in the first row and click the **Merge Cells** button [*Table Tools Layout* tab, *Merge* group].
   d. Select the cells in the second column in rows 2–4 and click the **Merge Cells** button. This step merges the cells in the second column to the right of the "Day 1" heading, "Highlights," and description content.
   e. Repeat step 4d to merge the three cells in the second column to the right of each day, highlights, and description cell in the first column. Continue this process through the cells that contain the "Day 8" heading, highlights, and description (Figure 7-106).

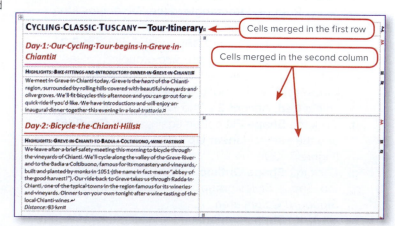

7-106 Cells merged in the first row and second column

5. Insert, resize, crop, modify, and align pictures.
   a. Place the insertion point in the cell in the second column to the right of the "Day 1" content.
   b. Insert the **Day1-07** picture [*Insert* tab, *Illustrations* group] from your student data files.
   c. Change the *Width* of the picture to **2.5"** [*Picture Tools Format* tab, *Size* group]. The height automatically adjusts to maintain the aspect ratio.
   d. Click the **Crop** drop-down arrow [*Picture Tools Format* tab, *Size* group], select **Crop to Shape**, and then select **Rounded Rectangle** in the *Rectangles* area (Figure 7-107). The picture is cropped to the size of the shape.
   e. Click the **Picture Effects** button [*Picture Tools Format* tab, *Picture Styles* group], select **Shadow**, and select **Offset Center** in the *Outer* area (Figure 7-108).

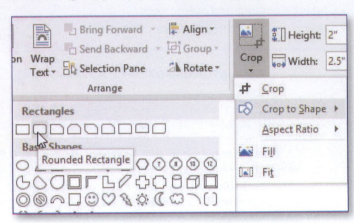

7-107 Crop picture to a shape

   f. With the picture selected, click the **Align Center** button [*Table Tools Layout* tab, *Alignment* group] to center the picture vertically and horizontally in the cell.
   g. Repeat steps 5b–f to insert and format the following pictures: **Day2-07**, **Day3-07**, **Day4-07**, **Day5-07**, **Day6-07**, **Day7-07**, and **Day8-07**. Don't be concerned about pagination at this point; you address this in the next step.

6. *AutoFit* the table to contents.
   a. Select the entire table.
   b. Click the **AutoFit** button [*Table Tools Layout* tab, *Cell Size* group] and select **AutoFit Contents**.

7. Draw, resize, and modify a shape.
   a. Go to the first page of the itinerary and **center** the text in the first row.
   b. Click the **Shapes** button [*Insert* tab, *Illustrations* group] and select **Rounded Rectangle** in the *Rectangles* area.
   c. Draw a shape around the text in the first row of the table.
   d. Change the *Height* to **0.35"** and the *Width* to **5.2"** [*Drawing Tools Format* tab, *Size* group].
   e. With the shape selected, click the **Shape Fill** button [*Drawing Tools Format* tab, *Shape Styles* group] and select **Red, Accent 2** in the *Theme Colors* area.
   f. Click the **Shape Fill** button again, select **Gradient**, and then select **Linear Up** in the *Dark Variations* area (Figure 7-109).
   g. Click the **Shape Outline** button [*Drawing Tools Format* tab, *Shape Styles* group] and select **Green** in the *Standard Colors* area.
   h. Click the **Shape Outline** button again, select **Weight**, and then select **2¼ pt**.

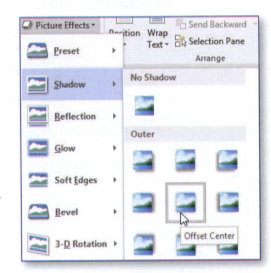

7-108 Apply a *Shadow* picture effect

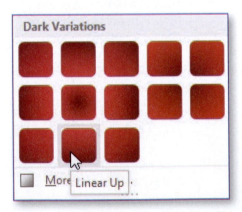

7-109 Apply a *Gradient* shape fill

8. Align and order a shape.
   a. With the shape selected, click the **Align** button [*Drawing Tools Format* tab, *Arrange* group] and select **Align to Margin**. The *Align to Margin* option should have a check to the left of it.
   b. Click the **Align** button again and select **Align Center**.
   c. Click the **Align** button again and select **Align Middle**.
   d. Click the **Send Backward** drop-down arrow [*Drawing Tools Format* tab, *Arrange* group] and select **Send Behind Text**.
   e. Select the text on top of the shape and change the font color to **White, Background 1**.

9. Place your insertion point before "Day 7" on page 2 and press **Ctrl+Enter** to insert a page break.

10. Save and close the document (Figure 7-110).

CYCLING CLASSIC TUSCANY—Tour Itinerary

Day 1: Our Cycling Tour begins in Greve in Chianti

HIGHLIGHTS: BIKE FITTINGS AND INTRODUCTORY DINNER IN GREVE IN CHIANTI

We meet in Greve in Chianti today. Greve is the *heart* of the Chianti region, surrounded by rolling hills covered with beautiful vineyards and olive groves. We'll fit bicycles this afternoon and you can go out for a quick ride if you'd like. We have introductions and will enjoy an inaugural dinner together this evening in a local *trattoria*.

Day 2: Bicycle the Chianti Hills

HIGHLIGHTS: GREVE IN CHIANTI TO BADIA A COLTIBUONO, WINE TASTING

We leave after a brief safety meeting this morning to bicycle through the vineyards of Chianti. We'll cycle along the valley of the Greve River and to the Badia a Coltibuono, famous for its monastery and vineyards, built and planted by monks in 1051 (the name in fact means "abbey of the good harvest!"). Our ride back to Greve takes us through Radda in Chianti, one of the typical towns in the region famous for its wineries and vineyards. Dinner is on your own tonight after a wine tasting of the local Chianti wines.
Distance: 83 km

Day 3: Bicycle Greve in Chianti to San Gimignano

HIGHLIGHTS: CASTELLINA IN CHIANTI AND SAN GIMIGNANO

Our first stop today is Castellina in Chianti, perhaps the most famous town in the region. Stroll around town and/or visit the fortress before beginning a long downhill bike ride out of the Chianti Hills into the valley of the Elsa River ("Val d'Elsa" in Italian). A loop along the river valley and adjacent hills then takes us up to San Gimignano, one of the best preserved medieval villages in Italy. You can pick up picnic supplies in Poggibonsi and enjoy a view back on the Chianti hills under a shade tree while you eat. We'll be in delightful San Gimignano for two nights.
Distance: 70 km

American River Cycling Club | Page 1 of 3

7-110 Word 7-3 completed (page 1 of 3 with table gridlines visible)

Independent Project 7-4

For this project, you modify a memo detailing the weekly expenses of Life's Animal Shelter. You convert text to a table, add formulas, modify the table, insert a picture, crop and modify the picture, and insert and modify a shape.
[Student Learning Outcomes 7.1, 7.2, 7.3, 7.4, 7.5]

Files Needed: ***WeeklyExpenses-07.docx*** and ***LASfamily.jpg*** *(student data files are available in the* Library *of your SIMnet account)*
Completed Project File Name: *[your initials] Word 7-4.docx*

Skills Covered in This Project

- Convert text to a table.
- Insert rows and columns and merge cells.
- Insert *SUM* and *AVERAGE* formulas.
- Create a table style.
- Apply a custom table style to a table.

- Insert, crop, and resize a picture.
- Crop a picture to a shape and apply a border.
- Position a picture in the document.
- Compress a picture.
- Draw, resize, and modify a shape.
- Add text to a shape and format the text.

1. Open the ***WeeklyExpenses-07*** document from your student data files.

2. Save the document as [your initials] Word 7-4.

3. Convert text to a table and modify the table.
   a. Select the lines of tabbed text below the body of the memo, convert the text to a table, and **AutoFit to contents** the table.
   b. Insert one column to the right of the last column.
   c. Insert two rows below the last row.
   d. Type Totals in the last cell in the first row.
   e. Type Totals in the next to the last cell in the first column.
   f. Type Averages in the last cell in the first column.
   g. Insert a row above the first row and merge the cells in this row. If there is a paragraph symbol in this row, delete it.
   h. **Center** and type Life's Animal Shelter Weekly Expenses in the new first row.

4. Insert formulas to add and average expenses.
   a. In rows 3–8 in the last column, use the **SUM** function to add the numbers to the left and apply the **$#,##0.00;($#,##0.00)** number format. You can use "LEFT" as the range for the *SUM* functions (=SUM(LEFT)).
   b. In the next to the last row, use the **SUM** function to add the numbers above and apply the **$#,##0.00;($#,##0.00)** number format. You can use "ABOVE" as the range for the *SUM* functions.
   c. In the last row, use the **AVERAGE** function to calculate the average of the amounts in rows 3–8 above and apply the **$#,##0.00;($#,##0.00)** number format. Type the cell reference range to average (for example =AVERAGE(B3:B8)). Don't include the *Totals* row in the range. The letter reference for the column changes in each of these formulas.

5. Create and customize a new table style.
   a. Create a **New Table Style** and name the new table style LAS Expenses.
   b. Base the new table style on **Grid Table 5 Dark - Accent 3**.

c. Apply formatting to the **Whole table** and change the font size to **10 pt**.

d. Open the *Table Properties* dialog box (*Format* drop-down list) and change the top and bottom cell margins to **0.02"** and the left and right cell margins to **0.1"** (*Hint: select* **Options**).

e. With the *Table Properties* dialog box still open, change the *Alignment* of the *Table* to **Center**.

6. Set the table style options, apply a custom table style, and modify the table format.

a. Select the table and set the *Table Style Options* to include the following: **Header Row**, **Banded Rows**, **First Column**, and **Last Column**.

b. Apply the **LAS Expenses** custom table style to the table.

c. **Center** the text in the first row of the table and change the font size to **12 pt**.

d. Apply **bold** formatting to the second row and the last two rows.

e. Change the alignment of all values and their corresponding column headings to **Align Top Right**.

7. Insert, crop, and modify a picture.

a. Insert the **LASfamily-07** picture at the bottom of the document.

b. Crop the picture so the edges are approximately ¼" from the individuals in the picture (Figure 7-111). Click the top half of the **Crop** button to accept the cropping changes.

7-111 Crop picture

c. Change the picture height to **2"** and maintain aspect ratio.

d. Crop the picture to the **Round Same Side Corner Rectangle** shape in the *Rectangles* area.

e. Apply an **Olive Green, Accent 3** picture border and change the picture border weight to **1 pt**.

f. Apply the **Film Grain** *Artistic Effect* to the picture.

g. Change the *Position* of the picture to **Position in Bottom Center with Square Text Wrapping** (Figure 7-112).

h. Compress the picture so the resolution is **Web (150 ppi)**.

8. Draw a shape, modify the shape, and add text to the shape.

a. Draw a **Wave** shape (*Stars and Banners* category) at the top of the document.

b. Change the height to **1"** and the width to **4"**.

c. Change the shape fill to **Olive Green, Accent 3**.

d. Change the shape fill gradient to **From Center** (*Light Variations* category).

e. Change the shape outline to **Olive Green, Accent 3** and the shape outline weight to **1½ pt**.

f. Apply the **Perspective Diagonal Upper Left** (*Perspective* category) shadow shape effect.

9. Position the shape and add text.

a. Use the *Position* tab in the *Layout* dialog box to change the *Horizontal* **Alignment** to **Centered** *relative to* **Page** and change the *Vertical* **Absolute Position** to **0.2"** below the **Page**.

b. Add text (not a text box) to the shape and type Life's Animal Shelter.

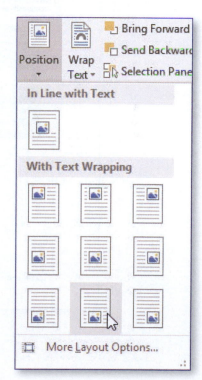

7-112 Position picture in the document

c. Select the text in the shape and apply the following changes:
Change the text color to **Olive Green, Accent 3, Darker 50%**.
Change the font size to **22 pt**.
Apply **bold** *and* **small caps** *formatting.*
Change the *After* paragraph spacing to **0 pt**.

10. Save and close the document (Figure 7-113).

LIFE'S ANIMAL SHELTER

TO: Life's Animal Shelter staff and volunteers

FROM: Kelly Sung, Director of Services

DATE: March 2, 2018

SUBJECT: Weekly Expenses

Thank you for the time you have spent volunteering at Life's Animal Shelter. Our staff and volunteers have contributed countless hours making this shelter a safe environment for animals and providing adoption services for families in our community. You have been a part of hundreds of animal rescues and adoptions over the past year. Families throughout our region are enjoying their new pets thanks to your dedication and work at Life's Animal Shelter.

I'm providing you with our expenses update for the last week. Our operating funds come through donations and pet adoption fees. Thank you for your help in keeping our expenses at a moderate level. Because of you, we are able to offer reasonable adoption fees to animal lovers in our community.

Again, thank you for all of your hard work. Because of you, Life's Animal Shelter valuably serves our community by providing shelter and adoption services.

Life's Animal Shelter Weekly Expenses							
Expenses	Mon	Tue	Wed	Thurs	Fri	Sat/Sun	Totals
Food	340.45	344.05	350.51	340.01	341.48	359.75	$2,076.25
Medicine	525.33	529.31	535.25	524.59	527.99	543.39	$3,185.86
Wages	675.21	580.91	575.88	579.55	680.81	750.05	$3,842.41
Heat	25.75	26.01	28.05	25.03	25.99	62.30	$ 193.13
Equipment	199.03	209.25	198.90	229.05	245.09	351.98	$1,433.30
Electricity	19.45	20.09	21.75	19.02	19.99	48.56	$ 148.86
Totals	$1,785.22	$1,709.62	$1,710.34	$1,717.25	$1,841.35	$2,116.03	$10,879.81
Averages	$ 297.54	$ 284.94	$ 285.06	$ 286.21	$ 306.89	$ 352.67	$1,813.30

Life's Animal Shelter   Weekly Expenses

7-113 Word 7-4 completed

Independent Project 7-5

For this project, you modify a document of Microsoft Outlook shortcuts from Courtyard Medical Plaza. You convert text to a table, include tabs and indents in the table, modify the table, modify a table style, repeat header rows, insert and modify pictures, draw and modify a shape, and align and group objects.
[Student Learning Outcomes 7.1, 7.2, 7.3, 7.4, 7.5]

Files Needed: *OutlookShortcuts-07.docx, CMP-logo-07.png*, and *Email-07.png* (student data files are available in the Library of your SIMnet account)
Completed Project File Name: *[your initials] Word 7-5.docx*

Skills Covered in This Project

- Change margins.
- Convert text to a table.
- Customize tabs and indents in the table.
- Insert a row and merge cells.
- Apply a table style.
- Modify a table style.
- Repeat header rows.
- Insert and resize a picture.
- Align and group pictures.
- Draw, resize, and modify a shape.
- Group selected objects.
- Edit a footer.

1. Open the **OutlookShortcuts-07** document from your student data files.

2. Save the document as [your initials] Word 7-5.

3. Change all margins to **0.5"**.

4. Convert text to a table.
   a. Select all of the text in the document and **Convert Text to Table**.
   b. Apply **AutoFit to window**.
   c. Separate text at **Paragraphs**.
   d. Change the number of columns to **2**.

5. Change tabs and indents in the table.
   a. Select the first column and set a **2.5" left** tab stop with a **broken line leader** (leader 3).
   b. Select the second column, set a **0.25" left indent** (*Paragraph* dialog box), and set a **2.6" left** tab stop with a **broken line leader**.

6. Add a row to the table and add text to the row.
   a. Add a row above the first row and type Microsoft Outlook Shortcuts in the first cell in the new row.
   b. Merge the cells in the new first row and change the *Left* indent to **0"**.

7. Change table style options and apply a table style.
   a. Select the table and set the *Table Style Options* to include a **Header Row** and **Banded Rows**.
   b. Apply the **List Table 4 - Accent 2** table style to the table (Figure 7-114).

7-114 Apply a table style

8. Modify the table style.
   a. Modify the **List Table 4 - Accent 2** table style.
   b. Apply the following formatting changes to the table style to the **Whole table**:
      Change the font size to **9 pt**.
      Change the text alignment to **Align Center Left**.
      Change the top and bottom cell margins to **0.02"** *(Hint: open the* Table Options *dialog box from the* Table Properties *dialog box).* Don't change the left and right cell margins.
   c. Apply the following formatting changes to the table style to the **Header row**:
      Change the font size to **16 pt**.
      Change the text alignment to **Align Center**.
   d. Apply the following formatting change to the table style to the **Odd banded rows**:
      Change the *Fill Color to* **White, Background 1, Darker 5%**.
   e. Click **OK** to accept the changes and modify the table style.

9. Select the first row of the table and **Repeat Header Rows** [*Table Tools Layout* tab, *Data* group]. The header row repeats at the top of each page.

10. Insert and resize pictures.
    a. Place the insertion point at the end of the document and insert the **CMP-logo-07** picture.
    b. Change the text wrapping to **Square** and drag the picture so it is approximately one inch below the table and one inch to the right of the left side of the table.
    c. Place the insertion point at the end of the document and insert the **Email-07** picture.
    d. Change the height of the email picture to **1.5"** and maintain aspect ratio.
    e. Change the text wrapping to **Square** and drag the email picture so it is approximately one inch below the table and one inch to the left of the right side of the table.

11. Align and group the pictures.
    a. Select both pictures.
    b. Use the **Align** drop-down list [*Picture Tools Format* tab, *Arrange* group] to apply the following alignment changes:
       Select **Align to Page**
       Select **Distribute Horizontally**
       Select **Align Selected Objects**
       Select **Align Middle**
    c. **Group** selected objects.

12. Draw and modify a shape.
    a. Draw a **Rounded Rectangle** shape (*Rectangles* category) around the grouped objects.
    b. Change the height to **2"** and the width to **6"**.
    c. Select **Send to Back** so the shape displays behind the pictures.
    d. Select the shape and apply the **Subtle Effect - Black, Dark 1** from the *Shape Styles* gallery (Figure 7-115).

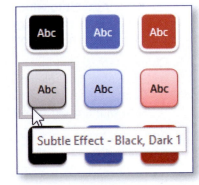

7-115 Apply a shape style

13. Align and group the objects.
    a. Select the shape and the grouped objects inside the shape.
    b. Use the **Align** drop-down list [*Picture Tools Format* tab, *Arrange* group] to apply the following alignment changes:
       Select **Align Selected Objects**
       Select **Align Center**
       Select **Align Middle**.
    c. **Group** selected objects.
    d. Use the *Position* tab in the *Layout* dialog box to change the *Horizontal* **Alignment** to **Centered** *relative to* **Margin** and change the *Vertical* **Absolute Position** to **7.5"** below the **Page**.

14. Edit the footer.
   a. Edit the footer, clear the existing right tab stop (6.5"), and set a **7.5" right** tab stop.
   b. Apply **bold** and **small caps** formatting to all of the text in the footer and then close the footer.

15. Save and close the document (Figure 7-116).

7-116 Word 7-5 completed

Independent Project 7-6

For this project, you create a cycling event calendar for the American River Cycling Club. You insert a table, modify the table structure, apply a table style, format and align text in the table, draw and modify shapes, add text to shapes, align shapes, and insert and modify a picture.
[**Student Learning Outcomes 7.2, 7.3, 7.4, 7.5**]

File Needed: ***ARCC-logo-07.png*** *(student data files are available in the* Library *of your SIMnet account)*
Completed Project File Name: ***[your initials] Word 7-6.docx***

Skills Covered in This Project

- Change margins and page orientation.
- Insert a table.
- Customize row height.
- Merge cells.
- Type and align text in a table.
- Apply a table style.
- Insert and modify a shape.
- Add text to a shape and modify text.
- Align shapes.
- Insert and modify a picture.
- Position a picture in the table.

1. Open a new blank Word document.

2. Save the document as [your initials] Word 7-6.

3. Change the page orientation to **Landscape**.

4. Change the top and bottom margins to **0.75"** and the left and right margins to **0.5"**. If you receive an error message about the margin settings, click **Ignore**.

5. Insert a table, modify table structure, and add text.
   a. Insert a **7×7** table.
   b. Change the row height to **1"** on all of the rows.
   c. Merge the cells in the first row and type June.
   d. Change the row height of the second row to **0.3"**
   e. Type the days of the week beginning with Sunday in the cells in the second row.
   f. Beginning in the *Wednesday* column in the third row, type the day numbers beginning with 1. June has 30 days.

6. Set the table style options and apply a table style.
   a. Select the table and set the *Table Style Options* to include a **Header Row** and **Banded Rows**. All other options should be deselected.
   b. Apply the **Grid Table 4 - Accent 6** table style to the table.

7. Format text and text alignment in the table.
   a. Change the font size of the text in the first row to **72 pt**.
   b. Select the second row, change the font size to **14 pt.**, apply **bold** and **small caps** formatting, and change the text alignment to **Align Center** (center vertically and horizontally).
   c. Select rows 3–7, apply **bold** formatting, and change alignment to **Align Top Right**.

8. Add shapes to the table.
   a. Draw a **Folded Corner** shape (*Basic Shapes* category) in the *Monday, June 6* cell.
   b. Change the height to **0.8"** and the width to **1"**.
   c. Apply the **Subtle Effect - Green, Accent 6** shape style (Figure 7-117).
   d. Add text to the shape (not a text box), type Morning Ride, press **Enter**, and type 6-8 a.m. You might not be able to see all of the text you type; you format the text in the next step.
   e. Select the text in the shape (**Ctrl+A**), change the font size to **10 pt.**, apply **bold** formatting, and change the after paragraph spacing to **0 pt**.
   f. Copy the shape and paste it in the three cells below.
   g. Select the four shapes and, using the **Align** drop-down list, select **Align to Margin**, select **Align Left**, and select **Align Top**.

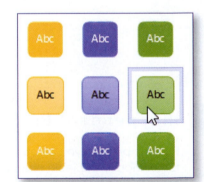

7-117 Apply a shape style

9. Add shapes to the table.
   a. Draw a **Plaque** shape (*Basic Shapes* category) in the *Wednesday, June 1* cell.
   b. Change the height to **0.8"** and the width to **1"**.
   c. Apply the **Subtle Effect - Blue, Accent 1** shape style.
   d. Add text to the shape, type River Ride, press **Enter**, and then type 6-8 p.m.
   e. Select the text in the shape (**Ctrl+A**), change the font size to **10 pt.**, apply **bold** formatting, and change the after paragraph spacing to **0 pt**.
   f. Copy the shape and paste it in the four cells below.
   g. Select the five shapes, select **Align to Margin**, select **Align Left**, and then select **Align Top**.

10. Add shapes to the table.
   a. Draw a **Pentagon** shape (*Block Arrows* category) in the *Friday, June 3* cell.
   b. Change the height to **0.8"** and the width to **1"**.
   c. Apply the **Subtle Effect - Black, Dark 1** shape style.
   d. Add text to the shape, type Time Trial, press **Enter**, and then type 5-6 p.m.
   e. Select the text in the shape (**Ctrl+A**), change the font size to **10 pt.**, apply **bold** formatting, and change the after paragraph spacing to **0 pt**.
   f. Copy the shape and paste it in the three cells below.
   g. Select the four shapes, select **Align to Margin**, select **Align Left**, and then select **Align Top**.

11. Add shapes to the table.
   a. Draw a **Flowchart: Document** shape (*Flowchart* category) in the *Saturday, June 4* cell.
   b. Change the height to **0.8"** and the width to **1"**.
   c. Apply the **Subtle Effect - Gold, Accent 4** shape style.
   d. Add text to the shape, type Hilly Ride, press **Enter**, and then type 8-11 a.m.
   e. Select the text in the shape (**Ctrl+A**), change the font size to **10 pt.**, apply **bold** formatting, and change the after paragraph spacing to **0 pt**.
   f. Copy the shape and paste it in the three cells below.
   g. Select the four shapes, select **Align to Margin**, select **Align Left**, and then select **Align Top**.

12. Insert a picture into the table.
   a. Insert the ***ARCC-logo-07*** picture in the first row.
   b. Change the height to **0.75"** and maintain the aspect ratio.
   c. Change the text wrapping to **In Front of Text**.
   d. Use the **Picture Effects** drop-down list to apply an **Offset Top** effect (*Shadow, Outer* category).
   e. Use the *Layout* dialog to position the picture using the following settings:

      Horizontal **Alignment** *to* **Right** *relative to* **Margin**

      Vertical **Absolute position 0.3"** *below* **Margin**
   f. Select the first row of the table and change the *Font Color* to **Green, Accent 6, Lighter 80%**.

13. Save and close the document (Figure 7-118).

7-118 Word 7-6 completed

Improve It Project 7-7

For this project, you improve a buyer escrow checklist from Emma Cavalli at Placer Hills Real Estate. You split a table, convert a table to text, use bullets in the table, create a table style, apply a custom table style, and insert and modify pictures.
[**Student Learning Outcomes 7.1, 7.2, 7.3, 7.4**]

Files Needed: ***BuyerEscrowChecklist-07.docx, PHRE-logo-07.png***, and ***Checkmark-07.png*** *(student data files are available in the* Library *of your SIMnet account)*
Completed Project File Name: *[your initials] Word 7-7.docx*

Skills Covered in This Project

- Split a table.
- Convert a table to text.
- Modify tab settings.
- Insert columns and merge cells.
- Change text direction.
- *AutoFit* a table to contents.
- Create a table style.
- Apply a custom table style.
- Modify column widths.
- Apply bullets to text in a table.
- Modify indents in a table.
- Insert and modify a picture.
- Group, align, and position pictures.

1. Open the **BuyerEscrowChecklist-07** document from your student data files.

2. Save the document as [your initials] Word 7-7.

3. Split the table at the "Task" row. "Task" should be in the first row of the second table.

4. Select the first table and convert the table to text (**Convert to Text** [*Table Tools Layout* tab, *Data* group]) using paragraph marks to separate text.

5. Modify the text at the beginning of the document.
   a. Select the first five lines of text and change the font size to **12 pt**.
   b. Change the after paragraph spacing to **18 pt**.
   c. On the selected lines of text, clear the existing tab stop and set a **4.75" right** tab stop with a **solid underline leader** (4).

6. In the table, add one column to the left of the first column and three columns to the right of the last column.

7. Merge cells, add text, and change text direction.
   a. Merge the cells in the first column. If paragraph symbols display in this column, delete them.
   b. Type BUYER ESCROW CHECKLIST in the first column.
   c. Change the text direction to vertical from bottom to top.
   d. Select the first column and change the font size to **28 pt**.

8. Add text to the table and *AutoFit* the table.
   a. Type Date in the first row of the third column, press **Enter**, and then type Completed.
   b. Type Initials in the first row of the fourth column.
   c. Type Notes in the first row of the fifth column.
   d. Apply **AutoFit Contents**.

9. Create a table style.
   a. Create a table style named PHRE that is based on the **Grid Table 5 Dark** table style.
   b. Apply the following changes to the **Whole table** in the new table style:
      Change the text alignment to **Align Center Left**.
      Change the top and bottom cell margins to **0.07"**.
      Change the left and right cell margins to **0.1"**.
      Change the cell spacing to **0.04"**.
      Change the table alignment to **Center**.

10. Set table style options and apply a table style.
    a. Select the table and set the *Table Style Options* to include a **Header Row** and **First Column**. All other options should be deselected.
    b. Apply the **PHRE** custom table style to the table.

11. Change the column widths in the table.
    a. Change the second column width to **3"**.
    b. Change the third column width to **1"**.
    c. Change the fifth column width to **1.2"**.

12. Apply bullets and change indents in the text in the table.
    a. Apply an open square bullet (*Wingdings*, character code 113) to the text in the second column below the column heading.
    b. Change the left indent of the bulleted list to **0"**.
13. Change font size and text alignment in the table.
    a. Select the first column and change the text alignment of the *First column* to **Align Center**.
    b. Select the column headings in the first row (don't include the first column), change the font size to **12 pt**., and change the text alignment to **Align Bottom Center**.
14. Delete the blank line between the tabbed text and the table.
15. Insert and modify pictures.
    a. Insert the ***PHRE-logo-07*** picture at the top of the document.
    b. Change the text wrapping to **Tight** and drag the picture to the right of the tab leaders.
    c. Apply the **Offset Diagonal Bottom Right** shadow picture effect (*Outer* category).
    d. Insert the ***Checkmark-07*** picture at the top of the document.
    e. Change the height to **1.5"** and maintain the aspect ratio.
    f. Change the text wrapping to **Tight** and drag the picture to the right of the tab leaders and below the logo picture.
    g. Apply the **Offset Diagonal Bottom Right** shadow picture effect (*Outer* category).
    h. Apply the **Pencil Grayscale** artistic effect.
16. Align and group pictures.
    a. Select both pictures.
    b. Using the *Align* drop-down list, select **Align Selected Objects** and select **Align Center**.
    c. Group the two pictures.
    d. Position the grouped object using the following settings:
       Horizontal **Absolute position 6.2"** *to* **Right** *to the right of* **Page**.
       Vertical **Absolute position 0.3"** *below* **Page**
17. Save and close the document (Figure 7-119).

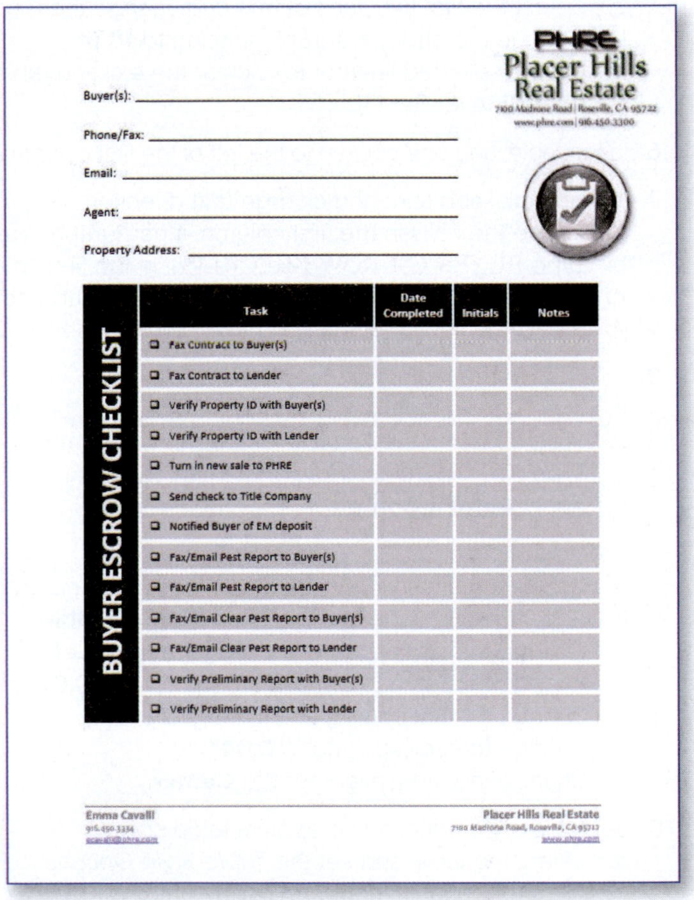

PHRE
Placer Hills Real Estate
7100 Madrone Road | Roseville, CA 95722
www.phre.com | 916-450-3300

Buyer(s): ______________________________

Phone/Fax: ______________________________

Email: ______________________________

Agent: ______________________________

Property Address: ______________________________

	Task	Date Completed	Initials	Notes
BUYER ESCROW CHECKLIST	❑ Fax Contract to Buyer(s)			
	❑ Fax Contract to Lender			
	❑ Verify Property ID with Buyer(s)			
	❑ Verify Property ID with Lender			
	❑ Turn in new sale to PHRE			
	❑ Send check to Title Company			
	❑ Notified Buyer of EM deposit			
	❑ Fax/Email Pest Report to Buyer(s)			
	❑ Fax/Email Pest Report to Lender			
	❑ Fax/Email Clear Pest Report to Buyer(s)			
	❑ Fax/Email Clear Pest Report to Lender			
	❑ Verify Preliminary Report with Buyer(s)			
	❑ Verify Preliminary Report with Lender			

Emma Cavalli
916-450-3334
ecavalli@phre.com

Placer Hills Real Estate
7100 Madrone Road, Roseville, CA 95722
www.phre.com

7-119 Word 7-7 completed

Challenge Project 7-8

We all look forward to vacations, and planning a vacation builds excitement and expectations. A travel itinerary helps you plan and estimate a budget for your vacation. Create a travel itinerary and budget for an upcoming vacation, a trip, or your dream vacation.
[Student Learning Outcomes 7.1, 7.2, 7.3, 7.4, 7.5]

File Needed: None
Completed Project File Name: *[your initials] Word 7-8.docx*

Create a new blank document and save it as [your initials] Word 7-8.

A travel itinerary and budget can include, but is not limited to, the following elements:

- Overall travel schedule
- Daily list of activities
- Description of activities
- To-do list
- Travel and accommodation information
- Pictures of destinations and hotels
- Estimated expenses

Create a travel itinerary and budget with tables, pictures, and shapes. Modify your document according to the following guidelines:

- Set up your itinerary and budget in table format.
- Merge and split cells as needed.
- Apply and modify a table style or create a table style.
- Modify borders, shading, alignment, cell margins and spacing, and text direction.
- Use formulas as desired to calculate totals.
- Include bulleted and/or numbered lists.
- Insert pictures of destinations or places to visit.
- Crop, resize, modify, and align pictures.
- Insert shapes around objects or text, or add text to shapes.
- Resize, modify, and position shapes.

Challenge Project 7-9

Most organizations prepare a calendar of events, or you might keep a personal calendar of upcoming assignments, tests, and projects for your classes. For this project, you create a monthly or weekly calendar of upcoming events for an organization you belong to or are familiar with, such as a non-profit organization, a professional organization, a student group, a school or work project team, a religious organization, or a sports team. Or, you can create a calendar for school work that is due in the next month.
[Student Learning Outcomes 7.1, 7.2, 7.3, 7.4, 7.5]

File Needed: None
Completed Project File Name: *[your initials] Word 7-9.docx*

Create a new blank document and save it as [your initials] Word 7-9.

Using tables, pictures, and shapes, create a calendar of events for one of your organizations or upcoming class work. Modify your document according to the following guidelines:

- Set up your events calendar in table format.
- Merge and split cells as needed.
- Resize columns and rows as needed.
- Add and align text.
- Apply and modify a table style or create a table style.
- Modify borders, shading, alignment, cell margins and spacing, and text direction.
- Insert shapes around objects or text, or add text to shapes.
- Resize, modify, and position shapes.
- Insert an organization logo picture, picture of team members, or other appropriate pictures.
- Crop, resize, modify, and align pictures.

Challenge Project 7-10

Searching for a new car, motorcycle, bicycle, cell phone, cell phone plan, or any other expensive item can be a time-consuming task. When shopping for these high-cost items, researching product features and costs provides the information you need in order to make a decision. Create a product feature and cost comparison table to organize your research about a future purchase.
[Student Learning Outcomes 7.1, 7.2, 7.3, 7.4, 7.5]

File Needed: None
Completed Project File Name: *[your initials] Word 7-10.docx*

Create a new blank document and save it as [your initials] Word 7-10.

Your product feature and cost analysis can include, but is not limited to, the following elements:

- Product names
- Product features

- List of pros and cons for each product
- Cost comparison
- Cost of additional features
- Pictures of products

Create a document comparing the features and costs of different versions of a product you plan to purchase in the future. Include at least three comparable products. Modify your document according to the following guidelines:

- Set up your product comparison in table format.
- Merge and split cells as needed.
- Apply and modify a table style or create a table style.
- Modify borders, shading, alignment, cell margins and spacing, and text direction.
- Use formulas as needed to calculate totals.
- Include bulleted and/or numbered lists.
- Insert pictures of products you plan to purchase.
- Crop, resize, modify, and align pictures.
- Insert shapes around objects or text, or add text to shapes.
- Resize, modify, and position shapes.

CHAPTER 8

Using Desktop Publishing and Graphic Features

CHAPTER OVERVIEW

In addition to being the leading word processing software on personal and business computers, Microsoft Word is also a powerful desktop publishing application. You can use Word to create professional-looking newsletters, brochures, advertisements, invitations, and a variety of documents that incorporate pictures, tables, columns, charts, text boxes, and other desktop publishing features. In this chapter, you learn about available desktop publishing features including, text boxes, custom themes, *SmartArt*, charts, and indexes.

STUDENT LEARNING OUTCOMES (SLOs)

After completing this chapter, you will be able to:

SLO 8.1 Apply desktop publishing features to a Word document (p. W8-463).

SLO 8.2 Customize an existing theme and create a custom theme (p. W8-472).

SLO 8.3 Insert and customize a built-in text box and create a custom text box (p. W8-473).

SLO 8.4 Insert and customize a *SmartArt* graphic (p. W8-479).

SLO 8.5 Insert and customize a chart (p. W8-484).

SLO 8.6 Mark index entries and insert and customize an index page (p. W8-493).

CASE STUDY

In the Pause & Practice projects in this chapter, you use desktop publishing features to enhance a handout given to the students in a freshman composition course at Sierra Pacific Community College District.

Pause & Practice 8-1: Enhance a document using custom page settings, a drop cap, page color, a watermark, and hyphenation.

Pause & Practice 8-2: Use and customize a built-in text box, create a text box building block, draw and customize a text box, and modify an existing theme to create a custom document theme.

Pause & Practice 8-3: Insert and modify a *SmartArt* graphic and a chart.

Pause & Practice 8-4: Mark index entries in a document and create and customize an index page.

Using Desktop Publishing Features

Word's desktop publishing features allow you to create engaging documents. For example, you can apply custom page settings, insert a drop cap, use page color, insert and customize a watermark, capture and insert a screenshot, use line numbering, and apply hyphenation to text. By moderately incorporating desktop publishing visual elements, you improve document readability and layout without overwhelming readers with too many formatting bells and whistles.

Custom Page Settings

In addition to changing margins, page orientation, and page size, you can apply a variety of custom page settings to multiple-page documents. ***Gutter margins*** and ***mirror margins*** are options for multi-page documents that you plan to print and bind on the left, right, or top. You can also change page settings to create ***2 pages per sheet*** or apply ***book fold*** to create a booklet. The following table lists and describes custom page settings:

Custom Page Settings

Page Setting	Description
Gutter margins	Use to add extra margin space to the left or top of the document when you are planning to bind a document at the left or top. Gutter margins ensure text on bound edges displays correctly and margin spacing is even on multiple-page bound documents.
Mirror margins	Use on multi-page documents that print on both sides and have a binding at the left or right. You can use a gutter margin with mirror margins to ensure you have additional space for binding the document.
2 pages per sheet	Use to split a page horizontally into two pages.
Book fold	Use to split a page vertically into two pages. Use book fold to create a booklet, menu, or invitation. When you use book fold, the page orientation of your document automatically changes to landscape.

▶ HOW TO: Apply Custom Page Settings

1. Click the **Margins** button [*Layout* tab, *Page Setup* group].
2. Select **Custom Margins** to open the *Page Setup* dialog box (Figure 8-1).
3. Change the **Gutter margin** setting and change the **Gutter position** to *Left* or *Top* in the *Margins* area on the *Margins* tab.
4. Click the **Multiple pages** drop-down list and select from the options.
   - You can adjust page gutter margins after you select a *Multiple pages* option.
   - The *Preview* area displays how your document will appear.
5. Click the **Apply to** drop-down list and select the part of the document where you want to apply the settings.
   - Your options include *Whole document, This point forward*, or *Selected text*.
   - If you select *This point forward* or *Selected text*, Word inserts a section break to control page formatting.
6. Click **OK** to close the *Page Setup* dialog box.

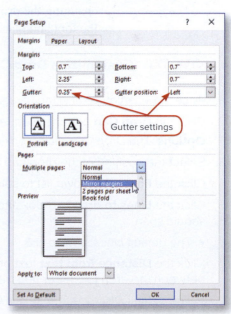

8-1 *Page Setup* dialog box

Drop Caps

A *drop cap* emphasizes the first letter of a paragraph (Figure 8-2). When you use this feature, the first letter of the paragraph becomes a graphic object, and you can customize its appearance and placement. You can also apply the drop cap format to the entire first word (not just the first letter) at the beginning of a paragraph.

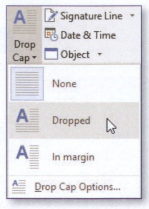

8-2 Drop cap applied to the first letter of a paragraph

▶ HOW TO: Insert a Drop Cap

1. Place the insertion point in the paragraph where you want the drop cap to appear.
   - By default, drop cap applies to the first letter of a paragraph.
   - Alternatively, select the first word of the paragraph and apply drop cap formatting to the first word of the paragraph rather than just the first letter.
2. Click the **Drop Cap** button [*Insert* tab, *Text* group] to display the list of drop cap choices (Figure 8-3).
3. Select a drop cap to apply to the first letter of the paragraph.
   - To remove an existing drop cap, click the **Drop Cap** button and select **None** from the drop-down list.

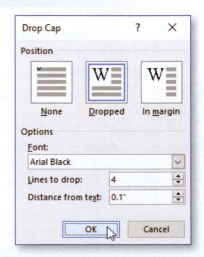

8-3 *Drop Cap* drop-down list

Drop Cap Options

After applying drop cap formatting to a letter or word in a paragraph, you can customize its appearance. Format the drop cap letter or word the same way you format text in a document by changing the drop cap's font, size, color, and style. Use the *Drop Cap dialog box* to customize the font and placement of the drop cap.

▶ HOW TO: Customize a Drop Cap

1. Place the insertion point in the paragraph with the drop cap or select the drop cap.
2. Click the **Drop Cap** button [*Insert* tab, *Text* group] and select **Drop Cap Options**. The *Drop Cap* dialog box opens (Figure 8-4).
3. Select the position of the drop cap in the *Position* area.
4. Click the **Font** drop-down list to select a different font for the drop cap.
5. Click the **Lines to drop** text box and select the number of lines the drop cap should span.
   - The default *Lines to drop* is *3*.
6. Click the **Distance from text** text box and change the amount of space between the drop cap letter and the surrounding text.
   - The default *Distance from text* is 0".
7. Click **OK** to close the *Drop Cap* dialog box.

8-4 *Drop Cap* dialog box

Page Color

By default, a Word document has no page color. In previous chapters, you used shading and fill colors with borders, shapes, and other graphic objects. You can similarly change the **page color** of a document. When you apply a page color, it applies to the entire document. Select a page color from theme colors or standard colors, or apply a gradient, texture, pattern, or picture as the background of a document.

> **HOW TO: Apply and Customize Page Color**
>
> 1. Click the **Page Color** button [*Design* tab, *Page Background* group] to display the drop-down list of options (Figure 8-5).
> 2. Select from *Theme Colors* or *Standard Colors* to apply a page color.
> 3. Click the **More Colors** button to open the *Colors* dialog box to select from a variety of *Standard* or *Custom* colors.
> 4. Click the **Fill Effects** button to open the *Fill Effects* dialog box. Apply a *Gradient*, *Texture*, *Pattern*, or *Picture* as a page background for the document as desired (Figure 8-6).
>   - Click the **Gradient** tab to select gradient *Colors*, *Transparency*, and *Shading* styles.
>   - Click the **Texture** tab to select a *Texture* to apply as the page background.
>   - Click the **Pattern** tab to select a *Pattern* and change the *Foreground* and *Background* pattern colors.
>   - Click the **Picture** tab to select a picture to use as the page background.
> 5. Click **OK** to close the *Fill Effects* dialog box and apply the fill as the page background.
>   - Remove the page color by clicking the **Page Color** drop-down list and selecting **No Color**.

8-5 *Page Color* drop-down list

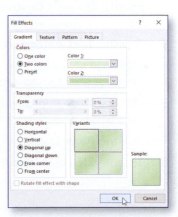

8-6 *Fill Effects* dialog box

Watermarks

A **watermark** is text or a picture that appears behind the text on every page in a document (Figure 8-7). For example, you might want the words "Draft" or "Sample" to appear behind the text as a notation for readers. A watermark text or picture does not affect the placement or wrapping of text or other objects in your document. Watermarks are typically in a lighter color than the other text in your

8-7 **Watermark applied to a document**

document and semitransparent so as not to affect the readability of the document. You can insert a built-in watermark or a custom watermark.

Built-In Watermarks

Word provides a variety of built-in watermarks to insert into your documents easily and quickly. Built-in watermarks display in categories on the *Watermark* drop-down list (Figure 8-8). Click the **Watermark** button in the *Page Background* group on the *Design* tab and select the built-in watermark to insert into your document.

Custom Watermarks

Alternatively, you can create your own custom watermark. A custom watermark can be text or a picture. You can change the font, size, color, and layout of the custom watermark.

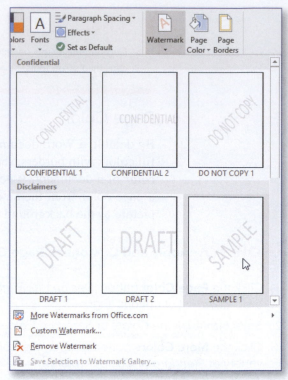

8-8 Insert a built-in watermark

▶ **HOW TO:** Insert a Custom Watermark

1. Click the **Watermark** button [*Design* tab, *Page Background* group] and select **Custom Watermark**. The *Printed Watermark* dialog box opens (Figure 8-9).

2. Click the **Text watermark** radio button.
   - You can also select the *Picture watermark* radio button and choose a picture to apply as a watermark.

3. Click the **Text** drop-down list and select from the text options in the list or type custom text for the watermark.

4. Click the **Font** drop-down list to select the font.

5. Click the **Size** drop-down list to select the font size.
   - *Auto* is the default font size, but you can choose a specific font size.

6. Click the **Color** drop-down list to select a color.
   - By default, the *Semitransparent* check box is selected. Deselect this check box to darken the watermark.

7. Select the **Diagonal** or **Horizontal** radio button in the *Layout* area.

8. Click **Apply** to apply the watermark to your document.

9. Click **Close** to close the dialog box.

8-9 *Printed Watermark* dialog box

> **MORE INFO**
>
> You can also use the *Printed Watermark* dialog box to customize a built-in watermark.

Create a Watermark Building Block

Built-in watermarks are building blocks stored in the *Watermark* gallery. You can create your own **watermark building block** similar to how you create a *Quick Part* or *Footer* building block. For example, you can save a club or company logo or a company name as a watermark building block to use in other documents.

If you insert text or a picture as a custom watermark, you can select and save it in the *Watermark* building block gallery. Open the header or footer to select an existing watermark in a document.

▶ HOW TO: Create a Watermark Building Block

1. After you insert a custom watermark (see *How To: Insert a Custom Watermark*), right-click the header or footer and select **Edit Header** or **Edit Footer** to open the header or footer.

2. Select the watermark in the document.

3. Click the **Watermark** button [*Design* tab, *Page Background* group] and select **Save Selection to Watermark Gallery**. The *Create New Building Block* dialog box opens (Figure 8-10).

4. Type the *Name* and *Description* for your building block.

5. Click the **Category** drop-down list and select a category or create a new category.

6. Click the **Save in** drop-down list and select the location to save the building block.

7. Click **OK** to create the watermark building block.

8. Click the **Close Header and Footer** button [*Header & Footer Tools Design* tab, *Close* group].

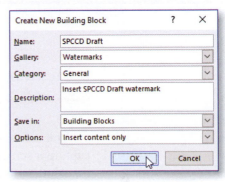

8-10 Create watermark building block

Remove a Watermark

A watermark is typically used on a sample or draft document, and when the review process is complete, you can remove the watermark. To remove a watermark, click the **Watermark** button [*Design* tab, *Page Background* group] and select **Remove Watermark** (Figure 8-11). You can also remove a watermark by selecting the **No watermark** radio button in the *Printed Watermark* dialog box (see Figure 8-9).

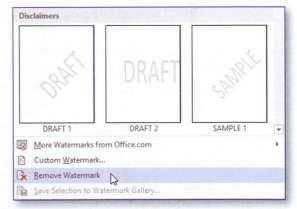

8-11 Remove a watermark

Screenshots

In Chapter 7, you inserted and customized pictures in documents. A similarly useful Word feature is **Screenshot**. Screenshot allows you to capture an open window on your computer such as an open document or an Internet browser window. This screenshot becomes a picture that displays in your document, and you can resize, crop, arrange, and customize the screenshot.

1. Open the file or Internet browser window that you want to use as a screenshot in your document.

2. Open the Word document and place your insertion point where you will insert the screenshot.

3. Click the **Screenshot** button [*Insert* tab, *Illustrations* group] to display the drop-down list of available windows (Figure 8-12).

4. Select from the *Available Windows* to capture as a screenshot.

   - The screenshot displays as a picture in your document.
   - Resize, move, and customize the picture as desired.

8-12 **Select window to capture as a screenshot**

▶ **MORE INFO**

To save a picture that is in your document, right-click the picture and select **Save as Picture**.

You can also capture a portion of a window, which is called a ***screen clipping***. When you capture a screen clipping, your pointer becomes a selection crosshair to select the portion of the window to capture.

▶ **HOW TO:** Insert a Screen Clipping

1. Open the window that contains the content you want to capture.

2. Place your insertion point in the Word document at the location to insert the screen clipping.

3. Click the **Screenshot** button [*Insert* tab, *Illustrations* group] and select **Screen Clipping** from the drop-down list.

   - The window behind the Word document opens, and your pointer becomes a selection crosshair.

4. Click and drag over the region to capture as a screen clipping (Figure 8-13).

5. Release the pointer to capture the screen clipping.

   - The screen clipping displays as a picture in your document.
   - Resize, move, and customize the picture as desired.

TUESDAY, JANUARY 31

Conquer Your Inbox and E-mail Etiquette

After settling back into a routine in this new year, it's now a good time to think about how to more effectively manage that overflowing e-mail *Inbox* of yours. For most of us, the volume of e-mails received each day (both personal and business-related) can be overwhelming. Below are some tips to help you control your *Inbox* rather than letting it control you.

Inbox Management Tips

- **Read**: Select a couple chunks of time throughout your day to dedicate to reading your e-mails. After reading each e-mail, take action on it. The content and context of the message will determine what to do with it: *reply*, *reorganize*, and/or *remove*.
- **Reply**: Not all e-mails need a response, but to those that do, try to respond to as quickly as possible. This will not only make you more responsive to others, but also complete a task that will most likely have to be done at some point in the future.
- **Reorganize**: Decide whether or not a message needs to be kept and then use one or more the of following Outlook features to keep your e-mail organized.
   - *Follow Up Flags*: Flag a message requiring further action. Click here for more about follow up flags.

Selection crosshair   8-13 **Select screen clipping**

Hyphenation

Hyphenation is a desktop publishing feature used to divide words at the right margin of a column or page to balance line endings and use the space on each page more effectively. Word can automatically hyphenate your document, or you can manually choose the placement of the hyphen at the end of a line of text. Hyphenation is typically used when using multiple columns in a document. The following are basic hyphenation guidelines:

- Divide words between syllables.
- Don't hyphenate one-syllable words.
- Leave at least two letters and the hyphen at the end of a line and three letters on the carryover line.
- Don't divide proper nouns or proper adjectives.

Word applies these hyphenation guidelines when you automatically hyphenate text, but it is a good idea to check your document for proper hyphenation.

▶**HOW TO:** Automatically Hyphenate Text in a Document

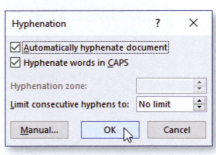

8-14 *Hyphenation* dialog box

1. Place the insertion point at the beginning of the document.
2. Click the **Hyphenation** button [*Layout* tab, *Page Setup* group].
3. Select **Automatic** to automatically hyphenate the entire document.
   - Click **Hyphenation Options** from the *Hyphenation* drop-down list to open the *Hyphenation* dialog box where you customize hyphenation settings (Figure 8-14).
   - To remove hyphenation, click the **Hyphenation** button and select **None**.

Line Numbers

When reviewing or editing a long document with a team or in a meeting, it can be time consuming to locate specific text in the document and ensure everyone is viewing the same information. *Line numbers* display at the left side of each line and are a helpful reference when editing and reviewing a long document.

▶**HOW TO:** Turn on Line Numbering

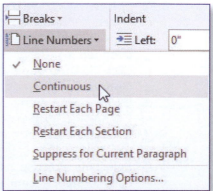

8-15 Insert line numbers

1. Click the **Line Numbers** button [*Layout* tab, *Page Setup* group].
2. Select from the drop-down list of options (Figure 8-15).
   - *Continuous*: Numbers lines consecutively throughout the document.
   - *Restart Each Page*: Numbers the lines on each page beginning with 1 and restarts each page with 1.
   - *Restart Each Section*: Numbers the lines in each section beginning with 1 and restarts each section with 1.
   - *Suppress for Current Paragraph*: Turns off numbering on selected paragraph.
   - *Line Numbering Options*: Opens the *Page Setup* dialog box with the *Layout* tab displayed. Click the **Line Numbers** button to open the *Line Numbers* dialog box where you customize line-numbering options.
3. Turn off line numbers by clicking the **Line Numbers** button and selecting **None**.

For this Pause & Practice project, you modify a handout Sierra Pacific Community College District gives to all its freshman composition students. You change margins, add a gutter margin, apply a drop cap, apply a page color, create a custom watermark, save a watermark as a building block, and apply hyphenation.

File Needed: **AddEmphasis-08.docx** *(student data files are available in the Library of your SIMnet account)*
Completed Project File Name: *[your initials] PP W8-1.docx*

1. Open the **AddEmphasis-08** document from your student data files.
2. Save the document as [your initials] PP W8-1.
3. Change the margins and add a gutter margin.
   a. Change the *Top*, *Bottom*, and *Right* margins to **0.7"**.
   b. Change the *Left* margin to **2.25"**.
   c. Change the *Gutter* to **0.25"** and the *Gutter position* to **Left**.
4. Apply styles to selected text.
   a. Apply the **Heading 1** style to all bolded (but not underlined) section headings. Don't apply the *Heading 1* style to the title.
   b. Apply the **Heading 2** style to all underlined headings.
   c. Apply the **List Paragraph** style to the two bulleted lists.
5. Add a gradient page color to the document.
   a. Click the **Page Color** button [*Design* tab, *Page Background* group] and select **Fill Effects**. The *Fill Effects* dialog box opens, and the *Gradient* tab displays (Figure 8-16).
   b. Click the **Two colors** radio button in the *Colors* area.
   c. Click the **Color 1** drop-down list and select **Green, Accent 6, Lighter 80%**.
   d. Click the **Color 2** drop-down list and select **Green, Accent 6, Lighter 60%**.
   e. Select the **Diagonal up** radio button in the *Shading styles* area.
   f. In the *Variants* area, select the upper left option.
   g. Click **OK** to close the dialog box and apply the page color.
6. Apply and customize a drop cap.
   a. Place the insertion point in the first paragraph below the title.
   b. Click the **Drop Cap** button [*Insert* tab, *Text* group] and click **Dropped**.
   c. Click the **Drop Cap** button again and select **Drop Cap Options**. The *Drop Cap* dialog box opens (Figure 8-17).
   d. Click the **Font** drop-down list and select **Arial Black**.
   e. Change the *Lines to drop* to **4**.
   f. Change the *Distance from text* to **0.1"**.
   g. Click **OK** to close the *Drop Cap* dialog box.
   h. Select the drop cap in the document and change the font color to **Blue, Accent 1, Darker 50%**.
   i. Deselect the drop cap.
7. Create a custom watermark.
   a. Click the **Watermark** button [*Design* tab, *Page Background* group] and select **Custom Watermark**. The *Printed Watermark* dialog box opens (Figure 8-18).
   b. Click the **Text watermark** radio button.

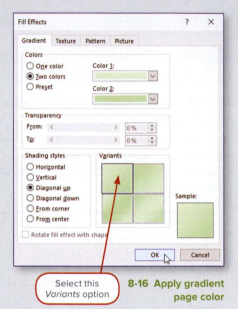

Select this *Variants* option

8-16 Apply gradient page color

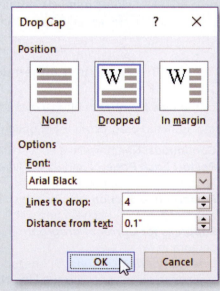

8-17 Modify drop cap options

c. Delete the existing text in the *Text* area, and type SPCCD Draft as the watermark text.
d. Click the **Font** drop-down list and select **Arial Black**.
e. Click the **Size** drop-down list and select **Auto** if it is not already selected.
f. Click the **Color** drop-down list and select **Dark Red** in the *Standard Colors* area.
g. Check the **Semitransparent** box and select the **Diagonal** radio button if they are not already checked and selected.
h. Click **Apply** to insert the watermark.
i. Click **Close** to close the dialog box.

8-18 Create custom text watermark

8. Save the custom watermark as a building block.
a. Edit the header on the first page.
b. Select the watermark on the page.
c. Click the **Watermark** button [*Design* tab, *Page Background* group (not *Header & Footer Tools Design* tab)] and select **Save Selection to Watermark Gallery**. The *Create New Building Block* dialog box opens (Figure 8-19).
d. Add the following properties for the new building block:
   Name: SPCCD Draft
   Gallery: **Watermarks**
   Category: **General**
   Description: Insert SPCCD Draft watermark
   Save in: **Building Blocks**
   Options: **Insert content only**
e. Click **OK** to close the dialog box and create the new building block.
f. Close the header if it is still open.

8-19 Create watermark building block

9. Click the **Hyphenation** button [*Layout* tab, *Page Setup* group] and select **Automatic** to automatically hyphenate the entire document.

10. Save and close the document (Figure 8-20). Click **Yes** if prompted to save changes to building blocks.

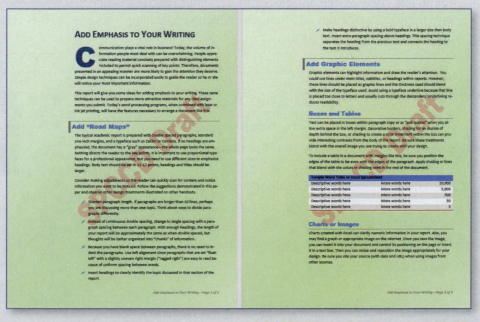

8-20 PP W8-1 completed (pages 1 and 2 of 3)

SLO 8.2

Customizing and Creating Themes

In *SLO 2.7: Using Styles and Themes*, you learned about themes and how a document theme controls the fonts, sizes, colors, line and paragraph spacing, and styles in a document. You can apply a *theme* to a document, customize an existing theme, or create a custom theme.

Theme Colors, Fonts, and Effects

When you apply a theme to a document, Word automatically changes the *theme colors*, *theme fonts*, and *theme effects* to match the theme you select. Although the document theme controls the theme colors, fonts, and effects, you can customize a document theme by selecting different theme colors, fonts, and effects.

► **HOW TO:** Customize a Theme

1. Click the **Themes** button [*Design* tab, *Document Formatting* group] and select a theme from the drop-down list to apply to your document.
2. Click the **Colors** button [*Design* tab, *Document Formatting* group] and select a theme color set (Figure 8-21).
3. Click the **Fonts** button [*Design* tab, *Document Formatting* group] and select a theme font set.
4. Click the **Effects** button [*Design* tab, *Document Formatting* group] and select a theme effects set.

8-21 Select theme colors

Create Custom Theme Colors and Fonts

In addition to applying preset theme colors and fonts to an existing theme, you can also create your own custom theme colors and fonts. You can select specific colors and fonts and save these custom color and font sets, which you can apply to a document or document theme.

► **HOW TO:** Create New Theme Colors

1. Click the **Colors** button [*Design* tab, *Document Formatting* group].
2. Select **Customize Colors** from the drop-down list. The *Create New Theme Colors* dialog box opens (Figure 8-22).
3. Change the color of any item by selecting a color from the drop-down list in the *Theme colors* area.
   - The *Sample area* displays the theme colors.
4. Click the **Name** text box and type a name for the new theme colors.
5. Click **Save** to close the dialog box.
   - The new custom *Theme Colors* displays in the *Colors* drop-down list in the *Custom* category, and you can apply it to other documents or themes.

8-22 *Create New Theme Colors* dialog box

The procedure to create new theme fonts is similar to creating new theme colors. Theme fonts contain two font sets: *Heading font* and *Body font*. Customize the new theme fonts and save the changes for future use (Figure 8-23).

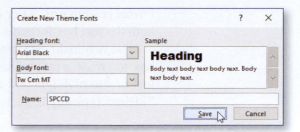

8-23 *Create New Theme Fonts* dialog box

Create a Custom Theme

After modifying theme fonts, colors, or effects, you can save these changes as a new document theme. Custom themes display in the *Themes* drop-down list, and you can apply a custom theme to other documents. Custom themes help to create consistency among documents and save you time.

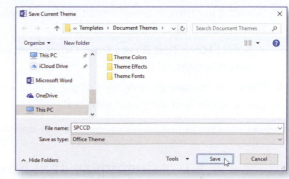

▶ HOW TO: Create a Custom Theme

1. Apply a theme to a document.

2. Change the theme colors, fonts, and effects as desired.

3. Click the **Themes** button [*Design* tab, *Document Formatting* group] and select **Save Current Theme**. The *Save Current Theme* dialog box opens (Figure 8-24).

4. Type a name for the new theme in the *File name* area.

   - The new theme will be saved in the *Document Themes* folder on your computer. If you save the new theme in a different location, it will not be available in the drop-down list of themes in your documents.
   - The file type for a theme is *Office Theme*.

5. Click **Save** to close the dialog box and save your custom theme.

   - The new custom theme displays in the *Custom* category in the *Themes* drop-down list, and you can apply it to any Word document (Figure 8-25).

8-24 *Save Current Theme* dialog box

> **MORE INFO**
>
> To delete a custom theme, right-click the custom theme in the *Themes* drop-down list and select **Delete**.

8-25 Custom theme in the *Themes* drop-down list

Using Text Boxes

A ***text box*** is a useful desktop publishing feature that draws attention to information in a document. Word includes many built-in text boxes, or you can draw your own text box. A text box is a graphic object that you can resize, arrange, and customize like a shape or picture. You can customize text in a text box and create a custom text box building block.

Built-In Text Boxes

When you insert a ***Built-in text box***, the text box is preformatted with custom borders, fill, and effects. Built-in text boxes contain placeholder text in a ***content control field*** that you can replace with your own text. A content control field is a Word field where you can insert and format custom text. After inserting a built-in text box into your document, you can customize both the text box format and the text box content.

The two main categories of built-in text boxes are *quotes* and *sidebars*. Use a quote text box to create a pull quote. A pull quote is content you "pull" from the text and insert in a text box to highlight and emphasize a point. Use sidebars to display additional information. Sidebars typically align at the left, right, top, or bottom of a page.

▶ HOW TO: Insert a Built-In Text Box

1. Place the insertion point in your document where you want to insert a text box.

2. Click the **Text Box** button [*Insert* tab, *Text* group].

3. Select a text box to insert from the drop-down list of built-in text boxes (Figure 8-26).

   - Select **More Text Boxes from Office.com** to view additional text box options.

4. Click the content control field of the text box and replace the placeholder text with your own text.

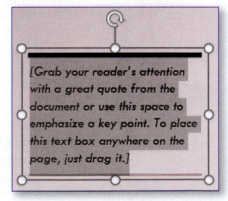

8-26 Built-in text boxes

Customize Text Box Content

After inserting a built-in text box, replace the placeholder text with custom content. You can type your information in the content control field or remove the content control field and type your text directly in the text box. Format text in the text box the same way you format text in your documents, changing the font, size, style, color, line spacing, and paragraph spacing with the font and spacing options on the *Home* tab. You can also use the text options in the *WordArt Styles* and *Text* groups on the *Drawing Tools Format* tab to customize the appearance of your text.

▶ HOW TO: Customize Text Box Content

1. Click the placeholder text in the text box to select it (Figure 8-27).

2. Type text to replace the placeholder text or copy text from a document and paste it in the content control field.

   - To remove the content control field, right-click the field and select **Remove Content Control** field from the context menu.

3. Select the text in the text box and change the font, size, style, color, line spacing, or paragraph spacing as desired.

4. In the *Text* group [*Drawing Tools Format* tab], change the *Text Direction*, *Align Text*, or *Create Link*.

   - The *Create Link* option links text from one text box to another text box.

5. In the *WordArt Styles* group [*Drawing Tools Format* tab], modify the *WordArt Style*, *Text Fill*, *Text Outline*, and *Text Effects*.

   - Click the **Word Art Styles** launcher to open the *Format Shape* pane and to customize text.
   - Adjust the text layout and internal margins in the *Text Options* area of the *Format Shape* pane.

8-27 Select placeholder text in the text box

Customize Text Box Format

Customizing the format of a text box is similar to customizing the format of other shapes. When you insert a text box in your document, the context-sensitive *Drawing Tools Format* tab displays to customize the shape style, shape outline, shape fill, or shape effects of the text box. Use the *Position* and *Wrap Text* buttons in the *Arrange* group to customize the size and position of the text box and to control text wrapping around the text box.

▶ HOW TO: Customize Text Box Format

1. Click the border of the text box to select it. The *Drawing Tools Format* tab is available on the *Ribbon*.

2. Customize the shape of your text box by modifying the *Shape Style*, *Shape Fill*, *Shape Outline*, or *Shape Effects* in the *Shape Styles* group [*Drawing Tools Format* tab].

   - Click the **Shape Styles** launcher to open the *Format Shape* pane and apply formatting changes to the shape of the text box shape (Figure 8-28).

3. Change the *Height* and *Width* of the text box shape in the *Size* group [*Drawing Tools Format* tab].

   - You can also use the sizing handles to resize the text box shape.

4. Customize the text box by choosing from the *Position*, *Wrap Text*, *Align*, *Group*, or *Rotate* options in the *Arrange* group [*Drawing Tools Format* tab]. Use the *Bring Forward* or *Send Backward* options to customize the arrangement.

   - Click the **Size** launcher to open the *Layout* dialog box to customize *Position*, *Text Wrapping*, and *Size* of the text box.
   - Alternatively, click the **Layout Options** button to the right of the text box (see Figure 8-29) and select a text wrapping option.

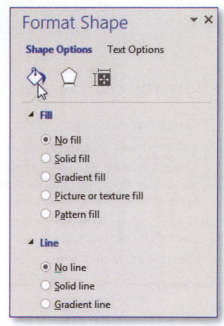

8-28 *Format Shape* pane

Draw a Text Box

Another way to insert a text box into a document is to draw the text box. You can draw a text box any shape you want anywhere in the document. After you draw a text box, you can insert and format text in the box and customize the text box shape.

▶ HOW TO: Draw a Text Box

1. Click the **Text Box** button [*Insert* tab, *Text* group].

2. Select **Draw Text Box** from the drop-down list. Your pointer becomes a drawing crosshair pointer.

3. Draw a text box in the document by dragging diagonally down and to the right (Figure 8-29). The insertion point displays in the text box.

4. Type or paste text in the text box.

5. Format the text in the text box as desired.

6. Use the *Drawing Tools Format* tab to customize the text box shape, alignment, text wrapping, size, and position.

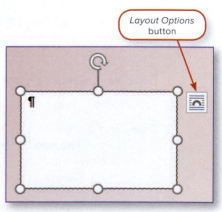

8-29 **Draw a text box**

Text Box Building Blocks

All built-in text boxes are building blocks in the *Text Box* gallery. Just like creating a watermark, header, footer, or table building block, you can create a text box building block. Once you have stored a custom text building block, you can insert it in other documents.

▶ **HOW TO:** Create a Text Box Building Block

1. Create and customize a text box.
   - Alternatively, insert and customize a built-in text box.
2. Select the text box, click the **Text Box** button [*Insert* tab, *Text* group], and select **Save Selection to Text Box Gallery**. The *Create New Building Block* dialog box opens (Figure 8-30).
3. Type or select the *Name, Category, Description, Save in* area, and *Options* for the building block.
4. Click **OK** to create the text box building block.

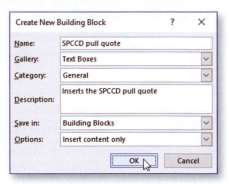

8-30 Create text box building block

PAUSE & PRACTICE: WORD 8-2

For this Pause & Practice project, you modify the document you worked with in *Pause & Practice 8-1*. You customize an existing theme, create new theme fonts, create a new theme, insert and customize a built-in text box, draw and customize a text box, and create a text box building block.

File Needed: ***[your initials] PP W8-1.docx***
Completed Project File Name: ***[your initials] PP W8-2.docx***

---

1. Open the ***[your initials] PP W8-1*** document you completed in *Pause & Practice 8-1*.

2. Save the document as [your initials] PP W8-2.

3. Apply and customize a theme.
   a. Click the **Themes** button [*Design* tab, *Document Formatting* group] and select **Wisp** from the drop-down list.
   b. Click the **Colors** button [*Design* tab, *Document Formatting* group] and select **Orange Red** from the drop-down list.
   c. Click the **Effects** button [*Design* tab, *Document Formatting* group] and select **Subtle Solids** from the drop-down list.

4. Create new theme fonts.
   a. Click the **Fonts** button [*Design* tab, *Document Formatting* group].
   b. Select **Customize Fonts** from the drop-down list. The *Create New Theme Fonts* dialog box opens (Figure 8-31).
   c. Click the **Heading font** drop-down list and select **Arial Black**.
   d. Click the **Body font** drop-down list and select **Tw Cen MT**.
   e. Type SPCCD in the *Name* area.
   f. Click **Save** to create the new theme font and apply it to the current document theme.

5. Create a new document theme.
   a. Click the **Themes** button [*Design* tab, *Document Formatting* group].
   b. Select **Save Current Theme** to open the *Save Current Theme* dialog box (Figure 8-32).
   c. Type SPCCD in the *File name* area. Don't change the save location.
   d. Click **Save** to close the dialog box and save the custom theme.

8-31 *Create New Theme Fonts* dialog box

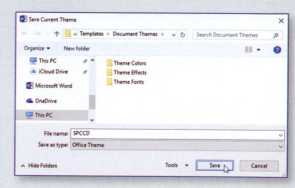

8-32 *Save Current Theme* dialog box

6. Insert and customize a built-in text box.
   a. Place the insertion point at the beginning of the first paragraph in the "Add "Road Maps"'" section.
   b. Click the **Text Box** button [*Insert* tab, *Text* group] and select **Motion Quote**.
   c. Select the last sentence in the first paragraph on the first page ("**Simple design techniques . . .**") and copy it. Don't include the paragraph mark at the end of the sentence when selecting it.
   d. Click the placeholder text in the text box to select it and press **Ctrl+V** to paste the copied text, which replaces the placeholder text.
   e. Select the text in the text box and apply **italic** formatting.
   f. Change the *Height* of the text box to **1.4"** and the *Width* to **1.9"** [*Drawing Tools Format* tab, *Size* group].
   g. Click the **Shape Effects** button [*Drawing Tools Format* tab, *Shape Styles* group], select **Preset**, and choose **Preset 2**.
   h. Click the **Position** button [*Drawing Tools Format* tab, *Arrange* group] and select **More Layout Options**. The *Layout* dialog box opens.
   i. Set the *Horizontal* **Absolute position** at **0.3"** to the right of **Page** and set the *Vertical* **Alignment** to **Centered** relative to **Page**.
   j. Click **OK** to close the *Layout* dialog box.

7. Create a text box building block.
   a. Select the text box you created in step 6 (Figure 8-33).
   b. Click the **Text Box** button [*Insert* tab, *Text* group] and select **Save Selection to Text Box Gallery**. The *Create New Building Block* dialog box opens.
   c. Add the following properties for the new building block:

   Name: SPCCD pull quote
   Gallery: **Text Boxes**
   Category: **General**
   Description: Inserts the SPCCD pull quote
   Save in: **Building Blocks**
   Options: **Insert content only**

   d. Click **OK** to close the dialog box and create the new building block.

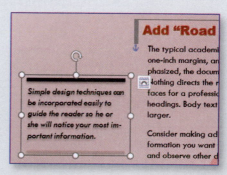

8-33 **Text box positioned in the document**

8. Insert and customize a text box building block.
   a. Place the insertion point at the beginning of the first paragraph on the last page ("In writing, content . . .").
   b. Click the **Text Box** button [*Insert* tab, *Text* group] and select the **SPCCD pull quote** (Figure 8-34).
   c. Select the last sentence on the last page and copy it. Don't select the paragraph mark at the end of the sentence.
   d. Select the existing text in the text box, click the **Paste** button [*Home* tab, *Clipboard* group], and select the **Merge Formatting** paste option.
   e. Change the *Height* of the text box to **1.2"**.

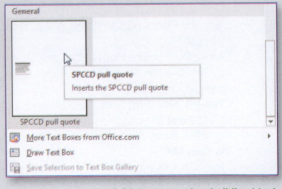

8-34 **Insert text box building block**

9. Draw a text box and customize the content.
   a. Place the insertion point near the middle of the second page.
   b. Click the **Text Box** button and select **Draw Text Box**. Your pointer becomes a drawing crosshair pointer.
   c. Draw a text box (approximately 1" tall and 5" wide) over the second paragraph in the "Boxes and Tables" section.
   d. Change the *Height* to **0.8"** and the *Width* to **5.25"**.
   e. Type the following text in the text box:

   This is an example of a text box that was drawn between two paragraphs. Remember to adjust the text box's internal margins to leave space between the text and the text box. The format of this text box has been customized.

10. Customize the text box format.
   a. Select the text box.
   b. Click the **Shape Styles** drop-down list [*Drawing Tool Format* tab, *Shape Styles* group] and select **Subtle Effect – Dark Red, Accent 2**.
   c. Click the **Shape Styles** launcher to open the *Format Shape* pane.
   d. Click **Layout & Properties** and select **Text Box** to expand this area (Figure 8-35).
   e. Change the *Vertical alignment* to **Middle**.
   f. Set the *Left*, *Right*, *Top*, and *Bottom* internal margins to **0.1"**.
   g. Click the **X** in the upper right corner of the *Format Shape* pane to close it.
   h. Change the text wrapping to **Tight**.
   i. Drag the text box between the first and second paragraphs in the "Boxes and Tables" section.
   j. Click the **Align** button [*Drawing Tools Format* tab, *Arrange* group] and select **Align to Margin** (if it's not already selected).
   k. Click the **Align** button again and select **Align Left**.
   l. Use the up or down keyboard arrow key to align the text box between the first and second paragraph, if necessary.

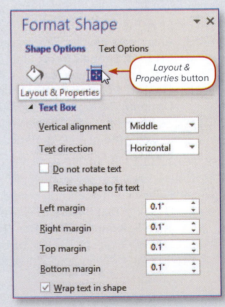

8-35 *Format Shape* pane

11. Click at the beginning of the "Write Vertical Lists" heading and insert a **page break** (**Ctrl+Enter**).

12. Position the text box on the last page.
   a. Select the text box on the last page.
   b. Click the **Position** button [*Drawing Tools Format* tab, *Arrange* group] and select **More Layout Options**. The *Layout* dialog box opens.
   c. Set the *Vertical* **Absolute position** at **0.9"** below **Margin**. Don't change the horizontal position.
   d. Click **OK** to close the *Layout* dialog box.

13. Save and close the document (Figure 8-36).

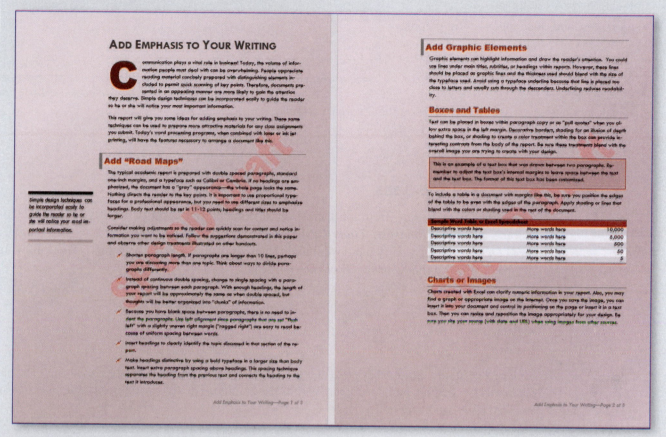

8-36 PP W8-2 completed (pages 1 and 2 of 3)

SLO 8.4

Using SmartArt

A *SmartArt* graphic is an excellent way to visually display information in a document. *SmartArt* graphics are a collection of customized shapes, lines, and text. Now that you have experience working with shapes and text boxes, you can apply your knowledge to customize *SmartArt* graphics.

Insert a SmartArt Graphic

Word provides a variety of *SmartArt* categories, and each category has many built-in *SmartArt* graphics to insert in your document. Once you select and insert your *SmartArt*, add text, customize the design, and customize the individual objects in the *SmartArt*.

▶ HOW TO: Insert a SmartArt Graphic

1. Place your insertion point in the document where you want to insert a *SmartArt* graphic.

2. Click the **SmartArt** button [*Insert* tab, *Illustrations* group] to open the *Choose a SmartArt Graphic* dialog box (Figure 8-37).

3. Select a category of *SmartArt* graphics on the left to view the options in that category.

4. Select a *SmartArt* graphic.
   - A preview and description of the graphic appears on the right.
   - The preview is the basic structure of the graphic; you can add to or remove graphic objects from this structure.

5. Click **OK** to close the dialog box and insert the *SmartArt* graphic.

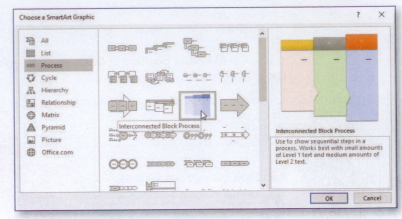

8-37 *Choose a SmartArt Graphic* dialog box

SmartArt Tools Tabs

When you insert a *SmartArt* graphic into your document, two context-sensitive *SmartArt* tabs become available: **SmartArt Tools Design** and **SmartArt Tools Format**. Use the *SmartArt Tools Design* tab to modify the design and structure of the *SmartArt* graphic. The following groups display on the *SmartArt Tools Design* tab:

- *Create Graphic*
- *Layouts*
- *SmartArt Styles*
- *Reset*

Use the *SmartArt Tools Format* tab to format the shapes, text, arrangement, and size of the *SmartArt* graphic and the objects within the graphic. The following groups display on the *SmartArt Tools Format* tab:

- *Shapes*
- *Shape Styles*
- *WordArt Styles*
- *Arrange*
- *Size*

Customize SmartArt Text

After you insert a *SmartArt* graphic into your document, customize the graphic by adding shapes and bulleted text or removing these items. You can type text directly in the *SmartArt* graphic or use the ***Text pane*** to enter and organize text. The *Create Graphic* group on the *SmartArt Tools Design* tab includes options to add a shape or bullet, promote or demote the level of items, move items up or down, switch the layout from right to left, or modify the layout.

Modify the text in the *SmartArt* graphic the same way you modify other text using the *Font* and *Paragraph* groups on the *Home* tab. You can also customize the text in the *SmartArt* graphic with the *WordArt Styles*, *Text Fill*, *Text Outline*, and *Text Effects* options in the *WordArt Styles* group on the *SmartArt Tools Format* tab.

▶ **HOW TO:** Customize SmartArt Text

1. Select and insert a *SmartArt* graphic into your document.

   • Click the **Text Pane** button [*SmartArt Tools Design* tab, *Create Graphic* group] to toggle on/off the *Text* pane to the side of the *SmartArt* graphic (Figure 8-38).

   • Alternatively, open and close the *Text* pane by clicking the **Text pane control**.

2. Type text in the *Text* pane or directly in the objects in the *SmartArt* graphic.

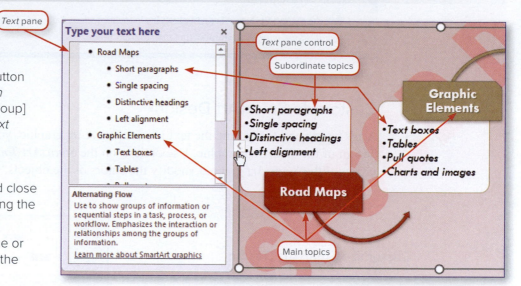

8-38 *SmartArt* graphic with *Text* pane displayed

3. Click the **Add Shape** drop-down button [*SmartArt Tools Design* tab, *Create Graphic* group] to add a shape after, before, above, or below the selected shape in the graphic (Figure 8-39).

   • The shapes and text in the graphics automatically resize when you add shapes to the *SmartArt* graphic.

   • Delete a shape or text by selecting it and pressing **Delete**.

4. Click the **Add Bullet** button [*SmartArt Tools Design* tab, *Create Graphic* group] to add a subordinate topic to the list of topics.

   • Alternatively, press **Enter** at the end of a bulleted topic in the graphic or *Text* pane to add another bullet.

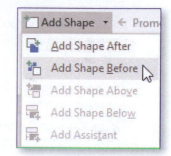

8-39 Add shape to *SmartArt* graphic

5. Click the **Promote** or **Demote** button [*SmartArt Tools Design* tab, *Create Graphic* group] to change a main topic to a subordinate topic or to change a subordinate topic to a main topic (Figure 8-40).

6. Click the **Move Up** or **Move Down** button [*SmartArt Tools Design* tab, *Create Graphic* group] to arrange topics in a list.

   • You can also select and drag or cut and paste topics in the *Text* pane to arrange them.

8-40 *Create Graphic* group on the *SmartArt Tools Design* tab

7. Click the **Right to Left** button [*SmartArt Tools Design* tab, *Create Graphic* group] to switch the layout of the *SmartArt* graphic from left to right or right to left.

8. Click the **WordArt Styles**, **Text Fill**, **Text Outline**, or **Text Effects** button to customize the appearance of the text [*SmartArt Tools Format* tab, *WordArt Styles* group] (Figure 8-41).

   • When customizing text, always select the text before applying formatting options.

9. Click the **Text Pane** button [*Table Tools Design* tab, *Create Graphic* group] or the **X** in the upper right corner of the *Text* pane to close it.

8-41 *WordArt Styles* group on the *SmartArt Tools Format* tab

Customize SmartArt Design

After typing and formatting the text in your *SmartArt* graphic, you can customize the overall design of the *SmartArt* graphic. Use options on the *SmartArt Tools Design* tab to change the layout of the *SmartArt* graphic, modify the colors of the objects, or apply a *SmartArt* style.

HOW TO: Customize SmartArt Design

1. Select the *SmartArt* graphic and use the *Layouts* group [*SmartArt Tools Design* tab] to select a different *SmartArt* layout.
   - Click the **More** button in the *Layouts* group [*SmartArt Tools Design* tab] to display additional options in the *Layouts* gallery.
   - In the *Layouts* gallery, select **More Layouts** to open the *Choose a SmartArt Graphic* dialog box to change the *SmartArt* layout.
2. Click the **Change Colors** button [*SmartArt Tools Design* tab, *SmartArt Styles* group] to change the color of your *SmartArt* (Figure 8-42).
3. Select a style to apply to your *SmartArt* graphic from the *SmartArt Styles* area [*SmartArt Tools Design* tab].
   - *SmartArt Styles* apply custom fill, outlines, and effects to your *SmartArt* graphic.
   - Click the **More** button [*SmartArt Tools Design* tab, *SmartArt Styles* group] to display additional style options.

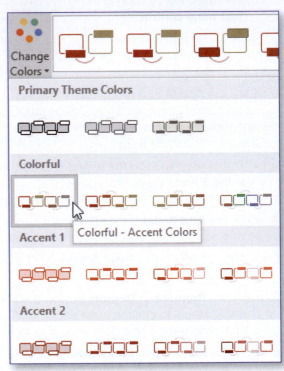

8-42 Change color of SmartArt graphic

Customize SmartArt Objects

In addition to modifying *SmartArt* text and design, you can also customize individual objects within the *SmartArt* graphic. You can change the size or shape of individual objects in your *SmartArt* graphic, apply a shape style, or customize a shape fill, outline, or effects. Apply changes to the individual objects in a *SmartArt* graphic similar to how you customize shapes.

▶ **HOW TO:** Customize SmartArt Objects

1. Select the object to customize.
   - Use the **Ctrl** key to select multiple objects in your *SmartArt* graphic if you want to apply changes to more than one object.
   - You can also use the *Selection* pane [*SmartArt Tools Format* tab, *Arrange* group] to select objects in your *SmartArt* graphic.
2. Click the **Change Shape** button [*SmartArt Tools Format* tab, *Shapes* group] to select a different shape for the selected objects (Figure 8-43).

   - You don't have to draw a new shape; Word automatically applies the selected shape to the selected objects and adjusts the size of the text if needed.

8-43 *Shapes group on the SmartArt Tools Format tab*

3. Click the **Larger** or **Smaller** button [*SmartArt Tools Format* tab, *Shapes* group] to change the size of the selected objects.
   - Alternatively, change the size of an object by using the sizing handles or the *Size* group [*SmartArt Tools Format* tab].

4. Select a shape style from the *Shape Styles* gallery to apply to selected objects (Figure 8-44).

8-44 *Shape Styles group on the SmartArt Tools Format tab*

5. Click the **Shape Fill**, **Shape Outline**, or **Shape Effects** button to customize the selected shapes.
   - You can also click the **Shape Styles** launcher to open the *Format Shape* pane to customize selected shapes.
6. Use the **Bring Forward**, **Send Backward**, **Align**, **Group**, and **Rotate** buttons [*SmartArt Tool Format* tab, *Arrange* group] to arrange selected objects in your *SmartArt* graphic.

Resize, Align, and Position SmartArt

The final step is to customize the size, text wrapping, alignment, and position of the *SmartArt* graphic. When you adjust the size of your *SmartArt* graphic, Word automatically resizes the objects and text in the graphic.

▶ **HOW TO:** Resize, Align, and Position SmartArt

1. Select the *SmartArt* graphic and use the *Size* group [*SmartArt Tools Format* tab] or the sizing handles to change the height and width of the graphic.
   - The sizing handles on a *SmartArt* graphic are the small circles on the sides and corners of the *SmartArt* frame.
2. Click the **Wrap Text** button [*SmartArt Tools Format* tab, *Arrange* group] to select a text wrap option.
3. Click and drag the frame of the *SmartArt* graphic to position it in your document.
   - When you place your pointer on the frame of the *SmartArt* graphic, your pointer becomes a four-pointed move pointer.
   - You can also click the **Align** or **Position** button [*SmartArt Tools Format* tab, *Arrange* group] to align your *SmartArt* graphic in relation to the page or margins.

▶ **MORE INFO**

Click the **Size** launcher [*SmartArt Tools Format* tab, *Size* group] to open the *Layout* dialog box to modify the position, text wrapping, and size.

Using Charts

Use **Charts** to graphically display numerical data in Word documents, Excel worksheets, and PowerPoint presentations. In Word, you can insert a variety of different chart types and customize the data presented in the chart, the layout and elements of the chart, the chart design, and the format of the chart and specific chart elements.

Insert a Chart

When inserting a chart in your document, determine the type of chart that best displays the data you are presenting. The most common types of charts are *Column*, *Line*, *Pie*, and *Bar*. Word also offers other charts such as *Area*, *X Y (Scatter)*, *Stock*, *Surface*, *Doughnut*, *Bubble*, and *Radar*.

When you insert a chart, a sample chart displays in the Word document. Also, a **Chart in Microsoft Word worksheet** opens in a new window and displays generic data. The information in the *Chart in Microsoft Word* worksheet displays in columns and rows, similar to a table (see Figure 8-46). As you edit the data in the worksheet, the chart in the Word document updates automatically.

▶ HOW TO: Insert a Chart

1. Place the insertion point at the location where you want to insert the chart.
2. Click the **Chart** button [*Insert* tab, *Illustrations* group]. The *Insert Chart* dialog box opens (Figure 8-45).
3. Select the chart type to insert into your document.
   - Chart categories display on the left.
   - The thumbnail graphics at the right display each chart structure, and a preview of a chart displays below the thumbnails.
4. Click **OK** to close the dialog box and insert the chart.
   - The chart displays in the document and a *Chart in Microsoft Word* worksheet window opens (Figure 8-46).

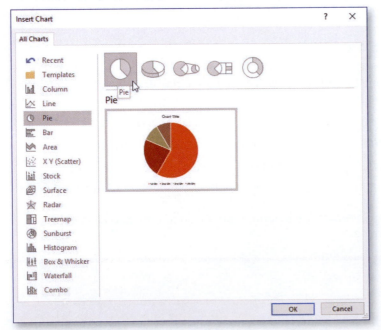

8-45 *Insert Chart* dialog box

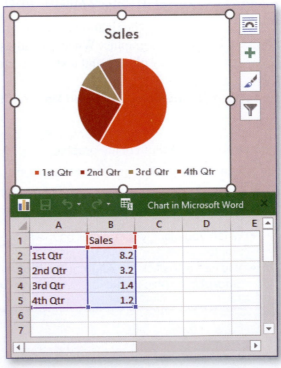

8-46 Chart inserted and *Chart in Microsoft Word* worksheet displayed

Customize Chart Data

After you insert a chart, the first step is to customize the data for the chart, which is in the *Chart in Microsoft Word* worksheet (see Figure 8-46). Sample data displays in the worksheet when you insert a chart. Replace the sample data with your own data. Column and row headings describe the data, which you can use as axes and legend labels.

The ***chart data range*** is the information in the *Chart in Microsoft Word* worksheet. A border displays around the chart data range as shown in Figure 8-47. Type data in this worksheet, add rows or columns of data in the worksheet, and adjust the chart data range if necessary. You can also remove data and adjust the chart data range. The information in the chart data range displays in the chart in the document.

▶**HOW TO:** Customize Chart Data

1. Type the chart data in the *Chart in Microsoft Word* worksheet (see Figure 8-47).

   - As you edit the *Chart in Microsoft Word* worksheet, the data in the chart updates automatically.
   - Include column and row headings to describe the data in the table. Columns are vertical, and rows are horizontal.
   - Drag the title bar of the *Chart in Microsoft Word* worksheet to reposition the window if needed.

2. Click and drag the **chart data range** handle (bottom right corner of the chart data range) to change the size of the chart data range.

   - Verify that the chart data range contains no blank rows or columns. Blank rows or columns within the data range border display in the chart in the Word document.

3. Click the **X** in the upper right corner of the *Chart in Microsoft Word* worksheet to close the window when you finish editing the chart data.

   - To edit the chart data after closing the *Chart in Microsoft Word* worksheet, click the **Edit Data** button [*Chart Tools Design* tab, *Data* group] to open the *Chart in Microsoft Word* window.
   - You can also edit chart data in a Microsoft Excel 2016 worksheet. Click the **Edit Data** drop-down list and select **Edit Data in Excel**.

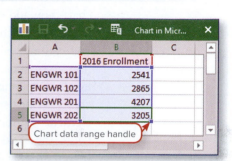

8-47 Edit chart data in the *Chart in Microsoft Word* worksheet

---

Chart Tools Tabs, Format Pane, and Format Buttons

When you insert a chart into your document, two context-sensitive ***Chart Tools tabs*** display on the *Ribbon*: ***Chart Tools Design*** and ***Chart Tools Format***. Both of these contextual tabs include options to customize the design and format of the chart and the elements within the chart. The following are the *Chart Tools* tabs and the groups available on each tab:

- ***Chart Tools Design***: *Chart Layouts, Chart Styles, Data,* and *Type*
- ***Chart Tools Format***: *Current Selection, Insert Shapes, Shape Styles, Word Art Styles, Arrange,* and *Size*

The ***Format "Chart Element" pane*** opens when you click the **Shape Styles** or **WordArt Styles** launcher on the *Chart Tools Format* tab (Figure 8-48). The name of the *Format* pane changes depending on the chart element selected (for example *Format Chart Area, Format Chart Title*). Click the **Chart Elements** drop-down list to select a chart element. The *Format* pane provides format categories (*Fill & Line*, *Effects*, *Layout & Properties*) and options within each category. The format categories and options vary depending on the chart element you select.

Additionally, four format buttons display on the right of a selected chart: *Layout Options*, *Chart Elements*, *Chart Styles*, and *Chart Filters*. These format buttons provide another method to customize chart design and format. Click any of these format buttons to display a list of options (Figure 8-49).

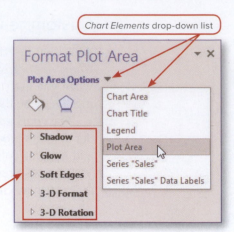

8-48 *Format "Chart Element" pane*

Customize Chart Layout

After you insert the chart and customize the data to display in the chart, you add or modify the elements of the chart. For example, you can add or modify the chart title, axis titles, legend, and data labels. Depending on the type of chart you are using, different chart element options are available. Click the **Add Chart Element** button on the *Chart Tools Design* tab in the *Chart Layouts* group to display the drop-down list of chart elements. The following table lists and describes the common chart elements:

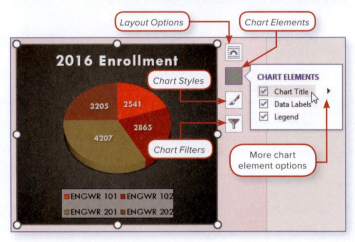

8-49 **Chart format buttons**

Chart Elements

Chart Element	Description
Axes	The horizontal axis (x-axis) and vertical axis (y-axis) that appear on charts. You can customize the scale and format of both axes.
Axis Titles	Text that describes the horizontal axis (x-axis) and vertical axis (y-axis).
Chart Title	Text that describes the chart's content and purpose.
Data Labels	Numerical labels on columns, bars, lines, or pie segments that display the number or percent for each value on the chart.
Data Table	A table below the chart that displays the data values.
Error Bars	Bars that display margins of error and standard deviations at a glance.
Gridlines	Vertical and horizontal lines that appear in the chart plot area to help readers distinguish values and data.
Legend	Text that describes the data represented in the chart and typically displays on the right or at the bottom of the chart.
Lines	Vertical lines that drop from data points to the x-axis or display vertical lines between high and low data points on line charts.
Plot Area	The area of the chart where the columns, bars, or lines display chart data.

Chart Element	Description
Trendline	A line that charts the trend between data points.
Up/Down Bars	Bars that display between data points on a line chart.
Walls and Floors	Side and back walls and floors that display when using a 3-D chart.

You can apply a *Quick Layout* to a chart. A *Quick Layout* adds common chart elements such as data labels or a data table. You can also change the chart type after you insert a chart.

▶**HOW TO:** Customize Chart Layout

1. Click the **Add Chart Element** button [*Chart Tools Design* tab, *Chart Layouts* group], select the chart element to add or modify, and select an option within the chart element (Figure 8-50).

   - Most of the chart elements have a *More "Chart Element" Options* selection (for example *More Data Label Options*). This selection opens the *Format "Chart Element"* pane where you can further modify the chart element (Figure 8-51).
   - You can also click the **Chart Elements** button on the right of a chart and select or deselect a chart element (see Figure 8-49). Click the triangle on the right of each chart element in this menu to further customize each chart element.

2. Click the **Quick Layout** button [*Chart Tools Design* tab, *Chart Layouts* group] and select an option from the drop-down list to apply a *Quick Layout* to a chart.

3. Change the chart type by clicking the **Change Chart Type** button [*Chart Tools Design* tab, *Type* group] to open the *Change Chart Type* dialog box and selecting a different chart type.

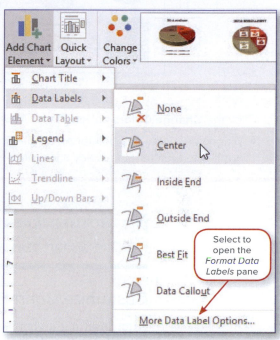

8-50 *Add Chart Element* **drop-down list**

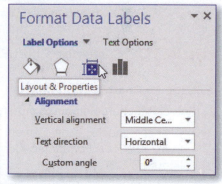

8-51 *Format Data Labels* **pane**

Apply a Chart Style and Quick Color

After customizing the layout of your chart, you can apply a *Chart Style* and *Quick Colors*. A *Chart Style* is a combination of colors and chart elements applied to a chart with one click. *Quick Colors* are color sets that apply to the chart. The two different categories of *Quick Colors* are *Colorful* and *Monochromatic*. Both *Chart Styles* and *Quick Colors* apply to an entire chart.

▶ HOW TO: Apply a Chart Style and Quick Color

1. Select the chart and click the **Chart Tools Design** tab.
2. Click the **More** button in the *Chart Styles* group to display the *Chart Styles* gallery (Figure 8-52).
   - When you place your pointer on a selection in the *Chart Styles* gallery, the chart style is temporarily applied to the chart to display a live preview of the style.

8-52 *Chart Styles* gallery

3. Click the **Change Colors** button [*Chart Tools Design* tab, *Chart Styles* group] and select a *Quick Color*.
   - When you place your pointer on a selection in the *Quick Colors* drop-down list, the color set temporarily applies to the chart to display a live preview of the *Quick Color*.

> ### ▶ ANOTHER WAY
> Click the **Chart Styles** button on the right of a chart to apply a *Chart Style* or *Quick Color*.

Customize Chart Elements

After inserting a chart and customizing the data, layout, and design, you can apply styles, fills, outlines, and effects to specific chart elements. For example, apply a fill color to the entire chart area, change the color of a column, apply an outline to the legend, or change the font on your data labels.

▶ HOW TO: Customize Chart Elements

1. Click the **Chart Tools Format** tab.
2. Select the chart element to modify.
   - Click the specific chart element in the chart or click the **Chart Elements** drop-down list [*Chart Tools Format* tab, *Current Selection* group] and select a chart element (Figure 8-53).

8-53 Select chart element

3. Click the **Shape Styles** drop-down list [*Chart Tools Design* tab, *Shape Styles* group] to apply a *Shape Style* to the chart element (Figure 8-54).
4. Click the **Shape Fill**, **Shape Outline**, or **Shape Effects** button [*Shape Styles* group] to apply a fill, outline, or effect to the chart element.
   - Click the **Shape Styles** launcher to open the *Format* pane, which gives you more customization options. For example, if you select the chart data labels and click the *Shape Styles* launcher, the *Format Data Labels* pane opens (see Figure 8-51).

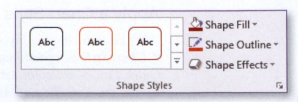

8-54 *Shape Styles* group on the *Chart Tools Format* tab

- You can also right-click a chart element and select **Format "Chart Element"** from the context menu to open the *Format "Chart Element"* pane.

5. Click the **WordArt Styles**, **Text Fill**, **Text Outline**, or **Text Effects** button [*WordArt Styles* group] to customize the chart element text (Figure 8-55).

- Click the **WordArt Styles** launcher to open the *Format* pane to customize the chart element.

8-55 *WordArt Styles* group on the *Chart Tools Format* tab

> ANOTHER WAY
>
> Use the arrow keys on the keyboard to scroll through and select chart elements.

Resize, Align, and Position a Chart

The final step is to customize the size, text wrapping, alignment, and position. Customizing the size and arrangement of the chart is similar to customizing *SmartArt* graphics, pictures, or shapes. Word automatically resizes chart elements when you adjust the size of your chart.

▶ **HOW TO: Resize, Align, and Position a Chart**

1. Select the chart.

2. Use the *Size* group [*Chart Tools Format* tab] or the sizing handles to change the height and width of the chart (Figure 8-56).

3. Click the **Wrap Text** button [*Chart Tools Format* tab, *Arrange* group] to select a text wrap option.

4. Click and drag the frame of the chart to position it in your document.

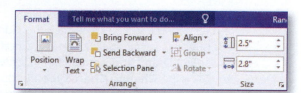

8-56 *Arrange* and *Size* groups on the *Chart Tools Format* tab

- When you place your pointer on the frame of the chart, it becomes a four-pointed move pointer.
- Click the **Align** or **Position** button [*Chart Tools Format* tab, *Arrange* group] to align your chart relative to the page or margins.
- Click the **Size** launcher [*Chart Tools Format* tab, *Size* group] to open the *Layout* dialog box to modify the position, text wrapping, and size of the chart.

PAUSE & PRACTICE: WORD 8-3

For this Pause & Practice project, you modify the document you created in *Pause & Practice 8-2*. You insert a chart and customize the chart data, layout, design, and format, and you insert a *SmartArt* graphic and customize the *SmartArt* text, design, and objects.

File Needed: ***[your initials] PP W8-2.docx***
Completed Project File Name: ***[your initials] PP W8-3.docx***

1. Open the ***[your initials] PP W8-2*** document you completed in *Pause & Practice 8-2*.

2. Save the document as [your initials] PP W8-3.

3. Insert a chart and customize the chart data.
   a. Place the insertion point at the end of the last paragraph on the second page.
   b. Click the **Chart** button [*Insert* tab, *Illustrations* group]. The *Insert Chart* dialog box opens (Figure 8-57).
   c. Click **Pie** on the left, select the **Pie** chart, and click **OK** to insert the chart and open the *Chart in Microsoft Word* worksheet window. Don't be concerned with chart placement at this point; you will modify the placement later.
   d. Type the data shown in Figure 8-58 in the *Chart in Microsoft Word* worksheet.
   e. Click the **X** in the upper right corner of the *Chart in Microsoft Word* worksheet window to close it.

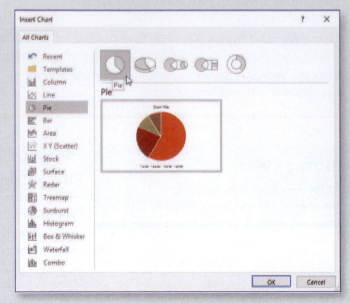

8-57 Insert pie chart

4. Modify the chart layout and design.
   a. With the chart selected, click the **Add Chart Element** button [*Chart Tools Design* tab, *Chart Layouts* group], select **Data Labels**, and select **Center**.
   b. Click the **Change Chart Type** button [*Chart Tools Design* tab, *Type* group] to open the *Change Chart Type* dialog box.
   c. Select **3-D Pie** and click **OK** to close the dialog box and change the chart type.
   d. Select **Style 7** in the *Chart Styles* gallery [*Chart Tools Design* tab, *Chart Styles* group]. You might need to click the **More** button in the *Chart Styles* group to display the *Chart Styles* gallery.

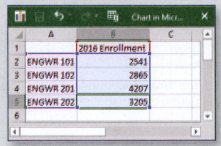

8-58 Edit chart data

5. Customize chart elements.
   a. Click the **Chart Elements** drop-down list [*Chart Tools Format* tab, *Current Selection* group] and select **Series "2016 Enrollment" Data Labels** (Figure 8-59).
   b. Apply **bold** formatting (**Ctrl+B**) to the selected data labels.
   c. Click the **Text Effects** button [*Chart Tools Format* tab, *WordArt Styles* group], select **Shadow**, and select **Offset Diagonal Bottom Right** in the *Outer* category (Figure 8-60).
   d. Click the title of the chart to select it and apply the **Offset Diagonal Bottom Right** shadow text effect.
   e. Press the **down arrow** key to select the legend (rectangle box below the pie). You might have to press the down arrow key more than once.

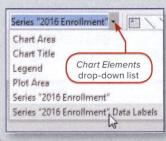

8-59 Select chart element

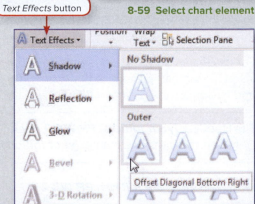

8-60 Apply a *Shadow* text effect

f. Click the **More** button [*Shape Styles* group] to display the *Shape Styles* gallery and select **Subtle Effect - Black, Dark 1** (Figure 8-61).

g. Click the **Shape Styles** launcher to open the *Format* pane at the right.

h. Click the **Chart Elements** drop-down list and select **Plot Area**.

i. Click the **Effects** button if it is not already selected and click **3-D Rotation** to open the *3-D Rotation* options area in the *Format Plot Area* pane (Figure 8-62).

j. Change the *Y Rotation* to **50°** and close the *Format Plot Area* pane.

8-61 Apply a *Shape Style*

6. Resize, change text wrapping, and position the chart.

a. Click the border of the chart to select the chart area. The tool tip displays *Chart Area* when you place your pointer on the border of the chart.

b. Change the *Height* to **2.5"** and the *Width* to **2.8"** in the *Size* group [*Chart Tools Format* tab].

c. Click the **Wrap Text** button [*Chart Tools Format* tab, *Arrange* group] and select **Tight**. The chart moves to the top of the second page.

d. Click the **Position button** [*Chart Tools Format* tab, *Arrange* group] and select **More Layout Options** to open the *Layout* dialog box.

e. Change the *Horizontal* **Alignment** to **Right** *relative to* **Margin**.

f. Change the *Vertical* **Absolute position** to **7.4"** *below* **Page**.

g. Click **OK** to close the dialog box. The chart is near the bottom right of the second page.

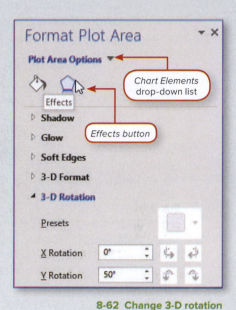

8-62 Change 3-D rotation

7. Insert a *SmartArt* graphic and add text.

a. Position the insertion point at the end of the document (**Ctrl+End**).

b. Click the **SmartArt** button [*Insert* tab, *Illustrations* group] to open the *Choose a SmartArt Graphic* dialog box (Figure 8-63).

c. Click the **Process** button at the left.

d. Select **Interconnected Block Process** and click **OK** to insert the *SmartArt* graphic.

e. Click the first main heading bullet in the *Text* pane of the *SmartArt* graphic and type Road Maps. If the *Text* pane does not display, click the **Text Pane** button [*SmartArt Tools Design* tab, *Create Graphic* group].

f. Click the next bullet to move to the first subordinate topic bullet and type the following text, pressing **Enter** after each topic to add a new subordinate topic:

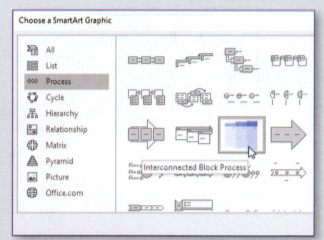

8-63 Insert a *SmartArt* graphic

Short paragraphs
Single spacing
Distinctive headings
Left alignment

g. Add the remaining main and subordinate topics shown in Figure 8-64.

h. Click the **X** in the upper right corner of the *Text* pane to close the *Text* pane.

8. Change *SmartArt* layout and customize design.
   a. Click the border of the *SmartArt* graphic to select it if it is not already selected.
   b. Click the **More** button in the *Layouts* group [*SmartArt Tools Design* tab] to open the *Layouts* gallery.
   c. Select the **Alternating Flow** layout (Figure 8-65).
   d. Click the **Change Colors** button [*SmartArt Tools Design* tab, *SmartArt Styles* group] and select **Colorful - Accent Colors** from the *Colorful* category.
   e. Click the **More** button in the *SmartArt Styles* group [*SmartArt Tools Design* tab] to open the *SmartArt Styles* gallery and select **Intense Effect** (Figure 8-66).

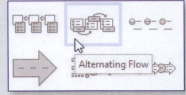

8-65 Change *SmartArt* layout

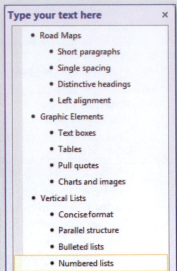

8-64 Add text using the *Text* pane

8-66 Apply *SmartArt* style

9. Modify *SmartArt* objects.
   a. Press and hold the **Ctrl** key and click the border of the three main topics ("Road Maps," "Graphic Elements," and "Vertical Lists") to select all three.
   b. Click the **Change Shape** button [*SmartArt Tools Format* tab, *Shapes* group] and select the **Snip Diagonal Corner Rectangle** shape (Figure 8-67).
   c. With the three shapes still selected, apply **bold** formatting.
   d. With the three shapes still selected, click the **Text Effects** button [*SmartArt Tools Format* tab, *WordArt Styles* group], select **Shadow**, and select **Offset Diagonal Bottom Right** in the *Outer* category.
   e. Click the border of the *SmartArt* graphic to deselect the three shapes.
   f. Select the three subordinate topic shapes (bulleted items) and apply **italic** formatting (**Ctrl+I**).

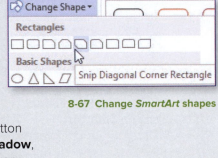

8-67 Change *SmartArt* shapes

10. Resize the *SmartArt* graphic.
    a. Click the frame of the *SmartArt* graphic to select it.
    b. Change the *Height* to **3"** and the *Width* to **5"** in the *Size* group [*SmartArt Tools Format* tab].

11. Save and close the document (Figure 8-68).

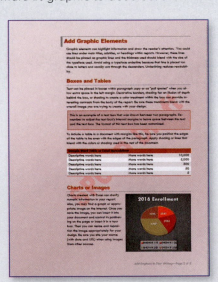
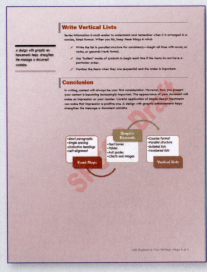

8-68 PP W8-3 completed (pages 2 and 3)

<table>
<tr><td>SLO 8.6</td></tr>
</table>

Creating an Index

An *index page* is a list of topic references in a long report or technical document. Using an index, readers are able to look up the location of key words in a document. You can mark *index entries* in your document and use these index entries to create an index page for the document. Word can automatically generate an index page that displays index entries and page numbers based upon index entries in your document. In this section, you learn how to insert an index entry, an index subentry, a cross-reference to an index entry, and an index page.

Mark an Index Entry

Before creating an index page, you must first mark index entries in your document. You can select specific text to mark as an index entry or insert an index entry at a specific location in your document. When you mark an index entry, Word inserts an *index field code* and automatically turns on *Show/Hide* if it is not already on so you can see the index field codes in your document.

An index field code displays in braces following the index entry (Figure 8-69). When creating index entries, spelling and capitalization are very important to maintain accuracy and consistency of index entries.

Add·"Road·Maps{·XE·"Road·Maps"·\b·}"¶

The·typical·academic·report·is·prepared·with·double·spaced·paragraphs,·standard·
one-inch·margins,·and·a·typeface·such·as·Calibri·or·Cambria.·If·no·headings·are·em-

8-69 Index field code displayed in document

▶ HOW TO: Mark an Index Entry

1. Select the text or place the insertion point in your document where you want to insert an index entry.

2. Click the **Mark Entry** button [*References* tab, *Index* group]. The *Mark Index Entry* dialog box opens (Figure 8-70).

   - If you select text before clicking the *Mark Entry* button, the text displays in the *Main entry* text box.
   - If you did not select text, the *Main entry* text box is empty.
   - You can edit the text in the *Main entry* text box, which is the text that will display on the index page.

3. Edit the text in the *Main entry* text box if necessary.

4. Verify the **Current page** radio button in the *Options* area is selected.

5. Check the **Bold** or **Italic** box in the *Page number format* area to apply formatting to the page number on the index page.

   - For example, you can apply bold formatting to all main index entries.

6. Click the **Mark** or **Mark All** button. The index field code displays in braces following the index entry (see Figure 8-69).

   - *Mark* inserts an index field code on the selected text or location.
   - *Mark All* inserts an index field code on all instances of the word or words in the *Main entry* text box so you don't have to manually mark each instance of the same index entry.
   - The *Mark Index* entry dialog box remains open so you can continue marking index entries in your document.

7. Click the **Close** button when you finish marking index entries.

8-70 *Mark Index Entry* dialog box

SLO 8.6 Creating an Index **W8-493**

> **MORE INFO**
>
> When *Show/Hide* is on, the index field codes affect pagination; don't be concerned about this. When *Show/Hide* is off, these hidden field codes do not affect pagination.

Mark an Index Subentry

An index *subentry* is useful to index items within a main index entry. For example, you can mark "Boxes," "Tables," and "Pull Quotes" as subentries for the main index entry of "Graphic Elements." When you mark subentries, these entries display with an indent on the index page to visually indicate they are subentries to a main index entry.

▶ **HOW TO:** Mark an Index Subentry

1. Select the text or place the insertion point in your document at the location to insert the index subentry.

2. Click the **Mark Entry** button [*References* tab, *Index* group] to open the *Mark Index Entry* dialog box (Figure 8-71).

3. Type the main entry in the *Main entry* text box.

   • It is very important to spell the main index entry correctly because Word uses the exact spelling to index text on the index page.

4. Type the subentry in the *Subentry* text box.

5. Click **Mark** or **Mark All**.

6. Continue marking index entries or click **Close** to close the dialog box.

8-71 Mark an index subentry

Cross-Reference an Index Entry

A *cross-reference index entry* references another index entry rather than a page number. You can cross-reference a main index entry or a subentry. Figure 8-72 shows an index page with a cross-reference index entry (*See* Sample SmartArt).

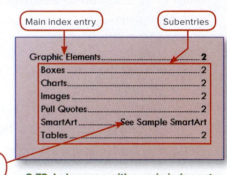

8-72 Index page with a main index entry, subentries, and a cross-reference index entry

▶ **HOW TO:** Mark a Cross-Reference Index Entry

1. Select the text or place the insertion point in your document where you want to create a cross-reference index entry.

2. Click the **Mark Entry** button [*References* tab, *Index* group] (Figure 8-73).

3. Type the main entry in the *Main entry* text box.

   • If you are cross-referencing a subentry, type the subentry in the *Subentry* text box also.

W8-494

4. Select the **Cross-reference** radio button in the *Options* area.

5. Click the *Cross-reference* text box after "*See*" and type the cross-reference text.

   • "*See*" automatically displays in the *Cross-reference* text box.

6. Click **Mark**.

7. Continue marking index entries or click **Close** to close the dialog box.

8-73 Create a cross-reference index entry

Insert an Index Page

After you finish marking index entries in your document, insert an ***index page***. Word provides a variety of index page formats. You can also customize the index page format to change the number of columns or page number alignment. It is usually best to insert the index page on a separate page at the end of your document.

▶ HOW TO: Create an Index Page

1. Place the insertion point in your document where you want to insert the index page.

   • Use a page break (**Ctrl+Enter**) to insert a blank page at the end of your document.
   • If you want a title on your index page, type it before you insert the index page.

2. Click the **Insert Index** button [*References* tab, *Index* group] to open the *Index* dialog box (Figure 8-74).

3. Click the **Formats** drop-down list and select an index page format.

   • A sample index page displays in the *Print Preview* area.

4. Check the **Right align page numbers** box if you want to align page numbers at the right.

5. Click the **Tab leader** drop-down list to select a tab leader.

6. Select the **Indented** or **Run-in** radio button in the *Type* area.

   • *Indented* places each subentry with an indent on a new line below the main entry. This is the default setting.
   • *Run-in* lists subentries on the same line. The document margins control how subentries wrap to the next line.

7. Type the number of columns in the *Columns* area.

8. Click the **OK** button to close the dialog box and to insert the index page (Figure 8-75).

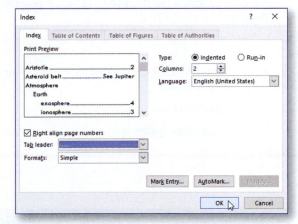

8-74 *Index* dialog box

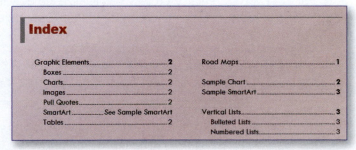

8-75 Index page

Update an Index Page

After inserting an index page, you can add, remove, or edit index entries. When you modify index entries or apply changes to your document that affect the pagination, update your index page to ensure index entries and page numbers are correct. Remember to turn off **Show/Hide** before you update your index page. Update your index page using one of the following methods:

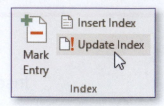

- Select the index page and click the **Update Index** button in the *Index* group on the *References* tab (Figure 8-76).
- Right-click the index page and **Update Field** from the context menu.
- Select the index page and press **F9**.

8-76 Update index page

Delete an Index Entry

If you want to remove an index entry, delete the index field code. When deleting an index entry, be very specific to select only the index field code and surrounding braces.

▶ **HOW TO:** Delete an Index Entry

1. Turn on **Show/Hide**.
2. Select the **index field code** to remove and press **Delete** (Figure 8-77).

8-77 Delete index field code

- Select both braces and the text between them ({XE "Road Maps" \b}).
- After you delete the index entry, check your document to ensure you did not delete any other text, spaces, or paragraph marks.

3. Turn off **Show/Hide**.
4. Click the **Update Index** button [*Reference* tab, *Index* group] to update your index page.

---

3. Mark main index entries.
   a. On the first page, select "**Road Maps**" in the first section heading; don't include the quotation marks.
   b. Click the **Mark Entry** button [*References* tab, *Index* group] to open the *Mark Index Entry* dialog box (Figure 8-78). The text "Road Maps" appears in the *Main entry* text box.
   c. Check the **Bold** check box in the *Page number format* area.
   d. Click **Mark All** to mark all instances of this text as a main index entry. Leave the *Mark Index Entry* dialog box open so you can mark additional index entries. You can drag the title bar of the *Mark Index Entry* dialog box to move it if needed.
   e. Select "**Graphic Elements**" in the main section heading on the second page of your document; don't include the paragraph mark.
   f. Click the **Main entry** text box to display the selected text, confirm the **Bold** box is checked, and click **Mark All**.
   g. Select "**Vertical Lists**" in the "Write Vertical Lists" section heading.
   h. Click the **Main entry** text box to display the selected text, confirm the **Bold** box is checked, and click **Mark All**.
   i. Leave the *Mark Index Entry* dialog box open to mark additional index entries. The index field codes affect pagination; this will be fixed later.

8-78 *Mark Index Entry* **dialog box**

4. Mark index subentries.
   a. Select "**Boxes**" in the first subheading of the "Add Graphic Elements" section.
   b. Delete the existing text in the *Main entry* text box, type Graphic Elements, and then type Boxes in the *Subentry* text box (Figure 8-79).
   c. Deselect the **Bold** check box and click **Mark All**.
   d. Repeat steps 4 a–c to mark the following index subentries in the "Add Graphic Elements" section. Type Graphic Elements as the *Main entry* for each subentry.

      Tables ("Boxes and Tables" heading)
      Pull Quotes (in the first sentence in the "Boxes and Tables" section)
      Charts ("Charts or Images" heading)
      Images ("Charts or Images" heading)

   e. Place the insertion point at the end of the second bulleted item in the "Write Vertical Lists" section.
   f. Type Vertical Lists in the *Main entry* text box, type Bulleted Lists in the *Subentry* text box, and click **Mark**.
   g. Place the insertion point at the end of the third bulleted item in the "Write Vertical Lists" section.

8-79 **Mark index subentry**

h. Type Vertical Lists in the *Main entry* text box, type Numbered Lists in the *Subentry* text box, and then click **Mark**.

i. Click **Close** to close the *Mark Index Entry* dialog box.

5. Mark an area and an object as index entries.
   a. Place the insertion point at the end of the body paragraph in the "Charts or Images" section.
   b. Click the **Mark Entry** button [*References* tab, *Index* group] to open the *Mark Index Entry* dialog box (Figure 8-80).
   c. Type Sample Chart in the *Main entry* text box, check the **Bold** box, and click **Mark**. Leave the *Mark Index Entry* dialog box open to mark an additional index entry.
   d. Select the *SmartArt* graphic in the "Conclusion" section.
   e. Type Sample SmartArt in the *Main entry* text box, check the **Bold** box, and click **Mark**. Leave the *Mark Index Entry* dialog box open to mark an additional index entry.

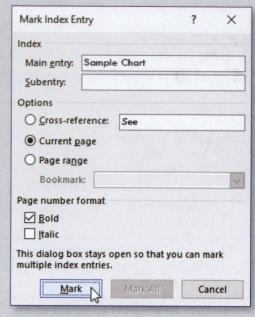

8-80 Mark a chart as an index entry

6. Create a cross-reference index entry.
   a. Select the word "**Images**" in the "Charts or Images" subheading.
   b. Type Graphic Elements in the *Main entry* text box and type SmartArt in the *Subentry* text box (Figure 8-81).
   c. Select the **Cross-reference** radio button and type Sample SmartArt after the word "*See*" in the text box.
   d. Deselect the **Bold** check box and click **Mark**.
   e. Click **Close** to close the dialog box.

7. Insert and customize an index page at the end of the document.
   a. Move to the end of the document (**Ctrl+End**) and insert a **page break** (**Ctrl+Enter**).
   b. Type Index, apply the **Heading 1** style, and press **Enter**.
   c. Click the **Insert Index** button [*References* tab, *Index* group] to open the *Index* dialog box (Figure 8-82).

8-81 Create a cross-reference index entry

d. Click the **Formats** drop-down list and select **Simple**.

e. Check the **Right align page numbers** box.

f. Click the **Tab leader** drop-down list and select the **dot leader**.

g. Confirm the *Type* is **Indented** and the number of *Columns* is **2**.

h. Click **OK** to close the dialog box and insert the index.

8. Update the index page.

a. Click the **Show/Hide** button [*Home* tab, *Paragraph* group] to turn it off.

b. Place the insertion point in the index and click the **Update Index** button [*References* tab, *Index* group].

9. Format the title of the document.

a. Select the title of the document.

b. Change the font to **Arial Black**.

c. Change the left indent to **−2"** (negative 2").

10. Save and close the document (Figure 8-83).

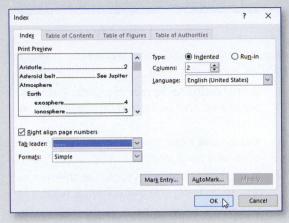

8-82 *Index* dialog box

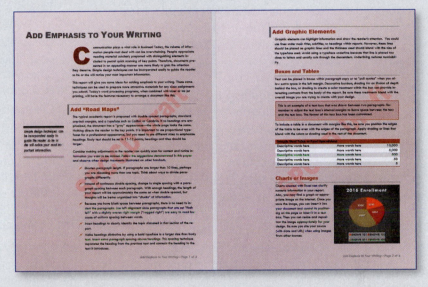

8-83 PP W8-4 completed

Chapter Summary

8.1 Apply desktop publishing features to a Word document (p. W8-463).

- ***Gutter margins***, ***mirror margins***, ***2 pages per sheet***, and ***book fold*** customize page layout.
- A ***drop cap*** emphasizes the first letter or first word of a paragraph.
- Customize a drop cap to adjust the number of lines to drop and the distance from text.
- Add ***page color*** to the document and customize page color with a fill color, gradient color, texture, pattern, or picture.
- A ***watermark*** is text or a picture that appears behind the text in the document without affecting the layout of the document. You can apply a built-in watermark, create a custom watermark, or use a picture as a watermark.
- Create a ***watermark building block*** to save and use in other documents.
- A ***screenshot*** or ***screen clipping*** captures and inserts a window or portion of a window as a picture in your document.
- The ***hyphenation*** feature automatically or manually hyphenates an entire document.
- Use ***Line numbering*** to insert line numbers on each line of a document. Line numbers are helpful when you are editing a long document or working with a group on document review.

8.2 Customize an existing theme and create a custom theme (p. *W8-472*).

- Apply a ***theme*** and customize ***theme colors***, ***theme fonts***, and ***theme effects***.
- Save a custom theme, theme colors, theme fonts, and theme effects to use in other documents.

8.3 Insert and customize a built-in text box and create a custom text box (p. *W8-473*).

- ***Text boxes*** are shapes that display text.
- Insert built-in text boxes or draw custom text boxes.
- Customize text boxes by applying a ***shape style***, ***fill***, ***outline***, or ***effect***.

- Save a text box as a ***building block*** to use in other documents.

8.4 Insert and customize a *SmartArt* graphic (p. *W8-479*).

- ***SmartArt*** graphics are shapes and text that graphically present information in a document.
- Use the *SmartArt* ***Text pane*** to type information in the *SmartArt* graphic or type information directly in the graphic objects.
- You can add shapes and text in the shapes. Text in a *SmartArt* graphic can be reordered, promoted, or demoted.
- Customize the *SmartArt* graphic design by changing the layout, colors, or applying a *SmartArt* style using the ***SmartArt Tools Design*** tab.
- Customize the individual objects and text in a *SmartArt* graphic using the ***SmartArt Tools Format*** tab.
- Resize and arrange *SmartArt* graphics in your document in the same way you resize and arrange pictures and shapes.

8.5 Insert and customize a chart (p. W8-484).

- Charts visually present numerical data.
- When you insert a chart, a ***Chart in Microsoft Word*** window opens where you type the chart data and set the ***chart data range***.
- The contextual ***Chart Tools Design*** and ***Chart Tools Format*** tabs allow you to customize the chart and its elements.
- Add and customize chart elements such as ***chart title***, ***axis titles***, ***legend***, ***data labels***, ***data table***, and ***gridlines***. You can also customize chart ***axes***, ***plot area***, ***chart wall***, ***chart floor***, and ***3-D rotation***.
- Preset options are available for all chart elements, and you can further customize each element using the contextual ***Format "Chart Element" pane***.
- Resize and arrange charts in your document in the same way you resize and arrange *SmartArt* graphics, pictures, and shapes.

8.6 Mark index entries and insert and customize an index page (p. W8-493).

- When you mark an *index entry* in your document, Word inserts an *index field code*.
- Use the *Mark Entry* dialog box to create a *main entry*, *subentry*, and a *cross-reference* index entry. You can customize the page number format and mark an individual entry or mark all instances of specific text.

- An *index* lists all index entries with a page number.
- You can customize the layout and format of the index page.
- After adding or deleting index entries, update the index when content or pagination changes.

Check for Understanding

The SIMbook for this text (within your SIMnet account) provides the following resources for concept review:

- Multiple choice questions
- Matching exercises
- Short answer questions

W8-501

Guided Project 8-1

For this project, you convert a document about teen substance abuse from Courtyard Medical Plaza into a booklet. You adjust page setup and margins, apply desktop publishing features, insert and customize text boxes, apply and modify a theme, insert and modify a *SmartArt* graphic, and mark index entries and create an index page.
[Student Learning Outcomes 8.1, 8.2, 8.3, 8.4, 8.6]

File Needed: **SubstanceAbuse-08.docx** *(student data files are available in the* Library *of your SIMnet account)*
Completed Project File Name: *[your initials] Word 8-1.docx*

Skills Covered in This Project

- Use book fold layout and change margins.
- Apply, customize, and save a theme.
- Apply page color and hyphenation.
- Insert and customize a built-in text box.

- Insert and customize a *SmartArt* graphic.
- Use the *Find* feature.
- Mark index entries.
- Create an index page.
- Update an index.

---

1. Open the **SubstanceAbuse-08** document from your student data files.

2. Save the document as [your initials] Word 8-1.

3. Change page setup and margins.
    a. Open the *Page Setup* dialog box.
    b. Click the **Multiple pages** drop-down list and select **Book fold**.
    c. Click the **Sheets per booklet** drop-down list and select **All**.
    d. Change the *Top*, *Bottom*, *Inside*, and *Outside* margins to **0.5"**.
    e. Change the *Gutter* to **0.25"**.
    f. Click **OK** to close the *Page Setup* dialog box. Click **Ignore** if a dialog box opens informing you the margins are outside the printable area.

4. Apply and customize a theme.
    a. Apply the **Integral** theme [*Design* tab, *Document Formatting* group].
    b. Click the **Colors** button [*Design* tab, *Document Formatting* group] and select **Aspect**.
    c. Click the **Colors** button again and select **Customize Colors**. The *Create New Theme Colors* dialog box opens (Figure 8-84).
    d. Click the **Accent 1** drop-down list and select **Red, Accent 2, Darker 25%**.
    e. Click the **Hyperlink** drop-down list and select **Red, Accent 2**.

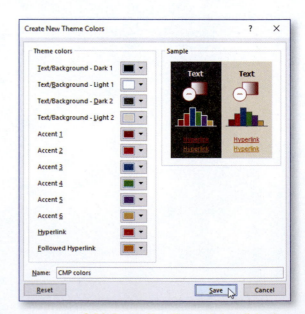

8-84 *Create New Theme Colors* dialog box

   f. Type **CMP colors** in the *Name* area

   g. Click **Save** to close the dialog box and save the new theme colors.

   h. Click the **Themes** button and select **Save Current Theme**. The *Save Current Theme* dialog box opens.

   i. Type **CMP** in the *File name* area and click **Save** to save the custom theme. Don't change the save location.

5. Click the **Page Color** button [*Design* tab, *Page Background* group] and select **White, Background 1, Darker 5%**.

6. Click the **Hyphenation** button [*Layout* tab, *Page Setup* group] and select **Automatic** to hyphenate the entire document.

7. Insert and customize a built-in text box.

   a. Place your insertion point at the end of the first paragraph in the "Why Do Teens Abuse Drugs and Alcohol?" section.

   b. Click the **Text Box** button [*Insert* tab, *Text* group] and select **Simple Quote**.

   c. Copy the last three sentences (don't include the paragraph mark) in the first paragraph of the "What Is Teen Substance Abuse?" section.

   d. Click the placeholder text in the text box to select it and press **Ctrl+V** to paste the text in the text box.

   e. Select the text in the text box, apply **italic** formatting, change the line spacing to **1.5**, and change the *After* paragraph spacing to **0 pt**.

   f. Click the **Shape Effects** button [*Drawing Tools Format* tab, *Shape Styles* group], select **Soft Edges**, and select **2.5 Point**.

   g. Change the *Height* and *Width* to **1.6"** [*Drawing Tools Format* tab, *Size* group].

   h. Click the **Position** button [*Drawing Tools Format* tab, *Arrange* group] and select **Position in Middle Right with Square Text Wrapping** (Figure 8-85).

   i. Turn on **Show/Hide**, and if there is a blank line in the "Why Do Teens Abuse Drugs and Alcohol?" section, delete it.

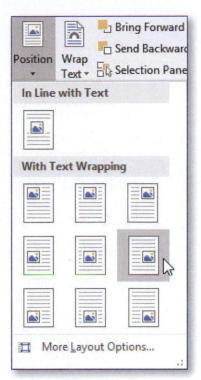

8-85 Position text box on the page

8. Insert and customize a built-in text box.

   a. Copy the first two sentences in the "What Should You Do If Your Teen Is Using?" section on the second page.

   b. Place your insertion point at the end of the last paragraph in the "What Should You Do If Your Teen Is Using?" section.

   c. Insert the **Simple Quote** built-in text box.

   d. Click the placeholder text in the text box to select it and press **Ctrl+V** to paste the text in the text box.

   e. Select the text in the text box, apply **italic** formatting, change the line spacing to **1.5**, and change the *After* paragraph spacing to **0 pt**.

   f. Apply a **2.5 Point** *Soft Edges* shape effect.

   g. Change the *Height* and *Width* to **1.8"** [*Drawing Tools Format* tab, *Size* group].

   h. Click the **Position** button [*Drawing Tools Format* tab, *Arrange* group] and select **Position in Bottom Right with Square Text Wrapping**.

9. Place your insertion point at the beginning of the "Can Teen Substance Use and Abuse Be Prevented?" section and insert a **page break**.

10. Insert and customize a *SmartArt* graphic.

   a. Place your insertion point at the end of the document.

   b. Click the **SmartArt** button [*Insert* tab, *Illustrations* group] to open the *Choose a SmartArt Graphic* dialog box.

c. Click **Cycle** on the left, select **Continuous Cycle**, and click **OK** to close the dialog box and to insert the *SmartArt* graphic (Figure 8-86).

d. Beginning at the top and going clockwise, type the following text in the *SmartArt* graphic boxes:

Expectations
Activities
House Rules
Communication
Know Friends

e. Select **Moderate Effect** in the *SmartArt Styles* gallery [*SmartArt Tools Design* tab] (Figure 8-87).

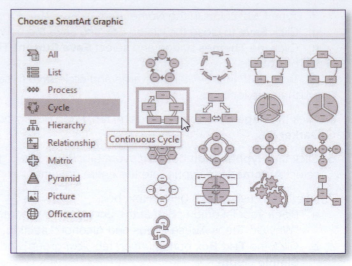

8-86 Insert a *SmartArt* graphic

11. Mark index entries.

a. Click the **Find** button [*Home* tab, *Editing* group] to open the *Navigation* pane to the left of the Word window.

b. Type alcohol in the text box at the top of the *Navigation* pane to find all instances of this word.

c. Select the first occurrence of "**alcohol**" in the body of the document.

d. Click the **Mark Entry** button [*References* tab, *Index* group] to open the *Mark Index Entry* dialog box. The word "alcohol" appears in the *Main entry* text box (Figure 8-88).

e. Capitalize the "A" in "alcohol" in the *Main entry* text box.

f. Click the **Mark All** button to mark all instances of this word as an index entry.

g. Continue this process to mark the following words as index entries. Capitalize the first letter of the first word in the *Main entry* text box.

8-87 Apply *SmartArt* style

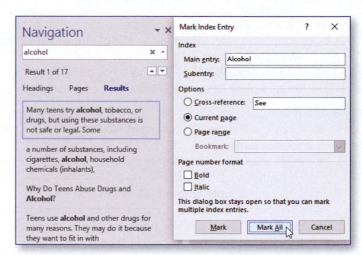

8-88 Find text in the *Navigation* pane and mark index entries

Tobacco
Drugs
Drug abuse
Marijuana
Risk
Treatment

h. Click **Close** to close the *Mark Index Entry* dialog box and close the *Navigation* pane.

12. Create an index page.

a. Place the insertion point at the end of your document (**Ctrl+End**) and insert a page break (**Ctrl+Enter**).

b. Type Index, apply the **Heading 1** style, and press **Enter**.

c. Click the **Insert Index** button [*References* tab, *Index* group] to open the *Index* dialog box (Figure 8-89).

d. Click the **Formats** drop-down list and select **Simple**.

e. Check the **Right align page numbers** box.

f. Click the **Tab leader** drop-down list and select the **dot leader**.

g. Confirm the *Type* is **Indented** and *Columns* is **2**.

h. Click **OK** to close the dialog box and insert the index.

13. Update the index page.

a. Turn off **Show/Hide** [*Home* tab, *Paragraph* group].

b. Place the insertion point in the index and click the **Update Index** button [*References* tab, *Index* group].

14. Save and close the document (Figure 8-90).

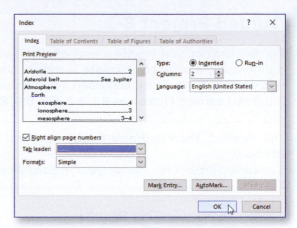

8-89 *Index* dialog box

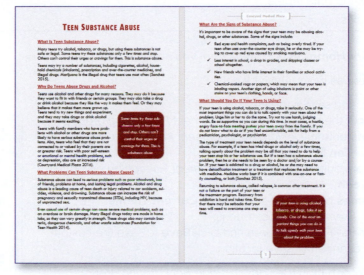

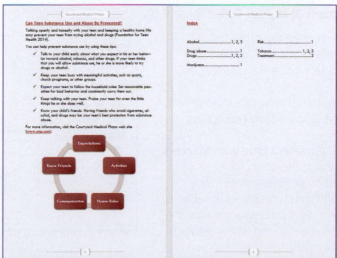

8-90 **Word 8-1 completed**

Guided Project 8-2

For this project, you modify a promotional flyer for Placer Hills Real Estate. You apply and modify a theme, apply a page color, create and customize a chart, insert and modify a *SmartArt* graphic, insert and customize a text box, and insert and position a watermark.
[Student Learning Outcomes 8.1, 8.2, 8.3, 8.4, 8.5]

File Needed: ***YourFirstHome-08.docx*** *(student data files are available in the* Library *of your SIMnet account)*
Completed Project File Name: *[your initials] Word 8-2.docx*

Skills Covered in This Project

- Apply, customize, and save a theme.
- Apply page color.
- Insert a chart and customize chart data.
- Insert an axis title and data labels.
- Modify a vertical axis.

- Customize chart elements.
- Resize a chart.
- Insert and customize a *SmartArt* graphic.
- Resize and arrange the *SmartArt* graphic.
- Insert, customize, and align a built-in text box.

1. Open the ***YourFirstHome-08*** document from your student data files.

2. Save the document as [your initials] Word 8-2.

3. Apply, customize, and save a theme.
   a. Apply the **Facet** theme [*Design* tab, *Document Formatting* group].
   b. Click the **Fonts** button [*Design* tab, *Document Formatting* group] and select **Tw Cen MT**.
   c. Click the **Colors** button [*Design* tab, *Document Formatting* group] and select **Green**.
   d. Click the **Themes** button and select **Save Current Theme**. The *Save Current Theme* dialog box opens.
   e. Type PHRE in the *File name* area and click **Save** to save the custom theme. Don't change the save location.

4. Click the **Page Color** button [*Design* tab, *Page Background* group] and select **Lime, Accent 3, Lighter 80%** (Figure 8-91).

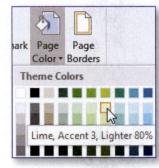

8-91 Apply a page color

5. Insert a chart and customize the chart data.
   a. Place your insertion point on the blank line below the "Fixed Mortgage Rate Averages" heading.
   b. Click the **Chart** button [*Insert* tab, *Illustrations* group]. The *Insert Chart* dialog box opens (Figure 8-92).
   c. Click **Line** at the left, select **Line with Markers**, and click **OK** to insert the chart.
   d. Type the information in Figure 8-93 in the *Chart in Microsoft Word* worksheet to replace the sample chart data. If necessary, resize the worksheet window by clicking and dragging the bottom right corner.

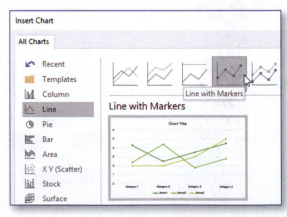

8-92 Insert a line chart

e. Click and drag the **chart data range** handle so it appears around the chart data you typed (see Figure 8-93). You don't have to delete the data in column D.

f. Click the **X** in the upper right corner of the *Chart in Microsoft Word* window to close it.

6. Add and customize chart elements.

a. Click the "**Chart Title**" and type Historic Mortgage Rates and Points to replace the existing text.

b. Click the **Add Chart Element** button [*Chart Tools Design* tab, *Chart Layouts* group], select **Axis Titles**, and select **Primary Vertical**.

c. Delete the placeholder text in the vertical axis title text box and type Percent in the text box.

d. Click the **Add Chart Element** button, select **Data Labels**, and select **Above**.

e. Right-click the vertical axis numbers and select **Format Axis**. The *Format Axis* pane opens.

f. Click the **Axis Options** button if it is not already selected (Figure 8-94).

g. Type 1.0 in the *Minor* text box in the *Units* area.

h. Click the **Tick Marks** heading.

i. Click the **Minor type** drop-down list and select **Cross**.

j. Close the *Format Axis* pane.

7. Customize chart elements.

a. Click the **Chart Elements** drop-down list [*Chart Tools Format* tab, *Current Selection* group] and select **Vertical (Value) Axis** to select the vertical axis.

b. Change the font size to **8 pt.** [*Home* tab, *Font* group].

c. Select the following chart elements and change the font size to **8 pt.**: **Horizontal (Category) Axis**, **Series "Rate" Data Labels**, **Series "Points" Data Labels**, and **Legend**.

d. Select the **Plot Area**, click the **Shape Fill** button [*Chart Tools Format* tab, *Shape Styles* group], and select **Lime, Accent 3, Lighter 80%**.

e. Select the **Chart Area**, click the **Shape Outline** button [*Chart Tools Format* tab, *Shape Styles* group], and select **Green, Accent 1**.

f. Click the **Shape Outline** button again, select **Weight**, and select **1½ pt**.

g. Click the **Shape Effects** button [*Chart Tools Format* tab, *Shape Styles* group], select **Shadow**, and select **Offset Diagonal Bottom Right** in the *Outer* category.

h. Select the **Chart Area** and change the *Height* to **3"** and the *Width* to **6.5"** [*Chart Tools Format* tab, *Size* group].

8. Insert and customize a *SmartArt* graphic.

a. Place the insertion point at the end of the document (**Ctrl+End**).

b. Click the **SmartArt** button [*Insert* tab, *Illustrations* group]. The *Choose a SmartArt Graphic* dialog box opens (Figure 8-95).

c. Click **Process** on the left, select **Circle Process**, and then click **OK**.

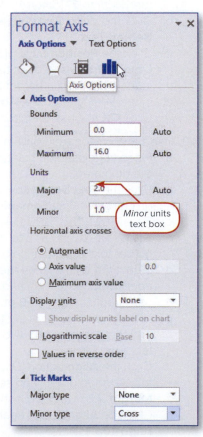

	A	B	C	D
1	Year	Rate	Points	Series 3
2	1975	9.19	1.2	2
3	1980	11.2	1.6	2
4	1985	13.88	2.5	3
5	1990	10.32	2.1	5
6	1995	8.38	1.8	
7	2000	7.44	1	
8	2005	5.84	0.7	
9	2010	5.04	0.7	
10	2015		0.8	
11				

Chart data range handle

8-93 Type chart data and select chart data range

Format Axis

Axis Options ▼   Text Options

Axis Options

▲ **Axis Options**

Bounds

Minimum   0.0   Auto

Maximum   16.0   Auto

Units

Major   2.0   Auto

Minor   1.0   *Minor* units text box

Horizontal axis crosses

⦿ Automatic

◯ Axis value   0.0

◯ Maximum axis value

Display units   None ▼

☐ Show display units label on chart

☐ Logarithmic scale   Base   10

☐ Values in reverse order

▲ **Tick Marks**

Major type   None ▼

Minor type   Cross ▼

8-94 *Format Axis* pane

d. Click the **Add Shape** button [*SmartArt Tools Design* tab, *Create Graphic* group] three times to add three more shapes to the graphic.

e. Beginning at the left, add the following text to the shapes:
Be patient
Be sure you are ready
Determine what you can afford
Get your credit in shape
Save for a down payment
Get mortgage pre-approval

f. Click the **Change Colors** button and select **Dark 2 Fill** in the *Primary Theme Colors* category.

g. Click the **SmartArt Styles** drop-down list and select **Inset** in the *3-D* category.

h. Click directly above the text in the first text box to select the text box and then use **Ctrl+click** to select the other five text boxes.

i. Apply **bold** formatting to the selected text boxes.

9. Resize and arrange the *SmartArt* graphic.

a. Click the frame of the *SmartArt* graphic to select it and change the *Height* to **1.8"** and the *Width* to **7"** [*SmartArt Tools Format* tab, *Size* group].

b. Click the **Wrap Text** button [*SmartArt Tools Format* tab, *Arrange* group] and select **Behind Text**.

c. Click the **Position** button [*SmartArt Tools Format* tab, *Arrange* group] and select **More Layout Options** to open the *Layout* dialog box.

d. In the *Horizontal* area, set **Absolute position** at **0.7"** *to the right of* **Page**.

e. In the *Vertical* area, set **Absolute position** at **8"** *below* **Page**.

f. Click **OK** to close the dialog box.

10. Insert and customize a built-in text box.

a. Place your insertion point at the beginning of the document.

b. Click the **Text Box** button [*Insert* tab, *Text* group] and select **Semaphore Quote**.

c. Type **HOME BUYING INFO FROM PLACER HILLS REAL ESTATE** to replace the place-holder text in the text box.

d. Select the text, change the font size to **14 pt.**, apply **bold** formatting, and change the After paragraph spacing to **0 pt**.

e. Change the *Height* of the text box to **0.8"** and the *Width* to **2.8"** [*Drawing Tools Format* tab, *Size* group].

f. Click the **Align** button [*Drawing Tools Format* tab, *Arrange* group] and select **Align to Margin**. *Align to Margin* should be checked.

g. Click the **Align** button again and select **Align Top**.

h. Turn on **Show/Hide**. If there is a blank line above the first line of text in the body of the document ("Learn about Mortgages"), delete it.

11. Save and close the document (Figure 8-96).

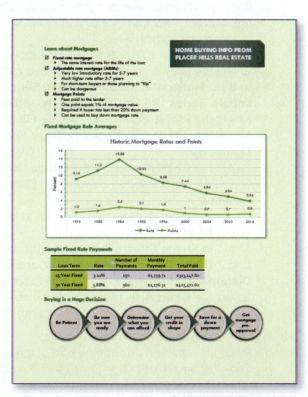

8-95 Insert *SmartArt* graphic

8-96 Word 8-2 completed

Guided Project 8-3

For this project, you create a draft of a newsletter for Central Sierra Insurance. You apply and modify a theme, apply hyphenation, insert a watermark, customize and apply a drop cap, use *WordArt*, insert and customize text boxes, and create and customize a chart.
[Student Learning Outcomes 8.1, 8.2, 8.3, 8.5]

File Needed: ***CSINewsletter-08.docx*** *(student data files are available in the* Library *of your SIMnet account)*
Completed Project File Name: ***[your initials] Word 8-3.docx***

Skills Covered in This Project

- Apply, customize, and save a theme.
- Set tab stops.
- Apply a border and shading to selected text.
- Apply automatic hyphenation.
- Insert a built-in watermark.
- Apply and customize a drop cap.
- Insert, resize, and arrange *WordArt*.
- Draw a text box around selected text.
- Customize text box style and arrangement.
- Insert a chart and customize chart data.
- Resize and position a chart.
- Insert a chart title and data labels.
- Modify a vertical axis.
- Customize chart elements.

1. Open the ***CSINewsletter-08*** document from your student data files.

2. Save the document as [your initials] Word 8-3.

3. Apply, customize, and save a theme.
   a. Apply the **Integral** theme [*Design* tab, *Document Formatting* group].
   b. Click the **Colors** button [*Design* tab, *Document Formatting* group] and select **Yellow Orange**.
   c. Click the **Themes** button and select **Save Current Theme**. The *Save Current Theme* dialog box opens.
   d. Type CSI in the *File name* area and click **Save** to save the custom theme. Don't change the save location.

4. Set tab stops and apply a border and shading to selected text.
   a. Turn on **Show/Hide**.
   b. Select the second paragraph ("Issue No. XVII . . .") and apply **bold** formatting.
   c. Set a **center** tab stop at **3.75"** and a **right** tab stop at **7.5"**.
   d. Use the *Borders and Shading* dialog box to apply a **Box** border, change the *Width* to **1 pt.**, and change the *Color* of the border to **Orange, Accent 1**.
   e. Click the **Shading** tab and select **Orange, Accent 1, Lighter 80%** as the *Fill* color.

5. Select the third paragraph ("CSI's Cost-Effective . . ."), change the font size to **22 pt.**, and apply **bold** formatting.

6. Click anywhere in the document to deselect the text, click the **Hyphenation** button [*Layout* tab, *Page Setup* group], and select **Automatic**.

7. Click the **Watermark** button [*Design* tab, *Page Background* group] and select **Draft 1** in the *Disclaimers* category.

8. Apply a drop cap to the first letter in a paragraph.
   a. Place the insertion point at the beginning of the first paragraph in the section with two columns ("Now you can have . . .").

b. Click the **Drop Cap** button [*Insert* tab, *Text* group] and select **Drop Cap Options** to open the *Drop Cap* dialog box (Figure 8-97).

c. Select **Dropped** in the *Position* area.

d. Change the *Lines to drop* to **2** and change the *Distance from text* to **0.1"**.

e. Click **OK** to close the dialog box and to apply the drop cap.

9. Apply *WordArt* to the title and position the title.

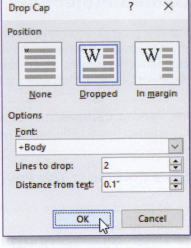

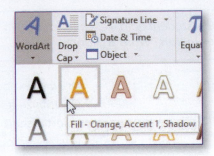

a. Select "**Central Sierra Insurance Newsletter**" at the top of the document.

b. Click the **WordArt** button [*Insert* tab, *Text* group] and select **Fill - Orange, Accent 1, Shadow** (Figure 8-98).

8-98 Apply *WordArt* to selected text

8-97 Customize and apply a drop cap

c. Click the **Wrap Text** button [*Drawing Tools Format* tab, *Arrange* group] and select **Tight**.

d. Click the **Position** button [*Drawing Tools Format* tab, *Arrange* group] and select **More Layout Options** to open the *Layout* dialog box.

e. In the *Horizontal* area, set **Alignment** at **Centered** *relative to* **Page**.

f. In the *Vertical* area, set **Absolute position** at **0.1"** *below* **Page**.

g. Click **OK** to close the dialog box.

10. Draw text boxes around selected text and customize the text boxes.

a. Select the paragraph of text beginning "**Picture mid-summer with temps . . .**"

b. Apply **bold** and **italic** formatting to the selected text.

c. Click the **Text Box** button [*Insert* tab, *Text* group] and select **Draw Text Box**. A text box appears around the selected text.

d. Click the **Shape Styles** drop-down list [*Drawing Tools Format* tab, *Shape Styles* group] and select **Subtle Effect - Orange, Accent 1** (Figure 8-99).

e. Change the *Width* of the text box to **7.5"** [*Drawing Tools Format* tab, *Size* group].

f. Select all of the text in the second column.

g. Click the **Text Box** button [*Insert* tab, *Text* group] and select **Draw Text Box**. A text box appears around the selected text.

h. Click the **Shape Styles** drop-down list [*Drawing Tools Format* tab, *Shape Styles* group] and select **Subtle Effect - Orange, Accent 1**.

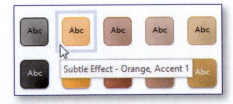

8-99 Apply shape style to text box

11. Insert a chart and customize the chart data.

a. Place your insertion point at the end of the document (**Ctrl+End**).

b. Click the **Chart** button [*Insert* tab, *Illustrations* group] to open the *Insert Chart* dialog box.

c. Click **Column** on the left, select **Clustered Column**, and click **OK** to insert the chart. A *Chart in Microsoft Word* worksheet also opens.

d. Type the information in Figure 8-100 in the *Chart in Microsoft Word* window to replace the sample chart data. Resize column width by clicking and dragging the right edge of a column heading.

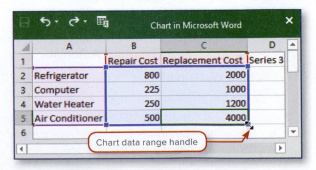

8-100 Type chart data and select chart data range

e. Click and drag the **chart data range** handle around the chart data you typed (see Figure 8-100).

f. Click the **X** in the upper right corner of the *Chart in Microsoft Word* window to close it.

12. Customize the position and size of the chart.

a. Select the border of the chart, click the **Position** button [*Chart Tools Format* tab, *Arrange* group] and select **Position in Bottom Center with Square Text Wrapping**.

b. Change the *Height* of the chart to **2.8"** and the *Width* to **6"** [*Chart Tools Format* tab, *Size* group].

13. Customize the layout of the chart.

a. Select the "**Chart Title**" and type Estimated Repair and Replacement Costs to replace the existing text.

b. Click the **Add Chart Element** button [*Chart Tools Design* tab, *Chart Layouts* group], click the **Data Labels** button, and select **Outside End** to align data labels above each column.

14. Customize chart elements and design.

a. Right-click the vertical axis numbers and select **Format Axis**. The *Format Axis* pane opens (Figure 8-101).

b. Click the **Number** heading.

c. Click the **Category** drop-down list and select **Currency**.

d. Change *Decimal places* to 0 and confirm that the *Symbol* is **$**.

e. Close the *Format Axis* pane.

f. Select **Style 14** from the *Chart Styles* gallery [*Chart Tools Design* tab, *Chart Styles* group].

g. Click the **Chart Elements** drop-down list [*Chart Tools Format* tab, *Current Selection* group] and select **Plot Area** to select the chart plot area.

h. Click the **Shape Fill** button [*Chart Tools Format* tab, *Shape Styles* group] and select **White, Background 1, Darker 5%**.

i. Select the **Chart Area** from the *Chart Elements* drop-down list, click the **Shape Outline** button [*Chart Tools Format* tab, *Shape Styles* group], and select **Orange, Accent 1**.

j. Click the **Shape Outline** button again, select **Weight**, and then select **2 ¼ pt**.

k. Click the **Shape Effects** button [*Chart Tools Format* tab, *Shape Styles* group], select **Shadow**, and then select **Offset Center** in the *Outer* category.

15. Save and close the document (Figure 8-102).

8-101 Customize vertical axis number format

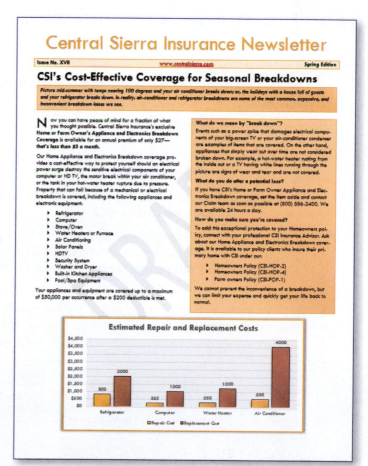

8-102 Word 8-3 completed

Independent Project 8-4

For this project, you customize a draft of a report for Sierra Pacific Community College District. You apply desktop publishing features, apply and customize a theme, insert and customize text boxes, insert and customize a *SmartArt* graphic and a chart, mark index entries, and create an index page.
[Student Learning Outcomes 8.1, 8.2, 8.3, 8.4, 8.5, 8.6]

File Needed: **OnlineLearning-08.docx** *(student data files are available in the Library of your SIMnet account)*
Completed Project File Name: **[your initials] Word 8-4.docx**

Skills Covered in This Project

- Adjust document margins and gutter settings.
- Apply, customize, and save a theme.
- Use and customize a drop cap.
- Create and apply a custom watermark.
- Apply automatic hyphenation.
- Insert a built-in watermark.
- Insert and customize a *SmartArt* graphic.

- Insert a chart and customize chart data.
- Insert a chart title and data labels.
- Modify a vertical axis.
- Apply a shape style to a chart.
- Resize a chart.
- Insert, customize, and position built-in text boxes.
- Mark index main entries and subentries.
- Create and update an index page.

1. Open the **OnlineLearning-08** document from your student data files.

2. Save the document as [your initials] Word 8-4.

3. Adjust margins and gutter settings.
   a. Change the top, bottom, left, and right margins to **0.75"**.
   b. Change the gutter to **0.25"** and the gutter position to **Left**.

4. Apply and customize a theme.
   a. Apply the **Retrospect** theme.
   b. Change the theme *Colors* to **Grayscale** and the theme *Fonts* to **Gil Sans MT**.
   c. Save the current theme as SPCCD 2.

5. Apply a **Dropped** drop cap to the first letter in the paragraph below the "PURPOSE OF THIS PLAN" heading and modify the lines to drop to **2**.

6. Create and apply a custom text watermark.
   a. Insert a custom text watermark and type OL Draft as the watermark text.
   b. Change the size to **120 pt**. and change the layout to **Diagonal**.

7. Insert and customize a *SmartArt* graphic.
   a. Place your insertion point at the end of the paragraph in the "PURPOSE OF THIS PLAN" section.
   b. Insert the **Horizontal Bullet List** *SmartArt* graphic (*List* category).
   c. Type the information shown in Figure 8-103 in the *SmartArt* graphic.
   d. Select the *SmartArt* border and change the height of the *SmartArt* graphic to **1.5"** and the width to **6.5"**.

8-103 *SmartArt* **graphic and text**

e. Change the *Colors* to **Colorful - Accent Colors**.
f. Apply the **Polished** *SmartArt* style (*3-D* area).
g. **Bold** the text in the three main headings of the *SmartArt* graphic.
h. Place the insertion point at the end of the paragraph above the *SmartArt* graphic and press **Enter**.

8. Insert and customize a chart.
a. Place your insertion point at the end of the last paragraph in the "Course Offerings and Programs" section on the second page.
b. Insert a **Clustered Column** chart.
c. Type the information in Figure 8-104 in the *Chart in Microsoft Word* worksheet to replace the sample chart data.
d. Adjust the chart data range as needed and close the *Chart in Microsoft Word* worksheet.
e. Type SPCCD Course Offerings as the chart title.
f. Apply data labels to the **Outside End** of the columns.
g. Apply the **Style 11** chart style.
h. Format the vertical axis and change the number format to **Number** with **0** decimal places and a **1000 separator**.
i. Select the **Chart Area** and apply the **Subtle Effect - Light Gray, Accent 1** shape style.
j. Change the height of the chart to **2.5"** and the width to **6.5"**.
k. Place the insertion point at the end of the paragraph above the chart and press **Enter**.

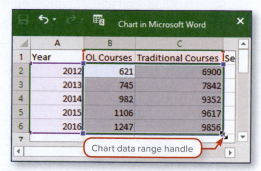

8-104 Type chart data and select chart data range

9. Insert and customize text boxes.
a. Place your insertion point at the end of the paragraph in the "Planning Process" section on the first page and insert the **Austin Quote** built-in text box.
b. Copy the second sentence in the paragraph in the "PURPOSE OF THIS PLAN" section and paste (**Ctrl+V**) it in the text box to replace the placeholder text.
c. Select the text box and apply the **Subtle Effect - Black, Dark 1** shape style.
d. Change the height of the text box to **1.25"** and the width to **3.4"**.
e. Set the *Position* [*Drawing Tools Format* tab, *Arrange* group] as **Position in Bottom Right with Square Text Wrapping**.
f. Place your insertion point at the top of the third page and insert the **Austin Quote** built-in text box.
g. Copy the first and second sentences in the first paragraph in the "Tech Support Services" section and paste it in the text box to replace the placeholder text.
h. Select the text box and apply the **Subtle Effect - Black, Dark 1** shape style.
i. Change the height of the text box to **1.6"** and the width to **2.3"**.
j. Set the *Position* as **Position in Middle Right with Square Text Wrapping**.

10. Insert **page breaks** before the "Program Selection" and "Student Support Services" headings.

11. Mark index entries.
a. Select and mark the four main section headings as a **Main entry**. Use **bold** page number format and click **Mark** (not *Mark All*).
b. Select each of the types of online courses in the "ONLINE LEARNING MODES" section and mark each as **Subentry**. Type Online Learning Modes as the *Main entry* and the online course type as the *Subentry*. Do not use bold page number format.
c. Select each of the subheadings in the "PLANNING PROCESS" section and mark as **Subentry**. Type Planning Process as the *Main entry* and the subheading as the *Subentry*. Do not use bold page number format.
d. Select each of the subheadings in the "SPCCD ONLINE LEARNING" section and mark as **Subentry**. Type SPCCD Online Learning as the *Main entry* and the subheading as the *Subentry*. Do not use bold page number format.
e. Select the chart and create an index entry. Type SPCCD Online Learning as the *Main entry* and Course Offerings Chart as the *Subentry*. Do not use bold page number format.

12. Create and update an index page.
    a. Place the insertion point at the end of the document and insert a **page break**.
    b. Type Index, apply the **Heading 1** style, and then press **Enter**.
    c. Insert an index and use **Simple** format, **right align page** numbers, use a **dot leader**, and use **1** column.
    d. Turn off **Show/Hide** and update the index.

13. Save and close the document (Figure 8-105).

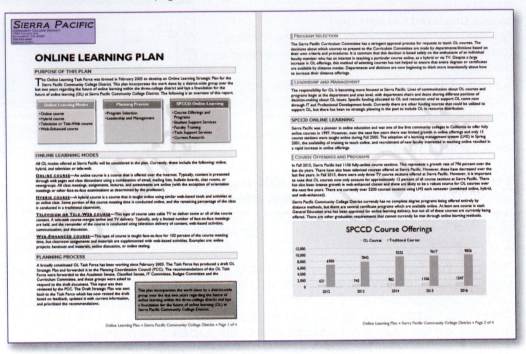

8-105 Word 8-4 completed

Independent Project 8-5

For this project, you customize an informational flyer for the Skiing Unlimited program. You apply desktop publishing features, apply and customize a theme, insert and customize a text box, and insert and customize a *SmartArt* graphic and chart.
[**Student Learning Outcomes 8.1, 8.2, 8.3, 8.4, 8.5**]

Files Needed: ***SkiingUnlimited-08.docx*** and ***Snow-08.png*** *(student data files are available in the Library of your SIMnet account)*
Completed Project File Name: *[your initials] Word 8-5.docx*

Skills Covered in This Project

- Customize and save a theme.
- Use a picture as a page color.
- Insert and customize a built-in text box.
- Insert a chart and customize chart data.
- Insert data labels.
- Modify chart elements.
- Apply a chart and shape style to the chart.
- Resize the chart.
- Insert and customize a *SmartArt* graphic.
- Resize and arrange a *SmartArt* graphic.

---

1. Open the ***SkiingUnlimited-08*** document from your student data files.

2. Save the document as [your initials] Word 8-5.

3. Create a custom theme.
   a. Change the theme *Colors* to **Red**, theme *Fonts* to **Candara**, and theme *Effects* to **Grunge Texture**.
   b. Save the current theme as Skiing Unlimited.

4. Apply a picture as the page color.
   a. Apply a **Page Color** and use **Fill Effects**.
   b. Select the **Picture** tab of the *Fill Effects* dialog box and select the **Snow-08** picture from your student data files.

5. Insert and customize a built-in text box.
   a. Place your insertion point at the top of the document and insert the **Grid Quote** built-in text box.
   b. Type SKIING UNLIMITED, press **Enter**, and type LOOKING BACK . . . LOOKING FORWARD to replace the placeholder text in the text box.
   c. Change the height of the text box to **1.5"** and the width to **8.4"**.
   d. Select "**SKIING UNLIMITED**" in the text box, change the font size to **40 pt.**, apply **bold** formatting, turn off italic formatting, and **left** align text.
   e. Select "**LOOKING BACK. . .LOOKING FORWARD**," change the font size to **16 pt.**, and **right** align text.
   f. Use the *Position* tab in the *Layout* dialog box to change the *Horizontal* **Alignment** to **Centered** relative to **Page** and change the *Vertical* **Alignment** to **Top** relative to **Page**.
   g. Turn on **Show/Hide**, and if there is a blank line above the first body paragraph, delete it.
   h. Apply **10 pt.** *Before* paragraph spacing on the first body paragraph below the text box.

6. Insert and customize a chart.
   a. Place your insertion point at the end of the first body paragraph in the document.
   b. Insert a **Clustered Bar** chart.
   c. Type the information in Figure 8-106 in the *Chart in Microsoft Word* worksheet to replace the sample chart data.

◢	A	B	C
1		Participants	Volunteers
2	2014	41	104
3	2015	53	138
4	2016	61	186
5	2017	74	231

8-106 Type chart data and select chart data range

d. Adjust the chart data range and close the worksheet.

e. Type Skiing Unlimited to replace the existing text as the chart title.

f. Add data labels to the **Outside End** of the bars.

g. Apply the **Style 12** chart style.

h. Select the **Chart Area** and apply the **Subtle Effect – Black, Dark 1** shape style.

i. Apply **bold** formatting to the data labels (participants and volunteers), vertical axis, horizontal axis, and legend.

j. Select the chart area and change the height of the chart to **2.5"** and the width to **6.5"**.

k. Place the insertion point at the end of the paragraph above the chart and press **Enter**.

7. Insert and customize a *SmartArt* graphic.

   a. Place your insertion point at the end of the second body paragraph.

   b. Insert the **Circle Arrow Process** *SmartArt* graphic (*Process* category).

   c. Type the following information in the *SmartArt* graphic. Add shapes and use the *Text* pane as needed.

   January 20
   January 27
   February 10
   February 17
   February 24

   d. Apply **bold** formatting and **8 pt**. font size to the text in the *SmartArt* graphic.

   e. Select the border of the *SmartArt* and change the height to **3.5"** and the width to **2"**.

   f. Change the color of the *SmartArt* graphic to **Dark 2 Fill**.

   g. Apply the **Subtle Effect** *SmartArt* style.

   h. Change the text wrapping to **Tight**.

   i. Drag the *SmartArt* graphic to the bottom right of the first page. Use the alignment guides for placement.

   j. Use the *Position* tab in the *Layout* dialog box to change the *Horizontal* **Absolute position** to **6"** *to the right of* **Page** and change the *Vertical* **Absolute position** to **7"** *below* **Page**.

8. Save and close the document (Figure 8-107).

8-107 Word 8-5 completed

Independent Project 8-6

For this project, you customize a weekly expense report for Life's Animal Shelter. You apply desktop publishing features, apply and customize a theme, insert and customize text boxes, and insert and customize a chart. **[Student Learning Outcomes 8.1, 8.2, 8.3, 8.5]**

File Needed: **WeeklyExpenses-08.docx** (student data files are available in the Library of your SIMnet account)
Completed Project File Name: **[your initials] Word 8-6.docx**

Skills Covered in This Project

- Customize and save a theme.
- Apply and customize a drop cap.
- Insert and customize built-in text boxes.
- Insert a chart and customize chart data.
- Customize the chart title.
- Modify chart elements.
- Apply a chart and shape style to the chart.
- Resize a chart.

1. Open the **WeeklyExpenses-08** document from your student data files.

2. Save this document as [your initials] Word 8-6.

3. Change the bottom margin to **0.5"**.

4. Create a custom theme.
   a. Change the theme *Colors* to **Median**, theme *Fonts* to **Corbel**, and theme *Effects* to **Banded Edge**.
   b. Save the current theme as LAS.

5. Apply a **Dropped** drop cap to the first letter in the first body paragraph, modify it to drop **2** lines, and set the distance from text to **0.1"**.

6. Insert and customize a built-in text box.
   a. Place your insertion point at the top of the document and insert the **Grid Sidebar** built-in text box.
   b. Change the height to **11"** and the width to **2.5"**.
   c. Use the *Position* tab in the *Layout* dialog box to change the *Horizontal* **Alignment** to **Right** *relative to* **Page** and change the *Vertical* **Alignment** to **Top** *relative to* **Page**
   d. Type Life's Animal Shelter to replace the first placeholder text ("Sidebar Title").
   e. Select "**Life's Animal Shelter**" in the text box, change the font size to **28 pt.**, apply **bold** formatting (if not already applied), and apply the **Offset Diagonal Top Right** shadow text effect.
   f. Click the second placeholder text and type the following, pressing **Enter** after each line except the last line:

      3429 Second Avenue North
      Park Rapids, MN 56470
      218.240.7880
      www.lifesanimalshelter.com
      "Serving our community through animal rescue and pet adoption"
      (Don't press *Enter* after this last line.)

   g. Select the address and phone number lines and change the *After* paragraph spacing to **0 pt**.
   h. Select the quoted text including the quotation marks ("**Serving our community . . .**"), change the line spacing to **1.5**, and apply **italic** formatting.
   i. Turn on **Show/Hide**, and if there is a blank line above the first body paragraph, delete it.

7. Insert and customize a chart.
   a. Place your insertion point at the end of the second body paragraph.
   b. Insert a **3-D Clustered Column** chart.

c. Type the information in Figure 8-108 in the *Chart in Microsoft Word* worksheet, to replace the sample chart data.

d. Adjust the chart data range and close the worksheet.

e. Change the height of the chart to **3"** and the width to **4.5"**.

f. Type Daily Expenses to replace the existing text in the chart title.

g. Apply the **Style 6** chart style.

h. Select the **Chart Area** and apply the **Brown, Text 2** shape fill color.

i. In the *Gradient* area on the *Shape Fill* drop-down list, select the **From Center** gradient in the *Dark Variations* category.

j. Apply **bold** formatting to the legend and the horizontal axis.

k. Place your insertion point at the end of the second body paragraph and press **Enter**.

	A	B	C
1		Daily Total Expenses	Daily Average Expenses
2	Mon	1785	298
3	Tue	1709	285
4	Wed	1710	285
5	Thurs	1717	286
6	Fri	1841	307
7	Sat/Sun	2116	353

8-108 Type chart data and select chart data range

8. Insert and customize a built-in text box.

a. Select the last body paragraph (not including the paragraph mark) and cut (**Ctrl+X**) it from the document.

b. Insert the **Motion Quote** built-in text box and paste (**Ctrl+V**) the cut text in the text box to replace the placeholder text.

c. Select the text in the text box and change text alignment to **Center** [*Home* tab, *Paragraph* group].

d. Apply the **Preset 2** shape effect.

e. Change the width of the text box to **4.5"**.

f. Set the position as **Position in Bottom Left with Square Text Wrapping**.

9. Save and close the document (Figure 8-109).

8-109 Word 8-6 completed

Improve It Project 8-7

For this project, you customize a document from American River Cycling Club. You apply desktop publishing features, apply and customize a theme, and insert and customize text boxes, a *SmartArt* graphic, and a chart.
[Student Learning Outcomes 8.1, 8.2, 8.3, 8.4, 8.5]

File Needed: ***HeartRate-08.docx*** *(student data files are available in the* Library *of your SIMnet account)*
Completed Project File Name: *[your initials] **Word 8-7.docx***

Skills Covered in This Project

- Adjust margins.
- Apply and customize a drop cap.
- Customize and save a theme.
- Draw and customize a text box.
- Align and group a picture and text box.
- Insert and customize a *SmartArt* graphic.

- Insert a chart and customize chart data.
- Resize a chart.
- Insert a chart title, axis titles, and data labels.
- Apply a chart and shape style to the chart.
- Modify chart elements.
- Insert, customize, and position a built-in text box.

1. Open the ***HeartRate-08*** document from your student data files.

2. Save the document as [your initials] Word 8-7.

3. Change the top margin to **0.75"**, the bottom margin to **0.5"**, the left margin to **1.75"**, and the right margin to **0.75"**.

4. Apply a **Dropped** drop cap to the first letter in the first body paragraph and modify it to drop **2** lines.

5. Create a custom theme.
   a. Change the theme *Colors* to **Green Yellow** and theme *Fonts* to **Gil Sans MT**.
   b. Save the current theme as ARCC.

6. Draw a text box and customize it.
   a. Draw a text box down the left side of your document.
   b. Change the height to **11"** and the width to **1.3"**.
   c. Apply the **Lime, Accent 1, Lighter 80%** shape fill.
   d. Remove the shape outline (**No Outline**).

7. Resize a picture and align and group a picture with a text box.
   a. Select the picture (logo) at the top of the document and change the width to **8.5"**. The height automatically adjusts.
   b. With the picture selected, **Rotate Left 90°**.
   c. Drag the picture on top of the text box at the left and **Bring to Front** [*Picture Tools Format* tab, *Arrange* group].
   d. Use the **Ctrl** key to select the text box and picture.
   e. Align selected objects at **Align Center** and **Align Middle**.
   f. Confirm both objects are still selected and **Group** the two objects.
   g. Use the *Position* tab in the *Layout* dialog box to change the *Horizontal* **Absolute position** to **0"** *to the right of* **Page** and change the *Vertical* **Alignment** to **Top** *relative to* **Page**.

8. Insert and customize a *SmartArt* graphic.
   a. Place your insertion point at the end of the second body paragraph ("Example: a 40-year-old's . . .").
   b. Insert the **Equation** *SmartArt* graphic (*Process* category).

 c. Type the following information in the *SmartArt* graphic:

  220
  Age
  Max Heart Rate

 d. Select the **Plus** shape and change it to a **Minus** shape [*SmartArt Tools Format* tab, *Shapes* group].

 e. Select the border of the *SmartArt* graphic and change the height to **1"** and the width to **4"**.

 f. Apply the **Intense Effect** *SmartArt* style.

 g. Change the text wrapping to **Top and Bottom**.

 h. Use the *Position* tab in the *Layout* dialog box to change the *Horizontal* **Alignment** to **Centered** *relative to* **Margin** and change the *Vertical* **Alignment** to **Top** *relative to* **Line**.

 i. Select the sentence below the *SmartArt* graphic and **center** it.

9. Insert and customize a chart.

 a. Select the tabbed text below the paragraphs and delete it.

 b. Place your insertion point on the blank line below the last body paragraph and insert a **Line with Markers** chart.

 c. Type the information in Figure 8-110 in the *Chart in Microsoft Word* worksheet to replace the sample chart data.

 d. Adjust the chart data range and close the worksheet.

 e. Change the height of the chart to **3.3"** and the width to **6"**.

 f. Type **Max and Target Heart Rates** in the chart title to replace the existing text.

 g. Add a **Primary Horizontal** axis title and type **Age** in the text box.

 h. Add a **Primary Vertical** axis title and type **Heart Rate** in the text box.

	A	B	C
1	Age	Max Heart Rate	Target Heart Rate (75%)
2	20	200	150
3	25	195	146
4	30	190	143
5	35	185	139
6	40	180	135
7	45	175	131
8	50	170	128
9	55	165	124
10	60	160	120

8-110 Type chart data and select chart data range

10. Modify chart elements.

 a. Apply the **Style 2** chart style.

 b. Select the **Chart Area** and apply the **Subtle Effect – Lime, Accent 1** shape style.

 c. Change the shape outline weight to **1" pt**.

 d. Apply the **Offset Center** shadow shape effect (*Outer* category).

 e. Select the legend and apply the **Subtle Effect – Lime, Accent 1** shape style.

11. Insert and customize a text box.

 a. Place your insertion point at the end of the first paragraph in the "What Is Target Heart Rate?" section and insert the **Austin Quote** built-in text box.

 b. Copy the first sentence in the second paragraph in the "What Is Target Heart Rate?" section and paste it in the text box to replace the placeholder text.

 c. Change the height of the text box to **1.6"** and the width to **2"**.

 d. Select the text box and apply the **Subtle Effect – Lime, Accent 1** shape style.

 e. Change the text wrapping to **Tight**.

 f. Use the *Position* tab in the *Layout* dialog box to change the *Horizontal* **Absolute position** to **5.9"** *to the right of* **Page** and change the *Vertical* **Absolute position** to **3.4"** *below* **Page**.

 g. Select the text in the text box, apply **italic** formatting, and change the text alignment to **center**.

 h. Turn on **Show/Hide**, and if there is a blank line above the first body paragraph in the "What is Target Heart Rate" section, delete it.

12. Save and close the document (Figure 8-111).

American River Cycling Club

info@arcc.org

Cycling...a way of life

www.arcc.org

WHAT IS MAXIMUM HEART RATE?

Maximum heart rate is the highest your pulse rate can get. To calculate your predicted **maximum heart rate**, use this formula:

(Example: a 40-year-old's predicted maximum heart rate is 180)

Your actual maximum heart rate can be determined by a graded exercise test. Please note that some medicines and medical conditions might affect your maximum heart rate. If you are taking medicines or have a medical condition (such as heart disease, high blood pressure, or diabetes), always ask your doctor if your maximum heart rate/target heart rate will be affected.

WHAT IS TARGET HEART RATE?

You gain the most benefits and decrease the risk of injury when you exercise in your target heart rate zone. Usually this is when your exercise heart rate (pulse) is 60 percent to 85 percent of your maximum heart rate. Do not exercise for an extended amount of time above 85 percent of your maximum heart rate. This increases both cardiovascular and orthopedic risk and does not add any extra benefit.

> When beginning an exercise program, you might need to gradually build up to a level that is within your target heart rate zone, especially if you have not exercised regularly before.

When beginning an exercise program, you might need to gradually build up to a level that is within your target heart rate zone, especially if you have not exercised regularly before. If the exercise feels too hard, slow down. You will reduce your risk of injury and enjoy the exercise more if you don't try to over-do it.

To find out if you are exercising in your target zone (between 60 percent and 85 percent of your maximum heart rate), use your heart rate monitor to track your heart rate. If your pulse is below your target zone (see the chart below), increase your rate of exercise. If your pulse is above your target zone, decrease your rate of exercise.

The following chart displays maximum and target heart rates for different ages. Remember, these are estimated heart rates and will vary depending of fitness level and other physiological factors.

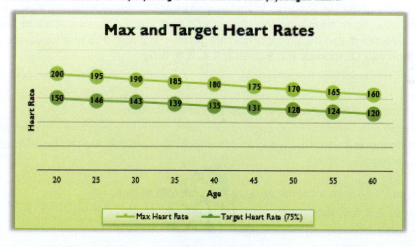

8-111 Word 8-7 completed

Challenge Project 8-8

It is important to plan and budget for your college education. Create an education plan and budget using desktop publishing and graphics features discussed in this chapter. Use a *SmartArt* graphic to plan your courses for your remaining semesters and use a chart to visually display your estimated expenses.
[Student Learning Outcomes 8.1, 8.2, 8.3, 8.4, 8.5]

File Needed: None
Completed Project File Name: *[your initials] Word 8-8.docx*

Create a new blank document and save it as [your initials] Word 8-8. Create an education plan and budget using the Word features you learned about in this chapter. Modify your document according to the following guidelines:

- Use a *SmartArt* graphic to display your education plan.
- Use a chart to display your estimated expenses.
- Apply and customize a theme and create a custom theme.
- Customize the *SmartArt* graphic and chart layout and design.
- As appropriate, include a drop cap, page color, watermark, screenshot, and/or hyphenation.
- Insert a built-in text box or draw a text box and customize as needed.

Challenge Project 8-9

Apply desktop publishing features to improve readability and enhance the appearance of a report from one of your classes or from your job. Apply and customize a theme, mark index entries, and create an index page. You can also include a *SmartArt* graphic, a chart, and text boxes as appropriate.
[Student Learning Outcomes 8.1, 8.2, 8.3, 8.4, 8.5, 8.6]

File Needed: None
Completed Project File Name: *[your initials] Word 8-9.docx*

Open an existing report and save it as [your initials] Word 8-9. Modify your document according to the following guidelines:

- Apply and customize a theme and create a custom theme.
- Mark index entries, subentries, and cross-reference index entries.
- Create and customize an index page.
- Use built-in text boxes for pull quotes to emphasize important information in the report.
- Insert and customize a *SmartArt* graphic and/or chart as appropriate to visually display information.
- Include a drop cap, page color, watermark, screenshot, and/or hyphenation, as appropriate.

Challenge Project 8-10

Create a flyer, announcement, or invitation to an upcoming event for a student group or organization on campus, such as a blood drive, community service event, or food bank collection. Use desktop publishing and graphic features to enhance this document.
[Student Learning Outcomes 8.1, 8.2, 8.3, 8.4, 8.5]

File Needed: None
Completed Project File Name: *[your initials] Word 8-10.docx*

Create a new blank document and save it as [your initials] Word 8-10. Create a flyer, announcement, or invitation using Word features you learned in this chapter. Modify your document according to the following guidelines:

- Apply and customize a theme and create a custom theme.
- Appropriately include a drop cap, page color, watermark, screenshot, and/or hyphenation.
- Insert and customize text boxes to emphasize information in pull quotes.
- Insert and customize a *SmartArt* graphic and/or chart, as appropriate, to visually display information.
- Customize your *SmartArt* graphics and chart layout and design.

Working Collaboratively and Integrating Applications

CHAPTER OVERVIEW

Microsoft Word provides tools that allow you to work collaboratively on documents. *Comments* and *Track Changes* are two valuable collaboration tools that you use to edit documents. In addition to working with multiple users, you can also work with multiple applications. When preparing documents, you can incorporate content from other Microsoft Office applications. For example, you can insert a PowerPoint slide, a chart from Excel, or a table from Access in your Word documents. You can also merge data from Outlook, Excel, and Access into a Word document.

STUDENT LEARNING OUTCOMES (SLOs)

After completing this chapter, you will be able to:

SLO 9.1 Enhance collaboration by using advanced comments and track changes features and sharing documents (p. W9-525).

SLO 9.2 Use Word collaboration features to compare, combine, and protect documents (p. W9-531).

SLO 9.3 Embed and link content from other Microsoft Office applications into a Word document (p. W9-542).

SLO 9.4 Use mail merge rules to customize how data merges into a Word document from other Office applications (p. W9-551).

SLO 9.5 Insert bookmarks into a document (p. W9-553).

CASE STUDY

In the Pause & Practice projects in this chapter, you use collaboration and integration features available in Word to enhance an informational document from Hamilton Civic Center about their yoga classes.

Pause & Practice 9-1: Use advanced *Comments* and *Track Changes* features to edit a document and review a document that has comments and edits marked with tracked changes.

Pause & Practice 9-2: Prepare a document to be shared, combine changes in two documents, and protect a document.

Pause & Practice 9-3: Embed and link objects from PowerPoint and Excel into a Word document.

Pause & Practice 9-4: Add a bookmark to a document, merge recipients from Excel into a Word document, and use rules to customize a mail merge.

WORD

Advanced Collaboration Features

In *Chapter 3: Collaborating with Others and Working with Reports*, you learned how to use comments and tracked changes to collaborate on a document. In this chapter, you will learn how to customize these features and use advanced collaboration features. You can customize how comments and tracked changes display in a document, lock tracking, collaborate on an online document, and print document markup.

> ### MORE INFO
>
> Review comments and track changes in *SLO 3.1: Using Comments* and *SLO 3.2: Using Track Changes and Sharing*.

Customize Comment and Markup Color

Comments and tracked changes appear in a default color when you insert a comment or change a document using *Track Changes*. If multiple reviewers are commenting on the same document, Word uses a different color for each reviewer. You can select a color to use for comments and markup in the ***Track Changes Options*** dialog box.

▶ HOW TO: Customize Comment and Markup Color

1. Click the **Tracking** launcher [*Review* tab, *Tracking* group] to open the *Track Changes Options* dialog box.

2. Click the **Advanced Options** button to open the *Advanced Track Changes Options* dialog box (Figure 9-1).

3. Click the **Insertions Color**, **Deletions Color**, or **Comments** drop-down lists and select a color for comments and markups.
   - All existing and new comments and markup change to the selected color.
   - By default, Word uses the *By author* option, which uses a different color for each author.

4. Click **OK** to close the *Advanced Track Changes Options* dialog box.

5. Click **OK** to close the *Track Changes Options* dialog box.

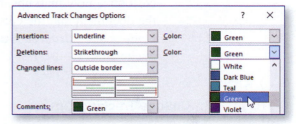

9-1 Change comment and markup color in the *Advanced Track Changes Options* dialog box

Customize Show Markup Options

You can customize which markups display, how they display, and which reviewers' markups display.

▶ HOW TO: Customize Show Markup Options

1. Click the **Show Markup** button [*Review* tab, *Tracking* group] to display the list of markup options.

2. Select the markup options to display or hide (*Comments*, *Ink*, *Insertions and Deletions*, and *Formatting*).
   - A check mark indicates a markup option displays.

3. Click **Balloons** and select one of the three balloons options: **Show Revisions in Balloons**, **Show All Revisions Inline**, or **Show Only Comments and Formatting in Balloons** (Figure 9-2).
   - *Show Only Comments and Formatting in Balloons* is the default setting.
4. Click **Specific People** to display a list of reviewers and select or deselect reviewers as desired (Figure 9-3).
   - When you deselect a reviewer, his or her comments and revisions do not display in the document.
   - A check mark indicates a reviewer's comments and revisions display in the document.

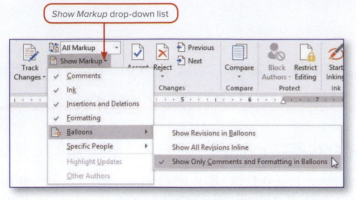

9-2 Customize *Show Markup* options

9-3 Select or deselect reviewers

Change Tracking Options

The **Track Changes Options** and **Advanced Track Changes Options** dialog boxes provide you additional control over how changes and comments appear in your document. You can customize how markups, moves, table cell highlighting, formatting, and balloons display in the document and the color for each of these changes. Changes made in the *Track Changes Options* and *Advanced Track Changes Options* dialog boxes are global changes that affect all documents that use *Track Changes*.

▶**HOW TO:** Change Tracking Options

1. Click the **Tracking** launcher [*Review* tab, *Tracking* group] to open the *Track Changes Options* dialog box.
2. Click the **Advanced Options** button to open the *Advanced Track Changes Options* dialog box (Figure 9-4).
3. Click the **Insertions**, **Deletions**, **Changed lines**, **Comments**, or **Color** drop-down list and change the appearance as desired.
4. Select or deselect the **Track moves** check box to determine if Word marks moved content as a tracked change.
   - Use the drop-down lists to customize how *Moved from* and *Moved to* display in your documents.
   - Also in this area, customize how *Inserted cells*, *Deleted cells*, *Merged cells*, and *Split cells* display.
5. Select or deselect the **Track formatting** check box to determine if Word marks formatting changes as a tracked change.
   - In this area, customize how formatting changes display in the document and the *Markup* area.

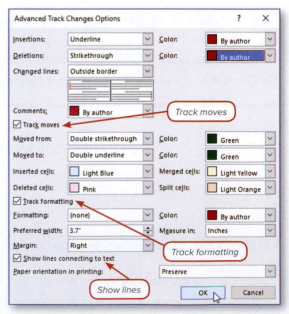

9-4 *Advanced Track Changes Options* dialog box

6. Select the **Show lines connecting to text** check box to display a line connecting the formatting change in the *Markup* area with highlighted text in the document.
7. Click **OK** to close the *Advanced Track Changes Options* dialog box.
8. Click **OK** to close the *Track Changes Options* dialog box.

Lock Tracking

If you are working on a document with multiple users, you can *Lock Tracking* so other users cannot turn off *Track Changes* without a password. Use this feature to ensure that all changes made by users are tracked.

▶ HOW TO: Lock Tracking

1. Click the bottom half of the **Track Changes** button [*Review* tab, *Tracking* group] and select **Lock Tracking**. The *Lock Tracking* dialog box opens (Figure 9-5).
2. Type a password in the *Enter password* text box.
   - If you don't type a password, users can turn off *Lock Tracking* without a password.
3. Type the same password in the *Reenter to confirm* text box.
4. Click **OK** to close the dialog box and lock tracking.

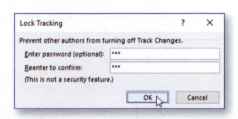

9-5 *Lock Tracking* dialog box

Real-Time Collaboration on a Shared Document

When a document is saved on *OneDrive*, an online storage area connected to your Microsoft account, you can share this document with others and collaborate online rather than emailing a document to others. Users can now simultaneously edit shared documents using the desktop version of Word 2016 or using *Word Online*. Previously, editing of shared document was limited to *Word Online*.

Sharing a document online allows multiple users to edit a document and add comments. *Real-time collaboration* immediately displays changes users make on a shared document. The owner of the document can accept or reject changes made by other users.

▶ HOW TO: Share a Document on OneDrive

1. Open a file saved on *OneDrive* or save a file to *OneDrive*.
2. Click the **Share** button in the upper right of the Word window (Figure 9-6).
   - The *Share* pane opens on the right of the Word window (Figure 9-7).
   - Alternatively, click the **Share** button on the *Backstage* view and click **Share with People** to open the *Share* pane.
3. Type the email address of the person(s) with whom you want to share the document.
   - Use a semi-colon to separate two or more email addresses.
   - Click the **Address Book** button on the right to select recipients from your Outlook address book.

9-6 *Share* button

4. Click the drop-down list and select **Can edit** or **Can view**.

   - Choose **Can edit** to allow recipients to edit the shared document.
   - Choose **Can view** to allow recipients to view or download the document. This option restricts recipients from editing the original document.

5. Type a message to the recipient(s) in the *Message* area.

6. Click **Share** to send a sharing email.

   - Alternatively, click **Get a sharing link** to open an area of the *Share* pane where you can choose to get an *Edit link* or *View-only link* that you can send to recipients.
   - You also have the option to *Send as Attachment*, which emails the file as either a Word document or PDF file.

9-7 *Share* pane

> **MORE INFO**
>
> Sharing documents on *OneDrive* using Word Online is discussed further in *Chapter 12: Customizing Word 2016 and Using OneDrive and Office Online*.

Print Document Markup

When you are working with a document containing tracked changes and comments, you have the option to print these markups in the documents.

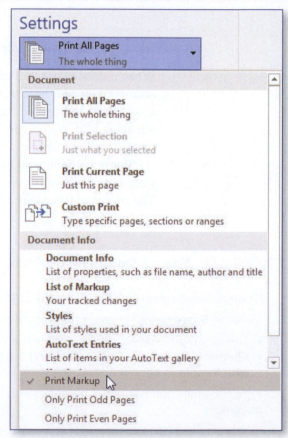

9-8 *Print Markup* option in the *Settings* area

> **HOW TO:** Print Document Markup

1. Click the **File** button to open the *Backstage* view.
2. Click the **Print** button on the left.
3. Click the first drop-down list in the *Settings* area and select **Print Markup** (Figure 9-8).
4. Click the **Print** button to print the document with markup.

For this Pause & Practice project, you work with two documents from Hamilton Civic Center. In the first document, you change user name and initials, add comments, and revise the document using *Track Changes*. In the second document, you review tracked changes, accept or reject changes, and delete comments.

Files Needed: ***Yoga-09a.docx*** and ***Yoga-09b.docx*** *(student data files are available in the* Library *of your SIMnet account)*
Completed Project File Names: ***[your initials] PP W9-1a.docx*** and ***[your initials] PP W9-1b.docx***

1. Open the ***Yoga-09a*** document from your student data files.

2. Save the document as [your initials] PP W9-1a.

3. Change user name and initials.
   a. Click the **Tracking** launcher [*Review* tab, *Tracking* group] to open the *Track Changes Options* dialog box.
   b. Click the **Change User Name** button to open the *Word Options* dialog box.
   c. In the *Personalize your copy of Microsoft Office* area, type your first and last name in the *User name* text box and type your first and last initials in lowercase letters in the *Initials* text box.
   d. Check the **Always use these values regardless of the sign in to Office** box.
   e. Click **OK** to close the *Word Options* dialog box.
   f. Click **OK** to close the *Track Changes Options* dialog box.

4. Change tracking and comment display options.
   a. Click the **Show Markup** drop-down list [*Review* tab, *Tracking* pane], click **Balloons**, and select **Show Revisions in Balloons**.
   b. Click the **Tracking** launcher to open the *Track Changes Options* dialog box. Confirm that all of the boxes in the *Show* area are checked. Check any boxes that are not checked.
   c. Click the **Advanced Options** button to open the *Advanced Track Changes Options* dialog box.
   d. Change the *Color* of *Insertions*, *Deletions*, and *Comments* to **Green** (Figure 9-9).
   e. Click **OK** to close the *Advanced Track Changes Options* dialog box and click **OK** to close the *Track Changes Options* dialog box.
   f. Click the **Display for Review** drop-down list [*Review* tab, *Tracking* group] and select **All Markup** if it is not already selected (Figure 9-10).

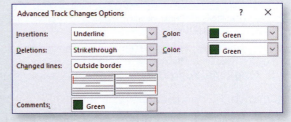

9-9 Change settings in the *Advanced Track Changes Options* dialog box

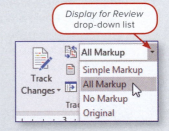

9-10 Change *Display for Review* view

5. Add comments to the document.
   a. Select the words "**Registered Yoga Teacher**" in the first paragraph.
   b. Click the **New Comment** button [*Review* tab, *Comments* group] to open a new comment (Figure 9-11).
   c. Type What is Amanda's level of certification? in the comment balloon.

9-11 New comment inserted

    d. Place your insertion point in the first word in the last sentence of the last paragraph ("**We**").

    e. Click the **New Comment** button and type Is this closing okay? in the comment balloon.

6. Turn on *Track Changes* and revise the document.

    a. Click the top half of the **Track Changes** button [*Review* tab, *Tracking* group] to turn on track changes (or press **Ctrl+Shift+E**).

    b. Select the word "**lot**" in the first sentence of the first paragraph.

    c. Type variety to replace the selected word. Confirm one space appears after the word.

    d. Select and delete the first sentence in the last paragraph (**"Register at the front desk or by phone."**), including the space after the period.

    e. Type the following sentence as the first sentence in the last paragraph: Register at the front desk, by phone (615-822-4965), or online (www.hccenter.org). Confirm one space appears after the period.

    f. Delete the **comma** after the first instance of "members" in the second sentence in the last paragraph.

7. Lock the tracked changes in the document.

    a. Click the bottom half of the **Track Changes** button and select **Lock Tracking** to open the *Lock Tracking* dialog box (Figure 9-12).

    b. Type HCC in the *Enter password* text box and type HCC again in the *Reenter to confirm* text box.

    c. Click **OK** to close the *Lock Tracking* dialog box.

9-12 *Lock Tracking* dialog box

8. Save and close the document (Figure 9-13).

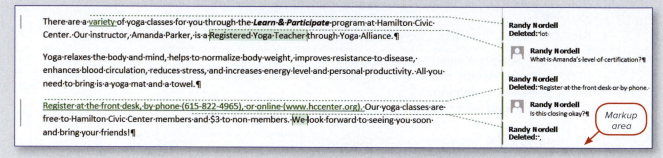

9-13 **PP W9-1a completed**

9. Open the **Yoga-09b** document from your student data files.

10. Save the document as [your initials] PP W9-1b.

11. Click the **Display for Review** drop-down list [*Review* tab, *Tracking* group] and select **All Markup** if it is not already selected.

12. Turn on the *Reviewing* pane and reject changes.

    a. Click the **Reviewing Pane** drop-down arrow [*Review* tab, *Tracking* group] and select **Reviewing Pane Vertical**. The *Reviewing* pane displays on the left side of the Word window.

    b. In the *Reviewing* pane, find where "reduces stress," was inserted.

    c. Right-click "**Rachel Gonzalves Inserted reduces stress**," and select **Reject Insertion** from the context menu (Figure 9-14).

    d. In the *Reviewing* pane, find where "reduces stress," was deleted.

    e. Right-click "**Rachel Gonzalves Deleted reduces stress**," and select **Reject Deletion** from the context menu.

    f. Click the **X** in the upper right corner of the *Reviewing* pane to close it.

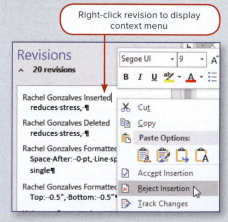

9-14 **Reject an insertion in the** *Reviewing* **pane**

13. Accept changes in the document and delete comments.
   a. Move to the top of the document (**Ctrl+Home**).
   b. Click the **Next** button [*Review* tab, *Changes* group] to select the first change.
   c. Click the top half of the **Accept** button [*Review* tab, *Changes* group] to accept the change and move to the next change.
   d. Click the bottom half of the **Accept** button and select **Accept All Changes** from the drop-down list (Figure 9-15). All of the remaining changes in the document are accepted.
   e. Click the bottom half of the **Delete** button [*Review* tab, *Comments* group] and select **Delete All Comments in Document** from the drop-down list to delete all comments.

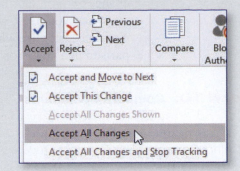

9-15 Accept all changes in the document

14. Save and close the document (Figure 9-16).

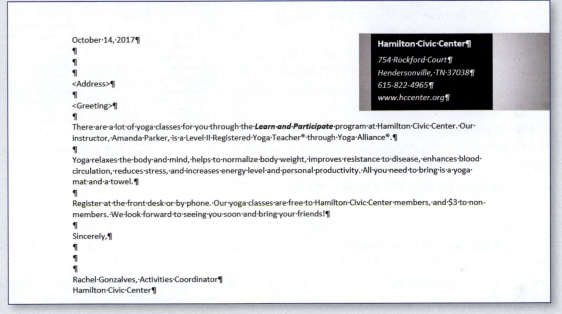

9-16 PP W9-1b completed

Using Other Collaboration Features

In addition to *Comments* and *Track Changes*, Word has other features to help you manage documents when collaborating with others. For example, you can incorporate editing changes from multiple documents using the compare and combine features. Also, when finalizing a document, you can mark it as final, encrypt it with a password, restrict editing, and add a digital signature.

Compare Documents

Compare is a collaboration feature that compares the content of different versions of a document and displays the differences as changes that are marked with *Track Changes*. You can then review and accept or reject the tracked revisions. You can compare different versions of a document after changes have been accepted or rejected or documents that include tracked changes.

When you use *Compare*, you compare an ***original document*** with a ***revised document***. You can customize which editing changes Word compares, and display the results of the comparison in a new Word document, the original document, or the revised document.

▶ **HOW TO:** Compare Documents

1. Click the **Compare** button [*Review* tab, *Compare* group] and select **Compare**. The *Compare Documents* dialog box opens (Figure 9-17).
   - If the documents you are comparing are open, save the documents before comparing.

2. Click the **Original document** drop-down list and select the original document or click the **Browse** button to locate the file.
   - When you click the **Browse** button, the *Open* dialog box opens where you select a document.

3. Click the **Revised document** drop-down list and select the revised document or click the **Browse** button to locate the file.
   - Type or change the reviewer name in the *Label changes with* text boxes.

4. Click the **More** or **Less** button to display more or fewer settings.

5. Select the check boxes in the *Comparison settings* area for the revisions you want to compare and mark.

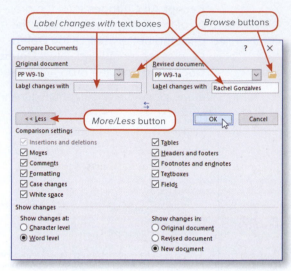

9-17 *Compare Documents* dialog box

6. Select either **Character level** or **Word level** in the *Show changes at* area.
   - When comparing documents, Word can display comparison results by individual character or by word.

7. Select **Original document**, **Revised document**, or **New document** in the *Show changes in* area. This determines where the results of the comparison display.
   - *New document* is the default setting, so your original and revised documents do not change when you compare documents.

8. Click **OK** to close the dialog box and compare the documents.

   - If tracked changes are in either document, a dialog box opens (Figure 9-18).
   - Tracked changes in either document are accepted when the comparison is performed.
   - Click **Yes** to continue the comparison.
   - The differences between the two documents display as tracked changes. You can accept or reject these proposed changes.

9. Save the compared document.

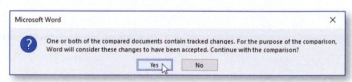

9-18 Accept changes before comparing documents

Show or Hide Source Documents

After comparing two documents, you can choose whether to show one or both of the source documents in the Word window or hide both source documents. If you show one or both source documents, they display on the right of the Word window. You can't edit the source documents when they display in a compared document; they display for review only in the *Reviewing* pane.

▶ HOW TO: Show or Hide Source Documents

1. Click the **Compare** button [*Review* tab, *Compare* group].

2. Select **Show Source Documents** and select from one of the four options: **Hide Source Documents**, **Show Original**, **Show Revised**, or **Show Both** (Figure 9-19).

   - The last setting you choose applies the next time you compare documents.

3. Click the **X** in the upper right corner of a source document to close it.

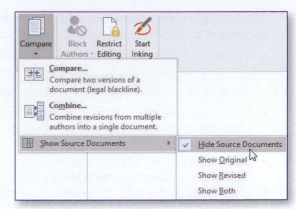

9-19 *Show Source Documents* options

Combine Documents

The **Combine** feature combines tracked changes from two documents into a single document. Whereas the *Compare* feature looks for just the *differences* between documents, the *Combine* feature incorporates *all* tracked changes from both documents into one document. You can then accept or reject the changes in the combined document. You can combine all of the tracked changes in a new document, the original document, or the revised document.

> **MORE INFO**
>
> You can compare and combine only two documents at a time. If you are comparing or combining more than two documents, perform the feature multiple times.

▶ HOW TO: Combine Documents

1. Click the **Compare** button [*Review* tab, *Compare* group] and select **Combine**. The *Combine Documents* dialog box opens (Figure 9-20).

   - When combining documents that are open, save the documents before combining.

2. Click the **Original document** drop-down list and select the original document or click the **Browse** button to locate the file.

3. Click the **Revised document** drop-down list and select the revised document or click the **Browse** button to locate the file.

   - Type or change the reviewer name in the *Label unmarked changes with* text boxes.

4. Click the **More** or **Less** button to display more or fewer settings.

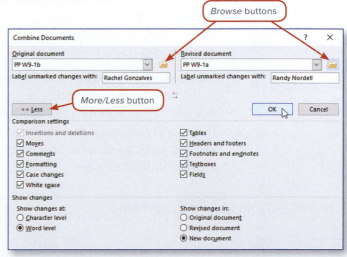

9-20 *Combine Documents* dialog box

5. Select the check boxes in the *Comparison settings* area for the revisions you want to compare and mark.

6. Select either **Character level** or **Word level** in the *Show changes at* area.

   - When combining documents, Word can display comparison results by individual character or by word.

7. Select **Original document**, **Revised document**, or **New document** in the *Show changes in* area. This determines where the results of the combined documents display.

   - *New document* is the default setting, so your original and revised documents do not change when you combine documents.

8. Click **OK** to close the dialog box and combine the documents.

   - If you have formatting changes in one or both documents, a dialog box opens where you select which formatting changes you want to keep (Figure 9-21).
   - Select the document containing the formatting changes to keep and click **Continue with Merge**.
   - The changes in the two documents combine and display as tracked changes. You can accept or reject these proposed changes.

9. Save the combined document.

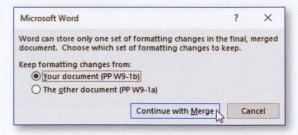

9-21 Keep formatting changes from a specific document

> **MORE INFO**
>
> Showing or hiding source documents functions the same when using either the *Compare* or *Combine* feature.

Check for Issues

When you share a document with other users, Word provides tools to alert you to potential problems that might occur when the document is shared with and modified by multiple users. You can inspect your document, check accessibility, and check compatibility. All of these options display on the *Backstage* view (Figure 9-22).

9-22 *Check for Issues* on the *Backstage* view

Inspect Document

The **Inspect Document** feature examines a document for hidden content, properties, or personal information that might create compatibility issues. When you use the *Inspect Document* feature, Word generates a report, and you can choose to remove properties or hidden information from your document before sharing with other users.

▶ **HOW TO:** Inspect a Document

1. Click the **File** tab to open the *Info* area on the *Backstage* view.
2. Click the **Check for Issues** button and select **Inspect Document** from the drop-down list. The *Document Inspector* dialog box opens (Figure 9-23).
3. Select the document content you want to inspect.

   - All of the document content areas are selected by default.

4. Click **Inspect**. The results displays in the *Document Inspector* dialog box (Figure 9-24).

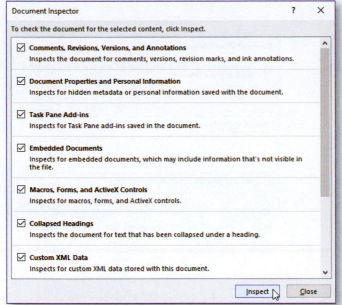
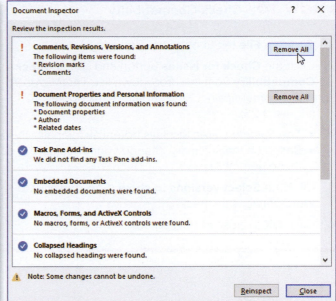

9-23 *Document Inspector* dialog box   9-24 Document inspection results

5. Click the **Remove All** button if you want to remove information from your document.

6. Click the **Reinspect** button if you want to inspect the document again after you remove content.

7. Click the **Close** button to close the *Document Inspector* dialog box.

Check Accessibility

The ***Check Accessibility*** feature checks for potential issues that users with disabilities may have with your document. For example, users with visual impairments use document or screen readers to read the text in the document. A screen reader may not properly read objects in Word. The *Check Accessibility* feature alerts you to potential issues and provides you with solutions in the ***Accessibility Checker pane***.

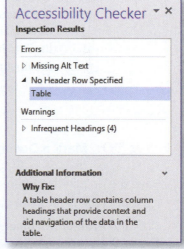

9-25 *Accessibility Checker* pane

▶**HOW TO:** Check Accessibility

1. Click the **File** tab to open the *Backstage* view.

2. Click the **Check for Issues** button and select **Check Accessibility** from the drop-down list. The *Accessibility Checker* pane opens (Figure 9-25).

3. Select one of the results in the *Inspection Results* area.

   • The *Additional Information* area displays why and how to fix the problems.

Check Compatibility

The ***Check Compatibility*** feature searches for compatibility issues between the version of Word that you are using and older or newer versions. This feature is useful if you are sharing documents with others who might have a different version of Word.

▶ HOW TO: Check Compatibility

1. Click the **File** tab to open the *Backstage* view.
2. Click the **Check for Issues** button and select **Check Compatibility** from the drop-down list. The *Microsoft Word Compatibility Checker* dialog box opens (Figure 9-26).
   - The *Summary* area displays potential compatibility issues.
   - Based on the summary, change your document to correct these potential issues.
3. Click the **Select versions to show** drop-down list to select Word versions to check.
4. Click **OK** to close the dialog box.

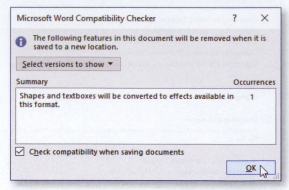

9-26 *Microsoft Word Compatibility Checker* dialog box

Protect Document

After you share a document and make editing changes, you can finalize and protect your document. ***Protect Document*** options include *Mark as Final*, *Encrypt with Password*, *Restrict Editing*, and *Add a Digital Signature*. All of these options are available on the *Backstage* view (Figure 9-27).

Mark as Final

The ***Mark as Final*** feature marks a document as a final version and protects it from being edited. When a user opens a document that has been marked as final, the *Info* bar displays a message informing the user that the document has been marked as final.

9-27 *Protect Document* options

▶ HOW TO: Mark a Document as Final

1. Save the document before marking it as final.
2. Click the **File** tab to open the *Backstage* view.
3. Click the **Protect Document** button and select **Mark as Final** (see Figure 9-27).
4. Click **OK** in the dialog box that opens and informs you that the document will be marked as final and saved (Figure 9-28). Another dialog box opens.
5. Click **OK** in the dialog box that provides information about the final version (Figure 9-29).

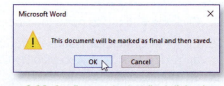

9-28 Confirm marked as final dialog box

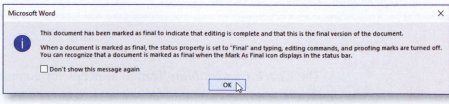

9-29 Marked as final informational dialog box

- Check the **Don't show this message again** box if you don't want this informational dialog box to appear again.
- On the *Backstage* view, a notation stating the document has been marked as final appears in the permissions area (Figure 9-30).

6. Click the **Back** arrow to close the *Backstage* view and return to the document.

- The *Info* bar between the *Ribbon* and the *Ruler* displays a notation indicating the document is marked as final (Figure 9-31).
- The *Ribbon* is collapsed and the document is protected from editing.

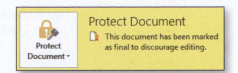

9-30 *Marked as Final* notation on the *Backstage* view

9-31 *Marked as Final* notation in the *Info* bar

When a document is marked as final, users can edit the document by turning off *Mark as Final*. Select one of the following to turn off *Mark as Final*:

- Click the **Edit Anyway** button in the *Info* bar (see Figure 9-31).
- Click the **File** tab to open the *Backstage* view, click the **Protect Document** button, and select **Mark as Final**.

Encrypt with Password

Use the **Encrypt with Password** feature to prevent users from opening and editing a document. When a document is encrypted with a password, a user receives a prompt to enter a password to open the document.

▶ **HOW TO:** Encrypt a Document with a Password

1. Click the **File** tab to open the *Backstage* view.
2. Click the **Protect Document** button and select **Encrypt with Password**. The *Encrypt Document* dialog box opens (Figure 9-32).
3. Type a password in the *Password* area and click **OK**. The *Confirm Password* dialog box opens.
   - Passwords are case sensitive.
4. Type the password in the *Reenter password* area and click **OK**.
   - On the *Backstage* view, a notation stating a password is required to open the document displays in the permissions area.
5. Click the **File** tab to close the *Backstage* view and return to the document.

9-32 *Encrypt Document* dialog box

▶ **MORE INFO**

Store document passwords in a secure location.

When reopening a document encrypted with a password, you are prompted to enter the password (Figure 9-33). Type the password in the dialog box and click **OK** to open the document.

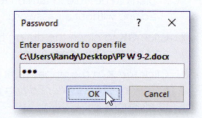

9-33 *Password* dialog box

You can remove a document password after you have opened a document that is encrypted with a password.

▶ **HOW TO:** Remove a Document Password

1. Open the password encrypted document and type the password to open the document.

2. Click the **File** tab to open the *Backstage* view.

3. Click the **Protect Document** button and select **Encrypt with Password**. The *Encrypt Document* dialog box opens (Figure 9-34).

4. Delete the password in the *Password* text box and leave this text box blank.

5. Click **OK** to close the dialog box and to remove the password.

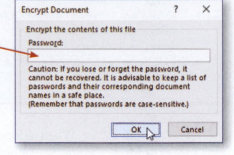

9-34 **Remove a document password**

Restrict Editing

Another way to protect a document is to *restrict editing* of a document. This feature enables you to restrict what a user can do in a document. Users can open the document without a password, but you control what they can and cannot change in the document. For example, you can restrict the editing of the entire document so the document becomes a read-only document, or you can allow users to add comments or use *Track Changes*.

▶ **HOW TO:** Restrict Editing of a Document

1. Click the **File** tab to open the *Backstage* view.

2. Click the **Protect Document** button and select **Restrict Editing**. The *Restrict Editing* pane opens on the right side of the Word window (Figure 9-35).

3. Check the **Allow only this type of editing in the document** box in the *Editing restrictions* area.

4. Click the drop-down list and select what type of editing you wish to allow.

   - *No changes* restricts users from making any editing changes.
   - You can allow users to insert *Tracked changes*, insert *Comments*, or allow *Filling in forms*.

5. Click the **Yes, Start Enforcing Protection** button. The *Start Enforcing Protection* dialog box opens (Figure 9-36).

6. Select the **Password** radio button and enter and reenter the password.

   - Passwords are case sensitive.
   - Leave the password text boxes blank to be able to turn off *Restrict Editing* without a password.

7. Click **OK** to close the dialog box and protect the document.

8. Click the **X** in the upper right corner of the *Restrict Editing* pane to close it.

9-36 *Start Enforcing Protection* dialog box

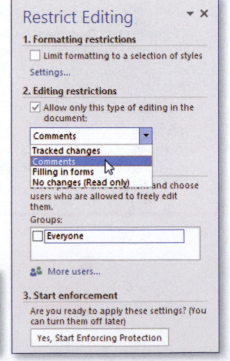

9-35 *Restrict Editing* pane

You can remove restrictions on a document by clicking the **Stop Protection** button in the *Restrict Formatting and Editing* pane and entering the password.

Add a Digital Signature

The ***Add a Digital Signature*** feature ensures the integrity of a document by adding an invisible digital signature to the document. When you add a digital signature to your document, Word saves your document and marks it as final. This feature is useful when you are working with highly sensitive documents. This advanced security feature requires a digital ID that employers may provide. Third-party vendors also provide this security service.

Manage Versions

When you are working on a document, Word automatically saves your document every 10 minutes. You can use these ***autosaved versions*** to recover previous information or a previous version of your document. If Word or your computer crashes while working on a document, Word uses the most recent autosaved version to recover your document. The different saved versions of your document display in the *Versions* area in the *Backstage* view.

▶ **HOW TO:** Recover Autosaved Versions of a Document

1. Click the **File** tab to open the *Backstage* view.
2. Select one of the autosaved versions of your document in the *Versions* area (Figure 9-37). The autosaved document opens.
   - The *Info* bar of the autosaved document give you two options: *Compare* and *Restore* (Figure 9-38).

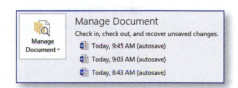

9-37 Autosaved versions of a document

3. Click the **Compare** button to compare this document with the most current version of the document.
   - A new document automatically opens with the most current version of your document so you can compare it to the previous version.

9-38 Version options on an autosaved document

4. Click **Restore** to revert to a previous version of the document.
   - A dialog box opens informing you that you are about to overwrite the last saved version of the document (Figure 9-39).
   - Click **OK** to overwrite the last saved version.

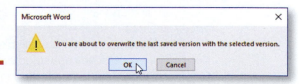

9-39 Overwrite most recent version with previous version

▶ **MORE INFO**

Customize the frequency of autosave in the *Save* area of the *Word Options* dialog box.

For this Pause & Practice project, you combine the two documents from *Pause & Practice 9-1* into a new document. You inspect the new document, check compatibility, restrict editing, encrypt the document with a password, and mark it as final.

Files Needed: ***[your initials] PP W9-1a.docx*** and ***[your initials] PP W9-1b.docx***
Completed Project File Name: ***[your initials] PP W9-2.docx***

1. Open a document and turn off *Lock Tracking*.
   a. Open the ***[your initials] PP W9-1a.docx***. If the document opens in *Reading* view, click the **View** tab in the upper left and select **Edit Document**.
   b. Click the bottom half of the **Track Changes** button [*Review* tab, *Tracking* group] and select **Lock Tracking** to open the *Unlock Tracking* dialog box.
   c. Type HCC in the *Password* text box and click **OK** to turn off *Lock Tracking*.
   d. Save and close the document.

2. Create a new blank Word document.

3. Combine documents.
   a. Click the **Compare** button [*Review* tab, *Compare* group] and select **Combine**. The *Combine Documents* dialog box opens (Figure 9-40).
   b. Click the **Browse** button in the *Original document* area to display the *Open* dialog box.
   c. Locate and select the ***[your initials] PP W9-1b*** document and click **Open**.
   d. Type Rachel Gonzalves in the *Label unmarked changes with* text box in the *Original document* area.
   e. Click the **Browse** button in the *Revised document* area, select the ***[your initials] PP W9-1a*** document, and click **Open** to select the document.

   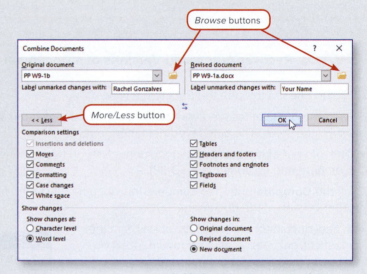

   9-40 *Combine Documents* dialog box

   f. Type your first and last name in the *Label unmarked changes with* text box in the *Revised document* area.
   g. Click the **More** button (if it is available) to display all settings options.
   h. Confirm all check boxes are selected In the *Comparison settings* area.
   i. Select the **Word level** radio button in the *Show changes at* area.
   j. Select the **New document** radio button in the *Show changes in* area.

   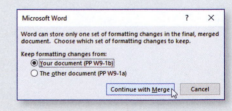

   9-41 *Keep formatting changes from a specific document*

   k. Click **OK** to close the dialog box and combine the documents into a new document. A dialog box opens and prompts you to keep the formatting changes from one of the documents (Figure 9-41).
   l. Select the **Your document (PP W9-1b)** radio button and click **Continue with Merge**. The two documents are combined in a new Word document.

4. Save the combined document and hide source documents.
   a. Save this combined document as **[your initials] PP W9-2**.
   b. If the source documents display on the right, click the **Compare** button, select **Show Source Documents**, and select **Hide Source Documents**.

5. Accept changes and delete comments.
   a. Click the bottom half of the **Accept** button and select **Accept All Changes** to accept the remaining changes in the document.
   b. Click the bottom half of the **Delete** button [*Review* tab, *Comments* group] and select **Delete All Comments in Document** to delete all comments.
   c. Close the *Revisions* pane if it is open.
   d. Save the document.

6. Inspect the document.
   a. Click the **File** tab to open the *Backstage* view.
   b. Click the **Check for Issues** button and select **Inspect Document** to open the *Document Inspector* dialog box.
   c. Deselect the **Document Properties and Personal Information** check box.
   d. Click **Inspect**. The *Document Inspector* dialog box opens and displays the inspection results (Figure 9-42). No issues should display.
   e. Click **Close** to close the dialog box and click the **Back** button to return to the document.
   f. Save the document.

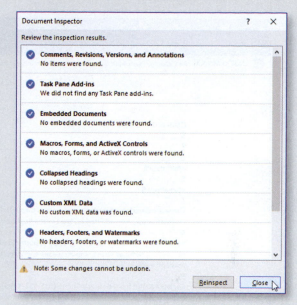

9-42 *Document Inspector* with inspection results displayed

7. Check the compatibility of the document.
   a. Click the **File** tab to open the *Backstage* view.
   b. Click the **Check for Issues** button and select **Check Compatibility**. The *Microsoft Word Compatibility Checker* dialog box opens.
   c. Review the compatibility issues and click **OK** to close the dialog box.

8. Restrict editing of the document.
   a. Click the **File** tab to open the *Backstage* view.
   b. Click the **Protect Document** button and select **Restrict Editing**. The *Restrict Editing* pane appears on the right.
   c. Check the **Allow only this type of editing in the document** box in the *Editing restrictions* area (Figure 9-43).
   d. Click the drop-down list and select **Comments**.
   e. Click the **Yes, Start Enforcing Protection** button. The *Start Enforcing Protection* dialog box opens (Figure 9-44).
   f. Type **HCC** in the *Enter new password* area.
   g. Type **HCC** in the *Reenter password to confirm* area.
   h. Click **OK** to close the dialog box.
   i. Close the *Restrict Editing* pane.

9-43 Restrict editing to only comments

9. Encrypt the document with a password and mark the document as final.
   a. Click the **File** tab to open the *Backstage* view.
   b. Click the **Protect Document** button and select **Encrypt with Password**. The *Encrypt Document* dialog box opens.

9-44 Set protection password

c. Type **HCC** in the *Password* text box and click **OK**. The *Confirm Password* dialog box opens.

d. Type **HCC** in the *Reenter password* text box and click **OK**.

e. Click the **Protect Document** button on the *Backstage* view and select **Mark as Final**.

f. Click **OK** in the dialog box that informs you that the document will be marked as final and saved.

g. Click **OK** to close the next informational dialog box.

h. Click the **Back** arrow to close the *Backstage* view and return to the document.

10. Close the document (Figure 9-45).

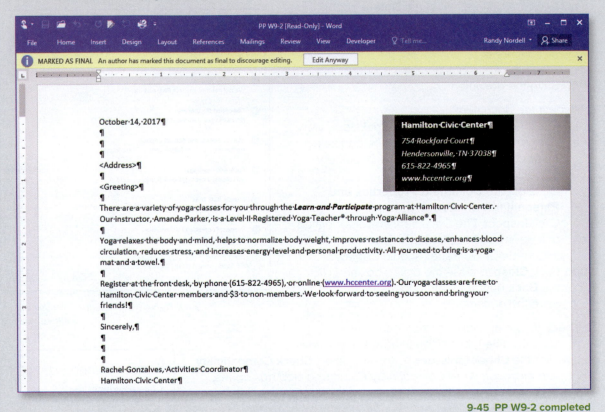

9-45 PP W9-2 completed

Integrating Office Applications

Microsoft Office 2016 provides you the ability to integrate information between the different applications. For example, you can use data from an Excel worksheet in a Word document or PowerPoint presentation, export data from an Access database to use in an Excel worksheet or Word document, or insert slides from a PowerPoint presentation into a Word document.

Object Linking and Embedding

Object linking and embedding, also known as *OLE*, refers to Microsoft Office's ability to share information between the different Microsoft Office applications. The following is terminology that is important to know when using *OLE*:

- *Source program*: The Office application where you create the content.
- *Destination program*: The Office application where you insert the object.
- *Source file*: The file where the content is stored.
- *Destination file*: The file where you insert the object.

When you are using *OLE* to insert content from an Office application into a Word document, you insert the content as an object and modify it in the Word document. Embedding and linking are two different ways to insert content from one application into another.

Embed an Object

Embedding inserts an object from one application into another. You can modify the object in the destination file independently of the source file. Use embedding when the source and destination files do not need to remain the same. When you embed an object into a Word document, the object retains the formatting from the source program.

Usually when you embed an object into a Word document, you embed a portion of the file, such as a chart from an Excel worksheet or a slide from a PowerPoint presentation. To embed a portion of a file, copy the content to embed from the source file and then use the *Paste Special* dialog box to control how the object embeds into the destination file. Using this method, you select the file format of the object to embed into the destination file.

▶ HOW TO: Embed an Object in a Document

1. Open the source file.

   • Use the source program to open the file or open the file from the *File Explorer* folder, which opens the source program and file.

2. Select the portion of the document you want to embed as an object (Figure 9-46).

   • To embed a chart, click the chart frame to select the *Chart Area*.
   • To embed a PowerPoint slide, select the entire slide by clicking a slide thumbnail in the *Navigation* area on the left.

3. Copy the selected information.

4. Close the source file and program.

5. Place your insertion point in the destination file at the location to embed the object.

6. Click the bottom half of the **Paste** button [*Home* tab, *Clipboard* group] and select **Paste Special** (Figure 9-47). The *Paste Special* dialog box opens (Figure 9-48).

7. Select the **Paste** radio button.

8. Select the file type in the *As* area.

   • If you select the source program file type, the object retains the connection with the source program and you can edit the object.
   • If you choose a different file type, such as a *Picture* or *Microsoft Office Graphic Object*, the object does not retain connection with the source program, but rather connects to the destination program. You can edit this type of embedded object as you would a picture or graphic in Word.

9. Click **OK** to close the *Paste Special* dialog box and to embed the object in the destination file.

9-46 Copy PowerPoint slide to embed as an object

9-47 Open the *Paste Special* dialog box

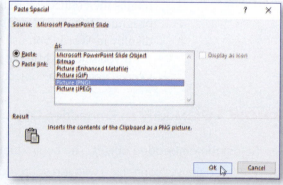

9-48 *Paste Special* dialog box

Embed a File

You can also embed an entire file into a destination file. For example, you can embed an entire Excel worksheet or an entire PowerPoint presentation. When you embed a file into a Word document, the file retains the formatting from the source program.

► **HOW TO:** Embed a File

1. Place your insertion point in your document at the location where you want to insert the embedded file.
2. Click the **Object** button [*Insert* tab, *Text* group]. The *Object* dialog box opens.
3. Click the **Create from File** tab and click the **Browse** button to select a file to embed (Figure 9-49). The *Browse* dialog box opens.
4. Select the file to embed and click **Insert**.
5. Click **OK** to close the *Object* dialog box and embed the file.

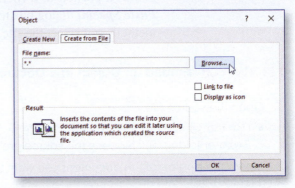

9-49 *Object* dialog box

Modify an Embedded Object

You modify an embedded object similarly to how you modify other graphic objects in Word. The file type you select when you embed an object determines how the object is edited. For example, if you select the source program as the file type for the embedded object, the object retains the connection to the source program and you edit it using the *Ribbon* from the source program. When you double-click the object, the *Ribbon* and tabs from the source program display in Word. You use these to modify the embedded object.

If you select a different file type for the embedded object, such as a picture or Microsoft Office Object, you edit the object using the contextual tabs in Word for the object type you choose.

► **HOW TO:** Modify an Embedded Object

1. Select the embedded object. The contextual tab(s) associated with the object display.
   - If the object is connected with the source program, double-click the object to open the *Ribbon* from the source program.
2. Modify the size, text wrapping, and arrangement of the object.
   - On some objects, you can also edit the elements within the object.
3. Click outside the object area to deselect it.

Link an Object

Linking inserts an object from one application into another and creates a link between the object in the source and destination files. You can edit an embedded object independently of its source file, but changes to a linked object change the information in the source file as well. In addition, if you change the source file, the linked object in the destination file is also changed. Linking is useful when you want the object in the source and destination files to remain the same in both locations.

To link to a portion of a file, copy the selected portion of the source file, and use the *Paste Special* dialog box to link it to the destination file.

▶ HOW TO: Link to an Object to a Document

1. Open the source file.
   - Use the source program to open the file or open the file from the *File Explorer* folder, which opens the source program and file.
2. Select the portion of the source file to link as an object and copy it (Figure 9-50).
   - To link a chart, click the chart frame to select the *Chart Area*.
   - To link a PowerPoint slide, select the entire slide by clicking a slide thumbnail in the *Navigation* area on the left.
   - You can also create a link to an entire file. To link an entire file, use the *Object* dialog box.
3. Place your insertion point in the destination file at the location to insert the linked object.
4. Click the bottom half of the **Paste** button [*Home* tab, *Clipboard* group] and select **Paste Special**. The *Paste Special* dialog box opens (Figure 9-51).
5. Select the **Paste link** radio button.
6. Select the file type in the *As* area.
7. Click **OK** to close the *Paste Special* dialog box and to insert the linked object in the destination file.

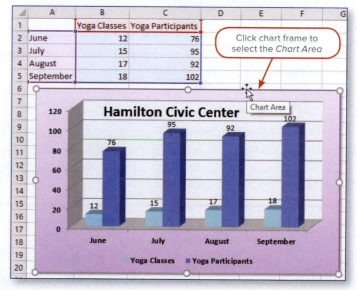

9-50 Select object to link

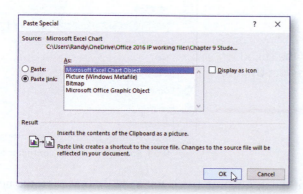

9-51 *Paste link* using the *Paste Special* dialog box

▶ ANOTHER WAY

When embedding or linking an object, you can select from one of the *Paste Options* available in the *Paste* drop-down list or context menu.

Open a Document Linked to an Object

When you open a document containing one or more linked object, Word prompts you to update the links in the document, which updates the linked content in the destination file to match the content in the source file. A dialog box opens and prompts you to update the links in the document (Figure 9-52). Click **Yes** to update the link(s).

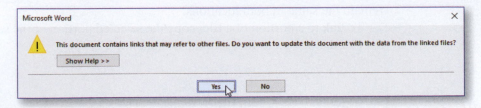

Microsoft Word ✕

⚠ This document contains links that may refer to other files. Do you want to update this document with the data from the linked files?

Show Help >>

Yes   No

9-52 Update links in the document

Modify the size, text wrapping, and arrangement of a linked object the same way you modify other graphic objects. In addition, you can modify the content of the linked object, modify the links in the document, or break the link between the linked object and the source file.

Modify Linked Object Content

A linked object in a Word document links directly to the source file. When you edit the linked object, the source file opens, and you can edit it. When you save the source file, the linked object in the destination file updates to reflect the current data from the source file.

▶ **HOW TO:** Modify Linked Object Content

1. Double-click the linked object to open the source program and file.
   - Alternatively, right-click the linked object, select **Linked [*object type*] Object**, and select **Edit Link** or **Open Link** to open the source program and file (Figure 9-53).
2. Edit the source file.
3. Save and close the source file.
   - Because both files are open, the linked object updates. If the linked object does not update, right-click the linked object and select **Update Link** from the context menu.

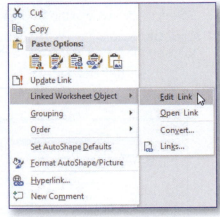

9-53 *Edit Link* from the context menu

You can also change the source file if the destination file is not open. In that case, the next time you open the destination file with the linked object, you will be prompted to update the linked objects in the document.

Modify a Link to an Object

A linked object in the destination file links to the source file on your computer. If you change the location of the source or destination file, Word cannot find the source file to update the linked object in the destination file. To change a link to a file you have moved, edit the link to the file using the *Links* dialog box.

▶ HOW TO: Modify a Link to an Object

1. Open the destination file.
   - Word prompts you to update links in the document; click **Yes** to update links.
2. Click the **File** tab to open the *Backstage* view.
3. Click **Info** on the left.
4. Click **Edit Links to Files** below the document properties on the right (Figure 9-54). The *Links* dialog box opens (Figure 9-55).
5. Select the source file of the linked object in the *Source file* area.
   - If you have multiple linked objects in a document, multiple source files display in the *Source file* area.

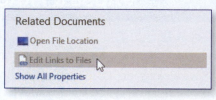

9-54 *Edit Links to Files* on the *Backstage* view

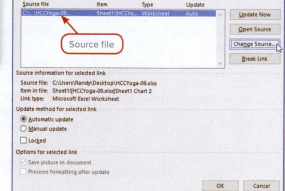

9-55 Change the source file in the *Links* dialog box

6. Click the **Change Source** button to open the *Change Source* dialog box.
7. Select the source file for the linked object and click **Open** to close the *Change Source* dialog box.
8. Click **OK** to close the *Links* dialog box.
9. Click the **Back** arrow to return to the document.

Break a Link to an Object

If you no longer want a linked object to connect to the source file, you can break the link between the object and source file. When you do this, the linked object converts to an embedded object and no longer links directly to the source file. You can modify the embedded object without modifying of the source file.

▶ HOW TO: Break a Link to an Object

1. Open the destination file containing the linked object.
2. Click the **File** tab to open the *Backstage* view.
3. Click the **Info** button on the left.
4. Click **Edit Links to Files** (see Figure 9-54). The *Links* dialog box opens (see Figure 9-55).
5. Select the source file of the linked object in the *Source file* area.
   - If you have multiple linked objects in a document, multiple source files display in the *Source file* area.
6. Click the **Break Link** button. A dialog box opens asking if you want to break the selected link (Figure 9-56).
7. Click **Yes**. The *Links* dialog box closes automatically.
8. Click the **Back** arrow to return to the document.

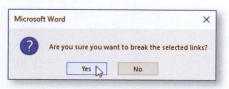

9-56 Confirm breaking links

PAUSE & PRACTICE: WORD 9-3

For this Pause & Practice project, you modify the document from *Pause & Practice 9-2*. You remove the document password and protection, insert a PowerPoint slide as an embedded object, modify the embedded object, insert an Excel chart as a linked object, and modify the linked object.

Files Needed: **[your initials] PP W9-2.docx, YogaPPT-09.pptx**, and **HCCYoga-09.xlsx** *(student data files are available in the* Library *of your SIMnet account)*
Completed Project File Name: **[your initials] PP W9-3.docx** and **[your initials] HCCYoga-09.xlsx**

1. Open the **[your initials] PP W9-2** document you saved in *Pause & Practice 9-2*.

2. Type HCC when prompted to enter a password and click **OK**. The open document is marked as final.

3. Click the **Edit Anyway** button on the *Info* bar to turn off *Mark as Final*.

4. Save the document as [your initials] PP W9-3.

5. Remove the document encryption password and disable restrict editing.
   a. Click the **File** tab to open the *Backstage* view.
   b. Click the **Protect Document** button and select **Encrypt with Password** to open the *Encrypt Document* dialog box (Figure 9-57).
   c. Delete the password in the *Password* text box and click **OK**.
   d. Click the **Protect Document** button again and select **Restrict Editing**. The *Restrict Editing* pane opens on the right.
   e. Click the **Stop Protection** button, type HCC in the *Password* text box, and click **OK**.
   f. Close the *Restrict Editing* pane.

9-57 Remove document encryption password

6. Insert a PowerPoint slide as an embedded object.
   a. Open your student data files from the *File Explorer* window and double-click **YogaPPT-09.pptx** to open this file in PowerPoint. Click the **Enable Editing** button on the *Message* bar if the file opens in *Protected* view.
   b. Select **slide 3** on the left in the *Slides* area, **copy** the slide, and close PowerPoint.
   c. Place your insertion point at the end of the third body paragraph in the **[your initials] PP W9-3** document.
   d. Click the bottom half of the **Paste** button [*Home* tab, *Clipboard* group] and select **Paste Special** to open the *Paste Special* dialog box (Figure 9-58).

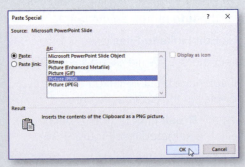

9-58 Paste embedded object

e. Click the **Paste** radio button.

f. Select **Picture (PNG)** in the *As* area

g. Click **OK** to close the dialog box and to insert the slide as an embedded object.

7. Resize and position the embedded object.

a. Select the picture and change the *Height* to **2.5"** [*Picture Tools Format* tab, *Size* group]. The width automatically changes.

b. Change the *Position* to **Position in Middle Right with Square Text Wrapping**.

c. Save the document.

8. Insert an Excel chart as a linked object.

a. Open your student data files from the *File Explorer* window and double-click **HCCYoga-09.xlsx** to open this worksheet in Excel. Click the **Enable Editing** button on the *Message* bar if the file opens in *Protected* view.

b. Save this file to your desktop and name it [your initials] HCCYoga-09.xlsx.

c. Select the frame of the chart to select the *Chart Area* (Figure 9-59) and **copy** the chart.

d. Return to your *[your initials] PP W9-3* document and place your insertion point at the end of the third body paragraph.

e. Press **Alt+Ctrl+V** to open the *Paste Special* dialog box (Figure 9-60).

f. Click the **Paste link** radio button.

g. Select **Microsoft Excel Chart Object** in the *As* area.

h. Click **OK** to close the dialog box and insert the chart as a linked object.

9. Modify size, text wrapping, and position of the embedded chart.

a. Right-click the chart and select **Picture** to open the *Format Object* dialog box.

b. Click the **Size** tab, and in the *Height* area, change the **Absolute** size to **3"**, and press **Tab**. The width automatically adjusts.

c. Click the **Layout** tab and click the **Advanced** button to open the *Layout* dialog box.

d. Select **Tight** on the **Text Wrapping** tab.

e. Click the **Position** tab, and in the *Horizontal* area, set **Alignment** to **Centered** *relative to* **Margin**.

f. In the *Vertical* area, set **Alignment** to **Bottom** *relative to* **Margin**.

g. Click **OK** to close the *Layout* dialog box.

h. Click **OK** to close the *Format Object* dialog box.

i. Save the document.

10. Modify linked object content.

a. Right-click the chart, select **Linked Worksheet Object**, and select **Edit Link** (or **Open Link**) to open the source file (*[your initials] HCCYoga-09.xlsx*) in Excel.

b. In the "September" row (row 5), change the number of *Yoga Classes* to 20 and the *Yoga Participants* to 115 (Figure 9-61).

c. Save the Excel worksheet and leave the file open.

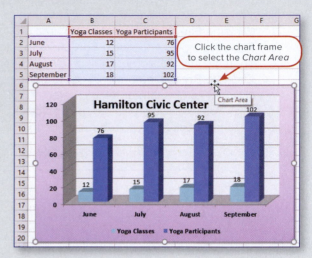

9-59 Select chart to copy

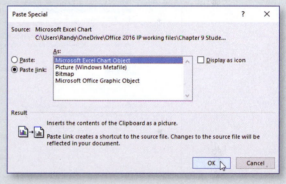

9-60 Paste link to an object

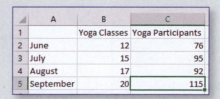

9-61 Change data in source file

d. Return to the Word document, right-click the linked chart in the Word document, and select **Update Link** from the context menu. The values in the chart update to reflect the changed data in the source file.
   e. Save the Word file.

11. Break the link between the linked chart and the source file.
   a. Click the **File** tab to open the *Info* area on *Backstage* view and select **Edit Links to Files** to open the *Links* dialog box (Figure 9-62).
   b. Click the **Break Link** button. A dialog box opens asking if you want to break the selected link.
   c. Click **Yes** to break the link to the source file.
   d. Click the **Back** arrow to return to the document.

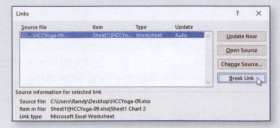

9-62 Break link to source file

12. Save and close the Word document (Figure 9-63). Also, save and close the Excel file.

9-63 PP W9-3 completed

Using Mail Merge Rules

In Chapter 5, you learned about mail merge and how to merge information from other Microsoft Office applications into a Word document (*SLO 5.4, 5.5,* and *5.6*). In Chapter 6, you learned how to insert custom content into a document using Word field codes (*SLO 6.6*). This section reviews the merge process and presents advanced merge features using rules. You can use rules, which are Word merge field codes, to customize and control the merge process.

Mail Merge Review

When merging content into a Word document, you can use the *Mailings* tab or the *Mail Merge Wizard* to create and customize your merge. The following are the six steps in the merge process:

1. *Select the type of merge*: Create merged letters, email messages, envelopes, labels, or a directory.
2. *Select the document*: The main document is where you insert merge fields and merge the records from the data source.
3. *Select the recipients*: Select a data source such as an Excel worksheet, Access database, or Outlook contacts that contains the recipient information. You can also create and save a new data source.
4. *Insert merge fields*: Insert individual fields from the recipient data source into your main document or insert an address block or a greeting line, which combines individual fields into one merge field. You can customize the address block and greeting line fields to match your data source.
5. *Preview the merge results*: Display how the information from your data source will appear in your document when you perform the merge.
6. *Complete the merge*: Merge information from your data source into the main document. You can send the merged document to the printer or to a new document that you can save and modify before printing.

Mail Merge Rules

Previously, you used Word field codes to automatically insert and update content in a document. For example, you learned how to insert the current date that updates automatically, insert index entries and an index page with automatic page numbering, and insert document properties. You can use Word field codes to customize the merge process, which are called *rules*. The following are rules that customize the results of a merge:

Mail Merge Rules

Rule	Field Code	Description
Ask	*Ask*	Prompts the user for text to assign to a bookmark
Fill-in	*Fill-in*	Prompts the user for text to insert into a document
If. . .Then. . .Else	*If*	Displays information in a merged document based on a logical condition being true or false
Merge Record #	*MergeRec*	Inserts the number of the current merge record
Merge Sequence #	*MergeSeq*	Inserts the merge record sequence number
Next Record	*Next*	Moves to the next record in the mail merge
Next Record If	*NextIf*	Moves to the next record in the mail merge if a condition is met
Set Bookmark	*Set*	Assigns new text to a bookmark
Skip Record If	*SkipIf*	Skips a record in the mail merge if a condition is met

For example, when creating a merged document, you can use the *If. . .Then. . .Else* rule to insert a specific sentence if the recipient is a member of the club and insert a different sentence if the recipient is not currently a member. Or, if you are creating a targeted mailing, you can use the *Skip Record If* rule to skip all records of individuals who do not live in a specific city.

Use the *Rules* button in the *Write & Insert Fields* group on the *Mailings* tab to insert merge rules into the main document that you will merge with recipients, or use the *Field* dialog box to insert a merge rule field.

▶ HOW TO: Add a Rule to a Mail Merge

1. Place your insertion point in the main mail merge document at the location to insert the rule.
   - Word populates field codes sequentially in your document starting at the beginning, so it is important to place the rule in the correct location.

2. Click the **Rules** button [*Mailings* tab, *Write & Insert Fields* group] and select the rule you want to insert (Figure 9-64). The *Insert Word Field: [Rule]* dialog box opens (Figure 9-65).

3. Enter the conditions for the rule.
   - Depending on the rule you are using, you may not need to fill in all conditions of the rule.

4. Click **OK** to close the dialog box and to insert the rule (field code).
   - Some field codes are hidden and do not display in your document; in the next section, you learn how to view field codes in your document.

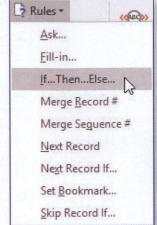

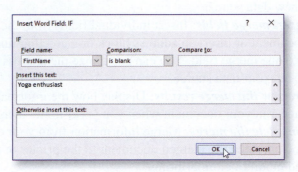

9-65 *Insert Word Field: IF* dialog box

9-64 Insert rule

View Merge Field Codes

Fields codes display differently in your document and some field codes are hidden. For example, index field codes only appear when *Show/Hide* is turned on, property field codes display the text of the document property, and an address block field code displays "<<AddressBlock>>". The following are two ways to view field codes in your document:

- *View all field codes*: Press **Alt+F9** (Figure 9-66). **Alt+F9** toggles field code display on/off.
- *View an individual field code*: Right-click the field and select **Toggle Field Codes** from the context menu. Repeat to toggle off the field code.

When editing a document, it is helpful to see the location of field codes. You can delete or move field codes the same way you delete and move text or objects in your document.

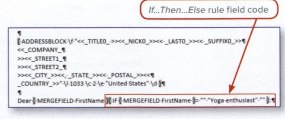

9-66 View merge field codes

Using Bookmarks

When working with documents, you can add a ***bookmark***, which marks a location, selected text, or object in the document. After you insert a bookmark, you can create a hyperlink or a cross-reference to the bookmark to quickly move to this location in the document, or index the bookmark to include on an index page.

Add a Bookmark

Use a bookmark to mark a specific location, a word, selected text, or object.

▶ HOW TO: Add a Bookmark

1. Position the insertion point or select the text you want to bookmark.
2. Click the **Insert** tab.
3. Click the **Bookmark** button [*Links* group] to open the *Bookmark* dialog box (Figure 9-67).
4. Type the name of the bookmark.
   - Bookmark names cannot contain spaces.
5. Click **Add** to add the bookmark and close the dialog box.

9-67 *Bookmark* dialog box

Display Bookmarks in a Document

When you insert a bookmark, by default the bookmark is not visible in your document. But you can display bookmarks in Word by changing a setting in the ***Word Options*** dialog box.

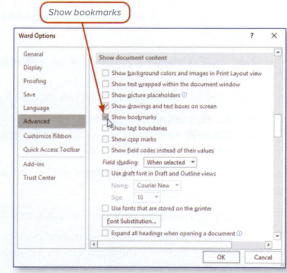

▶ HOW TO: Display Bookmarks in a Document

1. Click the **File** tab to open the *Backstage* view.
2. Click the **Options** button to open the *Word Options* dialog box.
3. Select **Advanced** on the left of the *Word Options* dialog box (Figure 9-68).
4. Check the **Show bookmarks** check box in the *Show document content* area.
5. Click **OK** to close the dialog box.

9-68 Display bookmarks in document

When you show bookmarks, a gray I-beam marks the specific location of the bookmark (Figure 9-69), and gray brackets mark selected text (Figure 9-70).

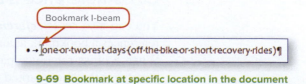

9-69 **Bookmark at specific location in the document**

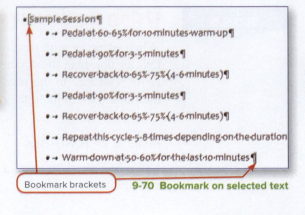

9-70 Bookmark on selected text

Go To a Bookmark

The following are methods to quickly move
to a bookmark in your document:

- *Insert Bookmark* [*Insert* tab, *Links*
  group]: Open the *Bookmark* dialog box,
  select the bookmark, and click **Go To**.
- *Find and Replace*: Click the **Find**
  drop-down arrow [*Home* tab, *Editing*
  group] and select the **Go To** tab. Select
  Bookmark in the *Go to what* area,
  select the bookmark, and click **Go To**
  (Figure 9-71).

9-71 Use *Go To* to find a selected bookmark

Hyperlink to a Bookmark

You can create a *hyperlink* in your document that takes the reader to the bookmark.

HOW TO: Create a Hyperlink to a Bookmark

1. Select the text on which to create a hyperlink to a bookmark.
2. Click the **Hyperlink** button [*Insert* tab, *Links* group] or
   press **Ctrl+K**. The *Insert Hyperlink* dialog box opens
   (Figure 9-72).
3. Choose **Place in This Document** in the *Link to* area.
4. Select the bookmark.
5. Click **OK** to insert the hyperlink and to close the dialog box.
   - The selected text is blue and underlined.
   - Press **Ctrl** and click the hyperlink to move to the bookmark.

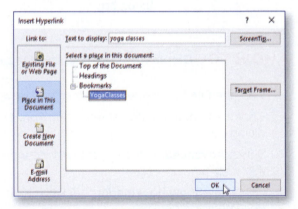

9-72 Insert hyperlink to a bookmark

Cross-Reference a Bookmark

You can also *cross-reference* a bookmark. For example, you can insert a page number that
references a bookmark at another location in the document ("Schedule rest days (*see page 3*)").
When a cross-reference page number links to a bookmark, the page number automatically
updates if the bookmarked text moves to a different page.

1. Position the insertion point at the location to insert the cross-reference to a bookmark.

2. Click the **Cross-reference** button [*Insert* tab, *Links* group]. The *Cross-reference* dialog box opens (Figure 9-73).

3. Select **Bookmark** in the *Reference type* area.

   - Check the **Insert as hyperlink** check box if you want the cross-reference to function as a hyperlink to the bookmark.

4. Select the type of reference from the drop-down list in the *Insert reference to* area.

   - You can reference a page number, the bookmarked text, or the words "above" or "below."
   - If you choose *Page number*, you can also include the words "above" or "below" after the page number (for example *"see page 3 above"*).

5. Select the bookmark in the *For which bookmark* area.

6. Click **Insert** to insert the cross-reference.

7. Click **Close** to close the dialog box.

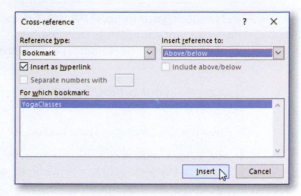

9-73 Insert cross-reference to a bookmark

Use a Bookmark in a Formula

Bookmarks can also be variables in formulas. If you have a bookmark in your document that is a value, you can insert the bookmark into a formula. Click the **Paste bookmark** drop-down list in the *Formula* dialog box to display the available bookmarks in your document.

Delete a Bookmark

When you delete a bookmark from a document, Word does not remove hyperlinks or cross-references associated with this bookmark. You must manually remove a hyperlink or cross-reference to a bookmark.

▶ **HOW TO:** Delete a Bookmark

1. Click the **Bookmark** button [*Insert* tab, *Links* group]. The *Bookmark* dialog box opens.

2. Select the bookmark to delete and click **Delete**.

3. Click **Close** to close the *Bookmark* dialog box.

PAUSE & PRACTICE: WORD 9-4

For this Pause & Practice project, you add a bookmark, create a hyperlink and cross-reference to the bookmark, and merge the document from *Pause & Practice 9-3* with recipient data from an Excel worksheet. You select the type of merge, select recipients, insert merge fields, sort records, create rules, and share the document with your instructor.

Files Needed: ***[your initials] PP W9-3.docx*** and ***HCCAddresses-09.xlsx*** *(student data files are available in the* Library *of your SIMnet account)*
Completed Project File Names: ***[your initials] PP W9-4.docx*** and ***[your initials] PP W9-4 merged.docx***

1. Open the ***[your initials] PP W9-3*** you completed in *Pause & Practice 9-3*.

2. Save the document as [your initials] PP W9-4.

3. Add a bookmark and display bookmarks in a document.
   a. Click the picture of the PowerPoint slide on the middle right of the document.
   b. Click the **Bookmark** button [*Insert* tab, *Links* group] to open the *Bookmark* dialog box (Figure 9-74).
   c. Type YogaClasses in the *Bookmark name* text box (no space between words).
   d. Click **Add** to add the bookmark.
   e. Click the **File** tab to open the *Backstage* view.
   f. Click **Options** to open the *Word Options* dialog box and click **Advanced** on the left.
   g. Check the **Show bookmarks** box in the *Show document content* area (Figure 9-75).
   h. Click **OK** to close the *Word Options* dialog box.

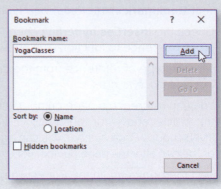

9-74 Add a bookmark

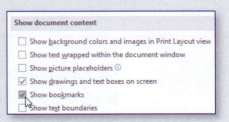

9-75 Show bookmarks in the document

4. Insert a hyperlink to a bookmark.
   a. Select "**yoga classes**" in the first sentence in the first body paragraph.
   b. Click the **Hyperlink** button [*Insert* tab, *Links* group] to open the *Insert Hyperlink* dialog box (Figure 9-76).
   c. Click **Place in This Document** on the left.
   d. Select the **YogaClasses** bookmark. If needed, click the plus sign (+) to the left of *Bookmarks* to display the bookmark.
   e. Click the **ScreenTip** button, type Types of yoga classes as the *ScreenTip*, and click **OK** to close the *Set Hyperlink ScreenTip* dialog box.
   f. Click **OK** to insert the hyperlink to the bookmark.

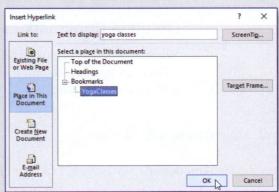

9-76 Insert hyperlink to a bookmark

5. Insert a cross-reference to a bookmark.
   a. Place the insertion point after the space after the "yoga classes" hyperlink.
   b. Type (see and **space** once.
   c. Click the **Cross-reference** button [*Insert* tab, *Links* group] to open the *Cross-reference* dialog box (Figure 9-77).
   d. Click the **Reference type** drop-down list and select **Bookmark**.
   e. Check the **Insert as hyperlink** box and select **YogaClasses** in the *For which bookmark* area.
   f. Click the **Insert reference to** drop-down list and select **Above/below**.

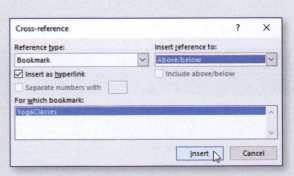

9-77 Insert cross-reference to a bookmark

g. Click **Insert** and then click **Close**.

h. Type **)** after "below" and **space** once. Confirm proper spacing before and after the text in parentheses.

6. Start the mail merge, select recipients, and sort records.

a. Click the **Start Mail Merge** button [*Mailings* tab, *Start Mail Merge* group] and select **Letters**.

b. Click the **Select Recipients** button and select **Use an Existing List** to open the *Select Data Source* dialog box.

c. Select the ***HCCAddresses-09*** file from your student data files and click **Open**. The *Select Table* dialog box opens.

d. Select **MailingList** and click **OK**.

e. Click the **Edit Recipient List** button to open the *Mail Merge Recipients* dialog box.

f. Click the **LastName** column heading drop-down list, select **Sort Ascending**, and click **OK** to close the dialog box.

7. Insert an address block and greeting line field codes.

a. Turn on **Show/Hide** if it is not already on.

b. Select the **"<Address>"** placeholder and delete it. Don't delete the paragraph mark after the text.

c. Click the **Address Block** button [*Mailings* tab, *Write & Insert Fields* group] to open the *Insert Address Block* dialog box (Figure 9-78).

9-78 Insert *Address Block* merge field

d. Select **Mr. Josh Randall Jr**. as the recipient's name format and click **OK** to close the dialog box and insert the address block.

e. Select the **"<Greeting>"** placeholder and delete it. Don't delete the paragraph mark after the text.

f. Type Dear and **space** once.

g. Click the **Insert Merge Field** drop-down list, select **FirstName**, and type **:** (colon).

8. Create a rule to insert custom greeting if the recipient's first name is not available in the data source.

a. Place your insertion point between the *<<FirstName>>* field and the colon.

b. Click the **Rules** button [*Mailings* tab, *Write & Insert Fields* group] and select **If. . .Then. . .Else** from the drop-down list. The *Insert Word Field: IF* dialog box opens (Figure 9-79).

c. Click the **Field name** drop-down list and select **FirstName**.

d. Click the **Comparison** drop-down list and select **is blank**.

e. Type Yoga enthusiast in the *Insert this text* area.

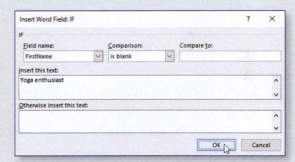

9-79 Insert *If. . .Then. . .Else* rule

f. Click **OK** to close the dialog box and to insert the rule. This is a hidden field code and is visible only when field codes display.

g. Press **Alt+F9** to display field codes in the document and confirm that the *If* field code is between the *<<FirstName>>* field and the colon. If you are using a laptop computer, you may have to press **Fn+Alt+F9**.

h. Press **Alt+F9** again to toggle off field codes.

9. Create a rule to merge only those recipients from Hendersonville.

a. Place your insertion point in front of the *<<AddressBlock>>* field.

b. Click the **Rules** button and select **Skip Record If** from the drop-down list. The *Insert Word Field: Skip Record If* dialog box opens (Figure 9-80).

c. Click the **Field name** drop-down list and select **City**.

d. Click the **Comparison** drop-down list and select **Not equal to**.

e. Type Hendersonville in the *Compare to* area.

f. Click **OK** to close the dialog box and to insert the rule. The rule displays in front of the *<<AddressBlock>>* field code.

9-80 Insert *Skip Record If* rule

10. Create a rule to insert a custom sentence based on the recipient's membership status.

a. Delete the last sentence in the last body paragraph of the letter ("We look forward . . ."). Don't delete the paragraph mark after the sentence.

b. Confirm that your insertion point is after the space after the period at the end of the third body paragraph.

c. Click the **Rules** button and select **If. . .Then. . .Else** from the drop-down list. The *Insert Word Field: IF* dialog box opens (Figure 9-81).

d. Click the **Field name** drop-down list and select **MembershipDate**.

e. Click the **Comparison** drop-down list and select **is not blank**.

f. Type We look forward to seeing you again in our yoga classes. Next time you come, please feel free to bring your friends who are not yet members. in the *Insert this text* area.

9-81 Insert *If. . .Then. . .Else* rule

g. Type We hope you will try one or more of our yoga classes. in the *Otherwise insert this text* area.

h. Click **OK** to close the dialog box and insert the rule. If the condition is true, the sentence displays in the document (see step 10f). When the document is merged, this sentence will change if the condition is false (no membership date).

11. Select the date line (first line of the document) and apply **18 pt**. *Before* paragraph spacing.

12. Preview and finish the merge.

a. Click the **Preview Results** button [*Mailings* tab, *Preview Results* group] to preview the merged document. *(Note: The* Skip Record If *rule is not applied until you finish the merge.)*

b. Click the **Next Record** button [*Mailings* tab, **Preview Results** group] to preview the letters in the merge.

c. Click the **Preview Results** button again to hide the recipient information and display the merge field codes.

d. Save the document.

e. Click the **Finish & Merge** button [*Mailings* tab, *Finish* group] and select **Edit Individual Documents**. The *Merge to New Document* dialog box opens.

f. Click the **All** radio button and click **OK** to finish the merge. A new document opens, and the recipient information merges into the document. The document should contain four letters.

13. Save the merged document as [your initials] PP W9-4 merged (Figure 9-82).

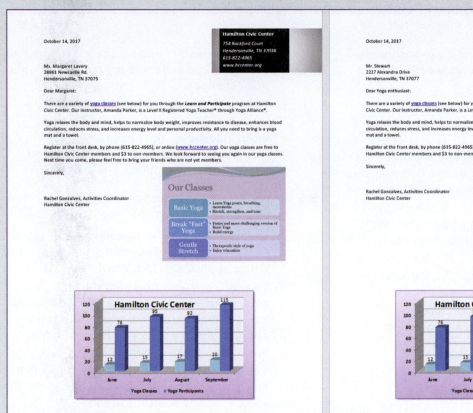
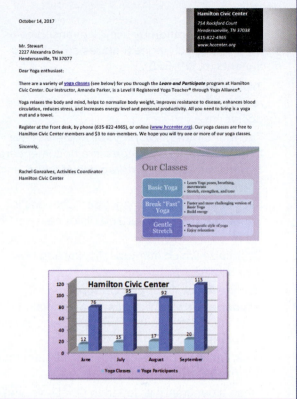

9-82 PP W9-4 merged completed (pages 1 and 2 of 4)

14. Share the document with your instructor.
    a. Save this document on *OneDrive* if you haven't already. If you don't have the ability to save to *OneDrive*, skip all of step 14.
    b. Click the **Share** button in the upper right of the Word window to open the *Share* pane.
    c. Type your instructor's email address in the *Invite people* text box.
    d. Select **Can edit** in the drop-down list below the email address.
    e. Type a brief message to your instructor and click the **Share** button. If Word is not connected to your Microsoft account this *Share* feature may not work properly. Alternatively, click **Get a sharing link** at the bottom of the *Share* pane, click **Create an edit link**, click the **Copy** button, and email the sharing link to your professor.
    f. Click the **X** in the upper right corner of the *Share* pane to close it.

15. Save and close both documents.

Chapter Summary

9.1 Enhance collaboration by using advanced comments and track changes features and sharing documents (p. W9-525).

- *Track Changes* is a collaboration tool that reviewers use to edit and track changes in a document.
- The four different *Display for Review* views to display tracked changes in a document are **Simple Markup**, **All Markup**, **No Markup**, and **Original**.
- Each change made using *Track Changes* is attributed to a reviewer and his or her user name.
- Customize which markups display and how they display.
- Use the *Track Changes Options* and *Advanced Track Changes Options* dialog boxes to customize how tracked changes and comments appear in your document.
- *Lock Tracking* prevents others from turning off the *Track Changes* feature.
- When a document is saved to OneDrive, you can share this document with others and collaborate on the document.
- *Real-time collaboration* immediately displays changes users make on a shared document when multiple users edit the shared document at the same time.
- When you print a document, you can choose to print comments and markup.

9.2 Use Word collaboration features to compare, combine, and protect documents (p. W9-531).

- The *Compare* feature compares two versions of a document and displays the differences as tracked changes.
- The *Combine* feature combines two versions of a document.
- Word provides you with the following features to prepare your document for sharing with others: **Inspect Document**, **Check Accessibility**, and **Check Compatibility**.
- *Mark as Final* marks the document as a final version and protects it from editing.
- *Encrypt with Password* requires users to enter a password to open a document.
- When you use *Restrict Editing*, a user can open the document but is restricted from editing it.

- When you restrict editing, you can restrict all editing or allow users to only use comments, track changes, or fill in forms.
- You can also *Add a Digital Signature* to a document to enhance security.
- Word autosaves your document at set intervals. You can access previous *autosaved versions* of a document.

9.3 Embed and link content from other Microsoft Office applications into a Word document (p. W9-542).

- *Object linking and embedding (OLE)* allows users to embed or link information from other Office applications into Word.
- You can copy an embedded object from a *source file* and paste it into a *destination file*. You can modify the embedded object independently of the object in the source file.
- You can also *link* an object from a source file a destination file, and the linked object in the destination file retains its connection with the source file and source program.
- You can edit a linked object in the source file and update the object in the destination file to reflect the changes in the source file.
- Use the *Paste Special* dialog box to paste an embedded or linked object into the destination file.
- The process for resizing, arranging, or modifying embedded or linked objects in your Word document is similar to working with pictures, charts, *SmartArt*, or shapes.
- You can modify or break the link between the object in the source and destination files.

9.4 Use mail merge rules to customize how data merges into a Word document from other Office applications (p. W9-551).

- You can use mail merge to merge recipient information from other Office applications into a Word document.
- *Rules* are Word field codes that you can use to customize the output of a mail merge.
- View Word field codes in your document by pressing **Alt+F9**.

9.5 Insert bookmarks into a document (p. W9-553).

- Use a *bookmark* to mark a specific location or selected text in a document.

- Use the **Word Options** dialog box to control how bookmarks display in your documents.
- Use **Go To** to move to a bookmark in the document.
- You can add a **hyperlink** to a bookmark; this takes users to the bookmark when they click the hyperlink.
- Press **Ctrl** and click a hyperlink to navigate to the linked area or object.
- You can add a **cross-reference** to a bookmark; this provides the page number for the bookmark or a general location in the document.

Check for Understanding

The SIMbook for this text (within your SIMnet account) provides the following resources for concept review:

- Multiple choice questions
- Matching exercises
- Short answer questions

Guided Project 9-1

For this project, you edit a document from Kelly Sung at Life's Animal Shelter. You change how markup displays, accept and reject changes, review comments, edit the document, link and format slides from a PowerPoint presentation, finalize the document, and share the file with your instructor.
[Student Learning Outcomes 9.1, 9.2, 9.3]

Files Needed: ***LASSupportLetter-09.docx*** and ***LASSupportPPT-09.pptx*** (student data files are available in the Library of your SIMnet account)
Completed Project File Names: ***[your initials] Word 9-1.docx*** and ***[your initials] LASSupportPPT-09.pptx***

Skills Covered in This Project

- Change user name and initials.
- Change how markup displays.
- Change the color of insertions, deletions, and comments.
- Turn on *Track Changes* and edit a document.
- Review and delete comments.
- Reject and accept tracked changes.
- Insert the current date.
- Change the display for *Review* view.

- Accept and reject changes in a document.
- Link slides from a PowerPoint presentation to a Word document.
- Update text in a source file.
- Update a linked object in a destination file.
- Break links in the document.
- Resize and align pictures.
- Inspect a document and remove information.
- Mark a document as final.
- Share a file.

1. Open the ***LASSupportLetter-09*** document from your student data files.

2. Save the document as [your initials] Word 9-1.

3. Change user name and initials. Skip the following steps if your user name and initials are already in Word.
   a. Click the **Tracking** launcher [*Review* tab, *Tracking* group] to open the *Track Changes Options* dialog box.
   b. Click the **Change User Name** button to open the *Word Options* dialog box.
   c. Type your first and last name in the *User name* area, type your initials in lowercase letters in the *Initials* area, and check the **Always use these values regardless of sign in to Office** box.
   d. Click **OK** to close the *Word Options* dialog box and click **OK** to close the *Track Changes Options* dialog box.

4. Change how markup displays and the color of comments and markup.
   a. Click the **Display for Review** drop-down list [*Review* tab, *Tracking* group] and select **All Markup**.
   b. Click the **Show Markup** drop-down list [*Review* tab, *Tracking* group], click **Balloons**, and select **Show Revisions in Balloons**.
   c. Click the **Tracking** launcher to open the *Track Changes Options* dialog box.
   d. Click **Advanced Options** to open the *Advanced Track Changes Options* dialog box.

e. Change the *Color* of *Insertions*, *Deletions*, and *Comments* to **Red** (Figure 9-83).

f. Click **OK** to close the *Advanced Track Changes Options* dialog box and click **OK** to close the *Track Changes Options* dialog box.

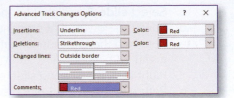

9-83 Change the color of insertions, dele-tions, and comments

5. Review comments and edit the document.
    a. Click the top half of the **Track Changes** button [*Review* tab, *Tracking* group] to turn on *Track Changes*.
    b. Click the **Next** button [*Review* tab, *Comments* group] to move to the first comment.
    c. Read the comment and click the **Delete** button [*Review* tab, *Comments* group] to delete the comment.
    d. Select "**[Insert Current Date]**", delete it, and insert the current date so it updates automatically. Use January 1, 2018 as the format for the date.
    e. Click the **Next** button to move to the next comment and read the comment.
    f. Click the **Delete** button to delete the comment.

6. Accept and reject tracked changes.
    a. Click the top half of the **Track Changes** button to turn off *Track Changes*.
    b. Move to the top of the document (**Ctrl+Home**).
    c. Click the **Display for Review** drop-down list [*Review* tab, *Tracking* group] and select **No Markup** to see how the final document will look with proposed changes accepted.
    d. Click the **Display for Review** drop-down list again and select **All Markup**.
    e. Click the **Next** button [*Review* tab, *Changes* group] to move to where the words "Kelly Sung," were deleted. You have to click the **Next** button more than once to get to this deletion.
    f. Click the top half of the **Reject** button [*Review* tab, *Changes* group] to reject the deletion of the words "Kelly Sung,".
    g. Click the bottom half of the **Accept** button and select **Accept All Changes** to accept the remaining changes in the document.

7. Link slides from a PowerPoint presentation to the Word document.
    a. Open a *File Explorer* window, browse to your student data files, and open the ***LASSupportPPT-09. pptx*** PowerPoint presentation. Click the **Enable Editing** button on the *Message* bar if the file opens in *Protected* view.
    b. Save this file to your desktop and name it [your initials] LASSupportPPT-09.
    c. Select **slide 5** on the left and copy it.
    d. Return to your Word document and place the insertion point on the blank line below the last body paragraph.
    e. Click the bottom half of the **Paste** button [*Home* tab, *Clipboard* group] and select **Paste Special** to open the *Paste Special* dialog box (Figure 9-84).
    f. Click the **Paste link** radio button, select **Microsoft PowerPoint Slide Object** in the *As* area, and click **OK** to insert the linked slide. The slide is placed on page 2; you will fix this later.
    g. Place the insertion point on the bottom right of the linked slide and press **Enter** once.
    h. **Copy** and insert a link to **slide 6**, repeating step 7f.

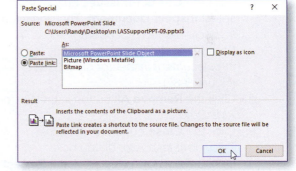

9-84 Paste copied slide as a linked object

8. Modify content on the linked slides.
    a. Return to the PowerPoint presentation and select **slide 5** on the left.
    b. Select the title in the working area of PowerPoint (on the right) and change the text to Donate to Life's Animal Shelter (Figure 9-85).

Donate to Life's Animal Shelter

9-85 Edit the slide title in the source file

c. Select **slide 6** and change the title of the slide to Volunteer with Life's Animal Shelter.

d. Save the PowerPoint presentation and leave it open.

e. Return to the Word document, right-click the first slide, and select **Update Link** from the context menu.

f. Right-click the second slide and select **Update Link** from the context menu.

g. Return to the PowerPoint presentation, save the presentation, and close PowerPoint.

9. Break the links between the source and destination files.

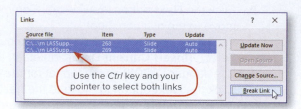

a. Return to the Word document, click the **File** tab to open the *Backstage* view, and click **Info** on the left if it is not already selected.

b. Click the **Edit Links to Files** button to open the *Links* dialog box (Figure 9-86).

c. Press the **Ctrl** key and click both of the items in the *Source file* area to select both items.

d. Click the **Break Link** button. A dialog box opens confirming you want to break the selected links.

e. Select **Yes** to break the links.

f. Click the **Back** arrow to return to the document.

9-86 Break links using the *Links* dialog box

10. Format the slide pictures in the document.

a. Select the first slide and change the *Height* to **2.5"** [*Picture Tools Format* tab, *Size* group]. The width automatically adjusts.

b. Select the second slide and change the *Height* to **2.5"**.

c. Click the first slide and click the **Center** alignment button [*Home* tab, *Paragraph* group].

d. **Center** the second slide. Both slides display on the first page.

11. Save the document.

12. Inspect the document and mark as final.

a. Click the **File** tab to open the *Backstage* view.

b. Click the **Check for Issues** button and select **Inspect Document**. The *Document Inspector* dialog box opens.

c. Click **Inspect**. The results display in the *Document Inspector* dialog box (Figure 9-87).

d. Click the **Remove All** button in the *Custom XML Data* area.

e. Click the **Close** button to close the *Document Inspector* dialog box.

f. On the *Backstage* view, click the **Protect Document** button and select **Mark as Final**. A dialog box opens informing you that the file will be saved and marked as final.

g. Click **OK** to close the dialog box and click **OK** to close the next informational dialog box.

h. Click the **Back** arrow to return to the document.

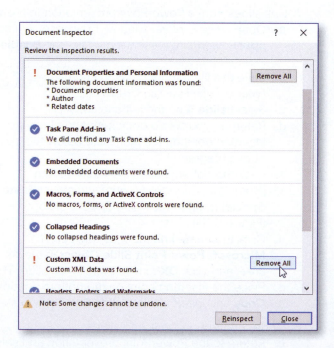

9-87 Inspection results displayed in the *Document Inspector* dialog box

13. Share the document with your instructor.
    a. Save this document on *OneDrive* if you haven't already. If you don't have the ability to save to *OneDrive*, skip all of step 13.
    b. Click the **Share** button in the upper right of the Word window to open the *Share* pane.
    c. Type your instructor's email address in the *Invite people* text box.
    d. Select **Can edit** in the drop-down list below the email address.
    e. Type a brief message to your instructor and click the **Share** button. If Word is not connected to your Microsoft account this *Share* feature may not work properly. Alternatively, click **Get a sharing link** at the bottom of the *Share* pane, click **Create an edit link**, click the **Copy** button, and email the sharing link to your professor.
    f. Click the **X** in the upper right corner of the *Share* pane to close it.

14. Close the document (Figure 9-88).

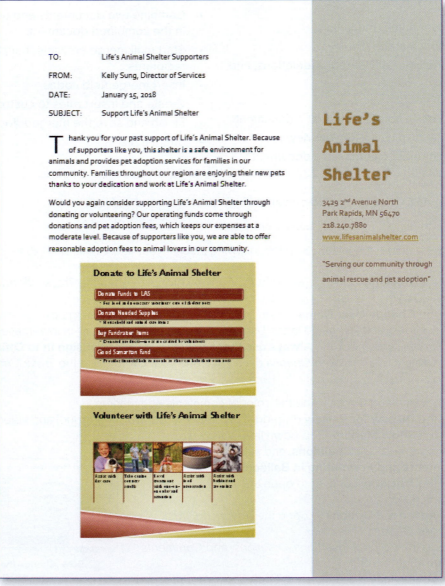

9-88 Word 9-1 completed

W9-565

Guided Project 9-2

For this project, you edit two documents from American River Cycling Club. You revise a document and add comments, review and accept changes, combine two documents and accept changes, merge the combined document with an Access database table, create rules to customize the merge, and share the document with your instructor.
[**Student Learning Outcomes 9.1, 9.2, 9.4**]

Files Needed: ***ARCCCoaching-09a.docx***, ***ARCCCoaching-09b.docx***, and ***ARCC-09.accdb*** *(student data files are available in the* Library *of your SIMnet account)*
Completed Project File Names: *[your initials]* **Word 9-2a.docx**, *[your initials]* **Word 9-2b.docx**, *[your initials]* **Word 9-2 combined.docx**, and *[your initials]* **Word 9-2 merged.docx**

Skills Covered in This Project

- Change user name and initials.
- Change how markup displays.
- Change the color of insertions, deletions, and comments.
- Insert comments.
- Turn on *Track Changes* and edit a document.
- Change the display for *Review* view.
- Accept and reject changes in a document.
- Review and delete comments.
- Combine two documents and accept changes in the combined document.
- Start mail merge and select and edit recipients.
- Insert merge field codes.
- Create and insert rules to customize a merge.
- Finish and save the merged document.
- Share a file.

1. Open the ***ARCCCoaching-09a*** document from your student data files.

2. Save the document as [your initials] Word 9-2a.

3. Change user name and initials. Skip the following steps if your user name and initials are already in Word.
   a. Click the **Tracking** launcher [*Review* tab, *Tracking* group] to open the *Track Changes Options* dialog box.
   b. Click the **Change User Name** button to open the *Word Options* dialog box.
   c. Type your first and last name in the *User name* area, type your initials in lowercase letters in the *Initials* area, and check the **Always use these values regardless of sign in to Office** box.
   d. Click **OK** to close the *Word Options* dialog box and click **OK** to close the *Track Changes Options* dialog box.

4. Change how markup displays and the color of comments and markup.
   a. Click the **Display for Review** drop-down list [*Review* tab, *Tracking* group] and select **All Markup**.
   b. Click the **Show Markup** drop-down list [*Review* tab, *Tracking* group], click **Balloons**, and select **Show Only Comments and Formatting in Balloons**.
   c. Click the **Tracking** launcher to open the *Track Changes Options* dialog box.
   d. Click **Advanced Options** to open the *Advanced Track Changes Options* dialog box.
   e. Change the *Color* of *Insertions*, *Deletions*, and *Comments* to **Blue** (Figure 9-89).
   f. Click **OK** to close the *Advanced Track Changes Options* dialog box and click **OK** to close the *Track Changes Options* dialog box.

9-89 Change the color of insertions, deletions, and comments

5. Insert comments and track changes in the document.
   a. Select the first word in the first body paragraph ("**There**") and click the **New Comment** button [*Review* tab, *Comments* group] to insert a new comment.
   b. Type Merge this letter with our database in the comment balloon.
   c. Select the first word in the last bulleted item ("**Be**") and click the **New Comment** button.
   d. Type Type a paragraph about the coach and include the coach's info in a table in the comment balloon.
   e. Click the top half of the **Track Changes** button [*Review* tab, *Tracking* group] to turn on *Track Changes*.
   f. Select and delete "**time trial, or century**." in the first body paragraph (don't delete the paragraph mark) and type or time trial. (include the period).
   g. Select and delete "**General Guidelines**" including the paragraph mark.
   h. In the first bulleted item, delete the space between "off" and "season" and type **-** (hyphen).
   i. Turn off **Track Changes**.

6. Save and close the document.

7. Open the ***ARCCCoaching-09b*** document from your student data files. Click the **Enable Editing** button on the *Message* bar if the file opens in *Protected* view.

8. Save the document as [your initials] Word 9-2b.

9. Review comments and changes and accept changes.
   a. Click the **Display for Review** drop-down list [*Review* tab, *Tracking* group] and select **Simple Markup** to display the document with proposed changes.
   b. Click the **Display for Review** drop-down list again and select **All Markup**.
   c. Click the bottom of the **Accept** button [*Review* tab, *Changes* group] and select **Accept All Changes**.
   d. Click the bottom half of the **Delete** button [*Review* tab, *Comments* group] and select **Delete All Comments in Document**.
   e. Save the document.

10. Combine the two edited documents.
    a. Click the **Compare** button [*Review* tab, *Compare* group] and select **Combine**. The *Combine Document* dialog box opens (Figure 9-90).
    b. Click the **Browse** button in the *Original document* area. The *Open* dialog box opens.
    c. Select the ***[your initials] Word 9-2a*** document and click **Open**.
    d. Click the **Browse** button in the *Revised document* area, select the ***[your initials] Word 9-2b*** document, and click **Open**.
    e. Click the **More** button if necessary to display more options and confirm all boxes are checked.
    f. Select the **Word level** and the **New document** radio buttons In the *Show changes* area.
    g. Click **OK** to close the dialog box and combine the documents. The combined document displays in a new Word window.

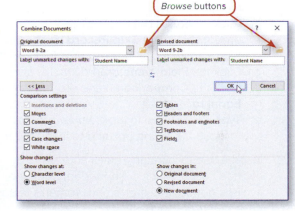

9-90 *Combine Document* dialog box

11. Save the combined document as [your initials] Word 9-2 combined.

12. Hide source documents, accept changes, and delete comments.
    a. If source documents display, click the **Compare** button, click **Show Source Documents**, and select **Hide Source Documents**.
    b. Click the bottom of the **Accept** button and select **Accept All Changes and Stop Tracking**.
    c. Click the bottom half of the **Delete** button and select **Delete All Comments in Document**.
    d. Close the *Reviewing* pane if it is open.

13. Return to the ***[your initials] Word 9-2b*** document and save and close the document.

14. Start a merge and select recipients from an Access database.
    a. Return to the *[your initials] Word 9-2 combined* document, click the **Start Mail Merge** button [*Mailings* tab, *Start Mail Merge* group], and select **Letters**.
    b. Click the **Select Recipients** button [*Mailings* tab, *Start Mail Merge* group] and select **Use an Existing List**. The *Select Data Source* dialog box opens.
    c. Select the *ARCC-09* database from your student data file and click **Open**.
    d. Click the **Edit Recipient List** button [*Mailings* tab, *Start Mail Merge* group] to open the *Mail Merge Recipients* dialog box.
    e. Click the **Last** column heading drop-down list and select **Sort Ascending**.
    f. Deselect the **check box** next to the following names so they are not included in the merge: Roy Baxter, Rick Hermenn, and Kelsey Kroll.
    g. Click **OK** to close the *Mail Merge Recipients* dialog box.

15. Insert merge fields.
    a. Select and delete **<Name and address>**. Don't delete the paragraph mark after these words.
    b. Click the **Address Block** button [*Mailings* tab, *Write & Insert Fields* group]. The *Insert Address Block* dialog box opens.
    c. Select **Joshua Randall Jr**. as the recipient's name format and click **OK** to close the dialog box and to insert the *Address Block* merge field code.
    d. Place your insertion point after the space after "Dear".
    e. Click the **Insert Merge Field** drop-down list [*Mailings* tab, *Write & Insert Fields* group] and select **First** from the drop-down list.
    f. Place your insertion point in the first cell in the second row of the table.
    g. Click the **Insert Merge Field** drop-down list and select **Coach**.

16. Insert a rule to skip cyclists who are not racers.
    a. Place your insertion point in front of the *<<AddressBlock>>* merge field code.
    b. Click the **Rules** button [*Mailings* tab, *Write & Insert Fields* group] and select **Skip Record If**. The *Insert Word Field: Skip Record If* dialog box opens (Figure 9-91).
    c. Click the **Field name** drop-down list and select **Level**.
    d. Click the **Comparison** name drop-down list and select **Equal to**.
    e. Type Recreational in the *Compare to* text box and click **OK** to close the dialog box and to insert the rule.

9-91 Insert a *Skip Record If* rule

17. Insert a rule to insert the email address of the cyclist's coach, which is dependent upon the cyclist's gender (the men's and women's teams have different coaches).
    a. Place your insertion point in the third cell in the second row of the table.
    b. Click the **Rules** button and select **If. . .Then. . .Else**. The *Insert Word Field: IF* dialog box opens (Figure 9-92).
    c. Click the **Field name** drop-down list and select **Gender**.
    d. Click the **Comparison** name drop-down list and select **Equal to**.
    e. Type Female in the *Compare to* area.
    f. Type coachkelsey@arcc.org in the *Insert this text* area.
    g. Type coachrick@arcc.org in the *Otherwise insert this text* area.
    h. Click **OK** to close the dialog box and to insert the rule. An email address displays in this cell.

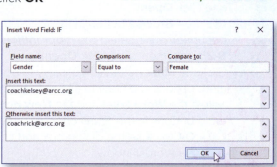

9-92 Insert an *If. . .Then. . .Else* rule

18. Create a rule to insert the phone number of the cyclist's coach dependent upon the cyclist's gender.
    a. Place your insertion point in the fourth cell in the second row of the table.

b. Click the **Rules** button and select **If. . .Then. . .Else**.

c. Click the **Field name** drop-down list and select **Gender**.

d. Click the **Comparison** name drop-down list and select **Equal to**.

e. Type Female in the *Compare to* area.

f. Type 916-453-2845 in the *Insert this text* area.

g. Type 916-451-9879 in the *Otherwise insert this text* area.

h. Click **OK** to close the dialog box and to insert the rule. A phone number displays in this cell.

i. Save the document.

19. Preview the results and finish the merge.

a. Click the **Preview Results** button [*Mailings* tab, *Preview Results* group] to preview your document.

b. Click the **Preview Results** button again to turn off preview.

c. Click the **Finish & Merge** button [*Mailings* tab, *Finish* group] and select **Edit Individual Documents**. The *Merge to New Document* dialog box opens.

d. Click the **All** radio button and click **OK** to finish the merge.

e. Save the merged document as [your initials] Word 9-2 merged (Figure 9-93). The document should contain 13 letters.

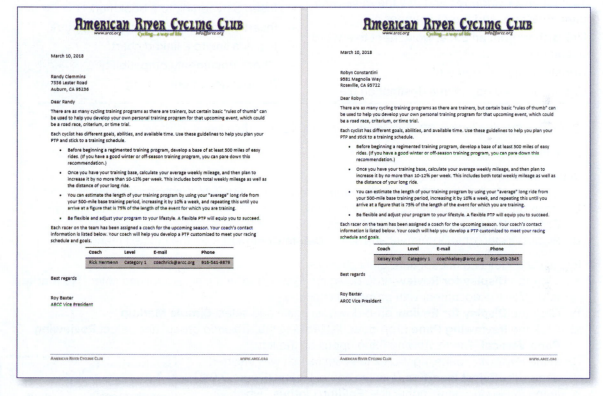

9-93 Word 9-2 merged completed (pages 1 and 2 of 13)

20. Share the document with your instructor.

a. Save this document on *OneDrive* if you haven't already. If you don't have the ability to save to *OneDrive*, skip all of step 20.

b. Click the **Share** button in the upper right of the Word window to open the *Share* pane.

c. Click **Get a sharing link** at the bottom of the *Share* pane, click **Create an edit link**, and click **Copy**.

d. Click the **X** in the upper right corner of the *Share* pane to close it.

e. Open the email account you use for this course, create an email to your instructor, and type an appropriate subject line and a brief message to your instructor.

f. Paste (**Ctrl+V**) the sharing link in the body of the email and send the email.

21. Save and close all open documents.

Guided Project 9-3

For this project, you edit a document from Sawyer Petrosky at Courtyard Medical Plaza. You review the document to accept and reject changes, review comments, edit the document, link and embed objects from Excel and PowerPoint, add a bookmark, create a hyperlink and cross-reference to a bookmark, prepare the document for sharing, and protect the document.
[Student Learning Outcomes 9.1, 9.2, 9.3, 9.5]

Files Needed: ***StayingActive-09.docx***, ***EstimatedCalories-09.xlsx***, and ***CMPStayingActive-09.pptx***
(student data files are available in the Library *of your SIMnet account)*
Completed Project File Names: ***[your initials] Word 9-3.docx*** and ***[your initials] EstimatedCalories-09.xlsx***

Skills Covered in This Project

- Review and delete comments.
- Turn off *Track Changes* and use the *Reviewing* pane to accept and reject changes.
- Link a chart from an Excel worksheet to a Word document.
- Update data in a source file.
- Update a linked object in a destination file.

- Embed and format PowerPoint slides.
- Remove a watermark.
- Add a bookmark.
- Insert a hyperlink to a bookmark.
- Insert a cross-reference to a bookmark.
- Break a link to a linked chart.
- Check document compatibility.
- Restrict document editing.

1. Open the ***StayingActive-09*** document from your student data files.

2. Save the document as [your initials] Word 9-3.

3. Review and delete comments.
   a. Click the **Next** button [*Review* tab, *Comments* group] to move to the first comment.
   b. Read both of the comments in the document.
   c. Click the **Delete** button to delete the comment.
   d. Right-click the other comment and select **Delete Comment** from the context menu.

4. Review changes and accept and reject changes.
   a. Click the **Display for Review** drop-down list [*Review* tab, *Tracking* group] and select **No Markup** to display the document with proposed changes.
   b. Click the **Display for Review** drop-down list again and select **Simple Markup**.
   c. Click the **Reviewing Pane** drop-down list [*Review* tab, *Tracking* group] and select **Reviewing Pane Vertical**. The *Reviewing* pane opens on the left.
   d. In the *Reviewing* pane, right-click the comma that was inserted and select **Reject Insertion** from the context menu (Figure 9-94).
   e. In the *Reviewing* pane, right-click "**Folding clothes**," which was deleted, and select **Reject Deletion** from the context menu.
   f. Click the bottom half of the **Accept** button [*Review* tab, *Changes* group] and select **Accept All Changes** to accept the remaining changes.
   g. Click the **Reviewing Pane** button to close the *Reviewing* pane.

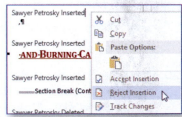

9-94 Reject an insertion

5. Paste a chart from an Excel worksheet as a link in the Word document.
   a. Open a *File Explorer* window, browse to your student data files, and open the ***EstimatedCalories-09*** Excel worksheet. Click the **Enable Editing** button on the *Message* bar if the file opens in *Protected* view.

b. Save this file to your desktop and name it **[your initials] EstimatedCalories-09**.
c. Select the frame of the chart and copy it.
d. Return to your Word document and place your insertion point on the blank line above the "Keep Exercise Fun and Interesting" heading.
e. Click the bottom half of the **Paste** button [*Home* tab, *Clipboard* group] and select **Paste Special**. The *Paste Special* dialog box opens (Figure 9-95).
f. Click the **Paste link** radio button and select **Microsoft Excel Chart Object** in the *As* area.
g. Click **OK** to close the dialog box and insert the linked chart.
h. Click the chart to select it and **Center** [*Home* tab, *Paragraph* group] the chart horizontally.

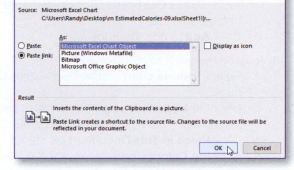

9-95 Paste Special dialog box

6. Edit the source file and update the linked chart.
   a. Right-click the chart, click **Linked Worksheet Object**, and select **Edit Link**. The linked Excel file opens.
   b. Click the **Moderately Active Male 31-50** cell (**C7**), type 2400, and press **Enter**.
   c. Click the **Moderately Active Male 51+** cell (**C8**), type 2300, and press **Enter**. (Figure 9-96)
   d. Save the **[your initials] EstimatedCalories-09** worksheet.
   e. Return to the Word document, right-click the chart, and select **Update Link**. The data in the chart updates to match the source file.
   f. Return to the Excel file, save the file, and exit Excel.

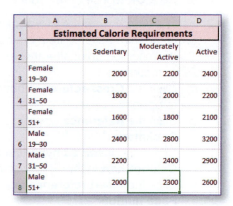

9-96 Edit the source file

7. Embed slides from a PowerPoint presentation into the Word document.
   a. Open a *File Explorer* window, browse to your student data files, and open the **CMPStayingActive-09** PowerPoint presentation.
   b. Select **slide 2** on the left and copy it.
   c. Return to your Word document and place your insertion point on the blank line at the end of the second page.
   d. Click the bottom half of the **Paste** button [*Home* tab, *Clipboard* group] and select **Paste Special**. The *Paste Special* dialog box opens.
   e. Click the **Paste** radio button and select **Picture (PNG)** in the *As* area.
   f. Click **OK** to close the dialog box and insert the embedded picture.
   g. Press **Ctrl+End** to move to the end of the document and press **Enter**.
   h. Repeat steps 7b–f to copy and embed **slide 8** below slide 2. Slide 8 displays on the third page.
   i. Return to PowerPoint and exit PowerPoint.

8. Resize and format the embedded slides.
   a. Return to the Word document, select the first slide (on second page), and change the *Height* to **3"** [*Picture Tools Format* tab, *Size* group]. The width automatically changes.
   b. Click the **Drop Shadow Rectangle** picture style in the *Picture Styles* gallery [*Picture Tools Format* tab, *Picture Styles* group] and **Center** [*Home* tab, *Paragraph* group] the picture horizontally.
   c. Select the second slide and repeat steps 8a–b.

9. Click the **Watermark** button [*Design* tab, *Page Background* group] and select **Remove Watermark** from the drop-down list.

10. Add a bookmark to a chart.
    a. Select the chart at the bottom of the first page.
    b. Click the **Bookmark** button [*Insert* tab, *Links* group] to open the *Bookmark* dialog box (Figure 9-97).
    c. Type **CalorieChart** in the *Bookmark name* text box (no space between words).
    d. Click **Add** to add the bookmark.

9-97 Add a bookmark

11. Insert a hyperlink to a bookmark.
    a. Select "**calorie chart**" in the third bulleted item on the second page.
    b. Click the **Hyperlink** button [*Insert* tab, *Links* group] to open the *Insert Hyperlink* dialog box (Figure 9-98).
    c. Click **Place in This Document** on the left.
    d. Click the **CalorieChart** bookmark. If necessary, click the plus sign (+) to the left of *Bookmarks* to display the bookmark.
    e. Click **OK** to insert the hyperlink to the bookmark.

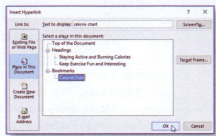

9-98 Insert hyperlink to a bookmark

12. Insert a cross-reference to a bookmark.
    a. In the third bulleted item on the second page, place the insertion point after the space after "page" in the parentheses.
    b. Click the **Cross-reference** button [*Insert* tab, *Links* group] to open the *Cross-reference* dialog box (Figure 9-99).
    c. Click the **Reference** type drop-down list and select **Bookmark**.
    d. Check the **Insert as hyperlink** box and select **CalorieChart** in the *For which bookmark* area.
    e. Click the **Insert reference to** drop-down list and select **Page number**.
    f. Click **Insert** and then click **Close**.

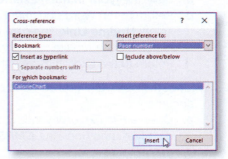

9-99 Insert cross-reference to a bookmark

13. Check document compatibility.
    a. Click the **File** tab to open the *Backstage* view.
    b. Click the **Check for Issues** button and select **Check Compatibility**. The *Microsoft Word Compatibility Checker* dialog box opens and displays potential compatibility issues. No issues should display.
    c. Click **OK** to close the dialog box.

14. Break the link between the source and destination files.
    a. Click the **File** tab to open the *Backstage* view and click **Info** on the right if it is not already selected.
    b. Click the **Edit Links to Files** button to open the *Links* dialog box (Figure 9-100).
    c. Select the link and click the **Break Link** button. A dialog box opens confirming you want to break the link.
    d. Select **Yes** to break the links.
    e. Click the **Back** arrow to return to the document.

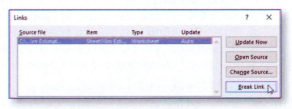

9-100 Break a link using the *Links* dialog box

15. Save the document.

16. Restrict editing of the document.
    a. Click the **File** tab to open the *Backstage* view.
    b. Click the **Protect Document** button and select **Restrict Editing**. The *Restrict Editing* pane opens on the right (Figure 9-101).
    c. Check the **Allow only this type of editing in the document** box in the *Editing Restrictions* area.
    d. Click the drop-down list below the check box and select **Comments**.
    e. Click the **Yes, Start Enforcing Protection** button. The *Start Enforcing Protection* dialog box opens.
    f. Type **CMP** in the *Enter new password* text box.
    g. Type **CMP** in the *Reenter password to confirm* text box.
    h. Click **OK** to close the dialog box and begin enforcing protection.
    i. Close the *Restrict Editing* pane.

17. Save and close the document (Figure 9-102).

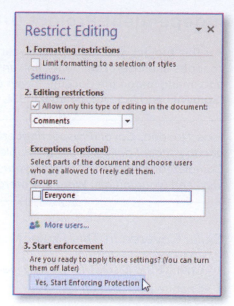

9-101 *Restrict Editing* pane

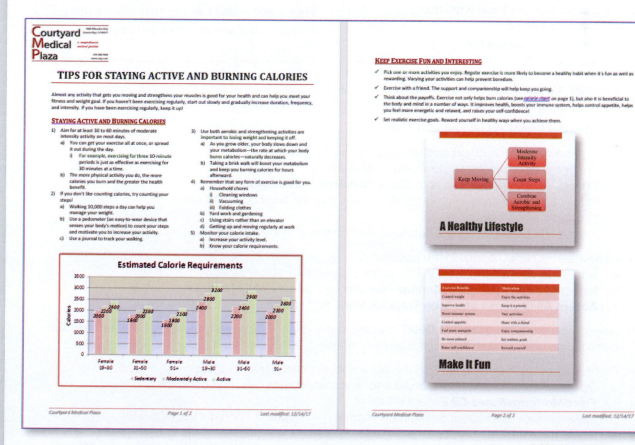

9-102 Word 9-3 completed

Independent Project 9-4

For this project, you edit a prospecting letter from Emma Cavalli at Placer Hills Real Estate. You track changes and insert comments, link an object from source file, insert a bookmark, create a hyperlink to a bookmark, merge the document with data source, apply merge rules, and encrypt the document.
[Student Learning Outcomes 9.1, 9.2, 9.3, 9.4, 9.5]

Files Needed: **CavalliProspectingLetter-09.docx**, **FixedMortgageRates-09.xlsx**, and **CavalliPHRE-09. accdb** (student data files are available in the Library of your SIMnet account)
Completed Project File Names: *[your initials] Word 9-4.docx*, *[your initials] FixedMortgageRates-09. xlsx*, and *[your initials] Word 9-4 merged.docx*

Skills Covered in This Project

- Change the *Display for Review* view.
- Change how markup displays.
- Review and delete comments.
- Turn off *Lock Tracking*.
- Accept changes in a document.
- Link a chart from an Excel worksheet to a Word document.
- Update data in a source file.

- Update a linked object in a destination file.
- Break a link to a linked chart.
- Add a bookmark.
- Insert a hyperlink to a bookmark.
- Start the mail merge and select and edit recipients.
- Insert merge field codes.
- Create and insert rules to customize a merge.
- Encrypt a document with a password.

1. Open the **CavalliProspectingLetter-09** document from your student data files. If this document opens in *Reading* view, click the **View** tab and select **Edit Document**.

2. Save the document as [your initials] Word 9-4.

3. Change how markup displays and review and delete comments.
   a. Change the *Display for Review* view to **All Markup**.
   b. Change how markup displays to **Show Revisions in Balloons**.
   c. Read each of the comments in the document. Use the **Next** button to move through the comments.
   d. After reading the comments, delete all the comments in the document.

4. Review and accept changes in the document.
   a. Turn off **Lock Tracking**; type PHRE as the password.
   b. Review the changes in **No Markup** view and then return to **All Markup** view.
   c. **Accept All Changes and Stop Tracking** in the document.

5. Select and delete the "**[Current Date]**" placeholder text (don't delete the paragraph mark), insert the current date in proper business letter format (January 1, 2018), and set it to update automatically.

6. Paste an Excel worksheet chart into the Word document as a linked object.
   a. Open a *File Explorer* window, browse to your student data files, and open the **FixedMortgageRates-09** Excel worksheet.
   b. Save the Excel file to your desktop and name it [your initials] FixedMortgageRates-09.
   c. Select the chart and copy it.
   d. Return to the Word document and place your insertion point on the blank line below the "Fixed Mortgage Rate Averages" heading on the second page.
   e. **Paste link** as a **Microsoft Excel Chart Object**.

7. Update the source file for the linked chart.
   a. Return to the *[your initials] FixedMortgageRates-09* worksheet, change the *2016 Rate* to 3.58 and the *Points* to 0.6 and then save the worksheet.
   b. Update the chart in the destination Word file.
   c. Close Excel.
   d. Return to the Word document and break the link between the source file and the destination file.

8. Add a bookmark and create a hyperlink to a bookmark.
   a. Select the "**Sample Fixed Rate Payments**" heading on the second page.
   b. Add a bookmark and type SamplePayments as the *Bookmark name*.
   c. Change the *Word Options* to **Show bookmarks** (*Advanced* area of the *Word Options* dialog box).
   d. Select "**Sample Fixed Rate Payments**" in the second sentence of the second body paragraph on the first page.
   e. Create a hyperlink to the **SamplePayments** bookmark.

9. Start the mail merge.
   a. Select **Letters** as the type of mail merge.
   b. Select the *CavalliPHRE-09* Access database as the recipients.
   c. Edit the recipient list and sort in ascending order by last name.

10. Insert merge field codes.
   a. Delete the "**<Address>**" placeholder text on the first page. Don't delete the paragraph mark.
   b. Insert the **Address Block** merge field code and select the **Mr. Joshua Randall Jr**. format.
   c. Delete the "**<Greeting>**" placeholder text. Don't delete the colon.
   d. Insert the **Title** merge field code after "Dear," **space** once, and insert the **Last** merge field code. Confirm one space appears after "Dear" and between the *Title* and *Last* merge field codes and a colon displays after the *Last* merge field code.
   e. Delete the "**<City>**" placeholder text in the first sentence in the first body paragraph.
   f. Insert the **City** merge field code.
   g. Check to ensure proper spacing around the merge field codes.

11. Insert rules to customize the merge.
   a. Place your insertion point on the blank line above the <<*AddressBlock*>> merge field code.
   b. Insert a **Skip Record If** rule to skip records where **City** is **Equal to** Roseville.
   c. Insert another **Skip Record If** rule to skip records where **City** is **Equal to** Rocklin.
   d. Insert another **Skip Record If** rule to skip records where **Status** is **Equal to** Sold.
   e. Delete "**has recently expired**" in the first sentence of the first body paragraph.
   f. Confirm there is one space after the <<*City*>> merge field code and place your insertion point after the space and before the period.
   g. Insert an **If. . .Then. . .Else** rule and use the following settings for the rule: if the *Field name* **Expired** is **Equal to** True, insert has recently expired in the textbox; otherwise, insert will expire soon in the text box.

12. Preview the merge results to see how the records will appear in your letter. Remember, the *Skip Record If* rule does not apply until you complete the merge.

13. Turn off the merge preview and save the Word document.

14. Finish the merge.
   a. Merge all the records to edit individual letters. The document should contain five letters (10 pages total).
   b. Save the new merged document as [your initials] Word 9-4 merged and close it (Figure 9-103).

15. Encrypt the *[your initials] Word 9-4* document with a password. Use PHRE as the password.

16. Save and close the document.

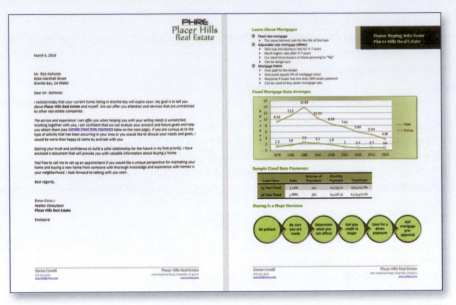

9-103 Word 9-4 merged completed (pages 1 and 2 of 10)

Independent Project 9-5

For this project, you edit an insurance renewal letter from Eva Skaar at Central Sierra Insurance. You use track changes and comments, the combine feature, a bookmark, a hyperlink and cross-reference to a bookmark, merge and merge rules, and document protection.
[Student Learning Outcomes 9.1, 9.2, 9.4, 9.5]

Files Needed: **CSIRenewalLetter-09a.docx**, **CSIRenewalLetter-09b.docx**, and **SkaarCSIRenewals-09. accdb** (student data files are available in the Library of your SIMnet account)
Completed Project File Names: **[your initials] Word 9-5a.docx**, **[your initials] Word 9-5b.docx**, **[your initials] Word 9-5 combined.docx**, and **[your initials] Word 9-5 merged.docx**

Skills Covered in This Project

- Change how markup displays.
- Turn on *Track Changes* and edit a document.
- Insert comments.
- Remove a document encryption password.
- Review and delete comments.
- Change the *Display for Review* view.
- Accept changes in the document.
- Combine documents.

- Add a bookmark.
- Insert a cross-reference and hyperlink to a bookmark.
- Start the mail merge and select recipients.
- Insert merge field codes.
- Create and insert rules to customize a merge.
- Inspect a document and remove *Custom XML Data*.
- Merge to a new document.
- Mark a document as final.

1. Open the **CSIRenewalLetter-09a** document from your student data files.

2. Save the document as [your initials] Word 9-5a.

3. Change how markup and comments display.
   a. Change user name and initials to your name and initials.
   b. Use the *Advanced Track Changes Options* dialog box to change the insertions, deletions, and comments color to **Violet**.
   c. Change how markup displays to **Show Revisions in Balloons**.

4. Edit the document using *Track Changes* and add a comment.
   a. Turn on **Track Changes**.
   b. Type Central Sierra Insurance is to replace "I am" at the beginning of the first body paragraph.
   c. Delete the last sentence in the second body paragraph including the space at the beginning of the sentence. Don't delete the paragraph mark at the end of the sentence.
   d. In the last body paragraph, place your insertion point after the space after "do not hesitate to call," type (780-886-2464), and **space** once.
   e. Select the first word in the second body paragraph ("**Central**"), insert a comment, and type Insert a table with renewal information below this paragraph in the comment balloon.
   f. View the document with **Simple Markup** to review your revisions.
   g. Turn off **Track Changes** and save and close this document.

5. Open an encrypted document, remove password encryption, and save the document.
   a. Open the **CSIRenewalLetter-09b** document from your student data files.
   b. Use CSI as the password for this encrypted document.
   c. Remove the password encryption from the document using the **Protect Document** button on the *Backstage* view.
   d. Save the document as [your initials] Word 9-5b.

6. Review comments and accept tracked changes.
   a. View the document with **No Markup** and then change the view back to **All Markup**.
   b. Read the comments in the document and then delete them.
   c. Accept all the changes in the document.
   d. Save the document.

7. Combine documents and review changes.
   a. Open the *Combine Documents* dialog box, select *[your initials] Word 9-5b* as the *Original* document, and select *[your initials] Word 9-5a* as the *Revised* document.
   b. Combine the documents into a **New document**.
   c. Hide source documents if they display.
   d. Accept all the changes in the document and delete all comments in the document.
   e. Save the combined document as [your initials] Word 9-5 combined.
   f. Save and close *[your initials] Word 9-5b*.
   g. Return to the *[your initials] Word 9-5 combined* document.

8. Add a bookmark and create a cross-reference and hyperlink to a bookmark.
   a. Select the words "**Discounted Premium**" in the last cell of the first row of the table.
   b. Add a bookmark and type DiscountedPremium as the bookmark name.
   c. Place your insertion point at the end of the second body paragraph ("cost-effective renewal") and before the period.
   d. **Space** once, type (see, and **space** once again.
   e. Insert a cross-reference to the **DiscountedPremium** bookmark, **Insert as a hyperlink**, and *Insert reference to* **Above/Below**. Insert the cross-reference and close the *Cross-reference* dialog box.
   f. Type) after "below."
   g. Select "**cost-effective renewal**" near the end of the second body paragraph and add a hyperlink to the **DiscountedPremium** bookmark.
   h. Save the document.

9. Start the mail merge and select recipients.
   a. Select **Letters** as the type of mail merge.
   b. Select the **SkaarCSIRenewals-09** Access database as the recipients.
   c. Edit the recipient list and sort in ascending order by last name.

10. Insert merge field codes.
    a. Delete the **"<Address>"** placeholder text, insert the **Address Block** merge field, and use the **Mr. Joshua Randall Jr**. format.
    b. Delete the **"<Salutation>"** placeholder text, insert the **Greeting Line** merge field, and use **Dear Mr. Randall**: as the format.
    c. Delete the **"<Policy Number>"** placeholder text and insert the **Policy_Number** merge field.
    d. Delete the **"<Company>"** placeholder text and insert the **Company** merge field.
    e. Delete the **"<Insurance Company>"** placeholder text and insert the **Insurance_Company** merge field.
    f. Delete the **"<First Name>"** placeholder text and insert the **First_Name** merge field.
    g. Place your insertion point in the first cell in the second row of the table and insert the **Policy_ Description** merge field.
    h. Place your insertion point after the "$" in the second cell in the second row of the table and insert the **Premium_Basis** merge field.
    i. Place your insertion point after the "$" in the third cell in the second row of the table and insert the **Rate_per_1000** merge field.
    j. Check to ensure proper spacing around the merge field codes.

11. Preview the merge results to see how the records will appear in your letter and then turn off preview.

12. Insert a rule to skip recipients who have paid online.
    a. Place your insertion point on the blank line above the <<AddressBlock>> merge field code.
    b. Insert a **Skip Record If** rule to skip records where **Paid_Online** is **Equal to** True (*Compare to* text box).
    c. Save the document.

13. Finish the merge.
    a. Merge all the records to edit individual letters. The document should contain five letters.
    b. Save the new merged document as [your initials] Word 9-5 merged and close it (Figure 9-104).

14. Mark the *[your initials] Word 9-5 combined* as final and then close the document.

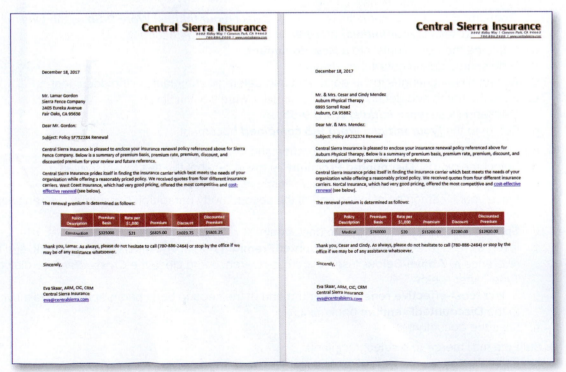

9-104 Word 9-5 merged completed (pages 1 and 2 of 5)

Independent Project 9-6

For this project, you edit a fax cover sheet for Kelly McFarland, director of Skiing Unlimited. You review the document to accept and reject changes, review comments, and edit the document, link a chart from Excel, protect the document, and share the file with your instructor.
[Student Learning Outcomes 9.1, 9.2, 9.3]

Files Needed: **SkiingUnlimitedFax-09.docx** and **SkiingUnlimitedParticipation-09.xlsx** (student data files are available in the Library of your SIMnet account)
Completed Project File Names: **[your initials] Word 9-6.docx** and **[your initials] SkiingUnlimited-Participation-09.xlsx**

Skills Covered in This Project

- Turn off *Lock Tracking*.
- Use the *Reviewing* pane to reject and accept changes.
- Turn off *Track Changes* and edit a document.
- Review and delete comments.
- Link a chart from an Excel worksheet to a Word document.
- Update data in the source file.
- Update a linked object in the destination file.
- Break links between documents.
- Encrypt a document with a password.
- Share a file.

1. Open the **SkiingUnlimitedFax-09** document from your student data files. If this document opens in *Reading* view, click the **View** tab and select **Edit Document**.

2. Save the document as [your initials] Word 9-6.

3. Review comments and changes.
   a. Turn off **Lock Tracking**. Use CMP as the password.
   b. Turn off **Track Changes**.
   c. Use the *Reviewing* pane to locate where "1" was deleted from the "PAGES" area and reject this deletion.
   d. Accept all remaining changes in the document.
   e. Read the two comments in the document and then delete them.
   f. Close the *Reviewing* pane.

4. Edit the document.
   a. Select the current date in the "*[Pick the date]*" field.
   b. Type Seth Uribe after "TO:".
   c. Type 916.450.9525 after "FAX:" in the first column of the second table.
   d. Type 916.450.9515 after "PHONE:" in the first column of the second table.
   e. Type your name in the "FROM:" area.

5. Paste a chart from an Excel worksheet as a linked object.
   a. Open a *File Explorer* window, browse to your student data files, and open the **SkiingUnlimitedParticipation-09** Excel worksheet.
   b. Save the Excel to your desktop and name it [your initials] SkiingUnlimitedParticipation-09.
   c. Select the chart and copy it.
   d. Return to the Word document and place your insertion point on the blank line below the second table.
   e. Paste the chart as a link as a **Microsoft Excel Chart Object**.

6. Edit the source file and update the chart in the destination file.
   a. Return to the Excel worksheet and change the 2017 participants to 74 and the volunteers to 231.
   b. Save the Excel worksheet.

  c. Return to the Word document and update the linked chart.

  d. Change the horizontal alignment of the chart in the destination file to **center**.

  e. Close the Excel worksheet.

7. Break the link between the chart in the destination file and the source file.

8. Encrypt the document with a password. Use **CMP** as the password.

9. Share the document with your instructor.

  a. Save this document on *OneDrive* if you haven't already. If you don't have the ability to save to *OneDrive*, skip all of step 9.

  b. Open the *Share* pane, **Get a sharing link**, **Create an edit link**, copy the link, and close the *Sharing* pane.

  c. Open the email account you use for this course, create an email to your instructor, and type an appropriate subject line and a brief message to your instructor.

  d. Paste (**Ctrl+V**) the sharing link in the body of the email and send the email

10. Save and close the document (Figure 9-105).

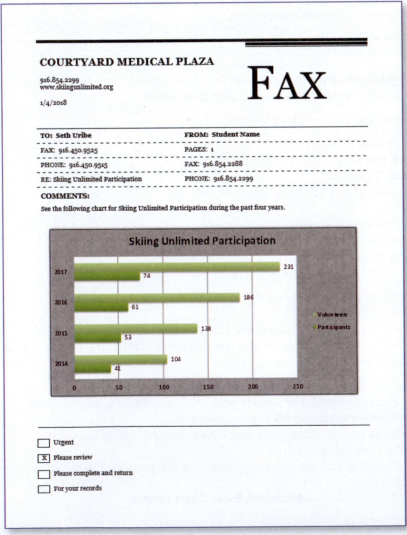

9-105 Word 9-6 completed

Improve It Project 9-7

For this project, you edit an insurance newsletter for Central Sierra Insurance. You use *Track Changes*, edit the document, accept changes, embed an Excel chart, format the chart, add a bookmark, insert a hyperlink to a bookmark, prepare the document for sharing, and mark the document as final.
[Student Learning Outcomes 9.1, 9.2, 9.3, 9.5]

Files Needed: ***CSINewsletter-09.docx*** and ***EstimatedCosts-09.xlsx*** *(student data files are available in the Library of your SIMnet account)*
Completed Project File Name: ***[your initials] Word 9-7.docx***

Skills Covered in This Project

- Open a password-encrypted document.
- Remove a document password.
- Review and delete comments.
- Turn on *Track Changes* and edit a document.
- Change the *Display for Review* view.
- Change user name and initials.
- Change color of insertions, deletions, and comments.

- Accept and reject changes in a document.
- Embed and format a chart from an Excel worksheet to the Word document.
- Add a bookmark.
- Insert a hyperlink to a bookmark.
- Inspect a document.
- Mark a document as final.

1. Open the ***CSINewsletter-09*** document from your student data files.
   a. This document is encrypted with a password. The password is CSI.
   b. Remove the encryption password from this document.

2. Save the document as [your initials] Word 9-7.

3. Read the comments in the document and delete all comments.

4. Use *Track Changes* and edit the document.
   a. Turn on **Track Changes**.
   b. Change the user name and initials to your name and initials.
   c. Change the color of insertions, deletions, and comments to **Dark Red**.
   d. Change the *Display for Review* view to **Simple Markup**.
   e. Select the bordered text directly below the newsletter title ("Issue No. XVII. . .") and apply **White, Background 1, Darker 5%** shading.
   f. Change hyphenation to **None**. This change will not be marked as a tracked change.
   g. Select the bulleted list in the first column and sort paragraphs in **ascending** order.
   h. In the second paragraph in the first column, select "**Home Appliance and Electronics Breakdown coverage**" and apply **bold** formatting.
   i. In the text box in the second column, apply **small caps** formatting and **0 pt**. *After* paragraph spacing to each of the three bolded headings.

5. Accept and reject changes.
   a. Change the *Display for Review* view to **All Markup**.
   b. Reject the three **Space After: 0 pt**. formatting changes.
   c. Accept all other changes and stop tracking.

6. Select the text box in the second column and change the *Height* to **4.9"**.

7. Paste a chart from an Excel worksheet as an embedded object.
   a. Open a *File Explorer* window, browse to your student data files, and open the ***EstimatedCosts-09*** Excel worksheet.

b. Select the chart and copy it.

c. Close the Excel worksheet.

d. Return to the Word document and place your insertion point on the blank line below the text box in the second column.

e. Paste the copied chart as a **Picture (PNG)**.

8. Format the chart.

a. Select the chart picture and change the text wrapping to **In Front of Text**.

b. Use the *Layout* dialog box to change the *Horizontal* **Alignment** to **Centered** *relative to* **Page** and change the *Vertical* **Alignment** to **Bottom** *relative to* **Margin**.

c. Change the *Width* of the chart picture to **7.5"**. The height adjusts automatically.

9. Add a bookmark and insert a hyperlink to a bookmark.

a. Select the chart and add a bookmark.

b. Type EstimatedCosts as the bookmark name.

c. Select "**cost-effective**" in the first sentence of the second paragraph in the first column.

d. Insert a hyperlink to the **EstimatedCosts** bookmark.

10. Inspect the document and **Remove All** *Custom XML Data* and *Headers, Footers, and Watermarks*.

11. Save the document.

12. Mark the document as final and close the document (Figure 9-106).

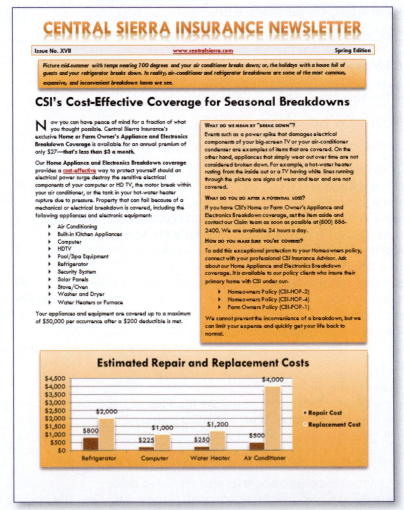

9-106 Word 9-7 completed

Challenge Project 9-8

People often work collaboratively with coworkers or classmates on projects. Use the Word collaboration tools in this chapter to work with others to modify a report, project, or document.
[**Student Learning Outcomes 9.1, 9.2, 9.5**]

File Needed: None
Completed Project File Name: *[your initials] Word 9-8.docx*

Open an existing document you are working on with others and save it as [your initials] Word 9-8. Modify your document according to the following guidelines:

- Customize your user name and initials.
- Insert comments.
- Use *Track Changes* to mark content and formatting changes.
- View the document in different *Display for Review* views.
- Customize tracking options.
- Add a bookmark to the document.
- Insert a hyperlink and/or a cross-reference to a bookmark.
- Prepare the document for sharing by inspecting the document, checking accessibility, and checking compatibility.
- Protect the document by using one or more of the protect document features. If you use a password to encrypt your document or restrict it from editing, send your instructor the password.

Challenge Project 9-9

For this project, you use the Word mail merge features to create a merged document. You can create mailing labels, a merged customized fax cover sheet, a merged letter, an invitation, or other document that you can merge with recipients from a data source. You can use an existing data source for recipients or create a new one. Use mail merge rules to customize your mail merge.
[**Student Learning Outcome 9.1, 9.3, 9.5**]

File Needed: None
Completed Project File Names: *[your initials] Word 9-9.docx* and *[your initials] Word 9-9 merged.docx*

Open a new or existing document and save it as [your initials] Word 9-9. Save your merged document as [your initials] Word 9-9 merged. Modify your documents according to the following guidelines:

- Use track changes and comments as necessary.
- Change track changes options.
- Edit the recipient list.
- Insert the *Address Block* and/or *Greeting Line* merge field codes.

- Insert individual merge fields.
- Use rules to customize the merge.
- Preview results and finish the merge.
- Inspect the main document and check accessibility.
- Mark the main document as final and encrypt with a password.

Challenge Project 9-10

Track changes, use comments and bookmarks, and link and embed objects to modify and enhance a document. For example, link your budget from an Excel worksheet to a Word document, embed your work or school schedule into a Word document, or link or embed slides from a PowerPoint presentation to a Word document to prepare a notes sheet for an upcoming presentation.
[Student Learning Outcome 9.1, 9.3, 9.5]

File Needed: None
Completed Project File Name: ***[your initials] Word 9-10.docx***

Open a new or existing document and save it as [your initials] Word 9-10. Use the Word object linking and embedding features. Modify your document according to the following guidelines:

- Use track changes and comments.
- Customize how tracked changes and comments display.
- Embed an object from another application in a Word document.
- Link an object from another application to a Word document.
- Resize, arrange, and format linked or embedded objects.
- Update the source file and update the linked object.
- Break the object link between the source and destination files.
- Add a bookmark and insert a hyperlink and/or cross-reference to a bookmark.

Automating Tasks Using Templates and Macros

CHAPTER OVERVIEW

Microsoft Word provides many tools to automate routine tasks and work more efficiently. Templates store a common document structure, such as an agenda, check list, or company letterhead. Once you create a template, you can open a document based upon the template, modify the content, and save it with a new file name. The original template remains unchanged. Another tool available in Word is a macro. A macro is a stored set of instructions applied with a single command. Like templates, macros save you time and add consistency to your documents.

STUDENT LEARNING OUTCOMES (SLOs)

After completing this chapter, you will be able to:

SLO 10.1 Create, save, and use a template to generate commonly used documents (p. W10-586).

SLO 10.2 Customize template content using a variety of Word fields and styles (p. W10-589).

SLO 10.3 Record a set of instructions as a macro and run and delete a macro (p. W10-596).

SLO 10.4 Copy and edit an existing macro using Visual Basic and add a keyboard and button shortcut to run a macro (p. W10-605).

SLO 10.5 Create and use a macro-enabled template to automate common tasks and copy a macro to another document (p. W10-612).

CASE STUDY

In the Pause & Practice projects in this chapter, you customize and use an agenda template for the student government at Sierra Pacific Community College District. You also create and use macros to automate common tasks used in Word documents.

Pause & Practice 10-1: Create and customize an agenda template and create a document based upon the template.

Pause & Practice 10-2: Create macros to store commonly used instructions and use these macros in the agenda template.

Pause & Practice 10-3: Edit existing macros, copy macros, assign a keyboard shortcut to a macro, and add macro buttons to the *Quick Access* toolbar.

Pause & Practice 10-4: Create a macro-enabled template, copy macros from another file, delete a macro, and create a document based upon the macro-enabled template.

WORD

W10-585

Creating and Saving Templates

A *template* includes content and formatting and is used to create new documents quickly and with consistent format. You can create and customize new documents based on a template without modifying the structure and content of the original template file. For example, you can create an agenda template with formatting and placeholder text to use as the structure for a new agenda for each meeting. By using a template, you avoid having to recreate a new agenda from scratch each time, and your agendas have a consistent format.

A template file is a specific type of Word file that is different from a regular Word document. Template files have a *.dotx* file name extension, while regular Word document files have a .docx extension. You can save a new or existing document as a template or use a Word online template. Templates can also store styles, building blocks, and macros (macros are covered later in this chapter). The following table lists the types and extensions of the different Word files that you will be using in this chapter:

Word Files

Word File Type	File Name Extension
Word Document	.docx
Word Template	.dotx
Word Macro-Enabled Document	.docm
Word Macro-Enabled Template	.dotm

Save a Document as a Template

When you create a new Word document, the document is, by default, a regular Word document (with a .docx extension). You can customize this new document and save it as a template file (with a .dotx extension). You can also save an existing document as a template file and create new documents based upon the template file.

▶ HOW TO: Save a Document as a Template

1. Create a new document or open an existing document.
2. Click the **File** tab to open the *Backstage* view.
3. Click **Save As** on the left and click the **Browse** button to open the *Save As* dialog box (Figure 10-1).
4. Type the document name in the *File name* area.
5. Click the **Save as type** drop-down list and select **Word Template**.
6. Browse to the location where you want to save your file.
   - When you select *Word Template* as the file type, the save location changes to the default location for templates. Be very specific where you save template files.
7. Click the **Save** button to close the dialog box and save the template.

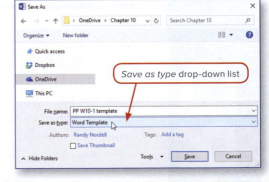

10-1 *Save As* dialog box

> ▶ **ANOTHER WAY**
>
> Press **F12** to open the *Save As* dialog box (if you're using a laptop computer, you might have to press **Fn+F12**).

Personal Templates

You can also save templates in the *Custom Office Templates* folder, which is the default folder when saving a template file. When you save a template in this folder, it is available in the *Personal* templates area on the *Backstage* view. To view your personal templates, click the **File** tab to open the *Backstage* view, click **New** on the left, and select **Personal** to view templates you previously saved in the *Custom Office Templates* folder. Click a personal template to create a document based upon that template.

Online Word Templates

In addition to creating your own templates, Word provides you with a variety of online templates. Online templates are available in the *New* area on the *Backstage* view. You can create a document based on an online template and customize it to meet your needs. Common templates are pinned to the list of templates in the *New* area. Search for other online templates by typing key words in the *Search for online templates* text box or clicking one of the links for suggested searches. You can unpin templates from the existing list of templates, or, when you search for templates, you can pin a template to your template list.

When you select an online template, a new window opens that provides details about the template. When you create a template, it is downloaded as a regular Word document based on the template. You can save the document as a template, regular Word document, or a different file type.

▶ **HOW TO:** Use an Online Template

1. Click the **File** tab to open the *Backstage* view.
2. Click the **New** button on the left and click **Featured** to view the available online templates (Figure 10-2).
3. Search for online templates by clicking the **Search for online templates** text box and typing key words.
   - Alternatively, click one of the **Suggested searches** links to display related templates.
4. Select an online template to open a preview window (Figure 10-3).
   - A preview of the template appears on the left.
   - Details about the template appear on the right.
   - Click the **Previous** or **Next** button on the left or right to scroll through other online templates in the same category.
   - Click the **pin** icon to pin a template to the *New* area on the *Backstage* view.
5. Click the **Create** button.
   - The online template opens as a Word document in a new window.
   - When you create a document based on an online template, the template is attached to the document.
6. Save the document as a template file or regular Word document.

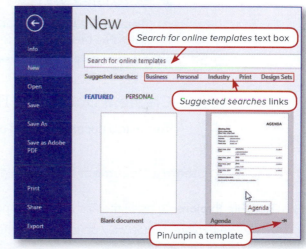

10-2 Online template in the *New* area on the *Backstage* view

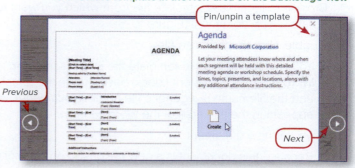

10-3 Template displayed in preview area

Edit a Template

When you work with templates or documents based on templates, the procedure to open a file is very important. The method you use to open a file determines whether a file opens as a template or a document based on a template. You can open, edit, and customize a template file, or you can create a document based on a template (see the next section, *Create a Document Based on a Template*).

▶ HOW TO: Edit a Template

1. Click the **File** tab to open the *Backstage* view.
2. Click the **Open** button on the left.
3. Click **Browse** to open the *Open* dialog box (Figure 10-4).
   - The file icon for a template is different from the icon for a regular Word document. This helps to distinguish between the two types of files.
4. Locate and select the template you want to edit.
5. Click the **Open** button to open the template file for editing.
   - When you open a Word file, the file name appears in the title bar at the top center of the Word window.

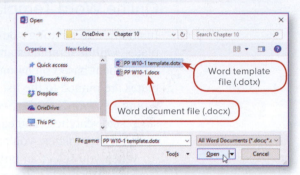

10-4 Open a template from the *Open* dialog box

▶ ANOTHER WAY

Press **Ctrl+F12** to open the *Open* dialog box (if you're using a laptop computer, you might have to press **Fn+Ctrl+F12**).

Create a Document Based on a Template

To create a document based on a template, always open the file from a *File Explorer* window.

▶ HOW TO: Create a Document Based on a Template

1. Click **File Explorer** to open the *File Explorer* window.
   - The *File Explorer* button may be located on the Windows *Taskbar* or on the *Start* menu.
2. Browse to locate the template file from which you want to create a new document (Figure 10-5).
3. Double-click the template file.
   - You can also select the template file and press **Enter**.
   - Word opens a document (.docx) based upon the template, and the file name is a generic file name (*Document1*), which appears in the title area of the Word window.
4. Save the new document.
   - Because this document is a new file based on a template, you are prompted to save the document before you close it.

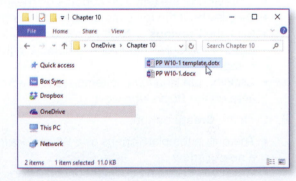

10-5 Open a document based on a template from a *File Explorer* window

SLO 10.2

Customizing and Using Templates

When you create a new document from an online template, content and formatting display in the document. You can customize the template content and format to meet your needs. You may want to create a document based on a template, but other times you may want to attach a template to an existing file so the styles and building blocks in the template are available in the document. You can also copy styles from one template to another template or document.

Customize Template Content

Some online templates provide a basic structure and sample text in the template, while others have content control fields, Word fields, and document property fields to control the content. You can add content to or customize existing fields in a template. You can also add document properties or Word fields to a template.

Content Control Fields

Many available online templates include ***content control fields***. Content control fields are placeholders where users can type custom content. Some of content control fields are for text. In others, users select a date or check a box. When you enter text in the content control field, the content control field is removed and replaced by the text you type. You can move, copy, or delete these fields.

▶ **HOW TO:** Use Content Control Fields

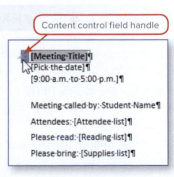

1. Open the template or document with content control fields.
2. Click the **handle** of the content control field to select it (Figure 10-6).
3. Type your custom text in the content control field.
   - The content control field is removed from the document when you type your text.
4. Click the content control field handle and drag the field to a new location, copy it, or delete it.
   - You can also right-click a content control field and select **Remove Content Control** to delete the field.
5. Deselect a content control field by pressing the **left** or **right** keyboard arrow key.

10-6 Content control field

Document Property Fields

Online templates typically include *document property fields*. You can add or remove document property fields to an existing template or to a new template you create. Document property fields are populated with content from document properties. If there is no content in document properties for a document property field in the template, the field displays the document property field name.

▶ **HOW TO:** Customize and Insert Document Property Fields

1. Click the **handle** of the document property field to select it (Figure 10-7).
2. Type the content in the document property field.
   - The content you type populates the document property in the document.
   - You can also click the **File** tab to open the *Backstage* view and type content in the document properties. This information appears in document property fields in the document.
3. Insert a document property field by placing the insertion point in the document at the desired location, clicking the **Quick Parts** button [*Insert* tab, *Text* group], clicking **Document Property**, and selecting the document property field to insert.
4. Remove a document property field by right-clicking the field and selecting **Remove Content Control**.
   - Alternatively, delete a document property field by selecting the field handle and pressing **Delete**.

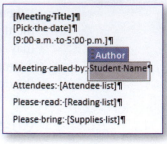

10-7 Document property field

Word Fields

Use Word fields in a template to automatically insert content. For example, you can use Word fields to automatically insert the last date the document was saved (*SaveDate*), add user name (*UserName*) or user initials (*UserInitials*), or include the file name of the document (*FileName*). Another useful field for templates is the ***Fill-in*** field. The *Fill-in* field prompts a user for information when a template or document based on a template opens.

▶ **HOW TO:** Insert a Fill-in Field

1. Place your insertion point in the template at the location to insert the *Fill-in* field.
2. Click the **Quick Parts** button [*Insert* tab, *Text* group] and select **Field**. The *Field* dialog box opens (Figure 10-8).
3. Select **Fill-in** in the *Field names* area.
4. Click the **Prompt** text box and type the prompt for the user.
5. Check the **Default response to prompt** check box in the *Field options* area and type a default response for the prompt.
   - The default response is the text that displays in the document if the user does not type a response to the fill-in prompt.
6. Click **OK** to close the dialog box and to insert the field. A prompt dialog box opens (Figure 10-9).

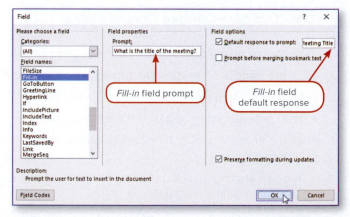

10-8 Insert a *Fill-in* field

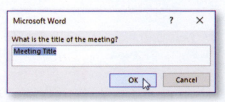

10-9 *Fill-in* field prompt dialog box

7. Click **OK** to close the prompt dialog box and to insert the default text.
   - The default text displays in the *Fill-in* field (Figure 10-10). When creating or modifying a template, it is best to include the default response to the prompt for this field.
   - When you create a document based on this template, the prompt dialog box opens (see Figure 10-9), and the user types the text to replace the default response and to populate the *Fill-in* field.

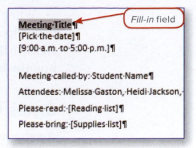

Meeting·Title¶   *Fill-in* field
[Pick·the·date]¶
[9:00·a.m.·to·5:00·p.m.]¶

Meeting·called·by:·Student·Name¶
Attendees:·Melissa·Gaston,·Heidi·Jackson,·
Please·read:·[Reading·list]¶
Please·bring:·[Supplies·list]¶

10-10 *Fill-in* **field in the template**

> ### MORE INFO
> You can insert multiple *Fill-in* fields in a document. An individual dialog box opens for each *Fill-in* field prompting the user to enter information.

Attach a Template to a Document

When you create a document based on a template, the template automatically attaches to the document. Another way to connect a template to a document is to manually attach the template to the document. When you attach a template to a document, the styles, building blocks, and macros stored in the template become available in the document. In addition, you can set the document to automatically update whenever changes are made to the template file.

▶HOW TO: Attach a Template to a Document

1. Open the document on which you want to attach a template.
2. Click the **Document Template** button [*Developer* tab, *Templates* group]. The *Templates and Add-ins* dialog box opens (Figure 10-11).
   - If the *Developer* tab does not display on the *Ribbon*, click the **File** tab to open the *Backstage* view, select **Options** on the left to open the *Word Options* dialog box, click **Customize Ribbon**, check the **Developer** box on the right, and click **OK**.
3. Click the **Attach** button in the *Document template* area to open the *Attach Template* dialog box.
4. Select the template to attach and click **Open** to attach the template.
5. Check the **Automatically update document styles** box.

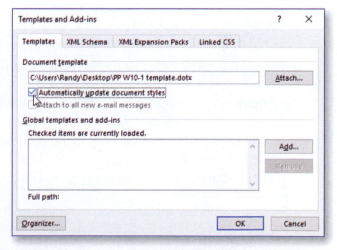

10-11 Attach a template to a document

   - If this box is checked, the styles in the document are updated each time styles are modified in the template.
   - If this box is not checked, the styles in the document are not updated when the styles in the template are modified.
6. Click **OK** to close the *Templates and Add-ins* dialog box and attach the template to the document.

When you create a document based on a template, the template file automatically attaches to the document, but, by default, styles in the document do not automatically update when the styles in the template are modified. You can change this setting by checking the **Automatically update document styles** box in the *Templates and Add-ins* dialog box.

Styles Organizer

Another way to automate tasks and create consistency in documents is to copy styles from one document to another.

MORE INFO

You cannot attach a template to a template file.

For example, you might not want to attach a template to a document or create a document based on a template, but you want to use styles that already exist in a template or other document. In situations like this, use the *Organizer* dialog box to copy styles from a template or document to another template or document. This process saves you the time of recreating these styles.

▶HOW TO: Copy Styles into a Document

1. Open the document or template into which you want to copy styles.
2. Click the **Document Template** button [*Developer* tab, *Templates* group] to open the *Templates and Add-ins* dialog box.
3. Click the **Organizer** button to open the *Organizer* dialog box (Figure 10-12).
   - The open document displays on the left, and the styles in that document display below the file name.
   - The template on which the document is based displays on the right. By default, new blank Word documents are based on the *Normal* template.
4. Click the **Close File** button below the styles in the document on the right.
   - This closes the template on which the document is based, and the *Close File* button becomes the *Open File* button.
5. Click the **Open File** button. The *Open* dialog box opens.
6. Browse and select the file that contains the styles you want to copy. This file is called the source file.
7. Click **Open** to open the source file. The source file styles display on the right.
8. Select the styles on the right to copy to the document on the left (Figure 10-13).
   - Press the **Ctrl** key and use your pointer to select non-adjacent styles.
   - Press the **Shift** key and use your pointer to select a range of adjacent styles.
9. Click the **Copy** button to copy the selected styles.
   - If the same style(s) exist in the document where you are copying the styles, a dialog box opens. Click **Yes** or **Yes to All** to overwrite the existing style(s).
10. Click the **Close** button to close the *Organizer* dialog box.
    - The copied styles display in the *Styles* gallery and *Styles* pane.

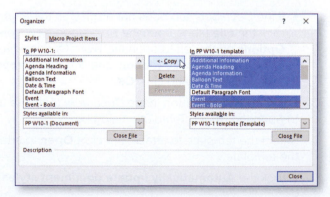

10-12 *Organizer* dialog box

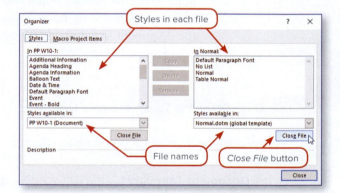

10-13 *Copy selected styles*

PAUSE & PRACTICE: WORD 10-1

For this Pause & Practice project, you create and modify a template for Sierra Pacific Community College student government meeting agendas. You save a document as a template, customize document property and content control fields, insert *Fill-in* fields, and create a document based on the template.

File Needed: **SPCCDAgenda-10.docx** *(student data files are available in the* Library *of your SIMnet account)*
Completed Project File Names: **[your initials] PP W10-1 template.dotx** and **[your initials] PP W10-1.docx**

1. Open the **SPCCDAgenda_10** document from your student data files.

2. Save the document as a Word template named [your initials] PP W10-1 template.

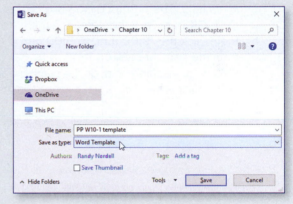

   a. Open the *Save As* dialog box (Figure 10-14).
   b. Type [your initials] PP W10-1 template in the *File name* area.
   c. Click the **Save as type** drop-down list and select **Word Template**.
   d. Browse to the location where you want to save your file.
   e. Click **Save** to save the template.

   10-14 Save document as a Word template file

3. Customize the title.
   a. Select "**agenda**" and delete it. Don't delete the paragraph mark.
   b. Type SPCCD Student Government Agenda as the title.

4. Add content to document property and content control fields.
   a. Click the "**Author**" (*Student Name*) document property field handle to select the field (Figure 10-15).
   b. Type your first and last name to replace the existing document property.
   c. Select the "**Attendee list**" content control field and type the following text: Melissa Gaston, Heidi Jackson, Rachel Sanchez, Peter Zanko, Ron Costa, Roietta Molden, and Ravi Kumar.
   d. In the table, select the "**Introduction**" content control field and type Welcome and Meeting Overview to replace the placeholder text.
   e. Select the "**Wrap-up**" content control field and type Wrap-up and Adjourn to replace the placeholder text.

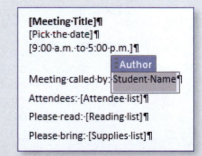

   10-15 Document property field

5. Customize the table content.
   a. Place your insertion point on the blank line above the content control field in the third cell in the first row of the table (above "[Rainier Room]").
   b. Type Location as the heading.
   c. Select "**Location**" and apply the **Event – Bold** style [*Home* tab, *Styles* group].

6. Insert *Fill-in* fields.
   a. Select the "**Meeting Title**" content control field handle to select it and press **Delete** to remove the content control field.
   b. Place your insertion point on the blank line above the "Pick the date" field, click the **Quick Parts** button [*Insert* tab, *Text* group], and select **Field** to open the *Field* dialog box (Figure 10-16).
   c. Select **Fill-in** in the *Field names* area.
   d. Type What is the title of the meeting? in the *Prompt* area.
   e. Check the **Default response to prompt** box and type Meeting Title in the text box.

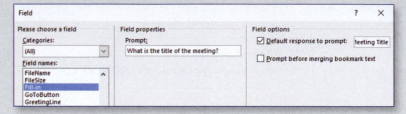

   f. Click **OK** to close the *Field* dialog box and to insert the *Fill-in* field. The prompt dialog box opens.

10-16 Insert *Fill-in* field

   g. Click **OK** to accept the default response to the *Fill-in* prompt.
   h. Right-click the "**9:00 a.m. to 5:00 p.m.**" content control field and select **Remove Content Control** from the context menu.
   i. Place your insertion point on the blank line below the "Pick the date" field and insert another **Fill-in** field.
   j. Type What is the time of the meeting? as the prompt and Meeting Time as the default response to the prompt.
   k. Click **OK** to close the *Field* dialog box and click **OK** to accept the default response to the *Fill-in* prompt.

7. Save and close the template.

8. Open a *File Explorer* window, browse to the location of the *[your initials] PP W10-1 template* file, and double-click it to open a document based on the template.

9. Type custom content for *Fill-in* field prompts.
   a. Type Fall Welcome Day and click **OK** at the first prompt.
   b. Type 3 to 5 p.m. and click **OK** at the second prompt.

10. Save the document as a Word document and name it [your initials] PP W10-1. If prompted to save changes to the document template, click **Yes**.

11. Customize agenda content.
   a. Click the "**Pick the date**" field and select next Tuesday.
   b. Type the highlighted text from Figure 10-17 in the content control fields. Type your first and last name to replace "Your Name" in the first row of the table. Don't highlight the highlighted text.

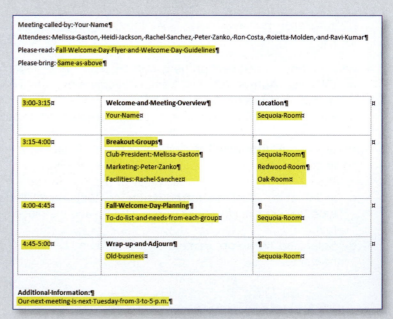

10-17 Type text in content control fields

12. Change the document so styles are updated automatically if the template is modified
    a. Click the **Document Template** button [*Developer* tab, *Templates* group] to open the *Templates and Add-ins* dialog box.
    b. Check the **Automatically update document styles** box and click **OK** to close the dialog box.

> ▶ **MORE INFO**
>
> If the *Developer* tab does not display on your *Ribbon*, click the **File** tab to open the *Backstage* view, select **Options** to open the *Word Options* dialog box, click **Customize Ribbon**, and then check the **Developer** box on the right.

---

13. Save and close the document. If prompted to save changes to the document template, click **Yes**.

14. Modify styles in the template file.
    a. From within Word, open the *[your initials] PP W10-1 template* file.
    b. Select the title, change the font size to **28 pt.**, apply **bold** and **small caps** formatting, change line spacing to **Single** (1), and change the *Before* paragraph spacing to **12 pt**. and the *After* paragraph spacing to **0 pt**.
    c. With the title selected, right click the **Agenda Heading** style [*Home* tab, *Styles* group] and select **Update Agenda Heading to Match Selection** to update this style.
    d. Modify the **Event – Bold** style to apply **small caps** formatting. Each of the headings in the table changes to small caps.

15. Save and close the template file.

16. Open the *[your initials] PP W10-1* file. The style changes in the template (*Agenda Heading* and *Event - Bold* styles) automatically apply to this document based on the template (Figure 10-18).

17. Save and close the document. If prompted to save styles and building blocks, click **Don't Save**.

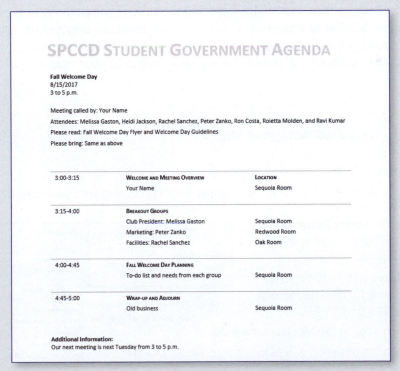

10-18 PP W10-1 completed

Creating and Running Macros

SLO 10.3

A *macro* is a combination of instructions and keystrokes that you store and use in documents. Macros save you time by recording and saving instructions you regularly use. For example, you can create a macro to insert and customize a header, to insert an *AutoText* building block, or to insert a custom watermark. Insert macros quickly into a document by assigning and using a keystroke combination or a button on the *Quick Access* toolbar. You can store macros and use them in multiple documents.

Plan a Macro

When creating a macro, it is important to plan what your macro will do, where you will store your macro, and how you will run your macro. Before you create a macro, ask yourself the following questions:

1. ***What will my macro do?*** Macros store keystrokes and button clicks. Carefully plan the macro keystrokes and commands before recording your macro.
2. ***Where should I save my macro?*** Macros can be stored in templates or documents. If your macro is stored in a document, it is only available in that document. If you store your macro in a template, the macro is available in the template and all documents based on that template. You can also store your macro in the *Normal* template where it will be available in all new documents you create.
3. ***How will I run my macro?*** Macros can be assigned to a shortcut key such as **Ctrl+Shift+Alt+H** or a button on the *Quick Access* toolbar. You can also run macros from the *Macros* dialog box.

Record a Keyboard-Activated Macro

Creating a macro is actually recording the actions you perform to apply commands to a document. Similar to recording a video on your phone or a movie on your DVR, a macro stores and plays back what you record. After you plan what your macro will do, where it will be stored, and how it will run, you are ready to record your macro.

▶HOW TO: Record a Keyboard-Activated Macro

1. Place your insertion point in the document where you want the macro to run.
   - If you are inserting text or an object, it is important to begin recording with your insertion point in the specific location.
   - If you are inserting a header, footer, or watermark, it is not important where your insertion point is located.
2. Click the **Record Macro** button [*Developer* tab, *Code* group] (Figure 10-19). The *Record Macro* dialog box opens (Figure 10-20).
3. Type a name for the macro in the *Macro name* area.
   - You cannot use spaces between words in a macro name. Use an underscore to separate words if necessary.
   - Macro names can include letters, numbers, and the underscore.

10-19 *Record Macro* button on the *Developer* tab

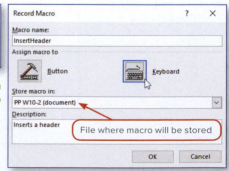

10-20 *Record Macro* dialog box

4. Click the **Store macro in** drop-down list and select the document or template where the macro will be stored.

5. Type a brief description for the macro in the *Description* area.

6. Click the **Keyboard** button. The *Customize Keyboard* dialog box opens (Figure 10-21).

7. Click the **Save changes in** drop-down list and select the document or template where the keyboard shortcut will be saved.

8. Place your insertion point in the **Press new shortcut key** text box and press the keyboard sequence to use as the shortcut key for the macro.

   - You can use a combination of **Ctrl**, **Shift**, **Alt**, and a letter or number as the shortcut key.
   - If the shortcut key is assigned to another command or macro, Word displays the macro or command to which shortcut key is assigned in the *Currently assigned to* area.
   - If you assign a keyboard sequence that is already used, your keyboard sequence for the macro replaces the existing shortcut.
   - You can choose a different shortcut key if the one you select is already assigned to another command shortcut.

9. Click the **Assign** button to assign the keyboard sequence as the shortcut to run the macro.

10. Click the **Close** button to close the dialog box and to begin recording your macro. Your pointer changes to a macro-recording pointer (Figure 10-22).

11. Perform the actions to record as a macro.

    - For example, you could edit a header, insert and format text in the header, and then close it.
    - You can click the **Pause Recording** button [*Developer* tab, *Code* group] to pause the recording if you need to perform an action you don't want recorded in the macro.

12. Click the **Stop Recording** button [*Developer* tab, *Code* group] to stop recording the macro (Figure 10-23).

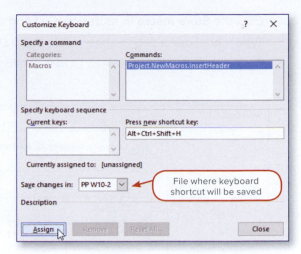

10-21 *Customize Keyboard* dialog box

10-22 Record macro pointer

10-23 Stop recording the macro

> ▶ **ANOTHER WAY**
>
> Click the bottom half of the **Macros** button [*View* tab, *Macros* group] and select **Record Macro**, or click the **Macros** button on the *Status* bar to open the *Record Macro* dialog box.

Record a Button-Activated Macro

You can also create a button-activated macro. When you assign a button to a macro, the button appears on the *Quick Access* toolbar. You can run the macro by clicking this button. Recording a button-activated macro is similar to recording a keyboard-activated macro.

▶ **HOW TO:** Record a Button-Activated Macro

1. Place your insertion point in the document where you want the macro to run.

2. Click the **Record Macro** button [*Developer* tab, *Code* group]. The *Record Macro* dialog box opens.

3. Type a name for the macro In the *Macro name* area.

   - You cannot use spaces between words in a macro name. If needed, use an underscore to separate words.

4. Click the **Store macro in** drop-down list and select the document or template where the macro will be stored.

5. Type a brief description for the macro in the *Description* area.

6. Click **Button** to open the *Word Options* dialog box (Figure 10-24).

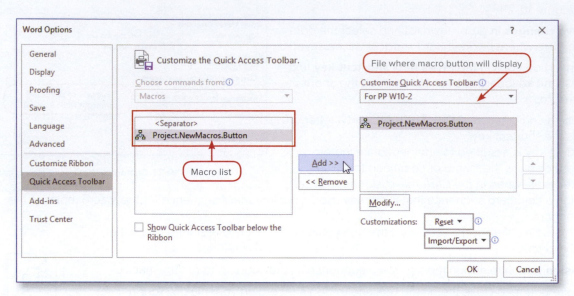

10-24 Add a macro to the *Quick Access* toolbar

7. Click the **Customize Quick Access Toolbar** drop-down list on the right and select the document where the macro button will be stored.

8. Select the **macro** in the list on the left (for example, **Project.NewMacro. Button**) and click the **Add** button (see Figure 10-24).

9. Click the **Modify** button. The *Modify Button* dialog box opens (Figure 10-25).

10. Type a name for the button in the *Display name* area.

11. Select the icon to use as the button. Word provides you with a variety of button icon options.

12. Click **OK** to close the *Modify Button* dialog box.

13. Click the **OK** button to close the *Word Options* dialog box and begin recording your macro. Your pointer changes to a macro-recording pointer.

14. Perform the actions to record as a macro.

15. Click the **Stop Recording** button [*Developer* tab, *Code* group] to stop recording the macro.

   • The macro button appears on the *Quick Access* toolbar (Figure 10-26).

10-25 *Modify Button* dialog box

10-26 Macro button on the *Quick Access* toolbar

> **MORE INFO**
>
> You can record a macro that is not assigned to a keyboard shortcut or button on the *Quick Access* toolbar. In this case, run the macro from the *Macros* dialog box.

Save a Macro-Enabled Document

When you create a macro in a document, you must save the document as a macro-enabled document in order for the macro to be stored in the document. When you save a document containing macros, Word prompts you to either save the document as a *Word Macro-Enabled Document* or remove the macros from the document. A Word macro-enabled document has a *.docm* file extension.

MORE INFO

If a document contains macros and you don't save it as a macro-enabled document, the macros in the document are removed.

▶ **HOW TO:** Save as a Macro-Enabled Document

1. Press **Ctrl+S** or click the **Save** button on the *Quick Access* toolbar to save a document containing a macro.
   - When you save a document that contains a macro, a dialog box opens and informs you the document contains macros (Figure 10-27).

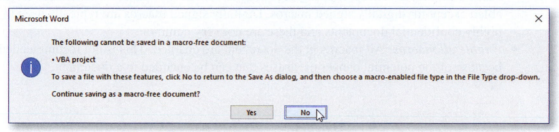

10-27 Dialog box prompting you to save as a macro-enabled document

2. Click **No** to open the *Save As* dialog box (Figure 10-28).
   - If you click *Yes*, the document is saved, and the macros are removed from the document.
3. Type a file name in the *File name* area.
4. Click the **Save as type** drop-down list and select **Word Macro-Enabled Document**.
   - Saving a document as a macro-enabled template is covered in *SLO 10.5: Creating and Using Macro-Enabled Templates*.
5. Click the **Save** button.

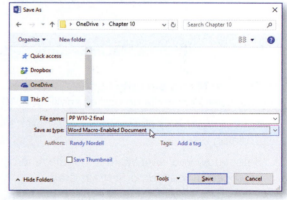

10-28 Save as a Word macro-enabled document

If you are creating a document that will contain macros, it is best to save the document as a macro-enabled document when you first save the document.

MORE INFO

The file icon for a macro-enabled document is different from the icon for a regular Word document and other Word file types.

Macro Security Settings

Because a macro is actually a program that runs within your document, Word provides security settings to control the action of macros when you open a document containing macros. The following are four different macro settings:

- ***Disable all macros without notification***: All macros in the document are disabled without notifying you.
- ***Disable all macros with notification***: All macros in the document will be temporarily disabled and a security warning appears in the *Info* bar when you open the document (Figure 10-29). Click the **Enable Content** button to enable macros in the document. This is the default setting and the best setting to use.

10-29 Click *Enable Content* to enable macros

- ***Disable all macros except digitally signed macros***: All macros in the document are disabled except for digitally signed macros. Digitally signed macros are typically used in highly confidential documents and these are not very common.
- ***Enable all macros***: All macros in the document are enabled. This is not recommended because of the potential danger of viruses that can be encoded in a document.

> ### MORE INFO
>
> When you open a document containing macros, you are usually prompted to enable the macros. Click the **Enable Content** button in the *Info* bar (see Figure 10-29).

▶ HOW TO: Change Macro Security Settings

1. Click the **Macro Security** button [*Developer* tab, *Code* group]. The *Trust Center* dialog box opens (Figure 10-30).
   - Alternatively, open the *Trust Center* from the *Word Options* dialog box.
2. Select how you want Word to handle macros in documents you open in the *Macro Settings* area.
3. Click **OK** to close the *Trust Center* dialog box.

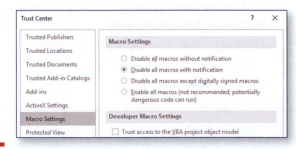

10-30 Macro settings in the *Trust Center* dialog box

Run a Macro

When you run a macro, you insert the recorded macro actions into the document. Depending on how a macro is recorded and saved in a document, you can run a macro in a variety of ways. Run a keyboard-activated macro by pressing the keyboard shortcut key. Run a button-activated macro by clicking the macro button on the *Quick Access* toolbar. You can also run a macro from the ***Macros*** dialog box.

▶ HOW TO: Run a Macro from the Macros Dialog Box

1. Click the **Macro** button [*Developer* tab, *Code* group] to open the *Macros* dialog box (Figure 10-31).
2. Select the macro you want to run in the *Macro name* area.
3. Click the **Run** button.
   - The *Macros* dialog box automatically closes when you run a macro.

> ▶ **ANOTHER WAY**
>
> **Alt+F8** opens the *Macros* dialog box.

10-31 *Macros* dialog box

Create an AutoMacro

Word also provides **AutoMacros** that automatically run when you perform a specific action. For example, you can create an *AutoMacro* to insert the current date each time you open a document or remove a watermark when you save and close a document. Each of these macros uses a specific macro name that Word recognizes as an *AutoMacro*. Because *AutoMacros* run automatically when you perform an action, you don't have to assign the macro to a button or keyboard shortcut. The following table lists *AutoMacros* and a description of each:

Types of AutoMacros

AutoMacro	Description
AutoExec	Runs when you open Word.
AutoOpen	Runs each time you open a Word document.
AutoNew	Runs each time you create a new Word document.
AutoClose	Runs each time you close a Word document.
AutoExit	Runs when you exit Word.

▶ HOW TO: Create an AutoMacro

1. Click the **Record Macro** button to open the *Record Macro* dialog box (Figure 10-32).
2. Type the *AutoMacro* name in the *Macro name* area.
3. Click the **Store macro in** drop-down list and select the document where you want to store the macro.
4. Type a brief description of the macro in the *Description* area.
5. Click **OK** to begin recording the macro.
   - You don't have to assign a button or keyboard sequence to an *AutoMacro* because the macro runs automatically when you perform an action such as open or close a document.

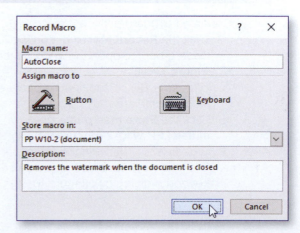

10-32 Record an *AutoMacro*

6. Perform the actions to be recorded in the *AutoMacro*.
7. Click the **Stop Recording** button [*Developer* tab, *Code* group].
   - The *AutoMacro* runs the next time you perform the specified action.
   - The *AutoMacro* displays in the *Macros* dialog box.

Delete a Macro

If you make a mistake when recording macro or if you want to delete a macro from a document, delete the macro using the *Macros* dialog box.

▶ **HOW TO:** Delete a Macro

1. Click the **Macros** button [*Developer* tab, *Code* group] to open the *Macros* dialog box.
2. Select the macro you want to delete from the list of macros in the *Macro name* area.
3. Click the **Delete** button. A dialog box opens asking if you want to delete the macro (Figure 10-33).
4. Click **Yes** to delete the macro.

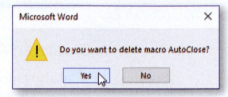

10-33 Delete a macro

PAUSE & PRACTICE: WORD 10-2

For this Pause & Practice project, you modify the agenda document you created based on an agenda template. You create a macro to insert a header, create an *AutoMacro* to remove a watermark, save the agenda as a macro-enabled document, and delete a macro.

File Needed: *[your initials] PP W10-1.docx*
Completed Project File Names: *[your initials] PP W10-2.docx* and *[your initials] PP W10-2 final.docm*

1. Open the *[your initials] PP W10-1* document completed in *Pause & Practice 10-1*.

2. Save the document as [your initials] PP W10-2 (regular Word document).

3. Create a keyboard-activated macro.
   a. Click the **Record Macro** button [*Developer* tab, *Code* group] to open the *Record Macro* dialog box (Figure 10-34).
   b. Type InsertHeader (no spaces between words) in the *Macro name* area.
   c. Click the **Store macro in** drop-down list and select **[your initials] PP W10-2 (document)**.
   d. Type Inserts a header in the *Description* area.
   e. Click the **Keyboard** button to open the *Customize Keyboard* dialog box (Figure 10-35).

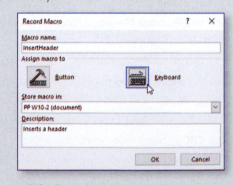

10-34 Record a keyboard-activated macro

f. Click the **Save changes in** drop-down list and select **[your initials] PP W10-2**.

g. Place your insertion point in the **Press new shortcut key** text box and press **Alt+Ctrl+ Shift+H**.

h. Click the **Assign** button to assign the keyboard shortcut to the macro.

i. Click the **Close** button to close the *Customize Keyboard* dialog box and to begin recording the macro.

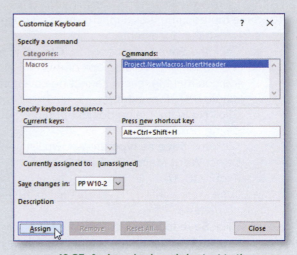

10-35 Assign a keyboard shortcut to the macro

4. Record a macro to insert a header in the agenda.
    a. Click the **Header** button [*Insert* tab, *Header & Footer* group] and select **Edit Header** from the drop-down list to open the header.
    b. Click the **Bold** button [*Home* tab, *Font* group].
    c. Type SPCCD Student Government Agenda and press **Tab** two times to move the insertion point to the right margin.
    d. Type Last updated: and **space** once.
    e. Click the **Date & Time** button [*Header & Footer Tools Design* tab, *Insert* group] to open the *Date and Time* dialog box.
    f. Select the number date format (1/1/2018), check the **Update automatically** box, and click **OK** to close the dialog box and to insert the date.
    g. Click the **Borders** drop-down button [*Home* tab, *Paragraph* group] and select **Bottom Border**.
    h. Click the **Close Header and Footer** button [*Header & Footer Tools Design* tab, *Close* group] to close the header.
    i. Click the **Stop Recording** button [*Developer* tab, *Code* group].

5. Test the macro.
    a. Edit the header, delete all of the information in the header, and close the header.
    b. Press **Alt+Ctrl+Shift+H** to run the macro. The header displays in the document.

6. Click the **Watermark** button [*Design* tab, *Page Background* group] and select the **Draft 1** watermark.

7. Create an *AutoClose* macro that runs each time you close the document.
    a. Click the **Record Macro** button [*Developer* tab, *Code* group] to open the *Record Macro* dialog box (Figure 10-36).
    b. Type AutoClose (no spaces between words) in the *Macro name* area.
    c. Click the **Store macro in** drop-down list and select **[your initials] PP W10-2 (document)**.
    d. Type Removes the watermark when the document is closed in the *Description* area.
    e. Click the **OK** button to close the *Record Macro* dialog box and begin recording the macro.

8. Record a macro to remove a watermark.
    a. Click the **Watermark** button [*Design* tab, *Page Background* group] and select **Remove Watermark** from the drop-down list.
    b. Click the **Stop Recording** button [*Developer* tab, *Code* group].

9. Click the **Watermark** button and select the **Draft 1** watermark to insert it.

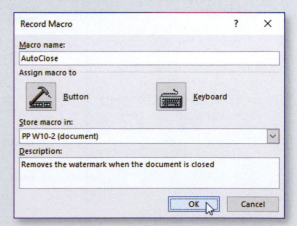

10-36 Record an *AutoClose* macro

10. Save the document as a macro-enabled document and close the document.
    a. Click the **Save** button or press **Ctrl+S** to save the document. A dialog box opens informing you that the macro cannot be saved in a macro-free document.
    b. Click **No** in the dialog box to open the *Save As* dialog box.
    c. Click the **Save as type** drop-down list and select **Word Macro-Enabled Document** (Figure 10-37).
    d. Type [your initials] PP W10-2 final in the *File name* area.
    e. Click **Save** to save the document. If prompted to save changes to the template, click **Yes**.
    f. Close the document. The watermark is removed and you are prompted to save the document.
    g. Click **Save** to save and close the document.

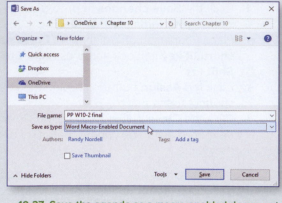

10-37 Save the agenda as a macro-enabled document

11. Open a macro-enabled document and enable the macro content.
    a. Open the *[your initials] PP W10-2 final* document. If this document does not display in the location where you saved the file, select **All Files** from the file type drop-down list (above the *Open* button) in the *Open* dialog box.
    b. Click **Enable Content** in the *Info* bar to enable the macros in the document (Figure 10-38) if a security warning displays in the *Info* bar. Notice that the watermark has been removed.

10-38 Enable macros in the document

12. Delete the *AutoClose* macro.
    a. Click the **Macros** button to open the *Macros* dialog box.
    b. Select the **AutoClose** macro and click the **Delete** button. A dialog box opens asking if you want to delete the macro.
    c. Click **Yes** to delete the macro.
    d. Click **Close** to close the *Macros* dialog box.

13. Save and close the document (Figure 10-39). If prompted to save changes to the template, click **Yes**.

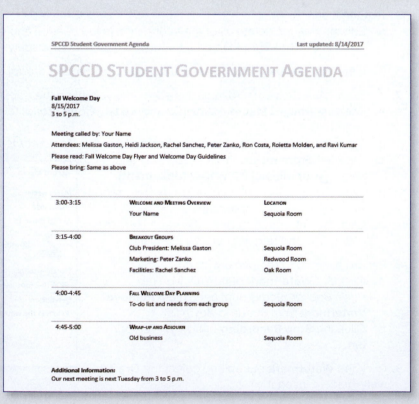

10-39 PP W10-2 final completed

<table>
<tr><td>**SLO 10.4**</td><td></td></tr>
</table>

Copying and Editing Macros

Macros are programs that run within Word, and they are coded in *Visual Basic* programming language. When you record a macro, Word automatically creates and stores the Visual Basic code in the macro. You can copy a macro and edit it rather than creating another macro. The *Microsoft Visual Basic editor* is the program used to edit or copy a macro. You don't need knowledge of Visual Basic programming to copy a macro and do simple editing.

Copy a Macro

Copying a macro can save you time if the macro you are copying is similar to the one you want to create. For example, you can copy a macro that inserts a header and edit it so it inserts a footer instead. This section explains how to copy a macro and the next section explains how to edit a macro. Copy a macro when you want to create a macro that is similar to the original macro. If you are creating a macro that is very different from an existing macro, it is easier to record a new macro.

▶ HOW TO: Copy a Macro

1. Click the **Macros** button [*Developer* tab, *Code* group] to open the *Macros* dialog box.
2. Select the macro to copy and click the **Edit** button. The *Microsoft Visual Basic* editor opens.
3. Select the Visual Basic code for the macro and click the **Copy** button or press **Ctrl+C** to copy it (Figure 10-40).
   - A macro begins with "Sub" and the name of the macro.
   - A macro ends with "End Sub."
   - The green text near the top is the macro name and description.
   - The coding in the middle describes the actions the macro performs.
4. Place your insertion point on the blank line below "End Sub."
5. Click the **Paste** button or press **Ctrl+V** to paste the copied macro.
   - The copied macro appears below the original macro. A horizontal line separates the macros.
6. On the copied macro, change the name of the macro after "Sub" (Figure 10-41).
   - Don't delete the beginning and ending parentheses ( ) after the macro name.
   - The name of the macro is the macro name that appears in the *Macros* dialog box.
7. Press **Ctrl+S** or click the **Save** button to save the macros.
8. Click the **File** menu in the upper left corner and select **Close and Return to Microsoft Word** to return to your document.

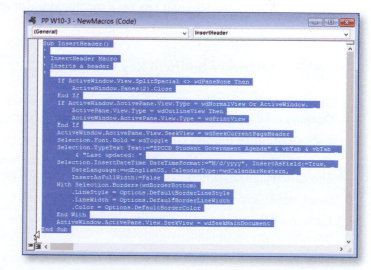

10-40 Copy a macro in the Microsoft Visual Basic editor

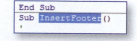

10-41 Change the macro name

Edit a Macro

After copying a macro, edit the macro using the Microsoft Visual Basic editor. You can also edit an existing macro. For example, change text in a macro, change the macro name or description, change a header to a footer, or change a border.

▶ HOW TO: Edit a Macro

1. Click the **Macros** button [*Developer* tab, *Code* group] to open the *Macros* dialog box.

2. Select the macro you want to edit and click the **Edit** button. The Microsoft Visual Basic editor opens (Figure 10-42).

3. Edit the existing code to customize the macro.

   - In Figure 10-42, edits to the macro are high-lighted in yellow to more easily identify the changes.
   - When you edit a macro, changes are not highlighted.

4. Press **Ctrl+S** or click the **Save** button to save the macros.

5. Click the **File** menu in the upper left corner and select **Close and Return to Microsoft Word** to return to your document.

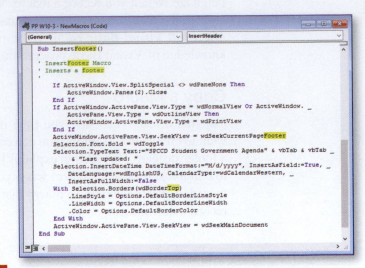

10-42 Edit the macro

Assign a Shortcut Key to a Macro

If you create a macro and do not assign a shortcut key to the macro, or if you want to change the shortcut key on a macro, you can add or change the shortcut keys for your macros using the **Customize Keyboard** dialog box.

▶ HOW TO: Assign a Shortcut Key to a Macro

1. Click the **File** tab to open the *Backstage* view and select **Options** on the left to open the *Word Options* dialog box.

2. Click **Customize Ribbon** on the left.

3. Click the **Customize** button in the *Keyboard shortcuts* area. The *Customize Keyboard* dialog box opens (Figure 10-43).

4. Scroll down and select **Macros** in the *Categories* area.

5. Click the **Save changes in** drop-down list and select the document where the macro is stored.

6. Select the macro in the *Macros* list that you want to add a shortcut key to.

7. Place your insertion point in the *Press new shortcut key* text box.

8. Press the shortcut key (for example, **Alt+Ctrl+Shift+F**) to assign to the selected macro.

9. Click the **Assign** button.

   - After you click the **Assign** button, the shortcut key appears in the *Current keys* area.
   - If a selected macro already has a shortcut key, it displays in the *Current keys* area.
   - You can remove a shortcut key by selecting it in the *Current keys* area and clicking the **Remove** button. After removing an existing shortcut key from a macro, you can add a new one.

10. Click **Close** to close the *Customize Keyboard* dialog box.

11. Click **OK** to close the *Word Options* dialog box.

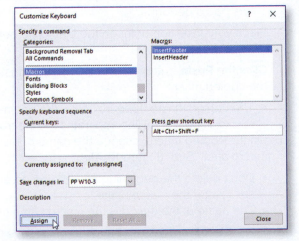

10-43 Assign a shortcut key to a macro

Add a Macro Button to the Quick Access Toolbar

Recall that you can run a macro using a button on the *Quick Access* toolbar. If you didn't create a button-activated macro when you originally recorded the macro, you can add a macro button to the *Quick Access* toolbar, or you can edit an existing macro button to change the icon or display name.

> **HOW TO:** Add a Macro Button to the Quick Access Toolbar

1. Click the **File** tab to open the *Backstage* view and select **Options** on the left to open the *Word Options* dialog box.
2. Click **Quick Access Toolbar** on the left to display the *Customize the Quick Access Toolbar* area (Figure 10-44).

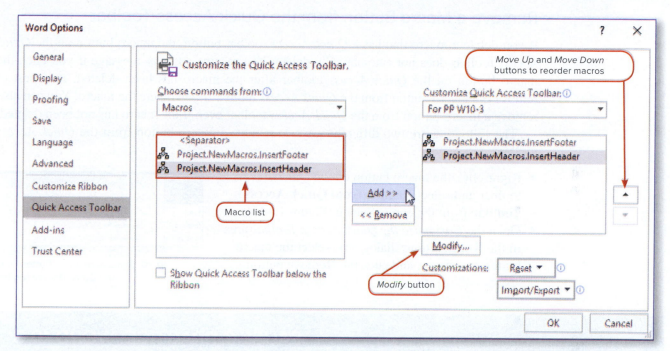

10-44 Add a macro button to the *Quick Access* toolbar

3. Click the **Choose commands from** drop-down list and select **Macros**.
4. Click the **Customize Quick Access Toolbar** drop-down list and select the document where the macro is stored.
5. From the list of macros at the left, select the macro that you want to add to the *Quick Access* toolbar and click the **Add** button.
   - After adding macros to the *Quick Access* toolbar, you can reorder macros using the *Move Up* and *Move Down* buttons to the right of *Customize Quick Access* toolbar area.
6. Click the **Modify** button to open the *Modify Button* dialog box (Figure 10-45).
   - If a macro already has a *Quick Access* toolbar button assigned to it, you can modify the display name or button icon.
7. Type the display name for the macro in the *Display name* area.
   - The display name is the tag that appears when you place your pointer on the button on the *Quick Access* toolbar.
8. Select the icon you want to use as the button on the *Quick Access* toolbar.

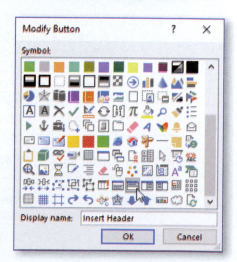

10-45 Modify the macro button and display name

9. Click **OK** to close the *Modify Button* dialog box.

10. Click **OK** to close the *Word Options* dialog box.
   - The macro button appears on the *Quick Access* toolbar.

> **ANOTHER WAY**
>
> Click the **Quick Access toolbar** drop-down list and select **More Commands** to open the *Customize the Quick Access Toolbar* area in the *Word Options* dialog box. You can also right-click the **Ribbon** and select **Customize Quick Access Toolbar** or **Customize the Ribbon** to open the *Word Options* dialog box.

Remove a Macro Button from the Quick Access Toolbar

If you delete a macro that has a *Quick Access* toolbar button, the macro button on the *Quick Access* toolbar does not automatically delete. You receive an error message if you click the macro button on the *Quick Access* toolbar after the macro has been deleted. It is best to remove the macro button from the *Quick Access* toolbar if you delete the macro. You can also remove a macro button from the *Quick Access* toolbar even if the macro has not been deleted.

The following are two different ways to remove a macro button from the *Quick Access* toolbar:

- Right-click the macro button on the *Quick Access* toolbar and select **Remove from Quick Access Toolbar** from the context menu (Figure 10-46).
- Open the *Customize the Quick Access Toolbar* area in the *Word Options* dialog box, select the macro button to remove, and click the **Remove** button.

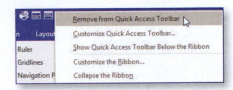

10-46 Remove a macro button from the *Quick Access* toolbar

PAUSE & PRACTICE: WORD 10-3

For this Pause & Practice project, you modify the macro-enabled agenda document you created in *Pause & Practice 10-2*. You copy and edit a macro using the Microsoft Visual Basic editor, add a keyboard short-cut to a macro, and add macro buttons to the *Quick Access* toolbar.

File Needed: *[your initials] PP W10-2 final.docm*
Completed Project File Name: *[your initials] PP W10-3.docm*

1. Open the *[your initials] PP W10-2 final* macro-enabled document completed in *Pause & Practice 10-2*. If a security warning appears in the *Info* bar, click **Enable Content**.

2. Save the document as a **Word Macro-Enabled Document** named [your initials] PP W10-3. If prompted to save changes to the template, click **Yes**.

3. Copy the *InsertHeader* macro using the Microsoft Visual Basic editor.
   a. Click the **Macros** button [*Developer* tab, *Code* group] to open the *Macros* dialog box.
   b. Click the **Macros in** drop-down list and select **[your initials] PP W10-3 (document)**.
   c. Select the **InsertHeader** macro and click the **Edit** button. The *Microsoft Visual Basic* editor opens.

d. Select the Visual Basic code for the macro beginning with "**Sub InsertHeader ( )**" and ending with "**End Sub**" (Figure 10-47).
e. Click the **Copy** button or press **Ctrl+C** to copy the code for the macro.
f. Place your insertion point on the blank line after "End Sub."
g. Press **Ctrl+V** to paste the copied macro. The copied macro displays below the original macro, and a horizontal line separates the two.
h. On the copied macro below the *InsertHeader* macro, change the name of the macro after "Sub" to InsertFooter (Figure 10-48).

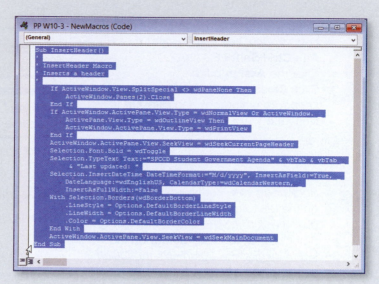

10-47 Select and copy macro Visual Basic code

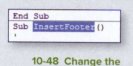

10-48 Change the macro name

i. Press **Ctrl+S** or click the **Save** button to save the macros.

4. Edit the *InsertFooter* macro.
a. Edit the macro to include the four changes highlighted in Figure 10-49.
b. Press **Ctrl+S** or click the **Save** button to save the macros.
c. Click the **File** menu and select **Close and Return to Microsoft Word** to return to your document.
d. Save the document.

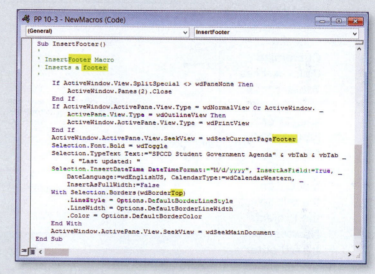

10-49 Edit the *InsertFooter* macro Visual Basic code

5. Test the *InsertFooter* macro.
a. Click the **Macros** button to open the *Macros* dialog box.
b. Select the **InsertFooter** macro and click the **Run** button. A footer with a top border displays in the document.
c. Edit the header and footer and delete all content in the header and footer.
d. Close the header and footer area.

6. Add a keyboard shortcut to the *InsertFooter* macro.
a. Click the **File** tab to open the *Backstage* view.
b. Select **Options** on the left to open the *Word Options* dialog box.
c. Click **Customize Ribbon** on the left.
d. Click the **Customize** button in the *Keyboard shortcuts* area. The *Customize Keyboard* dialog box opens (Figure 10-50).
e. In the *Categories* area, scroll down and select **Macros**.
f. Click the **Save changes in** drop-down list and select **[your initials] PP W10-3**.
g. Select the **InsertFooter** macro in the *Macros* list.

h. Place your insertion point in the *Press new shortcut key* text box and press **Alt+Ctrl+Shift+F**.

i. Click the **Assign** button.

j. Click **Close** to close the *Customize Keyboard* dialog box and click **OK** to close the *Word Options* dialog box.

7. Add macro buttons to the *Quick Access* toolbar.

a. Click the **File** tab to open the *Backstage* view and select **Options** on the left to open the *Word Options* dialog box.

b. Select **Quick Access Toolbar** on the left to display the *Customize the Quick Access Toolbar* area (Figure 10-51).

c. Click the **Choose commands from** drop-down list and select **Macros**.

d. Click the **Customize Quick Access Toolbar** drop-down list and select **For [your initials] PP W10-3**.

e. In the list of macros on the left, select the **Project. NewMacros. InsertFooter** macro and click the **Add** button.

f. Select the **Project.NewMacros.InsertHeader** macro and click the **Add** button.

g. In the list on the right, select the **Project.NewMacros. InsertHeader** macro and click the **Modify** button to open the *Modify Button* dialog box (Figure 10-52).

h. Type Insert Header in the *Display name* area, select the icon shown in Figure 10-52, and click **OK** to close the *Modify Button* dialog box.

i. In the list on the right, select the **Project.NewMacros. InsertFooter** macro and click the **Modify** button.

j. Type Insert Footer in the *Display name* area, select the icon shown in Figure 10-52, and click **OK** to close the *Modify Button* dialog box.

k. Click **OK** to close the *Word Options* dialog box. The two macro buttons display on the *Quick Access* toolbar.

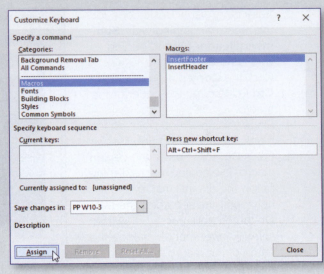

10-50 Add a shortcut key to the *InsertFooter* macro

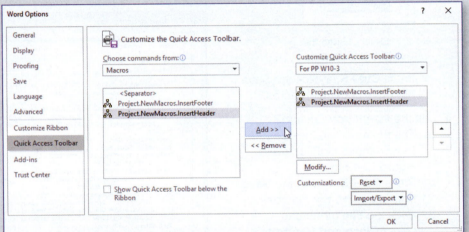

10-51 Add macro buttons to the *Quick Access* toolbar

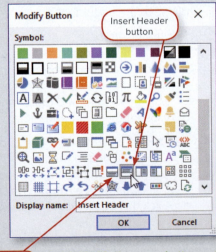

Insert Header button

Insert Footer button

10-52 Modify the macro button and display name

8. Test a macro button and macro keyboard shortcut.
   a. Click the **Insert Header** button on the *Quick Access* toolbar to insert the header in the document (Figure 10-53).
   b. Press **Alt+Ctrl+Shift+F** to insert the footer.
   c. Delete the header content from the document and close the header area.

10-53 *Insert Header* macro button on the *Quick Access* toolbar

9. Save and close the document (Figure 10-54). If prompted to save changes to the template, click **Yes**. If prompted to save styles and building blocks, click **Don't Save**.

SPCCD STUDENT GOVERNMENT AGENDA

Fall Welcome Day
8/15/2017
3 to 5 p.m.

Meeting called by: Your Name
Attendees: Melissa Gaston, Heidi Jackson, Rachel Sanchez, Peter Zanko, Ron Costa, Roietta Molden, and Ravi Kumar
Please read: Fall Welcome Day Flyer and Welcome Day Guidelines
Please bring: Same as above

3:00-3:15	WELCOME AND MEETING OVERVIEW	LOCATION
	Your Name	Sequoia Room
3:15-4:00	BREAKOUT GROUPS	
	Club President: Melissa Gaston	Sequoia Room
	Marketing: Peter Zanko	Redwood Room
	Facilities: Rachel Sanchez	Oak Room
4:00-4:45	FALL WELCOME DAY PLANNING	
	To-do list and needs from each group	Sequoia Room
4:45-5:00	WRAP-UP AND ADJOURN	
	Old business	Sequoia Room

Additional Information:
Our next meeting is next Tuesday from 3 to 5 p.m.

SPCCD Student Government Agenda   Last updated: 8/14/2017

10-54 **PP W10-3 completed**

Creating and Using Macro-Enabled Templates

You can store macros in a template to further automate tasks. When you create a document based on a template or open a document that has a template attached, the macros stored in the template are available in those documents. You can also copy macros from a template or document to another template or document so you don't have to recreate macros that exist in another file.

Save a Macro-Enabled Template

Similar to a Word document containing macros (macro-enabled document), a template that contains macros must be saved as a *macro-enabled template* (*.dotm*) in order for the macros to function in the template and in documents that you create based on the template.

▶ HOW TO: Save a Macro-Enabled Template

1. Open the file you want to save as a macro-enabled template or create a new document.
2. Open the *Save As* dialog box (Figure 10-55).
3. Type the name of the template in the *File name* area.
4. Click the **Save as type** drop-down list and select **Word Macro-Enabled Template**.
5. Browse to the location on your computer where you want to save the template.
   - Be specific when selecting the save location for templates because Word, by default, selects the default template location when you save a template file.
6. Click **Save** to close the dialog box and save the macro-enabled template.

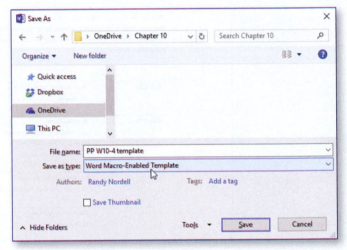

10-55 Save as a macro-enabled template

If you create macros in a template that is not macro-enabled and then save the template, a dialog box opens informing you that the document cannot be saved in a macro-free environment. In this dialog box, click **No** to open the *Save As* dialog box and save the document as a **Word Macro-Enabled Template** so the macros are available in the document.

Copy a Macro to Another File

A time-saving feature in Word is the ability to copy macros from one document or template to another. Copying macros is similar to copying styles. You use the *Organizer* dialog box to select the file you want to copy the macros to and the file from which you will copy the macros. When you copy macros from one file to another, you copy the entire **macro project item**, which are all of the macros stored in the file. After you have copied macros into a document, you can delete unwanted macros using the *Macros* dialog box.

▶HOW TO: Copy Macros to Another Document

1. Open the document or template where you want to copy the macros.
2. Click the **Macros** button [*Developer* tab, *Code* group] to open the *Macros* dialog box.
3. Click the **Organizer** button. The *Organizer* dialog box opens and displays the *Macro Project Items* tab.
   - Your document displays on the left and the *Normal* template displays on the right.
4. Click the **Close File** button on the right to close the *Normal* template.
5. Click the **Open File** button on the right to open the *Open* dialog box (Figure 10-56).
6. Click the **File type** drop-down list to the right of the *File name* text box and select **All Word Documents**.
7. Browse to locate and select the file containing the macros and click **Open** to close the dialog box.
   - The opened file appears on the right in the *Organizer* dialog box.
8. Select the macro project item (on the right) to copy to your open document (on the left) and click the **Copy** button (Figure 10-57).
   - The macro project item is copied to your document.

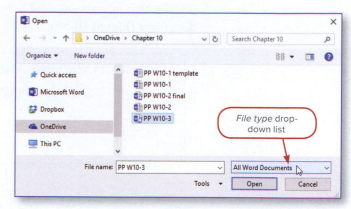

10-56 Open the document containing the macros

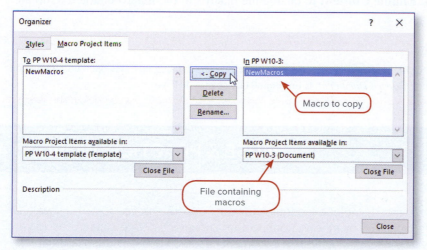

10-57 Copy macros from one file to another

9. Click the **Close** button to close the *Organizer* dialog box.
   - In your document, click the **Macros** button to open the *Macros* dialog box and display the copied macros.

> ▶ **MORE INFO**
>
> You can also use the *Organizer* dialog box to delete and rename macro project items.

Use a Macro-Enabled Template

Using a macro-enabled template is similar to using a template. When you create a new document based on a macro-enabled template, the macros in the template are available in the new document. The following describes how to create a new document based on a macro-enabled template and how to edit an existing macro-enabled template.

- **Create a new document based on a macro-enabled template**: Open a *File Explorer* window, locate the macro-enabled template, and double-click the file. A new document based on the macro-enabled template opens. A security warning appears in the *Info* bar informing you that macros are disabled. Click **Enable Content** to enable the macros in the new document (Figure 10-58).

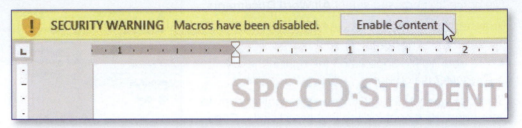

10-58 Enable macros in the document

- **Edit a macro-enabled template**: Open the macro-enabled template from within Word. Because the macro-enabled template contains macros, a security warning appears in the *Info* bar. Click **Enable Content** to enable the macros in the macro-enabled template.

> **MORE INFO**
>
> If you store your files on *OneDrive* or another online location, a dialog box may open prompting you to make the file a *Trusted Document*. If this dialog box opens, click **Yes**.

PAUSE & PRACTICE: WORD 10-4

For this Pause & Practice project, you modify the agenda template from *Pause & Practice 10-1*. You save the template as a macro-enabled template, copy macros from another document, delete a macro, assign a keyboard shortcut to a macro, create a macro, and create a document based on a macro-enabled template.

Files Needed: *[your initials] PP W10-1 template.dotx*, *[your initials] PP W10-3.docm*, and
SPCCDlogo-10.png *(student data files are available in the Library of your SIMnet account)*
Completed Project File Name: *[your initials] PP W10-4 template.dotm*

1. From within Word, open the *[your initials] PP W10-1 template* Word template completed in *Pause & Practice 10-1*.

2. Save the template as a macro-enabled template.
   a. Open the *Save As* dialog box.
   b. Type [your initials] PP W10-4 template in the *File name area*.
   c. Click the **Save as type** drop-down list and select **Word Macro-Enabled Template**.
   d. Browse to the location on your computer where you want to save the macro-enabled template.
   e. Click **Save** to close the dialog box and save the macro-enabled template.

3. Copy macros from a macro-enabled document into your macro-enabled template.
   a. Click the **Macros** button [*Developer* tab, *Code* group] to open the *Macros* dialog box.
   b. Click the **Organizer** button to open the *Organizer* dialog box.
   c. Click the **Close File** button on the right to close the *Normal* template.
   d. Click the **Open File** button on the right to open the *Open* dialog box.
   e. Click the **File type** drop-down list to the right of the *File name* text box and select **All Word Documents**.
   f. Browse to locate and select the **[your initials] PP W10-3** macro-enabled document and click **Open** to close the dialog box and return to the *Organizer* dialog box.
   g. Select the **NewMacros** macro project item (on the right) and click the **Copy** button (Figure 10-59).
   h. Click the **Close** button to close the *Organizer* dialog box.

10-59 Copy macros from a macro-enabled document to a macro-enabled template

4. Delete the *InsertHeader* macro.
   a. Click the **Macros** button [*Developer* tab, *Code* group] to open the *Macros* dialog box.
   b. Click the **Macros in** drop-down list and select **PP W10-4 template (template)**.
   c. Select the **InsertHeader** macro and click the **Delete** button.
   d. Click **Yes** in the dialog box that opens and confirms the deletion of the macro.
   e. Click **Close** to close the *Macros* dialog box.

5. Add a keyboard shortcut to the *InsertFooter* macro.
   a. Click the **File** tab to open the *Backstage* view and select **Options** on the left to open the *Word Options* dialog box.
   b. Click **Customize Ribbon** on the left and then click the **Customize** button in the *Keyboard shortcuts* area. The *Customize Keyboard* dialog box opens.
   c. In the *Categories* area, scroll down and select **Macros**.
   d. Click the **Save changes in** area and select **[your initials] PP W10-4 template**.
   e. Select the **InsertFooter** macro in the *Macros* list.
   f. Place your insertion point in the **Press new shortcut key** text box and press **Alt+Ctrl+Shift+F**.
   g. Click the **Assign** button.
   h. Click **Close** to close the *Customize Keyboard* dialog box, and click **OK** to close the *Word Options* dialog box.

6. Create a keyboard-activated macro.
   a. Place your insertion point after the content control field below the "Additional Information" heading and press **Enter** two times.
   b. Click the **Record Macro** button [*Developer* tab, *Code* group] to open the *Record Macro* dialog box.
   c. Type InsertPicture (no spaces between words) in the *Macro name* area.
   d. Click the **Store macro in** drop-down list and select **Documents Based On [your initials] PP W10-4 template**.
   e. Type Inserts a picture in the *Description* area.

f. Click the **Keyboard** button to open the *Customize Keyboard* dialog box.

g. Click the **Save changes in** drop-down list and select **[your initials] PP W10-4 template**.

h. Place your insertion point in the **Press new shortcut key** text box and press **Alt+Ctrl+Shift+P**.

i. Click the **Assign** button to assign the keyboard shortcut to the macro.

j. Click the **Close** button to close the *Customize Keyboard* dialog box and to begin recording the macro.

7. Record a macro to insert a company logo picture.

   a. Click the **Pictures** button [*Insert* tab, *Illustrations* group] to open the *Insert Picture* dialog box.

   b. Browse to your student data files, select the **SPCCDlogo-10** picture, and click **Insert**.

   c. Click the **Stop Recording** button [*Developer* tab, *Code* group].

8. Select the inserted picture and delete it.

9. Save and close the macro-enabled template.

10. Create a document based on the macro-enabled template to confirm the template works properly.

    a. Open a *File Explorer* window, locate the **[your initials] PP W10-4 template** macro-enabled template, and double-click the file to create a new document based on the template.

    b. Click **OK** to accept the default responses to the two *Fill-in* field prompt dialog boxes.

    c. Click **Enable Content** on the security warning to enable the macros in the new document. If prompted to save styles and building blocks, click **Don't Save**.

    d. Press **Alt+Ctrl+Shift+F** to run the *InsertFooter* macro.

    e. Press **Ctrl+End** to move to the end of the document.

    f. Press **Alt+Ctrl+Shift+P** to run the *InsertPicture* macro.

    g. Examine the document to confirm both macros are inserted (Figure 10-60).

11. Close the document without saving.

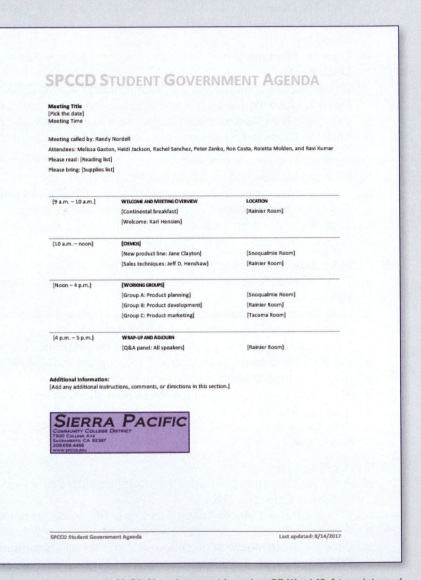

10-60 New document based on PP Word 10-4 template and macros inserted

Chapter Summary

10.1 Create, save, and use a template to generate commonly used documents (p. W10-586).

- A **template** is a type of Word file that stores content and formatting; you can create a document based on the contents of a template.
- A template file has a **.dotx** file name extension.
- You can save an existing or new document as a template.
- A variety of online templates are available in Word in the *New* area on the *Backstage* view. You can also search for templates using key words.
- To edit a template, open the template file from within Word.
- To create a document based on a template, double-click the template file in a *File Explorer* window.
- A new document based on a template has a generic file name such as "*Document1.*"

10.2 Customize template content using a variety of Word fields and styles (p. W10-589).

- A document based on an online template includes a combination of **Word fields**, **content control fields**, and **document property fields**.
- You can customize the content in the fields and copy, move, or delete fields.
- Templates also use formatting and styles that you can modify and apply to other areas of the template or a document based on the template.
- When you attach a template to a document, the styles in the template are available in the document.
- When you attach a template to a document, you can set the document to update each time styles are changed in the template.
- Use the **Organizer** dialog box to copy styles from one template to another template or document.
- Use a **Fill-in field** to prompt a user for information to insert into a document.

10.3 Record a set of instructions as a macro and run and delete a macro (p. W10-596).

- A **macro** is a combination of instructions and keystrokes that you can store and run in a document.

- Before creating and recording a macro, plan what the macro will do, where you will store the macro, and how you will run the macro.
- Use the **Record Macro** dialog box to create the macro and name it.
- You can create a **keyboard-activated macro** or a **button-activated macro**. A keyboard-activated macro runs when you press a shortcut key. A button-activated macro runs when you click the macro button on the *Quick Access* toolbar.
- You must save a document that contains macros as a **Word Macro-Enabled Document** in order for the macros to be stored in the document. A macro-enabled document has a **.docm** file name extension.
- When you open a document containing macros, a security warning appears in the *Info* bar. Click the **Enable Content** button to enable macros in the document.
- Use the **Macros** dialog box to run a macro or delete a macro.
- **AutoMacros** are macros that run automatically when you perform a specific action such as open or close a document.

10.4 Copy and edit an existing macro using Visual Basic and add a keyboard and button shortcut to run a macro (p. W10-605).

- Macros are recorded in **Visual Basic**, which is a programming language.
- To duplicate an existing macro in a document, you can copy a macro using the **Microsoft Visual Basic editor**.
- You can edit the macro code in the Microsoft Visual Basic editor to change an existing or copied macro.
- You can edit the shortcut key assigned to a macro or add a shortcut key to a macro in the **Customize Keyboard** dialog box.
- You can add to, change, or delete a macro button from the *Quick Access* toolbar in *the Word Options* dialog box.

10.5 Create and use a macro-enabled template to automate common tasks and copy a macro to another document (p. W10-612).

- When you use a macro in a template, you must save the template as a macro-enabled template.

- A *macro-enabled template* has a *.dotm* file name extension.
- You can copy a macro from one file to another using the *Organizer* dialog box.
- When you copy macros from one file to another, you copy the *macro project item*, which is the set of macros stored in a file.
- A security warning displays in the *Info* bar when you open a template containing macros or a document based on a macro-enabled template.

Check for Understanding

The SIMbook for this text (within your SIMnet account) provides the following resources for concept review:

- Multiple choice questions
- Matching exercises
- Short answer questions

Guided Project 10-1

For this project, you create a macro-enabled template from an existing Courtyard Medical Plaza document. You insert *Fill-in* fields, record a macro, assign a button to the macro, and create a document based on the template.
[Student Learning Outcomes 10.1, 10.2, 10.3, 10.4, 10.5]

File Needed: ***PrivacyNotice-10.docx*** *(student data files are available in the* Library *of your SIMnet account)*
Completed Project File Names: *[your initials] **Word 10-1 template.dotm*** and *[your initials] **Word 10-1.docm***

Skills Covered in This Project

- Save a document as a macro-enabled template.
- Insert a *Fill-in* field.
- Create a keyboard-activated macro.
- Add a macro button to the *Quick Access* toolbar.

- Create a new document based on a macro-enabled template.
- Insert information in a *Fill-in* field prompt dialog box.
- Enable the macro content in the document.
- Run a macro using the macro button on the *Quick Access* toolbar.

1. Open the **PrivacyNotice-10** document from your student data files.

2. Save the document as a macro-enabled template.
   a. Open the *Save As* dialog box.
   b. Type [your initials] Word 10-1 template in the *File name* area.
   c. Click the **Save as type** drop-down list and select **Word Macro-Enabled Template**.
   d. Browse to the location on your computer where you want to save the file.
   e. Click **Save** to close the dialog box and save the macro-enabled template.

3. Turn on **Show/Hide** if needed and delete the information to the right of the tab on each line in the shaded heading area at the top of the document; don't delete the tab (Figure 10-61).

4. Insert *Fill-in* fields to prompt users for information when a document is created based on the template.
   a. Place your insertion point after the tab and before the paragraph mark in the first line of the heading ("Name:").
   b. Click the **Quick Parts** button [*Insert* tab, *Text* group] and select **Field** from the drop-down list to open the *Field* dialog box (Figure 10-62).
   c. Select **Fill-in** in the *Field names* list.
   d. Type What is the employee's name? in the *Prompt* area.
   e. Check the **Default response to prompt** box and type Employee Name in the text box.

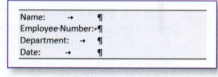

10-61 Remove text in the heading

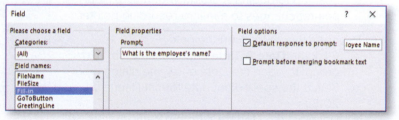

10-62 Insert *Fill-in* field

f. Click **OK** to close the *Field* dialog box and to insert the *Fill-in* field. A dialog box opens prompting you for the employee's name.

g. Click **OK** to accept the default response to the prompt (Figure 10-63).

h. Place your insertion point after the tab on the second heading line ("Employee Number:") and insert another **Fill-in** field.

i. Type What is the employee's number? as the prompt and type Employee Number as the default response to the prompt.

j. Click **OK** to close the *Field* dialog box and **OK** to accept the default response at the prompt.

k. Place your insertion point after the tab on the third heading line ("Department:") and insert another **Fill-in** field.

l. Type What is the employee's department? as the prompt and type Employee Department as the default response to the prompt.

m. Click **OK** to close the *Field* dialog box and **OK** to accept the default response at the prompt (Figure 10-64).

10-63 *Fill-in* **field prompt dialog box**

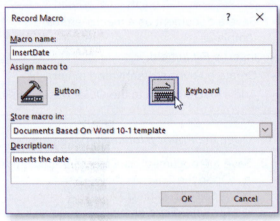

10-64 *Fill-in* **fields inserted in the document**

5. Record a keyboard-activated macro.

a. Place your insertion point after the tab on the fourth heading line ("Date:").

b. Click the **Record Macro** button [*Developer* tab, *Code* group]. The *Record Macro* dialog box opens (Figure 10-65).

c. Type InsertDate in the *Macro name* area.

d. Click the **Store macro in** drop-down list and select **Documents Based On [your initials] Word 10-1 template**.

e. Type Inserts the date in the *Description* area.

f. Click the **Keyboard** button. The *Customize Keyboard* dialog box opens (Figure 10-66).

g. Click the **Save changes in** drop-down list and select **[your initials] Word 10-1 template**.

h. Place the insertion point in the **Press new shortcut key** text box and press **Alt+Ctrl+Shift+D**.

i. Click the **Assign** button to assign the keyboard shortcut to run the macro.

j. Click the **Close** button to close the dialog box and to begin recording your macro. Your pointer changes to a macro-recording pointer.

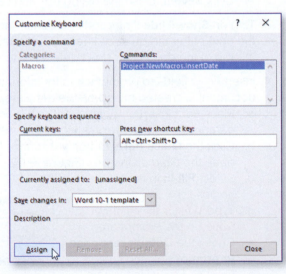

10-65 **Record a keyboard-activated macro**

6. Record a macro to insert the date.

a. Click the **Date & Time** button [*Insert* tab, *Text* group] to open the *Date and Time* dialog box.

b. Select the spelled out date format (January 1, 2018).

c. Deselect the **Update automatically** check box.

d. Click **OK** to close the dialog box and to insert the date.

e. Click the **Stop Recording** button [*Developer* tab, *Code* group] to stop recording the macro.

10-66 **Assign a shortcut key to the macro**

7. Test the macro to confirm it works properly.
   a. Delete the date that was inserted in fourth heading line; don't delete the tab.
   b. Press **Alt+Ctrl+Shift+D** to run the macro.
   c. Delete the date you just inserted.

8. Add a macro button to the *Quick Access* toolbar.
   a. Click the **File** tab to open the *Backstage* view and select **Options** on the left to open the *Word Options* dialog box.
   b. Click **Quick Access Toolbar** on the left to display the *Customize the Quick Access Toolbar* area (Figure 10-67).
   c. Click the **Choose commands from** drop-down list and select **Macros**.
   d. Click the **Customize Quick Access Toolbar** drop-down list and select **For [your initials] Word 10-1 template**.
   e. Select **Project. NewMacros. InsertDate** in the list of macros on the left and click the **Add** button.

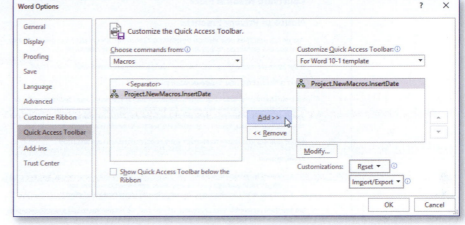

10-67 Add a macro button to the *Quick Access* toolbar

   f. Click the **Modify** button to open the *Modify Button* dialog box (Figure 10-68).
   g. Type Insert Date in the *Display name* area.
   h. Select the icon shown in Figure 10-68 to use as the button on the *Quick Access* toolbar.
   i. Click **OK** to close the *Modify Button* dialog box.
   j. Click **OK** to close the *Word Options* dialog box.

9. Save and close the macro-enabled template.

10. Create a new document based on *[your initials] Word 10-1 template*.
   a. Open a *File Explorer* window and browse to locate the *[your initials] Word 10-1 template* file.
   b. Double-click the file to open a new document based on the template.
   c. Type Mrs. Karen Draper in the first prompt dialog box and click **OK**.
   d. Type 0001484 in the second prompt dialog box and click **OK**.
   e. Type Marketing in the third prompt dialog box and click **OK**.
   f. Click the **Enable Content** button in the security warning in the *Info* bar to enable the macro in the document. If prompted to save changes to the template, click **Save**.

11. Save the document as a **Word Macro-Enabled Document** named [your initials] Word 10-1. If prompted to save changes to the template, click **Yes**.

10-68 Modify the macro button and display name

12. Run the macro to insert the date.
   a. Place your insertion point after the tab on the fourth line of the heading ("Date:").
   b. Click the **Insert Date** macro button on the *Quick Access* toolbar to insert the date.

13. Save and close the document (Figure 10-69).

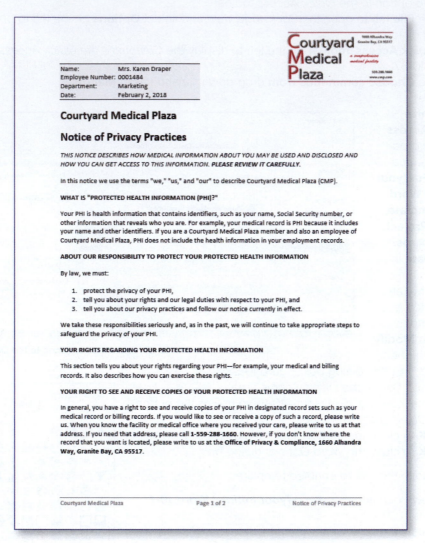

10-69 Word 10-1 completed (page 1 of 2)

Guided Project 10-2

For this project, you open an online Word template and create a letter template for Emma Cavalli at Placer Hills Real Estate. You customize content control fields, delete content control fields, insert text from another file, create a document based on the template, and customize the document.

[**Student Learning Outcomes 10.1, 10.2**]

Files Needed: ***Business Letter* online Word template** and ***CavalliLetter-10.docx*** *(student data files are available in the* Library *of your SIMnet account)*
Completed Project File Names: *[your initials] Word 10-2 template.dotx* and *[your initials] Word 10-2.docx*

Skills Covered in This Project

- Create a document based on an online Word template.
- Save a document as a template.
- Customize a content control field.
- Delete a content control field.
- Copy text from a document to paste into a template.
- Create a new document based on a template.
- Customize a document based on a template.

1. Open an online Word template.
   a. Click the **File** button to open the *Backstage* view.
   b. Click the **New** button to display the Word templates.
   c. Type business letter apothecary in the *Search for online templates* text box and press **Enter**.
   d. Select **Business letter (Apothecary design)**. A preview window opens (Figure 10-70).
   e. Click the **Create** button to create a document based on this template.
   *Note: If this template is not available in Word, open the **BusinessLetter-10** file from your student data files.*

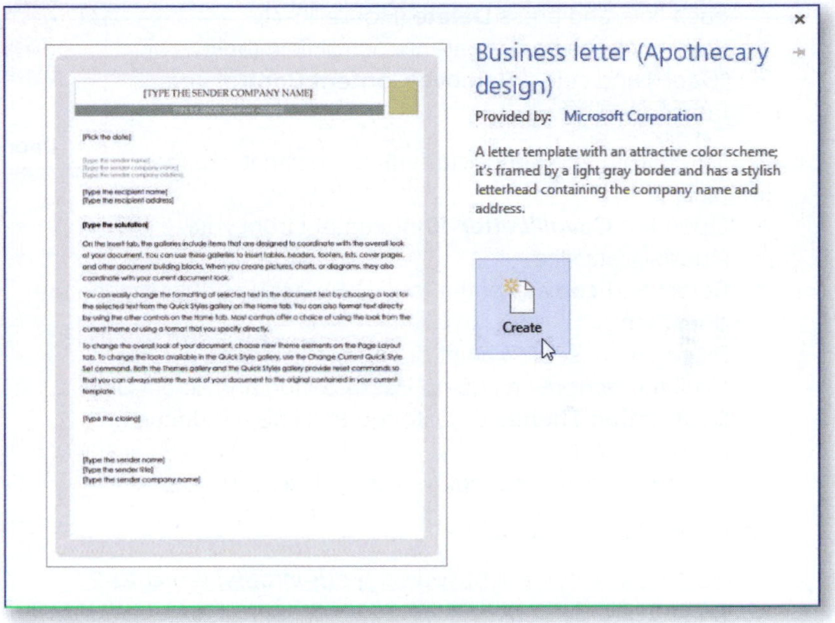

10-70 Create a document based on an online template

2. Save this document as a template.
   a. Open the **Save As** dialog box.
   b. Save the document as a **Word Template** named [your initials] Word 10-2 template.
   c. Browse to the location on your computer where you want to save the template and click the **Save** button. If prompted to save the document in the most current version of Word, click **OK**.

3. Customize content control fields.
   a. Click the "**TYPE THE SENDER COMPANY NAME**" content control field at the top, and type in all caps PLACER HILLS REAL ESTATE.
   b. Click the "**TYPE THE SENDER COMPANY ADDRESS**" content control field at the top and type in all caps 7100 MADRONE ROAD, ROSEVILLE, CA 95722.
   c. Click the "**Type the salutation**" content control field above the body and type Dear and **space** once.
   d. Click the "**Type the closing**" content control field at the bottom and type Best regards in the field.

e. In the author name content control field below "Best regards", type Emma Cavalli to replace the existing author name if there is one.

f. Click the "**Type the sender title**" content control field near the bottom and type Realtor Consultant.

4. Add text to the document.

a. Place your insertion point after the company name at the bottom and press **Enter**.

b. Type ecavalli@phre.com and press **Enter**.

c. Type 916.450.3334 as the phone number.

5. Delete content control fields.

a. Select the three content control fields below the date including the paragraph mark at the end of each line, and press **Delete** (Figure 10-71).

b. Right-click the body content control field (below "Dear") and select **Remove Content Control** from the context menu.

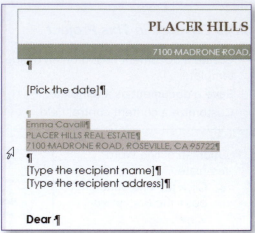

10-71 Delete content control fields

6. Copy text from another document and paste it into the template.

a. Open the ***CavalliLetter-10*** document from your student data files.

b. Select and **copy** all of the text in the document and close the document.

c. Place your insertion point on the blank line below "Dear."

d. Click the bottom half of the **Paste** button and select **Use Destination Theme** to paste the text into the document (Figure 10-72).

e. Delete the blank line below the pasted body text.

7. Save and close the template.

8. Create a new document based on ***[your initials] Word 10-2 template***.

a. Open a *File Explorer* window and browse to locate the ***[your initials] Word 10-2 template*** file.

b. Double-click the file to open a new document based on the template.

10-72 Paste text using the destination theme

9. Save the file as a **Word Document** named [your initials] Word 10-2. If prompted to save the template file, click **Yes**.

10. Customize the document based on the template.

a. Click the "**Pick the date**" content control field and select the current date.

b. Click the "**Type the recipient name**" content control field and type Mr. and Mrs. Robert McCartney.

c. Click the "**Type the recipient address**" content control field and type 7105 High Street, press **Enter**, and type Folsom, CA 93714.

d. Place your insertion point after the space after "Dear" and type Robert and Lanita.

e. Confirm that "Emma Cavalli" is the author name that appears in the content control field near the bottom. If it is not, change it to Emma Cavalli.

f. Right-click the email address near the bottom and select **Remove Hyperlink** from the context menu.

11. Save and close the document (Figure 10-73). If prompted to save the template file, click **Yes**.

PLACER HILLS REAL ESTATE
7100 MADRONE ROAD, ROSEVILLE, CA 95722

4/22/2018

Mr. and Mrs. Robert McCartney
7105 High Street
Folsom, CA 93714

Dear Robert and Lanita

I noticed today that your current home listing has recently expired. My goal is to tell you about **Placer Hills Real Estate** and myself. We can offer you attention and services that are unmatched by other real estate companies.

The service and experience I can offer you when helping you with your selling needs is unmatched. Working together with you, I am confident that we can analyze your present and future goals and help you obtain them. If you are curious as to the type of activity that has been occurring in your area or you would like to discuss your needs and goals, I would be more than happy to come by and talk with you.

Gaining your trust and confidence to build a solid relationship for the future is my first priority. I have enclosed a document that will provide you with valuable information about buying a home.

Feel free to call me to set up an appointment if you would like a unique perspective for marketing your home and buying a new home from someone with thorough knowledge and experience with homes in your neighborhood. I look forward to talking with you soon.

Best regards

Emma Cavalli
Realtor Consultant
PLACER HILLS REAL ESTATE
ecavalli@phre.com
916.450.3334

10-73 Word 10-2 completed

Guided Project 10-3

For this project, you modify a template and document for Sierra Pacific Community College District. You save a template as a macro-enabled template, record and edit a macro, copy and modify a macro, and attach a template to a document.
[Student Learning Outcomes 10.1, 10.2, 10.3, 10.4, 10.5]

Files Needed: ***SPCCDtemplate-10.dotx*** and ***SPCCDValues-10.docx*** *(student data files are available in the* Library *of your SIMnet account)*
Completed Project File Names: ***[your initials] Word 10-3 template.dotm*** and ***[your initials] Word 10-3.docm***

Skills Covered in This Project

- Save a template as a macro-enabled template.
- Create a button-activated macro.
- Edit a macro in Visual Basic.
- Copy and modify a macro using the Visual Basic editor.

- Add a keyboard shortcut to a macro.
- Save a document as a macro-enabled document.
- Attach a template to a document.
- Enable macro content in the document.
- Run a macro in a document.

1. From within Word, open the ***SPCCDtemplate-10*** template from your student data files. If you don't find this file in your student data files, click the **File type** drop-down list in the *Open* dialog box and select **All Word Documents** to display all Word files.

2. Save the document as a macro-enabled template.
   a. Open the **Save As** dialog box.
   b. Save as a **Word Macro-Enabled Template** named [your initials] Word 10-3 template.
   c. Browse to the location on your computer where you want to save the macro-enabled template and click the **Save** button.

3. Create a button-activated macro.
   a. Place your insertion point anywhere in the words "*Two Columns*" in the document.
   b. Click the **Record Macro** button [*Developer* tab, *Code* group] to open the *Record Macro* dialog box (Figure 10-74).
   c. Type TwoColumns in the *Macro name* area.
   d. Click the **Store macro in** drop-down list and select **Documents Based On [your initials] Word 10-3 template**.
   e. Type Change to two columns in the *Description* area.
   f. Click the **Button** button to open the *Customize the Quick Access Toolbar* area of the *Word Options* dialog box.
   g. Click the **Customize Quick Access Toolbar** drop-down list and select **For [your initials] Word 10-3 template**.
   h. Select the **TemplateProject. NewMacros.TwoColums** macro and click the **Add** button (Figure 10-75).
   i. Click the **Modify** button to open the *Modify Button* dialog box.
   j. Type Two Columns in the *Display Name* text box and select the icon as shown in Figure 10-76.
   k. Click **OK** to close the *Modify Button* dialog box and click **OK** to close the *Word Options* dialog box and to begin recording the macro.

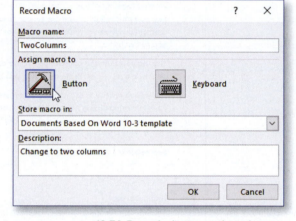

10-74 Record a button-activated macro

10-75 Add a macro button to the *Quick Access* toolbar

4. Record a macro to change the number of columns to two.
   a. Click the **Columns** button [*Layout* tab, *Page Setup* group] and select **Two** from the drop-down list.
   b. Click the **Stop Recording** button [*Developer* tab, *Code* group].
   c. **Save** the macro-enabled template.

5. Edit a macro so it will work on documents with different margins and page layout.
   a. Click the **Macros** button to open the *Macros* dialog box.
   b. Select the **TwoColumns** macro and click the **Edit** button. The Microsoft Visual Basic editor opens.
   c. Select "**.Width = InchesToPoints(6.5)**" and **delete** it. It is okay if there is a blank line where you deleted the code (Figure 10-77).
   d. Press **Ctrl+S** to save the macro code and leave the Microsoft Visual Basic editor open.

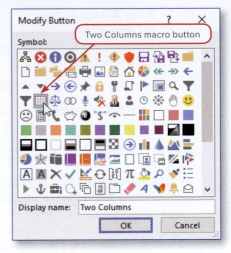

10-76 Modify the macro button and display name

6. Copy the macro and modify it to apply three-column format.
   a. Select the *TwoColumns* macro code beginning with "**Sub TwoColumns ( )**" and ending with "**End Sub**" and press **Ctrl+C** to copy the code.
   b. Place your insertion point below "End Sub" and press **Ctrl+V** to paste the copied macro code.
   c. Edit the copied macro to include the four highlighted changes in Figure 10-78.
   d. Press **Ctrl+S** to save the macro code.
   e. Click the **File** menu and select **Close and Return to Microsoft Word**.

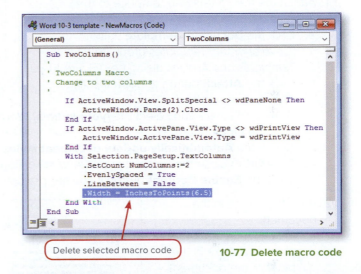

10-77 Delete macro code

7. Assign a keyboard shortcut to a macro.
   a. Click the **File** tab to open the *Backstage* view and select **Options** on the left to open the *Word Options* dialog box.
   b. Click **Customize Ribbon** on the left.
   c. Click the **Customize** button in the *Keyboard shortcuts* area. The *Customize Keyboard* dialog box opens (Figure 10-79).
   d. In the *Categories* area, scroll down and select **Macros**.
   e. Click the **Save changes in** drop-down list and select **[your initials] Word 10-3 template**.
   f. Select the **ThreeColumns** macro in the *Macros* list.
   g. Place your insertion point in the **Press new shortcut key** text box and press **Alt+Ctrl+Shift+3** (*Alt+Ctrl+#* displays as the keyboard shortcut).

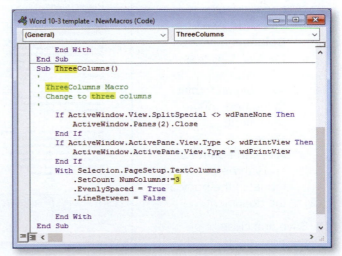

10-78 Modify the macro code

h. Click the **Assign** button.

i. Click **Close** to close the *Customize Keyboard* dialog box and click **OK** to close the *Word Options* dialog box.

8. Save and close the macro-enabled template.

9. Open the ***SPCCDValues-10*** document from your student data files.

10. Save this document as a macro-enabled document.

   a. Open the **Save As** dialog box.

   b. Save as a **Word Macro-Enabled Document** named [your initials] Word 10-3.

   c. Browse to the location on your computer where you want to save the document and click the **Save** button.

11. Attach the macro-enabled template to the document.

   a. Click the **Document Template** button [*Developer* tab, *Templates* group] to open the *Templates and Add-ins* dialog box (Figure 10-80).

   b. Click the **Attach** button to open the *Attach Template* dialog box.

   c. Browse to locate and select the *[your initials] Word 10-3 template* macro-enabled template and click the **Open** button.

   d. Check the **Automatically update document styles** box.

   e. Click **OK** to close the *Templates and Add-ins* dialog box and to attach the template.

   f. Click the **Enable Content** button if you are prompted to enable the macros in the document.

12. Run the macros in the document.

   a. Place your insertion point anywhere in the body of the document below the title.

   b. Press the **Two Columns** button on the *Quick Access* toolbar to apply two-column format to the body of the document.

   c. Press **Alt+Ctrl+Shift+3** to apply three-column format to the body of the document.

13. Save and close the document (Figure 10-81).

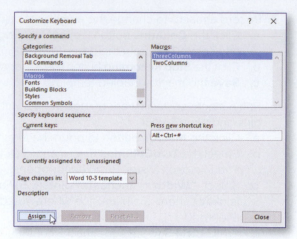

10-79 Add a shortcut key to a macro

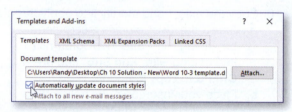

10-80 Attach a template to a document

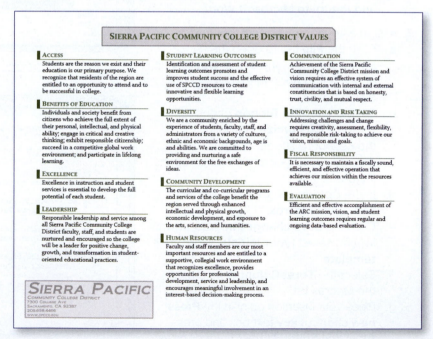

10-81 Word 10-3 completed

Independent Project 10-4

For this project, you create a fax template for American River Cycling Club from an online Word template. You save the template as a macro-enabled template, modify the template format and structure, customize the template content, insert *Fill-in* fields, record and copy macros in the template, and create a macro-enabled document based on the template.
[**Student Learning Outcomes 10.1, 10.2, 10.3, 10.4 10.5**]

Files Needed: ***Fax cover sheet (rust)*** **online Word template** and ***ARCClogo-10.png*** *(student data files are available in the* Library *of your SIMnet account)*
Completed Project File Names: *[your initials]* **Word 10-4 template.dotm** and *[your initials]* **Word 10-4.docm**

Skills Covered in This Project

- Create a document based on an online Word template.
- Save a document as a macro-enabled template.
- Insert and resize a picture.
- Delete and customize a content control field.
- Modify the structure and format of a table in a template.
- Insert a *Fill-in* field.

- Record a button-activated macro.
- Copy and modify a macro.
- Add a macro button to the *Quick Access* toolbar.
- Create a document based on a template.
- Respond to a *Fill-in* field prompt.
- Enable the macro content in the document.
- Save a document as a macro-enabled document.
- Run a macro in the document.

1. Create a document from an online Word template.
   a. In the *New* area on the *Backstage* view, search for fax in the *Search for online templates* area.
   b. Select the **Fax cover sheet (Rust design)** online Word template and click **Create** to create a document based on this online template.
   c. If this online Word template is not available, open the **FaxCoverSheet-10** file from your student data files.

2. Save the document as a **Word Macro-Enabled Template** named [your initials] Word 10-4 template. Be sure to select the specific location to save the template. Click **OK** if prompted to upgrade the file to the newest format.

3. Replace the picture in the content control field, resize the picture, and delete other content control fields.
   a. Select the picture placeholder in the "Picture" content control field ("YOUR LOGO HERE").
   b. Change the picture and replace it with the **ARCClogo-10** picture from your student data files.
   c. Select the picture and change the width to **4"**. The height automatically adjusts.
   d. Delete the "**Your company slogan**" and "**Comments**" content control fields.

4. Modify the tables in the template.
   a. Turn on **View Gridlines** so you can see the tables in the template (this template contains four tables).
   b. Select the first table and change the bottom border color to **Olive Green, Accent 3**.
   c. Select the second table and change the font color to **Black, Text 1**.
   d. Select the third table and change the color of all borders to **Olive Green, Accent 3**.
   e. With the third table selected, change the font color to **Black, Text 1**.
   f. Delete the last two rows of the third table.
   g. In the third table, delete **FROM**: and type DATE:.
   h. Select the fourth table and change the color of all borders to **Olive Green, Accent 3**.
   i. Select the first row of the fourth table and change the shading fill color to **Olive Green, Accent 3**.

W10-629

5. Use the following information to customize the fax template content control fields in the second table.

Your Company Name: Kelly Weatherby

Street Address: P.O. Box 4472

City, ST ZIP Code: Sacramento, CA 95841

Phone: 916-450-3320

Fax: 916-450-3301

Email: kelly@arcc.org

6. In the third table, insert the date in the cell to the right of "DATE:". Use the spelled out date format (January 1, 2018) and set it to update automatically.

7. Insert *Fill-in* fields in the third table.
   a. In the cell to the right of "TO:", insert a **Fill-in** field. Type Who is the fax recipient? as the prompt and Fax Recipient as the default response to the prompt. When prompted, click **OK** to accept the default response.
   b. In the cell to the right of "FAX:", insert a **Fill-in** field. Type What is the recipient's fax number? as the prompt and Fax Number as the default response to the prompt. When prompted, click **OK** to accept the default response.
   c. In the cell to the right of "PAGES:", insert a **Fill-in** field. Type How many pages? as the prompt and Pages as the default response to the prompt. When prompted, click **OK** to accept the default response.

8. Record a button-activated macro to insert text.
   a. Place your insertion point in the second row of the fourth table (below "URGENT").
   b. Record a macro named MembershipReceipt and store it in **Documents Based On [your initials] Word 10-4 template**.
   c. Type Membership receipt text as the *Description*.
   d. Click **Button** to assign a button to this macro.
   e. Select **For [your initials] Word 10-4 template** as the *Quick Access* toolbar to customize and add the *MembershipReceipt* macro.
   f. Modify the macro button to use Membership Receipt as the display name and the **orange square** as the icon for the button.
   g. Begin recording the macro. With your insertion point in the second row of the fourth table, type Your membership receipt is included with this fax.
   h. Stop recording the macro and delete the text you just typed.
   i. Test the macro by clicking the **Membership Receipt** macro button on the *Quick Access* toolbar.
   j. Delete the text inserted by the macro.

9. Copy and modify a macro.
   a. Open the *Macros* dialog box and edit the **MembershipReceipt** macro.
   b. Copy the macro code and paste it below the existing macro.
   c. Edit the copied macro to include the highlighted changes in Figure 10-82.
   d. Save the macro code, and close and return to the Word document.

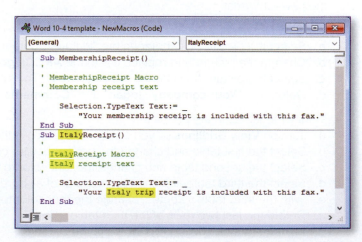

10-82 Modify the macro code

10. Customize the *Quick Access* toolbar for the **[your initials] Word 10-4 template** to add a macro button for the *ItalyReceipt* macro.
    a. Use Italy Receipt as the display name.
    b. Select the **yellow square** as the icon for the button.
    c. Place your insertion point in the second row of the fourth table and run the *ItalyReceipt* macro using the macro button on the *Quick Access* toolbar.
    d. Delete the text inserted by the macro.

11. Save and close the macro-enabled template.

12. Open a document based on the **[your initials] Word 10-4 template** (open from a *File Explorer* window).

13. Use the following information for the three *Fill-in* prompt dialog boxes.
    Recipient name: Rick Hermenn
    Recipient fax number: 916-452-9226
    Number of pages: 3

14. Enable the macro content in the document.

15. Save the document as a **Word Macro-Enabled Document** named [your initials] Word 10-4. If prompted to save styles and building block, click **Don't Save**. If prompted to save changes to the template, click **Yes**.

16. Place your insertion point in the second row of the fourth table and run the *ItalyReceipt* macro using the button on the *Quick Access* toolbar.

17. Save and close the document (Figure 10-83).

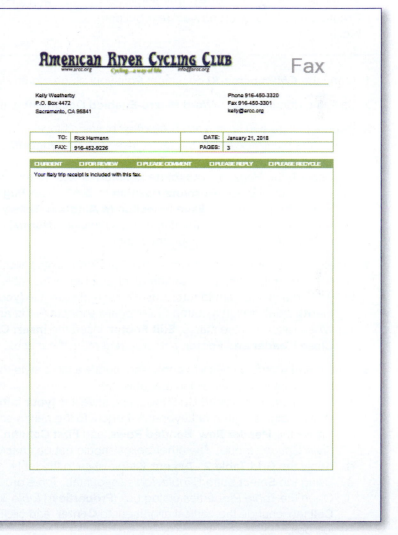

10-83 Word 10-4 completed

Independent Project 10-5

For this project, you modify a document from Courtyard Medical Plaza using macros you create in another document. You create macros in a document, copy and modify a macro, and copy macros to another document.
[Student Learning Outcomes 10.3, 10.4, 10.5]

Files Needed: ***CMPmacros-10.docx***, ***VaccinationSchedule-10.docx***, and ***CMPlogo-10.png*** *(student data files are available in the* Library *of your SIMnet account)*
Completed Project File Names: ***[your initials] Word 10-5 macros.docm*** and ***[your initials] Word 10-5.docm***

Skills Covered in This Project

- Save a document as a macro-enabled document.
- Insert and arrange a picture.
- Save a picture as an *AutoText* building block.
- Create a macro to insert an *AutoText* building block.

- Create a macro to apply and modify a table style.
- Copy and modify a macro.
- Use the *Organizer* dialog box to copy a macro from one file to another.
- Run a macro in a document.

1. Open the ***CMPmacros-10*** document from your student data files.

2. Save the document as a **Word Macro-Enabled Document** named [your initials] Word 10-5 macros.

3. Insert a picture and save it as an *AutoText* building block.
   a. On the blank line below the table, insert the ***CMPlogo-10*** picture.
   b. Change the text wrapping to **Tight**.
   c. Change the *Horizontal* **Absolute position** to **0.3"** *to the right of* **Page**.
   d. Change the *Vertical* **Absolute position** to **9.6"** *below* **Page**.
   e. Select the picture and **Save Selection to AutoText Gallery**.
   f. Use Insert CMP logo as the name and save in the **Normal** template.
   g. Delete the picture from your document.

4. Create and record a macro to insert the *AutoText* building block into the footer of the document.
   a. Place your insertion point on the blank line below the table.
   b. Record a macro named InsertLogoFooter and save it in **[your initials] Word 10-5 macros (document)**. Don't assign a button or keyboard shortcut to the macro and don't include a description.
   c. When recording the macro, **Edit Footer**, insert the **Insert CMP logo** *AutoText* building block, **Close Header and Footer**, and stop recording the macro.

5. Create and record a macro to apply and modify a table style to the table.
   a. Place your insertion point in the table.
   b. Record a macro named GridTable2 and save it in **[your initials] Word 10-5 macros (document)**. Don't assign a button or keyboard shortcut to the macro and don't include a description.
   c. Check the **Header Row**, **Banded Rows**, and **First Column** boxes [*Table Tools Design* tab, *Table Style Options* group]. The other boxes should not be checked.
   d. Apply the **Grid Table 2 - Accent 2** table style to the table.
   e. Using the **Select** button [*Table Tools Layout* tab, *Table* group], select the entire table.
   f. Open the *Table Properties* dialog box (**Properties**) [*Table Tools Layout* tab, *Table* group], click the **Cell** tab, change the vertical alignment to **Center**, and click **OK** to close the *Table Properties* dialog box.
   g. Stop recording the macro.

6. Copy and modify a macro.
   a. Open the *Macros* dialog box and edit the **GridTable2** macro.
   b. Copy the *GridTable2* macro code and paste it below the *GridTable2* macro.
   c. Edit the copied macro to include the highlighted changes in Figure 10-84.

```
Sub GridTable5()
'
' GridTable5 Macro
'
'
    Selection.Tables(1).ApplyStyleHeadingRows = Not Selection.Tables(1). _
        ApplyStyleHeadingRows
    Selection.Tables(1).ApplyStyleRowBands = Not Selection.Tables(1). _
        ApplyStyleRowBands
    Selection.Tables(1).ApplyStyleFirstColumn = Not Selection.Tables(1). _
        ApplyStyleFirstColumn
    Selection.Tables(1).Style = "Grid Table 5 Dark - Accent 2"
    Selection.Tables(1).Select
    Selection.Cells.VerticalAlignment = wdCellAlignVerticalCenter
End Sub
```

10-84 Modify the macro code

   d. Save the macro code and close and return to the Word document.

7. Place your insertion point in the table and run the **GridTable5** macro using the *Macros* dialog box.

8. Save and close the macro-enabled document.

9. Open the ***VaccinationSchedule-10*** document from your student data files.

10. Save this document as a **Word Macro-Enabled Document** named [your initials] Word 10-5.

11. Copy the macros from the ***[your initials] Word 10-5 macros*** document to ***[your initials] Word 10-5***.
    a. Open the *Macros* dialog box and then open the *Organizer* dialog box (Figure 10-85).

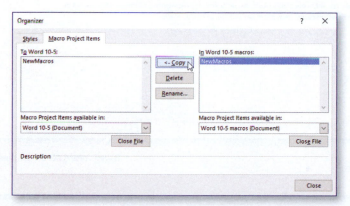

10-85 Copy macros from one file to another

    b. Close the *Normal* template on the right and open the ***[your initials] Word 10-5 macros*** document. In the *Open* dialog box, select **All Word Documents** in the file type drop-down list to display all Word documents if necessary.
    c. Select the **NewMacros** macro project item from ***[your initials] Word 10-5 macros*** (on the right) and copy to ***[your initials] Word 10-5*** (on the left).
    d. Close the *Organizer* dialog box.

12. Open the *Macros* dialog box and run the **InsertLogoFooter** macro to insert the footer into the document.

13. Place your insertion point in the table and run the **GridTable5** macro.

14. Place your insertion point in the table and run the **GridTable2** macro.

15. Save and close the document (Figure 10-86).

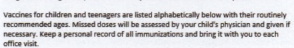

VACCINATION SCHEDULE

Think of vaccines as a coat of armor for your child. To keep it shiny and strong, you have to make sure your child's immunizations are up to date. Timely vaccinations help to prevent disease and keep your family and the community healthy. Some immunizations are given in a single shot, while others require a series of shots over a period of time.

Vaccines for children and teenagers are listed alphabetically below with their routinely recommended ages. Missed doses will be assessed by your child's physician and given if necessary. Keep a personal record of all immunizations and bring it with you to each office visit.

Don't neglect your vaccinations!

RECOMMENED VACCINATION SCHEDULE

Name of Vaccine	When It's Recommended	Total Doses
Chickenpox (varicella)	At 12 months and 4-6 years	2
Diphtheria, tetanus, and pertussis (DTaP)	At 2, 4, 6 and 12-15 months, and 4-6 years	5
Haemophilus influenzae type b (Hib)	At 2, 4, 6, and 12 months	4
Hepatitis A (HepA)	At 12 and 18 months	3
Hepatitis B (HepB)	At birth, 1-2 months, and 6 months	3
Human papillomavirus (HPV)	3-dose series for girls at age 11-12 years	3
Inactivated influenza (flu shot)	Annually starting at age 6 months	Annually
Inactivated poliovirus (IPV)	At 2, 4, 6 months, and 4-6 years	4
Live intranasal influenza	Annually starting at age 2 years	Annually
Measles, mumps, and rubella (MMR)	At 12 months and 4-6 years	2
Meningococcal conjugate (MCV)	At 11-12 years	1
Pneumococcal conjugate (PCV)	At 2, 4, 6, and 12 months	4
Pneumococcal polysaccharide (PPSV)	At 2, 4, 6, and 12 months	4
Rotavirus (RV)	At 2, 4, and 6 months	3
Tetanus and diphtheria (Td)	At 11-12 years	1

These recommendations are for generally healthy children and teenagers and are for information only. If your child has ongoing health problems, special health needs or risks, or if certain conditions run in your family, talk with your child's physician. He or she may recommend additional vaccinations or schedules based on earlier immunizations and special health needs.

Courtyard Medical Plaza
a comprehensive medical facility

1000 Alhambra Way
Granite Bay, CA 95117

559.288.1660
www.cmp.com

10-86 Word 10-5 completed

Independent Project 10-6

For this project, you create an insurance renewal letter template for Central Sierra Insurance. You create a macro-enabled template, insert *Fill-in* fields, record a macro, copy and modify a macro, and create a document based on the template.

[Student Learning Outcomes 10.1, 10.2, 10.3, 10.4, 10.5]

File Needed: **CSIPolicyRenewal-10.docx** (student data files are available in the Library of your SIMnet account)
Completed Project File Names: **[your initials] Word 10-6 template.dotm** and **[your initials] Word 10-6.docm**

Skills Covered in This Project

- Save a document as a macro-enabled template.
- Insert a *Fill-in* field.
- Create a keyboard-activated macro to insert the closing lines of a letter.
- Copy and modify a macro.
- Assign a keyboard shortcut to a macro.
- Create a document based on a macro-enabled template.
- Respond to a *Fill-in* field prompt.
- Enable the macro content in the document.
- Save a document as a macro-enabled document.
- Update formulas in a table.
- Run a macro in a document.

1. Open the **CSIPolicyRenewal-10** document from your student data files.

2. Save the document as a **Word Macro-Enabled Template** named [your initials] Word 10-6 template.

3. Insert *Fill-in* fields in the document.
   a. Use the following information for the five *Fill-in* fields to replace the bracketed placeholder text. Delete placeholder text and brackets.
   b. Accept the default response as you create each *Fill-in* field.

Placeholder Text	Prompt	Default Response to Prompt
[Name and Address]	Type name, company, and address.	Name/Company/Address
[First Name]	Type client's first name.	First Name
[Insurance Company]	Type name of insurance company.	Insurance Company
[Premium Basis]	What is the premium basis?	Premium Basis
[Rate per $1000]	What is the rate per $1000?	Rate per $1000

4. Create and record a macro to insert the closing lines of the letter.
   a. Place your insertion point on the last blank line in the document.
   b. Record macro a named GretchenClosing and store the macro in **Documents Based On [your initials] Word 10-6 template**.
   c. Type Inserts Gretchen Souza closing lines as the description. Don't assign a keyboard shortcut or button to the macro.
   d. Record the following lines of text as the macro:
      Sincerely and press **Enter** four times
      Gretchen Souza, ARM, CIC, CRM and press **Enter**
      Central Sierra Insurance and press **Enter**
      gretchen@centralsierra.com
   e. Stop recording the macro and delete the text you just typed. Confirm two blank lines display below the last paragraph in the letter.

5. Copy and modify a macro.
   a. Use the Microsoft Visual Basic editor to copy the *GretchenClosing* macro and paste it below the last line of macro code.
   b. Edit the copied macro to include the highlighted changes in Figure 10-87.
   c. Save and close the macro and return to Microsoft Word.

6. Assign a keyboard shortcut to the two macros.
   a. Open the *Customize Keyboard* dialog box and select **Macros** in the *Categories* area.
   b. Save changes in the [**your initials**] **Word 10-6 template**.
   c. Select the *GretchenClosing* macro and assign **Alt+Ctrl+Shift+G** as the keyboard shortcut.
   d. Select the *JuanClosing* macro and assign **Alt+Ctrl+Shift+J** as the keyboard shortcut.
   e. **Close** the *Customize Keyboard* dialog box and click **OK** to close the *Word Options* dialog box.

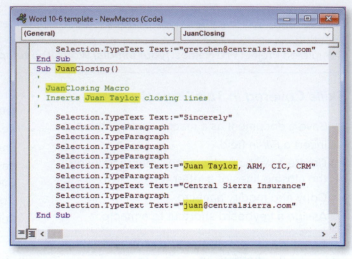

10-87 Modify the macro code

7. Test the macro and finalize the template.
   a. Use the keyboard shortcut to test the *GretchenClosing* macro.
   b. Delete the inserted macro text. Confirm two blank lines display below the last paragraph in the letter.
   c. Use the keyboard shortcut to test the *JuanClosing* macro.
   d. Delete the inserted macro text. Confirm two blank lines display below the last paragraph in the letter.

8. Check the spacing in the document around the *Fill-in* fields to ensure proper spacing.

9. Save and close the template.

10. Open a *File Explorer* window and create a new document based on [**your initials**] **Word 10-6 template**.

11. Use the following information for the *Fill-in* field prompts:

    Name/Company/Address:
    Mr. Lamar Gordon
    Sierra Fence Company
    2405 Eureka Avenue
    Fair Oaks, CA 95636
    First Name: Lamar
    Insurance Company: West Coast Insurance
    Premium Basis: $325,000
    Rate per $1000: $21

12. Enable the macro content in the document. If prompted to save the template, click **Save**.

13. Save the document as a **Word Macro-Enabled Document** named [**your initials**] **Word 10-6**. If prompted to save the template, click **Yes**.

14. Update the formulas in the last three cells in the second row of the table.

15. Place your insertion point on the second blank line below the body and run the *JuanClosing* macro.

16. Save and close the document (Figure 10-88). If prompted to save the template, click **Save**.

10-88 Word 10-6 completed

Improve It Project 10-7

For this project, you create an invoice template for Eller Software Services from an online Word template. You save the template as a macro-enabled template, customize the template content, insert a *Fill-in* field, record macros in the template, and create a macro-enabled document based on the template.
[Student Learning Outcomes 10.1, 10.2, 10.3, 10.5]

Files Needed: ***Invoice* online Word template** and ***ESSlogo-10.png*** *(student data files are available in the Library of your SIMnet account)*
Completed Project File Names: *[your initials] Word 10-7 template.dotm* and *[your initials] Word 10-7.docm*

Skills Covered in This Project

- Create a document based on a Word online template.
- Save a document as a macro-enabled template.
- Insert, resize, and arrange a picture.
- Customize a content control field.
- Delete a row from a table.
- Insert a *Fill-in* field.
- Insert a formula in a table.
- Record a button-activated macro.
- Create a document based on a template.
- Respond to a *Fill-in* field prompt.
- Enable the macro content in the document.
- Save a document as a macro-enabled document.
- Run a macro in a document.

1. Create a document from an online Word template.
    a. Search for online templates in the *New* area on the *Backstage* view and use invoice as the keyword.
    b. Select the **Invoice (Red design)** online Word template and create a document based on this template. If this template is not available in Word, open the ***Invoice-10*** file from your student data files.

2. Save the document as a **Word Macro-Enabled Template** named [your initials] Word 10-7 template.

3. Change the existing logo picture and resize and arrange the picture.
    a. Change the sample logo picture and replace it with ***ESSlogo-10*** from your student data files.
    b. Change the height to **0.6"** while maintaining the aspect ratio.
    c. Change the text wrapping to **In Front of Text** and **Align Right** and **Align Top** relative to the margins.

4. Customize the content of the template.
    a. Type Eller Software Services in the "Company" content control field.
    b. Type 3421 East Avenue, Saint Cloud, MN 56301 in the "Street Address, City, ST ZIP Code" content control field.
    c. Type Payment is due within 30 days after the invoice date. in the "Add additional instructions" content control field.
    d. Edit the footer, type the following information in the content control fields, and then close the footer:
        Telephone: 320.675.4100
        Fax: 320.675.4101
        Email: info@ellerss.com
        Web: www.ellerss.com
    e. In the third table in the body of the document, delete the next to the last row ("Shipping & Handling").

5. Insert a *Fill-in* field.
   a. Delete the content control field below "To" and insert a **Fill-in** field.
   b. Type What is the client's name, company, and address? as the prompt and Client Info as the default response to the prompt.
   c. Accept the default response to the prompt.

6. Insert formulas in the table.
   a. Insert a formula in the cell to the right of "Subtotal" to **SUM** the cells **ABOVE** (Figure 10-89). Use the number format shown.
   b. Insert a formula in the cell to the right of "Sales Tax" to multiply cell **D13** by **7.5%** and use the same number format.
   c. Insert a formula in the cell to the right of "Total Due By [Date]" to add cells **D13** and **D14** and use the same number format.

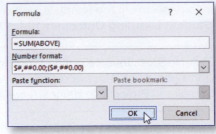

10-89 Insert formula to add the cells above

7. Record a button-activated macro to insert a product into the invoice.
   a. Place your insertion point in the cell below "Quantity" in the table.
   b. Record a macro named ESS_Software and store it in **Documents Based On [your initials] Word 10-7 template**.
   c. Type Inserts ESS Accounting Software package as the *Description*
   d. Assign the macro to a button and add the macro to the *Quick Access* toolbar **For [your initials] Word 10-7 template**.
   e. Modify the button to use **ESS Software** as the display name, and select the button icon shown in Figure 10-90.

8. Record the macro.
   a. Type the following information in the first row of the table, pressing **Tab** to move from cell to cell:

   1   ESS Accounting Software $875.00 $875.00

   b. Stop recording the macro.
   c. Delete the text you typed in the table.

9. Record another button-activated macro to insert a product into the invoice.
   a. Place your insertion point in the cell below "Quantity".
   b. Record a macro named ESS_Support and store it in **Documents Based On [your initials] Word 10-7 template**.
   c. Type Inserts ESS Accounting Software Support package as the *Description*.
   d. Assign the macro to a button and add the macro to the *Quick Access* toolbar **For [your initials] Word 10-7 template**.
   e. Modify the button to use **ESS Support** as the display name, and select the button icon shown in Figure 10-90.

ESS Software macro button

Modify Button

10-90 Assign a button to a macro

ESS Support macro button

10. Record the macro.
   a. Type the following information in the first row of the table, pressing **Tab** to move from cell to cell:

   8 hrs   ESS Accounting Software Support $75.00 $600.00

   b. Stop recording the macro.
   c. Delete the text you typed in the table.

11. Save and close the macro-enabled template.

12. Open a *File Explorer* window and create a new document based on the ***[your initials] Word 10-7 template***.

13. Use the following information for the *Fill-in* field prompt:

    Ms. Amanda Mendez
    Paradise Lakes Resort
    1256 Raymond Drive
    Cass Lake, MN 56633

14. Enable macro content in the document. If prompted to save styles and building blocks, click **Don't Save**.

15. Save the document as a **Word Macro-Enabled Document** named [your initials] Word 10-7. If prompted to save the template, click **Yes**.

16. Customize content control fields.
    a. Type ESS2305 in the invoice number content control field on the left ("[0000]").
    b. In the "Click to select date" content control field, select the current date.
    c. In the "Date" content control field ("Total Due By [Date]") at the bottom of the second table, select the date one month from today.

17. Run macros.
    a. Place your insertion point in the cell below "Quantity" and run the **ESS Software** macro using the button on the *Quick Access* toolbar.
    b. Place your insertion point in the first cell in the next row and run the **ESS Support** macro.

18. Update the three formulas in the table beginning with the "Subtotal" formula and continuing down.

19. Save and close the document (Figure 10-91).

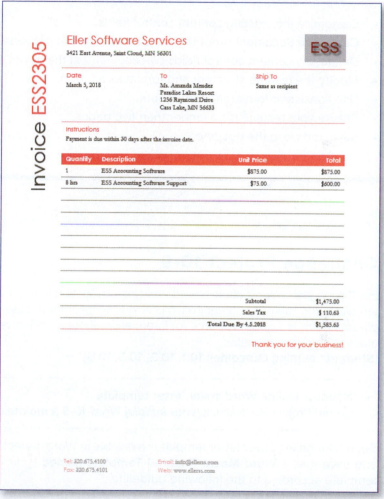

10-91 Word 10-7 completed

Challenge Project 10-8

For this project, you create a résumé based on an online Word template. You can use content from a previous résumé to customize the new résumé. Your college career center is a good resource for information about an effective résumé.
[Student Learning Outcomes 10.1, 10.2]

File Needed: **Online Word resume template**
Completed Project File Name: *[your initials] Word 10-8.docx*

Search the online résumé templates available in Word. Select the résumé template of your choice and save the document as [your initials] Word 10-8. Modify your document according to the following guidelines:

- Customize the existing content control fields.
- Customize document properties and add document property fields as needed.
- Delete any content control fields placeholder text that is not needed.
- Modify the résumé structure and format as needed.
- Use consistent formatting throughout.
- Ensure your résumé is no longer than two pages.
- Save and close the document.

Challenge Project 10-9

For this project, you create a cover letter (job application letter) template based on an online Word template. You can use content from a previous cover letter to customize the new cover letter. Your college career center is a good resource for information about an effective cover letter. Use *Fill-in* fields and macros in your cover letter.
[Student Learning Outcomes 10.1, 10.2, 10.3, 10.5]

File Needed: **Online Word cover letter template**
Completed Project File Names: *[your initials] Word 10-9 template.dotm* and *[your initials] Word 10-9.docm*

Search for online cover letter templates available in Word. Select the cover letter template of your choice and save it as a **Word Macro-Enabled Template** named [your initials] Word 10-9 template. Modify your template according to the following guidelines:

- Customize the existing content and control fields.
- Customize document properties and add document property fields as needed.
- Delete any content control fields placeholder text that is not needed.
- Use *Fill-in* fields for the recipient's name and address and the salutation.
- Record macros for paragraphs of information in the body of the letter. Store these macros in the template so you can customize future cover letters with information from the macros.

- Modify the cover letter structure and format as needed.
- Use consistent formatting throughout and fit the cover letter on one page.
- Save and close the template.

Create a document based on your cover letter template. Customize information in the *Fill-in* field prompts and enable macro content. Insert content from macros as needed. Save the document as a macro-enabled document named [your initials] Word 10-9.

Challenge Project 10-10

Most of your classes have homework assignments, and your professors usually want you to turn in these assignments in a specific format. For example, you might have to include a header with your name, your professor's name, and the name of the assignment. In this project, create a macro-enabled template that you can use for your homework assignments.
[Student Learning Outcomes 10.2, 10.3, 10.4, 10.5]

Files Needed: None
Completed Project File Name: *[your initials] Word 10-10 template.dotm*

Create a new document and save it as a Word Macro-Enabled Template named [your initials] Word 10-10 template. Modify your template according to the following guidelines:

- Plan the macros you want to include in this document.
- Create and record macros for content to insert into your homework assignment document.
- If the macros are similar, copy and edit them to create new macros.
- Assign the macros to a button or keyboard shortcut.
- Include *Fill-in* fields as needed.
- Run macros to confirm they work properly.
- Include a heading to label each macro content in the document.

CHAPTER 11

Working with Forms and Master Documents

CHAPTER OVERVIEW

In previous chapters, you used content control fields in templates and cover pages. In this chapter, you learn how to insert and customize a variety of content control fields. You can use content control fields and templates together to create fill-in forms. You can also group or protect forms so users can only edit the content control fields, which preserves the formatting of your fillable forms.

In Chapter 3, *Collaborating with Others and Working with Reports*, you worked with reports and long documents. In this chapter, you also learn how to manage long documents using a master document and subdocuments. *Outline* view and heading styles are useful tools when you are working with a master document and subdocuments.

STUDENT LEARNING OUTCOMES (SLOs)

After completing this chapter, you will be able to:

SLO 11.1 Insert, customize, and arrange a variety of content control fields (p. W11-643).

SLO 11.2 Insert and customize advanced content control fields where a user selects from a list of choices (p. W11-651).

SLO 11.3 Edit a content control field to change the format and lock content, and use *Design* mode to edit placeholder text (p. W11-653).

SLO 11.4 Group content control fields, protect and edit a form, create a form based on a template, fill in a form, and save a form based on a template (p. W11-659).

SLO 11.5 Manage a long document using a master document that contains subdocuments (p. W11-663).

CASE STUDY

In the first three Pause & Practice projects in this chapter, you create a registration form for Central Sierra Insurance using content control fields. In *Pause & Practice 11-4*, you manage a long report using a master document that contains subdocuments.

Pause & Practice 11-1: Customize a registration form using basic content control fields.

Pause & Practice 11-2: Insert and customize advanced content control fields where users select from options.

Pause & Practice 11-3: Group content control fields, save a form as a template, and create a new document based on the template.

Pause & Practice 11-4: Use a master document containing subdocuments to manage a long report.

WORD

Using Content Control Fields

You are familiar with customizing information in content control fields from *SLO 3.6: Inserting a Cover Page* and *SLO 10.2: Customizing and Using Templates*. In this section, you learn how to insert and customize basic content control fields where users enter information such as their name and company, check a check box, pick a date, or insert a picture. Each content control field has a title and properties associated with it, and you can arrange fields in a document using a variety of formatting methods.

Content Control Fields

Recall that **content control fields** are containers for information or objects. Each content control field is designed to contain a specific type of information. The following table lists basic content control fields and a description of each type:

Content Control Fields

Content Control Field	Use
Rich Text	User types text and the text can be formatted.
Plain Text	User types text and all the text is formatted the same way.
Check Box	User selects or deselects a check box.
Date Picker	User selects a date from a calendar thumbnail.
Picture	User inserts a picture into the content control field.

The size of *Rich Text* and *Plain Text* content control fields adjusts as a user types text in the fields. These content control fields can contain a few words or paragraphs of text. *Check Box* content control fields can be checked or unchecked by a user and do not change in size. *Date Picker* content control fields automatically adjust in size to fit the date format you select. *Picture* content control fields automatically resize to accommodate the picture a user inserts.

Control Content Control Field Arrangement

When you use content control fields in a document or form, the first step is to plan the arrangement of the fields in the document. You can use **tab stops** and **indents** to control the location of the fields in the document and to control how the text wraps to the next line when you are using *Rich Text* or *Plain Text* content control fields.

Tables are also an effective way to arrange content control fields in a document. You can insert one or more content control fields in a cell and use horizontal and vertical alignment to align them in a cell. Use tab stops and indents to arrange content control fields in the cells of a table.

Insert a Rich Text Content Control Field

For an open-ended response from a user, use a **Rich Text content control field** where the user enters a single word, a sentence, or paragraphs of text. Users can also copy text and paste it in a *Rich Text* content control field and apply formatting to individual words in the content control field. In other words, not all text has to be formatted the same. For example, you can apply bold and italic formatting to a specific word or to all of the text entered into the field.

▶HOW TO: Insert a Rich Text Content Control Field

1. Place your insertion point in the document where you want to insert the content control field.

2. Click the **Rich Text Content Control** button [*Developer* tab, *Controls* group] (Figure 11-1). A *Rich Text* content control field displays in the document (Figure 11-2).

   - Click the **handle** of the content control field to select it.
   - Press the **left** or **right** keyboard arrow key to deselect the content control field and move the insertion point to the left or right of the content control field.

11-2 *Rich Text* content control field

11-1 Insert *Rich Text* content control field

   - Move a content control field by selecting the content control field handle and dragging it to a new location.
   - You can also select a content control field, copy it, and paste it in another location.

▶ **ANOTHER WAY**

To copy a content control field, press and hold the **Ctrl** key and drag the content control field to another location.

Content Control Field Properties

After inserting a content control field, add a *title* and a *tag* to the content control field using the **Content Control Properties** dialog box so each content control field has a unique identifier. The content control field title appears on the handle of the field, such as *Name*, *Address*, *Company*, or *Email*. A tag is a unique identifier that is used when the form is connected to a database, and information from the form automatically populates fields in the database. Both *Title* and *Tag* fields are optional.

11-3 *Content Control Properties* dialog box

▶HOW TO: Customize Content Control Field Properties

1. Select the content control field and click the **Properties** button [*Developer* tab, *Control* group]. The *Content Control Properties* dialog box opens (Figure 11-3).

2. Click the **Title** text box and type a title for the content control field.

3. Click the **Tag** text box and type a tag for the content control field.

   - You do not have to include a tag unless you are connecting your form to a database.

4. Click **OK** to close the *Content Control Properties* dialog box.

- The title of the content control field appears on the handle of the field (Figure 11-4).

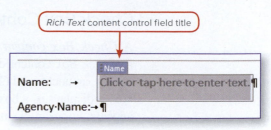
MORE INFO

See *SLO 11.3: Editing Content Control Fields* for additional information about customizing content control fields.

11-4 Content control field title displayed on the handle

Plain Text Content Control Field

The main differences between a *Rich Text* and a **Plain Text content control field** is how the text is formatted in the field and how multiple paragraphs of text display in these fields. Text in a *Plain Text* content control field is all formatted the same. You can apply bold or italic formatting, but all of the text in the field will have the same formatting. In a *Rich Text* content control field, individual words can be formatted independently of other words in the field.

In addition, *Plain Text* content control fields, by default, can contain only one paragraph of text. You can change the properties of the *Plain Text* content control field to allow users to use *Enter* to type text on a new line or include multiple paragraphs of text. Word automatically inserts a line break (*Shift+Enter*) rather than a paragraph break (*Enter*) when the user presses **Enter**.

▶**HOW TO:** Insert and Customize a Plain Text Content Control Field

1. Place your insertion point in the document where you want to insert the content control field.

2. Click the **Plain Text Content Control** button [*Developer* tab, *Controls* group] to insert a *Plain Text* content control field (Figure 11-5).

11-5 Insert *Plain Text* content control field

3. Select the content control field and click the **Properties** button [*Developer* tab, *Control* group] to open the *Content Control Properties* dialog box (Figure 11-6).

4. Click the **Title** text box and type a title for the content control field.

5. Allow users to type multiple lines of text by checking the **Allow carriage returns (multiple paragraphs)** box.

- Check this box if you want users to be able to use *Enter* to insert a paragraph break between lines or paragraphs of text.

6. Click **OK** to close the *Content Control Properties* dialog box.

11-6 Allow multiple lines of text in a *Plain Text* content control field

MORE INFO

Plain Text and *Rich Text* fields appear the same when inserted in a document.

Check Box Content Control Field

A **Check Box content control field** allows users to select an option by clicking a check box. A *Check Box* content control field limits users to only two options: checked or unchecked. By default, an unchecked *Check Box* content control field is an open box, and when the user checks the box, it displays as a box with an **X** in it. You can customize how the unchecked and checked box appears. For example, use a check mark symbol for the checked *Check Box* content control field.

▶**HOW TO:** Insert and Customize a Check Box Content Control Field

1. Place your insertion point in the document where you want to insert the content control field.

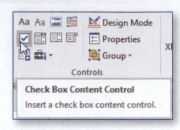

2. Click the **Check Box Content Control** button [*Developer* tab, *Controls* group] to insert a *Check Box* content control field (Figure 11-7).
   - A *Check Box* content control field is, by default, unchecked.

3. Select the content control field and click the **Properties** button [*Developer* tab, *Control* field] to open the *Content Control Properties* dialog box.

11-7 Insert *Check Box* content control field

4. Click the **Title** text box and type the title of the content control field.

5. Change the checked or unchecked symbol by clicking the **Change** button (Figure 11-8). The *Symbol* dialog box opens (Figure 11-9).

11-8 Change check box content control symbol

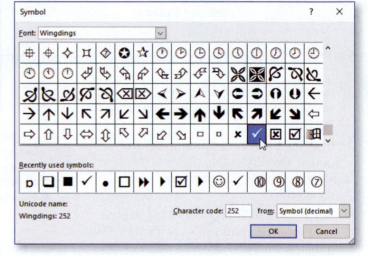

6. Click the **Font** drop-down list, select a font set, and select a symbol to use.
   - Alternatively, you can select a symbol from the *Recently used symbols* area.

7. Click **OK** to close the *Symbols* dialog box.

8. Click **OK** to close the *Content Control Properties* dialog box.

11-9 *Symbol* dialog box

Content control field drop-down arrow

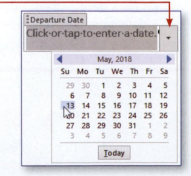

Date Picker Content Control Field

The **Date Picker content control field** provides a calendar thumbnail where the user selects a date rather than typing a date (Figure 11-10). This ensures consistency in how dates display in the document. You can control the format of the date in the *Content Control Properties* dialog box.

11-10 *Date Picker* content control field

1. Place your insertion point in the document where you want to insert the content control field.

2. Click the **Date Picker Content Control** button [*Developer* tab, *Controls* group] to insert a *Date Picker* content control field (Figure 11-11).

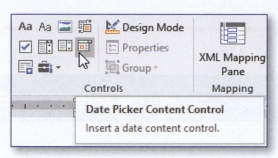

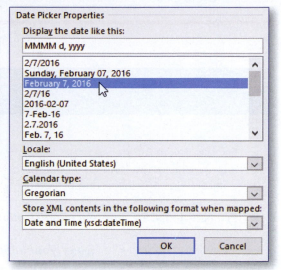

11-11 Insert *Date Picker* content control field

3. Select the content control field and click the **Properties** button [*Developer* tab, *Control* group] to open the *Content Control Properties* dialog box.

4. Click the **Title** text box and type a title for the content control field.

5. Select the date format from the list in the *Date Picker Properties* area in the *Content Control Properties* dialog box (Figure 11-12).

6. Click **OK** to close the *Content Control Properties* dialog box.

11-12 Select the date format

Picture Content Control Field

A ***Picture content control field*** allows the user to insert a picture at a specific location in the document (Figure 11-13). For example, you might use this type of content control field in a real estate listing template where a picture of the home displays in a specific location in the template. A *Picture* content control field automatically resizes to fit the selected picture. You can arrange a *Picture* content control field in a document the same way you arrange a picture with text wrapping and alignment.

When you use a *Picture* content control field, it is important to consider how the inserted picture will affect the layout of the existing text and content in the document. Position the *Picture* content control field in a location that does not negatively affect other text and fields in the document.

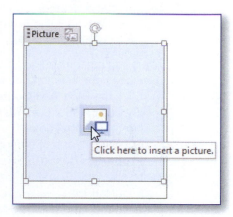

11-13 *Picture* content control field

1. Place your insertion point in the document where you want to insert the content control field.

2. Click the **Picture Content Control** button [*Developer* tab, *Controls* group] to insert a *Picture* content control field (Figure 11-14).

11-14 Insert *Picture* content control field

3. Select the content control field and click the **Properties** button [*Developer* tab, *Control* group] to open the *Content Control Properties* dialog box.

4. Click the **Title** text box and type a title for the content control field.

5. Click **OK** to close the *Content Control Properties* dialog box.

For this Pause & Practice project, you modify an existing document from Central Sierra Insurance to create a fill-in registration form for a conference. You set a tab stop and indents to control alignment of content control fields and insert and customize content control fields.

File Needed: ***CSIConferenceRegistration-11.docx*** *(student data files are available in the* Library *of your SIMnet account)*
Completed Project File Name: *[your initials] PP W11-1.docx*

1. Open the ***CSIConferenceRegistration-11*** document from your student data files.

2. Save the document as a Word document named [your initials] PP W11-1.

3. Add a tab stop and set a hanging indent.
   a. Check the **Ruler** box [*View* tab, *Show* group] to display the ruler if it is not already displayed.
   b. Select the "**Name:**" and "**Agency Name:**" paragraphs and set a **1" left** tab stop.
   c. Select the next two paragraphs of text ("**Yes**, . . ." and "**No**, . . ."), set a **0.25" hanging** indent, and set a **0.25" left** tab stop.

4. Insert and customize *Rich Text* content control fields.
   a. Place your insertion point after "Name:" and press **Tab**.
   b. Click the **Rich Text Content Control** button [*Developer* tab, *Controls* group] to insert a *Rich Text* content control field.
   c. Select the content control field and click the **Properties** button [*Developer* tab, *Controls* group] to open the *Content Control Properties* dialog box (Figure 11-15).
   d. Click the **Title** text box, type Name, and click **OK** to close the dialog box.
   e. Place your insertion point after "Agency Name:" and press **Tab**.
   f. Insert a **Rich Text** content control field.
   g. Click the **Properties** button to open the *Content Control Properties* dialog box, type Agency Name as the *Title*, and click **OK**.
   h. Place your insertion point after "Arrival Time:" in the "Travel" section of the document and press **Tab**.
   i. Insert a **Rich Text** content control field.
   j. Open the *Content Control Properties* dialog box, type Arrival Time as the *Title*, and click **OK**.
   k. Place your insertion point after "Departure Time:" and press **Tab**.
   l. Insert a **Rich Text** content control field.
   m. Open the *Content Control Properties* dialog box, type Departure Time as the *Title*, and click **OK**.

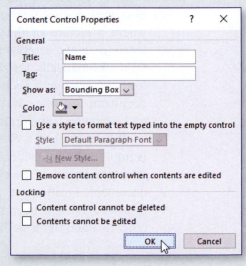

11-15 Add a title to the content control field

5. Insert *Check Box* content control fields, customize the properties, and change the symbol.

   a. Place your insertion point before "Yes, . . ." and click the **Check Box Content Control** button [*Developer* tab, *Controls* group] to insert a *Check Box* content control field.

   b. Open the *Content Control Properties* dialog box and type Attending as the *Title* (Figure 11-16).

   c. Click the **Change** button to the right of *Checked symbol*. The *Symbol* dialog box opens (Figure 11-17).

   d. Click the **Font** drop-down list and select **Wingdings**.

   e. Select the **check mark** symbol (character code 252).

   f. Click **OK** to close the *Symbol* dialog box and click **OK** to close the *Content Control Properties* dialog box.

   g. Press the **right** arrow key two times to deselect the *Check Box* content control field and position the insertion point between the content control field and the text.

   h. Press **Tab**.

   i. Place your insertion point before "No, . . ." and insert a **Check Box** content control field.

   j. Open the *Content Control Properties* dialog box and type Not Attending as the *Title*.

   k. Click the **Change** button to the right of *Checked symbol*, select the **check mark** symbol (*Wingdings* character code 252), click **OK** to close the *Symbol* dialog box, and click **OK** to close the *Content Control Properties* dialog box.

   l. Press the **right** arrow key two times to deselect the content control field and position the insertion point between the content control field and the text and press **Tab**.

11-16 Change symbol for check box content control field

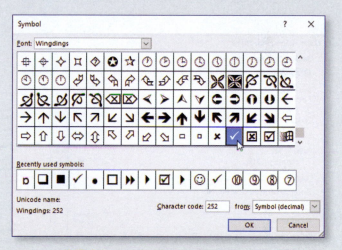

11-17 Select symbol for check box content control field

6. Insert and customize *Check Box* content control fields.

   a. Place your insertion point before "I will be staying . . .", insert a **Check Box** content control field, and customize the content control properties to include Staying at Northgate as the *Title*. For all of the *Check Box* content control fields in step 6, *don't* change the *Checked symbol* as you did in step 5.

   b. Use the **right** arrow key to deselect the content control field and position the insertion point between the content control field and the text, and press **Tab** (Figure 11-18).

   c. Place your insertion point before "I will not be staying . . .", insert a **Check Box** content control field, and customize the content control properties to include Not Staying at Northgate as the *Title*.

   d. Deselect the content control field and **Tab** between the content control field and the text.

   e. Place your insertion point before "I will be driving . . .", insert a **Check Box** content control field, and customize the content control properties to include Driving as the *Title*.

   f. Deselect the content control field and press **Tab** between the content control field and the text.

   g. Place your insertion point before "I will be flying . . .", insert a **Check Box** content control field, and customize the content control properties to include Flying as the *Title*.

   h. Deselect the content control field and press **Tab** between the content control field and the text.

i. Place your insertion point between the tab and "I need a shuttle . . .", insert a **Check Box** content control field, and customize the content control properties to include Shuttle as the *Title*.

j. Deselect the content control field and press **Tab** between the content control field and the text.

k. Compare your document with Figure 11-18 to confirm the correct placement of the check box content control fields.

7. Insert and customize a *Date Picker* content control field.

a. Place your insertion point after "Departure Date:" and press **Tab**.

b. Click the **Date Picker Content Control** button.

c. Open the *Content Control Properties* dialog box and type Departure Date as the *Title*.

d. Click the **Display the date like this** text box, delete the existing text, and type MMMM d to display the month and day only (Figure 11-19).

e. Click **OK** to close the dialog box.

11-18 *Check Box* content control fields inserted

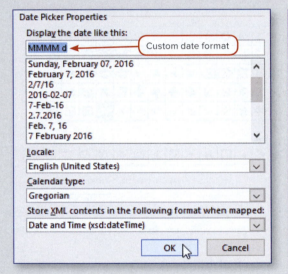

11-19 **Type specific date format**

8. Confirm none of the *Check Box* content control fields are checked.

9. Save and close the document (Figure 11-20).

11-20 **PP W11-1 completed**

SLO 11.2   Using Advanced Content Control Fields

In addition to the content control fields you learned about in *SLO 11.1: Using Content Control Fields*, other content control fields allow users to select from pre-defined options. The *Combo Box* and *Drop-Down List* content control fields allow users to choose from a list of choices that you create. These content control fields limit the responses of users and save users time by allowing them to select an option from the list rather than typing a response. The *Building Block Gallery* content control field lets users insert a building block. *Legacy Tools* are form fields that are available in older versions of Word.

Combo Box Content Control Field

A **Combo Box content control field** lists user options in the form of a drop-down list (Figure 11-21). When you insert a *Combo Box* content control field, you create the list of options in the *Content Control Properties* dialog box. This type of content control field also

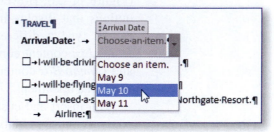

11-21 *Combo Box* content control field

allows users the option of typing their own responses in the field. For example, create a list of dates from which users can choose, but they also have the option of typing a different date.

▶ **HOW TO:** Insert and Customize a Combo Box Content Control Field

1. Place your insertion point in the document where you want to insert the content control field.

2. Click the **Combo Box Content Control** button [*Developer* tab, *Controls* group] to insert a *Combo Box* content control field (Figure 11-22).

3. Select the content control field and click the **Properties** button [*Developer* tab, *Controls* group] to open the *Content Control Properties* dialog box.

4. Click the **Title** text box and type a title for the content control field.

5. Click the **Add** button in the *Drop-Down List Properties* area (Figure 11-23). The *Add Choice* dialog box opens (Figure 11-24).

6. Click the **Display Name** text box and type a choice.

   - The *Value* field automatically displays the same text that you type in the *Display Name* area.
   - You can change the *Value* text so it is different from the *Display Name*, but normally these two fields are the same.

7. Click **OK** (or press **Enter**) to close the *Add Choice* dialog box.

   - Use the **Add** button to insert additional drop-down list options to the *Combo Box*.
   - Alternatively, press **Enter** two times to add a choice and to open the *Add Choice* dialog box.

8. Customize the drop-down list to modify, remove, or reorder drop-down list choices.

   - Select an item in the list and click **Modify** to change an option in the list.
   - Select an item in the list and click **Remove** to remove an option from the list.

11-22 Insert *Combo Box* content control field

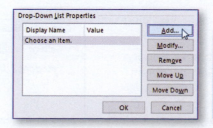

11-23 *Drop-Down List Properties*

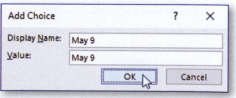

11-24 *Add Choice* dialog box

- Select an item in the list and click **Move Up** or **Move Down** to reorder the list.
- You can remove the "Choose an item" option.

9. Click **OK** to close the *Content Control Properties* dialog box.

Drop-Down List Content Control Field

A ***Drop-Down List content control field*** is similar to a *Combo Box* content control field (Figure 11-25). However, users are limited to the options that display in the drop-down list; they cannot type a different response in the *Drop-Down List* content control field. *Drop-Down List* and *Combo Box* content control fields display the same in a document.

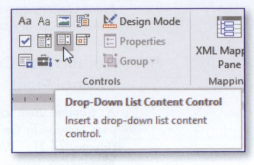

You insert and customize a *Drop-Down List* content control field the same way you insert and customize a *Combo Box* content control field. See *How To: Insert and Customize a Combo Box Content Control Field* on the previous page.

11-25 Insert *Drop-Down List* content control field

Building Block Gallery Content Control Field

A ***Building Block Gallery content control field*** allows users to insert a building block from the building block gallery you specify. The advantage of using a *Building Block Gallery* content control field rather than just inserting a building block is that you control where the building block displays in the document. For example, if you create a form letter, you could save paragraphs of text as individual building blocks in *the AutoText* building block gallery and then insert a *Building Block Gallery* content control field. Users would then select the appropriate *AutoText* building block from the *Building Block Gallery* content control field to insert the building block in a specific location in the document.

▶ **HOW TO:** Insert and Customize a Building Block Gallery Content Control Field

1. Place your insertion point in the document where you want to insert the content control field.

2. Click the **Building Block Gallery Content Control** button [*Developer* tab, *Controls* group] to insert a *Building Block Gallery* content control field (Figure 11-26).

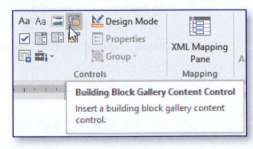

3. Select the content control field and click the **Properties** button [*Developer* tab, *Controls* group] to open the *Content Control Properties* dialog box.

4. Click the **Title** text box and type a title for the content control field.

11-26 Insert *Building Block Gallery* content control field

5. Click the **Gallery** drop-down list to select a building block gallery (Figure 11-27).

- *Quick Parts* is the default building block category when you insert a *Building Block Gallery* content control field.
- To limit the user's choice to building blocks from a specific category, click the **Category** drop-down list and select a category.

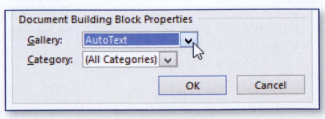

11-27 Select the *Building Block* gallery and category

6. Click **OK** to close the *Content Control Properties* dialog box.

    • Users click the drop-down list in the *Building Block Gallery* content control field to select a building block to insert (Figure 11-28).

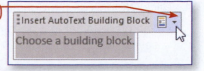
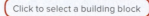

11-28 *Building Block Gallery drop-down list*

Legacy Tools

Legacy tools are a set of form fields from previous versions of Word that can still be used in current versions (Figure 11-29). Whereas content control fields function in both documents and templates even if the document or template is not protected, legacy tools function only in protected templates.

Legacy tools include *Legacy Forms* and *ActiveX Controls* fields. You can insert legacy form fields into forms, and they are very similar to content control fields (but they only function in a protected template). *ActiveX* control fields require macros to function and are usually used in web pages.

11-29 Legacy tools

SLO 11.3

Editing Content Control Fields

After you create your form and insert content control fields, you can change the color of the content control fields, how the content control fields display in the document, or how content control fields display after users enter information. You also have the option to lock content control fields and the content in these fields. Use *Design* mode to change the placeholder text for content control fields.

Apply a Style to a Content Control Field

When you insert content control fields where users type text (*Rich Text* or *Plain Text*) or select an item from a list (*Combo Box*, *Drop-Down List*, or *Date Picker*), the text users type or select displays with the style of the paragraph where the content control field is located.

For example, if you insert a *Rich Text* or *Plain Text* content control field in a paragraph that is formatted with the *Normal* style, the text you type or select is formatted in *Normal* style. You can change the style that is applied to the text typed in a content control field.

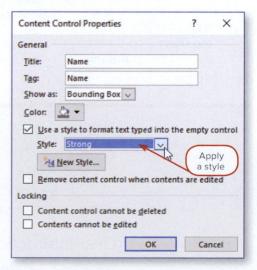

11-30 Apply a style to content control field contents

▶ **HOW TO:** Apply a Style to a Content Control Field

1. Select the content control field to modify and click the **Properties** button [*Developer* tab, *Controls* group] to open the *Content Control Properties* dialog box (Figure 11-30).

2. Check the **Use a style to format text typed into the empty control** box.

3. Click the **Style** drop-down list and select a style to apply to the contents of the content control field.

    • Alternatively, you can click **New Style** to create a new style to apply.

4. Click **OK** to close the *Content Control Properties* dialog box.
   - The placeholder text does not display in the selected style; the selected style applies only to text users type or select.

Change Content Control Display and Color

You can change how content control fields display in your document and the color of the content control field. When you insert a content control field, it is, by default, shown as a ***bounding box***, which displays with a border and handle. You can change the settings so the content control field displays with ***start and end tags***, so the content control fields are more visible in the document. Content control fields can also display with no border or start and end tags, which is the *None* option. The *None* option displays the content control field with only shading.

▶ HOW TO: Change Content Control Display and Color

1. Select the content control field you want to modify and click the **Properties** button [*Developer* tab, *Controls* group] to open the *Content Control Properties* dialog box (Figure 11-31).

2. Click the **Show as** drop down list and select from the three options: **Bounding Box** (Figure 11-32), **Start/End Tag** (Figure 11-33), or **None** (Figure 11-34).

3. Click the **Color** drop-down list and select a color for the content control field.
   - By default, the theme of the document controls the color of content control fields.
   - To change the content control field back to the theme color after you have changed it, click the **Color** drop-down list and select **Automatic**.

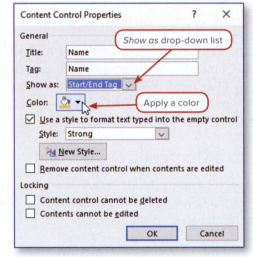

11-31 Modify content control field display and color

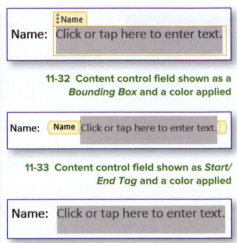

11-32 Content control field shown as a *Bounding Box* and a color applied

11-33 Content control field shown as *Start/End Tag* and a color applied

11-34 Content control field shown as *None* and a color applied

4. Click **OK** to close the *Content Control Properties* dialog box.

User Interaction with Content Control Fields

When working with content control fields, you control what happens to the content control field when a user interacts with it. By default, the content control field remains in a document when a user types or selects text. However, you can customize a content control field so it is removed from the document when a user edits the contents of the field. In other words, the text replaces the content control field. For example, in many online templates, content control fields are removed when a user types text or selects an option.

If you check the **Remove content control when contents are edited** box, the text a user types or selects in the content control field replaces the control field (Figure 11-35). When this happens, only the text or selection remains in the document. If this box is not checked, the content control field remains in the document after the user edits the contents of the content control field. When using grouping or protection on forms (covered in *SLO 11.4: Using Forms*), do not check the *Remove content control when contents are edited* box in the *Content Control Properties* dialog box. Checking the box prevents users from typing information in these fields.

11-35 Remove content control when contents are edited

Lock a Content Control Field

When using content control fields in a document, you have the ability to lock a field so the user cannot delete and/or edit it. Locking a content control field so it cannot be deleted prevents users from inadvertently deleting a content control field. If a content control field is locked so users cannot delete it, the user can still edit the contents of the content control field. You can also lock a content control so users cannot edit the contents of the field.

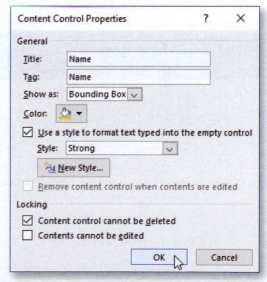

11-36 Lock a content control field

▶**HOW TO:** Lock Content Control Fields

1. Select the content control field to modify and click the **Properties** button [*Developer* tab, *Controls* group] to open the *Content Control Properties* dialog box (Figure 11-36).

2. Check the **Content control cannot be deleted** box in the *Locking* area to prevent users from deleting the content control field.

3. Check the **Contents cannot be edited** box to prevent users from editing the content control field.

4. Click **OK** to close the *Content Control Properties* dialog box.

Design Mode

Use **Design mode** to view and edit content control fields in your document. When you insert a content control field in a document, Word automatically inserts placeholder text (such as "Click or tap here to enter text.") in the field (with the exception of *Picture* and *Check Box* content controls). In *Design* mode, you can customize the placeholder text and easily view the content control fields in your document.

▶HOW TO: Use Design Mode to Edit Placeholder Text

1. Click the **Design Mode** button [*Developer* tab, *Controls* group] to turn on *Design* mode.
   - Start and end tags display in *Design* mode.
2. Click the content control field **start tag** to select the placeholder text to modify (Figure 11-37).
3. Type the new placeholder text.
4. Click the **Design Mode** button to turn off *Design* mode.

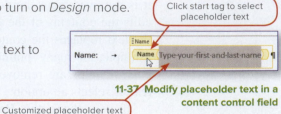

Click start tag to select placeholder text

Customized placeholder text

11-37 Modify placeholder text in a content control field

> **MORE INFO**
>
> When you use *Design* mode, the formatting and layout of your document may display differently. When you turn off *Design* mode, the formatting and layout displays correctly.

Delete a Content Control Field

When customizing a document or form containing content control fields, you might need to delete an existing content control field. The following are two different ways to remove a content control field:

- Click the handle of the content control field to select it and press **Delete**. This method deletes the content control field and the contents of the field.
- Right-click the content control field and select **Remove Content Control** from the context menu. This method removes the content control field but not the contents of the field if the contents have been edited. The contents of field remain in the document.

PAUSE & PRACTICE: WORD 11-2

For this Pause & Practice project, you work with the form from *Pause & Practice 11-1*. You insert content control fields, modify the properties of the content control fields, and use *Design* mode to change the placeholder text.

File Needed: *[your initials] PP W11-1.docx*
Completed Project File Name: *[your initials] PP W11-2.docx*

1. Open the *[your initials] PP W11-1* you completed in *Pause & Practice 11-1*.

2. Save the document as [your initials] PP W11-2.

3. Insert and customize a *Drop-Down List* content control field.
   a. Place your insertion point on the blank line below "Type of Room" and click the **Drop-Down List Content Control** button [*Developer* tab, *Controls* group] to insert a *Drop-Down List* content control field.
   b. Click the **Properties** button [*Developer* tab, *Controls* group] to open the *Content Control Properties* dialog box (Figure 11-38).

c. Type *Room Type* in the *Title* area.
d. Check the **Content control cannot be deleted** box.
e. Click the **Add** button to open the *Add Choice* dialog box.
f. Type *Non-Smoking* in the *Display Name* area and press **Enter** (or click **OK**) to close the *Add Choice* dialog box.
g. Press **Enter** again (or click **Add**) to open the *Add Choice* dialog box.
h. Type *Smoking* in the *Display Name* area and press **Enter** to close the *Add Choice* dialog box.
i. Select **Choose an item** in the *Drop-Down List Properties* area and click the **Remove** button to remove this option from the list (see Figure 11-38).
j. Click **OK** to close the *Content Control Properties* dialog box.
k. Use the **right** arrow key to deselect the *Drop-Down List* content control field and press **Tab** to position your insertion point centered below "Type of Bed."

4. Insert another *Drop-Down List* content control field.
a. With your insertion point below "Type of Bed," insert a **Drop-Down List** content control field.
b. Open the *Content Control Properties* dialog box, type *Bed Type* as the *Title*, and check the **Content control cannot be deleted** box.
c. Add the following choices: *King*, *Queen*, and *Two Doubles*.
d. Remove **Choose an item** from the list of choices and click **OK** to close the dialog box.
e. Press the **right** arrow key to deselect the *Drop-Down List* content control field and press **Tab** to position your insertion point below "Number of Nights".

5. Insert *Combo Box* content control fields.
a. With your insertion point below "Number of Nights", insert a **Combo Box** content control field.
b. Open the *Content Control Properties* dialog box, type *Number of Nights* as the *Title*, and check the **Content control cannot be deleted** box.
c. Add the following choices: *1*, *2*, *3*, and *4*.
d. Remove **Choose an item** from the list of choices and click **OK** to close the dialog box.
e. Place your insertion point after "Arrival Date:", press **Tab**, and insert a **Combo Box** content control field.
f. Open the *Content Control Properties* dialog box, type *Arrival Date* as the *Title*, and check the **Content control cannot be deleted** box.
g. Add the following choices: *May 9*, *May 10*, and *May 11*.
h. Remove **Choose an item** from the list of choices and click **OK** to close the dialog box.
i. Place your insertion point after "Airline:", press **Tab**, and insert a **Combo Box** content control field.
j. Open the *Content Control Properties* dialog box, type *Airline* as the *Title*, and check the **Content control cannot be deleted** box.
k. Add the following choices: *American*, *Delta*, *Southwest*, and *United*.
l. Remove **Choose an item** from the list of choices and click **OK** to close the dialog box.

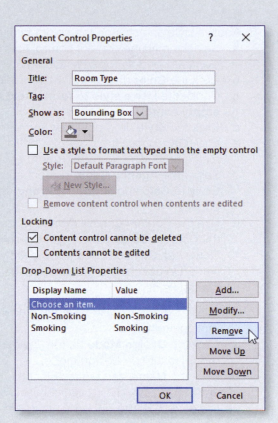

11-38 Insert and customize a *Drop-Down List* content control field

6. Apply a style and change the color of content control fields.
   a. Select the **Name** content control field and open the *Content Control Properties* dialog box (Figure 11-39).
   b. Click the **Color** drop-down list and select **Gold**.
   c. Check the **Use a style to format text typed into the empty control** box.
   d. Click the **Style** drop-down list and select **Strong**.
   e. Click **OK** to close the *Content Control Properties* dialog box.
   f. Select the **Agency Name** content control field change the *Color* to **Gold** and apply the **Strong** style (see steps 6b–e above).
   g. Use the *Content Control Properties* dialog box to change the *Color* to **Gold** on all of the remaining *Rich Text*, *Drop-Down List*, *Combo Box*, and *Date Picker* content control fields. Do not change the color on the *Check Box* content control fields.

7. Use *Design* mode to customize the placeholder text on content control fields.
   a. Click the **Design Mode** button [*Developer* tab, *Controls* group] to turn on *Design* mode.
   b. Click the **Name** start tag to select the placeholder text and type Type your first and last name as the placeholder text (Figure 11-40).
   c. Use the following information to customize the placeholder text on other content control fields.
   Agency Name: Type your agency name
   Room Type: Select room type
   Bed Type: Select bed type
   Number of Nights: Select or type # of nights
   Arrival Date: Select or type arrival date
   Airline: Select or type airline
   Arrival Time: Type arrival time
   Departure Time: Type departure time
   Departure Date: Select departure date
   d. Click the **Design Mode** button to turn off *Design* mode.

8. Save and close the document (Figure 11-41).

11-39 Change the color and add a style to a content control field

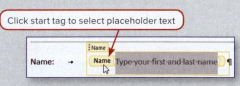

11-40 Customize placeholder text using *Design* mode

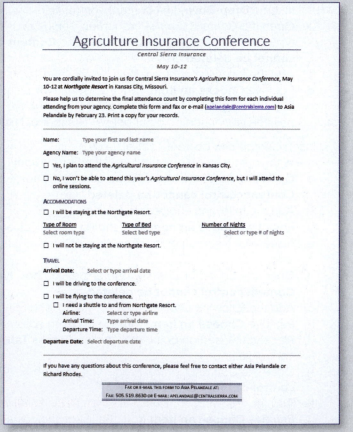

11-41 PP W11-2 completed

SLO 11.4

Using Forms

After you insert and customize content control fields to create a form, you need to determine how to set up your form so others can use it. In Chapters 5 and 10, you learned how to create and use a template, which is an excellent way to save a form. Saving the form as a template allows users to create a new document based upon the form template so the original form is not modified.

When you create a form, usually you want the users to fill in only the contents of the form fields without modifying the structure of the form. Grouping form fields prevents the form from being modified while allowing editing of content control fields. You can also use the protect feature to allow editing of content control fields while protecting other parts of the form.

Group Content Control Fields

The *Group* feature protects the content and format of a document containing content control fields but still allows users to edit the contents of content control fields. The *Group* feature locks all parts of a document except content control fields. An advantage of using the *Group* feature with content control fields in a document is that users can fill in these fields, and you do not need to save a document as a template. For example, you can create a fillable registration form, save it as a document, and group the content control fields. You can then email this registration form to users, who can edit only the contents of the form fields and save and return the form.

▶HOW TO: Group Content Control Fields

11-42 Group content control fields

1. Open the document containing the content control fields.
2. Select the entire document (**Ctrl+A**).
3. Click the **Group** button [*Developer* tab, *Controls* group] and select **Group** from the drop-down list (Figure 11-42).
   - Grouping protects the text and formatting in the document but still allows users to edit the contents of content control fields.
   - To turn off grouping, select the entire document, click the **Group** button, and select **Ungroup**.

Save a Form as a Template

Grouping content control fields is useful when the form is not going to be used again by the same person. Saving a form as a ***template*** is a good idea if the form is going to be reused. For example, a business can create an expense form that users complete each week to report expenses. In this case, it is best to save the form as a template so the form can be reused, and users can create a new expense report document based upon the template each week. This preserves the original template.

▶HOW TO: Save a Form as a Template

1. Open the form you want to save as a template.
2. Open the *Save As* dialog box.
3. Type a file name for the template in the *File name* area.
4. Click the **Save as type** drop-down list and select **Word Template**.
5. Browse to the location on your computer or *OneDrive* where you want to save the document.
6. Click **Save** to close the dialog box and save the template.

Protect a Form

Like grouping, using **Restrict Editing** is another way to protect a form. *Restrict Editing* is commonly used with forms that are saved as templates and controls what areas of the document or template can be edited. You can use *Restrict Editing* to allow users to fill in forms while protecting the content and layout of the document.

▶ **HOW TO:** Protect a Form

1. Open the form you want to protect.

2. Click the **Restrict Editing** button [*Developer* tab, *Protect* group]. The *Restrict Editing* pane opens on the right (Figure 11-43).

3. Check the **Allow only this type of editing in the document** box.

4. Click the drop-down list and select **Filling in forms**.

5. Click the **Yes**, **Start Enforcing Protection** button. The *Start Enforcing Protection* dialog box opens (Figure 11-44).

   - Protecting the document with a password is optional.
   - If you want to use a password, type a password in the *Enter new password* text box and type it again in the *Reenter password to confirm* text box.
   - If you don't want to use a password, leave both of the text boxes blank.

6. Press **OK** to close the *Start Enforcing Protection* dialog box.

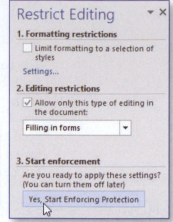

11-43 Restrict Editing pane

11-44 Start Enforcing Protection dialog box

To turn off restrict editing, click the **Stop Protection** button in the *Restrict Editing* pane (Figure 11-45). If you used a password to restrict editing, Word prompts you to type the password in the *Unprotect Document* dialog box to turn off restrict editing.

▶ **MORE INFO**

When using grouping or protection on forms, do not check the *Remove content control when contents are edited* box in the *Content Control Properties* dialog box. Checking the box prevents users from typing information in these fields.

11-45 Stop protecting a document

Open and Fill in a Form

After you finish creating your form, inserting and customizing content control fields, and grouping content control fields or protecting the form, you are ready to fill out the form by editing the contents of content control fields.

▶ HOW TO: Open and Fill in a Form

1. Open a form containing the content control fields.
   - If the form is a document, open from within Word.
   - If the form is a template, open a *File Explorer* window and double-click the template file to create a document based on the template.
2. Select a content control field and type information, check a box, or select from a drop-down list.
3. Press the **Tab** key to move from field to field or click the next field.
   - Don't press *Tab* after typing information in a *Rich Text* or *Plain Text* content control field, which inserts a tab after the text you typed. Instead, click the next field to fill in information.
   - On *Check Box* content control fields, click the box or press the **spacebar** to select or deselect the check box.
   - On *Combo Box*, *Drop-Down List*, *Date Picker*, and *Building Block Gallery* content control fields, click the **drop-down arrow** on the right to view selections (Figure 11-46).
   - On *Picture* content control fields, click the **icon** in the middle to select a picture to insert.
4. Save and close the document when you finish filling in the form.

11-46 Filling in a form

Edit and Save a Form

You can add, copy, or move content control fields in an existing form. You can also customize the properties of each content control field or use *Design* mode to change the placeholder text. To edit a template, open the template from within Word, so you open the template file rather than creating a document based on the template. If you have grouped content control fields or restricted editing of the document, use **Ungroup** to ungroup content control fields or **Stop Protection** to edit the content control fields in the document. After editing your form, group content control fields or restrict editing of the document, and then save the document.

PAUSE & PRACTICE: WORD 11-3

For this Pause & Practice project, you finalize the form you modified in *Pause & Practice 11-2*. You save the form as a template, group content control fields, create a document based on the form template, and fill in content control fields.

File Needed: ***[your initials] PP W11-2.docx***
Completed Project File Names: ***[your initials] PP W11-3 form.dotx*** and ***[your initials] PP W11-3.docx***

1. Open the ***[your initials] PP W11-2*** file you completed in *Pause & Practice 11-2*.

2. Save the document as a **Word Template** named [your initials] PP W11-3 form and select the location to save the template.

3. Group content control fields.
   a. Select the entire document (**Ctrl+A**).
   b. Click the **Group** button [*Developer* tab, *Controls* group] and select **Group** from the drop-down list.

4. Save and close the template.

5. Create a new document based upon a template and save the new document.
   a. Open a *File Explorer* window and locate the ***[your initials] PP W11-3 form*** template.
   b. Double-click the template file to create a document based on the template.
   c. Save this new document as a *Word Document* named [your initials] PP W11-3. If prompted to save changes to the template, click **Yes**.

6. Fill in the conference registration form.
   a. Type Jennie Owings in the *Name* field.
   b. Type Central Sierra Insurance in the *Agency Name* field.
   c. Check the **Attending** box ("Yes, I plan to attend. . .").
   d. Check the **Staying at Northgate** box.
   e. Click the **Room Type** drop-down list and select **Non-Smoking**.
   f. Click the **Bed Type** drop-down list and select **King**.
   g. Click the **Number of Nights** drop-down list and select **4**.
   h. Type May 8 in the *Arrival Date* field. Since "May 8" is not a selection in the drop-down list, you must type the arrival date.
   i. Check the **Flying** and **Shuttle** boxes.
   j. Click the **Airline** drop-down list and select **United**.
   k. Type 9:45 a.m. in the *Arrival Time* field.
   l. Type 6:20 p.m. in the *Departure Time* field.
   m. Click the **Departure Date** *Date Picker* field and select **May 12**.

7. Save and close the document (Figure 11-47). If prompted to save changes to the template, click **Yes**. If prompted to save styles and building blocks, click **Don't Save**.

11-47 PP W11-3 completed

SLO 11.5

Working with a Master Document

When you are working with a long document, you may want to combine multiple documents into one ***master document***. A master document can contain existing text and includes text from one or more ***subdocuments***. A subdocument is a file you insert and link to a master document. For example, you might work on a report with others where each person is responsible for writing a section of the report. You can insert and link each person's contributions as a subdocument in the master document.

Outline View

You have worked extensively with heading styles in previous chapters. Recall that in Chapters 2 and 6, you applied styles to headings, such as *Heading 1* and *Heading 2*, to organize long documents and to create a table of contents based on the document headings. Apply heading styles to show the outline structure of your document. ***Outline view*** displays your document as an outline so you can easily rearrange sections of your document. For example, change a heading level by promoting it to a higher-level heading or demoting it to a lower-level heading. You can also add, delete, or edit text in *Outline* view. When you use *Outline* view, the ***Outlining tab*** displays. When working with master and subdocuments, use *Outline* view.

> ▶ **HOW TO:** Use Outline View

1. Click the **Outline** button [*View* tab, *Views* group] to display the document in *Outline* view and to open the *Outlining* tab (Figure 11-48).
   - Text with a heading style applied has a ***section selector*** (plus icon) to the left.
   - Text with *Normal* style (*Body* style) or other styles applied has an open circle bullet to the left of the first line.

2. Click the **section selector** (plus icon) to the left of a heading to select the heading and text in that section.

3. Click the **Promote** or **Demote** button to change the level of a selected heading.
   - Alternatively, you can click the **Outline Level** drop-down list and select a heading level to apply or click the **Promote to Heading 1** or **Demote to Body Text** button.

4. Click the **Move Up** or **Move Down** button to move selected text up or down in the outline.

5. Click the **Expand** or **Collapse** button to expand or collapse a section.
   - Alternatively, double-click the **section selector** to the left of a heading to expand or collapse a section.

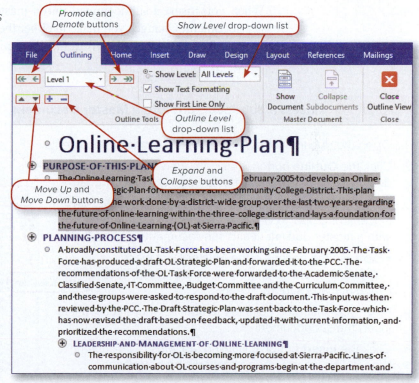

11-48 Using *Outline* view and the *Outlining* tab

6. Click the **Show Level** drop-down list to select which levels display in the outline.
   - By default, all levels display.
7. Check the **Show Text Formatting** check box to display the style formatting.
   - If this check box is not selected, text in the outline displays without styles applied.
8. Check the **Show First Line Only** box to display only one line of text for each heading in the outline.
9. Click the **Close Outline View** button to close *Outline* view.

Insert a Subdocument into a Master Document

You can use any document as a master document. When you insert subdocuments into a document, that document becomes the master document. When you are working with master and subdocuments, you use *Outline* view. An advantage of working with a master document and subdocuments is the ability to apply consistent style formatting across documents. When you insert a subdocument, the styles from the master document apply to the subdocument even if the styles in the subdocument are different.

When you insert a subdocument into a master document, the subdocument links to the master document. Changes you make in either the master document or subdocument automatically update in the linked file. Word inserts section breaks before and after a subdocument.

▶ **HOW TO:** Insert a Subdocument into a Master Document

1. Open the document that will become the master document.
2. Click the **Outline** button [*View* tab, *Views* group] to display the document in *Outline* view and to open the *Outlining* tab.

11-49 Master Document group on the Outlining tab

3. Click the **Show Document** button [*Outlining* tab, *Master Document* group] to view the options available for working with a master document and subdocuments (Figure 11-49).
   - You use the options in the *Master Document* group on the *Outlining* tab to insert, create, and manage subdocuments.
4. Place your insertion point in the outline where you want to insert the subdocument.
5. Click the **Insert** button [*Outlining* tab, *Master Document* group]. The *Insert Subdocument* dialog box opens.
6. Select the subdocument to insert and click **Open**. The subdocument displays in the master document (Figure 11-50).
   - If the subdocument has heading styles applied, a dialog box opens asking if you want to rename the style(s) in

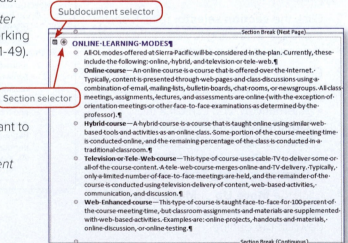

11-50 Subdocument inserted into a master document

the subdocument. Click **Yes** or **Yes to All** to rename the styles in the subdocument to match the styles in the master document. Click **No** or **No to All** if you do not want the styles in the subdocument to be renamed.

- A next page section break displays before and a continuous section break displays after the subdocument.
- You can remove these section breaks in *Outline* view or in *Print Layout* view.
- A border displays around the subdocument in the outline. This border does not display in *Print Layout* view.
- A subdocument selector displays to the left of the first line of the subdocument. Click this icon to select the entire subdocument.

7. Click the **Insert** button to insert another subdocument into the master document.
8. Click the **Close Outline View** button to close *Outline* view.

Create a Subdocument

In addition to inserting an existing subdocument file into a master document, you can create a subdocument in the master document in *Outline* view. When you create a subdocument in the master document, Word actually creates a separate file that is saved in the same location as the master document. You can type the subdocument text in the master document or open the subdocument file and modify it.

▶ **HOW TO:** Create a Subdocument

1. Open the master document and click the **Outline** button [*View* tab, *Views* group] to display the document in *Outline* view.
2. Place your insertion point in the outline where you want to create the subdocument.

   - You can only create a subdocument in the master document at a heading level (for example *Heading 1* or *Heading 2*), not at the body level. You receive an error message if you try to create a subdocument at the body level.

3. Click the **Create** button [*Outlining* tab, *Master Document* group] to create a new subdocument (Figure 11-51).

   - The new subdocument is blank.
   - Section breaks display before and after the new subdocument and a border displays around the subdocument in *Outline* view.

4. Type content in the subdocument.

   - You can use the **Promote** or **Demote** button to change heading levels.

5. Save the master document.

   - When you save the master document, all subdocuments are also saved.

11-51 Create a new subdocument in the master document

Merge Subdocuments

After you insert subdocuments into your master document, you have the option of merging two or more adjacent subdocuments into one subdocument. For example, if you are working on two smaller adjacent subdocuments, you can merge them into one subdocument. The new merged subdocument is saved with the file name of the first subdocument. The other subdocument file remains on your computer, but it no longer links to the master document.

1. Open the master document and click the **Outline** button [*View* tab, *Views* group] to display the document in *Outline* view.

2. Select the subdocuments to merge.

    *   Press the **Shift** key and click the **subdocument selectors** to select multiple subdocuments (Figure 11-52). Alternatively, click and drag to select subdocuments.
    *   You can merge more than two subdocuments.
    *   You cannot merge a subdocument with text in the master document or merge non-adjacent subdocuments.

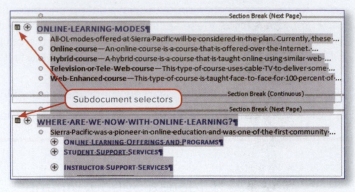

11-52 Select subdocuments to merge

3. Click the **Merge** button [*Outlining* tab, *Master Document* group].

    *   The section breaks between subdocuments are not removed.

4. Save the master document.

    *   The contents of the merged subdocument save in the first subdocument file.
    *   The other subdocument file(s) no longer links to the master document, but the files remain in their original location.

Split a Subdocument

If you have a large subdocument in your master document, you can select a portion of the subdocument and split it into a separate subdocument. When you split a subdocument, a new linked subdocument file is created and the selected text is removed from the original linked subdocument.

▶ **HOW TO:** Split a Subdocument

1. Open the master document and click the **Outline** button [*View* tab, *Views* group] to display the document in *Outline* view.

2. Select the portion of the subdocument to split into a new subdocument.

    *   You cannot split a part of the master document to create a new subdocument.

3. Click the **Split** button [*Outlining* tab, *Master Document* group] to split the selected text into a new subdocument (Figure 11-53).

    *   Section breaks display before and after the new subdocument.

4. Save the master document.

    *   The new subdocument saves as a new file. The first heading of the new subdocument becomes the subdocument file name.

11-53 Split selected content into a separate subdocument

Unlink a Subdocument

You can ***unlink*** a subdocument from the master document to break the connection between the two documents. When you unlink a subdocument, the text of the subdocument remains in the master document, but since the documents are no longer linked, changes made in the subdocument file are not updated in the master document. The text from the unlinked subdocument becomes part of the master document.

▶ **HOW TO:** Unlink a Subdocument

1. Open the master document and click the **Outline** button [*View* tab, *Views* group] to display the document in *Outline* view.

2. Click the **Show Document** button [*Outlining* tab, *Master Document* group] to display the borders around the subdocuments.

3. Click the **subdocument selector** or place your insertion point within a subdocument.

4. Click the **Unlink** button [*Outlining* tab, *Master Document* group] to unlink the subdocument from the master document (Figure 11-54).

11-54 Unlink a subdocument from the master document

- When you unlink a subdocument, it becomes part of the master document.
- After you have unlinked a subdocument from the master document, you cannot merge or split the text that was previously a subdocument.

Arrange Text in an Outline

After you insert, merge, and split subdocuments, you can easily move subdocuments or sections within a subdocument or the master document in *Outline* view. Use the **Move Up (Alt+Shift+Up)** or **Move Down (Alt+Shift+Down)** button to move a selected subdocument or section up or down in the outline (Figure 11-55). You can also select a section and drag it to a different location in the outline.

11-55 Use the *Move Up* or *Move Down* button to arrange sections of subdocuments

> ▶ **MORE INFO**
>
> When you move the contents of a subdocument into the master document text, the link between the subdocument and the master document is removed.

If you are working on a long document, you can collapse sections of the document. By collapsing them, the text below a heading does not display in *Outline* view, so it easier to rearrange subdocuments and selected sections. Check the **Show First Line Only** box (see Figure 11-55) to display only the first line of text on each heading and body level so the document is less cluttered and easier to edit. Click the **Show Document** button to view borders around the subdocuments.

Lock a Subdocument

You can lock a subdocument so changes cannot be made to the subdocument in the master document while using *Outline* view or *Print Layout* view. After you lock a subdocument, you can still change the original subdocument file, and those changes update in the master document.

▶ **HOW TO:** Lock a Subdocument

1. Open the master document and click the **Outline** button [*View* tab, *Views* group] to display the document in *Outline* view.

2. Click the **Show Document** button [*Outlining* tab, *Master Document* group] to display the borders around the subdocuments.

3. Click the **subdocument selector** or place your insertion point within a subdocument.

4. Click the **Lock Document** button [*Outlining* tab, *Master Document* group] to lock the subdocument in the master document.

- A lock icon appears below the subdocument icon (Figure 11-56).

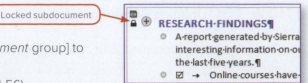

11-56 Locked subdocument

When a master document and a subdocument are both open in Word, the subdocument in the master document automatically locks in the master document. Changes to the subdocument can only be made in the subdocument file, not in the master document. When you close the subdocument file, the subdocument in the master document unlocks.

Save and Reopen a Master Document

When you save a master document, all of the linked subdocuments also save. If you make changes to any of the subdocuments in the master document, those changes will save in the subdocument files when you save the master document. This ensures that your linked subdocument files are consistent with the subdocument content in the master document.

You can modify subdocument files when the master document is closed. When you open the master document, the updated content from the subdocument files displays in the master document. When you reopen a master document, the subdocuments display as hyperlinks (Figure 11-57). Click a subdocument link to open the subdocument file. Click **Expand Subdocuments** in *Outline* view to display the text of the subdocuments.

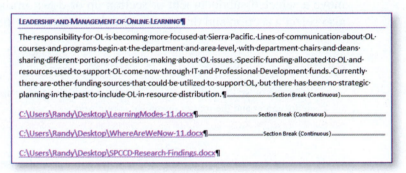

11-57 Subdocuments displayed as hyperlinks in the master document

▶ **HOW TO:** Reopen a Master Document and Display Subdocuments

1. Open the master document and click the **Outline** button [*View* tab, *Views* group] to display the document in *Outline* view.

- Linked subdocuments by default display as hyperlinks in both *Print Layout* and *Outline* views (see Figure 11-57).

2. Click the **Show Document** button [*Outlining* tab, *Master Document* group].

3. Click the **Expand Subdocuments** button [*Outlining* tab, *Master Document* group] to display the contents of the subdocuments (Figure 11-58).

- This button toggles between *Expand Subdocuments* and *Collapse Subdocuments*.
- When subdocuments are expanded, the options in the *Master Document* group become active.
- Click **Collapse Subdocuments** to display hyperlinks to subdocuments.
- Click a subdocument hyperlink to open the subdocument file.

4. Click **Close Outline View** to return to your document.

11-58 Expand subdocuments to display subdocument text in the master document

PAUSE & PRACTICE: WORD 11-4

For this Pause & Practice project, you work with a master document and subdocuments. You insert subdocuments into a master document, split a subdocument, arrange subdocuments, modify subdocuments, reopen a master document, and unlink documents.

Files Needed: **OnlineLearning-11.docx**, **LearningModes-11.docx**, and **WhereAreWeNow-11.docx** (student data files are available in the Library of your SIMnet account)
Completed Project File Names: **[your initials] PP W11-4.docx** and **SPCCD Research Findings** (split subdocument)

1. Open the **OnlineLearning-11** file from your student data files.

2. Save the document as [your initials] PP W11-4.

3. Open a File Explorer window, locate the **LearningModes-11** and **WhereAreWeNow-11** files from your student data files, and **copy** the files to the same location as your **[your initials] PP W11-4** file.

4. Use Outline view to change heading level and arrange sections.
   a. Return to the **[your initials] PP W11-4** document in Word and turn on **Show/Hide** [Home tab, Paragraph group] if it is not already on.
   b. Click the **Outline** button [View tab, Views group] to display the document in Outline view.
   c. Click the **section selector** (plus icon) to the left of the "ONLINE COURSE AND PROGRAM SELECTION" heading to select the heading and body text.
   d. Click the **Demote** button [Outlining tab, Outline Tools group] to demote the heading to Level 2 (Figure 11-59).
   e. Click the **section selector** to the left of the "Leadership and Management of Online Learning" heading to select the heading and body text.
   f. Click the **Move Down** button twice [Outlining tab, Outline Tools group] (see Figure 11-59) to move this section below the "Online Course and Program Selection" heading and body text in the outline.

5. Insert subdocuments into the master document.
   a. Place your insertion point on the blank line below the last body paragraph in the outline.
   b. Click the **Show Document** button [Outlining tab, Master Document group].
   c. Click the **Insert** button [Outlining tab, Master Document group] to open the Insert Subdocument dialog box.
   d. Browse to the location where your master document and subdocuments are saved.
   e. Select the **LearningModes-11** file and click **Open** to insert the subdocument.
   f. Select the "**Online Learning Modes**" line in the subdocument.
   g. Click the **Outline Level** drop-down list [Outlining tab, Outline Tools group] and select **Level 1** (Figure 11-60).

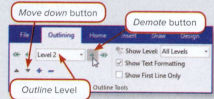

11-59 Demote heading to *Level 2*

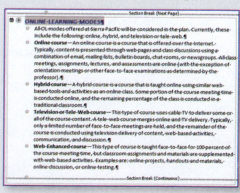

11-60 Subdocument inserted into the master document

h. Place your insertion point on the last blank line in the outline.
i. **Insert** the **WhereAreWeNow-11** file as a subdocument.
j. Click **Yes to All** in the dialog box asking if you want to rename styles in the subdocument (Figure 11-61).

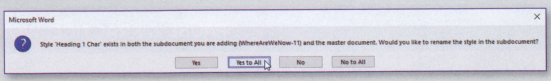

11-61 Rename styles in the subdocument file

6. Split a subdocument.
   a. Check the **Show First Line Only** box [*Outlining* tab, *Outline* Tools group] to display only the first line of text at each level.
   b. Click the **section selector** to the left of the "Research Findings" section in the second subdocument.
   c. Click the **Split** button [*Outlining* tab, *Master Document* group] to split the section into a new subdocument.
   d. Click the **section selector** to the left of the "Research Findings" section and click the **Promote** button once. The "Research Findings" heading changes to *Level 1*.
   e. Place your insertion point in front of the "RESEARCH FINDINGS" heading, type SPCCD, and **space** once (Figure 11-62).
   f. Click the **Close Outline View** button.

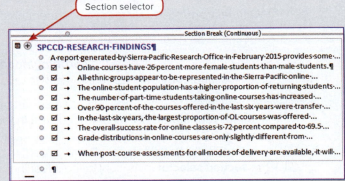

11-62 Split subdocument and promote heading

7. Save and close the *[your initials] PP W11-4* master document.

8. Modify a subdocument.
   a. Open the **WhereAreWeNow-11** document from the location where your master document and subdocuments are located.
   b. Change "Tech" to Instructor in the last subheading of this document ("Tech Support Services").
   c. Save and close the document.

9. Open the *[your initials] PP W11-4* master document.

10. Arrange a subdocument.
    a. Change to *Outline* view. The subdocuments display as hyperlinks.
    b. Click the **Show Document** button and the **Expand Subdocuments** button [*Outlining* tab, *Master Document* group].
    c. Click the **subdocument selector** to the left of "ONLINE LEARNING MODES" to select the entire subdocument (Figure 11-63).
    d. Use the **Move Up** button to move this subdocument above the "PLANNING PROCESS" section. You will press the *Move Up* button multiple times. The moved subdocument becomes part of the master document and is no longer linked to the subdocument file.

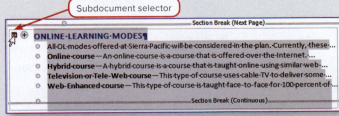

11-63 Select subdocument

11. Unlink subdocuments from the master document.
    a. Click the **subdocument selector** to the left of "WHERE ARE WE NOW WITH ONLINE LEARNING" to select the entire subdocument.
    b. Click the **Unlink** button [*Outlining* tab, *Master Document* group] to unlink this document from the subdocument file.
    c. Place your insertion point in the last subdocument ("SPCCD RESEARCH FINDINGS").
    d. Click the **Unlink** button to unlink this document from the subdocument file.

12. Remove section breaks from the document.
    a. Deselect the **Show First Line Only** check box [*Outlining* tab, *Outline Tools* group] to display the entire outline.
    b. Place your insertion point on each of the section break indicators and press **Delete** to remove each of the section breaks in the document (including the section break at the end of the outline). Be careful not to delete any text.
    c. Confirm no blank lines display between sections.
    d. Close *Outline* view and return to *Print Layout* view.

13. Insert **page breaks** before the "Online Course and Program Selection" and "Student Support Services" headings to keep the headings with the text that follows.

14. Save and close the document (Figure 11-64).

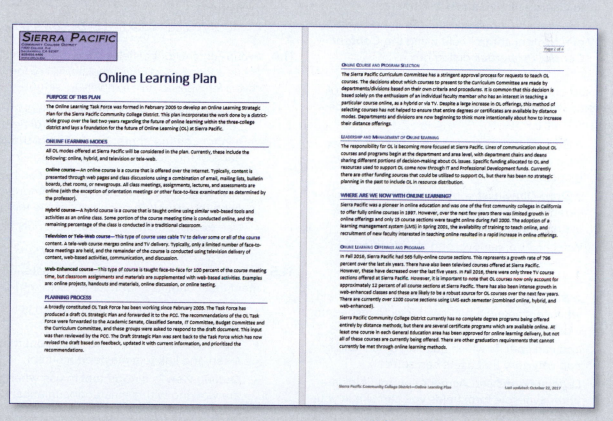

11-64 PP W11-4 completed (pages 1 and 2 of 4)

Chapter Summary

11.1 Insert, customize, and arrange a variety of content control fields (p. W11-643).

- **Content control fields** are containers in a document where users enter or select information.
- Use **tab stops**, **indents**, and **tables** to align and arrange content control fields in a document.
- Use **Rich Text** and **Plain Text** content control fields for open-ended responses from users.
- In a *Rich Text* content control field, users can apply formatting to specific text.
- A **Check Box** content control field enables a user to select or deselect a check box.
- Users select (or enter) a date in a **Date Picker** content control field.
- A **Picture** content control field prompts a user to insert a picture into a document.
- You can add a **title** and modify the properties of a content control field using the **Content Control Properties** dialog box.

11.2 Insert and customize advanced content control fields where a user selects from a list of choices (p. W11-651).

- A **Combo Box** content control field provides a list of choices or users can type their own responses.
- A **Drop-Down List** content control field provides a list of choices. In a *Drop-Down List*, users cannot type their own responses.
- You can add, remove, and modify users' choices in both *Combo Box* and *Drop-Down List* content control fields.
- A **Building Block Gallery** content control field lets users select a building block to insert into a document.
- You can specify which building block gallery and category that users can select.
- **Legacy Forms** and **ActiveX** control fields are other available form fields you can use in your Word documents.

11.3 Edit a content control field to change the format and lock content, and use *Design* mode to edit placeholder text (p. W11-653).

- You can apply a style to the contents of a content control field. Select from an existing style or create a new style.

- You can also change the color of content control fields. By default, the content control field color is controlled by the theme of the document.
- A content control field displays in the document as a **bounding box**, with **start and end tags**, or not shown at all (the *None* option). By default, content control fields display as bounding boxes.
- Set up a content control field so the field remains in the document when a user enters information or set it so the field is removed when a user enters information.
- *Lock* content control fields so the field cannot be deleted, or lock a field so it cannot be edited by users.
- You can copy, move, or delete content control fields.
- Modify placeholder text in **Design mode**.

11.4 Group content control fields, protect and edit a form, create a form based on a template, fill in a form, and save a form based on a template (p. W11-659).

- **Group** content control fields so users enter or select information in content control fields but cannot edit the content or format of the other parts of the document.
- Save a form as a **template** so you can base a new document on the template without modifying the structure or content of the template.
- Use **Restrict Editing** so users can only fill in content control fields in forms.

11.5 Manage a long document using a master document that contains subdocuments. (p. W11-663)

- A **master document** is useful when you are working with long documents.
- A **subdocument** is a Word document that you insert and link to a master document.
- **Outline view** is a good tool to use when you are working with a master document and subdocuments.
- **Expand** or **collapse** and **promote** or **demote** headings using the **Outlining tab** in *Outline* view.
- **Merge** subdocuments to combine multiple subdocuments into one subdocument file.
- **Split** a portion of a subdocument to create a new subdocument.

- After you **unlink** a subdocument from a master document, the changes made in the subdocument are not updated in the master document.
- You can move subdocuments and sections of text in subdocuments and the master document in *Outline* view.
- **Lock** a subdocument to prevent subdocument text from being edited in the master document.

Check for Understanding

The SIMbook for this text (within your SIMnet account) provides the following resources for concept review:

- Multiple choice questions
- Matching exercises
- Short answer questions

Guided Project 11-1

For this project, you create a form template for Emma Cavalli at Placer Hills Real Estate. You use content control fields, customize content control fields, protect the form, and create a new document based on the form template.
[Student Learning Outcomes 11.1, 11.2, 11.3, 11.4]

Files Needed: **PHREAuthorizationLetter-11.docx** and **BurgessHome-11.jpg** *(student data files are available in the* Library *of your SIMnet account)*
Completed Project File Names: **[your initials] Word 11-1 form.dotx** and **[your initials] Word 11-1.docx**

Skills Covered in This Project

- Save a document as a template.
- Set a tab stop to align text and content control fields.
- Insert and customize *Date Picker, Combo Box, Rich Text, Plain Text,* and *Picture* content control fields.
- Use *Design* mode to customize placeholder text.
- Protect a form.
- Create a document based on a template.
- Fill in a content control field.

1. Open the **PHREAuthorizationLetter-11** document from your student data files.

2. Save the document as a **Word Template** named [your initials] Word 11-1 form.

3. Set tab stops to align text and content control fields.
   a. Turn on **Show/Hide** [*Home* tab, *Paragraph* group] if it is not already on.
   b. Select the lines of text beginning with "**Loan Application Date**" and ending with "**Street Address**" and set a **1.5" left** tab stop.
   c. Select the "**City**" line of text and set the following **left** tab stops: **0.4"**, **1.5"**, and **1.8"**.
   d. Place your insertion point after "City:", press **Tab** twice, and type ZIP:.
   e. Select the line of text that contains "**Sincerely**," and set a **center** tab stop at **5.25"**.

4. Insert and customize a *Date Picker* content control field.
   a. Place your insertion point after "Loan Application Date:" and press **Tab**.
   b. Click the **Date Picker Content Control** button [*Developer* tab, *Controls* group] to insert a *Date Picker* content control field (Figure 11-65).
   c. Click the **Properties** button [*Developer* tab, *Controls* group] to open the *Content Control Properties* dialog box.
   d. Type Application Date in the *Title* text box.
   e. Select the spelled out date format (January 1, 2018) in the *Date Picker Properties* area.
   f. Click **OK** to close the *Content Control Properties* dialog box.

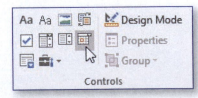

11-65 Content control form fields

5. Insert and customize *Combo Box* content control fields.
   a. Place your insertion point after "Financial Institution:" and press **Tab**.
   b. Click the **Combo Box Content Control** button [*Developer* tab, *Controls* group] to insert a *Combo Box* content control field.

c. Click the **Properties** button to open the *Content Control Properties* dialog box.

d. Type Financial Institution in the *Title* text box.

e. Click the **Add** button in the *Drop-Down List Properties* area to open the *Add Choice* dialog box.

f. Type Bank of America in the *Display Name* area and press **OK** to close the dialog box and add the choice.

g. Add two more choices: Chase Bank and Wells Fargo Bank.

h. Select **Choose an item** and click the **Remove** button (Figure 11-66).

i. Click **OK** to close the *Content Control Properties* dialog box.

j. Place your insertion point after the first tab after "City:" and insert a **Combo Box** content control field.

k. Open the *Content Control Properties* dialog box and type City as the *Title*.

l. Add Lincoln, Loomis, Rocklin, and Roseville as the choices, remove **Choose an item**, and click **OK** to close the dialog box.

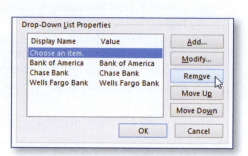

11-66 Add choices to the *Combo Box* and remove a choice

6. Insert and customize *Rich Text* content control fields.

a. Place your insertion point after "Loan Number:" and press **Tab**.

b. Click the **Rich Text Content Control** button [*Developer* tab, *Controls* group] to insert a *Rich Text* content control field.

c. Open the *Content Control Properties* dialog box and type Loan Number as the *Title* (Figure 11-67).

d. Click the **Show as** drop-down list and select **None**.

e. Check the **Use a style to format text typed into the empty control** box.

f. Click the **Style** drop-down list and select **Book Title**.

g. Click **OK** to close the dialog box.

h. Place your insertion point after "Borrower Name(s):" and press **Tab**.

i. Insert a **Rich Text** content control field.

j. Open the *Content Control Properties* dialog box, type Borrower Name as the title, and repeat steps 6d–g to customize the content control field.

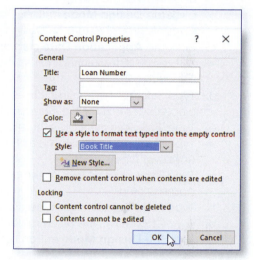

11-67 Customize *Rich Text* content control field

7. Insert and customize *Plain Text* content control fields.

a. Place your insertion point after "Street Address:" and press **Tab**.

b. Click the **Plain Text Content Control** button [*Developer* tab, *Controls* group].

c. Open the *Content Control Properties* dialog box and type Street Address as the *Title*.

d. Click the **Show as** drop-down list, select **None**, and click **OK** to close the dialog box.

e. Place your insertion point after "ZIP:" and press **Tab**.

f. Insert a **Plain Text** content control field.

g. Open the *Content Control Properties* dialog box, type ZIP Code as the *Title*.

h. Click the **Show as** drop-down list, select **None**, and click **OK** to close the dialog box.

8. Insert and customize a *Picture* content control field.

a. Place your insertion point after "Sincerely," press **Tab**, and type Picture of the Property.

b. Place your insertion point on the blank line below the phone number at the end of the document.

c. Click the **Picture Content Control** button [*Developer* tab, *Controls* group] to insert a *Picture* content control field.

d. Open the *Content Control Properties* dialog box, type Property Picture as the *Title*, and click **OK** to close the dialog box.

e. Click the **Position** button [*Picture Tools Format* tab, *Arrange* group] and select **More Layout Options** from the drop-down list to open the *Layout* dialog box.

f. Click the **Size** tab and change the *Height* and *Width* to **2.5"**.

g. Click the **Text Wrapping** tab and select **Tight**.

h. Click the **Position** tab and set the *Horizontal* **Alignment** to **Right** relative to **Margin** and the *Vertical* **Absolute position** at **5.7"** below **Page** (Figure 11-68).

i. Click **OK** to close the *Layout* dialog box.

9. Use *Design* mode to customize placeholder text.

a. Place your insertion point at the beginning of the document.

b. Click the **Design Mode** button [*Developer* tab, *Controls* group] to turn on *Design* mode.

c. Click the **Application Date** start tag and type **Select date of loan application** as the placeholder text (Figure 11-69).

d. Type **Select or type financial institution** as the placeholder text for the *Financial Institution* field.

e. Type **Type loan number** as the placeholder text for the *Loan Number* field.

f. Type **Type borrower name(s)** as the placeholder text for the *Borrower Name* field.

g. Type **Type street address** as the placeholder text for the *Street Address* field.

h. Type **Select or type city** as the placeholder text for the *City* field.

i. Type **ZIP code** as the placeholder text for the *ZIP Code* field.

j. Click the **Design Mode** button to turn off *Design* mode.

10. Protect the form template.

a. Click the **Restrict Editing** button [*Developer* tab, *Protect* group] to display the *Restrict Editing* pane on the right (Figure 11-70).

b. Check the **Allow only this type of editing in the document** box in the *Editing restrictions* area.

c. Click the drop-down list and select **Filling in forms**.

d. Click **Yes, Start Enforcing Protection.** The *Start Enforcing Protection* dialog box opens.

e. Click **OK** to protect the document without a password.

f. Close the *Restrict Editing* pane.

11. Save and close the form template.

12. Open a *File Explorer* window, locate the **[your initials] Word 11-1 form** template, and double-click the file to create a new document based on the template.

13. Save the document as **[your initials] Word 11-1**. If prompted to save changes to the template, click **Yes**.

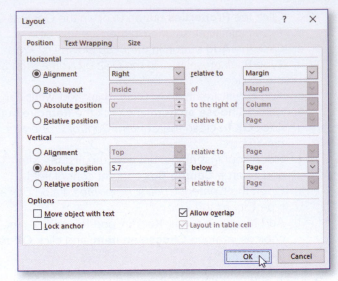

11-68 Customize the layout of the *Picture* content control field

11-69 Customize field placeholder text

11-70 Restrict editing to *Filling in forms*

14. Use the following information to fill in the content control fields:
    Application Date: Select the previous Monday
    Financial Institution: Chase Bank
    Loan Number: CB2003476
    Borrower Name(s): John and Robyn Burgess
    Street Address: 85741 Auberry Road
    City: Roseville
    ZIP Code: 95722

15. Insert a picture in the *Picture* content control field.
    a. Click the **icon** in the center of the *Property Picture* content control field to open the *Insert Pictures* dialog box.
    b. Select **From a file** to open the *Insert Picture* dialog box.
    c. Select the ***BurgessHome-11*** picture from your student data files and click **Insert**.

16. Save and close the document (Figure 11-71).

Placer Hill Real Estate

AUTHORIZATION LETTER TO LENDER

Loan Application Date: March 5, 2018

Financial Institution: Chase Bank

Loan Number: *CB2003476*

Borrower Name(s): *John and Robyn Burgess*

Street Address: 85741 Auberry Road

City: Roseville ZIP: 95722

Please consider this my/our authorization to you to provide any and all information regarding our above referenced loan to Emma Cavalli, Placer Hills Real Estate as per my/our request.

BORROWER SIGNATURE(S)

Sincerely,

Emma Cavalli
Placer Hills Real Estate
ecavalli@phre.com
916-450-3334

Picture of the Property

Placer Hills
Real Estate
7100 Madrone Road | Roseville, CA 95722
www.phre.com | 916.450.3300

11-71 Word 11-1 completed

Guided Project 11-2

For this project, you use a master document and subdocuments to create a training guide for the Skiing Unlimited program. You insert subdocuments into a master document, split and merge subdocuments, change heading levels, and arrange sections of a subdocument.
[Student Learning Outcome 11.5]

Files Needed: *SkiingUnlimitedTrainingGuide-11.docx*, *DevelopmentallyDisabled-11.docx*, *FourTrackand ThreeTrack-11.docx*, and *VisuallyImpaired-11.docx* (student data files are available in the Library of your SIMnet account)
Completed Project File Name: *[your initials] Word 11-2.docx*

Skills Covered in This Project

- Use *Outline* view.
- Insert subdocuments into a master document.
- Promote and demote headings.
- Arrange sections in a subdocument.
- View different levels in *Outline* view.

- Modify subdocument text.
- Merge two subdocuments.
- Split a subdocument into two subdocuments.
- Unlink subdocuments.
- Delete a section break.
- Insert a page break.

1. Open the **SkiingUnlimitedTrainingGuide-11** document from your student data files.

2. Save the document as [your initials] Word 11-2 and turn on **Show/Hide** [*Home* tab, *Paragraph* group] if it is not already on.

3. Open a *File Explorer* window, locate the **DevelopmentallyDisabled-11**, **FourTrackandThree Track-11**, and **VisuallyImpaired-11** files, and **copy** these to the same location as your *[your initials] Word 11-2* file. These are your subdocument files.

4. Use *Outline* view to change a heading level.
   a. Return to the *[your initials] Word 11-2* document open in Word and click the **Outline** button [*View* tab, *Views* group] to display the document in *Outline* view.
   b. Place your insertion point in "**Introduction**" and click the **Promote to Heading 1** button [*Outlining* tab, *Outline Tools* group] (Figure 11-72).

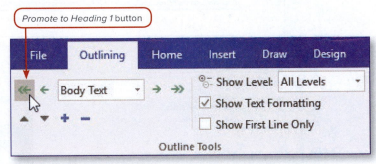

11-72 *Promote to Heading 1* button

5. Insert and modify a subdocument.
   a. Place your insertion point on the blank line below the last line of text in the outline.
   b. Click the **Show Document** button [*Outlining* tab, *Master Document* group].
   c. Click the **Insert** button to open the **Insert Subdocument** dialog box.
   d. Browse to the location where the *[your initials] Word 11-2* document and subdocuments are located.
   e. Select the **DevelopmentallyDisabled-11** file and click **Open** to insert the subdocument into the master document.

f. Click **Yes to All** in the dialog box that opens and asks if you want to rename styles in the subdocument (Figure 11-73).

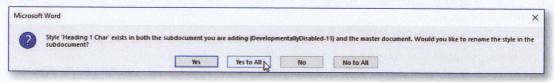

11-73 Rename styles in the subdocument file

g. Click the **section selector** to the left of "Disabilities" to select the heading and the text below the heading.

h. Click the **Demote** button [*Outlining* tab, *Outline Tools* group] to change the selected heading to *Level 2*.

i. **Demote** to *Level 2* each of the next three headings in the subdocument.

6. Insert and modify another subdocument.
a. Place your insertion point on the last blank line in the outline.
b. **Insert** the ***VisuallyImpaired-11*** file and click **Yes to All** in the dialog box that opens and asks if you want to rename styles in the subdocument.
c. Click the **Show Level** drop-down list and select **Level 2** to display two levels of headings in the outline (Figure 11-74).
d. Select the "**Disabilities**" section in the second subdocument and click the **Move Up** [*Outlining* tab, *Outline Tools* group] button to move this section above the "Physical Evaluation" section.

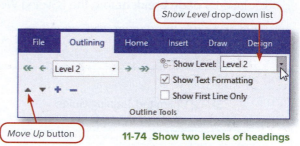

11-74 Show two levels of headings

7. Insert and modify another subdocument.
a. Click the **Show Level** drop-down list and select **All Levels** to display all the text in the outline.
b. Place your insertion point on the last blank line in the outline.
c. **Insert** the ***FourTrackandThreeTrack-11*** file and click **Yes to All** in the dialog box that opens and asks if you want to rename styles in the subdocument.
d. Select the "**Four-Track and Three-Track**" section heading at the top of this subdocument and **promote** to *Level 1*.
e. Select the "**Bi-Ski and Mono-Ski**" section in this subdocument and **promote** to *Level 1*.

8. Modify subdocuments.
a. Click the **Show Level** drop-down list and select **Level 2**.
b. In the first subdocument ("Developmentally Disabled (DD)"), place your insertion point before "Disabilities," type **Common**, and then **space** once.
c. In the second subdocument ("Visually Impaired (VI)"), place your insertion point before "Disabilities," type **Common**, and then **space** once.

9. Merge subdocuments.
a. Click the **subdocument selector** for the first subdocument, press the **Shift** key, and click the **subdocument selector** for the second subdocument to select both subdocuments (Figure 11-75).
b. Click the **Merge** button [*Outlining* tab, *Master Document* group] to merge the two subdocuments.

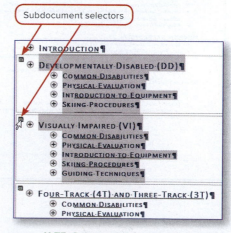

11-75 Select subdocuments to merge

W11-679

10. Split a section of a subdocument to create a new subdocument.
    a. Select the "**Bi-Ski and Mono-Ski**" section.
    b. Click the **Split** button [*Outlining* tab, *Master Document* group] to split the selected section into a new subdocument.
    c. Save the ***[your initials] Word 11-2*** master document.
11. Unlink subdocuments and remove section breaks.
    a. Select the first subdocument ("Developmentally Disabled (DD)", which also now includes the merged "Visually Impaired (VI)" section) and click the **Unlink** button [*Outlining* tab, *Master Document* group] to break the link between the master document and the subdocument file.
    b. **Unlink** the other two subdocuments.
    c. Click the **Show Level** drop-down list and select **All Levels**.
    d. Move to the top of the outline, click the first section break, and press **Delete**.
    e. Delete all remaining section breaks in the document.
    f. Delete any blank lines between sections and at the end of the document.
12. Click the **Close Outline View** button [*Outlining* tab, *Close* group] and view the document in *Print Layout* view.
13. Insert page breaks to keep text with headings.
    a. Insert a **page break** before the "Introduction to Equipment" section at the bottom of page 4.
    b. Insert a **page break** before the "Gliding Wedge Turns" section at the bottom of page 5.
14. Save and close the document (Figure 11-76).

Skiing Unlimited Training Guide

INTRODUCTION

Courtyard Medical Plaza works closely with the Society for Handicapped Children and Adults of Sacramento County to run the Skiing Unlimited program for individuals with developmental challenges. The Skiing Unlimited programs is solely donor funded and is run by volunteers who give of their time and energy to provide snow skiing opportunities to those who would otherwise not be able to participate in this wonderful sport.

This training guide is designed to help volunteers understand the different types of disabilities and the equipment used for the Skiing Unlimited program.

DEVELOPMENTALLY DISABLED (DD)

COMMON DISABILITIES

Below is a summary of some of the DD participants we will work with throughout the ski season.

- Brain injury (Organic—physical; Inorganic—psychiatric)
- Autism
- Cerebral Palsy (Diplegia—All limbs, but legs more severely; Hemiplegia—Limbs on one side, Quadriplegia—All limbs affected)
- Fetal Alcohol Syndrome (Usually physical and mental impairment)
- Fragile X Syndrome
- Downs Syndrome (Always ask if they are C-1 or C-2 instable)

PHYSICAL EVALUATION

A physical evaluation should always be performed prior to selecting equipment. Parents are a wonderful source of information during this process.

- Determine strength, coordination, balance, range of motion, sensory and motor abilities.
- Cognitive Assessment: determine the developmental age, learning style, motivation, social skills, and communication abilities of the participant.
- Always ask if prone to seizures. What medications?

INTRODUCTION TO EQUIPMENT

- Be sure student's boots fit properly with only one pair of socks.
- Poles may be used, but they may also be inappropriate.
- Have participant feel equipment to get familiar with it. Be sure to warn student about sharp ski edges and powerful binding springs.
- Explain the uses of the adaptive equipment that may be used to assist the participant.

SKIING PROCEDURES

- Follow standard ATS progression for skier levels 1 through 9.
- Establish emergency commands.
- Establish procedure for student and instructor in case of separation on the hill.
- Be aware of cognitive and behavioral challenges the student may have. Be in a position to intervene should the student stray from the task at hand physically and/or mentally.

Skiing Unlimited Training Guide Page 1 of 6

VISUALLY IMPAIRED (VI)

COMMON DISABILITIES

Below is a list of common conditions for those who are visually impaired and a brief explanation of each.

- Albinism—Oversensitive to light possible poor vision due to imperfect retina
- Cataracts—Cloudiness similar to looking through a dirty windshield (Worse in sunlight)
- Color Blindness—Poor color vision
- Congenital Visual Impairment or Eye trauma—Any degree of visual impairment
- Diabetic Retinopathy—Patchy vision may change from day to day, Bring Candy
- Glaucoma -Tunnel vision, Lack of peripheral vision
- Head injury or cardiovascular accident—Any visual impairment, check for seizures
- Macular Degeneration—Poor visual acuity lack of detail good peripheral vision
- Monocular vision—Poor depth perception but generally good acuity
- Multiple Sclerosis—Blurred or Double vision
- Nystagmus—Inability to focus causes rapid eye movement
- Retinitis Pigmentosa—Night Blindness

PHYSICAL EVALUATION

A physical evaluation should always be performed prior to selecting equipment. Parents are a wonderful source of information during this process.

- Determine strength, coordination, balance, range of motion, sensory and motor abilities.
- Cognitive Assessment: determine the developmental age, learning style, motivation, social skills, and communication abilities of the participant.
- Test Vision thoroughly including: visual acuity, range of vision, depth of vision, outdoor vision vs. indoor vision, peripheral vision, and light and color sensitivity.
- Always ask if prone to seizures. What medications?

INTRODUCTION TO EQUIPMENT

- Be sure student's boots fit snugly with only one pair of socks.
- Be sure to get poles if student is able to use them. They can be used like a cane for feeling nearby objects and to provide sensory input while skiing.
- Have student feel equipment to get familiar with it. Be sure to warn student about sharp ski edges and powerful binding springs
- Blind Skier and Guide Bibs, Ski tip connector, Reins, Bamboo poles or ski pole, Climbing harness, and Cants and lifts.

SKIING PROCEDURES

- Follow standard ATS progression for skier levels 1 through 9.
- Find out from the student which guiding technique they prefer. It is easier for the able bodied instructor to adjust to the students preferred method than it is for the student to adjust to the instructors preferred method.
- Establish emergency commands.
- Establish procedure for student and instructor in case of separation on the hill.

GUIDING TECHNIQUES

- Guiding from in front, rear, and side
- Horse and buggy from the front and the rear
- Bamboo pole

Skiing Unlimited Training Guide Page 2 of 6

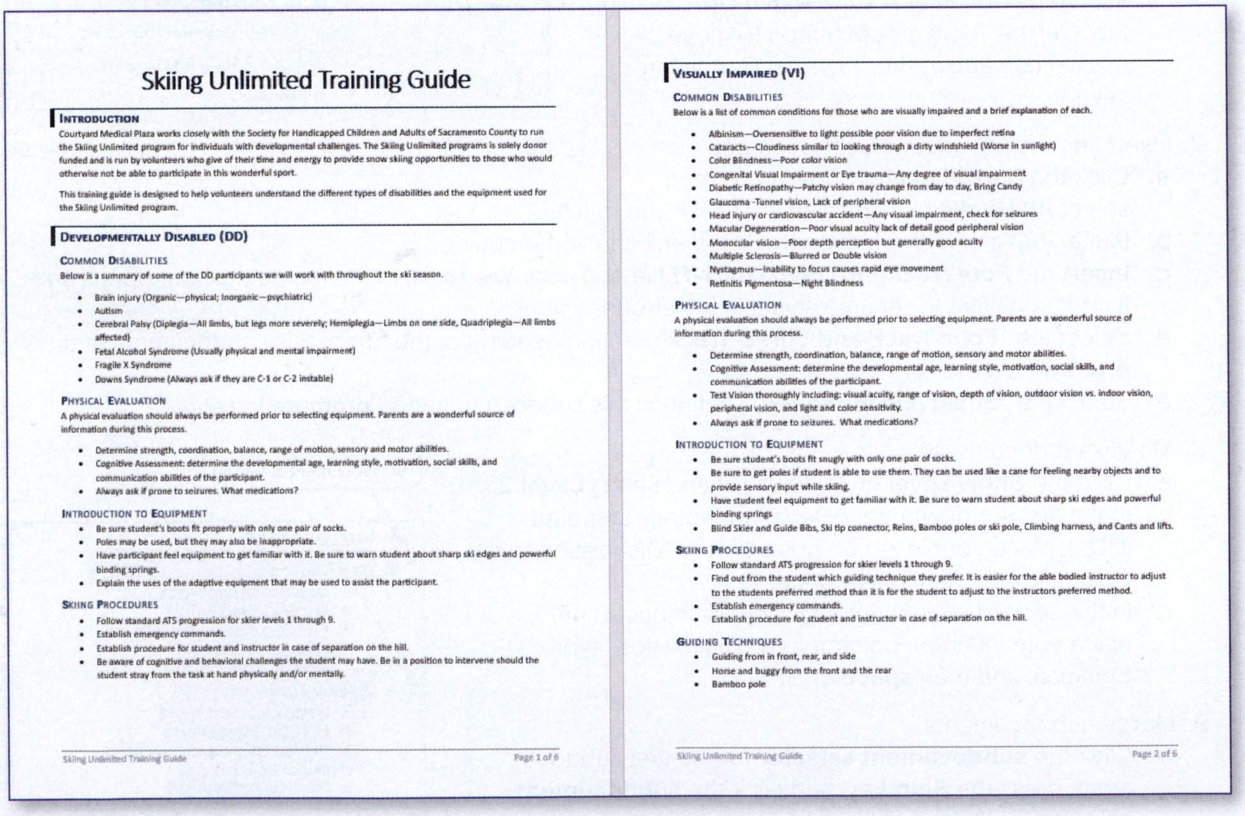

11-76 Word 11-2 completed (pages 1 and 2 of 6)

Guided Project 11-3

For this project, you create a volunteer form for Life's Animal Shelter. You insert content control fields, customize content control fields, group content control fields, and create a new document based on the form template.
[Student Learning Outcomes 11.1, 11.2, 11.3, 11.4]

File Needed: ***LASVolunteerForm-11.docx*** *(student data files are available in the* Library *of your SIMnet account)*
Completed Project File Names: *[your initials]* **Word 11-3 form.docx** and *[your initials]* **Word 11-3.docx**

Skills Covered in This Project

- Set a tab stop to align text and content control fields.
- Change table row height and text alignment.
- Insert and customize *Rich Text*, *Plain Text*, *Check Box*, *Drop-Down List*, and *Combo Box* content control fields.

- Copy and customize a content control field.
- Use *Design* mode to customize placeholder text.
- Group content control fields.
- Fill in a content control field.

1. Open the ***LASVolunteerForm-11*** document from your student data files.

2. Save the Word document as [your initials] Word 11-3 form.

3. Set a tab stop to align text and content control fields and modify the table.
   a. Select the last four rows of the table and set a **0.25" left** tab stop.
   b. Place your insertion point before the text in the fourth row of the table ("Yes, I can volunteer . . .") and press **Ctrl+Tab** to insert a tab before the text.
   c. Use **Ctrl+Tab** to insert a tab before the text in the last three rows of the table.
   d. Select the entire table, change the row height to **0.3"**, and change the text alignment to **Align Center Left**.

4. Insert and customize a *Rich Text* content control field.
   a. Place your insertion point in the second cell in the first row.
   b. Click the **Rich Text Content Control** button [*Developer* tab, *Controls* group] to insert a *Rich Text* content control field.
   c. Click the **Properties** button to open the *Content Control Properties* dialog box (Figure 11-77).
   d. Type Name as the *Title*.
   e. Click the **Color** drop-down list and select **Indigo**.
   f. Check the **Use a style to format text typed into the empty control** box.
   g. Click the **Style** drop-down list and select **Strong**.
   h. Check the **Content control cannot be deleted** box in the *Locking* area.
   i. Click **OK** to close the dialog box.

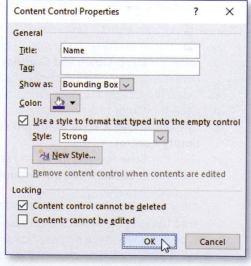

11-77 Customize a *Rich Text* content control field

5. Insert and customize *Plain Text* content control fields.
   a. Place your insertion point in the second cell in the second row.
   b. Click the **Plain Text Content Control** button [*Developer* tab, *Controls* group] to insert a *Plain Text* content control field.

c. Open the *Content Control Properties* dialog box and type Email Address as the *Title*.
d. Click the **Color** drop-down list and select **Indigo**.
e. Check the **Content control cannot be deleted** box in the *Locking* area.
f. Click **OK** to close the dialog box.
g. Place your insertion point in the second cell in the third row and insert a **Plain Text Content Control** field.
h. Open the *Content Control Properties* dialog box and type Phone Number as the *Title*.
i. Click the **Color** drop-down list and select **Indigo**, check the **Content control cannot be deleted** box, and click **OK** to close the dialog box.

6. Insert and customize *Check Box* content control fields.
   a. Place your insertion point before the tab in front of "Yes, I can volunteer . . ."
   b. Click the **Check Box Content Control** button [*Developer* tab, *Controls* group] to insert a *Check Box* content control field.
   c. Open the *Content Control Properties* dialog box and type Volunteer as the *Title*.
   d. Click the **Color** drop-down list and select **Indigo**.
   e. Click the **Change** button in the *Checked symbol* area (Figure 11-78) to open the *Symbol* dialog box.
   f. Click the **Font** drop-down list and select **Wingdings**.
   g. Select the **smiley face** icon (character code 74) and click **OK** to close the *Symbol* dialog box.
   h. Click **OK** to close the *Content Control Properties* dialog box.
   i. Place your insertion point before the tab in front of "Yes, I would like to donate . . ." and insert a **Check Box Content Control** field.
   j. Open the *Content Control Properties* dialog box and type Donate as the *Title*.
   k. Change the *Color* to **Indigo**, change the *Checked symbol* to the **smiley face** icon (character code 74), and click **OK** to close the *Symbol* dialog box.

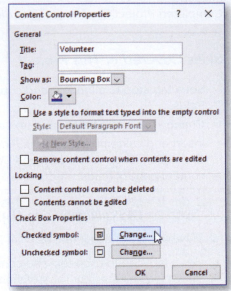

11-78 Customize a *Check Box* content control field

7. Insert and customize a *Drop-Down List* content control field.
   a. Place your insertion point after "Hours per week I can volunteer:" and **space** once.
   b. Click the **Drop-Down List Content Control** button [*Developer* tab, *Controls* group] to insert a *Drop-Down List* content control field.
   c. Open the *Content Control Properties* dialog box and type Volunteer Hours as the *Title*.
   d. Click the **Color** drop-down list and select **Indigo**.
   e. Check the **Use a style to format text typed into the empty control** box.
   f. Click the **Style** drop-down list and select the **Strong** style.
   g. Check the **Content control cannot be deleted** box in the *Locking* area.
   h. Click the **Add** button in the *Drop-Down List Properties* area to open the *Add Choice* dialog box.
   i. Type 1-5 hours in the *Display Name* area and press **OK** to close the dialog box and add the choice.
   j. Add three more choices: 6-10 hours, 11-15 hours, and 16-20 hours.
   k. Select **Choose an item** and click the **Remove** button (Figure 11-79).
   l. Click **OK** to close the *Content Control Properties* dialog box.

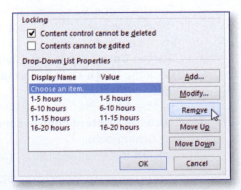

11-79 Add and remove choices from a *Drop-Down List* content control field

8. Insert and customize a *Combo Box* content control field.
    a. Place your insertion point after "Amount:" and **space** once.
    b. Click the **Combo Box Content Control** button [*Developer* tab, *Controls* group] to insert a *Combo Box* content control field.
    c. Open the *Content Control Properties* dialog box and type Donation Amount as the *Title*.
    d. Click the **Color** drop-down list and select **Indigo**.
    e. Check the **Use a style to format text typed into the empty control** box.
    f. Click the **Style** drop-down list and select the **Strong** style.
    g. Check the **Content control cannot be deleted** box in the *Locking* area.
    h. Add the following choices: $10, $25, $50, and $100.
    i. Select **Choose an item** and click the **Remove** button.
    j. Click **OK** to close the *Content Control Properties* dialog box.

9. Use *Design* mode to customize placeholder text.
    a. Click the **Design Mode** button [*Developer* tab, *Controls* group] to turn on *Design* mode.
    b. Click the **Name** start tag and type Type first and last name as the placeholder text (Figure 11-80).
    c. Type Type email address as the placeholder text for the *Email Address* field.
    d. Type Type phone number as the placeholder text for the *Phone Number* field.
    e. Type Select hours as the placeholder text for the *Volunteer Hours* field.
    f. Type Select or type donation amount as the placeholder text for the *Donation Amount* field.
    g. Click the **Design Mode** button to turn off *Design* mode.

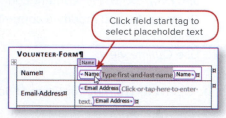

11-80 Customize field placeholder text

10. Group content control fields to lock the text in the document.
    a. Select the entire document (**Ctrl+A**).
    b. Click the **Group** button [*Developer* tab, *Controls* group] and select **Group** from the drop-down list.
    c. Click anywhere in the document to deselect the selected text.

11. Save the document, but do not close it.

12. Save the Word document as a different file name. Save it as [your initials] Word 11-3.

13. Use the following information to fill in the content control fields in the table:
    Name: Cammi Acevedo
    Email Address: cammi@live.com
    Phone Number: 218.285.3776
    Check the **Yes, I can volunteer. . .** box.
    Volunteer Hours: 6-10 hours
    Check the **Yes, I would like to donate. . .** box.
    Donation Amount: type $40

14. Save and close the document (Figure 11-81).

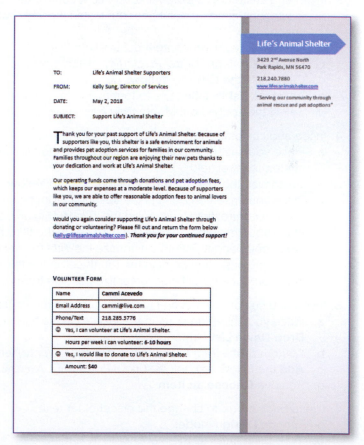

11-81 Word 11-3 completed

Independent Project 11-4

For this project, you create a training log form for American River Cycling Club and then insert the form into a master document. You will insert and customize content control fields, copy and paste content control fields, insert a subdocument into a master document, and modify the contents of the master document.
[Student Learning Outcomes 11.1, 11.2, 11.3, 11.4, 11.5]

Files Needed: ***TrainingLogForm-11.docx*** and ***TrainingLog-11.docx*** *(student data files are available in the Library of your SIMnet account)*
Completed Project File Names: ***[your initials] Word 11-4 form.docx*** and ***[your initials] Word 11-4.docx***

Skills Covered in This Project

- Insert and customize *Date Picker*, *Rich Text*, and *Drop-Down List* content control fields.
- Copy, paste, and modify a content control field.
- Use *Outline* view.
- Insert a subdocument into a master document.
- Remove a section break in an outline.
- Unlink a subdocument.
- Use *Design* mode to customize placeholder text.
- Group content control fields.

1. Open the ***TrainingLogForm-11*** document from your student data files.

2. Save the Word document as [your initials] Word 11-4 form.

3. Insert and customize a *Date Picker* content control field.
   a. Place your insertion point after the text in the first row of the table ("TRAINING LOG. . .") and **space** once.
   b. Insert a *Date Picker* content control field.
   c. Use the *Content Control Properties* dialog box to customize the *Title* to Training Week
   d. Customize the *Color* to **Yellow**.
   e. Apply the **Table Title** style to format the contents of the content control field.
   f. Select the spelled out Month, Day, Year date format (January 1, 2018).

4. Insert and customize *Rich Text* content control fields.
   a. Place your insertion point in the first cell in the third row (below "Miles") and insert a **Rich Text** content control field.
   b. Customize the *Title* to Miles and the *Color* to **Yellow**.
   c. Place your insertion point in the second cell in the third row (below "Duration"), insert a **Rich Text** content control field, customize the *Title* to Duration, and change the *Color* to **Yellow**.
   d. Place your insertion point in the third cell in the third row (below "Average Speed"), insert a **Rich Text** content control field, customize the *Title* to Average Speed, and change the *Color* to **Yellow**.
   e. Place your insertion point in the fourth cell in the third row (below "Average HR"), insert a **Rich Text** content control field, customize the *Title* to Average HR, and change the *Color* to **Yellow**.

5. Insert and customize a *Drop-Down List* content control field.
   a. Place your insertion point in the last cell in the third row (below "How I Felt") and insert a **Drop-Down List** content control field.
   b. Customize the *Title* to How I Felt and the *Color* to **Yellow**.
   c. **Add** the following choices: Like a Pro, Strong, Average, and Tired.
   d. Remove **Choose an item**.

6. Use *Design* mode to change the placeholder text:
   a. Turn on **Design** mode.
   b. Type Enter miles as the placeholder text for *Miles*.

c. Type **Enter hours** as the placeholder text for *Duration*.

d. Type **Enter avg. speed** as the placeholder text for *Average Speed*.

e. Type **Enter avg. HR** as the placeholder text for *Average HR*.

f. Type **Select how I felt** as the placeholder text for *How I Felt*.

g. Turn off **Design** mode.

7. Copy and paste content control fields.

a. Select the **Miles** content control field handle and copy the field.

b. Paste the content control field in each of the six cells that are below its current location.

c. Repeat the above steps for the remaining content control fields in the other columns (Figure 11-82).

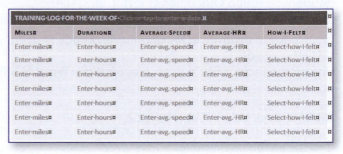

8. Save and close the document.

11-82 Copy and paste content control fields

9. Open the *TrainingLog-11* document from your student data files.

10. Save the Word document as [your initials] Word 11-4.

11. Insert a subdocument into this master document, unlink subdocument, and change heading level.

a. Change to **Outline** view.

b. Place your insertion point on the blank line at the end of the outline.

c. **Insert** the *[your initials] Word 11-4 form* as a subdocument. Click **Yes to All** when prompted to rename styles in the subdocument.

d. Select and **Unlink** the subdocument from the master document.

e. Delete the section breaks in the outline.

f. Change the "Training Intensity and Heart Rate" heading to **Level 1**.

g. Close the *Outline* view and return to *Print Layout* view.

12. Select the entire document and **Group** the content controls fields.

13. Save and close the document (Figure 11-83).

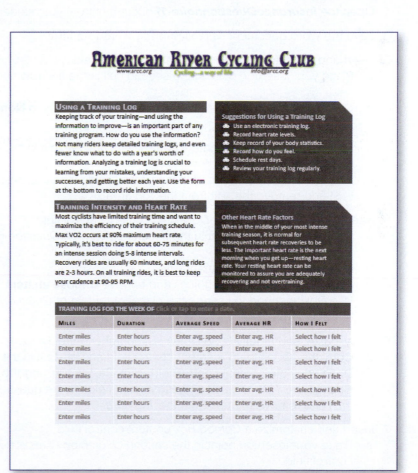

11-83 Word 11-4 completed

Independent Project 11-5

For this project, you create an insurance questionnaire for Central Sierra Insurance. You insert and customize content control fields, copy and modify content control fields, protect the document, create a new document based on the questionnaire, and fill in content control fields.
[Student Learning Outcomes 11.1, 11.2, 11.3, 11.4]

File Needed: ***InsuranceQuestionnaire-11.docx*** *(student data files are available in the* Library *of your SIMnet account)*
Completed Project File Names: *[your initials]* **Word 11-5 form.docx** and *[your initials]* **Word 11-5.docx**

Skills Covered in This Project

- Insert and customize *Rich Text*, *Drop-Down List*, *Combo Box*, and *Date Picker* content control fields.
- Change the display for a content control field.
- Apply a style to a content control field.

- Copy, paste, and customize a content control field.
- Use *Design* mode to customize placeholder text.
- Restrict editing to filling in forms.
- Fill in a content control field.

1. Open the ***InsuranceQuestionnaire-11*** document from your student data files.

2. Save the Word document as [your initials] Word 11-5 form.

3. Insert and customize a *Rich Text* content control field.
   a. Place your insertion point in the second cell in the first row and insert a **Rich Text** content control field.
   b. Customize the *Title* to Question 1 and change *Show as* to **None**.

4. Copy, paste, and modify *Rich Text* content control fields.
   a. Copy the "Question 1" content control field and paste it in the second column for questions 2–5.
   b. Change the *Title* on each of these pasted fields to the question number (*Question 2, Question 3, etc.*) and remove the text from the *Tag* area.

5. Insert and customize a *Drop-Down List* content control field.
   a. Place your insertion point in the second column on *Question 6* and insert a **Drop-Down List** content control field.
   b. Customize the *Title* to Question 6.
   c. **Add** Yes and No as the choices and remove **Choose an item**.
   d. Use *Design* mode to change the placeholder text of *Question 6* to Select Yes or No and then turn off *Design* mode.

6. Copy, paste, and modify *Drop-Down List* content control fields.
   a. Copy the "Question 6" content control field and paste it in the second column for questions 7–10. Don't copy the content control field to 7a, 8a, 9a, 10a, and 10b.
   b. Change the *Title* on each of these pasted fields to the question number (*Question 7, Question 8, etc.*) and remove the text from the *Tag* area.

7. Insert and customize a *Combo Box* content control field.
   a. Place your insertion point in the second column on *Question 7a* and insert a **Combo Box** content control field.
   b. Customize the *Title* to Question 7a.
   c. Apply the **Emphasis** style to format the contents of the content control field.
   d. **Add** N/A as the choice and remove **Choose an item**.

e. Use *Design* mode to change the placeholder text to Type a response or select N/A and then turn off *Design* mode.

8. Copy, paste, and modify *Combo Box* content control fields.
   a. Copy the "Question 7a" content control field and paste it in the second column for *Questions 8a, 9a, 10a,* and *10b*.
   b. Change the *Title* on each of these pasted fields to the question number (*Question 8a, Question 9a,* etc.) and remove the text from the *Tag* area.

9. Insert and customize a *Date Picker* content control field.
   a. Place your insertion point after "Date of Application:", **space** once, and insert a **Date Picker** content control field.
   b. Customize the *Title* to Application Date and select the spelled out date format (January 1, 2018).
   c. Use *Design* mode to change the placeholder text to Select date of application and then turn off *Design* mode. Remember, content temporarily shifts when using *Design* mode and returns to normal when you turn off *Design* mode.

10. Restrict editing of the questionnaire.
    a. Allow only **Filling in forms**.
    b. Start enforcing protection and don't use a password. Close the *Restrict Editing* pane.

11. Save the document, but do not close it.

12. Save the Word document as a different file name. Save it as [your initials] Word 11-5.

13. Use the information in the following table to fill in the questionnaire:

Question 1	Tish Waterson
Question 2	95002 North Avenue, Loomis, CA 96885
Question 3	916-528-6861
Question 4	CA3775409
Question 5	18
Question 6	Yes
Question 7	Yes
Question 7a	15%
Question 8	No
Question 8a	N/A
Question 9	No
Question 9a	N/A
Question 10	No
Question 10a	N/A
Question 10b	N/A
Application Date	Select current date

14. Save and close the document (Figure 11-84).

11-84 Word 11-5 completed

Independent Project 11-6

For this project, you use a master document and subdocuments to create a report for Courtyard Medical Plaza. You insert subdocuments into a master document, split and merge subdocuments, change heading levels, unlink subdocuments, and arrange sections of a subdocument.
[**Student Learning Outcome 11.5**]

Files Needed: *TeenSubstanceAbuse-11.docx*, *SubstanceAbuse1-11.docx*, *SubstanceAbuse2-11.docx*, *SubstanceAbuse3-11.docx*, and *SubstanceAbuse4-11.docx* (*student data files are available in the* Library *of your SIMnet account*)
Completed Project File Name: *[your initials] Word 11-6.docx*

Skills Covered in This Project

- Use *Outline* view.
- Insert a subdocument into a master document.
- Promote and demote headings.
- Merge subdocuments.

- Split a subdocument into two subdocuments.
- Show different levels in *Outline* view.
- Arrange sections in a subdocument.
- Unlink subdocuments.
- Delete a section break.
- Insert a page break.

---

1. Open the **TeenSubstanceAbuse-11** document from your student data files.

2. Save the document as [your initials] Word 11-6.

3. Open a *File Explorer* window, locate the **SubstanceAbuse1-11.docx**, **SubstanceAbuse2-11.docx**, **SubstanceAbuse3-11.docx**, and **SubstanceAbuse4-11.docx** files from your student data files, and **copy** these to the same location as your **[your initials] Word 11-6** file. These are your subdocument files.

4. Return to the **[your initials] Word 11-6** document and display the document in *Outline* view.

5. Select the "**What Is Teen Substance Abuse?**" heading and change it to **Level 1**.

6. Insert subdocuments into the master document.
   a. Place your insertion point on the blank line at the end of the outline.
   b. Insert the **SubstanceAbuse1-11** file. This file should be located in the same folder as **[your initials] Word 11-6** document.
   c. Insert each of the following subdocuments on the last blank line of the outline: **SubstanceAbuse2-11.docx**, **SubstanceAbuse3-11.docx**, and **SubstanceAbuse4-11.docx**.

7. Change heading levels in the subdocuments.
   a. **Show First Line Only** in the outline.
   b. In the first subdocument, change the "What Problems Can Teen Substance Abuse Cause?" heading to **Level 2**.
   c. In the second subdocument, change the "What Are the Signs of Substance Abuse?" heading to **Level 2**.
   d. In the third subdocument, change the "Why Do Teens Abuse Drugs and Alcohol?" heading to **Level 1**.
   e. In the fourth subdocument, change the "What Should You Do if Your Teen Is Using?" and "Bibliography" headings to **Level 1**.
   f. In the fourth subdocument, change the "Can Teen Substance Use and Abuse Be Prevented?" and "What Are the Treatment Options?" headings to **Level 2**.

8. Merge and split subdocuments.
   a. Select the first three subdocuments and **merge** them into one subdocument. Use the **Shift** key and the **subdocument selectors** to select multiple subdocuments.
   b. Select the "**Bibliography**" section and **split** it into a separate subdocument.

9. Arrange sections in subdocuments, unlink subdocuments, and remove section breaks.
   a. Change the *Show Level* to display **Level 2**, which displays *Levels 1* and *2* in the outline.
   b. In the first subdocument, move the *Level 1* heading ("Why Do Teens Abuse. . .") above the *Level 2* headings.
   c. In the second subdocument, move the second *Level 2* heading ("What Are the Treatment Options?") above the first *Level 2* heading ("Can Teen Substance Use. . .") in that subdocument.
   d. **Unlink** the three subdocuments from the master document and show **All Levels**.
   e. Remove all section breaks from the master document.

10. Save the document.

11. Close *Outline* view and display the document in *Print Layout* view.

12. Finalize the document and insert page breaks.
    a. If a section break displays at the end of the bibliography, delete it.
    b. Place your insertion point in front of the "Bibliography" heading and insert a **page break**.
    c. Place your insertion point in front of "Can Teen Substance Use and Abuse Be Prevented?" and insert a **page break**.
    d. If any blank lines display in the document, delete them.

13. Save and close the document (Figure 11-85).

TEEN SUBSTANCE ABUSE

WHAT IS TEEN SUBSTANCE ABUSE?

Many teens try alcohol, tobacco, or drugs, but using these substances is not safe or legal. Some teens try these substances only a few times and stop. Others can't control their urges or cravings for them. This is substance abuse.

Teens may try a number of substances, including cigarettes, alcohol, household chemicals (inhalants), prescription and over-the-counter medicines, and illegal drugs. Marijuana is the illegal drug that teens use most often (Sanchez, 2015).

WHY DO TEENS ABUSE DRUGS AND ALCOHOL?

Teens use alcohol and other drugs for many reasons. They may do it because they want to fit in with friends or certain groups. They may also take a drug or drink alcohol because they like the way it makes them feel. Or they may believe that it makes them more grown up. Teens tend to try new things and take risks, and they may take drugs or drink alcohol because it seems exciting.

Teens with family members who have problems with alcohol or other drugs are more likely to have serious substance abuse problems. Also, teens who feel that they are not connected to or valued by their parents are at greater risk. Teens with poor self-esteem or emotional or mental health problems, such as depression, also are at increased risk (Courtyard Medical Plaza, 2016).

What Problems Can Teen Substance Abuse Cause?

Substance abuse can lead to serious problems such as poor schoolwork, loss of friends, problems at home, and lasting legal problems. Alcohol and drug abuse is a leading cause of teen death or injury related to car accidents, suicides, violence, and drowning. Substance abuse can increase the risk of pregnancy and sexually transmitted diseases (STDs), including HIV, because of unprotected sex.

Even casual use of certain drugs can cause severe medical problems, such as an overdose or brain damage. Many illegal drugs today are made in home labs, so they can vary greatly in strength. These drugs also may contain bacteria, dangerous chemicals, and other unsafe substances (Foundation for Teen Health, 2014).

What Are the Signs of Substance Abuse?

It's important to be aware of the signs that your teen may be abusing alcohol, drugs, or other substances. Some of the signs include:

- Red eyes and health complaints, such as being overly tired. If your teen often uses over-the-counter eye drops, he or she may be trying to cover up red eyes caused by smoking marijuana.
- Less interest in school, a drop in grades, and skipping classes or school altogether.
- New friends who have little interest in their families or school activities.
- Chemical-soaked rags or papers, which may mean that your teen is inhaling vapors. Another sign of using inhalants is paint or other stains on your teen's clothing, hands, or face.

WHAT SHOULD YOU DO IF YOUR TEEN IS USING?

If your teen is using alcohol, tobacco, or drugs, take it seriously. One of the most important things you can do is to talk openly with your teen about the problem. Urge him or her to do the same. Try not to use harsh, judging words. Be as supportive as you can during this time. In most cases, a hostile, angry face-to-face meeting pushes your teen away from the family. If you do not know what to do or if you feel uncomfortable, ask for help from a pediatrician, psychologist, or psychiatrist.

What Are the Treatment Options?

The type of treatment your teen needs depends on the level of substance abuse. For example, if a teen has tried drugs or alcohol only a few times, talking openly about the problem may be all that you need to do to help your teen stop his or her substance use. But if a teen has a substance abuse problem, then he or she needs to be seen by a doctor and/or by a counselor. If your teen is addicted to a drug or alcohol, he or she may need to have detoxification treatment or a treatment that replaces the substance with medicine. Medicine works best if it is combined with one-on-one or family counseling, or both (Sanchez, 2015).

Returning to substance abuse, called relapse, is common after treatment. It is not a failure on the part of your teen or the treatment program. Recovery from addiction is hard and takes time. Know that there may be setbacks that your teen will need to overcome one step at a time.

Courtyard Medical Plaza—Teen Substance Abuse

11-85 Word 11-6 completed (pages 1 and 2 of 4)

Improve It Project 11-7

For this project, you create a buyer escrow checklist form for Placer Hills Real Estate. You convert text to a table, modify the table, insert and customize content control fields, copy and modify content control fields, and group content control fields.
[Student Learning Outcomes 11.1, 11.2, 11.3, 11.4]

File Needed: **BuyerEscrowCheckList-11.docx** *(student data files are available in the* Library *of your SIMnet account)*
Completed Project File Name: *[your initials] Word 11-7.docx*

Skills Covered in This Project

- Set tab stops to align text.
- Convert text to a table.
- Apply a table style.
- Modify row height and column width and change text alignment.

- Insert and customize *Rich Text*, *Plain Text*, *Combo Box*, and *Date Picker* content control fields.
- Change color and apply a style to a content control field.
- Copy, paste, and customize a content control field.
- Use *Design* mode to customize placeholder text.
- Group content control fields.

1. Open the ***BuyerEscrowCheckList-11*** document from your student data files.

2. Save the Word document as [your initials] Word 11-7.

3. Select the five lines beginning with "**Buyers(s):**" and ending with "**Property Address:**" and set **left** tab stops at **0.75"** and **1.25"**.

4. Convert text to a table and modify the table.
   a. Select the lines of text beginning with "**Task**" through the last line of the document.
   b. Convert the text to a table with **4** columns and **AutoFit to window**.
   c. With the entire table selected, change the font size to **10 pt**.
   d. Apply the **Grid Table 2** table style and set the table options to include a **Header Row**, **Banded Rows**, and **First Column**.
   e. With the table selected, change the row height of the entire table to **0.3"** and change the text alignment to **Align Center Left**.
   f. Select the first column, change the width to **2.8"**, and set a **0.25" left** tab stop.
   g. Change the width of the second and third columns to **1"** and change the text alignment to **Align Center**.
   h. Change the width of the fourth column to **1.6"**.

5. Insert and customize a *Rich Text* content control field.
   a. Insert a **Rich Text** content control field after the tab following "Buyer(s):".
   b. Change the title to Buyer, change the color to **Green**, and apply the **Book Title** style.

6. Insert and customize a *Plain Text* content control field.
   a. Insert a **Plain Text** content control field after the tab following "Phone:".
   b. Change the title to Phone and change the color to **Green**.

7. Copy and modify *Plain Text* content control fields.
   a. Copy the *Plain Text* content control field ("Phone") and paste it after the tab following "Email" and "Property Address."
   b. Change the titles to Email and Address respectively and remove the text from the *Tag* field.
   c. Copy and paste the *Plain Text* content control field ("Phone") in cells below "Initials" and "Notes" in the table (copy only to the second row of the table).
   d. Change the titles to Initials and Notes respectively and remove the text from the *Tag* field.

8. Insert and customize a *Combo Box* content control field.
   a. Insert a **Combo Box** content control field after the tab following "Agent:".
   b. Change the title to Agent and change the color to **Green**.
   c. Add Emma Cavalli, Ames Bellah, Hudson Alves, and Simon Bidou as the choices and remove **Choose an item**.
   d. Use the **Move Up** and **Move Down** buttons to arrange these choices alphabetically by last name.

9. Insert and customize a *Date Picker* content control field.
   a. Insert a **Date Picker** content control field in the cell below "Date Completed" in the table.
   b. Change the title to Date Completed, change the color to **Green**, and select the number date format (1/1/2018).

10. Insert *Check Box* content control fields.
    a. Insert a **Check Box** content control field before "Fax Contract to Buyer(s)."
    b. Use the **right** arrow key to deselect the content control field and press **Ctrl+Tab** to insert a tab between the *Check Box* content control field and the text.
    c. Repeat steps 10a and b above on each of the remaining cells in the first column.

11. Use *Design* mode to customize the placeholder text.
    a. Turn on **Design** mode and customize the placeholder text on the following fields:

    > *Buyer*: Type buyer's name(s)
    > *Phone*: Type phone number
    > *Email*: Type email address
    > *Agent*: Select or type agent's name
    > *Property Address*: Type property address
    > *Date Completed*: Select date
    > *Initials*: Type initials
    > *Notes*: Type notes

    b. Turn off **Design** mode.

12. Copy each of the content control fields in the second, third, and fourth columns of the table to the cells below to fill the table with content control fields.

13. Select the second and third columns of the table and **Align Center**.

14. Select the fourth column of the table and **Align Center Left**.

15. Select the entire document and **group** the content control fields.

16. Save and close the document (Figure 11-86).

Buyer Escrow Checklist

Buyer(s): Type buyer's name(s)

Phone: Type phone number

Email: Type email address

Agent: Select or type agent's name

Property Address: Type property address

Task	Date Completed	Initials	Notes
☐ Fax Contract to Buyer(s)	Select date	Type initials	Type notes
☐ Fax Contract to Lender	Select date	Type initials	Type notes
☐ Verify Property ID with Buyer(s)	Select date	Type initials	Type notes
☐ Verify Property ID with Lender	Select date	Type initials	Type notes
☐ Turn in new sale to PHRE	Select date	Type initials	Type notes
☐ Send check to Title Company	Select date	Type initials	Type notes
☐ Notified Buyer of EM deposit	Select date	Type initials	Type notes
☐ Fax/Email Pest Report to Buyer(s)	Select date	Type initials	Type notes
☐ Fax/Email Pest Report to Lender	Select date	Type initials	Type notes
☐ Fax/Email Clear Pest Report to Buyer(s)	Select date	Type initials	Type notes
☐ Fax/Email Clear Pest Report to Lender	Select date	Type initials	Type notes
☐ Verify Preliminary Report with Buyer(s)	Select date	Type initials	Type notes
☐ Verify Preliminary Report with Lender	Select date	Type initials	Type notes

Emma Cavalli
916-450-3334
ecavalli@phre.com

Placer Hills Real Estate
7100 Madrone Road, Roseville, CA 95722
www.phre.com

11-86 Word 11-7 completed

Challenge Project 11-8

Before each semester begins, you have a variety of tasks to accomplish so you are ready when classes begin. For example, you may need to register and pay for classes, complete financial aid paperwork, buy books and supplies, download and read your course syllabi, check professors' web sites, or log into learning management systems.

For this project, you create a form using content control fields to manage tasks you need to accomplish before the semester begins.
[**Student Learning Outcomes 11.1, 11.2, 11.3, 11.4**]

File Needed: None
Completed Project File Names: *[your initials] Word 11-8 check list.dotx* and *[your initials] Word 11-8.docx*

Create a new document and save it as a template named [your initials] Word 11-8 checklist. Modify your document according to the following guidelines:

- List the text and content control fields you will need in this checklist based on the tasks you need to complete before the semester begins.
- Use tab stops, indents, and/or a table to control alignment of text and content control fields.
- Insert text and content control fields for the tasks you need to complete before the semester begins.
- Customize content control fields to include titles. Change the color and how the field displays, apply a style, and add choices to *Combo Box* and *Drop-Down List* content control fields.
- Copy and modify content control fields as needed.
- Use *Design* mode to customize placeholder text.
- Group the content control fields.

Create a new document based on the checklist template and save it as [your initials] Word 11-8.

- Fill in the content control fields.
- Save and close the document.

Challenge Project 11-9

For this project, you create a form to use for an upcoming conference or workshop or a membership form for a club or organization. Insert a variety of text and content control fields in this form.
[**Student Learning Outcomes 11.1, 11.2, 11.3, 11.4**]

File Needed: None
Completed Project File Name: *[your initials] Word 11-9 form.dotx*

W11-693

Create a new document and save it as a template named [your initials] Word 11-9 form. Modify your document according to the following guidelines:

- List the text and content control fields you will need in this form.
- Use tab stops and indents to control alignment of text and content control fields.
- Insert text and content control fields for your form.
- Customize content control fields to include a title. Change the color and how the field displays, apply a style, and add choices to *Combo Box* and *Drop-Down List* content control fields.
- Copy and modify content control fields as needed.
- Use *Design* mode to customize placeholder text.
- Restrict editing of the document and protect with a password.

Challenge Project 11-10

It is important to create a budget and live within it. You need to track what you're spending in order to create an accurate budget and effectively control your finances. For this project, you create an expenditure template to track your weekly spending, and then create a document based upon the expenditure template.
[Student Learning Outcomes 11.1, 11.2, 11.3, 11.4]

File Needed: None
Completed Project File Names: *[your initials] Word 11-10 template.dotx* and *[your initials] Word 11-10.docx*

Create a new document and save it as a template named [your initials] Word 11-10 template. Modify your template according to the following guidelines:

- List the text and content control fields you need in your weekly expenditure template.
- Use a table to control alignment of text and content control fields.
- Insert text and content control fields for expenses.
- Customize content control fields to include a title. Change the color and how the field displays, apply a style, and add choices to *Combo Box* and *Drop-Down List* content control fields.
- Copy and modify content control fields as needed.
- Use *Design* mode to customize placeholder text.
- Insert a formula at the bottom of the table to total your expenditures for the week.
- Group the content control fields.

Create a new document based on the expenditure template and save it as [your initials] Word 11-10.

- Fill in your weekly spending in the content control fields.
- Update the formula in the table to total expenses. Ungroup content control fields if necessary to update the formula.
- Save and close the document.

Customizing Word and Using OneDrive and Office Online

CHAPTER OVERVIEW

Now that you know how to use the many features of Word 2016, you can customize Word settings to personalize your working environment. In addition to being customizable, Office 2016 also integrates "cloud" technology, which allows you to use your Office files in *OneDrive* and *Office Online*. These different cloud services enable your files and Office settings to roam with you and allows you to share *OneDrive* files with others. With these online features, you are not limited to using Office on only one computer, and you don't have to save your files on a USB drive or portable hard drive to have access to your files.

STUDENT LEARNING OUTCOMES (SLOs)

After completing this chapter, you will be able to:

SLO 12.1 Customize Word options, the *Ribbon,* and the *Quick Access* toolbar to personalize your working environment (p. W12-696).

SLO 12.2 View and modify Office account settings and install an Office add-in (p. W12-706).

SLO 12.3 Use *OneDrive* to create, upload, move, copy, delete, and download files and folders (p. W12-712).

SLO 12.4 Share *OneDrive* files and folders (p. W12-717).

SLO 12.5 Use *Office Online* to edit, create, share, collaborate, and comment on a document (p. W12-722).

SLO 12.6 Explore other *Office Online* products and productivity tools (p. W12-729).

Case Study

For the Pause & Practice projects in this chapter, you customize your Word settings and use Microsoft cloud services to save, edit, and share documents for Courtyard Medical Plaza.

Pause & Practice 12-1: Customize the Word 2016 working environment and Office account settings and install an Office add-in.

Pause & Practice 12-2: Use *OneDrive* and *Word Online* to save, create, edit, and share documents.

Pause & Practice 12-3: Create and share a survey using *Office Online* and *OneDrive*.

Customizing Word 2016

In this book, you have used many Word features to customize a variety of documents. You can also customize Word settings, which are global Word settings that apply to all files you work with in Word. Customize Word settings in the **Word Options** dialog box, which you open from the *Backstage* view. Once implemented, these options apply to all the documents you create and edit in Word.

Word Options

In the *Word Options* dialog box, the settings display in categories. Within each category, you can change individual settings by selecting or deselecting a check box or selecting from a drop-down list. Buttons in the *Word Options* dialog box open a dialog box to display additional customization settings. The following list includes the different categories in the *Word Options* dialog box:

- *General*
- *Display*
- *Proofing*
- *Save*
- *Language*
- *Advanced*
- *Customize Ribbon*
- *Quick Access Toolbar*
- *Add-Ins*
- *Trust Center*

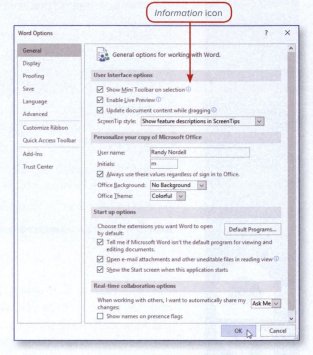

▶**HOW TO:** Customize Word Options

1. Click the **File** tab to open the *Backstage* view.
2. Click the **Options** button on the left to open the *Word Options* dialog box (Figure 12-1).
3. Click an options category on the left to display the available customization options on the right.
4. Change options using check boxes, text boxes, drop-down lists, or buttons.
   - When you click a button, a dialog box with additional option settings opens.
5. Click **OK** to close the *Word Options* dialog box and apply the settings.

12-1 *Word Options* dialog box

General

The *General* category includes the following areas: *User Interface options, Personalize your copy of Microsoft Office, Start up options,* and *Real-time collaboration options* (see Figure 12-1).

In the *User Interface options* area, you can show/hide the mini toolbar display, enable/disable live preview, and turn on/off document content while dragging. You can also customize the *ScreenTip* style.

In the *Personalize your copy of Microsoft Office* area, you can change your user name and initials and change the Office background and theme. To use the current user name and initials as the default setting for all users, check the **Always use these values regardless of sign in to Office** box.

In the *Start up options* area, you can set the default program, choose how email attachments display, and determine whether or not the *Start* screen displays when Word opens. The *Start* screen displays your recent documents and Word templates.

In the *Real-time collaboration options* area, choose how changes are made and marked when collaborating with others on an online document. Sharing is covered in *SLO 12.4: Sharing OneDrive Files and Folders* and *SLO 12.5: Using Office Online* later in this chapter.

Display

The *Display* options category controls how document content displays on the screen and when it is printed (Figure 12-2). In the *Page display options* area, you can show or hide white space between pages in *Print Layout* view, highlighter marks, and document tooltips.

In the *Always show these formatting marks on the screen* area, select the formatting marks to display when *Show/Hide* is turned on. By default, object anchors and all formatting marks display. To customize which formatting marks display, deselect **Show all formatting marks** and check the individual marks next to the formatting marks you want *Show/Hide* to display.

In the *Printing options* area, customize which elements do or don't print. You can also set Word to update fields and linked data before printing.

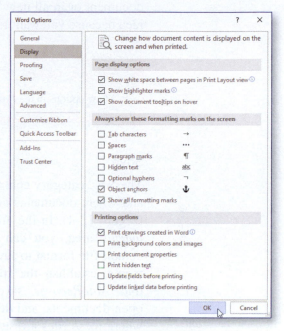

12-2 *Display* options in the *Word Options* dialog box

Proofing

The *Proofing* category controls how Word corrects and formats your text (Figure 12-3). Click the **AutoCorrect options** button to open the *AutoCorrect* dialog box and change options in the *AutoCorrect, Math AutoCorrect, AutoFormat As You Type, AutoFormat,* and *Actions* categories.

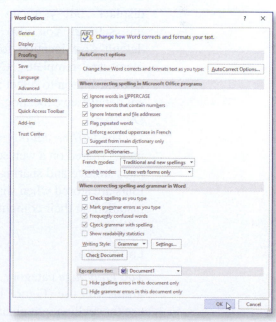

12-3 *Proofing* options in the *Word Options* dialog box

In the *When correcting spelling in Microsoft Office programs* area, Word is, by default, set to ignore words in uppercase, words that contain numbers, and Internet and file addresses. Click the **Custom Dictionaries** button to open the *Custom Dictionaries* and add, edit, or delete words from the custom dictionary.

In the *When correcting spelling and grammar in Word* area, you control how and when the spelling and grammar check functions. You can also turn on ***readability statistics*** to display statistics about your document after you finish checking spelling and grammar.

By default, Word checks spelling and grammar, but not style. To check grammar and style, click the **Settings** button to customize grammar and style settings.

In the *Exceptions for* area, you can hide spelling and grammatical errors in a selected document or in all new Word documents. Hiding spelling and grammar errors is not a good idea because you want to be able to see and correct your errors.

> **MORE INFO**
>
> Many options in the *Proofing* category apply to all Office applications and files.

Save

The *Save* category controls how and where documents are saved (Figure 12-4). In the *Save documents* area, you can set the default file format to save documents, establish the frequency that *AutoRecover* saves your open documents, and determine where these files are stored. By default, when you press **Ctrl+O** or **Ctrl+S** to open or save a document, the *Backstage* view displays, but you can change this setting. You also set the default save location for documents and templates. Click the **Browse** button to select a different default save location, such as *OneDrive*.

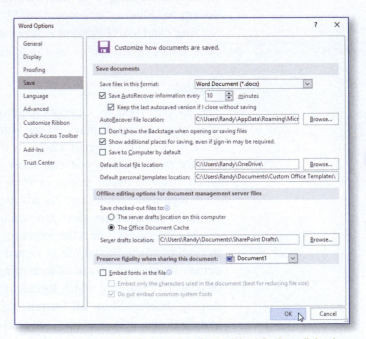

12-4 *Save* options in the *Word Options* dialog box

The *Offline editing options for document management server files* area pertains to documents shared on a web server (such as *OneDrive for Business*), which is a location that facilitates storage and sharing of files. *Preserve fidelity when sharing this document* controls how fonts are stored when sharing a document between users who may not have all the same fonts installed on their computers. Neither of these customization options is common.

Language

The *Language* category controls the language preferences in Word and the other Office programs you use (Figure 12-5). In the *Choose Editing Languages* area, select the language to use for spelling, grammar, dictionaries, and sorting. You can add a new language, set a different default language, or remove a language.

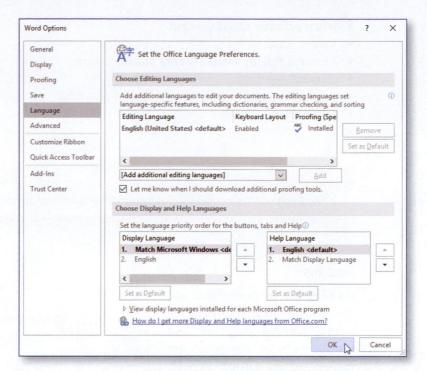

12-5 *Language* options in the *Word Options* dialog box

In the *Choose Display and Help Languages* area, you can set the language for display tabs, buttons, and *Help*.

> **MORE INFO**
>
> The language settings in Office are determined by the default language you selected when you installed Windows.

Advanced

The *Advanced* category provides you with a variety of customization options (Figure 12-6). The following is a list of the different options in the *Advanced* category. Scroll through each of these areas to familiarize yourself with the different customization options available.

- *Editing options*
- *Cut, copy, and paste*
- *Pen*
- *Image Size and Quality*
- *Chart*
- *Show document content*
- *Display*
- *Print*

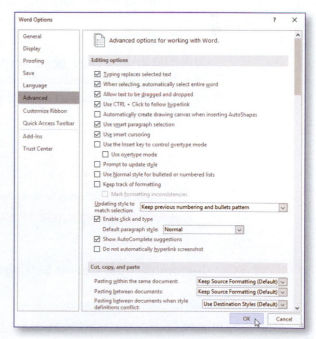

12-6 *Advanced* options in the *Word Options* dialog box

- *When printing this document*
- *Save*
- *Preserve fidelity when sharing this document*
- *General*
- *Layout options*
- *Compatibility options*

> **MORE INFO**
>
> The *Customize Ribbon* and *Quick Access Toolbar* options are covered later in this section.

Add-Ins

Add-ins are programs that add functionality to your Office programs. Certain programs you install on your computer are recognized by Office as add-in programs such as Google Desktop or Snag-It.

In the *Add-Ins* category in the *Word Options* dialog box, view the add-in programs that interact with Office (Figure 12-7). Enable or disable add-ins by clicking the **Manage** drop-down list, selecting a category, and clicking **Go**. A dialog box opens where you enable or disable add-ins.

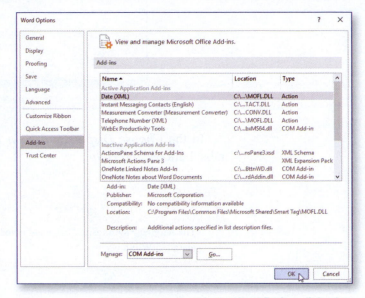

12-7 *Add-Ins* options in the *Word Options* dialog box

Trust Center

The *Trust Center* helps keep your files safe and prevents your files and computer from becoming infected with viruses. You can customize many different areas in the *Trust Center* dialog box. It is generally recommended that you use the default settings in the *Trust Center*.

> **MORE INFO**
>
> For more information on macros and the *Trust Center*, see *SLO10.3: Creating and Running Macros*.

HOW TO: Customize Trust Center Settings

1. Click the **File** tab to open the *Backstage* view.
2. Click the **Options** button on the left to open the *Word Options* dialog box.
3. Click the **Trust Center** button on the left.

4. Click the **Trust Center Settings** button to open the *Trust Center* dialog box (Figure 12-8).

5. Click the different categories on the left to view the available options and apply changes.

6. Click **OK** to close the *Trust Center* dialog box.

7. Click **OK** to close the *Word Options* dialog box.

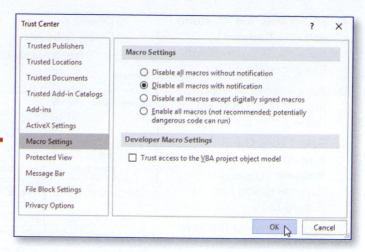

12-8 *Trust Center* dialog box

Customize the Ribbon

The Word *Ribbon* includes many of the common commands you use, but not all available commands display on the *Ribbon*. You can customize the *Ribbon* to add a new group to a tab or to add commands you commonly use. For example, you can create a new group on the *Home* tab that includes a button to open the *Tabs* dialog box or create a custom tab with groups containing commonly used commands.

> **MORE INFO**
>
> You can add commands to custom groups, but you cannot add or remove commands in existing groups.

▶ HOW TO: Add a Tab, Group, and Commands to the Ribbon

1. Right-click anywhere on the **Ribbon** and select **Customize the Ribbon** from the context menu. The *Word Options* dialog box opens and displays the *Customize Ribbon* area (Figure 12-9).
   - Alternatively, click the **File** tab to open the *Backstage* view, click the **Options** button to open the *Word Options* dialog box, and select **Customize Ribbon**.
   - The left side lists available commands and groups, and the right side lists the existing tabs and groups that display on the *Ribbon*.
   - The drop-down lists at the top of each of the lists provide you with other commands and tabs to display in these lists.

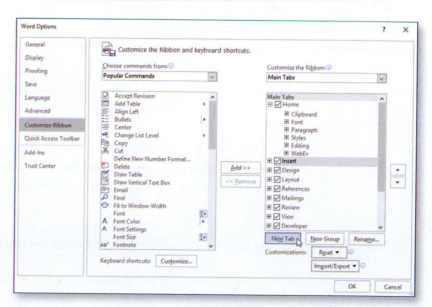

12-9 *Customize Ribbon* area of the *Word Options* dialog box

2. Click a tab on the right where you want to insert a new tab.

3. Click the **New Tab** button. A new custom tab and group display below the selected tab.

4. Select **New Tab (Custom)** and click **Rename** to open the *Rename* dialog box (Figure 12-10).

5. Type a name for the new tab and click **OK** to close the *Rename* dialog box.

6. Select **New Group (Custom)** and click **Rename** to open the *Rename* dialog box (Figure 12-11).

7. Type a name for the new group in the *Display name* area, select a symbol (optional), and click **OK** to close the *Rename* dialog box.

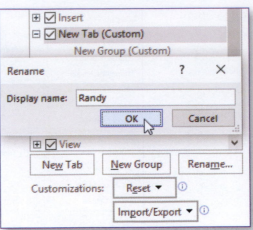

12-10 Rename a new tab

12-11 Rename a new group

8. Select a custom group on the right where you want to add a command.

   • Click the plus or minus sign by a tab or group to expand or collapse it.

9. Click the **Choose commands from** drop-down list on the left side and select **All Commands** to display all the available commands.

10. Select a command on the left to add to the custom group on the right and click the **Add** button to add the command to the group (Figure 12-12).

11. Click **OK** to close the *Word Options* dialog box.

   • The new tab and group display on the *Ribbon* (Figure 12-13).

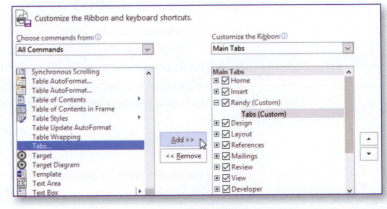

12-12 Add a command to a custom group

12-13 Custom tab, group, and commands on the *Ribbon*

You can also rearrange tabs on the *Ribbon,* groups on a tab, and commands in a custom group. You cannot rearrange existing commands within existing groups.

▶ **HOW TO: Rearrange Tabs, Groups, and Commands on the Ribbon**

1. Right-click anywhere on the **Ribbon** and select **Customize the Ribbon** from the context menu. The *Word Options* dialog box opens and displays the *Customize Ribbon* area.

2. Select the command, group, or tab you want to rearrange.

3. Click the **Move Up** or **Move Down** button to rearrange the selected item (Figure 12-14).

4. Click **OK** to close the *Word Options* dialog box.

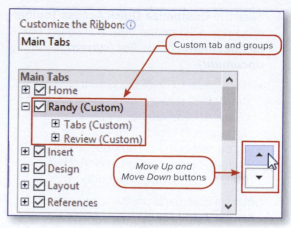

12-14 Rearrange a tab on the *Ribbon*

Customize the Quick Access Toolbar

In *Chapter 10: Automating Tasks Using Templates and Macros,* you added macro buttons to the *Quick Access* toolbar. You can also add commands you frequently use to the *Quick Access* toolbar. By default, the *Save, Undo, Redo,* and *Touch/Mouse Mode* (if the computer has a touch screen) commands display on the *Quick Access* toolbar. Add commonly used commands from the *Customize Quick Access Toolbar* drop-down list (Figure 12-15) or add other commands in the *Quick Access Toolbar* area in the *Word Options* dialog box. When customizing the *Quick Access* toolbar, changes, by default, apply to all documents, but you can apply changes to the current document only.

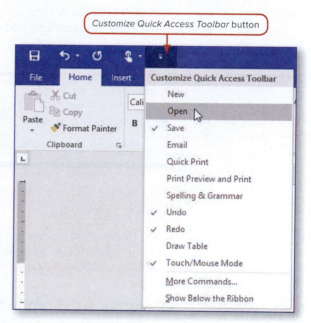

12-15 Add a command to the *Quick Access* toolbar

▶ **HOW TO:** Customize the Quick Access Toolbar

1. Click the **Customize Quick Access Toolbar** drop-down list on the right edge of the *Quick Access* toolbar (see Figure 12-15).

2. Select a command to add to the *Quick Access* toolbar. The command displays on the *Quick Access* toolbar.
   - Items on the *Customize Quick Access Toolbar* drop-down list with a check mark are commands that display on the *Quick Access* toolbar.

3. Add a command that is not listed on the *Customize Quick Access Toolbar* by clicking the **Customize Quick Access Toolbar** drop-down list and selecting **More Commands**.
   - The *Word Options* dialog box opens and displays the *Quick Access Toolbar* area (Figure 12-16).

4. Click the **Customize Quick Access Toolbar** drop-down list on the right and select **For all documents** or the **For [current document]**.

- If you select *For all documents* (which is the default setting), changes apply to the *Quick Access* toolbar for all documents you open in Word.
- If you select the current document, changes apply to the *Quick Access* toolbar in that document only.

5. Select a command on the left to add and click the **Add** button.

- Click the **Choose commands from** drop-down list and select **All Commands** to display more command options.

6. Rearrange commands on the *Quick Access* toolbar by selecting the command to move and clicking the **Move Up** or **Move Down** button.

7. Click **OK** to close the *Word Options* dialog box.

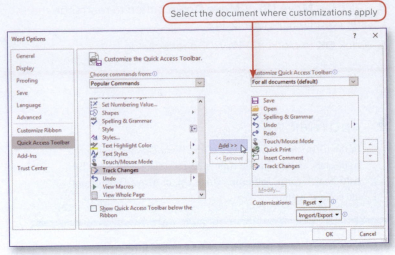

Select the document where customizations apply

12-16 Customize the *Quick Access* toolbar

> **ANOTHER WAY**
>
> Right-click a command on the *Ribbon* and select **Add to Quick Access Toolbar** from the context menu.

> **MORE INFO**
>
> To display the *Quick Access* toolbar below the *Ribbon,* click the **Customize Quick Access Toolbar** drop-down list and select **Show Below the Ribbon**.

Remove a Command from the Quick Access Toolbar

You might want to remove an existing command from the *Quick Access* toolbar or remove a command you added.

▶ **HOW TO:** Remove Commands from the Quick Access Toolbar

1. Right-click the item to remove on the *Quick Access* toolbar.

2. Select **Remove from Quick Access Toolbar** from the context menu (Figure 12-17).

- Alternatively, click the **Customize Quick Access Toolbar** drop-down list and click a checked command to deselect it, which removes it from the *Quick Access* toolbar.
- You can also remove commands from the *Quick Access* toolbar by opening the *Word Options* dialog box, selecting **Quick Access Toolbar**, selecting a command on the right, and clicking the **Remove** button.

12-17 Context menu to remove a command from the *Quick Access* toolbar

Remove an Item from the Ribbon

To remove custom tabs, groups, or commands from the *Ribbon,* use the *Customize Ribbon* area of the *Word Options* dialog box. You cannot remove existing default tabs from Word, but you can deselect one or more tabs in the *Customize the Ribbon* area so they are hidden and do not display on the *Ribbon.* You can remove existing groups from a tab, but you cannot delete individual commands from an existing default group.

▶ HOW TO: Remove an Item from the Ribbon

1. Right-click anywhere on the **Ribbon** and select **Customize the Ribbon** from the context menu. The *Word Options* dialog box opens and displays the *Customize Ribbon* area (Figure 12-18).

   • You can also click the **File** tab to open the *Backstage* view, click the **Options** button to open the *Word Options* dialog box, and select **Customize Ribbon**.

2. Hide a tab by clicking the check box to the left of the tab name to deselect the tab.

   • The tab still exists in the list, but it does not display on the *Ribbon.*

3. Select a custom tab, group, or command on the right and click the **Remove** button.

   • Click the plus or minus sign to the left of a tab or group to expand or collapse the tab and group.
   • You can also right-click a tab or group and select **Remove** from the context menu.

4. Click **OK** to close the *Word Options* dialog box.

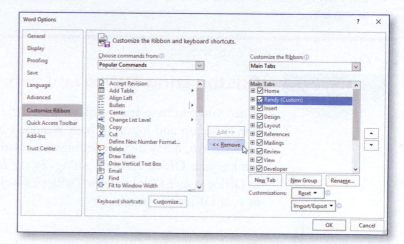

12-18 Remove a custom tab from the *Ribbon*

Reset the Ribbon and Quick Access Toolbar

You can reset the *Ribbon* and the *Quick Access* toolbar to their original settings. When resetting the *Ribbon,* you can reset a specific tab or all *Ribbon* customizations. Use the *Word Options* dialog box to reset the *Ribbon* or *Quick Access* toolbar.

▶ HOW TO: Reset the Ribbon and Quick Access Toolbar

1. Open the *Word Options* dialog box and select either **Customize Ribbon** or **Quick Access Toolbar**.

2. Click the **Reset** button at the bottom right and select from the available options (Figures 12-19 and 12-20).

   • To reset a specific tab, select the tab to reset before clicking the *Reset* button.

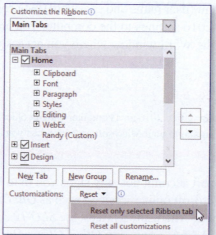

12-19 Reset the *Ribbon*

12-20 Reset the *Quick Access* toolbar

- If you are resetting the *Ribbon,* select **Reset only selected Ribbon tab** or **Reset all customizations**.
- If you are resetting the *Quick Access* toolbar, select **Reset only Quick Access Toolbar** or **Reset all customizations**.
- If you select **Reset all customizations**, Word resets both the *Ribbon* and the *Quick Access* toolbar.

3. Click **Yes** if a dialog box opens to confirm you want to delete customizations (Figure 12-21).

4. Click **OK** to close the *Word Options* dialog box.

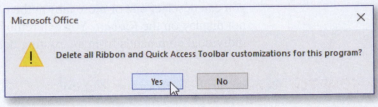

12-21 Confirm to delete all customizations

SLO 12.2 Customizing Office and Installing Office Add-Ins

When you purchase and install Office 2016 or 365, you use your Microsoft account information to set up and log in to both Windows and Office. If you upgrade from Office 2013 to Office 2016, many of your settings automatically transfer to the new version. View and customize your Office account settings in the *Backstage* view. You can add connected services to Office such as LinkedIn or Twitter as well as add Office add-ins, which add functionality to your Office programs.

> **MORE INFO**
>
> If you don't have a Microsoft account, you can create a free account at the following web site: https://signup.live.com

Microsoft Account Information

One of the features of Office 2016 and 365 is the portability of your documents and account settings. Your Office settings and files can travel with you, which means that you are not restricted to using just a single computer. For example, you can now log in to Office 2016 on a computer at a computer lab on your college campus, at a public library, or on a friend's computer, and your Office 2016 settings apply to that computer.

When you sign in to your computer using Windows 10, it is best to log in with your Microsoft account (user name and password). Microsoft Office uses this information to transfer your Office 2016 settings to the computer you are using. Your name displays in the upper right corner of the Word window where you access your account settings.

> **MORE INFO**
>
> If you are using Office 2016 on a computer with an older version of Windows, you might be prompted to sign in to your Microsoft account when you open an Office 2016 application or file.

Your Microsoft account not only signs you in to Windows and Office but also signs you in to other free Microsoft online services, such as *OneDrive* and *Office Online*. For more information on these online Microsoft services, see *SLO 12.3: Using OneDrive, SLO 12.5: Using Office Online,* and *SLO 12.6: Exploring Other Office Online Applications.* Create a free Microsoft account at https://signup.live.com if you don't already have a Microsoft account.

1. Click your name or the log on area in the upper right corner of the Word window (Figure 12-22).

2. Click the **Account settings** link to open the *Account* area on the *Backstage* view (Figure 12-23).

   - You can also click the **File** tab and select **Account** on the left.
   - Your account information displays in this area.

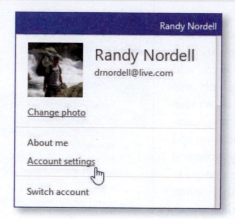

12-22 **Microsoft account information**

12-23 *Account* area on the *Backstage* view

3. If you are not signed in to Office with your Microsoft account, click the **Sign in** link in the upper right of the Word window or on the *Backstage* view to open the *Sign in* dialog box.

   - Type your Microsoft account email address and click **Next**. Another *Sign in* dialog box opens (Figure 12-24).
   - Type your password and click **Sign in**.
   - If you don't have a Microsoft account, click the **Create one** link to take you to a web page where you create a free Microsoft account.
   - You also use your Microsoft account to log in to *OneDrive* where you can create store and share files and use *Office Online*.

12-24 **Sign in to Office using a Microsoft account**

> **MORE INFO**
>
> If you are using a public computer, be sure to click the **Sign out** link in the *Account* area on the *Backstage* view to log out of your Microsoft account.

Office Background and Theme

You can change the *Office Background* and *Office Theme* in the *Account* area on the *Backstage* view or in the *General* category in the *Word Options* dialog box. Click the **Office Background** or **Office Theme** drop-down list and select a background or theme (Figure 12-25). The background displays a graphic pattern in the upper right corner of the Word window. The theme controls the colors of the working *Ribbon*, the *Backstage* view, and dialog boxes. The background and theme you select apply to all Office applications you use. The new default *Office Theme* for Office 2016 is *Colorful*.

12-25 **Change *Office Background* or *Office Theme***

Connected Services

Office 2016 has added many features to allow you to connect to online services. In the *Account* area on the *Backstage* view, add online services you regularly use by clicking the **Add a service** drop-down list and selecting a service (Figure 12-26). When you add a service, you are usually prompted to enter your user name and password to connect to the online service. The services you are currently connected to are listed in the *Connected Service* area.

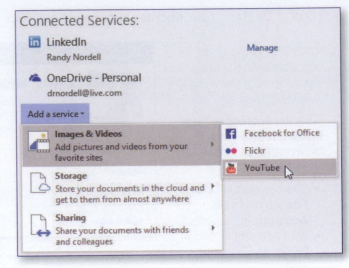

12-26 Add an online service to your Office account

All of the connected services in your account travel with you when you log in to Office on another computer. The following services are currently available, and Microsoft continues to add new services:

- *Images & Video: Facebook for Office, Flickr,* and *YouTube*
- *Storage: Office365 SharePoint* and *OneDrive*
- *Sharing: LinkedIn* and *Twitter*

Office Add-Ins

Another feature in Office 2016 is the ability to install ***Office add-ins*** to your Office 2016 programs. Similar to apps on your smart phone, Office add-ins are applications that add functionality to your Office software. For example, you can add a dictionary, encyclopedia, a news feed, or maps. When you add and open an Office add-in, the add-in opens in a pane at the right of the Word window.

▶ HOW TO: Install an Office Add-In

1. Click the **Store** button [*Insert* tab, *Add-ins* group] to open the *Office Add-ins* dialog box (Figure 12-27).

2. Select a category on the left to display the available add-ins.

   - Use the search text box to type keywords and search for matching add-ins.
   - Click the **My Add-ins** link at the top of the dialog box to display previously installed Office add-ins.

3. Select an add-in to display information about the add-in.

4. Click the **Add** button to install the add-in.

   - An *Add-in* pane opens on the right (Figure 12-28).

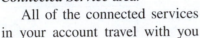

12-27 *Office Add-ins* dialog box

- Depending on the app you select, you may be taken to a web site to add the app.

5. Click the **X** in the upper right corner to close the pane.

12-28 *Add-in* pane

MORE INFO

Regularly check the *Office Add-ins* store for new and featured add-ins. New add-ins are added regularly.

Open and Manage Office Add-ins

After installing apps in Office, you can view the add-ins you have installed, open an add-in in the pane at the right, and manage which add-ins are visible.

▶**HOW TO:** Open and Manage Office Add-Ins

1. Click the **My Add-ins** button [*Insert* tab, *Add-ins* group] to open the *Office Add-ins* dialog box (Figure 12-29).

2. Select an add-in to open and click **OK**. The add-in opens in a pane to the right of the Word window (see Figure 12-28).

   - You can also click the **My Add-ins** drop-down button [*Insert* tab, *Add-ins* group] to display *Recently Used Add-ins*.

3. Manage available add-ins by clicking the **My Add-ins** button [*Insert* tab, *Add-ins* group] to open the *Office Add-ins* dialog box.

   - Right-click an add-in (or click the ellipses in the upper right corner) and select **Remove** to remove an add-in.
   - You can also view add-in details or rate and review the add-in from this context menu.
   - Click the **Store** link at the top of the dialog to search for and install other add-ins.

12-29 Open an Office add-in

4. Click the **Manage My Add-ins** link in the *Office Add-ins* dialog box to open an Internet browser window that displays your add-ins.

   - Click the **Hide** link to hide an add-in.
   - Click the **Hidden** link in the upper right to display hidden add-ins. Click **Retrieve** to make the add-in visible again.

PAUSE & PRACTICE: WORD 12-1

For this project, you customize Word options, add items to the *Ribbon* and the *Quick Access* toolbar, customize your Office account settings, and add an Office add-in.
Note: You need a Microsoft account (https://signup.live.com) to complete this project.

File Needed: ***StayingActive-12.docx*** *(student data files are available in the* Library *of your SIMnet account)*
Completed Project File Name: ***[your initials] PP W12-1.docx***

1. Open the **StayingActive-12** document from your student data files.

2. Save this document as [your initials] PP W12-1.

3. Log in to Office using your Microsoft account. Skip this step if you are already logged in with your Microsoft account.
   a. In the upper right corner of the Word window, log in to Office using your Microsoft account.
   b. If you don't have a Microsoft account, go to https://signup.live.com and follow the instructions to create a free Microsoft account.

4. Customize Word options.
   a. Click the **File** tab to open the *Backstage* view and select **Options** to open the *Word Options* dialog box.
   b. Select **General** on the left, type your name and initials in the *User name* and *Initials* areas if they are not already there, and check the **Always use these values regardless of sign in to Office** box.
   c. Select **Display** on the left and check the **Update fields before printing** and **Update linked data before printing** boxes in the *Printing options* area.
   d. Select **Save** on the left and check the **Don't show the Backstage when opening or saving files** box in the *Save documents* area.
   e. Select **Advanced** on the left and check the **Show bookmarks** box in the *Show document content* area if it is not already checked.
   f. Click **OK** to close the *Word Options* dialog box and apply the changes.

5. Add and rename a custom tab and group.
   a. Right-click anywhere on the **Ribbon** and select **Customize the Ribbon** from the context menu to open the *Word Options* dialog box and display the *Customize Ribbon* area.
   b. Click the **Home** tab on the right (under *Main Tabs*) and click the **New Tab** button. A new tab and group are inserted below the *Home* tab.
   c. Select **New Tab (Custom)** and click the **Rename** button to open the *Rename* dialog box.
   d. Type your first name and click **OK** to close the *Rename* dialog box.
   e. Select **New Group (Custom)** and click the **Rename** button to open the *Rename* dialog box (Figure 12-30).
   f. Select the smiley face symbol, type Common Commands in the *Display name* area, and click **OK** to close the *Rename* dialog box.

12-30 Rename new custom group

6. Add commands to a custom group on the *Ribbon*.
   a. Select the new **Common Commands** group on the right.
   b. Click the **Choose commands from** drop-down list on the left side and select **All Commands** to display all the available commands in the list on the left.

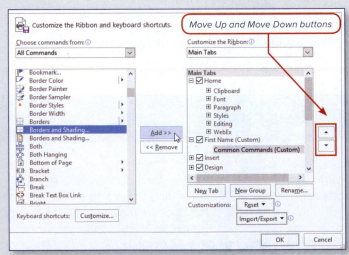

12-31 Add a command to a custom group

c. Scroll down and select the **Borders and Shading** command (the first one listed) and click the **Add** button to add the command to the group (Figure 12-31).

d. Select and add the **Tabs** and **Custom Margins** commands to the *Common Commands* group.

e. Use the **Move Up** or **Move Down** button on the right to arrange the commands in alphabetical order.

f. Click **OK** to close the *Word Options* dialog box.

g. Click the *[your first name]* tab on the *Ribbon* (Figure 12-32).

12-32 New tab and group

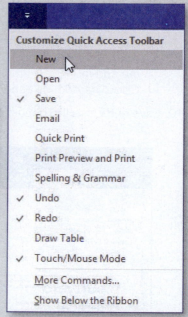

12-33 Add a command to the *Quick Access* toolbar

7. Add commands to the *Quick Access* toolbar.

a. Click the **Customize Quick Access Toolbar** drop-down list and select **New** (Figure 12-33).

b. Add **Open** and **Quick Print** to the *Quick Access* toolbar from the *Customize Quick Access Toolbar* drop-down list.

c. Click the **Customize Quick Access Toolbar** drop-down list and select **More Commands** to open the *Word Options* dialog box and display the *Quick Access Toolbar* area.

d. Scroll down the list on the left, select **Insert Comment**, and click the **Add** button (Figure 12-34).

e. Select **Quick Print** on the right and use the **Move Up** button to rearrange it so it appears after *Save* in the *Quick Access* toolbar list of commands.

f. Click **OK** to close the *Word Options* dialog box.

8. Customize your Office account settings.

a. Click the **File** tab and select **Account** to display your account information on the *Backstage* view.

b. Click the **Office Background** drop-down list and select a background of your choice.

c. Click the **Office Theme** drop-down list and select a theme of your choice.

d. Click the **Add a service** drop-down list, select **Images & Videos**, and click **YouTube**. YouTube is added in the *Connected Services* area.

e. Click the **Back** arrow to close the *Backstage* view.

9. Add an Office add-in. You must be logged in to your Microsoft account to add an add-in.

a. Click the **Store** button [*Insert* tab, *Add-ins* group] to open the *Office Add-ins* dialog box. (Figure 12-35).

b. Click **Editor's Picks** in the *Category* area to display the add-ins.

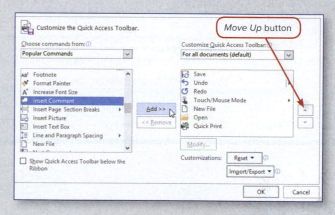

12-34 Add a command to the *Quick Access* toolbar

12-35 Add an Office add-in

c. Select an add-in to display information about the add-in.
   d. Click **Add** to add the add-in. The add-in opens in the pane on the right. If the add-in does not automatically load in the *Add-ins* pane, click the **exclamation point** in the upper left corner of the *Add-ins* pane to display information about the add-in, and then click the **Start** button to activate the add-in.
   e. Close the *Add-ins* pane.

10. Save and close the document (Figure 12-36).

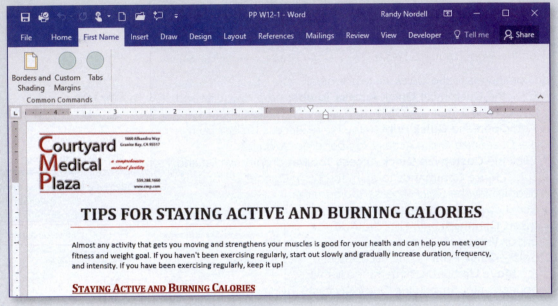

12-36 PP W12-1 completed (page 1 and customized *Ribbon* and *Quick Access* toolbar displayed)

SLO 12.3

Using OneDrive

Windows and Microsoft Office work in conjunction with Microsoft's **OneDrive** to provide online access to your files from any computer. *OneDrive* is a "cloud" storage area where you can securely store files in an online location and access them from any computer.

When you have a Microsoft account (Live, Hotmail, MSN, Messenger, Outlook.com, or other Microsoft service account), you also have a *OneDrive* account. Your *OneDrive* account is a private and secure online location. Use *OneDrive* to store files, create folders to organize stored files, and share files with others. You can access your *OneDrive* files from a *File Explorer* window on your computer or access *OneDrive* online from any computer using an Internet browser. If you don't have a Microsoft account, create a free account at https://signup.live.com.

> **MORE INFO**
>
> While *OneDrive* is secure and requires a user name and password to log in, no online accounts are 100 percent secure. Highly sensitive and confidential documents should not be stored online.

Use OneDrive in a File Explorer Window

When using Windows 10, *OneDrive* is one of your storage location folders, similar to your *Document* or *Pictures* folders (Figure 12-37). Your **OneDrive folder** looks and functions similarly to other Windows folders. You can save, open, and edit documents from the *OneDrive* folder. You can also create folders and rename, move, or delete files from your *OneDrive* folder. When you open the *Save As* or *Open* dialog box in Word, *OneDrive* is one of the available folders. In *Word Options,* you can set *OneDrive* as the default save location.

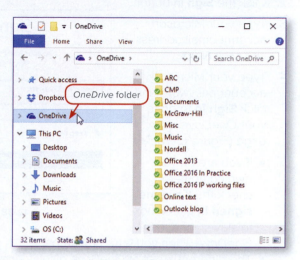

12-37 *OneDrive* folder displayed in a *File Explorer* window

The primary difference between the *OneDrive* folder and other Windows folders is the physical location where files are stored. If you save a document in your *Documents* folder, the file is stored only on the hard drive on your computer, and you have access to this file only when you are working on your computer. When you save a document in your *OneDrive* folder, the file is stored on your computer and the *OneDrive* cloud, and you have access to the file from your computer *and* any other computer with Internet access.

> **MORE INFO**
>
> To access your *OneDrive* folder on your computer, you must be logged in using your Microsoft account.

> **MORE INFO**
>
> If you are using Windows 7 or a previous version of Windows, you need to download and install the free *OneDrive desktop app for Windows* on your computer. After you do this, the *OneDrive* folder is available when you open a *File Explorer* window. Search the Internet to find, download, and install the *OneDrive desktop app.*

Use OneDrive Online

The main benefit of using *OneDrive* to store your files is the freedom it gives you to access files from any computer with Internet access. In addition to accessing your *OneDrive* files from a *File Explorer* folder on your computer, you can access your *OneDrive* files from a web page using an Internet browser. You sign in to the *OneDrive* web page using your Microsoft account.

> **MORE INFO**
>
> Depending on the Internet browser you use (Chrome, Edge, or Firefox), the user interface, button options, and dialog boxes might be slightly different. Also, the *OneDrive* online environment changes regularly, so figures in this book might be slightly different from what is currently available.

▶ HOW TO: Use OneDrive Online

1. Open an Internet browser window and go to the *OneDrive* web site (www.onedrive.live.com), which takes you to the *OneDrive* sign in page.
   - You can use any Internet browser to access *OneDrive* (Microsoft Edge, Google Chrome, or Mozilla Firefox).

2. Click the **Sign in** button.

3. Type your Microsoft account email address and click **Next**.

4. Type your Microsoft account password and click **Sign in** to go to your *OneDrive* web page (Figure 12-38).

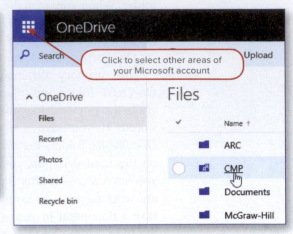

12-38 Sign in to *OneDrive*

12-39 *OneDrive* online environment

   - If you are on your own computer, check the **Keep me signed in** check box to stay signed in to *OneDrive* when you return to the page.
   - The different areas of *OneDrive* display under the *OneDrive* heading on the left corner (*Files, Recent, Photos, Shared*) (Figure 12-39).

5. Choose from the sort and view options in the *OneDrive* page in the upper right corner of the window (Figure 12-40).

   - Click the **Sort** drop-down list to select a sort option.
   - Click the **View** button to toggle between *List, Tiles, and Photo* views. Figure 12-39 displays *OneDrive* folders in *List* view.

12-40 *OneDrive* sort and display options

6. Click the **Files** button on the left to display your folders and files in the *Files* area on the right.

7. Click the **circle** to the left of a file or folder to select it (Figure 12-41).

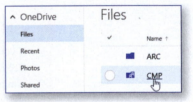

   - Use the buttons and drop-down menus at the top to perform actions on selected files and folders.

12-42 Open a *OneDrive* folder

8. Click a file or folder to open it (Figure 12-42).

12-41 Select a *OneDrive* folder

   - If you click an Office file, the file opens in *Office Online* (see *SLO 12.5: Using Office Online*).
   - If you click a folder, the folder opens and displays the contents of the folder. Click **Files** on the left or at the top to return to all *OneDrive* files.

9. Click your name or picture icon in the upper right corner and select **Sign out** to sign out of *OneDrive*.

▶ MORE INFO

If you're using a public computer, do not check the *Keep me signed in* check box. You do not want your *OneDrive* files available to the next person who uses the computer.

Create a Folder

In *OneDrive* online, you can create folders to organize your files in a way that is similar to how you organize Windows folders.

▶ HOW TO: Create OneDrive Folders

1. Click the **Files** button on the left to display the contents of your *OneDrive* folder in the *Files* area on the right.

2. Click the **New** button and select **Folder** from the drop-down list (Figure 12-43). A new folder window opens.

3. Type the name of the new folder and click **Create**.

4. Click a folder to open it.

   - You can create a new folder inside an existing folder, or you can upload files to the folder (see the following *Upload a File* section).

5. Click **Files** on the left to return to the main *OneDrive* folder.

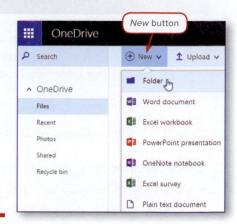

12-43 Create a new *OneDrive* folder

> ▶ **MORE INFO**
>
> When you upload files or create folders online in *OneDrive,* these changes also apply to your Windows *OneDrive* folder on your computer.

Upload a File or Folder

You can upload files to your *OneDrive* from a folder on your computer or a portable storage device. When you upload files to your *OneDrive,* you are not removing the files from the original location, but actually copying them to *OneDrive*.

▶ HOW TO: Upload a File or Folder to OneDrive

1. Click **Files** on the left to display your files and folders in the *Files* area on the right.

   - If you are uploading a file to a specific folder, click the folder to open it.

2. Click the **Upload** button and select **File** or **Folder** (Figure 12-44).

   - The actions for this button may vary slightly depending on the Internet browser you use. Some browsers open a dialog box when you click the *Upload* button rather than displaying the *File* and *Folder* options.
   - The dialog box that opens varies depending on the browser you use and the upload choice you make.

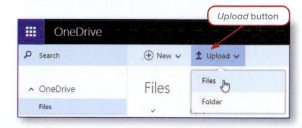

12-44 Upload a file to *OneDrive*

3. Select the file(s) or folder to upload to *OneDrive* and click **Open** (Figure 12-45).

   - You may have to click **OK** or **Select Folder** depending on the browser you use and whether you are uploading a file or folder.
   - You can upload more than one file at a time. Use the **Ctrl** key to select non-adjacent files, the **Shift** key to select a range of files, or **Ctrl+A** to select all files in a folder.
   - An upload status indicator appears in the upper right corner when you are uploading files.
   - The files you upload appear in the files and folders area of *OneDrive*.

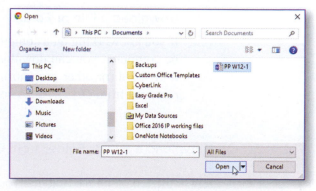

12-45 Select a file to upload to *OneDrive*

Move, Copy, or Delete a File or Folder

You can also move, copy, and delete files and folders online in *OneDrive*. When you move a file or folder, it is removed from its current location and moved to the new location you select. When you copy a file or folder, it is copied to the new location you select, and the file or folder also remains in its original location.

▶ **HOW TO:** Move, Copy, or Delete OneDrive Files

1. Check the **circle** to the left of the file or folder you want to move or copy.
   - Move multiple items by selecting the check boxes of all of the items to move.
2. Click the **Move to** or **Copy to** button at the top (Figure 12-46). A *Move item to* or *Copy item to* pane opens on the right (Figure 12-47).

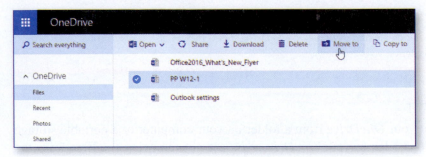

12-46 Move a *OneDrive* file

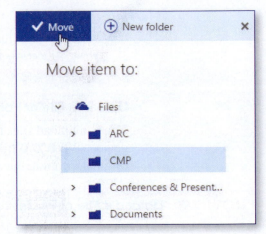

12-47 Select folder where you will move selected item(s)

3. Select the folder where you want to move or copy the selected items and click the **Move** or **Copy** button.
   - You can place selected items in an existing folder or click **New folder** to create a new folder.
   - Press **Esc** on the keyboard or click the **X** in the upper right corner of the pane to cancel the move or copy process and close the pane.
4. Delete a file or folder by checking the **circle** to the left of the items(s) to delete and clicking the **Delete** button at the top.

Download a File or Folder

If you are working on a computer in a computer lab on your college campus or any other public computer, you can download a file or folder from your *OneDrive* folder so you can open it in Word (or other program). When you download a file or folder from *OneDrive*, it is not removed from *OneDrive*. A copy of the file or folder is downloaded.

▶ **HOW TO:** Download a File or Folder from OneDrive

1. Check the **circle** to the left of the file or folder you want to download.
   - If you select more than one file or a folder to download, a compressed (zipped) folder downloads with the files/folders you selected.
   - If you select a single file, *OneDrive* downloads the file.

2. Click the **Download** button at the top. Depending on the Internet browser you use, the download actions differ slightly.

- *Google Chrome:* Click the **Download** button and the *Save As* dialog box opens (Figure 12-48).
- *Microsoft Edge:* Click the **Download** button and the file automatically downloads to the *Downloads* folder on your computer.
- *Mozilla Firefox:* Click the **Download** button and the *Opening [File name]* dialog box opens where you can select to open or save the file or folder.

3. Select the location where you want to save the downloaded items.

4. Type a file name in the *File name* area if you want to rename the file.

5. Click the **Save** button to close the *Save As* dialog box and download the selected items.

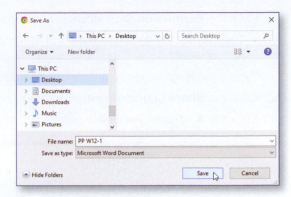

12-48 Save downloaded file from *OneDrive*

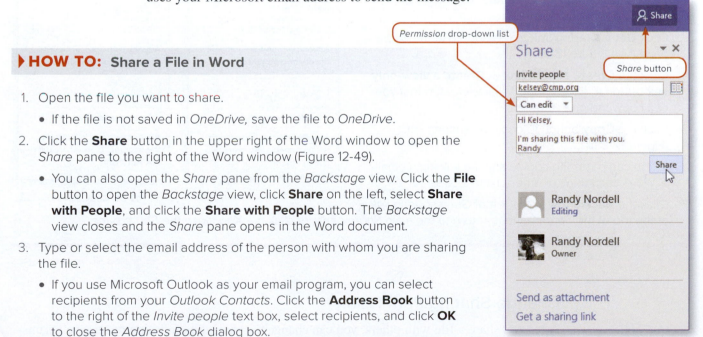

SLO 12.4

Sharing OneDrive Files and Folders

In addition to being able to access all of your *OneDrive* files from any computer or mobile device, you can also share files and folders. Sharing provides you the ability to collaborate with others on individual files, or you can share a folder where others can upload and edit files. When sharing files and folders, you control users' level of access. You can give them permission to view files or edit files, and you can remove sharing permission.

Share a File in Word

You can share any files stored on *OneDrive.* If you try to share a file that is not saved in *OneDrive,* you are prompted to save your document to *OneDrive* before sharing it. In the **Share** pane, you can type or select the recipients, set the permission level of the shared file, and type a message recipients receive through email. Word uses your Microsoft email address to send the message.

▶**HOW TO:** Share a File in Word

1. Open the file you want to share.
   - If the file is not saved in *OneDrive,* save the file to *OneDrive.*

2. Click the **Share** button in the upper right of the Word window to open the *Share* pane to the right of the Word window (Figure 12-49).
   - You can also open the *Share* pane from the *Backstage* view. Click the **File** button to open the *Backstage* view, click **Share** on the left, select **Share with People**, and click the **Share with People** button. The *Backstage* view closes and the *Share* pane opens in the Word document.

3. Type or select the email address of the person with whom you are sharing the file.
   - If you use Microsoft Outlook as your email program, you can select recipients from your *Outlook Contacts.* Click the **Address Book** button to the right of the *Invite people* text box, select recipients, and click **OK** to close the *Address Book* dialog box.
   - If typing multiple email addresses, separate each with a semicolon.

12-49 Share a *OneDrive* file

4. Click the **Permission** drop-down list and select **Can edit** or **Can view**.
   - The *Permission* drop-down list and *Message* area do not display until you type an email address in the *Invite people* area.
5. Type a message to recipient(s) in the *Message* area.
6. Click the **Share** button. An email is sent to people you invited.
7. Click the **X** to close the *Share* pane.

> ANOTHER WAY
>
> You can also send a file as an attachment through email. Click the **Send as attachment** link at the bottom of the *Sharing* pane. You have the option to send the file as a Word document or PDF file.

Create a Sharing Link

You can also choose to create a sharing link (hyperlink) to share a file with others rather than sending an email through Word. You can get a sharing link, copy it, and email it to others as another way of sharing. You have the option of generating an *Edit link* or a *View-only link*.

▶ **HOW TO:** Create a Sharing Link

1. Open the file you want to share.
   - If the file is not saved in *OneDrive,* save the file to *OneDrive.*
2. Click the **Share** button in the upper right of the Word window to open the *Share* pane to the right of the Word window.
3. Click **Get a sharing link** at the bottom of the *Share* pane (see Figure 12-49).
4. Click the **Create an edit link** or **Create a view-only link** button (Figure 12-50). A link is created that you can copy and give to others.
5. Click the **Copy** button to copy the sharing link (Figure 12-51).
   - You can paste the copied sharing link in an email, Word document, or other online location.
6. Click the **Back** arrow to the left of *Get a sharing link* at the top of the *Share* pane to return to the main *Share* pane, or click the **X** to close the *Share* pane.

12-50 Create a sharing link   **12-51 Copy a sharing link**

Change Sharing Permission

After you share a file with others, you can change the sharing permission or remove permission to edit the file. If you created a sharing link, you can disable the sharing link.

▶ **HOW TO:** Change Sharing Permission

1. Open the shared file.
2. Click the **Share** button in the upper right of the Word window to open the *Share* pane.
3. Right-click a name of one person with whom you have shared the document.
4. Select **Remove User** or **Change permission to: Can view** (or **Can edit**).
5. Right-click the sharing link and select **Disable Link** (Figure 12-52).
   - You can also click **Copy Link** to copy and share the link with others.
6. Click the **X** to close the *Share* pane.

Right-click to display sharing options

12-52 Disable or copy a sharing link

Other Sharing Options in Word

Word also provides other ways to share files. You can email a file to others, email a PDF version of the file, present the file online, or post the file to a blog (web log). Click the **Share** button on the *Backstage* view to display and use the other sharing options.

- *Email:* Click the **Email** button in the *Share* area on the *Backstage* view to display the different email options (Figure 12-53). You can *Send as Attachment, Send a Link, Send as a PDF, Send as XPS,* and *Send as Internet Fax.* For the first four options, Microsoft Outlook must be set up on your computer for these options to function. To *Send as Internet Fax,* you must first sign up with a fax service provider.

12-53 Share a file through email

- *Present Online*: Click **Present Online** in the *Share* area of the *Backstage* view and then click the **Present Online** button to share this document with others via an Internet browser. Check the **Enable remote viewers to download the document** box to give others the ability to download the file. This option is particularly useful when sharing PowerPoint files.
- *Post to Blog*: Click **Post to Blog** in the *Share* area of the *Backstage* view and then click the **Post to Blog** button to create a new blog post to popular blog sites such as SharePoint Blog, WordPress, or Blogger. You must have an account for the blog service to which you are posting the blog.

Share a File or Folder in OneDrive

You can also share a file or folder from within *OneDrive* online. When you share files or folders with others, you choose if users can only view or edit shared files and folders. When you share a file or folder in your *OneDrive,* you have the option to send an email with a link to the shared item or generate a hyperlink to share with others that gives them access to the shared file. If your Windows account is connected to LinkedIn, Facebook, or Twitter, you can also post a link to a shared file in one or more of these social networking sites.

> **MORE INFO**
>
> Microsoft regularly updates *OneDrive* online. Figures in this chapter may appear slightly different from how *OneDrive* displays in your Internet browser. The figures in this section display *OneDrive* using Google Chrome web browser.

▶ HOW TO: Share a OneDrive File or Folder

1. Open an Internet browser and log in to your *OneDrive* account (www.onedrive.live.com).

2. Select (check the circle) the file or folder you want to share.
   - If you share a folder, shared users have access to all of the files in the folder.

3. Click the **Share** button at the top. A sharing window opens with two different sharing options: *Get a link* and *Email* (Figure 12-54).
   - By default, recipients can edit shared files.
   - To change the sharing permission, click the **Anyone with this link can edit this item** link and deselect the **Allow editing** check box.

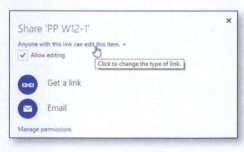

12-54 Sharing options

4. Create a sharing link to send to others by clicking **Get a link**.
   - Click **Copy** to copy the sharing link (Figure 12-55). You can email this link to others or post it in an online location.
   - To display more sharing options, click the **More** link where you can share the file on Facebook, Twitter, or LinkedIn.

5. Send a sharing email by clicking **Email** (see Figure 12-55).
   - Type the email address(es) in the first text box. Press **Tab** after typing an email address to add another recipient.

12-55 Copy a sharing link in *OneDrive*

- Type a brief message in the body area (second text box).
- Click the **Share** button to send the sharing invitation email (Figure 12-56). The people you have chosen receive an email containing a link to the shared file or folder.

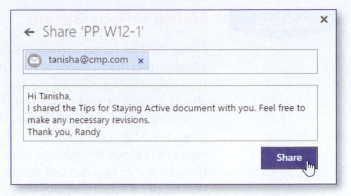

Change OneDrive Sharing Permission

You can change the sharing permission or remove sharing on a file or folder from within OneDrive. The *Information pane* on the right displays properties of the selected file or folder.

▶**HOW TO:** Change or Remove OneDrive Sharing

1. Select the shared file or folder in *OneDrive* online.
2. Click the **Information** button in the upper right corner to open the *Information* pane on the right (Figure 12-57).
   - The *Sharing* area in the *Information* pane lists those who have permission to view or edit the selected item and the available sharing links.
3. Click the **Add People** button to open a sharing window where you can get a link or send a sharing email to others.
4. Change sharing permission or stop sharing by clicking the **Permission** drop-down list and selecting **Change to view only**, **Allow edit**, or **Stop Sharing**.
5. Copy a sharing link by clicking the link and pressing **Ctrl+C**.
6. Remove a sharing link by clicking the **X** to the right of the sharing link and clicking **Remove link** in the *Remove link* dialog box (Figure 12-58).

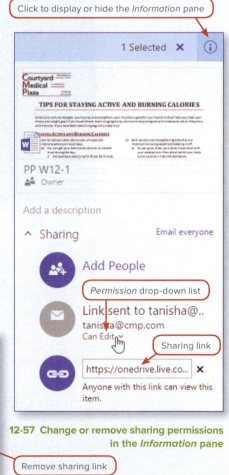

12-57 Change or remove sharing permissions in the *Information* pane

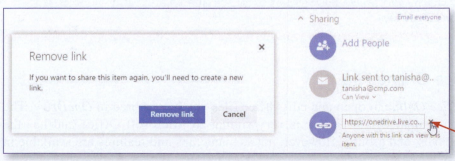

12-58 Remove a sharing link

7. Click the **Information** button again to close the *Information* pane.

Using Office Online

Office Online is free online software from Microsoft that works in conjunction with your Microsoft account and online *OneDrive* account. With *Office Online,* you can work with Office files online *without* having the desktop version of Office 2016 installed on the computer you are using, such as when you use a friend's computer that does not have Office 2016 installed.

Office Online is available from your Microsoft account web page (www.office.live.com) (Figure 12-59). *Office Online* is a scaled-down version of Office 2016 and not as robust in terms of features, but you can use it to create, edit, print, share, and insert comments on files. If you need more advanced features, you can open *Office Online* documents in the desktop version of Office 2016.

12-59 *Office Online* **web page**

> ### MORE INFO
>
> Microsoft regularly updates the *Office Online* products and online environment. Figures in this chapter may appear slightly different from how *Office Online* displays in your Internet browser. The figures in this section display *Office Online* using Google Chrome web browser. Also, Microsoft Access is not available in *Office Online*.

Edit an Office Online File

You can use *Office Online* to open and edit Office files you have stored in *OneDrive*. The working environment in *Office Online* is very similar to Microsoft Office and has the familiar *Ribbon,* tabs, and groups. However, not as many tabs and features are available in *Office Online*.

When you initially open an Office file from *OneDrive,* the file displays in **read-only mode** in the browser window where you view the document. When you edit the file in the browser window, *Office Online* opens your file in **edit mode** in the appropriate program. For example, if you open a Word document stored in *OneDrive,* your document opens in **Word Online**.

▶ HOW TO: Edit an Office Online File

1. Log in to your *OneDrive* account in an Internet browser window (www.onedrive.live.com).

2. Click an Office file (the file name, not the circle on the left) to open from *OneDrive* (Figure 12-60). The file displays in *read-only* mode in an *Office Online* tab on your browser.

   - If you are prompted to install an extension for your Internet browser, click the **Get the extension** button.
   - You can add comments to an *Office Online* file in *read-only* mode.
   - You cannot edit the file in *read-only* mode.
   - You can also select a file (check circle), click the **Open** drop-down list, and select **Open in Word Online** or **Open in Word**.

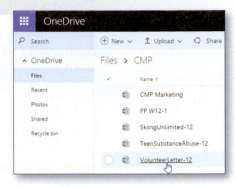

12-60 Open a document in *Office Online*

3. Click the **Edit Document** drop-down list and select **Edit in Browser** to edit the file in *Office Online* (Figure 12-61).

   - You can also open an *Office Online* file in the desktop version of Microsoft Office. To do this, Microsoft Office must be installed on your computer. Click **Edit in [Office application]** (for example **Edit in Word**) to open the file in the appropriate Office desktop application (see Figure 12-61).

4. Edit and apply formatting changes in *Office Online* (Figure 12-62).

12-61 Change from *read-only* mode to *edit* mode in *Word Online*

   - When using *Office Online,* advanced formatting such as text boxes, pictures, charts, and *SmartArt* might not display as they do when you open the file in the desktop version of Office 2016.
   - *Word Online* automatically saves changes to the file.
   - Click **Edit in [Office application]** (for example **Edit in Word**) if you want to open the file in the desktop version of the Office application (see Figure 12-62).

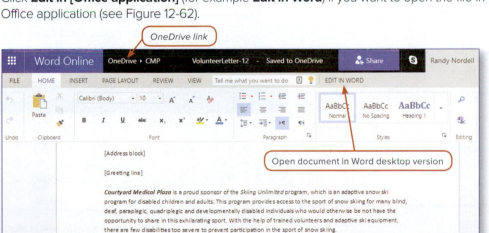

12-62 Edit a document in *Word Online*

5. Close the browser tab to close the *Office Online* document.

   - When you open a file in *Office Online,* the file opens in a new tab and *OneDrive* remains open in the previous browser tab.
   - You can also click the **OneDrive** link in the top left to return to your *OneDrive* folders and files (see Figure 12-62).

Create an Office Online File

You are not limited to editing existing documents in *Office Online*; you can create a new Word document, Excel workbook, PowerPoint presentation, OneNote notebook, Excel survey, or a plain text document. When you create an *Office Online* file, the document saves in your *OneDrive*.

▶ **HOW TO:** Create an Office Online File

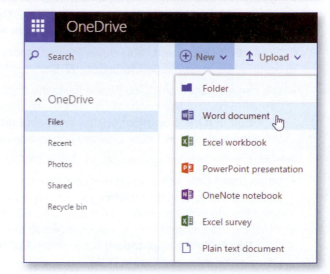

1. Select the location in *OneDrive* where you want to create a new file.

2. Click the **New** button and select the type of file to create (**Word document, Excel workbook, PowerPoint presentation, OneNote notebook, Excel survey,** or **Plain text document**) (Figure 12-63). A new file opens in *edit* mode.

3. Type information in the file and apply formatting as desired.

4. Rename the file by clicking the default file name in the *Title* bar and typing a new file name (Figure 12-64).

    • You can also click the **File** tab and select **Save As** for other saving options.

5. *Office Online* automatically saves changes to the file.

6. Close the browser tab to close the *Office Online* file.

    • You can also click the **OneDrive** link in the top left to return to your *OneDrive* folders and files (see Figure 12-64).

12-63 Create a *Word Online* document

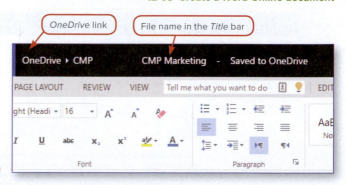

12-64 Rename a document in *Word Online*

Share an Office Online File

In addition to sharing a file from *OneDrive,* you can also share a file you are previewing or editing in *Office Online*. You have the option to send a sharing email or get a link to share the file. The process for sharing a file in *Office Online* is similar to sharing a file or folder in *OneDrive.*

▶**HOW TO:** Share an Office Online File

1. Open a file in *Office Online*.
2. Click the **Share** button in the upper right corner (available in both *read-only* and *edit* modes). The *Share* window opens with different options.
   - You can either *Invite people* (send an email) or *Get a link*.
3. Send a sharing email by clicking **Invite people** on the left (Figure 12-65).
   - Type the recipient's email address(es). Press **Tab** after typing an email address to add another recipient.
   - Type a brief message.
   - Click the **Recipients can edit** link below the message and select **Recipients can only view** or **Recipients can edit** to select the permission setting.
   - You can also require recipients to sign in to their Microsoft account to view or edit the file by selecting **Recipients need to sign in with a Microsoft account** from the drop-down list.
   - Click the **Share** button to send the sharing invitation email. Recipients receive an email containing a link to the shared file.
   - Click **Close** to close the *Share* window and to return to the *Office Online* document.
4. Alternatively, create a sharing link to send to others by clicking **Get a link** on the left (Figure 12-66).

12-66 Create a sharing link in *OneDrive*

   - Select **Edit** or **View only** from the *Choose an option* drop-down list and click the **Create link** button.
   - Copy the sharing link and paste in an email or online location to share the file.
   - Click **Close** to close the *Share* window and to return to the *Office Online* document.

Collaborate in Office Online

Use *Office Online* to collaborate with others who have permission to edit the shared Office file. If two or more users are working on the same file in *Office Online*, collaboration information displays in the upper right corner of the *Office Online* window (Figure 12-67). You are alerted of available updates and told how many people are editing the file. Changes to the file automatically save and apply to the file, and all changes are marked with the name of the person who made the change.

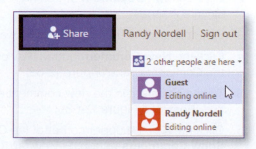

12-67 List of users collaborating on a shared file

Use Comments in Office Online

In *Office Online*, you can add comments to a file, review comments from others, reply to comments, mark comments as done, and delete comments. When reviewing a document in *Word Online*, you can insert comments in both *edit* and *read-only* modes.

▶ HOW TO: Add a Comment in Office Online in Read-Only Mode

1. Open a file in *Office Online* in *read-only* mode.
2. Select an area of the file where you want to insert a comment.
3. Click the **Comments** button at the top right to open the *Comments* pane on the right (Figure 12-68).

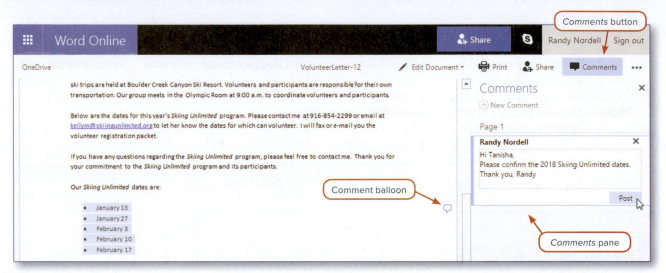

12-68 *Post* a comment in *Office Online*

4. Click **New Comment** to add a new comment to the selected area.
5. Type a comment in the new comment area in the *Comments* pane and click **Post**.
   - A comment balloon displays to the right of the area you selected in the document.
6. Click the **Comments** button or **X** in the upper right corner of the *Comments* pane to close the pane.

You can also add a comment in *edit* mode in *Office Online*. Use the *Review* tab to add a comment to an *Office Online* file in *edit* mode.

▶ HOW TO: Add a Comment in Office Online in Edit Mode

1. Open a file in *Office Online*.
2. Click the **Edit Document** button and select **Edit in Browser** to open the file in *edit* mode.
3. Select an area of the file where you want to insert a comment.
4. Click the **New Comment** button [*Review* tab, *Comments* group] to open the *Comments* pane (Figure 12-69).
5. Type a comment in the new comment area in the *Comments* pane and click **Post** (see Figure 12-68).
6. Click the **X** in the upper corner of the *Comments* pane or click the **Show Comments** button [*Review* tab, *Comments* group] to close the pane.

12-69 Insert a *New Comment* in *edit* mode

Review Comments in Office Online

When reviewing your own comments or comments from others, click a comment balloon in the document to open the *Comments* pane on the right (Figure 12-70). You can perform the following actions on existing comments:

- Click the **Reply** button to reply to a comment.
- Click the **Mark as Done** button to mark a comment as done after you have acted on the comment or when it is no longer relevant.
- Click the **Delete** button to delete a comment.

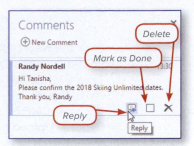

12-70 *Reply* to a comment

For this project, create a folder in *OneDrive*, upload files to *OneDrive*, edit a document in *Word Online*, create a *Word Online* document, and share a *OneDrive* folder.

***Note to Instructor and Students*:**

For this project, you use your Microsoft account, OneDrive, and Word Online. If you don't have a Microsoft account, you can create a free account at https://signup.live.com. See the Microsoft Account Information *section in* SLO 12.2: Customizing Office and Installing Office Add-Ins.

Microsoft regularly updates the Office Online *products and* OneDrive *online environment. Instructions and figures in this project may differ slightly from how* Office Online *and* OneDrive *display in your Internet browser. The Google Chrome web browser is used for instructions and figures in this project.*

Files Needed: *[your initials] PP W12-1.docx*, *SkiingUnlimited-12.docx*, *TeenSubstanceAbuse-12.docx*, and *VolunteerLetter-12* (student data files are available in the Library of your SIMnet account) Completed Project Folder and File Names: **CMP** *OneDrive* folder containing the following five files: **CMP Marketing**, *[your initials] PP W12-2.docx*, *SkiingUnlimited-12.docx*, *TeenSubstanceAbuse-12.docx*, and *VolunteerLetter-12.docx*

---

1. Log in to *OneDrive* online using your Microsoft account.
   a. Open an Internet browser window and go to the *OneDrive* web site (http://www.onedrive.live.com), which takes you to the *OneDrive* sign in page. You can use any Internet browser to access *OneDrive* (Microsoft Edge, Google Chrome, or Mozilla Firefox).
   b. Click the **Sign in** button.
   c. Type your Microsoft account email address and click **Next**.
   d. Type your Microsoft account password and click **Sign in** to go to your *OneDrive* web page (Figure 12-71).

2. Create a new folder, upload files, and rename a file.
   a. Click **Files** on the left to display the contents of your *OneDrive* folder.
   b. Click the **View** button in the upper right to display your folders and files in *List* view if they do not already display as a list (Figure 12-72).

12-72 *View* button in *OneDrive*

12-71 Sign in to *OneDrive*

c. Click the **New** button at the top and select **Folder** from the drop-down list (Figure 12-73).

d. Type CMP as the name for the new folder and press **Create**.

e. Click the *CMP* folder to open the folder.

f. Click the **Upload** button (also select **Files** if it is an option) at the top to open an upload dialog box. Remember, the name of this dialog box varies depending on the Internet browser you are using.

g. Select the *[your initials] PP W12-1* file from *Pause & Practice 12-1* and click **Open** to upload this file to the *CMP* folder.

h. Repeat the above process to upload the *SkiingUnlimited-12*, *TeenSubstanceAbuse-12*, and *VolunteerLetter-12* files from your student data files (use the **Ctrl** key to select non-adjacent files). There should be four files in your *CMP* folder in *OneDrive*.

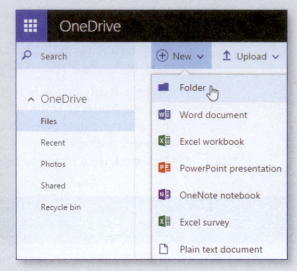

12-73 Create a new folder in *OneDrive*

i. Check the circle to the left of the *[your initials] PP W12-1* and click the **Rename** button to open the *Rename* dialog box.

j. Change the file name to [your initials] PP W12-2 and click **Save**.

3. Edit a file in *Word Online*.

a. Click the *VolunteerLetter-12* file in the *CMP* folder to open it in *Word Online* in *read-only* mode. When you open a document in *Word Online,* by default it opens in *read-only* mode. If you are prompted to install an extension for your Internet browser, click the **Get the extension** button and follow the steps to install *Office Online* for your browser..

b. Click the **Edit Document** button in the top right and select **Edit in Browser** from the drop-down list. The document opens in *Word Online* in *edit* mode.

c. Replace the ski dates placeholder text and brackets in the bulleted list with the following dates:

January 13

January 27

February 3

February 10

February 17

4. Add a comment to the document and close the document.

a. Select the items in the bulleted list.

b. Click the **New Comment** button [*Review* tab, *Comments* group] to open a new comment in the *Comments* pane on the right.

c. Type Please confirm these dates with Tanisha in the new comment area and click **Post** (Figure 12-74).

12-74 Add a comment

d. Click the **X** in the upper right corner of the *Comments* pane to close the pane.

e. Click the **X** on the *VolunteerLetter-12* tab of the browser to close the *VolunteerLetter-12* document (Figure 12-75).

5. Create a new Word document in *Word Online*.

a. Confirm the *CMP* folder is open in *OneDrive* in the browser window. If not, open it.

b. Deselect the *VolunteerLetter-12* if it is selected (checked).

12-75 Close a *Word Online* document

c. Click the **New** button and select **Word document**. A new document opens in *Word Online*.

d. Click the file name at the top, type CMP Marketing as new file name, and press **Enter**.

e. Place your insertion point in the document, type CMP Marketing on the first line of the document, and press **Enter**.

f. Click the **Bullets** button [*Home* tab, *Paragraph* group] to turn on bullets and type the following three bulleted items:

Skiing Unlimited (January and February)

Healthy Lifestyle Workshops (April and October)

Substance Abuse Prevention Conference (June)

g. Select "**CMP Marketing**," apply the **Heading 1** style, and **bold** formatting (Figure 12-76).

h. Close this document and return to the **CMP** folder in *OneDrive*. You should now have five files in your **CMP** folder in *OneDrive*.

CMP Marketing
- Skiing Unlimited (January and February)
- Health Lifestyle Workshops (April and October)
- Substance Abuse Prevention Conference (June)

12-76 CMP Marketing document in Word Online

6. Share the **CMP** folder with your instructor.

a. Click **Files** on the left to return to your *OneDrive* folders and files.

b. Check the circle to the left of the **CMP** folder to select the folder.

c. Click **Share** at the top to open the *Share* window.

d. Click the **Anyone with this link can edit this item** link and deselect the **Allow editing** check box.

e. Click **Get a link**.

f. Click **Copy** to copy the sharing link (Figure 12-77).

g. Click the **X** in the upper right to close the *Share* window.

12-77 Create and copy a sharing link

7. Email the sharing link to your professor.

a. Open the email account you use for your course.

b. Create a new email and type your instructor's email address in the *To* area.

c. Type Your Name | Course code | PP W12-2 as the subject line.

d. Type a brief message in the body of the email.

e. Paste (**Ctrl+V**) the sharing link below the message and type your name below the link.

f. Send the email.

8. Return to *OneDrive* and sign out of your account. Figure 12-78 displays files in the **CMP** folder.

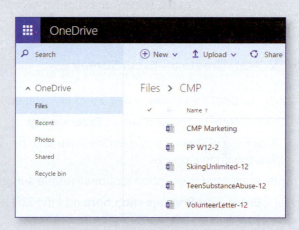

12-78 PP W12-2 completed (CMP folder in OneDrive)

Exploring Other Office Online Applications

With your Microsoft account, you have access to many Microsoft online applications in addition to *OneDrive* and *Word Online*. In *Office Online*, you have access to the main applications in Office 2016 (except Access) and additional programs not available in the desktop version of Office 2016 such as **Excel Survey** and **Sway**. You also have **Outlook.com** for email, **People** to store your contacts, and **Calendar** to organize your schedule.

Office Online

Office Online gives you online access to the most popular Office applications. All of these programs are free with your Microsoft account, and you don't need the desktop version of Office 2016 installed on your computer to use these applications. Each of these applications have the look and feel of the desktop version but don't have as many features as the desktop version of Office 2016.

You log in to Office Online (www.office.live.com) using your Microsoft account. Click the **List of Microsoft Services** button (Figure 12-79) in the upper left corner of the *Office Online* or *OneDrive* browser window to display and choose from the list of services (this button is available in all areas of *Office Online*).

12-79 List of Microsoft online services

Excel Survey

Excel Online provides users the ability to create an **Excel Survey** that can be used to gather data. An *Excel Survey* is shared via email or posted in an online environment. Respondents complete the online survey in an Internet browser window, and responses to the survey are automatically added to the *Excel Survey* file, which is an *Excel Online* worksheet. The creator of the survey does not get overwhelmed with email responses to the survey, but can easily and quickly view results of the survey on *OneDrive*.

▶ **HOW TO:** Create an Excel Survey

1. Log in to *OneDrive* online using your Microsoft account.
2. Click the **New** button and select **Excel survey**.
   - A new Excel file is created in *OneDrive* and the *Edit Survey* window opens.
3. Enter a title and description (optional) for the survey.
4. Click **Enter your first question here** and the *Edit Question* dialog box opens (Figure 12-80).
5. Type the question text and subtitle (optional)
6. Click the **Response Type** drop-down list and select the type of question.
   - The following response types are available: *Text, Paragraph Text, Number, Date, Time, Yes/No,* and *Choice.*
   - Check the **Require** box to require a response to the question.
   - Type a *Default Answer* if you want (optional).
7. Click **Done** to add the question.
8. Click **Add New Question** to continue adding questions to the survey.
   - Click the **Edit Question** button to edit an existing question.
   - Click the **Delete Question** button to delete an existing question.
   - Drag a question up or down to reorder questions.

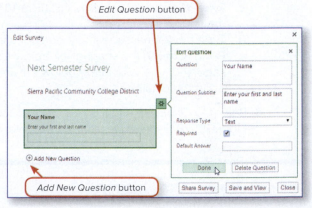

12-80 Add a question to an *Excel Survey*

9. Click **Save and View** to (see Figure 12-80) save and preview your survey (Figure 12-81).

10. Click **Share Survey** to get a link for the online survey.

   - Click **Create Link**.
   - Copy the survey link (**Ctrl+C**) and paste it in an email or online location.
   - Click **Done** (Figure 12-82).

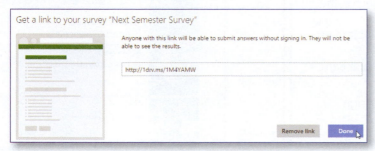

12-82 Get a sharing link for an *Excel Survey*

12-81 *View Survey* window

11. Click the file name at the top of the *Excel Survey* to rename the survey file.

12. Click the **X** on the browser tab to close the *Excel Survey*.

13. View responses to the survey by opening the survey in either *Excel Online* or Excel (desktop version).

   - To edit the survey, click the **Survey** button [*Home* tab, *Tables* group] (in *Excel Online* only) and select **Edit Survey** from the drop-down list. You can also *View Survey, Delete Survey,* and *Share Survey* from this drop-down list.

Sway

Sway is an online digital presentation application that is similar to PowerPoint and Prezi and is only available online through your Microsoft account. In *Sway,* you can type text, import text or another file (Word, PowerPoint, PDF), add pictures, videos, charts, tweets, or embed links to other online sources. Each object in a *Sway* is called a ***card***, and cards can be combined into a ***group***. Share a *Sway* with others similar to how you share a *OneDrive* or *Office Online* file.

▶ HOW TO: Create a Sway

1. Log in to *OneDrive* online using your Microsoft account.
2. Click the **List of Microsoft Services** button and select **Sway**.
3. Click **Create New** or **Import** (Figure 12-83).

   - If you select *Import,* an *Open* dialog box displays where you can select a file to import.
   - If you select *Create New,* a new blank *Sway* opens where you can add information.
   - The main working area of *Sway* is the *Storyline*. Cards and groups display in the *Storyline*.

12-83 Import information into a new *Sway*

4. Click the **Insert** menu button to select content to add to a card.

   - *Sway* displays suggested content, but you can also search for content or select from *OneDrive* or social media sites.

5. Click the **Cards** menu button to insert a card or group (Figure 12-84).

- Alternatively, click the **Insert Content** button between cards in the *Storyline* area to display the type of card to add (*Heading, Text, Picture,* or *Upload*).
- You can type text directly on a card.
- Select a card to display the edit options at the top of the card. The edit options vary depending on the type of card.
- Reorder cards or groups by dragging the object up or down.
- Click the **Delete** button in the upper right of a card to delete a card.

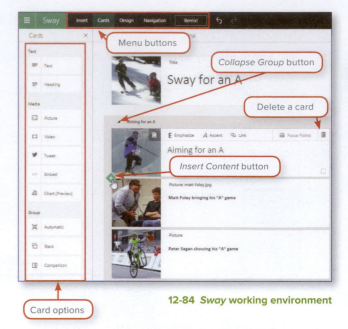

12-84 *Sway* working environment

6. Click the **Design** menu button to select a design to apply to your *Sway* or customize a design.

- A design applies color, typography, and texture to your *Sway*.
- You can customize an existing design.

7. Click the **Navigation** menu button to customize how your *Sway* displays when viewed.

- A *Sway* scrolls vertically or horizontally, or displays optimized for a presentation.

8. Click the **Remix** menu button to quickly cycle through different combinations of design and navigation.

9. View your *Sway*.

- Click **Preview** in the upper right to view your *Sway* (Figure 12-85).
- Click the **Storyline** arrow to return to your *Sway* cards and groups.
- Click **Play** to view your *Sway* with navigation and animation. Click the **Edit** button (pencil icon) to return to the *Storyline*.

10. Click the **Share** button in the upper right to view the available share options.

11. Click the **X** on the browser tab to close the *Sway*. Your *Sway* automatically saves.

12-85 *Sway* view and share options

> **MORE INFO**
>
> Click the **Tutorial** button in the upper right corner of *Sway* to view an online tutorial video of this application. *Sway* is also available as a free app for Windows 10 from the Windows Store.

Outlook.com

Outlook.com is Microsoft's online email application. If you have a Microsoft email address (Live, Hotmail, Outlook.com, or MSN), your email is available in *Outlook. com* (Figure 12-86). You can create, read, and respond to emails in *Outlook.com*. Organize your email by adding new folders, creating rules, and using categories.

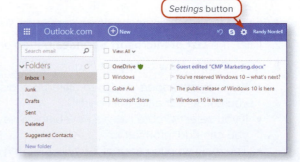

12-86 *Outlook.com* working environment

Click the **Settings** button to display a drop-down list of options. Select **Options** from the *Settings* drop-down list to manage your account, add additional email accounts, and set preferences for writing and reading emails, preventing junk email and customizing *Outlook.com*. You can add additional email accounts in *Outlook.com*.

People

People is an online area to store your contacts. Add individuals and companies and include details such as phone numbers, email addresses, addresses, birthday, anniversary, and job title (Figure 12-87). The contacts in *People* are used in conjunction with *Outlook.com* to send emails.

You can create a contact group that contains multiple contacts and email the contact group rather than

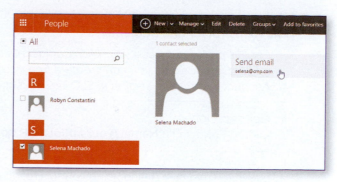

12-87 A contact selected in *People*

selecting individual contacts. You can import contacts from other applications such as Outlook, Gmail, or Yahoo! You can also export your contacts to Outlook or other email programs.

Calendar

Calendar can be used to store your appointments and events online (Figure 12-88). After items are added to the calendar, you can easily edit the item or drag it to a new location on the calendar. When you create a new calendar item or open an existing calendar item, click the **View details** link to display more detailed options for the calendar item.

You can create different calen-

12-88 *Calendar* displayed in *Month* view

dars and have a separate calendar for birthdays. Calendar views include: *Month, Week, Day, Agenda,* and *Task.* A *Calendar* can be shared with others so they can view your calendar.

OneNote Online

OneNote Online is a powerful note-taking application that integrates with other Office 2016 applications. *OneNote* is organized into *Notebooks, Sections,* and *Pages* (Figure 12-89). You can insert text, pictures, links, and tables. *OneNote* uses text formatting features similar to those in Word. *OneNote* is also available as an Office 2016 desktop application and an app for phones and tablets. Your *OneNote* syncs across all devices when connected to your Microsoft account.

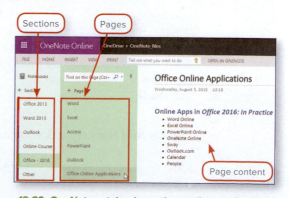

12-89 *OneNote* notebook, section, and page displayed

When you open *OneNote Online* for the first time, you are prompted to create a new notebook. Each subsequent time you log in, you are prompted to select the notebook to open. Click the **+ Section** or **+ Page** button to add a section or page to your notebook. You can share your notebook to collaborate with others.

For this project, you create an *Excel Survey* and share it with your professor and others.

Note to Instructor and Students:

For this project, you use your Microsoft account, OneDrive, and Excel Online. If you don't have a Microsoft account, you can create a free account at https://signup.live.com. *See the* Microsoft Account Information *section in* SLO 12.2: Customizing Office and Installing Office Add-Ins.

File Needed: None
Completed Project File Name: ***[your initials] PP W12-3.xlsx***

1. Log in to *OneDrive* online using your Microsoft account.
   a. Open an Internet browser window and go to the *OneDrive* web site (www.onedrive.live.com), which takes you to the *OneDrive* sign in page. You can use any Internet browser to access *OneDrive* (Microsoft Edge, Google Chrome, or Mozilla Firefox).
   b. Click the **Sign in** button.
   c. Type your Microsoft account email address and click **Next**.
   d. Type your Microsoft account password and click **Sign in** to go to your *OneDrive* web page.

2. Create an *Excel Survey* and add a question.
   a. Click the **New** button and select **Excel Survey**. A new Excel file is created in *OneDrive* and the *Edit Survey* window opens.
   b. Type Next Semester Survey as the title for your survey.
   c. Type Sierra Pacific Community College District as the description for your survey.
   d. Click **Enter your first question here** and the *Edit Question* dialog box opens.
   e. Type Your Name in the *Question* area, and type Enter your first and last name in the *Question Subtitle* area.
   f. Click the **Response Type** drop-down list and select **Text**.
   g. Check the **Required** box and leave the *Default Answer* area blank.
   h. Click **Done** (Figure 12-90).

3. Add a *Yes/No* question.
   a. Click the **Add New Question** button.
   b. Type Will you enroll in classes next semester? in the *Question* area. Leave the *Question Subtitle* blank.
   c. Click the **Response Type** drop-down list and select **Yes/No** and check the **Required** box.
   d. Click the **Default Value** drop-down list and select **Yes**.
   e. Click **Done**.

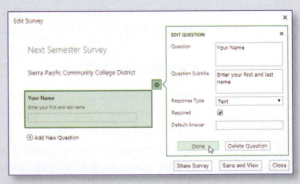

4. Add a *Choice* question.
   a. Click the **Add New Question** button.
   b. Type How many units will you take? in the *Question* area, and type Select from the options below in the *Question Subtitle* area.

12-90 Add a question to an *Excel Survey*

c. Click the **Response Type** drop-down list and select **Choice** and check the **Required** box.
d. Delete the existing choices in the *Choices* area and type the following choices (press **Enter** after each choice except the last one):

None
1-3 units
4-6 units
7-9 units
10-12 units
More than 12 units

e. Click **Done** (Figure 12-91).

5. Save, view, rename, and share the *Excel Survey*.
    a. Click the **Save and View** button to save and preview your survey (Figure 12-92).
    b. Click **Close** to close the *View Survey* window and return to the Excel file in *Excel Online*.

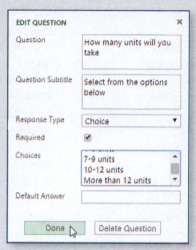

12-91 Add a *Choice* question to an *Excel Survey*

12-92 View the *Excel Survey*

c. Click the title at the top of the *Excel Online* file, type [your initials] PP W12-3 as the file name, and press **Enter**.
d. Click the **Survey** drop-down list [*Home* tab, *Tables* group] and select **Share Survey**. A sharing window opens.
e. Click **Create Link**.
f. Select and copy (**Ctrl+C**) the survey link and click **Done** (Figure 12-93).
g. Click the **X** on the browser tab to close the *[your name] PP W12-3* file.
h. Click the **X** in the upper right corner of the browser window to close the Internet browser.

6. Email the *Excel Survey* sharing link to your professor and yourself.
    a. Open the email program you use and create a new email.
    b. Add your instructor's and your email addresses to the recipient list.

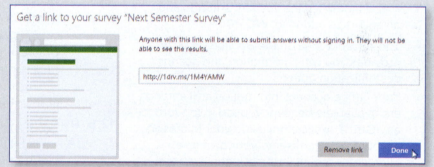

12-93 Get a sharing link for the *Excel Survey*

c. Type [your name] Excel Survey PP W12-3 as the subject.
d. Type a brief message in the body of the message.
e. Paste (**Ctrl+V**) the copied survey link below the message in the body of the email.
f. Type your name below the survey link.
g. Send the email message.

Chapter Summary

12.1 Customize Word options, the *Ribbon,* and the *Quick Access* toolbar to personalize your working environment (p. W12-696).

- Use the **Word Options** dialog box to customize global settings in Word. Certain Word option settings apply to all Office programs.
- The *Word Options* dialog box features the following categories: *General, Display, Proofing, Save, Language, Advanced, Customize Ribbon, Quick Access Toolbar, Add-Ins,* and *Trust Center.*
- Use the *Word Options* dialog box to customize the *Ribbon.* Create a new tab or group, add commands to custom groups, rearrange existing tabs and groups, and rename existing and custom tabs and groups.
- Quickly customize and add commands to the *Quick Access* toolbar using the *Customize Quick Access Toolbar* drop-down list or add other commands using the *Word Options* dialog box.
- Both the *Ribbon* and the *Quick Access* toolbar can be reset to return them to their original settings. You can reset the *Ribbon* or the *Quick Access* toolbar individually or reset all customizations, which resets both the *Ribbon* and the *Quick Access* toolbar.

12.2 View and modify Office account settings and install an Office add-in (p. W12-706).

- The *Account* area on the *Backstage* view provides you with information and account customization options.
- Your Office account information and settings are available whenever you log in to Word (or any Office application) using your Microsoft account. You can create your own free Microsoft account (https://signup.live.com).
- Change the **Office Background** in the *Account* area on the *Backstage* view.
- You can add **Connected Services** to your account to access online services for **Images & Videos**, **Storage**, and **Sharing**.
- **Add-ins** are applications that provide additional functionality to Office. Office add-ins are available in the *Store,* and add-ins previously installed display in the *My Add-ins* area.

12.3 Use *OneDrive* to create, upload, move, copy, delete, and download files and folders (p. W12-712).

- **OneDrive** is a cloud storage area that provides you with online storage space for your files. If you have a Microsoft account (Live, Hotmail, MSN, Messenger, or other Microsoft service account), you have access to *OneDrive.*
- If you don't have a Microsoft account, you can create a free Microsoft account (https://signup. live.com).
- You can access your *OneDrive* files from any computer that has Internet access.
- Log in to *OneDrive* using your Microsoft account.
- If you use Windows 10, *OneDrive* is one of your storage options. You can save and edit *OneDrive* files using a Windows folder or online using an Internet browser.
- In *OneDrive,* you can add files, create folders, and move, copy, delete, and download files.

12.4 Share *OneDrive* files and folders (p. W12-717).

- You can share *OneDrive* files with others. You determine the access other users have to view and/or edit your *OneDrive* files.
- You can email a sharing request to others or create a sharing link that can be emailed, shared in a document, or posted to an online location.
- Other sharing options include **Email**, **Present Online**, and **Post to Blog**.
- Change sharing permission to view or edit a *OneDrive* file or folder or remove sharing permission.

12.5 Use *Office Online* to edit, create, share, collaborate, and comment on a document (p. W12-722).

- **Office Online** is free online software that works in conjunction with your Microsoft account and is available from your *OneDrive* web page.
- *Office Online* is similar to Microsoft Office 2016 but less robust in available features.
- You can use *Office Online* without having Office 2016 installed on your computer.
- You can edit existing files from your *OneDrive* account in *Office Online* and create new Office files using *Office Online.*

- You can share *Office Online* files with others.
- More than one user can edit an *Office Online* file at the same time, which allows real-time collaboration on documents.
- You can add comments, reply to comments, mark a comment as done, or delete comments on *Office Online* files.

12.6 Explore other *Office Online* products and productivity tools (p. W12-729).

- *Office Online* contains additional online productivity tools in addition to **Word Online**, **Excel Online**, and **PowerPoint Online**.
- **Excel Survey** allows users to create a survey that can be shared with others. The survey collects data and stores it in an Excel file on *OneDrive*.
- **Sway** is an online presentation application available in *Office Online* and connected to your Microsoft account.

- **Outlook.com** is an online email program connected to your Microsoft account.
- **People** is an area of *Office Online* where you store information about your contacts.
- **Calendar** is an online calendar where you create and store appointments and events. The *Calendar* can be shared with others.
- **OneNote** is a note-taking program that is available in both *Office Online* and the desktop version of Office 2016.

Check for Understanding

The SIMbook for this text (within your SIMnet account) provides the following resources for concept review:

- Multiple choice questions
- Matching exercises
- Short answer questions

Guided Project 12-1

For this project, you work on documents from American River Cycling Club using *OneDrive, Word Online,* and *Excel Survey.*
[Student Learning Outcomes 12.1, 12.2, 12.3, 12.4, 12.5, 12.6]

Note to Instructor and Students:

> *For this project, you use your Microsoft account, OneDrive, and Word Online. If you don't have a Microsoft account, you can create a free account at https://signup.live.com. See the* Microsoft Account Information *section in* SLO 12.2: Customizing Office and Installing Office Add-Ins.

> *Microsoft regularly updates the* Office Online *products and* OneDrive *online environment. Instructions and figures in this project may differ slightly from how* Office Online *and* OneDrive *display in your Internet browser. The Google Chrome web browser is used for instructions and figures in this project.*

Files Needed: *TrainingLog-12.docx, ARCCCyclingCalendar-12.docx, FlexibilityExercises-12.docx,* and ***HeartRate-12.docx*** *(student data files are available in the* Library *of your SIMnet account)*
Completed Project Folder and File Names: *ARCC* *(OneDrive* folder) containing the following files: ***ARCCCyclingCalendar-12.docx, FlexibilityExercises-12.docx, HeartRate-12.docx, [your initials] Word 12-1 survey.docx,*** and *[your initials] Word 12-1.docx*

Skills Covered in This Project

- Reset customizations to the *Ribbon* and *Quick Access* toolbar.
- Customize the *Quick Access* toolbar for the current document.
- Apply an Office background and theme.

- Log in to *OneDrive* and create a folder.
- Upload a file to your *OneDrive* folder.
- Open a document in *Word Online.*
- Add a comment to a *Word Online* document.
- Create and share an *Excel Survey.*
- Share a *OneDrive* folder.

1. Open the ***TrainingLog-12*** document from your student data files.

2. Save this document as [your initials] Word 12-1.

3. Reset the *Ribbon* and *Quick Access* toolbar.
   a. Click the **Customize Quick Access Toolbar** drop-down list and select **More Commands** to open the *Word Options* dialog box and display the *Quick Access Toolbar* area (Figure 12-94).
   b. Click the **Reset** button and select **Reset all customizations**. A confirmation dialog box opens.
   c. Click **Yes** to delete all *Ribbon* and *Quick Access* toolbar customizations.

4. Add commands to the *Quick Access* toolbar for this document only.
   a. With the *Word Options* dialog box still open and displaying the *Quick Access Toolbar* area, click the **Customize Quick**

12-94 Reset *Ribbon* and *Quick Access* toolbar customizations

Access Toolbar drop-down list on the right and select **For [your initials] Word 12-1** (Figure 12-95).

b. Select **Quick Print** in the list on the left and click **Add**.

c. Also add **Spelling & Grammar** and **Open** to the *Quick Access* toolbar.

d. Click **OK** to close the *Word Options* dialog box.

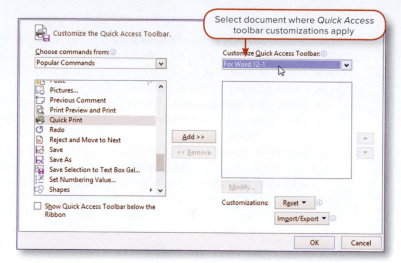

12-95 Add commands to the *Quick Access* toolbar on this document only

5. Apply an Office background and theme.

a. Click the **File** tab to display the *Backstage* view and click **Account** on the left.

b. Click the **Office Background** drop-down list and select a background of your choice.

c. Click the **Office Theme** drop-down list and select a theme of your choice.

d. Click the **Back** arrow to return to your document.

6. Save and close the document and exit Word.

7. Log in to *OneDrive* online using your Microsoft account.

a. Open an Internet browser window and go to the *OneDrive* web site (www.onedrive.live.com), which takes you to the *OneDrive* sign in page. You can use any Internet browser to access *OneDrive*.

b. Click the **Sign in** button, type your Microsoft account email address, and click **Next**.

c. Type your Microsoft account password and click **Sign in** to go to your *OneDrive* web page.

8. Create a folder and upload files to your *OneDrive*.

a. Click the **Files** button on the left to display your *OneDrive* folders and files.

b. Click the **View** button in the upper right to display your folders and files in *List* view if they are not already displayed as a list.

c. Click the **New** button and select **Folder** from the drop-down list.

d. Type **ARCC** as the name of the new folder and click **Create**.

e. Click the **ARCC** folder to open it.

f. Click the **Upload** button and click **Files** to open an upload dialog box.

g. Locate and select **[your initials] Word 12-1** and click **Open** to upload this file to the **ARCC** folder.

h. Upload the following files to the **ARCC** folder from your student data files: **ARCCCyclingCalendar-12**, **FlexibilityExercises-12**, and **HeartRate-12**.

9. Add a comment to a document in *Word Online*.

a. Click the **ARCCCyclingCalendar-12** document to open it in *Word Online*. If you are prompted to install an extension for your Internet browser, click the **Get the extension** button.

b. Select "**June**" at the upper left and click the **Comments** button to open the *Comments* pane at the right.

c. Click **New Comment** to add a comment to the document.

d. Type **Please email the June Cycling Calendar to ARCC members** in the comments area and click **Post**.

e. Click the **X** at the upper right of the *Comments* pane to close the pane.

f. Click the **X** on the browser tab to close the **ARCCCyclingCalendar-12** document and return to **ARCC** folder in *OneDrive*.

10. Create an *Excel Survey*.
    a. Deselect the **ARCCCyclingCalendar-12** if it is selected (check mark on the left).
    b. Click the **New** button and select **Excel survey** from the drop-down list.
    c. Type American River Cycling Club as the title of the survey.
    d. Type Cycling Survey as the description of the survey.
    e. Click **Enter your first question here** to display the *Edit Question* area.
    f. Type Your Name in the **Question** area, select **Text** as the *Response Type,* check the **Required** box, and click **Done**.
    g. Click **Add New Question**, type Are you racing this year? in the **Question** area, select **Yes/No** as the *Response Type,* check the **Required** box, select **Yes** as the *Default Value,* and click **Done**.
    h. Click **Add New Question**, type What is your racing category? in the *Question* area, select **Choice** as the *Response Type,* and check the **Required** box.
    i. Delete the existing choices in the *Choices* area and type the following:
    Pro/1/2
    3
    4
    5
    N/A
    j. Leave the *Default Answer* area blank and click **Done**.

11. View, rename, and share an *Excel Survey*.
    a. Click the **Save and View** button to view your survey (Figure 12-96).
    b. Click **Close** to close the *View Survey* window and return to the Excel file in *Excel Online*.
    c. Click the title at the top of the *Excel Online* file, type [your initials] Word 12-1 survey as the file name, and press **Enter**.
    d. Click the **Survey** drop-down list [*Home* tab, *Tables* group] and select **Share Survey**. A sharing window opens.
    e. Click **Create Link**.
    f. Select and copy (**Ctrl+C**) the survey link and click **Done** (Figure 12-97).
    g. Click the **X** on the browser tab to close the [your initials] *Word 12-1 survey* file and return to the **ARCC** folder in *OneDrive*.

12-96 View the *Excel Survey*

12-97 Get a sharing link for the *Excel Survey*

12. Email the *Excel Survey* sharing link to your professor and yourself.
    a. Open the email program you use and create a new email.
    b. Add your instructor's and your email addresses to the recipient list.
    c. Type [your name] Word 12-1 survey as the subject.
    d. Type a brief message in the body of the message.
    e. Paste (**Ctrl+V**) the copied survey link below the message in the body of the email.
    f. Type your name below the survey link.
    g. Send the email message.

13. Share a *OneDrive* folder with your instructor.
    a. Return to *OneDrive* in the Internet browser and click **Files** at the left to display your *OneDrive* files.
    b. Click the **circle** to the left of the ***ARCC*** folder to select it and click **Share** at the top to open the *Share* window.
    c. Click **Email**.
    d. Type your instructor's email address in the first text box and type a brief message in the body area (Figure 12-98).
    e. Click **Share** to send the sharing email to your instructor.

14. Close the browser window (Figure 12-99).

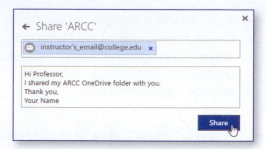

12-98 Share a *OneDrive* folder

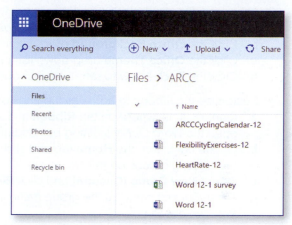

12-99 Word 12-1 completed (*ARCC* folder in *OneDrive*)

Guided Project 12-2

For this project, you use *OneDrive* and *Word Online* to customize a document for Hamilton Civic Center.
[Student Learning Outcomes 12.1, 12.2, 12.3, 12.4, 12.5]

Note to Instructor and Students:

> *For this project, you use your Microsoft account, OneDrive, and Word Online. If you don't have a Microsoft account, you can create a free account at https://signup.live.com.* See the Microsoft Account Information *section in* SLO 12.2: Customizing Office and Installing Office Add-Ins.

> *Microsoft regularly updates the* Office Online *products and* OneDrive *online environment. Instructions and figures in this project may differ slightly from how* Office Online *and* OneDrive *display in your Internet browser. The Google Chrome web browser is used for instructions and figures in this project.*

File Needed: ***YogaClasses-12.docx*** *(student data files are available in the* Library *of your SIMnet account)*
Completed Project Folder and File Name: ***HCC*** *(OneDrive folder) containing the following file:* **[your initials]
Word 12-2.docx**

Skills Covered in This Project

- Apply an Office background and theme.
- Create a new group on the *Home* tab.
- Add and arrange commands in the custom group.
- Arrange a group on a tab.

- Upload a file to *OneDrive*.
- Create a folder in *OneDrive*.
- Move a file to a *OneDrive* folder.
- Edit a document in *Word Online*.
- Add a comment to a document in *Word Online*.
- Get a sharing link to a *OneDrive* file.

---

1. Open the **YogaClasses-12** document from your student data files.

2. Save this document as [your initials] Word 12-2.

3. Apply an Office background and theme.
   a. Click the **File** tab to display the *Backstage* view and click **Account** on the left.
   b. Click the **Office Background** drop-down list and select a background of your choice.
   c. Click the **Office Theme** drop-down list and select a theme of your choice.
   d. Click the **Back** arrow to return to your document.

4. Customize the *Ribbon* to add a group and commands.
   a. Right-click anywhere on the **Ribbon** and select **Customize the Ribbon** from the context menu to open the *Word Options* dialog box and display the *Customize Ribbon* area.
   b. On the right, click the **Home** tab and click the **New Group** button. A new group appears below the existing groups on the *Home* tab.
   c. Select **New Group (Custom)** and click **Rename** to open the *Rename* dialog box.
   d. Type your first name as the group name in the *Display name* area, and click **OK** to close the *Rename* dialog box.
   e. On the right, select the *[your first name]* **(Custom)** group.
   f. Click the **Choose commands from** drop-down list on the left side and select **All Commands** to display all the available commands in the list on the left (Figure 12-100).

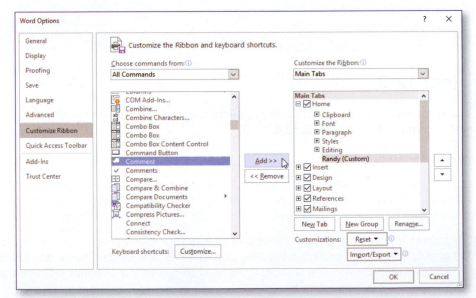

12-100 Add a custom group and commands to the *Home* tab

   g. Select the **Comment** command and click the **Add** button between the two lists to add the command to the group.

h. Add the **Tabs**, **Custom Margins**, and **Borders and Shading** (first one) commands to the *[your first name]* group.
i. Use the **Move Up** and **Move Down** buttons to arrange the commands in alphabetical order.
j. Select the *[your first name]* **(Custom)** group and click the **Move Up** button so it appears between the *Styles* and *Editing* groups.
k. Click **OK** to close the *Word Options* dialog box.
l. Click the **Home** tab to view your custom group (Figure 12-101).

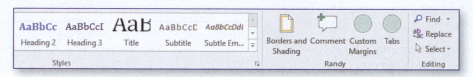

12-101 Custom group displayed on the *Home* tab

5. Save and close the document and exit Word.

6. Log in to *OneDrive* online using your Microsoft account.
    a. Open an Internet browser window and go to the *OneDrive* web site (www.onedrive.live.com), which takes you to the *OneDrive* sign in page.
    b. Click the **Sign in** button.
    c. Type your Microsoft account email address and click **Next**.
    d. Type your Microsoft account password and click **Sign in** to go to your *OneDrive* web page.

7. Upload a file in *OneDrive,* create a folder, and move a file.
    a. Click the **Files** button on the left to display your *OneDrive* folders and files.
    b. Click the **Upload** button and select **Files** from the drop-down list to open an upload dialog box.
    c. Select *[your initials]* **Word 12-2** from your solutions files and click **Open** to upload this file to the *OneDrive* folder.
    d. Click the **New** button and select **Folder** from the drop-down list.
    e. Type HCC as the name of the new folder and click **Create**.
    f. Click the **circle** to the left of *[your initials]* **Word 12-2** to select this file.
    g. Click the **Move to** button at the top to open the *Move* pane at the right.
    h. Click the **HCC** folder and click **Move** to close the dialog box and move the file to the selected folder (Figure 12-102).

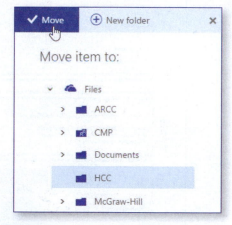

12-102 Move a file to a folder in *OneDrive*

8. Edit a document in *Word Online* and add a comment.
    a. Click the **HCC** folder to open it.
    b. Click the *[your initials]* **Word 12-2** file to open it in *Word Online*. If you are prompted to install an extension for your Internet browser, click the **Get the extension** button.
    c. Click the **Edit Document** button and select **Edit in Browser**. The text box that was in the upper right corner does not display correctly, and text wrapping around the picture might not display correctly. Don't try to fix these in *Word Online*.
    d. Place your insertion point at the end of the second body paragraph ("... yoga mat and towel.") and press **Enter** two times.
    e. Type Our yoga classes are taught on the following days and times: and press **Enter** two times.

f. Click the **Bullets** button [*Home* tab, *Paragraph* group] and type the following three bulleted lines:

Monday, Wednesday, and Friday at 6 and 8 a.m.

Tuesday and Thursday at 7 a.m. and 12:30 p.m.

Saturday and Sunday at 9 a.m.

g. Select the sentence before the bulleted list.

h. Click the **Comment** button [*Insert* tab, *Comments* group] to open the *Comments* pane on the right.

i. Type Rachel, please confirm with Amanda the days and times of the yoga classes in the new comment and click **Post**.

j. Click the **X** at the upper right of the *Comments* pane to close the pane.

9. Share a file on *OneDrive* with your instructor.

a. With the document still open in *Word Online*, click the **Share** button at the top right to open the *Share* dialog box.

b. Click **Get a link** on the left, select **Edit** from the *Choose an option* drop-down list, and click **Create link** (Figure 12-103).

c. Select and copy (**Ctrl+C**) the sharing link.

d. Click **Close** to close the sharing dialog box.

e. Click the **X** on the browser tab to close the *[your initials] Word 12-2* file (Figure 12-104).

f. Close **X** in the upper right corner of the browser window to close the Internet browser.

12-103 Create a sharing link to a *OneDrive* file

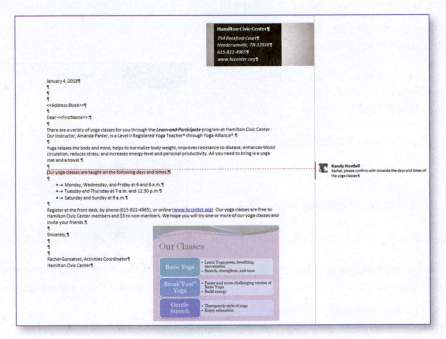

12-104 Word 12-2 completed (displayed in the desktop version of Word)

10. Email the sharing link to your professor and yourself.

a. Open the email program you use and create a new email.

b. Type your instructor's and your email addresses in the *To* area.

c. Type *[your name]* Word 12-2 as the subject.

d. Type a brief message in the body of the message (be sure to include your name) and paste (**Ctrl+V**) the sharing link.

e. Send the message.

Guided Project 12-3

For this project, you customize your working environment in Word and use *OneDrive* and *Word Online* to modify files for Placer Hills Real Estate.
[Student Learning Outcomes 12.1, 12.2, 12.3, 12.4, 12.5]

Note to Instructor and Students:

> For this project, you use your Microsoft account, OneDrive, and Word Online. If you don't have a Microsoft account, you can create a free account at https://signup.live.com. See the Microsoft Account Information *section in* SLO 12.2: Customizing Office and Installing Office Add-Ins.

> Microsoft regularly updates the Office Online *products and* OneDrive *online environment. Instructions and figures in this project may differ slightly from how* Office Online *and* OneDrive *display in your Internet browser. The Google Chrome web browser is used for instructions and figures in this project*.

Files Needed: ***ExpirationLetter-12.docx*, *EscrowChecklist-12.docx*, and *HomeBuying-12.docx*** (student data files are available in the Library of your SIMnet account)
Completed Project Folder and File Names: ***PHRE*** (*OneDrive* folder) containing the following files: ***EscrowChecklist-12.docx*, *HomeBuying-12.docx*, and *[your initials] Word 12-3.docx***

Skills Covered in This Project

- Change default save location in Word.
- Reset the *Quick Access* toolbar.
- Add and rearrange commands on the *Quick Access* toolbar.

- Create a *OneDrive* folder.
- Upload files to a *OneDrive* folder.
- Edit a document in *Word Online*.
- Share a *OneDrive* folder.

1. Open the ***ExpirationLetter-12*** document from your student data files and save the file as [your initials] Word 12-3.

2. Change default save location in Word.
   a. Click the **File** tab to open the *Backstage* view and click **Options** to open the *Word Options* dialog box.
   b. Click **Save** on the left to display save options (Figure 12-105).
   c. Click the **Browse** button to the right of *Default local file location*. The *Modify Location* dialog box opens.
   d. Select the **OneDrive** folder on the left and click **OK** to close the *Modify Location* dialog box and change the default save location. Leave the *Word Options* dialog box open. If the *OneDrive* folder is not available on the computer you are using, skip this step.

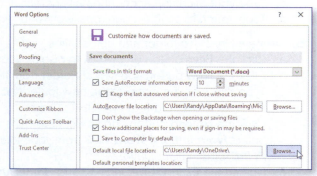

12-105 Change the default save location

3. Reset and modify the *Quick Access* toolbar.
   a. Select **Quick Access Toolbar** on the left in the *Word Options* dialog box.
   b. Click the **Reset** button and select **Reset only Quick Access Toolbar**. *Note: If your* Quick Access *toolbar is already at its original settings, the* Reset only Quick Access Toolbar *option is not active, and you can skip both this step and step 3c.*
   c. Click **Yes** in the dialog box that opens to confirm the reset.

d. On the right, click the **Customize Quick Access Toolbar** drop-down list and select **For *[your initials]* Word 12-3**.

e. In the list of commands on the left, select **Email** and click the **Add** button to add it to the *Quick Access* toolbar.

f. Add **Insert Comment**, **Quick Print**, and **Open** to the *Quick Access* toolbar.

g. Select **Open** on the right and use the **Move Up** button to position it above *Quick Print* (Figure 12-106).

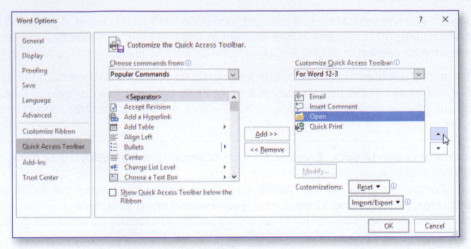

12-106 Add and rearrange commands on the *Quick Access* toolbar

h. Click **OK** to close the *Word Options* dialog box.

i. Save and close the document and exit Word.

4. Log in to *OneDrive* online using your Microsoft account.

a. Open an Internet browser window and go to the *OneDrive* web site (www.onedrive.live.com), which takes you to the *OneDrive* sign in page. You can use any Internet browser to access *OneDrive* (Microsoft Edge, Google Chrome, or Mozilla Firefox).

b. Click the **Sign in** button.

c. Type your Microsoft account email address and click **Next**.

d. Type your Microsoft account password and click **Sign in** to go to your *OneDrive* web page.

5. Create a *OneDrive* folder and upload files.

a. Click the **Files** button on the left to display your *OneDrive* folders and files.

b. Click the **New** button and select **Folder** from the drop-down list.

c. Type **PHRE** as the name of the new folder and click **Create**.

d. Click the ***PHRE*** folder to open it.

e. Click the **Upload** button and select **Files** from the drop-down list to open an upload dialog box.

f. Select ***[your initials]* Word 12-3** from your solutions files and click **Open** to upload this file to the ***PHRE*** folder in *OneDrive*.

g. Upload the ***EscrowChecklist-12*** and ***HomeBuying-12*** files from your student data files to the ***PHRE*** folder in *OneDrive*.

6. Edit a document in *Word Online*.

a. Click the ***[your initials]* Word 12-3** file to open it in *Word Online*. If you are prompted to install an extension for your Internet browser, click the **Get the extension** button.

b. Click the **Edit Document** button at the top and select **Edit in Browser**.

c. Replace the "*<Address Block>*" placeholder text with the following recipient address:

Mr. Rick DePonte

8364 Marshall Street

Granite Bay, CA 95863

d. Replace the *"<Salutation>"* placeholder text (don't delete the colon) with Mr. DePonte as the salutation.

e. Click the **X** on the browser tab to close the *[your initials] Word 12-3* file and return to the *PHRE* folder in *OneDrive*.

7. Share a folder on *OneDrive* with your instructor.

a. Click **Files** at the left to return to your *OneDrive* files.

b. Click the **circle** to the left of the *PHRE* folder to select it and click **Share** at the top to open the *Share* window.

c. Click **Email**.

d. Type your instructor's email address in the first text box (Figure 12-107).

e. Type a brief message and your name in the second text box.

f. Click **Share** to send the sharing email to your instructor.

8. Close **X** in the upper right corner of the browser window to close the Internet browser. (Figure 12-108).

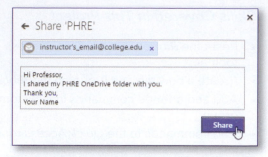

12-107 Share a *OneDrive* folder

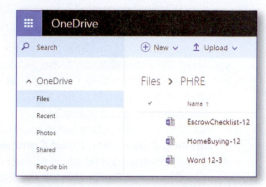

12-108 Word 12-3 completed (*PHRE* folder in *OneDrive*)

Independent Project 12-4

For this project, you customize the working environment in Word and use *OneDrive* and *Word Online* to create, store, edit, and share documents for Sierra Pacific Community College District.
[Student Learning Outcomes 12.1, 12.2, 12.3, 12.4, 12.5]

Note to Instructor and Students:

> For this project, you use your Microsoft account, OneDrive, and Word Online. If you don't have a Microsoft account, you can create a free account at https://signup.live.com. See the Microsoft Account Information *section in* SLO 12.2: Customizing Office and Installing Office Add-Ins.

> Microsoft *regularly updates the* Office Online *products and* OneDrive *online environment. Instructions and figures in this project may differ slightly from how* Office Online *and* OneDrive *display in your Internet browser. The Google Chrome web browser is used for instructions and figures in this project.*

Files Needed: **OnlineLearning-12.docx**, **EmergencyProcedures-12.docx**, and **WritingTips-12.docx** (student data files are available in the Library of your SIMnet account)
Completed Project Folder and File Names: **SPCCD** (OneDrive folder) containing the following files: **EmergencyProcedures-12.docx**, **[your initials] Word 12-4a.docx**, **[your initials] Word 12-4b.docx**, and **WritingTips-12.docx**

Skills Covered in This Project

- Reset the *Ribbon* and the *Quick Access* toolbar.
- Create a new tab and group on the *Ribbon*.
- Add and arrange commands in a custom group.
- Add commands to the *Quick Access* toolbar.
- Customize *Word Options*.
- Apply an Office background and theme.
- Create a *OneDrive* folder and upload files.
- Create a document in *Word Online* and apply formatting.
- Add a comment to a *Word Online* document.
- Share a *OneDrive* folder.

---

1. Open the **OnlineLearning-12** document from your student data files and save this file as [your initials] Word 12-4a.

2. Reset and customize the *Ribbon* and the *Quick Access* toolbar.
   a. Reset all customizations to the *Ribbon* and the *Quick Access* toolbar.
   b. Create a new tab after the *Home* tab.
   c. Rename the new tab to SPCCD.
   d. Rename new group in the *SPCCD* tab to Frequent Commands.
   e. Add the following commands (in *Popular Commands*) to the *Frequent Commands* group: **Save As, Spelling & Grammar, Insert Comment, Page Setup, Paragraph,** and **Insert Picture.**
   f. Arrange these commands in alphabetical order.
   g. Add **Open** and **Quick Print** to the *Quick Access* toolbar and click **OK** to close the *Word Options* dialog box.

3. Customize Word options.
   a. Open the *Word Options* dialog box and display the **General** area.
   b. Confirm that your *User name* and *Initials* are correct. Change them if necessary.
   c. Select an *Office Background* and *Office Theme* of your choice.
   d. Select the **Advanced** category on the left and check the **Expand all headings when opening a document** check box in the *Show document content* area.
   e. Click **OK** to close the *Word Options* dialog box.

4. Save and close the document and exit Word.

5. Create a *OneDrive* folder and upload files.
   a. Open an Internet browser and log in to your *OneDrive* account (www.onedrive.live.com).
   b. Create a new folder named SPCCD in the *Files* area.
   c. Open the **SPCCD** folder and upload the *[your initials] Word 12-4a* file.
   d. Upload the following files from your student data files: **EmergencyProcedures-12** and **WritingTips-12**.

6. Create a new Word document in *Word Online* and add a comment.
   a. In the **SPCCD** folder, create a new **Word document** using *Word Online* and name it [your initials] Word 12-4b. If you are prompted to install an extension for your Internet browser, click the **Get the extension** button.
   b. Refer to Figure 12-109 and enter the information in the new document.
   c. Apply **Heading 1** style, **bold** format, and **12 pt**. *After* paragraph spacing to the first line.
   d. Apply **Bullets** to the list if you have not already done so.
   e. Select the bulleted list and insert a comment.
   f. Type Please confirm these dates are correct in the comment and **Post** the comment.

SPCCD Fall Semester Important Dates

- August 22: Classes Begin
- August 30: Last Day to Register
- October 1: Apply for Fall Graduation
- November 8: Last Day to Drop
- December 14-18: Final Exams

12-109 Data for document in *Word Online*

g. Close the *[your initials] Word 12-4b* document and return to your **SPCCD** folder in *OneDrive* (Figure 12-110).

7. Share the **SPCCD** folder on *OneDrive* with your instructor.
   a. Select the **SPCCD** folder and **Share** the folder.
   b. Use **Email** as the sharing option.
   c. Type your instructor's email address in the recipient area and type a brief message in the body area.
   d. **Share** the folder with your instructor.

8. Sign out of *OneDrive* and close the Internet browser window.

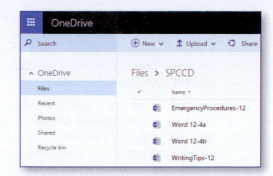

12-110 Word 12-4 completed (*SPCCD* folder in *OneDrive*)

Independent Project 12-5

For this project, you use *OneDrive* and *Word Online* to customize, store, edit, and share documents for Life's Animal Shelter. You also create and share an *Excel Survey*.
[**Student Learning Outcomes 12.3, 12.4, 12.5, 12.6**]

Note to Instructor and Students:

> *For this project, you use your Microsoft account, OneDrive, and Word Online. If you don't have a Microsoft account, you can create a free account at https://signup.live.com. See the* Microsoft Account Information *section in* SLO 12.2: Customizing Office and Installing Office Add-Ins.

> *Microsoft regularly updates the* Office Online *products and* OneDrive *online environment. Instructions and figures in this project may differ slightly from how* Office Online *and* OneDrive *display in your Internet browser. The Google Chrome web browser is used for instructions and figures in this project.*

Files Needed: **LASExpenses-12.docx** and **LASSupportForm-12.docx** (*student data files are available in the* Library *of your SIMnet account*)
Completed Project Folder and File Names: **LAS** (*OneDrive* folder) containing the following files: **LASExpenses-12.docx**, **LASSupportForm-12.docx**, **[your initials] Word 12-5.docx**, and **[your initials] Word 12-5 survey.xlsx**

Skills Covered in This Project

- Create a *OneDrive* folder.
- Upload a file to a *OneDrive* folder.
- Edit a document in *Word Online*.
- Mark a comment as done.
- Create a document in *Word Online* and apply formatting.
- Create and share an *Excel Survey*.
- Share a *OneDrive* folder.

1. Create a *OneDrive* folder and upload files to the *OneDrive* folder.
   a. Open an Internet browser and log in to your *OneDrive* account (www.onedrive.live.com).
   b. Create a new folder name LAS in the *Files* area.
   c. Open the **LAS** folder and upload the **LASExpenses-12** and **LASSupportForm-12** files from your student data files to the **LAS** folder.

2. Edit a *Word Online* document and mark a comment as done.
   a. Open the **LASExpenses-12** document in *OneDrive* and **Edit in Browser**. The text and graphic objects in the document may not align properly; don't try to fix alignment. If you are prompted to install an extension for your Internet browser, click the **Get the extension** button.
   b. Change the date in the "DATE" line to the current date.
   c. Click the **comment balloon** to the right of the date line to open the *Comments* pane.
   d. Click the **Mark as Done** check box on the comment and close the *Comments* pane.
   e. Close the **LASExpenses-12** document and return to your **LAS** folder in *OneDrive*.

3. Create a new document in *Word Online*.
   a. Create a new *Word Online* document in the **LAS** folder and type [your initials] Word 12-5 as the file name.
   b. Refer to Figure 12-111 to enter information in the new document.
   c. Type the title and then insert a table and type the body information. Edit the email address so the first letter is not capitalized if necessary.

   New LAS Supporters

Name	Email	Phone
Jennie Solara	jennies@live.com	208-773-2519
Ramon and Mary Clifton	cliftonrm@gmail.com	208-836-9914
Trevor Andrews	tandrews@outlook.com	208-228-3498

   12-111 Data for document in *Word Online*

   d. In the *Table Style Options* group [*Table Tools Design* tab], confirm **Header Row** and **Banded Rows** are selected, and deselect other options.
   e. Apply the **Grid Table 5 Dark – Accent 1** table style.
   f. Select the title ("**New LAS Supporters**"), apply **Heading 1** style, **bold** formatting, and **6 pt**. *After* paragraph spacing.
   g. Close the document and return to your **LAS** folder in *OneDrive*.

4. Create and view an *Excel Survey*.
   a. Deselect any selected (checked) files in the **LAS** folder if any files are selected.
   b. Create a new **Excel Survey** and use the following information:
   Title: Life's Animal Shelter
   Description: Volunteer Survey
   c. Add a question using the following information:
   Question: Your name
   Question Subtitle: leave blank
   Response Type: **Text**
   Required: yes (checked)
   Default Answer: leave blank
   d. Add another question using the following information:
   Question: I can volunteer at Life's Animal Shelter
   Question Subtitle: Select Yes or No
   Response Type: **Yes/No**
   Required: yes (checked)
   Default Answer: **Yes**
   e. Add another question using the following information:
   Question: Hours per week I can volunteer
   Question Subtitle: Select hours per week
   Response Type: **Choice**
   Required: no (unchecked)

Choices:
1-5 hours
6-10 hours
11-15 hours
16-20 hours
Default Answer: leave blank

    f. **Save and View** the survey (Figure 12-112).
    g. **Close** the *View Survey* window to return to *the Excel Survey* in *Excel Online*.

5. Rename and share an *Excel Survey*.
    a. Rename the survey and use [your initials] Word 12-5 survey as the file name.
    b. Share the survey [*Home* tab, *Tables* group].
    c. **Create link**, copy (**Ctrl+C**) the sharing link, and close the sharing window.
    d. Close the *[your initials] Word 12-5 survey* browser tab.
    e. Using your email, create a new email message to your instructor and use [your name] Word 12-5 survey as the subject line.
    f. Type a brief message in the body, paste (**Ctrl+V**) the survey link in the body of the email message, and send the message.

6. Share the **LAS** folder in *OneDrive* with your instructor.
    a. Return to *OneDrive* and select the **LAS** folder.
    b. **Share** the **LAS** folder and use **Email** as the sharing option.
    c. Type your instructor's email address in the recipient area and type a brief message in the body area.
    d. **Share** the folder with your instructor.

7. Sign out of *OneDrive* and close the Internet browser window (Figure 12-113).

12-112 View the *Excel Survey*

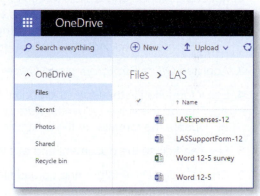

12-113 Word 12-5 completed (*LAS* folder in *OneDrive*)

Independent Project 12-6

For this project, you customize the working environment in Word and use *OneDrive* and *Word Online* to customize, store, edit, and share documents for Central Sierra Insurance.
[**Student Learning Outcomes 12.1, 12.2, 12.3, 12.4, 12.5**]

Note to Instructor and Students:

For this project, you use your Microsoft account, OneDrive, and Word Online. If you don't have a Microsoft account, you can create a free account at https://signup.live.com. See the Microsoft Account Information *section in* SLO 12.2: Customizing Office and Installing Office Add-Ins.

Microsoft regularly updates the Office Online *products and OneDrive online environment. Instructions and figures in this project may differ slightly from how* Office Online *and* OneDrive *display in your Internet browser. The Google Chrome web browser is used for instructions and figures in this project.*

Files Needed: **RenewalLetter-12.docx** and **ConferenceRegistrationForm-12.docx** *(student data files are available in the* Library *of your SIMnet account)*
Completed Project Folder and File Names: **CSI** *(OneDrive* folder) containing the following files: **ConferenceRegistrationForm-12.docx** and *[your initials]* **Word 12-6.docx**

Skills Covered in This Project

- Reset the *Ribbon* and the *Quick Access* toolbar.
- Add commands to the *Quick Access* toolbar.
- Apply an Office background and theme.
- Edit a document and update formulas.

- Log in to *OneDrive* and create a folder.
- Upload a file to a *OneDrive* folder.
- Delete and add a comment to a document in *Word Online*.
- Share a *OneDrive* folder.

1. In Word, open the **RenewalLetter-12** document from your student data files and save this file as [your initials] Word 12-6.

2. Reset the *Ribbon* and *Quick Access* toolbar and customize the *Quick Access* toolbar.
   a. Reset all *Ribbon* and *Quick Access* toolbar customizations.
   b. Add **Open**, **Quick Print**, and **Spelling & Grammar** to the *Quick Access* toolbar from the *Customize Quick Access Toolbar* drop-down list.

3. Apply an *Office Background* and *Office Theme* of your choice.

4. Edit information in the table and update formulas.
   a. Change the value below the *Rate per $1,000* column heading in the table to $19.50.
   b. Update the formulas in the next three cells.

5. Save and close the document and exit Word.

6. Create a *OneDrive* folder and upload files to a *OneDrive* folder.
   a. Open an Internet browser and log in to your *OneDrive* account (www.onedrive.live.com).
   b. Create a new *OneDrive* folder named CSI.
   c. Open the **CSI** folder and upload the *[your initials]* **Word 12-6** file.
   d. Upload the **ConferenceRegistrationForm-12** file from your student data files to the **CSI** folder.

7. Use *Word Online* to delete a comment and add a comment.
   a. In your **CSI** folder in *OneDrive,* open the *[your initials]* **Word 12-6** document in *Word Online* in *read-only* mode. If you are prompted to install an extension for your Internet browser, click the **Get the extension** button.
   b. Open the *Comments* pane, delete the comment in the document, and close the *Comments* pane.
   c. Close the *[your initials]* **Word 12-6** document and return to the **CSI** folder in *OneDrive*.
   d. Open the **ConferenceRegistrationForm-12** file in *Word Online* in *read-only* view and select the title of the document.
   e. Add a new comment, type Please email this conference registration form to all CSI sales staff in the comment area, and post the comment.
   f. Close the **ConferenceRegistrationForm-12** document and return to your *OneDrive* folder.

8. Share the **CSI** folder in *OneDrive* with your instructor.
   a. Select the **CSI** folder and **Share** the folder.
   b. Select **Email** as the sharing option.

c. Type your instructor's email address in the recipient area and type a brief message in the body area.

d. **Share** the folder with your instructor.

9. Sign out of *OneDrive* and close the Internet browser window (Figure 12-114).

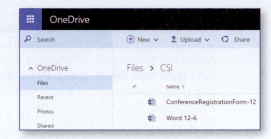

12-114 Word 12-6 completed (*CSI* folder in *OneDrive*)

Improve It Project 12-7

For this project, you customize the working environment in Word and use *OneDrive* and *Word Online* to customize, store, edit, and share documents for Skiing Unlimited.
[**Student Learning Outcomes 12.1, 12.2, 12.3, 12.4, 12.5**]

Note to Instructor and Students:

> *For this project, you use your Microsoft account, OneDrive, and Word Online. If you don't have a Microsoft account, you can create a free account at https://signup.live.com. See the* Microsoft Account Information *section in* SLO 12.2: Customizing Office and Installing Office Add-Ins.

> *Microsoft regularly updates the* Office Online *products and* OneDrive *online environment. Instructions and figures in this project may differ slightly from how* Office Online *and* OneDrive *display in your Internet browser. The Google Chrome web browser is used for instructions and figures in this project.*

Files Needed: *VolunteerLetter-12.docx*, *SkiingUnlimited-12.docx*, and *TrainingGuide-12.docx* *(student data files are available in the* Library *of your SIMnet account)*
Completed Project Folder and File Names: *Skiing Unlimited* *(OneDrive folder)* containing the following files: ***SkiingUnlimited-12.docx*, *TrainingGuide-12.docx*, and *[your initials] Word 12-7.docx***

Skills Covered in This Project

- Create a *OneDrive* folder.
- Reset the *Ribbon* and *Quick Access* toolbar.
- Create a new group on an existing tab.
- Add commands to a custom group.
- Arrange a group on a tab.

- Add commands to the *Quick Access* toolbar.
- Create a *OneDrive* folder and upload a file.
- Edit a document in *Word Online*.
- Reply to and delete a comment in *Word Online*.
- Share a document in *OneDrive*.
- Customize group options.

1. In Word, open the **VolunteerLetter-12** document from your student data files and save this file as [your initials] Word 12-7.

2. Reset and customize the *Ribbon* and the *Quick Access* toolbar.
   a. Reset all *Ribbon* and the *Quick Access* toolbar customizations.
   b. Create a new group on the *Home* tab.
   c. Rename the new custom group as Skiing Unlimited and select a symbol of your choice.

d. Add the following commands to the *Skiing Unlimited* group: **Page Setup**, **Insert Comment**, **Track Changes**, **Paragraph**, and **Add Table**.
e. Arrange these commands in alphabetical order.
f. Move this group up so it appears between the *Paragraph* and *Styles* groups.
g. Add **New File**, **Open**, **Quick Print**, **Save As**, and **Track Changes** to the *Quick Access* toolbar for this document only (use the *Customize the Quick Access Toolbar* area in the *Word Options* dialog box).

3. Apply an *Office Background* and *Office Theme* of your choice.

4. Save the document and exit Word.

5. Create a *OneDrive* folder and upload files.
   a. Open an Internet browser and log in to your *OneDrive* account (www.onedrive.live.com).
   b. Create a new *OneDrive* folder named Skiing Unlimited.
   c. Open the **Skiing Unlimited** folder and upload the *[your initials] Word 12-7* file.
   d. Upload the **SkiingUnlimited-12** and **TrainingGuide-12** files from your student data files to the **Skiing Unlimited** folder.

6. Edit a document in *Word Online*.
   a. Open the *[your initials] Word 12-7* document and edit the document in *Word Online*. If you are prompted to install an extension for your Internet browser, click the **Get the extension** button.
   b. Replace the placeholder text in the bulleted list with the following dates:

      January 13
      January 27
      February 3
      February 10
      February 17

   c. Close the *[your initials] Word 12-7* document and return to your **Skiing Unlimited** folder in *OneDrive*.

7. Edit comments in *Word Online*.
   a. Open the **SkiingUnlimited-12** document in *read-only* mode in *Word Online*.
   b. Reply to the existing comment, type The dates are correct in the comment area, and post the comment.
   c. Close the **SkiingUnlimited-12** document and return to your **Skiing Unlimited** folder in *OneDrive*.
   d. Open the **TrainingGuide-12** document in *read-only* mode in *Word Online*.
   e. Delete the existing comment.
   f. Close the **TrainingGuide-12** document and return to your *OneDrive* folder.

8. Share the **Skiing Unlimited** folder in *OneDrive* with your instructor using a sharing link.
   a. Select the **Skiing Unlimited** folder in *OneDrive* and share the folder.
   b. **Share** the folder, use **Get a link** as the sharing option, and **Copy** the sharing link.
   c. Using your email, create a new email message to your instructor and use [your name] Word 12-7 as the subject line.
   d. Type a brief message in the body, paste (**Ctrl+V**) the sharing link in the body of the email message, and send the email message.

9. Sign out of *OneDrive* and close the Internet browser window (Figure 12-115).

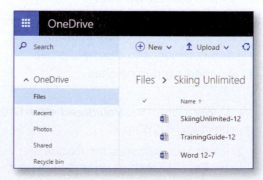

12-115 Word 12-7 completed (*Skiing Unlimited* folder in *OneDrive*)

Challenge Project 12-8

OneDrive is an excellent online storage area to organize your school work. You can create a *OneDrive* folder and subfolders to store files from all of your classes and share files or folders with your classmates and instructors. Remember, it is recommended that you do not store files with highly sensitive information in online locations.
[**Student Learning Outcomes 12.3, 12.4, 12.5**]

Note to Instructor and Students:

> *For this project, you use your Microsoft account and OneDrive. If you don't have a Microsoft account, you can create a free account at https://signup.live.com. See the* Microsoft Account Information *section in* SLO 12.2: Customizing Office and Installing Office Add-Ins.

File Needed: None
Completed Project File Name: New *OneDrive* folder, subfolder, and files

Create a *OneDrive* folder to store all files for all of your classes. Modify your *OneDrive* folder according to the following guidelines:

- Create a *OneDrive* folder and give it your school name.
- Create subfolders for each of your classes and any other folders needed (for example "Financial Aid," "Clubs," "Internships," etc.).
- Upload files to each of the folders.
- Share the folder for this class with your instructor.

Challenge Project 12-9

Now that you are familiar with many of the features and the working environment in Word, you can customize the working environment to meet your needs. For this project, you customize the *Ribbon,* the *Quick Access* toolbar, and Word options to personalize your working environment in Word.
[**Student Learning Outcomes 12.1, 12.2**]

File Needed: None
Completed Project File Name: *[your initials] Word 12-9*

Create a new document and save it as [your initials] Word 12-9. List the top ten new Word features you have learned in this class and create your *Word Top 10* list. Customize Word options, the *Ribbon,* and the *Quick Access* toolbar as desired. Modify your document according to the following guidelines:

- Create your *Word Top 10* list of new features you have learned in this class.
- Apply formatting and design principles you have learned to attractively format and arrange this document.
- Modify Word options to meet your needs.
- Reset the *Ribbon* and the *Quick Access* toolbar.
- Create a new tab and/or group and rename them.
- Add and arrange commands in the group.
- Add commands to your *Quick Access* toolbar.

Challenge Project 12-10

Office Online has many other applications you can use online to increase your personal productivity. For this project, create either an *Excel Survey* or a *Sway*.
[Student Learning Outcomes 12.3, 12.5, 12.6]

Note to Instructor and Students:

> *For this project, you use your Microsoft account, OneDrive, and Office Online. If you don't have a Microsoft account, you can create a free account at https://signup.live.com. See the* Microsoft Account Information *section in* SLO 12.2: Customizing Office and Installing Office Add-Ins.

File Needed: None
Completed Project File Name: New *Excel Survey* or *Sway*

Create a new *Excel Survey* or *Sway* for a club, organization, work team, or student group. Modify your *Excel Survey* or *Sway* according to the following guidelines:

- Create a new *Excel Survey* or *Sway*.
- Customize the content.
- Preview the results.
- Share the *Excel Survey* or *Sway* with your instructor and classmates.

appendices

- **APPENDIX A:** Office 2016 Shortcuts
- **APPENDIX B:** Business Document Formats (online resource)

APPENDIX A

Office 2016 Shortcuts

Using Function Keys on a Laptop

When using a laptop computer, function keys perform specific Windows actions on your laptop, such as increase or decrease speaker volume, open Windows *Settings*, or adjust the screen brightness. So when using a numbered function key in an Office application, such as **F12** as a shortcut to open the *Save As* dialog box, you may need to press the ***function key*** (**Fn** or **fn**) on your keyboard in conjunction with a numbered function key to activate the Office command (Figure Appendix A-1). The *function key* is typically located near the bottom left of your laptop keyboard next to the *Ctrl* key.

Appendix A-1
Function key

Common Office 2016 Keyboard Shortcuts

Action	Keyboard Shortcut
Save	**Ctrl+S**
Copy	**Ctrl+C**
Cut	**Ctrl+X**
Paste	**Ctrl+V**
Select All	**Ctrl+A**
Bold	**Ctrl+B**
Italic	**Ctrl+I**
Underline	**Ctrl+U**
Close *Start* page or *Backstage* view	**Esc**
Open *Help* dialog box	**F1**
Activate *Tell Me* feature	**Alt+Q**
Switch windows	**Alt+Tab**

Word 2016 Keyboard Shortcuts

Action	Keyboard Shortcut
File Management	
Open a new blank Word document	**Ctrl+N**
Save	**Ctrl+S**
Open *Save As* dialog box	**F12**
Open an existing document from the *Backstage* view	**Ctrl+O**
Open an existing document from the *Open* dialog box	**Ctrl+F12**
Close a document	**Ctrl+W**
Editing	
Toggle on/off *Show/Hide*	**Ctrl+Shift+8**

(continued)

Action	Keyboard Shortcut
Copy	Ctrl+C
Cut	Ctrl+X
Paste	Ctrl+V
Bold	Ctrl+B
Italic	Ctrl+I
Underline	Ctrl+U
Double underline	Ctrl+Shift+D
Small caps	Ctrl+Shift+K
All caps	Ctrl+Shift+A
Left align text	Ctrl+L
Center text	Ctrl+E
Right align text	Ctrl+R
Justify text	Ctrl+J
Single line spacing	Ctrl+1
Double line spacing	Ctrl+2
1.5 line spacing	Ctrl+5
Left Indent	Ctrl+M
Remove Left Indent	Ctrl+Shift+M
Undo	Ctrl+Z
Repeat/redo	Ctrl+Y
Insert line break	Shift+Enter
Insert page break	Ctrl+Enter
Insert column break	Ctrl+Shift+Enter
Insert non-breaking space	Ctrl+Shift+spacebar
Copy formatting	Ctrl+Shift+C
Paste formatting	Ctrl+Shift+V
Increase font size	Ctrl+Shift+. (Ctrl+>)
Decrease font size	Ctrl+Shift+, (Ctrl+<)
Insert an endnote	Alt+Ctrl+D
Insert a footnote	Alt+Ctrl+F
Update field	F9
Open Panes and Dialog Boxes	
Print area on the *Backstage* view	Ctrl+P
Open *Font* dialog box	Ctrl+D
Open *Spelling and Grammar* pane	F7
Open *Thesaurus* pane	Shift+F7

(continued)

Action	Keyboard Shortcut
Open *Navigation* pane	**Ctrl+F**
Open *Find and Replace* dialog box with the *Replace* tab selected	**Ctrl+H**
Open *Find and Replace* dialog box with the *Go To* tab selected	**Ctrl+G or F5**
Open *Insert Hyperlink* dialog box	**Ctrl+K**
Open Word Help dialog box	**F1**
Selection and Navigation	
Select all	**Ctrl+A**
Turn selection on (continue to press F8 to select word, sentence, paragraph, or document)	**F8**
Move the insertion point to the beginning of the document	**Ctrl+Home**
Move the insertion point to the end of the document	**Ctrl+End**
Move the insertion point to the beginning of a line	**Ctrl+left arrow**
Move the insertion point to the end of a line	**Ctrl+right arrow**
Switch window	**Alt+Tab**

glossary

.docx The file format of a Word 2016 document.

2 pages per sheet Custom page setting that splits a page horizontally into two pages.

A

Add Text Inserts text on a shape object.

Add-in Third-party application users can add to Office application programs to provide enhanced functionality.

Address Block Single merge field that groups individual merge fields to make a complete mailing address in mail merge.

alignment guides Vertical and horizontal green lines that appear when you drag a graphic object; help to align the object to margins, text, or other objects.

All apps An area of the *Start* menu in Windows 10 that displays all apps (applications) on the computer.

***All Markup* view** The *Display for Review* view that displays all tracked changes and comments in a document.

alternative text (alt text) Information tag that appears when a reader places the pointer on a table or graphic object; also used with screen readers to accommodate those with visual impairments.

app Short for application; software program or Windows 10 application or accessory.

Artistic Effects Built-in formatting that can be applied to a picture.

ascending order Sort order that arranges data from lowest to highest for a numeric field or from A to Z for a text field.

aspect ratio The ratio of width of height; affects picture and object sizing.

AutoComplete Feature that fills in the complete day, month, or date as you type.

***AutoComplete* tag** The notation that displays and predicts what will be typed, such as a day, month, or date. When the tag appears, press **Enter** to automatically insert the text.

AutoCorrect Feature that corrects commonly misspelled words.

***AutoCorrect Options* smart tag** Tag that appears by a word that has been automatically corrected.

AutoFit Formatting option that automatically adjusts column width to adjust the width of a table.

AutoFormat Feature that controls the formatting of items such as numbered and bulleted lists, fractions, ordinal numbers, hyphens and dashes, quotes, indents, and hyperlinks.

AutoMacro A macro that automatically runs when an action, such as opening or closing a document, occurs.

AutoText Building block gallery where you store information; you can insert *AutoText* building blocks in a document.

axis (pl. axes) Vertical or horizontal boundary on the plot area of line, column, and bar charts.

axis title Chart element that names the horizontal and vertical axes using placeholders or textboxes.

B

***Backstage* view** Area of an Office application where you perform common actions, such as *Save, Open, Print,* and *Share,* and change application options; document properties are displayed here.

balloon Object where comments display.

Banded Columns *Table Style* option featuring columns that have alternating colors.

Banded Rows *Table Style* option featuring rows that have alternating colors.

bar chart Chart type that is similar to a column chart with bars shown horizontally.

bar tab stop Tab that inserts a vertical line at the tab stop.

bibliography List of the sources used in a report.

bibliography style Style that determines the formatting of sources and citations in a report.

block format letter All parts of the letter begin at the left margin. No lines are indented or centered. Block format can be used on either business or personal business letters.

Book fold Custom page setting that splits a page vertically into two pages.

bookmark Location in a document that is electronically marked and can be linked to a hyperlink or cross-reference.

border Line around text, paragraph, page, cell, table, or graphic object.

Border Painter Pointer used to draw borders on a table.

Border Sampler Tool that applies an existing border style on a table to other areas of a table; similar to the *Format Painter.*

Border Style Built-in border color, weight, and format applied to selected boundaries of a table.

building block Text, formatting, and/or object that is saved and can be inserted into a document; there are a variety of different building block galleries (e.g., *Quick Parts, AutoText, Header, Footer,* or *Tables*).

***Building Block Gallery* content control field** Word field in which users insert a building block into the content control field.

bulleted list Unordered list of items; a bullet symbol precedes each item, and a left and hanging indent controls left alignment.

button Use to apply a command or open a dialog box in Office applications.

button-activated macro A macro that runs when a button on the *Quick Access* toolbar or *Ribbon* is pressed.

C

caption Descriptive text that appears above or below a graphic.

cell Intersection of a column and a row.

cell address Letter of the column and number of the row that represents the location of a cell; also referred to as a cell reference.

cell margins Space around the top, bottom, left, and right of the text inside a table cell.

cell reference Column letter and row number that represents the location of the cell; also referred to as a cell address.

cell spacing Amount of space between cells in a table.

center tab stop Tab that centers text at the tab stop.

Change Case Button used to change text from the case shown to a different case such as uppercase to lowercase.

Change Colors Gallery that lists different color combinations for *SmartArt* layouts that are based on theme colors.

character spacing Space between letters and words.

***Character* style** Style that applies to selected text.

chart Object that displays numeric data in the form of a graph to compare data values or display data trends.

chart area One of several chart background elements; background area where the entire chart is displayed in a frame.

chart element One of the components that make up a chart, such as chart floor, chart area, data series, chart wall, etc.

chart floor Horizontal bottom area of a 3-D chart.

chart label A title, legend, or data table used to organize chart data.

chart object An object that represents a chart in a workbook.

Chart Styles Gallery that lists preset effects for chart elements.

chart title Chart element that names the chart using placeholders or text boxes.

chart type Category of charts that represent data using various shapes and subtypes.

chart walls Vertical side and back areas of a 3-D chart.

Check Accessibility Examines a document for potential issues that users with disabilities might have when using a screen reader or other adaptive resources.

check box Box that allows you to choose one or more from a group of options.

Check Box content control field Word field in which users select or deselect a check box.

Check Compatibility Examines a document for potential version compatibility issues.

child table Table inside parent table.

citation Abbreviated source information in the body of a report that credits the source of information referred to in the document.

Clear Formatting Command that removes formatting from selected text and formats the text in *Normal* style.

clip art Electronic graphical image.

Clipboard Location where multiple copied items from an Office file or other source such as a web page are stored.

Clipboard pane Pane that displays the contents of the *Clipboard*.

column Vertical grouping of cells in a table or a vertical area of text in a document.

column break Formatting option that ends a column and pushes subsequent text to the next column.

column selector Pointer that selects a column of a table.

Combine Tool that merges an original document and a revised document and displays differences between the two documents as marked changes.

Combo Box content control field Word field in which users select from a list of options or type in their own response.

Comment Word collaboration feature that allows users to add notations to a document without affecting text or objects in the document.

Compare Tool that reviews an original document and a revised document and displays differences between the two documents as marked changes.

Compress Picture Feature that reduces the resolution and file size of a picture or all pictures in a document.

connected services Third-party services users can add to Office application programs, such as Facebook, LinkedIn, and YouTube.

Content Control Display Options that control how content control fields are shown in the document; there are three display (*Show as*) options: *Bounding Box*, *Start/End Tag*, and *None*.

content control field Word field in which you type custom information such as the date or year.

Content Control Field Properties Unique identifiers, content, and format of a content control field.

context menu Menu of commands that appears when you right-click text or an object.

context-sensitive Describes menu options that change depending on what you have selected.

continuous section break Formatting option that divides a document into different sections on the same page so sections can be

formatted independently of each other; can also be used at the end of columns to balance column length.

copy Duplicate text or other information.

Cortana The help feature in Windows 10 that responds to both keyboard and voice commands. *Cortana* searches not only the computer but also the Internet and displays search results in the *Cortana* menu.

crop Trim unwanted areas of a selected picture.

cropping handles Black handles that appear on the corners and sides of pictures that you can drag to remove part of the picture.

crosshair Large plus sign tool used to draw a shape.

cross-reference Note in a document that directs readers to another location in a document.

cross-reference index entry Index entry that references another index entry rather than a page number.

custom dictionary Location in Office where words that you add to the dictionary are stored.

cut Remove text or other information.

D

data label Numerical value on data plotted in a chart.

database An organized collection of integrated and related tables.

Date Picker content control field Word field in which users select a date from a calendar.

decimal tab stop Tab that aligns text at the decimal point at the tab stop.

default Setting that is automatically applied by an application unless you make specific changes.

descending order Sort order that arranges data from highest to lowest for a numeric field or from Z to A for a text field.

Design mode Setting that allows users to edit placeholder text in content control fields.

destination file File where an object is inserted.

destination program Office application where an object is inserted.

dialog box Window that opens and displays additional features.

Different First Page Formatting option that imposes first-page header or footer content that differs from the other headers and footers in a document.

Different Odd & Even Pages Formatting option that imposes headers and/or footers that differ on odd and even pages.

Display for Review View options that show tracked changes and comments in a document; there are four *Display for Review* views: *Simple Markup*, *All Markup*, *No Markup*, and *Original*.

Distribute Columns Table option that evenly distributes column width.

Distribute Rows Table option that evenly distributes row height.

document property Information about a file such as title, author name, subject, etc.

document property field Word field that displays the document property contents in the body, header, or footer of a document.

drag and drop A method to copy or move select text or an object.

Drop Cap Feature that changes the first letter or word of a paragraph to a larger font, graphic object.

drop-down list List of options that displays when you click a button.

Drop-Down List content control field Word field in which users select from a list of options and are limited to those selections; users cannot type in their own response as they can in a *Combo Box* content control field.

E

Edit link A hyperlink used when sharing a file with others that allows users to edit a shared file.

edit mode Office Online view where users can edit and save a file.

Effect Formatting feature such as shadow, glow, or soft edges added to an element.

embed Insert an object from an Office application into another file; an embedded object is no longer connected to the original file and can be modified independently without affecting the original object.

Enable Content Button that activates content blocked by Word macro security settings.

Encrypt with Password Protects a document from being opened and edited; a password is required to open the document.

endnote Reference, citation, or other text that appears at the end of a document.

eraser Pointer used to erase parts of a table.

extract Create a regular folder from a zipped folder.

F

field handle Area to select a document property of content control field.

field name Label associated with each field in a database or recipient list in mail merge.

File Explorer Window where you browse for, open, and manage files and folders (formerly called Windows Explorer).

file name extension A series of letters automatically added to a file name that identifies the type of file (e.g., *.docx, .dotx, .docm,* and *.dotm*).

fill Color or pattern used as a background.

Filter Feature used to select records in a recipients list that match specific criteria.

Find Feature that searches a file to locate specific text and/or formatting.

first line indent Horizontal space between the first line of a paragraph and the left margin.

folder A Windows feature used to store and organize files in a specific location.

font Named design of type for characters, punctuation, and symbols.

font color The color applied to selected text.

font face Specifies the shape of text.

font size Specifies the size of text.

font style Formatting applied to create bold, italics or underlined text.

footer Displays content at the bottom of a document page or object.

footnote Reference, citation, or other text that appears at the bottom of a page.

Format Painter Tool that duplicates formatting choices, such as font, font size, line spacing, indents, bullets, numbering, styles, etc., from one selection to another selection.

formula Mathematical syntax in a cell that calculates and updates results.

function Predefined formula that performs a specific task (e.g., *SUM* or *AVERAGE*).

function keys The numbered command keys (i.e., F1, F2, etc.) located near the top of the keyboard. Function keys can perform both Windows and Office application commands. Some laptops require the user to press the *Function key* (*Fn* or *fn*) on the keyboard in conjunction with a numbered function key to activate an Office command.

G

gallery Group of options on a tab.

Go To The feature that moves the insertion point to a specific location in a file, such as a page, bookmark, footnote, comment, or heading level.

Gradient Option that blends two or more colors or light and dark variations of the current fill color in different directions.

graphics Visual objects such as pictures, clip art, shapes, *SmartArt,* charts, and *WordArt.*

grayscale A range of shades of black in a display or printout.

Greeting Line Single merge field that groups individual merge fields to make a complete salutation in a business letter in mail merge.

gridlines Lines that visually frame rows and columns in a table.

group Area on a tab that contains related commands and options.

Group/Ungroup *Group* combines multiple graphic objects; *Ungroup* separates previously grouped objects into separate objects; also used with content control fields to restrict editing of a document and allow editing only of content control fields.

Gutter **margins** Custom page settings that add extra margin space at the top or left of a document to accommodate binding.

H

hanging indent Additional horizontal space between second and carry-over lines of a paragraph and the left margin.

header Displays content at the top of each page of a document.

header row First row of a table.

Highlight Merge Fields Feature used in mail merge to shade all merge fields in a document to visually identify the location of the merge fields.

horizontal alignment Content positioning option that aligns material in relation to the left, center, right, or middle (justified) of the margins, column, or cell; can also refer to the position of objects in relation to each other.

hyperlink Text or an object that a reader can click to be taken to another location in the document, to a web page, or to a different file.

Hyphenation Feature that automatically hyphenates text in a document; facilitates tighter text wrapping at the right margin.

I

Import/Export Styles Tool that copies styles from one document to another.

index Alphabetical list of key words with page number references for where they can be found in a document, typically found at the end of a document; also called an index page.

index entry Text, bookmark, or location in a document that is marked with a field code and is used to generate an index page.

index field code Word field code that marks an index entry.

insert control Button that allows you to quickly insert a row or column into a table.

Inspect Document Examines a document for hidden content, properties, or personal information that might create document compatibility issues.

J

justified alignment Content positioning option that aligns material with both the left and right margins.

K

Kerning Space between letters in a proportional font.

keyboard shortcut Key or combination of keys that you press to apply a command.

keyboard-activated macro A macro that runs when a keystroke combination is pressed.

L

Labels Pre-defined table format used to arrange information so it prints correctly on a sheet of labels; can be used to create individual labels, a full sheet of the same label, or in mail merge.

landscape orientation Page layout option in which the page is oriented so it is wider than it is tall.

leader Series of dots or lines that fills the blank space between text and a tab stop.

left indent Horizontal space between a paragraph and the left margin.

left tab stop Tab that aligns text at the left of the tab stop.

Legacy Tools Content control fields available in previous versions of Word.

legend Descriptive text in a table that describes a data series and identifies it by color.

line break Formatting option that controls where lines begin and end; can be used to keep lines together in a bulleted or numbered list.

Line Numbers Feature that automatically numbers lines in a document; facilitates collaborative editing and reviewing process.

line spacing Amount of space between lines of text within a paragraph.

link Insert an object from an Office application file into another file; linking maintains a connection between the source file and the destination file, and when the original object is modified, the linked object updates automatically.

Linked style Style that applies to selected text or an entire paragraph.

List style Style that applies a numbered or bulleted list style to selected paragraphs.

live layout Feature that automatically and instantly rearranges text and other objects when you drag a graphic object to a different location.

live preview Display option that allows you to temporarily apply and view a style or formatting feature.

lock a subdocument Protect a subdocument from being modified within a master document; users can edit the original subdocument file, and changes are reflected in the master document.

Lock Tracking Keeps *Track Changes* turned on so all changes reviewers make are marked.

M

macro Recorded combination of instructions and keystrokes that are saved and can be inserted in other documents.

Macro Security Settings Options that control how macros are handled when a user opens a document.

macro-enabled document Word document that contains macros.

macro-enabled template Word template that contains macros; a document based on a macro-enabled template contains the macros that are stored in the template.

Mail Merge Feature that combines information from a recipient list into a main document, such as a letter or labels.

mail merge rule Controls the results of a mail merge by applying a condition and action to the merge.

Mail Merge Wizard Step-by-step instructions to guide a user to create a mail merge.

main document Document where a mail merge is performed, such as a letter or labels.

Manage Versions Allows users to recover a previous version of a document.

margin Blank space at the top, bottom, left, or right of a document; in a text box, the space between the outside of the box and the text within the box; in a table, the space between a cell border and the cell text.

Mark as Final Saves a document and prevents it from being edited.

markup area Area outside the right margin of a document where comments and tracked changes display.

master document File containing links to one or more subdocuments.

Match Fields Feature used in mail merge to select fields from a recipient list to match corresponding fields in an address block or greeting line.

mathematical order of operations Set of rules that establishes the sequence that operations are performed in multiple-operation expressions and formulas.

maximize Increase the size of the window of an open Office file so it fills the entire computer monitor.

Merge Completes a mail merge by inserting information from the recipient list into the merge fields in the main document.

Merge Cells Command that combines two or more cells in a row or column.

merge field An individual piece of information from a recipient list, such as first name, last name, or company name, that is inserted in the main document during a mail merge.

merge subdocuments Combine two or more subdocuments in a master document.

Microsoft Access The database software in the Microsoft Office suite of applications.

Microsoft account User profile used to log in to Windows and Microsoft Office; this free account also provides access to *OneDrive* and Office Online.

Microsoft Excel The spreadsheet software in the Microsoft Office suite of applications.

Microsoft Office 2016 The suite of Microsoft productivity software that typically includes Microsoft Word, Excel, Access, PowerPoint, OneNote, and Outlook.

Microsoft Office 365 The subscription version of Microsoft Office where users pay a monthly or yearly fee to install and use the Microsoft Office applications on a computer.

Microsoft OneNote The note-taking software in the Microsoft Office suite of applications.

Microsoft Outlook The personal information management software in the Microsoft Office suite of applications that includes email, calendar, contacts, and tasks.

Microsoft PowerPoint The presentation software in the Microsoft Office suite of applications.

Microsoft Store The online store where users can purchase and download a variety of apps (applications).

Microsoft Word The word processing software in the Microsoft Office suite of applications.

Microsoft Visual Basic editor Program used to edit macro code.

mini toolbar Toolbar listing formatting options that appears when you select text or right-click.

minimize Place an open Office file on the *Taskbar* so it is not displayed on the desktop.

Mirror margins Margin settings for multi-page documents that are printed on both sides; ensures consistent margin space when the document is bound on the left.

mixed punctuation Use a colon after the salutation (e.g., "Dear Ms. Vasquez:") and a comma after the complimentary close (e.g., "Best regards,"). Mixed or open punctuation can be used on either business or personal business letters.

modified block format letter Type the date line and closing lines [complimentary close, writer's name, writer's title, and return address (on personal business letters)] beginning at the horizontal midpoint. Typically, set a left tab stop at 3.25". Modified block format can be used on either business or personal business letters.

multilevel list Customized list that includes a combination of numbers, letters, or bullets.

N

Navigation pane (Windows File Explorer) The area on the left side of a *File Explorer* window that displays the different storage areas of the computer.

Navigation pane (Word) The pane at the left side of the Word window when the *Find* command is selected. The *Navigation* pane displays headings, pages, and search results.

nested table A table inside another table; the main table is the parent table, and tables inside the parent table are child tables.

No Markup view The *Display for Review* view that displays the final document with changes applied.

non-breaking space Formatting option that keeps words together so they are not separated by word wrap at the end of a line.

Normal template Predesigned and ready-to-use document that includes default fonts, font sizes, line and paragraph spacing, styles, and margins; new blank document.

numbered list List that arranges items in order; a number or letter precedes each item, and a left and hanging indent controls left alignment.

NumPages field Word field that lists the number of pages in a document.

O

Object Linking and Embedding (OLE) Integration feature to insert content from other Office application files into a Word document.

Office Background Graphic image display in the working environment of Word.

Office Clipboard Storage location for cut or copied data shared by all Office applications.

Office desktop apps The version of Microsoft Office that users download and install on a PC or Apple computer.

Office Online The online version of Microsoft Office that is available through a web browser.

Office universal apps The version of Microsoft Office that users download and install on tablets or mobile phone devices.

Office Theme Color of the working environment in Word.

OneDrive Online (cloud) storage area that is a part of your Microsoft account where you can store and access documents from any computer with an Internet connection.

OneDrive folder Windows folder that displays folders and files stored on a user's *OneDrive* account; synchronizes folders and files stored in the *OneDrive* folder with *OneDrive* cloud storage.

online Word template Preset template available on Office.com that users can use to create documents and customize content.

open punctuation Punctuation after the salutation and complimentary close are omitted. Mixed or open punctuation can be used on either business or personal business letters.

operating system Software that makes a computer function and controls the working environment.

operator Mathematical symbol used in formulas.

Original view The *Display for Review* view that displays the original document with none of the tracked changes applied.

outdent Negative indent that lines up information outside the left or right margins.

outline Border around selected element.

Outline view View option used to arrange and edit subdocuments in a master document.

P

page break Formatting option that controls where text on a page ends.

Page Color Fill color, color gradient, picture, or texture applied to the entire page(s) of a document.

page number field Word field that lists the page number.

page orientation The direction of the page. The two different orientation options are *Portrait* and *Landscape*.

paragraph alignment Formatting option that determines how a paragraph is positioned horizontally on the page.

paragraph break Formatting option that you insert when you press *Enter* at the end of a word, line, or paragraph.

paragraph spacing Amount of spacing before and after a paragraph.

Paragraph style Style that applies to an entire paragraph.

paragraph symbol Icon that indicates a paragraph break.

parent table The main table that has child tables inside of it.

Paste Place text or other objects that have been stored on the *Clipboard* in a new location.

Paste Options Gallery of choices for how data is copied.

Paste Special Dialog box that allows users to choose how a copied object or text is inserted into a document.

PDF (portable document format) File format used to convert a file into a static image.

pen Pointer used to draw a table or add columns, rows, or cells.

picture anchor Location in a document where an object connects to text.

Picture content control field Word field in which users insert a picture into the field.

Picture Correction Options Feature that sharpens, softens, or changes the brightness or contrast of a picture by a percentage of its original resolution.

Picture Effects Command used to apply effect options, such as *Shadow* or *Glow,* to pictures.

Picture Fill *Shape Fill* option that fills the *WordArt* or shape with a picture from a file or from the Office.com clip art collection.

placeholder Text that temporarily marks a spot in a document where a citation is missing and needs to be completed.

Plain Text content control field Word field in which users can type text; all of the text in the field is formatted the same way.

plot area Area of a chart that displays chart data.

pointer Small icon, such as a block plus sign, thin black plus sign, or white arrow, that appears and moves when you move your mouse or touch your touchpad.

points Font measurement of 1/72 of an inch.

portrait orientation Page layout option in which the page is oriented so it is taller than it is wide.

Position A character-spacing option that raises or lowers text by a designated number of points.

Preview Mail Merge Displays information from the recipient list in the merge fields in a main document in mail merge.

program options Area in each Office application where you can make changes to the program settings.

protection Layer of security you can apply to a document for form fields that allows various areas to be accessible while others are not.

Q

Quick access (Windows *File Explorer*) The area at the top of the *Navigation* pane in a *File Explorer* window that displays folders or locations on a computer so users can quickly access these item. Users can pin folders or locations on a computer to the *Quick access* area of a *File Explorer* window.

Quick Access toolbar Area located above the *Ribbon* with buttons you use to perform commonly used commands.

Quick Parts Building block gallery where you store information; you can insert *Quick Parts* building blocks in a document.

Quick Tables Gallery of built-in and custom table building blocks.

R

radio button Round button you click to choose one option from a list.

range Group of cells.

read-only mode *Office Online* view where users can view and add comments to a file.

Real-time collaboration The Word 2016 feature that allows multiple users to simultaneously edit a shared filed stored in an online location, such as *OneDrive*.

recipients Data that can be merged into a main document from an external source, such as an Excel worksheet, Access database, or text file, used in mail merge.

record Collection of related data fields used in mail merge.

Recycle Bin Location where deleted files and folders are stored.

Redo Repeat an action.

reference marker Number, letter, or symbol that marks a footnote or endnote in the body of a document.

Repeat The command to automatically repeat the previous command used.

Replace Feature that searches a file to locate specific text and/or formatting and replace it with specified replacement text and/or formatting.

Reset Picture Command used to restore a picture's original characteristics and dimensions.

resize pointer Pointer that resizes a graphic object or a table column or row.

restore down Decrease the size of the window of an open Office file so it does not fill the entire computer monitor.

Restrict Editing Protects an entire document or portions of a document; a user can customize to allow comments or tracked changes.

reviewer User who inserts comments and changes in a document; a document can have multiple reviewers.

Reviewing pane Area to the left of the Word window where tracked changes and comments display.

Ribbon Bar that appears at the top of an Office file window and displays available commands.

Ribbon Display Options A button is the upper right corner of an Office application window that controls how the *Ribbon* displays. The options include *Auto-hide Ribbon, Show Tabs,* and *Show Tabs and Commands.*

Rich Text content control field Word field in which users can type and format some or all of the text.

right indent Horizontal space between a paragraph and the right margin.

right tab stop Tab that aligns text at the right of the tab stop.

rotation handle A circular arrow used to rotate a graphic object.

row Horizontal grouping of cells.

row height Top to bottom measurement of a row.

row selector Pointer that selects a row of a table.

Ruler Vertical or horizontal guide that displays measurements within the margins of a document.

S

sans serif font One of several font typefaces with letters that do not include structural details (flair).

Scale Character-spacing option that changes spacing by a designated percentage.

screen clipping A capture of a portion of an open window on your computer as a graphic object.

screenshot A capture of an open window on your computer as a graphic object.

ScreenTip Descriptive information about a button, drop-down list, launcher, or gallery selection that appears when you place your pointer on the item.

section break Formatting option used to break a document into different sections so sections can be formatted independently of each other.

Select Recipients Feature used in mail merge to choose the recipients that will be merged into the main document.

selection handle Four-pointed arrow that selects and moves objects.

Selection pane Window that displays graphic objects in a document; used to select, rearrange, group, or hide objects.

serif font One of several font typefaces with letters that feature structural details (flair).

Settings (Windows 10) The area of Windows 10 used to customize computer settings. The *Settings* area in Windows 10 is similar to the *Control Panel* in previous versions of Windows.

shading Fill color applied to text, paragraph, page, cell, table, or graphic object.

Shadow Style effect option that provides dimension by inserting a shadow behind or below text or an object.

shape Graphic object that can be drawn, such as a line, arrow, circle, or rectangle.

shape adjustment handle Yellow circle handle that changes the contour of a shape.

Shape Effects Command used to apply effect options, such as *Shadow, Reflection,* or *Glow,* to a graphic object.

Shape Fill Color, gradient color, picture, or texture applied to a graphic object.

Shape Outline Border, border color, and border weight applied to a graphic object.

Shape Style Set of built-in formats for shapes that include borders, fill colors, and effect components.

share Allow other users access to a file or folder saved in an online location, such as *OneDrive.*

Share (Windows 10 File Explorer) The feature in a *File Explorer* window that allows users to share files stored online with other users.

Share pane The pane at the right side of the Word, Excel, or PowerPoint window that displays options to share a file.

Show/Hide Button that displays or hides paragraph breaks, line breaks, spaces, tabs, and other formatting symbols in a document.

Simple Markup view The *Display for Review* view that displays the document with all tracked changes applied and a line at the left side of the document indicating where changes are made.

sizing handles Circles on the corners and sides of an object that resize the object.

Smart Lookup The feature that displays the definition and additional information from the Internet of a selected word or words.

Smart Lookup pane The pane on the right side of the Office application window that displays the definition and additional information from the Internet of a selected word or words when the *Smart Lookup* feature is used.

SmartArt graphics Diagram layouts used to illustrate concepts such as processes, cycles, or relationships.

SmartArt Styles Gallery that displays different effects for emphasizing shapes within *SmartArt* layouts.

Snap Assist The Windows feature that allows users to fill half or a quarter of the computer screen with an open application or window and select another open application or window to fill a different half or quadrant of the computer screen.

Soft Edges Style effect option that creates a feathered edge, which gradually blends into the background color.

soft page break Formatting option that allows text to flow to the next page when it reaches the bottom margin of a page.

Sort Feature that arranges text, table rows, or records in alphabetical or numerical order.

source Complete bibliographic reference for a book, journal article, or web page.

source data Cell range with values and labels graphed in a chart.

source documents The two documents (original and revised) used when comparing and combining documents.

source file File where linked content is stored.

source program Office application where content is created.

Spelling Feature that identifies misspelled words and gives the user word choice options to correct spelling.

split a subdocument Create a new subdocument from a portion of a subdocument.

split button Use to apply a command or display a drop-down list of additional commands depending on where you click the button.

Split Cells Command that divides a single cell into two or more cells.

Split Table Command that splits an existing table into two tables.

Start button (Windows 10) The button located on the left of the Windows *Taskbar* that opens the Windows *Start* menu.

Status bar The area at the bottom of an Office application that displays certain file information and application commands.

style Set of built-in formats, which include a variety of borders, shading, alignment, and other options.

Style gallery Collection of preset effects for text, shapes, pictures, or other objects.

Style Set Group of styles and formatting applied to an entire document.

style template Word template used to store styles; a new document based upon a style template contains the styles in the styles template; a style template can be attached to a document so styles are available and update automatically.

Styles Organizer Dialog box that allows users to copy styles from one document or template to another document or template; also referred to as the *Organizer* dialog box.

Styles pane Window that opens on the right and displays styles in a document where you can insert or modify styles.

subdocument File inserted into and linked to a master document.

subentry Index entry that is subordinate to a main index entry.

syntax Rules that dictate how the various parts of a formula must be written.

T

tab Area on the *Ribbon* that lists groups of related commands and options; also a keyboard button that moves the insertion point to the next tab stop.

tab selector Button at the top of the vertical *Ruler* where you select the type of tab stop you want to set on the *Ruler*.

tab stop Marker that controls where the insertion point stops when *Tab* is pressed.

table Information arranged in columns and rows.

Table building block An entire table saved as a building block that can be inserted in a document; table building blocks are stored in the *Quick Tables* gallery.

table of contents List of topics in a document; lists headings in the document and related page numbers.

Table properties Alignment, text wrapping, size, and position options for an entire table.

table selector handle Handle that appears at the upper left of a table when the pointer is on a table.

Table Style Options Tool that applies table style formatting to specific areas of a table, such as header row, first column, or banded rows.

Table Styles Built-in formats for tables, which include a variety of borders, shading, alignment, and other options.

Tablet mode The Windows feature that optimizes the computer for use with a touch screen.

target frame Window where a reader is directed when a hyperlink document or web site opens.

task pane Area at the left or right of an Office application window where you can perform tasks.

Task View The feature in Windows 10 that displays all open windows as tiles on the desktop, and users can select an item to display as the active window on the desktop.

Taskbar Horizontal area at the bottom of the Windows desktop where you can launch programs or open folders.

Tell Me The new help feature in Office applications that displays both application commands and information about commands.

template Predesigned and ready-to-use file upon which other Word documents can be created and modified; a Word template has a .dotx file name extension.

text box Graphic object where you can type text; also an area in a dialog box where you can type text.

Text Effects Command used to apply effect options, such as *Shadow* or *Glow*, to text.

Text pane Area where you enter text for *SmartArt* shapes.

text wrapping Formatting option that controls how text wraps around a graphic.

Theme Collection of fonts, colors, and effects that you can apply to an entire document, workbook, or presentation; provides consistent background graphics.

Theme Colors Set of background and accent colors.

Theme Fonts Pair of fonts used in headings and body text.

Thesaurus Resource tool that lists synonyms for a selected word.

thumbnail Small picture of an image or layout.

tick marks Symbols that identify the categories, values, or series on an axis.

Touch Mode The Office applications feature that optimizes the software for use with a touch screen.

Track Changes Word feature that marks text and formatting changes in a document.

Track Changes Options Settings that customize how changes and comments are tracked and displayed in a document.

U

Undo Reverse an action.

unlink a subdocument Break the links between the master document and the subdocument file.

Update Labels Feature used in mail merge to insert merge fields that were inserted into the first label into the remaining labels.

V

value Number that you type in a cell for numbers, currency, dates, and percentages.

value axis (Y axis) Vertical border in the plot area that measures charted data.

vertical alignment Content positioning option that aligns material in relation to the top, bottom, or middle of the page; can also refer to the position of objects in relation to each other.

View-only link A hyperlink used when sharing a file with others that allows users to only view or download a shared file.

Visual Basic Programming language used to record and store macros.

W

watermark Background text or image that appears on every page of a document.

Watermark **building block** Saved watermark object that you can insert from the *Watermark* gallery.

Weight Thickness of an line or border measured in points.

white space Blank space around text and objects in a document; improves the readability of a document and prevents the document from appearing cluttered.

Windows 10 Operating system software that controls computer functions and the working environment.

Windows desktop Working area in Windows.

Windows *Start* **menu** Menu that displays when the *Start* button in the bottom left corner of the screen is clicked. Open applications and Windows features from the *Start* menu.

Word field Code inserted in a document that controls content display (e.g., a document property field, formula field, or page number field).

Word Options Dialog box that allows users to customize global Word settings.

word wrap Formatting option that ensures that text automatically continues to the next line when a line ends at the right margin.

WordArt Graphic object that visually enhances text.

worksheet Individual sheet within an Excel workbook; also referred to as a sheet; comparable to a page in a book.

wrap points Locations on a graphic object that function as boundaries for an object and determine where text wraps around the object; you can adjust wrap points for precise text wrapping.

Wrap Text Formatting tool that enables you to display the contents of a cell on multiple lines.

X

X axis Axis displayed horizontally, usually on the bottom of a chart; also called the category axis.

Y

Y axis Axis displayed vertically, usually on the left of a chart; also called the value axis.

Z

zip The Windows feature that combines files and/or folders into one compressed folder; also called a compressed folder.

zipped (compressed) folder Folder that has a reduced file size and can be attached to an email.

Zoom Change file display size.

Index

SYMBOLS

*, W2-99
?, W2-99
=, W7-394
− (subtraction), W7-394
( ), W7-394
^ (exponent), W7-394
+ (addition), W7-394
÷ (division), W7-394

A

Accessibility Checker pane, W9-535
Account area (Backstage view), W12-707, W12-708
Account settings link, W12-707
ActiveX Controls, W11-653
Add a Digital Signature, W9-539
Add Bullet button, W8-481
Add Chart Element button, W8-486, W8-487
Add Chart Element drop-down list, W8-487
Add Choice dialog box, W11-651
Add-ins, W12-700. See also Office add-ins
Add New Placeholder, W3-153
Add New Source, W3-151, W3-152
Add People button, W12-721
Add Shape drop-down button, W8-481
Add Text, W7-428
Add to Style Gallery, W6-333
Add to the Styles gallery check box, W6-332, W6-333
Addition (+), W7-394
Address Block button, W5-291
Address block field code, W9-552
Address Block merge field, W5-291
Address Book button, W9-527, W9-528
Address list, W5-288 to W5-290
Advanced category (Word Options dialog box), W12-699 to W12-700
Advanced collaboration features, W9-525 to W9-531. See also Collaboration features
Advanced Properties, W1-37
Advanced Track Changes Options dialog box, W9-525, W9-526
Align button
   chart, W8-489
   graphics, W4-236
   picture, W7-416
   SmartArt, W8-483
Align drop-down list, W7-416
Align Text button, W7-428
Alignment
   graphics, W4-236
   paragraph, W1-29
   shapes, W7-430
   table, W4-216
   vertical, W2-68
Alignment buttons, W7-397
Alignment guides, W7-416
All caps, W1-22
All Markup view, W3-138, W9-530
Allow carriage returns (multiple paragraphs) check box, W11-645

Allow editing check box, W12-720
Allow only this type of editing in the document check box, W11-660
American Psychological Association (APA) style, W3-150
Anyone with this link can edit this item, W12-720
APA style, W3-150
Arithmetic operators, W4-238
Arrange group, W8-489
Artistic Effect Options, W7-422
Artistic Effects button, W7-422
Artistic picture effects, W7-422
Ask rule, W9-551
Aspect ratio, W7-417
Aspect Ratio, W7-418
Assign button, W10-606
Asterisk (*), W2-99
Austin, W2-84
Author, W3-135
AutoClose, W10-601
AutoComplete, W1-9
AutoComplete tag, W1-9
AutoCorrect, W1-9
AutoCorrect dialog box, W1-10, W12-697
AutoCorrect options button, W12-697
AutoCorrect Options dialog box, W1-9
AutoCorrect Options smart tag, W1-9
AutoExec, W10-601
AutoExit, W10-601
AutoFit, W4-215
AutoFormat, W1-9
AutoMacro, W10-601 to W10-602
Automatic capitalization, W1-9
Automatically resize to fit contents box, W7-403
Automatically update document styles check box, W6-344, W10-591, W10-592
AutoNew, W10-601
AutoOpen, W10-601
AutoRecover, W12-698
Autosaved versions, W9-539
AutoText building block, W6-351 to W6-353
AVERAGE function, W7-395
Axis titles, W8-486

B

Backstage view, W12-698
Balancing columns, W4-229, W4-230
Balloon
   comments, W3-134
   track changes, W3-137
Balloons, W9-526
Banded rows/columns, W4-223
Bar tab, W2-69
Bevel, W7-420
Bibliography button, W3-156
Bibliography gallery, W6-348
Bibliography/references/work cited
   Add New Source, W3-151, W3-152
   bibliography style, W3-150, W3-151
   create bibliography/references/work cited pages, W3-155 to W3-156
   current/master list, W3-154
   definitions, W3-149, W3-150

edit citations and sources, W3-155
   insert a citation, W3-152, W3-153
   manage sources, W3-153 to W3-154
   placeholder, W3-153
   report styles, W3-149 to W3-150
   Source Manager dialog box, W3-153, W3-154
   table of contents, W3-155
   Update Citations and Bibliography, W3-156
Bibliography style, W3-150, W3-151
Bing Image Search, W4-233, W7-423
Bitmap (BMP), W4-232
Blank document, W1-3
Block arrows, W4-238
Blogger, W12-720
Blue wavy underline, W1-33
BMP (.bmp), W4-232
Body font, W8-473
Bold, W1-20, W1-22
Bold and Italic, W1-22
Book fold, W8-463
Bookmark
   add, W9-553
   cross-reference, W9-554 to W9-555
   delete, W9-555
   display, W9-553
   formula, W9-555
   go to, W9-554
   hyperlink, W9-554
   I-beam, W9-553
Bookmark brackets, W9-554
Bookmark button, W9-553, W9-555
Bookmark dialog box, W9-553, W9-554, W9-555
Bookmark I-beam, W9-553, W9-554
Border
   built-in, W2-100
   customize, W2-100 to W2-101
   default setting, W2-100
   page, W2-102 to W2-103
   picture, W7-419 to W7-420
   remove, W2-100
   table, W4-221, W7-405 to W7-407
Border and Shading Options dialog box, W2-101
Border Painter, W7-405 to W7-406
Border Painter button, W7-406, W7-407
Border sampler, W7-406 to W7-407
Border Sampler button, W7-406
Border Styles button, W7-407
Border Styles gallery, W7-406
Borders and Shading dialog box, W2-100, W2-101, W2-102, W2-103, W4-221, W7-407
Borders button, W2-101
Borders drop-down list, W2-100, W4-221
Borders launcher, W7-407
Bottom, W2-68
Bounding box, W11-654
Break Link button, W9-547
Bring Forward, W7-415, W7-429, W7-430
Building block. See Building blocks
Building block galleries, W6-348
Building Block Gallery Content Control button, W11-652
Building Block Gallery content control field, W11-652 to W11-653

Building Block Gallery drop-down list, W11-653
Building block template, W6-350
Building blocks
    AutoText, W6-351 to W6-353
    Building Blocks Organizer, W6-348, W6-349
    built-in galleries, W6-348
    create, W6-349 to W6-350
    defined, W6-348
    delete, W6-351
    edit, W6-350 to W6-351
    insert, W6-350
    new category, W6-351
    Quick Parts, W6-357 to W6-359
    Quick Tables, W7-410 to W7-411
    summary/review, W6-366
    text box, W8-476
    watermark, W8-467
Building Blocks Organizer, W6-348, W6-349, W6-366, W7-410
Building Blocks Organizer dialog box, W6-348, W6-349
Built-in borders, W2-100
Built-in building block galleries, W6-348
Built-in cover page, W3-164
Built-in headers/footers, W2-84, W3-168
Built-in page numbers, W2-84, W3-168
Built-in style, W2-93
Built-in table of contents, W3-162
Built-in text box, W8-473 to W8-474
Built-in watermarks, W8-466
Bullet and numbering formatting, W6-340
Bullet Library, W2-88, W2-89
Bulleted list, W2-88 to W2-90, W7-398
Bullets button, W7-398
Bullets drop-down list, W2-88
Button-activated macro, W10-597 to W10-598

C

Calendar, W12-733
Callouts, W4-238
Can edit, W9-528
Can view, W9-528
Capitalization, W1-9
Capitalize Each Word, W1-20
Caption, W4-236 to W4-237, W7-429
Caption dialog box, W4-237
Card, W12-731
Category drop-down list, W11-652
Cell, W4-210, W7-394. See also Table
Cell address, W7-394
Cell margins, W4-216, W7-403
Cell Margins button, W7-403
Cell reference, W7-394
Cell selector, W4-212
Cell spacing, W7-403
Center
    paragraph alignment, W1-29
    vertical alignment, W2-68
Center tab, W2-69
Change Case, W1-20
Change Chart Type button, W8-487
Change Colors button, W8-482, W8-488
Change default
    font, W1-25
    font size, W1-25
    paragraph alignment and spacing, W1-32
    tab stops, W2-73
Change document layout radio button, W5-299
Change document style set, W6-333 to W6-334

Change List Level drop-down list, W2-90, W7-398
Change Picture, W7-422 to W7-423
Change Picture button, W7-423
Change Shape button, W8-483
Change Source button, W9-547
Change Source dialog box, W9-547
Change text direction, W7-396 to W7-397
Change tracking options, W9-526 to W9-527
Change User Name button, W3-135
Character level, W9-532, W9-533
Character Spacing, W1-23
Character style, W6-329
Chart, W8-484 to W8-489
    align, W8-489
    arrow keys, W8-489
    Chart in Microsoft Word worksheet, W8-485
    Chart Tools Design tab, W8-485
    Chart Tools Format tab, W8-485
    common chart elements, W8-486 to W8-487
    customize chart data, W8-485
    customize chart elements, W8-488 to W8-489
    Format "Chart Element" pane, W8-485 to W8-486
    insert, W8-484
    layout, W8-486 to W8-487
    position, W8-489
    Quick Colors, W8-487 to W8-488
    Quick Layout, W8-487
    resize, W8-489
    ScreenTip, W8-487
    styles, W8-487 to W8-488
    text wrapping, W8-489
    types, W8-484
    Word Options dialog box, W12-699
Chart button, W8-484
Chart data range, W8-485
Chart data range handle, W8-485
Chart elements, W8-486 to W8-487, W8-488
Chart Elements button, W8-487
Chart Elements drop-down list, W8-485, W8-486, W8-488
Chart format buttons, W8-486
Chart in Microsoft Word worksheet, W8-484, W8-485
Chart styles, W8-487 to W8-488
Chart Styles button, W8-488
Chart Styles gallery, W8-488
Chart title, W8-486
Chart Tools Design tab, W8-485, W8-486, W8-488
Chart Tools Format tab, W8-485, W8-488, W8-489
Check Accessibility, W9-535
Check Box Content Control button, W11-646
Check Box content control field, W11-646
Check Compatibility, W9-535 to W9-536
Check for Errors button, W5-294
Check for Issues, W9-534 to W9-536
Check for Issues button, W9-534, W9-536
Checking and Reporting Errors dialog box, W5-294
Chicago reporting style, W3-150
Child table, W7-404
Choose a SmartArt Graphic dialog box, W4-240, W8-480
Choose from Outlook Contacts, W5-289
Choose Profile dialog box, W5-289
Circle, W4-238
Citation, W3-149. See also Bibliography/references/work cited

Clear All Formatting, W1-25
Clear All Formatting button, W6-333
Clear all styles, W6-339 to W6-340
Clear formatting, W6-333
Clear Formatting of Instances, W6-341
Clip art, W7-415. See also Picture
Clipboard, W1-17
Clipboard launcher, W1-17
Clipboard pane, W1-17
Close Header and Footer button, W8-467
Collaboration features
    change tracking options, W9-526 to W9-527
    check accessibility, W9-535
    check compatibility, W9-535 to W9-536
    check for issues, W9-534 to W9-536
    combine documents, W9-533 to W9-534
    comment and markup color, W9-525
    comments. See Comments
    compare documents, W9-531 to W9-532
    digital signature, W9-539
    encrypt with password, W9-537
    inspect document, W9-534 to W9-535
    lock tracking, W9-527
    manage versions, W9-539
    mark as final, W9-536 to W9-537
    Office Online, W12-725
    print document markup, W9-528
    protect document, W9-536 to W9-539
    real-time collaboration, W3-140 to W3-141, W9-527
    remove document password, W9-538
    restrict editing, W9-538 to W9-539
    shared document, W9-527 to W9-528
    show markup options, W9-525 to W9-526
    show or hide source documents, W9-532 to W9-533
    summary/review, W9-560
    track changes. See Track Changes
Collapse button, W11-663
Collapse Heading, W6-342
Collapse Subdocuments, W11-668, W11-669
Color
    charts, W8-487 to W8-488
    comments, W9-525
    content control field, W11-654
    font, W1-20, W1-21, W1-22
    markups, W9-525
    page, W8-465
    picture, W7-421
    theme, W2-94, W6-334, W8-472
    transparent, W7-421
Colored wavy underline. See Wavy underline
Colors button, W6-334, W7-421
Colors dialog box, W7-420
Column, W4-227
    balancing, W4-229 to W4-230
    convert text to columns, W4-228 to W4-229
    customize, W4-228
    ends/breaks, W4-229
    horizontal text wrapping, W4-229
    preset column settings, W4-227
    table, W4-210. See also Table
Column break, W2-87, W4-229
Column selector, W4-212
Column width, W7-402
Columns button, W4-227
Columns dialog box, W4-228
Combine, W9-533
Combine documents, W9-533 to W9-534
Combine Documents dialog box, W9-533
Combo Box Content Control button, W11-651

Combo Box content control field, W11-651 to
    W11-652
Command shortcuts
    drag and drop. *See* Drag and drop
    keyboard shortcuts. *See* Keyboard
        shortcuts
    right-click. *See* Right-click
Comments. *See also* Collaboration features
    balloon, W3-134
    color, W9-525
    delete, W3-136, W3-137
    Display for Review view, W3-134
    edit, W3-136
    insert, W3-134
    Mark Comment Done, W3-136
    New Comment button, W3-134
    Next/Previous buttons, W3-135 to W3-136
    Office Online, W12-726 to W12-727
    reply (Reply To Comment), W3-136
    review/display, W3-135 to W3-136
    right-click, W3-136
    Show Comments button, W3-138
    user name, W3-135
Comments balloon, W3-134
Compare, W9-531
Compare button, W9-532, W9-533, W9-539
Compare documents, W9-531 to W9-532
Compare Documents dialog box, W9-532
Compatibility options, W12-700
Compress pictures, W7-422
Compress Pictures button, W7-422
Compress Pictures dialog box, W7-422
Connected Services, W12-708
Contacts folder, W5-287
Content control cannot be deleted check box,
    W11-655
Content control field
    basic control fields, W11-643
    bounding box, W11-654
    Building Block Gallery, W11-652 to W11-653
    Check Box, W11-646
    color, W11-654
    Combo Box, W11-651 to W11-652
    copy, W11-644
    cover page, W3-166
    Date Picker, W11-646 to W11-647
    delete, W11-656
    Design mode, W11-655 to W11-656
    dialog box. *See* Content Control Properties
        dialog box
    display, W11-654
    Drop-Down List, W11-652
    edit placeholder text, W11-655 to W11-656
    grouping, W11-659
    indent, W11-643
    lock, W11-655
    Picture, W11-647 to W11-648
    Plain Text, W11-645
    remove control control when contents
        edited, W11-655
    Rich Text, W11-643 to W11-644
    Show As drop-down list, W11-654
    start and end tags, W11-654
    style, W11-653 to W11-654
    summary/review, W11-672
    tab stops, W11-643
    table, W11-643
    tag, W11-644
    template, W10-589
    text box, W8-473 to W8-474
    title, W11-644
    user interaction, W11-654 to W11-655
Content control field drop-down arrow,
    W11-646

Content control field handle, W10-589, W11-644
Content Control Properties dialog box
    apply style to content control field, W11-672
    Building Block Gallery content control field,
        W11-652
    Check Box content control field, W11-646
    Combo Box content control field, W11-651
    customize content control field properties,
        W11-644
    Date Picker content control field, W11-647
    lock content control field, W11-655
    modify content control field display and
        color, W11-654
    Picture content control field, W11-648
    Plain Text content control field, W11-645
Contents cannot be deleted check box,
    W11-655
Context menu. *See also* Right-click
    bibliography, W3-155
    caption, W7-429
    change list level, W7-398
    copy, W1-16
    Customize Ribbon, W12-703
    cut and paste, W1-15
    edit field, W6-362
    edit formula, W7-396
    edit link, W9-546
    graphics, W4-233, W4-238
    numbered list, W2-91
    Paste drop-down list, W9-545
    removing content control field, W5-273
    shapes, W7-428
    Smart Lookup, W1-33
    spelling, W1-33
    table, W4-213, W4-216, W4-217
    update field, W6-362
    update formula, W7-396
    update index page, W8-496
    view field codes, W9-552
Context menu numbering options, W2-91
Continue with Merge, W9-534
Continuous block process, W4-240
Continuous section break, W2-86, W2-87,
    W3-167, W4-229, W4-230
Convert Notes, W3-147 to W3-149
Convert Notes dialog box, W3-148
Convert Table to Text dialog box, W4-225,
    W7-393
Convert Text to Table dialog box, W4-224,
    W7-392
Convert to Endnote, W3-149
Convert to Footnote, W3-149
Convert to Text button, W7-392
Copy, W1-15, W1-16, W12-699
Copy styles into document, W10-592
Corrections button, W7-421
Cover page, W3-164
    built-in, W3-164
    content control fields, W3-166
    customize, W3-164 to W3-165
    document property fields, W3-165 to
        W3-166
    Office.com (more cover pages), W3-164
    remove, W3-166 to W3-167
    theme, W3-165
Cover Pages gallery, W6-348
Create from File tab, W9-544
Create New Building Block dialog box,
    W6-349, W6-350, W8-467, W8-476
Create New Style from Formatting dialog box,
    W6-331, W6-332
Create New Theme Colors dialog box,
    W8-472
Create New Theme Fonts dialog box, W8-473

Create Source dialog box, W3-151, W3-154
Crop, W4-235, W7-417 to W7-418
Crop button, W7-418
Crop to Shape, W7-418
Cropping options, W7-418
Cross-reference a bookmark, W9-554 to
    W9-555
Cross-reference button, W9-555
Cross-reference dialog box, W9-555
Cross-reference index entry, W8-494 to
    W8-495
Current list of sources, W3-154
Custom Dictionaries button, W1-35, W12-698
Custom document properties, W6-359
    to W6-362
Custom document property field, W6-359 to
    W6-360
Custom Office Templates folder, W10-587,
    W10-589
Custom page settings, W8-463 to W8-464
Custom watermarks, W8-466
Customize
    AutoCorrect entry, W1-10
    border, W2-100 to W2-101
    bulleted list, W2-89 to W2-90
    columns, W4-228
    cover page, W3-164 to W3-165
    document properties, W1-36 to W1-37
    footnotes and endnotes, W3-146 to W3-147
    header and footer content, W2-81
    margins, W2-67
    numbered list, W2-90 to W2-91
    table of contents, W3-162 to W3-163
    Word dictionary, W1-34
Customize button, W10-606
Customize Colors, W8-472
Customize Columns button, W5-288
Customize Keyboard dialog box, W10-597,
    W10-606
Customize Quick Access Toolbar button,
    W12-703
Customize Quick Access Toolbar drop-down
    list, W10-598, W10-607, W12-703,
    W12-704
Customize Ribbon area, W12-701. *See also*
    Ribbon
Cut and paste, W1-15, W12-699

D

Dash tab leader, W2-73
Dashes, W7-420
Data labels, W8-486
Data source, W5-305
Data table, W8-486
Database terminology, W5-287
Date and time, W2-82 to W2-83
Date Picker Content Control button, W11-647
Date Picker content control field, W11-646 to
    W11-647
Date Picker Properties window, W11-647
Decimal tab, W2-69
Decrease Indent button, W2-75, W7-398
Default page layout settings, W2-66
Default response to prompt check box,
    W10-590
Default return address, W5-281
Default settings
    Before and After paragraph spacing, W1-30
    borders, W2-100
    cell margins, W4-216
    default folder (saving template file),
        W10-587

Default settings—*Cont.*
  font, W1-25
  font size, W1-25
  generally, W1-29
  graphics, W4-235
  margins, W2-66
  page orientation, W2-66
  paper size, W2-66
  show comments and revisions, W9-526
  SUM formula, W4-223
  tabs, W2-73
  text wrapping, W7-415
  theme, W6-328
  vertical alignment, W2-66
Default wrapping option, W7-415
Define New Bullet dialog box, W2-89
Define New Multilevel list dialog box, W2-92
Define New Number Format dialog box, W2-91
Delete index field code, W8-496
Delete Table, W4-214
Demote button, W8-481, W11-663
Design mode, W11-655 to W11-656
Design Mode button, W11-656
Desktop publishing
  custom page settings, W8-463 to W8-464
  drop cap, W8-464 to W8-465
  hyphenation, W8-468 to W8-469
  line numbers, W8-469
  page color, W8-465
  screen clipping, W8-468
  screenshot, W8-467 to W8-468
  watermark, W8-465 to W8-467
Destination file, W9-542
Destination program, W9-542
Dialog box launcher, W1-17
Dictionary, W1-34
Different first page, W2-80, W3-169 to W3-170
Different Odd & Even Pages, W3-170
Digital ID, W9-539
Digital signature, W9-539
Display for Review drop-down list, W9-530
Display for Review view, W3-134, W3-138
Display options, W12-697, W12-699
Distance from text box, W8-464
Distribute rows/columns, W4-215
Division (÷), W7-394
.doc, W1-4, W5-270
.docm, W1-4, W10-586, W10-599
DocProperty field, W6-361
Document
  blank, W1-3
  create, W1-3
  different versions, W1-5
  export, W1-7
  master. *See* Master document
  new, W1-3
  open, W1-6
  pin, W1-6
  save, W1-4, W1-5
  share, W1-7
Document Formatting group, W6-334
Document Info button, W2-83
Document Inspector dialog box, W9-534,
    W9-535
Document password, W9-537, W9-538
Document properties, W1-36, W1-37, W6-359
    to W6-362
  add, W1-37
  advanced properties, W1-37
  Backstage view, W3-165
  body of document, W2-84
  cover page, W3-165, W3-166
  Document Info button, W2-83
  header and footer, W2-83, W2-84

print, W1-38
  Properties button, W1-37
  Properties dialog box, W1-37
Document Property, W10-590
Document property field, W6-359 to W6-362,
    W10-590
Document Template button, W6-344, W10-591,
    W10-592
Document Template dialog box, W6-343
Document theme, W2-94
.docx, W1-4, W5-270, W10-586
.dot, W5-270
Dot tab leader, W2-72, W2-73
.dotm, W10-586, W10-612
.dotx, W1-4, W5-270, W10-586
Double strikethrough, W1-22
Double underline, W1-22
Drag and drop, W1-15, W1-16
Draw table, W7-405
Draw Table button, W7-405
Draw Text Box, W8-475, W8-476
Draw Text Box button, W7-428
Drawing crosshair, W4-238, W7-427
Drawing Tools Format tab, W4-242, W7-426
Drop cap, W8-464 to W8-465
Drop Cap button, W8-464
Drop Cap dialog box, W8-464
Drop Cap Options, W8-464
Drop-Down List content control field, W11-652
Drop-Down List Properties window, W11-651

E

Edit Anyway button, W9-537
Edit Citation dialog box, W3-155
Edit Data in Excel, W8-485
Edit Field, W6-362, W7-396
Edit Hyperlink dialog box, W2-105
Edit in Word, W12-723
Edit Individual Documents, W5-294
Edit link, W3-141, W9-528, W9-546,
    W12-718
Edit Links to Files, W9-547
Edit Points, W7-427
Edit Properties button, W6-351
Edit Recipient List button, W5-290
Edit Shape button, W7-427
Edit Shape drop-down list, W7-427
Edit Source dialog box, W3-154, W3-155
Edit Wrap Points, W7-417
Editing options, W12-699
Editing restrictions, W9-538
Effects button, W7-419, W7-428
Embed and link
  break link to an object, W9-547
  embed a file, W9-544
  embed an object, W9-543
  link an object, W9-545
  modify embedded object, W9-544
  modify link to an object, W9-546 to W9-547
  modify linked object content, W9-546
  object linking and embedding (OLE),
    W9-542 to W9-543
  open document linked to an object,
    W9-546
  summary/review, W9-560
  terminology, W9-542
Enable Content button, W10-600,
    W10-614
Enable remote viewers to download the docu-
    ment check box, W12-720
Encrypt Document dialog box, W9-537,
    W9-538

Encrypt with Password, W9-537
Endnote, W3-144. *See also* Footnote and
    endnote
Endnote Text style, W3-147
Envelope Options dialog box, W5-280,
    W5-281
Envelope printing options, W5-281
Envelope size drop-down list, W5-280
Envelopes and labels
  add envelope to existing document,
    W5-281
  create envelope, W5-280
  create full page of same label, W5-283 to
    W5-284
  create individual labels, W5-282 to W5-283
  create labels, W5-282
  default return address, W5-281
  envelope options, W5-280
  envelope printing options, W5-281
  label options, W5-282
  update labels, W5-293
Envelopes and Labels dialog box, W5-280,
    W5-283, W5-284
Envelopes button, W5-280
Equals sign (=), W7-394
Equation shapes, W4-238
Equations gallery, W6-348
Eraser, W7-405
Eraser button, W7-405
Error bars, W8-486
Even Page section break, W2-86, W2-87
Excel Survey, W12-730 to W12-731
Expand button, W11-663
Expand/Collapse button, W3-161,
    W6-342
Expand/collapse documents, W11-668,
    W11-669
Expand/collapse headings, W6-342
Expand Subdocuments button, W11-668
Exponent (^), W7-394
Export, W1-7
Eyedropper, W7-407

F

Facebook for Office, W12-708
Field, W5-287. *See also* Word fields
Field code, W9-551, W9-552
Field dialog box, W2-82, W6-360, W6-361,
    W7-395, W10-590
Field handler, W3-166
Field name, W5-287
FieldName field, W6-361
File Explorer button, W10-588
File Explorer window, W10-588, W12-713
File icon (macro-enabled document), W10-599
File name extensions, W1-4, W5-270, W5-271,
    W10-586
Fill Effects dialog box, W8-465
Fill Effects option, W8-465
Fill-in field, W10-590, W10-591
Fill-in field prompt dialog box, W10-590
Fill-In rule, W9-551
Fill & Line button, W7-419, W7-420,
    W7-428
Filter and Sort dialog box, W5-290
Find, W2-97 to W2-99
Find and Replace, W2-98 to W2-99
Find and Replace dialog box, W2-98, W2-99,
    W9-554
Find and replace styles, W6-341
Find Style dialog box, W6-341
Find whole words only, W2-99

Finish & Merge button, W5-294
First line indent, W2-74, W2-75 to
   W2-76
Flickr, W12-708
Flowchart shapes, W4-238
Folder Options dialog box, W5-271
Font, W1-18, W1-19
Font Color, W1-20, W1-21, W1-22
Font dialog box, W1-21, W1-22
Font drop-down list, W1-19
Font Effects, W1-22
Font formatting, W6-340
Font group, W1-20
Font size, W1-18, W1-19
Font size drop-down list, W1-19
Font styles, W1-19, W1-20, W1-22
Font tab, W1-21
Fonts button, W6-334
Footer. See Header and footer
Footers gallery, W6-348
Footnote and endnote, W3-144
   Convert Notes, W3-147 to W3-149
   customize, W3-146 to W3-147
   delete, W3-149
   format, W3-147
   Go To, W3-146
   insert a footnote, W3-144 to W3-145,
      W3-147
   insert an endnote, W3-145, W3-147
   move, W3-149
   Next Footnote button, W3-146
   reference marker, W3-144
   Show Notes button, W3-146
   styles, W3-147
   summary/review, W3-178
   view/display, W3-145 to W3-146
Footnote and Endnote dialog box, W3-146,
   W3-147
Footnote Text style, W3-147
Form, W11-653, W11-659 to W11-661
   content control fields. See Content
      control field
   edit and save, W11-661
   filling in the form, W11-661
   open, W11-661
   protect (group content control fields),
      W11-659
   protect (restrict editing), W11-660
   save form as template, W11-659
Format "Chart Element" pane, W8-485 to
   W8-486
Format Data Labels pane, W8-487, W8-488
Format Painter, W1-24
   bulleted list, W2-91
   numbered list, W2-91
Format Picture pane, W7-419, W7-420,
   W7-421, W7-422
Format Plot Area, W8-486
Format Shape pane, W7-428, W8-475,
   W8-482, W8-483
Format Text Effects dialog box, W1-23, W1-24
Formatting restrictions, W9-538
Formula, W4-223, W4-224, W7-394 to W7-396
   bookmark, W9-555
   create, W7-395
   edit, W7-396
   equals sign (=), W7-394
   function, W7-395 to W7-396
   operators, W7-394
   syntax, W7-394
   update, W7-396
   values, W7-394
Formula dialog box, W4-224, W7-395,
   W7-396, W9-555

Formula operators, W7-394
Formula syntax, W7-394
Four-pointed move pointer, W8-489
Full page of the same label radio button,
   W5-284
Function, W7-395 to W7-396

G

Gallery drop-down list, W11-652
General
   Advanced category, W12-700
   Word Options dialog box, W12-696 to
      W12-697
Get a sharing link, W9-528
GIF (.gif), W4-232
Glow, W1-20, W1-23, W7-420
Go To, W2-99, W9-554
Gradient tab, W8-465
Grammar and style settings, W12-698
Grammar pane, W1-34
Grammatical errors, W1-33, W12-698
Graphics
   Align options, W4-236
   Bing Image Search, W4-233
   caption, W4-236 to W4-237
   context menu, W4-233, W4-238
   crop, W4-235
   Drawing Tools Format tab, W4-242
   grouping graphic objects, W4-237 to
      W4-238
   insert a picture, W4-232 to W4-233
   insert an online picture, W4-233
   layout options, W4-235
   picture. See Picture
   Picture Tools Format tab, W4-235, W4-236
   positioning, W4-236
   resize, W4-234
   shapes. See Shapes
   SmartArt. See SmartArt
   special characters, W4-242
   styles, W4-242
   summary/review, W4-246 to W4-247
   symbols, W4-242
   text wrapping, W4-234 to W4-235
   types of graphic formats, W4-232
   WordArt, W4-241 to W4-242
Greeting Line button, W5-291
Greeting Line merge field, W5-291
Grid tables, W7-407
Gridlines, W4-222, W8-486
Group, W4-237 to W4-238
   combine multiple objects, W7-431
   content control fields, W11-659
   ribbon, W12-701 to W12-703
   Sway, W12-731
Group button, W11-659
Gutter margins, W8-463
Gutter position, W8-463

H

Hanging indent, W2-74, W2-75
   to W2-76
Header and footer
   built-in headers, footers, page numbers,
      W2-84, W3-168
   cover page, W3-172
   customize, W2-81, W3-168 to W3-169
   date and time, W2-82, W2-83
   document properties, W2-83, W2-84
   link to previous, W3-170 to W3-171

navigation buttons, W3-172
number of pages field, W2-82
odd and even pages, W3-170
page and section breaks, W3-167
page number. See Page number
remove, W3-172
summary/review, W3-179
tab stops, W2-82
Header and footer navigation buttons, W3-172
Header and Footer Tools Design
   tab, W2-81
Headers gallery, W6-348
Heading font, W8-473
Heading styles, W3-161
Hide. See Show/Hide
Hide button, W7-429
Hide extensions for known file types check
   box, W5-271
Hide Source Documents, W9-533
Highlight Merge Fields button, W5-293
Horizontal alignment guide, W7-416
Horizontal line, W2-103
Horizontal ruler, W2-69
Hyperlink, W2-100, W2-104 to W2-106,
   W9-554
Hyphenation, W8-468 to W8-469
Hyphenation button, W8-469
Hyphenation dialog box, W8-469

I

I-beam, W9-553
If…Then…Else rule, W9-551
Image Size and Quality, W12-699
Import/Export button, W6-338, W6-339,
   W6-342
In Line with Text, W4-235, W7-415
Increase Indent button, W2-75, W7-398
Indent
   content control field, W11-643
   first line, W2-75 to W2-76
   hanging, W2-75 to W2-76
   increase/decrease indent buttons, W2-75
   left, W2-74, W2-75
   remove, W2-76
   right, W2-74, W2-75
   table, W7-397
   types, W2-74
Indented radio button, W8-495
Index
   cross-reference, W8-494 to W8-495
   delete index entry, W8-496
   indented or run-in style, W8-495
   Index dialog box, W8-495
   index page, W8-495
   insert index page, W8-495
   mark index entry, W8-493
   mark index subentry, W8-494
   Show/Hide, W8-494, W8-496
   tab leader, W8-495
   update index page, W8-496
Index dialog box, W8-495
Index entry, W8-493
Index field code, W8-493, W8-494,
   W9-552
Index page, W8-493, W8-495
Index subentry, W8-494
Information button, W12-721
Information icon, W12-696, W12-697
Information pane, W12-721
Insert Address Block dialog box, W5-291,
   W5-301
Insert as hyperlink check box, W9-555

Insert Caption, W7-429
Insert Captions button, W4-237
Insert Cells dialog box, W4-212, W4-213
Insert Chart dialog box, W8-484
Insert Citation button, W3-152, W3-153
Insert Endnote button, W3-145
Insert Footnote button, W3-144
Insert Greeting Line dialog box, W5-291
Insert Hyperlink dialog box, W2-104, W9-554
Insert Index button, W8-495
Insert Merge Field button, W5-292
Insert Merge Field dialog box, W5-292
Insert Pictures dialog box, W2-89, W4-232,
    W4-233, W7-423
Insert References page, W3-156
Insert row control, W4-212
Insert Table dialog box, W4-210, W4-211
Insert Table drop-down list, W4-210
Insert Word Field: If dialog box, W9-552
Insert Word Field: Skip Record If dialog box,
    W9-557, W9-558
Insights pane, W1-32
Inspect Document, W9-534 to W9-535
Integrating Office applications, W9-542 to
    W9-550. See also Embed and link
Italic, W1-20, W1-22

J

JPEG (.jpeg/.jpg), W4-232
Justified (vertical alignment), W2-68
Justify (paragraph alignment), W1-29

K

Keep Source Formatting, W1-16
Keep Text Only, W1-16
Kerning, W1-23
Keyboard-activated macro, W10-596 to
    W10-597
Keyboard button, W10-597
Keyboard shortcuts, A-2 to A-4
    bold, W1-20
    bulleted list, W2-89
    column break, W4-229
    copy, W1-15
    copy/move rows/columns (table), W4-213
    cut and paste, W1-15
    expanding/collapsing documents, W11-669
    Find, W2-98
    Find and Replace, W2-99
    font color, W1-21
    Font dialog box, W1-21
    font size, W1-19
    footnotes and endnotes, W3-145
    go to, W9-554
    Go To, W2-99
    hyperlink, W2-104, W2-105
    Insert Hyperlink dialog box, W2-105
    italic, W1-20
    line spacing, W1-30
    list level (table), W7-398
    Macros dialog box, W10-601
    move up/down, W11-667
    new blank document, W1-3
    non-breaking space, W1-11
    Open dialog box, W1-6, W10-588
    page break, W2-87, W3-167
    paragraph alignment, W1-29
    Paste Special dialog box, W9-544
    redo/repeat, W1-18
    reverse automatic correction, W1-9
    Save As dialog box, W10-586

save/save as, W1-5
select text, W1-8
Show/Hide, W1-8
sort rows/columns (table), W4-218
Spelling and Grammar pane, W1-34
Styles pane, W6-329
tab stops (table), W7-397
Thesaurus pane, W1-36
track changes, W3-137
underline, W1-20
undo, W1-18
update field, W6-362
update formula, W7-396
update index page, W8-496
view field codes, W9-552

L

Label Options dialog box, W5-282
Labels. See Envelopes and labels
Labels button, W5-282, W5-283
Landscape, W2-67
Language, W12-698 to W12-699
Launcher, W1-17
Layout dialog box, W4-234, W4-235
    chart, W8-489
    layout options, W7-415
    picture, W7-415, W7-416, W7-417,
        W7-418
    resize picture, W7-417
    rotate picture, W7-418
    SmartArt, W8-483
    text box, W8-475
    text wrapping options, W7-416
Layout options, W12-700
Layout Options button, W4-235, W7-415
Layout Options menu, W7-415
Layout & Properties button, W7-419,
    W7-428
Layout tab, W2-74
Leaders, W2-72, W2-73
Left align, W1-29
Left indent, W2-74, W2-75
Left tab, W2-69
Legacy Forms, W11-653
Legacy tools, W11-653
Legend, W8-486
Ligatures, W1-20, W1-23
Line, W4-238, W8-464
Line and Paragraph Spacing, W1-30, W1-31
Line break, W1-11, W1-31
Line Numbering Options, W8-469
Line numbers, W8-469
Line Numbers button, W8-469
Line spacing, W1-29, W1-30
Line Style drop-down list, W7-406
Line Weight drop-down list, W7-406
Lines, W4-238, W8-486
Lines to drop box, W8-464
Link to Previous button, W3-171
Linked "object type" Object, W9-546
Linked style, W6-329
LinkedIn, W12-708
Linking, W9-545. See also Embed and link
Links dialog box, W9-546, W9-547, W9-548
List
    bullet. See Bulleted list
    multilevel, W2-91, W2-92
    number, W2-90, W2-91
List Library, W2-91
List of Microsoft Services button, W12-730
List style, W6-329
Live layout, W7-416
Live preview, W4-241

Lock
    aspect ratio, W4-234
    content control field, W11-655
    subdocument, W11-667 to W11-668
Lock Document button, W11-668
Lock Tracking, W9-527
Lock Tracking dialog box, W9-527
Locked subdocument, W11-668
Long documents. See Master document
Lowercase, W1-20

M

Macro
    AutoMacro, W10-601 to W10-602
    button-activated, W10-597 to W10-598
    copy, W10-605
    copy, to another document, W10-612 to
        W10-613
    defined, W10-596
    delete, W10-602
    edit, W10-605 to W10-606
    file icon, W10-599
    keyboard-activated, W10-596 to W10-597
    questions to ask, W10-596
    Quick Access toolbar, W10-598, W10-607,
        W10-608
    run, W10-600 to W10-601
    save, W10-599
    security settings, W10-600
    shortcut key, W10-606
    summary/review, W10-617 to W10-618
    template, W10-612 to W10-614
    Visual Basic, W10-605
Macro-enabled template, W10-612 to W10-614
Macro project item, W10-612
Macro Security button, W10-600
Macro security settings, W10-600
Macros button, W10-597, W10-602, W10-605,
    W10-606, W10-613
Macros dialog box
    copy macro, W10-605
    copy macro to another document, W10-612
        to W10-613
    delete macro, W10-602
    edit macro, W10-606
    keyboard shortcut, W10-601
    run macro, W10-598, W10-601
Mail merge, W5-269
    Address Block merge field, W5-291
    address list, W5-288 to W5-290
    create new recipient list, W5-288
    database terminology, W5-287
    edit recipient list, W5-290
    filtering, W5-290
    finish the merge, W5-294
    Greeting Line merge field, W5-291
    highlight merge fields, W5-293
    individual merge field, W5-292, W5-293
    Mailings tab, W5-287 to W5-298
    main document, W5-286
    match fields, W5-291 to W5-292
    open existing mail merge document,
        W5-295
    Outlook contacts, W5-289
    preview the document, W5-293 to W5-294
    recipients, W5-286, W5-288, W5-290
    rules, W9-551, W9-552
    sorting, W5-290
    start the merge, W5-287
    summary/review, W5-305, W9-551
    type of merge, W5-286
    update labels, W5-293
    use existing recipient list, W5-289

view merge field codes, W9-552
wizard. *See* Mail Merge Wizard
Mail Merge pane, W5-299 to W5-302
Mail Merge Recipients dialog box, W5-289, W5-290
Mail Merge rules, W9-551, W9-552
Mail Merge Wizard. *See also* Mail merge
  address block, W5-301
  complete the merge, W5-302
  document type, W5-299
  go back to any previous step, W5-302
  labels, W5-301
  merge fields, W5-301
  preview the document, W5-301
  recipients, W5-300
  starting document, W5-299 to W5-300
  steps in process, W5-299
Mailing labels, W5-280. *See also* Envelopes and labels
Mailings tab, W5-280, W5-287 to W5-298. *See also* Mail merge
Main document, W5-286
Manage Document, W9-539
Manage My Add-ins link, W12-709
Manage sources, W3-153, W3-154
Manage Styles button, W6-338, W6-342
Manage Styles dialog box, W6-338, W6-339
Manage versions, W9-539
Manual for Writers of Research Papers, Theses, and Dissertations (reporting style), W3-150
Margin settings, W2-66, W2-67
Margins button, W8-463
Margins drop-down list, W2-66
Mark as Final, W9-536 to W9-537
Mark Comment Done, W3-136
Mark Entry button, W8-493, W8-494
Mark Index Entry dialog box, W8-493
Markup area, W3-134
Markups. *See also* Comments; Track Changes
  color, W9-525
  display options, W9-525 to W9-526
  print, W9-528
Master document
  create subdocument, W11-665
  insert subdocument, W11-664 to W11-665
  lock subdocument, W11-667 to W11-668
  merge subdocuments, W11-665 to W11-666
  move subdocuments/sections up or down, W11-667
  Outline view, W11-663 to W11-664
  reopen master and display subdocuments, W11-668
  save, W11-668
  shortcut keys, W11-664
  split subdocument, W11-666
  summary/review, W11-672 to W11-673
  unlink subdocument, W11-666 to W11-667
Master list of sources, W3-154
Match Case, W2-99
Match Fields, W5-291 to W5-292
Match Fields button, W5-292
Match Fields dialog box, W5-292
.mdb, W5-288
Merge. *See* Mail merge
Merge Cells button, W4-213
Merge Formatting, W1-16
Merge Record # rule, W9-551
Merge records radio button, W5-294
Merge Sequence # rule, W9-551
Merge to New Document dialog box, W5-294

Merge to Printer dialog box, W5-294
Metafile (WMF), W4-232
Microsoft Access database table, W5-287
Microsoft account, W12-706
Microsoft account information, W12-706 to W12-707
Microsoft Office Address Lists file (.mdb), W5-288
Microsoft Visual Basic editor, W10-605
Microsoft Word Compatibility Checker dialog box, W9-536
Mini toolbar, W1-19, W1-20. *See also* Right-click
  Bullets drop-down list, W2-90
  crop, W7-418
  Numbering drop-down list, W2-90
  picture style, W7-419
  shapes, W7-428
  style, W2-93
  table, W4-212
  update a style, W6-331
Mirror margins, W8-463
MLA style, W3-150
Modern Language Association (MLA) style, W3-150
Modify Building Block dialog box, W6-351, W6-353
Modify Button dialog box, W10-598, W10-607
Modify Style dialog box, W2-94, W3-148, W6-330, W7-408
Modify Table Style, W7-408
More/Less button, W9-532, W9-533
More Outline Colors, W7-420
Move Down button, W8-481, W11-663
Move text, W1-15
Move Up button, W8-481, W11-663
Multilevel list, W2-91, W2-92
Multiplication (x), W7-394
My Add-ins link, W12-708, W12-709

N

Navigation
  headers and footers, W3-172
  table, W4-211
Navigation pane, W2-97
Nested table, W7-404
New Address List dialog box, W5-288
New Comment button, W3-134
New document, W1-3
New Document button, W5-284
New Entry button, W5-288
New Label button, W5-282
New style, W6-331 to W6-332
New Style button, W6-331
New Tab (Custom), W12-702
New Tab button, W12-701
New Table Style, W7-409
Next Footnote button, W3-146
Next Page section break, W2-86, W2-87, W3-167
Next Record If rule, W9-551
Next Record rule, W9-551
No Border, W2-100
No Markup view, W3-138, W9-530
No watermark radio button, W8-467
Non-breaking space, W1-11
Normal template (Normal.dotm), W1-3, W1-25, W5-270, W6-332
Normal template default settings, W1-29
Number format drop-down list, W2-81, W7-395, W7-396
Number of pages field, W2-82
Number Styles, W1-20, W1-23

Numbered list, W2-90 to W2-91, W7-398
Numbering button, W7-398
Numbering Library, W2-90
NumPages, W2-82, W6-361

O

Object button, W9-544
Object dialog box, W9-544
Object linking and embedding (OLE), W9-542 to W9-543
Odd & Even Pages, W3-170
Odd Page section break, W2-86, W2-87
.odt, W1-4
Office add-ins, W12-708. *See also* Add-ins
Office Add-ins dialog box, W12-708, W12-709
Office Background, W12-707
Office.com, W3-164, W4-240
office.live.com, W12-722
Office Online
  Calendar, W12-733
  collaborate with others, W12-725
  comments, W12-726 to W12-727
  create Office Online file, W12-724
  edit Office Online file, W12-722 to W12-723
  Excel Survey, W12-730 to W12-731
  List of Microsoft Services button, W12-730
  OneNote Online, W12-733
  open document, W12-723
  Outlook.com, W12-732 to W12-733
  People, W12-733
  read-only mode/edit mode, W12-722 to W12-724
  rename document in Word Online, W12-724
  ribbon, W12-724
  share Office Online file, W12-724 to W12-725
  summary/review, W12-736 to W12-737
  Sway, W12-731 to W12-732
  what is it?, W12-722
Office Online Ribbon, W12-724
Office 365 SharePoint, W12-708
Office Theme, W12-707
Offline editing options for document management server files area, W12-698
OLE. *See* Object linking and embedding (OLE)
OneDrive, W9-527, W12-712 to W12-721
  create folder, W12-714 to W12-715
  download file or folder, W12-716 to W12-717
  File Explorer window, W12-713
  move, copy, or delete file or folder, W12-716
  OneDrive online, W12-713 to W12-714, W12-720
  Permission drop-down list, W12-717, W12-718, W12-721
  picture, W7-423
  Post to Blog, W12-720
  Present Online, W12-720
  share file in Word, W12-717 to W12-718
  share file through email, W12-719
  share OneDrive file or folder, W12-720 to W12-721
  sharing link, W12-718
  sharing permission, W12-718 to W12-719, W12-721
  sign in page, W12-714
  summary/review, W12-736
  Trusted Document, W10-614
  upload file or folder, W12-715
OneDrive desktop app for Windows, W12-713
OneDrive link, W12-723, W12-724
onedrive.live.com, W12-714, W12-720, W12-723
OneDrive online, W12-713 to W12-714, W12-720

OneDrive online environment, W12-713, W12-714
OneNote Online, W12-733
Online Pictures button, W4-233
Online services, W12-708
Online templates, W5-271 to W5-272, W10-587
Only in this document check box, W6-332
Open, W1-6, W5-277
Open dialog box, W1-6, W10-588, W10-613
Open Link, W9-546
Operators, W7-394
Options button, W12-696. *See also* Word Options dialog box
Ordering shapes, W7-429 to W7-430
Organizer button, W6-344, W10-592, W10-613
Organizer dialog box, W6-338, W6-342, W6-343, W6-344, W10-591, W10-593, W10-613
Orientation button, W2-67
Original document, W9-532
Original document drop-down list, W9-532, W9-533
Original view, W3-138, W9-530
Outline, W1-20, W1-23
Outline button, W11-663, W11-667
Outline Level drop-down list, W11-663
Outline view, W11-663 to W11-664. *See also* Master document
Outlining tab, W11-663
Outlook.com, W12-732 to W12-733
Outlook contacts, W5-289
Overwrite last saved version, W9-539

P

Page border, W2-102, W2-103
Page break, W2-86 to W2-88, W3-167
Page color, W8-465
Page Color button, W8-465
Page Color drop-down list, W8-465
Page display options area, W12-697
Page layout settings, W2-66
Page number
    built-in, W2-84, W3-168
    cover page, W3-172
    different first page, W2-80, W3-169 to W3-170
    edit, W2-79, W2-80
    format, W2-80 to W2-81, W3-171
    insert, W2-79
    remove, W2-81
Page Number drop-down list, W2-81
Page Number Format dialog box, W2-80, W3-171
Page Numbers gallery, W6-348
Page orientation, W2-66, W2-67
Page Setup dialog box, W2-66, W2-67, W2-68, W8-463, W8-464
Page Setup group, W2-68
Page Setup launcher, W8-464
Page size, W2-68
Paper size preset options, W2-68
Paragraph, W1-10, W1-11
Paragraph alignment, W1-29
Paragraph break, W1-10
Paragraph dialog box, W1-29, W1-30, W1-31, W1-32, W2-75, W2-76, W7-397
Paragraph group, W1-31
Paragraph launcher, W7-397
Paragraph level formatting, W6-340
Paragraph spacing, W1-30, W1-31, W6-334
Paragraph Spacing button, W6-334
Paragraph style, W6-329

Paragraph symbol, W1-10
Parent table, W7-404
Parentheses ( ), W7-394
Password, W9-527, W9-537, W9-538
Password dialog box, W9-537
Paste, W1-15, W1-16, W1-17
Paste bookmark drop-down list, W9-555
Paste button, W9-543, W9-545
Paste drop-down list, W9-545
Paste function drop-down list, W7-396
Paste link radio button, W9-545
Paste options, W1-16
Paste radio button, W9-543
Paste Special dialog box, W9-543, W9-544, W9-545
Pattern tab, W8-465
Pause Recording button, W10-597
.pdf, W1-4
Pen, W7-405, W12-699
Pen Color drop-down list, W7-406
People, W12-733
Permission drop-down list, W3-140, W12-717, W12-718, W12-721
Personal template, W10-587
Personalize Microsoft Office, W6-361 to W6-362
Personalize your copy of Microsoft Office area, W12-697
Photo, W7-415. *See also* Picture
Picture, W4-231, W7-415 to W7-423. *See also* Graphics
    alignment guides, W7-416
    anchor, W7-417
    artistic effects, W7-422
    aspect ratio, W7-417
    border, W7-419 to W7-420
    caption, W7-429
    change, W7-422 to W7-423
    color, W7-421
    compress, W7-422
    corrections, W7-421
    crop, W7-417 to W7-418
    effects, W7-420 to W7-421
    Format Picture pane, W7-419
    layout options, W7-415
    live layout, W7-416
    page background, W8-465
    Picture Tools Format tab, W7-415
    reset, W7-423
    resize, W7-417
    resolution, W7-422
    rotate, W7-418
    Save as Picture, W8-468
    styles, W7-419
    summary/review, W7-434
    text wrapping, W7-415 to W7-416
    wrap points, W7-416 to W7-417
Picture adjustments, W7-421
Picture anchor, W7-417
Picture Border button, W7-420
Picture border options, W7-420
Picture borders, W7-419 to W7-420
Picture color options, W7-421
Picture Content Control button, W11-647
Picture content control field, W11-647 to W11-648
Picture correction options, W7-421
Picture effects, W7-420, W7-420 to W7-421
Picture Effects drop-down list, W7-420
Picture resolution, W7-422
Picture styles, W7-419
Picture Styles gallery, W4-241, W7-419
Picture Styles launcher, W7-419, W7-420

Picture tab, W8-465
Picture Tools Format tab, W4-235, W4-236, W7-415
Picture wrap points, W7-416 to W7-417
Pin/unpin template, W10-587
Pinned document, W1-6
Placeholder, W3-153
Placeholder text, W11-655 to W11-656
Plain tables, W7-407
Plain Text Content Control button, W11-645
Plain Text content control field, W11-645
Plot area, W8-486
PNG (.png), W4-232
Points (pt.), W1-18
Portrait, W2-67
Position (character spacing), W1-23
Position button
    chart, W8-489
    graphics, W4-236
    SmartArt, W8-483
Positioning button, W7-402
Post to Blog, W12-720
Preferred width box, W7-401
Present Online, W12-720
Preserve fidelity when sharing this document, W12-698, W12-700
Preset, W7-420
Preset margin settings, W2-66
Press new shortcut key text box, W10-597
Preview Mail Merge, W5-293 to W5-294
Preview Results button, W5-294
Print
    envelope, W5-281
    mail merge, W5-294
    markups, W9-528
    Word Options dialog box, W12-699, W12-700
Print background colors and images box, W8-465
Print document properties, W1-38
Print Documents, W5-294
Print Markup, W9-528
Printed Watermark dialog box, W8-466, W8-467
Printing options area, W12-697
Professional looking documents. *See* Desktop publishing
Promote button, W8-481, W11-663
Proofing category (Word Options dialog box), W12-697 to W12-698
Properties button, W1-37, W7-401, W7-402, W11-644. *See also* Content Control Properties dialog box; Document properties
Properties dialog box, W1-37, W6-359
Property field code, W9-552
Protect Document button, W9-536, W9-537, W9-538

Q

Question mark (?), W2-99
Quick Access toolbar, W1-17, W1-18
    add a command, W12-703 to W12-704
    display toolbar below Ribbon, W12-704
    macros, W10-598, W10-607, W10-608
    remove a command, W12-704
    reset to original settings, W12-705 to W12-706
Quick Colors, W8-487 to W8-488
Quick Layout, W8-487
Quick Layout button, W8-487
Quick Parts building block, W6-357 to W6-359, W11-652

Quick Parts button, W2-84, W6-351, W6-360, W10-590
Quick Tables, W7-410 to W7-411
Quick Tables gallery, W7-411

R

Range, W7-395, W7-396
Re-order object, W7-430
Readability statistics, W12-698
Real-time collaboration, W3-140 to W3-141, W9-527
Real-time collaboration options area, W12-697
Recipients, W5-286, W5-288, W5-290
Recommended styles, W6-339
Record, W5-287
Record button-activated macro, W10-597 to W10-598
Record keyboard-activated macro, W10-596 to W10-597
Record Macro button, W10-596, W10-597, W10-601
Record Macro dialog box, W10-596, W10-601
Record macro pointer, W10-597
Rectangles, W4-238
Red wavy underline, W1-33
Redo, W1-18
Reference marker, W3-144
References page, W3-156, W3-160. See also Bibliography/references/work cited
Reflection, W1-20, W1-23, W7-420
Related Documents, W9-547
Remove Content Control, W5-273, W8-474, W10-589, W10-590, W11-656
Remove content control when contents are edited check box, W11-655, W11-660
Remove document password, W9-538
Remove from Style Gallery, W6-333
Remove Watermark, W8-467
Repeat, W1-18
Repeat header rows, W7-404 to W7-405
Repeat Header Rows button, W7-404, W7-405
Replace, W2-98, W2-99
Replace All, W2-98
Replace Style dialog box, W6-341
Reply To Comment, W3-136
Report styles, W3-149, W3-150
Reset picture, W7-423
Reset Picture options, W7-423
Reset Picture & Size, W7-423
Reset Ribbon/Quick Access toolbar, W12-705 to W12-706
Resize
    chart, W8-489
    crop, W4-234
    graphics, W4-234
    picture, W7-417
    rows/columns (table), W4-214, W4-215, W7-402
    shapes, W4-239
    SmartArt, W8-483
    table, W7-401
Resizing pointer, W4-214
Resolution, W7-422
Restrict Editing, W9-538 to W9-539, W11-660
Restrict Editing button, W11-660
Restrict Editing pane, W9-538, W11-660
Restrict Formatting and Editing pane, W9-539
Return address, W5-281, W5-284
Reviewer, W3-135, W9-526
Reviewing pane, W3-140, W9-530, W9-532
Revised document, W9-532

Revised document drop-down list, W9-532, W9-533
Revisions, W3-140, W9-526
Ribbon
    add a tab, group, or command, W12-701 to W12-702
    Office Online, W12-724
    rearrange tabs, groups, and commands, W12-702 to W12-703
    remove an item, W12-705
    reset to original settings, W12-705 to W12-706
Rich Text Content Control button, W11-644
Rich Text content control field, W11-643 to W11-644
Rich Text content control field title, W11-645
Right align, W1-29
Right align page numbers box, W8-495
Right-click
    bibliography, W3-156
    comments, W3-136
    context menu, W1-16. See also Context menu
    delete custom theme, W8-473
    hyperlink, W2-106
    Links dialog box, W9-548
    Mini toolbar, W1-19. See also Mini toolbar
    Modify Building Block dialog box, W6-351, W6-353
    Remove Content Control, W11-656
    Save as Picture, W8-468
    table of contents, W3-164
    track changes, W3-139
Right indent, W2-74, W2-75
Right tab, W2-69
Right to Left button, W8-481
Rotate drop-down list, W7-418
Rotation handle, W4-239, W7-418, W7-427
Rotation options, W7-418
Row, W4-210. See also Table
Row height, W4-214, W4-215, W4-216, W7-402
Row selector, W4-212
.rtf, W1-4
Ruler, W2-69
    first line indent, W2-76
    hanging indent, W2-76
    horizontal, W2-69
    left/right indent, W2-75
    remove indent, W2-76
    tab stops, W2-71
    vertical, W2-69
Rules, W9-551, W9-552
Rules button, W9-552
Run-in radio button, W8-495

S

Sans serif font, W1-18
Save, W1-4, W1-5, W12-698, W12-700
Save Address List dialog box, W5-288
Save As dialog box, W1-4, W1-5
    create template from blank document, W5-276
    macro-enabled template, W10-612
    save document as template, W10-586
    save form as template, W11-659
Save as Picture, W8-468
Save as type drop-down list, W10-612
Save changes in drop-down list, W10-597
Save Current Theme dialog box, W8-473
Save macro-enabled document, W10-599
Save Selection to Watermark Gallery, W8-467
SaveDate field, W6-361
Scale, W1-23

Screen clipping, W8-468
Screenshot, W8-467 to W8-468
Screenshot button, W8-468
ScreenTip, W2-104
Search for online templates, W5-271, W10-587
Section break, W2-86 to W2-88, W3-167
Section selector, W11-663, W11-664
Security
    digital signature, W9-539
    document password, W9-537, W9-538
    macro, W10-600
    protect document, W9-536 to W9-539
Select
    table, W4-211 to W4-212
    text, W1-8
Select button, W4-212
Select Contacts dialog box, W5-289
Select Data Source dialog box, W5-289
Select drop-down list, W4-212
Select how list is sorted drop-down list, W6-340
Select or deselect reviewers, W9-526
Select Recipient button, W5-288, W5-289
Select styles to show drop-down list, W6-340
Selection crosshair, W8-468
Selection/move pointer, W4-239
Selection pane, W7-429
Send as Attachment, W9-528, W12-718, W12-719
Send Backward, W7-415, W7-429, W7-430
Send Email Messages, W5-294
Sentence case, W1-20
Serif font, W1-18
Set As Default, W1-25
Set Bookmark rule, W9-551
Set for All Levels dialog box, W2-92
Set Hyperlink ScreenTip dialog box, W2-105
Set Numbering Value dialog box, W2-91
Set Target Frame dialog box, W2-105
Set Transparent Color, W7-421
Shading, W2-101 to W2-102, W4-222
Shading drop-down list, W2-102
Shadow, W1-20, W1-23, W7-420
Shape. See Shapes
Shape Adjustment handle, W4-239, W7-427
Shape Alignment options, W7-430
Shape Effects, W4-239, W7-428, W8-483
Shape Fill, W4-239, W7-427, W8-483
Shape Outline, W4-239, W7-428, W8-483
Shape styles, W7-427 to W7-428
Shape Styles drop-down list, W8-488
Shape Styles gallery, W7-427
Shape Styles group, W8-483
Shape Styles launcher, W7-428, W8-475, W8-482, W8-483, W8-488
Shapes, W4-238 to W4-239, W7-426 to W7-431. See also Graphics
    add text to shape, W7-428
    alignment, W7-430
    caption, W7-429
    customize, W7-427
    Drawing Tools Format tab, W7-426
    edit, W7-427
    Format Shape pane, W7-428
    group, W7-431
    insert, W7-427
    ordering/re-ordering, W7-429 to W7-430
    Selection pane, W7-429
    styles, W7-427 to W7-428
    summary/review, W7-435
    text box, W7-428 to W7-429
Shapes button, W4-238, W7-427
Shapes drop-down list, W4-238
Share, W1-7

OneDrive. *See* OneDrive
Preserve fidelity when sharing this
    document, W12-698, W12-700
Share an online file, W3-140 to W3-141
Share button, W9-527
Share pane, W3-140, W9-527, W9-528
Share with People, W9-527
Shared document, W9-527 to W9-528
SharePoint Blog, W12-720
Sharing link, W3-141
Shortcut commands
    drag and drop. *See* Drag and drop
    keyboard shortcuts. *See* Keyboard
        shortcuts
    right-click. *See* Right-click
Show All Properties, W6-359
Show As drop-down list, W11-654
Show Below the Ribbon, W12-704
Show bookmarks check box, W9-553
Show Both, W9-533
Show Comments button, W3-138
Show Document button, W11-664, W11-667,
    W11-668
Show document content, W12-699
Show/Hide, W1-7 to W1-8, W2-86, W4-229
    headings, W6-342
    index, W8-494, W8-496, W9-552
    keyboard shortcut, W1-8
    mail merge, W5-293
    source documents, W9-532 to W9-533
Show Level drop-down list, W11-663, W11-664
Show lines connecting to text check box,
    W9-527
Show Markup button, W9-525
Show Markup drop-down list, W9-526
Show markup options, W9-525 to W9-526
Show Notes button, W3-146
Show Original, W9-533
Show recommended styles only check box,
    W6-338, W6-339
Show Revised, W9-533
Show Source Documents, W9-533
Sign in dialog box, W12-707
Sign out, W12-707
Sign up now, W12-707
signup.live.com, W12-706, W12-712
Simple Markup view, W3-138, W9-530
Size group, W7-417, W8-489
Size launcher, W8-483, W8-489
Sizing handles, W4-234, W4-239, W7-417,
    W7-427. *See also* Resize
Sizing pointer, W4-234
Skip Record If rule, W9-551
Small caps, W1-22
Smart Lookup, W1-32, W1-33
SmartArt, W4-239 to W4-240, W8-479 to
    W8-483
    align, W8-483
    design, W8-482
    insert, W8-479 to W8-480
    objects, W8-482 to W8-483
    position, W8-483
    preview, W8-482
    resize, W8-483
    SmartArt Tools Design tab, W8-480
    SmartArt Tools Format tab, W8-480
    text, W8-480 to W8-482
    text wrapping, W8-483
SmartArt button, W8-480
SmartArt Tools Design tab, W4-240, W8-480
SmartArt Tools Format tab, W4-240, W8-480
Soft Edges, W1-24, W7-420
Soft page break, W2-86
Solid underline tab leader, W2-73

Sort, W4-217 to W4-218, W7-393
Sort dialog box, W4-217, W7-393
Source, W3-149. *See also* Bibliography/refer-
    ences/work cited
Source file, W9-542
Source Manager dialog box, W3-153, W3-154
Source program, W9-542
Spacebar, W1-11
Spacing
    character, W1-23
    line, W1-29 to W1-30
    paragraph, W1-30 to W1-31
Special characters, W4-242
Specific People, W9-526
Specify height box, W7-401
Spelling context menu, W1-33
Spelling errors, W1-33, W12-698
Spelling & Grammar button, W1-34
Spelling pane, W1-34
Split button, W11-666
Split cells, W7-403 to W7-404
Split Cells button, W4-213, W7-404
Split Cells dialog box, W7-404
Split table, W7-403
Split Table button, W7-403
Square, W4-238
Stars and banners, W4-238
Start and end tags, W11-654
Start enforcement, W9-538
Start Enforcing Protection dialog box, W9-538,
    W11-660
Start Mail Merge button, W5-287, W5-299
Start up options area, W12-697
Step-by-Step Mail Merge Wizard, W5-299. *See
    also* Mail Merge Wizard
Stop Protection button, W9-539, W11-660
Stop Recording button, W10-597, W10-598,
    W10-602
Store link, W12-708, W12-709
Store macro in drop-down list, W10-597, W10-
    598, W10-601
Straight line, W4-238
Strikethrough, W1-20, W1-22
Style. *See* Styles
Style dialog box, W3-147
Style for following paragraph drop-down list,
    W6-332
Style gallery, W2-92, W3-161, W6-328, W6-332
    to W6-333
Style pane options, W6-339 to W6-340
Style Pane Options dialog box, W6-340
Style sets, W6-333 to W6-334
Style Sets gallery, W6-333
Style types, W6-329
Styles, W6-327 to W6-347
    built-in style, W2-93
    change document style set, W6-333 to
        W6-334
    chart, W8-487 to W8-488
    clear formatting, W6-333, W6-340 to
        W6-341
    content control field, W11-653 to W11-654
    copy, W6-344
    create new style from selected text,
        W6-332
    defined, W2-92, W6-328
    delete, W6-344
    edit, W6-338
    expand/collapse headings, W6-342
    export, W6-342 to W6-343
    find and replace, W6-341
    footnotes and endnotes, W3-147
    gallery, W6-328, W6-332 to W6-333
    graphics, W4-241

    import, W6-342 to W6-343
    Manage Styles dialog box, W6-338,
        W6-339
    mini toolbar, W2-93
    modify, W2-93 to W2-94, W6-330
    new, W6-331 to W6-332
    Organizer dialog box, W6-342, W6-344
    picture, W7-419
    recommended, W6-339
    rename, W6-344
    Select how built-in style names are shown,
        W6-340
    sets, W6-333 to W6-334
    shape, W7-427 to W7-428
    style pane options, W6-339 to W6-340
    summary/review, W6-366
    table, W4-222 to W4-223, W7-407 to
        W7-410
    template, W6-343 to W6-344
    types, W6-329
    update, W6-330 to W6-331
    Update Style to Match Selection, W2-93
Styles drop-down arrow, W6-329
Styles launcher, W6-328, W6-331, W6-339
Styles organizer, W10-592
Styles pane, W6-328 to W6-329
Styles template, W6-343
Stylistic Sets, W1-20, W1-23
Subdocument, W11-663. *See also* Master
    document
Subdocument selector, W11-664, W11-666,
    W11-667, W11-668
Subscript, W1-20, W1-22
Subtraction (−), W7-394
SUM function, W4-223, W7-395
Superscript, W1-20, W1-22
Suppress for Current Paragraph, W8-469
Sway, W12-731 to W12-732
Symbol button, W4-241
Symbol dialog box, W2-89, W4-241, W11-646
Symbols, W4-242
Synonyms, W1-35
Syntax, W7-394

T

Tab leader, W2-72 to W2-73, W8-495
Tab leader drop-down list, W8-495
Tab selector, W2-71
Tab stop position, W2-70
Tab stops
    content control field, W11-643
    default, W2-73
    header and footer, W2-82
    leaders, W2-72 to W2-73
    move, W2-71 to W2-72
    remove, W2-72
    ruler, W2-71
    set, W2-70 to W2-71
    table, W7-397
    types, W2-69
Table
    add rows/columns, W4-212
    alignment and positioning, W7-402
    AutoFit, W4-215
    banded rows/columns, W4-223
    borders, W4-221, W7-405 to W7-407
    bulleted list, W7-398
    cell margins and spacing, W4-216, W7-403
    change text direction, W7-396 to W7-397
    child, W7-404
    column width, W7-402
    content control field, W11-643

context menu, W4-213, W4-216, W4-217
convert table to text, W4-225, W7-392 to
  W7-393
convert text to table, W4-224, W7-392
copy rows/columns, W4-213 to W4-214
definitions, W4-210
delete rows/columns, W4-214
Delete Table option, W4-214
distribute rows/columns, W4-215
draw, W7-405
formatting, W4-215, W4-220 to W4-222
formula, W4-223, W4-224, W7-394
  to W7-396
grid, W7-407
gridlines, W4-222
indents, W7-397
insert, W4-210 to W4-211
merge cells, W4-213
mini toolbar, W4-212
move rows/columns, W4-213 to W4-214
multiple pages, display column headings,
  W7-404 to W7-405
navigation, W4-211
nested, W7-404
numbered list, W7-398
parent, W7-404
plain, W7-407
positioning, W7-402
Quick Tables, W7-410 to W7-411
repeat header rows, W7-404 to W7-405
resize rows/columns, W4-214 to W4-215,
  W7-402
row height, W4-214, W4-215, W4-216,
  W7-402
select text/table, W4-211, W4-212
shading, W4-222
Shift cells right, W4-213
size, W7-401
sort, W4-217 to W4-218, W7-393
split table and cells, W4-213, W7-403
  to W7-404
styles, W4-222 to W4-223, W7-405,
  W7-407 to W7-410
SUM formula, W4-223
summary/review, W4-246, W7-434
tab stops, W7-397
Table Properties dialog box, W4-217
Table Tools Design tab, W4-220, W7-392
Table Tools Layout tab, W4-211, W7-392
text alignment, W4-216
Table alignment and position, W7-402
Table Alignment options, W7-402
Table borders, W4-221
Table building blocks, W7-410 to W7-411
Table button, W7-405
Table drawing tool, W7-405
Table of contents, W3-161
  bibliography, W3-155
  built-in, W3-162
  custom/customize, W3-162 to W3-163
  heading styles, W3-161
  modify, W3-163
  remove, W3-164
  summary/review, W3-179
  theme, W3-161
  title, W3-162
  update, W3-163 to W3-164
Table of Contents dialog box, W3-163
Table of Contents gallery, W6-348
Table of contents title, W3-162
Table Options dialog box, W4-216, W7-403
Table Positioning dialog box, W7-402
Table Properties dialog box, W4-217, W7-401,
  W7-402, W7-403

Table selection tools, W4-211 to W4-212
Table selector handle, W4-211, W7-401
Table shading, W4-222
Table size, W7-401
Table sizing handle, W7-401
Table style, W6-329
Table Style Options group, W4-223
Table Styles, W4-222 to W4-223, W7-405,
  W7-407 to W7-410
Table Styles gallery, W7-407
Table Styles Options group, W7-407
Table Tools Design tab, W4-220, W7-392
Table Tools Layout tab, W4-211, W4-212,
  W4-215, W4-217, W7-392
Tables gallery, W6-348
Tabs, W2-69. See also Tab stops
Tabs button, W7-397
Tabs dialog box, W2-70, W2-72, W7-397
Tag, W11-644
Target frame, W2-104
Template, W5-269
  attach template to a document, W6-343 to
    W6-344, W10-591 to W10-592
  content control fields, W10-589
  create document based on template,
    W5-277, W10-588
  create template from blank document,
    W5-276
  Custom Office Templates folder, W10-589
  customize template content, W10-589
    to W10-591
  defined, W10-586
  document property fields, W10-590
  edit, W5-278, W10-588
  file name extension, W10-586
  insert template content, W5-272
  macro-enabled, W10-612 to W10-614
  modify content and format, W5-274
  Normal, W5-270
  online, W5-271 to W5-272, W10-587
  Organizer dialog box, W10-591
  personal, W10-587
  pin/unpin, W10-587
  remove template content, W5-273
    to W5-274
  save document as template, W5-276 to
    W5-277, W10-586
  save form as template, W11-659
  styles, W6-343
  summary/review, W5-305, W10-617
  Word fields, W10-590 to W10-591
Templates and Add-ins dialog box,
  W10-591, W10-592
Text
  copy, W1-15, W1-16
  enter, W1-7
  move, W1-15
  paste, W1-16
  select, W1-8
Text alignment buttons, W7-397
Text box
  building block, W8-476
  built-in, W8-473 to W8-474
  content, W8-474
  draw, W7-428 to W7-429, W8-475
    to W8-476
  format, W8-475
Text Box building blocks, W8-476
Text Box button, W8-474
Text Boxes gallery, W6-348
Text Direction button, W7-397
Text Effects, W1-23, W8-481
Text Fill, W8-481
Text Fill & Outline, W1-24

Text Highlight Color, W1-20, W1-22
Text Outline, W8-481
Text pane, W8-480
Text pane button, W8-481
Text pane control, W8-481
Text watermark radio button, W8-466
Text wrapping
  column, W4-229
  graphics, W4-234, W4-235
  page break, W2-87
  picture, W7-415 to W7-416
  Wrap Text options, W4-235
Texture tab, W8-465
Theme, W2-92, W2-94, W3-161
  Colors button, W8-472
  create new theme colors, W8-472
  create new theme fonts, W8-473
  custom, W8-473
  default setting (Office), W6-328
  delete custom theme, W8-473
  Effects button, W8-472
  Fonts button, W8-472
  what is it?, W6-328
Theme colors, W2-94, W6-334, W8-472
Theme Effects, W2-94, W8-472
Theme Fonts, W2-94, W6-334, W8-472,
  W8-473
Themes button, W8-472, W8-473
Themes drop-down list, W8-473
Thesaurus, W1-35, W1-36
Thick underline with color, W1-22
3-D Format, W1-24
3-D Rotation, W7-420
TIFF (.tiff), W4-232
Time (date & time), W2-82, W2-83
Title page, W3-164. See also Cover page
Toggle Case, W1-20
Toggle Field Codes, W9-552
Top, W2-68
Track Changes, W3-137. See also
  Collaboration features
  accept/reject changes, W3-138 to
    W3-139
  balloon, W3-137
  change tracking options, W9-526 to
    W9-527
  Display for Review view, W3-138
  lock tracking, W9-527
  on/off toggle, W3-137
  Reviewing pane, W3-140
  Show Comments button, W3-138
  turn on the feature, W3-137
Track Changes balloon, W3-137
Track Changes button, W9-527
Track Changes Options dialog box, W3-135,
  W9-525, W9-526
Track formatting check box, W9-526
Track moves check box, W9-526
Tracking launcher, W9-525, W9-526
Transparent color, W7-421
Trendline, W8-487
Trust Center, W12-700 to W12-701
Trust Center button, W12-700
Trust Center dialog box, W10-600,
  W12-700, W12-701
Trust Center Settings button, W12-701
Trust It button, W12-708
Trusted document, W10-614
Turabian reporting style, W3-150
Tutorial button, W12-732
Twitter, W12-708
2 pages per sheet, W8-463
.txt, W1-4
Type a New List, W5-288

U

Underline, W1-20, W1-22
Underline color, W1-21
Underline style, W1-21
Underline Words only, W1-22
Undo, W1-17
Ungroup, W4-237, W4-238, W7-431, W11-659
Unlink button, W11-667
Unlink subdocument, W11-666 to W11-667
Unprotect Document dialog box, W11-660
Up/down bars, W8-487
Update all Labels button, W5-301
Update Citations and Bibliography, W3-156
Update Field, W6-362, W7-396
Update Index button, W8-496
Update index page, W8-496
Update labels, W5-293
Update Labels button, W5-293
Update Link, W9-546
Update [style name] to Match Selection, W6-331
Uppercase, W1-20
Use a style to format text typed into the empty control check box, W11-672
Use Alignment Guides, W7-416
Use an Existing List, W5-289
Use return address check box, W5-284
User Interface options area, W12-696
User name, W3-135
UserInitials field, W6-361
UserName field, W6-361
Using other Office applications, W9-542 to W9-550. See also Embed and link

V

Version options (autosaved document), W9-539
Vertical alignment, W2-68
Vertical alignment guide, W7-416
Vertical ruler, W2-69
View Gridlines, W4-222
View-only link, W3-141, W9-528, W12-718
View Survey window, W12-731
Visual Basic programming language, W10-605

W

Walls and floors, W8-487
Watermark, W8-465 to W8-467
Watermark building block, W8-467
Watermark button, W8-466, W8-467
Watermarks gallery, W6-348
Wavy underline
    blue, W1-33
    red, W1-33
Webdings, W4-241
Weight, W7-420
White space, W2-66
Wildcards, W2-99
Windows Bitmap (BMP), W4-232
Windows Metafile (WMF), W4-232
Wingdings, W4-241
WMF (.wmf), W4-232
Word Count, W1-36
Word Count dialog box, W1-36
Word dictionary, W1-34
Word document. See Document
Word fields, W6-359 to W6-362, W10-590
Word level, W9-532, W9-533
Word macro-enabled document, W10-599
Word Macro-Enabled Template, W10-612
Word Online, W9-527, W9-528, W12-722 to W12-724. See also Office Online
Word Options dialog box, W1-34, W3-135
    Add-ins, W12-700
    add macro button to Quick Access toolbar, W10-607
    Advanced category, W12-699 to W12-700
    assign shortcut key to macro, W10-606
    autosave, W9-539
    bookmark, W9-553
    customize the ribbon. See Ribbon
    Display options category, W12-697
    General category, W12-696 to W12-697
    Language category, W12-698 to W12-699
    list of categories, W12-696
    page color, W8-465
    personalize Microsoft Office, W6-362
    Proofing category, W12-697 to W12-698
    Quick Access toolbar. See Quick Access toolbar
    Save category, W12-698
    summary/review, W12-736
    Trust Center, W12-700 to W12-701
Word Template, W5-276
Word wrap, W1-7
WordArt, W4-241 to W4-242
WordArt gallery, W4-240
WordArt Styles group, W8-481, W8-489
WordArt Styles launcher, W8-474, W8-482, W8-489
WordPress, W12-720
Works Cited, W3-150. See also Bibliography/references/work cited
Wrap points, W7-416 to W7-417
Wrap text. See Text wrapping
Wrap Text button, W7-415, W7-416, W7-417, W8-483, W8-489

X

x (multiplication), W7-394
X-axis, W8-486

Y

Y-axis, W8-486
Yes, Start Enforcing Protection button, W9-538, W11-660
YouTube, W12-708